"Lapidus is concerned not with defining an essential Islam, but rather with mapping the role of Islamic beliefs, institutions, and identities in particular historical contexts."
– *International Journal of Middle East Studies*

"The value of *A History of Islamic Societies* lies in its sheer comprehensiveness. In one volume a vast amount of material is synthesized and presented in a clear and effective style. There is nothing else like it. For the first time the worldwide history of Islamic societies is made accessible to the interested reader."
– *The Journal of Asian Studies*

"I do not think that any other world civilization can boast a comparable general account of such substance and quality. This is a great deal more than a textbook. It is a product of learning, intellect and style of an extremely high order."
– *Journal of the Royal Asiatic Society*

A HISTORY OF
ISLAMIC SOCIETIES

In the second edition of this now classic work, Ira Lapidus explores the origins and evolution of Muslim societies, across the world. His overarching vision brings perspective and coherence to a rich and diverse history, which has been updated and revised. The book is divided into three parts. The first covers the formative era of Islamic civilization from the revelation of the Quran to the thirteenth century, and examines the transformation of Islam from a complex of doctrines and cultures into the organizing principles of Middle Eastern societies. The second traces the creation of similar societies in the Balkans, North Africa, Central Asia, China, India, Southeast Asia and sub-Saharan Africa. The third part explores the reaction of these societies to European imperialism, and describes how they emerged at the beginning of the twentieth century as independent states with fledgling economies. The concluding chapters consider Islam's most recent history, the formation of Islamic revival movements in their religious, community-building and political dimensions, and global Islamic identities and organizations.

Throughout, the author engages with the social structures of these societies, their families and communities, religious congregations and political regimes. The richness of Islamic civilisation is illustrated through its language, theology, philosophy and law, through its art and architecture.

Since it was first published this book has become essential reading for students and for all those seeking to understand the Muslim peoples, their history and their civilization. In these troubled times, this book is an education and an illumination.

IRA M. LAPIDUS is Professor Emeritus of History, University of California at Berkeley. He is one of the most distinguished and highly regarded scholars writing Islamic history today. His many articles and books include *Islam, Politics and Social Movements* (edited with Edmund Burke, 1988) and *Contemporary Islamic Movements in Historical Perspective* (1984). The first edition of *A History of Islamic Societies* was published in 1988 as a supplement to *The Cambridge History of Islam* (1970). Since publication, the book has become a classic work of history. The second edition brings this definitive and best-selling book to a new generation of readers.

A HISTORY OF
ISLAMIC SOCIETIES

SECOND EDITION

IRA M. LAPIDUS

Emeritus, University of California, Berkeley

CAMBRIDGE
UNIVERSITY PRESS

PUBLISHED BY THE PRESS SYNDICATE OF THE UNIVERSITY OF CAMBRIDGE
The Pitt Building, Trumpington Street, Cambridge, United Kingdom

CAMBRIDGE UNIVERSITY PRESS
The Edinburgh Building, Cambridge CB2 2RU, UK
40 West 20th Street, New York, NY 10011–4211, USA
477 Williamstown Road, Port Melbourne, VIC 3207, Australia
Ruiz de Alarcón 13, 28014 Madrid, Spain
Dock House, The Waterfront, Cape Town 8001, South Africa

http://www.cambridge.org

First published 1988
13th printing 1999
Second edition first published 2002

Printed in Singapore by Craft Print

Typeface Garamond (*Adobe*) 10/12 pt.   *System* QuarkXPress®   [PK]

A catalogue record for this book is available from the British Library

National Library of Australia Cataloguing in Publication data
Lapidus, Ira M. (Ira Marvin).
A history of Islamic societies.
2nd ed.
Bibliography.
Includes index.
ISBN 0 521 77056 4.
ISBN 0 521 77933 2 (pbk.).
1. Islam – History. 2. Islamic countries – History.
Title.
909.097671

ISBN 0 521 77056 4 hardback
ISBN 0 521 77933 2 paperback

CONTENTS

Part II THE WORLDWIDE DIFFUSION OF ISLAMIC SOCIETIES FROM THE TENTH TO THE NINETEENTH CENTURIES

THE MIDDLE EASTERN ISLAMIC SOCIETIES

ISLAM IN CENTRAL AND SOUTHERN ASIA

ISLAM IN AFRICA

PART III THE MODERN TRANSFORMATION: MUSLIM PEOPLES IN THE NINETEENTH AND TWENTIETH CENTURIES

NATIONALISM AND ISLAM IN THE MIDDLE EAST

ILLUSTRATIONS

Every effort has been made to trace and acknowledge copyright. The author and
publisher would be pleased to hear from copyright owners they have been unable
to trace.

MAPS

TABLES AND FIGURES

TABLES

FIGURES

PREFACE AND ACKNOWLEDGMENTS
TO THE FIRST EDITION

Islam is the religion of peoples who inhabit the middle regions of the planet from the Atlantic shores of Africa to the South Pacific, from the steppes of Siberia to the remote islands of South Asia: Berbers, West Africans, Sudanese, Swahili-speaking East Africans, Middle Eastern Arabs, Turks, Iranians, Turkish and Persian peoples of Central Asia, Afghans, Pakistanis, many millions of Indians and Chinese, most of the peoples of Malaysia and Indonesia, and minorities in the Philippines – some one-and-a-quarter billion people adhere to Islam. In ethnic background, language, customs, social and political organization, and forms of culture and technology, they represent innumerable variations of human experience. Yet Islam unites them. Though Islam is not often the totality of their lives, it permeates their self-conception, regulates their daily existence, provides the bonds of society, and fulfills the yearning for salvation. For all its variousness, Islam forges one of the great spiritual families of mankind.

This book is the history of how these multitudes have become Muslims and what Islam means to them. In this book we ask: What is Islam? What are its values? How did so many peoples, so different and dispersed, become Muslims? What does Islam contribute to their character, to their way of living, to the ordering of their communities, and to their aspirations and identity? What are the historical conditions that have given rise to Islamic religious and cultural values; what are the manifold ways in which it is understood and practiced? To answer these questions we shall see how religious concepts about the nature of reality and the meaning of human experience, embedded at once in holy scripture and works of commentary, and as thoughts and feelings in the minds and hearts of Muslim believers, have given shape to the lifestyles and institutions of Muslim peoples, and how reciprocally the political and social experiences of Muslim peoples have been given expression in the values and symbols of Islam. Our history of Islam is the history of a dialogue between religious symbols and everyday reality.

This history will be presented in two dimensions: one historical and evolutionary, an effort to account for the formation of Islamic societies and their change over time; the other analytic and comparative, which attempts to understand the variations among them. Three methodological and historical assumptions underlie this approach. The first is that the history of whole societies may be presented in terms of their institutional systems. An institution, whether an empire, a mode of economic exchange, a family, or a religious practice, is a human activity carried out in a patterned relationship with other human beings as defined and legitimized in the mental world of the participants. An institution encompasses at once an activity, a pattern of social relations, and a set of mental constructs.

The second assumption is that the history of Islamic societies may be told in terms of four basic types of institutions: familial, including tribal, ethnic, and other small-scale community groups; economic, the organization of production and distribution of material goods; cultural or religious concepts of ultimate values and human goals and the collectivities built upon such commitments; and political, the organization of conflict resolution, defense, and domination.

The third assumption is that the institutional patterns characteristic of Islamic societies had their origin in ancient Mesopotamia in the third millennium BC. The constellation of lineage and tribal, religious, and political structures created by the Mesopotamian city-states and empires set the foundations for the later evolution of Middle Eastern societies before and during the Islamic era, and was either reproduced or diffused from the Middle East to other Islamic societies. Thus the Middle Eastern Islamic society was based upon the infusion of more ancient institutions with an Islamic cultural style and identity. These Middle Eastern Islamic institutions in turn interacted with the institutions and cultures of other world regions to create a number of variant Islamic societies. In the modern era these variant societies were again transformed, this time by interaction with Europe. Modern Islamic countries are each the product of the interaction of a particular regional form of Islamic society with different forms of European imperial, economic, and cultural influences. The variation among modern Islamic societies may be traced to older patterns.

Part I examines the formative era of Islamic civilization from the revelation of the Quran to the thirteenth century. It begins with the Prophet Muhammad, and continues with the classical Islamic era which gave rise to Arabic literature, Islamic religious teaching, and cosmopolitan artistic achievements – a tripartite complex of tribal–ethnic, religious, and courtly–aristocratic cultures from which all later versions of Islamic civilization derive. It attempts to explain the development of this civilization in terms of the relationship of Islamic cultures to past patterns of Middle Eastern societies, and in terms of the cultural effects of the formation of new empires, urbanization, and social change. It concludes with the history of Iraq and Iran from the tenth to the thirteenth centuries, to explain the transformation of Islam from a complex of doctrines and cultural systems into the operative principles of a Middle Eastern society. In this period, Muslim peoples formed new state and communal institutions (Shiʻi "sects," Sunni schools of law, and Sufi brotherhoods), and defined the relations of political regimes to religious bodies. This was the age in which Islam became the religion of the masses of Middle Eastern peoples.

In its turn the Islamic version of Middle Eastern society became a paradigm for the creation of similar societies in other parts of the world. Part II traces the diffusion of the Middle Eastern Islamic paradigm. From the seventh to the nineteenth centuries, Islam became the religion of peoples in the Arab Middle East, Inner Asia and China, India, Southeast Asia, Africa, and the Balkans. It considers the forces behind the diffusion of Islam, and the interaction between Islamic religious values and existing cultures and societies. It also examines the consolidation of Islamic regimes including the Mughal, Ottoman, and Safavid empires, and Islamic states in Southeast Asia, Africa, and elsewhere, and their varied ways of integrating political regimes, Islamic religious institutions, and non-Islamic values and forms of community.

By the eighteenth century the Middle Eastern paradigm for an Islamic society had been replicated, multiplied, and modified into a worldwide family of societies. Each was a recognizable variant upon an underlying structure of familial–communal, religious, and state institutions. Each also represented a version of the various ways in which Islamic belief, culture, and social institutions have interacted with the still broader complex of human organization – including the non-Islamic institutions of political regimes, systems of economic production and exchange, non-Islamic forms of kinship, tribal, and ethnic communities, and pre-Islamic or non-Islamic modes of culture. Here we explore the degree to which the Middle Eastern paradigm was transferred to new Islamic societies. What was the relation of Islamic to pre-Islamic institutions in these regions? What were the similarities and differences among these numerous Islamic societies?

The transformation of Islamic societies from the eighteenth century to the present tests the resilience of the historical templates and the identity of the Islamic world system. In part III we see how Islamic societies were profoundly disrupted by the breakup of Muslim empires, economic decline, internal religious conflict, and by the establishment of European economic, political, and cultural domination. These forces led to the creation of national states, to the modernization of agriculture, to industrialization, to major changes in class structure, and to the acceptance of secular nationalist and other modern ideologies. In the course of these changes Islamic thought and Islamic communal institutions have been radically altered.

The legacy of eighteenth- and nineteenth-century historical change, however, is not a unilinear movement toward "modernization," but a heritage of continuing conflict in Muslim countries over political, economic, and cultural goals. Political decline and European intervention have led to a struggle among political elites, scholarly (*'ulama'*) and mystical (Sufi) religious leaders, and revivalist movements for political and social power. While secularized political elites tend to favor modernization in Western forms, and the redefinition of Islam to make it consistent with modern forms of state and economy, religious reformers espouse the revitalization of moral values and the formation of new political communities on Islamic principles. By examining the historical forms of political and religious organization, the impact of European imperialisms, and the political and ideological struggles of competing elites in Muslim countries, this book will attempt to interpret the development of present-day societies.

Has the impact of the West and of modern technical civilization generated a new form of society or do the historical political and religious templates still regulate the destiny of new Muslim nations? Do present conditions reflect the cultural and political qualities of the imperial, sectarian, and tribal societies of the eighteenth century or have the nineteenth- and twentieth-century transformations of economy, class structure, and values generated a new evolutionary stage in the history of Islamic societies?

This is not, it should be clear, an effort to define an essential Islam, but rather an attempt to develop a comparative method of assessing the role of Islamic beliefs, institutions, and identities in particular historical contexts. The mechanism I have adopted to do this – the expository framework – is based on the assumptions that Islamic societies are built upon institutions and that these institutions are subject to internal variation, to variations in the relationships among them, and to variations over time. The limited number of institutional factors imposes a constraint that allows us to conceive this large subject in some ordered way, but also allows for the depiction of individual societies as concrete and different entities. By exploring the variation of institutions in differing contexts, we may be able to comprehend why Islamic societies are similar in general form and yet differ so much in specific qualities.

In this volume primary emphasis will be placed upon the communal, religious, and political institutions of Islamic societies rather than upon technologies and economies. I subordinate economic to non-economic institutions because the distinctive historical developments in Islamic societies in the last millennium have been cultural and political; and because differences of culture and institutions differentiate Islamic societies from each other and from other human civilizations. In Muslim societies the basic forms of economic production and exchange were set down in the pre-Islamic era. The forms of agricultural and pastoral production, handicrafts, manufacturing, prevailing systems of exchange, and technological capacities are all older than, and continue through, the Islamic era in their inherited forms. This is not to deny that there has been considerable variation in economic activity in and among Muslim societies, such as in the relative role of pastoral, agricultural, commercial, and manufacturing activities, or in degrees of poverty and prosperity, or in the distribution of wealth; or that these differences have important cultural and political implications, or that economic considerations are an essential aspect of all human values and social action. Still, the fundamental modes of economic production and exchange were basically unaltered until the modern era, and economic and technological changes were not the primary sources of political and cultural variation or of changes in class structure and social organization. Until the modern era economic activity remained embedded in communal and political structures, and class divisions in society did not determine, but were inherent in, state and religious organizations. Even in the nineteenth and twentieth centuries, when European capitalism and profound economic and technological changes have influenced Islamic societies, economically derived classes such as merchants and proletariats were weakly developed in Muslim countries, and political and religious elites, institutions, and cultural values played a predominant role in the development of these societies. While cultural and sociopolitical institutions and economic and technological forces can each be an autonomous causal factor in historical change, in the history of Islamic societies the former have been the significant locus of historical individuation. Whether twentieth-century technological and economic change now call into question the existence of an Islamic group of societies is a moot point.

These assumptions derive from a variety of historical, social scientific, and philosophic sources. As a historian, however, my primary interest is not in theory but in the adaptation of the theory to the needs of a coherent and meaningful exposition. The central problem of this book is how to present a history of enormous diversity – the history of societies that to sight and sound are utterly different – and yet preserve some sense of their historical and institutional relatedness. For the reader this book is intended to provide a coherent overview of Islamic history. As a teacher I think that the endless everyday flow of events and news confuses rather than enlightens us, and that a large "map" of the subject as a whole is essential to the understanding of particular occurrences. Only from an overall point of view can we acquire the poise, distance, and perspective that make it possible to identify basic structural factors and long-term historical trends, and distinguish them from accidental and short-term considerations.

A few comments about the organization of the book may help readers find their way through this large volume. First, the reader should be cautioned that the factual narrative approach of this book conceals great uncertainties of historical judgment, incomplete knowledge, conflicts of opinion and interpretation among experts, and constantly changing research which brings new knowledge and new points of view to the fore. Little has been said about the degree of reliability or the margin of error in the presentation of information, but the book is based upon the most reliable research and interpretation, though the reader should be aware that parts of the work are provisional and exploratory in nature, and represent the author's best judgment about particular subjects.

The book is divided into three parts, each of which has an introduction and conclusion which deal with the organizing concepts upon which the book is based and summarize the important themes that come up in the narrative chapters. For an overview of the evolution of Islamic societies, these introductory and concluding chapters may be read separately or in conjunction with selected period or regional histories.

Each of the three main divisions deals with a particular epoch in Islamic history – the origins, diffusion, and modern transformation of Islamic societies. This means that Islamic culture, arts, literatures, and religious values are discussed primarily in part I, and are only referred to in a summary way in parts II and III. Regional histories also are ordinarily divided into two or three sections. The history of Middle Eastern Islamic societies is divided among all three parts; the histories of other Islamic societies feature in parts II and III. There are, however, a number of exceptions. While part I deals generally with the formation of Middle Eastern Islamic societies from the seventh to the thirteenth centuries, for narrative convenience the early histories of the Arab Middle East, North Africa, and Spain are grouped with their regional histories in part II; portions of these chapters may usefully be read in conjunction with part I. Similarly, the entire history of the Arabian peninsula, Libya, the Caucasus, Afghanistan, and the Philippines is found in part III rather than being scattered through the volume. The history of all these societies concludes around 2000.

The definition of geographic regions also requires some arbitrary simplifications. Muslim world areas are by and large defined in regional terms such as Middle East, North Africa, Indian subcontinent, Southeast Asia, West and East Africa, and so on. For convenience of reference, and despite the obvious anachronism, these areas or parts of them are commonly identified by the names of present national states such as India, Indonesia, or Nigeria. This is to simplify identification for readers unfamiliar with the geography of these vast regions and to avoid such cumbersome locutions as "areas now part of the state of —," but it should be clear that the use of these terms does not necessarily imply any similarity of state and social organization or of cultural style between pre-modern and contemporary times. It should also be noted that I have placed the history of Libya in the chapter on North Africa and the Sudan in East Africa though these countries also belong to the Arab Middle East. Finally, not all Muslim regions are covered in this book. Some Muslim minorities, as in mainland Southeast Asia and Ceylon, are not discussed.

Transliterations from the numerous native languages of Muslim peoples have been simplified for the convenience of English readers. In general I have tried to follow standard scholarly usage for each world area, modified by the elimination of diacritical marks and sometimes adapted to give a fair sense of pronunciation. Certain standard Arabic terms and names are given in their original, usually Arabic, literary form despite actual variations in spelling and pronunciation the world over. Dates are given in the Christian era.

ACKNOWLEDGMENTS

In the preparation of the book I have been greatly aided by my students, research assistants, and colleagues. They have helped me, depending upon their skills and my background in a given world area, in the following ways: by the preparation of bibliographies; reading, review, and preparation of digests on relevant literatures; research into particular themes and topics in both secondary and source materials; summaries or translations of materials in languages I do not read, and discussion of historiographical or methodological problems in their particular fields or disciplines. They have made an important contribution to my understanding of the role of Islam in several world areas, and have enormously facilitated the completion of the book.

I would like to thank David Goodwin, Margaret Malamud, Ann Taboroff, Sahar von Schlegell (Islamic history and Sufism); James Reid (Iran); Corrine Blake (Arab Middle East); Elaine Combs-Schilling (North Africa); Sandria Freitag and David Gilmartin (India); Mary Judd and Allan Samson (Indonesia); William McFarren and Leslie Sharp (Africa); Rose Glickman and Mark Saroyan (Russian Inner Asia); and John Foran and Michael Hughes (modernization and political economy). I am also grateful for the bibliographical help of Melissa MacCauly and Susan Mattern.

For the selection of illustrations, I benefited from the advice and assistance of Guitty Azarpay, Jere Bacharach, Sheila Blair, Jonathan Bloom, Herbert Bodman, Gordon Holler, Thomas Lentz, Kim Lyon, Amy Newhall, and Labelle Prussin. I warmly thank the individuals and institutions by whose kind permission they are reproduced here. I am grateful to Cherie A. Semans of the Department of Geography, University of California, Berkeley, for the preparation of the designs and sketch maps upon which the maps in this volume are based.

Many friends and colleagues have read portions or even the whole of the manuscript and have given me invaluable corrections, suggestions, and reflective thoughts. Each of them has enriched this volume, though none of them is responsible for the remaining faults. It gives me great pleasure to thank Jere Bacharach, Thomas Bisson, William Brinner, Edmund Burke III, Elaine Combs-Schilling, Shmuel Eisenstadt, Sandria Freitag, David Gilmartin, Albert Hourani, Suad Joseph, Barbara Metcalf, Thomas Metcalf, Martha Olcott, James Reid, Richard Roberts, William Roff, Allan Samson, Stanford Shaw, David Skinner, Ilkay Sunar, Ilter Turan, Abraham Udovitch, Lucette Valensi, and Reginald Zelnik. As much as the writing, the friendship and generosity of these people have blessed many years of work.

Several colleagues have had a particularly strong effect on the development of my understanding and have generously shared with me their views and unpublished work on various aspects of this book. In particular I would like to thank Barbara Metcalf (India), Elaine Combs-Schilling (North Africa), Suad Joseph (women's studies), Martha Olcott (Soviet Inner Asia), James Reid (Iran and Inner Asia), Allan Samson (Indonesia), Warren Fusfeld (for his dissertation on the Naqshbandiya in India), and Sandria Freitag and David Gilmartin (India). Morris Rossabi has graciously allowed me to see a copy of an unpublished article by Joseph Fletcher on the Naqshbandiya in China.

I am equally indebted to the many people who have helped prepare the manuscript and the published book. The staff of the Center for Advanced Studies in the Behavioral Sciences, Stanford, California prepared an early draft of the manuscript. Muriel Bell edited several of the chapters. Lynn Gale helped to arrange the transmission of this material to the word processor of the Institute of International Studies at Berkeley, where Nadine Zelinski and Christine Peterson worked with great skill on the preparation of the manuscript and have given me endless friendly support; they are among the close collaborators to whom I owe this book. The staff of Cambridge University Press, Elizabeth Wetton, editor, Susan Moore, subeditor, and Jane Williams, designer, have been especially helpful. Finally, but not least, I am grateful to my wife, Brenda Webster, for her amazed, and amazing, patience as this book grew larger and larger, for her suggestions and criticism, and above all, for her faith in the work.

The research for this project has been generously supported by the Institute of International Studies of the University of California, Berkeley. I would like to express my thanks to Professor Carl Rosberg, Director of the Institute, to Mrs Karin Beros, Management Services Officer of the Institute, and to the Institute staff, who have been generous and gracious in their support. The preparation of this volume has also been made possible by a year in residence at the Center for Advanced Studies in the Behavioral Sciences, Stanford, California, with the support of the National Endowment for the Humanities, and by a research grant from the Hoover Institution, Stanford University. The completion of this work has been made possible by a grant from the Division of Research of the National Endowment for the Humanities, an independent federal agency. To these institutions I express my deep appreciation for affording me the opportunity to concentrate upon research and writing.

Information and ideas for the maps in this book are derived from R. Roolvink, *Historical Atlas of the Muslim Peoples*, Cambridge, Mass., 1957; J. L. Bacharach, *A Middle East Studies Handbook*, Seattle, Wash., 1984; W. C. Bryce, *An Historical Atlas of Islam*, Leiden, 1981; F. Robinson, *Atlas of the Islamic World*, Oxford, 1982; J. D. Fage, *An Atlas of African History,* New York, 1978.

With the permission of the publishers extensive passages have been quoted or adapted from my previous publications:

"Adulthood in Islam: Religious Maturity in the Islamic Tradition," *Daedalus*, Spring 1976, pp. 93–108.

"Islam and the Historical Experience of Muslim Peoples," *Islamic Studies: A Tradition and its Problems*, ed. Malcolm H. Kerr, Malibu, Calif.: Undena Publications, 1980, pp. 89–102.

"Arab Settlement and Economic Development of Iraq and Iran in the Age of the Umayyad and Early Abbasid Caliphs," *The Islamic Middle East, 700–1900: Studies in Economic and Social History*, ed. A. L. Udovitch, Princeton: Darwin Press, 1981, pp. 177–208.

"The Arab Conquests and the Formation of Islamic Society," *Studies on the First Century of Islamic Society*, ed. G. H. A. Juynboll, Carbondale, Ill.: Southern Illinois University Press, 1982, pp. 49–72.

"Knowledge, Virtue and Action: The Classical Muslim Conception of Adab and the Nature of Religious Fulfillment in Islam," *Moral Conduct and Authority in South*

Asian Islam, ed. Barbara Metcalf, Berkeley: University of California Press, 1984, pp. 38–61. © 1984, The Regents of the University of California.

Contemporary Islamic Movements in Historical Perspective, Policy Papers No. 18, Institute of International Studies, University of California, Berkeley, 83.

"Mamluk Patronage and the Arts in Egypt," *Muqarnas*, 11, 1984, New Haven, Conn.: Yale University Press, pp. 173–81.

IRA M. LAPIDUS
University of California, Berkeley
1985

PREFACE AND ACKNOWLEDGMENTS
TO THE SECOND EDITION

This book was first published in 1988 on the basis of research that extended to about 1980. At that time the contemporary Islamic revival was in an early stage. There had been an Islamic revolution in Iran, but whether it would spread to other, and Sunni, Muslim countries was much debated. After a long phase of secularization in politics and law, and the beginnings of an economic development process not connected to Islam, the revival reaffirmed the importance of Islam in the contemporary construction of Muslim societies. The beginnings of the Islamic revival made it possible to see that Muslim societies worldwide shared a common heritage and elements of a common identity. The evidence of their relatedness, however tenuous at the time, enabled us to look for the evolutionary origin of that common identity and to see the processes of the formation of Islamic societies as a historical whole. Thus in the first edition we were able to see the origins of Islamic civilizations in the ancient Near East and in the teachings of the Prophet Muhammad, and see the successive phases of historical development. In the first phase an Islamic culture and society was formed in the Middle East. In the second phase the Middle Eastern Islamic culture was carried by conquerors, missionaries, and merchants to other parts of the world, where Islamic institutions again interacted with local ones to form new groups of different, but related, societies. Each of these societies was the product of two parent cultures, one Muslim and the other local. In the next phase of development each of these societies had a fateful encounter with European imperialism, economic power and cultural influences, and each responded in a unique way to form its mid-twentieth-century configuration.

After twenty more years, we are in a fourth phase. The third is not yet complete, but in this phase many of the "grandchildren" Islamic societies have reaffirmed their shared religious heritage. The revival is manifested in a wave of reformist, Salafi- or Wahhabi-type movements, which teach a return to the teachings of the Quran and the Prophet. It is manifest in widespread missionary, educational, and community-building movements, and above all it is manifest in political action. Muslim politics varies from pacific and cooperative to oppositional and violent, but the hallmark of the revival is the drive to create Islamic states in place of the failed secular states of the mid- and late twentieth century.

The rise of these movements has made it useful to prepare a second edition of this book. While there has been a wealth of scholarship on the early periods, I believe that the narrative and analysis presented in parts I and II of the first edition remains fundamentally sound. It is the third part that requires updating. The story of the burgeoning of these movements and their impact on Muslim communities and states must not only be brought to the present, but requires us to reevaluate recent history. Thus, in part III each chapter on national and regional histories has been brought up to date, and the story reintegrated to see the full sweep of developments from the middle of the century to the present. In the conclusion I have tried to reassess the balance of power between the secular legacy of the late nineteenth and early twentieth centuries and the contemporary revival.

While the Islamic revival occupies much of our attention, it is not the only force operative in Muslim societies today. In the revised version I consider the continuing importance of secularization, the formation of modernist–Islamist hybrids, the maturation of new and more complex Islamic–national identities, and the emergence of a global Muslim identity. With so many forces in play, the Islamic revival is not likely to be the final phase in the evolution of Islamic societies.

In the course of revising the book, I have also filled a few important lacunae. There are new sections on Afghanistan and the Philippines, and expanded chapters on Islam in the Caucasus and Central Asia. There is a new chapter on Muslim peoples in Europe and America. The concluding section on women and gender has been enlarged and brought up to date, and there is a new discussion of the emergence of global Islamic identities and movements, including the recent terrorist events. The bibliography has been enlarged to include works dealing with the last two decades. While there are a number of smaller Muslim communities not considered in the text, the history is again up to date and comprehensive in its coverage.

In preparing the new edition I have again been blessed with the help of many friends and colleagues. To Marigold Acland, my Cambridge editor, I owe the inspiration for a new edition, the determination to awaken me to my duty, and helpful interventions throughout the process of revision. Murat Dagli tracked down data, maps, photos and bibliography. Scott Strauss helped with the research on Africa. Nancy Reynolds prepared a first draft of the new parts of the revised chapter on Islam in South Asia. Renate Holub and Laurence Michalak gave me good insights and helped correct the text for the chapter on Muslims in Europe and America. David Yaghoubian read through the whole of revised Part III and gave me innumerable suggestions for improvements. Saba Mahmood thoughtfully reviewed the conclusion. The chapter on women and gender has been revised with the help of and co-authored with Lisa Pollard. She has provided good counsel, insights, corrections, and new textual material. Nadine Ghammache skillfully prepared the manuscript.

Mary Starkey did very thoughtful and tasteful work in her copy editing, and Bennett Katrina Brown carefully checked part of the proofs. The Cambridge University Press editorial staff, Paul Watt and Karen Hildebrandt, have generously given their indispensable help in the preparation of the text. I am deeply grateful to each of them for their work, their collegiality, and their support. To my wife, Brenda Webster, I owe the happiness and peace of mind that allowed me to undertake this venture.

Maps 36 and 37 are based on maps printed in *Le Monde diplomatique*, November 2001. I would also like to thank the publishers of my previous work for their permission to print extracts and adaptations from the following articles:

"A Sober Survey of the Islamic World," *Orbis*, 40, 1996, pp. 391–404.

"The Middle East's Discomforting Continuities," *Orbis*, 42, 1998, pp. 619–30.

"Between Universalism and Particularism: The Historical Bases of Muslim Communal, National, and Global Identities," *Global Networks*, 1, 2001, pp. 19–36.

Ira M. Lapidus
Berkeley, California
2002

PUBLISHER'S PREFACE

The Press Syndicate originally commissioned Ira Lapidus to write *A History of Islamic Societies* as a supplement to *The Cambridge History of Islam*, which was published in 1970 in two volumes. His would be a unique enterprise, a monumental work with the status of a Cambridge History, but by one hand and integrated by one coherent vision. Since its publication in 1988, it has surpassed all expectations. The book has become a classic work of history. This second edition brings this definitive and bestselling book to a new generation of readers.

PART I

THE ORIGINS OF ISLAMIC CIVILIZATION: THE MIDDLE EAST FROM c. 600 TO c. 1200

1 The Pilgrimage to the Kaʿba

INTRODUCTION: MIDDLE EASTERN SOCIETIES
BEFORE THE ADVENT OF ISLAM

Islamic societies were built upon the framework of an already established and ancient Middle Eastern civilization. From the pre-Islamic Middle East, Islamic societies inherited a pattern of institutions which would shape their destiny until the modern age. These institutions included small communities based upon family, lineage, clientage, and ethnic ties, agricultural and urban societies, market economies, monotheistic religions, and bureaucratic empires. The civilization of Islam, though born in Mecca, also had its progenitors in Palestine, Babylon, and Persepolis.

Islamic societies developed in an environment that since the earliest history of mankind had exhibited two fundamental, and persisting, qualities. The first was the organization of human societies into small, often familial, groups. The earliest hunting and gathering communities lived and moved in small bands. Since the advent of agriculture and the domestication of animals, the vast majority of Middle Eastern peoples have lived in agricultural villages or in the tent camps of nomadic pastoralists. Even town peoples were bound into small groups by ties of kinship and neighborhood with all that implies of strong affections and hatreds. These groups raised the young, arranged marriages, arbitrated disputes, and formed a common front vis-à-vis the outside world.

The second was an evolutionary tendency toward the creation of unities of culture, religion, and empire on an ever-larger scale. In prehistoric times this tendency was manifested in the expansion of trade and the acceptance of common decorative styles and religious ideas, but its most important early manifestation was the emergence of the city-state in ancient Mesopotamia (3500 BC–2400 BC). The formation of cities in lower Iraq was a revolution in the history of mankind: it brought about the integration of diverse clans, villages, and other small groups into a single society. It led to new cultural and artistic achievements such as the invention of writing, the creation of great works of myth and religion, the construction of architectural masterpieces, and the fashioning of sensuous sculpture.

The first cities developed from the integration of small village communities into temple communities built upon shared commitment to the service of the gods. The Sumerians, the people of southern Iraq, believed that the lands they inhabited were the property of the gods, and that their primary duty was the construction of a great temple to worship the forces of the universe. The priests who presided over the worship were also judges and "political" chiefs. Moreover, the temple-cities were necessarily communities of economic as well as religious interests. The construction of the great temples required contributions of labor and the organization of masses of workers; their rituals required specialists in administrative, professional, and artisanal activities. The earliest cities were then communities in which religious leaders and religious ideas governed the economic and political affairs of the temples' adherents.

ANCIENT EMPIRES

Beginning about 2400 BC, the temple-cities of Mesopotamia were superseded by new unifying institutions – kingship and empires. Kingship in ancient Mesopotamia emanated from two sources: the warrior or warlord houses of the ancient Sumerian cities and the tribal peoples of northern Mesopotamia. Between 2700 and 2500 BC, city kings established ephemeral states among their neighbors. About 2400 BC, Sargon of Akkad, the chief of pastoral peoples in northern Mesopotamia, founded the first of the world's empires. Sargon's empire soon failed, and the temple-cities temporarily regained their independence. From Sargon to Hammurapi, the great lawgiver (d. 1750 BC), Mesopotamian empires rose and fell, but each one, though relatively short lived, reinforced the institutions of kingship and of multi-city regimes.

Kingship as it developed from Sargon to Hammurapi increasingly assumed a sacred aura. Kings usurped the authority of priests and became the chief servants of the gods. They took over the priestly functions of mediating between the gods and the people. Ever after, in Middle Eastern conceptions, kingship was justified as the expression of the divine plan for the ordering of human societies. Sacralized political power, as well as religious community, became a vehicle for the unification of disparate peoples.

The successive empires of this ancient period also established the institutions that would henceforth be the medium for imperial rule. At the center was the ruler's household, the king surrounded by his family, retainers, soldiers, servants, and palace administrators. Standing armies were founded; feudal grants of land were awarded to loyal retainers. Governors, administrators, and spies were assigned to control cities and provinces.

The superimposition of empires upon smaller communities transformed local life. Temples were reduced to cogs in the imperial machine, and priests lost their judicial and political authority. The empires also intervened in small communities by freeing individuals from their commitments to clans and temples. To defend, administer, and maintain communications across wide territories required some decentralization of authority and greater mobility and autonomy for individuals. Warriors and administrators were assigned land and became independent proprietors. Merchants became entrepreneurs working with their own capital. Craftsmen began to work for the market rather than for the temple or royal household. A market economy emerged to facilitate exchanges among independent producers and consumers and progressively supplanted the older forms of household redistributive economy. The spread of markets and the introduction, by the seventh or sixth century BC, of money as the medium of exchange transformed the economic structures of the ancient world. For increasing numbers of people the cash nexus replaced patrimonial authority as the mechanism that regulated the way they earned a living.

Empires also fostered the emergence of social individuality by providing the linguistic, religious, and legal conditions that freed individuals from absorption into clans, temples, and royal households, enabling them to function in a more open society. The language of the dominant elites became the language of the cosmopolitan elements of the society; the remote and powerful gods of the king and the empire – the gods of the cosmos, organized into a pantheon – superseded the intimate gods of individual localities. Imperial law regulated the distribution of property, economic exchange, and relations between the strong and the weak. Ancient empires, then, were not only political agencies, but provided the cultural, religious, and legal bases of society. Alongside religion they were a powerful force for the cultural integration of Middle Eastern civilization.

For ancient peoples, the empires symbolized the realm of civilization. The function of empires was to defend the civilized world against the barbarians and to assimilate them into the sphere of higher culture. For their part, the barbarians, mostly nomadic peoples, wanted to conquer empires, share in their wealth and sophistication, and win for themselves the status of civilized men. Empires commanded allegiance because they were a coalition of civilized peoples against the darkness without. They commanded allegiance because kingship was thought of as a divine institution and the king was a divinely selected agent, a person who, if not himself a god, shared in the aura, magnificence, sacredness, and mystery of the divine. The ruler was God's agent, his priest, the channel between this world and the heavens, designated by the divine being to bring justice and right order to men so that they might in turn serve God. The king thus assured the prosperity and well-being of his subjects. Magically he upheld the order of the universe against chaos.

From these earliest empires to the eve of the Islamic era, the history of the Middle East may be summarized as the elaboration and expansion of the institutions formed in this early period. While parochial communities and local cultures were a continuing force in Middle Eastern society, empires grew progressively larger, each wave of expansion and contraction bringing new peoples into the sphere of imperial civilization. Empires came and went, but the legacy of interchange of populations – the movement of soldiers, administrators, merchants, priests, scholars, and workers – left a permanent imprint of cosmopolitan culture and a heritage of shared laws, languages, scripts, and social identity.

From Sargon to Hammurapi, Middle Eastern empires were restricted to Mesopotamia, but later Hittite, Kassite, and other "barbarian" empires brought Mesopotamia, Anatolia, and Iran into a common network. The empire of Assyria (911–612 BC) brought Iraq, western Iran, and, for a time, Egypt into a single state. The Achaemenid empire (550–331 BC) incorporated eastern Iran and formed the first universal Middle Eastern empire – the first to include all settled peoples from the Oxus River to the Nile and the Dardanelles.

With the destruction of the Achaemenid empire by Alexander the Great, the Middle East was divided into two empires. Iraq and Iran as far as the Oxus River belonged to the Persian or eastern empires – the Parthian empire (226 BC–AD 234) and its successor, the Sasanian empire (AD 234–634). In the west the successor states to the empire of Alexander became part of the Roman empire. The Late Roman empire, called the Byzantine empire, governed southern Europe, the Balkans, Anatolia, northern Syria, and parts of Mesopotamia, Egypt, and North Africa.

RELIGION AND SOCIETY BEFORE ISLAM

The development of more encompassing empires and empire-wide civilizations was paralleled by the transformation of religions. The earliest religions were religions of nature and place, associated with small communities. The gods of Middle Eastern peoples were, in ancient times, the gods of families, tribes, villages, and towns, but with the growing connections between peoples, universal gods came to be recognized. The gods of empires, the gods of dominant peoples, the gods of conquerors, travelers, merchants, and priests whose activities were not circumscribed by a single locality came to be worshiped over large areas. The tendency toward syncretism and unification was also expressed by the conception of a pantheon and hierarchy of gods, which allowed different peoples to share in the same universe while preserving local cults and forms of worship.

From the universal supremacy of the great gods it was but one step, an inspired leap, to the revelation that there was but one God, who was the God of the whole universe and of all mankind. The oneness of God was preached first by the prophets of ancient Israel and then, in the seventh century BC, by the Iranian prophet Zoroaster. Christianity, and later Islam, would also teach the unity of God, the universality of his sway, and the obligation of all of mankind to acknowledge his glory. The missionary force of the new ideas and doctrines, the widening net of contacts among Middle Eastern peoples, and the support of the great empires made Judaism, Zoroastrianism, and Christianity the religions of almost all peoples in the Roman–Byzantine and Sasanian empires. Some of Iraq and all of Iran adhered to the Zoroastrian religion, including its main heresies, Manichaeanism and Mazdaism. Parts of Iraq and all the regions of the Byzantine empire to the west adhered to one of the several forms of Christianity. The Coptic Church was the church of Egypt; the Jacobite was the church of Syria; the Nestorian Church prevailed in Iraq. The population of Armenia followed the Armenian Church, while the populations of Anatolia and the Balkans adhered in the main to the Greek Orthodox Church. Numerous Jewish communities and a few pagan enclaves were scattered throughout the area.

The monotheistic faiths held similar beliefs. Judaism taught that there was a single God of the universe who commanded his people, Israel, to fulfill his holy law, and who would judge them in this world and the next. Zoroastrianism held to a belief in a supreme God, Ahura Mazda, the creator of the world, a God of light and truth. The destiny of the world was thought to be decided by God's struggle with the forces of evil and darkness. Man was a part of this struggle: he had the obligation to contribute to the victory of the Good and Light by his actions and beliefs, and would be judged at the day of judgment. Zoroastrianism, like Judaism, was a religion of individual ethical responsibility. While Christianity held many similar beliefs, it was a religion of a different type. The central Christian doctrine is faith in a triune God – God the Father, the Son, and the Holy Spirit, the Son being the *logos*, Christ incarnate, who was crucified so that believers may be saved. Christianity has a strong ethical strand, but its central aspiration was salvation through faith in Christ from the evil and suffering that is inherent in man's nature.

Though different in orientation, Judaism, Zoroastrianism, and Christianity had certain basic features in common. All were transcendental. They held that beyond the world of this life there is a higher world, the realm of the divine, to be attained either through ethical action or through faith in God. Through sacrifice, prayer, and sacrament, they sought salvation from sin and death, and entrance for men into the eternal reality beyond the ephemeral appearances of this world. Furthermore, they were universal religions, believing that God had created and continued to govern the whole universe and all men. Before God, believers are individually responsible for their faith and their ethical character. Believers are thus brothers in a common religious way of life and a common quest for salvation.

This sense of identity and the common ways of life were more than sentiments. Religious belief inspired the formation of religious associations of which the best examples were the Christian churches. A church was a spiritual and administrative hierarchy in which the highest authority in both doctrinal and organizational matters belonged to a supreme head, who communicated with the body of believers through a territorially organized hierarchy. Popes and patriarchs held supreme authority. They appointed the bishops who administered the districts called dioceses, and the bishops appointed the parish priests. The Zoroastrians had their *mobads* or fire priests, and at some time in the third century acquired a chief mobad, and thus a similar hierarchy of clergy. These hierarchies integrated different localities into a common body, and defined the doctrines and principles by which they lived.

The parish implemented the church's principles at the local level. At this level Christian churches wielded considerable authority in the lives of their communicants in what we would now consider secular as well as religious matters. Church courts had jurisdiction in many areas of civil law such as family, property, commerce, and even in some matters of criminal law. The church was also an important educational institution. Bishops were sometimes the governors and administrators of the cities in which their dioceses were located. With bishops as its magistrates, a church was an organization for the management of communal life, a kind of civic corporation based on religion. The churches did not separate the secular from the religious, but religion provided the overarching concepts by which man could comprehend the social and natural universe that surrounded him, and was the institution through which the needs of worship, justice, education, and local administration could be served.

Jewish communities were also organized as the equivalent of local parishes. They also combined belief and worship with the civil administration of law, education, and charity. The heads of the Jewish communities represented them before the state authorities. Jews, however, did not have a hierarchical ecclesiastical organization, but were linked together by informal ties to and respect for the great academies of learning. Both the organized Christian churches and the decentralized Jewish communities were precedents for the later organization of Muslim religious associations.

On the eve of Islam, then, the Middle East was divided into two great realms of polity and culture, Byzantine and Sasanian, and two overlapping spheres of religious belief, Christian and Zoroastrian. Despite profound differences, the two realms of Middle Eastern civilization shared certain underlying similarities in the organization of empires, in religious beliefs, and in the structures of religious and communal life. Within each civilization, a myriad of small communities retained their social and cultural distinctiveness. Their headmen, chiefs, and elders mediated their integration into the overarching realms of common religion and empire. Religion and empire were also closely related. The empires sustained, patronized, endowed, and enforced the organized worship of the churches. The Sasanian empire, however, was by and large tolerant of the various religions under its jurisdiction while the Byzantine empire insisted on religious unity and persecuted schismatic churches. In turn the religious communities legitimized the emperors' reigns and helped govern the subjects in their name.

The two political and religious regions, with their common institutional forms, would soon be drawn into a single Middle Eastern civilization. The Arab conquests of the seventh century and the Islamic era that followed preserved the continuity of Middle Eastern institutions. Family, lineage, clientele, and ethnic communities continued, despite historical change, to be the building blocks of society. The regional ecology continued to be based upon agrarian and urban communities, and the economy functioned on the basis of marketing and money exchanges. The basic forms of state organization, including bureaucratic administration, and the predominant style of religious life, focusing upon universal and transcendental

Table 1. *Islam in world history*

Early village farming communities	c. 7000 BC
Cities	c. 3000 BC
Empires	c. 2400 BC
Axial-age and monotheistic religions	c. 800 BC
Muhammad	c. 570–632
Middle Eastern Islamic societies	622–c. 1200
Worldwide diffusion of Islam	c. 650 to present
Rise of European world empires	1200–1900
Modern transformation of Islamic societies	1800 to present

beliefs and a parish-like community organization, were also maintained. Islam, however, redefined the religious beliefs and the cultural and social identity of Middle Eastern peoples and reorganized the empires that ruled them.

This transformation took place in three main phases: first, the creation of a new Islamic community in Arabia as a result of the transformation of a peripheral region with a predominantly lineage society into a Middle Eastern type of monotheistic and politically centralized society. The second phase began with the conquest of the Middle East by this new Arabian-Muslim community, and led to the generation, in the period of the early Caliphate (to 945), of an Islamic empire and culture. Finally, in the post-imperial or Sultanate period (945–c. 1200) the institutional and cultural prototypes of the Caliphal era were transformed into new types of Islamic states and institutions. In this era Islam became the religion and the basis of communal organization of the mass of Middle Eastern peoples. In the first phase we see the emergence of Islam in a tribal society. In the second we consider Islam as it becomes the religion of an imperial state and urban elite. In the third phase we see how Islamic values and elites transformed the masses of Middle Eastern peoples.

THE PREACHING OF ISLAM

CHAPTER 1

ARABIA

On the eve of the Islamic era, Arabia stood on the periphery of the Middle Eastern imperial societies in a state of development equivalent to the ancient rather than the evolved condition of the rest of the region. Here the primary communities remained especially powerful, while urban, religious, and royal institutions, though not absent, were less developed. Whereas the imperial world was predominantly agricultural, Arabia was primarily pastoral. While the imperial world was citied, Arabia was the home of camps and oases. Whereas the imperial peoples were committed to the monotheistic religions, Arabia was largely pagan. While the imperial world was politically organized, Arabia was politically fragmented.

At the same time, Arabia was always in close contact with and strongly under the influence of the imperial regions. There were no physical boundaries between Arabia and the Middle East proper. No rigid ethnic or demographic frontier isolated Arabia from the rest of the region; nor did great walls or political boundaries. Arabian peoples migrated slowly into the Middle East and made up much of the population of the desert margins of Syria and Iraq. Arabs in the fertile crescent region shared political forms, religious beliefs, economic connections, and physical space with the societies around them. Arabia was further connected to the rest of the region by itinerant preachers, who introduced monotheism into the largely pagan peninsula; by merchants who brought textiles, jewelry, and foodstuffs such as grain and wine into Arabia and stimulated the taste for the good things of life; and by the agents of the imperial powers who intervened diplomatically and politically to extend their trading privileges, protect sympathetic religious populations, and advance their strategic interests. The Byzantines and the Sasanians disputed control of Yemen, and both were active in creating spheres of influence in North Arabia. They also exported military technique to the Arabs. From the Romans and the Persians the Arabs obtained new arms, and learned how to use armor. They learned new tactics, and the importance of discipline. This seepage of military technique came through the enrollment of Arabs as auxiliaries in the Roman or Persian

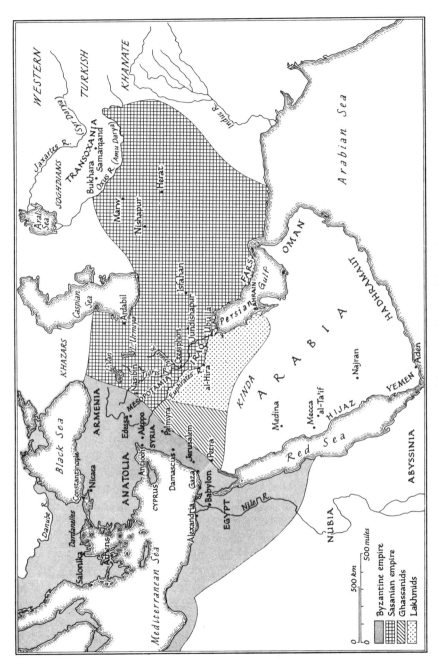

Map 1 The Middle East on the eve of the Muslim era

armies, and sometimes through the unhappy experience of being repulsed by superior forces on the frontiers of the empires.

Thus the civilization of the Middle Eastern empires was seeping into Arabia as happened everywhere where developed empires maintained frontiers with politically and culturally less organized societies. These influences and the need to mobilize the power and resources required to maintain political autonomy, or to carry on trade with empires, stimulated in less developed societies the same processes of stratification, specialization, and of community and identity formation by which the empires had themselves come into being. They generated in peripheral areas just those conditions that allowed for the eventual amalgamation of empire and outside areas into a single society. By the late sixth century, however, these inducements to evolutionary change had not gone so far as to absorb Arabia into the general civilization of the Middle East, or to inspire in it the birth of a new civilization.

CLANS AND KINGDOMS

From the beginning of camel domestication and the occupation of the central Arabian desert in the thirteenth and twelfth centuries BC until the rise of Islam in the seventh century, the balance between parochial elements and the unifying forces of religion and empire lay heavily on the side of small, relatively isolated communities. Families and clans, often pastoralists and camel herders, and the confederations built upon them, were the basic units of society. The bedouins raised camels and migrated seasonally in search of pasturage. They also provided caravans with animals, guides, and guards. They passed the winter in desert reserves, migrating to seek spring pasturage at the first signs of rain. In the summer they usually camped near villages or oases, where they exchanged animal products for grain, dates, utensils, weapons, and cloth.

The migratory peoples lived in tight-knit kinship groups, patriarchal families formed of a father, his sons, and their families. These families were further grouped into clans of several hundred tents, which migrated together, owned pasturage in common, and fought as one in battle. Each clan was fundamentally an independent unit. All loyalties were absorbed by the group, which acted as a collectivity to defend its individual members and to meet their responsibilities. If a member was harmed, the clan would avenge him. If he did harm, it would stand responsible with him. As a consequence of this group solidarity, called *'asabiya*, the bedouin clan regarded itself as a complete polity and recognized no external authority. Each clan was led by a *shaykh* (chief) who was usually selected by the clan elders from one of the prominent families and who always acted in accordance with their counsel. He settled internal disputes according to the group's traditions, but he could not legislate or command. The shaykh had to be wealthy and show generosity to the needy and to his supporters; he had to be a man of exquisite tact and prudence – forbearing, resolute, and practical. Above all, he had to have the good judgment to avoid antagonizing his sensitive followers.

The clan defined the mental universe of the bedouin. Poetry expressed a fundamental devotion to the prestige and security of the group; without the clan, the individual had no place in the world, no life of his own. The language of the bedouins offered no way to express the concept of individuality or personality. The term *wajh* (face), although applied to the chief, was really a concept designating the persona of the group rather than the individuality of the shaykh as a person.

In certain conditions the bedouins could be integrated into more inclusive, often stratified, bodies. At the points of contact between the fertile parts of Arabia and the desert, at oases in Yemen, and in the northern margins where the Arabian desert touches the fertile crescent, confederations organized caravans and trade. The formation of a *haram*, a common sanctuary, also allowed for worship of the same gods, economic exchange, sociability, and political bargaining.

Monarchies and kingdoms took shape on the peripheries. In South Arabia, royal authority was first established about 1000 BC and lasted until the Muslim era. By the fifth century BC, Yemen was organized into kingdoms encompassing agricultural, trading, and pastoral peoples, with monarchs, landed elites, a religious pantheon, and organized temple worship of the gods. The political elite was drawn from aristocratic tribes and controlled extensive landed estates. Temples also had substantial holdings, while the commoners were organized into clans that were obliged to provide agricultural and military services to the elites. Tributary and vassal tribes extended the power of the Yemeni kingdoms well into the interior of Arabia. In the north, kingdoms were less fully institutionalized. The Nabatean kingdom (sixth century BC–AD 106) was ruled by a king but really depended on a supporting coalition of clan and tribal chiefs. From 85 BC, the Nabateans, with their capital at Petra, controlled much of Jordan and Syria, and traded with Yemen, Egypt, Damascus, and the coastal cities of Palestine until it was destroyed by the Romans in AD 106. Palmyra succeeded Petra, extending monarchical control over the deserts and surrounding border areas. An urban capital, elaborate temples, wide commercial networks, and a strong Hellenistic culture marked Palmyran supremacy. These kingdoms maintained economic and political order throughout the peninsula by bringing the bedouins of the desert interiors into the political, commercial, and cultural frameworks of the periphery.

The balance of power between the clans of the desert interior and the large-scale societies of the periphery was historically variable. From about 1000 BC until about AD 300 Yemen, the Hijaz, and the northern periphery successfully organized the interior of the peninsula and kept bedouin life subordinate to the agricultural and commercial economies of the settled kingdoms, but the opening of sea routes for international trade in the first century BC brought financial and political disaster to Yemen. Political power in the south further weakened with the failure of overland routes; bedouins interfered in internal conflicts, pushed in against agricultural areas, and cut off Yemeni influence in the Hijaz and in central Arabia. In AD 328, Imru al-Qays b. 'Amr, king of the Arabs, took control of Najran. In the north, Palmyra was destroyed in AD 271 – the victim, as were the Nabateans, of Roman efforts to incorporate northern Arabia directly into the empire. By the end of the third century, the peripheral kingdoms had lost control of the center of the peninsula.

From the early fourth century to the end of the sixth century, there were several efforts to reestablish the dominance of peripheral kingdoms, restore order in the desert, and protect trade and oasis cultivation. In Yemen, the Himyarite kingdom was reestablished, and its influence, mediated by the tribal confederation of Kinda, extended over the bedouins of the Hijaz and central Arabia. After the destruction of Petra and Palmyra, the Romans attempted to defend these provinces by recruiting Arab confederates to guard them against other Arabs and the Sasanians. At the end of the fifth century the Ghassan, an Arab-Christian people, defended Syria and Palestine against the bedouins and the Persians. The Sasanian empire also maintained a buffer state – the kingdom of Lakhm, a coalition of Aramean and Christian tribes along the border between Iraq and the desert, organized under the leadership of the Lakhm family whose capital was at al-Hira, on the lower reaches of the Euphrates. The new peripheral regimes, however, were less powerful than their predecessors, and in the course of the sixth century they all disintegrated. The South Arabian economy crumbled, and political unity was completely lost. In the North, the Romans and Persians removed their vassals and attempted to partition north Arabia and absorb it into their respective empires. In the early seventh century the Byzantine and Sasanian empires engaged in mutually exhausting wars. Thus, the middle-period confederations had been destroyed by outside powers who could not replace even their limited contributions to political and economic order.

In the sixth century, only Mecca stood against the trend towards political and social fragmentation. A religious sanctuary whose shrine, the Ka'ba, attracted pilgrims from all over Arabia, Mecca became the repository of the various idols and tribal gods of the peninsula, and the destination of an annual pilgrimage. The pilgrimage also entailed a period of truce, which served not only for religious worship, but also for the arbitration of disputes, the settlement of claims and debts, and, of course, trade. The Meccan fairs gave the Arabian tribes a common identity and gave Mecca moral primacy in much of western and central Arabia.

These fairs were the origin of Mecca's commercial interests. The people called the Quraysh, who took control of Mecca in the fifth century, became a skilled retailing population. In the sixth century they found a place in the spice trade as well, as difficulties with other international trade routes diverted traffic to the overland Arabian route. Byzantine sea power in the Red Sea and the Indian Ocean was on the decline; piracy was endemic in the Red Sea. At the same time, the Persian Gulf–Tigris–Euphrates route was harassed by Sasanian exploitation, and was frequently disrupted by Lakhm, Ghassan, and Persian–Roman wars. By the mid-sixth century, as heir to Petra and Palmyra, Mecca became one of the important caravan cities of the Middle East. The Meccans carried spices, leather, drugs, cloth, and slaves which had come from Africa or the Far East to Syria, and returned money, weapons, cereals, and wine to Arabia. The trade required treaties with Byzantine officials and with the bedouins to assure safe passage of the caravans, protection of water and pasture rights, and guides and scouts. Such arrangements eventually gave Mecca a sphere of political as well as commercial influence among the nomads and created a confederation of client tribes. In association with the Tamim tribes, a loose Meccan diplomatic hegemony was established in the desert. With the decline of Abyssinia, Ghassan, and Lakhm, Meccan influence was about the only integrative political force in late sixth-century Arabia.

In most of Arabia, however, the failure of the border powers led to bedouinization. As bedouin communities were set free of the political and commercial controls once exerted by the border kingdoms, violent conflicts between clans and tribes became more frequent. In the fourth, fifth, and sixth centuries, bedouin marauders harassed the caravan trade, and bedouin migrations converted marginal regions in Yemen and on the borders of Iraq and Syria back to pasturage. The bedouinization of Arabia did not, of course, occur all at once. It was a gradual and cumulative process, shifting the ever-delicate balance between organized polities and clan societies in favor of the latter.

In the late sixth century, the confrontation between strengthened small communities and trading and religious confederacy was reflected in the cultural as well as the political life of Arabia. Just as the political realm was beset by the tension among different types of political and economic organization, cultural life was beset by incompatible visions of human life, human society, and conflicting concepts of the cosmos and the gods.

POETRY AND THE GODS

The poetic and religious culture of the clans remained a fundamental element in bedouin life. The Arabian bedouin was an animist and a polytheist who believed that all natural objects and events were living spirits who could be either helpful or harmful to man. The universe of the Arabs was peopled with *jinn* (demons), who had to be propitiated or controlled and defeated by magic. By magical practices, the bedouin might determine his fate or coerce these forces, but he had no sympathetic relation with them. They were another tribe, not his own. The bedouins also worshiped ancestors, moon and star gods, and gods in the form of stones or trees placed in protective sanctuaries. Otherwise, their religion did not entail a philosophic vision of the universe, though it expressed their sense of the sacred as vested mysteriously in the plethora of forces that dominated the natural world and the being of man.

The religions of the politically more complex confederations and kingdoms were also polytheistic, but they expressed a more differentiated concept of the divine, the natural, and the human worlds. The tribal harams and the temples of archaic kingdoms were devoted to regularized cultic worship. The Meccan Ka'ba, for example, the center of a pilgrimage, was the sanctuary of numerous gods arranged in a hierarchy. These gods were no longer simply identified with nature; they were defined as distinct persons separate from the natural forces that, as willful beings, they controlled. Such gods had to be propitiated by sacrifices; one could communicate with them as persons.

In an environment of shared sanctuaries, new conceptions of collective identity emerged. The annual trade and religious fairs at Mecca and other places of pilgrimage brought the numerous families and tribes of the peninsula together, focused the worship of tribal peoples upon common cults, allowed them to observe each other's mores, and standardized the language and customs by which they dealt with each other. Awareness of common religious beliefs and lifestyles, recognition of aristocratic tribes and families, agreed institutions regulating pasturage, warfare, commerce, alliance and arbitration procedures, a poetic *koine* used by reciters of poems throughout Arabia – marked the development of a collective identity transcending the individual clan.

Still, there was a profound similarity between the cultic confederation of Mecca and the fragmented life of the bedouin clans. The bedouin mentality and Meccan polytheism both held the same view of the person, society, and the universe. This view afforded no coherent conception of the human being as an entity. In ancient Arabic there was no single word meaning the person. *Qalb* (heart), *ruh* (spirit), *nafs* (soul), and wajh (face) were several terms in use, none of which corresponds to the concept of an integrated personality. The plurality of the gods reflected and symbolized a fragmented view of the nature of man, of society, and of the forces that governed the cosmos. In the pagan view the self was without a center, society without wholeness, and the universe without overall meaning.

The monotheistic religions stood for something other. They were introduced into Arabia by foreign influences: Jewish and Christian settlements, traveling preachers and merchants, and the political pressure of the Byzantine empire and Abyssinia. By the sixth century, monotheism already had a certain vogue. Many non-believers understood the monotheistic religions; others, called *hanif* in the Quran, were believers in one God but not adherents of any particular faith. Christians settled in Yemen, in small oases, and in the border regions of the north; they were a minority but were profoundly influential and, to many people, deeply appealing, both by the force of their teaching and by force of representing what was felt to be a more powerful, more sophisticated, and more profound civilization. These new religions taught that there was a single God who created the moral and spiritual order of the world; a God who made men individually responsible for their actions and faith; a God who made all men brethren, whatever their race or clan; and a God who made their salvation possible.

Thus, the monotheists differed profoundly from the polytheists in their sense of the unity of the universe and the meaningfulness of personal experience. Whereas the polytheists could see only a fragmented world, composed of numerous, disorderly, and arbitrary powers, the monotheists saw the universe as a totality grounded in, and created and governed by, a single being who was the source of both material and spiritual order. Whereas the polytheists envisaged a society in which people were divided by clan and locality, each with its own community and its own gods, the monotheists imagined a society in which common faith made men brothers in the quest for salvation. Whereas in the polytheistic view the human being was a concatenation of diverse forces without any moral or psychic center, a product of the fates, in the monotheistic view he was a moral, purposive creature whose ultimate objective was redemption. In the view of the monotheistic religions, God, the universe, man, and society were part of a single, meaningful whole.

Nowhere was this confrontation of world-views more important than in Mecca. Mecca was one of the most complex and heterogeneous places in Arabia. Here society had grown beyond the limitations of the clan and tribe to afford some complexity of political and economic ties. Mecca had a council of clans (*mala*), although it held only a moral authority, with non-independent powers of enforcement. Mecca was also one of the few places in Arabia to have a floating, non-tribal population of individual exiles, refugees, outlaws, and foreign merchants. The very presence of different peoples and clans – people belonging to no clan, foreigners, people with diverse religious convictions, differing views of life's purposes and values – moved Meccans away from the old tribal religions and moral conceptions. New conceptions of personal worth and social status and new social relationships were fostered in this more complex society. On the positive side, the imperatives of commercial activity, and Arabia-wide contacts and identifications set individuals free from the traditions of their clans and allowed for the flourishing of self-conscious, critical spirits, who were capable of experimenting with new values, and who might conceive a universal God and universal ethics. On the negative side, society suffered from economic competition, social conflict, and moral confusion. Commercial activities brought in their wake social stratification on the basis of wealth, and morally inassimilable discrepancies between individual situations and the imperatives of clan loyalty. The Quran would condemn the displacement of tribal virtues by the ambition, greed, arrogance, and hedonism of the new rich. Mecca, which had begun to give Arabia some measure of political and commercial order, was losing its moral and social identity.

Arabia was in ferment: a society in the midst of constructive political experiments was endangered by anarchy; strong clan and tribal powers threatened to overwhelm the fragile forces of agricultural stability, commercial activity, and political cohesion. It was a society touched by imperial influences but without a central government; marked by the monotheistic religions but without an established church; susceptible to Middle Eastern ideas but not permeated by them. Arabia had yet to find its place in the Middle Eastern world. Here Muhammad was born, was vouchsafed the Quran, and here he became the Prophet of Islam.

CHAPTER 2

THE LIFE OF THE PROPHET

Prophecy is a rare phenomenon, and all the more extraordinary is the prophet whose influence permanently transforms the lives of his people and leaves as a legacy one of the world's great religions. Thus the life of Muhammad and the rise of Islam have to be understood in terms of both religious vision and worldly impact. Compared with the founders of other great religions, the sources of our knowledge of the Prophet's life are abundant. We have the Quran itself, Muslim scripture, believed by Muslims to have been revealed by God through the angel Gabriel to Muhammad – the direct revelation of God's word and will, the ultimate source of Muslim belief, and the inspiration to live in the way God requires of human beings. In the Muslim view the Quran is the final revelation and supersedes the previous Jewish and Christian dispensations. The Prophet himself probably began the process of compiling a written scripture by dictating to scribes and instructing them on how to order the verses of the revelation. The Quran was fully compiled after the Prophet's death and an official version promulgated by the Caliph 'Uthman (644–56). Because of various problems of script and variant non-'Uthmanic traditions, small points of detail remained in dispute until the tenth century, when Muslim scholars agreed to consider seven variant readings equally valid.

The *hadith,* or sayings of the Prophet, are a second source. In the Muslim view, these are Muhammad's own inspired utterances, as opposed to Quranic utterances. Hadith deal mainly with ritual, moral, and other religious matters. The third principal source of the Prophet's life is the biography compiled by Ibn Ishaq (d. 768–69) on the basis of oral tradition and partial written accounts and then edited and revised by Ibn Hisham (d. 833–34). Materials not included in Ibn Hisham's edition are found in later Muslim sources.

From these sources we know that the Quran was revealed over the last two decades of Muhammad's life, from about 610 until his death in 632. As it unfolded over time, the Quran dealt with specific historical circumstances; later Muslim commentators have provided us with information about the events associated with

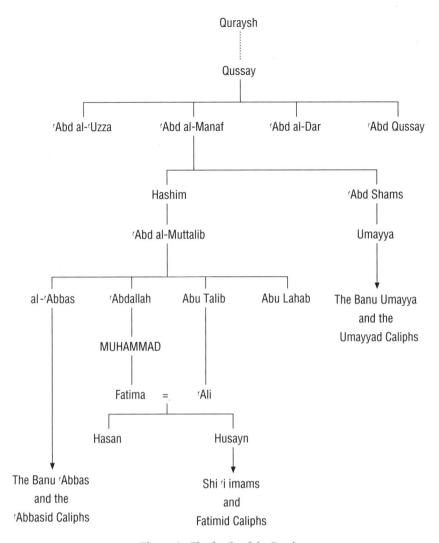

Figure 1   The family of the Prophet

particular revelations. Verses of the Quran deal with Muhammad's debate with the Meccans and his handling of political and social problems in Medina, and provide concrete guidance for ritual, moral, legal, and political matters. The Quran, viewed as a historical document, shows how Muhammad's vision developed in direct response to concrete circumstances. In his biography we do not see him propounding a fixed system of belief. He was a judge rather than a legislator, a counselor rather than a theorist. We see the Prophet as a man to whom the revelation has given a new direction in life, a direction whose implications and possibilities constantly unfold before him.

MUHAMMAD IN MECCA

Muhammad was born around AD 570 into the once-prominent clan of Banu Hashim. His ancestors had been guardians of the sacred well of Zamzam in Mecca, but by his time the clan, though engaged in commerce, was not among the most influential. Muhammad's father died before he was born. He was raised by his grandfather and then by his uncle, Abu Talib. Muhammad worked as a caravaner, and at twenty-five married his employer, Khadija, a rich widow. They had four daughters and several sons; all the boys died in infancy. In the years before the revelations Muhammad was wont to retreat to the mountains outside Mecca to pray in solitude. A tradition reported as coming from Ibn Ishaq but not found in the recension of Ibn Hisham indicates that Muhammad received advice and support from a hanif – an Arabian monotheist, a believer in one God though not a Jew or a Christian – who taught him about the futility of worshiping idols.

About the year 610, the seeker after religious truth received his first revelations. They came upon him like the breaking of dawn. The first words revealed to him were the opening five lines of *sura* (chapter) 96: "Recite: In the Name of thy Lord who created, created Man of a blood-clot. Recite: And thy Lord is the Most Generous, who taught by the Pen, taught Man that he knew not." His consciousness of the presence of the divine brought awe, fear, and foreboding.

In the early years the content of these revelations was the vision of a great, just God, Allah, who would on the day of judgment weigh every man's works and consign him to bliss or damnation. The early revelations emphasized the fear of the last judgment, piety and good works, and warnings against neglect of duties and heedlessness of the final day of reckoning. Opposed to the worship of God and fear of the last judgment were presumption, pride in human powers, and attachment to the things of this world. This was the false pride of the Meccans, which led them to the sin of avarice – neglect of almsgiving and the poor. In addition to preaching these ideas, Muhammad instituted ritual prayer. Eschatological piety, ethical nobility, and prayer formed the basis of early Islam.

The revelation in the Quran bore important similarities to Christianity and Judaism. For Muhammad the revelations came from the same source. Christian parallels are evident in the articulation of Muhammad's vision of the last judgment – the prediction that it would come with thunder, trumpets, and earthquakes, that the world would be destroyed and the dead resurrected, that it would be a terrifying moment when, one by one, all men passed before God, the angels interceding only for the good. These details were found in the preaching of itinerant Syrian monks and missionaries at the fairs of Arabia. Ideas similar to Judaism, such as uncompromising monotheism, belief in written revelations, the conception of a prophet sent to a chosen people, and certain specific religious practices are also prominent in the Quran. Yet Muhammad's inspiration and the language in which it was couched were original. He had been vouchsafed a personal knowledge of God's being and will, and must have understood his revelation in the sense of the Arabian monotheists, who believed in a transcendent God but were neither Jews nor Christians.

For three years after the first revelations, Muhammad remained a private person, coming to terms with God's message. He related his experiences to his family and friends, and the force of his inspiration and the compelling language in which it was clothed persuaded them that his visions were indeed divine revelations. A small group of people accepted his ideas and gathered around him to hear and recite the Quran. These were the first converts, and they included his wife Khadija, Abu Bakr and 'Ali, later to be Caliphs (the Prophet's successors as leaders of the Muslims), and others.

After three years the time had come for a public mission. In about 613 Muhammad received the revelation that begins "Rise and warn." He began to preach publicly, a first step toward injecting religious ideas into the actualities of social and political life. Significantly, the first converts were rootless migrants, poor men, members of weak clans, and younger sons of strong clans – those people most dissatisfied with the changing moral and social climate of Mecca, for whom the Prophet's message proved a vital alternative.

Still, apart from his small following, Muhammad's preaching met with almost universal opposition. From the Quran we know that the Quraysh, the traders who dominated Meccan life, belittled Muhammad's revelations. They scoffed at the bizarre notion of a last judgment and resurrection, and asked for miracles as proof of the truth of his message. Muhammad's only response – still the Muslim response – was that the Quran itself, with its unique beauty of language, is a miracle and a sign of revelation. Nonetheless the Quraysh denounced Muhammad as a *kahin*, a soothsayer, a disreputable sort of magician or madman. Then came insults, harassment of Muhammad and his followers, and an economic boycott that extended to keeping the Muslims from purchasing food in the markets.

This opposition was couched in religious terms, but Muhammad's preaching was in fact an implicit challenge to all the existing institutions of the society – worship of gods and the economic life attached to their shrines, the values of tribal tradition, the authority of the chiefs and the solidarity of the clans from which Muhammad wished to draw his followers. Religion, moral belief, social structure, and economic life formed a system of ideas and institutions inextricably bound up with one another. To attack them at any major point was to attack the whole society root and branch.

The revelations of the Quran provided Muhammad with a response to this opposition. He was justified in his preaching because he was sent by God to rescue his people from ignorance and guide them on the path to righteousness. He was a prophet in the long succession of Old and New Testament and Arabian prophets; he was a prophet sent to declare God's will in Arabic. At this stage Muhammad included Christians and Jews, as well as pagans, in his mission. Only later did it become clear that his preaching would establish a new religion alongside Judaism and Christianity.

As Muhammad's mission unfolded it became clear that it involved not only the presentation of the Quranic revelation, but the leadership of the community. Prophecy implied eschatological vision and knowledge of God's will, which in turn entailed right guidance and social leadership. We have a concrete sign that as early as 615 Muhammad had become the leader of a community, and that those who believed in his teachings constituted a group set apart from other Meccans. In that year, a group of his followers departed for Abyssinia. For the sake of religion people were willing to leave their families and clans and take up life together in a foreign land. The bonds of common belief were stronger than the bonds of blood. In this way, the new religion threatened to dissolve the old order of society and create a new one.

The opposition to Muhammad revealed yet another dimension of the relations between religion and society. It exposed the extent to which Muhammad's very survival in Mecca, to say nothing of his preaching, depended on his uncle, Abu Talib, and his clansmen, the Banu Hashim who protected him because he was their kinsman. With their support, Muhammad could, despite harassment, continue preaching. But from about 615 or 616, he no longer made many converts. He had by then about a hundred followers, but the Meccan boycott had made it clear that to join Muhammad was to invite hardship. The truth of his message and his oratorical, poetical, and personal qualities were no longer as persuasive because the man himself was insulted, hounded, and ostracized. For his mission to succeed, Muhammad would have to be in a more powerful position. People would not be moved by ideas alone, only by ideas propounded with commanding prestige.

In 619, Muhammad resolved to seek support outside Mecca. By then his situation had become precarious. His wife Khadija and his uncle Abu Talib were dead; the support of his clan had diminished. He finally decided to go to al-Ta'if, a nearby oasis, and call on the people there to accept him as Prophet. This venture proved naive. Muhammad was ridiculed and driven out. He also tried to find support among the bedouins, but again met with no success. Now Muhammad understood that to protect himself and his followers, to overcome the resistance of the Quraysh, and to gain a hearing from Arabians beyond the small circles spontaneously attracted to him, some kind of political base was necessary.

At this juncture, the situation of the agricultural oasis of Medina was a godsend. Like Mecca it was inhabited by various clans rather than by a single tribe, but unlike Mecca it was a settlement racked by bitter and even anarchic feuding between the leading tribal groups – the Aws and the Khazraj. Prolonged strife threatened the safety of men in the fields and called into question Medina's very existence. Unlike the bedouins, Medinans had to live as neighbors, and could not move from place to place.

Moreover, like Mecca, Medina was undergoing social changes that rendered the underlying bedouin form of kinship society obsolete. Agricultural rather than pastoral needs governed its economy. Its social life came increasingly to be dictated by spatial proximity rather than by kinship. Also, Medina had a large Jewish population, which may have made the populace as a whole more sympathetic to monotheism.

THE MEDINA YEARS

At a crucial impasse in his own life Muhammad made his first converts in Medina, and after a protracted set of negotiations was invited to come to the troubled city. In 620 six men of Khazraj accepted him as Prophet. In 621 a dozen men representing both Khazraj and Aws pledged to obey Muhammad and to avoid sin, and in 622 a delegation of seventy-five Medinans paved the way for his coming to Medina by taking the pledge of al-ʿAqaba – the pledge to defend Muhammad.

Behind these agreements lie both acceptance of the Quranic revelation and Arabian precedents. In a society with no common law or government and no authority higher than the chiefs of individual clans, feuding clans often selected someone reputed to have religious vision and to be just, politic, tactful, and disinterested to be their arbitrator, or *hakam*. Because the hakams had no means of enforcing their decisions, it was common practice for a potential hakam to interview the disputants and assure himself that they would accept his decisions.

With the guarantees provided by the pledge, Muhammad and his followers made the journey to Medina – the most dramatic event in Muslim history. The community of Islam originated at that moment; the Muslim calendar dates the Christian year 622 as the year 1. The journey is called the *hijra,* which simply means "migration." For Muslims the word has come to mean not only a change of place, but the adoption of Islam and entry into the community of Muslims. The hijra is the transition from the pagan to the Muslim world – from kinship to a society based on common belief.

In Medina Muhammad and his Medinan hosts also came to a formal political agreement. Muhammad and his Meccan followers were to form one political group with the clans of Medina, called an *umma* – still the word for the community of Muslims. Meccans and Medinans would act as one in the defense of Muhammad and of Medina against outsiders. No clan would make a separate peace. No one would aid the Quraysh of Mecca, the presumptive enemy. The charter specified that all disputes would be brought before Muhammad. For Muhammad, moreover, the agreements were the first step toward converting political followers into religious believers. Without unity or effective leadership, his opponents were too divided to resist the consolidation of his power. The pagan clans were converted to Islam.

A crucial step in the consolidation of Muhammad's power was the elimination of the Jewish clans. In his early vision of himself as a prophet, Muhammad was sent by God to all Arabians – Jews and Christians as well as pagans – to restore the purity of the faith already revealed, preach a renewal, and end the corruption that had crept into daily life. Thus in Medina Muhammad had at first wanted to include

the Jews in his nascent community. Religious practices such as an equivalent to the
Jewish Day of Atonement and Jerusalem as the direction of prayer were meant to
appeal to the Jews. The Jewish clans, however, rejected Muhammad's claim to
being a prophet in the Hebrew tradition. They disputed his accounts of sacred history. In the course of this struggle new revelations denounced the Jews for having
broken their covenant. They revealed that Abraham was the prophet par excellence, the first hanif, the builder of the Ka'ba, and the father of the Arabs. The Quran
now stressed that Muhammad was sent to restore the pure monotheism of Abra-
ham. Bypassing the Jewish and Christian scriptural legacy, Muhammad's community would no longer include Jews and Christians, but would be a distinct religion
superseding Judaism and Christianity. To carry out his mission, Muhammad went
on to exile two of the Jewish clans, execute the male members of a third, and seize
their property for his followers. By winning over the Medinan pagans and destroying his opponents, including the Jewish clans, Muhammad made all of Medina a
Muslim community under his rule.

In the years that followed, Muhammad worked to create a community based on
shared religious beliefs, ceremonies, ethics, and laws – a community which would
transcend the traditional social structure based on families, clans, and tribes and
would unite disparate groups into a new Arabian society. This work proceeded on
several levels. First, the Quran set down the rituals of Islam. These include the five
pillars of the faith: *salat* (ritual prayer); *zakat* (almsgiving); *hajj* (pilgrimage); the
fast of Ramadan; and *shahada* (the obligation to bear witness to the unity of God
and the Prophethood of Muhammad). The five pillars were derived from Arabian,
Christian, and Jewish precedents and were public rituals that, when collectively performed, reinforced the collective awareness of the Muslim community and its members' consciousness of a special destiny. Brothers in religion shared alms just as
clan brothers shared their livelihoods. Prayer, fasting, and the bearing of witness
humbled men before God and made them open to his will. The pilgrimage was
derived from an ancient Arabian rite. Almsgiving was a symbol of the renunciation
of selfish greed and acceptance of responsibility for all members of the community
of faith.

The Quran also defined the social norms of the new community. Its teachings
on family law were the crux of a social and metaphysical revolution. In pre-Islamic
Arabian society, the basic family unit was the patriarchal agnatic clan, a group of
people descended directly in the male line from a common ancestor and under the
authority of the eldest male or chief member of the family. This was an extended
family of several generations, and several groups of married couples and their offspring, with collaterals and clients, were all considered part of one household.
Status, duties, and rights stemmed entirely from the clan. Property was regulated
by the customs of the group. Marriages were arranged by the heads of the families
with a view to the interests of the families rather than the wishes of the couple to
be married. Women were of inferior status and were not full members of the group.

A good marriage brought honor to the clan; if its female members were violated, the clan was dishonored. The group was responsible for defending the other members and making restitution in case of any crime committed by a member.

However, alongside the agnatic clan, various forms of polyandrous marriage of one woman to several men with varying degrees of permanence and responsibility for paternity, including temporary "marriages," were also known in Arabia. Polygamous arrangements varied from multiple wives in one residence to arrangements in which a man had several wives living with their own tribes whom he would visit on a rotating basis. No single norm was universally accepted. It was increasingly difficult to hold people to the ideal obligations regarding the distribution of property, the protection of women, or the guardianship of children.

In these confused conditions, Quranic teachings attempted to strengthen the patriarchal agnatic clan. The Quranic rules against incest were crucial for the viability of group life, for biological heredity, and for the creation of marriage bonds between families. Divorce, though still relatively easy, was discouraged. Polyandrous marriages were condemned because they undermined patriarchal family stability. Since the family descended through its male heirs, the Quran provided rules to assure knowledge of paternity. For example, in the event of divorce, a woman could only remarry after having three menstrual periods.

The family ideal was buttressed by a clear definition of its collective duties in the all-important matter of responsibility for crimes. As in pre-Islamic times, all the male kin were held responsible for the protection of family members, but the Quranic teachings tried to reduce the devastating effects of the blood feuds that often resulted from this obligation. They urged that the aggrieved party accept compensation in money rather than blood, and ruled that if blood retaliation were insisted upon, only the culprit himself could be slain, rather than any male relative. This modification did not end the law of blood revenge or the strong common responsibilities of family members to one another, but by restricting feuds it gave security to families, who no longer had to fear that the indiscretion of one member would in the end destroy them all.

Furthermore, in the context of the patriarchal family the Quran provided for moral and spiritual reform and introduced a new freedom and dignity to individual family members. In particular, it enhanced the status of women and children, who were no longer to be considered merely chattels or potential warriors but individuals with rights and needs of their own. For the benefit of women, marriage was recognized as having important spiritual and religious values. It was a relationship sanctioned by the will of Allah. The Quran urged respect for their modesty and privacy, that they be treated as feeling persons. The Quran also granted women certain specific rights that they did not enjoy in pre-Islamic Arabia. A woman was now able to hold property in her own name, and was not expected to contribute to the support of the household from her own property. She was given the right to inherit up to a quarter of her husband's estate, and, in case of divorce, retained the agreed-upon bridal gift. In addition, the Quran tried to protect women from hasty and willful divorces, by urging delay, reconciliation, and mediation by the families. The waiting period following a divorce also served to assure a woman of interim support and of support for a future child if she were pregnant. Finally, at least some possibility was opened for a divorce on the woman's initiative.

Nonetheless, despite the emphasis on the security and status of women, the Quran did not establish equality of rights for men and women. While the spirit of its teaching encouraged mutuality between husband and wife, and a greater sensitivity to the personal and moral worth of individuals, the prerogatives of males were left fundamentally intact. The Quranic ideal and Muhammad's example were probably much more favorable to women than was later Arab and Muslim practice.

This idea of the family was at the core of the Muslim conception of the individual person and the umma, the community of believers. The family ideals reinforced the concept of individuality by stressing the religious importance of individuals as God's creatures rather than as mere objects in the clan system of society, and by stressing the individual's responsibility for moral relations within the family. This sense of individuality was essential for a true appreciation of the Quranic teachings about the oneness of God and the responsibility of human beings before him at the last judgment. Only an ethical individual who acted out of inner choices could comprehend the transcendence and unity of God. Thus, the family teachings were essential to ethical individuality, which was in turn the basis of religious insight. Conversely, religious insight cultivated ethical responsibility, which in turn influenced the organization and conduct of family life. The teachings of the Quran, in contrast to the pagan view, cultivated a sense of the wholeness of the world, the unity of society, and the integrity of the person as aspects of a single transcendent vision of reality.

Apart from family laws and morals, the Quran dealt with many other communal problems. Norms for business transactions were set down – injunctions to deal justly, honor contracts, give true witness, and not take usurious interest. These norms were often couched in ethical rather than legal terms. For example, the prohibition of usury did not specify a maximum rate of interest on loans, but taught that no one should exploit people in need. Such norms were also given for the conduct of war, the treatment of prisoners, and the distribution of booty. There were moral prohibitions against gambling and the consumption of intoxicating beverages.

Thus, one dimension of Muhammad's work was to communicate the shared beliefs, common social norms, and common rituals that were the basis of a community transcending the clan and tribe. The other aspect of his work in Medina was to build the political confederation that would extend his reforms to Mecca and to the rest of Arabia. This was part of Muhammad's religious ambition, but it was also a matter of political necessity. If Mecca were opposed to Muhammad, she could eventually crush him in Medina. However, to bring Mecca under his influence required controlling the tribes of Arabia as well. Meccan wealth and power derived from trading operations which depended on the cooperation of the Arabian tribes. In short, both religious ambition and the political logic of Muhammad's removal to Medina required an Arabian as well as a Medinan confederation.

TRIUMPH AND THE RETURN TO MECCA

Muhammad's policy toward Mecca began with unremitting hostility. From the very first, small parties of the *muhajirun*, the exiled Meccans, raided Meccan trade caravans for booty. At first only Meccans were involved in the raids, but by 624 Muhammad's boldness, and the temptations of booty, enabled him to assemble a large force of Meccan exiles and Medinan supporters to attack an important Meccan caravan. At the battle of Badr, Muhammad defeated a larger Meccan force, decimated Mecca's leadership, and won tremendous prestige everywhere in Arabia. The battle was widely taken to be a sign of divine favor, and led to the defection of some of the bedouin tribes that protected Mecca's caravan lines, thus cutting the major trade routes between her and the north.

In the following years the initiative passed to the Meccans, who twice attacked Muhammad and Medina, first at the battle of Uhud (625) and then at the battle of the Ditch (627). The former was a defeat for Muhammad and the latter a stalemate, but Muhammad profited from both battles. He had survived the worst Mecca could do, and even managed on each occasion either to exile or execute some of the remaining Jewish clans, confiscate their property, and expand his influence over the desert tribes.

From this point, however, Muhammad relaxed rather than intensified the pressure on Mecca, for his object was not to fight Mecca to the death but to convert her people to Islam. In 628 Muhammad and a large group of followers made the pilgrimage to the Ka'ba, and proposed adopting it as part of Islam. They did this to show that Islam was an Arabian religion and would preserve the pilgrimage rites in which Mecca had so great a stake. The Meccans, however, were wary of Muhammad's intentions and intercepted him at a place called al-Hudaybiya. There Muhammad concluded a truce in which the Meccans agreed to admit the Muslims for the pilgrimage, but Muhammad had to drop his demand that he be recognized as the Prophet of God. Further, he even agreed to an unequal arrangement whereby children who left Mecca to become Muslims would have to be returned if they did not have parental consent, while Muslim apostates would not be returned. At one level the treaty was an embarrassment to Muhammad, but at another he made tremendous gains. Meccan hostility was allayed, and the treaty confirmed what Meccan failures at the battles of Uhud and the Ditch had shown – that Muhammad was a power to contend with and that Mecca had given up her efforts to defeat him. Sniffing the wind, Arabian tribes continued to throw in their lot with Muhammad.

Two years later, in 630, Muhammad completed his triumph over Mecca. A dispute between client tribes of Mecca and Medina broke the truce, but Meccan leaders surrendered the city. Muhammad gave amnesty to almost everyone and generous gifts to the leading Quraysh. The idols of the Ka'ba were destroyed, and it was declared the holiest shrine of Islam.

The victory over Mecca was also the culmination of Muhammad's tribal policy. Throughout the eight-year struggle, Muhammad had tried to gain control of the tribes in order to subdue Mecca. Missionaries and embassies were sent throughout Arabia, factions loyal to Muhammad were supported, and tribes were raided to compel them to pay allegiance and zakat, the alms tax, to Muhammad. He regarded the tax as a sign of membership in the Muslim community and acceptance of himself as Prophet. The bedouins looked on it as a tribute plain and simple, and conspired to evade it as soon as they could. Muhammad's successes had resulted in the cutting off of Mecca's trade. Then, with Mecca finally subdued, many Arabian tribes accepted Islam. By the end of his life Muhammad had created, for the first time in centuries, a large-scale Arabian federation of oases and tribes, and had provided a solution to the destructive anarchy of Arabian life.

THE OLD WORLD AND THE NEW RELIGION

By the time of his death in 632, Muhammad had provided his followers with the design for a political community based on religious affiliation, and a conception of a way of life grounded in the vision of the oneness of God. Muhammad was the agent of a great historical change. In the revelations of the Quran he synthesized Arabian religious concepts, Judaism, and Christianity, along with distinctly Islamic ideas, into a new monotheism. Eschatological piety and fear of hellfire recall Syriac monastic preaching. The role of a prophet, the significance of written revelations, obedience to God's commands, and stress on communal life as the context of religious fulfillment all parallel Judaic ideas. Though elements of the Quranic teaching resembled Jewish and Christian beliefs, Muhammad's unique religious vision and the formation of a community based upon that vision made Islam a new religion. The stress on God's utter transcendence, majesty, omnipotence and untrammeled will, and upon the submission of one's own will to God's, surrender to God's commands, and acceptance of God's judgment gave Quranic teachings a special originality within the framework of the monotheistic religions. The new religion was affiliated with the old, but it claimed to be the final revelation of God's full and correct will. In the realm of society, the early teachings of Islam at first involved Jews and Christians as well as pagans; but in the end it was redirected toward pagan Arabians, with the object of establishing a new community.

The translation of monotheistic values into the principles of a reformed Arabian society, and the formation of a new community with its own congregational life and ritual and legal norms, made Islam a new religious community alongside the old. This was the umma, the brotherhood that integrated individuals, clans, cities, and even ethnic groups into a larger community in which religious loyalties encompassed all other loyalties without abolishing them, and in which a new common law and political authority regulated the affairs of the populace as a whole. In a fragmented society he integrated otherwise anarchic small clans into a larger confederacy and built a "church"-like religious community and an incipient imperial organization. Thus the Quranic revelation and Muhammad's leadership brought to a hitherto marginal region the same type of religious beliefs and sociopolitical organization as those characteristic of the Middle East as a whole. While Arabia maintained a unique identity it was becoming a society of a Middle Eastern type – committed on the basis of a familial or lineage structure to a universal confessional religion and to political unity.

Radical as this was, it was still an adaptation of traditional Arabian concepts. The umma redefined the meaning of the tribe as a group that defended its brothers to include religious as well as blood brothers. It also came under the leadership of a shaykh, a person who had the prestige to arbitrate because he represented the divine will rather than custom, and was governed by a new *sunna* – the authoritative example of the Prophet – rather than tribal tradition. The law of blood revenge was accepted, but now the umma as a whole was substituted for the clan. Within the umma Muhammad counseled restraint, forgiveness, and the mediation and control of the shaykh. In family life, the patriarchal clan was reaffirmed as the ideal Muslim family, but redefined to include a new concern for women and children, the stability of marriages, individuality, and decency.

In the realm of individual morality, a similar reshaping of values took place. The traditional Arab virtues were vested with new Islamic meanings. Bedouin courage in battle, reckless bravery in defense of one's tribe, became persistent dedication to the new faith of Islam and the capacity for disciplined sacrifice in the name of the new community. Patience in the face of adversity (*sabr*) became unshakable faith in God in the face of trials and temptations. Generosity was shorn of its impulsive quality, of the penchant for showing off and display, and was transmuted into the virtue of almsgiving and care for the weak and the poor as part of a pious and restrained, but regular, commitment. The Quranic teachings and Muhammad's leadership extracted the virtues of the bedouin culture from the context of *jahl* (passion, ignorance, and thoughtlessness), to reestablish them on the basis of *hilm* (self-control) and *'aql* (rational judgment), based on *islam* (submission to Allah).

Thus, the new religion reaffirmed the Arabian moral tradition. But in a society that had already failed to realize its own ideals, this could only be accomplished through new concepts of brotherhood and authority. Islam gave to traditional virtues and social institutions a new meaning that could command allegiance and elicit participation. By giving old concepts new meaning, it made possible a new religious sensibility and the integration of disparate peoples into a new community. When one looks at Arabian society before and after Muhammad, the outward movement was small, but the inner journey was immeasurable.

What made Muhammad so rare a figure in history, what made him a prophet, was his ability to convey his vision to people around him so that concepts long known to everyone took on the power to transform other people's lives as they had transformed his. This was accomplished by direct preaching about God, and also by changing family life and institutions, and by introducing new ritual practices, social mores, and political loyalties. Muhammad was a prophet who caused a religious vision to operate in the body of a whole society.

In the Quran and Muhammad's teachings and example, Muslims have ever after found a revelation of the spiritual reality of God's transcendence and man's humble place in the universe. They find a revelation of the laws by which people should live in a community of believers, dedicated to the care of the weak and the poor, to education, and to social reform. Equally they are dedicated to a political community organized to administer justice, to defend itself, and to wage war in the name of the true faith. Islam proved particularly effective in unifying tribal societies and in motivating militant struggle in the interests of the umma as a whole. To this day, to be a Muslim implies a combination of personal religious belief and membership in the community of fellow believers.

THE ARAB-MUSLIM IMPERIUM (632–945)

CHAPTER 3

THE ARAB CONQUESTS AND THE SOCIO-ECONOMIC BASES OF EMPIRE

Within a decade the new Arab-Muslim community had conquered much of the Middle East and created an arena for the construction of a new form of Islamic civilization – not only in the peripheral region of Arabia but in the core areas of already developed Middle Eastern civilization. The conquests began the long historical process that culminated in the absorption of both the Sasanian empire and the eastern regions of the Byzantine empire into an Islamic empire, and the eventual conversion of the majority of Jewish, Christian, and Zoroastrian peoples to Islam. In the first instance the conquest led to the formation of a new regime, to the migration and settlement of large numbers of Arabians in the cities and towns of the Middle East, and to extensive urbanization and economic development. Arab settlement also promoted social change and the progressive but partial integration of Arab and non-Arab populations into new cosmopolitan communities. Urbanization, economic change, and the formation of new communities generated resources for the organization of a new and powerful empire; the elites of city and empire gave birth to new forms of Islamic religious and imperial culture. Islamic civilization, then, was the cultural expression of the elites thrown up by the forces of economic and social change generated by the Arab conquests.

THE ARAB CONQUESTS

The Arab conquests are popularly understood to have been motivated by a lust for booty or a religious passion to subdue and convert the world to Islam. Whatever the motives involved, they were in part the outcome of deliberate state policy and in part accidental. Upon Muhammad's death in 632 the whole of his life's work was threatened. In the absence of an agreement with regard to a successor, the Muslim community, a conglomeration of diverse elements, threatened to break up. The Khazraj of Medina decided to elect their own chief. Other Muslims, especially exiled Meccans, weaker Medinan clans, and many individuals who had abandoned their clans to join Muhammad, saw that this would lead to the resumption of feuding. They tried to head off the Khazraj, and in the course of an all-night debate the idea of a succession was born. Abu Bakr, one of Muhammad's closest associates and his father-in-law, was elected as Caliph. He was a successor to the Prophet, but was not himself a prophet. He was rather to be a shaykh or chief, who led the collectivity, arbitrated disputes, and followed the precedents set by Muhammad. Selected by a minority with no special competence, Abu Bakr had his nomination ratified the following day by the community as a whole. In the mosque Abu Bakr said simply that he would obey the Sunna (precedent) of the Prophet and that people should obey him as long as he obeyed it.

Having preserved its existence, the Muslim community asserted its authority in the rest of Arabia. At Muhammad's death many of the Arabian tribes that had been forced into his confederation sought to regain their independence; some of them put forth prophets and religions of their own. The claim of Islam to be the only true religion of the Arabs was in jeopardy. Abu Bakr refused any concessions to demands for relief from taxes, waged war on recalcitrant tribes, forced them into subjection, and even expanded the sphere of Muslim power beyond what it had been in Muhammad's time. At the battle of al-Aqraba (633) the Muslims defeated a rival tribal confederation and extended their power over eastern Arabia.

The immediate outcome of the Muslim victories was turmoil. Medina's victories led allied tribes to attack the non-aligned to compensate for their own losses. The pressure drove tribes as far as Hadhramaut and Yemen in the south, Bahrain and Oman in the east, and then across the imperial frontiers. The Bakr tribe, which had defeated a Persian detachment in 606, joined forces with the Muslims and led them on a raid in southern Iraq to Ubulla and al-Hira, the former Lakhm capital. A similar spilling over of tribal raiding occurred on the Syrian frontiers. Abu Bakr encouraged these movements, for they no doubt corresponded to Muhammad's intentions and helped recruit bedouins for campaigns in the north.

At first the small tribal groups were mainly searching for booty, but when Arab raids forced the Byzantines to send a major expedition into southern Palestine, the raiding parties had to concentrate their forces east of Gaza, and there, under the leadership of Khalid b. al-Walid, sent by Abu Bakr from Iraq to take the generalship of the Arab clans, they defeated a Byzantine army at the battle of Ajnadayn (634). This was the first battle in which the Arabs acted as an army rather than as separate raiding parties. With this victory their ambitions became boundless; they were no longer raiders on the soil of Syria seeking booty, but contenders for control of the settled empires. What began as inter-tribal skirmishing to consolidate a political confederation in Arabia ended as a full-scale war against the two empires.

In the wake of the battle of Ajnadayn, the Arabs moved against the Byzantine province of Syria. They took Damascus in 636. Baalbek, Homs, and Hama soon surrendered. The rest of the province, however, continued to resist. Only in 638 was Jerusalem taken. Caesarea fell in 640. Finally, in 641, the Arabs took the northern Syrian and Mesopotamian towns of Harran, Edessa, and Nasibin. The conquest of Syria took so long because victories over Byzantine armies did not necessarily bring about the surrender of fortified towns, which had to be reduced one by one. The next Byzantine province to fall to the Arabs was Egypt. Egypt's attractions were its position as the granary of Constantinople, its proximity to the Hijaz, important naval yards, and a strategic location for further conquests in Africa. The Arab general 'Amr b. al-'As, on his own initiative, began the conquest of the province in 641. Within the year he had taken Heliopolis and Babylon, and the whole of the country except Alexandria, which capitulated in 643. Because Egypt was politically centralized and scarcely urbanized, the conquest was virtually instantaneous. The next Arab objective was North Africa. Tripoli was taken in 643, but the subjugation of all of North Africa took another seventy-five years. Instead of sudden, dramatic victories, painfully prolonged wars were waged to establish Arab suzerainty.

Within a decade the Arabs had captured Syria and Egypt, but the Byzantine empire retained its richest and most populous provinces, Anatolia and the Balkans, and would engage in almost continuous border warfare on land and on sea, always threatening to retake territories that had for hundreds of years been part of the Roman and Christian world. The survival of Byzantium left the Arabs with a contested and dangerous frontier and a permanent barrier to their expansion.

The Sasanian empire, by contrast, was utterly destroyed. The Arabs defeated the Persians at the battle of Qadisiya (637), seized the capital of the empire, Ctesiphon, and forced the last emperor, Yazdagird, to flee to the protection of Turkish princes in Inner Asia. All Iraq fell into Arab hands. With the collapse of the empire, the Arabs were faced in Iran with a number of small and weak but inaccessible principalities, protected by mountains and deserts. The problem in conquering Iran was not a strong resisting state, but the large number of remote areas that had to be invaded, absorbed, and occupied. It took decades to subdue all the quasi-independent principalities that had comprised the Sasanian empire. From the garrison base of Kufa the Arabs moved north, occupying Mosul in 641. Nihawand, Hamadhan, Rayy, Isfahan, and all the main cities of western Iran fell by 644. Azarbayjan, to the west of the Caspian Sea, was captured about the same time. Other forces operating from Basra captured Ahwaz (Khuzistan) in 640, but took until 649 to complete the conquest of Fars. Only then did the conquest of more outlying regions, such as Armenia and Khurasan, begin. Khurasan was conquered in 654.

This first wave of conquests was followed several decades later by new campaigns on a grand scale. To the west, North Africa was conquered between 643 and 711; Spain was absorbed by the Arabs between 711 and 759. In the north, the Arabs attacked Anatolia and launched three great but failed expeditions in 660, 668, and 717 to capture Constantinople. They fought against the Khazars in the Caucasus. The capitals of Transoxania, Bukhara and Samarqand, fell in 712 and 713. For the first time in history the Arabs conquered the whole of the Middle East, and incorporated North Africa, Spain, and Transoxania into their empire as well. Thus they established the geographical arena for the eventual diffusion of a common culture and a common sociopolitical identity in the name of Islam.

The reasons for the relatively rapid success of the Arab-Muslim conquests are not hard to find. The Byzantine and Sasanian empires were both militarily exhausted by several decades of warfare prior to the Arab-Muslim invasions. The Christian populations – the Copts in Egypt, the Monophysites in Syria, and the Nestorians in Iraq – all had long histories of troubled relations with their Byzantine and Sasanian overlords. Their disaffection was important in the cases where Christian-Arab border tribes and military auxiliaries joined the conquerors and where fortified cities capitulated. The conquests, then, were due to victories over militarily weakened powers, and were consolidated because local populations were content to accept the new regime. The conquests were further secured by a large migration of Arabian peoples. With the defeat of the Byzantine and Sasanian empires, a frontier between populations broke down, leading to a massive movement of peoples from Arabia into the lands of the Middle East.

THE ADMINISTRATION OF THE NEW EMPIRE

Responsibility for controlling the Arabian migrants, and for governing and exploiting the conquered sedentary peoples, fell to the new Caliphs and the aristocracy of Meccan and Medinian merchants and soldiers who were the mainstay of the Muslim regime. From the outset, the chiefs of the Islamic community in Medina sought to channel the bedouin migrations for both their own and the common advantage. Medinians decided on the two basic principles of the post-conquest government: that the bedouins would be prevented from damaging the agricultural society; and that the new elite would cooperate with the chiefs and notables of the conquered population. The necessary arrangements between conqueror and conquered were implemented in the reign of the second Caliph, 'Umar (634–44).

The first principle of 'Umar's settlement entailed the transformation of the Arab conquerors into an elite military caste who garrisoned the subdued areas and carried on further conquests. To prevent the bedouins from raiding indiscriminately, to forestall the destruction of the productive agricultural lands, and to segregate the Arabs from the conquered peoples, the bedouins were settled in garrison cities (*amsar*, sing. *misr*). The three most important were new cities founded in Iraq and Egypt. Basra, at the head of the Persian Gulf, was strategically located for easy communication with Medina and for Arab expeditions into southern Iran. Kufa, on the Euphrates River to the north of the marshes near al-Hira, became the administrative capital of northern Iraq, Mesopotamia, and northern and eastern Iran. Fustat, the new capital of Egypt, was located just below the delta of the Nile, and served as the base for Arab expansion into North Africa until Qayrawan (in Tunisia) was founded in 670. In other provinces the Arabs did not usually found new cities, but settled in towns, suburbs, and villages on the outskirts of existing towns. Important

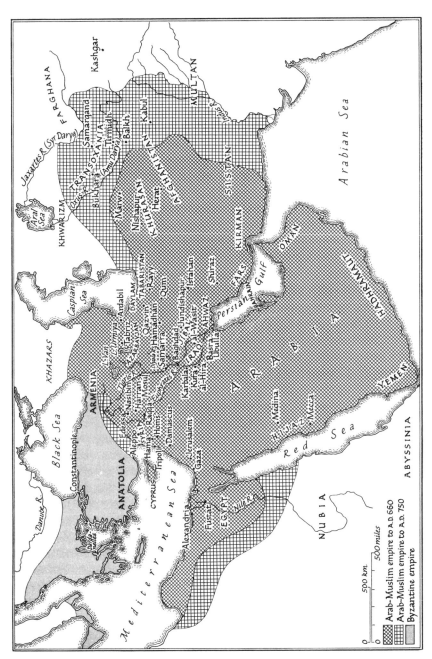

Map 2 The Arab–Muslim empire to AD 750

Arab bases in Iran were Hamadhan, Isfahan, and Rayy. A new eastern garrison was established at Marw in 670.

The amsar served not only to house the bedouin migrants and organize the armies, but to distribute the spoils of victory. As conquerors, the Arabs were entitled to a stipend paid out of the taxes collected from peasants and the tribute paid by townspeople. In principle Arab soldiers and clans were not permitted to seize landed property as their own. Conquered property (*fay*) was considered the permanent possession of the community; the revenues, but not the land, could be given to the conquerors. These arrangements both protected the cultivated areas from pillaging and distributed the spoils of victory more equitably. Islam was a crucial factor in the formation of the great garrisons, not because it motivated people to conquer, but because the faith made strangers willing to cooperate in a common cause. Islam facilitated acceptance of the Caliphate and justified its authority.

The second principle of 'Umar's settlement was that the conquered populations should be disturbed as little as possible. This meant that the Arab Muslims did not, contrary to reputation, attempt to convert conquered peoples to Islam. Muhammad had set the precedent of permitting Jews and Christians in Arabia to keep their religions, if they paid tribute; the Caliphate extended the same privilege to Middle Eastern Jews, Christians, and Zoroastrians, whom they considered protected peoples (*ahl al-dhimma*), "Peoples of the Book," the adherents of earlier written revelations. At the time of the conquest, Islam was meant to be a religion of the Arabs, a mark of caste unity and superiority. When conversions did occur, they were an embarrassment because they created status problems and led to claims for financial privileges.

Just as the Arabs had no interest in changing the religious situation, they had no desire to disturb the social and administrative order. The Caliphate sent governors to oversee the collection of tributes and taxes, supervise the distribution of tax revenues as salary to the troops, and lead the Arabs in war and in prayer, but otherwise local situations were left in local hands. The old elites and the administrative machinery of the Byzantine and Sasanian empires were incorporated into the new regime. Iranian, Aramean, Coptic, and Greek scribes and accountants worked for their new masters as they had for the old. The old landowners, chiefs, and headmen kept their authority in the villages and assisted in collecting taxes. The whole of the former social and religious order was left intact.

In practice, the relationship established between the Arabs and local elites varied from region to region, depending on the circumstances of the Arab conquests and on the available social and administrative machinery. Some provinces came under direct bureaucratic administration, but many others retained their autonomy. Places that had stubbornly resisted Arab incursions forced the invaders to concede favorable terms in return for local compliance. Hosts of formal treaties were made with the notables of towns or the chiefs and princes of small provinces, promising to leave the old elites in power, and respecting their property and their religion, in return for the payment of a tribute, usually a fixed sum, which the notables could continue to collect from their subjects. In these cases, the Arabs simply collected taxes from sub-rulers who were their vassals. In the citied areas of upper Mesopotamia and Syria, in Khurasan and elsewhere, the Arabs were remote suzerains.

However, the arrangements made in the wake of the conquests were not permanent. As the Arabs consolidated their power, they sought to increase their control over local affairs. In Iraq and Egypt, they set the bureaucratic machinery of the old regimes to work for the new. In Iraq, the Caliph 'Umar confiscated the land that once had belonged to the Sasanian crown, along with the estates of notables who had fled with the defeated Sasanian emperor, and made them part of the Caliphal domains. In Egypt, the Arabs simplified the administrative system by abolishing the fiscally independent estates (*autopragia*) and municipalities as separate units of administration. In Mesopotamia and Syria, uniform administration superseded special treaties as the Arabs refused to renegotiate tribute and insisted on payment of taxes in direct proportion to the populations and resources of the areas. The Arab regime also separated town and rural administration. Since classical antiquity the Mediterranean region had been divided into self-governing city-states. Though the municipalities eventually became cogs in the machine of the Roman bureaucracy, the city-state with its surrounding rural area had continued as a basic element in Roman administration. Now the Arabs destroyed the city-state as a political form and placed Syria and Mesopotamia under a territorial bureaucracy. In Khurasan and other parts of Iran, however, only the loosest suzerainty and tributes were imposed, and virtually complete autonomy was conceded to local peoples.

In each province the Arabs adopted the system of taxes already in use. In Iraq they adopted the Sasanian system of collecting both a land tax (*kharaj*) and a poll tax (*jizya*). The land was measured and a tax was fixed for every *jarib* (2,400 square meters). The actual rate of taxation per jarib varied with the quality of land, the crop, the expected productivity, and the estimated value of the produce. The rates also varied with distance from market, availability of water, type of irrigation, transportation, and so on. In addition everyone was expected to pay a poll tax in gold coins. In Syria and Mesopotamia, land taxes were levied on the basis of the *iugum*, or the amount of land that could be worked by one man and a team of animals in a day. A special poll tax was levied on urban, non-farming populations. In Egypt too there were both land and poll taxes but the poll tax was assessed on the whole village population and then divided up internally by the villagers. For provinces such as Khurasan, where there was no centralized administration, and taxation and tribute payments were left in the hands of local notables, we have no conclusive information about the nature of the tax system.

The economic repercussions of taxation were considerable everywhere. Taxes on peasants often reached 50 percent of the value of their produce, and at such levels the incidence of taxation determined whether life for the mass of the people would be tolerable. Taxation affected the attention given to the soil and the level of investment to maintain productivity. It influenced the choice of crops. It determined whether or not the peasants would stay in the villages and work the land, or flee, leaving their homes and lands to decay. Furthermore, taxation defined social structure. Taxes were duties levied on some classes of the population for the support of others. Peasants, workers, and merchants paid taxes. Landowners, administrators, clergymen, soldiers, and emperors collected them. To pay taxes was not only an economic burden, it was a sign of social inferiority.

The Arab conquests thus followed a pattern familiar from past nomadic conquests of settled regions. The conquering peoples became the military elite, and the settled societies were exploited to support them. The governing arrangements were a compromise between the elites of the conquering peoples and those of the conquered or settled peoples, in which the interests of the former in military power and adequate revenues were assured in exchange for permitting the latter to retain their local political, religious, and financial autonomy. Both, of course, leaned on the tax-paying peasantry.

ECONOMIC CHANGE AND THE NEW URBAN SOCIETIES

Despite conservative intentions, the Arab conquests, the settlement of large Arab populations in numerous garrisons, and the consolidation of a new imperial regime set in motion vast changes in patterns of international trade, urban commerce, and agriculture. The unification of the former Sasanian and Byzantine parts of the Middle East into one polity removed political and strategic barriers to trade, and laid the foundations for a major commercial revival. The Euphrates frontier between the Persian and the Roman worlds disappeared, and Transoxania, for the first time in history, was incorporated into a Middle Eastern empire. However, a new frontier was drawn between Syria and Anatolia, which had formerly been part of a single state. Commercial considerations inspired Arab expansion in Inner Asia and India and city development in northern Syria, Iraq, Iran, and Transoxania. Basra and (later) Baghdad became two of the leading trading cities in the world. Samarqand, Bukhara, and Nishapur prospered.

The conquests also had dramatic effects on agriculture and regional development. Iraq, on the eve of the Arab conquests, suffered from neglect of irrigation, exploitative taxation, and severe wars with the Roman empire. In southern Iraq the irrigation works had been allowed to degenerate, and in 627–28, on the eve of the Arab conquests, a major agricultural disaster took place. In a year of high water flow, the dikes in the Tigris River system of canals burst, and there was a major shift in the river bed. The Tigris flowed westward through the canals into the Euphrates at a point to the north and west of its previous channel, creating a desert in the east, but flooding the lower course of the Euphrates, which remains a marsh to the present day. Agricultural production also declined seriously in the Diyala region, which depended upon state-maintained irrigation.

Arab rule, however, provided a stable government and encouraged recovery. Wherever the Arabs established administrative capitals and garrison towns, as at

Basra, Kufa, Mosul, al-Wasit, and other places, efforts were made to stimulate agricultural output and develop fresh sources of food for the new cities. The swamps around Kufa were drained and brought under cultivation. In the early eighth century areas in the upper Euphrates region were irrigated. Basra was planted with date-palm forests. To the east of Basra salt marshes were reclaimed by Caliphs, Arab governors, and rich tribal shaykhs, encouraged by a policy of land and tax concessions. Caliphs and governors in particular sought to generate private revenues apart from taxation. To work the new lands, they imported slaves from East Africa in large numbers, thus creating the only plantation-type economy in the Middle East. These investments, however, were highly selective and favored new areas to the detriment of old areas of production whose revenues were already assigned to peasants, local landowners, and the garrison armies. The net effect of the Arab effort was to restore regions in Iraq that had Arab settlements and allow others to decay. Nonetheless, the total output of Iraq was probably below the best levels of Sasanian times.

In Iran, the Arab conquest and migrations also favored urban and agricultural development. Security, trade, a new population, and Arab policies regarding settlement, city building, and irrigation stimulated economic growth. In Iran, the Arabs did not found new cities, but settled in already established places. Important places such as Hamadhan, Isfahan, Qazvin, Rayy, Nishapur, and Marw received Arab garrisons. These were usually housed in newly constructed quarters, and in villages surrounding the town centers.

Moreover, in Iran, construction and settlement continued beyond the initial conquest. Throughout the seventh and eighth centuries Caliphs and governors added new quarters to the old cities. Each important governor imported his own clientele of guards, soldiers, and administrators, and built new quarters, palaces, mosques, barracks, gardens, and canals. Surrounding agricultural lands were brought into cultivation. Later Caliphs also constructed walls and defined administrative jurisdictions, and thus converted groups of quarters and villages into cities. By this process, Isfahan, Rayy, and Qazvin became large cities. Qum grew from a simple complex of agricultural villages into a major town. Whole regions – such as the districts around Samarqand and Bukhara, favored with new quarters and villages, irrigation works, and walls to defend them against Turkish nomads – prospered. Khwarizm, the delta of the Oxus River, which before the Arab conquests had contained small hamlets and farmsteads interspersed with feudal castles, became highly urbanized and densely settled.

Not all provinces flourished. In Syria, Mesopotamia, and Egypt the Arab conquest adversely affected the long-term prospects for economic development. For a time the location of the Caliphate at Damascus increased the prosperity of Syria, but the creation of a new frontier with Anatolia stifled its economy. The region north of Aleppo, formerly a center of olive growing and the manufacture of olive oil, was abandoned because Syria was cut off from its markets in Anatolia. The region east of a line from Raqqa to Damascus to 'Aqaba, which specialized in grape growing and wine making, similarly declined owing to the loss of export markets in Anatolia and the end of Christian pilgrimages to Palestine. The migration of Arab bedouins also damaged the economies of northern Syria and Mesopotamia. In most places, Arab migrants had been forced to settle in cities, quarters, or villages, but in this region bedouins were allowed to occupy unused steppe lands. Soon the nomads began to attack towns and villages. Agriculture and commerce were seriously set back by pastoralism. In Egypt exploitative taxation led to serious peasant revolts in 697, 712, and 725–26, which represented both economic protest and Coptic resistance to Muslim rulers. Thus, the net effect of the Arab conquests and empire was prosperity in Iran, a redistribution of the pattern of development in Iraq, and the economic decline of Mesopotamia, Syria and Egypt.

CLIENTS, CONVERTS, AND COMMUNITIES

Under pressure of war, migration, and intensive economic change the fundamental assumption of the conquest empire – that Arab and non-Arab populations would be segregated, with the former serving as a military elite and the latter as producers and taxpayers – proved untenable, and gave way to a mutual assimilation of conquered and conquering peoples on the basis of new communities and new Islamic identities. Sedentarization itself created pressures for the assimilation of Arabs into the surrounding societies. At Isfahan, Marw, Nishapur, and Balkh, the Arab garrisons were settled in villages and rapidly became landowners or peasants. Of the 50,000 families initially settled in Marw in 670, only 15,000 were still in active military service by 730. Most of the Arab army had by then left active service for civilian occupations. In Azarbayjan, parties of Arabs from Basra and Kufa seized lands and villages and established themselves as a local landowning aristocracy. In Kirman, Arab migrants reclaimed abandoned lands, founded new villages, and settled as a peasant population. In Iraq, Arab chiefs from Basra and Kufa became landowners. In all these provinces an Arab landowning elite came into being, and Arabs refused to take up military duties and to live isolated from other peoples, and found themselves, though in principle an elite caste, in fact absorbed into the occupations of the subject population. Furthermore, in Iran occupational assimilation was accompanied by social assimilation. While some Persians were converted to Islam, the Arabs by and large assimilated to the Persian milieu. Arabs spoke Persian, dressed like Persians, celebrated Persian holidays, and married Persian women.

Furthermore, the garrison towns themselves became centers of social change. Out of the matrix of Arabian kinship and lineage societies came a more socially stratified, occupationally differentiated, and communally organized Arab urban society which was assimilated into non-Arab populations to form a new type of cosmopolitan community. Basra, for example, founded as a camp city for migrant bedouin soldiers, proved to be a melting pot of peoples. Each major clan or tribal group originally had its own quarter, mosque, cemetery, and meeting place. Over time, however, the tent dwellings were replaced by reed huts; the huts were rein-forced with earthen walls and then replaced with mud-brick houses. The bedouins, used to moving whenever the climate proved unpropitious, found themselves immured in brick.

The military and administrative systems also generated profound changes. They required that the natural units of Arabian society be rearranged into artificial groups. To make uniform regiments and pay units of about a thousand men, big clans were subdivided and smaller ones combined. In 670, tens of thousands of families were removed from Basra and Kufa to garrison Marw in Khurasan, and all the remain-ing groups had to be reorganized. Also, newcomers who came in continuous streams to partake in the Arab wars had to be integrated into the basic units. Even though the military units kept their clan and tribal names, and may have kept a kin-ship core, they no longer represented the pre-Islamic Arabian social structure.

Furthermore, class distinctions divided the chiefs and ordinary tribesmen. The existence of privately owned palaces and agricultural estates suggests that the chiefs were enjoying wealth, privileges, and a style of life far removed from that of the mass of their clansmen. Military and administrative functions widened the gap between the chiefs and their followers. The military elites began to form a new class stratum, fortified by marriage ties. Tribal society was breaking down in favor of a society stratified on the basis of wealth and power.

Settlement also entailed the transformation of bedouins and soldiers into an eco-nomically differentiated working population. As Basra developed as an important administrative capital and center of cloth manufacturing and as a trading city con-nected with Iran, India, China, and Arabia, Arab settlers became merchants, traders, artisans, and workers, supplementing their meager military allotments with new incomes. Similarly, the new religion of Islam offered opportunities for social mobil-ity through careers in teaching, scholarship, and legal administration.

At the same time, settlement also helped to break down the barriers between Arab and non-Arab populations. As a capital and commercial center, Basra attracted non-Arab settlers. The soldiers and administrators of the old regime came to seek their fortune with the new. Iranian regiments were enlisted en masse. Arab gover-nors brought back troops from the east to serve as police and bodyguards. Clerks, tax collectors, estate managers, and even village chiefs and landowners flocked to the center of government. In addition, both merchants in lucrative, long-distance trade and humble workers, including bath attendants, weavers, and spinners, migrated to the new town. Slaves – captured and purchased – itinerant construc-tion workers, and fugitive peasants and migrant laborers, seeking employment and relief from the harshness of the countryside, flooded the new city. This non-Arab population was extremely diverse. The most important elements were Iranians and Arameans, the people of Iraq. Most of them were originally Nestorian Christians. Many were Jews. Indians, Malays, Gypsies, Africans, and Turks also came in small numbers from remote areas.

The absorption of this non-Arab population had important repercussions on Arab society. The Arabs tried to absorb the newcomers into the old clan structure as clients (*mawali*, sing. *mawla*). The concept of clientship was inherited from pre-Islamic Arabia, where a client was an inferior associate of an Arab clan. Very often, he was a former slave who was freed and then raised to the level of client, though many people were adopted directly into the status. The client was almost a member of the clan; his heirs were also clients. Mawali could expect support and protection, and would be helped in arranging marriages. The protection of the powerful was exchanged for the loyalty of the subordinates. However, as they absorbed mawali, Arab clans ceased to be kin units and became stratified political and economic groups built around a kinship core. The gap between aristocratic and plebeian clans widened. For example, in the Tamim tribe, the noble clans acquired former Persian cavalry units as their clients, while others had slave laborers and weavers as theirs.

Clientage also generated class conflicts between the mawali and their overlords. Even mawali who carried on skilled professions in war, administration, commerce, medicine, and religious life were held to be social inferiors. They were exploited economically, and could not intermarry with the Arabs or inherit equally. The active soldiers resented exclusion from the military payrolls (*diwans*), for enrollment was not only a financial benefit, but a symbol of social privilege. The mawali wanted to be recognized as part of the elite, but to the Arabs this was unthinkable. They clung to their status and privileges and resented the importance of the clients in the army and administration, their religious precocity, their commercial skill, and the shadow they cast over Arab primacy.

Thus, within fifty years the founding of new cities, and the transfer of economic opportunities and political power to new peoples and new places, stimulated the interpenetration of Arab and non-Arab peoples. Non-Arabs permeated the Arab-Muslim military caste as converts and associates, and Arabs became landowners, merchants, and settlers. The pressures generated by sedentarization and urbanization, by the teachings of Islam and by contact with other Middle Eastern peoples, broke down the lineage structure of the old tribal society, fostered new group and communal structures, intensified the stratification of society and the division of labor, and led to the formation of new mixed Arab and non-Arab communities. Social change also made possible the formation of new religious associations built around family chiefs descended from the Prophet, charismatic preachers, Quran readers, scholars, and mystics.

Social change took cultural expression through conversions to Islam and acceptance of Arabic or Persian as shared languages. Conversion, however, was a very slow process. Though the original assumption of Muslim and Western writers was that the Middle East was quickly and massively converted to Islam, nowhere in the Arab sources is there explicit information about the conversion of large numbers of people, and certainly not of whole villages, towns, and regions.

The available evidence points, rather, to a slow and uneven process of social and religious adjustment.

The earliest converts to Islam were those Christian-bedouin tribes living on the margin of the fertile crescent who were swept up in the great migrations. Later in the first century of Arab rule other Mesopotamian Arab tribes also accepted Islam, but many such tribes remained Christian. Once the Arab conquests were secure, elites of the former Sasanian empire – soldiers, officials, and landowners – made common cause with the conquerors and accepted Islam. Converts were made among client soldiers and scribes serving the Arab elite, and among other strata of the population attracted to the Arab garrisons. Conversions implied the ratification of old privileges and paved the way for entry into the dominant elite. In these cases, conversions seemed to involve mobile individuals and not classes or whole communities.

At the very beginning of the Islamic era, the Arab-Muslim elite assumed that they would form a dual society in which the conquerors would constitute an aristocracy and the conquered peoples a subject population: the former Muslim, the latter not. Thus, the early Muslim regime was not only tolerant of the non-Muslim populations but actually helped reorganize Christian churches. The Nestorian Church in Iraq resumed its roles in the educational, judicial, and even political administration of the Christian population. In Egypt, the Muslim authorities took a paternalistic attitude toward the Coptic Church. Christian scribes served in the administration of both Iraq and Egypt. For the sake of political inclusiveness and effective administration, the empire collaborated with non-Muslim elites, permitted them partial access to power, and protected them against disruptive social and economic changes.

Only after a century was this attitude reversed. By then widespread Arab assimilation into the general population had led many Arabs to accept the equality of Arabs and non-Arabs, and to value Muslim as well as Arab identifications. Thus 'Umar II (717–20) changed the standing policy of the Caliphate and sought to put the empire on a Muslim, rather than a strictly Arab, basis. He accepted the fundamental equality of all Muslims, Arab and non-Arab, and promulgated new laws giving fiscal equality to Muslims regardless of origin. The wars in Transoxania reinforced this reversal of attitude. Protracted struggles against local princes and Turkish rivals for control of the region prompted the Caliphate to offer fiscal benefits to converts. Though this policy was eventually abandoned as politically unfeasible, the sporadic attempts at encouraging conversion to Islam marked a turning point in the ongoing integration of Arabs and conquered peoples. By the middle of the eighth century, there was a steady progress of conversions in Iraq, Egypt, Syria, Khurasan, and Transoxania. Significant numbers of converts were to be found in and around the Muslim garrison centers. However, outside the garrison towns the mass of Middle Eastern peoples remained non-Muslims.

Along with conversion to Islam, common languages emerged. In general, Arabic became the language of written communication in administration, literature, and religion. It also became the predominant spoken dialect in the western parts of the Middle East – Egypt, Syria, Mesopotamia, and Iraq – where languages close to Arabic, such as Aramaic, were already spoken. The spread of Arabic was faster than the diffusion of Islam, but this is not to say that the process was rapid or complete. For example, Coptic was still spoken in Fustat in the eighth century. In Syria and Iraq there continued to be Aramaic-speaking populations. In western Iran Arab settlers were absorbed into the local populations and became bilingual. In Khurasan, where the Arabs were assimilated to Persian manners, mores, and dress, they used local Persian dialects. Not only did Arabs learn Persian, but the Arab-Muslim conquest became the vehicle for the introduction of Persian as the lingua franca of the peoples east of the Oxus. In Transoxania, Persian, the spoken language of Arabs in eastern Iran, replaced Soghdian as the common language for Arabs, Persians, and Soghdians.

Thus within a century of the Arab-Muslim conquests, the basic principles on which the empire was organized were no longer valid. In the nomadic kingdom organized by the Caliph 'Umar, Arabian peoples were to constitute a "nation in arms," settled in garrison centers, segregated from the subject peoples, restricted to military activities, and barred from commerce and agriculture. Membership in Islam was their prerogative. Non-Arab peoples were to keep their communal ties and religions and continue to work in the productive occupations that enabled them to support the ruling elite.

Nonetheless, in the course of the first Muslim century, the Arabs changed from a clan or tribal people into an "urban" people; they mingled with non-Arab peoples, abandoned military affairs, took on civilian occupations, and lost their monopoly on Islam. Correspondingly, non-Arab peoples entered the military and government services, converted to Islam, adopted the Arabic language, and claimed a place in the government of the empire in which they were initially subjects. Economic and social change in the garrison centers, conversions, and shared languages paved the way for the society of the future, no longer divided between Arab conqueror and conquered peoples, but united on the basis of their commitment to Islam, sharing an Arabic and/or Persian linguistic identity. This mutual assimilation of peoples and the emergence of Islamic Middle Eastern communities took place, however, only in a restricted number of garrison centers. Although the rest of the Middle Eastern population remained outside the influence of the new societies, still bound to their more ancient heritage, the cosmopolitan communities set the tone of Middle Eastern politics and culture for centuries to come.

CHAPTER 4

THE CALIPHATE

In the first century of Arab-Muslim rule the Caliphate was transformed from a coalition of nomadic conquerors into a new form of Middle Eastern empire defined and legitimized in Islamic terms. Its transformation was driven by intense conflicts within the Arab elites and between Arabs and non-Arabs. A central issue was the tension between the precepts of religion and the actualities of political power. Under these pressures the Caliphate went through several phases coinciding with the *rashidun,* or Rightly Guided Caliphs (632–61), the Umayyad dynasty (661–750), the early 'Abbasid empire (750–833), and the 'Abbasid empire in decline (833–945). In this chapter we shall follow the changing concept and practice of empire until the mid-ninth century.

FROM NOMADIC KINGDOM TO SYRIAN MONARCHY

The Rightly Guided Caliphs

The first phase in the construction of the Caliphal regime was the period of the Rashidun, in which the companions of the Prophet, Abu Bakr (632–34), 'Umar (634–44), 'Uthman (644–56), and 'Ali (656–61), ruled by virtue of their personal connection with the Prophet, and the religious and patriarchal authority derived from loyalty to Islam. The conquests made the Caliphs the military and administrative chiefs of the newly conquered lands. In this role they claimed to be the deputies of God.

The early Caliphate was politically based on the Muslim community of Arabia and upon the Arab tribal forces that conquered its Middle Eastern empire. This elite was divided among those who held a Muslim and those who held an Arab concept of the Caliphate. In organizing the new empire the Caliph 'Umar pursued an "Islamic" policy, favoring the Meccan companions of the Prophet and the *ansar* – his Medinan helpers, and the clans who had supported Medina in the Arabian wars and had been early participants in the conquest of Iraq. 'Umar appointed these

Table 2. *Outline chronology of early Islamic history*

Muhammad	c. 570–632
Rashidun Caliphs	632–61
First civil war	656–61
Umayyad Caliphs	661–750
Reign of Mu awiya	661–80
Second civil war	680–92
Reign of Abd al-Malik	685–705
Reconstruction of regime	685–744
Third civil war	744–50
Abbasid Caliphs	750–1258
Consolidation of empire	750 –c. 850
Reign of al-Ma mun	813–33
Breakup of empire	c. 835–945
Independent succession states	945– c. 1220
Mongol invasions	c. 1220–c. 1260

people to governorships, generalships, and administrative posts, gave them the highest stipends, and allowed them to administer the *sawafi* – the abandoned Sasanian crown lands – in their own interest. The opposition was equally powerful. In Medina and Mecca, the Quraysh aristocracy chafed under 'Umar's policies. In the provinces, large and prestigious Arabian clans, and even the former chiefs of the earlier tribal opposition now converted to Islam, claimed their share of power. By the end of 'Umar's reign a fierce conflict of interests had already developed.

'Uthman, who succeeded 'Umar, was a Meccan aristocrat of the Umayya clan. He reversed 'Umar's policies and favored Umayyad and other Meccan interests – and the large migrant clans – at the expense of the companions of the Prophet and the Medinans. To accomplish this redistribution of power, 'Uthman increased central control over provincial revenues. He also took initiatives in religious matters, including the promulgation of a standard edition of the Quran, which was resented by those Muslims who felt themselves to be the custodians of the holy book. 'Uthman thus stood for a reassertion of the pre-Islamic coalition of Meccan and Arabian tribal aristocrats against the new elements produced by Islam, and claimed an enlarged authority for the Caliph to effect social, economic, and religious changes.

In implementing these policies, 'Uthman provoked bitter opposition, conspiracies, and, eventually, civil war. In 656 he was murdered by a party of about five hundred Arabs from Fustat. In the wake of this murder, 'Ali was elected Caliph. He opposed the centralization of Caliphal control over provincial revenues, and favored an equal distribution of taxes and booty among the Arabs. As the cousin and son-in-law of Muhammad as well as one of the earliest converts to Islam, 'Ali had claimed the Caliphate on the basis of his devotion to Muhammad and Islam, but now he compromised himself by coming to power with the support of 'Uthman's assassins.

'Ali's accession led to factional fighting. First he was opposed by a faction led by the Meccan aristocrats Talha and Zubayr, and the Prophet's favorite wife, 'A'isha, whom he defeated at the battle of the Camel in 656. He was then challenged by Mu'awiya, 'Uthman's cousin and the governor of Syria, who refused 'Ali's demands for allegiance and called for revenge for 'Uthman and the punishment of his killers. The opponents and their armies met at the battle of Siffin (657), where after months of desultory confrontation and negotiations, the moderates forced an agreement to arbitrate the question of whether 'Uthman's murder was justified. Some of 'Ali's supporters, called the Kharijis (secessionists), saw his willingness to submit to arbitrate as a defeat for their own hopes of his Caliphate and a violation of religious principles. They turned against him, and were defeated in battle, but this new round of bloodshed further alienated Muslim support.

The arbitrators met at Adhruh in January 659, and agreed that the murder of 'Uthman was unjustified, and that a *shura*, or council, should be called to elect a new Caliph. 'Ali rejected the outcome, but his coalition disintegrated. Moreover, the protracted struggle had begun to threaten the security of the empire and the flow of revenues. As rebellions in eastern Iran cut off the payment of taxes to the tribesmen of Basra and Kufa, Arab opinion favored the succession of Mu'awiya to the Caliphate because he was backed by disciplined forces, and because it seemed that he could maintain order within the Arab-Muslim elite and Arab control over the empire. After 'Ali's assassination by a Khariji, Mu'awiya declared himself Caliph and was accepted by the dominant interests. He was the founder of the Umayyad dynasty (661–750).

The Umayyad monarchy

The civil war created permanent divisions within the Muslim community. Henceforth, Muslims were divided over who had the legitimate right to occupy the Caliphate. Muslims who accepted the succession of Mu'awiya and the historical sequence of Caliphs after him are called the Sunnis. Those who held that 'Ali was the only rightful Caliph and that only his descendants should succeed him are called the Shi'a. The Shi'a tended to stress the religious functions of the Caliphate, and to deplore its political compromises, while the Sunnis were inclined to circumscribe its religious role and to be more tolerant of its political involvements. The Kharijis held that the Caliphate should not be determined by descent, but that the Caliph should be elected by the community of Muslims at large and hold his position only so long as he was sinless in the conduct of his office. As these early differences were vested with ever-widening religious importance, Sunnis, Shi'a, and Kharijis developed separate versions of Islam and formed distinct religious bodies within the community as a whole.

Upon coming to power, Mu'awiya (661–80) began a new cycle of efforts to reconstruct both the authority and the power of the Caliphate, and to deal with factionalism within the ruling elite. Mu'awiya began to change a coalition of Arab tribes into a centralized monarchy. He expanded the military and administrative powers

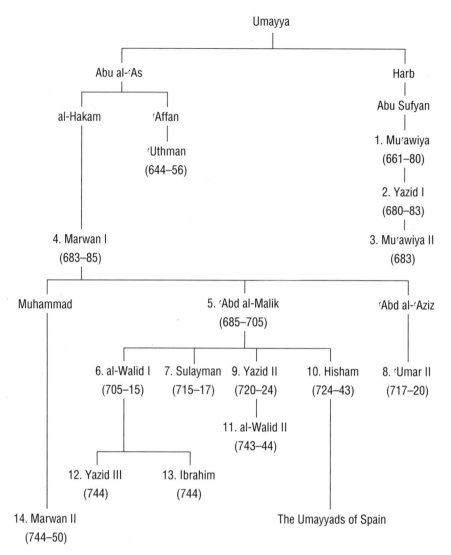

Figure 2 The Banu Umayya and the Umayyad Caliphs

of the state, and devised new moral and political grounds for loyalty to the Caliphate. To satisfy the interests of the tribal chiefs, the conquests were resumed in North Africa and eastern Iran. On the Syrian front Mu'awiya kept peace with the Byzantine empire so that he could hold Syrian forces in reserve for purposes of internal policing. Further, he sought to build up the revenues from private incomes, from confiscated Byzantine and Sasanian crown lands, and from investments in reclamation and irrigation. He also emphasized the patriarchal aspects of the Caliphate; his growing police and financial powers were cloaked by the traditional Arab virtues of conciliation, consultation, generosity, and respect for the forms of tribal tradition.

Mu'awiya's personal qualities were more important than any institutions. He is legendary for his hilm, a talent for dealing with his followers so that they cooperated without feeling that their dignity had been offended. It meant clemency and patience, and the power to do harm restrained by forbearance. If the Caliphate of 'Umar fundamentally rested on his closeness to Muhammad and religious integrity, Mu'awiya's reign was based upon centralized state power, his networks of clientele ties, and his unsurpassed ability to exemplify the Arab tribal patriarch.

Nonetheless, the decades of Mu'awiya's rule did not do away with the causes of the first civil wars. Medinans resented the Quraysh for usurping their place. The Shi'a aspired to control the Caliphate. Arab factional conflict simmered beneath the surface. When he died, civil war broke out again. This time it lasted from 680 to 692.

The second Arab civil war was a maelstrom of conflicting interests. It turned on three issues: the struggle among Arab aristocrats for control of the Caliphate, factional rivalries, and sectarian religious rebellions. At Mu'awiya's death, his son and successor, Yazid (680–83), fought against Meccan rivals led by 'Abdallah b. al-Zubayr. 'Ali's son Husayn attempted to move from Medina to Kufa to take up the leadership of his followers, but his small party was intercepted at Karbala (in Iraq) and destroyed. At the time the episode had few repercussions, but Husayn's death gradually assumed the significance of martyrdom. Today Husayn's shrine at Karbala is one of the great pilgrimage sites of the Muslim world. Along with the defeat of his father, Husayn's death at the hands of the Umayyads divides Muslims more than any dispute over law or theology or any antipathy between tribes, races, and linguistic groups. 'Ali is the ancestor of Shi'ism; Husayn is its martyr.

Apart from these direct challenges to the Umayyad Caliphate, the civil war period was marked by widespread factional fighting among Arab groups. Whereas the factions of the first civil war were based on Islamic versus tribal loyalties, the new factions were based upon ad hoc alliances between clans that had come together in the insecure and changing societies of the garrison towns. Though defined in tribal terms the warring coalitions were probably composed of older- and younger-generation migrants. The Syrian tribal coalitions, which had for decades been the mainstay of Mu'awiya's reign, divided into two warring coalitions called Yemen (or Kalb) and Qays. The fighting spread to Iraq, where the factions were called Mudar and Tamim; and to Khurasan where they were called Qays and Rabi'a.

In the meantime, the Kharijis who had repudiated 'Ali after the battle of Siffin also rebelled. The Kharijis formed small bands, usually of between thirty and a hundred men. Each group was at once a terrorist band and a fanatical religious sect. They were held together by the conviction that they were the only true Muslims, and that their rebellions had profound religious justification. A group of Kharijis, called Najda, controlled a good part of Arabia including Bahrain, Oman, Hadhramaut, and Yemen before they were finally crushed. These Khariji bands were most likely formed by uprooted individuals looking for communal affiliation through sectarian movements.

In the end the Umayyads prevailed by force of arms. The Caliph 'Abd al-Malik (685–705), backed by Syrian Yemeni armies, eventually crushed his numerous opponents. The new Caliph and his successor, al-Walid (705–15), now faced with endemic messianic religious opposition – both Shi'a and Khariji – and tribal factionalism provoked by the stress of social change in the garrison cities, had to devise a new strategy. Their solution was to centralize political power even further. In foreign policy, the freshly consolidated Caliphal regime resumed the Arab conquests on a massive scale. The early conquests, which made use of tribal migrations and the annual campaigns of Arab forces based in the garrison cities, were inspired by imperial ambitions and entailed planned attacks on remote places, carried out with the aid of non-Arab forces. These new wars were not fought for tribal expansion, but were imperial wars waged for world domination, and brought North Africa, Spain, Transoxania, and Sind into the Muslim empire.

In domestic policy 'Abd al-Malik demilitarized the Arabs in the garrison cities of Iraq. Henceforth, Syrian forces replaced Iraqi soldiers in all the eastern campaigns. A Syrian army policed Iraq from a new garrison town built at al-Wasit. The Arabs of Kufa and Basra were now treated as pensioned subjects of the empire they had founded. Al-Hajjaj, the governor of Iraq (692–715), no longer sought to conciliate the tribesmen, but threatened to make heads roll. The result of this draconian policy was forty years of internal peace.

In administration 'Abd al-Malik and al-Walid arranged for the translation of the tax registers from Greek and Persian into Arabic. Resumés, copies, and reports now appeared in Arabic. The changeover was made in 697 in Iraq, in 700 in Syria and Egypt, and shortly afterwards in Khurasan. The Caliphs then proceeded to reorganize the finances of various regions. Under 'Umar II (717–20), the Caliphate proposed a major revision of the rules and principles of taxation for the sake of greater uniformity and equity. The Caliph Hisham (724–43) tried to implement 'Umar's policies in Khurasan, Egypt, and Mesopotamia. Umayyad administration also began to develop an organizational identity. In the first decades of the Arab empire, administration had been carried on by Greek- and Persian-speaking officials inherited from the older empires. By 700, however, a new generation of Arab-speaking clients came to power. They and their descendants formed the secretarial backbone of the Arab-Muslim empire until the tenth century.

In line with these administrative developments, the Caliphal court was also reorganized. The days of Mu'awiya, when the Caliph was surrounded by Arab chiefs, were over. Now a court chamberlain kept visitors in order and regulated daily business. The officials of the chancery, the officer of the royal seal, guards and scribes, as well as Arab favorites, surrounded the ruler. Important governorships were still assigned to Arab leaders, but the business of government was conducted by professional administrators rather than by councils of Arab chiefs. The Caliphate had transformed itself from patriarchal rule into an imperial government.

The administrative and military dimensions of later Umayyad statism were backed by a new ideological policy. Whereas the early Caliphate had been a series of individual reigns deeply dependent upon the personal religious or patriarchal qualities of the Caliphs, now the state as an institution was made the focus of ideological loyalty. In the reign of 'Abd al-Malik, for the first time the Caliphate began to mint its own coins in place of Byzantine and Sasanian money. The new system did away with Christian and Zoroastrian symbolism, and introduced gold and silver coins with Arabic script to symbolize the sovereignty of the state – and its independence from, and superiority to – the previous empires. The state also symbolized its sovereignty by undertaking monumental constructions. Under 'Abd al-Malik, Jerusalem was appropriated as a holy place for Islam, and the Dome of the Rock was built on the site of the ancient Hebrew Temple. Under al-Walid, new mosques were built in Medina and Damascus. Their decoration symbolized the glory of the Arabs, the primacy of the state and its indispensability to Islam.

Despite the Islamic tone, however, the inspiration for this transformation was not purely Umayyad. The parallels between the measures taken by 'Abd al-Malik and al-Walid and the practices of the Byzantine and Sasanian empires are striking. In Syria and Egypt, the whole administrative apparatus, including the revenue administration, and even the form of chancery documents, was Byzantine in origin. Syrian military organization also followed Byzantine models. In Iraq, the Sasanian pattern of administrative organization, the fourfold division of finance, military, correspondence, and chancellery services, was adopted by Arab administrators. The sublimity of the emperor-Caliph, the official support of the state for religion, and the construction of monumental churches – or, in this case, mosques – was Byzantine in inspiration. The Umayyads borrowed Greek motifs and even Greek builders and artists to decorate their mosques, and took Sasanian designs and decorations for their palaces. Yet in borrowing the ideas of the previous empires, the Umayyads transformed the traditional motifs and provided old forms with a new content. The statist ideology derived from the previous empires, but its expression was characteristically Islamic.

The crisis of the dynasty and the rise of the 'Abbasids

The assertion of a new form of Arab-Muslim imperium, however, did not allay political and social unrest. The mawali who served as soldiers in the armies and as administrators in the government bureaucracy demanded equality of status and privilege with the Arabs. Peasant converts claimed the right to exemption from the taxes levied on non-Muslims.

Among the Arabs, bitter factional struggles continued. After the second civil war the Yemenis came to represent those demilitarized Arabs who were assimilated to civilian pursuits, and were becoming city dwellers engaged in trade, or village landowners and cultivators. They accepted the assimilation of Arab and non-Arab populations. They desired peace rather than continued wars of expansion, financial equality for Arabs and converts, and the decentralization of Caliphal power. They tended to stress Islamic rather than purely Arab identifications. By contrast, the Qays represented those Arabs who were actively engaged in the army and who

2   The Dome of the Rock

depended for their incomes on conquests, government administration, and tax revenues. They pushed for centralized political power, military expansion, and the
preservation of Arab privileges at the expense of sedentarized Arabs, converts, and
non-Muslim interests.

The struggle among these competing interests came to a head in the reign of
'Umar II (717–20). 'Umar realized that the domination of one ethnic caste over other
peoples was anachronistic. The peoples who filled the armies and staffed the
administration, the merchants and artisans who took a leading part in the propagation of Islam, would all have to be accepted as participants in the empire. The
antagonisms between Arabs and non-Arabs would have to be dissolved in a universal Muslim unity. As 'Umar saw it, the problem was not just to placate the converts while retaining Arab supremacy. Rather, he held that the empire could no
longer be an Arab empire, but had to be the imperium of all Muslims. He thus stood
for the conversion of all of the peoples of West Asia to Islam, and their acceptance
as equals of the Arabs.

In his actual policies, 'Umar showed a pragmatic approach enlightened by principle. He accepted the claim of the mawali that all active Muslim soldiers, Arabs or
not, were entitled to equal pay, and he also accepted the tax equality of all Muslims, but he implemented his decisions in ways that protected the interests of the

state. While converts claimed exemption from land and poll taxes as a form of equality with Arabs, 'Umar ruled that land taxes applied to all landowners regardless of social status, and that both Arab landlords and converts would have to pay them. The poll tax was to be paid only by non-Muslims, but Arab settlers and converts were expected to pay the *sadaqat*, or Muslim alms tax, which partially compensated the state for the loss of poll-tax revenues.

Later Caliphs attempted to implement these principles, but with very limited success. Throughout the late Umayyad period the interest in reconciliation and justice conflicted with the maintenance of the status quo, and Caliphal policy oscillated between tax concessions and cancellation of concessions.

These circumstances provoked opposition, and the stage was set for a third Muslim civil war. In Sunni religious circles there was deep suspicion of and hostility towards the Caliphate. While supporting the regime in principle as the expression of the Muslim community, many Sunni religious leaders were alienated by the military and administrative policies of the regime, by its evident assumption of a royal authority, and by its politically motivated intervention in religious affairs. Sunni thinkers wished to dissociate themselves from the regime and its political compromises, but not from the concept of the Caliphate and its religious significance.

The Shi'a nourished an unsatisfied desire for the family of 'Ali to lead the Muslim world. They claimed that the Caliphate rightly belonged to the members of this family, chosen by God to teach Islam and to rule the Islamic community. They raised the hopes of many disgruntled Arabs and converts that out of them a *mahdi*, a savior, would come. If Banu Hashim had borne Muhammad and 'Ali, might they not produce the messiah to come? Since the second civil war, however, the 'Alid branch of the family of the Prophet had scarcely been manifest in public, but various members were diligently organizing underground conspiracies against the Umayyads. Between 736 and 740, Shi'i agitation finally broke out in Kufa, and a number of Kufans were seized by the police and executed. In 740 Zayd b. 'Ali, a grandson of Husayn, rebelled and was promptly defeated.

Meanwhile, another branch of the Banu Hashim, the 'Abbasids, were biding their time. The 'Abbasids, like the 'Alids, were descended from an uncle of Muhammad, named 'Abbas; but their immediate claim to the Caliphate rested upon the allegation that a great-grandson of 'Ali, Abu Hashim, had bequeathed them leadership of the family and of the opposition movement. While the 'Alid branch of the family concentrated on Kufa with no success, the 'Abbasid branch proselytized in Khurasan, sending a succession of missionary or revolutionary organizers to create a popular front of all opponents of the Umayyads. 'Abbasid agents agitated for revenge for 'Ali, for the overthrow of the Umayyads, and for a new era of peace and justice. Over time, the leading 'Abbasid agent, Abu Muslim, built up an elaborate underground movement and organized military support in Khurasan.

At the death of the Caliph Hisham in 743 the Umayyad regime collapsed, and 'Alids, 'Abbasids, Kharijis, tribal factions, and disgruntled governors all entered the fray. The reasons for this outbreak lay in the military exhaustion of the Syrian state. The late Umayyad Caliphs had increasingly used the military power of Syria to control other Arabs and to stiffen the armies fighting on the frontiers of the empire with professional, battle-hardened troops. Garrison duties exposed Syrian troops in these areas to the brunt of warfare precisely at a time when the Arabs were suffering temporary setbacks. The Turks had driven the Arabs from Transoxania. The Khazars, a nomadic people living beyond the Caucasus, had broken through Arab defenses, defeated them at Ardabil, invaded Armenia, and penetrated as far as Mosul in 730. In 740 the Greeks won a decisive victory over Arab invaders at Acrazas in Anatolia, and destroyed a major Syrian army. Arab and Berber invaders were defeated in central France in 732, and Berber rebellions under the banner of Kharijism broke out in North Africa and destroyed a Syrian army of 27,000 men. What remained of this army made its way to Spain where parts of it helped establish the Spanish Umayyad dynasty. It took yet another Syrian army to quell these rebellions in 742. These defeats brought an end to the imperial phase of Arab empire building and left Syria militarily depleted. Having based a century of rule on the ever-increasing power of the state, the Umayyad dynasty now found itself without the military basis for effective central government. From 744 to 750, Shi'as, Kharijis, and tribal factions struggled to seize the throne. A few thousand troops might prevail.

By 747, the 'Abbasids were ready to move. In the villages of Khurasan, especially around Marw, Abu Muslim, the 'Abbasid agent, found the support he needed. These villages had been settled by the initial Arab conquerors of Khurasan who had become agriculturists, only to find themselves burdened with taxes and treated as a subject population. These were the people who had been promised tax reform by the Umayyads and had been betrayed. Now they were ready to fight. Khurasan was in a fever of political agitation and eschatological expectation. Popular apocryphal writings called *Jafr* and *al-Malahim* foretold fateful battles, the imminent end of the world, the coming of the mahdi, and the beginning of a new era of universal justice. In this atmosphere Abu Muslim rallied peoples aggrieved by loss of status and by unjust taxes, and, with only about three thousand fighting men, defeated rival factions and seized the Caliphate.

The 'Abbasid revolt was supported largely by Arabs, mainly the aggrieved settlers of Marw, with the addition of the Yemeni faction and their mawali. Further support came from Shi'as who were confused as to the identity of the 'Abbasid leadership and took up the cause as their own. They were later to be bitterly disappointed by the proclamation of Abu al-'Abbas, the head of the 'Abbasid house, as the new Caliph. Representing just one of a number of factions that had competed for the office, the 'Abbasids, on coming to power, would have to face the Umayyad problem of translating the title of Caliph into institutions of effective dynastic rule. How they would do this was still an open question in 750. The answer amounted to a revolution.

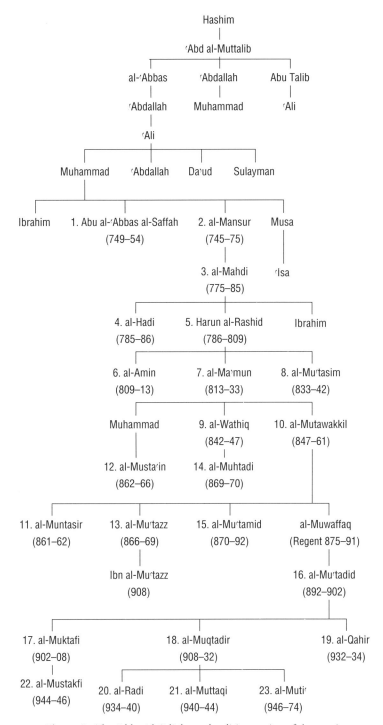

Figure 3 The 'Abbasid Caliphs to the disintegration of the empire

THE 'ABBASID EMPIRE: SOCIAL REVOLUTION AND POLITICAL REACTION

Baghdad

The first venture of the new regime was the creation of a new capital. From ancient times Middle Eastern rulers had built new cities as headquarters for their armies and administrative staff, and to symbolize the advent of a new order. The rulers of the Assyrian empire created the famous cities of Nineveh and Nimrud; the Sasanians founded Ctesiphon. In a strategic location on the main routes between Iraq, Iran, and Syria, in one of the most fertile parts of Iraq with ready access to the Tigris–Euphrates water system, the 'Abbasids built Baghdad to be their palace and administrative base.

Like its predecessors, Baghdad rapidly transcended the intentions of its founders, and grew from a military and administrative center into a major city. The very decision to build the administrative center, called the City of Peace (*madinat al-salam*), generated two large settlements in the vicinity. One was the extensive camp of the 'Abbasid army in the districts to the north of the palace complex, called al-Harbiya, and the other, to the south, was al-Karkh, inhabited by thousands of construction workers brought from Iraq, Syria, Egypt, and Iran. Here were markets to provision the workers and their families, workshops to produce their clothes, utensils, and tools, and factories to supply the building materials for the construction project. The original Baghdad, then, was a three-part complex – the troop settlement in al-Harbiya, the working populations in al-Karkh, and the administrative city itself, Madinat al-Salam. No sooner was Madinat al-Salam completed than the decisions of the Caliphs to build additional palace residences and administrative complexes in the immediate vicinity stimulated the growth of additional quarters. Across the Tigris the new palace district of al-Rusafa also promoted urban development.

Never had there been a Middle Eastern city so large. Baghdad was not a single city, but a metropolitan center, made up of a conglomeration of districts on both sides of the Tigris River. In the ninth century it measured about 25 square miles, and had a population of between 300,000 and 500,000. It was ten times the size of Sasanian Ctesiphon, and it was larger than all of the settled places – cities, towns, villages, and hamlets combined – in the Diyala region. It was larger than Constantinople, which is estimated to have had a population of 200,000, or any other Middle Eastern city until Istanbul in the sixteenth century. In its time, Baghdad was the largest city in the world outside China.

Its vast size is an index of its importance in the formation of the 'Abbasid empire, society, and culture. A capital city, Baghdad became a great commercial city for international trade and immensely productive textile, leather, paper, and other industries. Jews, Christians, and Muslims, as well as secret pagans, Persians, Iraqis, Arabs, Syrians, and Central Asians made up its cosmopolitan population. Soldiers and officials, the workers who built the new city, the people who lived in the surrounding villages, merchants from Khurasan and the East who engaged in the India traffic through the Persian Gulf, also settled in Baghdad. Basrans seeking intellectual

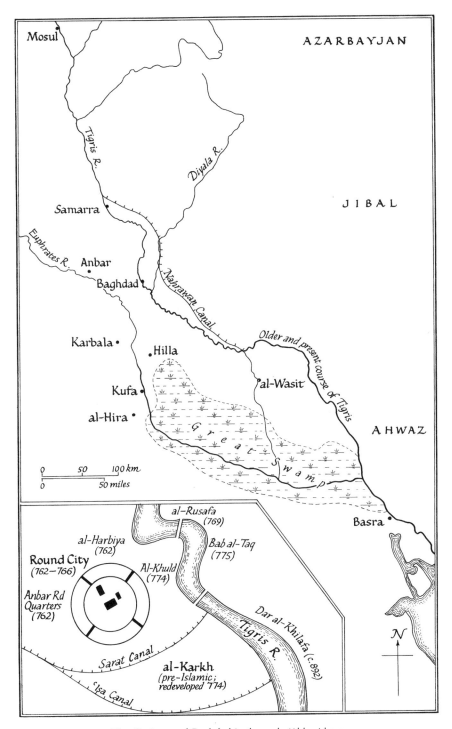

Map 3 Iraq and Baghdad in the early 'Abbasid era

contacts and business fortunes, notables and landowners from Ahwaz, cloth workers from Khuzistan, prisoners of war from Anatolia, scholars from Alexandria,
Harran, and Jundishapur, and Nestorian Christians from villages all over Iraq made
Baghdad their home. Baghdad, then, was the product of the upheavals, population
movements, economic changes, and conversions of the preceding century; the
home of a new Middle Eastern society, heterogeneous and cosmopolitan, embracing numerous Arab and non-Arab elements, now integrated into a single society
under the auspices of the Arab empire and the Islamic religion. It provided the
wealth and manpower to govern a vast empire; it crystallized the culture that became
Islamic civilization.

'Abbasid administration: the central government

The creation of Baghdad was part of the 'Abbasid strategy to cope with the problems that had destroyed the Umayyad dynasty, by building effective governing
institutions, and mobilizing adequate political support from Arab Muslims, converts,
and from the non-Muslim communities that paid the empire's taxes. The new
dynasty had to secure the loyalty and obedience of its subjects for a rebel regime
and justify itself in Muslim terms.

To deal with these problems the new dynasty returned to the principles of 'Umar
II. The 'Abbasids swept away Arab caste supremacy and accepted the universal
equality of Muslims. They did away with the anachronism of the Arab "nation in
arms," and frankly embraced all Muslims as their supporters. Arab caste supremacy
had lost its political meaning, and only a coalition regime, uniting Arab and non-
Arab elements, could govern a Middle Eastern empire. The propagation of Arabic
as a lingua franca, the spread of Islam and the conversion of at least some proportion of the population, the tremendous expansion of commercial activities, and
the economic and demographic upheavals that set people free from their old lives
and launched them on new careers in new cities such as Baghdad made possible
an empire-wide recruitment of personnel and of political support for the new
regime. Under the 'Abbasids the empire no longer belonged to the Arabs, though
they had conquered its territories, but to all those peoples who would share in Islam
and in the emerging networks of political and cultural loyalties that defined a new
cosmopolitan Middle Eastern society.

The new regime organized new armies and fresh administrative cadres. The
'Abbasids abolished the military privileges of the Arabs qua Arabs, and built up new
forces which though partly Arab were recruited and organized so that they would
be loyal to the dynasty alone, and not to tribal or caste interests. The Umayyads
had already begun to replace provincial Arab forces with Syrian troops, non-Arab
converts to Islam, mawali, and even local non-Arab, non-Muslim forces, as in
Khurasan and Transoxania, and tried to concentrate military and political power in
the hands of picked Syrian regiments loyal to the Caliphs. Yet they were never able
to declare in principle or to complete in practice the transition from the Arab "nation

in arms" to professional armies. Throughout the Umayyad period Arab forces were still needed for international conquests. Conversely, while the 'Abbasids continued to use Arab troops in Yemen, India, Armenia, and on the Byzantine frontiers, the end of the conquests meant that Arabs in Iraq, Khurasan, Syria, and Egypt could be retired from military service. The 'Abbasids no longer needed vast reserves of manpower. Rather, they required only limited frontier forces, and a central army to make occasional expeditions against the Byzantines, and to suppress internal opposition. For this purpose they used the army with which they had captured the state – the Khurasanian Arabs and their clients and descendants, a professional force loyal to the Caliphs who paid them.

The openness of the 'Abbasid regime was particularly evident in administration. Many of the scribes in the expanding 'Abbasid bureaucracy were Persians from Khurasan. Nestorian Christians were powerfully represented, probably because they made up a large proportion of the population of Iraq. Jews were active in tax and banking activities. Shi'i families were also prominent, and Arabs did not altogether lose their important place. The 'Abbasid dynasty was Arab; the 'Abbasid armies were composed of Arabs, and the judicial and legal life of Baghdad and other important cities was in Arab hands. The prominence of Arabs, however, was no longer a prescriptive right, but was dependent upon loyalty to the dynasty.

A revolutionary social policy was accompanied by the perpetuation of Umayyad administrative and governmental precedents. Just as the Umayyads had inherited Roman and Sasanian bureaucratic practices and even the remnants of the old organizations, the 'Abbasids inherited the traditions and the personnel of Umayyad administration. Clientele ties to the Caliphs themselves were the essence of government organization. At first the ministries were just the clerical staffs of the leading officials, and the Caliphs were consulted about everything. In time, however, the ad hoc, household character of the Caliphate was substantially (though by no means entirely) superseded by a more rationalized form of administration. The business of the government became more routinized and three types of services or bureaus (diwans) developed. The first was the chancery, the *diwan al-rasa'il*, the records and correspondence office. The second was the bureaus for tax collection, such as the *diwan al-kharaj*. Third, there were bureaus to pay the expenses of the Caliphs' armies, court, and pensioners; the army bureau, *diwan al-jaysh*, was the most important of these. As time went on, the conduct of business grew more elaborate and more specialized. Each function – revenue, chancery, disbursement – was subdivided into a host of offices, and each office was subdivided into divisions to carry on auxiliary activities.

Alongside the bureaucratic staffs, the Caliphs also appointed *qadis*, or judges. They were usually selected from among the leading scholars of Muslim law, and their duty was to apply this law to the civil affairs of the Muslim population. Other judicial officials dealt with state-related issues; customary law continued to be used in small communities.

With this elaboration of functions and offices, the Caliphs found themselves less and less able to supervise the business of the state. To keep the organization responsive to the will of the ruler they instituted internal bureaucratic checks. Financial affairs were watched by the *diwan al-azimma*, the controller's office, which was originally attached to each diwan but later evolved into an independent bureau of the budget. Correspondence had to go through the hands of the drafting agency, the *diwan al-tawqi'*, for countersignature, and the *khatam*, the keeper of the seal. In a special administrative court, the *mazalim*, the Caliphs, advised by leading judges, adjudicated fiscal and administrative problems. The *barid*, the official messenger and information service, spied on the rest of the government.

Finally, the office of the *wazir* was developed to coordinate, supervise, and check on the operations of the bureaucracy. Wazir was the title originally applied to the secretaries or administrators who were close assistants of the Caliphs and whose powers varied according to the wishes of their patrons. Under the Caliphs al-Mahdi (775–85) and Harun al-Rashid (786–809), the Barmakid family rose to particular prominence. Originally a Buddhist priestly family from Balkh, they were made generals and provincial governors, and served as the tutors of young princes. Still, however powerful, the Barmakids were not chiefs of the whole administration, but depended on the changing impulses of the Caliphs for their positions. In 803, Harun al-Rashid executed the leading members of the family. Not until the middle of the ninth century did the wazir become the chief of administration, with the combined duties of controlling the bureaucracy, nominating provincial officials, and sitting on the mazalim court.

The elaborate central government was the nerve center of the empire, and from Baghdad the Caliphs maintained communications with the provinces. But despite the propensities of the central administration, the provinces were not all governed in a bureaucratic manner. The degree of control ran from highly centralized administration to loosely held suzerainty. The empire was tolerant and inclusive rather than monolithic.

Provincial government

The directly controlled provinces were Iraq, Mesopotamia, Egypt, Syria, western Iran, and Khuzistan – the provinces physically closest to the capital. Khurasan was sometimes, but not always, included in this group. These provinces were organized to maximize the obedience of officials to the will of the central government and to assure the remittance of tax revenues from the provinces to the center. Governors' appointments were limited to a very short term so that their careers would be entirely at the mercy of the Caliphs. They were rapidly rotated to prevent them from developing local support they might use against the central government. In addition, the powers of provincial government were often divided among several officials. The governor was usually the military commander, and a different man was appointed by the central treasury to be in charge of taxation and financial affairs; yet another official headed the judiciary. These officials checked each other's powers, and all officials were subject to the supervision of the barid.

The ideal of frequent rotation of governors, separation of civil and military powers, and inspection by the barid was hard to implement. Governorships were often awarded in payment of political debts to warlords, generals, and members of the royal family who had acquiesced in the accession of a Caliph or in his succession plans, and Caliphs had to give these appointees wide latitude in the administration of their provinces. In such cases, frequent rotation and the separation of civil and military functions might be waived.

Outside the directly administered provinces were affiliated regions that were scarcely, if at all, controlled by the central government. Geographically these were the provinces of the Caspian highlands – Jilan, Tabaristan, Daylam, and Jurjan; the Inner Asian provinces – Transoxania, Farghana, Ushrusana, and Kabul; and most of North Africa. In some peripheral provinces the Caliphs appointed a supervising military governor and assigned a garrison to see to the collection of taxes and the payment of tribute. For example, until the middle of the ninth century, Armenia and Tabaristan had Arab governors who overawed the local rulers and collected tribute. These governors had no direct administrative contact with the subject people; the actual collection of taxes was in local hands.

In other cases, the Caliphate merely confirmed local dynasties as "governors of the Caliphs." Khurasan, which until 820 was directly ruled by Caliphal appointees, came under the control of the Tahirid family (820–73). Officially the Tahirids were selected by the Caliphs, but the Caliphs always confirmed the family heirs to the office. The Tahirids paid very substantial tributes, but no one from the central government intervened to assure the payments or to inspect their administration. Transoxania under the Samanids was governed in the same way. The Samanids had been a local ruling family since Sasanian times, but in the wake of the incorporation of Transoxania into the Islamic empire, they converted to Islam. In the Caliphate of al-Ma'mun (813–33), the ruling members of the family were named hereditary governors of Samarqand, Farghana, and Herat, without further supervision.

Local government

Local government was similarly varied. Iraq was divided into a hierarchy of districts, called *kura, tassuj*, and *rustaq*. The rustaq was the bottom unit in the hierarchy and consisted of a market and administrative town surrounded by a number of villages. The same hierarchy and even the same names were used in parts of Khurasan and western Iran. In Egypt the structure of administration was similar.

Local government was organized for taxation. Surveys were taken in the villages to determine the amount of land under cultivation, the crops grown, and their expected yield, and the information was passed up to the central administration. The taxes for whole regions would be estimated, the sums divided up for each district, and the demand notices sent out describing the responsibilities of each subdivision.

Each sub-unit received its bill and divided it among the smaller units. At the next stage, taxes were collected, local expenses deducted, and the balance passed upwards until the surplus eventually reached Baghdad.

This hierarchical administration did not encompass all cultivated lands. The crown lands, which included the estates of older Middle Eastern empires, church properties, reclaimed wastelands, and lands purchased or confiscated by the Caliphate, were not part of the usual provincial tax administration. Such lands were very extensive in Iraq and western Iran.

Other lands, called *iqta'*, were also cut off from regular provincial administration. One type of iqta', *iqta' tamlik*, was frequently, though not always, ceded out of wastelands, for the sake of stimulating agricultural investment. The concessionaire was expected to reclaim the land and assure its cultivation in return for a three-year grace period and a long-term reduction of taxes. Ultimately such lands became private property, since a concession holder could pass it on to his heirs.

A second type of iqta', called *iqta' istighlal*, resembled a tax-farm. In this case, lands already in cultivation and part of the general revenue administration were assigned to individuals who agreed to pay the treasury a fixed sum of money in return for the right to tax the peasantry. The assignee's payment was assessed at the *'ushr* or 10 percent rate, but he was permitted to exact from the peasants full taxes at the kharaj (land tax) rates, which usually amounted to a third or a half of the value of the crop. The benefit given the assignee was the difference between what the peasants paid him and what he paid the government.

There were several reasons for making these kinds of grants. Such lands were conceded as a way of paying off political debts to the 'Abbasid family, important courtiers, officials, and military officers who had claims on the state for rewards, pensions, or bribes for their support and cooperation. Such grants also simplified administration by obviating the need for collecting revenues in the provinces, bringing the specie to Baghdad, and redistributing the income through yet other bureaus. Instead of keeping surveys and records for large areas, all that was necessary was the description of the assignment and the amount due. Nevertheless, before the middle of the ninth century, iqta's were assigned with relative restraint, for they represented an important concession of state revenues and state powers. Never in this period were they assigned in lieu of payment of military salaries.

Furthermore, whatever the organizational forms of local government, local administration and tax collection posed delicate political problems. Despite the immense power of the bureaucratic organization, it was extremely difficult to make that power effective in the villages. The bureaucracy was admirably suited to the communication of orders and to clerical and financial tasks, but in the villages, the power of the state was limited by ignorance. How could the government tax the peasantry without knowing who owned the land, how much was produced, who had money, and who did not? How was the state to work its way through the millennia-old complications of land ownership, water rights, and other legal matters?

How was the state to know if crops were concealed? The state came to the villages with staffs of technical specialists such as surveyors to make land measurements, weighers and measurers to estimate the size of crops, and bankers and money changers to convert currencies or to give credits. It came with legal specialists, judges to adjudicate disputes, witnesses to transactions, registrars of deeds, and the like. Alongside the technicians, it came with specialists in violence, collectors, soldiers, police, extortionists, stool pigeons, and thugs. Fear was no small part of the business of tax collection.

Yet, with all this, the potential for passive resistance and the problem of inadequate information could not be solved without the cooperation of local people. These included family patriarchs, village headmen (such as the *ra'is* in Iran, or the *shaykh al-balad* in Egypt), and village landowners, who controlled a large part of the village land and were much richer than the average peasant, but not so wealthy as the great estate or iqta' holders. In Iraq and Iran, the *dihqans* included native elites and Arabs who had acquired land, village-dwelling and town-dwelling absentee landlords, grain merchants, and money changers who bought the peasants' crops, or lent them money to pay their taxes.

These notables played an important intermediary role in the taxation process. As the most powerful people connected with the villages, they handled negotiations, made a deal on behalf of the peasants, and paid the taxes. The arrangement suited everyone. The bureaucratic agents were never absolutely sure how much money they could raise, and wished to avoid the nuisance of dealing with individuals. The peasants did not have to confront the exorbitant demands of the tax collectors directly. The notables underestimated the taxes to the state, overestimated them to the peasants, and pocketed the difference. 'Abbasid officials understood perfectly well the importance of these people, whom they called their *a'wan* (helpers). They understood that for the ultimate tasks of assessment, division, and collection of taxes the bureaucracy had to depend on people who were not subordinates, who could not be given orders, but whose cooperation had to be enlisted nonetheless.

Thus, the 'Abbasid imperial organization was a complex bureaucracy highly elaborate at the center and in touch with provincial and local forces throughout the empire. Yet the arrangements between the central government and the provincial and local levels were not simply hierarchical. At each level, the business of administration was carried on by independent people. In some cases these were princes or independent governors who controlled whole provinces, while in others they were the local village chiefs and landowners without whom the central and provincial governments were helpless. Since the ties of government were not strictly hierarchical, a complex system of constraints and opportunities, obligations and loyalties, bound the central, provincial, and local notables to the regime.

These ties depended first of all upon the fact that the army, the police, and the inspectors of the barid could compel obedience. Also, self-interest dictated the collaboration of village chiefs and landowners because participation in the tax-collecting apparatus consolidated their local position. It increased their political importance, conferred upon them the prestige, authority, and respect accorded the state, and gave them financial opportunities. Apart from force and interest, class and clientele loyalties drew together central administrators and local elites. The officials of the central government were drawn from the provincial notable families. Provincial landowning and notable families sent their sons to careers in the central government. Merchant families maintained branches in Baghdad, and facilitated financial contacts between the administrative center and the provinces.

Patronage and clienteles were crucial to this system. Central administrators appointed their provincial representatives, and patronage – fortified by ethnic, religious, regional, and family affiliations – no doubt helped to smooth the operations of the ʿAbbasid state. For example, a governor of Khurasan, Tahir (820–22), explained that only he could govern the province because all the notable families were allied to him by marriage and clientship. Clientele ties also crossed religious lines. Converts to Islam at the center dealt with provincial cousins who remained Christians or Zoroastrians. Conversion to the new religion did not necessarily disrupt family, clientele, and regional ties. Thus, the ʿAbbasid policy of recruiting notables regardless of ethnic background not only soothed the conflicts that racked the Umayyad dynasty, but was essential if a centralized government was to be built at all. Insofar as effective administration was based upon sympathetic communication between central officials and local notables, the wider the recruitment, the greater the possibility for effective rule. The ʿAbbasid empire, then, was formed by a coalition of provincial and capital city elites, who agreed on a common concept of the dynasty and the purposes of political power, and who were organized through bureaucratic and other political institutions to impose their rule on Middle Eastern peoples.

Resistance and rebellion

This regime did not impose itself in a single moment, but only after decades of political struggle. The process of empire building was not smooth and uninterrupted, but depended on the forcible subjection of many dissident and unwilling populations. Mountainous provinces remote from Baghdad most easily resisted subordination. In the Caspian region the rulers of Tabaristan and Daylam, in Inner Asia the semi-independent provinces of Kabul, Ushrusana, and Farghana refused tribute or allegiance, obliging the Caliphs to send military expeditions to recover their suzerainty. By the reign of al-Maʾmun (813–33), however, most of these places were incorporated into the empire and their rulers and officials converted to Islam. In North Africa the tendency after 800 was toward independence, although local ruling houses recognized the suzerainty of the Caliphate.

Arab opposition was also important. The old military caste, deprived of employment, salaries and prestige, and displaced by a single professional army, sporadically resisted the ʿAbbasid settlement. Syrian Arabs rebelled in 760 and were defeated. In Egypt, the ʿAbbasids established their own garrisons at al-Askar near Fustat, provoking Arab tribal fighting (785) and rebellions (793–4). Bedouins in

Syria, Arabia, Sistan, Kirman, Fars, Khurasan, and most of all in upper Mesopotamia where Arab and Kurdish outbreaks were virtually incessant, rebelled against the consolidation of any government that might restrict their autonomy. Until the beginning of the ninth century bedouin rebels adopted Kharijism to articulate their opposition to the empire. From then on Shi'ism became the main expression of tribal opposition to centralized government.

In Iran, peasant villagers and mountaineers kept up their own staccato opposition to the 'Abbasid regime. Resistance to the Caliphate took the form of syncretistic sects, blending Shi'ism and Mazdaism, "heresies" from both Islam and Zoroastrianism. The first of these Iranian rebellions was the rebellion of Bihafarid, a peasant leader near Nishapur, which spread widely in Khurasan in 747–50, advocating a combination of Muslim ideas and the ancient worship of Ahura Mazda. The rebellion was put down by the 'Abbasid governor Abu Muslim – significantly, at the request of the Zoroastrian mobads, for it was a threat to the notables and to both Islamic and Zoroastrian beliefs.

This same Abu Muslim later became the symbol of religious and social opposition. His role in the 'Abbasid revolution made him, in the popular imagination, a precursor of the messiah and inspired Shi'i–Mazdaite syncretic heresies and rebellions in his name. The first of these broke out in the region of Nishapur under the leadership of a man named Sunpadh. Supported by the mountain peoples of Khurasan, it spread as far west as Rayy and Qum. Sunpadh preached that Abu Muslim was not dead, but lived on in the company of Mazdak and the mahdi and would return again. Similar outbreaks followed in Rayy, Herat, and Sistan. The most important of these was the movement led by a self-styled prophet called al-Muqanna, the veiled one. Al-Muqanna preached that he was God incarnate and that the spirit of God had passed from Muhammad to 'Ali to Abu Muslim to him. He would, he said, die and return to rule the world. His emphasis on the passage of the spirit and his return as imam was parallel to extremist Shi'i views, and he was accused of advocating the Mazdaite social doctrines – communism of money and community of women. Most of his support came from peasant villages.

Insofar as the 'Abbasid regime in Iran depended upon the collaboration of a Muslim imperial elite with local notables who were both Muslims and Zoroastrians, the empire presented itself as a kind of dual orthodoxy based upon a joint Muslim–Zoroastrian elite. Thus resistance to the consolidation of the empire was bound to cast itself in the form of syncretic religious heterodoxy. The unusual degree of religious ferment was also due to the fact that in the wake of the Arab invasions and decades of warfare in Transoxania, the older religions, Zoroastrian and Christian, were severely disorganized and the new faith, Islam, not yet organized. The eighth century was a time of unique freedom for religious invention as part of social and political conflict.

Throughout the 'Abbasid empire the most profound opposition to the Caliphate took the form of Shi'ism. The Shi'a had supported the 'Abbasid movement before it came to power, expecting that one of the heirs of 'Ali would succeed the

Umayyads, but the 'Abbasids disappointed these expectations by seizing the Caliphate for themselves. Thus in Basra, Kufa, Mecca, and Medina, the Shi'a generated a number of minor rebellions. A major Shi'i rebellion, backed by the bedouin tribes of upper Mesopotamia, took place between 813 and 816. In the early tenth century, the Isma'ili movement, an offshoot of Shi'ism, would provoke a new wave of anti-'Abbasid provincial resistance.

Thus, the 'Abbasid empire as a political system has to be understood in terms of its organization, its social dynamics, its political concepts, and also in terms of its opponents. As an empire it was a regime governing a vast territory composed of small communities. Each community was headed by its notables: headmen, landowners, and other men of wealth and standing, who characteristically were allied to superiors and patrons with positions in the provincial or central governments. Government organization, communication and tax collection was bureaucratic in form, but the social mechanism that made the organization work was the contacts between central officials and provincial elites. The bureaucracy mobilized the skills and social influence of prominent persons throughout the empire and put these assets at the disposal of Baghdad. This system of alliances was justified as an expression of God's will. By God's will, expressed both in Muslim and in pre-Islamic Middle Eastern terms, the exalted person of the Caliph reigned in expectation of passive obedience from all his subjects.

However, not all peoples and provinces of the empire would submit to the imperial order. Mountain peoples, semi-sedentarized villagers, peasants, nomads, and segments of the town populations, including strata of the upper as well as the lower classes, refused to accept the system. They denied its legitimacy, and rebelled against it, though they could not overthrow it. Nor could they be altogether repressed. The 'Abbasid regime was locked into constant struggle with its opponents.

CHAPTER 5

COSMOPOLITAN ISLAM:
THE ISLAM OF THE IMPERIAL ELITE

The Arab conquests and settlement, century-long processes of economic and social change, and the formation of cosmopolitan urban societies and of a vast empire, not only governed political events but were the bases for the emergence of an Islamic civilization. New forms of Islamic religion and culture emerged as the expression of the communities and of the empire brought forth by the Arab conquests.

Islam, of course, goes back to the Prophet Muhammad, the revelation of the Quran, and the first Muslim community in Medina and Mecca, but the Islamic religion, as we now know it, was the amplification of these teachings, carried out in later centuries, not only in the original home of Islam in Arabia, but throughout the whole of the vast region from Spain to Inner Asia conquered by the Arab Muslims. The Islamic religion in this sense encompassed not only the Quran and the example of Muhammad, but a vastly expanded range of religious study and practices including law, theology, and mysticism, developed in numerous schools and sub-communities. Islam in this sense refers to the whole panoply of religious concepts and communities through which the original inspiration was later expressed. Furthermore, Islamic ideas permeated the poetry and belles-lettres, arts and sciences that were also the cultural expressions of the new Muslim empire and societies. In this larger body of literature, arts, and sciences, religious and non-religious influences intermingled.

In the Umayyad and early 'Abbasid periods there were two foci of Islamic religious and cultural development. On the one hand, Islam expressed the political identity of the court, the Caliphate and the political elites; on the other, it expressed the religious, moral, and social values of the Muslim urban populations. Out of the two milieus came two different forms of early Islamic civilization. The court milieus contributed especially to Islamic art, architecture, philosophy, science, and Iranian and Hellenistic forms of literature in Arabic. The city milieus contributed the literatures of Quran interpretation, law, mysticism, and theology in conjunction with an

Arabic belles-lettres. Some subjects, such as poetry, theology, and history, were cultivated in both milieus.

To consolidate their regimes, the Umayyad and 'Abbasid dynasties attempted to give cultural legitimacy to the Arab-Muslim imperium and to weld the disparate elements of the governing class – the Caliph, his family and boon companions, Arab tribal chiefs and generals, Inner Asian soldiers, Iranian administrators, Christian ecclesiastics, and Muslim religious scholars – into a cohesive imperial elite. While accepting an Islamic identity the court and imperial versions of Islamic culture stressed the aspects of poetry, philosophy, science, art, and architecture that could help define the authority of the regime and the legitimacy of the ruling classes. A literary and philosophic culture was needed to present a vision of the universe as a whole, of the role of the state and the ruler in the divine plan and in the functioning of human society, and a concept of the nature of human beings and their destiny in this world and the next. In Umayyad and 'Abbasid societies this vision was expressed partly in Muslim terms and partly in literary and artistic terms inherited from the ancient cultures of the Middle East.

In the Umayyad period, this imperial culture included Arabic poetry, derived from pre-Islamic conventions and oral traditions concerning the history of the Arabs, the life of the Prophet, the origins of Islam, and the deeds of the early Caliphs. It also incorporated Byzantine and Sasanian artistic and literary materials. Thus, Umayyad mosques and palaces fused Christian and Byzantine decorative and iconographic motifs with Muslim uses and concepts to create new modes of Islamic architecture. The Umayyads also sponsored formal debates among Muslims and Christians which led to the absorption of Hellenistic concepts into Muslim theology.

The 'Abbasid dynasty enlarged this repertoire, and patronized Arabic poetry (in both old bedouin and new courtly genres), the translation into Arabic of Iranian literary classics (including works of history, polite literature, fables, political precepts, and manuals of protocol and behavior for scribes), and the mythic and scientific lore of Persia and India. Similarly, Syriac and Greek classics were translated into Arabic. The Caliph al-Ma'mun established an academy and observatory, the *bayt al-hikma*, to stimulate the translation of logical, scientific, and philosophical works into Arabic.

ART, ARCHITECTURE, AND THE CONCEPT OF THE CALIPHATE

The quintessential expression of this imperial program was court ceremony, art, and architecture. The court of the Umayyad Caliphs became a theater enacting the drama of royalty. The Caliph's residence was approached by ceremonial gates; its central feature was a longitudinal hall culminating in an absidal or domed room – a pattern found at Damascus, al-Wasit, Mushatta, and later Baghdad – derived from Hellenistic, Roman, Byzantine, and Sasanian patterns for the emperor's court. The Caliph held audience dressed in crown and royal robes, seated on a throne, and veiled from the rest of his audience by a curtain. His courtiers stood or sat on each side of the long hall. His day included consultations and receptions, prayer, and private entertainments – hunting, music, dancing girls, wine drinking, and poetry reading. A chamberlain controlled access to the royal person; everyone addressed him in submissive tones and with panegyric greetings.

The decorations of the court mirrored the royal way of life; representations of the Caliph depicted his majesty and power. In the desert palace at Qasr al-Khayr the Caliph appears in a formal, frontal pose; at Khirbat al-Mafjar he assumes a martial figure. Representations at Qusayr 'Amra portray the Caliph in a hieratic manner derived from Byzantine depictions of the Christ as Pantocrator. At Qusayr 'Amra his majesty also appears in its full triumph in a painting of the Shah of Iran, the Emperor of Byzantium, Roderic of Spain, the Negus of Abyssinia, the Emperor of China, and the Emperor of the Turks greeting the Caliph as their master. The family of kings is portrayed as deriving its authority from its new suzerain, the Islamic Caliph, whose power embraces not only Islam, but the whole world. Other scenes depict hunting and gardens, birds and animals, banquets, attendants, and dancing girls. The court with its domed room was the center of the universe; its decorations signified the gathering of the living cosmos to glorify the Caliph. The Caliph is majestic; his reign universal; his court paradise. Art was a narcissistic affirmation of royalty.

The array of court symbols conveyed the august majesty and unique rank of the Caliph among men. He was entitled to dress and furnishings, to ceremonies and amusements, and to gestures of respect that no other humans enjoyed. Court poetry glorified the ruler and surrounded him with a divine aura. The court poets addressed the Caliph as *khalifat allah* (the deputy of God). The panegyrics some-times imputed supernatural powers to him; his intercession brought rain. The *bay'a*, or oath of allegiance, became a gesture of the humble servitude of the courtier and subject before his overlord. Obedience and fidelity to an adored majestic person-age was a leading theme in Umayyad court life.

By contrast, the public art of the Umayyad Caliphs emphasized Islamic themes. The reign of 'Abd al-Malik inaugurated public displays with the construction of the Dome of the Rock in Jerusalem. The Dome of the Rock was built in the most sacred city of Judaism and Christianity in order to signify the political and religious appro-priation of the past by a new faith embodied in a new empire. It asserted the sov-ereignty of the Caliph as the conqueror of old religions and empires and the benefactor of Islam. The Dome of the Rock was built on the legendary site of Abra-ham's intended sacrifice of Ishmael, the favored son in Muslim tradition, for the Muslims meant to forge a direct connection to the common ancestor of mono-theism, thereby rendering Islam as venerable as the other religions. To appropriate and modify the Jewish temple area was to assert the primacy of Islam and its super-session of the previous monotheistic religions. The Islamic triumph was further cel-ebrated in the decoration of the building. Its ornamental motifs were borrowed from Byzantine and Persian forms, which expressed holiness and power, but were

3　The central portico of the Umayyad Mosque of Damascus

now used to show the sovereignty of Islam. Inscriptions proclaimed the mission of Islam, the truth of the new faith, and the surpassing of the old.

The Umayyad Mosque of Damascus expressed different themes. The mosque itself was built by the absorption of a pagan sanctuary, with its classical, Roman, Hellenistic motifs, and a Christian church, into a new and distinctly Muslim architecture. The mosaics showed idyllic buildings and landscapes which may represent heaven or may imply the subjection of the whole world to the new Caliphs and the new faith. Moreover, in constructing the mosque and its decorations, the Umayyads employed Greek craftsmen whom they solicited from the emperor of Constantinople. To the Greeks this implied the cultural and political superiority of Byzantium; the Muslims, however, construed it as an appropriation of Byzantine culture and power, a submission of Greek vassals to Muslim masters, and an exhibition of the ambition, triumph, and supersession of Byzantium by a Muslim imperium.

Similarly, the mosque of Medina bore witness to the victories of Islam. Umayyad Caliphs furnished this sacred place with the most exotic and luxurious spoils. They sent necklaces, ruby-encrusted crescents, cups, and thrones to emphasize the submission of non-Muslim peoples to Islam. The very structure of the mosque evoked the Caliph's glory. It was built in Hellenistic royal architectural design, and contained a longitudinal hall, absidal niche, and a *minbar* (pulpit) from which the official Friday sermon recognizing the sovereignty of the Caliph and important political announcements were made. The mosque also contained a box (*maqsura*) to seclude the Caliph from his subjects, much as he was secluded at court. These architectural features identified the faith of Islam with the Caliph and made the mosque itself a symbol of his prestige. In design, decoration, inscriptions, and ceremonial usage the mosque became a public version of the private court of the Caliph, witness to his triumphs and his primacy in Islam.

The Caliph as conqueror and endower treated religion as an intrinsic aspect of his own identity, and the mosque as a symbol of the compact union of the political and religious aspects of his rule. Before entering the mosque the Caliph al-Walid would change from perfumed and multicolored clothes to pure white garments. On returning to the palace he would again put on the worldly and splendid garb of the court. While the Caliphate took Islam into its political majesty, Islam absorbed the Caliph into the service of religion.

The 'Abbasid dynasty accepted this exalted position. Like its predecessor it adopted the court ceremony, protocol, and decorations depicting the majesty of the ruler, and the architectural monuments that expressed the semi-divine, cosmic, and universal importance of his person. The Caliphal conception of itself was further legitimized in non-Islamic Persian, Hellenistic, and other Middle Eastern terms. The Caliph was the vice-regent of God on earth. By his magical powers he upheld the order of the cosmos, providing for the rain and the harvests, keeping all persons in their places and seeing to it that they fulfilled their functions in society. He was the symbol of civilization: agriculture, cities, arts, and learning depended on his

4 Mosaics of the Damascus mosque (detail)

blessings. The poets approximated this awe as best they could. Court poets and court protocol elevated the Caliphs above angels and prophets, calling them the chosen of God, God's shadow on earth, a refuge for all of his lesser creatures. In the middle of the tenth century, a court chronicler reports that an unsophisticated provincial soldier, overcome by the splendor of the Caliph's appearance, momentarily thought he was in the presence of God.

Palaces and palace-cities also manifested the majesty of the Caliphate. Baghdad incorporated materials taken from the ruins of Sasanian palaces. Its design had symbolic implications. The Madinat al-Salam was a round city divided into quadrants by axial streets running from east to west and north to south, with the palace in the very center. The structure of the city reproduced the symmetry and hierarchy of society and the central position of the Caliph within it. It also symbolized the cosmic and heavenly world; the central placement of the Caliph signified his sovereignty over the four quarters of the world. Since ancient times the founding of a city had signified the creation of order out of chaos in the geographic, social, and cosmic levels of the universe. By the construction of a new city the Caliph became not only the upholder but also the creator of order in the otherwise formless, boundless, and threatening experience of mankind.

The 'Abbasids also reaffirmed the Muslim basis of their legitimacy. They claimed to be appointed by God to follow in the ways of the Prophet and to lead the Muslim community along the path of Islam. They had come to power on a current of messianic hopes, and their very titles stressed their role as saviors. Al-Mansur, al-Mahdi, al-Hadi, and al-Rashid claimed to be guided by God in righteous ways, to bring enlightenment, and to return the Muslims to the true path. They patronized scholars. They promoted the pilgrimage to Mecca by organizing the way stations, by providing military security in the desert, and by making gifts to the holy places. They themselves made the journey. The 'Abbasid Caliphs also tried to draw Muslim religious leaders into public service as judges and administrators. They created a judicial hierarchy and tried to use the judges as intermediaries to organize cadres of scholars, teachers, and legists under the jurisdiction as well as the patronage of the state.

Furthermore, the 'Abbasids intervened in doctrinal matters. Beginning in the reign of al-Mahdi, the Caliphs made themselves responsible for the defense of what they held to be Islamic orthodoxy against free thinkers and heretics. Al-Mahdi began the persecution of the *zanadiqa*. The word means Manichaeans or dualists who believed in the existence of two divine powers, one for good and one for evil, as opposed to the unitary conception of Islam, but the term was used more generally to justify the suppression of Arab poets, theologians, scribes, and others. The 'Abbasids really aimed at defining the boundaries of acceptable doctrine and unifying their cadres on common religious grounds. They had conceived the notion of a church hierarchy under state control as a foundation for political power.

This effort to bring Muslim religious life under state supervision descended from both Byzantine and Sasanian conceptions. Byzantine emperors did not have the right to make doctrine – only the church itself as represented by the collectivity of the bishops could do that – but they saw to it that the decisions taken suited imperial political interests as well as the convictions of the bishops. They presided over church councils and suggested formulas for the creed. The emperors also appointed the leading patriarchs, archbishops, and bishops.

The Sasanian system is less well known. However, we may take the early 'Abbasid scribe and translator of Sasanian literature into Arabic, Ibn al-Muqaffa', to represent the Sasanian view. He held that religious matters were of utmost importance to the state, and that uniformity in doctrine and control over religious organization were indispensable bases of power. He argued that the Caliphs could not afford doctrinal disputes in the administration and the army, and could not afford to permit the religious scholars and judges to be outside state control. Ibn al-Muqaffa' urged that the Caliphs promulgate doctrine, organize a hierarchical judiciary, and appoint the leading judges.

Thus, the 'Abbasids fostered ideological or religious loyalty to the Caliphate on both Muslim and traditional Middle Eastern grounds. No longer Arab princes, they appealed to Muslim sentiment to recognize them as the legitimate successors to the Prophet, and as the protectors and organizers of the Muslim faith, which they sought to channel in directions consonant with the political needs of the dynasty. At the same time, they directed their appeal to non-Muslims and converts for recognition as divinely selected rulers, exalted princes sent by God for the right ordering of worldly affairs. Ceremony, art, and architecture expressed an imperial ideal.

THE ARABIC HUMANITIES

Literature as well as art served the imperial program. Almost inseparable from Islam as a religion was the development of an Arabic literature covering linguistic, poetic, and historical subjects. Arabic literature was cultivated in both court and popular circles. It was strongly influenced by the heritage of pre-Islamic bedouin Arabia, by the interest of Arabs in the glorification of the conquests, and by the interest of the Caliphate in using Arabic poetry as an expression of their affinity with the mass of Arabs and an adornment of imperial rule.

In urban religious circles Arabic literary interests were pursued as an essential adjunct of Quranic studies. In the century following the founding of Basra, Kufa, and other Arab cities, the Arabic language evolved away from the Quran. An Arabic lingua franca emerged for the diverse tribes. Persian and Aramaic speakers contributed to rapid changes in vocabulary, grammatical usages, style, and syntax. As the Arabic language changed, religious scholars feared that they would lose touch with the Arabic of the Quran and thus lose the meaning of God's revelations. To prevent this, it was necessary to recapture the pure Arabic of Mecca and of the desert tribes, and create a classic form of Arabic. In eighth-century Basra, philosophical, lexicographical, and grammatical studies were undertaken to stabilize the usage of Arabic. The roots of words had to be specified, vocabulary selected and explained, and proper speech given rules of grammar and syntax. This linguistic effort persisted over a century, and produced what we know as classical Arabic. The great grammar of Sibawayh and the early dictionaries of Arabic were the products of this period.

The cultural ramifications of Quranic studies went beyond linguistic analysis. The basis of linguistic studies was the collection and gathering of all examples of old Arabic. Much in the manner of contemporary linguists or anthropologists, the scholars of Basra and Kufa sought out the bedouins and recorded their poems and sayings. Gradually, a large body of lore was accumulated, and cast from oral into written form. This lore included information on the life of the Prophet and the revelations of the Quran, the early conquests, and the behavior of the early leaders of the Muslim community. Most of what is known about this early period was collected in the eighth century. Religious studies thus became a guiding motif in the elaboration of a general Arabic culture.

Other segments of the Arab milieu, inspired by a more secular orientation, also contributed to its enrichment. Apart from the classical poetry of the desert, a new sort of poetry, reflecting the interests, entertainments, and the imagery of the urban and court environments, came into being. Historical studies had a similar secular inspiration. Caliphal, ethnic, and tribal pride in the conquests, the desire to glorify the Arab past and therefore their present importance, and the desire to defend their status against the claims of non-Arab peoples to be culturally superior, motivated historical scholarship.

The totality of this literary and religious culture was gathered, compiled, edited, and criticized in several encyclopedic collections during the eighth century. With the culmination of this literary effort, Islam as a religion was embedded in a general literary culture. Understanding the Quran depended on being versed in the Arabic language and its literary traditions. Conversely, Arab literary culture was itself shaped to reflect, elucidate, and be in conformity with the Quran. Arabic literary culture was not purely the heritage of the desert but was shaped in the early Islamic era out of Arabian elements, with a view toward the religious and historical concerns of the Umayyad and early 'Abbasid periods.

This dialectical relationship of religion and literary culture, sometimes expressing alternate religious and ethnic identities, sometimes merging the two, would ever after be the basis of Islamic civilization. Arabic culture, the product partly of the urban middle class and scholarly communities interested in Islam, partly of Arab tribal loyalties, and partly of the court and Caliphal patronage, had a crucial role to play in defining the political elite. Although Arab culture was subtly merged with Islamic culture, the development of Arabic literature preserved an ethnic and linguistic alternative to Islam. Arabism could stand apart from Islam as the foundation of political and cultural identity.

PERSIAN LITERATURE

Within the court milieus there were literary and cultural alternatives to both Islam and Arabism. In keeping with the recruitment of the late Umayyad and 'Abbasid political elites from all parts of the empire, Persian influences made themselves felt in Umayyad times. In the reign of Caliph Hisham (724–43), Persian court procedures were adopted, and the first translations of Persian political documents were made. Under the 'Abbasids, Persian scribes, merchants, workers, and soldiers saw to the translation of Persian manuals of behavior and protocol (*adab*) for scribes and administrators into Arabic. The manuals contained advice on how to conduct affairs of state, carry out the duties of various offices, and behave in the presence of rulers, and described the qualities required for different positions. This advice was embedded in tales and anecdotes about the great Persian rulers of the past.

With political advice came technical and scientific knowledge. Iran was an important transmitter of Indian and Hellenistic medical, mathematical, and astronomical ideas. Works on horsemanship and the care and use of weapons, practical knowledge about government, agricultural management, and irrigation were all translated into Arabic. So too were literary masterworks such as the fables of the *Kalila wa-Dimna* and some of the tales of the *Arabian Nights*.

The flourishing of Persian translations led to rivalry among Persian courtiers and their Arab counterparts. A literary movement, the Shu'ubiya, was formed to assert the cultural superiority of the Persians to the Arabs, and to influence the official culture of the 'Abbasid Caliphate. Persians emphasized the absolute and unlimited authority of the monarch, his divine selection, and his superiority in matters of religion as well as state. Persian literature also espoused a hierarchical view of society in which each person – ruler, noble, warrior, scribe, priest, merchant, worker, or peasant – had a fixed place. The duty of government was to preserve everyone in his place, giving each class its due prerogatives. These ideas differed profoundly from the prevailing sentiment in Arabic-Islamic circles. Arab-Muslim sentiment was more egalitarian and less hierarchical. Arab Muslims tended to deny the ruler authority in religious matters, and refused to accept that the ruler was a law unto himself. Arab sentiment clung to the feeling that the ruler was chosen by and was responsible to the community and its religion. Also embedded in Persian literature was a religious challenge to Islam. While Iranian administrators were Muslims, many were still sympathetic to Zoroastrianism; others may have been Manichaeans, gnostics, or even agnostics and atheists.

Arab scholars resisted Persian ideas, and attempted to meet the temptations of Persian literary sophistication on its own grounds. In response to Persian literature, Islamic literary culture was pushed into new directions for the sake of defending its old essence. In the ninth century Arabic writers began to synthesize the Arabic humanities with Persian adab. Ibn Qutayba (828–89) compiled treatises on such themes as government, war, nobility, scholarship, asceticism, love, friendship, and women. His selections were done in the manner of Arabic literature and included quotations from the Quran and hadith, and from Arabic histories of the early Caliphs and the Arab empire, but also enough borrowings from Persian adab works, Indian tales, and Aristotle's philosophy to attract the Persian elites. A second ninth-century writer, al-Jahiz (d. 869), who is often regarded as the finest prose stylist in the history of Arabic letters, also synthesized the literary interests of Arab- and Persian-minded elites. Out of the encyclopedic works of his predecessors he selected, adapted, edited, and made attractive a body of literature which would serve as a common culture for both Arabs and Arabic-speaking Persians. Arabic writers thus offered some of the fruits of Persian thought to Muslims, but obscured the elements that were in conflict with Islam and Arabic values. The flood of translations from Persian was diverted and rechanneled into the stream of a literature bearing a Persian imprint in manner, style, and subject, but firmly wedded to Arabic and Islamic ideas.

Thus, elements of the Persian heritage became an integral part of Islamic civilization. Still, Iranian political and religious ideas survived outside the Islamic synthesis. Persian political ideas continued to influence the practice of Middle Eastern governments; Persian gnosticism would return to inspire later Islamic religious developments.

HELLENISM

While Persian literature was screened and absorbed by Arabic writers, the heritage of Greek thought had a more complex and varied role in the formation of Islamic civilization. Greek culture as it became known in court circles was not the thought of ancient Greece, but rather Greek thought as preserved, understood, and interpreted in the late Roman empire. This culture was immensely variegated. Plato's ideas were represented by his political works and some of his dialogues. Aristotle's logical and scientific works, ethics, and metaphysics were also known. However, most of the materials attributed to Aristotle and Plato had actually been written in the centuries following the deaths of the two master philosophers, when they were reinterpreted in neo-Platonic terms as teachings of a path to spiritual salvation. The Greek heritage also included the scientific and medical ideas of Galen and the pseudo-science of the Hellenistic world, including alchemy and the semi-mystical, semi-scientific ideas of the neo-Pythagoreans and the Hermetics.

The transmission of Hellenistic literature depended on the survival of the ancient academies. The most important of these academies were originally located in Athens and Alexandria, but with the Christianization of the Roman empire in the fourth and fifth centuries, the pagan schools were dispersed. They found a haven in the Christian but non-Roman parts of the Middle East. The school of Athens was rescued by the Nestorian Church, which sponsored the translation of Greek works into Syriac in Edessa and Nasibin. In the sixth century, this school was transferred to Jundishapur, a Sasanian royal city in Fars. In the sixth and seventh centuries, Hellenistic philosophic and scientific studies flourished under the influence of Persian and Indian religious and occult conceptions, though the Jundishapur school and its personnel were still mainly Nestorian Christians. The transfer of this school to Baghdad marks the beginning of its direct influence on Arab-Muslim thinkers.

Alexandrian Hellenistic thought also came into the mainstream of the emerging Islamic culture. The Alexandrian school was moved to Antioch in Syria and then to Marw in Khurasan and Harran in Mesopotamia. Some of the scholars were Nestorian Christians, but others, at Harran, were pagans. From Mesopotamia, this school also moved to Baghdad at the end of the ninth and the beginning of the tenth centuries. Thus Greek thought survived under church and royal patronage and was transferred to 'Abbasid Baghdad.

Hellenistic thought first came to the attention of Muslims interested in theological questions. Debates between Muslims and Christians, which took place in the tolerant court of the Umayyad Caliphs, instructed Muslim thinkers in Greco-Christian or Hellenistic vocabularies, forms of rational argument, and literary methods. The early encounters at Damascus were followed by scientific research in Baghdad. At the Bayt al-Hikma, Syriac and Greek logical, scientific, and technical works were translated into Arabic. These included Aristotle's logical treatises, and the works of Galen and Hippocrates. The Bayt al-Hikma also contained an astronomical observatory.

By the middle of the ninth century, the Bayt al-Hikma was superseded by a school of translators under the guidance of Hunayn b. Ishaq. Hunayn and his school translated other scientific works of Galen and the philosophic and metaphysical works of Aristotle and Plato. The output of the translators was prodigious, and this school of philologically competent editors created a body of translations and a spirit of critical inquiry that made philosophical studies in the Islamic era rigorous and exacting. The translated works were then commented on and glossed by Muslim and Christian scholars, and lectures, compendiums, and texts were prepared to disseminate their ideas.

The most profound impact of Hellenistic culture upon the growth of Islamic civilization was in the realm of philosophy. Philosophy was a movement with a great variety of positions united by a shared vocabulary and by commitment to a rational program of investigations, including logic, natural science, and metaphysics. Philosophers in the Muslim era also dealt with theological issues such as the nature of God and his attributes, the theory of prophecy, ethics, and questions of the relationship of philosophy to scriptural revelation.

It was not, however, a neutral form of analysis, but was itself a kind of religion. Its ultimate goal was not only intellectual knowledge but the reabsorption of the human soul into the spiritual universe from which it had come. Philosophic teachings also differed from Islamic teachings on such questions as the resurrection and punishment of the body, the theory of the eternity or creation of the world, and God's knowledge of universals and particulars. Hellenistic philosophy thus represented a heritage of rational reflection upon metaphysical reality, the physical world, and human beings which posed a fundamental challenge to the Quranic revelation as a source of complete and infallible truth.

There were several responses to this challenge. One of the earliest Muslim specialists, the ninth-century philosopher al-Kindi, still believed in the primacy of the Quran, and of faith over reason as the way to the discovery of religious truths. He believed in the superiority of the Prophet to the philosophers in terms of knowledge of the divine world. The teachings of the Quran required no philosophic justification. Though he held that reason could clarify and even extend faith into areas left vague by Quranic pronouncements, he was not prepared to accept Platonic and Aristotelian opinions such as belief in creation *ex nihilo*.

Later Muslim philosophers (*falasifa*), however, gave primacy to philosophy as a means of finding truth, and regarded Islam as no more than an acceptable approximation. Al-Farabi (d. 950) established the broad outlines of philosophy and defined its relation to Muslim scripture. He believed in a supreme and eternal being who was the first cause of all existing things. He also believed that the supreme being was connected to the world by a hierarchical series of emanations, conceived of as intelligences, which constituted the structure of the spiritual world and gave form to the material world. The successive levels of intellect mediated between God and the material world.

Al-Farabi's view of the human condition was logically related to his view of the universe. The human being, like all created beings, was formed by the intelligences of the spiritual world, while at the same time constituting an object in the material world. Implanted in the human being was the faculty of reason, which is a counterpart of the spiritual intelligences. The destiny of humanity, then, is to cultivate rational intelligence to the utmost, and to use intellect and reason to control behavior and feeling so that the soul may be purified and returned to its ultimate destiny – knowledge of, vision of, and reintegration into spiritual reality.

Religion for al-Farabi was only an inferior and indirect way of symbolizing the truth, suitable for the masses. The imagination of the prophet, he believed, was inferior to the intelligence of the sage. To reconcile philosophy with Islam, al-Farabi held that Islam was indeed a true religion, and that Muhammad was the perfect sage and philosopher as well as a prophet who could express the truth in a fashion persuasive to ordinary people. Insofar as al-Farabi valued Muhammad, it was not as Prophet, but as philosopher. Thus, philosophers did not truly reconcile Greek thought to Islam; rather, they tried to rationalize their acceptance of Greek thought in terms of Islam. Their metaphysical and religious mentality was based on Greek opinions rather than Quranic tradition. Philosophy, they thought, was a higher vision, superior to the revealed but inferior version of truth known as Islam.

Other aspects of the Greek heritage remained the pursuits of a cosmopolitan aristocracy remote from the mainstream of Islamic religious and cultural trends. Muslim-era scientists showed a great talent for direct observation and experiment, and their contributions to astronomy, mathematics, medicine, chemistry, zoology, mineralogy, and meteorology often surpassed the received heritage of Greek, Persian, and Indian ideas. The occult sciences were also cultivated. Alchemy, occult physics, optics, and occult neo-Pythagorean mathematics, however, were not directed toward a scientific appraisal of the universe, but rather toward esoteric revelations. Neo-Pythagorean numbers, for example, were not mathematical entities but symbols of a higher and unseen reality which the occult scientist tried to conjure forth. In alchemy the object was not only to transform materials, but to discover the hidden relation of the material to the immaterial world. In place of Islam, which prescribed obedience to the law and devotion to the Quran, the occult sciences proposed another way to knowledge of the world beyond. Hellenistic thought in this mode introduced not an experimental endeavor or practical technology, but a non-theistic spiritual and religious conviction.

Persian and Greek thought were important in court circles because they introduced the ideal of aristocratic self-cultivation. The aristocratic ideal called upon the courtier, the administrator, and the servant of Caliphs to believe in God, and to be pious and conscious of the coming last judgment. Yet it also called upon them to be refined, cultivated, learned, and worldly gentlemen. The aristocrat had to be knowledgeable in all the sciences, literature, history, philosophy, and religion. He was to be gentlemanly in manners, gracious, and sensitive to the nuances of rank and honor. He should also be competent in finance, in letter writing, in horsemanship, and in technical matters of administration. The aristocrat's cultivation included Islamic virtues, but its essential quality was a worldly refinement which set him apart from the lowly and justified his claim to power. Indirectly the cultivation of Persian and Greek letters implied a common culture for a heterogeneous elite based upon the presumption of inherent aristocratic superiority.

Furthermore, all the court literatures served to propagate a pre-Islamic concept of the ruler and the empire. Interest in the secular aspects of Arabic literature, Persian adab, and Hellenistic philosophies and sciences signified the appropriation of a cultural heritage which could be used to legitimize Caliphal rule. They provided, in the Arabic case, an ethnic concept of political leadership; in the Persian case, a continuation of the heritage of ancient Middle Eastern kings; and in the Hellenistic case, a concept of the structure of the universe itself, in philosophic and scientific form, as the ultimate justification for imperial rule. The patronage of these several literatures implied that the Caliph, though a Muslim ruler, was legitimized by the non-Islamic heritage of the ancient Middle East.

CHAPTER 6

URBAN ISLAM:
THE ISLAM OF THE RELIGIOUS ELITES

The Caliphal version of Islamic civilization was inherently flawed. While Caliphs were considered the heirs of the Prophet's religious authority as well as his political leadership, they did not inherit Muhammad's prophethood. The Quran, the revealed book, stood apart from the Caliphs, and was available to every believer. At the core of their executive and symbolic primacy there was a void, for the Caliphs did not have the authority from which Muslim religious conceptions and practices were derived. Furthermore, the politicization of the Caliphal regime created severe tensions between its religious and political needs. The Umayyad dynasty provoked Shi'i, Khariji, and Yemeni Arab opposition in the name of religious principles. The 'Abbasid effort to build up a strong state apparatus, and to give the ruler a ceremonial grandeur that bordered on divinity, provoked rebellions and deep distrust even among their own followers.

In these conditions, a new and autonomous religious elite emerged within the garrison cities. The settlements fused Arab and non-Arab peoples into new communities of middle-class merchants, artisans, teachers, and scholars devoted to their newly defined Islamic identity. Some of these people were originally descended from Arab bedouins, but after a century of sedentarization they were thoroughly urbanized. Others were non-Arabs, converts and clients of the Arabs, who spoke Arabic and assimilated themselves into the tribal, religious, and literary traditions of the conquering elite. Within this milieu, students of religion who were without office, institutional means of support or priestly status, including the *qurra'* (the readers of the Quran), the *'ulama'* (religious scholars), and the Sufis (the ascetics), became the custodians of the Quran and of the teachings of the Prophet. Officially, the Muslim community was headed by the Caliph and his governors, but in fact the learned and pious people who held no official position, but who had acquired a reputation for knowledge of and devotion to the faith, were accepted by ordinary Muslims as the true authorities on Islam. These devotees of Islam formed circles of disciples and students dedicated to the study of hadith (accounts of the sayings and deeds of the Prophet), law, theology, or mysticism. The Muslim masses turned to them rather than to the Caliphs for moral instruction and religious guidance. Thus the development of religious authorities independent of the Caliphate was coupled with the emergence of "sectarian" bodies within the Islamic umma. The Caliphate and Islam were no longer wholly integrated.

The private religious scholars and their followers represented many different points of view. Some were supporters of the Caliphate; others were opponents. Some were concerned primarily with scripture, the study and explication of the Quran, the recollection of the sayings of the Prophet, and the elaboration of law; others were committed to theology or mysticism. Urban Islamic religious culture was ultimately the combined product of all of these orientations, and the outcome of the struggles among them and of those between them and the court and Caliphal versions of Islam.

SUNNI SCRIPTURALISM

The Quran is the fulcrum of Muslim faith, for it embodies the Muslim vision of the world. Muslims believe in the Quran as a book of guidance. It begins:

> In the Name of God, the Merciful, the Compassionate,
> Praise belongs to God, the Lord of all Being,
> the All-merciful, the All-compassionate,
> the Master of the Day of Doom.
> Thee only we serve; to Thee alone we pray for succor.
> Guide us in the straight path,
> the path of those whom Thou hast blessed,
> not of those against whom Thou art wrathful,
> nor of those who are astray.

At the center of the Quranic guidance is a vision of the reality of God's being. God is transcendent, eternal, utterly other, unfettered in will or action, almighty creator of the world and its creatures. Sent to convert men to Islam, the Quran carries strong exhortations to believe, warnings, proofs, threats of judgment, and appeals to gratitude to God. It requires belief in God and submission to his will. God will judge human beings at the end of days and mete out eternal reward or eternal punishment. The reality of the world to come is presented with potent eschatological symbols whose influence continues to be a living force in Islamic culture.

As guidance the Quran teaches what men should believe about God, nature, and history. It gives rules about what men should and should not do in religious rituals and in relation to their fellow men. It prescribes the basic beliefs of Islam and the five pillars: profession of faith, prayer, fasting, the giving of alms, and pilgrimage. It sets out laws of marriage, divorce, inheritance, and business matters. It

5 A page of an illuminated Quran

also presents the spiritual qualities that should infuse ritual, social, and legal obligations. These qualities include gratitude to God for one's existence, repentance, moral earnestness, fear of the last judgment, loyalty to the faith, sincerity, and truthfulness. It condemns arrogance, thanklessness, and pride.

Beyond precise specification is the moral spirit in which a man lives. The Quran leaves each man to judge what constitutes proper fulfillment of God's command. For example, the law defining the supererogatory night prayers are not given as a rule, but as permission to adapt the injunction to pray to individual circumstances:

> Therefore recite of the Koran so much as is feasible.
> He knows that some of you are sick, and others
> journeying in the land, seeking the bounty of God,
> and others fighting in the way of God.
> So recite of it so much as is feasible.[1]

Because the guidance is open, the boundaries of human responsibility become problematic. The prospects of achieving eternal reward are uncertain. Some passages in the Quran stress the full measure of human responsibility. God is just and he will weigh every deed and thought at the day of judgment on the scales of eternal reward and punishment. Other passages, however, stress God's power, his predetermination of all events, and man's helpless insufficiency before his majesty.

For early readers and commentators the Quran was more than a text. The scholars were eager to mold their own lives by it, and to infuse the lives of their contemporaries with the spirit and teachings of the holy book. They wanted the Quran to be the basis of a Muslim style of personal behavior, ritual, family, and business matters, and also of political questions such as the selection of rulers, justice, and taxation. They aspired to cast the whole of life in the mold of the Quran.

This interest in the application of the Quran led first to the commentary, exegesis, and criticism called *tafsir*. It also led to the accumulation and study of accounts of the sayings and deeds of the Prophet. Everything Muhammad said and did was of prime religious importance because his deeds and actions were authoritative examples of how a proper Muslim life was to be led. Hadith, which had been kept alive in oral tradition, began to be collected from the beginning of the eighth century, and in the ninth century an authoritative canon was compiled that stands alongside the Quran as Muslim scripture.

In the classical manuals and compilations hadith were organized by topic. In the *Sahih* of Bukhari they are organized under such headings as faith, purification, prayer, alms, fasting, pilgrimage, commerce, inheritance, wills, vows and oaths, crimes, murders, judicial procedure, war, hunting, and wine. In each chapter there are anecdotal descriptions of how the Prophet dealt with these matters.

---

[1] A. S. Arberry, *The Koran Interpreted*, London: Allen & Unwin, 1955, I, p. 29, II, pp. 309–10.

Table 3. *Early schools of law*

Founding father	Region	School
al-Awza i (d. 744)	Syria	Awza i
Abu Hanifa (d. 767)	Iraq	Hanafi
Malik b. Anas (d. 795)	Medina	Maliki
al-Shafi i (d. 820)	Egypt	Shafi i
Ibn Hanbal (d. 855)	Iraq	Hanbali
Dawud b. Khalaf (d. 883)	Iraq	Zahiri

Note. The four surviving schools of law are Hanafi, Maliki, Shafi i, and Hanbali.

Muslim believers read hadith in close relationship with the Quran. They clarify, supplement, and expand the range of specific guidance. They also constitute an open rather than a prescriptive text. The range of specific issues and advice is so great that no matter what a Muslim believes and does there are infinite aspects of the hadith that elude him. There is an endless tension among precepts fulfilled, precepts neglected, and precepts not understood.

A similar impulse to fashion a divinely guided way of life led to the development of Muslim law. Shari'a was not strictly speaking the revealed word of God, but it was widely taken by Muslims to be a divinely inspired extension of the teachings of the Quran and hadith. Muslim law had its origins in the efforts of seventh-century judges and scholars to reform existing legal practice and inspire it with Islamic ethical standards. This religio-judicial task was not the work of any single group, but was carried out in Basra, Kufa, Syria, Medina, and Mecca by men who formed in each place a "school of law." Beginning with actual practice in familial, commercial, and criminal law, administrative regulations, Sasanian, Byzantine, and Hellenistic popular maxims, the canon law of the Orthodox Church, Talmudic, Rabbinic, and old Babylonian law, the scholars sought to bring everything into conformity with God's will. Their discussions did not generate cold statute law, but a discursive body of rules laced with ethical, moral, and theological precepts.

Muslim law was divided into three substantive categories: *'ibadat* (ritual regulations); *mu'amalat* (rules of social relations); and *imama* (theory of collective organization). Under these categories the law dealt with prayer, almsgiving and fasting, matters of marriage, divorce, slavery, partnerships, debts, wills, and other legal and social concerns. In all these matters non-Islamic law and custom were reconciled to Islamic religious principles. The final corpus of the Shari'a thus represents custom and tradition transformed by Islamic ethical conviction.

Hadith and Shari'a represent different approaches to defining the will of God, but historically they evolved in intimate connection with each other. Toward the end of the eighth century the work of the legal scholars came under attack by the people of hadith. The people of hadith were those religious scholars, often minority members of the various law schools, who differed with the majority on specific issues, and about the proper sources of legal judgment. While most legal scholars believed in the traditions of their school and in a certain amount of personal discretion, the hadith-minded (*ahl al-hadith*) could not conceive of any legitimate source of law or morals other than the Quran itself and the sayings of the Prophet. They objected to the arbitrary personal opinions of their opponents.

Inevitably, the position of the people of hadith gained ground. The logic of accepting the views of the Prophet as a higher authority than the personal opinion of the legalists was irrefutable. Still, the legalists were not prepared to yield, and defended their position against unreliable hadith. Eventually, the jurist al-Shafi'i (767–820) found a *modus vivendi*. He accepted the authority of hadith as overriding, but sought to control them by holding that only the *ijma'*, or agreement of the qualified scholars, could decide which hadith were authentic and which were not. Al-Shafi'i reconciled the use of hadith with the legalists' methods of reasoning and discussion.

Reciprocally, under pressure of debate, the hadith supporters evolved their own internal criticism to guarantee the infallibility of hadith. In a society where the authority of the ancients counted for more than the opinions of contemporaries, no textual criticism or similar justification would do. One had to demonstrate simply and plainly that Muhammad's sayings were reported by a person of known probity, who in turn had heard them from earlier holy men. Chains of authorities, called *isnad*, were built up to guarantee the authenticity of hadith. The defense of the hadith-minded was to develop the logic of hadith to its utmost, without appeal or reference to external sources of appraisal or criticism. They relied only on whatever was dependably reported as having been said by the Prophet.

By the middle of the ninth century, the approaches of the legists and of the people of hadith were well consolidated. The outcome of the long struggle was to take two vaguely defined religious orientations and, by highlighting the implicit conflicts between them, to elaborate and systematize the law as a code of religious teaching based on Quran, hadith, the consensus of the learned, and analogical reasoning, and to assure the authenticity of hadith by some kind of external criticism. The long debate refined the shape of law and hadith, and persuaded Muslims that both corpuses of religious expression were the scriptures of Islam.

Nevertheless, concealed within this consensus was a profound disagreement over the meaning of a truly religious life. The proponents of hadith thought of Islam as a completely revealed faith, a religion of submission to the revealed word of God and acceptance of the words of Muhammad as an expression of God's guidance. The proponents of consensus of the community and of individual judgment as the bases of law held that Islam was a religion based on scripture, but one that must be adapted to changing circumstances by the agreement of the community and by human judgment about how the scripture should be applied. Implicit in the agreement that Islam was a religiously sanctified way of life lived in accordance with God's will as set out in scripture was profound disagreement about the boundaries between revealed truth and human interpretation, the requirements of faith and the use of reason, the degree of man's submission to God or his autonomy in living a Muslim life. The same outer life, as embodied in Quran and hadith, could imply radically different forms of spirituality.

THEOLOGY

Theological questions were first prompted by political disputes. The Kharijis had opposed 'Ali's reign on the grounds that he was a sinner. The supporters of Mu'awiya, however, did not want to open the personal religious qualifications of a Caliph to question, and held that all persons who professed Islam were *ipso facto* true Muslims. Political neutrals called Mu'tazila held that sinners were neither true Muslims nor infidels, but fell within an intermediate classification, and continued to belong to the Muslim community. Other neutrals called Murji'a crystallized the truly theological issue. In the Murji'a view, it was neither good deeds nor bad that made a man a true Muslim, but faith and intention. They introduced the problem of faith and works.

The Kharijis also broached the problem of free will and predestination. The question came up over the issue of whether children were automatically Muslims, or had they to elect membership in the community? The Kharijis held for election; it was consistent with their view that only a blameless person was a true Muslim, and by implication that every person had a choice and was responsible for his choices. The Murji'a and the Mu'tazila agreed, believing therefore in free will. Once this issue was broached, a host of theological subtleties followed. The question of free will or predestination raised the question of the meaning of God's attributes. What is to be understood by such Quranic phrases as "God's power" and "God's knowledge"? The question of attributes raised the further question of God's unity. Pious Muslims, debating the importance of faith versus works, or free will and predestination, or the nature of God and how his seemingly contradictory qualities should be understood, discovered that Greek philosophers and Christian theologians had already devised a tradition of argumentation upon which Muslim thinkers could draw to refine their conceptions. Converts introduced the earlier tradition into Muslim circles. Debates between Muslims and Christians at the court of the Umayyad Caliphs, and the translation of Greek and Syriac literature into Arabic, led Muslim thinkers to adopt Hellenistic vocabulary and Greco-Christian forms of rational argument. Theology was thus in part the product of Islamic urban milieus and in part that of the philosophic and religious interests of the Caliphal court.

In Muslim theological circles, the people most aggressively interested in Greek dialectics were the Mu'tazila. In the forefront of debate, competing with Christian trinitarianism, Manichaean dualism, pagan materialism, and even anthropomorphic conceptions widespread among Muslims, the Mu'tazila upheld God's unity and transcendence. They affirmed that there was but one God, who is pure, ultimate being. As pure being, God is not like any created matter, not like a human person, nor divided in any way. In the Aristotelian language adopted by the Mu'tazila, God's essence is his existence.

Other Mu'tazili doctrines were a corollary of their conception of God's transcendence and unity. For example, they held that the Quran was a created message inspired by God in Muhammad, and not part of God's essence or divine itself, as opposed to the Christian view that Christ, the Logos, the word of God, proceeds from God as part of his essence and is co-eternal with him. Other Muslims refused to accept this, and the issue became a *cause célèbre* in Muslim theology and the most important issue in the religious politics of the 'Abbasid Caliphate.

A corollary of the Mu'tazili conception of God's transcendence and unity was the doctrine of man's moral freedom and responsibility: men choose their own acts; they are not created by or determined by God. In holding this view, the Mu'tazila upheld God's justice, for he rightly punishes and rewards men for their deeds. They also upheld his goodness: men, not God, are the authors of evil. If men were not morally free, they argued, God would by implication be the cause of evil.

The main tenets of the Mu'tazila, though presented in terms of Greek thought, were profoundly Islamic in inspiration. Though other Muslims might disagree, their stress on God's unity and man's responsibility seemed to be the essence of Islam itself. Yet the Mu'tazila went beyond strictly Islamic issues to develop, on the basis of Greek thought, a metaphysics of being, a theory of the origin of the universe, a physics of created things, and a psychology of man, based on the teachings of Aristotle, Democritus, Empedocles, and other Greek philosophers. The crucial tenet in their philosophy was that God's being, the universe, and human nature are all rationally ordered and knowable to human reason. God is defined by his essence, which is reason. The created world functions according to its own rational laws and, once created, is independent of God and not changeable by him. Similarly, in moral matters, good and evil have an intrinsic value. They are not dependent on, or changed by, divine will. God's justice is constrained by the laws of good and evil. A natural corollary of the Mu'tazili position, though not necessarily drawn by all, was that revelation is of secondary importance, and can do no more than amplify or make the teachings of reason more specific. Revelation can complete, confirm, or complement reason, but no truths unknown, unknowable, or inconsistent with the dictates of reason can be revealed.

Though the Mu'tazila served Islam well in their defense of the unity of God and in their clarification of man's free will and responsibility, their larger philosophy, developed under the influence of Greek thought, was at odds with the majority sentiment of the Arab-Muslim milieu about the nature of God and his creation. For other Muslims, Muhammad and the Quran – not reason – were the central experiences of Islam. The Quran contained God's will for men and the duties he had assigned them, and Muhammad was the last messenger of God, bringing the last revelation. For most Muslims, man must submit to God, not presume to know better than God. The people of hadith, who had so severely criticized the legalists for the application of personal judgment to legal problems, were especially incensed that Muslim theologians were relying on reason for the discussion of religious matters. The hadith scholars rejected any accommodation with Greek methods of discussion. Reason had no place in religion at all, for the statements of the hadith were God's will, and not to be questioned. They rejected the siren song of Greek ideas as incompatible with complete and unassuming devotion to God and his revelations.

Thus, the hadith scholars opposed the Mu'tazili conception of *tawhid*, or unity of God. They insisted that the attributes of God, the independent existence of which was denied by the Mu'tazila, must exist because they are mentioned in the Quran. To deny or explain them away would be to derogate from God's own revelation of his being. They rejected the Mu'tazili notion of the createdness of the Quran, affirmed the contrary – its uncreatedness – and made this a fundamental tenet of faith, as a way of asserting the superiority of the Quran to all human reasoning and knowledge. Finally, they held that man's acts are predetermined by God alone. For hadith scholars, God's omnipotent power and his untrammeled inscrutable will, not his rationality or his justice, were the heartfelt attributes.

Thus by the ninth century two basic positions had emerged in Muslim theology. One was a rationalist-oriented position that emphasized the centrality of reason as an ordering principle of God's being in the human understanding of the universe, and in the governance of human behavior. The rationalist position had, as its corollary, belief in free will and individual responsibility for moral choices. A contrary position stressed the absolute omnipotence and inscrutability of the divine being, who can be known only insofar as he has chosen to reveal himself through the Quran. This view denied the utility of reason in religious or moral choices. All human action is ultimately an expression of the power of the creator rather than an autonomous exercise of free judgment and will.

Dissatisfied with the excesses of Mu'tazili rationalism, and appalled by the constricting literalism of the people of hadith, ninth and tenth century Muslim theologians tried to find a middle ground consistent with emphasis on the importance of hadith, but preserving some role for reason in the discussion of theological issues. Several such compromises were elaborated, but the most important in the history of Muslim theology was the work of al-Ash'ari (d. 935).

On doctrinal matters al-Ash'ari adopted the hadith scholars' views, but refined them to meet the higher standards of Mu'tazili reasoning. For example, on the problem of the createdness of the Quran, he held that it was uncreated but, adducing a philosophic distinction between essence and existence, pointed out that any particular copy of the Quran was created. On the question of free will, al-Ash'ari held that all human acts are decided or created by God, but that man, by *kasb* (acquisition), has a certain responsibility for them. God is the ultimate author of man's actions, but man is an instrument of and participant in these actions.

Thus, al-Ash'ari defended a theological viewpoint that stressed the overwhelming importance of the divine revelation and the humble quality of man's own will and rational faculties. Though he rejected rational metaphysics as a key to the nature of God and the universe, he used Greek concepts to defend his position. Reason, he allowed, can spell out the meanings embodied in the Quran and hadith, defend the truth against its adversaries, and can be used to persuade others of its validity. *Kalam* (theology) does not of itself discover truths, but reinforces belief in God and obedience to God's will by rational comprehension.

MYSTICS AND SUFISM

While the legists and the theologians concentrated upon finding out the rules that God had commanded to govern everyday life and sought a rational understanding of their beliefs, the mystics attempted to acquire an immediate and personal experience of God's reality. They sought to order their lives, channel their thoughts and feelings, and hone a language that would make possible a direct experience of the presence of a God who was otherwise acknowledged to be a transcendent and inaccessible being. In this quest language was particularly important, because only right language could unify the soul of the individual, break down the barriers between human and divine discourse, and enable the mystic to symbolize the reality he experienced. In religious terms this is a quest for unity with the divine being; in humanistic terms it is an effort to overcome the divided self, to realize the truths by which life must be lived, and to attain wholeness of being.

Islamic mysticism originated in the spiritual aspirations and religious practices of the Prophet Muhammad, his companions, and their successors. While the Arab-Muslim elite was engaged in conquest and empire, other Muslims questioned the value of a worldly life, and chose a piety that emphasized the memorization of the Quran, devotion to hadith and law, and the fulfillment of God's teachings in their daily lives. They questioned the value of marriage versus celibacy, wealth versus poverty, and active engagement versus retreat. Some chose an extreme asceticism, utmost poverty and isolation, constant watchfulness to avoid any sin, great or small, and yearning for the paradise promised true believers. Their lives were marked by fear of heedlessness, of temptation or sin, and of the last judgment. They wept for their sins and the punishment to come; they wept for the misery of the world. They taught that the only proper life for a good Muslim was one of humility and poverty; the only proper expression tears rather than laughter, and that silence was best of all. In silence one could concentrate on the recollection of God and on waiting for the last judgment. For others, however, the purgative way implied a more moderate asceticism and discipline of bodily desires. For still others, asceticism implied an attitude of emotional disinterest, of detachment, without requiring physical renunciation. Goodness in following the teachings of the Quran, avoidance of sin, and a humble, yearning attitude toward God was summed up in the word *zuhd* (renunciation). This form of piety, like Muhammad's own vision, echoes Eastern Christian spirituality.

Hasan al-Basri (d. 728) has come down through Muslim history as the exemplar of ascetic engagement in the world. He wept for his unworthiness and feared death, the last judgment, and the hellfire to come. He also taught obedience to the commands of the Quran and the strict practice of the rules of religion reinforced by ascetic devotions, patient acceptance of the trials of this world, submission to God's will, and constant anticipation of the last judgment. For Hasan, the cultivation of proper acts and attitudes was an individual responsibility. While accepting God's determination and guidance in all matters, he sought to reconcile the power of God with the responsibility of individuals through the mystical concept of *rida* (contentment), an attitude that brought the soul into harmony with God's will and thus reconciled freedom of choice with God's power to determine all things.

For Hasan ascetic renunciation and self-restraint were the bases of responsibility and moral conduct in communal and political affairs. He fought in the frontier wars to expand Islam, and held public office in Basra. He lived an active life devoted to *jihad* (holy war), teaching, preaching, and administration. He held it a responsibility of good Muslims to counsel ordinary believers on their obligations to God and to give moral advice to rulers. Even when rulers were unjust, the proper response was moral counsel and not violent rebellion. Paradoxically, renunciation of the world led back to the actual fulfillment of the divine law for both the individual and the community.

As the ascetics cultivated psychological, emotional, and spiritual awareness, Sufism, or Islamic mysticism, emerged in full flower. Recitation of the Quran, *dhikr* (the remembrance of God and repetition of his name), litanies, and meditation, coupled with the struggle to suppress inner vices, liberated the deepest capacities of the soul and prepared it for the vision of God. The Quran provided the Sufis with inspiration, guidance, and a vocabulary for this quest. Muqatil b. Sulayman (d. 767) developed a form of commentary that allowed the interpreter of the Quran to transcend its literal meaning and arrive at its spiritual meaning. Other writers such as Ja'far al-Sadiq (d. 765) taught that every passage of the Quran spoke on four levels of meaning, which could be appreciated by people having the requisite spiritual experience. These levels were *'ibara*, the physical words of the Quran; *ishara*, allusion to an outside object; *latifa*, the mysterious fruit within the Quran; and finally *haqiqa*, the truth or reality of the Quran.

A new level was reached when mystics no longer interpreted the vocabulary of the Quran directly, but developed their own language to express the stages of ascent toward God. Shaqiq al-Balkhi (d. 810) was one of the first Sufi writers to speak of four stages. The first was zuhd, renunciation of the appetites of the body; the second was fear of God and constant humility; the third was yearning for paradise; and the fourth was love of God. Later writers such as Abu Sa'id Kharraz (d. 890 or 899) described seven stages on the way to God in which the term *qurb*, or nearness, was the central metaphor. Each stage was partly a product of the Sufi's own disciplined efforts (*maqam*) and partly a gift of God's grace (*hal*).

As the stages of ascent became more elaborate, Sufis emphasized sabr, patience in accepting God's will and in renunciation of the world; *shukr*, gratitude; *tawakkul*, trust in God, which implied utter reliance upon God and acceptance of his will without recourse or hope in worldly things; and rida, acceptance of the vicissitudes of life and the reality of the divine decree with equanimity and even with joy and love. Love implied yearning for God, obedience to God's will, complete surrender, and dying to one's self in the hope of closeness to God. Rabi'a (d. 801), a female mystic, put into passionate poems her thirst, her desire to be joined to God. Some Sufis saw love as yearning; others understood it as union. Still others thought of love of God in terms of God's mercy and forgiveness upon which sinful man was always dependent. Love of God opened the way to a still higher stage, tawhid (unity), the loss of self and absorption in the divine being.

By the ninth century two broad tendencies had emerged within the Sufi movement. The Khurasanian tendency was characterized by emphasis on tawakkul, resignation to God's will expressed through voluntary poverty. This mysticism ruptured the ordinary pattern of Muslim religious activities and ignored obedience to Quranic law in search of a transcending religious self-realization. Abu Yazid al-Bistami (d. 873) epitomized the quest for an intoxicated, rapturous union with God. In al-Bistami's view, the mystic seeks annihilation of self and union with the divine names or attributes. The mystic's identification with God is expressed in *shath*, theopathic utterances, which are the voice of God speaking through his person. Al-Hallaj (d. 923), who lived as a preacher and missionary in Khurasan and Afghanistan, also sought loss of self and unity in God. As a manifestation of this union, al-Hallaj proclaimed, "I am the Truth," performed miracles, and claimed a religious authority greater than that of Caliphs and 'ulama' because it was the authority of the divine presence. His claims to miracles, usurpation of power, and doctrine of divine love and union led to prosecution for heresy and his execution in 923.

Other mystics held back from the radical implications of ecstatic Sufism and the concept of annihilation of the self in God. The Baghdadi tendency placed heavy stress on asceticism and renunciation of worldly things combined with the cultivation of practical virtues such as patience, trust, gratitude, and love of God. The Baghdadi tendency, however, as opposed to the Khurasanian, believed in observance of the Quran and conformity with Muslim law. Practically and intellectually, the Baghdadis were more closely integrated with ordinary Muslim religious practice and belief.

Al-Harith al-Muhasabi (781–857) was the leading ninth-century proponent of this position, but al-Junayd (d. 910) was the great master of the effort to integrate Sufism with other aspects of Islamic religious life. Al-Junayd laid stress upon renunciation, purification, and mental struggle in order to return to that pre-existent state in which the human being is a concept in the mind of God. Al-Junayd professed a two-stage concept of Sufi union. Beyond *fana'*, he found *baqa'*, or persistence in his own identity. He held that the mystic's goal was not the loss of self as the final end but, through a loss of self, a return to daily life transformed by the vision of God and ever after conducted in the presence of God. As opposed to the Khurasanians, al-Junayd taught that beyond the ecstasy of loss of self there was a sober persistence of the self in never-failing worldly devotion to God's will as expressed in the teachings of the Quran and the Prophet. For the Baghdadis, visionary insight into the reality of God's being was not an escape from but an intensification of the Sufi's commitment to the fulfillment of God's will in daily life. To Khurasanian intoxication al-Junayd opposed Baghdadi sobriety.

While mystics differed on the stages of the ascent toward God, they had by the end of the ninth century collectively articulated a theory of spiritual progress that combined the Quranic inspiration with the lived experience of generations of seekers. Later Sufis such as Niffari (d. 985) further perfected the language of Sufism. He employed symbols that came into being in the moment of mystic experience, and cultivated a language that condensed human experience with its transcendent reference. Through symbols, the mystic became familiar with the God who reveals himself in the language of men without compromising his transcendence. Symbolic language itself became a symbol of the mystic's absorption into the divine reality.

In addition to their pragmatic program, Sufis also cultivated a metaphysical, theosophical, and philosophical concept of the divine reality. By the early tenth century several metaphysical theories of the creation of the material world and the relation of human beings to God had been put forth. All of them in one form or another posited a transcendent God, but one whose spiritual radiance or emanation was implanted in human beings. A human being must overcome the bodily and animal forces with him, restore purity of will and intellect, and thus realize his inherently divine nature. Through this realization he returns to his origins in God.

One version of this was presented by Sahl al-Tustari (d. 896). In al-Tustari's view, God's essence is light, which is a single and transcendent illumination but which radiates from him to create the spiritual prototypes of the material world. Enshrined in this light are the prototypes of the prophets and of ordinary people who exist before their worldly birth as particles of the divine light. In this pre-existent state human beings recognize and testify to the oneness and the lordship of God, a primordial covenant. In the life of this world man attempts to reactualize this pre-existent covenant. In prayer he contemplates God's existence; in dhikr or Sufi ceremony, he attempts to recollect God's primordial self-revelation. To do this, he must purify the heart and make it triumph over the forces of the bodily self, following Quran and hadith with sincerity and repentance, living according to God's commands and prohibitions. Penitence and inner struggle free him from his bodily self (nafs) and allow him to realize his spiritual self, qalb (heart), 'aql (reason), or ruh (spirit). By the resurrection of this preexisting reality the mystic prepares himself for the vision of God and life eternal in the presence of the divine being.

With the translation of the Syriac and Greek classics into Arabic, the intellectual mysticism that stemmed from the thought of Plotinus (d. 270) provided a similar theosophical concept of the mystic way. Neo-Platonism introduced the idea that the universe radiated from the divine being in successive stages of spiritual and then material manifestation. Man, who stood at the juncture of the spiritual and material worlds, was capable by inner knowledge or illumination, of rising up in the hierarchy of being to the ultimate vision of God. By discovery of the inward truths of the heart, which correspond to the cosmological structure of the universe, the mystic ascends from his material state toward ever higher levels of spiritual being and the ultimate illuminative knowledge of God.

Thus, in several forms, early Sufi metaphysics combined a transcendentalist with an immanentist view of God's existence. God is utterly different from any created reality; yet he is also the source of spiritual illuminations which make it possible for human beings, in whom there dwells some aspect of the reality of God, to return from their material exile to their spiritual home.

Finally, there was a miraculous and magical aspect to Sufism. The individual who had achieved knowledge of God's being through his daily behavior and visionary insight was considered more than human. In his person he was an epiphany, a manifestation, of the divine being, and the vehicle of communication between man and God. The mystic was considered a healer, a magician, a worker of miracles, and a pillar of the universe. For many Muslim believers the Sufi was not only a person of great moral and spiritual quality but was a living expression of God's power in the world. Al-Tirmidhi (d. 932) advanced the theory that the Sufi adept was a saint who by his spiritual achievements upheld the order of the universe. Standing in the hierarchy of God's emanation, he was capable of miraculous deeds. Al-Tirmidhi's doctrine of sainthood became the basis of an almost universal Muslim belief in saints as intercessors with God, and of a veneration of saints and their descendants, disciples, and tombs as repositories of the divine presence. In metaphysical doctrine and in magical practice, the Sufis represented the possibility of salvation by entry into the presence of God.

Sufism, which began in the seventh century as the quest for individual spiritual redemption, became by the late eighth century a collective religious movement. By this period Sufis had developed a concept of themselves – the people of the coarse white wool garment – as initiates in a form of Muslim religious life that was different from the piety enshrined in scholarship and legal practice. Sufis gathered to recite the Quran and to sit in the presence of great masters. Collective retreats such as the *khanaqa* at Abadan helped give some coherence to Sufism as a movement. Combining ascetic renunciation with spiritual growth leading toward union with God, grounded in philosophical and metaphysical conceptions of God's being, and a doctrine of the venerable and miraculous nature of saints, Sufism had begun to develop both a social organization and a public mission. All of these trends would be consolidated and further developed in the centuries following the collapse of the 'Abbasid empire.

SHI'I ISLAM

Alongside the Sunni communities, the Shi'a developed their own concept of Islam. In the Shi'i view, the true source of belief in each generation was ultimately not the text of tradition, nor the consensus of the jurists, nor the piety of other Muslims, but loyalty to the Caliph 'Ali and his descendants. In the seventh and eighth centuries this led to a number of political movements in opposition to the Umayyad and 'Abbasid dynasties. Family loyalists tried again and again to seize the Caliphate. Defeat channeled many of the Shi'a from political activity into religious reflection. In the middle of the eighth century, two concerns governed the intensification of religious activity in Shi'i circles. First, since the Shi'a denied the legitimacy of the Sunni succession of Caliphs, Abu Bakr and 'Umar could no longer be accepted as authoritative sources of Muslim religious teaching. An independent hadith and law in which 'Ali was the prime authority was necessary. The Shi'a elaborated their own hadith and law, collected in the *Nahj al-Balagha* (Path of Eloquence), which differs from the Sunni versions only in matters of detail and in chains of transmission. The Shi'a were also in close touch with political sympathizers such as Mu'tazili theologians, and by the end of the ninth century also debated the questions of free will and God's attributes.

Second, the claims of the Shi'i imams to the Caliphate had to be defended. Ja'far al-Sadiq (d. 765), the sixth imam in the line of 'Ali, taught that the true Caliph and ruler of the Muslim community descended in the family of 'Ali by virtue of *nass* – the designation by each incumbent imam of his successor. Through nass the imam inherited a secret knowledge and exclusive authority to interpret the Quran and hadith and to elaborate the legal system of Islam. By the ninth century, Shi'i concepts of the imam came to include the notion that he was *ma'sum*, a sinless and infallible guide to religious truth. In the *ghulat* (extremist) view, which would become integral to later Shi'i thought, the imam was vested with an indwelling spirit of God and was the mahdi, the messiah chosen by God to restore the true faith of Islam and to establish justice and the kingdom of God in the world. He was the only legitimate ruler and teacher of the Muslims because he was an epiphany of the divine being. From this vantage point Shi'ism left a legacy of religious teachings similar to the Sunni types we have discussed, but it also moved toward a merger with Sufism in that the divinely graced imam became the example and teacher of a mystical reunion with God.

After Ja'far's death, the Shi'i community divided into two groups – the followers of his sons Musa and Isma'il. The followers of Musa and the ninth-century imams who were his descendants maintained a prominent position in Baghdad. Shi'a were important in merchant and scribal circles and had access to the 'Abbasid court. However, in 874, with the death of the eleventh imam, who left no heirs, this line of succession came to an end. The Shi'a then elaborated their concept of the hidden twelfth imam, who is not dead, but in retreat until he shall return as the mahdi, the messiah, at the end of days. In the absence of a living imam, the Banu Nawbakht, an important Shi'i family of Baghdad, took up the leadership of the community, and from 874 until 941 acted as agents of the hidden imam. This first period, in which the twelfth imam was hidden but still in direct touch with his agents, was called the lesser occultation. The period that followed, in which all direct contact

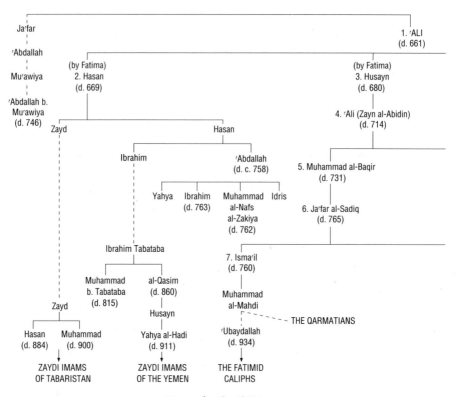

Figure 4   The Shi'i imams

was lost, is called the greater occultation. With an eschatological conception of the imamate and a doctrine of the historical succession of twelve imams culminating in the occultation of the twelfth imam, who would return as the messiah, the *ithna 'ashari* ("twelver"), or Imami, Shi'i community took its definitive historical form. In politics this meant that the "twelvers," though opposed to the 'Abbasid regime in principle, were willing to postpone their expectations of a Shi'i imam until the indefinite future.

The second branch of Shi'a were the followers of Ja'far's son Isma'il. The early Isma'ilis differed from Shi'a in recognizing Isma'il rather than Musa as the true imam. Moreover, their strong messianic orientation led to doctrinal changes and to political activism. In Isma'ili doctrine, the Quran revealed two truths – the *zahir*, or the external, literal truth of the divine message, and the *batin*, the inner, esoteric truth of the Quran, which could only be known by the proper exegesis of the Quranic text and by comprehension of the zahir as the symbol of an inner spiritual principle. For the Isma'ilis of the ninth century the doctrine implied a conception of the imam as the teacher and guide to the inner meaning of the Quranic revelation.

Isma'ilis also generated a historical and eschatological concept of the imam. According to their doctrine, prophetic revelation was always complemented by the

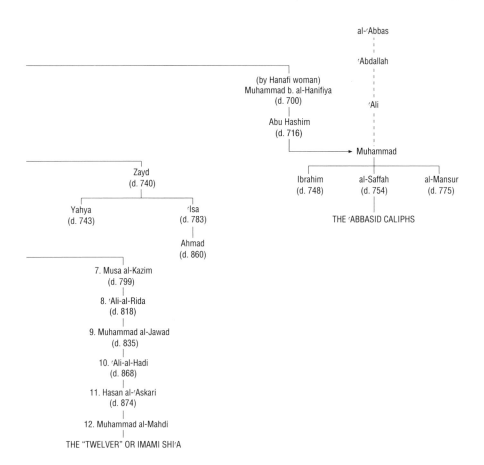

appearance of a *wasi*, who was the executor and interpreter of the inner meaning of the revelation. In history, there were to be seven prophets, each followed by a cycle of seven imams. Muhammad was the sixth prophet. His wasi was 'Ali, who was to be followed by a cycle of imams culminating in Muhammad the son of Isma'il, the mahdi, who would return as the seventh and final prophet to reveal the truth in its fullness and establish everlasting justice. Isma'ilism combined a historical cyclical concept of prophetology with eschatological messianism.

The Isma'ilis held further that the imams were figures in a universal hierarchy as well as participants in prophetic cycles. The prophet, the *natiq*, was superior to the imams, who in turn were superior to the *hujja*, the proof, who represented the imams in their absence and were in turn represented by *da'is*, or missionaries. This structure of communal authority was at once a hierarchy of leadership and the mark of successive stages of spiritual initiation.

The Isma'ilis of the ninth century were active missionaries and political organizers. While the Shi'a of Baghdad maintained their position in 'Abbasid society and government, the Isma'ilis set out to proselytize tribal and peasant peoples in Arabia, Syria, Iraq, North Africa, and the towns of Iran, preaching equality and justice, the need for reform, and the coming of the mahdi. Isma'ili da'is converted new peoples to their version of Islam and led extensive rebellions against the 'Abbasid Caliphate. Isma'ili dynasties were founded in North Africa, the Caspian region, Bahrain, Multan, and other places. While Imami Shi'ism was politically quietist, Isma'ili Shi'ism carried the banner of Islamic revolution.

In either form, Shi'ism was characterized by a religious mood which stressed messianic hopes and chiliastic expectations. The Shi'a believed in the return of the imam as a messiah, and that the historical world would come to an end with the fulfillment of successive cycles of prophets and imams in a cataclysmic era, out of which would come a reborn mankind and the establishment of a kingdom of God on earth. While Sunni and Shi'i Muslims did not vary much in the practice of their daily lives, they differed profoundly in the emotional mood through which they saw worldly reality.

CHAPTER 7

ISLAMIC CULTURE AND THE SEPARATION OF STATE AND RELIGION

The two principal versions of Islamic civilization, the courtly cosmopolitan and the urban religious, represented the political and religious elites thrown up by the Arab conquests. Each version also represented a selection and synthesis of the heritage of Middle Eastern Jewish, Christian, Hellenistic, Byzantine, and Sasanian cultures. The vast reach of the Islamic empires, the broad recruitment of the imperial elite, and the cosmopolitan quality of Baghdad brought the whole of the ancient Middle Eastern heritage into the purview of Islam. The new elites were impelled to generate a unified culture to provide a coherent way of life in their melting-pot cities, to integrate the disparate elements of the new elite, and to articulate the triumph, the legitimacy, and the permanence of the new order. These needs could only be fulfilled by the assimilation of the crucial elements of the ancient heritage.

The appropriation of the past was in part unconscious and in part deliberate. In the new era, the past was a living presence. The majority of Middle Eastern peoples remained Jews, Christians, or Zoroastrians. Family, village, neighborhood, tribal, and other forms of small-scale community organization were generally not affected by the Arab conquests and the Muslim empires. Despite geographical changes in the distribution of economic activity, the basic institutions of agricultural production and urban commerce remained unchanged. Byzantine and Sasanian imperial institutions, including the concept of the ruler and his responsibility for religion, were directly taken over by the Arab-Muslim Caliphate. Monotheistic religious beliefs and congregational forms of religious organization became the template for the newly forming Muslim religious communities. Converts brought their previous education, cultural style, and political identifications into the new faith. Christian eschatology and theology, neo-Platonic and Hellenistic philosophy, became part of Islamic theology and mysticism. Jewish scriptural, prophetic, ritual, and legal precedents were absorbed into Islamic law. Hellenistic science, Sasanian and Byzantine court ceremony, art and architecture, administrative precedents, and political concepts were assimilated by the Umayyad and 'Abbasid empires.

In historical retrospect Islam appears as a new guise for a more ancient civilization. The Islamization of the Middle East did not transform the basic institutions of
the economy, or of family, tribe, and empire. Rather, Islam seems to have infused
inherited institutions with a new vocabulary, concepts, and value preferences, as well
as a new definition of personal, social, and political identity. It redefined pre-Islamic
institutions in Muslim cultural terms. No matter how deliberate the appropriation of
Christian, Byzantine, and Sasanian artistic motifs, the resulting configuration was original and unmistakably Islamic. In literature, law, theology, mysticism, and philosophy, the materials of the past were reshaped. Islamic civilization had to find a
balance between the tendency to incorporate the past and the need to assert a new
identity; between the ancient religions of the Book and the new dispensation;
between the continuity of Middle Eastern imperial regimes and the novelty of the
Muslim Caliphate.

The process of forming Islamic civilization was not a passive assimilation but an
active struggle among the proponents of different views. Within court circles, representatives of Arabic, Persian, and Hellenistic literatures struggled to shape the
identity of the Caliphate. The proponents of Arabic and Persian identities fought
for a century until Arabic triumphed as the primary language of the empire, and
Persian and Hellenistic literatures were absorbed into Arabic literary forms.

Similarly, the Muslim urban communities embodied not one but a number of conflicting orientations. Some Muslims emphasized the authority of the scholarly tradition, others the teaching of the imams or the charismatic presence of the saints. The
Sunnis tended to stress the revealed text itself, the chain of commentary and interpretation going back through the generations directly to the Prophet, and the collective authority of learned men as the basis of Islamic belief and practice, but were
divided among those who emphasized good works and correct practice and those
who were concerned with doctrine and true belief; still others urged the importance
of direct experience of the being of God. The Shi'a emphasized personal loyalty to
the imams and their teachings. Urban Islam embodied fundamentalist, conservative,
puritanical, accommodationist, realist, and millenarian religious attitudes.

Each of these positions was formed by debate. We have seen how the scrip-
turalists held different views about the authority of the Quran, hadith, and law, and
differed over the boundaries of revelation and human judgment. By the middle of
the tenth century, hadith and law had been integrated, though new issues would
arise later. The theologians disputed the nature of God's being and his attributes,
free will and predestination; and the relative weight of revelation and reason, though
defined in terms of a limited use of reason, was yet to be resolved. The mystics were
divided by world-renouncing and world-accepting attitudes, and by ecstatic and
sober practices. Just as there were intense debates within each orientation over the
proper values of the religious life, there were intense conflicts among them. Scholars of law questioned the validity of mysticism. Theologians wrestled with the
hadith-minded commitment to revelation rather than reason. Proponents of law and

those of mysticism were still at odds. The relations of scripture, theology, mysticism, and philosophy would have to be reconsidered in a later era.

The most fateful confrontations, however, were between the court and the urban versions of Islam. Islamic court culture was visual, literary, philosophic, and scientific. As opposed to the courtly concern for symbols to articulate a vision of the universe that justified the authority of the Caliph and the supremacy of the dominant elite, the urban version of Islam emphasized individual piety in pursuit of an Islamic way of life. Those with pious tendencies set their concept of humbleness and devotion against aristocratic elegance and refinement. For the courtly milieu Islam was but an aspect of a cosmopolitan identity and worldview. For the urban milieus Islam defined the good life.

These differences led to conflict on several levels. The Shu'ubiya controversy over the supremacy of Arabic or Persian literary values was partly a court-centered dispute, but it also spilled over into a confrontation between court and urban milieus. While the proponents of Persian literature espoused political domination, social hierarchy, and aristocratic refinement, the urban 'ulama' affirmed religious equality, political accountability, and personal values based upon the Quranic revelation and the Arabic identity of the town populations.

An equally important struggle was waged over the legitimacy of Hellenistic thought. Hellenism represented both a reinforcement of and a challenge to the worldview of the urban 'ulama'. Court and urban theologians welcomed logical methods of argument to clarify Muslim perspectives and defend them against philosophic attack, but insofar as philosophy was conceived as an alternative source of divine truths, they rejected the primacy of reason in religious matters. Similarly, neo-Platonism was in one sense intrinsic to the philosophic vision and was therefore a court-sponsored alternative to urban Islam, but in another sense it reinforced an already existing strand of Muslim mysticism, and gave Sufi asceticism a rationale and a method for the mystical quest. Other aspects of Hellenistic teaching such as science, philosophy, and occult metaphysics, which were acceptable in court milieus, were rejected in urban 'ulama' Islam. Like Persian adab, Hellenistic culture was screened, adapted, and utilized to reinforce the basic moral and religious positions of the urban 'ulama'. Nonetheless, it continued to be sponsored in court circles as a part of cosmopolitan and aristocratic cultivation. In this guise Hellenistic philosophy and science would be preserved for future confrontations and interaction with Islamic religious thought and for eventual transmission to Christian Europe.

The conflict of worldviews also led to a struggle between the Caliphate and the urban 'ulama' over the content of Islamic belief and the role of the Caliphate in the governance of the Muslim community. From the very beginning the Caliphs had claimed to be the protectors of both the religious and the political interests of the Muslim umma. The 'Abbasid Caliph al-Mahdi (775–85) claimed to be the protector of Islam against heresy and arrogated the right to define acceptable doctrine. Later al-Ma'mun (813–33) tried to remake the religious foundations of the Caliphate in the wake of the disruptive civil war that brought him to power. He tried to win over his opponents by making a Shi'i imam, 'Ali al-Rida, the eighth descendant of 'Ali, heir to the Caliphate. The rapprochement with Shi'ism implied that al-Ma'mun accepted the Shi'i view of the Caliph as divinely chosen by God with the authority to define religious belief and law. 'Ali al-Rida, however, died within a year. Al-Ma'mun then tried to accomplish the same objective by adopting the Mu'tazili thesis that the Quran was created and not of the divine essence. This doctrine served to emphasize the religious importance of the Caliph by implying that the Quran, as a created thing, was, like all created things, subject to authoritative Caliphal interpretation. These were not idle claims. Al-Ma'mun initiated an inquisition to force Muslim scholars to accept this doctrine and his right to proclaim it.

Indeed, virtually all of the leading religious scholars capitulated. Among religious leaders, only Ahmad b. Hanbal refused to accept the Caliph's contentions. Ahmad, already reputed to be the greatest hadith scholar of his time, now emerged as the public leader of the urban 'ulama' point of view. He denied that the Quran was created, and affirmed the transcendent authority of the written word over its human interpreters. Islamic religious obligations, he argued, were not derived from Caliphal pronouncements, but from the fundamental texts known to the leading scholars. The Caliph was merely the executor of the Islamic community, and not the source of its beliefs. A protracted struggle between the Caliphate and the 'ulama' eventually ended with the victory of the latter. In 848–49 the Caliph al-Mutawakkil reversed the policy of his predecessors, abandoned the Mu'tazili thesis, and accepted the contention that the Quran was not the created word of God. The Caliph conceded both the point of doctrine and his claims to be the ultimate source of religious beliefs.

Despite this reversal, the damage done to Caliphal authority was irreparable. The claims of the Caliphate brought out a long-smoldering resentment. It had become suspect to the 'ulama' and other pious Muslims, who saw it as falling away from true religious principles. Insofar as the 'Abbasid empire had been built on the identity of Islam and the Caliphate, this loss of support was politically catastrophic. Though the Caliphate remained head of the umma and a symbol of Muslim unity, a gulf had opened between the state and religious communities. Henceforth, the Caliph would represent the administrative and executive interests of Islam while the scholars and Sufis defined Islamic religious belief. Islam began to evolve independently under the aegis of the religious teachers. The struggle over the "createdness of the Quran" confirmed the separateness of the two forms of early Islamic culture and community – the division of state and religious institutions, of court and urban 'ulama', and of cosmopolitan and religious forms of Islamic civilization. In the future they would develop along separate lines.

CHAPTER 8

THE FALL OF THE 'ABBASID EMPIRE

The very processes that gave rise to the early Islamic empire, its elites, and its cultural forms led to its collapse and transformation. The decline of the 'Abbasid empire began even in the midst of consolidation. While the regime was strengthening its military and administrative institutions, and encouraging a flourishing economy and culture, other forces were set in motion that would eventually unravel the 'Abbasid empire.

THE DECLINE OF THE CENTRAL GOVERNMENT

As early as the reign of Harun al-Rashid (786–809) the problems of succession had become critical. Harun bequeathed his elder son, al-Amin, the Caliphate, and the younger, al-Ma'mun, the governorship of Khurasan and the right to succeed his brother. With the death of Harun, al-Amin attempted to displace his brother in favor of his own son. Civil war resulted. Al-Amin was backed by the 'Abbasid army of Baghdad, while al-Ma'mun turned to the independent Khurasanian warlords. In a bitter civil war al-Ma'mun defeated his brother and assumed the Caliphate in 813.

Once in office, al-Ma'mun attempted to deal with his unreconciled opponents and subjects by means of a double policy. One goal, as we have seen in the previous chapter, was to restore the legitimacy of the Caliphate by manipulating Shi'i loyalties and Mu'tazili doctrines to give the Caliphate control over religious affairs. This policy failed, and failing, deprived the Caliphate of an important measure of popular support. Al-Ma'mun also adopted a new military policy. To win control of the Caliphate, he had depended on the support of a Khurasanian lord, Tahir, who in return was made governor of Khurasan (820–22) and general of 'Abbasid forces throughout the empire, with the promise that the offices would be inherited by his heirs. Despite the momentary usefulness of the arrangement, the concession of a hereditary governorship defeated the Caliphal objective of integrating provincial notables into the central government. Now the empire was to be governed by an alliance of the Caliph with the most important provincial lord.

To offset the power of the Tahirids and regain direct control of the provinces, the Caliphs were eager to create new military forces. Thus, al-Ma'mun and al-Mu'tasim (833–42) raised forces of two types. The first were *shakiriya*, intact units under the leadership of their local chiefs, from Transoxania, Armenia, and North Africa. Though the soldiers were not directly beholden to the Caliphs, they served as a counterweight to the Tahirids. The second type of force was Turkish slaves, called *ghilman* (pl.), who were purchased individually, but grouped into regiments. For the sake of efficiency and morale, and a balance of power between the regiments, each lived in its own neighborhood, had its own mosque and markets, and was trained, supplied, and paid by its commander. Thus slave regiments also became self-contained units which gave their primary loyalty to their officers rather than to the Caliphs.

The systematic recruitment, training, and employment of slave soldiers was a major innovation in Middle Eastern history, and the beginning of an institution that would characterize many later Muslim regimes. The pressing military and political need for loyal troops must have directed the attention of the Caliphs to long-established precedents for the employment of military forces from peripheral regions and marginal populations. Since Umayyad times the Caliphs and governors of the Arab-Muslim empire had raised supplementary troops in eastern Iran and had depended upon servile, client, and even slave troops, for their personal bodyguards. The new system of slave regiments was a rationalization of earlier practices now made the centerpiece of 'Abbasid military organization.

These new regiments strengthened the hand of the Caliphs, but the Transoxanian and Turkish soldiers soon ran afoul of the Baghdadi populace and of the former Arab soldiers in the Baghdadi army, and bloody clashes ensued. Eventually, the Caliph al-Mu'tasim built a new capital, Samarra, about 70 miles north of Baghdad, to isolate the troops from the masses. While Baghdad remained the cultural and commercial capital of the region, from 836 to 870 Samarra was the military and administrative headquarters of the Caliphate. However, the new city only created further difficulties. The Caliphs, who had hoped to avoid clashes between the populace and the troops, instead became embroiled in rivalries among the various guard regiments. The officers took civilian bureaucrats into their patronage, won control of provincial governorships, and eventually attempted to control succession to the Caliphate itself. Regimental rivalries led to anarchy. Between 861 and 870 all the leading officers were killed, and the troops fell out of control and turned to banditry. The employment of slave armies further alienated the Caliphate from the populace it ruled. While the early 'Abbasid empire had depended upon the military support of its own subjects, the late empire tried to dominate its peoples with foreign troops.

In the same period, changes in administrative organization also reduced the capacity of the central government to control the empire. These changes in administration were partly due to the interference of the army, and partly to the rise of independent provincial powers, but they were also due to overwhelming internal stresses inherent in the normal operation of the bureaucracy. In 'Abbasid government all high-ranking officers employed their personal followers to do their staff work. To learn the art of being an accountant or scribe a young man had to enter the service of a master, live in his household, and become a dedicated personal servant. He owed his master respect and obedience for life, and the patron was obliged not only to train him but to protect him and advance his career. In time the bureaucracy came to be dominated by cliques and factions, formed among the functionaries, whose main interest was to exploit bureaucratic office for private gain. The bureaucracy ceased to serve the interests of the ruler and the empire, and began to act on behalf of the personal and factional interests of the scribes.

By the late ninth century, the numerous small cliques attached to many leading officials had become polarized into two great factions, called the Banu Furat and the Banu Jarrah. Each of these factions was built around a wazir and his relatives and clients. The families also had a larger following based on social and ideological affiliations. The Banu Jarrah faction was composed mainly, though not exclusively, of Nestorian Christians or Christian converts, often educated in the monastery of Dayr Qunna in southern Iraq. By the middle of the ninth century, this faction had already grown powerful enough to influence state policy. In 852 al-Mutawakkil (847–61) was persuaded to assure Christians freedom of religion, freedom from military service, and the right to construct churches, and to give the Nestorian Catholicos full jurisdiction over all Christians. The Caliph also conceded the right of converts to inherit the property of parents who were still Christians, though Muslim law did not permit such transfers. These concessions, however, were soon revoked. The other major faction, the Banu Furat, were mainly Baghdadi Shi'a.

The chiefs of these factions eventually gained control of the whole government service. In the reign of al-Mutawakkil the wazirs were put in charge of all the administrative bureaus. While they could be appointed and removed by the Caliph at will, in practice the Caliphs rarely intervened in the routine operations of the bureaucracy. A wazir and his faction would come to power by intrigues and by bribing the Caliph and other influential courtiers. Their main concern then would be to exploit their offices, earn back the bribes, and prepare for future hard times by various frauds, such as padded payrolls, false bookkeeping, illegal speculations, and taking bribes. The officials regarded their positions as a property which they bought, sold, and exploited for private gain. When a faction had been in power and was known to have become rich, the Caliph and the opposing faction would be eager to seize the fortunes accumulated by the incumbents. The Caliph would then appoint a new wazir; a rival group would come to power, which would then confiscate the assets of the defeated party. Some of the money would go to the Caliph and back to the treasury, but some of it went into the pockets of the victorious faction. Special bureaus were set up to handle the reclaimed monies: the *diwan al-musadarat* for confiscated estates and the *diwan al-marafiq* for confiscated bribes. The Caliphate could maintain only a modicum of influence by rotating the leading factions in office and using each change of government as an occasion to extort the resources stolen by the faction last in power.

The cost, however, was extremely high, for the central government was forced to look to new administrative devices to make up the political and financial losses occasioned by a corrupt bureaucracy. One method was to distribute or sell iqta's to soldiers, courtiers, and officials, who collected the taxes ordinarily due from the peasants and paid a portion to the central government. While bringing in a short-term income, iqta's reduced long-term revenues, and subverted the normal operation of provincial and local administration. In addition, iqta's acted as crystals to collect and aggregate small holdings. Peasants, under pressure from the tax bureaus, would appeal for protection to the powerful iqta' holders and sign over their lands. The practice was called *taljia* (commendation), or *himaya* (protection). The growth of large landed estates further diminished the areas under routine administration. Instead of taxing peasants in a relatively direct way, the government found itself dealing more and more with powerful local landowning notables, who reduced the task of the administration to the collection of negotiated fees.

In addition to the sale of iqta's, the central government also introduced tax-farming in Iraq and western Iran. To obtain revenues in advance, the government sold the right to collect taxes to tax-farmers. Tax-farms were put up to annual auction, or were sold at an estimate of the likely yields based on past experience. The state was guaranteed a fixed revenue a year in advance of when it could normally be collected, and the tax-farmers profited by collecting taxes in excess of what they had to pay the state. To make the arrangement work to the benefit of the central government, strict inspection was essential.

Tax-farming, however, was not merely a financial arrangement; it was a substitute form of administration. The tax-farmer not only paid a sum to collect taxes, but also agreed to maintain local administration, meet all the government's local expenses, invest in irrigation, and support the local police. Though government inspectors tried to protect the peasants from abuse, the basic apparatus of local administration was being displaced by private governments. Through the distribution of iqta's and the sale of tax-farms, the government, in effect, forfeited its control over the revenue-bearing countryside.

PROVINCIAL AUTONOMY AND DISINTEGRATION

With the decline of the military and financial capacities of the central government, the provinces became increasingly independent. The peripheral provinces, governed by tributary rulers, freed themselves altogether from their subordination to the empire, and many of the core provinces, once directly administered by Baghdad, became peripheral provinces under the control of semi-independent governors. The devolution of provincial powers occurred in two main ways. In some cases, Turkish guard officers usurped provincial governorships and made themselves independent of the central government. For example, Egypt between 868 and 905 came under the control of the Tulunid dynasty. The founder of the dynasty, Ahmad b. Tulun (868–84), originally a sub-governor of Egypt, built up a private slave army, seized control of Egypt's finances, and established his own dynasty, all the while protected by patrons at the Caliphal court. In other areas, governors chipped away at the prerogatives of the central government. Some ceased to remit tax revenues. Others negotiated a fixed payment in return for their assignments.

Elsewhere, the decline of central authority allowed for popular resistance to central control. Iraq was the scene of a prolonged revolt of the Zanj slave laborers. In the middle of the ninth century, there was a mass uprising of *ghazis* (frontier soldiers) in Sijistan (southeastern Iran) under the leadership of the Saffarids. The Saffarids took control of Sijistan, Kirman, and northern India, seized Khurasan from the Tahirids, and then took western Iran and invaded Iraq. Though they were defeated in Iraq, the Caliphate had to recognize their control of Khurasan and most of western Iran. The Saffarid victory displaced the older landowning and administrative elites with ghazi leadership.

Despite the loss of Egypt and Iran, the Caliphate was able to reassert itself. In 900, the Samanid rulers of Transoxania defeated the Saffarids. The Samanid victory was a great gain for the 'Abbasids because the Samanids represented the same landowning and administrative notables as those who governed the 'Abbasid empire, and because they restored cooperation between a major independent provincial dynasty and the 'Abbasid central government. In 905 the Caliphs also managed to defeat the Tulunid dynasty in Egypt and Syria. The restoration of central authority, however, was only temporary. With the bureaucracy in disarray, the Caliphate could not use its temporary military victories to reorganize the empire. These victories were but a lull in a downward course which became headlong between 905 and 945.

In the early decades of the tenth century, Shi'ism again became the leading form of popular resistance to the 'Abbasid empire. Isma'ilism was preached in southern Iraq, Bahrain, Syria, Mesopotamia, Yemen, Daylam, eastern Iran, and North Africa. The Isma'ilis seem to have had a central directorate, but the Isma'ili missions tended to adapt to the prior religious convictions and understanding of the persons being proselytized. The Isma'ilis initiated their converts step by step, so that the true teachings of the faith were not fully presented to everyone. Moreover, the movement addressed itself to all classes of the population, whether peasants in Iraq and Syria, bedouins in Arabia, villagers in Iran, Berbers in North Africa, or the upper classes of eastern Iran.

Isma'ili religio-political agitation led to a series of rebellions called the Qarmatian movement. Around 900 there were peasant jacqueries in Iraq, and bedouin revolts in Syria and northeastern Arabia, which led to the formation of a Qarmatian state in Bahrain. In the 920s the Qarmatians attacked Basra and Kufa and threatened

Baghdad, cut the pilgrimage routes, pillaged Mecca, and made off with the black stone of the Ka'ba. In North Africa another offshoot of the Isma'ili movement founded the Fatimid dynasty (909) which conquered all of North Africa and Egypt by 969. The Fatimids claimed to be the rightful successors to the Prophet, not only for their own provinces, but for the whole of the Muslim world. They even adopted the title of Caliph, thus breaking the symbolic unity of the Muslim community. They were followed by the Umayyad dynasty in Spain and by other North African states (see part II) who thus debased the title, prestige, and legitimacy of the 'Abbasid dynasty.

Shi'ism also inspired resistance to the 'Abbasids in Mesopotamia, where Arab bedouins under the leadership of the Hamdanid family extended their influence southward from Mosul to Baghdad, westward into northern Syria, and northward into Armenia. In the Caspian province of Daylam, Shi'i refugees fleeing 'Abbasid persecution converted the local people to Islam. In 864 the Daylam Shi'a declared their independence of the Caliphate, forced out the 'Abbasid governor, and established an independent state. In the early tenth century, a local Daylamite ruler named Mardawij b. Ziyar conquered most of western Iran. When he was killed in 937, his empire was inherited by the Daylamite mercenaries in his service, led by the Buwayhid brothers, who established their dominion in the region.

Other governors and warlords also seized extensive territories. By 935 the Caliphate had lost control of virtually all of its provinces except the region around Baghdad. Administratively and militarily helpless, the Caliphs could only appeal for protection to one or another of the provincial forces, or play them off against each other. In 936, to stave off the enemies pressing in on Baghdad, the Caliphs created the post of *amir al-umara'* (general-in-chief) and divested themselves of all actual power save the formal right to select the most powerful of their subjects as chief of state. After a complex many-sided struggle, the Buwayhids took control of Baghdad in 945. The Caliphs were allowed to continue in nominal authority – indeed, the 'Abbasid dynasty lasted until 1258 – but they no longer ruled; the 'Abbasid empire had ceased to exist.

The disintegration of the 'Abbasid empire into a number of independent provincial regimes implied vast changes in the organization of society. The emergence of a slave military elite and the new iqta' form of administration assured not only the breakup of the empire but also the transfer of power from old to new elites. Early 'Abbasid government had been built upon a coalition of the central government staffs with provincial landowning and other notable families. The empire attracted into central government service the scions of provincial families whose contacts and goodwill served to unify the empire and make the central government effective in the provinces. Over time, however, the staffs of the central administration tended increasingly to be composed of the descendants of former scribes rather than being drawn from provincial families. As generations of scribes succeeded each other, the bureaucracy became a city-based organization, scarcely connected

Table 4. *Middle Eastern provincial regimes: Abbasid empire and post-imperial era*

	Iraq	Western Iran	Khurasan	Mesopotamia (Mosul)	Egypt	Syria
700	Abbasids 750–945	Abbasids 750–934	Abbasids 750–821	Abbasids 750–905	Abbasids 750–868	Abbasids 750–945
800			Tahirids 821–73 Saffarids 873–900		Tulunids 868–905	
900		Buwayhids 934–c. 1040	Samanids 900–99	Hamdanids 905–91	Abbasids 905–35 Ikhshidids 935–69	
	Buwayhids 945–1055		Ghaznavids 999–1040 (in Afghanistan, 961–1186)	Uqaylids (992–1096)	Fatimids (969–1171)	Partitioned between Hamdanids in Aleppo 945–1004 and Fatimids in Damascus 978–1076
1000		Saljuqs 1055–1194	Saljuqs 1038–1157			Mirdasids 1023–79 in Aleppo

Saljuq conquest 1078; Saljuqid states 1078–1183; crusader states 1099–1291 |
| 1100 | Saljuqs 1055–1194 | | | Zangids 1127–1222 | Conquest by Saladin 1169 Ayyubids 1169–1250 | Ayyubids 1183–1260 |
| 1200 | Mongols 1258 | | Nomadic invasions culminating in Mongols | | Mamluks 1250–1517 Ottomans 1517–1805 | Mamluks 1260–1517 Ottomans 1517–1918 |

to the provinces. It ceased to represent the diverse populations of the empire. More-over, the introduction of tax-farming, which required large investments, favored the interests of merchants wealthy from involvement in slave, grain, and international trade. Bankers who could raise the necessary sums and channel them into state investments became politically ever more important. Thus, a merchant elite, the product of the empire's fiscal centralization and tax-collecting methods, and a prod-uct of the opportunities it offered for worldwide trade, began to displace the scribal class, with its provincial contacts, as the political mainstay of the central government.

The decline of the central government brought in its wake the ultimate destruc-tion of the provincial landowning notables who had originally supported the 'Abbasid empire. The rise of military warlords and a new capital-city-based finan-cial and administrative elite, and the development of new forms of land tenure including iqta' assignments and tax-farms brought to the countryside a new elite, backed by the waning but still significant powers of the central government, to compete with the old provincial notables. In many regions a new class of large land controllers and landowners foisted upon the countryside by central government policies displaced the small-scale landholding notables of the villages.

These extensive political and social changes were accompanied by widespread economic regression. In the course of the late ninth and early tenth centuries, the economy of Iraq was ruined. For more than a century the Caliphate had neglected investment in irrigation and reclamation projects. Irrigation in the Tigris region was severely damaged by almost incessant warfare, and large districts became de-populated. The distribution of iqta's and the creation of tax-farms removed all incentives for maintaining rural productivity. In southern Iraq, the slave rebellions also led to agricultural losses. While the early Buwayhid rulers attempted to restore canals and to reclaim abandoned lands, political instability and fiscal exploitation ruined the countryside. Iraq, once the most prosperous of Middle Eastern regions, now became one of the poorest, and would not recover its agricultural prosperity until the twentieth century.

Iraq also suffered from declining international trade. The Qarmatian rebellions hurt the trade of the Persian Gulf and the trade between Arabia and Iraq. The dis-ruption of the Caliphate interfered with the international routes that brought goods from the Far East and South Asia to Baghdad for transshipment to the Mediter-ranean. In the late tenth century, the Fatimid regime helped to promote an alter-native international route through the Red Sea and Cairo, which also damaged the commercial prosperity of Iraq.

Other provinces were similarly in decline. Mesopotamia, which had been settled in the seventh century by large numbers of bedouins, suffered economically from the encroachment of pastoralism upon agriculture. In the late eighth century, peas-ants suffering from bedouin raids and excessive taxation began to abandon the land. In the course of the ninth century, there was a regression of sedentary life under nomadic pressure. The emergence of the Hamdanid dynasty ratified the dominance of pastoral over sedentary peoples. Egypt owed its decline to the exploitation of the peasantry. Iran, however, maintained its high levels of urban and agricultural development well into the eleventh century.

Thus, the breakup of the 'Abbasid empire was at once a political, a social, and an economic transformation. It led to the substitution of small states for a single, unified empire. The bureaucratic and small landowning elites who favored centralized government were replaced by large-scale landowners and military lords who opposed it. The overall decline of the economy further contributed to the weakening of the empire. Finally, the military, administrative, and cultural policies of the empire themselves led to its collapse, and the eventual formation of a new type of Middle Eastern state and society.

FROM ISLAMIC CULTURE TO ISLAMIC SOCIETY: IRAN AND IRAQ, 945–c.1200

CHAPTER 9

THE POST-'ABBASID MIDDLE EASTERN STATE SYSTEM

With the breakup of the 'Abbasid empire it is no longer possible to recount Middle Eastern history from a central point of view. The chaotic history of the period that follows is best understood by distinguishing the eastern parts of the Middle East, including Transoxania, Iran, and Iraq, from the western parts, consisting primarily of Syria and Egypt. In the east, the first generation of regimes that succeeded to the domains of the 'Abbasid empire included the Buwayhids in Iraq and western Iran (945–1055), the Samanids in eastern Iran and Transoxania (to 999), and the Ghaznavids in Afghanistan and Khurasan (to 1040). These regimes gave way to a succession of nomadic empires as the collapse of the 'Abbasid empire allowed the frontiers between the settled parts of the Middle East and Inner Asia to break down and Turkish nomadic peoples to infiltrate the region. In the tenth century, the Qarakhanids invaded and took control of Transoxania. In the eleventh century, the Saljuqs seized Iran and Anatolia. Ghuzz and Nayman followed in the twelfth century; the Mongols conquered most of the region in the thirteenth.

In the west, the Fatimids succeeded to the former 'Abbasid provinces of Egypt and parts of Syria, but the breakdown of political order in Syria permitted a succession of foreign invasions. In the tenth century, the Byzantine empire reoccupied the north, and even attempted to conquer Jerusalem. Byzantine armies were followed by Latin Crusaders, and finally by Saljuqs. With the establishment of Saljuq-derived regimes the western parts of the Middle East rejoined the stream of eastern developments. Here we shall consider the eastern regimes and reserve discussion of Syria, Egypt, and North Africa for part II.

IRAQ, IRAN, AND THE EASTERN PROVINCES

Iraq and Iran were the crucial centers for the formation of new state, communal, and religious institutions. In this region, no matter how numerous and ephemeral,

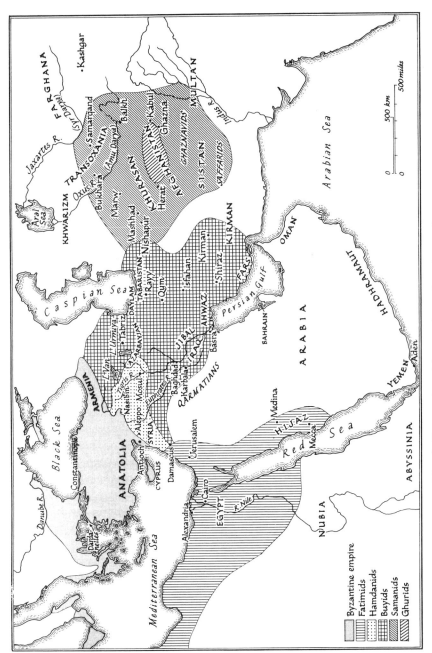

Map 4 The post-imperial succession regimes: late tenth century

Middle Eastern states came to be built around similar elites and institutions. Everywhere the old landowning and bureaucratic elites lost their authority and were replaced by nomadic chieftains and slave soldiers. Everywhere the cohesion of the state came to depend upon slave armies and a semi-feudal form of administration. Each state became the patron of a regional culture. In Iran a new Islamic civilization based on the Persian language and arts emerged. In the Arab provinces poetry, manuscript illumination, architecture, and minor arts developed. At the same time, the 'ulama' and the Sufis, who in the imperial age had been the informal spokesmen of Islam, became the heads of communal organizations. They presided over the conversion of Middle Eastern peoples, organized schools of law, Sufi brotherhoods and Shi'i sects, standardized Islamic religious teachings, and articulated an Islamic social and political ethic. Despite political fragmentation, a new form of Islamic state, community, and religion came into being.

The Buwayhids, who ruled western Iran, Iraq, and Mesopotamia, pioneered the new type of regime. They left the Caliphs in position as titular heads of state, recognized them as the chiefs of all Sunni Muslims, conceded their right to make appointments to religious offices, and accepted the idea that their own right to govern was based on Caliphal recognition. In practice the regime was based upon a family coalition in which each of the conquering brothers was assigned a province of Iran or Iraq as his appanage. The armies, composed partly of Daylamite infantry and partly of slave Turkish cavalry, were, like the forces of the latter-day Caliphate, organized into regiments loyal more to their own leaders and to their own ambitions for wealth and power than to the state itself. These regiments fought each other and encouraged conflicts among various Buwayhid princes. These conflicts further reduced the powers of the central government as the Buwayhids gave the soldiers the right to collect taxes from designated areas in lieu of salaries. To these new grants the old name iqta' was often applied. In Kirman, Fars, and Khuzistan, foreign Turkish and Daylamite mercenaries usurped ownership of the land, neglected investments in agriculture, and exploited the peasants for short-term gain. The result was further regression of the agricultural economy of Iraq and western Iran.

In eastern Iran and Transoxania, the Samanid dynasty maintained the 'Abbasid system for another half-century. The regime was administered by a bureaucratic elite which depended on the local notables and landlord families, while the attached provinces of Sijistan, Khwarizm, and Afghanistan were governed by tributary lords or slave governors. Like the 'Abbasids, the Samanids were the patrons of a fabulously creative Islamic culture. In the tenth century, Bukhara emerged as the center of a new Persian-Islamic literature and art as Arabic religious, legal, philosophic, and literary ideas were recast into Persian. For the first time the religion and culture of Islam became available in a language other than Arabic.

However, the Samanid regime disintegrated in the tenth century, and their domains in Khurasan and Afghanistan fell to Alptigin, a slave governor whose capital was Ghazna (Afghanistan). Alptigin founded a regime of slave soldiers who

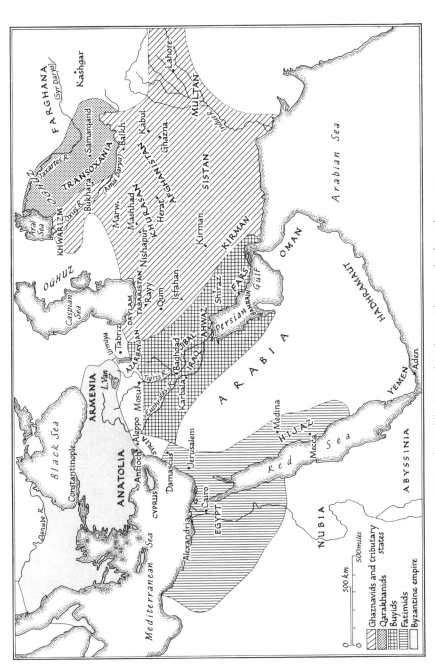

Map 5 The Middle East in the Ghaznavid era: early eleventh century

conquered and ruled Khurasan from 999 to 1040, and Afghanistan until 1186. They attacked Transoxania and western Iran, plundered Lahore in 1030, and occupied parts of northern India until 1187. Everywhere they destroyed established elites and replaced them with slave soldiers; the rulers were themselves former slaves. Like the Buwayhids they gave iqta's to their soldiers, but they also maintained the vestiges of Samanid bureaucratic administration to keep central control over the distribution of landed estates and to collect tributes, booty, and the revenues of crown estates. The Ghaznavids also started the policy of cultivating the support of Muslim religious leaders, by declaring allegiance to the Caliphate, and supporting Islamic education and a Persian literary revival. The slave army, decentralized administration, and patronage of Persian-Islamic culture were henceforth the defining features of Middle Eastern regimes.

By the middle of the eleventh century, Ghaznavid rule gave way to new forces which had their origin in Inner Asia. Inner Asia, between the borders of the Iranian and the Chinese empires, was inhabited by pastoral peoples who raised horses and sheep for their livelihood. These people generally lived in small bands, but they could form confederations to contest control of pasture lands and to attack settled areas. In the course of the seventh and eighth centuries, nomadic peoples on the eastern frontiers of China, prevented from entering China by the T'ang dynasty, began to push westward in search of pasturage. This started a wave of migrations pushing Inner Asian peoples into the region of the Aral Sea, Transoxania, Khwarizm, and Afghanistan.

These peoples were organized under the leadership of royal families and other chiefs. They entered regular commercial and cultural relations with the settled areas. From the settled peoples the nomads purchased grain, spices, textiles, and weapons. In return they sold livestock, hides, wool, and slaves. This lively exchange induced settled peoples to extend trading posts and towns out onto the steppes and involved Inner Asian nomads in the caravan traffic between Transoxania, the Volga and Siberian regions to the north, and China to the east.

Furthermore, nomadic peoples, in contact with Muslim merchants, scholars, and Sufis, were introduced to Islam. Originally they were pagans, who believed that the world, animate and inanimate, was peopled by living and vital spirits, and shamanists, who believed that some of their members had the capacity to separate body and soul, and, in ecstatic moments, rise up to heaven or descend to the underworld. Knowledge of the realms and powers beyond made the shamans healers and interpreters of dreams. Inner Asian peoples, however, were familiar with Nestorian Christianity, which had been preached on the steppes. Many were Buddhists; some were Manichaeans. In the middle of the tenth century, the Qarluq peoples who were to make up the Qarakhanid empire, were converted to Islam. Shortly before the end of the century, Oghuz peoples associated with the Saljuq family were also converted to Islam. Thus, by the end of the tenth century, Turkish–Inner Asian peoples had developed the capacity for large-scale coalitions, had stratified elites and royal institutions, had experience in trade, and had adopted the religious identity of the settled peoples. They would enter the Middle East with the political and cultural capacities to become a new imperial elite.

This leveling of political and cultural capacities opened the way for the breakdown of the frontier between steppe and sown. With the conversion of Inner Asian peoples, the settled frontier warriors or ghazis, who had hitherto resisted Turkish incursions on the grounds that they were defending their Muslim civilization against barbarians, gave up the jihad. With the conversion of the Turks, the whole rationale of the ghazi life was subverted and ghazis abandoned the eastern frontiers. Many made their way with the Ghaznavids into India; others moved to the Byzantine frontier. With the frontier defenses in disarray, Qarluq peoples, led by the Qarakhanid dynasty, took Bukhara in 992 and Samarqand in 999.

The Qarakhanid elites were quickly assimilated to the traditions of eastern Iranian-Islamic states. In Inner Asian fashion the new rulers divided their domains into a western Khanate which ruled Transoxania until 1211, and an eastern Khanate for Farghana and Kashgaria. The new rulers of Transoxania accepted the nominal authority of the 'Abbasid Caliphs and directly or indirectly promoted the spread of Islam among the populace of Transoxania, Kashgar, and the Tarim basin. The Qarakhanids also patronized the formation of a new Turkish literature, based upon Arabic and Persian models, which made it possible to recreate the religious and literary content of Islamic Middle Eastern civilization in Turkish dress. Just as the Samanids had presided over the formation of a Persian-Islamic culture, the Qarakhanids were the patrons of a new Turkish-Islamic civilization.

THE SALJUQ EMPIRE

While the Qarluq peoples occupied Transoxania, Oghuz peoples, under the leadership of the Saljuq family, crossed the Oxus River in 1025. In 1037 they took Nishapur; in 1040 they defeated the Ghaznavids and became the new rulers of Khurasan. This was the beginning of a Saljuq empire. The Saljuq chiefs, Tughril Beg and his brother Chagri Beg, led their followers into western Iran, defeated the Buwayhids, seized control of Baghdad and the Caliphate in 1055, and were named Sultans and rulers of a new Middle Eastern empire from Khurasan to Iraq. Nomadic bands pushed into Armenia, Azarbayjan, and Byzantine Anatolia, where, in 1071, at the battle of Manzikert, they defeated the Byzantine army, captured the emperor, and opened the whole of Asia Minor to Turkish penetration. The advancing Turkish peoples also entered Iraq and Mesopotamia, and extended Saljuq domination as far as the Mediterranean.

Thus the Saljuqs reunited most of the former 'Abbasid empire and rekindled the dream of Muslim unity and universal empire. They sought to rebuild bureaucratic forms of administration, and they sponsored Muslim religious activity as the basis of their legitimacy. But while the Saljuqs aspired to a unified Middle Eastern empire,

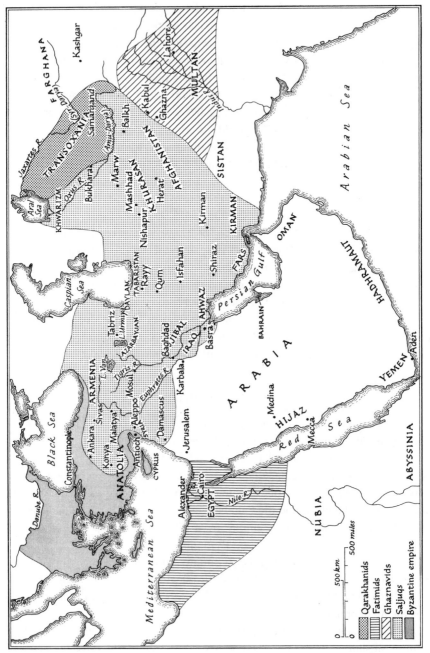

Map 6   The Saljuq empire in the late eleventh century

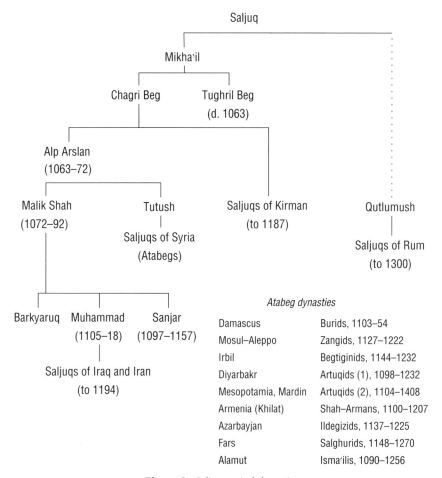

Figure 5   Saljuq-period dynasties

the organizational and institutional capacities needed to sustain a large empire were not available. The economy of Iraq could no longer support a centralized government; bureaucratic administration could not be effectively restored in a society dominated by the military landowners who had replaced the smallholding notables of the late Sasanian and 'Abbasid periods.

Moreover, the Saljuq nomadic heritage proved detrimental to their imperial ambitions. While nominally unified under the authority of a single Sultan, the Saljuqs had no fixed idea about legitimate succession, and considered the right to rule to be vested in the leading family as a whole. Thus members of the ruling house were entitled to share the family domains on behalf of the tribal subgroups whom they led. Furthermore, tribal tradition cherished the institution of the *atabeg*, who was a tutor or regent assigned to raise a minor prince and govern in his name. The atabeg was entitled to marry the mother of a ward who died, and become a governor in his own right. This was the start of many independent Saljuq-related principalities. Finally, tribal groups were entitled to regions for habitation and grazing. All these aspects of the nomadic heritage worked against imperial unity under the leadership of a single Sultan.

To overcome these inherent liabilities, the Saljuq Sultans adopted Buwayhid and Ghaznavid institutions. They tried to reduce their dependence on the Turkish peoples who had conquered the empire by creating slave armies of Turks, Greeks, Khurasanians, Kurds, Georgians, and others. They adopted the Buwayhid practice of granting lands as payment of the salaries of soldiers. Nonetheless, the unified empire lasted only from 1055 until the death of Malik Shah in 1092. His sons then divided the provinces among themselves, establishing independent dynasties in Iraq, Anatolia, Azarbayjan, Mesopotamia, Syria, Khuzistan, Fars, Kirman, and Khurasan. These proved to be ephemeral regimes, unable to consolidate power or defend their frontiers. The result was renewed nomadic invasions. In the late twelfth century, the Qarakhitay, a Mongol people who had ruled northern China in the eleventh century, took control of Transoxania from the Qarakhanids. Ghuzz peoples, displaced by the Qarakhitay, invaded Khurasan, and in 1153 destroyed the last Saljuq resistance to further nomadic incursion from Inner Asia. They were followed by the Naymans and the Mongols. These invasions had long-term demographic consequences. In the eleventh century, Armenia, Azarbayjan, and parts of Mesopotamia, which had been Iranian or Kurdish, became Turkish. The Greeks of Anatolia were in the process of being converted. Iran experienced an almost complete breakdown of state authority, unremitting nomadic invasions, and unprecedented destruction. The ultimate symbol of this chaotic era was the execution of the last ʿAbbasid Caliph in 1258.

THE SLAVE STATES AND ADMINISTRATION

Despite the numerous and short-lived provincial regimes, between 950 and 1200 a region-wide pattern of governmental institutions took shape. These institutions had their origin in the late ʿAbbasid concept of the Caliphate, in the use of slave military forces and the iqtaʿ forms of tax administration, and in nomadic concepts of family and state authority. This new order first took shape in the eastern provinces of the former ʿAbbasid empire under the aegis of the Buwayhids, the Ghaznavids, and the early Saljuqs.

With the demise of the ʿAbbasid empire a new concept of governmental authority was devised to accommodate the changing political realities. Though the ʿAbbasid dynasty continued in office until 1258, the Caliphs no longer possessed exclusive political authority. Other rulers in Egypt, North Africa, and Spain claimed their once-privileged title, and they lost effective military and administrative power. They retained, however, a role in judicial and religious affairs in that the Caliph was considered the head of the religious establishment and could suspend the administration of justice and worship. The Caliphs also retained an important moral authority and were able to intervene to temper the policies of the secular lords. Above all, they retained their symbolic standing as heads of the Muslim community; all provincial authorities were considered delegates of the Caliphs.

At the same time, the conquerors and reigning warlords sought to establish an independent basis for their authority. The Buwayhids, whose power was based upon the lifelong patronage of slaves in exchange for their loyal service, and sworn oaths exchanged among warriors and officials, still sought to generate a public aura of legitimacy. They revived an ancient Iranian titulature including the title *Shah-en-shah* (King of Kings), adopted sonorous-sounding Muslim names, practiced ceremonies to display royal insignias such as the crown and the throne, and cultivated a mystique of kingship suggesting divine selection revealed in dreams, miracles, and prophecies. The Buwayhids fabricated genealogies that connected them to ancient Iranian kings, and patronized public works, literature, and the arts as symbols of kingship. Similarly, the Ghaznavids sought recognition by the Caliphs, and implicitly assumed responsibility for the protection of Islam, but also glorified their reigns by the creation of splendid palace architecture and court ceremony, and by the erection of magnificent mosques and minarets as a sign of their service to the faith, to society, and to civilization. Like their predecessors, the Saljuqs professed to be the appointees of the Caliph, to serve Islam, and to support the institutions of religion. The first Saljuq ruler, Tughril Beg, adopted the title Sultan to assert supreme and exclusive power, though the title eventually became the ordinary name for Middle Eastern rulers.

The division of authority and power between Caliphs and Sultans was uncertain. As long as Saljuq Sultans were effective rulers, the Caliphs had a limited political position. Whenever the reigning Sultans were weak, however, the Caliphs were tempted to assert their political authority in Baghdad and the surrounding regions. Sultans, though dependent upon Caliphs for recognition of their legitimate rule, sought religious prestige by the patronage of Islamic religious life and by claims, in the Iranian fashion, to hold their authority and responsibility for the protection of their subjects directly from God. Thus in the course of the post-'Abbasid era, the Islamic aspect of political authority came more and more to the fore. Appointment by the Caliph was considered essential to legitimacy. Responsibility for Islamic institutions became the main justification of political authority, though ancient Iranian and Turkish concepts of rulership did not disappear.

New institutional arrangements as well as new concepts of government authority characterized the post-imperial era. All post-'Abbasid regimes were made up of an alien military elite. The Buwayhid, Ghaznavid, Qarakhanid, and Saljuq regimes were built by ethnic minorities, including mercenaries from the Caspian Sea and nomadic Turkish peoples from Inner Asia. These elites had no ethnic, cultural, linguistic, or historical connection with the peoples they ruled. Nomadic forces were supplemented by a praetorian guard of slave soldiers organized to offset the influence of the nomadic elites. These slaves were commonly purchased in Inner Asia while still young and then raised at the courts of their masters. Every regime followed a policy of pitting slave regiments against each other to maintain the authority of the ruler. Occasionally, as in the Ghaznavid case, the slaves seized control of the state and the leading generals became Sultans.

Military slavery and slave states were "peculiar" institutions. However, the translation of the word *ghulam* or *mamaluk* into English as "slave" carries inappropriate connotations. The concept of ghulam or mamaluk designated a binding personal obedience but not necessarily a humble situation in society. In its Arabic and Muslim sense the slave soldier was the personal property of a master and could be bought and sold. He was a servile retainer, depending upon the master for security and support. The social position of the slave, however, did not reflect his personal servitude, but rather the status of his master. The slave of the Sultan could be a general or minister of state, and the slave of a general, an officer in the army or administration. Furthermore, military slaves were eventually manumitted and became freedmen, clients of their former masters, which gave them limited legal rights to property, marriage, and personal security. In this institution the exclusive personal loyalty of the slave or client-soldier to his master was crucial.

THE IQTAʿ SYSTEM AND MIDDLE EASTERN FEUDALISM

The system of state fiscal administration was closely related to military organization. ʿAbbasid government had been based on bureaucratic methods of taxation and disbursements to the court and the army. The central government staffs collected revenues from the countryside and made payments in cash and kind to the officials and soldiers who served the state. With the decline of ʿAbbasid administration, the central bureaucracy progressively lost control of the countryside and, with the advent of the Buwayhid dynasty in 945, soldiers were for the first time assigned iqtaʿs in payment for military service. The Ghaznavids adopted a similar system and the Saljuqs extended this means of paying the army from Iraq and western Iran to Khurasan. They also introduced the system into Syria and eventually, under the Ayyubid dynasty, to Egypt. The terms of assignments varied considerably. In the Ghaznavid and early Saljuq cases a strong central government maintained control over the assigned lands. Assignees were held to their military responsibilities and rotated at the will of the ruler; hereditary succession was not permitted. Central government officials kept registers indicating the value of the tax assignment, the number of troops to be provided, and the terms of service.

In the later Saljuq period the central government was unable to maintain control. Iqtaʿs became hereditary, and the assignees usurped the land and turned their tax-collecting rights into private property. The assignees became landlords over peasants. Hereditary control of rural districts in the hands of military assignees gave rise to virtually independent principalities in Mesopotamia and Syria. The Saljuq practice of giving appanages to the members of the ruling family, the encourage-ment to independence inherent in the institution of the atabeg, the decline of central checks on the authority of provincial governors, the widespread assignment of salary iqta's, and the usurpation of iqta's tended to disperse political power. Saljuq administrative practices led to a drastic fragmentation of political power, and to the substitution of small principalities for large-scale states.

Many scholars have referred to this development as a period of Middle Eastern feudalism. The decline of the 'Abbasid empire may be seen as parallel to the breakup of the Roman empire, and the widespread distribution of iqta's in the Middle East as analogous to the widespread distribution of fiefs in Europe. In fact, however, the Middle Eastern development is different from the European. Euro-pean feudalism also had its origin in the breakup of a centralized state, the Caro-lingian empire, and the distribution of land to a multitude of small lords in France in the late tenth and eleventh centuries. However, the essence of feudalism did not lie in the decentralization of power and in the multiplication of numerous and rel-atively small principalities, but in certain characteristic institutions governing the relationships between the peasant populations and their lords, and the relation-ships among the lords themselves.

The relationship of peasant and lord was defined by the manor, an agricultural estate made up of the residence of the lord and his private properties surrounded by the small plots of the peasants. The manor, when assigned to a lord by his over-lord as a *benefice*, was a grant of the services of peasants, who became tenants of the lord and owed him economic dues for the use of the land. Benefices, more-over, were also conceded with immunity from central inspection. Then the lord was made judge and his tenants became his political subjects. Finally, and perhaps most important, they became his personal servitors as well. They could not leave the land and their heirs were automatically serfs. They had to work his lands; they were conveyable by him; they had to ransom the right to marry and to pass on their prop-erty. The economic powers of the landlord and the fiscal and jurisdictional rights of the state were united with the power of the patriarch over his household. The combination of powers defined the manor as a fief.

In the twelfth century some hierarchical order was brought into the distribution of fiefs, and they came to be considered as the concession of a higher lord to one of his vassals in return for military service. All lords of fiefs were in principle the vassals of higher-ranking lords. The king, highest lord of all, was the source of everyone's tenures and jurisdictions. In the feudal system the relationships between lords were not governmental relations of superior to subordinate, but were rela-tions of personal dependence. A vassal was the sworn client of his lord, exchang-ing service and devotion for protection and support. The relation between vassal and lord, moreover, was a contractual one, in which violation of the agreement on either side resulted in the termination of the contract, the dismissal or withdrawal of the vassal from service, and the return of the fief to the lord. One crucial aspect of this relationship was that disputes were judged in a court composed of other vassals. Every vassal, as part of his obligations and rights, had to attend his lord's court for the settlement of disputes between the vassals and the lord and the judgment of other matters.

Time and the weakness of lords in France favored the entrenchment of vassals in their fiefs. The fief ceased to be granted solely on condition of service but became a hereditary right. Eventually all connection with military service and clientage was dissociated from the possession of a fief, which became simply a hereditary governmental jurisdiction and personal property.

As inheritable property, the possession of a fief also defined the social status of the warrior class. A fief meant not only economic rights, personal servants, and governmental jurisdiction, but also conferred the privileges of nobility. Feudalism thus became not only a system that confounded public and private powers, but also a kind of society in which function or occupation, social status, political power, styles of life and culture, and economic wealth were all tied to the possession of land.

The Middle Eastern system was not feudal in this European sense. The collapse of the 'Abbasid empire indeed led to a decentralization of political authority, to the emergence of many petty rulers, and to the distribution of land in iqta's, but the situation differed in several ways. In the Middle East the idea of public authority and the distinctions between governmental powers and personal possessions and rights were never abandoned. However decentralized the powers of government, a subordinate was never considered a vassal, but always a delegate of the ruler. The ruler assigned a post to an official and he could unilaterally, at his pleasure, remove his agent from office. He made no contracts with his appointees and gave them no rights to be consulted. It was common in the Middle East for the governor to be a personal dependent of the Sultan, just as the vassal in Europe was a personal dependent, but still the relations were different. The vassal was a free man who contracted his dependency, while dependents in the Muslim world were slaves or freedmen. Also in the Middle East the personal relationship did not entirely substitute for the political relationship. It was not the personal relationship as such, but the designation of the ruler that conferred authority on a governor.

A second difference was the distinction between an iqta' and a fief. In principle, an iqta' was a grant of the right to collect taxes and to keep them in lieu of salary, a mechanism to decentralize the collection and disbursement of revenues due to the state. In principle, iqta's were conceded only on condition of military service being rendered, and were valid only for the lifetime of the incumbent. They could be increased or decreased, revoked or reassigned by the ruler. An iqta' was not a personal property. It could not be sold, leased, or willed. Nor was it a government jurisdiction. It brought no political, judicial, or personal powers over the peasants, who were considered subjects of the state, and not serfs or slaves of the iqta'-holder. Nor did the possession of an iqta' confer status privileges or legal rights. The status of the holder had nothing to do with the land, but was determined by his rank and duties as a soldier or administrator and his closeness to the ruler. Finally, iqta's could not be reassigned to subordinates. Officers were responsible for bringing men to service in proportion to the size of their iqta's, but in principle they did not pay their men by granting them iqta's in turn.

In practice certain powers not originally envisaged in the grants of an iqta' were usurped. Often an iqta' gave the holder enough local wealth to accumulate other properties and eventually, by merging his iqta' with other lands, to make it hereditary private property as well. Furthermore, iqta'-holders might force the peasants to surrender their land and to become personal dependents. In some cases iqta'-holders even acquired governmental powers by usurpation or immunities. When coupled with private power over land and peasants, this created a fief-like or "feudal" condition. Such aberrations, even though widespread in the Saljuq period, never became a recognized system of governmental relations. Muslim rulers always maintained substantial slave bodyguards and the bureaucratic staffs and records essential to the enforcement of obligations and the utilization of iqta's as a component of state power. While some iqta's became fiefs, a feudal system did not materialize. In the Middle East, then, decentralization entailed no fundamental institutional changes and could, in changed circumstances, be reversed. Imperial governments could and would be reconstructed by the later Mamluk, Ottoman, and Safavid empires.

Thus, from 950 to 1200, the unity of the 'Abbasid age was lost, and the successor states were short lived and provincial in scale. Still, despite the numerous different regimes, certain uniformities in the political concepts and institutions of the period emerged. The supremacy of the Caliphate and of Islamic principles was universally accepted, while effective political power was conceded to nomadic conquerors and slave warlords. Similar institutions of nomadic family practice, military slavery, and iqta' administration were developed, with variations, throughout the region. Everywhere the political concepts and military and administrative institutions adumbrated in the 'Abbasid age were integrated with the institutions and concepts of the nomadic conquerors and worked into a new system of government. In an era of unprecedented fragmentation of power and instability, these institutions were everywhere similar. They constituted, via numerous small experiments, an enduring legacy in the experience of Islamic government.

LOCAL COURTS AND REGIONAL CULTURES: ISLAM IN PERSIAN GARB

The new system of Middle Eastern states also opened a new era in the development of aristocratic and cosmopolitan Islamic culture. The post-imperial era reveals two dominant trends. One was the continuation of 'Abbasid tendencies toward the bifurcation of Islamic cosmopolitan and Islamic religious culture, though, in many respects, an intimate relationship was maintained between the two. While art and architecture, poetry, science, and certain forms of prose literature were expressions of court, regime, and governing elites, court patronage also extended to Islamic religious studies. Some genres such as history, political studies, and some forms of philosophy and theology were cultivated in both court and private urban milieus.

The second trend was toward regional diversity. As Baghdad dwindled, Samarqand and Bukhara, Nishapur and Isfahan, Cairo, Fez, and Cordova became the new capitals of Islamic civilization. In place of the single cosmopolitan court culture each capital generated its own blend of Islamic motifs and a local heritage. Islamic architecture now differed from region to region. Samanid brickwork, Ghaznavid minarets, Isfahan domes, and Fatimid shrines were emblematic of a new cultural diversity.

Within this diversity there was a tendency to divide the former regions of the 'Abbasid empire into two linguistic and cultural zones. In the western regions, including Iraq, Syria, and Egypt, and the lands of the far Islamic west including North Africa and Spain, Arabic became the predominant language of both high literary culture and spoken discourse. In the eastern lands, including Iran and Transoxania, Persian became the predominant literary language. Now the poems and epics of the east would be composed in Persian while the odes and quatrains of Baghdad and Cordova would be written in Arabic. The two cultural regions, however, continued to share a common system of religious values and institutions.

In the post-'Abbasid era Baghdad maintained its position as a capital of Islamic religious and Arabic literary studies. Baghdadi poetry continued to follow ninth-century forms; the *qasida* or panegyric and the *ghazal* or lyric were still the most important forms of poetic expression. Al-Mutanabbi (d. 965) and Abu al-'Ala al-Ma'arri (d. 1057) were the most important poets. Sufi poetry celebrated ecstatic experiences in the imagery of the intoxication of wine and love. In the tenth and eleventh centuries under the influence of Ibn Qutayba's compilations, anthologies of poetry, history, and other subjects were composed. Arabic letter writing and secretarial correspondence became an art of elaborate rhymed prose displaying great technical skill. The *Maqamat* of al-Hariri (d. 1122), done in virtuoso prose and with philological subtlety, was perhaps the greatest achievement of this type. Historical writing also flourished. Histories of the Caliphate were superseded by new world histories, local histories, collections of biographies and historical anecdotes written to entertain and enlighten. Arabic prose literature was profoundly influenced by a new literary criticism which insisted upon formal qualities in writing, and de-emphasized novelty or significance in content.

Persian culture developed in a multitude of places over a period of many centuries, but was nonetheless strikingly unified. In the ninth century, Sijistan, Khurasan, and Transoxania were the primary centers of the new Persian literary development. At the courts of the Tahirids of Nishapur and Marw, the Samanids of Bukhara, and the Ghaznavids the basis was laid for a new civilization. Only in the late tenth and the eleventh centuries did the new Persian language and literature created in eastern Iran become the literature of western Iran. In later generations Saljuqs, Ghurids, Ilkhanids, and Timurids produced their own contributions to the common culture. Persian culture not only became the characteristic style of Iran, it also had an important influence upon the development of Muslim culture in Inner Asia, India, and Indonesia. Persian literary and artistic styles superseded Arabic as the predominant cultural influence in the formation of the eastern Islamic world.

The development of new Persian was conditioned by two factors. One was the linguistic situation in eastern Iran just prior to the Arab conquests. In late Sasanian times, Parsi (Pahlavi) or Middle Persian was the official religious and literary language of the empire. Dari was the dialect version of this language spoken throughout much of Iran. Alongside formal Parsi and spoken Dari, poets and entertainers cultivated a popular oral literature for the amusement of the common people and the local lords, also expressed in a version of Dari. All three levels of Persian would contribute to the formation of the new Persian language.

The second factor was the Arab conquest. Under Arab rule, Arabic became the principal language for administration and religion. The substitution of Arabic for Middle Persian was facilitated by the translation of Persian classics into Arabic. Arabic became the main vehicle of Persian high culture, and remained such well into the eleventh century. Parsi declined and was kept alive mainly by the Zoroastrian priesthood in western Iran. The Arab conquests, however, helped make Dari rather than Arabic the common spoken language in Khurasan, Afghanistan, and the lands beyond the Oxus River. Paradoxically, Arab and Islamic domination created a Persian cultural region in areas never before unified by Persian speech.

A new Persian evolved out of this complex linguistic situation. In the ninth century the Tahirid governors of Khurasan (820–73) began to have the old Persian language written in Arabic script rather than in Pahlavi characters. At the same time eastern Iranian lords in the small principalities began to patronize a local court poetry in an elevated form of Dari. The new poetry was inspired by Arabic verse forms, so that Iranian patrons who did not understand Arabic could comprehend and enjoy the presentation of an elevated and dignified poetry in the manner of Baghdad. This new poetry flourished in regions where the influence of 'Abbasid Arabic culture was attenuated and where it had no competition from the surviving tradition of Middle Persian literary classics cultivated for religious purposes as in western Iran.

The new poetry borrowed both from Arabic literary forms and oral Iranian literature. The qasida became its chief form. Based on Arabic rhyming schemes, it was used mainly for panegyrics praising Iranian princes. Oral Persian poetry contributed a distinctive rhythmic pattern. The most important early poets in the new vein were the Samanid court poets, Rudaki (d. 940–41), who was considered the father of the new Persian poetry, and Daqiqi (d. c. 980), who was especially successful in conveying daily life in his poems. Bilingual poets translated Arabic poems into Persian and began to compose poems of their own in both Arabic and Persian.

The Persian literary heritage of stories, romances, fables, and dynastic histories also formed the basis of a new type of epic poetry. The Samanids revived Iranian interest in the ancient history of kings and in the literary collections of the Sasanian period. From the pen of Firdausi (d. 1020–21 or 1025–26) emerged an immense historical epic. His *Shah-name* or "Book of Kings" contains not only the court histories collected by the Sasanians, but also a cycle concerning the life of the great hero Rustam. For patrons who were attempting to legitimize their rule by virtue of their historical descent from ancient Iranian rulers and their emulation of ancient Iranian virtues, Firdausi composed a new epic preoccupied with sovereignty, feudalism, and the war of good and evil. The poem in new Persian language with a moderate influence of Arabic vocabulary became the literary standard of the new era.

Prose was equally important in the new Persian language. The historical works of al-Tabari were translated, and a small number of geographical, philosophic, and scientific works were written in Persian. Commentaries on the Quran, mystical treatises, legal and other religious texts were translated from Arabic. Such works were generally written in a utilitarian style without the elaborate literary pretensions of lyric and epic poetry. Under the influence of these translations and new compositions, Dari became more and more highly Arabized, and Persian evolved into "new Persian," heavily influenced by Arabic vocabulary and syntax.

The new language and literature flourished at other regional courts. Mahmud of Ghazna (988–1030) sought the help of poets to legitimize his regime. Mahmud patronized Unsuri (d. 1039–40), whose qasidas celebrated the court festivals, the changing of the seasons, the royal entertainments, and the pleasures of music and wine. Mahmud was also the patron of Firdausi, the scientist and geographer Biruni, and a host of historians who chronicled the events of the era. Poetry also flourished brilliantly in the Saljuq courts of the eleventh and twelfth centuries. The poets moved from court to court looking for patrons, giving continuity and unity to a literary activity carried on in numerous places throughout Iran.

Under Samanid and Ghaznavid patronage the new Persian literature favored several poetic and prose genres. Poetry was commonly composed in one of four metric forms. The ghazal, a lyric poem of some seven to fifteen lines on the theme of love, expressed private sentiments but in standard images and symbols, such as the nightingale in love with the rose. The *ruba'i,* or quatrain, was a lyric that usually expressed mystical or profane love. The *masnavi*, or rhyming couplet, was a loose form used for narratives such as tales, romances, legends, and histories. Persian literature was rich in such materials, including the tales of Sindbad, the heroic accounts of the life of Alexander the Great, the fables of *Kalila wa Dimna*, and the lives of saints. The characteristic product of court poets was panegyric poems produced for money in qasida, and sometimes in masnavi, form. Characteristically, the poems contained images of the king as ruler over cities, generous in gifts, noble in ancestry. The most important representative of this type of poetry was Anvari (1116–89) who lived at times in Marw, Nishapur, and Balkh. The Persian poets did not aim at self-expression, originality, creativity, or personal insight. Poetry was a public recitation, an adornment for court life, and the main value was virtuosity in handling familiar forms and content. This was a poetry of masks which wandered

6 An old woman petitions Sultan Sanjar

from theme to theme, so as to be a vehicle of sensuous appreciations or philosophical thoughts.

In Azarbayjan romantic poetry was favored. Courtly romances based not on personal experience but on literary convention told the stories of heroes consumed by physical passion and heroes who sublimated their love into an idealization of a perfect but inaccessible woman. Court poetry dwelt on the theme of the lover who suffers just for a glance, while his only comfort is wine. Perhaps the most important writer in this genre was Nizami (c. 1140–1209), who wrote the stories of Alexander's quest for the water of life; the love story of Shirin and the emperor Khusraw Parviz; and the story of Majnun, who became mad with longing for Layla whom he could never attain. Nizami's poetry brought a vernacular vocabulary into the high Persian poetic tradition.

In Sufi poetry images of wine, drinking, and love were adopted to express yearning for and love of God. The most important writer of this genre was Farid al-Din 'Attar (1142–1221), who was famous for his histories of the Sufis, his books of wisdom, the *Language of the Birds* and the *Book of God*, whose principal themes were renunciation of worldly desires and the soul's journey toward metaphysical vision. His works describe the forty stations of the visionary and cosmic passage by which the traveler progressively leaves behind this world in his quest for the world to come. Rumi (1207–73) was perhaps the greatest of the Persian mystical poets seeking the identification of the human self with the divine being. His *Mathnavi* combined impassioned lyrics with gentle storytelling, merging profane and mystical themes.

With the blossoming of Persian literature, Islam was relieved of its association with Arabic. Then, under the auspices of the Qarakhanids, who succeeded the Samanids as the rulers of Transoxania, Islamic culture was recreated in Turkish. A new Turkish language, developed first by translation and then by scholarly and literary recreation of Persian literature, became the bearer of Islamic civilization throughout Inner Asia. Islam was becoming a universal religion and civilization in several linguistic media.

An Iranian artistic style also emerged in the Saljuq period. In the ninth century, under the influence of Chinese wares, Nishapur and Samarqand produced white pottery decorated with Kufic writing. Pottery decorated with animals, birds, and vegetal elements was made to please an urban middle-class taste, and silver and gold objects were produced in imitation of Sasanian models. Kashan and Rayy produced new types of ceramics. One type was a blue-black or turquoise floral or calligraphic design under glaze; another was a polychrome painting over glaze in which court scenes or historic legends were depicted. The court scenes included hunting, polo, music, and dancing. The objects were illustrated with astronomical signs. Ceramics were often decorated with texts on the theme of love. Another type of ceramic depicted one or two persons sitting together, sometimes playing a musical instrument, perhaps an illustration of love or meditation. Ceramic manufacture of this sort continued until the middle of the fourteenth century.

The history of Iranian architecture followed a similar rhythm. In Iran the most important buildings were the tombs of holy men and rulers. These were covered by a dome and surrounded by a complex of buildings dedicated to worship and study. The most famous of these was the Samanid mausoleum at Bukhara built before 943 and the Gumbad-i Qabus dated 1006–07. Mosques with cupolas, round minarets, and monumental arcades derived from Iranian precedents were also built. By the middle of the eleventh century the characteristic features of Iranian architecture included brick construction, arcades, stalactite projections, and stucco decorated with geometric and vegetal designs to cover the surfaces of large buildings.

By the twelfth century a new standard form of mosque spread throughout Iran, and replaced the earlier Arab-inspired mosque built around a colonnaded courtyard. The new design consisted of a large central courtyard surrounded by arcades, the largest being on the qibla or Mecca side of the mosque and surmounted by a large dome. The mosques were built mainly of brick and with pointed barreled vaults. They also had *muqarnas* (stalactite-like projections) at the junctions between the domes and the substructures. In addition to mosques, numerous tower tombs and mausoleums with cupolas were built in the twelfth and thirteenth centuries, especially in Azarbayjan and Transoxania.

Royal patronage for poetry, literature, architecture, and art indicates a profound integration of the political and religious meaning of artistic composition. Kingship was justified by the construction and decoration of mosques, schools, tombs, minarets, and other religious buildings. Courtly arts and literature were intended to adorn, glorify, and justify the position of a ruler and a ruling elite and to inspire obedience. Similarly, the blending of profane and spiritual themes in Persian love poetry also bespeaks the inseparability of art and literature from religion.

In the post-imperial era the concept of an aristocratic culture was modified by the integration of secular and religious motifs. Whereas in the early 'Abbasid era, aristocratic culture maintained a certain distance from Islam, in the Saljuq era the education of an aristocrat combined literary or secular studies, such as poetry, belles-lettres, history, mathematics, and philosophy, with Islam. The secular aspects of the training were designed to develop the courtier as an elegant stylist, technician, and engineer who was competent in finance and public works as well as a refined and graceful adornment to the court of his king; the religious aspects were a moral and spiritual initiation intended to provide the deeper qualities of soul essential for the successful pursuit of a worldly career.

Yet from a strictly religious point of view, art remained suspect. Islamic sentiment was opposed to magic, to the display of riches, to the stimulation of the senses, and to myths that might rival the Quran. Islamic egalitarian and puritanical sentiment was also opposed to indulgence in wine, silk, music, and other riches; iconophobic, it opposed figural images which were a temptation to idolatry. The Shari'a provided no legitimization for the main forms of art. Thus, there was an ambiguity inherent in the royal sponsorship of art. While it was a contribution to the adornment and glory of Islam, especially in its political and communal aspects, it threatened Muslim religious beliefs.

This ambiguity influenced the whole stylistic development of Islamic art. While the arts served both a religious and a political purpose, the images and motifs employed in Islamic art avoided cosmological or mythical meanings. Sculpture was almost unknown; religious arts avoided the reproduction of human and animal figures. Islamic arts concentrated on purely visual or verbal demonstrations of richness, quality of craftsmanship, elaboration of invention, and compositional effects. The unifying element in Islamic art was the repetition of calligraphic motifs, arabesques, or geometric designs; when human figures were used they appeared as impersonal images rather than a human presence or hieratic symbol.

By avoiding cosmic myths and minimizing visual forms, Islamic art conformed to a Muslim theological and philosophic view of the universe as being without an overall pattern or causal interconnectedness. This world, created ex nihilo and maintained by continuous creation and recreation, is governed by God's will; its apparent regularity is not intrinsic in nature but is his bounty. This accords with a human ideal. Moral and spiritual qualities do not correspond to the ontological order of the world but derive from the fulfillment of God's will as expressed in the teachings of the Quran and the tradition. A human life is a sequence of actions correctly performed according to the divine command. Islamic art and literature, then, cultivated for the glory of the court, the ruler, and the elite were expressive of the universal aspects of Islamic religious culture. While they intruded the claims of the ruler upon Islamic religious sensibility, they were close enough to expressing that sensibility to be acceptable as an expression of the genius not only of regimes but of the whole civilization.

CHAPTER 10

MUSLIM COMMUNITIES AND MIDDLE EASTERN SOCIETIES

In the centuries following the collapse of the 'Abbasid empire, a new political elite of nomadic and slave warlords – and the ruin of local landowners and other notables – paved the way for far-reaching changes in the organization of town and village communities. The crucial change in this period was the crystallization of Muslim sectarian communities, including Shi'i sects, Sunni schools of law and theology, and Sufi brotherhoods. Bitter rivalries among them and strong state support for both Shi'i and Sunni movements hastened their diffusion. In the same period, the masses of Middle Eastern peoples were converted to Islam and absorbed into Muslim social bodies. Islam, originally the religion of a political and urban elite, became the religion and social identity of most Middle Eastern peoples.

The creation of an Islamic communal and religious identity apart from the Caliphate had already begun in the seventh and eighth centuries. In his ideal and early form, the Caliph was the sole ruler of a single community and custodian of both its religious principles and its political interests. From the outset, however, pious believers were disenchanted with the worldliness of the early Caliphal regimes. This disenchantment first expressed itself in the form of the Khariji, Shi'i, and 'Abbasid movements, which aimed to return the Caliphate to its ideal incumbents. With the victory of the 'Abbasids, and the defeat of both Khariji and Shi'i aspirations, the political opponents of the Caliphate began to evolve into religious sects.

THE SHI'I COMMUNITIES

The Shi'a were the earliest example of a new form of sectarian community. The early Shi'a were divided into different groups, depending upon their theory of the true succession of imams. One of these was the Baghdadi "twelver" community, which believed in the imamate of Ja'far's son Musa al-Kazim and his descendants; another was the believers in the imamate of Ja'far's son Isma'il and his descendants. From the time of Ja'far, the Baghdadi community denied in theory, but accepted in practice, the reign of the 'Abbasid Caliphs and concentrated more and more on religious teaching. In 873, however, the last of its living imams, the twelfth in line of succession, "disappeared," and in 941 direct communication with the imam was lost altogether. With the loss of direct divine guidance the Baghdadi Shi'a began to codify their religious and cultural heritage and organize a new communal life to compensate for the missing imam. In the late decades of the tenth century they began the public ritual cursing of Mu'awiya, the enemy of 'Ali, made a public holiday of mourning for the death of Husayn at Karbala ('ashura), and a day of celebration for Muhammad's adoption of 'Ali as his successor (ghadir khumm). Pilgrimage to the tombs of 'Ali at Najaf, Husayn at Karbala, and 'Ali al-Rida at Mashhad became important rituals. The passionate mourning for Husayn, identification with the suffering of the martyr, and the messianic hopes implicit in the commemoration of Karbala gave emotional and religious depth to "twelver" Shi'ism.

In the same period, "twelver" teaching in hadith, law, and theology also took definitive form. The first formal compilation of Shi'i hadith, ritual, and law was made by al-Kulayni (d. 940). The concept of the imam was reformulated in neo-Platonic and gnostic terms which provided a new metaphysical context and opened the way within imami Shi'ism for gnostic as well as ritual forms of religious experience. Later scholars debated whether their beliefs were based solely on the teachings of the imams or whether *ijtihad*, the exercise of individual judgment in matters of law, was permissible. The imam came to be understood as an emanation of the divine being, the *'aql al-kull*, the universal intelligence, and thus a bearer of direct knowledge of the secret truths and states of spirituality that lead to the reunion of the soul of man with God.

By the mid-eleventh century the imami Shi'a had created a worldly life lived in perpetual expectation of the world to come. In permanent opposition to the established political regimes, imamism had become a religion of salvation. This salvation might be attained by living in accordance with the hadith of the Prophet and the imams, by emotional absorption into their martyrdom, or by gnostic vision and mystical identification with the emanations of the divine being. With the consolidation of their doctrinal beliefs in written form, the development of a public ritual life, and political recognition by the reigning authorities, the Baghdadi Shi'a emerged as a sectarian community within the body of Islam.

THE SCHOOLS OF LAW AND SUNNI SECTARIANISM

The consolidation of the Baghdadi Shi'i community and the success of the Isma'ili missions stimulated the Sunni 'ulama' to further institutionalize their practice of Islam, and to make their schools of law and theology and Sufi brotherhoods the focus of community affairs. The schools of law had their origin in the late seventh century as groups of scholars committed to a common legal doctrine and method of legal analysis. By the ninth century the schools were well established as bodies of teachers and students and as agencies for legal administration. From their origins in Medina, Basra, Baghdad, and Fustat, they spread throughout the 'Abbasid realm. The travels of scholars and students in search of hadith and the appointment of judges with law-school affiliations introduced the schools into new provinces. The Hanafi school began in Iraq and was soon established in western Iran and Transoxania. The Hanbali school, Baghdadi in origin, spread to northern Iraq and Syria. Hanbali judges (qadis) were appointed in Damascus and Homs. Hanbalism also had its followers in the important cities of Iran. The Shafi'i school first developed in Egypt but, by the tenth century, was established in Syria, Baghdad, and in all of the important towns of western Iran, Khurasan, and Transoxania. The Maliki school was concentrated primarily in Egypt and North Africa. The schools were united by the travels of students, who came to study with great masters, and to obtain certificates certifying their knowledge of the books they had learned. Having acquired a wide range of learning from different teachers, a successful student would eventually settle down with a single professor, and in time succeed him. This international system of connections was informal, but was sufficient to maintain the identity of the major schools. Muslim theological schools also acquired a coherent social identity. Though they did not have judicial and administrative functions, the Mu'tazila and Ash'aris became important religious movements. The Karrami movement, which combined theological tenets and Sufi practices, appealing mainly to the lower classes, was influential in Khurasan, Transoxania, and Afghanistan.

In the course of the tenth and eleventh centuries, the early law schools found a new mode of organization. The *madrasa*, or formally organized college of legal studies, probably had its origins in Khurasan. Here Muslim law was originally taught in private homes, which were then converted into hostels for traveling scholars and students. In Baghdad, the madrasa was organized by combining the mosque in which the teaching was carried out, the *khan* or boarding house for students, private libraries, and the practice of community financial support. A madrasa then was a building used for study and as a residence for teachers and students, commonly provided with a library. Madrasas were also endowed with permanent sources of income, such as land or rent-bearing urban property, set aside in perpetuity. These *waqf*s paid the salaries of the faculty and stipends for students. By giving such gifts donors could preserve their property intact against fragmentation due to inheritance laws and appoint their heirs as administrators. Through salaries and the administration of endowments, the 'ulama' rose to the position of a rentier class.

In educational terms, the madrasa was an informal school. It did not have a program of specialized degrees or a graded curriculum. Rather, it was the preserve of its professor; the students were certified only to teach the texts they had studied with the master. The relationship of teacher and student was intensely personal, for the master communicated not only specialized learning but religious insight, and a stylized mode of behavior which signified the rank of scholar. The personal relationship between master and disciple, which could be traced generation by generation back to the Prophet himself, was the primary vehicle for the communication of Muslim truths.

The curriculum of the madrasas was therefore variable. Most, however, were academies of law, teaching the particular version of the professor's own *madhhab*, or school. Madrasas commonly taught the related subjects of Quran, hadith, and Arabic grammar; some professors taught theology or Sufism. In all cases there was an intense consciousness of the importance of training Muslim scholars to combat Shi'ism and Isma'ilism. Madrasas were not only colleges, but centers for religious propaganda and political action. The madrasa thus consolidated informal legal instruction into an institution with a physical center and permanently endowed funds, and made possible professional fulltime study of Muslim law and the expanded training of cadres of Muslim legal teachers and administrators. It became the standard Sunni Muslim way for the organization of religious and legal instruction, spreading from Iran throughout Samanid and Ghaznavid domains and then westward with the Saljuq conquests. Nizam al-Mulk, the leading vizier of the early Saljuq period (1063–92), endowed Hanafi and Shafi'i madrasas in all the major cities of the empire and made it the state's policy to support organized Muslim religious scholarship. The Hanbalis adopted the madrasa form of instruction early in the twelfth century.

As the madrasas became the centers of the schools of law, the schools themselves were becoming popular religious movements. Originally, each madhhab was built around a core of scholars and judges and their students, court functionaries, wealthy patrons, and local followers. Progressively, the leadership of the schools was extended to the masses, beginning with charitable, educational, and judicial services, and carrying on to informal social and political leadership.

The Hanbalis were the first to convert informal, popular influence and sympathy into a sectarian movement. As we have seen, they resisted the efforts of the 'Abbasid Caliphate to promulgate religious doctrine. They opposed al-Ma'mun's claims to authority, and held that while obedience was due to the Caliph in matters of state, authority in religion rested with the scholars of Quran and hadith. Preaching to their followers among former 'Abbasid soldiers and residents of the Harbiya quarter of Baghdad, the scholars mobilized popular support. Throughout the ninth and tenth centuries, Hanbali preachers raised popular demonstrations for or against Caliphal policy. The Hanbalis emerged as a vociferous popular party determined to enforce their own religious views. They organized groups of vigilantes, who attacked their opponents, and suppressed such immoral activities as wine drinking and prostitution. While the Shi'a organized public celebrations of their faith, the Sunnis similarly commemorated the reigns of the Rashidun Caliphs, Mu'awiya, and other symbols of Sunni identity. Hanbali preachers led anti-Shi'i riots, and opposed the Mu'tazili and the Ash'ari theological schools. Baghdad was frequently in turmoil because of the battles between the religious factions.

Thus, the Hanbalis created within the Sunni milieu the first Muslim community apart from the Caliphate, and contributed to the spread of religious factionalism. In eastern Iran the schools of law also turned into popular factions. In the tenth and eleventh centuries, Hanafi, Shafi'i, Karrami, and Isma'ili groups struggled for local political power. The schools had become *'asabiyat*, exclusive and mutually hostile small communities. In this guise, they resembled the neighborhood, lineage, or other parochial bodies into which Middle Eastern towns had always been divided. Religion now superseded tribal or quarter identifications.

The history of Nishapur in the eleventh and twelfth centuries is the best known example of the law schools as factions. Here the Hanafi school was built around leading merchant, official, and 'ulama' families who controlled the judiciary of the city, important waqf revenues, madrasas, and mosques. Their main opponents were the Shafi'is, who controlled most of the teaching positions in the madrasas, and also the revenues of important endowments. The Shafi'i following, however, was broader than the Hanafi, in that the Shafi'is were united with Ash'aris and Sufis, and seemed to have had mass support. The antagonism of the two schools of law spread from disputes over control of teaching and judicial positions to competition for governmental support and to pitched battles in which large segments of the town and the surrounding rural populace were mobilized to fight for their group. As a result, Nishapur had been physically and socially destroyed by the middle of the twelfth century.

SUFI BROTHERHOODS

The development of the Sufi movement paralleled the development of the schools of law. From the tenth to the fourteenth centuries, Sufis worked out their mystical practice and metaphysics, integrated their thought and practice with other forms of Islamic belief and worship, and reached maturity as a social movement. By the middle of the tenth century, they had become one of the Muslim groups pursuing the truth of Islam. While Sufism was highly individual, Sufi meeting houses gave them a collective identity. On the model of *ribats* – which were originally residences for Muslim warriors scattered along the frontiers of the Byzantine empire in North Africa and the frontiers of eastern Iran – similar meeting-houses were founded at Abadan, Damascus, and Ramla in the course of the eighth century. In imitation of Christian monks, there were grottoes in Khurasan. Ordinarily, Sufis met in private houses.

The term "khanaqa" appeared in the late ninth century, and came to be widely used for Sufi residences in Khurasan and Transoxania. The word was applied to residences for migrant individuals without a shared affiliation to a particular master, but the khanaqa was adapted to more sectarian purposes by the mystic and theologian Muhammad b. Karram (806–69), a student of hadith and an ascetic preacher in southern and eastern Iran, who taught a God-fearing way of life based on mortification of the flesh and pious devotion to God's will, and a theological doctrine emphasizing an anthropomorphic view of God, taking literally the Quranic usages that suggest that God has substance and a body. Ibn Karram won a large lower-class following in Transoxania, Afghanistan, and eastern Iran, and built khanaqas as centers of missionary activity.

Other Sufi masters followed his example. Shaykh Abu Ishaq Ibrahim al-Kazaruni (963–1033) cultivated a large following in his home district in western Iran, and converted numerous Zoroastrians and Jews to Islam. His warriors also fought on the Byzantine frontier. They built some sixty-five khanaqas in southwestern Iran as centers for teaching, missionary activity, and as places to distribute charity to the poor. His near contemporary Abu Sa'id b. Abi Khayr (967–1049), who was born and died in the region of Nishapur, was the first Sufi master to set up rules for worship and a code of behavior to regulate the communal life of the khanaqa. By the end of the eleventh century, in addition to their devotional, instructional, and missionary functions, the khanaqas came to be used as tombs for venerated Sufi masters and became sites of pilgrimage for ordinary believers.

From the tenth to the thirteenth centuries important changes in Sufi concepts reinforced the trend toward organized groups. A developing concept of the relations between masters and disciples paved the way for a more formal type of organization. In the ninth and tenth centuries a Sufi novice took lessons from his master. By the eleventh century he was a disciple who owed total obedience, just as any man owes obedience to God. By then the master was considered not only a teacher but a healer of souls and a repository of God's blessing. These new and deeper bonds were the basis of a more lasting loyalty of disciple to master and for the perpetuation of the authority of miraculous teachers over the generations.

New forms of Sufi ceremony emerged to symbolize the new relationships. In the earlier era a student had received an *ijaza*, or license to teach the subject he had learned from his master. In the new era, the *khirqa*, or cloak of the master was conferred upon him, and ceremonies of initiation were instituted to induct disciples of the same master into shared vigils, litanies, devotions, and other forms of worship. With the elaboration of the master's authority the spiritual genealogy of masters and disciples also became important. In the course of the twelfth and thirteenth centuries, chains of authority or *silsilas* reaching from the present masters across the generations to 'Ali and to the Prophet were formulated. The authority of Sufi teaching in any given generation was guaranteed by a chain of contacts which led from the present to the moment of revelation. Initiation into Sufism bore with it a spiritual power derived directly from the original revelation of Islam.

The origins of the Sufi brotherhood are shadowy, but we may surmise that the concept crystallized in the thirteenth and fourteenth centuries in the minds of the disciples of the great twelfth- and thirteenth-century masters. These Sufis attributed their practices and doctrine to famous earlier shaykhs or originating masters who were recognized as the transmitters of Sufi teaching and the founders of later Sufi brotherhoods. They were thought to have appointed the *khalifas*, or delegates, who established new chapters of the order and who would in turn appoint their lieutenants and successors to carry on the work of the *tariqa*, as the Sufi orders were called.

The known historical facts about the founding of these orders are few. The Suhrawardi order attributed to Abu Najib al-Suhrawardi was actually founded by

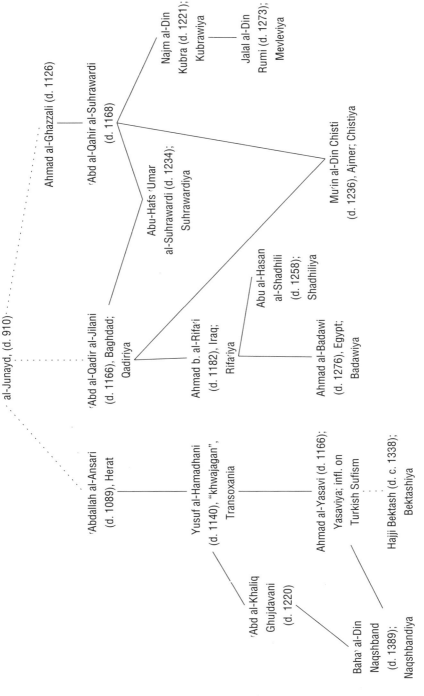

Figure 6 The early tariqat and their founders

al-Junayd, (d. 910)

Ahmad al-Ghazzali (d. 1126)

'Abd al-Qahir al-Suhrawardi (d. 1168)

Najm al-Din Kubra (d. 1221); Kubrawiya

Jalal al-Din Rumi (d. 1273); Mevleviya

Abu-Hafs 'Umar al-Suhrawardi (d. 1234); Suhrawardiya

Mu'in al-Din Chisti (d. 1236), Ajmer; Chistiya

'Abdallah al-Ansari (d. 1089), Herat

'Abd al-Qadir al-Jilani (d. 1166), Baghdad; Qadiriya

Ahmad b. al-Rifa'i (d. 1182), Iraq; Rifa'iya

Abu al-Hasan al-Shadhili (d. 1258); Shadhiliya

Ahmad al-Badawi (d. 1276), Egypt; Badawiya

Yusuf al-Hamadhani (d. 1140), "khwajagan", Transoxania

Ahmad al-Yasavi (d. 1166); Yasaviya; infl. on Turkish Sufism

Hajji Bektash (d. c. 1338); Bektashiya

'Abd al-Khaliq Ghujdavani (d. 1220)

Baha' al-Din Naqshband (d. 1389); Naqshbandiya

his nephew 'Umar al-Suhrawardi (1145–1234). 'Umar was appointed by the Caliph al-Nasir (1180–1225) to be the head of a group of ribats founded in Baghdad. 'Umar wrote a treatise on the behavior of Sufi novices and thus established a "monastic" rule. The Shadhili order, which was introduced into Egypt in the late thirteenth century, began in Morocco with the teachings of Abu Madyan (d. 1197). His student al-Shadhili (d. 1258) moved to Alexandria in 1244, gathered followers and disciples, and created the particular pattern of devotional activities, social life, and avoidance of close relations with government authorities that ever after characterized the order. The Qadiriya was at first a local chapter centered around the tomb of 'Abd al-Qadir al-Jilani in Baghdad, but a hospice for Qadiriya was founded in Damascus at the end of the fourteenth century. Later the order spread throughout the Arab world and sub-Saharan Africa. The order named after Najm al-Din Kubra was in fact organized in Iran by al-Simnani (d. 1336) and spread widely in Khurasan, Khwarizm, and Transoxania. Al-Simnani was the founder of a movement that emphasized the unity of the Islamic community. His following embraced both Sunnis and Shi'a, venerated the family of the Prophet, including 'Ali, along with the great Sunni masters, and appealed to Buddhists and pagans to convert to Islam. Sufism, in the view of this order, was an all-embracing form of Islam which transcended sectarian divisions.

By the end of the fourteenth century the Sufi tariqat were well established throughout the Middle East. In eastern Iran and Transoxania, the Kubrawiya was most important. In Iraq the Suhrawardiya was dominant. In Syria, the Qadiriya and the Rifa'iya were well established. In Egypt the Rifa'iya, the Qadiriya, the Shadhiliya, and the Badawiya were widespread. Sufi orders in Egypt enjoyed government patronage, the attendance of Sultans at Sufi devotions, and a considerable popular following.

The influence of Sufi teaching was considerable. In each community Sufis represented, in competition with the schools of law and theological sects, an alternative form of social affiliation. The alliance of Sufism with the ghazi commitment to holy war and its tradition of missionary activity made the peripheral rather than the historical regions of Islam – such as North Africa, Inner Asia, and India – centers of Sufi expansion. Still, Sufis were received at the courts of rulers and were called upon to give their blessings and counsel, and were allowed to intercede on behalf of their constituents. They also became integrated into the Shafi'i and the Hanbali schools of law. Most important, they exerted a vast influence upon the common people. The Sufi khanaqa was a center of public preaching, of religious instruction, and of shared worship for lay followers. Insofar as the khanaqa was also the tomb of a venerated saint, Muslims made pilgrimages to worship, to be cured, and to receive spiritual blessing and material aid. Worship at the tombs of saints, increasingly widespread in the thirteenth and fourteenth centuries, would become the main vehicle of the Sufi form of Islam.

Even though small discipleships had formed, the khanaqa had become a focus of collective life, and the concept of tariqa or brotherhood was institutionalized, individual Sufis with their followings of disciples and lay believers remained the heart of the Sufi movement. While the tariqat served to bring some uniformity into the teachings of the myriad of local Sufi masters and saints, Sufism was fundamentally the shared culture of individual teachers. Sufi insight was ultimately not the product of institutions but of other-worldly inspiration.

MUSLIM RELIGIOUS MOVEMENTS AND THE STATE

The religious and social roles of the Sunni schools of law, theological sects, Shi'i communities, and Sufi brotherhoods made them of the utmost importance to Middle Eastern military regimes. In the ninth and tenth centuries the rise of Shi'ism posed a challenge to Sunni dominance. The Buwayhids, the Hamdanids, and the Qarmatians were officially Shi'a. The Buwayhids authorized, patronized, and guided the organization of the imami community in Baghdad. The Fatimids were the sponsors of Isma'ili missions that reached from North Africa to Khurasan, Afghanistan, and Transoxania. The triumph of the Shi'i dynasties also permitted a literary and cultural renaissance in which Hellenistic, philosophic, and secularist views flourished. In response to these challenges the Sunni 'ulama' were led to strengthen their concept of Islam by a more rigorous definition of its content, and by the organization of a more closely knit community life.

Baghdad in the tenth and eleventh centuries became the focus of Sunni–Shi'i antagonism. The Caliph al-Qadir (991–1031) took the lead in the Sunni struggle against Shi'ism, and tried to organize a Sunni religious mission to restore the true practice of the faith. He helped the Sunnis set up their own festivals to rival the Shi'i celebrations; by official proclamation he made Hanbalism the official Muslim position. In an address in 1019 the Caliph condemned allegorical explanations of the Quran and the thesis that it was created, and proclaimed the excellence of the first four Caliphs in order of historical access to their office. His successor, al-Qaim (1031–75), renewed the effort to define Islamic orthodoxy in Hanbali terms and to mobilize popular support for Caliphal supremacy. In reaction to Shi'ism the Sunni revival of the eleventh century aspired not only to the definition of orthodoxy but to the restoration of the Caliphs as the heads of the Islamic community.

The advent of the Saljuqs in 1055 profoundly changed the relations between sectarian religious communities and the state. From the very beginning of their conquests in Khurasan, the Saljuqs became embroiled in religious controversy, and soon devised their own policy of alliance with selected Islamic movements. They espoused an uncompromising anti-Shi'i policy, and helped to suppress Shi'i activities throughout their domains. Their hostility was motivated partly by rivalry with the Fatimids and partly by Sunni anxiety over subversion by Shi'i movements. Saljuq opposition to Shi'ism was vigorously pursued in order to create Sunni solidarity and to promote the legitimacy of Saljuq states in the name of the true Islam.

The Saljuqs also took a position vis-à-vis the competing Sunni schools. First, they intervened in the Hanafi–Shafi'i and Hanbali–Ash'ari struggles, favoring the Hanafi school of law and forcibly suppressing Shafi'i and Ash'ari activity. In 1063,

however, Nizam al-Mulk, newly appointed as wazir, proposed to calm Sunni religious quarrels by patronizing both the Hanafis and the Shafi'is. The major instrument of this policy was the construction and endowment of madrasas in every
major city of the Saljuq domains. Saljuq support for madrasas created a broad base
for the education of Sunni religious teachers, for Sunni missions to the general
populace, and for opposition to Fatimid and Isma'ili claims. At the same time
Nizam al-Mulk probably aimed at state control over the Sunni movement, and
meant to use the major legal and theological schools as a vehicle for political influence over the masses.

After the death of Nizam al-Mulk, Saljuq policy oscillated between patronizing
the Hanafis and patronizing the Shafi'is. The late twelfth century, however, brought
a shift from sponsorship of individual schools to equal recognition of the four major
schools of law. Alongside the madrasas, which taught the legal doctrine of each of
the four main schools, a new type of college, called *dar al-hadith*, was created to
teach the sayings of Muhammad. The dar al-hadith, however, was not assigned to
a particular school of law but represented the common Muslim interest in the legacy
of the Prophet. In 1234, as a further expression of a pan-Sunni policy, a new
madrasa was founded in Baghdad to house all four of the law schools. In the course
of a century and a half, government policy had moved from identifying itself with
particular sectarian movements to a definition of Islamic orthodoxy including all
the major schools of law and the most prominent theological groups.

The Saljuqs endowed khanaqas as well as colleges. They brought the institution
to Baghdad, where these centers were known as ribats. Ribats housed scholars of
hadith, legists, and theologians, and were, in particular, residences for preachers
engaged in religious and political propaganda on behalf of the Saljuq Sultans.

Thus, by sponsorship of madrasas, schools of law, theological groups, and
khanaqas, Nizam al-Mulk initiated a state policy of seeking legitimacy and political
stability by patronage and sponsorship of Sunni religious institutions. State support
and sponsorship of religious schools helped overcome factional antagonisms and
helped establish a uniform system of legal organization and education. The
madrasas and khanaqas served as an organizational base for legal teaching, as a
vehicle for providing financial support for Muslim religious scholarship, as centers
for the training of religious and administrative cadres, and as bases for missionary
activity with the goal of achieving the universal acceptance of Sunnism. In return
for Sunni support and legitimization of state policy, the Saljuqs helped to realize
the Sunni ambition for a universal Muslim society.

ISLAMIC INSTITUTIONS AND A MASS ISLAMIC SOCIETY

The institutionalization of Shi'i sects, Sunni schools of law, and Sufi brotherhoods
was but one aspect of a larger process by which Middle Eastern communities were
absorbed into an "Islamic" type of society. The translation of Islamic institutions into

an Islamic type of society also depended upon the mass conversion of Middle Eastern peoples to Islam. Curiously, mass conversion was not achieved in the age of the 'Abbasid empire. The empire, which created the first forms of Islamic literary, religious, and court culture, never succeeded in making Islam the religion of the majority of Middle Eastern peoples. Despite numerous conversions, substantial Christian populations remained in Iraq, Mesopotamia, Syria, and Egypt; substantial Zoroastrian populations survived in Iran. While there were conversions among individuals who migrated to the Arab capitals and became Muslims, as late as two centuries after the conquests Muslims remained an elite minority among non-Muslim peoples.

The first mass conversion of a Middle Eastern population took place in Egypt in the middle of the ninth century. A massive Coptic peasant rebellion was crushed in 832. In the wake of the rebellion bedouins attacked Christian villages; money was extorted from the church. Under pressure of communal defeat, bedouin attack, and the impotence of the church, Christian loyalties were subverted. In regions that had been partially settled by an Arab population, such as the eastern Delta and parts of Upper Egypt, mass conversions to Islam took place. Other parts of Egypt, however, especially the western Delta, remained Christian.

Only with the breakup of the 'Abbasid empire, and the vast upheavals attendant upon the destruction of the established elites, did the masses of Middle Eastern people convert. Extensive warfare, rural insecurity, and the decline of the old elites and village communities allowed large numbers of Persians to convert to Islam. Sufi missionaries seem to have played a crucial part. In western Iran Shaykh al-Kazaruni and his followers converted numerous villages. Islamic missionary activity also had substantial success in eastern Iran, where Mu'tazili and Karrami missions made converts. The Caspian regions were converted by Shi'a fleeing from Baghdad. By the end of the tenth century Islam was the dominant religion in Iran. Sufis pushed out into Inner Asia where they converted Turkish peoples. By the eleventh century, as far as we can tell from exceedingly fragmentary evidence, Islam was no longer the faith of a dominant minority, but was the majority faith of Iraq and Iran. In northern Mesopotamia and Syria, however, the bulk of the population remained Christian until the late thirteenth century.

Just as Islam had served in the imperial era to define the identity of the political aristocracy and the dominant Arab-Muslim urban society, so in the new era it was progressively adapted to express the communal identity of the masses of Middle Eastern peoples. In the course of the tenth to the thirteenth centuries Islamic communal groups and religious leaders were able to take charge of Middle Eastern communities, and infuse them with Islamic identifications. This was possible because old landowning and office-holding notables lost their power to new military regimes dominated by slave soldiers or migratory nomadic chiefs. As foreigners with no historical ties to the societies they had conquered, warlords could restore provincial government, but they could not take the place of the old official and landowning classes and offer, on a local level, the protection, advice, and assistance that the powerful traditionally offered the poor. Faced with military elites unfamiliar with local traditions, the 'ulama' emerged as a new communal notability. The 'ulama' married into established merchant, administrative, and landowning families and merged with the older local elites to form a new upper class defined by religious qualifications. They took charge of local taxation, irrigation, judicial and police affairs, and often became scribes and officials in the Saljuq states. The 'ulama' thus developed from a purely scholarly and religious elite with judicial functions into a broad social and political elite. In many instances, given the instability of military regimes, they became the effective representatives, and even governors, of their towns and territories. Like tribal chiefs, local landowners, princes, and military governors, leading 'ulama' families sometimes ruled their towns in de facto independence from the military regimes. The families descended from Abu Burda governed Shiraz for centuries; the Mikalis family served as *ru'asa'* of Nishapur, and the Burhan family of Bukhara provided local governors who collaborated with the nomadic regimes that successively conquered eastern Iran and Transoxania. The acceptance of this new responsibility was a reversal of the earlier 'ulama' resistance to involvement in politics, and is explained by the dramatic breakdown of the Caliphate.

The authority of the 'ulama' was derived from achieved learning and a reputation for sanctity, since there was no central or church-like agency to ordain, license, or validate religious leadership. Authority was personal, grounded in the relationship of individual religious teachers to their disciples and followers. In the case of a Shi'i imam, the head of a school of law, or a Sufii shaykh, the personal relationship of layman to scholar, of worshiper to preacher, of sectarian to religious guide, of disciple to master, was crucial. Religious authority was validated by the recognition of other scholars and ordinary people. The influence of the 'ulama' with the general populace was further reinforced by the exercise of patronage, which bound ordinary people to the educated elite. The binding force in society was not a structure of offices and institutions, but the networks of personal ties that enabled the 'ulama' to uphold family, religious community, and umma as the essential expressions of an Islamic social order.

Shi'i sects, Sunni schools of law, and Sufi brotherhoods also served as cadres for local political organization. The schools – made up of study groups, teachers and students, interested members of the community and patrons, and legal functionaries such as deputies, witnesses, orderlies, and clerks grouped around the important judges – formed organized parties or factions. The 'ulama' had close ties to merchant families, bureaucrats, and officials. Their popular following was often found in the quarters where their mosques and schools were organized, among the people who sought their advice and protection. By the eleventh century, everyone was considered to be a member of one of the four schools of law on the basis of birth or the traditional membership of his quarter, city, or region. The common people belonged in that they looked to one or another of the schools for authoritative opinions on what they saw as the divinely commanded rules of behavior.

They went to the scholars of the law for judgments in uncertain cases, and to the witnesses and judges for commercial and legal matters.

While Muslim religious bodies became the usual organizing cadres for local communities, they were by no means the only ones. Primary groups including families, villages and town quarters defined by family, ethnic, or sectarian homogeneity, or by shared employment in some craft or trade, remained active forces. Young men's gangs – called *fityan, 'ayyarun,* or ghazis, made up of unmarried men of working-class background, separate from family, tribal, or craft organizations – espoused an ethic of bravery in sports and fighting, and played a complex role in the social life of towns and villages. An already venerable culture of masculine honor and social sanction for revenge helped reinforce the tendency to factionalism and feuds in Middle Eastern town and village communities. The 'ayyarun of Iraq and Iran were often gangs of criminals who sometimes served as strong-arm men for local notables, quarters or religious sects, sometimes acting as criminal predators, and sometimes defending their home communities. These factions made Middle Eastern towns quarrelsome places, but also gave them a limited capacity for organized resistance to nomadic and slave regimes.

The Muslim schools of law and Sufi brotherhoods played a double role. They were often parochial and factional bodies struggling for control of judicial offices and teaching positions, and often involved in pitched battles with rival schools over doctrine, prestige, and control of the streets. In other cases, the schools of law and the Sufi brotherhoods served to integrate disparate town populations and bring factional groups into a more embracing Muslim community. They transcended town, district, and local boundaries. Organized across the territories of states and empires, they were worldwide fraternities of students and scholars. Transcending loyalties to any particular place, membership in a school of law or a Sufi brotherhood created a sense of the umma as a whole, and was an important part of social consciousness. United by the travels of 'ulama', Sufis, merchants, and students, the schools of law and Sufi tariqat were crucial both in the formation of local community life and in linking each small locality to the worldwide brotherhood of Islam. Muslim communal loyalties were factional and parochial at the local level, but cosmopolitan and universal at the international level.

Towns and villages were thus segmentary societies made up of numerous groups, defined by neighborhood, or by religious sect, and sometimes by occupation, but never by economic class. This is not to deny that the notables formed an elite stratum or that lower-class groups could be independently organized. In Iranian towns the patriarchates, consisting of officials, professionals, landowners, and merchants, tended to dominate lower-class groups but, by and large, social and political groups were organized in communal rather than in class terms.

This pattern of social affiliations and identifications excluded one alternative pattern of communal organization – the corporation of citizens resident in a particular locality. The town or village from which a person hailed, however important in his consciousness, did not constitute a corporate body, had no territorial administration, and conveyed no political citizenship. No institutions corresponded to the social or psychological facts of town or village life. In this type of society with its combination of parochial and cosmopolitan identifications and its weak geographic solidarity, people depended upon the informal authority and mediation of the 'ulama' notables to cope with shared concerns. Informal consultation of respected notables and their networks of patronage ties allowed for mediation of local disputes, for mobilization across parochial group lines, and for the expression of shared religious and political interests.

Town and village societies of this type were not ordinarily self-governing. The 'ulama' notables were neither a military nor a territorial elite. They did not have the skills for warfare; nor did they control land and revenues. Middle Eastern localities lacked the technical, the organizational, and the economic bases for political independence. They lacked the internal cohesion necessary for political autonomy and they feared the breakdown of internal order more than the heavy hand of alien regimes.

This is not to say that the lack of political autonomy was their fault. Conquest by nomadic peoples and slave warlords who militarily and economically dominated both town and country precluded the possibility of communal independence. Only in interregnum periods, in the absence of strong military regimes, could mediation by 'ulama' and parochial clienteles give local forces temporary independence. When the ruling empires were weak, urban resistance to exploitation, revolts against unpopular governors, and protests against taxation were common. Town resistance based on religious leadership and 'ayyarun or ghazi forces could even settle the fate of empires. In 992 when the Samanids were faced with the advancing Qarakhanids, their last hope lay with the masses of Bukhara, whose religious spokesmen counseled neutrality. Similarly, the notables and the 'ulama' of Nishapur determined the success of the Saljuq invasion. Deciding that the Ghaznavids could no longer defend Khurasan, they surrendered to the Saljuqs and offered the services of a socially and administratively skilled elite to the new regime. Otherwise, empires reigned.

Thus, in the period between 950 and 1200 local elites and communities in Iran and Iraq had become Islamized. Through the schools of law, Sufi brotherhoods, and Shi'i sects, Islamic religious leaders provided the cadres of communal organization not only for a small sectarian following, but, in an age of conversions, for the masses of Middle Eastern peoples. Islam thus gave the post-imperial Middle East a new identity. While conquerors and regimes came and went, Islam became ever more firmly and widely entrenched as the basis of the social and political order.

CHAPTER 11

THE COLLECTIVE IDEAL

The new realities of state and religious institutions were reflected in an abundant literature of political theory. This theory had three principal branches: a Sunni theory of the Caliphate which was the work of the 'ulama', a Persian-inspired genre of mirrors for princes, and a philosophical theory of the ideal state composed by commentators on Plato and Aristotle. Each of them responded in part to the changing social universe, and in part to their own literary canons, but they also embodied a common perception of the ultimate significance of politics and community. The shared values and assumptions bring us to the core of the post-imperial conception of a Muslim society.

THE JURISTIC THEORY

The Sunni–Shari'a theory of the Caliphate was set forth in theological and juridical treatises. The Sunni writers tried to explain why there should be a Caliphate at all, what purposes the office served, what qualifications were required of its incumbents, how they were to be selected, and what were the obligations of subjects. The underlying assumption of the Sunni literature was that rulers held office to implement the Shari'a and maintain the existence of the Muslim community. Before the middle of the tenth century Muslim political debate turned on the question of who was qualified to hold this office. The Sunnis proposed certain personal qualifications combined with an electoral process to guarantee the legitimacy of a ruler. While Sunni authors discussed the formalities of assuming the office, including the formal act of designation, the consultation with the religious scholars, the oath of investiture, and the contract with the community, legal thinking in effect justified the actual pattern of succession, and especially the designation by the incumbent of his heir.

By the tenth and eleventh centuries it was clear that the Caliphs could no longer fulfill their political and religious roles. The Sultanates had stripped the Caliphate of its actual powers; sectarian quarrels diminished its religious authority. Sunni theorists accommodated to these realities. Al-Mawardi (d. 1058), a Sunni jurist, wrote the *Ahkam al-Sultaniya* (Principles of Government), to show that the primary duties of the Caliph are to maintain religion according to early precedents, enforce judicial decisions, and protect the people of Islam. For al-Mawardi the Caliphate was both a religious commitment and a political actuality. Thus, his theoretical views were supplemented with a discussion of the delegation of authority, the conditions of appointments and tenure for all classes of governmental officials, and the personal and moral qualities required of each office-holder. He described the organization of judicial administration, tax collection, government measures to stimulate agricultural production, and the application of legal penalties for criminal offenses. In effect he set out a comprehensive blueprint for the exercise of an Islamic government. Embedded in this elaborate literary exercise is a poignant mixture of scholarly devotion, religious idealism, and political ambition.

Al-Ghazzali (1058–1111) similarly combined allegiance to religious tradition with a pragmatic awareness of political realities. He too wanted to restore the Caliphate to its true function as the protector of the tradition of the Prophet and of Muslim law, to recapture the unity of Muslim peoples, and to restore their military and worldly might. To do this, he realized, it was necessary to assimilate the Turkish military aristocracy, subordinate them to the Caliphate, reform political administration, and above all to use the combined powers of Caliphs and reigning sultans to suppress the enemies of Islam, especially the Shi'a. Most important for al-Ghazzali was the need to inculcate in every individual Muslim true belief, true piety, and true practice of Muslim law. Despite his continuing commitment to the Caliphate, Al-Ghazzali was realistic enough to recognize that military commanders often appointed the Caliphs, who in turn legitimized their power. His theory conceived of Muslim government as a condominium of the authority of the Caliphs and the effective powers of the Sultans.

More important was the ever-increasing emphasis upon obedience. Obedience is counseled in the Quran and in hadiths. The Hanbali theologian Ibn Batta (d. 997) condemned armed revolt against an established government. He held that obedience was required of all subjects, but that this obedience was limited, in that the individual should refuse to disobey a command of God. Al-Ghazzali held that rulers should be obeyed because resistance, even to tyranny, was a worse alternative. He believed that in the absence of a strong government factional hostilities could lead to anarchy. These fears were not unrealistic. Under the pressure of political necessity Muslim jurists were led to accept any established government as legitimate and to put aside their insistence on the supremacy of the Caliphate.

With the demise of the Caliphate in 1258, Sunni political thinkers could finally articulate a concept of Islamic government based upon the collaboration of secular rulers and religious teachers. Just as the authority of Caliphs was based upon succession to the Prophet and on the presumption that they had the knowledge, understanding, and moral qualities essential to implement the revealed law, so the authority of the 'ulama' and Sufis was based upon a combination of personal achievements and the silsila, or chain of initiations going back to the Prophet. Thus the followers of the Caliphate, the students of the 'ulama', and the devotees of the Sufis respected the same essential principle – the transmitted presence of the Prophet. Political theorists assigned the 'ulama' an ever larger role in the government of Muslim communities as advisors and counselors to reigning princes. As early as the ninth century the Hanbalis had emphasized the Quranic injunction to "command the good and forbid the evil" as the basis of the responsibility of every scholar and of every Muslim to apply God's law in community affairs. With the rise to power of slave and nomadic chieftains, Hanbalis and other Muslim theologians also stressed the requirement for *nasiha*, or advising and admonishing the ruling elites to induce them to observe and implement Islam.

In both practice and theory Ahmad b. Taymiya (1263–1328) represented the epitome of the trend to focus Muslim religio-communal interests on the 'ulama'. Ibn Taymiya was an outstanding Hanbali scholar of Quran and hadith, and a prolific writer on a great variety of religious questions. Born in Harran in Mesopotamia, he fled from the Mongol invasions to Damascus. He first achieved notoriety in 1293 when he led a campaign to execute a Christian who was accused of insulting the Prophet. In sermons and speeches, legal responsa, and published creeds he violently denounced his religious enemies. He opposed the Ash'aris and speculative theology in all its forms; he opposed all forms of metaphysical Sufism; he denounced esoteric and antinomian religious views and the veneration of saints' tombs, and involved himself in violent controversies on legal matters such as the law of divorce. He took part in demonstrations to destroy cultic forms of worship, expeditions against the Isma'ilis in the mountains of the Lebanon, and led Muslim resistance to the Mongol invasions of Damascus. He insistently demanded that the Shari'a be a continuing and vital force in the everyday life of every Muslim.

In accordance with his own political role, Ibn Taymiya held that the 'ulama' were responsible for upholding the law by giving religious advice to rulers, teaching true principles to the community of Muslims, and "commanding the good and forbidding the evil." He set aside the traditional question of the Caliphate – arguing that true Caliphs had not ruled since the early days of Islam – and defined Muslim governments in terms of the actual ruling authorities, and their attention to the advice of the 'ulama'. His political activism thus embodied a new concept of state and society in which the 'ulama' rather than the Caliphs became the principal actors. Sunni political theory had shifted slowly to deemphasize the Caliphate and to accept the reality of Sultan and scholar as the key figures in the Muslim political order.

MIRRORS FOR PRINCES

While Sunni theory developed in Islamic religious circles, the mirror literature arose out of a Persian tradition of manuals of statecraft. The first works of this kind were

7   A youth prostrating himself before a ruler

translated into Arabic in the course of the eighth and ninth centuries to counsel the 'Abbasid Caliphs. The upheavals of the tenth and eleventh centuries led to a new wave of mirrors for princes, written by government officials and religious scholars, to define the rules of good government for their new Turkish overlords.

The most important treatise of this kind was *The Book of Government* by Nizam al-Mulk (d. 1092). *The Book of Government* urges the Sultan to do justice and gives him specific advice on the techniques of rule. The work is devoted to explicating the proper role of soldiers, police, spies, and finance officials; it tells anecdotes about the great ancient rulers to illustrate its lessons. Another important work, the *Qabus-name* of Kai Ka'us (d. 1082), was a compendium of the wisdom of an old king written for his favorite son, containing advice on the proper conduct of a household, agriculture, the professions, and government. The *Qabus-name* tries to teach a youth how to be a statesman, a gentleman, and a good Muslim. The *Book of Counsel for Kings* by al-Ghazzali is an altogether different kind of mirror. While Nizam al-Mulk concentrated upon pragmatic political questions, and Kai Ka'us was concerned with the education of an aristocrat, al-Ghazzali's *Book of Counsel* sets out the beliefs of Islam, the moral qualities and attitudes expected of a ruler, and his duty to uphold the true religion. The example of ancient Persian kings and the sayings of sages are quoted to illustrate these teachings, and to give a work with Muslim religious content a Persian literary flavor.

These works are strikingly diverse in tone and content, but they are all concerned with the ultimate ends of government and with the cultivation of rulers who have the vision, the character, and the technique to realize these ends. The purpose of government is to uphold justice and to preserve the Islamic tradition. In the work of Nizam al-Mulk, justice means that each class of the population – soldiers, administrators, merchants, and peasants – shall have its due; the weak shall be protected, and the productivity of the population assured. In concrete circumstances justice is defined by custom and by Muslim law. For these obligations a ruler is responsible to God. "Each of you is a shepherd and each one of you is answerable for his flock."

Al-Ghazzali's *Book of Counsel for Kings* also stresses the importance of justice. The ruler should understand that God loves a just Sultan and that God will judge him at the final day. The ruler should also see that his officers, servants, and slaves are disciplined. His most important responsibility is to shun heresy and evil actions, to keep to the tradition of the Prophet, and to reward virtuous people and condemn evil ones. For al-Ghazzali as well as for the secular writers, the principal function of kingship is to uphold order in society and the teachings of the true faith.

According to the implicit theory of the mirrors for princes the principal means for realizing justice is that the ruler himself be a just person. Though there are numerous pragmatic or political matters which must be managed, societies depend ultimately on the intellectual and moral qualities of their rulers. The good ruler must be a man of intelligence, knowledge, and experience, deliberate and circumspect, patient and self-restrained. This nobility must be expressed in a grave, dignified, and stern manner, for the ruler must inspire awe, loyalty, and good behavior in his subordinates. He must therefore avoid lying, avarice, anger, envy, and cowardice. If the ruler is a liar, men will have no fear; if he is avaricious, no hope. If he is angry, they will not confide in him. The most desirable trait is generosity: he must reward his servants and spend his treasure on those who help him. His good character not only wins the support of his subordinates but serves as an example and induces them to be good to the people. Thus the moral qualities of the ruler are at the heart of his capacity to make justice reign. For al-Ghazzali this essential goodness is based upon religious humility. The virtues of princes come from fear of God; for we are temporary sojourners in this world, and our ultimate destiny is in the world to come.

To achieve goodness the ruler must consult with the sages and the scholars. They will teach him what God requires; they will divert him from heresy and innovation; they will help make his soul into the image of a just ruler. The 'ulama' thus define the goodness incumbent upon the ruler and help instill it in him. The literature of the mirror for princes, then, trusts to personal virtue as the basis of social justice.

THE PHILOSOPHER-KING

A third genre of literature stems from the Greek heritage: the Islamic commentators on Plato and Aristotle, al-Farabi (d. 950), Ibn Sina (Avicenna, 980–1037), Ibn Rushd (Averroes, 1126–98), and others, who examine the ideal state and the ideal ruler. The highest goal in philosophic political theory is the perfection of the human speculative intelligence and the attainment of happiness through the rational contemplation of the divine reality. For the realization of this blessed state, the cooperation of human beings is essential.

Al-Farabi was the premier political theorist in the philosophic tradition. His *Madinat al-Fadila* (The Virtuous State) begins with a résumé of the principles covering the divine being, the emanation of the celestial intelligences, and the relation of human intelligence and imagination to the spiritual universe. His real purpose is to understand the nature of being and intellect and to attain a spiritual vision of reality; his principal concern is the person of the philosopher, who must know the truth and be responsible for actualizing it in human society. The philosopher who has attained a theoretical vision of the truth is the only person qualified to rule, instruct his people, form their character in accordance with moral principles, teach them practical arts, and rouse them to do good acts so that they in turn reach their highest possible perfection.

In the *Aphorisms of the Statesman*, al-Farabi explains that there are two levels of ideal state. One is the state ruled by the philosopher-prophet-prince, whose personal guiding presence is the inspiration for a virtuous society. The second type is the one ruled in accordance with the law set down by the original philosopher-prophet. In this state the ruler must have knowledge of ancient laws, good judgment about how to apply them, initiative in coping with new situations, and practical wisdom to handle matters where tradition does not suffice. The second type of ideal state corresponds to the Islamic society governed by the revealed law under the guidance of a ruler who implements the law – it is akin to the ideal Caliphate of Sunni legal theory.

Later political philosophers held much the same position. Ibn Rushd offered a comprehensive vision of the spiritual universe and the place of human society within it. This is presented in his commentary on Plato's *Republic*. The perfection of speculative intelligence is the highest goal of human existence; human society exists for the sake of this perfection. The ideal society requires a philosopher-king and law-giver who will create an order in which each person fulfills the tasks appropriate to his nature. When the virtues of the soul – intellect, temperament, and appetite – receive proper expression, there is justice in the society and in each person. The ruler establishes this perfect order by teaching philosophy to the elect and theology and poetry to the others. He trains the people by providing laws which guide them toward proper actions. Ibn Rushd, like al-Farabi, posits two levels of ideal society. One is established by the philosopher-prophet, who combines wisdom, intelligence, and the imaginative capacity to communicate the truth directly to the masses. The other is based upon law, which is a way of implementing the speculative truth known to philosophers, and is conducive to the perfection of the soul. In either case a good ruler is essential to the realization of a good society.

All three forms of Muslim political theory are ultimately grounded in the premise that the goal of the social order is the formation of individuals who live rightly in this world in accordance with the truth and are so prepared to achieve salvation in the world to come. Politics is but part of a larger quest for religious salvation. Nonetheless, in each theory the definition of that truth is somewhat different. In the Sunni theory the fulfillment of the law is the fulfillment of God's revealed will. In the mirror theory the substance of religious fulfillment is not discussed, but it is assumed that justice corresponds to the realization of religious principles. In the philosophical theory knowledge of the intelligences and the purification of the soul frees the human intellect to regain its visionary attachment to the spiritual world.

The three genres of Muslim political theory also agree that political society is essential to the realization of this perfection. In the philosophical theory a properly ordered society is necessary for the cultivation of souls who may comprehend the ultimate reality. In both philosophical and Sunni theory law is the essential device for instructing, educating, and forming the morals of human beings. In turn, the state is essential for the enforcement of laws and the protection of individuals from being harmed or doing harm. In all three theories society is necessary to enforce justice and order, sustain basic human needs, teach and instruct individuals in their moral duties, and support their spiritual quests.

All three genres insist that the proper social order requires a good ruler, whether he is a philosopher, Caliph, or Sultan. Happiness in society depends upon the person of the ruler. In all three forms of Muslim political literature the ruler symbolizes the integration or the orderly relation of human beings to the cosmos and to God. In the philosophical literature the ruler stands not only for personal religious fulfillment but for the harmony of the individual and society with the spiritual cosmos. The ruler who actualizes his rational potential brings his own soul into contact with the active intellect and the spiritual intelligences. He symbolizes in mythic terms the integration of man and God. In Sunni and mirror theory the ruler does not have a mythic function: the Caliph is not divine, or semi-divine, or an incarnate savior, or a perfect man. He is, however, God's vice-regent, God's shadow, his vehicle for the maintenance of order in society, and for fulfilling the conditions essential to the implementation of the Muslim law. The Caliph is seen as the upholder of order and justice in the image of God. He is mighty, capricious, inscrutable, and deserving of loyalty regardless of his actual deeds. An ordered society is unimaginable without a ruler, just as an ordered universe is unimaginable without God.

The ideal ruler is presented as ethical, just and God-fearing, but the unspoken motive for the composition of these literatures is that actual rulers are capricious, willful, self-serving, and tyrannical. The unspoken contrast symbolizes the deep conflict that is experienced in the soul of every individual and in the body of society – the conflict between the forces of unbridled passion and unrestrained exercise of power and the discipline of moderation and self-control. It also symbolizes the ever-present conflict in society generated by family antagonisms, tribal wars, factional struggles, conquests, and the rise and fall of regimes, as opposed to the hope for peace. The ruler signifies not merely order but the quest for order in a society composed of self-seeking human beings and groups.

The person of the ruler is so important that all of these works, with the partial exception of those of Nizam al-Mulk, neglect actual political institutions. The philosophical writers give no concrete description of the ideal city. They regard natural and revealed systems of law as a means of social discipline, but the content of social and ritual practice is never discussed. Society is described as organized into classes, but the classes are merely metaphors for the virtues of the well-ordered soul. In the Sunni theory the emphasis is upon the person of the Caliph, and not upon the mechanisms that could bring religious principles into practice. The mirror literatures are similarly vague about the meaning of justice and hierarchy. There is no concrete description of the classes of society, their rights and duties. In none of these literatures do economic issues have an important place.

There are several reasons for this emphasis upon the person of the ruler. One is that these literatures reflect the realities of their time. While modern political theory may focus upon institutions because of the highly bureaucratic and legalistic structure of modern societies, Muslim writers turned their attention to the ruler because authority was vested in patriarchal figures who depended upon the personal loyalty of their soldiers and officials to maintain their regimes. In a society that depended on men rather than institutions the only conceivable check upon the powers of rulers was their character as human beings.

Furthermore, the emphasis upon the ruler also reflects the weakness of organized institutions. Though ubiquitous in influence, the 'ulama' and the Sufis had no central organization. Urban communities were divided into factions. Landowners and other economic elites were divided by region and faction, and had no formal ways of generating solidarity. Apart from the small urban family or rural clans, lineages, and tribes, there was no organized political society. Even the state was often the household of the prince.

Finally, the person of the ruler was emphasized because the ruler symbolized not only the aspiration for political justice, but the hope for individual religious perfection. In the philosophic literature the ultimate concern of political theory is the education of the philosopher. Analogously, the ultimate concern of Sunni writers was not politics but religious and moral perfection to be attained by adherence to the law. The Caliph was a symbol of that perfection. Similarly, the mirror literature describes the ruler as a person in control of his own evil impulses and those of others. He is not an administrator but a model for how men should live. While addressing the question of the state, the underlying premise of Muslim "political literatures" is that the good state is the product of good human beings.

CHAPTER 12

THE PERSONAL ETHIC

The consolidation of a post-imperial Islamic society was accompanied by the consolidation of Islamic religious literatures, beliefs, and values and by the crystallization of an Islamic way of life. While the basic literatures of Quran commentary, hadith, law, theology, and mysticism had originated in an earlier era, in the tenth to the thirteenth centuries these literatures and mentalities were merged into the forms that we still recognize as classical Islam. The Sunni–scripturalist–Sufi orientation became the most commonly accepted version of Islam. Shi'ism, philosophy, theosophy, and popular religion were the alternatives to the Sunni consensus. The post-imperial era defined both the normative form of Islamic religious belief and practice and the alternatives, and thus defined the issues that would ever after constitute the *problématique* of Muslim religious discourse.

NORMATIVE ISLAM: SCRIPTURE, SUFISM, AND THEOLOGY

The Sunni consensus was grounded in scripture. In the post-imperial era the Quran was understood to require each person to do the good deeds commanded by God, be moderate, humble, kind, and just, and to be steadfast and tranquil in the face of his own passions. The true Muslim is the slave of God. He accepts his humble place in the world and takes no pride or consolation in human prowess, but recognizes the limited worth of all worldly things and the greater importance of pleasing God.

By the ninth century, hadith had also achieved a central place in Muslim religious life. Once the basic canons had been codified, hadith studies tended to concentrate on the criticism of isnads, or chains of authority, and on the compilation of anthologies garnered from the earlier canons. Sunni works of law, theology, and mysticism continued to quote proof-texts from the Quran and hadith, and the study of hadith was enshrined in the madrasa curriculum. By the twelfth century new colleges were dedicated to their study.

Table 5. *Central concepts in law*

fiqh	understanding, law
usul al-fiqh	sources of law: Quran, *hadith* (sayings of the Prophet); *ijma* (consensus of schools and community); *qiyas* (reasoning by analogy)
ilm	knowledge, especially of law, the learning of the *alim* (pl. *ulama*)
taqlid	imitation; following the established teachings
ijtihad	independent judgment of qualified legal scholar (*mujtahid*)
Shari a	the way, the total corpus of Muslim law and belief
fatwa	advisory opinion on a matter of law given by a *mufti* (jurisconsult)
qada	court judgment made by a qadi (judge) on the basis of Shari a

Shari'a was also a critical component of Islamic scripture. By the middle of the tenth century the schools of law had developed their basic jurisprudential procedures, and had elaborated a considerable body of legal materials. By then it was widely agreed that there were four major schools of jurisprudence, though there were also numerous independent scholars and small personal schools. By 1300 only the four major schools, the Hanafi, Shafi'i, Maliki, and Hanbali, had survived. Despite the consolidation of the schools of law there was still considerable legal development after 950. Islamic law became more logical and systematic. While the Hanafi, Maliki, and Shafi'i schools agreed that the "gate of ijtihad" or independent reasoning was closed and that scholars of later generations were not free to give personal or independent interpretations of the law, the Hanbalis and a minority of Shafi'i writers never accepted the principle of *taqlid*, or obedience to the traditional canon, and upheld the authority of every qualified legal scholar to use rational judgment in legal questions. Even the more conservative schools allowed for flexible accommodation of legal principles to custom and tradition. The application of the law to practical situations and the procedure of consulting scholars for legal opinions also allowed for the further evolution of law.

The Shari'a reached its definitive literary form with the *Hidaya* (Guide) of al-Marghinani (d. 1196). This work opened a new phase of compilation, repetition, and formalism in Islamic legal scholarship. The law took the form of a vast reservoir of case materials and precedents which could be used as the basis of judicial decisions but no longer offered a rigid set of rules for the regulation of social, familial, and commercial matters. In many cases the guiding principles of law were lost in favor of eclectic dependence on analogy from individual cases. The possibilities for individual interpretation and selection out of the repertoire of numerous jurists gave Islamic law almost boundless flexibility in practice.

Thus a peculiar contradiction arose. The authority of law was absolute but it was not adhered to in practice. While the literalists, such as the Hanbalis, stressed the necessity of adhering to every detail of law, most Muslims recognized that it was not necessarily precise. Legal rules were mixed with moral injunctions. Some actions were required, others were recommended; some were forbidden, others discouraged. In some matters the law was neutral. In many categories it did not provide sanctions and its application was left to conscience. Furthermore, custom often decided whether or not aspects of the law were applied. There were even legalistic devices (*hiyal*) to allow for exceptions to the principles of the law while keeping to its letter. This flexibility in practice was acceptable because the law was not only legislation, but a symbol of the meaningfulness of the world in its connection to God.

The problem of adherence points to a deep spiritual tension in Islam – a tension between ethical ideals and legal rules, between fulfillment in spirit and in letter, and between law as a symbol of truth and as a system of rules. Furthermore, embedded in the problem of adherence to the law was the question of its sources. Was law based on divine authority, the rational judgment of experts, or allegiance to the tradition and consensus of the community? Revelation, reason, consensus, and tradition all played a role in the formulation of religious judgments. Acceptance of scripture, then, implied faith in revelation, commitment to a specific way of life, and a search for personal realization of the moral and spiritual as well as the behavioral qualities implied in the Muslim revelation. In Quran, hadith, and law, we find not only prescriptive rules but the vocabulary of an open religious quest.

SUFISM IN THE POST-'ABBASID ERA

Sufism was another way of pursuing this quest. It devalued worldly things in the search for an ecstatic experience of God's being. It also carried with it a theosophical view of the universe which explained the structure of the cosmos and the possibility of religious ascent toward union with God. Finally, it encompassed belief in the miraculous powers of saints as channels for God's action in the world. Sufism thus encompassed piety and ethical behavior, ascetic and ecstatic practices, theosophical metaphysics, and magical beliefs. It embraced at once a scripturalist, an agnostic, and a miraculous concept of Islam. It led both toward and away from Islamic law and practice. Some forms of Sufism would be integrated with law, while others tended to gnosticism and the veneration of saints. Its ascetic and theosophical aspects were consistent with devoted practice of Islamic law, but the veneration of the magical powers of Sufi saints led rather to religious practices which were expected to produce miracles or to induce ecstatic visions. Sufism was thus not one but several forms of religious inspiration united under the same name.

By the end of the tenth century, Sufis had defined their movement as a science, parallel to that of law, capable of leading to true knowledge of God by virtue of correct doctrine, religious practices, and methods of mystical contemplation. Sufi writers worked out a technical vocabulary to define, defend, and standardize Sufi practice, integrate it with law and theology, and thus legitimize it within the framework of Islam.

In the tenth and eleventh centuries Sufi positions were expressed in a growing body of literature. Biographies linked Sufi initiates with a chain of teachers leading back through al-Junayd to Hasan al-Basri and the companions of the Prophet

Muhammad. Other Sufi treatises set forth the main ideas derived from Sufi experience, and tried to communicate the actual experiences of the masters through anecdotes and sayings. They illustrated the great piety and scrupulousness of Sufis, their trust in God, their unconcern for the things of this world, and their qualities of heart and soul. Such works included the *Qut al-Qulub* (The Food of Hearts) of al-Makki (d. 998), which set out Sufi prayers and recitations. The *Kashf al-Mahjub* (Unveiling of the Hidden) of al-Hujwiri (d. 1071) and the *Risala* (Epistle) of al-Qushayri (d. 1074) explained the meaning of key Sufi terms, discussed metaphysical and theological issues, and gave the biographies of famous masters.

The central motif of this literature is renunciation of individual will, of worldly concerns, and of everything except God. This renunciation, however, refers to an attitude of mind rather than a literal state of emptiness or vacuum. The Sufi lives with material things, but does not care about them. He owns things but does not derive his esteem from them.

Further, the Sufis taught that the true Islam is the submission of man's will to God's will. Al-Hujwiri says: "Divine grace is this – that God through His will should restrain a man from his own will and should overpower him with will-lessness, so that if he were thirsty and plunged into a river, the river would become dry." And further: "What we choose for ourselves is noxious to us. I desire only that God should desire for me, and therein preserve me from the evil thereof and save me from the wickedness of my soul … I have no choice beyond His choice." The Sufi does not wish his own wishes, but makes his wish whatever God has commanded; he is satisfied with whatever God decrees for his life; indeed, he embraces God's choices, doing God's will joyfully.

This does not mean that the Sufi does not have a "will" in the ordinary sense; it means he has fused the chaotic wishes of every person into his authentic will, his willing acceptance of God's command. In this, Sufism is consistent with the Quran, which sees that the unbeliever is one who gives free reign to unchecked passions, and who serves his apparent needs for wealth, honor, fame, power, or whatever. Controlling this false willfulness, obeying God's command, restraint, and modesty are the true Islam.

Sufism further teaches that the will is tamed by the love of God. The politicians would curb men by force; the moralists, by public opinion; the philosophers, by reason; the theologians, by faith. The Sufis teach that the true love of God is to love his will as one's own. They yearn to do God's will as a lover yearns to fulfill the wishes of his beloved. "God's choice for His servant with His knowledge of His servant is better than His servant's choice for himself with his ignorance of his Lord, because love, as all agree, is the negation of the lover's choice by affirmation of the Beloved's choice."[1] Love of God makes his every command the Sufi's own heartfelt wish.

---

[1] Al-Hujwiri, *The Kashf al-Mahjub*, trans. R. A. Nicolson, London: Luzac & Co., 1970, pp. 378–79.

The love of God was wedded to a profound Sufi determination to fuse personal religious experience with the practice of Islam according to law and tradition. Sufis of the tenth and eleventh centuries grappled with the tension between scripturalist Islam, a religion of external laws, rituals, moral and social norms required of all Muslims, and Sufism, a religion of the subjective being of man inculcating purity of heart, visionary knowledge, and love of God. Despite the efforts of generations of Sufis, including al-Junayd and al-Qushayri, and the growing rapprochement of law and Sufism in the tenth and eleventh centuries, the two forms of Islam continued to be taken as alternative paths to religious fulfillment. Shari'a still meant the conformity of outer behavior to legal requirements, while Sufism meant the purification of the heart for the sake of the vision of God. Finally, al-Ghazzali was able to combine the authority of scripture and historical tradition with the personal experience of the Sufi master. Seizing upon currents in philosophy, theology, law, and Sufi practice, he integrated Sufism and law in a way that has become definitive in Islamic civilization.

AL-GHAZZALI: HIS LIFE

Al-Ghazzali came to his vocation in a crisis of which he told in a memoir whose immediacy and poignancy is vivid to the present day. He studied law and theology in Tus and Nishapur. At the age of thirty-three he was appointed professor at the Nizamiya school in Baghdad, one of the most prestigious positions of the time. He wrote treatises on law and theology, mastered philosophy and esoteric subjects, gave authoritative legal decisions, and lectured to hundreds of students. He was widely regarded as living an exemplary Muslim life. Yet he was beset by doubts: "As I drew near the age of adolescence the bonds of mere authority [taqlid] ceased to hold me and inherited beliefs lost their grip upon me." At the time of his greatest success, his doubts flowed into a deep sense of unworthiness.

> Next I considered the circumstances of my life, and realized that I was caught in a veritable thicket of attachments. I also considered my activities, of which the best was my teaching and lecturing, and realised that in them I was dealing with sciences that were unimportant and contributed nothing to the attainment of eternal life.
>
> After that I examined my motive in my work of teaching, and realized that it was not a pure desire for the things of God, but that the impulse moving me ... was the desire for an influential position and public recognition.

Al-Ghazzali yearned to give up this false life, to sever the attachment to worldly things, leaving "wealth and position and fleeing from all-consuming entanglements." But he could not do it. The conflict absorbed his energies.

> One day I would form the resolution to quit Baghdad and get rid of these adverse circumstances; the next day I would abandon my resolution. I put one foot forward and

drew the other back. If in the morning I had a genuine longing to seek eternal life, by the evening the attack of a whole host of desires had reduced it to impotence.

One voice cried, "To the road. To the road." The other, "This is a passing mood … do not yield to it, for it will quickly disappear." It did not.

> For nearly six months beginning with Rajab 488 AH [July, AD 1095], I was continuously tossed about between the attractions of worldly desires and the impulses towards eternal life. In that month the matter ceased to be one of choice and became one of compulsion. God caused my tongue to dry up so that I was prevented from lecturing. One particular day I would make an effort to lecture in order to gratify the hearts of my following, but my tongue would not utter a single word nor could I accomplish anything at all.
>
> This impediment in my speech produced grief in my heart, and at the same time my power to digest and assimilate food and drink was impaired; I could hardly swallow or digest a single mouthful of food.

Al-Ghazzali had come to an emotional crisis. His doctors said wisely but helplessly: "This trouble arises from the heart … and from there it has spread through the constitution; the only method of treatment is that the anxiety which has come over the heart should be allayed."

His decision was made. He took up the life of a wandering Sufi. For ten years he pursued the mysteries of Sufism. His retreat, however, was neither total nor permanent. After ten years, he took up his public career again, returned to a professorship at Nishapur, and wrote his major treatises. He had resolved the doubt in his heart; he had come to certain knowledge of the truth of God's existence and of the nature of his obligations to him. He saw his return as a return to his old work in a new way.

> In myself I know that, even if I went back to the work of disseminating knowledge, yet I did not go back. To go back is to return to the previous state of things. Previously, however, I had been disseminating the knowledge by which worldly success is attained; by word and deed I had called men to it; and that had been my aim and intention. But now I am calling men to the knowledge whereby worldly success is given up and its low position in the scale of real worth is recognized.[2]

Al-Ghazzali did not renounce the world; he abandoned false goals in worldly activity.

Sufism brought al-Ghazzali to certain knowledge of God, and certain knowledge brought him back to Muslim beliefs, prayer, and teaching, to the Given Way of scripture and tradition. His master of theology, al-Juwayni, had already said:

> I had read thousands of books; then I left the people of Islam with their religion and their manifest sciences in these books, and I embarked on the open sea, plunging into the

---

[2] W. M. Watt, *The Faith and Practice of al-Ghazali*, London: Allen & Unwin, 1953, pp. 21, 56–76.

literature the people of Islam rejected. All this was in quest of the truth. At an early age, I fled from the acceptance of others' opinions [taqlid]. But now I have returned from everything to the word of truth. "Hold to the religion of the old women."[3]

AL-GHAZZALI: HIS VISION

In the *Ihya' 'Ulum al-Din* (Revivification of the Religious Sciences), al-Ghazzali gives his mature conception of the relationship between the outer and inner life, between Shari'a and Sufism. His position was rooted in a philosophic concept of the nature of the human being. In his view, the essence of the human being is the soul, which is a spiritual substance variously called qalb, ruh, nafs, or 'aql. In its original state, *al-fitra*, before it is joined to the body, it is a pure, angelic, eternal substance. In this state the soul possesses reason – the capacity to know the essence of things and the capacity for the knowledge of God. The highest good is the actualization of this inherent potential.

For this to be achieved the soul must be joined to the body, for the body is the vehicle that carries the soul on its journey to God. The body, however, necessarily corrupts the pure state of the soul. In the combined constitution of man, desire, anger, and *shaytaniya* (the inclination to do evil) are joined to the purely spiritual elements. The human being thus comes to possess both an animal soul made up of the faculties of desire and anger (nafs), and a divine soul (*rabbaniya*) possessing the faculties of reason and justice. To perfect the soul, every person must subordinate the animal faculties to the higher faculties and perfect the virtues – temperance, courage, wisdom, and justice – appropriate to each faculty. 'Aql has to prevail over nafs. The proper channeling of the animal parts, and the achievement of some harmony of faculties, is called justice in the soul. This does not mean, however, the destruction or abandonment of the lesser parts of the soul, but rather the dominance of reason over the other faculties. The goal is not to destroy, but to make use of nafs in the interest of 'aql.

The Sufi quest is aimed at such purification. The Sufis seek it by detachment from the world, by retreat to the khanaqa, where the Sufi can concentrate on renunciation of worldly attachments, and by dhikr – repetition and remembrance of the name of God – empty the mind of all distracting passions. As al-Ghazzali explains, the Sufi path to knowledge is to shut the gate on sense perception, sexual passion, and worldly ties; to shut the gate on the material side of the mind. To do this one does not need education or book learning – and here is the quarrel of Sufism with the 'ulama'. The certain knowledge of God does not come from learning but from piety.

Sufi detachment, however, is but an extreme tactic in a more broadly conceived reform of the heart. This reform has both an outer and an inner aspect. It involves the triad of good actions, virtues, and knowledge. According to the *Ihya'*, actions

---

[3] W. M. Watt, *A Muslim Intellectual: A Study of al-Ghazali*, Edinburgh: University Press, 1963, pp. 23–24.

come first. The first book of the *Ihya'*, after the introduction on knowledge, is entirely devoted to 'ibadat, ritual actions. These include ablutions, prayer, alms, fasting, pilgrimage, reading the Quran, dhikr, and *wird* (the continual remembering of God). Book II of the *Ihya'* is devoted to social actions – to table manners, marriage, earning a living, friendship, and journeys. These actions, ritual and social, are important precisely because they are God's revealed ways to cleanse the soul of passions and invoke the remembrance that is inherent in al-fitra – the original soul. The prescribed acts of themselves purify.

The second aspect of purification is a direct assault on the inner vices. The vices include the sins of speech – cursing, false promises, lying, slander, backbiting; they include anger, envy, greed, jealousy, gluttony, miserliness, ostentation, pride, love of wealth and power, and love of this world. These vices sully the heart and stand in the way of ultimate happiness, not to speak of ordinary well-being.

The elimination of these vices is a lifelong process. Children must be raised properly with praise and blame, reward and punishment, to discipline their desires, and habituate them to good acts. As children become adults, the discipline of society, the admonition of friends, the counsel of elders, and the imitation of good people is also helpful. In adulthood, however, the process of rooting out the vices becomes an individual responsibility. The individual must himself become aware that he is beset by vice, and self-awareness must be followed by inner struggle (*mujahada*), self-training (*riyada*), and habituation (*i'tiyad*), by sturdy resistance to any external expression of bad impulses in speech or action. Indeed, the individual must not only control his impulses, he must oppose his vices by deliberately acting contrary to them. He has to create in the soul a struggle between vices and their opposites so that the faculties are driven from extremes toward the virtuous mean.

The elimination of vices paves the way for a new level of inward achievement, the acquisition of the mystical virtues. Book IV is devoted to these virtues – the states and stations on the way to God. They include repentance, fear, asceticism, and patience, which are preliminary to gratitude, trust, love, and intimacy. In one sense, these virtues develop spontaneously. They flourish like flowers in a garden, when the garden is weeded. In another sense, they can only be won through God's guidance and grace (*rahma*). A good Muslim strives for ethical self-control, but the mystical virtues flourish only by passive acceptance of God's will.

Passive fulfillment is at the heart of al-Ghazzali's discussion of tawakkul, abandonment of self or trust in God. In the *Revivification of the Religious Sciences*, al-Ghazzali explains that trust in God means to leave everything to God and to have no will, initiative, or activity of one's own. There are three levels of this extraordinary state. One is akin to the trust of a man in the attorney who represents his interests. The man turns over his affairs to the management of another in whose honesty, energy, and ability he has confidence. This delegation, however, is limited to a particular case, and the subject does not surrender his awareness of what is going on, his judgment, or his ultimate right to make choices. This modest degree of trust may continue indefinitely.

The second degree of trust is akin to the dependence and confidence of a very small child in his mother. The infant cannot take care of himself; he knows only his mother, seeks refuge with her, and depends on her support. He has no capacity for initiative of his own, but he can cry, call for his mother, run after her, and tug her dress. At any distress, his first thought is of his mother; he has complete confidence that she will meet his needs. This is like the man who trusts entirely to God and has complete confidence that he will be nourished by the Almighty, to whom he addresses his prayers and petitions. This state of passivity may last a day or two, like a fever, before it passes and the mystic is returned to an everyday condition.

The third state is to be in the hands of God as a corpse in the hands of the washer. The mystic sees himself as dead, moved by God, certain that he does not move, or will, or know, save by God's decree. In this state, the mystic trusts completely that he will be sustained. He does not call out like a child or pray like an adult. This third state, al-Ghazzali says, lasts no longer than the pallor produced by fear.

These images convey the state of being that al-Ghazzali has in mind. The trust of the child in his mother is a man's trust in his basic security, his confidence that his being will be sustained. The trust of the corpse in the washer, that passivity that can only be communicated by images of death, whose interval is the moment of fear, lies beyond the infant's trust. To know it, one passes through the helplessness of infancy, through the fear of death, through the terror of nonexistence. This trust is known by the abandonment of one's own efforts and resources, by the testing of one's capacity to endure a total surrender of one's own life to the very ground of all life. To know this trust is to know that one's existence is assured without striving, effort, or will of one's own. It is assured as such.

Renunciation of the will, of the self, abandonment to God, and trust in God do not represent detachment in a physical sense from the ongoing life of the world, but moments that come to pass and return as part of the flow of man's psychic reality. These moments of passive grounding in trust become the basis of an active Muslim life and of the active virtues that pervade the scriptural and traditional imagery.

The third aspect of purification is knowledge. Knowledge has the most complex implications. It is at once a means and a goal to be attained. It is also a metaphor for the whole of the process by which religious vision is achieved. First, knowledge is basic. Knowledge of the principles of the faith, belief in God and his attributes, the angelic world, paradise, and the last judgment; knowledge of the character and actions of the Prophet, knowledge of which actions are commanded, which are prohibited; knowledge of the heart and how to cure evil impulses – all of this is essential. The scholar's knowledge – indeed, the knowledge contained in the volumes of the *Ihya* – is important information.

In another sense, knowledge for al-Ghazzali is not what is learned but what is experienced. It is precisely the insights impressed upon the heart by the actions and the inner traits of the person. Every action of the heart or the limbs, or inner movement of the soul, impresses itself as an image (*athar*) on the heart. Or, he sometimes says, the heart is like a mirror that reflects the *sura*, the form, the essence of the actions and dispositions it knows. Sometimes al-Ghazzali speaks of the heart as acquiring a hal, a condition, or a *sifa*, an attribute. In effect, every action implants a thought, an idea on the soul, for the essence of the soul is intellect. This knowledge of the heart is more than just information. It so impregnates the mind that all thinking runs by allusion from one passage of the Quran or Sunna to another, controlling the will and the actions of the believer totally. Such knowledge is a "disposition deeply rooted in the soul from which actions flow naturally and easily without means of reflection or judgment." Such knowledge is not only what we know but what we feel. It is knowledge that is not only known but meant. The fusion of knowing, feeling, and doing integrates the outer and the inner man.

Finally, this maturation of the soul through good deeds and virtues leads to knowledge in yet another sense, to mystical vision and love of God. Purification brings *kashf*, the lifting of veils and a vision of God as real beyond doubt. How is this to be interpreted? In one sense, it seems to mean that the soul once purified is set free from the trammels of the body and rises up to a transcending vision of God, but in fact al-Ghazzali does not allow any direct contact, vision, or unity between man and God. The vision, *ma'rifa*, means knowledge of the truths of religion known with utmost clarity without any intervening screen. In this sense, the vision of God is not another reality but a way of understanding reality, and the way of living life as a whole that results from the good deeds and virtues that impress themselves upon the heart as truth. Ma'rifa is not an extra experience but insight into the meaning of reality which rises from intellect and conviction, from behavior in the world and conformity to the principles of one's culture.

Actions, virtues, and knowledge are provisions for the eternal happiness of the soul. The three factors, however, are not cultivated successively or independently. They are altogether interrelated. In al-Ghazzali's view, doing good deeds establishes inner virtues. In turn, the virtues of the heart govern the actions of the limbs. As each act, each thought, each deed presses itself as an image upon the heart or becomes an attribute of the heart, the acquired attributes become all the more continuous, deeply rooted, and seemingly natural. Moreover, since the heart is the seat of knowledge this maturation of the soul through good deeds and virtues leads to mystical vision and love of God. Reciprocally, mystical vision is the source of virtue and channels all action according to God's will. What al-Ghazzali tells us about the relation of inward and outward deeds, of acts and knowledge, of the struggle for virtue and the vision of God, is that they are aspects of a single progressive achievement in the course of which the believer becomes more wise, more just, and more obedient at each step, until he achieves a totality of being which entails at once mystical vision and ordinary piety. This kind of Sufism reinforces the everyday fulfillment of the Muslim law by providing the believer with a still deeper insight into the reality of God's existence. Thus al-Ghazzali gives expression to a cultural ideal, the integration of Shari'a and Sufism, the outer and the inner way – an ideal which is manifest in his return from Sufi retreat to his work as teacher, advisor, and reformer of Muslims. In these terms al-Ghazzali unified Shari'a and Sufism and made them the normative form of Sunni Islam.

RATIONALITY AND THEOLOGY

Theology offered another option for the deepening of scriptural Islam. It arose out of the need to give rational expression to religious concerns. After the early debates over the proper understanding of the divine revelation, by the middle of the tenth century three basic positions had been accepted. The Mu'tazila and the philosophers emphasized the centrality of reason as an ordering principle in God's being, in the human understanding of the universe, and in the governing of human behavior. The rationalist position had as its corollary belief in free will and individual responsibility for moral choice. A contrary position stressed the absolute omnipotence and inscrutability of the divine being, who could be known only insofar as he had chosen to reveal himself through the Quran. Religious insight could only be attained by accepting the teachings of the Quran and hadith. By extension, all human action was ultimately an expression of the power of the creator rather than an autonomous exercise of free judgment and will, and reason was of no use for religious knowledge or moral choice. The Hanbalis, who held this position, rejected allegorical interpretation or rational speculation upon the text of the Quran or hadith.

The Ash'aris and the Maturidis steered a middle course between Mu'tazili rationalism and Hanbali literalism. Religious truths, according to the Ash'ari position, can only be known through revelation, though reason may play a subordinate role in defending the truth and persuading others. In moral matters all human action is governed by God's power but human beings acquire or participate in their own actions. From the tenth to the twelfth centuries, the Ash'aris continued to hold the intermediate position, but they evolved away from the thought of the master in the direction of a more philosophical form of theology. As the foremost opponent of philosophy, Ash'arism absorbed the strategies of the opposition. Philosophic methods and reasoning became an integral part of a new type of philosophical kalam.

In the work of al-Ash'ari, kalam argumentation was not methodical, like philosophical proofs, but indicative, in the sense of persuading or demonstrating the validity of a proposition. The main point of kalam was to attack and denounce all false religious views. It was the science of partisan dispute. Thus al-Baqillani (d. 1013) refuted Manichaean, Jewish, Christian, and heretical Muslim views and advanced his own demonstrations of the existence of God.

Al-Juwayni (d. 1085) and al-Ghazzali were key figures in the development of a new form of Ash'ari theology. In the prevailing mode of dialectical argumentation, the theologians reasoned by analogy to draw conclusions about new subjects.

Table 6. *The vocabulary of Sufism*

The anthropology of the soul	
al-fitra	pure state of being, before investment of soul in the body
qalb	heart, soul, seat of knowledge and conscience
aql	reasoning faculty, often equivalent of *qalb*
nafs	the passions and appetites to be subdued and ordered by reason
The spiritual path	
maqam	achieved status on the way to God
hal	state of rapture by grace of God
ibadat and mu amalat	ritual and social obligations
zuhd	piety, asceticism, renunciation
sabr	patience in accepting God's will
shukr	gratitude
tawba	repentance
tawakkul	trust in God
rida	contentment; acceptance of the divine will
islam	acceptance of God's will
ishq	love, yearning for God
fana	annihilation of the self
baqa	remaining in God
dhawq	tasting of divine reality
kashf	unveiling, revelation
ma rifa	immediate experience of truth
tawhid	unity of God and union in God

Al-Juwayni supplemented this form of argumentation by using the Aristotelian syllogism to deduce conclusions from universal principles or logical premises. Al-Juwayni shifted the meaning of kalam from rationalistic argumentation toward systematic philosophical discussion of the principles of religion. Al-Ghazzali further advanced the use of Aristotelian logic to improve the quality of kalam. Fakhr al-Din Razi (1149–1209) completed the integration of theology and philosophy. His *Muhassal* begins with an elaborate discussion of ontology and logic. In later manuals of theology, virtually two-thirds of the text was devoted to logic, natural philosophy, and ontology.

The absorption of a philosophic format did not imply a reconciliation of kalam with the principal teachings of philosophy. On the contrary: Ash'ari kalam, revitalized by a more sophisticated method of argument, was all the more vigorous in its condemnation of philosophic teachings that were contrary to the scriptural revelation. Al-Ghazzali's *Incoherence of the Philosophers* exposed the contradictions among philosophical writers, and affirmed that a transcendent God could not be known by rational insight. From this vantage al-Ghazzali denied the philosophic concept of the eternity of the world in favor of the Quranic idea of its creation in time, defended the doctrine of the resurrection of the body against the philosophic belief in the eternity of the soul, and affirmed God's knowledge of particulars against the philosophic belief that limited God's knowledge to universals. Al-Ghazzali employed Aristotelian logic and acknowledged the importance of philosophy in the study of nature and mathematics, but in religious matters he insisted on the primacy of God's revelation, the divine will, and God's command over human acts. For al-Ghazzali kalam was useful for the defense of religious truth against certain kinds of intellectual confusion, but it was not itself a way of confirming the reality of God's existence. Insight into religious truth could be found neither in philosophy nor in theology, but only in the direct religious experience provided by Sufism.

Through the synthesis of philosophy and theology, rational inquiry found an integral place in Islamic religious culture, but philosophy and theology continued to diverge despite the close alliance between them. While philosophy operated with the conviction that reason alone would reveal reality, most theologians held that reason alone without support of revelation could not address ultimate realities. What was believed could not be changed by rational speculation, nor could reason discover God's will in matters of good and evil, or control moral behavior. At best the knowledge that comes from divine revelation could be enlarged by rational insight and transformed from faith based on tradition to reasoned faith.

For Muslim theologians, faith was the key to religious fulfillment. Muslim faith, *iman*, means knowing the truth and believing in it. Faith begins in the intellect, knowing that God exists, knowing his attributes, his prophets, his will, and accepting this knowledge as the truth (*tasdiq*). Tasdiq is a conviction about what has been preached and recorded, which becomes the basis of a commitment to live one's life in accordance with that reality. It is an emotion of the heart as well as a thought in the mind. It is a state of devotion; it entails trust in and submission to God, fear and love of God, and above all love of what God wants men to do and hatred for what he has forbidden. Iman issues in devoted worship; every deed of everyday life is carried out as an expression of God's will.

Ibn Khaldun, a North African scribe and historian (1332–1406), explained the theological tradition. For Ibn Khaldun faith (tasdiq) had several degrees. First, faith is simply genuine belief in the teachings of Islam as traditionally defined: "the affirmation by the heart of what the tongue says." Beyond simple faith there is a higher degree of faith, perfect faith. Calling on Sufi thought, Ibn Khaldun defined perfect faith as knowledge of the oneness of God. This knowledge, however, is not merely a knowledge known, but knowledge which has become a built-in attribute (sifa), modifying the very nature of a man's being. The difference, Ibn Khaldun explained, between "'state' and knowledge in questions of dogma is the same as that between talking [about attributes] and having them." It is the difference between knowing that mercy for orphans is recommended and gladly giving alms.

This quality of faith can only be acquired by repeated affirmation of belief and by acts of worship and good deeds. Faith, like any habit, arises from actions, is perfected by action, and governs all actions.

> The highest degree is the acquisition, from the belief of the heart and the resulting actions, of a quality that has complete control over the heart. It commands the actions of the limbs.

Every activity takes place in submissiveness to it. Thus all actions, eventually, become subservient to this affirmation of faith, and this is the highest degree of faith. It is perfect faith. The believer who has it will commit neither a great nor a small sin.[4]

In the theological tradition the capacity for faith rather than reason sums up the human potential for religious salvation. Yet faith includes intellect, and devotion to scriptural truth implies acceptance of a rational dimension in human religiosity. Thus kalam transcended its purely apologetic functions and allowed an essential role for rational speculation in the elucidation of Islamic belief.

ALTERNATIVE ISLAM: PHILOSOPHY, GNOSTIC AND POPULAR SUFISM

Scripturalist Islam, integrated with theology and Sufism, defined the normative form of Islamic belief and practices. The supreme authority of scripture as revealed truth was integrated with rational judgment. Commitment to the fulfillment of God's command in everyday life was allied to the quest for spiritual insight. Within the purview of Islamic culture, however, there were alternative visions of human nature and religious salvation. They were embodied in intellectual form in philosophy and gnosticism; they were expressed in popular rituals and worship. These other forms of Islam overlapped with theology and Sufism, but they were at the same time profound challenges to Sunni–Shari'a–Sufi Islam.

Islamic philosophy and theosophy

Islamic philosophy was the work of a small group of scholars committed to rational inquiry and to the Hellenistic literary tradition. Al-Farabi defined philosophy as a comprehensive vision of the divine reality and the human condition. His successor, Ibn Sina (Avicenna), the great physician and metaphysician, was the son of a Persian official serving the Samanid regime near Bukhara, who by the age of eighteen was a master of logic, natural science, and medicine. He became a Samanid minister, but as a result of court intrigues was forced to flee from place to place. He lived for fourteen years in Isfahan and died at Hamadhan in 1037. A man of action, he produced numerous scholarly works. He contributed to all the natural sciences including physics, chemistry, astronomy, mathematics, and natural history, and composed the monumental *Qanun fi al-Tibb* (Canon of Medicine). The *Canon* includes an introduction to the general study of medicine and volumes on pharmacology of herbs, pathology of organs, fevers, surgery, and other books. His most important philosophical work was the *Kitab al-Shifa'* (Book of Remedy). Like his philosophic predecessors, Ibn Sina wrote on neo-Platonic metaphysics, natural science, and mysticism.

The core of Ibn Sina's teaching was his ontology, or doctrine of being. God is conceived as transcendent and prior to the universe. He stands utterly beyond all being. However, Ibn Sina allowed for a continuity between the necessary being and

---

[4] F. Rosenthal, *Ibn Khaldun, The Muqaddimah*, New York: Pantheon Books, 1958, III, pp. 31–33.

the contingent universe. Though distinct from him in essence, the universe is brought forth from God. As he conceived it, God is the necessary being whose essence is by definition inseparable from existence. All other beings are contingent, for their existence does not follow from their essence. They come into being, following the neo-Platonic tradition, by the self-contemplation of the necessary being. The first being brings forth the first intellect which, contemplating the essence of the necessary being and its own being, brings forth the second intellect. The process of contemplation proceeds until it brings forth the tenth intellect, which completes the celestial and spiritual universe. Thus, there are successive levels of heavenly being, each of which is an intellect emanating from the divine being, comprising a substance generated by the next higher level of being; each level includes an angel, a soul, and a heavenly sphere. The tenth or active intellect apprehends itself and forms ideas that bring into existence the concrete beings of the terrestrial realm. The tenth intellect also illuminates the minds of human beings and enables them to contemplate the universals existing in the angelic sphere.

This theory of creation also defines the ultimate relation of human beings to God. In Ibn Sina's view, the human soul is composed of several faculties. The rational faculty includes the theoretical or speculative faculty. This may be perfected through several stages until it reaches the level of intellect in which the human soul becomes an image of the spiritual world, receiving illumination from the active intellect. This religious vision is essentially an intellectual one, for there is no suggestion of direct union between the human being and the necessary being. In Ibn Sina's view, the highest level of interaction belongs to prophets, who come to know all things perfectly and directly from the active intellect and who communicate their knowledge in imaginative images to ordinary human beings. Prophets teach the existence of God and the practical and ritual aspects of religion. Religion, then, is an imaginative presentation of truths that are known in a pure form to the purely rational soul.

The *Recital of Hayy*, the *Recital of the Bird*, and the *Recital of Salmon and Absal*, three allegorized texts believed to have been written by Ibn Sina, develop the mystical aspects of his philosophical concepts. They recount how a beautiful stranger, an angel of initiation, leads the soul to the orient, to the source of light and the vision of God. This journey of the soul is at once an inward exploration of its own being and a progress through the cosmos. The consciousness which attains knowledge of itself attains knowledge of the successive levels of the divine emanation in the form of angels' souls and celestial spheres. This journey is motivated by love of the divine being and by the realization that the soul is a stranger in the world seeking to return to its origin. The method of this journey is *ta'wil*, interpretation of all existing things in a symbolic way so as to arrive at a new insight into reality. The study of the visionary recitals is then a psychic event leading the soul back to the experience that these texts symbolize.

This journey requires that the soul be detached from every worldly and corrupting influence. Like a steel mirror it must be polished to perfection to see the divine radiance reflected in itself. In this vision, the soul loses consciousness of itself as the medium of vision and retains consciousness only of the divine presence. This mode of union, however, is not a substantial union of the soul with God, but an intellectual vision of God as the necessary being who is the cause of the contingent world. By purifying imagination and by concentrating the intellect, the soul, driven by love of God, may lose itself in contemplation of the divine truth, but it has no prospect of merger with a transcendent God.

Ibn Sina's philosophy is thus a form of intellectual mysticism, which attempted to reconcile a Greek philosophic and theosophical point of view with the scriptural tradition. The doctrine of the necessary being attempts to be consistent with the scripturalist view of the transcendence of God and the separation of the created world from him. The concept of human salvation, while allowing for human intellectual and philosophic comprehension of divine reality, is presented in a way that maintains the ultimate distance between man and God.

While Ibn Sina tried to reconcile the scriptural vision of the transcending oneness and otherness of God with the philosophical and mystical conviction that God and humanity share the same spiritual essence, his effort was still out of tune with the scriptural tradition. His images and vocabulary come from Greek philosophy rather than the Quran. Some of his specific doctrines are actually heretical. His doctrine of the eternity of the world and its creation as a form of emanation from the divine being contradicts the revelation that the world was created ex nihilo. His emphasis upon the inherent rationality of human beings contradicts the scripturalist conviction that all that exists is the product of God's inscrutable will. His view that the soul survives by union with the spiritual world contradicts the Muslim view that man, constituted of both body and soul, will at the day of judgment be resurrected as an entity and rewarded or punished as such. His philosophy attempted to define positions in accordance with scripture, but its inspiration and religious vision remained profoundly alien to scripturalist Muslims.

Ibn Sina's metaphysical universe corresponded to gnostic Sufi visions of the structure of the cosmos and the nature of the quest for salvation. While the Shari'a forms of Sufism stressed the fulfillment of God's command to the very deepest levels of man's being as the way to salvation, the gnostic forms of Sufism sought spiritual fulfillment by bringing the human soul into complete harmony with God. The former was an active fulfillment of God's commands; the latter a contemplative state of being. Ibn Sina stands therefore not only as a central figure in philosophy, but as a precursor to Suhrawardi, Ibn al-'Arabi, and later philosophers and mystics of the sixteenth- and seventeenth-century Iranian school of *hikma* (wisdom). His concepts stand at the center of a long tradition of philosophic speculation and gnostic experimentation – a tradition which continues to appeal to intellectual and religious minorities in Muslim countries to the present day.

In the post-imperial era two figures stood out as the spokesmen of a theosophical and gnostic form of Sufism oriented toward metaphysical comprehension and ecstatic contemplation. Shihab al-Din Suhrawardi was born in 1153 and was executed for heresy in 1191. He combined the philosophical and theosophical aspects of Sufism with Ibn Sina's philosophy of emanations, and with ancient Zoroastrian, Platonic, and Hermetic symbols, and synthesized them into a new form of Islamic mysticism. In Suhrawardi's view, he was reviving an ancient esoteric wisdom, revealed to Hermes Trismegistus and then communicated in two streams of tradition, via Greece, Persia and Egypt, to Islam. He believed himself to be the spokesman of a universal wisdom known to the ancient sages of Iran, Greece, and India and now revealed once again in the Quran. Thus, Sufi gnosticism was fed by strong currents in Islamic philosophy, neo-Platonism, Isma'ili metaphysics, ancient Greek or Hermetic occult sciences, and other Middle Eastern religious ideas.

In his *Hikmat al-Ishraq* (Theosophy of the Orient of Lights) and other symbolic and mystical narratives, Suhrawardi taught that the divine essence was pure light, the source of all existence, and that the reality of all other things was derived from the supreme light. Degrees of light were associated with degrees of knowledge and self-awareness. For Suhrawardi, as for Ibn Sina, the emanation of light from the primary being established a hierarchy of angelic substances standing between God and this world. The angels were limitless in number. In Suhrawardi's vision there were two orders of angels: a vertical order in which each higher angel generated and dominated the lower ones and each lower angel loved the higher. The vertical order of angels gave rise to the celestial spheres, while the horizontal order of angels constituted the world of Platonic forms and archetypes, and gave rise to the angels who governed human souls.

In this spiritual universe the human soul stood in a privileged position. The soul was a heavenly body imprisoned in an earthly body. The imprisoned part sought to reunite with its angelic half and to escape its material and pitiful state. The souls who succeeded in freeing themselves would enjoy the proximity of the supreme light. In Suhrawardi's theosophy the hierarchy of being was a ladder of illumination along which the purified soul could return from the material world to the world of archetypes. In its own symbols this vision resembles neo-Platonic, Sufi, and Avicennan ideas.

Ibn al-'Arabi

The second great theosophist, Ibn al-'Arabi (1165–1240), born in Murcia in Spain and educated in Seville, made the pilgrimage to Mecca, where he had a vision of the spiritual universe. He saw the divine throne upheld by pillars of light. In the vision he was told that he was the seal of sainthood, the supreme figure in the hierarchy of saints who upheld the universe. As a result of these visions he wrote the *Meccan Revelations*. From Mecca he moved to Konya in Turkey and Damascus. In Damascus he wrote *The Bezels of Wisdom*, dictated to him by God through the angel Gabriel. This book was the masterpiece of esoteric sciences, for it synthesized Hermetic, neo-Platonic, Isma'ili, and Sufi influences into a religious vision for which Ibn al-'Arabi claimed an authority equivalent to that of the Prophet.

In Ibn Al-'Arabi's thought all reality is one. This is the doctrine of *wahdat al-wujud*, the unity of being. Everything that exists is God. The divine reality transcends all manifestations, but the manifested world is identical with him in essence. A hadith says: "I was a hidden treasure and I longed to be known so I created the world that I might be known." The reality of the universe is manifested on several planes, the lower planes being symbols of the higher. The highest is the absolute essence of God; there follow in the hierarchy of being the attributes and names of God, the actions and the presence of lordship, the world of spiritual existences, archetypes and forms, and finally, the world of senses and sensible experience.

The hierarchy of being is understood in terms of theophanies (*tajalliyat*). Each level of reality is a theophany of the divine names, which is brought into being by the self-consciousness of a higher level which, becoming conscious, generates another state of spiritual being. The process of creation is further imagined as the result of the divine breath just as words are formed by human breath. The creation is renewed at every breath of the Lord. Existence gushes out from the absolute being whose mercy and love of his own fulfillment bestows existence.

Ibn al-'Arabi's vision of the unfolding of the divine being and the creation of the material world follows in broad outline philosophic and neo-Platonic theory. To these theories he adds a rich and original vocabulary and corollary symbols. For example, in his vision, the first intellect of the philosophers, the primary manifestation of the divine being, is variously symbolized as the attributes and names of God, the Logos, the prototypes of creation, the *insan al-kamil*, or perfect man, and the *haqiqa muhammadiya*, or Muhammadan reality. The divine names symbolize at once the creation of the world, the revelation and the appearance of prophets, and the spiritual capacities of human beings. The prophets and the saints symbolize the fact that man himself is a manifestation of and ultimately an aspect of the absolute. The person who understands the nature of reality and the unity of existence is the perfect saint. Having discovered the truth he in turn becomes a guide for the rest of mankind. The symbols of the perfect man and the Muhammadan reality thus compress into a personified image the reality of the universe. This condensation of symbols also links the gnostic concept of spiritual reality to the Muslim concept of the historical actuality of the revelation and of Muhammad as Prophet.

Gnostic theosophy teaches that the world is one, and that all things participate in the chain of being, the continuous hierarchy of existence extending from God to the spiritual world to the lowliest beings. In this hierarchy man stands in a central position linked to both the world of spirit and the world of matter. Because each thing in the world is an analog of the spiritual reality, by understanding the symbolism of this reality human beings may pass from this world to the world beyond. Because the spiritual world is a hierarchy of intelligences, through the human capacity for knowledge we may participate in the divine reality. By contemplating the cosmos, we become one with the universe. Ultimately, the return to

God is motivated by love; it is driven by prayer and worship. In the vision of Ibn al-'Arabi, God is the mirror in which man contemplates his own reality and man is the mirror in which God knows his essence. Man needs God to exist, and God needs the world to know him.

The concept of a heavenly world, a realm of being which is the counterpart of the actual world, the archetype, the idea, the cause, and the governor of the world in which all humans live, welds the reality of the world and of the human mind. The intellectual and spiritual task assumed by Muslim gnostics was to understand the nature of symbolic discourse and its relation to concrete reality and to integrate the two by making speech and thought correspond to the physical and social actuality of the world. They attempted to achieve wholeness of being, to attain the truth which seems always to elude us because of the paradoxical relation of thought to actuality. In gnostic thought the intangible reality of meaning carried in language and conveyed between persons is a realm of reality separate from the physical world; yet it is the model of the physical world, the image of it, and the guide of our actions in it. Thought and language in the theosophy of Ibn al-'Arabi are ever the same and ever different from the actualities they define.

The doctrine of Ibn al-'Arabi was the culmination of centuries of Sufi gnostic and philosophical contemplation. His theoretical vision and his personal authority shaped for centuries to come the further development of Sufi theosophy and practice. His thought had profound, though unintended, implications for later Sufi practice and even for the daily life of Muslim believers. The doctrines of the perfect man and the invisible hierarchy of saints, the doctrine of the *qutb*, or pole of the universe around which the cosmos revolves, reinforced popular belief in miracles. By implication theosophical metaphysics diminished the importance of observance of Shari'a and Muslim ritual. For Sufis cosmic harmony became a justification for abandoning Muslim laws and for seeking states of intoxicated ecstasy. For many later Sufis it justified an antinomian morality. Such doctrines were also used to minimize the importance of communal loyalties, for truth is universal. Theosophical views increased the importance of dreams, visions and ecstasy rather than ordinary Muslim devotions. In some cases it was allied to the use of drugs and physical techniques to gain ecstatic vision. Though consistent in principle with the Shari'a-Sufi orientation, the theosophical doctrines of Ibn al-'Arabi allowed for religious practices and popular belief by which Muslims sought to short-circuit the trying discipline of the Shari'a way of life and to directly achieve spiritual redemption by contemplative, miraculous, and magical means. For the Sufi masters Sufism was a devotional practice or gnostic illumination. For ordinary believers it came to mean the veneration of saints and the tombs of saints.

The veneration of saints

This has its Muslim origin in the Quran and the hadith which mention the Prophet, the angels, the scholars, and holy men as potential intercessors between ordinary

8 A Sufi preaching

Muslim believers and God. The earliest form of Muslim veneration of human intermediaries was the cult of the Prophet. By the end of the eighth century his burial
place had become an important place for prayer. The story of his *mi'raj*, or ascension to heaven from Jerusalem, became a focus of popular piety and Sufi inspiration. Al-Bistami (d. 873) used the ascension as a model for his mystical journey, in
which the stages of the Prophet's ascent became equivalent to the stations of the
Sufis' progress toward God. Other Sufis wrote their own mi'rajes, modeled on that
of the Prophet, which organized the levels of heaven into stages corresponding to
the emotional levels of the journey toward unity. In the tenth and eleventh centuries the site of the Prophet's ascension in Jerusalem became a popular place for

Muslim worship. Already theologians were explaining that the Prophet was not of ordinary flesh and that he was immune from ordinary sins.

The Shi'a were probably the first to revere the family of the Prophet. In the early tenth century the Shi'i holy places were provided with elaborate tombs, and became centers of pilgrimage. Najaf, the burial place of 'Ali, became a hallowed cemetery; Mashhad, Karbala, and Qum became Shi'i shrines. The Fatimid Caliphs marked the Prophet's birthday (*mawlid*) with ceremonies and a procession of court dignitaries in the presence of the Caliph. The Fatimids also built a number of monumental shrines on the graves of descendants of the Prophet, which became the object of popular pilgrimage in the course of the twelfth century. In 1154 and 1155 the head of Husayn, the martyred son of 'Ali, was transferred to Cairo, where it became the focus of a popular Sunni cult lasting to the present day. By the end of the eleventh century the mawlid had also become a popular custom among Sunnis in Mesopotamia and Syria, and Saladin brought it back to Egypt as a popular festival.

Sunni veneration of the Prophet, the family of the Prophet, and of later Muslim martyrs and saints developed either in parallel with or in reaction to Shi'i pilgrimage and worship at the tombs of the family of 'Ali. In the eleventh century a mausoleum and school in the memory of Abu Hanifa, the founder of the Hanafi school of law, was reconstructed in Baghdad. In 1176 the Ayyubid dynasty rebuilt the college and tomb of al-Shafi'i in Cairo. It became customary for pilgrims to visit the tombs of companions of the Prophet, and to pray at the graves of holy men who martyred themselves for Islam or through whom miracles had been performed. By the beginning of the thirteenth century there were hundreds of sanctuaries all over the Muslim world. Guides and manuals were written to tell the miracles of the saints and to prescribe the rituals and prayers that would bring blessing upon the pilgrim. Early thirteenth-century guidebooks show shrines dispersed throughout Syria, Egypt, Turkey, Iraq, and Iran.

Formal theology and mystical writing gave support to popular belief. As early as the tenth century al-Tirmidhi (d. 932) developed a theory of sainthood as an explanation of the mysterious power of Sufis. Al-Baqillani (d. 1013) wrote that Sufi masters were friends of God who were capable of performing miracles and of interceding on behalf of ordinary Muslims. He elaborated a theological doctrine to distinguish saints from the Prophet and to define the nature of their miraculous powers. Al-Qushayri and al-Ghazzali accepted this doctrine and made it part of formal Muslim belief. Ibn al-'Arabi elaborated it into a cosmological doctrine of the hierarchy of saints who upheld the order of the universe. These teachings gave support to popular faith in Sufi ceremonies, belief in the efficacy of prayers performed at the tombs of saints, and the quest for ecstatic experiences. The equation of holy men and martyrs with the spiritual universe became an inherent aspect of Islamic religious culture. Whatever the legal, the intellectual, or the doctrinal basis of Sufism, its power and appeal to the masses of everyday Muslim believers came from faith in the miraculous power of saints.

THE DIALOGUES WITHIN ISLAM

Sunni Islamic beliefs and practices fell into certain patterns. By the ninth century, Sunnis accepted the Quran, hadith, and law as the core of Islam; schools of law and madrasas had become the central institutions. In Sunni Islam the main organizational impulse focused on schools of law, each of which had its own version of the Shari'a and its own jurisprudential methods. Though they varied in matters of detail there was widespread agreement upon basic religious issues.

With the consolidation of hadith and Shari'a as the central expression of Islamic identity, the great debates of the tenth to the thirteenth centuries turned on the relation of hadith and law to theology and Sufism. The debate over law and theology was especially complex, for it involved a debate over the role of rationalism, which was carried out at several levels. At one level there was a debate between philosophy and theology over reason and revelation. At another, there was a general debate between theology and scripturalism over the role theology itself would have in Islamic belief. The result of these debates was the integration of theological rationalism into the Shari'a religious mentality. Theology (kalam) became an acceptable adjunct of Islamic belief. Some scholars even regarded it as an exalted science which could prove the truth of revelation. Rational understanding of the truth, in their view, was essential to being a good Muslim. For many other scholars, however, theology was but a secondary concern limited to the defense of revealed truth, a kind of medicine for doubters. It was necessary that at least some members of the community pursue it, but it was not essential for all believers.

The schools of theology became closely linked to the schools of law. The Hanafi school of law harbored the Maturidi school of theology. The Shafi'i law school was the home of Ash'arism. However, not all legists in each school were committed to a theological position; nor was a theological position necessarily part of the teaching of the law schools. The legists treated theology as an enrichment of their intellectual and religious life rather than as the center of their scriptural position.

The Hanbalis, however, rejected rational speculation in any form. Hanbalism was thus simultaneously a school of jurisprudence, specifying hadith as the source of law, and a school of theology, affirming the overriding importance of revelation. At the same time, Hanbalism represented a conservative Sunni political tradition that insisted upon the legitimacy of all Caliphs, past and present. Thus by a broad, but not quite complete, consensus, theology in various forms was accepted as an important adjunct to Islamic religious faith and activity.

Sufism was similarly integrated with scripturalism. Sufis began with a religious community, and forms of worship separate from those of the schools of law. Progressively, however, there was a rapprochement between the legal and the Sufi approaches to Islam. Sufis accepted hadith and law as the basis of Muslim belief and practice. Legists recognized the importance of the inner life to the full realization of the law. As this rapprochement took place, the meaning of the term "Shari'a"

Table 7. *Muslim religious movements and sects*

Shi ism

Alid imams	Claim to be sole rightful leaders of Muslim community
Zaydis	Followers of Zayd; establish dynasties in the Caspian region and Yemen
Isma ilis	Militant, establish Fatimid and Qarmatian movements
Ithna ashari	"Twelvers," imamis, pacifist, primarily Iraq

Kharijism

Azariqa (684–c. 700)	Southwestern Iran: sinners must be excluded from the Muslim community; call for election of Caliph; declare war on all other Muslims
Ibadis	States founded in Oman, North Africa: sinners may remain Muslims with limited rights; permit political compromise

Theological schools

Qadaris	Hasan al-Basri (d. 728); discussed God's determination and human autonomy
Murji a	Defined good Muslims by faith rather than works; refused to judge between Uthman and Ali
Mu tazila	Neutral in the disputes over the proper succession to the Caliphate; affirm human free will and createdness of the Quran
Ash aris	al-Ash ari (d. 935); compromise between Mu tazili and Hanbali theological positions

Sufism

School of Khurasan	al-Hallaj (d. 923), ecstatic
School of Baghdad	al-Junayd (d. 910), sober

Sunni schools of law

Maliki
Hanafi
Shafi i
Hanbali (*ahl al-hadith*)

Falasifa

Hunayn b. Ishaq	Translator of Greek texts
al-Kindi (d. c. 866)	Accepts Mu tazili kalam
al-Farabi (d. 950)	Tradition of Alexandrian Hellenistic thought; superiority of reason to revelation
Ibn Sina (Avicenna, d. 1037)	Neo-Platonic philosophy and medicine
Ibn Rushd (Averroes, d. 1198)	Aristotelian, reconciliation with Shari a

progressively changed. In the eighth century it referred to the legal and moral norms for behavior specified in the Quran, hadith, and law. In the course of the tenth and eleventh centuries, Sufi lawyers and theologians gave Shari'a a comprehensive meaning implying not only legally correct behavior, but a rich intellectual, spiritual, and mystical life. While the term continued to be used in the narrow sense to mean revealed law as opposed to rational principles, or the law of external behavior as opposed to spiritual truths, the prevailing concept was all-inclusive.

Thus, law, theology, and Sufism shaped the Muslim consensus around belief in a transcendent God who had created the world and revealed his will to human beings through the agency of his prophets. Muslims believed in the authority of Muhammad and his Prophethood, and in the tradition of the community. They accepted the goodness of the companions, the genius of the imams of the law schools, and the piety of Sufi masters as the sources of right guidance. They accepted the literatures of law, theology, and mysticism as setting forth the beliefs, practices, and ethical and moral attitudes required of a good Muslim. The integrated concept of Islam thus combined the scriptural revelation of required actions with philosophical, theosophical, and mystical views of the nature of the universe and the meaning of human action within it.

The Sunni consensus presented a Muslim ideal of an individual who lives in society according to the rules he has been brought up to respect, according to the norms and laws of the Quran, hadith, law, and social custom, yet in harmony with his own inner knowledge, dispositions, choices, and feelings. This cultural ideal combined the practice of Shari'a and the cultivation of mystical knowledge. The Sunni–Shari'a–Sufi form of Islam sought salvation in the this-worldly conduct of the ritual and social prescriptions of Islam. For Sunni Muslims, a religious life was an active life, consisting of everyday occupations in politics and business, of marriage and family, intermixed with the practice of ritual and other religious obligations. For the Muslim merchant or artisan in the marketplace, the scholar at school, the scribe at court, or the mystic at worship, worldly action and fulfillment of religious commands were the soil in which intellectual and moral skills could grow. Religious knowledge and virtue could only be achieved by engaging in worldly affairs, though worldly activity has no ultimate value unless it is infused by religious purpose. The Sunni–Shari'a–Sufi tradition rejected worldly values pursued for their own sake; the enjoyment of family, economic well-being, and power is of secondary importance. It turned its back upon the *areté* of the warrior, the civic responsibility of the Greek citizen, the intellectualism of professionals, and the aestheticism of aristocrats. Still it did not embrace otherworldly detachment, such as the spirituality of the monk, the creativity of the romantic, or the abstract knowledge of the scientist. It was neither a surrender to the world nor an escape from it. It was a way of living in the world without being absorbed by it or fleeing from it. The goal of the Sunni–Shari'a–Sufi view of life was devotion to God as the basis of an active worldly personality.

The existence of a normative concept of Islam did not mean the formation of a new orthodoxy. The complex of views contained in Sunni-Shari'a-Sufi Islam never became a formal system. Islam has no master science as Christianity has in theology. Within the Sunni complex there were numerous collections of hadith, several equally valid versions of the law, several acceptable theological positions, and different schools of mysticism. Within the Sunni consensus the range of theological viewpoints could vary from sophisticated philosophical reasoning in theology and law to complete exclusion of the use of reasoning and literal reliance on scripture. Muslim mystics varied from strict adherence to the law to complete antinomian lack of interest in convention, ritual, and morality.

While the Sunni–Shari'a–Sufi consensus allowed considerable flexibility within itself, the Sunni community also permitted major religious positions to develop outside its framework. While devotional, rational Sufi positions were partly merged into the general position, philosophy, gnosticism, and popular religion maintained an independent stance, challenging the normative form of Islam. The availability of religious alternatives and the debates concerning their validity made up a more comprehensive program of Islamic religious discussions.

The most important religious alternative came from within Sufism. The gnostic and theosophical tradition influenced by philosophy, while partly accepted into the Sunni consensus, represented an altogether different view of human religious goals. While the scripturalist view insisted upon the fulfillment of God's command in worldly action, the gnostic goal, embodied in the Sufism, Isma'ilism, and philosophical literatures, was insight and contemplative union with the divine reality, to be achieved by purification of the soul and its detachment from bodily and material concerns.

The various forms of gnosticism, however, differed in their comprehension of the mechanism of this purification, vision, and union with God. The peripatetic philosophers stressed reason as the basis of knowledge of God and as the key to a total transformation of the soul which enabled the gnostic not only to comprehend but to enter into the divine presence. Some gnostics stressed reason as the essential aspect of the human soul and the metaphysical structure of the universe. Others stressed emotional forms of illumination; still others stressed the authority of imams and spiritual guides. In all its variations, gnosticism was a quest for a direct contemplative realization of the divine for which scripturalist symbols, rational dialectics, ritual practices, and ethical behavior were all secondary considerations. It was a religion of the visionary soul rather than the active person.

Another religious alternative within the Sunni tradition was popular Islam. Faith in direct divine intervention in human affairs put aside the whole of the Sunni effort to build a morally disciplined worldly life upon the teachings of the scriptural tradition. Popular faith held that the saints could intercede on behalf of human beings, and transmit God's miraculous powers into the world through the person of his saints and the physical things with which they had come into contact. The tombs of saints were considered especially potent.

Outside the Sunni fold there were also communal alternatives. For the Shi'a the critical issue was not law or mysticism but loyalty to the family of 'Ali. They believed that the divine spirit passed from imam to imam in each successive generation. This divine grace both entitled the 'Alids to the Caliphate and made them an infallible source of knowledge of the divine will. While Muhammad had revealed the Quran, its interpretation was vested in the infallible imams. In their view, the true source

Table 8. *Muslim worship*

Five pillars of Islam	
shahada	statement of faith. There is no God but God, and Muhammad is the Prophet of God
zakat	almsgiving
salat	prayer performed five times daily: before dawn, noon, mid-afternoon, before sunset, mid-evening
muezzin	stands in the minaret to summon worshipers to prayer
wudu	ritual ablutions prior to prayer
qibla	prayer performed facing in the direction of Mecca
masjid	mosque; place of prayer furnished with a *mihrab* (niche to mark direction of Mecca); *minbar* (pulpit); *maqsura* (box for Caliph)
imam	leader of prayer
Friday mid-day prayer	performed in *jami* (mosque for the whole community); sermon
khutba	preached by *khatib* from the *minbar*, in which the authority of the ruler is acknowledged
ramadan	ninth lunar month, dedicated to daytime fasting
laylat al qadr	27th of Ramadan: Night of Majesty commemorating first revelation of the Quran
id al-fitr	lesser *id*: festival celebrating the end of Ramadan
hajj	pilgrimage to Mecca
id al-adha	greater *id*: celebration and animal sacrifices to mark end of the pilgrimage
Optional festivals	
mawlid al-nabi	birthday of the Prophet
laylat al-mi raj	night of Muhammad's ascent to heaven from Jerusalem
ashura	10th of Muharram: Shi i festival commemorating martyrdom of Husayn

of belief in each generation was ultimately not the text of tradition, the consensus of the jurists, or the piety of other Muslims, but an imam descended from 'Ali. From this vantage point Shi'ism left a legacy of religious teachings similar to the Sunni types, but it also moved toward a merger with Sufism, in that the divinely graced imam became the example of a mystical reunion with God. Shi'ism is characterized by a religious mood which stresses hope in the return of the imam as a messiah who will redeem Muslims from the burdens of the world. Shi'ism is also chiliastic in believing that history will come to an end. The cycles of prophets and imams will culminate in a cataclysm, out of which will emerge a reborn mankind and the kingdom of God on earth.

The structures of Shi'i Islam are different from those of Sunni Islam. Instead of schools of law there are sects founded by the followers of the various imams. The "twelver" branch followed one line of succession; the Isma'ilis followed another. In time there would be more disagreements, each leading to the development of a new sect with different religious principles. Shi'i communities, often at war with their Sunni neighbors, were established throughout the Middle East.

With all these variations, what did it mean to be a Muslim? It meant that one believed in the truth of God's existence, in the revelation of the Quran, and that one adhered to at least some of the positions in a wide range of religious expression. Muslim believers clustered around one of several Sunni schools of law or one of several Shi'i sects. Islam, then, included a variety of religious positions sharing the same historical tradition. To be a Muslim meant to ponder these positions in the terms set down in the formative era of Islamic civilization.

CONCLUSION: THE MIDDLE EASTERN
ISLAMIC PARADIGM

The process of forming a Middle Eastern Islamic civilization occupied six hundred years, from the beginning of the seventh to the beginning of the thirteenth centuries. However innovative, Islamic civilization was constructed upon a framework of institutions and cultures inherited from the ancient Middle East. On the eve of the Islamic era Middle Eastern societies were organized on several levels. At the base there were numerous local, parochial communities built around factional, lineage, tribal, and village groups. These communities were integrated by market exchanges, and by great religious associations – Jewish, Christian, or Zoroastrian. The larger-scale economic networks and religious associations were in turn under the rule of the Byzantine and Sasanian empires. On the cultural level the ancient heritage included the monotheistic religions, imperial arts and literatures, and philosophy and science. This complex institutional and cultural heritage was carried over into the Islamic era. Despite the rise and fall of empires and shifts in economic activity, the fundamental aspects of technology, modes of production, and the relation of human communities to the natural environment continued unaltered. Also, the basic modes of state organization and family and religious association remained the same. The characteristic changes of the Islamic era were the formation of new political and social identities, the organization of new religious communities, and the generation, out of the elements of the past, of a new cultural style.

The process of creating a new political and religious identity for Middle Eastern societies began in Arabia. While under the influence of Byzantine and Sasanian civilizations, Arabia was not fully integrated into the rest of the region. It was basically a lineage society in which the conflicts of lineage and commercial communities, and the religious and cultural influences emanating from the rest of the Middle East, made possible the emergence of a new prophet, Muhammad, and the revelation of a new religion, Islam. To Muhammad God revealed a new monotheism, which differed in its specific teachings, eschatological consciousness, and literary qualities from Judaism and Christianity. The Prophet also organized a new community, the umma of the Muslims, parallel in form to Jewish and Christian religious associations. While the new society in principle resembled Middle Eastern forms of civilization, it differed in one crucial respect. Islam merged state and religious communal organizations, and did not, as did Byzantine-Christian and Sasanian-Zoroastrian/Christian societies, differentiate between the realm of Caesar and the realm of God.

The creation of a Muslim community in Mecca and Medina represented the formation of an overarching religiously defined community as an integrating force in a lineage society. The Prophet and his disciples transformed a segmentary society to make it serve the purposes of mediation among lineage groups, regulation of economy, state formation, and moral reform while maintaining its basic lineage structures. In Arabia the existence of the two levels of segmentary and religious organization resulted in a complex system of values. In principle the Quran introduced a concept of transcendent reality, as opposed to the aggrandizement of tribal groups and the areté of the tyrannical, boastful, and hedonistic warrior, and a community based on religious brotherhood and personal humility, modesty, and self-restraint. In practice, however, the family and lineage structures of Arabian peoples became part of Islamic society. Pagan virtues were preserved by being vested with new meaning as Islamic ethics, and bedouin identities persisted alongside Islamic loyalties. The ethos of the first Islamic society in Arabia was an amalgam of different levels of religious transcendence, modification of worldly reality, and acceptance of non-Islamic Arabian bedouin civilization. In its first guise the Islamic mission became a model for the way in which radical religious values and sectarian impulses would actually function in later lineage and tribal societies.

THE FORMATION OF IMPERIAL ISLAMIC SOCIETY

The next phase in the creation of a Middle Eastern Islamic society was the Arab conquests and migrations. They led to the creation of a new regime, the Caliphate, the settlement of new cities and towns, the formation of new urban communities, the rise of trade, and the growth of agriculture. In the garrison cities of the Middle East warrior-bedouin migrants were assimilated to non-Arab populations to form new mixed communities. The Arabs were transformed into an urban-dwelling, occupationally differentiated population which included workers, artisans, merchants, and a new religious elite of Quran readers, scholars of law and Arabic letters, and ascetic and charismatic preachers. The town populations were also stratified on the basis of political office-holding, landownership, and tribal chieftainship, and organized into new religious sects and political movements.

The new urban societies generated both the resources and the conflicts that would shape the Caliphate and the imperial regime. From the towns the Caliphate could draw skilled manpower and economic resources. The 'Abbasids in particular based their regime upon the diverse populations that flocked to Baghdad as well as other Arab cities. The pressures of urban social change also created new interest groups and classes, new forms of communal organization, and therefore conflict over political interests and over the Caliphate. The first Muslim century witnessed a series of civil wars. In the first the problem was factional divisions in the Arab elite, the balance of central and local power, and the role of religious versus political factors in the concept and identity of the regime. The major struggle was between factions united by commitment to Islam and Arab tribal coalitions. The second civil war was motivated by sectarian Khariji and Shi'i opposition, and by continuing factionalism within the Arab elite. The third civil war, which brought the 'Abbasids to power, was the product of the division between Arabs assimilated into the general society and those active in the military, a struggle marked by strong ideological conflict over Arab versus Muslim identity.

Each of the civil wars forced the Caliphate to develop the institutional mechanisms to keep political power and to legitimize dynastic rule. To consolidate its position the Caliphate adopted Byzantine and Sasanian institutions and concepts of imperial rule while giving them a new Islamic definition. The Umayyads adopted the bureaucratic administration of the older empires, and patronized architectural works which integrated Byzantine, Sasanian, and Christian symbols into Muslim designs. The 'Abbasids continued the Umayyad trend toward consolidation of an imperial regime and its definition in transmuted Middle Eastern terms. Their regime was centered on a royal court; they governed the provinces through clients and servants of the rulers, using a combination of bureaucratic tax-collecting methods and quasi-feudal forms of administration in which local princes and chieftains were confirmed in power and given status as servants of the Caliph. 'Abbasid administration depended upon a coalition of elites throughout the Middle East. The regime brought together Arab soldiers, Iraqi, Egyptian, and Iranian landlords, Nestorian scribes, Jewish merchants, Inner Asian warlords, and others to serve the central regime. These elites were united by loyalty to the Caliphate, by clientele and family ties linking the center and the provinces, and by common interests in the exploitation of the empire. These were the people made available by the extended period of economic change, social mobility, and urbanization that followed the Arab conquests. They transformed the Arab conquest kingdom into a universal Middle Eastern empire.

To legitimize their domination the 'Abbasids patronized cultural activities that made clear the historical roots of the regime and its cosmopolitan inclusiveness. The court culture signified the superiority of the Arab-Muslim imperium by borrowing the artistic and ceremonial themes of its ancestors and incorporating them into a new ritual of state. It signified its universality by patronizing the various Middle Eastern cultures: the poetic and historical traditions of the Arabs, the adab literature of Iran, and the Hellenistic philosophy and sciences of the Mediterranean. Imperial culture justified the exercise of power as a divine necessity, stressed the hierarchy of society, the responsibility of masters, and the subordination of the masses. The new culture gave the new elite a shared language, literary expression, and personal values based on the validation of worldly power and wealth. In the ancient debate over whether it was legitimate to enjoy the goods of this world the 'Abbasid imperial culture was resoundingly positive. As in the past, out of the formation of an empire came a new civilization. Empire was a moral and cultural entity as well as a system of political exploitation.

However, the very social processes that had made it possible to construct an empire extending over all the Middle East – the new urban centers, economic growth, and the formation of cosmopolitan communities – also created an independent urban population, led by religious chiefs and organized into sectarian communities, who would oppose the imperial vision with one of their own. The family or companions of the Prophet and their descendants, reciters of the Quran, scholars of Muslim law and history, and Sufi ascetics won over groups of disciples, students, and followers and thus generated numerous Shi'i and Khariji associations, Sunni schools of law, and, later, Sufi discipleships. Most of these groups were small, even esoteric, cults. Some of them acquired a mass following. In opposition to the Caliphs all of the groups claimed to embody the tradition of the Prophet and the true teachings of Islam. The Shi'a and the Kharijis at first violently opposed the Caliphate, but by the ninth century the "twelver" Shi'a and many Kharijis had renounced world-transforming political aspirations in favor of local community affairs and pious personal lives, and lived in an atmosphere of mourning for lost hopes and messianic dreams. Instead of trying to transform the world, they withdrew to a pious existence within it. Even the Sunnis, who supported the Caliphate in principle, withdrew from public commitments and concentrated on small-scale community life and personal piety. In the urban milieu, the crucial question was: what is the proper way to live the life of this world in view of the eternity to come? Was a good Muslim a person of good deeds or of inner faith, one who fulfilled his obligations to the law or who cultivated a spiritual contact with God? Between the seventh and the tenth centuries the Muslim urban response to these questions was elaborated in Quran commentary, hadith, law, theology, and mystical discourses which incorporated into Islam the heritage of Greece and Iran as well as of Arabia and Muhammad, and recast the historical religions of the Middle East into a new high cultural monotheistic vision.

The imperial and urban versions of Islamic culture were closely related. The court accepted the religious supremacy of the Quran, the validity of hadith, and the Muslim historical tradition. Law had important political and regulatory as well as moral functions; many legists and jurists were employed by the state. Mu'tazili theology was as much a court as an urban science. Similarly, urban 'ulama' and Sufis accepted many aspects of court culture. The symbols of palace and mosque, the legitimacy of the Caliph's authority, the cultural primacy of the Arabic language, poetry and history, and aspects of philosophy, neo-Platonism, and theology were all accepted in urban circles. Still, despite the interpenetration of cultural interests, the two milieus were in conflict over basic values. The Hanbalis, in particular, defied the religious authority of the Caliphs, and opened a chasm between the state and the religious communities. As a result of the ninth-century struggles between Caliph and 'ulama' it became clear that the Islamic mission was carried by two elites, Caliphate and court, 'ulama' and Sufis, and two distinct concepts of Islam – one imperial and one urban, one political and one communal, one worldly and one pietistic. Ever after, Islamic societies have been characterized, in fact, if not in culturally recognized principle, by separate state and religious institutions.

At the end of the ninth century the Islamic elites and their cultural vision still represented only a limited population, including the state elites and the populace of the Arab-Muslim towns and converted rural districts. The translation of these elite influences and cultural paradigms into a mass Islamic society began only with the disintegration of the 'Abbasid empire in the ninth and tenth centuries. The empire disintegrated not as the result of external shocks but as the outcome of the inherent evolution of its basic institutions. The Caliphate, caught in the dilemma of representing both worldly power and religious values, compromised its political authority and was forced to depend more and more upon military force. Both army and administration broke up into independent and self-serving factions; factional competition made it impossible for the Caliphate to maintain control over the central government and the provinces. The result was the rise to power of independent warlords and the outbreak of popular rebellions. By 945 the empire was no more. The process of disintegration, moreover, destroyed the bureaucratic and landowning classes which had controlled the empire and opened the way to power for nomadic elites, slave soldiers, local warlords, and others who had no interest in collaboration with a central government.

STATES AND COMMUNITIES IN A FRAGMENTED MIDDLE EAST

With the breakdown of the 'Abbasid empire, the separation of state and religious elites and institutions became more marked. The Middle East was conquered by Turkish nomadic warriors and by slave warlords. In the post-imperial era, the 'Abbasid Caliphs kept only nominal authority, while Buwayhid, Ghaznavid, and Saljuq Sultans organized the actual political regimes. The successor states to the 'Abbasid empire were secular regimes; Muslim religious associations independently took on the task of organizing the populace.

Under the Saljuqs a standard pattern of institutions developed, in which the power of the ruler was based upon a praetorian slave guard and the manipulation of nomadic tribal levies. Court bureaucrats and 'ulama' helped maintain administrative services; in the provinces the Sultans were represented by governors, garrisons, and fiscal inspectors. Iqta's were distributed widely, decentralizing control over rural revenues. These institutions did not suffice to provide a lasting political order. Disputes among competing members of aristocratic lineages, tribal lords, and slave generals prevented the centralization of power. The iqta' system of administration, in which tax-collecting privileges were parceled out among the military elite, also contributed to the fragmentation of power. Nevertheless, the institution of the Sultanate, slave military forces, and iqta' administration formed a pattern of government which would ever after constitute the norm.

The consolidation of these institutions was accompanied by the articulation of concepts to define, rationalize, and legitimize the exercise of power. In the Muslim view the Caliphate was the institution mandated by the Prophet to uphold Muslim law, protect the security of Muslim peoples, and wage jihad. All legitimate power was delegated from the Caliph to Sultans and from Sultans to their subordinates. Sultans were expected to uphold Islamic justice and education, patronize the 'ulama', and suppress heresy. If he upheld the Shari'a, a ruler was considered legitimate no matter how he had come to power. Government was also legitimized in personal terms. All regimes were built upon the loyalties of slaves, clients, and retainers to their masters and patrons. A subordinate officer did not conceive of himself as a functionary of the state, but as an elevated servant of the ruler. Slavery was but the most forceful expression of the personal bonds that complemented concepts of delegated authority. Furthermore, the state was identified with the person of the ruler. In all the political literatures of the time – Muslim, Persian, and Greek – the ruler was portrayed as the prototype of the perfected human being. He embodied wisdom and virtue, restrained the evil inclinations of his subordinates, and inspired goodness in his subjects. Government functioned as a consequence of personal ties and was considered legitimate because it was conducive to the fulfillment of religious ideals.

Finally, government was legitimized in terms of historical descent from ancient empires and of the fulfillment of cosmic and divine purposes. Architecture, art, and poetry, in Arabic or Persian regional variants, symbolized the attachment of the political regimes to the divinely given order of the universe, the inherent glory of the ruler, the rightness of the pursuit and exercise of power, and the legitimacy of aesthetic refinement and luxury. The Sultanal regimes patronized historical writing to trace the genealogical descent and mythic connection of present rulers to ancient Persian and Turkish kings. As God's own servant the ruler was entrusted with the care of the world, and given authority over men whose fate was confided to him. The ruler ordered society, promoted the construction of civilization, and even had magical powers, which could affect the course of nature. Despite the arbitrary exercise of powers, states were an image of the cosmos. They were vital not only to daily life but to the mythic wholeness of the social order. However damaged the great empires, however many military lords became independent, however much control of the land was distributed in iqta's, however much authority was conceded to local notables and local militias, the state continued to represent a commitment to a transcending order. Thus while the Sultanates had Islamic functions and identities, their Islamic aspect was paralleled by non-Islamic Persian and Turkish concepts of the nature of government. An "Islamic" state was also an expression of a non-Islamic territorial and cultural identity.

As states became militarized and secularized, Islamic religious associations became the almost universal basis of Middle Eastern communal organization. Until the ninth century Islam was the religion of the Arab populations and assimilated urban groups, but from the tenth to the thirteenth centuries the mass of Middle Eastern peoples were converted to Islam. This was due in part to the dissolution of the 'Abbasid empire, its replacement by foreign military elites, the ruin of the landowning and administrative classes, and their replacement by Muslim religious leaders, who converted the uprooted masses and provided them with leadership and religious organization through the Sunni schools of law, Sufi brotherhoods, Shi'i sects, and other Muslim groups. The schools of law were associations of scholars, teachers, and students adhering to the law codes developed by discussion among legal scholars in the eighth and ninth centuries. Through the law schools, the 'ulama' organized higher education, and trained teachers and judicial administrators; from the schools came consultants, notaries, and judges. The schools also gathered a popular following. The students considered themselves personal disciples of their masters; the communities in which the schools were located provided patrons and supporters, especially from the merchant and artisan classes. The Sufi brotherhoods were based on the disciples of each master and upon the groups of Sufis who lived in common residences called khanaqas. Tariqats or brotherhoods were formed when Sufi masters in the twelfth and thirteenth centuries began to reckon themselves the descendants of earlier teachers. Those who descended from the same teacher regarded themselves as perpetuating a common spiritual discipline and as units of a much larger religious movement accepting the same higher authority. Such formations grew beyond their local origins and became regional and even worldwide brotherhoods.

In an urban context the schools of law and Sufi brotherhoods served as confessional collectivities which could recruit individuals across the lines of existing community structures and unify smaller-scale family, clan, or residential collectivities into larger units. But Muslim religious associations could also operate wholly within the framework of existing collective units. Schools of law, Sufi brotherhoods, or Shi'i sects were often identified with particular neighborhoods, or occupational and ethnic minorities, and gave previously existing collectivities an Islamic identity.

COPING WITH THE LIMITS OF WORLDLY LIFE

The ethos of these associations varied on a spectrum ranging from other-worldly ecstatic, contemplative forms of Sufism to very worldly family and business orientations. There was a broad middle ground – the Sunni–Shari'a–Sufi position. This was represented by the Hanafi and Shafi'i schools of law, the Ash'ari and Maturidi schools of theology, and the "sober" Sufi tradition of al-Junayd, al-Qushayri, and al-Ghazzali. It attempted to integrate commitment to the principle of the Caliphate as the basis of the ideal Muslim community, devotion to the fulfillment of the teachings of the Shariʿa, belief in the limited use of reason for understanding religious truths, and the practice of Sufi ethical and meditational exercises. It was an attempt to combine the correct external forms of social and ritual behavior with internal emotional and spiritual awareness.

Sunnis with this orientation had a nuanced attitude to worldly actualities. They accepted existing regimes as legitimate by virtue of the inherent need for order in society and they worked out routine ways of collaborating with states. Political obedience was highly emphasized. The ʿulamaʾ reserved for themselves a consultative role and the right to admonish, educate, and give moral advice to rulers, and they expected rulers to give them control over legal administration and to patronize Muslim educational and charitable activities. Within this framework, however, Sunnis were not so much involved in politics as in community affairs. Their concern was to uphold public morality, to apply the Shariʿa to family and commercial affairs, to educate, to heal, and to mediate local conflicts.

Sunni Islam accepted the given clan, lineage, tribal, or clientele substructures of Middle Eastern societies, and with them inequalities of wealth and property. They regarded social and economic justice as matters of individual behavior. Sunni values were thus neutral with regard to different economic systems; there was no Muslim teaching on the proper structure of the economy, and no obvious correlation between Islamic beliefs and any particular economic organization. Furthermore, if we compare the Sunni attitude toward economic activity with later Protestant attitudes, we find that though Muslims were highly motivated in economic matters, they did not see such activity as a vehicle for the transformation of the world or of the individual. Sunni Islam did not try to mobilize people for economic ends, but called upon them to lead a pious life in the context of economic and other worldly activities.

Acceptance of the world was modified, however, by an attitude of detachment and a rejection of commitment. While many ʿulamaʾ and Sufis accepted the responsibilities of political power, held office, accumulated land and property, and served as spokesmen for the needs of their people, there was a deep strand of feeling opposed to such engagements. The companions of princes were regarded as morally corrupted. ʿUlamaʾ and Sufis characteristically refused official positions and turned down royal gifts. Disengagement was taken as a mark of piety and of the highest moral virtue. The refusal to give moral assent to the world as it is was accompanied by a nostalgia for the restoration of the true Caliphate and a yearning for the coming of the mahdi. Nostalgia expressed withdrawal from the actual world, but it also served to ratify things as they were.

The Hanbalis cultivated a more active stance. They undertook vigilante action to enforce morality, suppress alcohol and prostitution, and attack rival sects. They rallied Muslim volunteers for holy war and on occasion attempted to restore the political power of the Caliphate. This activism, however, was channeled mainly into pressuring existing political regimes to uphold Muslim morality rather than being aimed at changing the political order. Thus all Sunnis accepted the world as it was, yet withheld their full assent by refusing to be directly involved in politics, by actively campaigning to improve public morals, and by nostalgic reflection and eschatological yearning.

The reasons for this complex orientation can be understood when we consider that Muslim religious associations were partially but never fully differentiated from other socio-political institutions. The Sunni position reflects a transcendent religious vision embedded in sectarian associations, but these associations existed within the overall political framework of the Sultanal regimes, and they were interlocked with parochial lineage, residential, and other solidarities. Therefore the tension between religious and other commitments could not be absolute and the complex relationships among them had to be expressed in subtle modes of acceptance, detachment, and rejection.

Islamic organizations and identities were also institutionalized in rural societies, though on different terms. Throughout the Middle East clans, lineages, and village communities led by independent chieftains, legitimized in terms of tribal tradition and by the acceptance of an age-old pattern of culture, continued to be the backbone of the social order. The basic lineage and factional structures were reinforced by the Arab and Turkish migrations. In these societies Muslim religious leadership and Muslim symbols were used to unite factionalized peoples into more unified religious-political movements. The Arab-Muslim conquest is the prototypical case. In addition, Berbers in North Africa were united under Kharijism, Shi'ism, Sunni reformism, and later Sufism, into conquering religious movements such as the Fatimid, the Almoravid, and the Almohad. Kharijis in eastern Arabia, Qarmatis in the fertile crescent, and later the Safavids in western Iran are other examples of Muslim religious leaders and symbols becoming the basis of rural unification in the quest for the ever-elusive just Islamic society.

There is also evidence for the beginnings of widespread acceptance of Islamic identity by rural collectivities in the form of the veneration of Sufis and worship at shrines. Before the thirteenth century the doctrinal basis for the veneration of Sufis as intercessors between man and God had been established and pre-Islamic magical practices and superstitions were accepted as part of popular Islam. Sufis were commonly believed to be saints, and were venerated as intermediaries between the material and the spiritual worlds, as miracle workers, and as dispensers of blessings. On this basis they served to mediate disputes, facilitate the selection of chiefs, organize long-distance trade, teach the young, heal the sick, provide amulets, officiate at circumcisions, marriages, and funerals, celebrate festivals, do white magic, and otherwise uphold the tenuous connection of human beings with the world of the spirits and the divine. This type of Sufism also led to the veneration of the tomb, and the disciples and descendants of the holy man, and to a religious life of sacrifices and festivals around the tombs. In such cases Islam did not necessarily lead to the formation of an organized association capable of collective action, but served as a shared identity among diverse peoples who preserved their own kinship, territorial, linguistic, ethnic, and other bases of non-Islamic culture.

STATE AND RELIGION IN THE ISLAMIC PARADIGM

The crucial feature of this system of states and religious communities was the tacit collaboration of state military, local 'ulama', and Sufi elites. The nomadic and slave military elites needed the collaboration of the 'ulama' in order to govern. The Saljuqs were leaders of tribal groups with no experience in ruling an agriculturally based empire. Scribes, finance officials, estate managers, and other technicians were vital. Furthermore, the nomadic and slave elites needed the 'ulama', for both political and psychological reasons, to recognize the rightfulness of their regimes. The 'ulama' were the guardians of tradition, and to the Saljuqs, who were lacking in technical skills and literary and social knowledge, represented the epitome of a desired way of life. They looked to the 'ulama' to be tutored, educated, and guided in acceptable courses of action. Thus the conquerors were conquered by their subjects.

In return, the 'ulama' accepted the need for a military regime. Only a military regime could protect the trade routes and the agricultural villages from bedouins and bandits. The 'ulama' favored a strong state to repress factional strife and gang warfare and to act as an arbiter of disputes which the communities themselves could not regulate. Moreover, they were interested in an accommodation with military regimes because they could, by serving in the state administration, transform themselves from local elites into an imperial governing class. The state accorded them positions that could consolidate their local power. Finally, military elites could give valuable support to the Sunni social and educational mission.

To work out this tacit bargain the Ghaznavids and the Saljuqs restored mosques, built madrasas and khanaqas, endowed waqfs, and appointed members of the law schools to official positions. The Saljuqs suppressed Shi'ism and gave vigorous support to Sunni Islam. In return, the 'ulama' preached the legitimacy of established regimes, supported favored princes against their rivals, supplied cadres for the state administration, facilitated taxation, and accepted the nomadic and slave conquest states as part of the legitimate and necessary order of Islamic society. While the religious notables could mediate between military regimes and city populations, they lacked the ideological and economic bases to be fully independent. Thus, their inevitable collaboration with the state elites brought the rest of society under control.

In the post-imperial period, new forms of state organization, community life, and culture were integrated into a new order. The post-imperial system of government and society was profoundly different from that of the earlier era. The earlier 'Abbasid era had been characterized by a universal empire built upon the support of Middle Eastern landowning, bureaucratic, and merchant elites who forged a common religious and cultural identity. In the post-imperial period, the unity of the Middle East was no longer to be found in empire, but in the almost universal diffusion of certain forms of social and political organization and of allegiance to common values and symbols. For the first time in Middle Eastern history, the peoples of Iran and Iraq belonged, if not to the same empire, then at least to the same culture, religion, and type of political society. Islam had become a universal society without a universal empire.

The construction of this post-imperial Islamic society in Iran and Iraq marked the culmination of the formative period. In successive phases the historical societies of the Middle East had acquired an Islamic identity. An Islamic–tribal form of society had been created in Arabia under charismatic–prophetic leadership; conquest and urbanization gave rise to a universal empire and to the Caliphs, 'ulama', and Sufis who would be the bearers of Islamic high civilization. The disintegration of the empire allowed for a reconstruction of Middle Eastern societies into the Saljuq complex of state and socio-religious institutions and attendant Islamic identities.

This Middle Eastern Islamic society held a crucial place in the development of all later Islamic societies. It bequeathed a repertoire of cultural and religious ideas which remain operative in Islamic lands to the present day. From this era came the forms of Islamic orthopraxis contained in hadith and law, Sufi forms of ethical and spiritual self-cultivation, Shi'i concepts of religious leadership, ideals of mystical and gnostic transcendence, popular saint worship and magical practices, and a socially active and reformist Islamic ideal. This period also gave rise to the basic elements of Islamic social organization: states, schools of law, and Sufi tariqat. Finally, this era set the precedent for a separation between state institutions and Muslim religious communities. All the while, the persistence of non-Islamic modes of social and economic organization, and non-Islamic cultures, generated an endlessly rich variety of social and communal possibilities, and an abiding ambiguity as to what constituted an Islamic society. Wherever Islam was established, these institutions and cultural concepts would be combined and recombined and merged with local traditions to form new types of Islamic societies. Each of them would bear profoundly the imprint of the Middle Eastern origins of Islam.

THE WORLDWIDE DIFFUSION OF ISLAMIC SOCIETIES FROM THE TENTH TO THE NINETEENTH CENTURIES

9   The battle of the twelve heroes

INTRODUCTION: THE ISLAMIC WORLD AND THE RISE OF EUROPE

Between the seventh and the thirteenth centuries the historical institutions of Middle Eastern societies were recast in Islamic forms. New empires and states were organized under Islamic concepts of authority and symbols of legitimacy. Muslim religious elites including 'ulama' and Sufi holy men generated Islamic forms of worship, education, and legal administration. The majority of Middle Eastern peoples were converted to Islam; pastoral tribes, peasants, urban artisans and merchants, and state elites took on an Islamic identity. A new civilization, in part royal and artistic, in part urban and pietistic, came into being.

In subsequent eras, the Islamic system of institutions and its various cultures would continue to evolve in the already Islamized regions of the Middle East including Iran, Transoxania, and the Arab provinces. They would also serve as a paradigm for the establishment of Islamic societies in other parts of the world. From the seventh to the nineteenth centuries Islamic societies, based on the interaction of local institutions and cultures and Middle Eastern influences, were established in Anatolia and the Balkans, Inner Asia, South and Southeast Asia, and sub-Saharan Africa. The evolution of a world system of Islamic societies, however, was cut short in the eighteenth and nineteenth centuries by the growing political and economic power of Europe. The consolidation of European colonial rule in most of the Muslim world marks the end of the premodern era and the beginning of the modern transformation of Muslim societies.

CONVERSION TO ISLAM

The Middle East and North Africa

From the seventh to the tenth centuries, Islam was carried by the Arab conquests to North Africa, Spain, Sicily, and the Mediterranean coasts of Europe. Arab warriors and merchants brought it to Saharan and Sudanic Africa. Other Islamic societies were born from the conversion of Inner Asian Turkish peoples to Islam and their migrations, conquests, and empire building. From the tenth to the fourteenth centuries, Turkish peoples brought Islam westward into Anatolia, the Balkans, and southeastern Europe, eastward into Inner Asia and China, and southward into Afghanistan and the Indian subcontinent. They thus played a crucial historical role in the diffusion of Islam and in the founding of the Saljuq, Mongol, Timurid, Safavid, Ottoman, Uzbek, and Mughal empires. Finally, another cluster of Islamic societies originated from the expansion of Muslim merchants in the Indian Ocean. From Arabia Islam reached India and East Africa (tenth to twelfth centuries); from Arabia and India it reached the Malay peninsula and the Indonesian archipelago (thirteenth to fifteenth centuries); from the coastal zones it spread to the interior of the islands and continents.

The expansion of Islam involved different forces. In North Africa, Anatolia, the Balkans, and India, it was carried by nomadic Arab or Turkish conquerors. In the Indian Ocean and West Africa it spread by peaceful contacts among merchants or through the preaching of missionaries. In some cases the diffusion of Islam depended upon its adoption by local ruling families; in others, it appealed to urban classes of the population or tribal communities. Its appeal was couched in interwoven terms of political and economic benefits and of a sophisticated culture and religion.

The question of why people convert to Islam has always generated intense feeling. Earlier generations of European scholars believed that conversions to Islam were made at the point of the sword, and that conquered peoples were given the choice of conversion or death. It is now apparent that conversion by force, while not unknown in Muslim countries, was, in fact, rare. Muslim conquerors ordinarily wished to dominate rather than convert, and most conversions to Islam were voluntary.

Even voluntary conversions are suspect to European observers. Were they made out of true belief, or for opportunistic political or social reasons? Surely there are innumerable cases of conversion to Islam by the illumination of faith or by virtue of the perceived sanctity of Muslim scholars and holy men, as well as by calculation of political and economic advantage. In most cases worldly and spiritual motives for conversion blended together. Moreover, conversion to Islam did not necessarily imply a complete turning from an old to a totally new life. While it entailed the acceptance of new religious beliefs and membership in a new religious community, most converts retained a deep attachment to the cultures and communities from which they came. In the sections that follow, I will stress the historical circumstances that have induced large numbers of people to adhere to Islam rather than analyze the spiritual or material motives of individuals for becoming Muslims. This is not to diminish the centrality of belief and commitment in the subjective experience of individual converts, but to account on a historical basis for the responses of great numbers of human beings.

The first conversions to Islam occurred in the Middle East between the seventh and the thirteenth centuries. These took place in two phases, the first being the

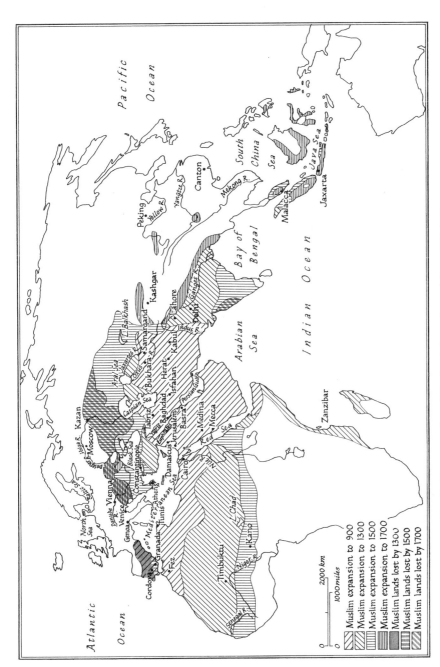

Map 7 The expansion of Muslim states and populations: 900–1700

Muslim expansion to 900
Muslim expansion to 1300
Muslim expansion to 1500
Muslim expansion to 1700
Muslim lands lost by 1300
Muslim lands lost by 1500
Muslim lands lost by 1700

2000 km
1000 miles

conversion of animists and polytheists belonging to the tribal societies of the Arabian desert and the periphery of the fertile crescent; the second was the conversion of the monotheistic populations of the Middle Eastern agrarian, urbanized, and imperial societies.

The conversion of Arabian populations was part of the process of transmitting the civilization of the sedentarized imperial societies to the nomadic periphery. Arabian peoples, standing on the margin of the agricultural and commercial zones of the Middle East, strongly influenced by Middle Eastern commerce and religious thought, found in Muhammad's teaching a way to formulate a kind of Middle Eastern monotheistic religion parallel to but distinct from the established Christian and Zoroastrian religions. The conversion of pagan Arabian peoples to Islam represented the response of a tribal, pastoral population to the need for a larger framework for political and economic integration, a more stable state, and a more imaginative and encompassing moral vision to cope with the problems of a tumultuous society. Conversion, then, was the process of integrating Arabians into a new cultural and political order defined in monotheistic religious terms.

The conversion of sedentary Middle Eastern peoples to Islam was a different process. In this case Islam was substituted for Byzantine or Sasanian political identity and for Jewish, Christian, or Zoroastrian religious affiliation. The transformation of identities among Middle Eastern peoples took place in two stages. In the first century of the Islamic imperium the Arab conquerors attempted to maintain themselves as an exclusive Muslim elite. They did not require the conversion as much as the subordination of non-Muslim peoples. At the outset, they were hostile to conversions because new Muslims diluted the economic and status advantages of the Arabs. Nonetheless, Muslim rule offered substantial incentives for conversion. It formed a protective umbrella over Muslim communities and conferred the prestige of the state on Muslim religious life. Political patronage allowed for the establishment of mosques, the organization of the pilgrimage, and the creation of Muslim judicial institutions. The establishment of an Arab empire made Islam attractive to elements of the former Byzantine and Sasanian aristocracies, including soldiers, officials, landlords, and others. Arab garrison cities attracted non-Arab migrants who found careers in the army and administration open to converts. Merchants, artisans, workers, and fugitive peasants seeking the patronage of the new elite were also tempted to accept Islam.

Despite these attractions, the mass of Middle Eastern peoples were not soon or easily converted. Only with the breakdown of the social and religious structures of non-Muslim communities in the tenth to the twelfth centuries did the weakening of churches, the awakening of Muslim hostility to non-Muslims, sporadic and localized persecution, and the destruction of the landed gentry of Iraq and Iran destroy the communal organization of non-Muslim peoples. Muslim teachers were then able to take the lead in the reconstruction of local communities on the basis of Islamic beliefs and identities. Large parts of Egypt and Iran were probably converted in the tenth and eleventh centuries. In northern Syria, however, Christian majorities survived through the twelfth century, until – compromised by their sympathies with and assistance to the Crusaders – they were put under severe pressure. Most converted in the thirteenth and fourteenth centuries, but substantial Christian minorities remained. Similarly, most of the remaining Christian population of Egypt adopted Islam in the fourteenth century. To adherents of the monotheistic and communalist faiths, Islam offered the same variety of intellectual, legal, theological, and mystical appeals. While Islam had a specific religious orientation toward the inscrutable and untrammeled will of Allah and the necessity for submission of spirit and actions to the will of God, its basic religious positions were fundamentally similar to those of the other monotheistic religions.

The conversion of North Africa also began with the Arab conquests, but was a different process because it primarily involved the adoption of Islam, notably in sectarian form, by the chiefs of Berber societies as the basis of tribal coalitions and state formation. Khariji states in Algeria and Morocco adopted Islam to help regulate tribal relations and long-distance trade. The process of Islamization of the masses of Christians and Jews is not known, but it may be related to the spread of ribats (forts manned by warriors for the faith), trade, and Sufis. In any case it seems to have been rapid compared with conversion in the Middle East.

Turkish conquests and conversions in Anatolia, the Balkans, the Middle East, Inner Asia, and India

The diffusion of Islam to regions beyond the Middle East involved analogous processes. The spread of Islam in Inner Asia, Anatolia, the Balkans, and India was closely tied to the conversion of pastoral Turkish, rather than Arab, peoples. The conversion of Turkish Inner Asian peoples began in the tenth century. Inner Asian peoples came into contact with Muslims through caravan trade and contacts with merchants who operated on the steppes as brokers between nomadic and settled populations. Muslim missionaries and Sufis also moved out to proselytize among the Turks. Political ambition prompted the Qarakhanid and Saljuq elites to take up the new religion. Later Inner Asian regimes, including the Mongols of the Golden Horde and the Chaghatay Khanates, also adopted Islam and brought it to the northern steppes and eastern Turkestan. In Inner Asia Islamization was important for the establishment of nomadic regimes over sedentary populations, for the creation of politically cohesive ethnic identities among Tatars, Uzbeks, Kazakhs, and other peoples, and for the organization of long-distance trade.

The spread of Islam into Anatolia and the Balkans paralleled the historical process of the spread of Islam in the Middle East. The Saljuq and Ottoman conquests of the eleventh to the fourteenth centuries led to Muslim regimes that patronized the Sunni law schools, Islamic judicial administration, the construction of schools and colleges, and other religious and communal facilities. They gave protection to 'ulama' and Sufis who founded centers for teaching and social services in the conquered territories.

The migration of a substantial Turkish population under the leadership of Muslim holy men uprooted Anatolian agricultural communities and replaced them with Turkish Muslim peoples. Nomadic conquests and the hostility of the Saljuq government to the Byzantine empire and the Greek Orthodox Church also led in Anatolia to the progressive reduction of church lands, administrative capacities, and authority. The weakening of the church deprived the Christian population of leadership and organization. In Anatolia, as in Inner Asia, India, and Africa, jihad-minded Sufi warriors and activist missionaries helped to establish Islam among a newly conquered peasant population. The assimilation of Anatolian peoples was facilitated on the cultural as well as the social level by the familiarity of Islamic religious concepts, which were easily adapted to the religious beliefs of the Christians. In Anatolia, as in the rest of the Middle East, the conjunction of Muslim state power, the decline of organized Christian societies, and the social and cultural relevance of Islam facilitated mass conversions to the new religion.

In the Balkans the factors favoring Islamization and conversion of local peoples were similar to those in Anatolia: the establishment of a regime that favored Islam and the migration and settlement of a substantial Turkish population. Islamization under these pressures was especially pronounced in the towns. In the Balkans, however, the spread of Islam was limited by the vitality of the Christian churches. It came at a later stage of Turkish conquests, at a time when Ottoman policy favored Christian nobles and churches as vehicles of Ottoman administration and so maintained – and, indeed, reinforced – the social structure of Balkan communities. Most Balkan peoples, buttressed by the continuity of organized Christian community life, remained loyal to their faith.

The history of Islam in India most closely resembles that of the Balkans. Islam was brought into India by a conquering Afghan and Turkish military elite which established the Delhi Sultanate in the thirteenth century. Conversions were made as a result of the political attraction of the dominant regime to both non-Muslim elites and dependent peasants and workers. Also, as in the Middle East, the construction of new cities favored the conversion of mobile peoples attracted to the centers of Muslim administration and trade. In most of India, however, as in the Balkans, the appeal of Islam was relatively restricted. Only in the Northwest Frontier, the Punjab, Sind, and Bengal were the populations converted en masse. In these regions the transition from hunter-gatherer and pastoral activities to settled agriculture was the occasion for a total reconstruction of society under Muslim leadership and for the development of new Islamic identifications. Conversion to Islam on a mass scale was most likely among disorganized populations.

In general, however, the assimilative capacity of Islam in the subcontinent was limited by the relative thinness of the Muslim elite. While Muslim rule in India attracted numerous warriors, administrators, and religious teachers, the Muslim conquest was not accompanied by massive migrations as in the cases of the Arab conquest of the Middle East or the Turkish conquest of Anatolia. Furthermore, the social structure of conquered peoples remained intact. Hindu Rajputs, for example, maintained their authority under Muslim suzerainty; nor were Brahmanic Hinduism and the caste system challenged by Muslim rule. Indeed, Hindu philosophy and popular religions were invigorated by Muslim competition. In the face of an ordered social and religious structure, conversions to Islam were inhibited.

When conversions did occur, Sufism played a considerable part. Following the scent of battle, Sufis streamed into India from Afghanistan, Iran, and Inner Asia. Many came as warriors to establish Muslim supremacy and convert the infidels. Some tied their fortunes to the state. Others fanned out in North India, establishing their influence by personal merit. Here too, the adaptability of Sufism to traditional religious cultures was important in the transition from Hindu and Buddhist identities to Islam. In India the boundary between Hindu and Muslim beliefs, ritual practices, and social loyalties was thin. As in the Middle East and the Ottoman empire, Islam was established under the auspices both of a political elite and of independent religious teachers.

Conversions in Southeast Asia and sub-Saharan Africa

The conversion of Malaya, Indonesia, and sub-Saharan Africa to Islam followed a different pattern. In these regions, Islam was not established by conquest, by the imposition of a single centralized state, or by the settlement of a substantial foreign Muslim population; nor was it associated with massive social change. It was, rather, due to the diffusion of Muslim merchants and missionaries who founded small communities, and sometimes induced (or forced) local elites interested in state formation, trade, and political legitimization to accept their religion. Islam spread as the result of commercial contacts, political and commercial rivalries, and by the progressive acceptance of new symbols of identity by ongoing societies.

Islam was first introduced into Indonesia at the end of the thirteenth century by merchants and Sufis from India, Arabia, and perhaps China. It appealed to the rulers of small coastal and riverine principalities who had close trading contacts with the Muslims and intense rivalries with Indonesian and Chinese traders. Acceptance of Islam by local merchant princes won them social and administrative support and an entrée into extensive trading networks. Portuguese and later Dutch intervention in the Indies further stimulated the acceptance of Islam. The struggle against the Portuguese and the Dutch made Islam desirable as a bond of solidarity in resistance to the efforts of Christian powers to establish trading monopolies. Local competition facilitated the further spread of Islam. The struggle of the coastal principalities with the interior states of Java led eventually to the establishment of Islam as the official religion of the whole of Java. As a result Indonesian state and elite culture was shaped, not by an aristocracy coming from the Middle East, but by a local elite which preserved its political and cultural continuity, and adopted Islam as an additional expression – or reinforcement – of its earlier legitimacy. Throughout Indonesia and Malaya, Islam was also integrated into popular culture.

Sufi missionaries and village teachers settled widely and made Islam part of folk culture and folk identity. In Southeast Asia, as opposed to India and the Balkans where it reached only a minority, Islam became the religion of great majorities of the population.

In most of Africa, Islam was established by processes more closely resembling those of Southeast Asia than the Middle East and India. Muslim merchants and missionary colonies, rather than conquest and empire, were central to Islamization. Arab and Berber traders and settlers in the Saharan and Sudanic regions, Arab and Persian settlers on the East African coasts, and Dyula communities in West Africa were the nuclei of Muslim influences. In Sudanic Africa, colonies of Muslim traders became allied with local political elites and induced the rulers of the states of Ghana, Mali, Kanem, Songhay, Hausaland, and Dogomba to accept Islam. It is possible that Muslims themselves seized kingships and created small states. Islam was adopted to consolidate political power, reinforce commercial contacts, recruit skilled personnel, and mobilize spiritual and magical powers in the interests of state elites. As in North Africa, acceptance of Islam provided an additional basis for legitimization of state regimes, coalition formation among disparate peoples, organization of trading networks, and the employment of skilled personnel. Under the auspices of Muslim states, a small scholarly elite of qadis, 'ulama', and imams was established, but no evidence for conversion of the lower classes is available. Islam was primarily the religion of the political and commercial elites.

In other parts of West Africa, the Islamic presence was established by Dyula traders, landowners, missionaries, and teachers scattered throughout the region, who created an Islamic presence without necessarily generating Islamic states and without attendant Islamization of the population. These family communities seem to have fitted into a highly stratified and subdivided society, whose internal divisions made it acceptable to have unassimilated communities, but were a barrier to the further diffusion of Islam.

Whereas in West Africa, Arab merchants inspired warrior elites to convert to Islam, in East Africa, Arab traders themselves took over the leadership of small states. In Somalia and Ethiopia, Arab merchants married into local lineages and assumed leadership of tribal coalitions which then adopted an Arab and Islamic identity. In the East African city-states, Arab settlers intermarried with local peoples and became the elites of the coastal Swahili society based on a new language and cultural style which symbolized the merger of populations. Muslim communities were consolidated by the integration of peoples and the formation of new cultural idioms. As the religion of the state and trading classes, Islam in Africa appeared in highly syncretic forms. Since African elites were not conquered and replaced, but converted and maintained in power, they brought with them a strong component of traditional, non-Islamic African practices.

In some cases, the formation of African-Muslim states was followed by the conversion of the masses. In Somalia, Mauritania, and other Saharan regions, the large numbers of Arab migrants, the close identification of pastoral peoples with Arab nomads, and the utility of holy leadership for the regulation of relations among tribal communities help to explain why Islam was so widely accepted. In the Funj and Darfur Sultanates, state elites adopted Islam as a result of trading contacts, and opened the way for a large influx of Sufi missionaries. Muslim holy men, supported by state grants of land, converted the common people to Islam. In the Sudan, the spread of Arabic and contacts with Egypt and the Middle East helped establish Islam among the common people.

By the eighteenth and nineteenth centuries, throughout West Africa, the spread of Muslim trading communities linked by lineage, trade, teaching, and Sufi affiliations had reached a critical mass which enabled Muslims to fight larger-scale political regimes. Motivated by a tradition of hostility to rulers among both trading and pastoral peoples, African-Muslim communities attempted to seize political power and to Islamize both state regimes and the masses of the African population. In Sudanic, savannah, and forest West Africa, the jihads were the equivalent of Islamic conquests in other parts of the world, and led indeed to the Islamization of northern Nigeria, Senegambia, and parts of the upper Guinea coast. However, even when colonial conquest put an end to Muslim jihads, Islam, without state support, served to express anti-colonialism and to unite uprooted peoples into new communal structures. In Africa the process of conversion was tied to a double mechanism of peaceful expansion of traders, settlers, and teachers, and to militant conquest. As in other parts of the world, the two could work either separately or in tandem.

If there is an underlying common factor in the worldwide diffusion of Islam it seems to be its capacity to generate religious fellowship, larger-order communities, and states among peoples otherwise living in highly factionalized or fragmented societies. Islam became the religion of tribal peoples and merchant groups seeking economic integration, and state elites seeking consolidated political power. In general, it seems to have been most effective when it gave a new social identity to peoples severed from traditional social structures.

Throughout the old world the diffusion of Islam led to the formation of new communities and states or to the redefinition of existing communities and empires in Islamic terms. In many parts of Africa and Inner Asia the introduction of Islam was the basis for conversions from animistic to monotheistic religions and for the construction of states in hitherto stateless societies. In most places, however, the advent of Islam inspired the reconstruction of societies that already had "higher" religions and state institutions.

In all these cases, the Middle Eastern experience served as a paradigm for the formation of the new societies. The Middle Eastern Islamic societies were built around three different types of collectivities: parochial groups, religious associations, and states. Parochial groups were based upon family, clan, lineage, tribal, clientele, and neighborhood ties. At the level of religious associations 'ulama' and Sufi elites were organized around schools of law, Sufi fraternities, and shrines. States were characterized by such institutions as nomadic or ethnic elite armies, slave or mercenary military forces, a combination of bureaucratic and quasi-feudal forms of administration, and a Muslim terminology for taxation. These components of the Middle Eastern societies involved a combination of Islamic and non-Islamic institutions and concepts. While religious associations and certain aspects of states were specifically Islamic, state bureaucratic, administrative, and feudal-like systems of taxation were not. Furthermore, the prevailing concepts of legitimacy were formulated in patrimonial, ethnic, historical, or cosmopolitan cultural terms as well as in Muslim symbols. Similarly, the social systems and cultural expressions of parochial communities owed little to Islam. Thus our template for "Islamic societies" by definition includes non-Islamic institutions and cultures.

In the diffusion of Islamic institutions and identities, Middle Eastern precedents were sometimes transmitted as a whole system, sometimes in parts, depending upon who were the bearers of Islam and what were the conditions of its diffusion and reception in different societies. For example, conquest by nomadic peoples as opposed to contact among small groups of merchants made a significant difference in the way in which Middle Eastern Islamic influences were transmitted and received. In all instances, however, the diffusion of Islam released tremendous artistic and cultural forces as each new Islamic state and society attempted to work out its own synthesis of Middle Eastern Islamic institutions and local traditions. The history of Islamic societies illustrates the originality of Muslim regimes the world over and yet reveals them to be variations upon an underlying pattern shaped by indigenous conditions in each part of the Muslim world.

MUSLIM ELITES AND ISLAMIC COMMUNITIES

In every Islamic society 'ulama' and Sufis were the teachers, exemplars, and leaders of Muslim communities. The 'ulama' were the scholars knowledgeable about Muslim hadith, law, and theology. Their primary function was instruction and judicial administration. In West Africa we find 'ulama' under the local names of *mallam* or *karamoko* teaching in villages and town quarters. In Indonesia they were the teachers in *pesantren*, sometimes called *kiyayi*. In Iran, Inner Asia, and the Ottoman empire they were the *mullahs*, who taught in Quran schools and higher-level madrasas. Despite important distinctions of knowledge, lineage, and wealth between higher- and lower-ranking 'ulama', there were rarely formal distinctions among them. Only in Bukhara and West Africa were 'ulama' graded by rank.

'Ulama' were commonly organized into schools of law, which were associations of scholars, teachers, and students adhering to the codes of law developed by discussion and debate among legal scholars in the eighth and ninth centuries. The principal Sunni schools were the Hanafi, Shafi'i, Maliki, and Hanbali, though the Shi'i 'ulama' of Iran were organized in an analogous fashion. Through the law schools, the scholars organized higher education and trained teachers and judicial administrators. From the law schools came *muftis*, or legal consultants, notaries, and judges.

These activities generated a popular or mass following for the scholars and their schools. The students usually considered themselves the personal disciples and loyal clients of their masters. In Africa and Indonesia they worked in their masters' employ to pay their tuition. They commonly married into their masters' families. As an organized following they could have a considerable local political importance. The students of Istanbul and Bukhara were ready to take to the streets to defend their collective interests. Patrons and supporters came from the merchant and artisan classes. In eastern Iran and Transoxania, under Mongol and Timurid suzerainty, and in West African Dyula settlements, the 'ulama' were political leaders as well.

The religious authority of the 'ulama', their expertise in law, and their social leadership made it important for states to control them. The Ottoman, the Safavid, and the Mughal empires, and the states of Tunisia and Bukhara provide, in differing degrees, examples of the bureaucratic organization of 'ulama'. In other North and Sudanic African states the 'ulama' were not bureaucratically organized but were still courtiers and clients of the political elites. By contrast, Hanbalis in Egypt and Syria, Malikis in North and West Africa, and Naqshbandis in India not only maintained their autonomy, but were the active opponents of state elites in the name of Islamic principles.

The 'ulama' performed different political roles, depending upon their class level and the type of political system in which they were embedded. Higher-ranking 'ulama' were commonly state functionaries, while lower-level teachers were often spiritual counselors for the common people. In the Ottoman empire, 'ulama' bureaucrats belonged to the state elites, and lower-ranking students and teachers to the opposition. In Iran, the Shi'i 'ulama' evolved from a position of subordination to the state to autonomy and leadership of the common people.

The most striking socio-religious development of post-thirteenth-century Islamic societies was the emergence of Sufism in innumerable variations as the principal expression of Islamic beliefs and communal identities. Personified in scholar-mystics, ardent reformers, ecstatic preachers, and miracle-working holy men, Sufism became the almost universal sign of the Muslim presence. It is difficult to characterize Sufism briefly, since the word was used to apply to extremely varied religious and social practices. In general, Sufism is Muslim mysticism, or the spiritual quest that leads to direct experience of the reality of God's being. With variations, the term covers two basic constellations of religious ideas. One kind of Sufism is a religious and ethical discipline built upon adherence to the teachings of the Quran, the hadith, and the law, supplemented by spiritual practices designed to cultivate an outward conformity to Muslim norms and an inner insight into the ultimate spiritual realities. Muslim holy men of this type cultivate religious knowledge, ethical discipline, and spiritual insight, and are commonly integrated with the 'ulama'. The ordinary Sufi of this type is at once a scholar and a spiritual master.

A second kind of Sufism emphasizes faith in Sufi saints, and seems to arise out of preexisting belief in the world of spirits and the magical powers of holy men. To many ordinary Muslims, a Sufi is a person who has attained a quality of inner consciousness that makes him close to God. The saint is directly connected to the cosmos because he participates in the essential forces of rational or spiritual power. The Sufi is considered by his followers to be a spiritual teacher, a miracle worker, a dispenser of blessings, and a mediator between men and God. This type of Sufism led to veneration of the person of the holy man, and the heirs of his *baraka* (power of blessing), in the form of his tomb or shrine, or his disciples and descendants. It led to a religious life of offerings, sacrifices, and communal festivals around the shrines of saints. Shrine-Sufism, then, is a religion of magical acquisition of divine powers rather than of ethical or emotional self-cultivation. Though both types of Sufism are called Islam, they represent profoundly contrasting concepts of the religious life.

In either case, the social organization of Sufism followed from the authority of the Sufi masters. The ultimate social unit was the individual Sufi surrounded by his disciples. The individual holy man and his disciples could also win lay followers among the people of his village, quarter, or camp. Such small communities might in turn be linked together in lineages or brotherhoods, sharing a common religious identity.

Holy lineages derived from a concept of Sufi authority built on a combination of knowledge of the Quran, mystical achievements, and inherited powers transmitted by spiritual and/or genealogical descent from an earlier saint or from the Prophet himself. In many respects this concept is parallel to that of the Shi'i imams. Just as the silsila, or chain of religious transmission, went back to the companions of the Prophet, the genealogies of Sufis were commonly traced back to the Caliphs and the Prophet. Such was the case for the *mirs*, *khwajas*, and *sayyids* of Transoxania and the *sharifs* of Morocco. The fusion of spiritual and genealogical descent was easy to make, for the Sufi was indeed a child of the Prophet; one who imitated his ways, recreated his life, and concentrated within himself the noble qualities, or the sura – the image of the Prophet. Given the widespread Muslim veneration for the holiness of ancestors, it was natural to identify present holiness with descent from superior beings.

In turn, the personal authority of the master was transmitted by silsilas, baraka, and genealogical descent to his descendants, to his disciples, and to his tomb. The descendants of a famous saint constituted a holy community based on inheritance of his spiritual qualities and lineage ties. Descent from the Prophet became particularly important in many regions in the fourteenth century and later. Certain lineages in Egypt, the khwajas of Bukhara and Kashgar, the sharifs of Morocco, Jakhanke lineages in West Africa, *evliadi* groups among Turkmens, and Berber *zawaya* lineages in Mauritania were identified as holy communities, every male member of which was a descendant of a saint and heir to his spiritual qualities.

More common was the organization of a tariqa, or Sufi brotherhood. A tariqa was formed when several Sufi masters considered themselves the disciples of an earlier common teacher, perpetuating a common spiritual discipline. Although the tariqa cells were independent of each other, they recognized the same higher authority, and became units of a larger-order association. Some of these associations were regional in scale. In India the introduction of the tariqa was the basis of a region-wide Islamic society. In West Africa the consolidation of such brotherhoods in the eighteenth and nineteenth centuries was in part the basis of the effort to create Muslim states. Some of these brotherhoods, such as the Naqshbandi, the Qadiri, and others, became worldwide.

Veneration of shrines also led to special forms of communal or political organization. As the tombs of saints became centers for worship, administered by their descendants, the tomb complexes became the focus of communities composed of all the people who believed that the saints could perform miracles. Shrines were endowed with agricultural estates to provide funds for their upkeep and for charitable activities. In such cases a Sufi order included not only the descendants of the saint and the active disciples, but all of the people who believed in the saint and worshiped at his tomb. This fellowship of believers, however, remained highly diffuse, segmented, and barely capable of organized group activity. Still, from the thirteenth to the end of the eighteenth centuries, the veneration of shrines and holy places became the most widespread form of Islamic religious life. The Sufis and shrines provided ritual and spiritual counsel, medical cures, and mediation among different groups and strata of the population. Sufis helped to integrate corporate bodies such as guilds and to form political organizations among diverse lineage groups.

Sufism embodied a great variety of religious and social practices. The individual Sufi may have subscribed to any of a wide variety of religious or theosophical beliefs, may have come from any walk of life, may have had multiple affiliations (including simultaneous membership in different schools of law and Sufi brotherhoods), and may have coupled his mystical insights and practices with any of a number of worldly vocations, combining the roles of Sufi and scholar, merchant, artisan, or political chieftain. Similarly, the disciples and followers, while united by their adherence to the master and to the religious practices of their order, represented every conceivable social milieu. Given all this variation, Sufism cannot generally be defined, but may only be described case by case. The underlying common factor is the exercise of religious insight, discipline, or authority in worldly affairs and a reputation for sanctity.

By the nineteenth century, Islamic societies the world over had acquired similar types of Muslim elites, beliefs, religious practices, and social organizations. In each Muslim region we find not one but several variant types of Islam. There were the 'ulama', who represented formal scholastic learning, organized education, and judicial administration, affiliated through schools of law. There were also the 'ulama'-cum-Sufis, who combined legal learning with mystical discipline and contemplation, in an effort to live their lives in imitation of the Prophet. Such religious teachers perpetuated a tradition of learning which combined law, theology, and

Table 9. *The social organization of Sufism*

The Sufi master	
shaykh	teacher
murshid, pir, ishan	guide
wali	friend of God, saint
arif	gnostic
khalifa	deputy, head of branch of Sufi order with authority to initiate new members
Sufi lineages	
ashraf, shurafa , zawaya, insilimen, evliad	descendants of the Prophet, of companions of the Prophet and of saints
Sufi brotherhoods	
murshid – khalifa – murid	hierarchy of members
silsila	chain of transmission of blessing from the Prophet to a present master
khirqa	the patched cloak of the master transmitted to the disciple as a sign of initiation
khanaqa, zawiya, tekke, dargah	residences and facilities of an order
waqf	endowed financial support
Tombs and shrines	
baraka	blessing, God's power communicated through the saints
karamat	miracles of saints
ziyara	visit to venerate a saint's tomb and seek his intercession before God
urs	celebration of the anniversary of the death of a saint, his marriage to God

Sufi wisdom representing Sunni–Shari'a–Sufi Islam. There were ecstatic visionary Sufis in the tradition of Ibn al-'Arabi and the gnostic forms of Islamic mysticism, as well as the popular forms of Sufi Islam expressed in veneration of saints, faith in their charismatic powers, and belief in the magic of their shrines. Throughout the Muslim world, Sufism in all its forms became the most widespread and popular form of Islam.

The seventeenth and eighteenth centuries witnessed the rise of a reformist (*tajdid*) movement opposed to the rigidities of the schools of law and the cultic aspects of shrine-Sufism – a reaction to the consolidation of the various types of 'ulama' and forms of Sufi Islam. In principle, the reformist mentality goes back to the early Hanbali movement which emphasized commitment to the hadith of the Prophet, rather than law or cultic worship, and to social activism to improve the quality of Muslim political and communal life. By the seventeenth century this position had new adherents outside Hanbali circles. Muslim scholars in the Ottoman empire and North Africa were again emphasizing the primacy of hadith. The Naqshbandi and Khalwati orders combined hadith and law with Sufi asceticism and meditation in opposition to shrine worship and festivals. Social reformers were active in India. The reformers stressed a combination of hadith and Sufism because their religious goal was not union with God but identification with the spirit and active life of the Prophet.

The various proto-reformist tendencies came together in seventeenth- and eighteenth-century Mecca and Medina, where scholars representing the new trends in Morocco, Iraq, India, and elsewhere combined hadith scholarship with neo-Sufi social action. They worked on the earliest possible texts of hadith rather than the later standard collections, and sought to eliminate religious practices that were not found in the Quran and in the teachings of the Prophet. They celebrated al-Ghazzali as the premier teacher of Sufism, and set the foundation for religious orders that would propagate the new devotional seriousness. The reformist position spread rapidly via informal contacts. Naqshbandi teachers brought the order from Yemen to Egypt, and from India to Syria. In Cairo al-Azhar emerged as an important center of the new tendency, communicating hadith scholarship and the teachings of al-Ghazzali while repudiating the tradition of Ibn al-'Arabi, and visiting North African scholars taught their doctrine of imitation of and union with the spirit of the Prophet rather than pantheistic union with God.

The first political expression of the reformist tendency was the Wahhabi movement in Arabia. The religious goal of Wahhabi teaching was the purification of the heart from vices and sin, and acknowledgment of the unity and transcendence of God. The Wahhabis rejected Sufism, the veneration of any human being, and any authority except the Prophet himself. Wahhabism thus set an example of militant moral and social reform.

In India, which was in continuous interaction with Arabia through the travels of merchants, the movements of scholars, and the journeys of pilgrims, reform movements took root in Delhi, the Northwest Frontier, and Bengal. Reformism inspired the Padri movement in Minangkabau in Sumatra. It would also become extremely important in Africa, where it inspired the Sanusiya, the Tijaniya, the jihad of al-Hajj 'Umar, and Sufi tariqat in the Sudan. The political breakdown of Muslim countries and the rise of European imperialism would give reformed Sufism a new role in the mobilization of Muslim peoples for defense against European domination.

THE SOCIAL STRUCTURE OF ISLAM

The various types of Muslim elites, beliefs, and associations gave Muslim societies a complex structure. On one level, Islam may be considered an international religion in which all Muslims were linked by a shared tradition of learning and belief, by travel and pilgrimage to common centers of learning and worship, and by membership in international schools of law and religious brotherhoods. For example, Istanbul was the religious capital, not only of the Ottoman empire and of many of the Arab provinces, but also of Inner Asia. Cairo drew students to al-Azhar from as far away as Indonesia and West Africa. Schools of law found their affiliates over broad regions. The Malikis were predominant in North and West Africa, the Hanafis in the Ottoman empire, Inner Asia, and India, and the Shafi'is in India, Southeast Asia, and East Africa. Similarly, the Sufi brotherhoods generated regional

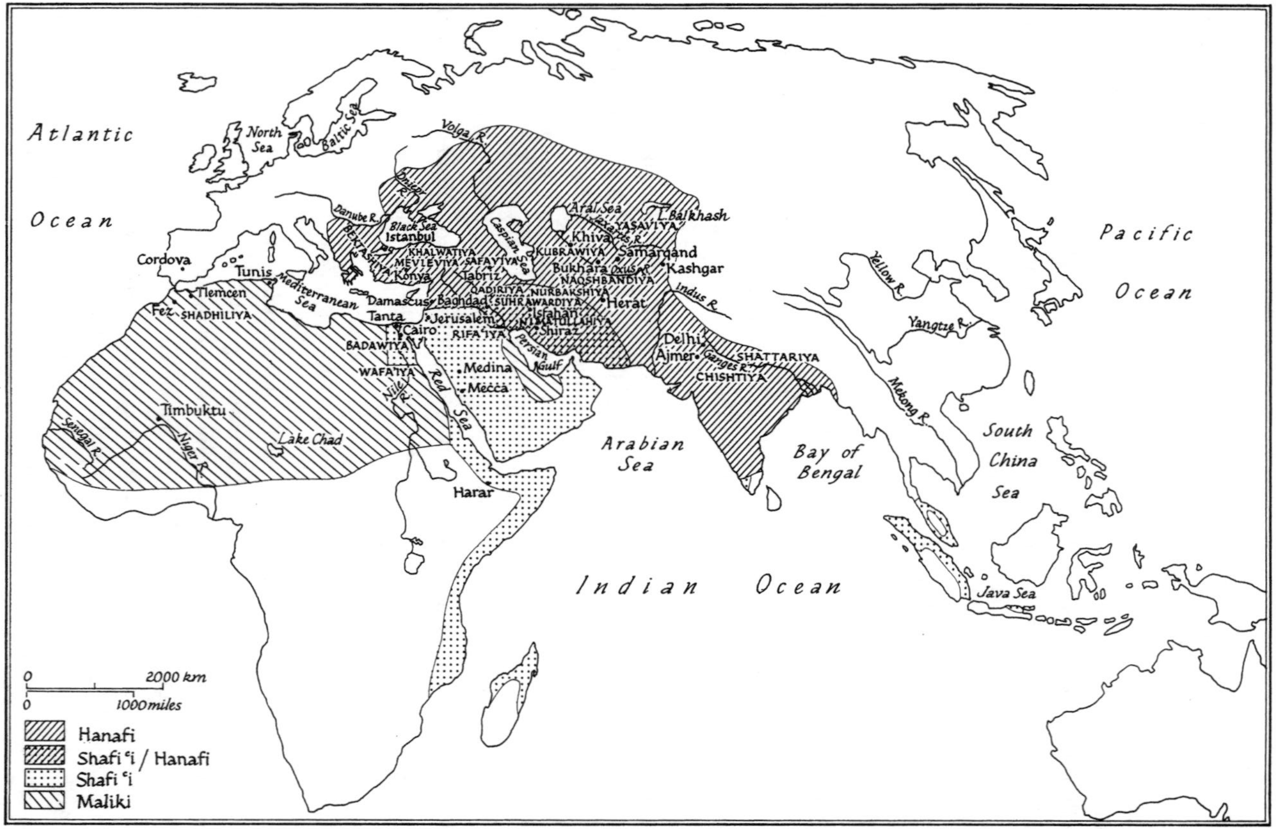

Map 8 Muslim schools of law and Sufi brotherhoods: c. 1500

and international loyalties. The Naqshbandis spread throughout India, Inner Asia, China, the Caucasus, and the Middle East. The Tijaniya in the eighteenth and nineteenth centuries became a North and West Africa-wide brotherhood with important branches in the Arab Middle East. The reform movement was centered upon Mecca and Medina, but radiated its influence to India, West Africa, Inner Asia, and China. This international Muslim community enables us to speak of "the Muslim world." Still, on another level, Islam remained intensely local, in that scholars and Sufis were embedded in particular communities and represented concepts and practices that were a fusion of the universal forms of Islam with local customs, beliefs, and lifestyles. Islam, then, has to be understood both as a universal religion and in its numerous particular contexts.

Islamic religious leadership and beliefs had a profound effect upon the social organization of Muslim peoples. In urban societies, which were commonly divided into strong family, clan, clientele, and residential groups, Islam could be the basis for the organization of neighborhood communities around a mosque, khanaqa, or college. Within the urban fabric there were schools of law, Sufi brotherhoods, or Shi'i sects identified with particular neighborhoods, occupations, or ethnic minorities. For example, in eleventh- and twelfth-century Iranian cities, neighborhood communities were closely identified with schools of law. In India and East Africa, merchant groups sometimes had a sectarian Isma'ili identity. Isma'ilis formed *jamatbandis*, or collective associations, which provided political leadership, and organized worship and instruction for a self-contained small community. Similarly, Dyula or Hausa merchant groups formed close-knit communities in West Africa. In these cases, the special trust and cohesion required for commercial activities came from religiously reinforced familial and ethnic loyalties.

Towns and cities, however, also provided a setting for social and political integration. This took place through markets, direct political negotiations among town notables, and the activities of 'ulama' and Sufis. Schools of law and Sufi tariqat drew diverse elements of the population into common religious bodies, and Islamic collectivities formed a superordinate community. Their integrative function was expressed in terms of allegiance to Shari'a. Through urban communities Islam also played an important role in creating regional and international trading networks, administrative organizations, and states.

In many village societies, Muslim identity was often superimposed upon preexisting village identity. In Minangkabau in Sumatra, peasant villages had a double social structure, in which family and property were treated on matriarchal lines while trade and politics were symbolized in patriarchal Muslim terms. In other cases, the merger of Islamic and non-Islamic cultural identity was expressed through shrine worship, festivals, belief in spirits, and shamanistic or magical curing practices which blended faith in the miraculous powers of Islamic holy men with pre-Islamic beliefs. Religious conviction was expressed through worship at shrines and holy places in an annual cycle of religious festivals, magical activities, and other rituals which incorporated non- or pre-Islamic concepts and ceremonies. Islamic belief, then, did not necessarily lead to the formation of an organized body of believers, but could serve as a shared identity among diverse peoples who preserved their own kinship, territorial, linguistic, ethnic, and other bases of non-Islamic culture in group organization and social relations.

After the thirteenth century Sufism became central to lineage societies. In lineage societies Muslim holy men appeared as individual charismatic teachers – sometimes the custodians of local shrines, sometimes affiliated with brotherhoods. They also appeared as members of holy lineages, as one lineage among others. Sufi lineages in Algeria, Morocco, southern Somalia, Mauritania, and Turkmenistan are among the many examples of groups tracing their descent to the Prophet or the early Caliphs, who were organized as separate communities within the framework of the surrounding tribal society. Similarly, African Dyula communities were made up of lineages or specialized occupational castes operating as components of complex, usually non-Muslim, segmented societies. The authority of these lineages was based in part on descent and in part upon Sufi qualities. Whether as individuals or lineages, Sufis served to facilitate the selection of chiefs, mediate disputes, and organize long-distance trade or other economic ventures.

Sufi leadership could also unite clans, lineages, and tribes into larger movements, tribal conquests, and the formation of states. In such cases, religious leadership and loyalties created a double structure of society in which religious elites represented the larger movement and secular tribal or group chieftains represented the smaller units. In these cases, the larger religious identity did not efface other aspects of ethnic, tribal, or clan loyalties, but rather was superimposed upon them. Movements created in this way were likely to fragment into their component parts.

The unification of pastoral or tribal peoples under Islamic religious leadership was a recurring phenomenon. The prime example is the original integration of Arabian bedouins into a conquering movement by the preaching of Islam. Later, in Oman, Arab tribesmen were united and governed by the Ibadi (Khariji) imams. In North Africa from the seventh to the thirteenth centuries, Berber peoples were united under Kharijism, Shi'ism, Sunni reformism, and Sufism to form the Fatimid, Almoravid, Almohad, and other movements. After the twelfth century, Sufism played a particularly important role in tribal unification. Rural populations throughout North Africa came to be organized in Sufi-led communities. In Morocco, the Sa'dian and the 'Alawi dynasties were based on Sufi-led coalitions of pastoral and mountain peasant peoples. The Safavids united individuals, clienteles, and clans to conquer and govern Iran. The conquerors of Anatolia and the Balkans, while under overall dynastic direction, were at the local level led by Sufis. In Inner Asia, the khwajas created coalitions of pastoral peoples. The tribes that occupied Somalia were united by allegiance to Sufis. The West African Fulani jihads of the eighteenth and nineteenth centuries were built on reform preaching.

Table 10. *Muslim religious officials*

Caliph	head of Sunni Muslim *umma*
Mosques	
imam	leader of prayer
khatib	preacher of official sermon
muezzin	crier of calls to prayer
Schools	
faqih or *alim* (pl. *ulama*)	scholar of law
mudaris	professor of *madrasa*
Legal administrators	
qadi	judge
mufti	jurisconsult
shaykh al-Islam	chief *mufti* and head of judicial establishment
muhtasib	market inspector and enforcer of morals
Sufi brotherhoods	
shaykh (*murshid*, etc.)	master and guide
khalifa	deputy
muqqadam	local headman in brotherhood
shaykh al-shuyukh	chief of Sufi shaykhs (Egypt)
sajjada nishin	successor, chief of shrine
Descendants of Prophet	
sayyid, sharif (pl. *ashraf, shurafa*)	
naqib al-ashraf	syndic of the descendants of the Prophet
Ithna ashari Shi a	
mujtahid	scholar of law qualified to give independent legal judgment
hujjatollah	proof of God: higher-ranking *mujtahid*
ayatollah	sign of God: highest-ranking *mujtahid*
marja i-taqlid	religious teacher to whom obedience is due
Isma ilis	
da i	missionary
hujja	proof-representative of imam
imams	successors to the Prophet and leaders of the Muslims

Thus many of the great "tribal" movements that led to the formation of Islamic states were built upon Muslim religious leadership or the integration of Muslim religious and secular chieftainship. In tribal societies Muslim leadership inspired millenarian revolts and radical opposition to established regimes. Before the modern era this was the principal expression of the Islamic impulse to transform the world and fashion a new human order.

MUSLIM STATES

Most Muslim societies were ruled by states, which operated in tandem with their 'ulama' and Sufi leadership. These states were often based upon similar concepts, institutions, and vocabularies. Generally, a Muslim ruler was the symbol of a legitimate regime, the guarantor that Muslim laws would be enforced, and the representative of the historical continuity of Muslim communities. Muslim states and empires were expected to maintain worship, education, and law. In times of war, they were to defend against infidel enemies; in times of peace, they patronized scholars and saints. The existence of a Muslim state assured its people that the civilized order of the world was being upheld.

Muslim states differed greatly as to the nature of their religious legitimization. In many cases, this legitimization was attached to the person of the ruler. The Umayyads of Damascus, 'Abbasids, Fatimids, Almoravids, Almohads, Umayyads in Spain, and the leaders of West African jihads in the nineteenth century all considered themselves hierocratic rulers. They were the heirs to the authority of the Prophet; they were at once teachers and rulers. Similarly, the khwajas of Kashgar, the Sufi masters of small Moroccan states, and the Safavids of Iran regarded themselves as the repository of religious as well as temporal authority. In Morocco, the legitimacy of the ruler depended upon his sharifian descent and Sufi qualities. The reform movements of the nineteenth century would bring a resurgence of the aspiration to unite religious and political leadership.

In other Muslim societies, legitimacy was attached directly to the state institutions. The Ottoman empire was legitimized by its reputation as a warrior regime that expanded the frontiers of Islam and defended Muslim peoples against the infidels. Even in the nineteenth century, when the Ottoman state was in decline and overwhelmed by European powers, its importance to Muslim security remained unquestioned.

Legitimization, more generally, depended upon a combination of Muslim and non-Muslim patrimonial, cosmopolitan, or cosmological symbols. The 'Abbasid regime and its Mamluk, Ottoman, Safavid, and Mughal successors appealed to genealogical descent from earlier Arab, Persian, or Turkish nobility to justify their rule. Each regime also patronized a cosmopolitan culture to define its political identity: the 'Abbasids and Ottomans, architecture; the Mughals, painting and music. Through their patronage of philosophy and science, Muslim regimes appealed to universal symbols as the basis of the political order. Muslim statecraft was also conceived of as being regulated by rules derived entirely from secular monarchical traditions. The state elites distanced themselves from Islamic commitments by cultivating artistic, literary, and scientific achievements that had little to do with Islam but were part of the historical political culture of the various Muslim regions. The multiple levels of legitimization responded to the need to win political support or acquiescence from the multi-ethnic, multi-religious populations who were commonly subjected to Muslim rule.

Furthermore, each regime showed originality in the selection of cultural and artistic styles, and in the degree of emphasis placed upon Islamic, cosmopolitan, cosmological, and patrimonial symbols. Thus the Arab regimes tended to be strongly Islamic, without noteworthy cosmopolitan symbols; the Indian Mughal empire was highly syncretic. Indonesian and Malayan regimes perpetuated a non-Islamic culture of imperium with little more than Islamic titles. By contrast, the nineteenth-century African jihads were dedicated to an Islamic utopia.

Muslim states tended to adopt similar political practices and to redefine local political precedents in Islamic terms. The militias of tribal-founded Muslim empires were commonly transformed into slave or client forces. This was especially important in the Middle East, where slave troops were recruited to supplement or to displace tribal levies, as in the cases of the 'Abbasid, Ghaznavid, Saljuq, Mamluk, Ottoman, and Safavid empires. Slaves were also used in North and West Africa. Slaves were generally recruited in Inner Asia and the Caucasus, but were also taken from non-Muslim populations in the Balkans, Georgia, and sub-Saharan Africa. Slaves commonly retained an ethnic and cultural identity based on their non-Muslim past.

In administration Muslim states also shared similar practices. The 'Abbasids inherited Byzantine and Sasanian practices in granting tax revenues for military services, and the Saljuqs molded the iqta' of late 'Abbasid times into a system of financial administration which, under various names, was later adapted by the Mongol, Timurid, Ottoman, Safavid, Uzbek, and Mughal empires. The iqta', *timar*, *tuyul*, and *jagir* (all names for grants of tax revenues) represent a similar principle of decentralized financial support for the state military elite. Other examples of administrative uniformities among Muslim states are taxation on a kharaj–jizya or land- and poll-tax basis, and the endowment of waqfs for religious purposes. In many cases, as in Inner Asia and North Africa, these uniformities were due to the direct transfer of Middle Eastern institutions, but in many others, they were due to the inheritance of similar institutions from earlier non-Muslim regimes, and to the adoption of a common Muslim terminology for separate precedents.

Alongside Islamic practices and symbols, Islamic states were defined by their relationship to the 'ulama' and the Sufis. The Ottoman, Safavid, and Bukhara monarchies were strongly supported by an organized 'ulama' bureaucracy which looked upon the state as indispensable to Islam. These states suppressed antagonistic Sufi brotherhoods, and appropriated the political functions of Sufis by endowing government officials with extensive powers to dispense justice, regulate economic matters, protect trade, and sponsor education. In these cases, 'ulama' commonly held the view that even a corrupt and evil state had to be accepted and obeyed, for any regime was better than none. In their view, the alternative to state control was anarchy and factional violence. In some African kingdoms, the 'ulama', while not highly organized by the state, were still the source of political legitimization – even from non-Muslim subjects, who accepted the superior magic of literate Muslim courtiers. In India the Mughals drew limited support and much criticism from the 'ulama'. In Indonesia, by contrast, Muslim elites had little or no role in the legitimization of regimes and were, if anything, the leaders of peasant resistance.

While the relations between states and 'ulama' tended toward interdependence, those between states and Sufis tended toward opposition. Some Sufi orders cooperated with central governments and transmitted governmental authority to the common people, as did the Suhrawardis of India and the Mevlevis of the Ottoman empire, but Sufism was usually apolitical, as in the case of the Chistis in India. Many

Sufi orders opposed governments, as in eighteenth-century Algeria and Morocco. In general, highly organized states regarded the 'ulama' as politically compatible, but considered the Sufis as political competitors to be suppressed or coopted.

Even in cases where Sufis were independent, there was an intimate connection between Sufis and the state authorities. Rulers patronized the Sufi masters in order to acquire some of the blessing attributed to the saints, and to transfer the legitimacy of the Sufis to the princes. In India the same rituals and ceremonies were observed in both the courts of the Sufis and the court of the ruler. Both courts were called by the same name – *dargah*. Conversely, the authority of Sufi masters was built around worldly success, power, and efficacy in daily affairs.

The Muslim aspects of these states were accompanied by shared non-Muslim factors. One of these was the incorporation of non-Muslim elites. "Muslim" state elites were often warriors for whom tribal identity was more salient than Muslim identity. Moreover, such tribal military forces were frequently supplemented or replaced by non-Muslim levies. The Mughal regime, for example, absorbed Hindu lords; North African regimes depended upon Catalan or Aragonese forces. The subordinate vassal principalities of large Muslim empires included non-Muslim tribal chiefs, feudal lords, and other local notables. These subordinate regimes were ordinarily legitimized in patriarchal or patrimonial terms and not by recourse to Islamic symbols or ideology.

Thus, Muslim regimes and empires were usually composite formations that embodied Islamic institutions in the matrix of a broader political culture. They carried an inherent ambiguity of identity. On one level, they were Muslim; on another, they were cosmopolitan patrons of a style of monarchical culture which, despite variations, gave a similar *gestalt* to Ottoman, Safavid, Mughal, and other Muslim state cultures. The production of illuminated manuscripts, the diffusion of Persian literary forms into Turkish and Urdu, the construction of domed architectural monuments, and many other features identify an imperial variant of Islamic civilization. On another level, the culture of Muslim regimes was also regional and derived from the pre-Islamic and non-Islamic substrates of the societies they ruled. Local languages, poetic traditions, literary forms, architectural motifs, musical motifs, and cultic practices made each Muslim regime an expression of a particular locality. The several interacting levels of universal Islamic, cosmopolitan imperial, and local cultural styles afforded each regime a distinctive identity.

CONFRONTATION WITH EUROPE

By the eighteenth century the worldwide system of Islamic societies had reached its apogee and begun its political decline. The Safavid state had been defeated by Afghan invaders and, deserted by its tribal vassals, disintegrated completely. The Ottoman empire went through a period of decentralization, though the concept of an imperial state was unimpaired. The Mughal empire disintegrated into numerous competing provincial and feudal regimes. In Southeast Asia, a centralized regime had never been established over the Indonesian archipelago or the Malay peninsula, and the largest Indonesian state, the Mataram empire of Java, came under direct Dutch economic and indirect Dutch political control. In North Africa, Muslim states were being subverted by their declining commercial position in the Mediterranean, and provincial, tribal, and Sufi resistance was on the increase. The Sudanic states had long passed the peak of their commercial prosperity, though Muslim communities were growing in influence in other parts of Africa. By this period much of the northern steppes of Inner Asia had come under Russian control and eastern Turkestan under Chinese rule.

Pluralistic European societies

The crucial common factor in the decline of Muslim regimes was the rising power of Europe. On the far western fringe of the Eurasian land mass European peoples were making a revolution in world history. From the late Middle Ages to modern times, European societies were developing the capacities to generate technological inventions, economic wealth, and military power. These developments would profoundly change the conditions of life not only for Muslims, but for all the world's peoples.

European world power had its origins in a set of intertwined socio-economic and cultural conditions that led to the formation of highly pluralistic societies. Unlike Middle Eastern societies, European societies were not organized upon the threefold template of kinship, religious community, and empire. Medieval European family structure, with some exceptions among the feudal nobility, did not tend to the formation of closed lineage groups, but rather to the formation of open and interlocking social networks based on bilateral connections of both husband and wife. With the fall of Rome and the failure of the Carolingian and Holy Roman empires, European states no longer had the all-embracing political and mythic importance they had held in the Middle East. In place of empires, feudal governments based on personal and contractual loyalties, governments by oath association, and communes or popular assemblies based on Roman or Germanic notions of popular sovereignty were accepted as legitimate.

Most important was the tendency toward separation of state and church. While in the Middle East Muslim symbols were becoming pervasive, European society was becoming secularized. The potentiality for secularization was implicit in the Christian church. The fact that the church was a highly organized, corporate institution governed under laws and norms appropriate to itself but not to lay society made it possible to define a profane realm – "the world" – outside the church, a world governed by non-church or non-canonical laws. At the same time, European society had independent sources of secular civic and cultural values. Greek and Roman political and legal ideas, and German communal and feudal concepts, defined a realm of legal authority and secular values which, though not Christian, were held to be legitimate. Not only were church and state separate institutions, but Christian and secular societies had separate foundations.

The historical trends of the twelfth and thirteenth centuries favored the enhancement of the pluralism implicit in European family, state, and religious organization. The growth of commerce, a money economy, and towns broke up village communities, favored the mobility of individuals, and promoted occupational specialization. New urban classes of landowning and capital-investing patricians, merchants and bankers, entrepreneurs in manufacturing, ship-building, or commerce, artisans, journeymen, and workers grew in size. With the growth of secular learning in literature, philosophy, law, and medicine, a non-clerical intelligentsia of poets, writers, physicians, lawyers, professors, administrators, and judges came into being. Thus, European society was divided into numerous social strata and classes: nobles, knights, clergy, and a bourgeoisie, subdivided again among merchants, artisans, intellectuals, lawyers, and other groups.

The differentiation of late medieval European society stimulated the formation of corporate groups to advance the interests of their members. Some groups served the need for political security. Feudal fiefdoms, aristocratic factions, church governments, peace associations, and communes all became active centers of political power. Within the church monastic orders and confraternities were formed to express new religious orientations. Merchant and artisan guilds and commercial companies organized economic activities. Universities were founded to carry on secular learning.

This pluralism was expressed in values as well as social organization. While Muslim societies maintained a holistic commitment to the law and umma, Europe recognized the legitimacy of several religious, ethical, or philosophic systems including feudal chivalry and romance, Roman law, philosophy, and bourgeois business ethics – each of which constituted a world of values independent of Christian beliefs. Each type of government, each stratum, each group operated in accordance with its own laws and regulations, its own moral concepts, and its own implicit idea of the nature of the human being and of human fulfillment.

This differentiation of activities and values was sustained by Christian, feudal, and urban humanistic commitments to the intrinsic worth of the human individual. Basic Christian values stressed the importance of the salvation of the individual soul. Medieval society recognized the inherent honor of the warrior – his areté, his prowess, and his right to express that prowess in conquest, chivalric daring and courtesy, vendetta, and the quest for love. The inherent genius of the warrior, and his rights and those of other honorable men to compete for wealth, power, and love, legitimized individual self-expression. Similarly, the new humanistic culture of the cities held the claims of the individual to be greater than those of society. Thirteenth-century Florentine society held the individual to be capable of personal refinement and redemption through Christian and chivalric love and through rhetorical and courtly instruction.

In this pluralistic society the relationship between the individual and society was different from that of the Middle East. Whereas in the Middle East individual obligations were defined in terms of participation in a religiously defined community, in Europe the individual was perceived on two levels. One was in terms of the specialized roles that individuals played in occupational, corporate, and office-holding situations; the other was in terms of an inherent spiritual identity. Society itself came to be conceived in terms of individuals fulfilling a function, a calling, a role in a corporate, pluralistic, and secular world.

The Renaissance and the Protestant Reformation seem to have exaggerated the underlying European tendency to pluralistic values and individual aggrandizement. In many parts of Europe the breakdown of agrarian feudal society, the growth of towns, and the ever-expanding system of commerce generated an extreme anxiety over personal security and ultimately over the worth of individuals and their capacity for salvation. Such forces were not uniform in their operation, but they were potent in critical milieus in England, France, Germany, and Switzerland where Protestant communities were organized in response to the aching need for order and communal association. In Protestant communities the anxieties of the age were reinforced by the doctrine of predestination, according to which it was impossible for a person either to know or to affect his prospects for salvation. Who were the sinners and who were the saved? Also, Protestant puritanism closed off the ordinary emotional and ritual outlets for inner stress. Protestant hostility to art, music and dance, sensuality and sexuality, religious pageantry and ritual, and to Catholic confession and absolution left few channels for the satisfaction of inner emotional needs.

These combined socio-economic, theological, and psychological pressures drove individuals to seek worldly signs of their salvation through methodical and devoted labor in their calling so as to curb inherent human wickedness and eliminate public sins and moral faults. Self-controlled, self-disciplined activity in God's service was the antidote to anxiety and anomie. Anxiety, then, could be relieved by the systematic acquisition of wealth as a demonstration of God's favor. The emergence of this cast of mind in people uprooted from organic communities, striving to form new formal associations, and capable of systematic behavior and the subordination of all extraneous considerations – personal, emotional, aesthetic, and even ethical – to the demand for a patterned way of living was what Max Weber called the spirit of capitalism. A similar systematic attitude could also be applied in politics, as in the English Puritan revolution, to the construction of a holy society. It could be applied to engineering, invention and scientific discovery, architectural and artistic design, and indeed to all realms of human endeavor. Weber saw that this capacity for impersonal, unemotional commitment to the inherent norms of an enterprise, and for pursuing specialized goals to their ultimate conclusions, was the basis of modern European civilization.

European trade and naval power

While it would be centuries before the full implications of Renaissance urban and Protestant culture would be realized, the new orientation was being applied to technical invention and to the pursuit of material well-being. By the thirteenth and fourteenth centuries the towns of Italy, Flanders, and the Baltic were already committed to commerce and industry, rather than agriculture, as sources of wealth. Out of these towns came novel techniques for investment, banking, and insurance, and other methods of economic organization and exchange. The pursuit of wealth and the sophisticated means to generate it led to a tremendous outward expansion of European city-states in search of exotic luxury products and of new sources of food, fuel, and raw materials for their growing and ambitious populations.

The trading impulse led by stages to a revolution in world commerce and politics. The first stage was the creation of a new worldwide pattern of trade. Venice and Genoa had already created extensive networks of colonies and trading posts in the eastern Mediterranean and the Black Sea where they could purchase spices, drugs, dyes, silk, and other exotic products of the East. When the rise of the Ottoman empire cut off the Italian city-states from their eastern sources, Genoa was forced to turn to the western Mediterranean and the Atlantic for its supplies of wool, sugar, alum, silk, cereals, dyes, and spices. The Portuguese undertook the search for a new route to the Indies which would bypass Middle Eastern routes and enable them to bring eastern products directly to Lisbon, and thus discovered an African route to the Indian Ocean. Spanish and Italian explorers discovered new continents. Portugal and Spain conquered empires in the southern seas and the New World, and brought home untold wealth.

The sixteenth century was occupied by the struggle to control the new world economy. The Ottomans and the French fought the Habsburgs in Italy, Eastern Europe, and the Mediterranean, and the Ottomans fought the Portuguese in the Indian Ocean. By the end of the sixteenth century the Ottomans had consolidated their position in the Balkans and North Africa, but the Spanish empire had fallen apart, ruining in its collapse the great commercial and banking houses of Italy, Germany, and Castile. Their demise opened the way for a new phase in the struggle to control the world economy. At the end of the sixteenth century Holland, England, and France emerged as the dominant forces in world trade. Each of them would create a worldwide commercial empire based on bourgeois initiative, sophisticated trading, advanced gunnery and sailing techniques, and utter ruthlessness in the pursuit of gain. Portugal, England, and Holland were tiny countries whose power came from technological and economic advantages, better ships and guns, more productive business enterprises, and more efficient use of human resources. The capacity to mobilize and organize men with maximum military and economic efficiency gave them a decisive advantage.

This advantage led not only to political and commercial dominance, but to the transformation of the basic structures of the world economy. While the discovery of new routes to the Orient did not close the traditional Middle Eastern international routes, they created a revolution in the distribution of wealth. Now Europe would prosper on the captured gold and silver, spices, and other products of the New

World and the old. The Baltic and the Atlantic replaced the Mediterranean and the Indian Ocean as the most important centers of world trade. The shift of international trading routes from the Mediterranean to the Atlantic meant not only a change of routes but also a change in the nature of the goods being exchanged. While the traditional trade was largely a trade in luxury goods, the modern trade was a trade in agricultural and industrial products – timber, grain, fish, salt – on a mass scale, and represented a new level of commodity production and division of labor in the world economy. The formation of the new commercial empires made possible a system of economic exploitation in which Europe became the principal beneficiary of a worldwide division of labor between colonies producing raw materials and metropoles producing high-value industrial goods and commercial services. European commercial dominance in the seventeenth and eighteenth centuries led ultimately to the emergence of a new form of capitalist industrial economy.

The rising power of Europe brought it into worldwide conflict with Muslim societies. While Islam was expanding from the Middle East into South and Southeast Asia, Africa, and Eastern Europe, the Atlantic and northern European powers began to assert their own ambitions, expanding on the northern and southern flanks of Islamic societies. While not strictly a society of the Western European type, Russia in the sixteenth century began its expansion across Inner Asia and Siberia to the Pacific. Russian expansion was primarily territorial, and involved the conquest and absorption of Muslim populations into a Russian empire. In the sixteenth century Russia absorbed the Tatar states in the Volga basin; by the nineteenth century most of the Kazakh population of the northern steppes was under Russian control. The Russian conquests culminated in the absorption of Transoxania and the Transcaspian regions in the late nineteenth century. At the same time China established its suzerainty in eastern Turkestan in the eighteenth century and made it a province of China in the late nineteenth. Russia and China took control of most of the Muslim populations of Inner Asia.

On the southern flanks of Islam, European expansion began with Portuguese, Dutch, and British merchant adventurers, who won naval and trading empires in the southern seas and ended by establishing colonial regimes. The Portuguese established a series of bases in the Indian Ocean and at Malacca in the early sixteenth century, but they were displaced by the Dutch, who took control of the Southeast Asian trade in the seventeenth century. The Dutch soon converted their commercial empire into a territorial one. They had made themselves suzerains of Java by the middle of the eighteenth century, and conquered the rest of the Indies in the course of the nineteenth.

The British also began by establishing trading bases, and ended by conquering an empire in India. After bitter rivalries with the French, the British took control of Bengal in the late eighteenth century and went on to dominate the Indian subcontinent in the early decades of the nineteenth. At the same time they also took full control of the Indian Ocean, with bases in Malaya, the Persian Gulf, the Red

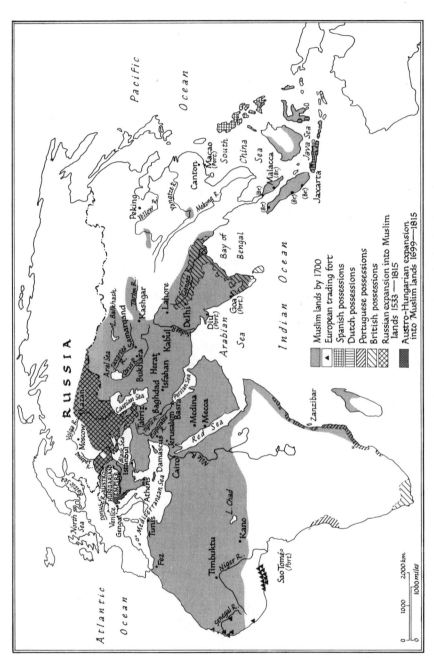

Map 9 European domination over Muslim and other lands: 1815

Muslim lands by 1700
European trading fort
Spanish possessions
Dutch possessions
Portuguese possessions
British possessions
Russian expansion into Muslim lands 1533 — 1815
Austro-Hungarian expansion into Muslim lands 1699—1815

RUSSIA

Pacific Ocean

South China Sea

Java Sea

Peking
Yellow R.
Yangtze R.
Mekong R.
Cantop.
Macao (Port.)
Malacca (Br.)
Jaxarta (Br.)

Indian Ocean

Bay of Bengal

L. Balkhash
Jaxartes R.
Oxur R.
Kashgar
Tarim R.
Samarqand
Bukhara
Herat
Kabul
Lahore
Delhi
Goa (Port.)
Diu (Port.)
Aral Sea
Kazan
Caspian Sea
Tabriz
Isfahan
Baghdad
Basra
Persian Sea
Arabian Sea

Moscow
Volga R.

Medina
Mecca
Red Sea
Jerusalem
Cairo
Damascus
Euphrates R.
Tigris R.
Nile R.

Zanzibar

AUSTRO-
HUNGARIAN
EMPIRE
Danube R.
Venice
Genoa
Istanbul
Black Sea
Athens
Tunis
Mediterranean Sea

Baltic Sea
North Sea
Atlantic Ocean

Fez
Timbuktu
Niger R.
Kano
L. Chad
Senegal R.
Sao Tomé (Port.)

0   1000   2000 km.
0   1000 miles

Sea, and East Africa. Europeans also established their commercial dominance in the Mediterranean and took territorial control of Egypt and North Africa. Africa was the last region with a large Muslim population to be subjected to colonial domination. Only the Ottoman empire and Iran maintained their political identity without experiencing direct colonial rule.

By the eighteenth century the reorganization of the world economy and the consolidation of European commercial and political dominance subverted Muslim societies, weakened Muslim states which depended on commercial revenues, and promoted factional strife and the exploitation of the peasantries. European ascendancy took a cultural as well as a political and economic form. By the nineteenth century, Europe was beginning to seize the imagination of Muslim peoples. The Ottomans, for example, were impressed with European military and technological efficiency, artistic style, and the morality of activism and individualism. European political – and especially nationalist – concepts and moral values began to influence Muslim populations. These influences opened a new era in the history of Muslim peoples. Part II concludes with the Muslim world on the eve of its modern transformation.

THE MIDDLE EASTERN
ISLAMIC SOCIETIES

CHAPTER 13

IRAN: THE MONGOL, TIMURID, AND
SAFAVID EMPIRES

From an earlier age, Iran inherited an agricultural civilization and a monarchical regime. The Saljuq empire had bequeathed its particular pattern of slave military elites and iqta' forms of administration; mixed Islamic and Iranian royal culture; Muslim religious associations in the form of Sunni schools of law, Sufi brotherhoods, and Shi'i sects; and strong local urban factions and rural clan communities.

THE MONGOLS

The Mongol invasions dealt a devastating blow to Iranian-Muslim civilization. The Mongol invasions originated with the formation of a confederation of Inner Asian peoples under the leadership of Chinggis Khan. Believing in a God-given destiny, the Mongols set out to conquer the whole of the known world, and brought East Asia, the Middle East, and the East European steppes under their rule. Within a few decades they ruled all of Eurasia from central Europe to the Pacific. This vast empire was divided among the four sons of Chinggis, partly for administrative convenience and partly because the conquered territories were considered the joint possession of the ruling family. Since there was neither a defined succession nor any way to assure unity, the descendants of Chinggis fought among themselves. Out of these disputes came several independent and even hostile Mongol states. These included Mongol regimes in Mongolia and China, the Golden Horde on the northern steppes, the Chaghatay Khanate in Transoxania and eastern Turkestan, and the Ilkhan regime in Iran and Anatolia.

The first impact of the Mongol invasions in Iran was disastrous, and amounted to a holocaust. The populations of many cities and towns were systematically exterminated. Whole regions were depopulated by invading armies and by the influx of Turkish and Mongol nomads who drove the peasants from the land. The conquerors plundered their subjects, made them serfs, and taxed them ruinously. The

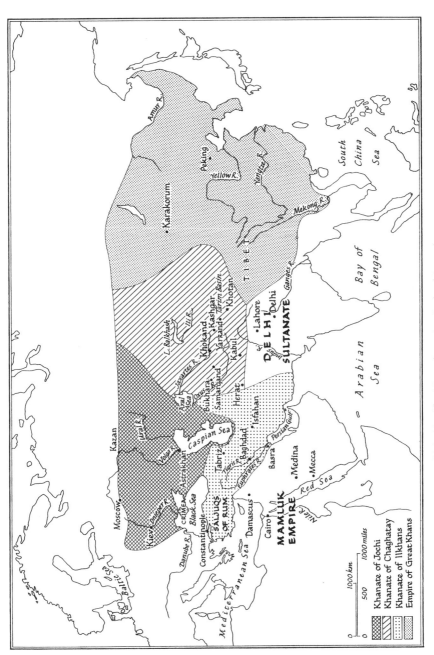

Map 10 The Mongol empires in the thirteenth century

Karakorum

Amur R.

Peking

Yellow R.

Yangtze R.

Mekong R.

South China Sea

T I B E T

Ganges R.

Bay of Bengal

Arabian Sea

L. Balkhash

Ili R.

Kashgar

Khokand

Tarim Basin

Khotan

Yarkand

Jaxartes R.

Kabul

Lahore

D E L H I

Delhi

SULTANATE

Indus R.

Aral Sea

Bukhara

Otrar

Samarkand

Herat

Isfahan

Kazan

Ural R.

Volga R.

Caspian Sea

Tabriz

Baghdad

Persian Gulf

ASTRAKHAN

Tigris R.

Euphrates R.

Basra

Medina

Mecca

Moscow

Kiev

Dnieper R.

CRIMEA

Black Sea

Constantinople

SALJUQS OF RUM

Damascus

Danube R.

Mediterranean Sea

MAMLUK EMPIRE

Cairo

Nile R.

Red Sea

Baltic Sea

1000 km.

0   500   1000 miles

0

Khanate of Jochi

Khanate of Chaghatay

Khanate of Ilkhans

Empire of Great Khans

result was a catastrophic fall in population, income, and state revenue. For over a century fine pottery and metalwares ceased to be produced. A period of urban autonomy and cultural vitality was brought to an end.

While the first century of Mongol rule wreaked havoc, the later Ilkhan regime resumed the historical trend toward state centralization of power and recreated the brilliance of Saljuq-period Turkic-Iranian monarchical culture. Beginning with the reign of Ghazan (1295–1304), the Ilkhans rebuilt cities, redeveloped irrigation works, and sponsored agriculture and trade in the familiar way of Middle Eastern empires. In particular they opened up Inner Asian trade routes to China.

The Mongol regime in Iran was a conquest state. It was made up of a single large army composed of a tribal military aristocracy allied to the ruling dynasty. This aristocracy conceived of itself as a privileged people whose right to dominate and tax its subjects was enshrined in its supreme law, the *yasa*. The Mongols ruled Iran by distributing the land to military chiefs for pasturage or for tax revenues. The chiefs, in turn, divided it among their followers. Pasture and plow lands were combined in estates called *tuyul*, a concept which combined Mongolian ideas about the distribution of pasturage and Iranian administrative concepts of the distribution of the right to collect taxes. Mongol rule, moreover, depended, as did the preceding Saljuq regimes, upon the support of local notable families. The Ilkhans allied themselves with Iranian urban bureaucrats, merchants, and 'ulama'. The 'ulama' continued or resumed their position as local elites. They filled the offices of qadi, preacher, market inspector, and other posts. Urban elites, whose prestige was based upon Islamic learning, whose social power was built on ownership of urban quarters, gardens, and village land and control of waqfs, and whose functions included financial and judicial administration, provided continuity in local government and buffered the impact of changing military regimes. They also provided the administrative personnel for the construction of successive Mongol and Timurid governments.

Despite their self-conscious superiority, however, the Ilkhans did not bring a new linguistic or religious identity to the Middle East. Unlike the Arabs, who changed both the language and the religion of the region, the Mongols were absorbed by Islam and Persian culture. They did, however, bring a new phase of creativity to that culture. In the reign of Ghazan, the Mongol and Turkish military elite was converted to Islam. Under Mongol sponsorship, history writing flourished, reflecting the Mongol sense of universal destiny. Al-Juvaini's (1226–83) *History of the World Conquerors* told the story of Chinggis Khan and the conquest of Iran. His near-contemporary Rashid al-Din (1247–1318), a physician and vizier, wrote the *Compendium of Histories*, integrating Chinese, Indian, European, Muslim, and Mongol history into a new cosmopolitan perspective on the fate of mankind. The Ilkhans, like other Turkish conquerors, were devoted to the construction of monumental tombs, and adapted older Iranian architectural forms for the monuments of Tabriz, Sultaniya, and Varamin. The most important of the Ilkhan constructions was the mausoleum of Oljeytu (1304–17) at Sultaniya, whose large central dome was a major technical achievement. Stucco, terracotta, and colored bricks or tiles were used to decorate the exterior surfaces.

The Mongol contribution to the revival of the glory of Iranian monarchy was most brilliantly expressed in the revival of painting and manuscript illustration. Tabriz became the center of a flourishing school. The historical works of Rashid al-Din were frequently copied and illustrated. So were the epic poems of the *Shah-name*, the *Life of Alexander*, and the fables of the *Kalila wa-Dimna*. Chinese influences were introduced by the travels of Mongol administrators, soldiers, and merchants across Inner Asia, and by the importation of Chinese silks and pottery. Chinese influences are evident in the artistic treatment of landscapes, birds, flowers, and clouds; in the composition of scenes that appear to be drawn on receding planes, and in new ways of grouping human figures. One type of human figure was aristocratic, elongated, motionless, with facial features precisely drawn, per-haps gesturing slightly with a movement of the head or finger; a second type was a caricature with highly exaggerated expressions of comedy or pain. Thus the Ilkhan regime continued the cosmopolitan aspect of Iranian monarchy, reinforced by Mongol concepts of authority and political destiny.

THE TIMURIDS

The Ilkhan regime lasted until 1336 when, like the Saljuq empire, it dissolved into competing provincial states. The small successor states were in turn absorbed into a new empire established by Timur (Tamerlane, 1370–1405) and his heirs, who introduced a new phase in the development of Iranian monarchical culture. Timur was a military adventurer who came to power by building up loyal bands of fol-lowers and defeating other chieftains. In 1370 he made Samarqand his capital, and thus became a successor to the Chaghatay branch of Mongol rulers in Transoxania. Timur was also supported by the local Muslim elites including the *Shaykh al-Islam* (chief jurisconsult) of Samarqand and the Sufis who became his spiritual advisors. Muslim religious leaders later served him as qadis, diplomats, and tutors for young princes. They may also have helped him rally support from both nomadic and town populations to legitimize his new regime.

Once in power Timur began his extraordinary conquests of the known world. From 1379 to 1402, zigzagging between east and west, he conquered Iran, north-ern India, Anatolia, and northern Syria. These conquests were made in the name of the Shari'a, on the pretext that his enemies were traitors to Islam. To administer his empire, Timur appointed his sons and grandsons as provincial governors, but he was careful to restrict their power by frequently rotating the gubernatorial assignments, appointing generals and tax collectors who were directly responsible to him, and assigning his personal representatives (*darughas*) to oversee their rule.

After Timur's death in 1405 his empire was divided into two realms, each of which became an important center of Iranian culture. Under Ulugh-beg (1404–49)

Table 11. *Iran: outline chronology*

Mongol conquests begin	1219
Ilkhanid dynasty	1256–1336
Iran partitioned among several local regimes	1336–
Conquest by Timur (Tamerlane)	1370–1405
Succession states	
Qara Qoyunlu, Azarbayjan	1380–1468
Aq Qoyunlu	1378–1508
Timurids of Herat	1407–1506
Safavids	
Sufi masters:	
Safi al-Din Ishaq	d. 1334
Sadr al-Din	d. 1391
Khwaja Ali	d. 1429
Ibrahim	d. 1447
Junayd	d. 1460
Haydar	d. 1488
Isma il I	d. 1524
Safavid conquest of Iran	1501–10
Safavid dynasty	1501–1722
Isma il I	1501–24
Abbas I	1588–1629
Afsharids	1736–95
Nadir Shah	1736–47
Zands	1750–94
Qajars	1779–1925
Pahlavis	1925–79
Islamic republic	1979–

Transoxania became a center of Muslim architectural, philosophic, and scientific achievement, and generated a new variant of Iranian-Islamic royal civilization. Great monuments were built at Samarqand, Bukhara, Herat, and Balkh, including the tomb complex of the Shah-i Zindah at Samarqand and the mausoleum of Timur, the Gur-i Mire, which is famous for its blue and turquoise tile decorations and gorgeous dome. Ulugh-beg presided over a court of musicians, poets, and singers. He was himself an astronomer and had a large observatory built for his studies.

The religious point of view was represented in Samarqand by the Naqshbandi Sufis and their merchant and artisan followers. In Bukhara the Sufi leaders led revolts against the political authorities, and Ulugh-beg sought to pacify them by endowing madrasas in both Bukhara and Samarqand. He also built a khanaqa for Sufis and a great new mosque. After the death of Ulugh-beg, local political power was assumed by Khwaja Ahrar (1404–90), a Naqshbandi holy man who denounced the lifestyle of the upper classes and had a strong influence on the army and the common people.

Herat was the second center of Muslim culture. Shah Rukh (1407–47) lived in an observant Muslim style, attended prayers, observed the fast of Ramadan, and heard readings from the Quran; he presided over a society in which the market inspectors were empowered to enter private houses and destroy wine. Sultan

Husayn (1469–1506), however, made Herat a center of Turkish literary culture. The great figure of his time was Mir 'Ali Shir Nava'i (1441–1501). Born in Herat of a bureaucratic family, he was a leading poet and patron of the arts and sciences. As a courtier he was an intermediary between the state and the town religious elites, and was initiated into the Naqshbandi order. He was most famous as a translator of Persian literature into Chaghatay and as the poet who made Chaghatay Turkish the principal language of Turkish-Islamic high culture.

Under the Timurids, Herat and Bukhara also became centers of manuscript illustration. The school of Bihzad (d. 1534–35 or 1536–37) at Herat, and later Tabriz, created a new style. Timurid-period paintings were composed in a way that broke up the surface of the painting into several scenes, each of which seemed to be independent of the others. Each wall, floor, or garden had its own self-contained pattern. Yet all the beautifully decorated objects within a painting – houses, gardens, tiles, carpets, animals, and human figures – were expected to form part of a larger ensemble. The ideal was not the single beautiful motif but the beauty of the whole. In Timurid paintings everything was subordinated to design. Even human figures were presented in a way that stressed graceful lines rather than conveying the feeling of a human presence. Faces were expressionless. The Timurid painter, like the court poet, wanted to adorn, delight the spectator, perhaps convey the glory of a patron, but not reveal emotional depths.

Sufi influences also had a powerful effect upon late fifteenth-century Persian painting. Classic Persian love stories, such as the story of Majnun and Layla, were depicted to suggest a spiritual ideal. The final meeting of the two lovers, which causes them to lose consciousness before they can consummate their love, is a symbol of the belief that the Sufi can only attain the object of his devotion after death. Physical features took on a spiritual meaning. For example, doorways and gates imply the movement from outer to inner worlds, the passage from the physical to the spiritual plane.

IRANIAN SOCIETY AND SUFI MOVEMENTS

While the Mongols and Timurids revived the Iranian monarchy, their rule saw profound changes in the structure of Iranian society. The Mongol invasions brought lasting demographic, economic, and political changes. In the twelfth and thirteenth centuries, large numbers of Turkish and Mongol peoples settled in northwestern Iran and eastern Anatolia, and, by the fourteenth century, a large Turkish population was also established in eastern Iran and in the Oxus region. Ever since, Turkish peoples have constituted about one-fourth of the total population of Iran. The Turkish presence radically changed the economy of Iran. Substantial territories were turned from agriculture into pasturage. Villagers were induced to take up a migratory existence, farming in valley bottoms and pasturing sheep in adjacent mountain highlands. Only in the reign of Ghazan (1295–1304) did the Ilkhans attempt to develop a more balanced relationship between agricultural and pastoral activities, and a system of property organization that maintained the position of both agricultural and pastoral peoples. The Ilkhans began to stabilize the division of Iran into two economic and cultural worlds – one, the world of the sedentary village; the other, that of the pastoral camp.

From Inner Asia also came new political institutions. To the Iranian legacy of monarchical and hierarchical institutions and Islamic communities were added Turkish and Mongolian political traditions. While the Iranian tradition conceived of society as governed by a regular system of hereditary rule, the Turkish conception of society was based upon military competition. Rulership in Turkish society was achieved by victory in battle, and was maintained by active struggle against rivals.

The crucial expression of chieftainship in the Turko-Mongolian societies was the *uymaq*, or household state. An uymaq was an elite military formation organized as a great household under the leadership of its chief. The chief was supported by his family and by other lesser chiefs and their followers whose support was won by delicate negotiations and/or by success in war. The uymaq chief used his military support to collect taxes from townsmen and peasants, and to establish, in effect, a local territorial government commonly based in a citadel or fortress. The powers of an uymaq chieftain could be reinforced by royal appointment to a position that gave him the right to tax and to supervise the local bureaucracy.

The uymaq, however, was generally unstable owing to the fact that it was based on the personal prowess of chiefs and upon semi-independent warriors, clans, and vassal groups who constantly calculated their relative advantage, bitterly competed for leadership, and regularly rebelled against the dominance of the great chiefs. The authority of an uymaq lord was always challenged by lesser chieftains. Competition among all these groups made the uymaq extremely volatile and led to rapid rises and falls of fortune. Thus, all post-Saljuq Iranian states acquired the dual heritage of an Iranian monarchical tradition and of Turkish uymaq polities. The Mongols, the Timurids, and the Safavids in succession had to struggle with the problems of maintaining a centralized monarchy and of coping with the tribal and military chiefs. Indeed, the later dynamic of Iranian history would turn on the relationship between state and uymaqs.

The shattering impact of the Mongol invasions, the succession of unstable and ruinous regimes, and the intrusion of Turkish pastoralists also provoked new forms of socio-religious organization among the common people of Iran. Islamic leadership in western Anatolia, northeastern Iran, and northern Mesopotamia passed into the hands of Sufi preachers, shamans, and sorcerers. These preachers performed miraculous cures, manipulated occult forces, and claimed a religious authority based upon esoteric knowledge vouchsafed through direct revelation or the interpretation of magical texts. They taught their followers that a savior would come to redeem ordinary people, and that the qutb, the pillar of the saintly world, would provide a haven for oppressed peoples.

Responding to the need for political protection and spiritual reassurance, the Sufis organized a number of local movements to unite rural populations and resist political oppression. In the thirteenth century the Kubrawi order in western Iran, named after Najm al-Din Kubra (1145/46–1221) but actually founded by al-Simnani (1261–1336), stood closest to high-culture Islam. Al-Simnani preached a doctrine that attempted to transcend sectarian divisions. The order appealed to both Sunnis and Shi'a, by venerating the family of the Prophet, including 'Ali, along with the great Sunni masters. Kubrawi mysticism was also intended to win Buddhists and pagan converts to Islam. The Hurufiya, founded by Fadlallah Astarabadi (d. 1394), represented a more populist version of Islam. Astarabadi claimed to be a hidden imam, the beneficiary of a direct revelation of God's will. He taught that it was possible to gain knowledge of secret and spiritual matters through the interpretation of the alphabet and the understanding of its implicit numerical values, for the letters of the alphabet are the microcosm of the divine reality. This secret knowledge would bring his followers salvation. Nurbaksh (1393–1465), like many other militant Sufi preachers, held that the true messiah must carry out jihad in the name of Islam. He led a rebellion in Kurdistan against the local Timurid rulers. Other millenarian movements looked forward to the ultimate confrontation between good and evil, the coming of a messiah and the redemption of mankind.

The Safavid movement, founded by Shaykh Safi al-Din (1252–1334), a Sunni Sufi religious teacher descended from a Kurdish family in northwestern Iran, also represented a resurgence of popular Islam in opposition to chaotic and exploitative military domination. The Safavid movement, however, unlike the others, led to the conquest of Iran and the establishment of a new dynasty which would reign from 1501 to 1722. The founder began by preaching a purified and restored Islam. His son, Sadr al-Din (r. 1334–91), made it into a hierarchical, politically sensitive, and propertied organization. He was the first head of the order to claim descent from the Prophet. He expanded the family compound in Ardabil, providing it with schools and residences, and broadened the movement's missionary activities. He organized the hierarchy of the *murshid* who was the head of the order, and the khalifas who were his direct agents, and supervised the missionaries, assistants, students, and novices.

In the fifteenth century, the Safavid movement became a powerful political force in northwestern Iran and eastern Anatolia. The Safavids took advantage of the breakup of the Timurid regime and of the bitter Turkish tribal conflicts to turn from preaching to militant action. Shaykh Junayd (1447–60) was the first murshid to fight Christian populations in Georgia and Trebizond. His wars against the Christians were soon turned against established Muslim states, which he denounced as infidel regimes.

The more militant Safavid policy depended upon active recruitment of both individuals and of uymaq and tribal groups. The Anatolian followers were individual soldiers and adventurers given political organization by the Safavid order.

The Iranian supporters were Turkish-, Kurdish-, and Luri-speaking pastoralists, peasants, artisans, and middle-level lineage chiefs who joined the Safavids to oppose the more powerful tribal lords. In addition, Shaykh Junayd married into the families of local princes to form military alliances and to recruit whole tribes to his cause. His recruits were called *Qizilbash*, after their distinctive red headgear, which showed that they were the disciples and warriors of the Safavid house. As exploited peasant populations flocked to the Sufi brotherhoods to find leadership in their struggle for existence and to give expression to their hope for redemption, the Safavids combined the forces of religious devotees and uymaq clients to establish a dynasty and an empire representing a new constellation of imperial, religious, and tribal forces.

The reorientation toward militant political action was accompanied by doctrinal elaboration. The Safavids declared their Shi'i allegiances, and Shah Isma'il (1487–1524) proclaimed himself the hidden imam, the reincarnation of 'Ali, and an epiphany of the divine being. Isma'il claimed to be descended from the seventh imam, and to be the seventh descendant in the Safavid line, each successive imam the bearer of the divine fire passed down from generation to generation. Isma'il, leaning on the religious syncretisms of almost two centuries of Sufi movements in northwestern Iran and Anatolia, and combining diverse religious influences including Shi'ism, Sunni messianism, Buddhism, and Zoroastrianism, also proclaimed himself the incarnation of Khidr, the bearer of ancient wisdom, and the spirit of Jesus. Illuminated by the divine pre-eternal fire, the fire that preceded the Quran and the creation of the universe, and which passed down in the family of the Prophet to its embodiment in Isma'il, he was messiah and Shah, possessor of both temporal power and mystical rulership. On the basis of these religious claims, the Safavid leaders called for absolute and unquestioning obedience from their Sufi and Qizilbash followers. To question the authority of the perfect master was tantamount to apostasy.

SAFAVID IRAN

In 1501 Isma'il occupied Tabriz and proclaimed himself Shah, and within a decade had conquered the rest of Iran. While the rival Ottoman empire to the west seized eastern Anatolia and the Shaybanid empire to the east took control of Transoxania as far as the Oxus River, Isma'il established the borders that have defined Iran until the present day. Political rivalries cut off the Ottoman empire from Islamic culture in Iran, and reinforced a growing cultural divide between Iran and Inner Asia. These borders divided the Middle East into separate realms of Turkish Ottoman, Iranian, and Inner Asian Muslim cultures.

The problems of rebuilding the Iranian state and society were formidable. Centuries of political upheaval had worn away the infrastructure of centralized imperial government. Agricultural and urban production had been undermined by nomadic invasions. Economic regression and a declining peasant population reduced the resources essential for a centralized state.

The first problem of the Safavid state was to consolidate the religious authority of the Shah and the military and administrative power of the central government over the Qizilbash uymaqs and the uymaq chieftainships that ruled over subject clans, tribal affiliates, and towns and villages. For example, the Mausillus controlled vast territories in western Iran. The chiefs held official positions in the Safavid government and received subsidies, allotments of infantry, soldiers, tax revenues, and economic rights which made them all the more powerful.

The fluid uymaq and tribal groups were not the only contenders for political power. Tribal-led, merchant-led, and Sufi-led peasant groups waged a multi-sided struggle for political and social power. The uymaqs were opposed by urban bourgeoisie and by peasants organized in secret religious societies. For example, in 1537 and 1538, there was a rebellion in Astarabad of local Persians against the Turkish elites, led by Muhammad Salih Bitikchi, who preached an egalitarian doctrine and promised the deliverance of oppressed peoples from the hands of evil masters. There were similar peasant rebellions in Mazandaran, Jilan, Azarbayjan, Fars, and Afghanistan. The reigning dynasty could only secure a limited degree of control. The Shahs were but suzerains over a society dominated on the local level by uymaqs and other groups battling to enlarge their power.

To fight this inherent dispersion of power, Shah Isma'il attempted to enhance the powers of Persian central officials vis-à-vis the Turkish military elites. The government was organized under the authority of a viceroy (*wakil*), who was also commander of the armies and head of the religious order. The civil administration was headed by a wazir. The military officers (*amirs*) were given land grants from which each had to pay a sum of money to the central government and support a contingent of troops. Isma'il also tried to control the army by appointing as generals men of lesser uymaq standing in order to limit the power of the great Qizilbash lords. A chief religious bureaucrat (*sadr*) supervised judicial appointments and charitable endowments. In the tradition of earlier Islamic regimes, the Safavids built up Georgian, Circassian, Armenian, and Turkish slave forces to offset the power of Turkish warlords.

The move to centralize political power was set back by several ineffectual reigns in the late sixteenth century, but the state-building program was resumed by Shah 'Abbas (1588–1629). 'Abbas began with the reconstruction of the army. He rallied loyal Qizilbash supporters called *shah-seven*, or lovers of the Shah. He supplemented these troops with Georgian and Armenian slaves. New musket and artillery units gave the Shah's armies modern fire power, and made them the equivalent of the Ottoman janissaries. The combination of Caucasian slaves and Persian infantry and artillery gave 'Abbas the military power to consolidate the frontiers of his realm and fortify his internal authority.

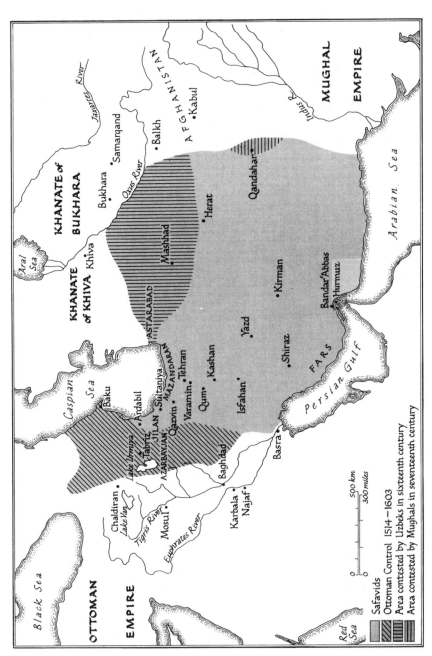

Map 11 Iran under the Safavids: seventeenth century

OTTOMAN
EMPIRE

Black Sea

Chaldiran•
Lake Van
Mosul•
Tigris River
Euphrates River
Karbala•
Najaf•
Baghdad•
Basra•

KHANATE of
BUKHARA

KHANATE
of KHIVA

Jaxartes River

Samarqand•
•Bukhara
Khiva•
Oxus River
•Balkh

A F G H A N I S T A N
•Kabul
Indus R.

MUGHAL
EMPIRE

*Aral
Sea*

*Caspian
Sea*

Baku•
•Ardabil
Tabriz•
Lake Urmiya
AZARBAYJAN
•Sultaniya
•Qazvin
JILAN
MAZANDARAN
•Tehran
Yaramin•
•Qum
•Kashan
Isfahan•

ASTARABAD

•Mashhad

•Herat

•Qandahar

•Kirman

•Yazd

•Shiraz

FARS

Bandar Abbas•
Hurmuz

Arabian Sea

Persian Gulf

500 km
300 miles
0

◻ Safavids
▨ Ottoman Control 1514–1603
▥ Area contested by Uzbeks in sixteenth century
▤ Area contested by Mughals in seventeenth century

*Red
Sea*

The financial basis of the slave armies was secured by seizing Qizilbash lands and turning them into crown lands. The wazirs were made responsible for putting these lands into cultivation. They were expected to invest in irrigation works, protect the peasants from oppression, and assure the collection of rents and taxes. Bureaucratic administration, however, was not completely centralized. In order to pay the salaries of the soldiers, 'Abbas reverted to the basic Islamic and Iranian practice of assigning iqta' or tuyul, which often became the private property of the assignees. Generally royal influence was used to tip the local balance of power against the great magnates in favor of lesser chieftains who would ally with the Shah. 'Abbas succeeded in reducing the power of the great magnates without changing the basic structure of the Turkish uymaq political system. Upon his death, the Iranian state continued to function by virtue of the shifting balance of power between the Safavid regime and the uymaq elites.

Shah 'Abbas's military and administrative reforms were partly financed by an elaborate mercantilist venture. By bringing Armenian merchants to Isfahan and making them intermediaries between the Shah and foreign customers, the royal court gained a strong position in Iranian trade. 'Abbas also established royal factories to produce luxury products for royal use and for international sale. Carpet making, which began as a cottage industry, was centralized in great factories in Isfahan. Silk making also became a royal industry, producing velvets, damasks, satins, and taffetas to be sold in Europe. Safavid ceramicists, with the help of imported Chinese workmen, produced their own "china" based on Chinese porcelains. Throughout Iran, trade was stimulated by the construction of roads and caravansaries.

Iran's opportunity to enter into international commerce came as a result of a British initiative. Ever since the Portuguese seized control of the Indian Ocean trade in the early sixteenth century, the British had been looking for opportunities to bypass Lisbon and find direct access to eastern spices and luxury goods. The first Englishmen to make their way to Iran were Anthony and Robert Sherley, merchant adventurers who arrived in 1598. In 1616, the English East India Company acquired the right to trade freely in Iran. In return, the English helped 'Abbas expel the Portuguese from the Persian Gulf port of Hurmuz and to create Bandar 'Abbas as a new port for the Persian–Indian Ocean trade. The British/Iranian victory encouraged the Dutch to enter the Iranian trade market, and by 1645 the English had been overrun by Dutch competition. The French East India Company entered the scene in 1664, but the first treaty between France and Iran was signed only in 1708, granting trading privileges and protection to Christian religious orders in Iran. Meanwhile Armenian merchants, in alliance with the British, the French, and the Dutch – and supported by the Shah – were competing with the Ottomans and Portuguese in the silk, wool carpet, shawl, and porcelain trades. By the late seventeenth century, however, European merchants were substantially in control of Iranian trade and the economic benefits of international trade were probably lost to Iran. In the

10   The Maydan of Isfahan

eighteenth and nineteenth centuries, the English reestablished their supremacy in the Indian Ocean and Persian Gulf.

The centerpiece of Shah 'Abbas's administrative and economic program was the creation of a great new capital city, Isfahan. It was essential to a centralized state and to the legitimization of the Safavid dynasty. The Safavids built the new city around the Maydan-i Shah, a huge square which measures about 160 by 500 meters. The square served as market, carnival place, and polo ground. It was surrounded by two-storied rows of shops and by principal buildings or arches on each of the cardinal sides. To the east the Masjid-i Shaykh Lutfallah, begun in 1603 and completed in 1618, was an oratory designed for the Shah's private worship. To the south stood the royal mosque, begun in 1611 and completed in 1629. On the west stood the 'Ali Qapu palace or Sublime Porte, which was the headquarters of the govern-

11   Persian court dress in the Safavid period: *(a)* male

ment. On the north side of the Maydan was the monumental arch which marked the entrance to the royal bazaar and its innumerable shops, baths, caravansaries, mosques, and colleges. From the Maydan, the Chahar Bagh avenue ran two-and-a-half miles to the summer palace in which the ruler gave audiences to ambassadors and held state ceremonies. On either side of the avenue were elaborate gardens, the Shah's harem, and residences for courtiers and foreign ambassadors. The whole ensemble was a masterpiece of Middle Eastern city planning.

Isfahan's bazaars were essential to the state economy, for they concentrated production and marketing and brought them under the taxing authority of the state. The new capital was a reservoir for recruits to the imperial armies and administration. It was equally important to the vitality of Iranian Islam. In 1666, Isfahan, according to

11   Persian court dress in the Safavid period: *(b)* female

a European visitor, had 162 mosques, 48 colleges, 182 caravansaries, and 273 public baths, almost all of them erected by 'Abbas I and 'Abbas II (1642–66).

Isfahan also symbolized the legitimacy of the dynasty. Its vast plazas and bazaars were a symbol of the ordering of the world by royal decree; its religious monuments signified royal sustenance for the faith; its gorgeous decoration was the universal sign of royal splendor. Safavid claims to legitimacy were broadened from their initial religious basis to include the traditional motifs of Iranian monarchical grandeur.

There were other signs of a new conception of monarchy. In 1510 the Timurid school of painting was transferred from Herat to Tabriz. Bihzad, the greatest painter of the time, was appointed Director of the Royal Library and supervisor of a workshop that produced illuminated manuscripts. Shah Tahmasp was also a great patron of the production of robes, silk hangings, and works in metal and ceramics. He kept these treasures as a private and courtly adornment, and devoted no attention to mosques, shrines, colleges, or other public expressions of imperial authority. The Timurid school produced an illuminated edition of the *Shah-name* (Book of Kings) which contains more than 250 paintings and is one of the great masterpieces of Iranian and Islamic illuminated manuscript art. 'Abbas I created the public style of royalty. Isfahan was his masterpiece, but he also patronized paintings of battles, hunting scenes, and royal ceremonies. After his death artistic effort turned to emotional expression and themes of private daily life: the great themes of the royal tradition were put aside in favor of more realistic and secular scenes, such as couples embracing, which may have appealed to an aristocracy of bureaucrats, landlords, and soldiers. Single-page drawings and paintings were made for inclusion in albums. The later seventeenth-century style combined sensuality and realism.

Under 'Abbas I the Safavid monarchy reached the height of its political power. His reign was a glorified household state, with the ruler surrounded by his personal servitors, soldiers, and administrators. He closely controlled the bureaucracy and tax collection, monopolized the manufacture and sale of important cloth goods and other products, built great cities, and maintained shrines and roads as an expression of his fatherly concern for the welfare of his people. Though his reign marked the apogee of the Iranian state, his achievement was flawed. He never succeeded in establishing a fully centralized regime. The military and administrative policies that reduced the power of Turkish lords did not succeed in replacing them. His commercial policies had only short-lived success; his religious and artistic efforts were eventually appropriated by others. Ultimately the rural elites proved too powerful, and urban merchant and rural landlord support too weak, to sustain a centralized state.

THE CONVERSION OF IRAN TO SHI'ISM

Parallel to the program of state formation, the Safavids created a religious establishment which would lend its authority and administrative services to the regime. Safavid religious appeals were first addressed to their Qizilbash and tribal supporters, to whom they promised messianic fulfillment. Shah Isma'il claimed to be the manifestation of God, the divine fire of the hidden imam, and the mahdi. He titled himself the Shadow of God on Earth, in the manner of Persian emperors. As the descendant of the seventh imam, an infallible leader, and an emanation of the divine being, his authority was absolute and unquestioned. This personal authority was reinforced by the cult of the Safavid ancestors at Ardabil and by direct Safavid patronage of the major Iranian shrines.

This absolute authority was communicated to his followers through his role as *murshid-i kamil*, or perfect master. The followers of Isma'il were supposed to adhere strictly to a code of conduct called *sufigare*; disobedience was punished by expulsion from the order and probably by execution. The devotion of the Qizil-bash, however, was a double-edged sword, for the millenarian impulses that had brought the Safavids to power could also be turned against them. Defeat by the Ottomans at the battle of Chaldiran in 1514 shattered the Qizilbash belief in the invincibility of their leader.

To cope with the complications of Qizilbash enthusiasm and the tepid response of the Iranian population, Isma'il's messianic claims were set aside in favor of "twelver" Shi'ism, a more institutionalized form of Shi'ism which was proclaimed the official religion of Iran. Isma'il, however, had little to build on; though there were pockets of Shi'a in Qum and Isfahan, the majority of the population was Sunni. Isma'il imported "twelver" Shi'i scholars from Syria, Bahrain, northeastern Arabia, and Iraq. 'Ali al-Karaki (1465–1534) founded the first Shi'i madrasa in Iran.

The Safavids then organized the 'ulama' into a state-controlled bureaucracy. The sadr was the liaison between the Shah and the religious establishment. He was initially responsible for the ritual cursing of the first three Caliphs, but his duties were gradually enlarged to include the appointment of judges and teachers and the administration of endowments. The office of *divan bagi* was created as a high court of appeal. Grants of land called *soyurghal* were also made to eminent religious families, and were allowed to pass from generation to generation immune from taxation. The religious elite became part of the Iranian landowning aristocracy. In the early period of Iranian Shi'ism, the administrative and moral authority of the Shahs over the religious establishment was virtually complete. This disposed the Shi'i 'ulama' to accept state authority and to stress those elements of the Shi'i tradition that affirmed the state order as a historical necessity.

To sustain the official religion, the Safavids embarked on a bold program to eliminate all rival forms of Islam in what had been a highly pluralistic society. "Twelver" Shi'ism was imposed by a wave of persecutions which has little or no parallel in other Muslim regions. The Safavids suppressed their messianic and extremist followers who seemed likely to turn their religious passion against them. Isma'il and Tahmasp executed religious enthusiasts who proclaimed them as messiahs. 'Abbas I massacred his Sufi disciples, who were accused of collaborating with the Ottomans and of failing to place the will of the master before all other concerns. Other chiliastic movements in northwestern Iran were also suppressed.

The dominance of Shi'ism was further assured by the violent suppression of Sunnism. The Safavids ritually insulted the memory of the first three Caliphs and violated the tombs of Sunni scholars. Sufi shrines were destroyed; Isma'il desecrated Naqshbandi tombs, and suppressed the Khalwatiya, Dhahabiya, and Nurbakhshiya orders. 'Abbas I later seized the Nimatullahi khanaqas and turned them over to youth organizations. The pilgrimage to Mecca was deemphasized in favor of ritual visits to the shrines of Shi'i imams. The persecution of Sunnis and Sufis continued sporadically throughout the sixteenth and seventeenth centuries until Muhammad Baqir al-Majlisi (d. 1699), the head of the Shi'i 'ulama', completed the suppression of Sunnism and expelled the remaining Sufis from Isfahan. However, despite persecution, individual Qalandaris, committed to a wandering life, rejecting all worldly connections, remained an important spiritual influence.

The Shahs were also hostile to non-Muslim communities. Decrees of 'Abbas I made it possible for a convert to Islam from Judaism or Christianity to claim the property of his relatives. In 1656, Shah 'Abbas II granted extensive powers to his wazirs to force Jews to become Muslims. Al-Majlisi persuaded Shah Husayn (1688–1726) to decree the forcible conversion of Zoroastrians. The Shi'i 'ulama', however, were less harsh in their treatment of Armenians. The Armenians maintained good relations with the Iranian regime because of their shared hostility to the Greek Orthodox Church. Also, Armenians and Georgians provided important recruits for the Shahs' military and commercial establishments.

Nonetheless, the success of "twelver" Shi'ism depended not only upon the power of the state, but upon its intrinsic religious appeal. Iranian Shi'ism integrated the legal, gnostic, and popular forms of Islam. The suppression of Sufism led to the incorporation, during the sixteenth and seventeenth centuries, of gnostic and philosophic ideas within the "twelver" establishment, and to the absorption of the popular veneration of Husayn, 'Ali, and other Shi'i imams as an integral part of Iranian Islam. A new school of philosophy, under the leadership of Mir Damad (d. 1631) and his disciple, Mulla Sadra (d. 1640), combined Shi'i scripture, theology, and mystical reflection to create a Shi'i version of Sufism and give a philosophic basis to individual religious consciousness and to Shi'i loyalty to the imams. The new school combined the illuminationism of Suhrawardi (see chapter 12) with the sayings of 'Ali and the imams, elements of Greek philosophy, and the teachings of Ibn al-'Arabi, and belonged to the neo-Platonic rather than the Aristotelian tradition of Greek and Muslim philosophy.

The central problem for Mir Damad was the creation of the universe and the place of the human being within it. He approached the classic issue of scholastic theology – whether the world is eternal or is created in time – by introducing an intermediary state. He divided temporal reality into three categories – *dahr*, *sarmad*, and *zaman*. Dahr means eternity and defines the divine essence, which is unitary and has no internal distinctions. The divine essence, however, is the source of the names and attributes that are integral to it and yet separate from it. The relationship between essence and attributes is characterized as sarmad. In turn, the names and attributes are the archetypes that generate the material and changeable world. The latter is characterized as zaman, or temporality. While existing in time, the created world is not purely temporal in its origin, for it is brought into being by archetypes which exist before the creation of the world and are themselves eternal. Like the neo-Platonists, Mir Damad tried to close the gulf between God and the creation and to reconcile the transcendence of God with his immanence in the created world.

For Mir Damad, as for the neo-Platonist and illuminationist philosophers, the human being stands in an intermediate position, a bridge between the world of eternity and the world of time. Man possesses qualities of perception, imagination, and intellect which link the visible and the invisible worlds. The soul both receives sensible perceptions from the material world and is illuminated by intelligible concepts from the spiritual world. The *'alam al-mithal*, or realm of archetypes, intermediate between material sense perception and intellectual abstraction, is the ontological basis for symbolic imagination, dream experience, and religious commitment. The emphasis upon this intermediary reality gave Shi'ism a rationalistic explanation of revealed truth, and defined the metaphysical meaning of the individual's quest for spiritual salvation.

Popular veneration for sacred figures was also part of Iranian Shi'ism. The great shrines of Mashhad and Qum were rebuilt in the reign of 'Abbas I, and were endowed with extensive properties. *Imamzadas* in memory of people born or related to imams, and *imambaras*, shrines devoted to Husayn and Hasan, replaced popular village shrines. The pilgrimage to Karbala was substituted for the pilgrimage to Mecca. *Ziyarat*, or ceremonial visits to the shrines of imams and their families, were promoted as an alternative to the veneration of Sufi shrines; imambaras replaced Sufi khanaqas as devotional centers, just as the hidden imam replaced the Sufi qutb as the object of religious veneration.

The festivals of the month of Muharram became the ceremonial center of the Shi'i religious calendar. Recitations of the heart-rending story of Husayn, and processions that included public flagellation, passion plays, sermons, and recitations of elegies, marked a period of mourning and atonement for his death. Neighborhood groups, youth gangs, and religious factions competed in their veneration of Husayn and often ended up in bloody struggles. Thus, Shi'ism seized hold of popular emotions in order to attach the Iranian populace to the religious establishment. By the late Safavid period, Shi'ism had duplicated the whole complex of religious sensibility already found within Sunnism. It thus became a comprehensive alternative version of Islam.

THE DISSOLUTION OF THE SAFAVID EMPIRE

The Safavid pattern of state, tribal, and religious institutions created by Shah 'Abbas I was profoundly altered in the late seventeenth and early eighteenth centuries. In this period, the Safavid regime was weakened and eventually destroyed by tribal forces, and Shi'i Islam was liberated from state control.

The decline of the central government was already manifest after the death of 'Abbas I. In order to prevent violent struggle among potential successors to the throne, succeeding generations of Safavid princes were confined to the harem and palace precincts, and were raised with a narrow education and without any experience of public life. No ruler after 'Abbas I duplicated his vision or authority. Furthermore, after the peace of 1639 with the Ottoman empire, the army was neglected and declined into a number of small and ill-disciplined regiments. By the end of the seventeenth century, the Safavid army was no longer a competent military machine. Central administration also fell apart, and the procedures for regulating taxation and distributing revenue were abandoned. The weakening of the central state permitted the revival of uymaq chieftainships and provincial revolts against Safavid authority. In the eighteenth century Iran fell into anarchy. The most important of the new competitors for political power were the Afghans, Afshars, Zands, and Qajars. Ghalzai Afghans took control of Isfahan, the Safavid capital, in 1722. Iran was then attacked by both its Ottoman and its Russian neighbors, who in 1724 agreed on a partition of Transcaucasia in which the Ottomans gained Armenia and parts of Azarbayjan and the Russians obtained the Caspian Sea provinces of Jilan, Mazandaran, and Astarabad.

With the Afghans in control of the south and the Russians and the Ottomans in control of the north, Nadir, an Afshar chieftain of Chaghatay descent, seized power. Nadir deposed the last of the Safavids and in 1736 named himself Shah of Iran. His actions were not merely a Bonapartist-like adventure, but harked back to an eastern-Iranian frontier tradition of Turkish resistance to an Iranian central government and to ethnic Persian rule. For centuries, a frontier population, closely resembling the Cossacks of the Russian steppes, had maneuvered between the larger powers and kept alive its aspirations to establish a new Khanate on the basis of a Chaghatay and Sunni identity.

In his short reign, Nadir restored the territory of the Iranian state, attempted to promote a reconciliation of Sunni and Shi'i Islam, and to integrate Afghan and eastern Iranian tribal peoples into the regime. He proposed to make Shi'ism a fifth school of law, called the Ja'fari school, equal in status to the four Sunni schools. He also weakened the Shi'i 'ulama' by confiscating properties, abolishing clerical positions in the government, and canceling the jurisdiction of religious courts. Nadir was succeeded by Karim Khan, the leader of a coalition of Zand tribal groups in western Iran, whose effective regime lasted from 1750 to 1779. In its turn it gave way to the Qajars, who were originally Turkish lords in Safavid service, and local governors in Mazandaran and Astarabad. In 1779 the Qajars defeated the Zand, and established a dynasty that was to last until 1924.

The destruction of the Iranian state in the eighteenth century had profound implications for the relations between state and religious elites. It allowed the latent claims to autonomy of the Shi'i 'ulama' to come to the fore. The first steps were taken with the reaffirmation of the Shi'i millenarian concept that the hidden imam would establish his personal rule only at the end of time, rather than in the era of Safavid authority. The 'ulama' withdrew from engagement in public affairs. By the seventeenth century religious motivation for worldly action was being replaced by a pious disdain for involvement in worldly affairs. The early fusion of the religious and political aspects of Safavid society was superseded by a separation of religion and politics and a devaluation of political action.

Moreover, by the late seventeenth century Shi'i scholars cast doubt upon the inherited authority of the Shah as the primary bearer of Shi'i Islam. This authority depended upon descent from the seventh imam, but in Shi'i theory biological inheritance was not sufficient. Testamentary designation (nass) was necessary to determine which of the descendants of a given imam had inherited his authority. The Safavid position was weak because they could not demonstrate designation by testament. Furthermore, according to "twelver" Shi'i belief, ever since the greater occultation of 941 the hidden imam was represented on earth by religious scholars. The 'ulama' thus asserted that the *mujtahids* (scholars capable of independent religious judgments) bore the highest religious authority. Several schools of 'ulama' elaborated upon the nature of that authority. The *usuli* school gave the mujtahids a wide latitude, for it saw their authority as based on such complex factors as knowledge of the Quran, the tradition of 'Ali, and the consensus of the community. The *akhbari* school restricted the authority of individual scholars by stressing the importance of literal adherence to the letter of the tradition passed down by the Prophet and the imams. That such a debate could take place was itself a demonstration of the autonomy of the religious establishment. The monolithic and all-absorbing religious establishment created by the Shahs was disengaging itself from the embrace of the state. In the nineteenth century it would become the leading opponent of the Iranian regime.

From the Mongol invasions to the collapse of the Safavid empire the history of Iran was marked both by continuity and transformation of the basic patterns of state, religion, and society inherited from the Saljuq era. From the Saljuq era the Mongols, Timurids, and Safavids inherited a tradition of centralized monarchy and sought to strengthen the power of the central state by subordinating the tribal or uymaq conquerors to slave military forces and a quasi-centralized administration. Nonetheless, the Turkish and Mongol invasions had permanently consolidated the parochial uymaq or tribal forces in Iranian society, and all Iranian monarchs were obliged to rely on the political cooperation of uymaq and tribal chiefs and on iqta' (or tuyul) forms of tax administration to effect their rule. Iranian states remained at best household or court regimes with limited powers in the countryside. Even when the state overcame the power of the uymaq lords and tribal chiefs, as in the reign of Shah 'Abbas I, it could not change the political system of Iran. With the weakening of the state in the eighteenth century, the uymaq lords again partitioned Iran and brought new dynasties to power.

Iran also went through extraordinary changes in the relationship between state and religion. In the Mongol and Timurid periods, rural Sufi movements organized popular opposition to brutal foreign regimes. Islam served, as it had in the era of the Prophet, to unite disparate peoples into larger moral and political movements. The Safavids originated as such a movement, but upon coming to power suppressed the millenarian forms of Sufi Islam in favor of a state-constructed 'ulama' establishment. The Safavids made "twelver" Shi'ism the official religion of Iran, and eliminated their own Sufi followers as well as the Sunni 'ulama'. Safavid-period Shi'ism absorbed philosophic and gnostic ideas and popular saint worship. Iran was virtually unique among Muslim societies in the degree to which the state controlled the religious establishment and in the extent to which it absorbed all religious tendencies found within the Muslim spectrum.

The eighteenth-century crisis brought to an end the pre-modern history of Iran. Whereas in most Muslim regions the pre-modern period ended with European intervention, conquest, and the establishment of colonial regimes, in this case the consolidation of European economic and political influence was preceded by the breakup of the Safavid empire and the liberation of the 'ulama'. Thus the Safavid regime left as its legacy to modern Iran a Persian tradition of glorified monarchy, a regime based on powerful uymaq or tribal principalities, and a cohesive, monolithic, and partially autonomous Shi'i religious establishment.

CHAPTER 14

THE TURKISH MIGRATIONS AND THE
OTTOMAN EMPIRE

THE MIGRATIONS AND TURKISH-ISLAMIC STATES IN ANATOLIA (1071–1243)

The migrations that gave rise to the Saljuq, Mongol, and Timurid empires in Iran also gave birth to a succession of great western Muslim empires. The Oghuz peoples, who established the Saljuq empire in Iran and Iraq, also pushed their way into Georgia, Armenia, and Byzantine Anatolia. At the battle of Manzikert in 1071, the Turks captured the Byzantine emperor, Romanos I. In the next century, they spread across Asia Minor, and established another Saljuq state and society. The migrating peoples were organized into small bands of warriors called ghazis under the leadership of chieftains (*beys*) or Sufi holy men (*babas*). Veneration of the chiefs and the desire to find rich pasturage, gather booty, and win victories against the infidels in the name of Islam held them together. The migrants destroyed agricultural enterprises, depopulated large territories, and cut off cities from their hinterlands and trading connections. Only a few fortified Byzantine towns remained as isolated islands in a sea of nomadic peoples. Greek and Armenian Christian populations, already decimated by previous invasions, were further reduced by warfare and migration, and by conversion to Islam. Turks became the majority in much of Anatolia.

Turkish expansion in Anatolia was soon counterbalanced by the formation of states that attempted to gain control over the nomadic peoples and the territory they had conquered, check their predatory adventures, and restore agricultural production. The formation of Turkish states toward the end of the eleventh century introduced the governing motif of Turkish, Anatolian, and Ottoman history for the next 500 years – the struggle between independent nomadic warriors and settled society. The history of Turkish Anatolia thus repeated the Saljuq experience in Iran and Iraq, in which states attempted to subordinate pastoral conquerors in the interests of sedentary societies.

The Saljuq state in central and southern Anatolia, with its capital at Konya, assiduously reconstructed the whole panoply of Turkish Saljuq Islamic government. To dominate the nomadic populations and the conquered Christian peoples, the Saljuqs built up a large standing army of Turkish and Christian slaves, and maintained detachments of Georgian and other Christian mercenaries. The administrative elite was composed of Iranian scribes. In the early thirteenth century a fiscal survey was made and iqta's were distributed in return for military service. The Saljuqs appointed provincial governors, made the chiefs subordinate officials of the regime, and even attempted to extract taxes from the pastoral population. Energetic efforts were made to sedentarize nomadic groups. The Saljuqs favored the sedentary economy by building caravansaries. Ocean traffic was encouraged from Saljuq-controlled seaports on the Black Sea, the Aegean, and the Mediterranean.

The Saljuqs also built up the whole infrastructure of Sunni Islam. Scholars from Iran were invited to settle in Anatolia. Qadis were appointed, colleges were endowed with waqfs, and funds were provided for the education of converts. The money came primarily from levies on Christian villages and appropriated ecclesiastical properties. The Saljuq regime also attempted to bring independent Sufi fraternities under government influence by providing them with schools, hospices, and endowments. Sufis were particularly important in Anatolia. Members of the Qalandariya, Rifaʿiya, and other Sufi brotherhoods migrated into Anatolia from Inner Asia and eastern Iran; others were driven westward by the Mongol invasions. The Sufi babas provided leadership for migrating Turkish peoples, and helped bring new territories into cultivation. They built hospices and mills, planted orchards, developed schools, provided for the safety of travelers, and mediated disputes among tribes. Thus they brought order into a fragmented warrior society.

Rural Sufis also adopted a tolerant attitude toward Christians and facilitated the conversion of Greek and Armenian peoples to Islam. Hajji Bektash (d. c. 1297), who was widely revered in Anatolia, preached a version of Islam that synthesized Sunni and Shiʿi beliefs and Muslim and Christian religious practices. He converted Tatar communities and arranged for them to perform military service in return for assignments of land. Urban religious fraternities called *akhis* (groups of unmarried young men devoted to the *futuwwa* [youth] ethic of bravery and hospitality), recruited from the artisan and merchant strata of the population, protected local populations from abuse and gave charity to strangers and the poor. The akhis were closely allied to the Mevlevi order, whose Friday prayers and common meals were a focus of town life.

The Mongol invasions destroyed the work of urbanization and sedentarization. In 1242–43 the Mongols defeated the Saljuqs, made them vassals, and tipped the balance of power in Anatolia from the central state to the pastoral warrior populations. The Mongols also opened the way to further Turkish migrations. Large numbers of new migrants entered Anatolia in the 1230s, and settled in the mountainous country on the frontiers of the Byzantine empire.

Small groups of warriors, nomads, refugees, adventurers, and bandits, eager to escape Mongol oppression, motivated by pressure of population and by the desire for pasturage, booty, and glory in the holy war, resumed the struggle against the Byzantine empire, and founded new principalities. The most important of these new states was the Karaman beylik in Cilicia, which in 1335 made Konya its capital and claimed to inherit Saljuq authority, the dynasty of Dulgadir in the northern reaches of the Euphrates River and Menteshe and Germiyan in the region of Kutahya.

THE RISE OF THE OTTOMANS (c. 1280–1453)

One of these frontier warrior states, led by Ertugrul (d. c. 1280) and his son Osman, was destined to attain greatness. The name of the Ottoman dynasty derived from Osman. Ertugrul had brought some 400 followers into Saljuq service. Struggling for control of pasturage, his son expanded onto the plains, and his grandson seized the important town of Bursa in 1326 and crossed the straits to Gallipoli (1345). Having established a foothold in Europe, the Ottomans invited masses of Turkish warriors into the Balkans, and occupied northern Greece, Macedonia, and Bulgaria. Ottoman control of the western Balkans was decisively established by their victory at the battle of Kosovo in 1389. On the basis of their European empire, the Ottomans began to annex rival Turkish principalities in western Anatolia and to plan for the conquest of Constantinople.

This ambitious plan was temporarily set back in 1402 by the invasion of Timur who, provoked by the eastward expansion of the Ottoman empire, made himself the defender of the Muslim principalities of Anatolia, defeated Bayazid I (1389–1402), and reduced the Ottoman state to vassalage. The Ottomans, however, survived this defeat, again annexed other Turkish principalities in Anatolia, and expanded Ottoman domains into Serbia.

The Ottoman conquests inspired a Europe-wide anxiety. To check Ottoman expansion, the European states mobilized latter-day Crusades. In 1396 a coalition organized by the papacy and Venice was defeated at the battle of Nicopolis. In 1444 the papacy and a coalition of powers including the kings of Hungary, Poland, and Naples, and the rulers of Transylvania, Serbia, Venice, and Genoa, launched another Crusade, only to be defeated at the battle of Varna. Nothing could prevent the conquest of Constantinople in 1453, a triumph which fulfilled an age-old Muslim ambition to inherit the domains of the Roman empire.

From Constantinople, the Ottomans pushed on to complete the absorption of the Balkans as far as the Danube and the Aegean. Mehmed II, the conqueror of Constantinople, pushed the Serbian frontiers to the Danube by 1449. In the next half century the Ottomans absorbed Greece, Bosnia, Herzegovina, and Albania. The Turkish advance was reinforced by the capacity of the Ottomans to gather political support from former Byzantine civil servants and Christian nobles who were integrated into the Ottoman armies and administration. The Ottomans also protected the Greek Orthodox Church in an effort to win the support of Balkan peoples.

The absorption of the former Byzantine empire by Turkish-Muslim conquerors led to the eventual conversion of Anatolia and thus added new territories to the

Table 12. *The Ottoman dynasty*

Accession date	
1281	Uthman I (Osman)
1324	Orhan
1360	Murad I
1389	Bayazid I
1402	interregnum
1413	Mehmed I
1421	Murad II
1444	Mehmed II the Conqueror
1446	Murad II (second reign)
1451	Mehmed II the Conqueror (second reign)
1481	Bayazid II
1512	Selim I
1520	Sulayman I ("the Law-giver" or "the Magnificent")
1566	Selim II
1574	Murad III
1594	Muhammad III
1603	Ahmad I
1617	Mustafa I (first reign)
1618	Uthman II
1622	Mustafa I (second reign)
1623	Murad IV
1640	Ibrahim
1648	Muhammad IV
1678	Sulayman II
1691	Ahmad II
1695	Mustafa II
1703	Ahmad III
1730	Mahmud I
1754	Uthman III
1757	Mustafa III
1774	Abd al-Hamid I
1789	Selim III
1807	Mustafa IV
1808	Mahmud II
1839	Abd al-Majid I
1861	Abd al-Aziz
1876	Murad V
1876	Abd al-Hamid II
1909	Muhammad V Rashid
1918	Muhammad VI Wahid al-Din
1922–24	Abd al-Majid II (as Caliph only)

domain of Islam. Before the Turkish migrations, the vast majority of the Greek, Armenian, Georgian, and Syrian populations of Anatolia had been Christian. By the fifteenth century more than 90 percent of the population was Muslim. Some of this change was due to the immigration of a large Muslim population, but in great part it was caused by the conversion of Christians to Islam.

These conversions were basically due to the breakdown of Anatolian Christianity through the weakening of the Byzantine state and the Greek Orthodox Church, and the collapse of Anatolian society in the face of Turkish migrations. In the late thirteenth and fourteenth centuries the Turks excluded bishops and metropolitans from their sees. Church revenues and properties were confiscated. Hospitals, schools, orphanages, and monasteries were destroyed or abandoned, and the Anatolian Christian population was left without leadership and social services. The remaining Christian clerics had to turn to Turkish authorities to handle internal disputes on terms that only further weakened Christian institutions.

At the same time, an ordered Islamic society was being built up to replace the dying Byzantine state and church. The Saljuq state and the Turkish emirates built palaces, mosques, colleges, caravansaries, and hospitals, supported by endowments and staffed with Persian and Arab scholars. A demoralized Christian population saw its defeat as a sign of punishment from God or even of the end of history, and Muslim holy men appealed to it by presenting Islam as a syncretism of Muslim and Christian religious beliefs. Christian holy places were taken over; Jesus was venerated by Muslims. Byzantine princes, lords, and administrators were tempted to convert to Islam in order to join the Ottoman aristocracy. By the end of the fifteenth century Anatolia was largely Muslim.

The Ottoman conquests in the Balkans also established Muslim hegemony over large Christian populations, but did not lead, as in Anatolia, to the substantial assimilation of the regional population to Islam. Several considerations seem to explain the difference. One is that the bulk of Turkish settlement took place in Anatolia rather than in the Balkans. The second is that Ottoman administrative policy in the Balkans favored the Christian churches. Until the conquest of Constantinople the churches in Anatolia, which were identified with the rival Byzantine empire, were harried and suppressed. After the conquest, the Orthodox Church in the Balkans was reorganized, confirmed in its jurisdictions and properties, and allowed to protect Christian communities.

In the Balkans, the Turkish-Muslim presence was first established by Turkish migrants who entered Thrace, the Maritsa Valley, northern Bulgaria, and Albania in the course of the fourteenth and fifteenth centuries. Hundreds of new villages were founded, often around Sufi hospices (*tekkes*); the major towns were settled by Muslims. In the Balkans, as in Anatolia, conversion was facilitated by the preaching of the Sufi orders, such as the Bektashis and the Mevlevis, and most probably occurred in rural areas. Though there were some cases of forced conversion in Serbia, Albania, and Bulgaria, there was no systematic persecution. Converts to Islam often brought with them Christian beliefs and practices. Baptism, worship of saints, the celebration of Easter, and belief in the healing efficacy of churches were taken from Christianity into Islam. In the Balkans Islam was also influenced by pagan practices which had remained a strong aspect of Balkan folk Christianity.

A census of 1520–30 showed that about 19 percent of the Balkan population was Muslim and 81 percent was Christian, with a small Jewish minority. The Muslim population of Bosnia, one of the highest, was 45 percent. In general, Muslims were concentrated in towns. For example, Sofia had a Muslim majority of 66.4 percent, whereas the surrounding district was only 6 percent Muslim. The town of Edirne was 82 percent Muslim in a district that was otherwise 74 percent Christian. The Muslim element was most numerous in Thrace, Macedonia, Thessaly, Bosnia, Herzegovina, and Silistria. A new wave of Islamization occurred between 1666 and 1690 in the Rhodope. Islam came to northern Albania and Montenegro in the seventeenth century. Greeks in southwestern Macedonia and Crete converted in the course of the seventeenth and eighteenth centuries.

THE OTTOMAN WORLD EMPIRE

The conquest of Constantinople and the Balkans was a turning point in Ottoman history. Rather than satisfying Turkish, Ottoman, and Muslim ambitions, it made them boundless. Mehmed II the Conqueror (1444–46, 1451–81) fused the Turkish interest in victories over the infidels with the imperial ambitions of both the Muslim Caliphate and the Roman empire. He saw himself as a successor to the Byzantine emperors, constructed vast formal palaces, and legislated new codes of law. Art and policy were adapted to symbolize the ambition for a universal empire. This empire would sweep eastward to the borders of Iran, and subsume the Arab provinces of the Middle East and North Africa and the holy places of Arabia. With the conquest of the former lands of the 'Abbasid Caliphate, the Ottomans would inherit Muslim world leadership. The absorption of Damascus, Cairo, Mecca, and Medina would bring a great influx of Muslim scholars to Istanbul. In addition to the title of ghazi or "Warrior for the Faith," the Ottoman rulers would take the titles of "Servitor of the Two Holy Sanctuaries" and "Defender of the Shari'a." Muslims the world over would appeal to them for military and political support. The Mamluks of Egypt and the Muslims of Gujarat and Acheh would invoke their aid in the Indian Ocean struggle against the Portuguese. Muslims in Spain would appeal for Ottoman help against the Christian Reconquista. Sunnis in Inner Asia would call to their Ottoman brothers to protect them against the Safavids and the Russians. From their dominant position in the Muslim East the Ottomans would also sweep northward and westward over central Europe and the Mediterranean. The sixteenth century was the period of the most aggressive expansion, the seventeenth century a period of maintenance; the eighteenth century would bring the first serious reversals to an expanding Ottoman empire.

The great eastern sweep began after the conquest of Constantinople. Ottoman successes in the Balkans were accompanied by campaigns to absorb the rival Turkish principalities in Anatolia. Ottoman expansion, exacerbated by Sunni–Shi'i religious antagonism, brought them into rivalry with the Safavids for control of eastern Anatolia and western Iran. The decisive battle of Chaldiran (1514) enabled the Ottomans to annex eastern Anatolia and northern Mesopotamia, and to take control of the important trade routes leading from Tabriz to Aleppo and Bursa. The

Ottoman struggle with Iran continued sporadically for more than a century, until the treaty of Qasr Shirin, which gave Baghdad and Iraq to the Ottomans and the Caucasus to Iran. This treaty confirmed the modern boundaries between Iraq and Iran. The Ottoman–Safavid rivalry cut the Ottoman empire off from the roots of Islamic culture in Iran and led to its Turkification. The schism between Iran and the Ottomans also reinforced Arab influence in the further development of Ottoman civilization. In the Arab regions, the Ottomans in 1516 and 1517 took over the Mamluk empire of Syria and Egypt and the Muslim holy places of Arabia.

As rulers of Egypt, the Ottomans became responsible for Muslim interests in the Indian Ocean. They fought European efforts to divert the international spice trade from the Mediterranean to Atlantic routes. By 1507 the Portuguese had established a series of bases in the Indian Ocean, cutting off commerce to the Red Sea and the Mediterranean, but after 1517 the Ottomans established their own bases in Arabia and East Africa including Sawakin, Aden, and Yemen. From these bases the Red Sea fleets under the leadership of Piri Re'is (1465–1554) reopened the routes to Alexandria and Aleppo. In the Persian Gulf region, they occupied Baghdad in 1534, Basra in 1538, and Bahrain in 1554.

In this epic struggle, the Portuguese and the Ottoman strategies were entirely different. The Portuguese relied upon maritime commerce and the control of trade. The Ottomans, by contrast, depended on the revenues of their vast territorial empire, and had only a defensive interest in the seas. Thus, the Ottoman commitment to the Indian Ocean was limited to some 25 ships and 4,000 men – merely a holding operation – and the Portuguese and the Ottomans could establish a frontier in the Indian Ocean based upon their respective interests. The moment had not yet come for the ultimate confrontation between Ottoman territorial and European naval power.

The conquest of the Balkans opened the way for a two-centuries-long struggle against the powers of Europe. In this war the Ottomans were primarily allied to France against their principal enemies, the Habsburg empire in Spain, the Netherlands, Austria and Hungary, and Tsarist Russia. The world war unfolded in three principal theaters. In central Europe the Ottomans pushed beyond the Danube and absorbed the Romanian principalities by 1504. They confirmed local princes in power, but maintained forts and garrisons and received a tribute of cereals, honey, hides, and cloth. The Hungarian monarchy, crippled by aristocratic factional quarrels and by unrest among the peasants, lost Belgrade in 1521, and was forced to accept Ottoman suzerainty in 1526. In 1529 the Ottomans besieged Vienna. Though the siege of Vienna failed, it assured the Ottomans control of Hungary. Still expanding, the Ottomans made Transylvania a vassal in 1559. Finally, the long war of 1593–1606 brought an end to Ottoman expansion. By the treaty of Zsitva Torok (1606), Ottoman rule over Romania, Hungary, and Transylvania was confirmed, but the Ottoman Sultans had to recognize the Habsburg emperors as their equals. The Ottomans had come up against the highly organized societies of central Europe, and at vast distances from their capital, Istanbul, could no longer make significant advances. Nevertheless, the struggle to break the stalemate went on and culminated in the last, and fruitless, Ottoman siege of Vienna in 1683.

The wars in central Europe were accompanied by an equally vast Ottoma–Habsburg struggle for control of the Mediterranean. In the early days of Ottoman expansion, the dominant naval powers in the Mediterranean were Venice and Genoa, each of which had established a series of fortified trading posts along the Mediterranean and Aegean coasts in order to sustain their commerce. When the conquest of Constantinople and consolidation of Ottoman rule in the Balkans put Byzantine maritime resources into the hands of the conquerors, Mehmed built a new navy based on Italian designs and Greek seamanship. The Ottomans pushed the Venetians out of the eastern Mediterranean and, after the conquest of Egypt in 1517, encouraged Muslim privateers in the western Mediterranean. Khayr al-Din Barbarossa led privateering operations out of Tunis, took Algiers in 1529, and was made Grand Admiral of the Ottoman fleets in 1533 – a clear expression of Ottoman aspirations to control the western Mediterranean.

Crucial to this ambition was the control of the straits between Sicily and Tunisia. The battles of Algiers (1529) and Tunis (1534–35) marked successful Ottoman advances. The Spanish Habsburgs counter-attacked by building a series of fortified posts along the coast of North Africa reaching as far as Tripoli in 1510 and La Goletta in 1535, but eventually the Ottomans seized Tripoli (1551), Bougie (1555), Jerba (1560), Malta (1565), and Cyprus (1570). This provoked the formation of a coalition among the papacy, Venice, and the Habsburgs, who defeated the Ottomans at the battle of Lepanto in 1571. Lepanto was celebrated as a triumph of Christian Europe over the Muslim Turks. The Europeans regained their confidence. In fact, the Ottomans restored their fleets and, in a resounding victory, seized Tunis in 1574. In 1580 the Mediterranean wars came to an end. Both the protagonists recognized that they could no longer change Mediterranean boundaries; the truce of 1580 confirmed the frontier between Christian and Muslim civilizations that has lasted to the present day.

Russia and the Ottoman empire were rivals for control of the regions north of the Black Sea and between the Black and the Caspian Seas. In the late fifteenth century the Ottomans established their suzerainty over Romania and the Crimean Tatars, but the Russians seized Kazan (1552) and Astrakhan (1556) and thus won control of the lower Volga. In response, the Ottomans determined on the bold strategy of building a channel between the Don and the Volga Rivers which would enable them to transfer ships from the Black to the Caspian Seas, block Russian expansion into the Caucasus, and keep open the trade and pilgrimage routes from Inner Asia. An Ottoman expedition of 1569–70, however, was defeated, and the Russians gradually increased their pressure on the Crimea and the Caucasus. Russian expansion led eventually to a three-way Polish, Russian, and Ottoman struggle for control of the Ukraine which culminated in 1676 with the Ottomans in control

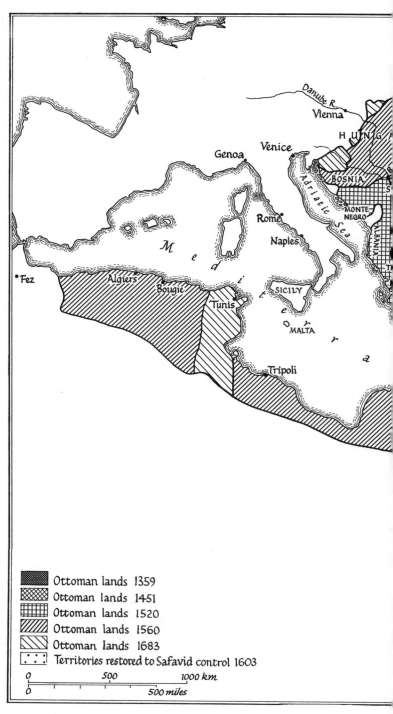

Ottoman lands 1359
Ottoman lands 1451
Ottoman lands 1520
Ottoman lands 1560
Ottoman lands 1683
Territories restored to Safavid control 1603

0   500   1000 km
0   500 miles

Map 12   The expansion of

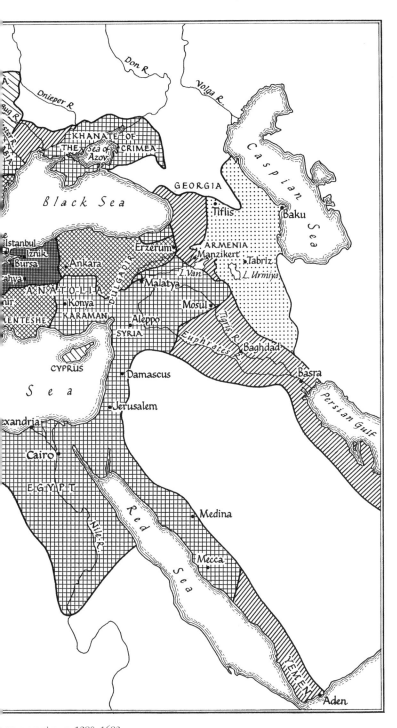

Don R.

Dnieper R

Volga R.

KHANATE OF
THE Sea of CRIMEA
Azov

GEORGIA

Black Sea

Tiflis

Baku

Caspian Sea

Istanbul
Iznik
Bursa
Ankara
Erzerum
ARMENIA
Manzikert
Tabriz
L. Van
L. Urmiya
ahya
ANATOLIA
Malatya
nir
Konya
Mosul
ENTESHE
KARAMAN
Aleppo
SYRIA
Tigris R
Euphrates
Baghdad
DULGADIR

CYPRUS

S e a
Damascus
Basra
Persian Gulf

Jerusalem

xandria

Cairo

EGYPT

Medina

Red Sea

Nile R.

Mecca

YEMEN

Aden

man empire: c. 1280–1683

of the Black Sea and part of the Ukraine. Thus the Ottomans reached the apogee of their expansion in northern Europe.

By the end of the seventeenth century the Ottomans had created a world-scale empire, reaching from the western Mediterranean to Iran and from the Ukraine to Yemen. The dynamism for the worldwide expansion of Ottoman rule came from the inner characteristics of Turkish and Ottoman society. The spearhead of Ottoman conquests were ghazi-warrior adventurers, united under the leadership of popular military chieftains or venerated holy men. Behind the holy war was an imperial state of exceptional organizational capacities, employing an advanced military technology based on cannons and massed infantry musket fire, tolerant and able to assimilate non-Muslim populations and reconcile them to Ottoman rule. This combination of qualities had no peer until the eighteenth century, when Europe generated the power to check and throw back the Ottoman advances.

Behind the conquests was a highly organized and efficient Ottoman state whose institutions were directly derived from the Saljuq state in Anatolia and indirectly from the Mamluk regime of Egypt and Syria. It had inherited the slave military corps and iqta' type of administration. It patronized the religious elites, protected trade and urban life, sponsored agricultural cultivation, and thus built up the infrastructure of a society that was capable of supporting an elaborate state apparatus and of suppressing predatory nomadic populations. Certain features of the Ottoman state, however, have no Middle Eastern antecedents. Administrative practices, architectural style, patronage of the Christian churches, the guild system, and controls over the provincial economy seem to stem from Byzantine rather than Islamic precedents.

THE OTTOMAN STATE

At the center of the Ottoman state was an elaborate court or palace apparatus. The Istanbul palace – the Topkapi Saray – was divided into an inner and an outer section. The inner section was the very heart of the empire. It included the residence of the Sultan and his harem, the privy chambers and treasury of the ruler, the royal kitchens, and the schools for the training of pages and slaves for the inner service. The outer service included the state offices for military, civil, and religious administration, kitchen staffs, artisans, and gardeners who maintained the palace grounds and performed military service.

Murad I (1360–89) was the first Sultan to use slave military units (*kapikullari*) organized either as infantry (the famous janissaries) or cavalry. The new troops were at first taken from prisoners and volunteers, but in 1395 the *devshirme* was instituted as a kind of "tax" in manpower taken on the Christian population of the Balkans. While the Mamluks of previous Middle Eastern regimes had been recruited from outside the territories of the empires they served, the Ottoman janissaries were taken from the subject population. This afforded a regular supply of manpower and perhaps a cheaper source of slaves, but it permitted the complication that the system had originally been designed to avoid: slaves recruited in the Balkans could resume family and social contacts in their home regions. The most promising of the slave recruits were educated in the palace schools to be pages in the royal household, or officers in the army or administration. They were given a Turkish, Arabic, and Islamic education, and were cultivated as gentlemen in the Ottoman style. Other recruits were apprenticed to Turkish officers in Anatolia, and were trained to operate as infantry in organized formations using firearms. New infantry tactics were devised in combination with the battlefield use of artillery to make the janissaries the most effective of Middle Eastern and European armies.

The janissary corps was complemented by provincial cavalry, most of whom were recruited from the free Turkish population, supported by timars, assignments of tax revenues in return for military service. In 1527 there were about 28,000 slave infantrymen and some 70–80,000 cavalrymen, of whom 37,500 were timar-holders. In addition, there were auxiliary garrison and frontier raiders who were financed by tax exemptions.

A bureaucracy was essential to the financing of the slave armies. Orhan (1324–60) appointed a wazir for the central administration, and military and civil governors for the conquered provinces. As the Ottoman empire expanded, provinces that had initially been tributaries were annexed and brought under routine administration. The largest provincial units, called *beylerbeyliks*, were subdivided into *sanjak beyliks* and further divided into *timarliks* which were the districts assigned to military officers in lieu of salary. In the sixteenth century the term *vali* was substituted for *beylerbey* to mean governor and the term *eyalet* was introduced to mean province. Some provinces were administered by salaried officials who collected taxes and sent the surplus to Istanbul; others were administered by timar-holders. For tax purposes cadastral surveys called *tahrirs* listed the villages, the households, and the adult males who were responsible for the payment of taxes, and their crops and other resources. The European provinces of Romania and Transylvania, the Crimea, and certain Anatolian districts in the control of Kurdish and Turkish peoples continued to be quasi-independent tributary provinces (*hukumet*).

The driving force in the slow evolution of Ottoman administration was the conflict between the Turkish or ghazi party, which was powerful in the provincial armies and the religious administration, and the slave or devshirme party, which was powerful in the imperial service and in the janissary corps. The frontier soldiers and the Turkish aristocracy favored expansion against Christian countries in Europe; the slave advisors of the Sultan preferred expansion in Anatolia and other Muslim regions. The ghazis wanted decentralized – as opposed to a strong patrimonial and central – government, and a Muslim and Turkish – as opposed to a cosmopolitan and imperial – cultural style. Successive Sultans favored the policies of one party or another, or manipulated them against each other. Bayazid I (1389–1402) consolidated the slave party by introducing the slave soldiers into administrative positions and by bringing the provinces under central control, but

Mehmed I (1413–21), in the wake of defeat by Timur, gave full support to the Turkish and ghazi elements. He removed Byzantine advisors from the court and made Turkish and Persian, rather than Greek, the official languages of administration.

Mehmed II returned power to the slave soldiers. He removed the Turkish nobility and all competing members of the Ottoman family from power, and reserved the most important positions in the central government for his own slaves. To maintain some balance of power, a functional division was made between the offices of the Grand Vizier, the religious notables, the treasury administration, and the chancery services, and some Turkish families were restored to favor and allowed to keep their properties. Mehmed also sought the support of the Greek Orthodox clergy by recognizing their civil as well as religious authority over the laity. He centralized government controls by taking tax surveys and absorbing independent vassal territories into the timar system, and he promulgated the first systematic legal codes dealing with the organization of the state and the obligations of subjects. By the reign of Sulayman I (1520–66), the dominance of the janissaries was uncontested. The centralizing program triumphed by defeating rival Ottoman claimants to the Sultanate, subduing the independent Turkish states in Anatolia, coopting noble Turkish families, and building an administrative apparatus based on slaves. Their victory, however, upset the internal balance of power and stimulated factionalism and harem intrigues.

Like the rulers of the ʿAbbasid and later Persian empires, the authority of the Ottoman Sultans combined patrimonial, Islamic, and imperial dimensions. The patrimonial authority of the Ottoman Sultan was foremost. The state was his household; the subjects his personal retainers. The soldiers were his slaves, loyal to him personally. The territory of the empire was his personal property, but much of it was given to members of the ruling class in the form of iqtaʿs.

At the core of this system based on absolute authority, however, was an ambiguity about the transmission of authority which subverted the effectiveness of Sultanal government. According to Turkish practice, the authority of the Sultan was passed on within the royal family, but the line of succession was not specified. Thus, the death of a reigning Sultan led to a struggle for power, usually among the surviving sons, which was ordinarily resolved by a test of military strength and sometimes by fratricide. A reigning Sultan might favor one of his sons by giving him an administrative or military position which would benefit him in the eventual struggle for power, but after 1595 all male relatives of the Sultan were imprisoned in the harem. Palace and harem intrigue became the road to power.

From the Islamic point of view, the Sultan's authority was derived from his role as executor of the Shariʿa, and in turn the subjects were responsible to him. Even a government that seized power by military force was regarded as legitimate as long as it recognized the sovereignty of the Shariʿa and respected the basic interests of the Muslim community. The Shariʿa, however, did not cover all aspects of Ottoman political and social life. In order to regulate the relations of the Ottoman aristocracy and subjects, and to define the status, duties, and dress codes of each, the Sultans were empowered to issue *firmans*. These decrees were gathered in codes called *kanun*, which were a form of secular and administrative law considered to be a valid extension of religious law as a result of the ruler's right to exercise legal judgment on behalf of the community. Mehmed II and Sulayman I the Magnificent created new law codes dealing with administrative and criminal justice, the discipline of officials, military affairs, and the organization of the religious hierarchy. In a broad range of issues not covered directly by Shari'a, systematic codification of law was probably inspired by the Codes of Justinian.

The authority of Ottoman Sultans was also based upon a cosmopolitan culture comprising Arab, Persian, Byzantine, and European elements. Mehmed II, a liberal patron of the arts, cultivated Persian poetry and European painting. At his court, Arab and Persian literati, Italian painters, and Greek and Serbian poets were welcome. Later regimes, however, moved away from Christian and European influences toward a more Muslim and Turkish style.

As at the courts of Arab and Persian princes, poetry was the principal expression of royal style. Court poetry was based on the *aruz*, a prosodic meter derived from Arabic meters, and was heavily infused with Arabic and Persian words. The basic poetic forms were those already pioneered in Persian court poetry – the qasida, the ghazal, the masnavi, and the ruba'i. The Ottoman poetic tradition began with Saljuq rulers who patronized Hoja Dehhani, a composer of panegyrics, and wine and love songs in the Persian manner. The greatest Ottoman poet of the classical period was Baki (1526–1600). Nef'i (1582–1636), a panegyrist and satirist, composed poetry celebrating power and struggle. Yahya Efendi (1552–1644) developed an original subject matter based on direct observation of life and nature and the expression of personal emotion.

Ottoman prose literature was strongly influenced by imperial ambitions. Early Ottoman historical writing was composed in Arabic and then translated into Turkish to legitimize the origin of the dynasty and its rise to power and to chronicle everyday court and military events. In the course of the sixteenth century, Ottoman world ambitions were given expression in the composition of universal histories. Mustafa 'Ali's (1541–99) *Kunh al-Akhbar* contained a history of the world from Adam to Jesus, a history of early Islam, a history of Turkish peoples up to the rise of the Ottomans, and a concluding part on the Ottoman empire. In the seventeenth century historians were employed to compile daily court chronicles. Geographical writing was stimulated by the expansion of Ottoman naval power. Piri Re'is, the Ottoman commander in the Indian Ocean, was the author of an important atlas. Evliya Chelebi's (1614–82) *Seyahat-name* (Book of Travels) contains a comprehensive description of journeys throughout the Ottoman empire and his observations of Ottoman society and economy.

Manuscript illustration also expressed the Ottoman sense of an imperial destiny. From the time of Mehmed II, the Ottoman regime maintained a court studio, or

12 Sultan Selim the First

nakkashhane, which employed calligraphers, painters, illuminators, and book-binders to produce manuscripts and to generate the designs for Ottoman ceramics, woodwork, metalwork, textiles, and carpets. Between 1451 and 1520, Persian precedents formed the basis of Ottoman manuscript art. Artists from Shiraz, Tabriz, and Herat were brought to Istanbul. The earliest works were illustrated copies of Persian classics such as 'Attar's *Language of the Birds,* the *Love Story of Khosraw and Shirin,* the *Khamsa* of Amir Khosraw, and the fables of the *Kalila wa-Dimna.* The history of Alexander's conquests and illustrated contemporary histories became staple products of the Ottoman workshop.

Sixteenth-century manuscripts turned from the illustration of classic literature to contemporary events such as the ceremonial reception of ambassadors, the collection of taxes, and the conquests of famous fortresses in the Balkans. Victories, descriptions of festivals, accessions, royal processions, battles, sieges, banquets, and celebrations were all the subject of manuscript illustrations. The *Shahinshah-name* of 1581 depicts the circumcision festivals held in Istanbul, athletic performances, guild parades, and other court events. Viziers, janissaries, cavalrymen, scholars, guildsmen, merchants, and Sultans appear in profusion. The *Shah-name-i Al-i Osman* (Book of Kings of the House of Osman) by Arifi (d. 1561–62) is one of the most famous productions of this period. By the end of the sixteenth century, illustrated history, celebrating the splendor of the Ottoman state and its conquests, had become a special Turkish contribution to the tradition of Middle Eastern and Muslim manuscript illumination. Ottoman manuscript art celebrated the self-consciousness of the Ottoman elite as a world historical force.

The Ottoman imperial sensibility was similarly reflected in architecture. Ottoman mosques and colleges expressed the close Ottoman tie to Islam, but Ottoman design features, such as single large domes, tall minarets, and colonnaded court-yards, showed the strong influence of Aya Sophia, the greatest of Byzantine churches. Ottoman mosques mimicked the great eastern Christian churches and expressed, like the Dome of the Rock in Jerusalem, the triumph of Islam over Christian rivals. Koja Sinan (1490–1578) was the master of this style of architecture.

In sum, the Ottoman regime, in both concept and practice, was derived from Turkish, Saljuq, and Mamluk Middle Eastern precedents. Christian and European influences were relatively limited. Yet the Ottoman regime was innovative and distinctive because of the refinement of the slave military organization and the importance of jihad. The Turkish warriors, royal slaves, court historians, and artists were all committed to an imperial vision of Islamic expansion; the Sultan was glorified as a warrior prince, as a Muslim Caliph, and as a conquering emperor.

RULERS AND SUBJECTS

To an unusual degree, the Ottoman regime dominated, controlled, and shaped the society it governed. A central Ottoman concept was the distinction between *askeri* and *re'aya* – rulers and ruled, elites and subjects, warriors and producers, tax collectors and tax payers. The chief attribute of the ruling elite was the right to exploit the wealth of the subjects. In addition, to be a member of the ruling class one had to be cultivated in the distinctive language and manners called "the Ottoman way." One could become an Ottoman either by birth or by education in the imperial, military, or Muslim religious schools.

The distinction between rulers and ruled was not the same as that between Muslims and non-Muslims. The ruling elites and the subject populations included both. Alongside Turkish soldiers and Arab and Persian scribes and scholars, the ruling elite included Balkan Christian lords and scribes. The patrician Greek families of the Phanar district of Istanbul, who were prominent merchants, bankers, and government functionaries, and the higher clergy of the Orthodox Church, may be considered part of the Ottoman elite. Jewish refugees from Spain also became important in Ottoman trade and banking in the fifteenth and sixteenth centuries. Joseph Nasi (1520–79), for example, a refugee descended from a Portuguese Jewish family which had moved to Antwerp and then to Italy after the expulsion of the Jews from Spain, came to Istanbul in 1554. Nasi had European business and diplomatic connections, and soon became a close adviser to Sulayman, played an influential role in French–Ottoman diplomatic relations, and in 1566 was made Duke of Naxos and given a monopoly on customs revenues and the export of wine. Nasi was also a patron of Jewish community life and of Jewish settlement in Palestine. Thus, the Ottoman system appears as a condominium of elites, some Muslim, some non-Muslim, who had partitioned the various dimensions of the political economy among ethnically or religiously defined sub-elites. Ottoman Muslims controlled the military and the bureaucracy; Armenians the banking system. Armenian *sarrafs* directed the flow of capital to the purchase of shares in tax-farms, linked provincial merchants to the ruling class, and provided the elites with credit. Greeks and Jews were active in tax-farming and international trade. Galata had big populations of Greek, Armenian, Jewish, and European as well as Muslim merchants. In the course of the sixteenth and seventeenth centuries, however, the Ottoman elite became more uniformly Muslim. Only the Phanar Greek financial aristocracy maintained its position, owing to its administrative and economic role in Romania.

The subjects, the re'aya, were organized into innumerable small communities. Ottoman society was an elaborate mosaic of territorial associations, religious fraternities, and corporate economic groups. From the Ottoman point of view, the religious communities organized to administer the educational, judicial, and charitable affairs of the subject population were fundamental. Most of the non-Muslim population were considered members of the Eastern Orthodox Church, which included Greek, Romanian, Slavic, and Arab believers. The Armenian Church was an administrative body, which included Monophysites in Syria and Egypt, Assyrians, and others. Maronites, Uniate Armenians, and Latin Catholics in Hungary, Croatia, and Albania had their own churches; Sephardi and Ashkenazi Jews their own synagogues.

The Ottomans, like previous Muslim regimes, considered their non-Muslim subjects autonomous but dependent peoples whose internal social, religious, and communal life was regulated by their own religious organizations, but whose leaders were appointed by, and responsible to, a Muslim state. Non-Muslim communities were called by the generic terms *dhimmi* (protected peoples), *ta'ifa* (group), or *jamat* (religious community). Minority leaders – sometimes ecclesiastics, sometimes laymen – represented their communities to the authorities, and dealt with ecclesiastical matters, internal disputes, and fines and taxes on a local basis. It is doubtful that these arrangements constituted an empire-wide "*millet*" system. Though the Greek Orthodox Church had its own concept of ecumenical authority, and may have attempted to convert the local authority of the Patriarch of Constantinople into an empire-wide authority, it was resisted by the churches of Ohrid (Bulgaria) and Pech (Serbia). The authority of the Patriarch of Constantinople was never clearly defined.

The Muslim masses, as a subject or re'aya population, were organized in a parallel way. The Muslim population was subdivided into numerous schools of law and Sufi brotherhoods, which the Ottomans were keen to bring under state control. They did this by extending their patronage to the 'ulama' and Sufi elites. Ottoman patronage led to the organization of an elaborate system of madrasa education. The first Ottoman madrasa was established in Iznik in 1331, when scholars were invited from Iran and Egypt to augment Muslim instruction in the new territories. Later Sultans founded colleges in Bursa, Edirne, and Istanbul. In the late fifteenth century these were arranged in a hierarchy which defined the career path for the promotion of leading scholars. The college built by Sulayman between 1550 and 1559 eventually became the highest ranking. Beneath it were ranked the colleges founded by previous Sultans, and beneath these the colleges founded by state officials and religious scholars. The madrasas were not only organized by rank but also were distinguished by their educational functions. The lowest-level madrasa taught Arabic grammar and syntax, logic, theology, astronomy, geometry, and rhetoric. The second-level kind stressed literature and rhetoric. The higher-level colleges taught law and theology.

A similar elaboration took place in judicial administration. The qadiships of Istanbul, Bursa, and Edirne were originally the most important appointments, but the hierarchy came to include judgeships in Damascus, Aleppo, Cairo, Baghdad, Medina, Izmir, and Konya. The judicial service was headed by two *qadi-askers,* one for the Balkans and one for Anatolia, and by the Shaykh al-Islam, the chief jurisconsult of Istanbul, who held the highest-ranking position in the system and had direct access to the Sultan. Ordinary mullahs, or judges, were also graded into several ranks, including qadis and their deputies who served as notaries public, registrars of deeds, and administrators of the properties of orphans and minors. Qadis supervised the administration of colleges and had an important role in certification of taxes, overseeing harvests, inspection of military forces, and supervision of the urban economy, including government regulations for artisan guilds and markets. An organization of muftis or jurisconsults paralleled the organization of judges, but muftis received no official salaries. The educational and the judicial hierarchies were interlocked. Appointments to judgeships required the attainment of appropriate levels in the educational system. The Ottoman state appointed all important judges, jurisconsults, and professors of law and thereby maintained a direct bureaucratic control over the religious establishment.

Sufis were also important to the Ottoman state because of their large role in Turkish rural society. Sufi babas mobilized bands of Turkish warriors and led them to holy war, protected travelers, and mediated in disputes. Wandering dervishes, called Malamatiya or Qalandariya, who openly disregarded the Shari'a and opposed contact with government authorities, were nonetheless venerated by rural people as bearers of God's blessings and of magical powers.

The rural Sufis were politically important because they could inspire resistance to the state. Eastern Anatolia, like northwestern Iran, was a breeding ground for Sufi messianic beliefs and Sufi-led revolts against state domination. For example, Bedreddin (d. 1416) denied the literal truth of heaven and hell, the day of judgment, the resurrection of the body, the creation of the world, and other basic tenets of Muslim belief. The Hurufiya (whose doctrine spread among both Muslims and Christians in Anatolia and Bulgaria at the end of the fourteenth century) preached that the only rightful income was that earned by manual work. Sufi-led rebellions also occurred in the late fifteenth century. In 1519 a preacher named Jelal took the name of Shah Isma'il, claimed to be the mahdi, and attracted Turkish cultivator and pastoralist opposition to the imposition of taxes. An early sixteenth-century wave of revolts was closely related to the Safavid agitation and the opposition of eastern Anatolian peoples to the Ottoman-Sunni regime.

Anatolian resistance was fostered by Turkish folk culture. Itinerant minstrel poets (*saz shairi*) toured the villages singing of the struggles of the Turks against the Georgians, Circassians, and Byzantines and celebrating the virtues of Turkish peoples. Epic poetry was then translated into the Karagoz; or shadow-play theater, which became another vehicle for Turkish folk culture. Sufi poets, of whom the most important was Yunus Emre (1238–1329), also kept popular literary and religious culture alive. Poets traveled with the soldiers, sang in the camps, entertained people at fairs, and conducted contests which were the basis of an Anatolian folk consciousness. The heritage of nomadic populations, independent states, and Sufi brotherhoods separated the Anatolian provinces from the capital city elites.

The Bektashis were among the most influential of these Sufis. Hajji Bektash, the founder of the order, probably lived toward the end of the thirteenth century. According to legend, he and some forty followers set up tekkes throughout eastern Anatolia and among Turkomans in Macedonia, Thessaly, and the Rhodope. Bektashis spread throughout Anatolia and the Balkans in the course of the fifteenth century. Around 1500, Balim Sultan organized the rituals of the order and perfected its system of tekkes.

The Bektashis were strongly influenced by both Shi'ism and Christianity. They took the sixth imam, Ja'far, as their patron saint, venerated the trinity of God, Muhammad, and 'Ali, offered bread and wine in initiation ceremonies, and required celibacy of their teachers. They taught that there were four levels of religious belief: Shari'a, adherence to the law; tariqa, initiation in special ceremonies to the Sufi order; ma'rifa, understanding of the truth; and haqiqa, the direct experience of the divine reality. Initiates were introduced progressively to the secret knowledge and ceremonies of the group.

Alongside the rural Sufis, urban religious orders also flourished in Anatolia and the Balkans. The Mevlevi leaders were spiritually descended from Mawlana Jalal al-Din Rumi (1207–73), and have become universally known, because of their ceremonial dancing, as the whirling dervishes. Apart from their ceremonial function, Mevlevi tekkes were also important for the study of Persian literature and Sufi thought, and for the education of the Ottoman bureaucratic elite. Naqshbandis and Khalwatis were also important.

In the course of the fifteenth and sixteenth centuries the Ottomans brought the Sufi orders under state control. The state coopted Sufi tekkes by providing them with permanent endowments and gifts for charitable purposes. The Bektashis, in particular, were taken under the wing of the Ottomans as chaplains to the janissaries. They lived and marched with the soldiers, and provided them with magical protection in battle. This enabled the order to spread throughout eastern Anatolia and among Turkish migrants in Macedonia and Albania. The Mevlevis were similarly tied to the Ottoman state; they acquired the right to gird a Sultan with a holy sword upon his accession. Thus the Ottomans succeeded in domesticating the major Sufi brotherhoods without entirely eliminating the independent influence of Sufi teachers.

The absorption of the 'ulama' and the Sufis into the state bureaucracy made religious controversies matters of state concern. Ottoman scholars assimilated the Arabic and Persian classics, including the madrasa curriculum, theology, and science. The translation of Arabic and Persian classics, including important works on literature, history, politics, astrology, medicine, the life of the Prophet and Sufi treatises, made the corpus of Muslim religious literature available to Turkish elites. In theology, al-Ghazzali and al-Razi were recognized as the master teachers, and the controversy between al-Ghazzali and Ibn Rushd (Averroes) was reopened. 'Ulama' committed to a narrow definition of Islamic religious studies focused on hadith and law soon found themselves opposed to 'ulama' interested in philosophy and science, and the Sufis who stressed personal religious experience rather than formal learning.

The narrow point of view progressively gained ground. As early as the 1540s theology and mathematics were losing popularity. In 1580 an observatory attached to the Sulaymaniya madrasa in Istanbul was destroyed. In the sixteenth and seventeenth centuries the more restrictive and puritanical forms of Islam asserted themselves against popular Sufi beliefs. Reform-minded religious scholars opposed popular ceremonies for the dead, entertainments such as dancing and singing, and the consumption of coffee and tobacco. Puritanical legalists, supported by madrasa students and tradesmen, won strong support for a more narrow definition of Islamic learning and practice. The supporters of Qadizade Mehmed Efendi (d. 1635) formed a party to control religious endowments and to persuade the authorities to enforce a Shari'a-oriented form of Islamic practice. Under the influence of this party tekkes were closed and Sufis were imprisoned. Finally, intellectual discussion was suppressed. The biographies of scholars show that, with the elaboration of a bureaucratic hierarchy, interest in careers outweighed genuine piety and learning. The influence of entrenched families enabled them to promote their children into the higher grades of the educational and judicial hierarchies without having reached the proper preliminary levels, while theological students who could not find patronage were excluded. In the course of the eighteenth century the 'ulama' became a powerful conservative pressure group. As servants of the state the 'ulama' no longer represented the interests of the people, nor protected them from the abuses of political power. No longer did they represent a transcendental Islamic ideal opposed to worldly corruption. Their integration into the Ottoman regime made them simply the spokesmen of Ottoman legitimacy.

THE OTTOMAN ECONOMY

The subject population was further controlled by state regulation of economic activity. From the Ottoman point of view, the economic well-being of the subjects was essential to the viability of the regime, and the early Ottoman conquests were directed to the control of trade routes and productive resources. Ottoman expansion in the Black Sea, the Aegean, and the Mediterranean was intended to wrest control of trade and naval resources from the Venetians and the Genoese. In wars which lasted from 1463 to 1479 and from 1499 to 1503, Venetian possessions in Greece and the Aegean were conquered. Cyprus was taken in 1571 and ceded by Venice in 1573; Crete in 1669. To bypass Venetian trade, the Ottomans also allied with the Adriatic port of Ragusa (Dubrovnic). After 1484 the Ottomans excluded foreigners from the Black Sea, with the exception of ships bringing wine from Crete or Chios. The Black Sea trade, in general, passed from the Genoese to Armenians, Jews, Greeks, Turks, and Romanians in the course of the fifteenth century.

Ottoman conquests in Iran, the Arab provinces, Egypt, and the Indian Ocean were also part of a program of channeling traffic in eastern goods through the Ottoman empire. Egypt imported silk, yarn, cotton, textiles, soap, and dried fruit from Syria, and exported rice, beans, wheat, sugar, and hides. From Anatolia, textiles, dried fruit, and wood were exported to Egypt, the Sudan, and India. From Syria, pistachios, dates, spices, and slaves were returned to Anatolia. The pilgrimage routes brought people from all over the empire to Mecca and Medina. Mecca was an emporium for spices, pearls, pepper, and coffee, and almost every pilgrim financed his journey by bringing goods to sell in Mecca and returning with goods to sell at home. The provisioning of the pilgrimage caravans in Damascus, Cairo, and Baghdad was an important business. Through Egypt, the Ottomans traded with the Sudan and with North and West Africa. The Red Sea ports of Arabia and of East Africa gave the Ottomans access to the Indian Ocean trade. Baghdad and Basra traded with Iran and India.

The Ottoman conquests also meant economic revival in Anatolia and the Balkans. The Ottomans stimulated land traffic by building bridges and caravansaries, digging wells, and garrisoning major road junctions. Population growth stimulated agricultural production in Anatolia, which in turn set free urban populations for the production of textiles, though by the end of the sixteenth century, excessive population growth had negative consequences in the cultivation of marginal lands, the substitution of barley for wheat, and the deterioration of security in the countryside.

In the course of the fifteenth and sixteenth centuries, Bursa and Izmir became the most important commercial centers in Anatolia. From Bursa, silks, spices, cotton, rice, iron, mohair, nuts, opium, vinegar, rugs, and other products were shipped across the Black Sea to the Crimea, whence they were carried into the Ukraine, Poland, and Russia. Bursa also had a large silk industry and a rich merchant elite whose fortunes were invested in specie, real estate, slaves, and cloth. Izmir, by contrast, was defined by its foreign and minority merchants. Izmir emerged in the seventeenth century as a rendezvous for European merchants with local Armenians, Jews, and Greeks to exchange the goods of Iran and western Anatolia. In the late seventeenth century, Portuguese Jews dominated tax-farming; Muslims controlled regional exchange; Greeks handled inter-regional trade; and Armenians predominated in international commerce, especially in the silk trade with Iran. In the eighteenth century, with European patronage, the Greeks emerged as the most important merchant community.

The European market also stimulated Ottoman exports from the Balkans. The riches of Edirne seem to have been based largely on the exploitation of the surrounding countryside and the export of raw materials. Salonika woolens were exported north of the Danube. Edirne had a "capitalist" population including money changers, jewelers, long-distance traders, local landowners growing wheat or raising cattle, and money lenders who invested in textiles or milling. Soldiers and government officials were prominent among the wealthy.

Ottoman policy was also important because of the endowment of *imarets* and of rural tekkes. An imaret was a complex of buildings, including a mosque, a college, a hospital, and a hospice for travelers and students, endowed with properties such as markets, mills, or kitchens to support its charitable activities. Sufi tekkes became centers of cultivation, trade, and local administration as well as educational and charitable activities. Numerous villages founded by Sufis in Anatolia and the Balkans were backed by state support. Endowment funds for mosques, colleges, hospitals, bridges, convents, soup kitchens, libraries, and other institutions were invested in baths, bazaars, shops, tenements, workshops, mills, presses, slaughterhouses, tanneries, and tile factories, and were an important source of capital for commerce and agriculture.

13 The Sultan Ahmed (Blue) Mosque, Istanbul

14 The Sultan Ahmed (Blue) Mosque, Istanbul; interior

The single greatest state project was the reconstruction of Istanbul to satisfy the glory of the Sultan and the needs of administration and trade. At the time of the conquest, Constantinople probably had a population of between 50,000 and 60,000 people. To repopulate it, the Ottoman government obliged Muslim merchants from Bursa, Konya, and other Anatolian places and the Balkans to move to Istanbul. The government gave land, houses, and tax concessions to the new migrants. Numerous villages in the vicinity of the city were laid out and settled with slaves, prisoners, and deportees from the Balkans. According to the census of 1478, there were about 9,000 Muslim, 3,100 Greek Christian, 1,650 Jewish, and about 1,000 Armenian and gypsy dwellings in Istanbul. Thus the population was about 60 percent Muslim, 20 percent Christian and 10 percent Jewish, and totaled less than 100,000. Within a century it would rise to over 700,000, more than twice the population of the largest European cities of the time.

The city was rebuilt by constructing public institutions such as schools, hospitals, baths, and caravansaries with attached bazaars, bakeries, mills, or factories in several districts. Each neighborhood was centered around an important religious and public institution and its attendant facilities. Between 1453 and 1481 alone, 209 mosques, 24 schools or seminaries, 32 public baths, and 12 inns or bazaars were built in Istanbul. Many thousands of houses and shops were constructed by waqf administrators in order to generate revenue.

In the Ottoman empire Istanbul was unique for the scale of its markets, the complexity of guild administration, and the financing of tax-farms. To provision Istanbul the government did not rely solely upon market forces. Strong government controls assured that the surplus of Anatolia and of other regions was directed toward the capital. The state required traders to guarantee delivery of wheat, rice, salt, meat, oil, fish, honey, and wax directly to the palace and the capital city at fixed prices. Merchants were thus made agents of the state to meet the fiscal and provisioning needs of the capital and the government establishment. Istanbul's demand led to an increased output of grain and cotton for thread and fabric. Adana, for example, became an important cotton-growing region. Istanbul's requirements stimulated the creation of *chiftliks*, or large estates, because of the profits to be made by supplying the market.

Guilds were the basic unit for the control of the urban populations. Merchants, craftsmen, transport workers, and even entertainers and prostitutes were organized into corporate bodies to enforce economic discipline and facilitate administration. The authorities regulated entry into trades, opening of new shops, and types and quality of merchandise produced. Maximum prices designed to protect consumer interests were set by the state. Weights and measures were regulated by government inspection. Guilds were expected to supply workers to accompany military campaigns and provide labor services. Egyptian, but not Turkish, guilds were also obliged to collect taxes from their members. A somewhat greater degree of administrative autonomy, however, was accorded guilds in Balkan cities.

The administrative apparatus that supervised the activity of professional corporations was elaborate. The Grand Vizier, the *agha* (chief) of the janissaries, qadis, and market inspectors enforced guild regulations. Shaykhs and other guild officials were appointed by the government in consultation with guild members in order to implement state rules. The chiefs of guilds acted through an informal body of guild elders, who were collectively responsible to the state.

Thus, Ottoman guilds were designed for state control, and were not the spontaneous expression of the interests of merchants and craftsmen. Nevertheless, they took on certain social and religious functions as an expression of the solidarity of the members. Guilds arbitrated disputes among their members and collected funds for mutual aid, religious ceremonies, and charities. They staged picnics and celebrations. The guilds were also religious confraternities with a patron saint and initiation ceremonies modeled on Sufi lines, which sponsored prayers and pilgrimages, and heard lectures on the value of sobriety and honesty. The internal solidarity of guilds was probably reinforced by the fact that they were confined to people of the same religious community. Only a minority of guilds had a mixed Muslim and Christian, or Muslim and Jewish, membership.

Some sectors of the Ottoman economy escaped direct administrative control. Merchants engaged in money changing and international trade were usually able to operate without close governmental supervision. Some merchants organized a putting-out system of manufacture in rural areas to compete with the monopolies of town guilds. Also, as janissaries penetrated into commerce and craft production in the seventeenth and eighteenth centuries, it became increasingly difficult for the government to regulate the artisan population.

PROVINCIAL ADMINISTRATION

Apart from the religious administrations and government regulation of the urban economy, control over the rural population was effected through provincial administration. All provinces were in principle subordinate to the central authority and subject to taxation. In western and central Anatolia and the eastern Balkans, the core provinces of the empire, the central government could exercise relatively close administrative control and channel the surplus of the regions to Istanbul, but in each region there was a tension between Ottoman control and local autonomy. Anatolia was the home of a bellicose pastoral population whose chieftains were important local political figures, and Sufi-led resistance was almost endemic. In the Balkans, fiscal surveys, supervised by central government officials, were the basis of a regular territorial administration with the ordinary apparatus for tax collection and police control. Ottoman rule tended for a time to perpetuate the social structure of Balkan populations. While the population was generally Greek, Serbian, Bulgarian, and Albanian, Turks and Muslims with some Jews, Armenians, and Greeks tended to concentrate in the towns. Urban communities were organized into quarters, bazaars, and guilds. Tribal groups, the Serbian *zadruga* or joint family, and independent churches such as the Serbian Patriarchate at Pech (between 1557 and 1766) were all permitted a quasi-autonomous existence. The Orthodox Church helped to preserve the ethnic and linguistic character of Greek and other Balkan peoples.

In peripheral areas, the state had to make further compromises with local chieftains and tribes. The Arab provinces were virtually subsidiary regions organized around their own capital cities: Cairo, Damascus, Aleppo, and Baghdad. Internal autonomy was accorded Romania, Transylvania, Albania, and Montenegro, where local non-Muslim aristocracies were allowed to consolidate their power under Muslim rule. The Greek aristocracy of Istanbul controlled church properties, taxfarms, and the commerce of much of the region. In the eighteenth century, leading Phanariot merchants were appointed as rulers of Romania.

Despite these zones of autonomy, the Ottoman regime was striking for the degree of centralization of state control over the subject societies. The Ottomans controlled vast territories and extracted from each village and locality the surplus wealth that supported the central government and sustained the wars of expansion. The state resisted the formation of independent loci of authority such as 'ulama' schools, Sufi brotherhoods, akhi fraternities, or independent merchant and artisan associations. The empire was not only assured its dominance through force but also through its hold on the minds of men. It stood for Islam and the arts of civilization. It won the cooperation of local chiefs, landlords, village headmen, and religious leaders, all of whom had to respect the power of the central regime, and all of whom benefited from being its accomplices. The state prevented organized elite resistance by manipulating factions and individuals, promoting some and not others, and inhibited the creation of patron–client ties in the provinces by rotating officials rapidly.

For a host of reasons peasants could never achieve sufficient solidarity to form rural alliances or revolt against the state. Family farming reduced village solidarity, and nomadic groups had different interests from and did not ally with peasants. Trust outside families was very limited. Tekkes might have provided solidarity across family and village lines, but the competition among dervishes was usually disruptive. Trade was focused on towns and controlled by the state, and so did not create solidarity among the people of nearby villages. Also, the government often provided relief for peasant grievances through the courts and the administration.

Still, in rural administration the absorptive and regulatory capacities of the regime reached its limits. Throughout rural Anatolia, tribal communities and mountain chiefs were able to maintain a degree of independence. In the Balkans this independence was underlined by the perpetuation of Christian identity. Moreover, the power of the central government was always limited because the people who served the state had ambivalent purposes. The men who made up the armies and the central administration always looked for ways to advance their private, familial, and factional interests. The local notables who supported the regime also resisted an excessive encroachment on their prerogatives. Nevertheless the Ottoman regime was vastly more powerful than the Safavid, and autonomous chiefs played a much smaller role in its history.

THE OTTOMAN EMPIRE IN DISARRAY

The weakening of the central state

In the seventeenth and eighteenth centuries there were profound alterations in the Ottoman system. The balance of power between center and periphery began to shift in favor of the provinces. With the end of Ottoman expansion, the state lost its administrative and military capacities, and the empire was beset by popular revolts, economic regression, and eventually military defeats. The long-latent struggle between central and provincial elites for control of the revenues of the tax-producing population came into the open, and power was transferred from the central government to janissaries, 'ulama', and Ottoman families who successfully established themselves in the provinces. From the point of view of the central government the devolution of power was regarded as a corruption of Ottoman institutions. From the point of view of provincial chieftains, officials, and merchants, it was a reduction of the exploitative capacities of the center and a gain in local autonomy.

These changes were in part due to the growing economic power of Europe. As early as the sixteenth century the Ottomans were competing with the Portuguese for control of the Indian Ocean trade. In the seventeenth and eighteenth centuries, however, the Dutch and the British supplanted the Portuguese as the dominant powers in the Indian Ocean and took control of the trade in Asia. The Black Sea trade was captured by Russia. There was some compensation to the Ottomans in the growth of trade in coffee which came from Yemen through Egypt to Istanbul and was then exported to Europe. European control of the Asian trade helped them build up a strong position in the Mediterranean as well. The Ottoman–French alliance against the Habsburg empire disposed the Ottomans to give France a monopoly of Ottoman trade. For a time all European ships had to sail under the French flag. The English, however, entered the Levant trade in 1580. British Ambassador Harbourne succeeded in 1583 in negotiating a trade treaty with the Ottoman empire which reduced the taxes on English goods to 3 percent. The English formed the Levant Company to export cloth and tin, essential to make brass for cannon founding, in return for silk, mohair, cotton, wool, carpets, drugs, spices, and indigo.

In the seventeenth and eighteenth centuries competition in the Mediterranean among the French, English, and Dutch was fierce. The Dutch and the English organized convoys and heavily armed their merchant ships. Armenians and Jews operated through Smyrna and Livorno, and the Venetians and Genoese were also active. Each of the competitors experienced wide fluctuations in trading activity and profits, but the overall volume of Mediterranean trade was probably declining, on account of the competition of direct shipments from South and Southeast Asia to Europe. Spices from the Indies, cloth from India, and Persian goods were coming to Europe over Atlantic routes. The British East India Company, buying Far Eastern goods at their source and bringing them into the Mediterranean via London, actually became a competitor of the British Levant Company which depended on the Persian Gulf and Red Sea routes.

The decline of the eastern trade shifted European interest from Turkey and the Arab provinces to the Balkans. European traders, with the participation of Jewish and Greek intermediaries, distributed imported products to the interior and gathered goods for export. From Salonika, European trade reached Bosnia, Albania, Serbia, and Bulgaria. The English imported luxury cloth; the French, middle-quality cloth. Venice sold silk, satin, and taffeta. The Germans brought paper, tin, iron, copper, sugar, and indigo. European merchants exported wood, cotton, silk, leather, tobacco, beeswax, and hides by sea; cattle went overland from Romania and Hungary into central Europe. Ordinarily the Ottomans prohibited the export of iron, lead, copper, and grain, but there was an active trade in contraband.

In the eighteenth century, the French become dominant over other Europeans in the Istanbul market, and set up their own corporate structure to strengthen their collective position. They used their influence with the Ottoman state to break the grip of Ottoman merchants and guilds over the local economy. They also attacked the local monopolies by allying with Jews against Greeks, and by mediating their relations with Muslims through the Armenian sarrafs. Ethnic factors became crucial to market positions.

The evidence concerning the impact of this trade on the Ottoman economy in the seventeenth and eighteenth centuries is very scattered, but it seems that some regions suffered while others prospered. The production of Bursa silk cloth and Ankara mohair woolens fell when Europeans began to replace Turkish textiles with their own manufactures. The output of pottery and tiles at Iznik and Kutahya also declined. In Izmir, however, there may have been an increase in cotton production. While there is no proof of a general decline in the Ottoman economy, clearly the balance of trade was shifting. In general, the Ottoman empire was importing manufactured goods and exporting raw materials. Ottomans began to prefer European textiles, glass, clocks, flowers, architectural adornments, and home furnishings. European commercial penetration subverted Ottoman control of trade, and helped transfer political and economic power from the Ottoman state to foreign commercial powers and provincial elites.

The decline of the central state apparatus directly contributed to decentralization. The removal of the Sultans from direct control of affairs of state, and the practice of confining young princes to the harem and preventing them from assuming active military and administrative positions, deprived successive generations of Ottoman princes of adequate education and worldly experience. Seventeenth-century Ottoman Sultans had no exposure to the realities of the political world beyond harem intrigues. The result was incompetence and a drastic decline of authority.

Furthermore, the discipline and loyalty of the janissaries broke down. The demoralization of the janissaries was due in part to the monopoly of state power acquired by the slave establishment in the sixteenth century and in part to falling incomes. As it ceased to expand, the empire ceased to acquire booty. After 1580, inflation, due to the influx of American silver, also reduced the value of Ottoman incomes. Inadequately paid soldiers and officials seized provincial lands and diverted the revenues for their private benefit. Janissaries also entered commerce and the crafts to supplement their income, married and established families, and then promoted their own children into the military corps. Close ties among janissaries, artisans, and 'ulama' made it politically impossible to control the soldiers. Discipline in the army was reduced to such an extent that there were pay riots in 1622 and 1631, accompanied by the looting of Istanbul. The abandonment of the devshirme in 1637 made it impossible to redress these trends. By the middle of the eighteenth century the traditional army corps were no longer useful. The Ottomans had to substitute peasant militias and ethnic auxiliaries, the private armies of provincial notables, and bandits. A critical development in the state system in the seventeenth century was the formation of mercenary *sekban* and *sarica* units armed with firearms. From the 1680s to the 1730s the Ottomans became dependent upon Albanian, Bosnian, Kurdish, Cossack, Tatar, Georgian, and Circassian auxiliaries. The new troops were not as well disciplined, trained, and armed as the traditional Ottoman corps and were all the more ineffective against their European enemies.

To support the new military units, the Ottomans revised the timar system. As firearms and organized infantry became ever more important, the Ottoman cavalry (*sipahis*) could no longer resist German riflemen, and their timars were given over to the new forces, fewer in number, but longer in tenure. Also, as the state increasingly needed ready cash to meet the demands of the soldiers, it converted the timars into tax-farms, and left a vacuum of administrative and police authority in the countrysides.

Provincial autonomy

The declining political effectiveness of the central government and increasing economic weakness meant that it was losing power in the provinces to its own officials. Provincial governors, soldiers, and others seized local power. Provincial notables built up armies and administrative staffs, developed local markets, and thus retained for local use an increasing part of the provincial surplus. To regain control, the central government started to rotate provincial governors more frequently, and began to assign provincial governorships to high courtiers in Istanbul. They in turn appointed deputies (*mutesellim*) to administer the provinces on their behalf, many of whom were local notables (*a'yan*). Some were descendants of slave army officers; some belonged to the families of important 'ulama'; others were tax collectors, owners of large estates, or rich merchants who had the financial resources to buy deputy governorships and build up independent military retinues. These officials converted tax-farms into life tenures (*malikane*) and ultimately into private properties, and built up private armies recruited among former janissaries, demobilized soldiers, and bandits. Janissaries serving in the retinue of provincial governors, assigned to garrison small towns, soon formed an exploitative class living off illegal tax revenues. Rival groups of janissaries, irregular soldiers, rebels, and bandits imposed their own illegal taxes.

The rise to power of independent local officials and notables was itself based on still more profound changes in Anatolian society. The growth of the Anatolian population in the course of the sixteenth century promoted the growth of provincial towns and intensified the competition for control of revenues. Population growth led to a great surplus of peasant laborers, unemployed soldiers, and students who migrated to the towns looking for work. The end of Ottoman conquests in Hungary and Iran also forced would-be soldiers to return to their villages and towns as unemployed drifters who sought to earn a living as retainers for local notables, often to oppress the peasants, as students with stipends, or as bandits. Banditry, however, was never a threat to the state or to the persistence of the social structure. Ottoman bandits did not try to undermine the state, but rather aimed at the benefits of incorporation, and the authorities managed them by alternating bargaining, payments, and suppression.

These developments also increased the power of the common people. Peasants were often permitted to arm themselves for defense against bandits, and with the consolidation of private estates, peasants increasingly moved into villages clustered around fortified manor houses. This concentration strengthened local community ties and encouraged the emergence of a stronger peasant leadership. In many parts of the Balkans, the breakdown of Ottoman central authority led to a three-way struggle for power among provincial office-holding and landowning notables, janissaries and artisans, and peasant bandits.

The decentralization of power and the rising influence of local officials contributed to the disruption of the traditional Ottoman economy. In an earlier era, the empire was able to channel the surplus produce of Anatolia to the benefit of the political elite and the populace of Istanbul. Now independent tax-farmers and local officials redirected the agricultural surpluses from the capital to provincial towns and markets controlled by the a'yan and their personal armies. Furthermore, increasing European demand for Ottoman products gave local notables, merchants, and estate owners an incentive for avoiding state regulations and exporting surplus produce to Europe. The export of grain, cotton, silk, and other raw materials in turn stimulated inflation in the Ottoman empire, and parts of western Anatolia and the Adana region went over to cash-crop farming. The combined

Istanbul, provincial, and international markets also increased the incentives for provincial notables to convert tax-farms into chiftliks, or private estates. Commercialization thus reinforced decentralization.

In the Balkans, the authority of the central government similarly declined and the power of local officials correspondingly rose. As in Anatolia, the janissary corps were corrupted, the rural cavalry evaded central control, and timar administration broke down. Tax-farms replaced timars and Ottoman officials acquired lifetime tax-farms and even private estates. In the course of the seventeenth and eighteenth centuries, a new landlord class made up of former Muslim governors and army officers, and rich non-Muslim merchants and other notables, emerged. These landlords were aggressively interested in the commercial prospects of their estates. They raised new crops such as maize, rice, and animals for export despite the fact that this was illegal under Ottoman regulations. In the Balkans, commercialization also stimulated the growth of towns. Absentee landlords, tax-farmers, rich notables, and import–export merchants formed a new urban aristocracy whose wealth was based upon agricultural production and marketing. Janissary-workers and peasant migrants flocked to the towns looking for work. Town populations tended to become less Turkish and to take on the ethnicity of the people living in the surrounding countrysides.

Such massive changes did not occur all at once or once and for all, but evolved over a period of more than two hundred years, marked by constant struggle between the central state and provincial elites and by constant changes in the balance of power between them. The seventeenth century was a period of open struggle for power marked by repeated "Jelali" rebellions led by lower-ranking military and administrative officers, often supported by mercenaries and bandits, seeking lucrative local positions. The new wave of revolts represented the ambitions of local contenders for power trying to force their way into the Ottoman elite. In the face of these pressures, the Ottoman empire repeatedly suppressed rebellions and attempted to reconsolidate its power. The Koprulu family of viziers attempted a complete reform. Mehmed Koprulu (1656-61), born of an Albanian Christian father and recruited through the devshirme, was appointed Grand Vizier with a reform mandate. Koprulu confiscated the properties of the chief qadis, and suppressed the religious orders and provincial rebellions. Nonetheless, by the end of the century Anatolia was again in the hands of rebellious local officials.

The first half of the eighteenth century was in general a period of consolidation. The vizierial and chancery services helped maintain effective discipline within the scribal corporation. In many provinces the Ottomans reorganized administration and appointed effective governors. Some semblance of order was also maintained by the self-interest of local officials and landowners, who wished to protect their estates and assure continued production.

By the end of the century, however, almost all of the Ottoman empire was in the control of independent officials. Councils of a'yan played a large role in administration. They won control over the appointment of deputy governors and judges, enforced guild regulations, prevented food shortages, and maintained public build-ings. By the laws of 1784 the procedures for appointment to councils and deputy governorships were regularized. In 1809 the a'yan extracted from the Sultan formal recognition of their rights and prerogatives. In the meantime, local dynasties entrenched themselves in power. The Karaosmanoglu dominated southwestern Anatolia, the Chapanoglu the central plateau, and the Pashaoglu the northeast. In the Balkans, 'Ali Pasha of Janina (1788–1822) had a small regional state in north-ern Albania and Greece; Osman Pasvanoglu (1799–1807) ruled western Bulgaria and parts of Serbia and Romania. Other Balkan lords occupied eastern Bulgaria and Thrace. In the Arab provinces, as we shall see, the governors of Damascus, Mosul, Baghdad, and Basra were substantially independent. Egypt was governed by the Mamluks. North Africa was autonomous. This was the high point of a'yan influence and political decentralization, and would be followed in the nineteenth century by strong government efforts to reestablish central control.

While the decentralization of power occurred throughout the Ottoman empire, it had very different implications in the different regions. Though Turkish and Arab societies escaped close central government control, the identity of local elites remained bound up with the Ottoman empire and with Islam. The Sultans contin-ued to be recognized as legitimate suzerains, and local officials continued to be Ottomans. Decentralization did not lead to the institutionalization of autonomy.

In the Balkans, however, autonomy was a harbinger of revolutionary change. Balkan peoples, predominantly Christians, never fully assimilated into Ottoman soci-ety, began to conceive of national independence. In its heyday, the Ottoman system had won general acceptance, but the breakdown of rural security turned Balkan populations against the empire. Rural lords, peasant bandits, and urban merchants released from Ottoman political control turned more and more to Europe. Further-more, while the Orthodox Church continued to ally itself with the Ottoman regime as a bulwark against European, Latin, and Catholic influences, its influence among its own people was diminishing. Orthodox Slavs were dissatisfied with Greek lead-ership. Middle-class townsmen began to look westward not only for economic exchange but for intellectual stimulation. Progressively, segments of the Balkan mer-cantile and landowning elites, prospering as exporters and middlemen in the trade with Europe, developed a new political consciousness. Elements of the Christian urban middle classes in Greece sponsored secular schools to replace church schools and patronized literary and intellectual movements which fostered secular and nationalist ideas. Increasing contacts with Europe led to the formation of movements for national independence. The decentralization of the Ottoman empire paved the way for the ultimate rejection of Ottoman rule.

European encroachment

While the Ottoman empire was becoming internally decentralized it was also falling behind the rising powers of Europe. For centuries the Ottomans and other Muslim powers had been competing with Europeans on a world scale. For centuries the Ottomans held the initiative, but in the sixteenth century the Ottomans and the Portuguese in the Indian Ocean, and the Ottomans and the Habsburgs in the Mediterranean, reached a stalemate. In the seventeenth century the immediate threat was Russian expansion. The Russians were moving south across the steppes to the Black and Caspian Seas. Though the Ottomans checked the Russian advance by their occupation of Podolia in 1676, Russia, under Peter the Great, with its armies newly modernized, took Azov in the Crimea in 1696. The Habsburgs seized most of Hungary north of the Danube between 1684 and 1687, and took Serbia in 1689. The Venetians seized Dalmatia and the Morea. Poland invaded Podolia. For the first time the European powers had pushed back the frontiers of the Ottoman empire.

The Ottomans were able to restore their territorial position in the early decades of the eighteenth century. By the peace of Passarowitz in 1718, they regained the Morea. In 1739 the Sava–Danube frontier was restored by the treaty of Belgrade. The Ottomans further consolidated their position in Romania by replacing the Hospodars with Phanariot Greek merchants from Istanbul. By the late eighteenth century, however, Russian expansion resumed. Between 1768 and 1774 the Russians occupied Romania and the Crimea, and by the treaty of Kuchuk Kaynarca (1774) achieved access to the Black Sea. A new series of wars, culminating in the Peace of Jassy (1792), allowed the Russians to advance to the Dniester, to establish a protectorate over Georgia, and to consolidate their position in the Crimea.

These Russian advances caused consternation in Istanbul, for the Ottomans were forced to recognize their military inferiority and the threat of still further Russian advances. Military and diplomatic pressure combined with the commercial penetration and provincial decentralization brought the empire to the nadir of its fortunes. While the Ottoman empire maintained its territorial domains, political resiliency, and cultural vitality, it was falling behind its European competitors.

Ottoman historians and court officials gave thoughtful attention to the problems of the regime, and wrote volumes of advice to rulers. In the seventeenth century, they saw the issue in terms of a restoration of traditional Ottoman institutions. The *Risale* of Mustafa Kochu Bey, written in 1631, advised the Sultan to return to the direct management of the government, restore the authority of the Grand Vizier, reconstruct the timars, and suppress factions. He warned against the oppression of the peasantry. Katip Chelebi analyzed the decline in terms of the abuse of peasants, the loss of production and revenues, and the flight to the cities, and called for the restoration of just taxation and lawful order. Mustafa Naima (1665–1716), an official historian of the Ottoman court, advised the government to balance its income and expenditures, pay stipends to the military, and purge the army of incompetent soldiers.

By the beginning of the eighteenth century, however, there was a reorientation of Ottoman perceptions. The treaty of Karlowitz (1699), the first time that the Ottomans lost territory to a European power, showed that European innovations in military technology, economic organization, and cultural style were a direct commercial and territorial threat to the Ottoman empire. The Ottomans cautiously began to import European advisors to implement military reforms. Between 1734 and 1738 de Bonneval taught mathematics and artillery techniques to Ottoman soldiers. In 1773 Baron de Tott provided up-to-date instruction in artillery and naval warfare. An Ottoman printing press was established to print European technical works dealing with military subjects, engineering, geography, and history.

The new political consciousness was expressed in literary style and the emulation of European fashions. Turkish poetry turned to themes of everyday life and adopted a more vernacular language. Turkish proverbs, puns, and jokes became part of the poetry of such writers as Ahmed Nedim (1681–1730). Mehmed Emin Belig (d. 1758) described the life of the artisans, the bazaars, and the baths.

Ottomans also became enamored of European architectural decoration and furniture. Ottoman mosques were decorated in baroque fashion. Summer palaces and water fountains, built on traditional Ottoman architectural lines, were decorated in a French-inspired rococo manner. European painting influenced Ottoman wall paintings which in this period showed battle and hunting scenes, dancing girls, and musical instruments. Ottoman writers reported on French theater and opera, dress and decorations, garden design, and the freer style of relations among the people. The craze for tulips in the reign of Ahmed III (1703–30) has become the emblem of this new sensibility. Ottoman art lost its hieratic quality; the taste for naturalistic and floral design replaced the formality of traditional geometric and Arabesque decoration. These changes indicate a shift from a self-conscious imperial style of culture to a more personal sensibility much in parallel with the evolution of Safavid taste in an era of imperial decline.

Decentralization and the changing international balance of power had mixed implications for the survival of the Ottoman system. In most of the empire, decentralization did not change the classic Ottoman arrangements. The concept of a legitimate state, its importance as the representative of Islam, and its authority as the overlord of local notables in Anatolia and the Arab provinces was unimpaired. The state maintained its dominance over the 'ulama' and the religious establishment despite the increased autonomy of tribal and other corporate groups. In the Balkans, however, European influence enhanced the autonomy of the Christian populations, and gave them new advantages in international trade that paved the way for the ultimate liberation of Balkan populations from Ottoman control.

Nevertheless, while other Muslim regimes succumbed to international pressures, or to European intervention, the Ottomans maintained dynastic continuity. At the end of the pre-modern era Ottoman-Islamic society was still built upon a strong state, legitimate in military, patrimonial, and cosmopolitan as well as Muslim terms, a well-organized and subordinate Muslim religious establishment, and an abiding acceptance of the concept of state control over parochial communities. These institutions would powerfully affect the modern development of Islamic societies in Turkey and other parts of the Middle East.

CHAPTER 15

THE ARAB MIDDLE EAST

The Arab provinces of the Middle East and North Africa now form a single cultural and ethnic unit. The region is interconnected by the Arabic language, by ethnic identity, and by the shared experience of Ottoman rule from the sixteenth to the nineteenth centuries. For the sake of narrative convenience, however, we have grouped the history of the Arab world into two successive chapters. In this chapter we shall deal with the history of Egypt and Syria. The following chapter deals with North Africa and Spain. Our account of the Arabian peninsula, which stood outside the framework of Middle Eastern developments, is reserved for part III.

The history of each region will be divided into three time frames. The first corresponds to the Arab conquests and the Caliphal phase in the history of the Middle East. It includes the Fatimid Caliphate in Egypt and North Africa, the Umayyad Caliphate in Spain, and the Almoravid and Almohad regimes in Morocco. The second phase or middle period was the era in which the Arab Middle East and North Africa came under the influence of Saljuq institutions, and developed new frameworks for state and religious organization which were variations upon the emerging universal Islamic pattern. This was the period of the Ayyubids and Mamluks in Egypt and Syria, the Hafsids in Tunisia, and the Marinids in Morocco. The third phase continues the history of the new institutions in the period of Ottoman domination from the sixteenth to the nineteenth centuries, and the Moroccan variant.

EGYPT AND SYRIA IN THE "CALIPHAL" AGE

Egypt and Syria were among the first Middle Eastern provinces to be absorbed into the Arab-Muslim Caliphate. They were both conquered in 641. Their populations rapidly adopted the Arabic language, though they were slow to accept Islam. Under the Umayyad and early 'Abbasid Caliphates, Egypt was a subsidiary province, but from the middle of the ninth century slave soldiers appointed by the 'Abbasids established short-lived dynasties. The Tulunids ruled Egypt from 868 to 905 and the

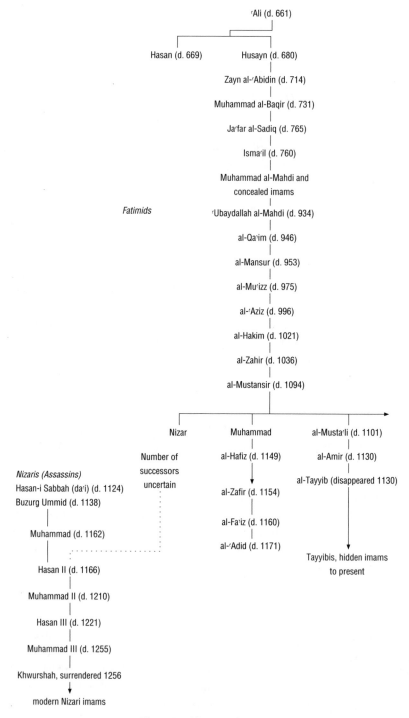

Figure 7   The Isma'ili imams

Ikhshidids from 935 to 969. In 969 the Fatimids conquered the country and established a new Caliphate which lasted until 1171.

The Fatimid dynasty was not merely an independent governorship, but was a revolutionary regime which claimed universal authority. It had its origin in the Isma'ili movement. The Qarmatians in the fertile crescent and Arabia roused peasant and bedouin opposition around 900. Similarly, the Fatimids incited Kitama Berbers to overthrow the Aghlabid regime of Tunisia in 909, and established a new government based on the claim of 'Ubaydallah to be the living imam. Under the leadership of the Fatimid imams, the Berbers conquered North Africa, Egypt, and parts of Syria. With the shattering of the 'Abbasid empire, Egypt emerged as a principal center of Arabic civilization.

The Fatimid dynasty (969–1171), like the 'Abbasid, laid claim to being the true leader of Islam. This claim was advanced in the multiple vocabularies of Mediterranean civilization. The Fatimids presented an Isma'ili, a philosophical, a Byzantine, and an 'Abbasid symbolism of political authority. They proclaimed that they were the true imams, the descendants of 'Ali; thus they broke with the prevailing Shi'i tradition that the imam was hidden and would return as the messiah. The declaration of a Fatimid imamate required a redefinition of the historical succession of imams and of the eschatological cycles of history. The Fatimids held that they were the continuation of the sixth cycle of imams, and that the coming of the messiah and the closure of the historical cycles was postponed to the indefinite future.

Under the auspices of the new theory, neo-Platonic and gnostic concepts were incorporated into Isma'ili thinking. At the beginning of the tenth century, al-Nasafi, an Isma'ili missionary in eastern Iran, taught that the universe was brought into being by divine emanations in the form of intellectual essences. The imams corresponded to these emanations. Through them the believers would be initiated into spiritual truth; by gnostic illumination they would become the Truth.

The Fatimid concepts of ruler and imperium were also expressed in court ceremony, art, and architecture. Emulating the rival 'Abbasid and Byzantine empires, the palace of the ruler was decorated with extraordinary splendor. Gold rafters supported the ceiling; rare birds and animals decorated the walls and the furniture; fountains of cascading water cooled the air. The ruler himself sat on a gold throne protected by a curtain in a fashion inspired by the 'Abbasids and resembling Byzantine enthronement. He was entitled to a special crown, sword, scepter, parasol, weapons, and other implements that were signs of his sovereignty. Court decorations, some the gifts of foreign ambassadors, some of Byzantine manufacture, and some 'Abbasid relics, depicted his glory. A huge silk hanging with a map of all the lands of the world and their rulers expressed the Fatimid claim to belong to the family of kings. Fatimid paintings and illuminated manuscripts showed the influence of the 'Abbasids' court at Samarra. Fatimid ceramics were decorated with vegetal and animal themes, which were symbols of good luck, and with hunters, musicians, dancers, and human figures who depicted court life. Their intent was to magically recreate the splendor of Fatimid rule.

The court decorations and utensils were housed in royal treasuries, for they were not only useful ornamentations but rare and exotic objects reserved for the sole use of the sovereign and the court. In 1067, however, in the course of a civil war, the Fatimid treasury was looted, and royal objects became accessible for imitation. Fatimid ceramics, metalworks, and woodcraft inspired an Egyptian craft culture based upon international imperial motifs.

Equally important in the palace symbolism was Islam. The palace contained halls for the teaching of Isma'ili beliefs. Judges, missionaries, reciters of the Quran, and prayer leaders were regularly present for court ceremonies. Formal religious processions symbolized the sublime importance of the monarchy. Audiences with the Caliph, reviews of the soldiers, receptions of ambassadors, Ramadan and New Year processions, and formal openings of the Nile canals brought the Caliph and his entourage to the mosques of the city where he delivered the sermon, celebrated the festivals, and displayed the magnificent and sacred objects of the Fatimid treasury. Thus the Caliph brought home to the populace the importance of the ruler both in the spheres of war and politics and in those of religion, nature, and magic.

The public architecture of the Fatimids was an extension of the ceremonial aspect of the royal court. The new Fatimid capital city, al-Qahira (Cairo), founded in 969, with its magnificent palaces and grand mosques, was an imperial city designed for imperial pageants. The principal mosques – al-Azhar and al-Hakim – were constructed with minarets and cupolas which symbolized the preeminence of the imam and recalled the holy places of Mecca and Medina as a way of glorifying the ruler in the service of God and Islam.

The Fatimids further cultivated religious glory by sponsoring the cult of the family of 'Ali; the cult of the living imam was replaced by the cult of the deceased family of the Prophet. The Fatimids constructed numerous mausolea over the supposed graves of the family of 'Ali in order to encourage pilgrimage and to inculcate a popular enthusiasm for shrines and relics. Quranic inscriptions encouraged obedience to the imam and called upon people to accept his authority as an expression of God's will. In 1153 the head of the martyr Husayn was moved from Ascalon, and a new mausoleum, Sayyidna al-Husayn, was constructed to house it. Pilgrims circumambulated the tomb, kissed his final resting place, wept, and begged the favor of the imam. The graves of Caliphs were also considered holy, but they were buried in the palace precincts and could be venerated only by court personnel. These constructions introduced artistic motifs, such as the muqarnas or stalactite decoration, facades with decorated gates and minarets, and the use of figural representation, which would become staple features of later Islamic art.

In their secular aspect the Fatimids were simply a conquest regime based on Berber tribal forces and Turkish and Sudanese slave regiments. They controlled Egypt by means of an efficient administration inherited from the 'Abbasids, staffed by Jewish and Christian officials. While the new regime made Isma'ilism the state religion, it made no effort to change the allegiances of the Egyptian population. The Muslim population of Egypt remained predominantly Sunni.

The rhythm of Fatimid history was similar to that of the 'Abbasids. The period from 969 to 1021 was one of political and religious consolidation. The second phase, from 1021 to 1073, saw a breakdown of political order, warfare between military factions, and the division of the country into iqta's, controlled by the leading military officers. This decline was arrested by the administration of Badr al-Jamali and his son, al-Afdal, from 1073 to 1121, in which the military chiefs replaced the Caliphs as the effective heads of government.

The internal decline of the Fatimid Caliphate accentuated the contradiction between its revolutionary pretensions and the actualities of its Egyptian political base. The decline of Caliphal authority led to schisms as the messianic and politically radical branches of the Isma'ili movement split off. In the Lebanon the Druze sect believed that the Caliph al-Hakim (d. 1021) was the last imam and was indeed God himself. At the death of the Caliph al-Mustansir in 1094, his son al-Musta'li succeeded him, but the missionary movement in Syria, Mesopotamia, and Iran, cut off from the Fatimids in Egypt, broke with the parent regime, recognized al-Mustansir's son Nizar as the true imam, and founded a new branch of Isma'ilism. The Nizari Isma'ilis later came to be known as the Assassins. They would carry on the Isma'ili challenge to Sunni Islam.

While the Fatimids ruled Egypt, Syria, a province characterized by numerous ecological and political zones – coastal, mountain, town, and desert – and exposed to multiple influences – from Anatolia, the Mediterranean, Egypt, and Iraq – was divided into numerous small states. The Fatimids established their authority in southern Syria and took control of Damascus from 978 to 1076. Northern Syria, after a brief interlude of Hamdanid, Buwayhid, and Byzantine warfare, came under Byzantine control from 968 to 1086. The balance of power between the Byzantine and Fatimid empires allowed for a proliferation of bedouin principalities in Mesopotamia and northern Syria under the aegis of the 'Uqaylid (990–1096), Marwanid (983–1085), and Mirdasid (1023–79) dynasties. Southern Syria was in the hands of Kalb tribes. Towns such as Tripoli became independent city-states. Mountain populations in the Lebanon preserved their autonomy. In this fragmented condition, Syria was overrun by the Saljuqs. They conquered Damascus in 1079, and took Antioch and Aleppo in 1085. Syria was then divided between two Saljuq succession regimes, one based in Aleppo and one in Damascus.

Syria was then exposed to yet another wave of invasions, this time by Latin Crusaders. The Crusades had their origin in a general European counter-attack against Muslim powers in the Mediterranean. Italian towns were pushing back Muslim pirates. The Reconquista had begun in Spain; by 1085 Toledo was in Christian hands. In 1087 Pisa and Genoa destroyed Mahdiya, the political and commercial capital of Muslim North Africa. The Normans conquered Sicily between 1061 and

Map 13   Egypt and Syria, showing the Crusader states in the twelfth century

1091 and moved on to attack the Byzantine empire. Furthermore, the papacy was eager to reconcile the Greek and Western churches, and to support the Byzantine empire against the Saljuq Turks. It wanted to establish new states under its auspices in the eastern Mediterranean in order to spread the influence of the Latin Church among Eastern Christian peoples. Alongside the political currents ran a strong passion for pilgrimage. Eleventh-century Christian feeling stressed penance and the quest for remission of sins. Jerusalem, the heavenly city, symbolized salvation. The Saljuq invasions raised European anxieties about access to Jerusalem and generated a passionate desire to secure the holy city in Christian hands.

These trends came together in 1096. Pope Urban II, speaking to an audience of restive warriors at Clermont in France, conscious of Papal policy needs, and influenced by the pilgrimage sensibility, broached the idea of an armed pilgrimage to capture the holy places from the infidels. To those who would undertake this mission, Urban offered protection of property at home, new lands in the east, plenary indulgences, and the total remission of all temporal punishments that might be imposed by the church for the commission of past sins. His audience probably heard this as a promise of absolution from sin and of salvation.

By sea and by land European warriors set out for the east. Between 1099 and 1109 they captured Edessa, Antioch, and Tripoli, and established the Latin Kingdom of Jerusalem. Baldwin was elected king, ruling as a feudal lord with the support of the Knights Templar and Hospitalers. Latin clergy took control of Christian administration in the holy land, but the Eastern Christian sects were not eliminated.

The Muslim response to the Crusades was slow to develop, but when it did it led eventually to the unification of Syria and Egypt into a single Muslim state. The initial Muslim reaction was, by and large, indifference. Syria was so fragmented as to preclude any unified opposition to the intruders; several more little states among many did not much disturb existing interests. The fact that these new states were Christian was not exceptional – the Byzantines had also ruled northern Syria, and there was a substantial, if not a majority, local Christian population.

Gradually, however, a Muslim counter-attack developed which may be described in three phases. From 1099 to 1146 was the phase of Mesopotamian leadership. The Saljuqid Atabegs of Mosul, who had nominal authority over Syria, wished to create their own small empire in Mesopotamia and northern Syria. In 1128 a new governor of Mosul, Zengi (c. 1127–46), seized Aleppo; in 1144 he managed by chance to capture Edessa. When Zengi died in 1146, however, Mosul and Aleppo were severed from each other to make independent principalities for his surviving sons. Throughout this period, the Mosul campaigns were not primarily directed against the Crusaders, but were aimed at winning territory from either Muslim or Christian rulers whenever possible. There was little consciousness of Muslim–Christian antagonism per se. In fact, Christian and Muslim princelings often allied to resist Zengi's encroachments. A second phase began with the succession of Nur al-Din (c. 1146–74), the son of Zengi, who inherited Aleppo.

Nur al-Din made the capture of Damascus his main goal. In 1147, he helped relieve the siege of Damascus by the second Crusade. In 1154, a local rebellion expelled the ruling Saljuqid governors, and the populace of the city turned it over to him. This unexpected turn of events reveals the underground growth of a new Muslim communal and religious spirit, frankly anti-Christian and opposed to the Crusader presence.

The Dome of the Rock had been built in Jerusalem by the Umayyad Caliphs to symbolize the Muslim appropriation of the sacred past of Judaism and Christianity. In the course of the eighth, ninth, and tenth centuries, Jewish and Christian ideas about Jerusalem were assimilated into Islamic teachings. Jerusalem was an axis of communication between this world and the next. It became venerable to Muslims as part of their own prophetic history because Muhammad was believed to have ascended to heaven from Jerusalem. Refugees waged a literary and religious campaign about the merits of Jerusalem and the importance of jihad. By the middle of the twelfth century this sentiment had become a popular force, and this helps to account for the surrender of Damascus to Nur al-Din, who was now seen as the Muslim prince who would redeem Jerusalem.

In fact, the reign of Nur al-Din in Damascus from 1154 to 1174 did not concentrate upon the redemption of Jerusalem but upon the consolidation of his little kingdom in Syria. He made treaties with the Byzantines and the Latins, and concentrated upon the conquest of Mosul, which he took in 1170, thus fulfilling a family ambition to reunite Syria and Mesopotamia; he also entered into the struggle for control of Egypt. With the Fatimid regime in total disarray, and Amalric, the Latin King of Jerusalem, maneuvering to seize the country, Nur al-Din sent his general Shirkuh and Shirkuh's nephew Salah al-Din (Saladin) with Muslim forces to take control of Egypt in 1169. In 1171 they removed the last of the Fatimid Caliphs, and established a Sunni regime. The histories of Egypt and Syria would be joined until the nineteenth century.

The advent of Saladin to the Sultanate of Egypt opened a third phase of the Muslim response to the Crusades. From Egypt, Saladin brought Syria and Mesopotamia into a unified Muslim state. In 1174 he took Damascus; in 1183, Aleppo; in 1186, Mosul. He then defeated the Crusaders at the battle of Hattin (1187) and brought an end to the Latin occupation of Jerusalem. At the siege of Acre (1192), however, Saladin made a truce with Richard the Lion-Heart which allowed the crusading principalities to maintain their foothold on the coasts of Palestine and Syria.

THE SALJUQ MODEL: STATE AND RELIGION

The conquest of Syria and then of Egypt by Turkish (and Kurdish) warriors and the establishment of Saljuqid regimes began a new era in the history of these regions. The Saljuqid era put an end to the legacy of Caliphal institutions and concepts, and introduced in the former western provinces of the 'Abbasid empire the system of state and religious organization that was being worked out in the eastern provinces. Under Nur al-Din, the system of state patronage for Muslim legal scholarship in the empire was transferred to Damascus. Under his patronage new colleges of law were founded and endowed with permanent funds. Stimulated by scholars from Iran and Spain, the influx of Hanafi and Shafi'i scholars integrated the Syrian provinces into what was becoming the prevalent system of education in the Middle East.

The conquest of Egypt by Saladin in 1171 opened the way for the installation of the Sunni schools in Egypt. The Shafi'i school had survived under Fatimid rule, but Saladin introduced the Hanafi school, endowed colleges of law, and recruited prominent teachers and judges from abroad. By the early thirteenth century, the Ayyubid government in Egypt adopted a pan-Sunni policy of equal recognition and equal sponsorship of all schools of law. The dar al-hadith al-Kamiliya was founded in 1222 to teach the points of law that were held in common among the schools. The madrasa al-Salihiya was founded in 1239 to house all four schools of law in the same building.

Similarly, the Saljuq sponsorship of khanaqas and ribats spread these institutions from eastern Iran to Baghdad and to the western Arab provinces. The first Syrian khanaqa was built in Aleppo in 1115. Nur al-Din established one in Damascus after 1154. Saladin founded a khanaqa in Egypt in 1173 as a hostel for foreign Sufis, and one in Jerusalem in 1189.

Upon Saladin's death in 1193, his family, the Ayyubid house, succeeded to the rule of Egypt (to 1250) and Syria (to 1260). The family divided his empire into the smaller kingdoms of Egypt, Damascus, Aleppo, and Mosul in accordance with the Saljuq idea that the state was the patrimony of the royal family. Nonetheless, the Ayyubids did not revert to the fragmentation of earlier regimes. The Sultan of Egypt usually managed to assert his suzerainty over the rest of the family and to make use of family loyalties to integrate the regime. The Ayyubids ruled Egypt and Syria through a military aristocracy composed of Kurdish and Turkish troops and some slave forces. They administered Egypt by the age-old bureaucratic system that prevailed in that country, and Syria by the distribution of iqta's to the leading military officers.

The Ayyubids were notably reluctant to continue the struggle against the remaining Crusader principalities. Having achieved a tenuous unity, and a prosperous Mediterranean trade between Syria and Egypt and the ports of Italy and Europe, the Ayyubids drew back from the struggle for Palestine, and gave priority to the protection of Egypt. Having realized that Egypt was the key to the recovery of the holy land, the Christians attacked it in 1197, 1217, 1229, and 1249. In 1217, to divert the Crusaders from Egypt, al-Kamil (1218–38) offered concessions in Palestine. In 1229, the Ayyubids negotiated a treaty with Frederick II, agreeing to return Jerusalem to Christian hands on the condition that the city would not be fortified and that the Temple area would remain open to Muslim pilgrims. Thus the Ayyubids gave preference to political and economic over religious and symbolic considerations. However deep Muslim anti-Christian sentiment might be, its effective expression still required that religious feeling correspond to the interests of the political elite.

In 1250 the Ayyubid house was overthrown by a rebellion of one of its Mamluk or slave regiments, which killed the last Ayyubid ruler of Egypt and named one of its own officers, Aybeg, as the new Sultan. The Mamluks defended Syria against the Mongols at the battle of 'Ayn Jalut in 1260, crushed the last of the independent Syrian principalities, expelled the remaining Crusader states by 1291, and expanded the boundaries of their empire into the Upper Euphrates Valley and Armenia. Thus they were able to unify Egypt and Syria until the Ottoman conquest in 1517. This was the longest-lived Muslim state in the Middle East between the 'Abbasid and the Ottoman empires.

The Mamluk era was noted for the perfection of the post-'Abbasid slave-military system. Before the Mamluk period, slave regiments had been employed in all Middle Eastern armies, but the Mamluks, like the Ghaznavids, were based entirely on the slave-military machine. The elite personnel of the regime, including the Sultan, were slaves or former slaves. In principle, though there were important exceptions, no one could be a member of the military elite unless he was of foreign origin, usually Turkish or Circassian, purchased and raised as a slave, and trained to be a soldier and administrator. No native of Egypt or Syria could ever belong to this elite, nor, in principle, could the sons of slaves and rulers. The raison d'être of this arrange-ment was that every man who served the regime belonged entirely to the state and was without any family or local ties to compromise his total dedication to his master and to the service of the military caste.

Mamluks were purchased from abroad at the age of ten or twelve, were con-verted to Islam and raised in barracks, where they not only learned military tech-nique but were imbued with loyalty to their masters and to their comrades-in-arms. Upon graduating from the barracks schools, the fully trained Mamluks served either in the Sultan's Mamluk regiment or as soldiers in the service of other leading offi-cers. The officers possessed their own personal slaves, apart from the regiments of the Sultan. A Mamluk army, then, may be imagined as a grouping of slave regi-ments, made up of the Sultan's troops and of the regiments loyal to individual offi-cers, who were in turn personally loyal to the Sultan. This army was not organized so much by hierarchy of rank as by personal allegiance.

To support the military elite, the bureaucratic tradition of Egypt and the iqta's of Syria were combined. The tax revenues of Egypt and Syria were assigned to pay the salaries of the Sultan and the Mamluk officers. In Egypt the amirs were assigned iqta' revenues, but the central bureaucracy kept close control over taxation. The bureaucracy made surveys to determine the available resources and to prevent the Mamluks from acquiring excessive revenues or other rights in the countryside. With the decline of the Mamluk state in the late fourteenth century, central controls became less effective.

The need to legitimize the regime led to a program of imperial and court cere-mony and cultural patronage designed to glorify the rulers. The presence at court

of the Caliph and the chief judges, the guardianship of the annual pilgrimage caravan to the holy places of Mecca and Medina, the formal presence of the Sultan in
the Hall of Justice, and the celebration of Islamic religious feasts emphasized the
religious importance of the regime. The magical as well as the religious aspects of
royal power were also celebrated. The ruler was revered as someone who had in
his control the powers of the cosmos. A good ruler could bring rain and abundant
harvests; a bad ruler could bring ruin. The tomb of al-Mansur Qala'un (1280–90)
copied features of the Dome of the Rock in Jerusalem to signify the Mamluk pre-
tension to be heirs to the glory of the first Islamic dynasty. In a similar spirit the
royal libraries were provided with copies of Persian illuminated manuscripts telling
of the conquests of Alexander the Great and the histories of Persian kings. Late
Mamluk-era culture was rich in Persian and Ottoman influences. The cosmopolitan
heritage of Mamluk Egypt was also reinforced by the migration of Iranian, Turkish,
Spanish, and Mesopotamian craftsmen and scholars, who brought with them metalwork, textile, ceramic, and building crafts, which were adopted by the Mamluks to
adorn the life of the court and the military aristocracy. The religious and cosmopolitan aspects of Mamluk court culture were tempered by a parochial ethnic and
military emphasis. The Mamluk court listened to Turkish and Circassian poetry. The
Mamluks also reveled in military reviews, tournaments, and displays of martial arts.
In the course of this effort to legitimize themselves, the Mamluks left a distinctive
Egyptian-Islamic artistic legacy.

The Ayyubids and the Mamluks also continued the Saljuq policy of strong state
support for and control of Islam. The decisive force behind Ayyubid- and Mamluk-
era Egyptian culture was the commitment of the state to Sunni rather than Shi'i
Islam. The early Mamluk period was dominated by intense Muslim religious feeling expressed in warfare against the Crusaders, the Mongols, and the Isma'ilis, and
hostility to Christians and Jews, coupled with pressures for the conversion of non-
Muslims to Islam. In addition, both the Ayyubids and the Mamluks sponsored a
revival of Sunni Islamic religious activity. In the Ayyubid period (1193–1260) there
were no fewer than 255 religious structures built in Damascus. This was followed
by an equally intense period of construction in the first century of Mamluk rule, at
the instance of governors, generals, judges, and rich merchants. The Ayyubids and
Mamluks also followed Fatimid precedents by constructing tombs for venerated
Muslim ancestors and for deceased rulers. One of the first Ayyubid projects was the
construction of a madrasa near the grave of al-Shafi'i, the founder of the principal
Egyptian school of law. Colleges and khanaqas came to be provided with mausoleums for the remains of their founders. A tomb advertised the sanctity of the
ruler, and his devotion to Islam.

A characteristic architectural design emerged for the religious architecture of
this period. Mosques, madrasas, and khanaqas were often built with an open central courtyard surrounded by four galleries or *liwans* on the principal sides of the
courtyard, with the intervening spaces filled in with rooms for students. The mausoleum itself was often topped by a dome, and the whole structure provided with

tall, slender minarets. Such buildings, clustered along main streets or in the cemeteries, created a vast visual display, shaped the physical fabric of the city, and symbolized the integral relation of the state, Islam, and the urban society. With strong state support the schools of law became the foci for the spread of Islamic teaching among the common people. In Damascus, lawyers issued legal advice, preachers exhorted the general populace, and religious manuals instructed the people.

In Syria and Egypt, the Saljuq succession states converted the routine patronage of the 'ulama' and Sufis into a system of state control. Nur al-Din selected the appointees to judicial and teaching offices and created a supervisory post for the administration of Sufi khanaqas. He pioneered a policy of making the 'ulama' and Sufis directly dependent upon state patronage and appointments. Saladin appointed a chief qadi and a chief shaykh for the Sufis. In 1263, Sultan Baybars (1260–77) appointed a chief qadi for each of the four major schools of law, a chief shaykh for the Sufis, and a syndic for the corporation of descendants of the Prophet (*naqib al-ashraf*). Under the Mamluks the state appointed judges, legal administrators, professors, Sufi shaykhs, prayer leaders, and other Muslim officials. They paid the salaries of religious personnel, endowed their schools, and thus brought the religious establishment into a state bureaucracy. Never did the state attempt to define the content of religious teaching. Thus, the Mamluks extended the Saljuq–Iranian pattern of organized religious life to Syria and Egypt. Owing to this strong support for Islam, Mamluk royal culture emphasized its Islamic rather than its cosmopolitan bases. It was thus typical of the tendency in the Arab provinces to legitimize states in Muslim rather than universalist terms.

THE OTTOMAN ERA

The Ottoman conquest of Egypt in 1517 perpetuated, with some modifications, the ongoing system of society. The Ottomans garrisoned Egypt with several corps of janissaries, and appointed military governors, inspectors, and finance officers to assure the collection of taxes and the remittance of the surpluses to Istanbul. The main functions of Ottoman administration were to pacify the country, control the bedouins, protect agriculture, irrigation, and trade, and thus assure the flow of tax revenues. In the course of the first century-and-a-half of Ottoman rule, the irrigation system of Egypt was rebuilt, cultivation increased, and trade restored by reopening the routes between India and Egypt. Egypt was also important to Ottoman control of the Red Sea, Yemen, Nubia, and Abyssinia, and the holy places in Arabia.

In many respects Egypt remained a separate political society. Beneath the top level of Ottoman administration the old institutional structure remained intact. The local Mamluk households continued to be militarily important, and were assigned taxable estates. While the Ottomans appointed a chief qadi and a chief syndic for the corporation of descendants of the Prophet from Istanbul, the rest of the 'ulama' establishment was of local origin. The muftis of the law schools, the chiefs of the holy lineages, and the rector of al-Azhar were the principal leaders of the religious establishment, and were responsible for the discipline of their followers. They managed the waqf revenues and, in the eighteenth century, the tax-farms assigned for their personal upkeep and the maintenance of the religious function of their schools and fraternities.

From the fifteenth century there were important changes in the character of Egyptian religious life. While in the early Mamluk period the schools of law and the madrasas had been the most important expression of Sunni Islam, now Sufism became increasingly important. The Khalwatiya, Shadhiliya, Ahmadiya, and other brotherhoods were organized under centralized leadership, and endowed with substantial properties. They were held in reverence by the military elites and the common people alike. The mawlids or birthdays of the Prophet and of famous Sufi saints were occasions for immense celebrations in which many thousands of people participated. Visits to the tombs or shrines of saints became a routine part of Egyptian religious life.

In Egypt, as in many other parts of the Muslim world, Sufism and shrine worship precipitated a religious reaction. Reformers in Mecca and Medina, Istanbul and Syria, Naqshbandis and others opposed the shrine forms of Sufism. In Egypt reform influences made themselves felt at al-Azhar, where hadith studies were revived. The Naqshbandis and the Khalwatis reinforced the trend. Reformism was especially appealing to, or indeed the expression of, the more scholarly, ethical, and puritanical spirit of merchant-'ulama' milieus with their wider range of commercial and intellectual contacts and their need for a more universal form of Islam as opposed to the parochial and localized forms of saint worship. In the late eighteenth century, Egypt seems to have maintained a variety of religious styles, including Shari'a, Sufi-Shari'a, shrine-Sufi, and reformist types of Islam.

Throughout this period, 'ulama' and Sufi leaders played an important political and social role. They were the intermediaries between the Mamluk elites and the common people. On the one hand, higher-ranking 'ulama' were often the clients of Mamluk regiments from whom they received waqfs, gifts, salaries, and fees for teaching and religious services. In the eighteenth century these ties enabled the leading 'ulama' to become extremely prosperous from the management of waqfs, control of tax-farms (*iltizams*), and other incomes. They served the Mamluks as negotiators and mediators in disputes among the factions, acted as bankers and tax collectors, and communicated the demands of the regime to the common people. On the other hand, they were also closely connected to the commoners. They married into merchant families, frequently invested in trade and real estate, managed schools, hospitals, and charities, and served as patrons for the people of their quarters. A leading scholar or Sufi would arbitrate in local disputes, feed the poor, and protect his people from abuse by the soldiers and the tax collectors. He could either organize or calm local resistance. Thus, in Egypt, the 'ulama' and Sufis played a critical role as intermediaries in the functioning of their society.

The late eighteenth century in Egypt was a period of violent warfare, exploitative taxation, a decline in irrigation, and rising bedouin power. As in many other parts of the empire, Ottoman governors lost authority, the Mamluks seized control of waqfs, and divided into factions. The Qasimiya and the Faqariya fought for political power until finally in 1786–87 the Ottomans defeated the Mamluk factions and restored central government control.

This was also a period of economic hardship due to inflation and a decline in commerce. In the sixteenth and seventeenth centuries Egypt lost some of its trade to Portuguese and then Dutch competition, but gained partial compensation from the coffee trade with Yemen. The eighteenth century, however, brought more severe European competition. European textiles, ceramics, and glass beat down Egyptian industries. Even coffee was imported into the Ottoman empire from the Antilles.

In the fertile crescent, the Ottomans also perpetuated the political society of the region. Unlike Egypt, which was a single province, the Ottomans ruled this region through the major towns, Damascus, Aleppo, Mosul, and Baghdad, which formed the territorial base for several Ottoman governorships. Ottoman administration had very limited means for centralizing political power. The Ottomans aimed at the minimum of governmental power needed to prevent officials from becoming independent and still allow them to maintain order, collect taxes, and remit the surplus to Istanbul. The primary concern in Istanbul was to make it difficult for its own appointees to defy central authority. Political authority was divided among military governors and independent civil and judicial officials. The army was divided into numerous units including regiments of janissaries and cavalry sent from Istanbul, the governor's private retainers, and local janissaries. Bedouin tribes served as auxiliary military units. The weakness of the state apparatus made it necessary to depend upon local notables. Their power was based upon control of taxation and waqfs, and upon the support they could rally from town quarters, artisan guilds, and local soldiers. In any case, control of the towns did not necessarily mean control of the countryside. Bedouins, especially in southern Iraq and along the Syrian margins of the north Arabian desert, and hill peoples in Kurdistan, northern Syria, and the Lebanon, maintained freedom from central control.

The notables differed in composition from city to city. In Damascus the 'ulama' were particularly important. Throughout the period of Ottoman rule a relatively small group of notable families controlled the posts of qadi, preacher, mufti, and teachers in the colleges and constituted a religious patriarchate. While Sufism was well established in Syria, it does not seem to have played so large a role as in Egypt. The 'ulama'–Sufi synthesis was less complete and the Syrian 'ulama' tended to be hostile to the less "orthodox" forms of Sufism. Sufi brotherhoods, khanaqas, shrines, and mawlids seem to have had a smaller place in Syrian religious life. The major exception to this was the veneration of the shrine of Ibn al-'Arabi in Damascus.

Aleppo is an example of both a provincial capital and a cosmopolitan caravan city. In the seventeenth century the Persian silk trade was Aleppo's primary industry. Armenians, Christian Arabs, Sephardic Jews, and merchants from Iran, India, and Europe were the principal actors in this trade. In the eighteenth century, the French surpassed the English as the predominant European merchant community, and many local Christians converted to Catholicism. Nonetheless, foreigners and minorities did not control or define the lifestyle of Aleppo as much as they did that of Izmir. Aleppo's hinterlands were as important in the political economy as trade. In the eighteenth century, the weakening of the central state allowed local notable families to control the rural hinterlands. Throughout the sixteenth century the Ottomans maintained a dominant position, but by the end of the century their position had deteriorated. Janissary units, aggrieved by the declining value of their salaries, rebelled against the central government, seized tax-farms, and turned them into life-tenure farms or private estates. Ottoman governors were reduced to manipulating the competing military factions. Then, in the first half of the eighteenth century, the Ottomans regained control of Damascus and Syria. In 1708 the newly appointed governor of Damascus was given direct authority over other administrative sub-districts of Syria, and was charged with responsibility for the pilgrimage. His job was to maintain the goodwill of the urban notables, and to curb the bedouins by offering them bribes and offices. After 1758, however, the central government was defeated by local forces. In the latter part of the eighteenth century, the Ottomans could no longer control the notables or protect the pilgrimage.

With Ottoman decline, governors established local dynasties. The 'Azm family ruled Damascus from 1724 to 1780; the heirs of Hasan Pasha governed Baghdad and Basra from 1704 until the early 1830s; the Jalili family governed Mosul from 1726 to 1834. In Palestine and the Lebanon, there were several small-scale regimes. Zahir al-'Umar took control of Acre in 1750 and established a local despotism based on efficient economic management. He encouraged the production of cash crops, established monopolies over production and foreign trade, and wooed European advisors. This short-lived regime ended in 1775, when the territory reverted to the governorship of Damascus. After 1780 Ahmad al-Jazzar succeeded to the control of Acre and Sidon, and also built up a personal domain based on a strong army, economic monopolies, and a lively European trade. This new type of despotism foreshadowed the nineteenth-century reform movement in Turkey and Egypt which led to a recentralization of power and to efficient government controls over the local economy.

The Lebanon posed special problems for Ottoman authority. In the north and in the Kisrawan region lived the Maronites. They had been Monothelite Christians until the period of the Crusades, when they accepted Catholic doctrine and Papal supremacy. Turkish Muslims also inhabited the north, but in the Gharb and the Shuf the population was largely Druze. Though the Lebanese peasants were affiliated with the religious communities, the local political order was not based on religion, but on allegiance to village and valley chiefs who were subordinate to feudal suzerains, in turn subordinate to the governor of Damascus and the Sultan in Istanbul. This hierarchy of authority was at best unstable. Between 1544 and 1697 the Ma'n family was the most powerful. The great ruler of this era, Fakhr al-Din (1603–35), governed by means of a Maronite and Druze peasant coalition. In 1697 the Ma'n were succeeded by the Shihabi, who ruled from 1697 to 1840.

In other parts of the fertile crescent, Ottoman power was subverted by bedouin opposition. The parts of Syria east of Hama and Homs were occupied by the Arab bedouins, who threatened agricultural settlement and the security of the pilgrimage route. Turkmen and Kurdish tribes occupied the regions north of Damascus. The northern Euphrates region was taken over by the 'Anaza confederation, and the southern reaches of the river were occupied by the Shamar.

In sum, the Arab Middle East was governed by an Ottoman elite with the cooperation of local intermediaries. In Egypt, these were Mamluk households and 'ulama'. In the fertile crescent, they were local janissaries, 'ulama', and mountain and bedouin chieftains. In the late eighteenth century, the balance of power between the central state and the provinces, and even between provincial capitals and their hinterlands, shifted in favor of the latter. Almost every local political power – Mamluk or janissary households, 'ulama', office-holders, tax-farmers, guildsmen, town quarters, bedouin tribes, and mountain communities – managed to increase its autonomy. Still the basic institutional structures of these societies and the historical system of ever-changing balances of power among state military, religious, and parochial elites continued to function.

On the horizon, however, the clouds of new forms of highly centralized states and of European commercial and political penetration were already visible. The whole structure of Muslim supremacy was being threatened by European trade and by the rising influence of Greek, Armenian, Maronite, and other Christian merchants who prospered under the protection of foreign powers while Muslim communities were in disarray. The decentralization of the late eighteenth century made it impossible to crystallize a regional political identity, or to protect the Muslims against the competition of local and foreign Christians. This political disarray would also make it extremely difficult to form stable national states in the twentieth century.

CHAPTER 16

ISLAMIC NORTH AFRICA AND SPAIN TO THE NINETEENTH CENTURY

Islamic civilizations in North Africa and Spain were initiated by the Arab conquests in the seventh and eighth centuries. The histories of these regions paralleled the Caliphal phase in Middle Eastern development, and were provincial variants of the Middle Eastern type of early Islamic civilization. In the twelfth and thirteenth centuries the Muslim states of North Africa took on an institutional configuration resembling that of the Saljuq empire in Iraq and Iran and the Mamluk empire of Egypt and Syria. In the sixteenth century, most of North Africa (with the exception of Morocco) came under Ottoman dominion. In the eighteenth and nineteenth centuries, these societies were undermined by European economic competition and brought under colonial rule.

STATE FORMATION IN THE "CALIPHAL" PHASE

The Arab conquest of both Berber peoples and Byzantine towns began with scattered raids from Egypt. Around 670, Tunisia was occupied and Arab garrisons were established in Qayrawan, Tripoli, Tunis, Tobna, and in numerous Byzantine forts or frontier ribats. From there the Arabs reached Morocco and Spain in 711. The people who manned these ribats were committed to Muslim holy war, and cultivated an ideology of piety and longing for martyrdom.

Arab-Islamic civilization in North Africa was based on the integration of Arab conquerors, Berber peoples, and Mediterranean cities. There were three zones of political and religious development – the desert margins and mountain regions, Tunisia, and Morocco. Scattered throughout North Africa small principalities were founded by Muslim chieftains with Berber support. The Berbers, known under the names of Masmuda, Sanhaja, and Zenata, were a diverse population including camel-herding nomads, pastoralists, and peasants. They shared a common culture, but they had rarely, if ever, formed states. After the Arab conquests, sedentarized Berbers at first remained Christians, but nomadic Berbers enlisted in the Arab armies, and helped

Table 13. *North Africa: outline chronology*

	Libya	Tunisia (Ifriqiya)	Algeria	Morocco	Spain
700	Arab conquests 643–				Arab conquest begins 711; the Umayyad dynasty, 756–1031
800		Aghlabids (Tunisia and eastern Algeria) (Qayrawan) 800–909	Rustamids (Tahert) 761–909	Idrisids (Fez) 789–926	
900		Fatimids 909– Zirids 972–1148	Fatimids	Fatimids 921–	First Caliph Abd al-Rahman III 912–61 Muluk al-Tawa if c. 1030–c. 1090 the party kings in Malaga, Seville, Cordova, Toledo, Valencia, Saragossa, etc.
1000	Hilali migrations 1052		Hammadids 1015–1152	Almoravids (Marrakesh) 1056–1147	Christian conquest of Toledo, 1085 Almoravid conquest, 1086–1106
1100		Almohads 1160–	Almohads 1147–	Almohads 1130–1269	Almohad conquest, 1145
1200		Hafsids (Tunisia and eastern Algeria) 1228–1574	Abd al-Wadids (Tlemsen) 1236–	Marinids 1196–1549 (take Marrakesh in 1269)	Defeat of Muslims, Las Navas de Tolosa, 1212 Christian conquest of Cordova, 1236, and Seville, 1248
1300					Nasrids of Granada 1230–1492

	Libya	Tunisia	Algeria	Morocco
1400				Portugese take Ceuta 1415; Wattasid Regency and Sultanate 1428–1549
1500	Ottoman conquests Ottomans 1551–1711	Ottomans capture Tunis 1574; Deys of Tunisia 1591–1705	Ottomans capture Algiers 1529, Tlemsen 1551	Sa dians 1511–1659
1600			Deys 1689–1830	Alawis 1631–present
1700	Qaramanlis 1711–1835	Beys 1705–1957		
1800	Ottomans 1835–1912 Sanusiya 1837–1902 (Cyrenaica)	French protectorate 1881	French occupation begins 1830	
1900	Italian conquest 1911 Independence 1951	Independence 1956	Independence 1962	French protectorate 1912–56 Independence 1956

spread Islam into Algeria, Morocco, and Spain. Others adopted Kharijism which allowed them to accept the new religion but to oppose Arab domination.

In the middle of the eighth century Berber-Khariji principalities were established at Tlemsen, Tahert, and Sijilmassa (Morocco). The Ibadi-Khariji kingdom of Tahert (761–909) was founded by 'Abd al-Rahman b. Rustam. The imam was elected by the notables and lived an ascetic life interpreting laws, rendering justice, and leading his warriors in battle. Life at Tahert was conducted in a perpetual state of religious fervor. The theocratic community enforced a high standard of social behavior by physical punishment and imprisonment.

For a time, these North African states maintained a flourishing economy. The countryside produced olives, grapes, and cereals; the towns had lively textile and ceramic industries. North African commerce with the Sudan, controlled by Qayrawan and by the Berber kingdoms, went from Qayrawan to Wargala, from Tripoli to the Fezzan, and through the Jerid to the Niger. Sijilmassa was linked to the Sudan and traded with Tahert, Tlemsen, and possibly Fez. On the Sudanic routes the principal products were slaves and gold. Trade with Europe, Egypt, and sub-Saharan Africa was crucial to this economy.

Tunisia

Tunisia was a natural center for an Arab-Islamic regime and society. Only Tunisia had the urban, agricultural, and commercial infrastructures essential for a centralized state. Arab governors of Tunis founded the Aghlabid dynasty which ruled Tunisia, Tripolitania, and eastern Algeria from 800 to 909. The Aghlabid military elites were drawn from the descendants of Arab invaders, Islamized and Arabized Berbers, and black slave soldiers. The administrative staffs comprised dependent client Arab and Persian immigrants, bilingual natives, and some Christians and Jews.

Tunisia flourished under Arab rule. Extensive irrigation works were installed to supply towns with water, irrigate royal gardens, and promote olive production. In the Qayrawan region hundreds of basins were built to store water to support horse raising. Important trade routes linked Tunisia with the Sahara, the Sudan, and the Mediterranean. A flourishing economy permitted a refined and luxurious court life and the construction of the new palace cities of al-'Abbasiya (809) and Raqqada (877).

Tunisia's prosperity, however, was undermined by political instability. The Fatimid movement which began as an offshoot of Isma'ili missionary resistance to the 'Abbasid dynasty conquered Sijilmassa, Tahert, and Qayrawan. The Fatimids went on to conquer much of the rest of North Africa and Egypt (969). Moving their capital to Cairo the Fatimids abandoned North Africa to local Zirid (972–1148) and Hammadid (1015–1152) vassals. North Africa was submerged by their quarrels. Political instability was connected to the decline of Tunisian trade and agriculture. The transfer of the Fatimid regime to Egypt favored eastern Egyptian and Spanish-patronized western routes to the Sahara. A growing agricultural and urban population made excessive demands upon reserves of water, pasturage, and forest.

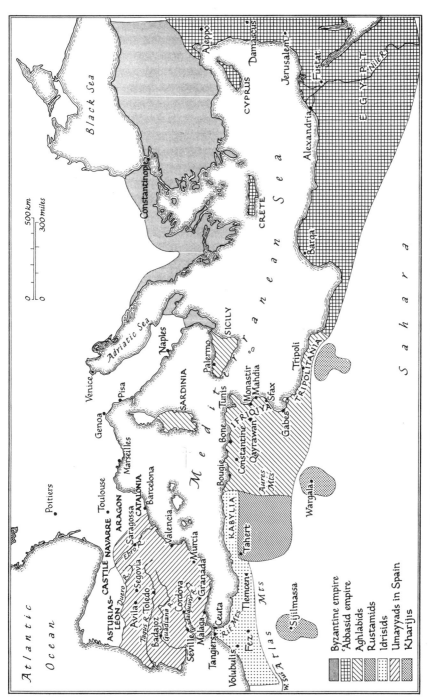

Map 14 North Africa, Spain, and the Mediterranean in the ninth century

European attacks further damaged Muslim North Africa. The Genoese and Pisans attacked Bone in 1034. The Normans conquered Sicily between 1061 and 1092, devastated Mahdiya in 1087, and between 1135 and 1153 conquered the coastal strip from Tripoli to Cape Bon.

The final blow was dealt by nomadic migrations from Arabia and Egypt in the eleventh and twelfth centuries. The Hilali bedouins defeated the Zirid and Hammadid states and sacked Qayrawan (1057). As the invaders took control of the plains, sedentary peoples were forced to take refuge in the mountains. In central and northern Tunisia, and later in Algeria and Morocco, farming gave way to pastoralism. Urban life declined as a result of the impoverishment of the countryside. Qayrawan and other cities, created by the first wave of Arab conquests, were ruined by the second. The decline of the Tunisian economy, then, was the result of a number of factors including Arab invasions, the internal weakness of local regimes, European assaults on coastal towns, and the shift of the Sahara trading economy to other routes.

The destruction, however, was not total. The coastal regions survived. Tripoli retained its palm, olive, fig, and other fruit plantations, and Tunis remained an important city for textiles, ceramics, glass, oil, soap, leather, and other urban manufactures. Moreover, some of the factors that led to decline in the east favored economic development in the Moroccan far west. The revival of western trade routes favored the exchange of salt and luxury products from the north for gold, slaves, hides, ivory, and wood from the south.

Morocco

Northern Morocco was the center of another cluster of Arab-Berber principalities, and eventually of a territorially defined Islamic state. The Idrisid regime was founded at the former Roman capital of Volubilis by a descendant of 'Ali and Fatima in 786. Idris formed a tribal coalition which quickly conquered northern Morocco. His son Idris II was the founder of Fez, built in 808. Despite its small size the Idrisid kingdom was the first Moroccan-Islamic state, and a center of active proselytization on behalf of Islam. The rest of Morocco was divided among a number of localized states including that of the Barghwata peoples, the followers of Salih b. Tarif, who declared himself a prophet, composed a "revealed book" in Berber, gave rules for fasting and prayer, and otherwise established a Berber version of Islam on the coastal plains of central Morocco. These regimes were islands of kingly rule in a sea of independent Berber peoples living in pre-state political communities.

Moroccan political unification was due to the Almoravid movement. Like the Fatimids, the Almoravids were a coalition of Berber peoples united by religious leadership and doctrine. The movement rose among Sanhaja Berbers in the western Sahara who were being pushed out of their trading livelihood by Zenata Berbers controlling the northern ends of the trans-Saharan trade routes, and by the Sudanic state of Ghana taking over the southern outlets of the trans-Saharan trade.

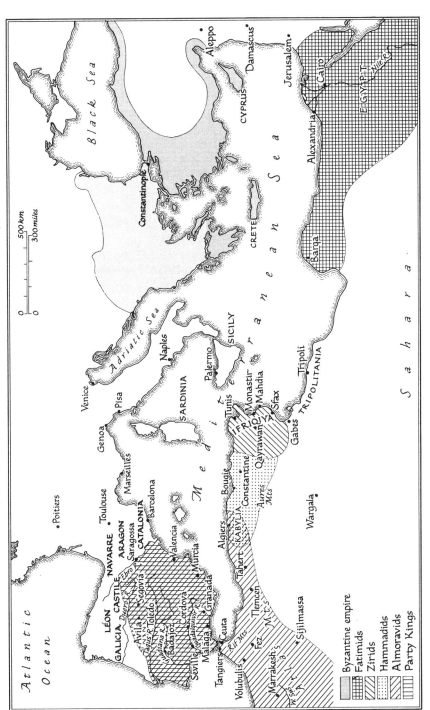

Map 15 North Africa, Spain, and the Mediterranean in the late eleventh century and the Almoravid conquests

Islam played an important role in the Sanhaja adaptation to these pressures. Returning from his pilgrimage to Mecca, a Sanhaja chieftain brought back a Moroccan student, 'Abdallah b. Yasin, who taught Quran, hadith, and law. Ibn Yasin called for repentance and warned that the last day was coming. He imposed a strict moral and religious discipline upon his followers. He closed taverns, destroyed musical instruments, abolished illegal taxes, and implemented Muslim laws for the distribution of booty. The inner jihad – the purification of body and soul – had to precede the warriors' outer jihad. The name of the movement he founded, al-Murabitun, was derived from the Quranic root *r-b-t*, referring to the technique of fighting in closed ranks, with infantry in front and camels and horsemen in the rear, rather than in the long, loose lines common to Berber battles. "Almoravid," then, refers to those who wage holy war in the Quranically prescribed fashion. In any case, 'Abdallah provided the religious cement for a Sanhaja counter-attack, under the leadership of the Lamtuna tribe, against pagan Sudanese kingdoms to the south and impious Zenata domination in the north.

The Almoravids went on to conquer Morocco, and founded Marrakesh around 1070 as their capital. Then, between 1086 and 1106, they conquered southern Spain. The Almoravids thus linked the Sahara, Morocco, and Spain into a new trading zone. Morocco, benefiting from trade and empire, became in the course of the eleventh to the thirteenth centuries a commercial and urbanized society.

The Almoravid regime was built around the Lamtuna tribal aristocracy, but the Almoravids also employed Spanish scribes, Christian mercenaries, and black slaves to form a cavalry bodyguard for the ruler, which gave him predominance over camel-riding Berber troops. The legitimacy of the regime was based on claims to religious purity. Almoravid rulers were titled *amir al-muslimin*. Scholars of Maliki law sat in executive council with the ruler and gave legal advice. The legalists condemned Muslim theology and opposed Sufism. Despite their narrow religious position the Almoravids laid the foundation for a flourishing North African civilization. They aided the final triumph of Sunni Islam and the Maliki school of law over Shi'i and Khariji rivals. North African rulers became patrons of Spanish scribes, philosophers, poets, and architects. The great mosque of Tlemsen, built in 1136, and the rebuilt Qarawiyin mosque of Fez were designed in the Andalusian manner.

By the middle of the twelfth century the Almoravid state began to unravel. In southern Morocco a new religious movement challenged its legitimacy. The Almohad movement (al-Muwahhidun) was founded by Muhammad b. 'Abdallah b. Tumart, who made the pilgrimage to Mecca and studied in Baghdad and Damascus. On his return he preached the transcendence and oneness of God, the supremacy of Quran and hadith over the law schools, and the need for moral reform. Grounding himself in the theology of al-Ash'ari, he rejected anthropomorphism and a physical interpretation of the attributes of God mentioned in the Quran. Ibn Tumart also denounced pagan Berber customs taken into Islamic practice and proscribed wine drinking, music, and the enjoyment of luxurious clothing.

He regarded himself as the heir of the Prophet, his career as a duplication of the Prophet's career, and his teaching an effort to restore the Islamic community as it had existed in the Prophet's lifetime. At Tinmal in southern Morocco he received the support of a local chieftain, Abu Hafs 'Umar, and declared himself mahdi, imam, and ma'sum, or infallible leader sent by God. Under his authority a new government was organized under a council of ten disciples, who in turn were advised by an assembly of fifty tribal delegates. Thus a religious hierarchy was superimposed upon a tribal society. After the death of Ibn Tumart, his successor, 'Abd al-Mu'min (1130–63), took the title Caliph of Ibn Tumart. The new ruler put his family in power but attached to each of its youthful members an Almohad shaykh as a teacher. He thus converted a religious oligarchy into a family-based monarchy.

'Abd al-Mu'min conquered Morocco, intervened in Spain, and invaded Algeria and Tunisia. His regime depended on a military aristocracy made up of the tribes that had originally supported the movement, backed up by slaves, Arab tribes, contingents of Turkish, Kurdish, and black soldiers as well as urban auxiliaries. An elaborate religious administration including a keeper of morals (*mizwar*), muezzins, and instructors in the Quran was also established. Among the duties of the mizwar were the destruction of musical instruments and the prohibition of alcohol. A civil bureaucracy of the Andalusian type was mobilized to support the government. Thus the Almohad regime was based on a combination of a royal household, a hierarchical religious organization, a tribal military elite with Berber and Arab tribal allies, and a Spanish-type administration.

Despite the power of the regime the Almohad doctrine was never successfully implemented. Alternative expressions of Islam, including that of the Maliki jurists, the popular cult of saints and Sufis, and the philosophy of Averroes, were always tolerated. Later rulers abandoned Almohad doctrine, and conflict within the ruling elite led in 1229 to the formal renunciation of the teachings of Ibn Tumart and a return to Maliki law. The Almohad empire, like its predecessors, soon dissolved. In 1212 the Almohads were defeated in Spain, and southern Morocco was invaded by Arab tribes of Banu Ma'qil who ruined the villages and undermined the authority of the central government. By the middle of the thirteenth century, however, Morocco had evolved from a region divided among Arab and Berber principalities into a unified state with a lasting territorial identity.

The collapse of the Almohad empire marked the conclusion of the "Caliphal" phase of state formation and Islamization in North Africa. In this era a succession of regimes – Rustamid, Idrisid, Fatimid, Almoravid, and Almohad – had used Islamic religious beliefs to legitimize new political elites and to unify Berber tribal peoples. Islam had become the basis of political solidarity among factious populations but the role of religion in the formation of these states varied. The Idrisid, Fatimid, Almoravid, and Almohad rulers all claimed an unmediated, divine authority based on their personal qualifications, and their descent in the family of the Prophet. In some respects these regimes were the ideological equivalents of the Caliphate. The

Khariji states of southern Tunisia and Algeria, however, stressed ideology rather than the person of the rulers. They were built upon an ascetic, egalitarian concept of the social order in which the imam was a representative of collective values rather than an embodiment of the divine mystery.

To build these states religious authority was joined to revenues from commerce and the support of a segmented tribal society. Yet the North African states were short lived, subject to changing patterns of trade, the rise of new tribal movements, and the breakdown of coalitions. Moreover, they did not fully control the territories under their nominal domain, but were suzerainties over independent peoples. Sometimes the states were no more than islands in a sea of autonomous and unorganized Berber populations.

'Ulama' and Sufis: the formation of Islamic religious communities

While Islamization was associated with state formation, as early as the eighth century religious elites separate from the state, and committed to Islamic values above state interests, had also come into being. Under Aghlabid patronage Qayrawan became the leading North African center of Sunni Islam and the Maliki school of law. Despite criticism that the Maliki school was rigid and literal-minded, it was not monolithic. Theological issues were hotly debated. Such topics as the creation of the Quran, free will and predestination, and the meaning of the Caliphate were debated as much in Qayrawan as in Baghdad. In the course of the tenth century Ash'arism was assimilated into the Maliki school, and was later transmitted to the Almohads. Maliki scholars were also students of grammar, philology, mathematics, astronomy, and medicine. Ibn al-Tabban (923–81) was a student of law, philology, grammar, mathematics, astronomy, medicine, and the interpretation of dreams. Al-Qabisi (935–1012) was a theologian who stressed hadith and mysticism, and an intensely pious religious practice. These men exemplified divergent orientations within the Maliki school parallel to those in the eastern Shafi'i school.

The schools of law were the vehicles for the mobilization of public opinion in the struggles among political regimes. In Qayrawan the Hanafis, representing an upper-class milieu, were favored by the Aghlabids and later collaborated with the Fatimids. The Malikis, by contrast, eschewed appointments to office and won popular support. Under Fatimid rule, the Malikis denounced Shi'ism, provoked anti-Shi'i riots and massacres in Qayrawan, and in 1049 forced the Zirids to accept Sunni allegiance and to recognize the 'Abbasid Caliphs. While Qayrawan and Tunis were the main centers of Maliki teaching, the Maliki position was also strongly supported in the coastal ribats, and spread to southern Morocco and West Africa.

Along with the Maliki school of law, Sufi asceticism – stressing sadness, silence, suffering, fear of God, attention to the coming of the last judgment, and the virtues of humility and charity – was cultivated in Qayrawan. The ribats combined holy war with pious devotions. The common people believed in saints who had the power to heal, bring rain, perform miracles, communicate with spiritual forces, interpret dreams, and otherwise act as intermediaries between men and God. Sufism in North

Africa, as in the Middle East, was not so much an organized religious movement as a religious sensibility.

In the eleventh and twelfth centuries, a new form of Sufism, based on both Spanish and eastern teachings, was introduced to North Africa, and spread in reaction to the Almoravid and Almohad conquests. Abu Madyan al-Andalusi (d. 1197) brought the Spanish form of Sufism which integrated ascetic mysticism with the study of law. His tomb became a venerated place of pilgrimage and his successors continued the tradition of combining the study of hadith and law with mystical practices. Sufi scholars were established in Tunisia at Tunis, Bone, and Qayrawan, and were represented in Morocco at Aghmat, Marrakesh, and other places. The Maliki school, the early ribats, Khariji teachers, and Sufis helped to diffuse Islam from its Tunisian base into southern Morocco. Traders and scholars also brought it to the Saharan region.

Unfortunately, our knowledge of this early period is too scattered to give an assured account of the rhythm of the diffusion of Islam. Libya appears to have been relatively quickly converted in the wake of the early conquests. Large numbers of Berbers accepted Khariji Islam, but Qayrawan, Tunis, Tripoli, Sfax, Mahdiya, Bougie, Bone, and other cities still had Christian communities in the eleventh and twelfth centuries. Nonetheless, the 200 bishoprics known in the seventh century had been reduced to 5 by 1053 and to 3 by 1076. The Almohads effectively put an end to Christianity in North Africa; Christians survived only in isolated villages. Jews were drastically reduced in number, and the cultural vitality of the Jewish communities was destroyed.

Thus, by the middle of the thirteenth century, the Arab invasions and the introduction of Islam had inspired a centuries-long wave of state construction culminating in the integration of Tunisia and Morocco into territorial states. At the same time Islam had been established as the dominant religion. Informal schools of legal instruction, theology, and mysticism emerged and Islamic religious teachers acquired a large popular following. Religious leadership and communal ties were differentiated from state institutions. As a result of state formation, the defeat of the great tribal and religious movements that sought to unify North Africa, and the formation of an autonomous Islamic religious elite, the way was prepared for a new historic phase of the relationships between state and Islam in North African societies.

SPANISH-ISLAMIC CIVILIZATION

Muslim Spain from the Arab conquest to the liquidation of the last Muslim possessions in Granada in 1492 represents yet another variant of the Caliphal type of early Islamic civilization. This civilization was built upon the assimilation of the Spanish and Berber populations to Arabic and Islamic culture, and was fostered by extraordinary economic prosperity. Muslim Spain bears an aura of glory. The great mosque of Cordova, the gardens, fountains, and courtyards of the Alhambra, the *muwashshahat* and *zajal* poetry with their Arabic verses and romance language refrains, the irrigated gardens of Seville and Valencia, the wisdom of philosophy and science – these are the monuments of Spanish Islam. Spain was the focal point for the transmission of Greek philosophy from the Arab world to Europe. No less important was the drama of the defeat of this brilliant Muslim civilization by its European enemies, the expulsion of the Arabs, and the reabsorption of Spain into Christian Europe.

For all its brilliance Muslim Spain was a province of the Arab Caliphate. Already overrun by successive waves of Alaric and Vandal invasions from the north, Spain was conquered by Arab and Berber forces from North Africa led by Tariq, who defeated the Visigothic King Roderic at the River Barbate in 711. The Arab advance into France was checked finally by Charles Martel at the battle of Poitiers in 732. Whereas in the East, Arab conquerors were generally forced to settle in garrison towns and villages, leaving the land in the direct control of its pre-conquest landlord elite and a tax-collecting bureaucracy, in Spain large territories were parceled out among Arab and Berber clans. This immediately led to factional quarrels. In the very first decades of Muslim rule, Berbers, allocated poor mountain lands in Galicia and Cantabria, rebelled against Arab governors. The rebellions were put down by Syrian Arabs and the new forces were in turn given fiefs. The Arabs themselves were divided into tribal factions called Qays and Yemen, representing the first-generation settlers and later immigrants.

Dispersed settlement, however, contributed enormously to the Arabization and Islamization of Spain. The Arabs took on clients, captured slaves, hired mercenaries, and married into local families. By the ninth century Arabic was widely used by the indigenous population and there were many converts (*muwalladun*). As converts multiplied, the distinction between the original Arab elite and assimilated Arabs blurred, and a more homogeneous Hispano-Arab society came into being.

This development was abetted by extraordinary economic prosperity in the ninth and tenth centuries. The introduction of irrigation agriculture based on eastern models led to the cultivation of valuable new crops including cherries, apples, pears, almonds, pomegranates, figs, dates, sugarcane, bananas, cotton, flax, and silk. A Damascus type of irrigation assigned water to each cultivator in proportion to the size of his land. A Yemeni type of irrigation, used in the oasis-like *huertas* of Valencia, distributed water by a fixed time flow. Irrigation was administered either by a town authority under the control of the *sahib al-saqiya*, who policed the distribution of water and assured equity, or by local communities, who selected their own irrigation managers. At the same time, Spain entered a phase of commercial prosperity due to the breakdown of Byzantine naval control over the western Mediterranean. Cities such as Seville and Cordova prospered on the bases of rich agricultural production and international trade.

The Caliphal era

The result of these social and economic changes was political consolidation. After a succession of weak governors appointed from North Africa, three great rulers built up the Spanish-Muslim state. 'Abd al-Rahman I (756–88), a grandson of the Umayyad Caliph Hisham, supported by Berbers from North Africa and by Syrian clients of the Umayyads, founded the Umayyad dynasty in Spain. The new regime followed the 'Abbasid pattern. It suppressed local revolts, and built up a client army of soldiers coming from north of the Pyrenees. 'Abd al-Rahman II (822–52) further centralized administration, brought into being a new secretarial class made up of merchants and clients, and created state monopolies and control of urban markets. 'Abd al-Rahman III (912–61) completed the consolidation of the central government. He built his army up from captives from northern Spain, Germany, and the Slavic countries. These troops, known as *saqaliba*, were later reinforced with detribalized professional Berber soldiers and local levies. A *hajib*, equal in rank to a vizier, was in charge of administration and taxation. Provincial tax collectors were appointed to raise revenues and send the surplus to Cordova. While twenty-one provinces were governed by appointees of the central government, frontier districts were managed by local *qa'ids* and hereditary petty lords. A chief qadi supervised judicial administration and managed the properties endowed for religious and charitable purposes.

'Abd al-Rahman III also sought a new basis for the legitimization of his regime by adopting Baghdadi 'Abbasid cultural forms. While Islamic culture in Spain assimilated some aspects of local culture, it was primarily an outpost of Middle Eastern Arabic-Islamic civilization. As in the East, court culture tried to integrate Muslim and cosmopolitan symbols. 'Abd al-Rahman adopted the title Caliph, or *amir al-mu'minin*, in reaction to the claims of the Fatimids in North Africa. Thus the precious title signifying the unity of the Muslim community was claimed by no fewer than three rulers in the early tenth century. 'Abd al-Rahman expanded the Cordova mosque, installed irrigation works, and waged jihad to check Christian attacks in northern Spain.

Poetry became the primary expression of Spanish cosmopolitan culture. Spanish poetry was originally based on Arabic models, which carried with them the warrior sentiments and factional interests of the Arab conquerors. The urbane Baghdadi style was introduced by bringing the poet and singer Ziryab (789–857) to Cordova. In early Hispano-Arabic poetry, the qasida, which praised the virtues of the ruler and served official purposes, was the dominant form. New Spanish forms, however, came into being. The new poems had Arabic strophes, and sometimes an additional *kharja*, or refrain, in Romance dialect, and were a synthesis of Arabic and Romance verse forms. The Arabic part, usually a love poem, was courtly in theme, masculine in tone; the kharja was usually the voice of the lower classes, or of a Christian slave girl, and feminine in inspiration. While the poems were composed in Arabic, the metrical system, the syllabic prosody, and the rhyme scheme all indicate a Romance influence.

Other literary activities flourished under Caliphal patronage. Eastern scholars emigrated to Spain, and the royal libraries were enlarged. Grammar and philology came from Iraq. Adab, or belles-lettres in eastern style, was first composed in Spain by Ibn 'Abd al-Rabbih (d. 940). Caliphal patronage broadened scientific learning. Aristotle's philosophy was introduced by the reception of the *Organon*; the *Republic*, the *Laws*, and the *Timaeus* of Plato were known. Galen became the standard medical author. A new translation of a classic work – Dioscorides' *Materia Medica* – was made in Spain. The earliest translations of astronomical and geometric works from Arabic into Latin were also made in the tenth century.

The architecture of the Caliphate, including mosques, palaces, and baths, was also eastern in inspiration. The mosque of Cordova was expanded and rebuilt by successive rulers. It was a vast hall divided by columns surmounted by horseshoe arches; a niche with a fluted shell-like vault and a horseshoe arch indicated the direction of prayer. Visigothic and Roman elements were built into the Muslim design. The mosque was redecorated between 961 and 966 by mosaic workers, who gave it a vivid and brilliant interior. The mosque of Cordova, like the mosque of Damascus, was a symbol of the incorporation of ancient values and their supersession by Islamic civilization. In the tenth century the Caliphs also built the royal city of Madinat al-Zahra, a city of splendid palaces, fountains, and gardens which imitated the palace complexes of Baghdad.

Under the auspices of the Umayyad regime, a Muslim as well as an Arab civilization came into being. The Syrian school of law, founded by al-Awza'i, favored by Syrian-Arab military lords, was imported into Spain, but the town populations favored the Maliki school from North Africa. From the East came Shafi'i's concepts. Hadith studies were introduced in the ninth century, and Muslim scholars were divided between the *shuyukh al-'ilm*, or students who favored hadith and theology, and the *shuyukh al-fiqh*, or scholars of law. This distinction may, as in Nishapur, have represented the division between Arab elites and later converts. Shafi'i scholars, however, had to accept Maliki law, and Malikism remained the primary religious identity of Muslim Spain. Muslim theology and Mu'tazilism were also introduced from Baghdad in the ninth century. Muhammad b. Masarra (883–931), whose father had studied in Basra, amalgamated neo-Platonic, Shi'i, and Sufi thought. The legal scholars, however, restricted the public expression of mystical tendencies.

Arabic-Islamic culture in Spain was associated with different social milieus and sociopolitical movements. Monumental architecture, formal poetry, and philosophic interests characterized the royal style of culture in Spain as in Baghdad. The scribal class was identified with Arabic belles-lettres. As in the East, the secretarial class, composed of Spanish converts, generated an Arabic literature which was intended to prove their equality with the Arab warrior elites. The *Risala* of Abu 'Amir b. Garcia provoked an avalanche of contemptuous Arabic poetry in response.

Important lower-class social movements were also connected with religious trends. In circumstances that still remain obscure, the 'ulama' of the Rabad quarter of Cordova led local rebellions in 805 and 818. They denounced the regime for corruption, fiscal exploitation, use of foreign military forces, and chronic insecurity.

Though the revolts were put down, the power of the religious leaders rose. 'Abd al-Rahman II created a religious council to demonstrate that he ruled in accordance with Islam. Thus the Umayyad princes sought to legitimize their rule by coopting the scholars of law. As in North Africa, Baghdad, and other parts of the Muslim world, the 'ulama' assumed political responsibilities and a voice in the direction of society. Sufis led a lower-class movement opposed to the exploitative accumulation of wealth by the upper classes, and espoused an ascetic, mystical, and communalist doctrine.

Arab-Muslim rule also had profound effects on the Christians. Christians under Muslim rule rapidly adopted the Arabic language, Arab customs and manners, and assumed the style of life led by the political elites. Thus the *mozarab* identity came into being. This assimilation of Christians was opposed by a priest named Eulogius, who called for a more purely Christian culture stripped of Arab influences. Between 850 and 859 he led a revolt of the mozarabs of Cordova in which Christians martyred themselves to protest against Arab-Muslim rule.

Like its 'Abbasid model, the Spanish-Muslim state was subverted by internal conflicts. The hostilities between provincial and urban mercantile elites, between townsmen and Berber troops, and converts and Arabs made it impossible to stabilize the regime. In the early eleventh century, the Caliphs lost control of the central government, provincial governors became independent, and Arab clans revolted. As in the history of the eastern Caliphate, a central imperial government was replaced by smaller provincial regimes. The Caliphate was abolished and Spain was divided into petty warring principalities, called the *muluk al-tawa'if*, or the party kings (1030–90). Arab, Slav, and Berber soldiers and local elites took power, and each province became an independent state with an army, court, and administration of its own. The Amirids – descendants of former Caliphal administrators – ruled the eastern coast of Andalus. The saqaliba settled Denia in the southeast. Regimes based on local Arab families were founded at Cordova, Seville, and Saragossa; Berber-dominated states were founded at Toledo, Badajoz, and Granada. In Granada the Berber ruling elite governed with the help of the Jewish Banu Naghrila family. This provoked intense Muslim hostility and a pogrom against Jews in 1066.

While the emergence of provincial regimes was a defeat for centralized government, Spanish society was not as fragmented as the political division of power would imply. Muslim law and a Muslim-Arab identity were universally accepted, and the 'ulama' continued to represent the urban populations. Spanish-Muslim society was also integrated by a flourishing regional and international commerce. Andalusia traded with Morocco, importing wood, alum, antimony, and cloth, and exporting cloth and copper. It traded with Tunisia and through Tunisia with Egypt, importing the wool, flax, and dyes that came to Egypt from Iran, Arabia, India, and China. Spanish Muslims also traded with the Christian north, where growing wealth and the rising power of new states created ever larger markets.

The Reconquista

Despite its great prosperity and cultivated urban life, the extreme degree of political fragmentation undermined Spanish-Islamic civilization. The initial Muslim advance had left a small belt of northern territories along the Pyrenees in Christian hands. In the course of the eighth and ninth centuries small kingdoms in this region began to reconquer and recolonize the Muslim areas of Spain. Christian sentiment was also expressed in the founding of Benedictine monasteries and the pilgrimage of Santiago de Compostela. Pope Gregory VII made the reconquest a religious duty of Christians as well as a territorial ambition of Spanish kings.

The disintegration of the Muslim states in the eleventh century allowed for the rapid expansion of the various Christian kingdoms. In 1085 Alfonso VI, on the strength of the unified kingdoms of Castile, Leon, and Galicia, conquered Toledo. This was a signal event in the struggle between Muslims and Christians, for a brilliant center of Muslim civilization, once the capital of Visigothic Spain, again fell into Christian hands. Christian migrants flocked to Toledo, but the Muslim and mozarab populations were allowed to remain. In the meantime the kingdom of Aragon captured Huesca (1096), Saragossa (1118), Tortosa (1148), and Lerida (1149). In the second half of the twelfth century the reconquest became institutionalized. Religious-military fraternities, such as the orders of Calatrava and Santiago, financed by landed estates, conquered and colonized Muslim territories.

The Christian advance was countered by the Muslims. In 1082 a delegation of 'ulama' urged the Almoravids to intervene on behalf of the Spanish-Muslim community. Thus in 1086 a Moroccan army crossed the straits and defeated Alfonso VI, and from 1090 to 1145 the North Africans conquered the Spanish-Muslim cities and governed Spain as a province of Marrakesh. Military commanders governed the cities in collaboration with the 'ulama'. Almoravid rule, however, increasingly incurred the hostility of the local population. There were Sufi-led revolts in Silves and Niebla, and 'ulama'-led revolts in Cordova and Valencia, which eventually overthrew Almoravid rule. The Almohads, who took Marrakesh in 1147, unhesitatingly accepted the concept of a Moroccan empire which included Spain. In turn, they took Seville and Cordova in 1149, and the rest of Muslim Spain by 1172.

A new Moroccan suzerainty was imposed upon Spain, but the Muslim position nonetheless continued to weaken under the combination of Christian pressures and regional anarchy. The Almohads were defeated in 1212 by the combined Christian forces of Leon, Castile, Navarre, and Aragon at the battle of Las Navas de Tolosa. With the defeat of the Almohads the Spanish-Muslim states again found themselves independent but helpless before the resumption of the Christian reconquest. The union of Castile and Leon in 1230 opened the way for the conquest of Cordova in 1236 and Seville in 1248. The Aragonese advanced along the coast to take Valencia in 1238 and Murcia in 1243. By 1249–50 the Portuguese had taken all of the lands west of the Guadiana River. By the middle of the thirteenth century only Granada remained in Muslim hands. It was protected by a large populace, a mountainous territory, and a productive economy which paid heavy tribute to the princes of Castile. Aragon had turned its interests to the Mediterranean, Castile was embroiled in civil wars, and the military orders were disbanded. Christian rulers gave no priority to the conquest of Granada until the union of Castile and Aragon opened the way for the final conquest of the last Muslim possession in Spain in 1492.

Hispano-Arabic civilization

The disintegration of the Caliphate and the centuries of struggles with the Christians did not disrupt Spanish-Muslim cultural life. With the decline of the Caliphate the patronage of art and culture shifted to the courts of the provincial rulers and merchants. In place of grand mosques, private palaces became the characteristic symbols of Hispano-Arabic civilization. In the late tenth century the muwashshahat poetry flourished, as city dwellers rediscovered the beauties of nature. Freed from religious restraints, qasidas devoted to descriptions of nature and gardens, wine and war, and love and passion were composed. Ibn Quzman (d. 1160) cultivated the zajal, a form of poetry in colloquial Arabic, whose themes were the life of towns and markets, the common people, and the underworld. This was a deliberately irreligious form of art. After a long period in which the Baghdadi style had dominated Arabic-Spanish literature, poetic interests were transferred from the political to the personal. Love and art for art's sake became the dominant themes.

Love was the central theme of the philosophy of Ibn Hazm (d. 1093). He taught that the attraction of two people was based on an eternal affinity, a timeless connection of souls. Ibn al-'Arabi later explained that a man loves a woman because she is the mirror that reveals his innermost true being – the spiritual being that transcends his animal reality. The love of a woman is the love of the original nature of the soul and therefore a reminder of God. Love stems from the creation of man in the image of God, and sexual love is a symbol of the extinction of the separate natures in the divine reality.

With the breakdown of Spanish-Islamic society, Sufism also became important. From Almeria came Abu al-'Abbas b. al-'Arif (1088–1141), whose writings described the stages of mystical ascent to the realization that only God exists. Ibn al-'Arabi, also from Spain, was probably the greatest Muslim mystical metaphysician.

Almohad rule also introduced theological and philosophic debates. While the Almoravids had favored strictly legal views, the Almohads were the patrons of Ibn Rushd (Averroes, 1126–98). Averroes took up the classic debate of theology and philosophy concerning human knowledge of spiritual realities. Al-Ghazzali taught that direct apprehension was the basis for the knowledge of the divine being, and that the Quran was a direct expression of God's being. Averroes held that reason was the basis of human knowledge of the divine being, and that the Quran was an allegory requiring rational interpretation.

From Spain, Islamic scientific and philosophical thought was transmitted to Europe. With the conquest of Toledo in 1085 and Saragossa in 1118, Hispano-Islamic culture had a strong and immediate influence upon Christian style. Nobles and churchmen built their houses in the Moorish manner and borrowed Hispanic-Islamic motifs for their heraldry. They dressed in Arab fabrics, and had Jewish and Muslim literatures translated into Castilian and Latin. Alfonso X arranged for the translation of the Bible, the Talmud, and the Quran into Castilian. The story of the mi'raj, the ascent of the Prophet into heaven, was translated into Castilian and then into old French and Latin, where it may have become available to Dante. In Toledo, Petrus Alphonsi, a Jewish convert to Christianity, and other translators under the patronage of Archbishop Don Raimundo, rendered Arabic works on astrology and astronomy into Castilian and then into Latin. The works of Ptolemy were translated. The Muslim philosophers al-Kindi, al-Farabi, and Avicenna were also translated into Latin, making the thought of Aristotle available to Europeans. Between 1160 and 1187 Gerard of Cremona translated into Latin some eighty-seven works, including the Quran, many books of Aristotle, and the *Qanun* of Avicenna. Between 1220 and 1250 Averroes's commentaries on Aristotle and the works of Maimonides were rendered into Latin, and were quoted by St. Thomas Aquinas. Thus Greek philosophic thought came through the Arab world to Europe.

Not even the Reconquista could extinguish the cultural vitality of Muslim Spain. Granada, the surviving Muslim enclave, maintained a sophisticated style of life. The city was adorned with patios, fountains, and pavements; Granada copied Eastern styles in bronzes, ivories, ceramics, and furniture. In order to meet its huge burden of tribute, Granada developed an export trade in ceramics, porcelains, silks, and weapons.

The Alhambra was one of the great achievements of Islamic urban art. It was first constructed as a fortress and royal residence in the eleventh century. By the thirteenth century it had been enlarged into a princely city. Like Baghdad and Cairo, it was a symbol of the power and aloofness of royalty. The Nasrid dynasty of Granada (1230–1492) built the famous Court of the Myrtles, the Court of the Lions, and innumerable gardens and pavilions. The palace complex was decorated with Islamic symbols and water motifs. It was embellished with Quranic inscriptions, and provided with a large mosque, an open prayer field, and a "Gate of the Law." Pools and fountains symbolized refuge, repose, and paradise. Inscriptions bore allusions to the legend of the glass floor built by King Solomon to resemble a pool of water – the Solomonic story linked Granada with the royal art of the ancient Near East and its later Islamic versions. It was a last echo of the courtly cosmopolitan civilization of the Arab East in the Mediterranean far West.

The Christian reconquest did not extinguish the Muslim presence. In the eleventh and twelfth centuries Muslim populations were found under Christian rule in Toledo and Saragossa. In the thirteenth century Muslims under Christian domination survived in Valencia. Apart from the small crusading principalities in Palestine, Lebanon, and Sicily, this was the first experience of Muslims under non-Muslim rule. James I of Aragon, who took Valencia in 1238, attempted to secure Christian hegemony by

15 Patio de los Leones, Alhambra (Granada, Spain)

bringing in new settlers, establishing religious orders, giving lands to Christian land-lords, and organizing a tax-collecting administration. Otherwise the Christians did not interfere with the Muslim population. Muslims kept their residences; merchants and artisans continued to flourish, and indeed took the lead in the overseas trade of Valencia. Small farmers, property owners, and tenants kept their tenures.

There was also substantial continuity in the social and political organization of the Muslim population. The kings of Aragon at first maintained the authority of the Muslim elites by treating them as vassals of the crown. They required oaths of loyalty and military service. The old rural social structure, consisting of small vil-lage or castle-scale communities governed by a qa'id, was maintained. In the cities, Muslims retained control of civil courts and of internal community matters. The qadi was the chief Muslim official, the *amin* the main administrator and tax collector, and the *sahib al-madina* was in charge of the police. The organized Muslim com-munities could thus both cooperate with and ward off state interference. Organized as a self-regulating religious community, the Muslims became – as the Christians had been – a protected population.

The terms of Muslim survival, however, would not always remain favorable. While the monarchy took a beneficent attitude, Christian nobles and churchmen sought to exploit their new subjects. Christian settlement and competition for trade and land led to rioting between Christians and Muslims. In 1276 Christians attacked the Muslim quarters in Valencia and other towns, and Muslims rebelled. In retalia-tion, Muslim property was seized, Muslim quarters were looted, and many people were sold into slavery.

By the middle of the fourteenth century the Muslim position had sharply deteri-orated: the Muslims acquired additional financial obligations; Muslim communities lost their internal autonomy; free Muslim peasants were pushed into servitude. Political control also led to a progressive restriction of Muslim religious liberties. In 1311 King James II prohibited the public call to prayer, though in 1357, in return for payment, it was permitted in a low voice. By the middle of the fourteenth cen-tury some 80 percent of judicial cases were heard in Christian rather than Muslim courts and were tried under Christian rather than Muslim law. The once organized and autonomous Muslim community had been subordinated to direct Christian rule.

Despite this deteriorating environment, the Valencian Muslims maintained their identity. While Aragonese Muslims who had been conquered centuries earlier lost their knowledge of Arabic and were fully assimilated to Christian rule, Valencian Muslims continued to speak Arabic, refused to learn the local Romance dialect, and did not interact with the Christian population. Valencia's Muslims continued to iden-tify with Granada and North Africa.

However, by the late fourteenth century Christians became actively interested in the conversion of the Jews and Muslims and the creation of religious uniformity in Spain. In 1391 Jews were forced to accept baptism. In 1478 the inquisition was inau-gurated, and offered Jews a choice of baptism or exile. In 1492 virtually the entire

Jewish population, once a flourishing commercial and cultural community, was expelled from Spain to other parts of Europe and the Ottoman empire. The Christian conquest of Granada in 1492 marked the beginning of the end of the Muslim population in Spain. While the treaty of surrender guaranteed Muslim religious liberty and property, in practice these rights were ignored. In 1501 Spanish law offered Muslims a choice between conversion and exile. Many Granadans became crypto-Muslims who tried to reconcile the secret practice of Islam with the outward profession of Christianity. In 1556 Arab and Muslim dress was forbidden, and in 1566 Philip II decreed that the Arabic language could no longer be used. Thus there emerged the *aljamiado* literature composed in Romance language but written in Arabic script and translating Arabic texts. Finally, in 1609 Philip III expelled the Muslims from Spain. They took refuge in North Africa where Andalusian communities once again contributed to a flourishing Islamic civilization.

Thus the first major Muslim experience of Christian rule showed how in the multi-ethnic and multi-religious societies of the Mediterranean, Middle Eastern and Muslim concepts of autonomous religious community could serve for a time to accommodate Muslims in a Christian society just as they had accommodated Christians in a Muslim society. In the long run, however, the Christian demand for religious homogeneity led to the forced assimilation or expulsion of the Jewish and Muslim populations.

THE TRIPARTITE REGIME: TUNISIA, ALGERIA, AND MOROCCO FROM THE THIRTEENTH TO THE NINETEENTH CENTURIES

While the Muslim presence in Spain was being liquidated, Islamic societies in North Africa were entering a new stage of development. With the collapse of the Almohads, North Africa began to take on a new configuration of state and society. While older claims to a "Caliphal" type of religious authority were carried into the new era, North African states increasingly moved toward the Saljuq (and Egyptian Ayyubid–Mamluk) type of Middle Eastern Islamic institutional structure. The states would be based upon client, slave, or mercenary armies and a small household bureaucracy, but would depend on a governing coalition of tribal forces. Inspired by developments in the eastern Muslim world and in Spain, Sufism took root throughout North Africa in the twelfth and later centuries. Sufi-led communities became an important form of social organization for rural populations. The states of the post-Almohad era would have to develop a new relationship with the religious notables. Some of them would surrender their claims to direct religious authority; all would accept the 'ulama' and Sufis as the bearers of Islamic legitimacy and as intermediaries in the government of their societies. In different forms they implemented the Eastern patronage concept of a Muslim state.

The power of these states vis-à-vis internal tribal and other political powers depended upon the trade routes that linked North Africa, the Sahara, the Sudan,

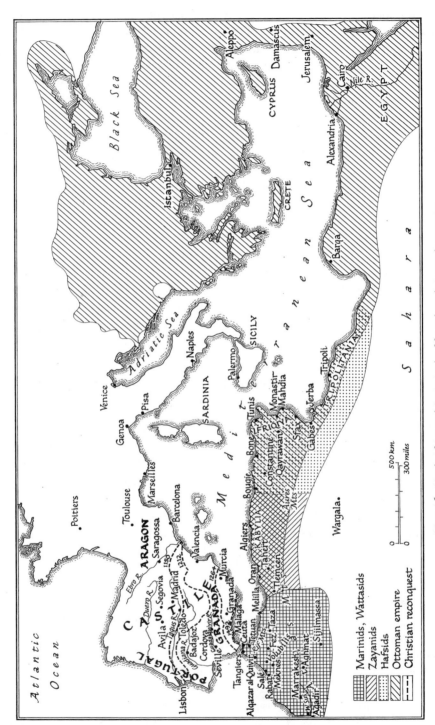

Map 16 North Africa and Spain in the fifteenth and sixteenth centuries

and Europe. All of them depended on revenues from European trade and sometimes on direct European military support. However, from the end of the fourteenth century, under pressure of tribal resistance and of Catalan, Portuguese, and Spanish expansion, centralized regimes broke down. The breakdown of these regimes shifted the balance of power in North Africa to Sufi-led tribal communities which united rural peoples to meet the needs of political order, defense, economic organization, mediation of disputes, and other essential functions. The growing importance of Muslim religious communities throughout North Africa linked the region to the wider Arab and Middle Eastern Islamic world.

The North African crisis also allowed for Ottoman intervention and opened a century-long struggle between the Ottoman and Habsburg empires for control of North Africa and the Mediterranean, a struggle that culminated in the imposition of Ottoman suzerainty on Libya, Tunisia, and Algeria, but confirmed the independence of Morocco. Ottoman suzerainty consolidated North African politico-religious institutions as variations upon Middle Eastern Islamic themes.

Tunisia

Tunisian society from the thirteenth to the nineteenth centuries was essentially a reconstruction of a past form of centralized state based on an urbanized economy and relatively close political control over rural and pastoral populations. The regime of the eighth and ninth centuries had lapsed under the pressure of the Hilali invasions and economic decline, but was rebuilt with significant innovations by the Hafsid dynasty (1228–1574). Despite repeated phases of consolidation and disintegration, the Hafsids defined the institutional complex of Tunisian society until the modern era.

In terms of political institutions the Hafsid regime grew directly out of the Almohad empire. The dynasty descended from an aristocratic Almohad family, and was built around the former Almohad elites. The Hafsid armies included Almohad tribes, Arab nomads, Berbers from the Constantine and Bougie regions, Turks and Kurds, black slaves, and a Christian militia whom the rulers of Aragon considered under their suzerain control. In the fifteenth century, the descendants of earlier generations of mercenaries continued to form a bodyguard for the rulers, though they had in the meantime become Arabized. The Hafsids also maintained a weak navy supplemented by privateers.

The civil administration was dominated by Andalusian scribes who provided the viziers of the army, finance, and chancery services. They were the principal officers for court affairs, governors of the royal palace, secretaries, chamberlains, and treasurers. The elites were supported by the distribution of iqta's to government officials, Almohad shaykhs, and tribal chiefs. The Hafsids tried to control nomadic tribes by influencing the choice of the chiefs, by putting them under military pressure, by winning favor through fiscal or territorial concessions, or by integrating tribal factions into the royal armies, but southern tribes were likely to be independent.

The relative strength of the state was related to the revenues of international trade. A series of thirteenth-century treaties with Sicily, Venice, Marseille, Genoa, and Florence helped revive Tunisian prosperity. At the end of the fourteenth century Tunis was exporting cereals, dried fruits, dates, olive oil, fish, salt, spices, sugar, wool, leather, cotton goods, coral, weapons, and slaves, and it was importing cereals, spices, wine, cloth goods, dyes, wood, metal, weapons, and jewelry. At the end of the fifteenth century the Portuguese discovery of a route to India and the aggressive expansion of Portugal and Spain along the coasts of North Africa undermined Tunisian trade.

Out of the broad possibilities afforded by the repertoire of Muslim, cosmopolitan, and patrimonial concepts of rule, the Hafsids chose to portray themselves as Muslim rulers. They took the titles of Caliph and amir al-mu'minin; the head of state was later called *malik al-sultan* in imitation of Mamluk Egyptian rulers. Succession was legitimized by the oath of allegiance and the recognition of the ruler in the Friday prayer. Solemn public processions accompanied by flags and drums were also prerogatives of the sovereign.

The rulers conducted state business in a formal court attended by tribal chiefs, soldiers, men of religion, intellectuals, and other courtiers. Mornings were reserved for military business; afternoons for civil administration; evenings for entertainment. The households of the rulers were not only centers of political administration but also of religious worship, with mosques and academies of learning. Scholars from all over North Africa and Spain gathered to instruct the rulers, minister to religious needs, and symbolize the religious credentials of the Sultans. The Hafsid court produced studies of the Quran, hadith, law, Arabic grammar, biographies of the Prophet and of saints, dictionaries of famous scholars, histories, and works of theology. The architectural style of the Hafsid period was derived from Morocco and Egypt. However, science and medicine languished.

Like the Mamluks in Egypt, the Hafsids sponsored Muslim law and a Maliki restoration. They maintained an Islamic religious administration under the authority of the *qadi al-jama'a*, a title which goes back to Umayyad Spain. Tunis had a second qadi who specialized in marriage law. A weekly council of qadis and muftis met to review important cases in the presence of the rulers. In 1257 the Hafsids endowed the al-Mustansiriya madrasa. The feast of the end of Ramadan and the feast of the conclusion of the pilgrimage were celebrated by massive public prayers led by the sovereign. The birthday of the Prophet, marked first in Egypt in the thirteenth century, and declared an official festival in Morocco in 1292, was accepted as an official feast in Tunisia at the end of the fourteenth century. The Sultans also sponsored the daily reading of hadith and of the biography of the Prophet in the great mosque of Tunis.

Gradually, however, Sufism began to displace law as the most important expression of Tunisian Islam. Between the eleventh and the thirteenth centuries, Sufism spread from the towns into rural areas. Al-Shadhili, who was born in Morocco, educated in Egypt, and died in Tunis in 1258, left numerous disciples who combined formal scholarship with mystical exercises. As friends of God, they were believed to perform miracles, know what would happen at a distance, see or dream the future, transport themselves magically over time and space, cure the sick, and intercede before God on behalf of ordinary believers. They gathered groups of disciples, sworn to absolute obedience, to whom they taught the special techniques that had given them their mystical powers, and whom they initiated by transmitting the khirqa, or cloak of the Sufi. The more puritanical Sufis deplored the common practices of visits to tombs and the use of music to achieve ecstasy.

From the late thirteenth century Sufi *zawiya*s (hospices) began to assume social and political functions. Sufis organized tribal coalitions to safeguard the trade routes, suppress brigandage, promote religious piety, and oppose illegal taxation. In the course of the fourteenth century Sufism was sufficiently consolidated for the political authorities to seek the favor of the Sufis. Territorial or fiscal concessions were given to the zawiyas. In Tunis a combination zawiya–madrasa, founded in 1399, marked the integration of urban Sufism and Maliki Islam. The breakup of the Hafsid state in the fourteenth century, its subsequent reconstruction in the fifteenth, and final decline in the sixteenth century allowed organized Sufi Islam to become the most powerful force in Tunisian society.

The Tunisian state was rebuilt by the imposition of Ottoman rule in the late sixteenth century. The Ottomans made Tunisia a province of their empire in 1574, and garrisoned Tunis with 4,000 janissaries recruited in Anatolia, reinforced by renegade Christians from Italy, Spain, and Provence. In 1591 the local janissary officers replaced the Sultan's appointee with one of their own men, called the Dey. While the Dey dominated Tunis, a Corsican-born Tunisian tax collector (Bey) named Murad (d. 1640), and his descendants, dominated the rest of the country. The struggle for power made allies of the Dey, the janissaries, and bedouin tribes against the Beys, the towns, and the fertile regions of the countryside. The Muradid Beys eventually triumphed, and ruled until 1705, when Husayn b. 'Ali came to power and established a dynasty which would reign until 1957. In theory Tunisia continued to be a vassal of the Ottoman empire – the Friday prayer was pronounced in the name of the Ottoman Sultan, money was coined in his honor, and an annual ambassador brought gifts to Istanbul – but the Ottomans never again exacted obedience.

Under Ottoman suzerainty Tunisia resumed the system of political control over the religious elites developed under the Hafsids. Under the Husaynids both Hanafi and Maliki qadis were appointed to high offices. The leading qadis and muftis participated in the Bey's council. The Bey could appoint and dismiss the judges, jurisconsults, teachers in madrasas, and Sufi shaykhs of zawiyas. The central government also controlled the rural tribes. It broke the power of the great tribal chiefs and left only lesser chieftainships and smaller units intact. Tunisia was ruled by some sixty qa'ids (district governors) and some two thousand local shaykhs. Much of the rural population, however, was quasi-independent on the basis of organized lineages, Sufi brotherhoods, and political alliances.

The migration of Spanish Muslims to North Africa reinforced the sedentary and commercial sectors of Tunisian society. After the fall of Granada in 1492, increasing Christian pressure on the Muslim population in Spain led to a steady emigration to North Africa, which reached its peak with the expulsion of the Moriscos at the beginning of the seventeenth century. Andalusian poets, scribes, scholars, and soldiers took refuge with the Hafsids. Many newcomers settled in the Zuqaq al-Andalus and other suburbs of Tunis. Numerous Andalusian villages were founded and produced olives, silk, and grapes. As cultivators, the Andalusians introduced new irrigation systems, mills, gardens, and vineyards in the Spanish fashion. The migrants were accorded autonomy in tax collections; an official spokesman, the Shaykh al-Andalus, represented them to the government. A cultured community, they continued to speak their own languages and founded mosques and colleges.

Until the late eighteenth and early nineteenth centuries the Tunisian economy functioned in the traditional way. It was divided into a sector of self-sufficient nomads and cultivators, and a sector attached to international trade. Tunisia exported meat, wool, olive oil, hides, beeswax, dates, and sponges, and imported European cloth and paper. The Beys entered the trade, gathering taxes of wheat and wool in kind which they sold to European merchants. In the eighteenth century 'Ali (1759–82) and Hammuda Pasha (1782–1813) seized the opportunities provided by European wars to enlarge Tunisian trade, improve ports, and encourage cloth production.

The felt-cap industry, introduced by Andalusians, was one of the most important. The *shashiya* was the standard cap worn throughout the Mediterranean by Christians, Jews, Armenians, and Muslims, and was widely sold throughout the Ottoman empire, the Balkans, and Iran. Hundreds of workshops were organized by merchant investors, and Tunisian production often reached 100,000 dozen hats per year. There were between 15,000 and 50,000 people engaged in the trade. The production of these caps also depended upon international trade. Wool came from Spain, vermilion from Portugal, and alum from Rome. The imports, however, were generally in the control of French merchants from Marseille and Jewish merchants from Livorno. Though Tunisians suffered from regulations imposed by the Bey of Tunis, European control of raw materials, a rigid corporate organization, and high costs of production, they had the advantage of understanding the market and producing an appropriate commodity.

In the late eighteenth century, however, the Tunisian economy went into decline. From 1784 to 1820 there were repeated crop failures and outbreaks of plague. Olive oil replaced wheat as the major export, and the shashiya was forced off the market by French competition. The industrial revolution and the tremendous increase of European production undermined the industry. By the middle decades of the nineteenth century the most profitable and highly capitalized Tunisian industry was in decline. At the same time the price of olive oil declined drastically, and Tunisia was left importing manufactured and luxury products with an unfavorable balance of payments.

In spite of economic decline, the government attempted to build up the army and the state apparatus. Rapid increases in taxes provoked a great peasant uprising in 1864. Even though the regime put down the revolt, it still did not have adequate revenues to maintain the army. Borrowing from European banks led to bankruptcy in 1867. In 1869 Tunisia had to submit to a French, British, and Italian commission to collect tax revenues and repay the bondholders. At the Congress of Berlin in 1878, the European powers encouraged France to establish a protectorate over Tunisia to divert her from the loss of Alsace-Lorraine and to compensate her for Russian gains in the Balkans and the British occupation of Cyprus. The protectorate was declared in 1881.

Algeria

While Tunisia had a long history of centralized states in addition to Khariji principalities and tribal dynasties, Algeria had no history of central states and no territorial identity. From the thirteenth to the fifteenth centuries it was generally under Hafsid suzerainty, but in the course of the fifteenth century Sufi teachers gathered followers, acquired large territories as gifts from local rulers or from their devotees, and became landowners, patrons, and spiritual counselors for multitudes of small cultivators. Henceforth the political structure of Algeria would be based upon tribal or lineage groups and Sufi-led communities.

An Algerian state first came into being as a result of the Ottoman conquest. With the help of Ottoman guns and janissaries Khayr al-Din Barbarossa captured Algiers in 1529. From 1529 to 1587 Algiers was ruled by a beylerbey (provincial governor), supported by janissaries, directly appointed by the Sultan in Istanbul. Against heavy odds the new Algiers regime carved out a North African empire. Turkish suzerainty was established in the rest of Algeria. Tunisia was taken under Ottoman control in 1574, but Ottoman efforts to impose suzerainty upon Morocco were defeated. North Africa from Egypt to the borders of Morocco came under Ottoman suzerainty.

Eventually, the agha of Algiers, the chief officer of the janissaries, made himself independent with the title of Dey. While tribute was sent to Istanbul in exchange for the Sultan's political and ideological support and the right to recruit janissaries in Anatolia, from 1659 to 1830 Algeria was ruled by the Deys and the local Turkish janissaries. The sons of Turkish soldiers and local women, called *kulughlis*, were in principle excluded from the janissary corps, but served as subordinate militias. The Dey was elected by the officers to administer the city of Algiers and its agricultural environs. The rest of the country was divided into three regions – Constantine, Mascara, and Titteri – governed by representatives of the Dey, who were called Beys. To sub-districts within their jurisdiction the Beys named qa'ids who controlled the local tribal leaders, levied taxes, settled judicial disputes, and presided over the markets. Apart from the judicial administration there is little evidence for a large 'ulama' establishment or for state sponsorship of a Muslim education system. There was no institution in Algeria comparable to the Qarawiyin college of Fez or the Zaytuna mosque of Tunis.

Apart from zones of direct administration, the Ottoman-Turkish regime organized the people under the authority of religious and tribal chieftains. Many of the local chiefs were Sufis. To win their support the Algerian regime accorded them respect, endowed mosques and tombs, appointed them to judicial positions, and gave them land and tax revenues. The Sufi-organized tribal communities were particularly important on the Moroccan frontier. The Turkish–Algerian regime also required all persons wishing to trade or work in the marketplace to have a permit issued by the agha of the janissaries. The Kabyle region, in particular, was dependent on these permits because it was overpopulated and relied upon the export of olive oil, figs, craft products, and surplus labor for survival. In southern Algeria the government controlled the movements of pastoralists by manipulating the price of grain and levying a tax on each camel load. To collect taxes the government also had recourse to a *mahalla*, or military expedition, to coerce the local population. Overall, some districts, such as the Kabyle, Aurès, and the Sahara, remained fully autonomous.

In the course of the sixteenth century privateering was a flourishing enterprise. Algerian corsairs seized European ships at sea, confiscated their goods, and sold their crews into slavery. Portions of the booty went to support the government and repay merchants who helped finance the ventures, but there was also a great increase in the number of mosques and pious foundations endowed by the earnings of the corsairs.

In the period of its ascendancy the Turkish regime managed to define the territorial identity of Algeria and to create a centralized state in the region between Tunisia and Morocco. The state apparatus was highly institutionalized in the Ottoman manner, but its control over the country was limited by independent rural communities. In the sixteenth and seventeenth centuries a small professional army could deal with dispersed tribal coalitions, but by the eighteenth century, as Algerian naval power and sea revenues declined, as fewer recruits came from Anatolia, and as modern weapons were more widely dispersed, the state's hegemony diminished. As the state depended increasingly upon Jewish, French, and English merchants, its legitimacy was compromised. In the decades between 1800 and 1830 there were Sufi-led rebellions by the Darqawa, the Qadiriya, and the Tijaniya. Since the various orders were confined to particular regions – the Rahmaniya to the Kabyle, the Tijaniya to the Sahara, and the Darqawa to the Oranie – the rebels were not able to present the regime with a united opposition. Though the Algerian state had long been a "sectored" regime, a regime effective only in part of its nominal domains, in the early nineteenth century the balance of power between this limited central government and the rest of Algerian society was turning against the Turkish state. This was the moment for the French invasion of 1830.

Morocco – the Marinid and Sa'dian states

The Almoravids and Almohads created the basis for a Moroccan territorial state. Morocco would go through successive cycles of political consolidation and decline as the Marinid, Sa'dian, and 'Alawi dynasties in turn captured the state and lost control to other forces.

The Marinids were the dominant group in a coalition of Zenata Berbers who overthrew the Almohads and conquered Morocco between 1244 and 1274. Their government was built around a court city and a small household administration. The Marinids built Fez Jadid in 1275 as a military and administrative residence for the ruler and his family, officials, and troops. Here were quartered Castilian or Catalonian militias. The dynasty was supported by a coalition of Moroccan tribes which included the Banu Marin, the Banu Ma'qil who controlled the territory south of the Atlas, and various Zenata-Berber chieftains in the Atlas region. Government control was effective on the plains of central and northern Morocco, but not in the mountain regions. To legitimize the regime, the Friday prayers were first said in the name of the Hafsid Caliphs; the Marinid princes claimed the title of amir al-muslimin. Gradually, however, they abandoned Almohad doctrine and simply claimed to be the protectors of Sunni Islam. They favored 'ulama' and madrasa forms of religious instruction. In 1437 they attempted to coopt the legitimacy attached to descendants of the Prophet by their discovery of the tomb of Idris II and the creation of a Marinid-sponsored cult around his tomb.

The Marinid regime, however, was undermined by a variety of economic problems. In the course of the fourteenth century there were profound changes in the pattern of international trade which were detrimental to Moroccan prosperity. The kingdom of Mali entered into competition for the southern sectors of the Sahara–Sudan routes, and helped revitalize competing trade routes via Tlemsen, Bougie, Tunis, and Egypt which substantially cut into Morocco's share of the profitable traffic. Throughout the fourteenth and fifteenth centuries, ships from Venice, Genoa, Pisa, Marseille, Catalonia, and Aragon regularly traded in Moroccan ports. Morocco imported metals, hardware, textiles, woolens, spices, and wine, and exported leather, hides, carpets, wool, coral, grain, slaves, and sugar, but from the beginning of the fifteenth century it was damaged by Portuguese efforts to establish their political and commercial supremacy in the western Mediterranean. In 1415 the Portuguese seized Ceuta and in 1471 Tangiers. Between 1486 and 1550 they established themselves on the Atlantic coast of Morocco. The Portuguese did not use their forts for further inland conquests. Rather, they moved along the African coast, opening the way for direct trade with Sudanic Africa.

Even in the short term, the Portuguese threat brought about both a crisis of economy and one of political legitimacy. Within Morocco the precarious balance between the state and tribal forces shifted in favor of the latter. Already Hilali Arabs had pushed their way into the Sus and Saharan regions of Morocco and done severe damage to agriculture. The Banu Ma'qil took control of Sijilmassa and created their own small empire south of the Atlas. Marrakesh fell into the control of tribal chiefs. The Wattasids, originally tribal allies of the Marinids, became regents for the dynasty in 1428 and then assumed the Sultanate from 1472 to 1549. Under the Wattasids the weakness of the central state allowed nomadic peoples to make further gains at the expense of peasant cultivation and permitted the Portuguese to seize and fortify numerous coastal ports.

The economic and political regression of Morocco in the Marinid and Wattasid periods led to the rise of Sufism. Moroccan Sufis were generally religious scholars living in village communities. A typical Moroccan Sufi of the fourteenth century combined knowledge of mysticism and law, literate scholarship, and esoteric practices. In the Moroccan ideal of the time the perfected Sufi was a symbol of the religious qualities of the Prophet, who was in turn a symbol of the reality of God. The Sufi was venerated not in his person but as a symbol of the *surat al-muhammadiya* – the laudable qualities that belong to the spiritual universe and are concentrated in the person of the Prophet. Sufis were affiliated with zawiyas as centers of worship and teaching, but in this period they did not have political functions.

In the fifteenth century, however, Sufism became crucial for organizing local self-defense and mobilizing popular resistance to the Portuguese. Sufis became the leaders of local tribal coalitions, and the scale of Sufi organization was greatly enlarged by the introduction of the tariqat. Under the inspiration of Abu 'Abdallah Muhammad al-Jazuli (d. 1465), master zawiyas created satellite communities, or combined into single brotherhoods based on shared spiritual lineages. Loyalty to the shaykhs, shared dhikrs, and ceremonies of initiation bound together the members of the brotherhoods.

Sufi authority was also buttressed by the acceptance of a new concept of religious authority. In addition to authority based on the imitation of the Prophet, descent was taken to assure religious sanctity. The descendants of the Prophet (*shurafa'*) were already a privileged caste in local society, supported by religious endowments, and organized under the leadership of a naqib, who acted as judge, maintained records, and represented the interests of the group. With the decline of the Marinid state the shurafa' claimed the right to oversee political affairs. Ever after, Moroccan Sufis and princes would claim sharifian descent.

The authority of the Sufis and the shurafa' challenged both tribal and state concepts of the political order and allowed for the creation of local coalitions on the basis of tribal allegiances to the Sufi orders. Henceforth, no Moroccan regime could come to power or maintain itself without integrating this new concept of authority and the organizational form in which it was embedded into its own political practice.

By the fifteenth century, then, Morocco, like Tunisia and Algeria, was a society with a central state regime and a Sufi-led rural population. In the course of the fifteenth and sixteenth centuries the central regime temporarily broke down and Sufi-led communities became the dominant force, but in the late sixteenth century the Moroccan state was seized by the Sa'dians and restored to a precarious sovereignty.

The Sa'dians had their origins in a local jihad against the Portuguese fortress of Agadir led by Muhammad al-Mahdi. The holy war gathered the support of Sufi and tribal chiefs and Muhammad was elected Amir of the Sus. From the Sus the Sa'dians conquered all of Morocco, protected in part by the balance of power between the Habsburgs and the Ottomans. The Sa'dians ruled Morocco from 1554 to 1659.

While Algeria and Tunisia were shaped by Ottoman institutions, the Sa'dians provided Morocco with another type of Islamic regime. Like that of the Ottomans, the authority of the new regime rested on its service to Islam in the holy war, but the Sa'dians claimed descent from the Prophet Muhammad and thus linked themselves to a concept that had, in the course of the fifteenth century, become central to Moroccan notions of political authority. This descent was conceived partly in genealogical terms, partly in terms of devotion to the teachings of the Prophet, and partly in terms of the symbolic embodiment of divine virtues. The Sa'dians linked themselves to the Sufis by moving the body of al-Jazuli to Marrakesh to symbolize the formation of a coalition of Sufi brotherhoods around the venerated tomb, and later made the birthday of the Prophet the premier Moroccan religious festival. The celebration of the Prophet's birthday gave added import to the political claims of the dynasty. It appealed to the Sufi brotherhoods because they too claimed physical and spiritual closeness to Muhammad, and it gave the common people a worshipful closeness to the principal figure in their religion. Sultan al-Mansur (1578–1603) also tried to embellish the ritual paraphernalia of his office by introducing a more elaborate court ceremonial. In the absence of Ottoman institutions the Sultans ruled not only by administrative means but also by the baraka (power of blessing) derived from sharifian descent, by dynastic inheritance, and by elective authority conferred by tribe, city, and the army. Thus the Sa'dian Sultanate represented Islamic religious unity and authority in a territory dominated by tribal and Sufi concepts of society. In this regard Moroccan authority resembled that of the Safavids rather than the Ottomans.

Al-Mansur emerged as the great organizer of the regime. He expanded the army from its Berber tribal base to include mercenaries from Spain, Turkey, and Africa who were competent in the use of firearms. In 1603 there were 4,000 European renegades, 4,000 Andalusians, and 1,500 Turks in an army of some 40,000. Modern artillery units were incorporated. Fortifications capable of mounting artillery were built at Taza, Fez, and Marrakesh. England and the Netherlands, in their shared enmity to Habsburg Spain, provided Morocco with ships, cannon, and powder. Loyal tribes enabled the regime to control the plains of northern Morocco and the Atlantic coastal regions.

Despite the favorable economic conditions, the Moroccan state broke down upon the death of al-Mansur. Sa'dian princes established separate regimes at Fez and Marrakesh; Sufi chiefs created independent principalities. In the ensuing struggles for power, the brothers Maulay Muhammad and Maulay Rashid, leaders of a sharifian faction in Tafilalt, triumphed over other factions and established the dynasty that governs Morocco to the present day.

The 'Alawi dynasty to the French protectorate

Like the Sa'dians, the 'Alawis came to power on the basis of the religious legitimacy provided by descent from the Prophet and war against the infidels. Maulay Isma'il (1672–1727) was the first great ruler of the dynasty. He reconstructed the centralized state by building up a professional army of some 30,000 to 50,000 slaves. These slaves were most probably recruited from the existing Moroccan slave population and from the subordinate, client tribes called *haratin*. The slave army was supplemented by the tribes who furnished troops in return for tax exemptions and rights to land. High government functionaries were recruited from the dominant tribes and from the town bourgeoisie, including the leading families of Fez and families of Andalusian descent. 'Ulama' filled the offices of judge, market inspector, administrator of intestate properties, and other posts. In the provinces the government was represented by qa'ids who varied in power from subordinate functionaries to independent local lords.

Despite the ostensible strength of the central government apparatus it had limited power in the provinces. While rural peoples did not question the Sultan's authority, in practice defiance of his power was the norm. In principle the Sufi leaders were also subordinate to the authority of the central government, but in fact they remained independent. Sufi chiefs played an important role in trade, and their headquarters were commonly located along trade routes or along the boundaries between tribal groups, where they could facilitate traffic and negotiate disputes. The zawiyas were also centers of agriculture, and provided educational and judicial services. A zawiya was at once a hotel, a hospital, a school, a market, a mosque, a court of law, and a refuge. Nonetheless, the 'Alawis tried to overcome Sufi influence by using the authority of the Sultan over religious activities. They took over the right to ratify succession to the chieftainship of a zawiya and the control of its properties, and conferred upon the Sufis both spiritual titles and control over land and revenues. The relation of the Sufi orders to governments was a complicated combination of antagonism and cooperation. In some cases the Sufi orders helped the state consolidate its authority; in others they resisted.

Sufi influence continued to expand as new brotherhoods were founded throughout the seventeenth, eighteenth, and nineteenth centuries. These included the Nasiriya, which claimed to represent the purest Islamic orthodoxy. Its rituals consisted of supplementary prayers and the recitation of the profession of faith, "There is no God but God," a thousand times a day. Its chiefs refused to use the name of the 'Alawi Sultan in the Friday prayers on the grounds that it was blasphemous to mention a human being in the course of divine supplication. The Darqawa, founded in the late eighteenth century, denounced the pointless repetition of prayers and sought to restore direct communication with the divine being through a prayer and dance designed to induce religious ecstasy.

The 'Alawis were able to consolidate their power with the help of economic resources gained from trade with Europe and the Sudan. They first captured the

Portuguese forts along the Atlantic coast, and then, in 1591, seized Timbuktu, and took control of the trans-Saharan region. Moroccan sugar was an important source of royal revenues. The industry was owned by the Sultans, managed by Jews and European Christians, and operated by slave labor. As early as the late thirteenth century Moroccan sugar was being exported to Flanders, Venice, and later to Spain, but in the seventeenth century new plantations in Madeira, the Canary Islands, and the Americas squeezed Morocco out of the international market.

In the eighteenth century Morocco was importing large numbers of slaves in return for cloth, leather, silk, jewelry, iron, lead, and weapons, and European-derived tea, coffee, sugar, paper, tin, copper utensils, and Indian spices. Britain and France were Morocco's principal trading partners, but dyes came from Spain, and woolen goods, other textiles, spices, and metals came from Holland. Italy supplied alum and artisanal products. From the eastern Mediterranean came silk, cotton, and opium. Salé was the most frequented port, but Agadir and then Mogador were important for the contacts between Europe, the Sus, and the Sudan. Trade, however, did not necessarily benefit the central government, because it could be organized by tribal confederations under religious protection. Local sharifs played an important part in providing the liaisons and guarantees of security for caravans. For example, descendants of Maulay Isma'il, residing in the fortresses of Tafilalt, had a monopoly on guiding caravan traffic to Touat.

In the nineteenth century European trade led to the economic penetration of the country. In 1856 Morocco was forced by British pressure to conclude a treaty which opened the country to free trade on the basis of a 10 percent customs duty. Also, Moroccan exports declined after the opening of the Suez Canal (1869) and the introduction of steamships and railroads which made it possible for American, Russian, and Australian producers to provide wheat and wool to European markets in competition with Moroccan products. The Moroccan Saharan trade also dwindled owing to French expansion in West Africa that drew Sudanic and Saharan goods to Atlantic ports. After the middle of the century the Europeans were no longer content to maintain a strictly commercial relationship, and tried to directly control the means of production. They began to purchase land, extend loans at high rates of interest, and take Moroccans under extraterritorial protection.

As a result, certain elements of the Moroccan population prospered while others suffered. A new Moroccan bourgeoisie, including the merchant intermediaries between the European and the local markets, and a host of petty traders and retailers, prospered. Customs officials and other functionaries also profited from trade, and acquired property and education. The merchants of Fez maintained their dominant position as Fassi families established colonies in Manchester, Marseille, Genoa, and French West Africa. The Fez textile industry survived European competition by cultivating new Middle Eastern, African, and domestic markets. The production of straw mats, rugs, carpets and wool blankets, and the building trades, also continued to prosper. Other Moroccan crafts suffered from European competition. Imported products destroyed cotton farming and manufacturing and the Moroccan shoe industry. The Moroccan state was among the economic losers.

Faced with declining revenues, power, and territory, Sultan Hasan (1873–95) attempted to reform the army by means of military instructors and weapons obtained from Europe, and to reform the state bureaucracy by a reorganization of provincial administration. He also proposed to improve the economic infrastructure of the country by building bridges and railroads and by establishing cotton and sugar plantations. These reforms had only a limited success. Most of the religious and political elite opposed them as infringements of tradition and law; the European powers were hostile to changes that might reduce their economic privileges.

As a result, in the course of the nineteenth century, Berbers pushed government forces out of the Middle and Central Atlas. The High Atlas was in the hands of the quasi-independent great qa'ids. By the end of the century the central government controlled scarcely a third of the land and about half of the population, concentrated in the plains of eastern Morocco, the Rif, Fez, and the Atlantic zones from Tangiers to the Atlas. Even in these regions local chieftains were often paramount. To maintain his influence the ruler commonly had to move a small army into non-complying or rebellious territory, camp, live off the resources of the country, and compel payment of taxes in arrears. The local people were thus put under pressure to save their crops; the Sultan, however, was also under pressure to conclude an agreement so that he could move on to another rebellious district. Religious chieftains would mediate between the tribes and the ruler until some kind of deal was made.

This kind of polity was scarcely able to resist European colonization. Between 1899 and 1912 the French occupied Morocco, abetted by diplomatic agreements with Italy, Spain, Britain, and eventually Germany. To consolidate their gains, the French manipulated the various players in the Moroccan political system. Thus in the region of Touat, faced with French intervention, local chiefs demanded that the Sultan wage jihad, but at the same time they resisted his efforts to collect taxes. The shortage of revenues made the Sultan dependent upon French financial support, and in turn he lost legitimacy in the eyes of local people, who then felt justified in yielding to French military superiority. The autonomy of local officials, religious leaders, and chiefs made it impossible for Morocco to put up a unified resistance to French aggression.

The Sultan's efforts to increase the power of the state only played into the hands of the French. From 1901 to 1903 Sultan 'Abd al-'Aziz tried to strengthen the central government by implementing a new tax on agriculture and livestock, and by the appointment of new officials to assure the collection of taxes. He proposed to tax tribes, religious leaders, government officials, and others hitherto exempt. The opposition of the rural notables and the 'ulama', however, was resolute, and 'Abd al-'Aziz was forced instead to mortgage the customs revenues and borrow heavily from the French. For this he was greeted with widespread revolt and a revolution which deposed him in favor of his brother 'Abd al-Hafiz.

The intervention of the 'ulama' was a novelty in Moroccan history. Traditionally the Moroccan 'ulama' were a group of officials but not an organized corporate body. The chief qadi of Fez named the professors of the major mosques and colleges, and controlled their endowed properties. For more than half a century, however, the government had been increasing its control over the appointment of judges and professors and of madrasa graduates who entered the state bureaucracy. Nonetheless, after 1900 many 'ulama' joined the opposition because they could not accept the collaboration of the Sultan with the French, his failure to protect Moroccan territory, and his tax reforms, loans, and European advisors. The result of 'ulama' and rural tribal opposition was the loss of independence and the declaration of French and Spanish protectorates in 1912.

STATES AND ISLAM: NORTH AFRICAN VARIATIONS

From the origins of the Islamic era to the nineteenth century, the history of North African society turned on two essential motifs: state formation and Islamization. Historically, families, hamlets, or groups of hamlets were the basic units of society. They were englobed in factional and tribal groups; class stratification, feudal dominance, and state power were generally weak. The economy was correspondingly based on small-scale grain, fruit, and olive gardening, stock raising by pastoral peoples, and limited urban-based textile and other small-scale manufacturing. While trade was important, the merchant middle class was not highly developed. Unlike the Middle East, North Africa did not have a long experience of imperial organization, monotheistic religious communities, and sedentarized agricultural and urban commercial development. It had a veneer of imperial and urban Christian civilization set down by the Phoenicians and Romans, and confined to relatively limited coastal territories.

The Arab conquest gave new impetus to state formation and to the organization of North African society into Muslim communities. Tunisia in the eighth century, Morocco in the eleventh, and Algeria in the sixteenth acquired territorial identity and state regimes. The conquests also led to the institutionalization of Islam for the masses of the population. From the eighth century, the Maliki school of law became rooted throughout North Africa and remained the mainstay of legal administration, education, and state legitimization until the nineteenth century. From about the twelfth century, Sufis became the chieftains of rural communities in Tunisia, Algeria, and Morocco and the leaders of tribal coalitions, in parallel with and in opposition to states. Much of the history of North Africa from the thirteenth to the nineteenth centuries may be defined in terms of the relations between state and Sufi forces. Finally, the Arab conquests also gave North Africa an Arab identity due to successive waves of Arab migration, and Arab dominance of states. Large parts of southern Tunisia, Algeria, and Morocco, however, were primarily Berber. Only in the twentieth century would Arabic become the universal language of societies that had been Muslim since the Almohad era.

Each society, however, exhibited its own variations upon state, religious, and tribal institutions. At the time of the Arab conquests, Tunisia was already the center of a developed civilization and remained throughout its history a society marked by a highly developed agricultural and commercial economy governed by an aristocracy of landowners, merchants, and urban intellectuals. Tunisia in the early Muslim era, like the Middle East, maintained its inherited institutional base but accepted an Islamic version of ancient civilization. Under the early Arab and Aghlabid governors a Caliphal type of administration and the Maliki school of law flourished. The Hafsid regime adopted the Sultanal type of administration and 'ulama' and Sufi forms of Islam. With the Ottoman conquest at the end of the sixteenth century, Ottoman janissary and administrative institutions and the Ottoman type of 'ulama' bureaucracy modified the structure of the Tunisian state. Throughout this era Tunisia maintained its state institutions, despite a large pastoral and tribal population in the southern parts of the country, and constant fluctuations in the balance of power between the state and the tribal parts of the society. Until the nineteenth century Tunisia was in all respects a provincial variant of the Middle Eastern Islamic world.

Algeria has a different history. As a whole it remained without state organization well into the Islamic era though it supported a number of local dynasties, such as the Hammadids, on the basis of a share of Saharan and European trade. These regimes, however, never controlled the whole of the territory and gave way readily to tribal opposition. A stable state was finally introduced by the Ottomans, who provided a ready-made military elite, administrative cadres who were supervised from Istanbul, and the rudiments of a religious bureaucracy. The concepts of jihad against Christians and of Sultanal authority served to legitimize this regime.

At first the Algerian regime was confined to the city-state of Algiers, and was based on privateering and on direct support from Istanbul, but progressively Algiers established its own administrative, tax-collecting, and judicial authority over a large territory. Ottoman-Turkish authority came to be recognized throughout Algeria though it was not uniformly effective. Provincial, tribal, and Sufi resistance, however, grew in the eighteenth and nineteenth centuries. Thus Algeria resembled Ottoman Syria and Iraq, where a centralized state governed a segmented society. The Ottoman-Algerian regime succeeded in creating an Algerian territorial and administrative identity, while the spread of Sufism among rural populations gave it Islamic identity.

The history of Morocco shows a third variation on the theme of Islam and state formation in a highly fragmented society. Though Volubilis was the capital of a Roman province, Morocco on the eve of the Arab conquests had neither territorial identity nor a history of centralized regimes. A number of local principalities emerged in the wake of the Arab conquests, based upon personal religious authority of the rulers, but from the eighth to the eleventh centuries the process of state formation was inhibited by internal fragmentation and external Fatimid and Umayyad interventions. The Almoravid conquests began the process of creating the territorial base for a Moroccan state. The Almoravids, the first of a series of conquest regimes set up by coalitions of tribal peoples from the south united on the basis of religious principles, were succeeded by the Almohads, the Marinids, the Sa'dians, and the 'Alawis, each of whom was legitimized by an appeal to the charismatic authority of the ruler, although this authority was articulated in different ways. In the Almoravid and Almohad cases the leaders were heads of reform movements. Later Sa'dian and 'Alawi rulers possessed the baraka of descent from the Prophet and were believed to have the charismatic powers of Sufi saints. They were also regarded as Caliphs, successors to the Prophet in the defense and administration of an Islamic society. The Sultan was at once Caliph, imam, sharif, wali, and mujtahid. He had important ritual roles at the Muslim holidays and shared in the national veneration for religious leaders.

Moroccan Sultans, however, did not have a monopoly of religious legitimacy, but shared sharifian descent and Sufi baraka with other religious leaders. This sharing of authority was both supportive and competitive. It was supportive in that the Sufis provided the Sultans with a cultural basis for their claims to worldly authority. It was competitive in that the sources of moral judgment and political authority were independent of the state and dispersed among many individuals in the society. This dispersion meant that Morocco could not easily create a unified national regime.

The highly personal nature of the Moroccan monarchy assured its legitimacy and historical continuity, but was also a source of weakness. Power was effected by means of personal contacts between the ruler and his clients. The highly personal nature of the state implied weak institutions. The central regime was supported by household administration and by mercenary and slave soldiers, but the *makhzan*, or coalition of independent, tribal, or Sufi power-holders supplying military forces to the regime, was crucial to its effectiveness. With the help of the makhzan the government could control the towns and the central plains, but not the mountains and the deserts. Morocco thus preserved a distinctive territorial and monarchical identity, based on the personal religious authority of the Sultans. This differed from Tunisia, which combined a Muslim statist concept of political legitimacy with centralized political administration, and from Algeria, which had a highly developed central government but a weak sense of political identity.

There are several reasons for the failure to consolidate a central Moroccan state. While Morocco was a relatively wealthy region, its agricultural and commercial sectors were small in comparison to its pastoral populations. Successive bedouin invasions destroyed peasant village life. Furthermore, the weakness of the state made it difficult to collect regular taxes. To supplement poor tax revenues the Sultans attempted to exploit long-distance trade, but rival Moroccan chiefs, and Sudanese, Algerian, and European competitors, appropriated important shares. While Moroccan dynasties often came to power on the basis of control of trade, it proved impossible to monopolize trade revenues for extended periods.

A related factor was the weakness of the urban bureaucratic, commercial, and intellectual elites. Andalusian minorities provided the cadres of administration. Without links to either the rural or urban masses, however, they could serve only as secretaries. The 'ulama', also, were merely a slim stratum of the population, dependent on the Sultans, restricted to the urban areas, and without politically potent ties to the common people. They also had to compete for religious prestige with the Sultans, the saintly lineages, and the Sufi brotherhoods.

The corollary of the weakness of the sedentary society was the strength of autonomous tribal and Sufi groups. Their independence was enhanced in the seventeenth and eighteenth centuries by their access to European weapons. The effort to control the tribes and Sufi coalitions was continually subverted by intra-elite struggles for power and by the need to make fiscal, territorial, and other concessions to pacify communities that could not be defeated. In any case, Moroccan tribes were themselves unstable constellations. They used the patrilineal idiom but they did not have a firm hierarchy or permanent constituencies. Tribal chieftainships were temporary positions subject to a constant competition for power. Sufi lineages and coalitions were similarly unstable, for the power of Sufis was personal rather than organizational, and depended on the voluntary adherence of the tribes to the saints.

The late eighteenth and nineteenth centuries were a period of protracted crisis for North African-Muslim societies. Their Ottoman suzerain could no longer protect them. Their states were no longer capable of exerting close political control or of generating large revenues and strong armies. Their economies were increasingly in bondage to Europe. The decline of economic power made them prey to French conquest and French protectorates.

ISLAM IN CENTRAL AND
SOUTHERN ASIA

CHAPTER 17

INNER ASIA FROM THE MONGOL CONQUESTS
TO THE NINETEENTH CENTURY

For millennia the central theme in the history of this vast and varied region was the relationship between nomadic-pastoral and sedentary peoples. While the great civilizations of the Middle East and China were primarily imperial and agricultural, the region between them was a zone of steppe lands and scattered oases. The population was predominantly pastoral, and lived by raising horses and sheep. It was also organized into clans and tribes, which were sometimes assembled into great confederations. The settled peoples lived primarily in the oasis districts of Transoxania, Khwarizm, Farghana, and Kashgar, and in scattered towns along the trade routes that linked China, the Middle East, and Europe. Settled and pastoral peoples had close relationships with each other, exchanging products and participating in caravan trade. Pastoral peoples also infiltrated the settled areas and became farmers or townsmen. Sometimes they conquered the agricultural oases and became rulers and landlords. Inner Asia was also the reservoir holding a sea of peoples who, organized into great confederations, from time to time conquered the Middle East and China. From the second millennium BC to the eighteenth century the history of the region may be told in terms of ever-repeated nomadic conquests, the formation of empires over oasis and settled populations, and the constant tension between pastoral and agricultural peoples.

The development of an Islamic civilization in Inner Asia was closely related to that of Iran. Islam first spread in this region as a result of the Arab conquests of Iran and Transoxania and the movement of Muslim traders and Sufis from the towns to the steppes. The two regions were also linked by the Turkish migrations of the tenth to the fourteenth centuries which brought Inner Asian peoples into Iran, and Iranian monarchical culture and Islamic civilization into Inner Asia. In the tenth and eleventh centuries Qarluq and Oghuz peoples were converted, and founded the Qarakhanid and Saljuq empires. Under the Qarakhanids, the Hanafi school of law and Maturidi school of theology were established in Transoxania, and a new Turkish literature inspired by Persian Islamic literature came into being. The Qarakhanids also favored the diffusion of Islam from Transoxania into the Tarim basin and the northern steppes. Sufi preachers, especially Shaykh Ahmad al-Yasavi (d. 1166), helped to spread Islam among nomadic peoples.

The connections between Iran and Inner Asia were reinforced by the Mongol invasions. In the thirteenth century non-Muslim Mongolian peoples established their suzerainty over the whole of Inner Asia, much of the Middle East, and China. The Mongol conquests brought the steppe regions north of the Black, Caspian, and Aral Seas into contact with Muslim peoples in Transoxania and Iran, and linked Muslim Transoxania with eastern Inner Asia and China.

The advent of Islam in this region led to the formation of three types of Islamic society. Among the Kazakhs, Islam became part of popular identity and belief, but not the basis of social organization. Among other tribal peoples and in some oasis communities such as Kashgar, Sufi masters or Sufi lineages mediated, organized, and sometimes governed. In large-scale urbanized societies such as Transoxania, state-organized Islamic societies of the Middle Eastern type were developed.

Eventually all of Inner Asia was brought under Russian and Chinese rule. As early as the sixteenth century Russia absorbed the Tatar states of the Volga region. In the eighteenth and nineteenth centuries Russia took control of the Crimea, the northern steppes, Turkestan, and Transcaspia. The Chinese occupied eastern Turkestan in the eighteenth century, and divided Inner Asia into spheres of Russian and Chinese rule. The rule of settled (and non-Muslim) empires brought to an end the ancient patterns of nomadic migration and empire formation.

THE WESTERN AND NORTHERN STEPPES

The semi-arid steppe region north of a line drawn across the top of the Black, Caspian, and Aral Seas and Lake Balkhash was inhabited predominantly by pastoral peoples whose livelihood depended upon raising cattle, horses, goats, sheep, camels, and yaks. The populace spoke Turkic-Altaic languages and was organized into families, clans, and confederations (hordes), with the clan being the basic unit of tax collection, military organization, adjudication of disputes, and other political activities. While small communities were based on lineage, a political or territorial concept was woven into the higher levels of organization.

The Mongol conquests gave this region a semblance of political unity. In 1236, under the leadership of Batu, Mongol and Turkish nomads conquered the regions north of the Aral and Caspian Seas, and established their capital on the Volga River. In one of the most extraordinary campaigns in world history the Golden Horde also conquered Russia, the Ukraine, southern Poland, Hungary, and Bulgaria, creating an empire that extended north to the forests of Russia, south to the Black Sea and the Caucasus, west to the Carpathians, and east to Khwarizm. Local princes were left in power as vassals of the Golden Horde and were used to extract tribute from the population. Moscow was the principal vassal of the Golden Horde; other Russian principalities were responsible to Moscow for the payment of tribute.

Amalgamating with the conquered peoples, the conquerors evolved over time into the Turkic-speaking "Tatar" population, and were eventually converted to Islam. Khan Berke (1257–67) was the first Muslim ruler, but only from the time of Uzbek Khan (1313–40) were the rulers routinely Muslims. The Islamic loyalties of the royal family were probably reinforced by contacts with the settled Muslim populations of Khwarizm and Transoxania, and perhaps by the absorption of the Bulgars who had been Muslims since the tenth century. Culturally the Golden Horde was dependent upon Egypt and Syria, which provided artists and artisans to produce wall paintings, mosaics, lamps, tombstones, and other artistic objects. In the steppes of northern Asia, the Golden Horde acquired aspects of Mediterranean-Islamic culture.

The empire of the Golden Horde maintained its suzerainty from the middle of the thirteenth to the middle of the fifteenth centuries, but gradually disintegrated under the pressure of Ottoman expansion (which cut off the Golden Horde from the Mediterranean), and the rise of Moscow, Moldavia, and Lithuania. Also, in the course of the fourteenth to the sixteenth centuries, the Golden Horde broke up into smaller principalities and became differentiated into separate Crimean Tatar, Volga Tatar, Uzbek, and Kazakh ethnic and political groups. The Khans of the Crimea, who claimed to be descendants of Chinggis Khan, declared themselves independent rulers in 1441. The Khans of Kazan, Astrakhan, and Siberia also established their autonomy. Each of these Khans had the right to conduct war and diplomacy and dispense justice, but their powers were checked by clan and tribal leaders, who had a voice in their succession. In the eastern steppes, from the Caspian–Ural region to the Tien-shan and Altai mountains, the Uzbeks probably originated as a coalition of warrior clans united under the leadership of the Shayban family and took their name from Uzbek Khan. The stability and political success of the Shaybanid confederation led gradually to the development of an Uzbek language and ethnic identity.

The Kazakhs formed a second confederation in the regions north of the Caspian and Aral Seas. The term "Kazakh" probably means free (of Uzbek authority?), and referred at first to a warrior stratum, then to a political confederation, and finally to an ethnic population. Kazakhs were organized into extended families called *aul* whose size was governed by the availability of pasture, and ranged between three and fifteen tents. Each aul had its own pasturage and migrated as a unit to exploit its grazing lands. The auls could also be grouped into larger units, called uymaqs, which were mixed groups of different clans. In the seventeenth century the Kazakhs formed the Great, Middle, and Little Hordes. A fourth horde, called the Bukey (Inner Horde), was formed at the beginning of the nineteenth century. The hordes took shape only when a Khan united them against a common enemy, or when larger states (such as Russia) used the Khans to control the nomads.

Table 14. *Inner Asia: outline chronology*

	Northern and western steppes			Turkestan		
	Volga	Northern Steppes	Crimea	Khwarizm	Transoxania	Eastern Turkestan
1200	*Mongol conquests* Chinggis Khan (1206–27)					
1300	Blue Horde, Batu ids (1227–1341) unites with White Horde to form Golden Horde (1378–1502)				Chaghatays 1227–1370 Timurid empire 1370–1500	
1400	Partitioned into several Khanates (fifteenth century)	Formation of Uzbek and Kazakh "nations" (fifteenth century)	Giray Khans 1426–1792			
1500	Kazan Khanate annexed by Moscow, 1552 Astrakhan Khanate, annexed 1556 Siberian Khanate, annexed 1598			Khans of Khiva 1515–1920	Shaybanids 1500–98	Chaghatays continue as nominal suzerains until 1678
1600					Astrakhanids 1599–1785	
1700						Kashgar, ruled by khwajas 1678–1756 Khokand, ruled by Khanate c. 1700–1876; Russian annexation, 1876

1800

1900

Russian annexation of Kazakhstan completed by 1868

Annexed by Russia, 1783

Russian protectorate, 1873

Mangits 1785–1920
Russian protectorate, 1868

Chinese conquest of Xinjiang, 1759

China annexes Xinjiang, 1884

In the fifteenth and sixteenth centuries Naqshbandi and Yasavi missionaries began to make converts among the Kazakhs. Islam, however, probably made little headway until the eighteenth century, when Tatar merchants, missionaries, secretaries, and teachers helped construct mosques and schools. Kazakh nomads accepted Muslim circumcision, marriage, and burial practices, and came to believe in the Muslim jinn as the equivalent of their spirit gods. They used Quranic amulets for protection and treated Muslim holy men as a kind of supplementary shaman. They worshiped at saints' tombs and observed Muslim holidays. Alongside Muslim festivals, however, the Kazakhs also maintained a folk culture in which wandering poets sang epic songs. Their style of Islam, like that of nomadic and rural peoples the world over, merged ancient folk beliefs and practices into the new religion. Thus the new Uzbek and Kazakh polities came into being when warrior or political elites built their power upon a confederation of families and clans, who in time assumed a genealogical relatedness and ethnic identity reinforced by Muslim beliefs and by a common language.

The decline of the Golden Horde opened the way for a multi-sided struggle for control of the western and northern steppes. In the fifteenth century, the Ottoman empire, Russia, Poland, Lithuania, and the Muslim states of Crimea, Kazan, and Astrakhan struggled for control of the Ural–Volga region. The ultimate outcome of these wars was that Russia freed itself from Tatar and Muslim domination and itself became master of the northern steppes and the Muslim populations. By 1535 Moscow claimed the right of investiture of Kazan rulers, and Muscovy chroniclers claimed that Kazan was "Russian land" which had to be recovered to reunite Russia. Church writers stressed the perfidy of the Tatars and the bitterness of the Christian–Muslim conflict. Amidst a growing sense of religious superiority and national mission, Moscow conquered Kazan in 1552 and Astrakhan in 1556. This gave it control of the Volga River and the north shore of the Caspian Sea, and paved the way for the submission of the Siberian Khanate in 1598.

Russian conquest of the Crimea, however, was delayed for almost two centuries. In the seventeenth century Moscow developed adequate frontier defenses against Ottoman and Crimean attack and began to colonize the southern steppes, which resulted ultimately in the Russian occupation of Azov in 1699. Peter the Great had to cede Azov to the Ottoman empire in 1711, but in 1774 the Russians defeated the Ottomans, and took full control of the Crimea in 1783. The Ottomans recognized the new sovereign in 1792.

From their dominant position in the Volga region the Russians set out to conquer the Kazakh steppes. Under Peter the Great, the Russians established a string of forts across the northern steppes from the Ural to the Irtysh Rivers, including Orenburg, Omsk, Barnaul, and Semipalatinsk. In 1723 the Kazakh Great Horde, and in 1730 the Kazakh Little Horde, were forced to accept Russian suzerainty. A century of slow consolidation was followed in 1822–24 by the abolition of the Kazakh Khanates and the submission of the Kazakhs to Russian control. In 1864 the

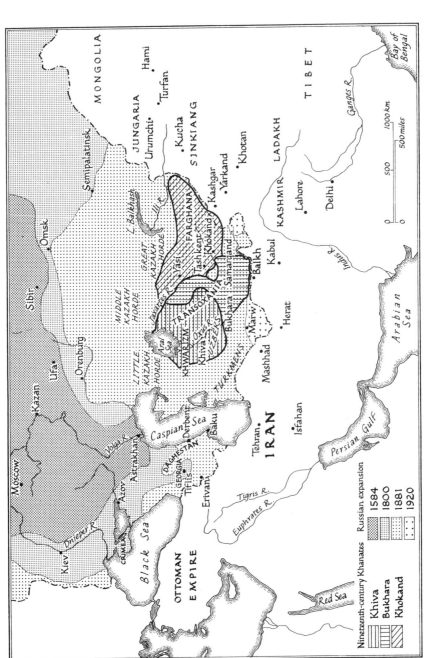

Map 17 Russian expansion in Muslim Inner Asia to 1920

Russians took the Syr–Darya region and completed the occupation of Kazakh territories. This victory was not easily won. Between 1783 and 1797 Batyr Srym led a series of counter-attacks, followed by some sixty years of Kazakh resistance. The Bukey Horde revolted between 1836 and 1838; Khan Kenesary Kasimov led Kazakh resistance between 1837 and 1847. The last revolt, in the name of Islam, was crushed in 1868. Thus Russia became the heir of the Golden Horde in the Ural–Volga region and on the northern and eastern steppes.

The Russian conquests were a disaster for Muslim peoples. Upon the conquest of Kazan and Astrakhan the Russians expelled the Tatars from the important cities, redistributed the land to Russian nobles and monasteries, and colonized the region with Russian artisans and peasants. Mosques were destroyed, Quran schools closed, and waqfs seized by the Russian treasury. The Russians aimed at no less than the complete conversion of the Tatars to Christianity. There was some success with Muslim nobles and their clients who were interested in collaboration with the Russians, but in general, Muslim resistance was fierce. From 1552 until 1610 there were repeated revolts by the Tatar nobility. Their defeat was followed by peasant uprisings from 1608 to 1615, and Tatar participation in Kazakh rebellions. Paradoxically, however, Russian conquest helped to spread Islam. Driven out of the major towns and deprived of land, Tatar nobles became merchants, colonized rural areas, built mosques and schools, and propagated Islam among the nomads.

In the seventeenth century the Russians suspended their efforts at assimilation and worked mainly to prevent the apostasy of converts, but in 1710 Peter the Great began a new campaign which lasted until 1764. Converts were transferred to purely Russian villages. Muslim children were sent to schools and adults were forced to accept baptism. Churches were constructed in Muslim villages. Yet after half a century there were only a small number of Tatar converts; many of these joined Pugachev's rebellion (1773–75).

To calm her eastern provinces Catherine the Great adopted a new policy in 1773. Aware of the importance of Tatar trading communities and eager to avoid further rebellions, Catherine ended religious persecution, gave Tatar nobles equal rights with Russian nobles, and encouraged Tatar merchants to trade between Russia and Transoxania. Decrees of 1782 and 1784 authorized the construction of mosques; in 1788 an Islamic spiritual administration was organized at Ufa under the leadership of a mufti. Under Catherine's peace, Tatar merchants flourished and invested in tanneries and in paper and woolen mills. Peasants developed cottage industries. Commercial success opened the way to European education, and eventually stimulated an intellectual enlightenment.

In the Crimea, Catherine guaranteed the nobility possession of their lands and the Muslim 'ulama' freedom of religion. A Muslim spiritual directorate for the Crimea was established in 1794; the mufti was nominated by the Tsar. In time, however, the Russians began to seize Tatar estates and waqfs for the benefit of the Russian aristocracy and European colonists who flocked to the country. Between 1783 and 1896 most of the Crimean Tatars were forced to migrate to the Ottoman empire; the remnant formed a minority in their own country.

TURKESTAN (TRANSOXANIA, KHWARIZM, AND FARGHANA)

While the northern steppes were the domain of the Golden Horde and later of settled Tatar and pastoral Kazakh peoples, Turkestan, the domain of the Chaghatays, was primarily agricultural and the site of numerous important oasis cities such as Bukhara and Samarqand. The commerce of these cities reached from China to the Black Sea, linking Iran, Afghanistan, India, China, and Russia. They were also important centers of Muslim religious learning. While nomadic peoples from the surrounding steppes time and again conquered the region, they accepted its city tradition and became patrons of its culture.

Throughout the period of the Caliphate and the Turkish and Mongol invasions, Turkestan was tied to eastern Iran. It was ruled in succession by the Qarakhanids, the Mongols, the Chaghatays, and the Timurids. The collapse of the Timurid empire, however, led to a permanent break between the two regions. Iran was conquered by the Safavids, and Transoxania (the principal part of Turkestan) by the Uzbeks. The trade routes that linked Transoxania to Iran were disrupted by Shaybanid–Safavid hostilities. Iran was converted to Shi'ism; Transoxania under Shaybanid rule remained Sunni. While Persians held sway in Iran, Turkish peoples and Chaghatay literary culture grew stronger in the east. Though it preserved a rich component of its Middle Eastern Islamic heritage, Transoxania under Uzbek rule was integrated once again into Inner Asia, and became the urban and agricultural center of Inner Asian-Islamic civilization.

Uzbek domination of Transoxania began with the Shaybanid dynasty (1500–98), and endured through successive dynasties until the establishment of a Russian protectorate in 1868. The Shaybanids were in many ways typical of Turkish conquest regimes. The conquering elite was divided between the ruling dynasty and its administrative, religious, and merchant supporters, and uymaq or tribal chiefs and their clients and retainers. The two segments of the elite struggled for their share of the spoils of power. The Khan himself kept a portion of the territory as state lands and a portion as *khasa* or private revenue estates which he controlled absolutely. A considerable portion of these lands was assigned as waqfs to Muslim religious leaders, and the rest was assigned to the nobility. It was divided into provinces called *wilayat*, and each wilayat was further subdivided into iqta's distributed to the supporters of the regional governors. The estates controlled by the members of the ruling family and the tribal chiefs (*beg*) were rated by *tumen*, probably a measure of the number of troops to be provided in return for the grant of revenues. Such grants of land tended to become hereditary, depriving the rulers of control. Strong rulers would seek to reestablish their power by seizing the iqta's, reducing the size of land grants, confiscating the excess properties of religious leaders, and paying

16 The Registan of Samarqand

their retainers in cash. In this respect the Shaybanid Khanate resembled the Safavid regime of Iran; the central rulers struggled against the uymaq and tribal forces that dominated the localities.

The Shaybanid Khanate, like earlier Muslim regimes, was legitimized by a combination of references to Sunni Islam and Persian literary culture. The Khans took the titles of *khalifat al-rahman* (Lieutenant of the Merciful God) and *imam al-zaman* (Ruler of the Times), quoted hadith to justify their rule, and became disciples of the Naqshbandi Sufi masters. Court poets wrote panegyrics, portraits were commissioned, and literary activity was patronized to depict the Shaybanids as Turkish–Persian princes. The *Shah-name* was translated into Turkish and many Iranian scholars came to Transoxania, where they found generous Uzbek patronage. Thus the Shaybanids maintained their own version of the Timurid heritage and created an Uzbek-dominated Irano-Islamic state.

The religious elites legitimized the regime. These elites included the qadis and the 'ulama' who taught in the madrasas, but ever since the Timurid period the leading position was held by the Naqshbandis. The Naqshbandis had their origin in the Tariqa-yi Khavajagan, or "way of the masters," founded by Yusuf Hamadhani (1048–1143). His disciple Ahmad al-Yasavi helped to spread Islam among Turkish peoples. Ahmad's tomb at Yasi was built by Timur as a gesture of obeisance to the Turkish Sufi tradition. His successor, 'Abd al-Khaliq Ghujdavani (d. 1220), a principal teacher of the Bukharan populace, introduced the crucial spiritual and social principle that later defined the Naqshbandi position: solitude in society – inner devotion expressed in outward social and political activity. The order then received its name from Baha' al-Din Naqshband (d. 1389). 'Ubaydallah (*khavaja*) Ahrar (1404–90), a wealthy farmer and merchant, who acquired a reputation for mysticism and magical powers, was the dominant figure in the late fifteenth century. He was an advisor of princes, a teacher of famous poets, and a revered master to the common people. He and other Sufis played a large political role in protecting Muslim populations from oppression, winning over the souls of kings, and defending the Muslim way of life. Sufis who had contacts in all reaches of society united the Inner Asian communities.

While Shaybanid rule constructed a variant form of Irano-Islamic state and society, larger historical forces were profoundly altering Inner Asia. For centuries the riches of Transoxania had been built upon trade and manufactures. Merchants, rich religious leaders, and government officials had participated in the trade with China and Russia. Bukhara, Samarqand, Tashkent, Yasi, and other towns were also centers of lively silk, cotton, leather, rug, jewelry, woodcarving, metal, and paper industries. Craft workers were organized into associations under the leadership of officials appointed by the rulers, but maintained a social and religious solidarity of their own based on the identification of guilds with patron saints, Sufi masters, and shared religious rituals.

In the course of the sixteenth century, however, the rise of the Safavids and the closure of Iranian routes to the Indian Ocean, the Russian conquest of the Volga region, and internal disorder and insecurity undermined the Inner Asian trade. The decline of Inner Asian routes was also hastened by the discovery of new sea routes between Europe and the Indies, and later by Russian expansion across Siberia to the Pacific which opened new routes to China. Inner Asia was cut off both from economic riches and from cultural stimulation. The roads that had once brought Buddhist, Christian, and other religious and cultural influences into the region fell into disuse. Once the links to the outside Muslim world were cut, provincialism, economic stagnation, and political fragmentation set in. The decline of Inner Asian trade compromised Shaybanid efforts to maintain a centralized state. It deprived the Khans of tax revenues, the merchants of profits, and the religious elites of investment opportunities. Power drifted into the hands of tribal and uymaq chieftains. From the end of the Shaybanid dynasty (1598) to the nineteenth century, centralized political administration was the rare and precarious achievement of exceptionally able rulers.

The nineteenth century, however, brought a revival. Bukhara (Transoxania), Khiva (Khwarizm), and Khokand (Farghana) each became the center of a newly flourishing Muslim society. In Bukhara, the Shaybanid dynasty had been succeeded by the Astrakhanid dynasty (1599–1785), which maintained only the barest continuity with Shaybanid traditions. It was in turn succeeded by the Mangit dynasty (1785–1920). Murad, the first ruler of the Mangit dynasty, ruled as Amir rather than Sultan, but also claimed an authority based on his conquests, his services as defender and executive of the Muslim community, and his personal charisma derived from being a descendant of the Prophet.

Under the Mangit dynasty Bukhara continued to follow the basic Shaybanid pattern. The state was ruled by the Amir who was served by a *qush begi*, or chief minister, and by Persian administrative officials. The territory was subdivided into wilayats and tax-collecting districts consisting of groups of villages or hamlets, each under the authority of an *aqsakal*, or elder. The territories and tax revenues were divided among the Amir and the leading notables. In the nineteenth century about 12 percent of the taxable land belonged to the ruler, 56 percent to the state, 24 percent to waqfs, and 8 percent to the rest of the population. State lands could be taxed in both cash and kind, the rates being adjusted to the unit of surface, the amount of water, and the type of crop, in order to approximate the value of the produce. State lands were commonly granted to tribal notables in return for which they promised to supply troops to the regime. They could also be given away as permanent rather than conditional gifts.

In the nineteenth century the Mangit dynasty struggled successfully to reduce the power of the tribal and uymaq chiefs. Amir Nasrallah (1826–60) removed hostile Uzbek chieftains from office and replaced them with Persian, Turkmen, and Arab functionaries. He also confiscated land, redistributed it to his supporters on a non-hereditary basis, and regulated the relations of landholders and peasants. This consolidation was aided by the sedentarization of Uzbek pastoralists which brought both men and land under the authority of the Amir. Still the local chiefs kept their castles, their retainers, and at least part of their revenues.

As in Iran and the Ottoman empire, Bukhara had a state-controlled religious administration under the authority of a Shaykh al-Islam (chief jurisconsult) and a *qadi kalan*, who was in control of judicial administration, colleges, elementary schools, and mosques. The qadis and sub-qadis were appointed to provincial districts. The muftis recorded evidence, interpreted the law, and sat in council to pass judgment on the conformity of state regulations to Muslim law. The scholars staffed more than 110 madrasas and taught in the elementary schools. They were organized in a hierarchy of three ranks under the titles *awraq, sadur*, and *sadr*, which were honorific distinctions given to scholars who had a madrasa education and who served as functionaries. People who held these ranks were entitled to *tankho* (rights to collect taxes) and gifts of land. A functionary called the ra'is served as the equivalent of the medieval *muhtasib*, enforcing honest market practices and good public morals. The ra'is could require delinquent Muslims to attend mosque or school in order to improve their religious practice and knowledge. Neighborhood religious life was under the direction of imams who presided over the recitation of prayers. The term "mullah" was applied to everyone who taught in schools, presided over prayers, and officiated at marriages, funerals, and other ceremonies. The whole of this elaborate religious organization was directly controlled by the Amir, who appointed the chief qadis and muftis, the professors in the madrasas, and other functionaries.

The social power of the 'ulama' of Bukhara was enhanced by their corporate organization. The religious establishment included privileged groups such as the sayyids, or descendants of the Prophet, the mirs, or descendants of the first three Caliphs, and the khwajas, or descendants of the early Arab conquerors. These groups formed endogamous lineages which were accorded popular veneration and religious prestige. Though not formally organized, the teaching 'ulama' also derived considerable political and social support from the mass of their students. Alongside the lineages, there were Sufi brotherhoods including the Naqshbandiya, the Qadiriya, and the Kubrawiya. The Sufi masters had a considerable following including their immediate disciples and the lay brothers attached to the orders. Sufis lived in khanaqas and worshiped at the shrines of venerated teachers. Sufi beggars, called Qalandaris, had their own community. Sufism was also important among the rural and nomadic populations, where it was strongly oriented to saint worship, healing, and use of amulets. Together, the holy lineages, the Sufi brotherhoods, and the student clienteles made a considerable force in Bukharan society.

Religious influence was also pervasive in the mentality of the Bukharan population. This was most commonly expressed in the veneration of tombs of saints. The relics of Timur in Samarqand were the object of pilgrimage, as were the tombs of the famous Naqshbandi teachers. When a shrine began to acquire a wide reputation it was commonly taken over by a Sufi order, which received the gifts of the pilgrims. The cult of 'Ali was widespread, even among Sunnis, for 'Ali was the patron saint of the canal-diggers and soldiers. Bibi Seshambeh (Lady Tuesday) and "Lady Solver of Problems" were the patron saints of women. Craft guilds were organized under patron saints and had collective rituals. Guild saints included

Noah, the saint of carpenters, and David, the saint of metalworkers. The Muslim populace also celebrated the *bayram* festivals (the 'ids of the sacrifice and of the end of Ramadan), and the birthday of the Prophet. Muslim spirituality, however, was tempered by a lively folk culture, which included secular entertainments by musicians, dancers, acrobats, jugglers, and gypsies. The populace also enjoyed tobacco, tea, and wine.

Despite the longevity of this state and society, important changes were taking place in the nineteenth century. First, the number of landless peasants was increasing and the state had difficulty in collecting taxes. As formerly nomadic Uzbeks were sedentarized, irrigation lagged behind the pace of settlement, partly because of the lack of skill among first-generation farmers, and partly because of political struggles over the control of water. While there were adequate lands for pasturage, lands suitable for cultivation were overpopulated.

The nineteenth-century consolidation of the Bukharan state also brought into being a new intermediary class between the ruling elites and the peasants and pastoralists. These included lower-ranking functionaries, scribes, secretaries, couriers, and policemen. Promoted by an active Bukharan commerce with Afghanistan, Iran, India, and Russia, the commercial bourgeoisie also became more important. Bukhara controlled the central Asian trade in raw silk and silk fabrics. Its merchants organized cotton industries and financed modest banking firms. With a growing merchant elite, private property and private land ownership became more important between 1840 and 1870.

Similarly, the territories of Farghana and Khwarizm were reorganized. Before the eighteenth century, Farghana had been divided into a number of small states governed by religious chiefs, but in the early eighteenth century migrant Uzbeks assumed power and forced surrounding Kazakh and Kirgiz tribes to submit to a new state with its capital at Khokand. The consolidation of the Khanate of Khokand was based on a flourishing economy in which irrigation agriculture, cotton and silk production, and trade with Kashgar, Bukhara, Khiva, and Russia were important sources of income. Khokand was the breakpoint where Russian and Chinese goods were sold and reshipped. The consolidation of state power, however, was inhibited by the struggle for control of land between the sedentary Persianized population and Qipchaq tribal peoples. Khwarizm went through a parallel phase of state consolidation and commercial development in the nineteenth century. However, the efforts of Muhammad Rahim I (1806–25) to centralize the Khwarizmian state were undermined by the constant struggle with the Turkmen nomadic population supported by Sufi holy men.

Undermined by conflicts among the ruling dynasties, uymaq and tribal chiefs, and pastoral and sedentary populations, the Inner Asian societies became prey to Russian expansion. The governing factors in Russian expansion were the ambitions of its generals and the willingness of the Tsars to tolerate their initiative and benefit from their successes. Motivated by the desire to secure its borders, control trade, and exploit rich agricultural lands, Russia had already absorbed the Tatar and

Kazakh steppes. Further expansion would give Russia political and trading advantages in relations with Iran, India, and China and enable her to forestall potential British rivalry.

From their bases on the Kazakh steppes the Russians occupied Tashkent in 1865, Samarqand in 1868, and forced Bukhara to pay indemnities and open up to Russian trade. Khokand was absorbed in 1876, the Transcaspian province in 1881, and the Pamirs were taken in 1895. Great Britain also took an interest in Inner Asia as a remote extension of its Indian sphere of influence. At the Congress of Berlin (1878) and by the treaty of 1907, Central Asia, Afghanistan, and India were divided into Russian and British spheres of influence. Thus, by the late nineteenth century the Russians had rounded out their Inner Asian empire and had become the masters of Tatar, Kazakh, Uzbek, and other Inner Asian peoples.

EASTERN TURKESTAN AND CHINA

Eastern Turkestan was also a region of nomadic peoples and important agricultural and oasis cities. From the time of the Mongol conquests, eastern Turkestan, parts of the northern steppes, and parts of Transoxania were the nominal domain of the Chaghatay Khans, successors of Chinggis Khan. In the middle of the fourteenth century the Chaghatays were restricted to eastern Turkestan. Chaghatay suzerainty was rarely more than nominal. Nomadic chieftains and the rulers of the oasis towns generally maintained their autonomy. Nonetheless, eastern Turkestan came into the domain of Turkish-Islamic culture. This was the result of a long, slow, and little-documented process in which Mongol peoples were converted to Islam and won over to the use of Turkish languages. Muslim rulers tried to use Islam as legitimization for warfare against non-Muslim peoples. By the time that Komul (Hami) came under Muslim rule in 1513, Sunni Islam was widely accepted in the Tarim basin and Chaghatay was spreading as a literary language. Mosques appeared along the trade routes between Inner Asia and China. Muslim expansion, however, was checked by Oirats (Mongols), who accepted Buddhism at the end of the sixteenth century. By then, however, much of the populace of Inner Asia outside Mongolia and Tibet was Muslim or under Muslim suzerainty.

The most striking manifestation of the influence of Islam was the role of khwajas, or Sufis who traced their biological as well as their spiritual lineage to the Prophet Muhammad or to the early Caliphs. The earliest of these figures were probably itinerant holy men, faith healers, and miracle workers who in the fourteenth century acquired local prestige, gained a livelihood from gifts of tithes and landed estates, and married into prominent families. In many ways they resembled the sharifs of Morocco by combining Sufi qualities with descent from the Prophet. The khwajas gradually attained a spiritual ascendancy over secular rulers, all of whom became their disciples. The descendants of Makhdum-i A'zam (d. 1540), the spiritual master of Bukhara, became the principal advisors to local rulers in Kashgar and Yarkand, and eventually the rulers of these cities. From 1678 to 1756 Kashgar was ruled by a dynasty of khwajas who claimed descent from Muhammad, headship of a Sufi order, and a blood relationship to Chinggis Khan. Thus the khwajas united spiritual and political authority. Nonetheless, the elites of these oasis cities were divided into bitterly hostile factions. Factional wars eventually led the khwajas to appeal to nomadic peoples for political support – a measure that eventually cost the oases their independence.

While Chaghatay Khans, khwajas, and tribal chiefs ruled eastern Turkestan, a new Oirat-Mongol empire called the Dzungarian Confederation, the last of the great Inner Asian nomadic empires, was being formed. The Dzungarian Confederation had its origins between 1400 and 1550, when Mongolian peoples were cut off from the markets of China and were forced to move westward and northward into eastern Turkestan, the northern steppes, and Transoxania. By the early seventeenth century an Oirat Khanate had come into existence – its power based on trade and dominance of peasants – and its leaders adopted Tibetan Lamaism as the religion of the confederation. Buddhism helped, as did Islam, to foster political unity among pastoral peoples, and to join them to sedentary populations. Expanding westward the Oirats attacked the Kirgiz and the Uzbeks, their competitors for pasture and access to cattle markets in Transoxania, and conquered the Tarim basin. Allied with the religious factions of Kashgar and Yarkand the Oirats took control of the oasis cities and appointed the khwajas as their vassals.

Oirat expansion, however, provoked Chinese intervention. China had long regarded Inner Asia as part of its inherent domain, and was concerned for the protection of its frontiers against barbarian incursions. The Chinese considered Inner Asian rulers as their vassals. In the guise of tributes and exchanges of gifts, China imported horses, furs, metals, and jade in exchange for paper, textiles, drugs, tea, and porcelain. The Chinese pursued their commercial and diplomatic policy under the assumption that they possessed cultural and political supremacy and considered all exchanges as a form of tribute. By 1759 the Chinese defeated the Dzungarians, took control of the oasis cities, drove out the khwajas, and absorbed eastern Turkestan. In addition the Chinese made the eastern Kazakhs and Khokand their tributaries. With these new vassals the Chinese exchanged silk, tea, and porcelain for horses, cattle, and Russian products.

The conquest of eastern Turkestan brought a new Muslim population under Chinese control. The earliest Muslims in China were Arab troops coming from Inner Asia and Muslim merchants who settled in Canton in the eighth century. Though permanent residents, these Muslims were considered foreigners, subjects of far-off Muslim rulers, and enjoyed an extraterritorial jurisdiction under their own officials. The Mongol conquests and the formation of the Yuan dynasty (1271–1368) reinforced the Muslim population. The Mongols employed Muslim administrators and tax collectors, encouraged trade between China and Inner Asia, and sponsored the migration and settlement of Muslims not only in northwestern but also in southwestern China and Yunnan. In many cities, Muslims, living under the leadership of their own Shaykh al-Islam and qadis, occupied separate quarters provided with mosques and bazaars. Under the Ming dynasty (1368–1644) Muslims served the emperor as astronomers, diviners, translators, postal officials, and caravaners.

In the Ming period the name Hui was applied to Chinese of Muslim faith, both to assimilated foreign Muslims and to Chinese converts to Islam. Muslims adopted the speech, names, manners, clothing, and other outward features of being Chinese. Muslim writers in this period attempted to show how Islam and Confucianism could be reconciled and how Chinese mythology and Islamic history were congruent. Still, Muslims retained an inner Muslim identity defined by their prayer rituals, Arabic names, and communal affiliations. Under the authority of an imam, Muslims had their own mosques, schools, charities, and endowments. Chinese Muslims, however, were not an organized group. There was no unity among the numerous different congregations, and the Hui were widely dispersed. The Manchu dynasty dealt with the Hui by assurances of protection and threats of punishment, and a pragmatic policy of suppressing resistance and tolerating religious differences. As long as Muslim identity did not interfere with their outward conformity it was acceptable to the Chinese. This coexistence lasted until the great Muslim revolts of the nineteenth century.

The newly conquered Muslim population of eastern Turkestan was very different from the assimilated Hui. Turkestani Muslims were mainly Uighurs and Kazakhs, and were not assimilated to the Chinese way of life. Under Chinese suzerainty, the Islamic identity of both the urban and the nomadic populations was fully maintained. Kashgar was the site of the much-venerated tomb of Hazrat Afaq and his family. Beggars and dervishes lived in the cemeteries; religious colonies surrounded the tomb. Pre-Islamic survivals such as fluttering flags, yak tails, and heaps of horns marked the reverence in which this place was held. While the Muslims of China proper had become a Chinese religious minority, the Muslims of Inner Asia remained a politically subordinate non-Chinese population.

The Chinese administration of eastern Turkestan was based on a superstructure of Chinese garrisons and administrative officers in the oasis towns of Komul, Urumchi, Kashgar, Khotan, and other places, who governed through local Muslim chieftains (begs). The begs collected taxes, controlled water supplies, administered justice, and maintained order. They were granted land and serfs to pay the costs of their offices, and then tried to increase these holdings and to convert them into private properties. Chinese rule introduced a period of security and commercial prosperity. By the 1820s the cultivated lands in the oasis district of Kashgar had doubled, and Chinese peasants were being brought in to reclaim wastelands.

Inner Asian Muslims, however, never fully accepted Chinese rule. A Muslim religious movement, the so-called New Teachings (Hsin-chiao), a variant of the Naqshbandi order, was introduced by Ma Ming-hsin, who came to China in 1761. He had studied in Yarkand and Kashgar, and propagated a form of Sufism expressed in loud chanting of the Quran, prayers with dance-like head-shaking and foot-stamping, belief in miracles and visions, and worship of saints. New sect members believed that faith was more important than family. They were reformers who were hostile to the old practices and to the political elites. Ma attracted a following in Kansu province, and, in 1781, rebelled against Chinese rule. The movement was soon repressed, but this provoked later revolts by Kirgiz warriors. The political unrest in eastern Turkestan tempted the khwajas, the former rulers of Kashgar who had taken refuge in Khokand, to try to regain their former possession. Between the 1820s and 1862 they led a series of attacks on Chinese territory, supported by Kirgiz and local Uighurs. The rulers of Khokand also aspired to a larger sphere of influence in eastern Turkestan. Chafing at Chinese political and trading restrictions, Khokand demanded the right to control the caravan trade and to appoint tax collectors in Kashgar. Chinese concessions only led to an expansion of Khokand's trade and influence in eastern Turkestan, and to covert Khokandi support for the aspirations of the khwajas.

The weakness of the Ch'ing dynasty (1644–1911) in eastern Turkestan was only a symptom of the general breakdown of the Chinese empire. Beset by the Taiping and numerous provincial rebellions, the Ch'ing were forced to allow their subjects to organize local military forces and yet had to press them for increased taxes. Chinese hostility to Muslims and demands for their assimilation also increased with the breakdown of the Ch'ing. Ch'ing misrule provoked Muslim rebellions in Yunnan, Shensi, Kansu, and eastern Turkestan. Hanafi law, which legitimizes rebellion if non-Muslim law is enforced or if non-Muslim territory separates Muslims from each other, provided a legal basis for secret societies and revolts. Muslim religious and political consciousness was stimulated by an outpouring of Islamic literature stressing the importance of emulating the teachings of the Prophet, ritual purity, and fulfilling God's commands. This nineteenth-century literature stressed the superiority of Islam and attacked Chinese civilization rather than attempting to be reconciled to it. Chinese Muslim scholars no longer insisted on the similarities of Islam and Confucianism, and urged Muslims to abide by Islamic law and to avoid Chinese customs. The nineteenth-century Muslim rebellions were also abetted by reformist Muslim influences coming from India or other parts of Inner Asia.

A series of Muslim rebellions in Yunnan culminated in the formation of an independent Muslim state from 1856 to 1873 under the leadership of Tu Wen-hsiu, who called himself Commander of the Faithful and Sultan. The principal Muslim rebellion in Shensi province was led by Ma Hua-lung, who represented the new teaching movement. Here Muslim secession took on a peculiarly Chinese quality. Ma Hua-lung adopted the name Tsung-ta A-hung or General Grand A-hung, which is a Muslim name, but when written in Chinese characters means "the horse became a dragon," and thus evoked Chinese as well as Muslim symbols. The new sect adopted Chinese popular symbols as the basis of a Muslim revivalism with separatist political implications. Under his leadership, Kucha and Ili rebelled, cutting off Chinese communications with Kashgar.

Taking advantage of Chinese weakness, the Khan of Khokand sent the surviving khwajas of Kashgar with a military subordinate named Ya'qub Beg to take control of Kirgiz and Uighur peoples. Ya'qub quickly conquered most of eastern Turkestan and the oasis states. He ruled in the name of the Shari'a, enforced Muslim law, and gave large gifts to mosques. However, he was dependent on Khokandis, Afghans, and others for his army. In a direct affront to Chinese authority, he recognized Ottoman suzerainty; the Ottomans acknowledged him as Amir in 1873.

Ya'qub's fate and that of the Muslim rebellions was linked to Russian and British maneuvers. In the nineteenth century eastern Turkestan was the object of Russian and British rivalry; both of them were interested in trading advantages and the protection of their respective territories in Russia and India. Generally the British planned to cooperate with friendly local rulers to check Russian advances, but in the late 1860s they backed China's efforts to suppress local rebellions, for fear that the dismemberment of China would hamper British access to Inner Asia. Russian occupation of the Ili province in 1871 led the British to see Ya'qub Beg as a potential buffer against the possibility of further Russian penetration of Inner Asia. In 1874 they supplied him with a small number of rifles. A revival of Chinese power under the leadership of Governor Tso Tsung-t'ang (1812–85) put an end both to Ya'qub and to British concerns. Tso reorganized Chinese forces, reconquered Shensi and Kansu, took Aksu and Kashgar by 1878, and suppressed the new teaching. In 1881 China and Russia negotiated a treaty which restored the Ili province to China and paved the way for the reorganization of eastern Turkestan as a province under civilian Chinese administration. Named Xinjiang, it became part of China in 1884. By then all of Inner Asia had come under either Russian or Chinese rule. It remained only to define the borders between Russia and China in 1892 and between Russia and Afghanistan in 1895. The expansion of the two great imperial powers brought an end to 3,000 years of nomadic migration and empires.

Thus, Inner Asian societies, until their conquest by Russia and China, exemplified several types of Muslim society. On the northern steppes and in eastern Turkestan Tatar, Uzbek, Kazakh, Kirgiz, Uighur, and other peoples were organized in family units and loose confederations. The uymaq or tribe, an alliance of family and clan units, was the effective political unit. Larger-order Khanates and hordes were fragile coalitions. Nevertheless, pastoral peoples conquered the sedentary areas. In the sedentarized districts of Transoxania, Farghana, Kashgaria, and other oases, they founded centralized states, legitimized partly in Muslim and partly in cosmopolitan cultural terms. In urban areas Islam was crucial to the viability of states. The Mangit dynasty was virtually the expression of the 'ulama' of Bukhara, who controlled judicial administration and education and whose organized bodies of sayyids, khwajas, mirs, Sufis, students, and guilds made up the body politic. In Kashgar, dynasties of khwajas ruled directly. Muslim society in sedentary Inner Asia was built around the tripartite division of power and authority among tribal, state, and religious elites, but Russian and Chinese rule would, as colonial rule did everywhere in the Muslim world, profoundly change this historical configuration.

CHAPTER 18

THE INDIAN SUBCONTINENT: THE DELHI SULTANATES AND THE MUGHAL EMPIRE

In the Indian subcontinent Islam was introduced into an already developed civilization defined by agriculture, urbanization, higher religions, and complex political regimes. India was defined by the caste system, by Brahmanic Hinduism and Buddhist religions, and by Rajput and other Hindu political elites. In the past there had been great empires, but on the eve of the Muslim invasion India was divided into numerous small states. The Muslim conquests brought a new elite and a new level of political integration, and began the process of generating a new culture blending universal Muslim concepts and symbols of statecraft, cosmopolitan artistic pursuits such as architecture and painting, and regional motifs. Muslim religio-communal orientations encompassed all of the principal varieties of 'ulama' scholasticism, Sufi–Shari'a synthesis, shrine worship, and reformism. In India, as opposed to Iran or the Ottoman empire, a pluralistic religious society escaped bureaucratization and state control. The special cultural qualities of Indian-Islamic civilization, and the autonomy and plurality of religious tendencies, made it a distinctive variant of the universal Islamic pattern.

THE MUSLIM CONQUESTS AND THE DELHI SULTANATES

The history of Islamic societies in the subcontinent goes back to the Arab invasions of 711–13 when Muslim rule was established in Sind, but the definitive Muslim conquest came from the post-'Abbasid military regimes in Afghanistan. The Ghaznavids captured Lahore in 1030 and plundered North India. In the late twelfth century, the Ghaznavids were replaced by local mountain chieftains under the leadership of the Ghurid dynasty, who began the systematic conquest of India. Between 1175 and 1192 they occupied Uch, Multan, Peshawar, Lahore, and Delhi. In 1206, one of the Ghurid generals, Qutb al-Din Aybeg, the conqueror of Delhi, made himself independent and founded the first of a succession of dynasties collectively known as the Delhi Sultanates (1206–1526). Each dynasty represented a different segment of

Table 15. *Muslim India: outline chronology*

Ghaznavids (begin the Muslim conquest of India)	
Afghanistan	977–1186
Khurasan	999–1040
Ghurids	
Afghanistan	1186–1215
India	1173–1206
Delhi sultanates	
Dynasty of Aybeg	1206–1290
Khalji	1290–1320
Tughluq	1320–1413
Sayyid	1414–1451
Lodi	1451–1526
Independent Muslim regimes	
Bengal	1356–1576
Kashmir	1346–1589
Gujarat	1407–1572
Jawnpur	1394–1479
Malwa	1401–1531
Deccan (Bahmanids)	1347–1527
Deccan (Faruqis)	1370–1601
Mughal empire	1526–1858
Suri dynasty	1540–1555
Akbar I	1556–1605
Aurangzeb	1658–1707
British victory at Plassey	1757
Britain becomes paramount power	1818
British Raj	1858–1947

the Afghan–Turkish Inner Asian military lords and their clients, the victors of the moment in the constant jockeying for power. The successive dynasties made continued efforts to centralize state power, but none of them achieved absolute political control; each was merely senior in a political society composed of numerous local Muslim and Hindu lords. Each dealt with the problem of establishing an Islamic state in a region of profound Hindu and Buddhist culture. Out of their collective achievement came a distinct kind of Muslim civilization.

Under 'Ala al-Din Khalji (1290–1316), the Delhi regime reestablished its imperial status, and extended its power to Gujarat, Rajasthan, the Deccan, and some parts of South India. 'Ala al-Din tried also to strengthen the agrarian administration. Before the Muslim conquest agrarian taxation was based on the principle that peasants had a duty to cultivate the land and to pay the ruler a share of the produce. The share extracted by the ruler could be assessed by measuring the land and taxing each measured unit by a fixed amount or by dividing the actual crop. Much less common was a contract under which peasants paid a fixed tax regardless of the size of the crop. Local rulers generally dealt with the villages as a unit, and collected the taxes with the assistance of local headmen who would assess the individual peasants. The ruler commonly assigned his tax rights to pay the salaries of his soldiers or administrative employees. In 1300, in the core areas of northern India, 'Ala al-Din Khalji fixed a new standard of revenue demand at one-half the produce, abolished the perquisites of local chiefs, and confiscated all existing land grants in an effort to deprive local lords of their military and financial power. He also controlled the grain market in Delhi, where grain was distributed at controlled prices to the soldiers and the urban population.

The Khalji regime barely survived the death of its founder; it was succeeded in 1320 by the Tughluq dynasty (1320–1413). Muhammad b. Tughluq (1325–51) attempted to counterbalance the political influence of well-established Muslim families by cultivating the support of newly immigrant Turkish warriors. He was the first Sultan to appoint non-Muslims to military and government offices, participate in local festivals, and permit the construction of Hindu temples. To maintain the Muslim credentials of his regime, Muhammad b. Tughluq followed a strong pro-Sunni policy. He stressed his identity as a Muslim warrior by defending India against the Mongols. He gave formal adherence to the Shari'a, accepted the 'Abbasid Caliph in Cairo as head of the Muslim umma, appointed a chief judge, and imposed the head tax on non-Muslims. He was generally favorable to the 'ulama'. His was the first Muslim regime to integrate Turkish warlords, Hindu feudatories, and Muslim scholars in the political elite.

The Tughluq empire, however, disintegrated rapidly under pressure of revolts by governors, local resistance in the Deccan, and the formation of independent Hindu kingdoms. In the early sixteenth century the struggles over the Delhi Sultanate led to the intervention of Babur (a descendant of Timur), a warrior adventurer and local lord in Farghana, who was for a short time ruler of Samarqand and then of Kabul, Herat, and Qandahar. In 1526 Babur defeated the Lodis at the battle of Panipat, and established himself as the ruler of Delhi. His son Humayun lost the throne to the Afghan lord Sher Shah (1540–55), but then reestablished himself in Delhi and Agra, and handed on his rule to Akbar. Akbar was the true founder of the Mughal empire.

For the Delhi Sultanate, an offshoot of Muslim expansion sustained by a small and factious military aristocracy that ruled over the vast Indian subcontinent, cultural and ideological cohesion was essential. To soothe the factional quarrels, maintain solidarity among the Muslims, and integrate the Hindu lords into the governing elite, the Delhi Sultanate elaborated its own cultural and political identity. This was at once Muslim and cosmopolitan, built upon both Persian and Indic languages, literature and arts, brought together into a new Indian-Islamic civilization.

This cultural policy, however, took time to develop. At the outset the Delhi Sultanate was aggressively Muslim. The first gesture of the Muslim conquest was to destroy major Hindu temples and replace them with great mosques, whose size, design, and inscriptions were symbols of Muslim domination. The mosque of Quwwat al-Islam in Delhi incorporated stones and iron pillars from Hindu monuments in order to symbolize that an Islamic order had superseded a Hindu one. The

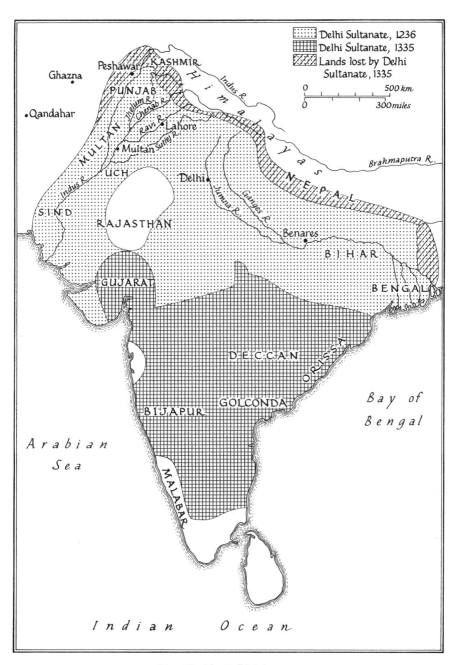

Map 18   The Delhi Sultanates

Qutb Minar, a towering brick structure, signaled the presence of a Muslim community. The Delhi regimes stressed allegiance to the Caliphate and support for the judicial establishment of the 'ulama'. Some rulers, such as 'Ala al-Din, sought Sufi rather than 'ulama' support for the Sultans, since the Sufis shared a hierarchical concept of political society. Just as the Sufi saints stood at the apex of the universal spiritual order, the Sultans stood at the head of secular society.

The Muslim concept of kingship derived substantially from the Iranian Muslim tradition. Barani's (d. c. 1360) treatise on kingship began with a section on the moral purpose of human existence. Men are created, he argued, with a mixture of vices and virtues; to cause the good to prevail, the ruler must change the dispositions of his subjects and help them act as true Muslims. He must himself follow the teachings of the Prophet, enforce the Shari'a, suppress rebellions, punish heretics, subordinate the unbelievers, and protect the weak against the strong. A Muslim king is responsible for order, for stability, and for the safety and prosperity of his subjects. Barani's moral principles were followed by practical advice on the management of the army, the treasury, and the subordinate officials. The ruler, he said, must appoint to office people who have the requisite virtues; rank should be determined by moral qualifications, for the ruler and his servants set an example of good behavior for all subjects and create the conditions that make it possible for them to fulfill their religious duties. Thus, his political theory aimed at the creation of a social order that brought men into accord with God's command by cultivating moral virtues in the governing authorities.

The Delhi regime also inherited pre-Islamic Persian concepts of kingship that allowed for the exaltation of rulers, and prompted them to demonstrate their authority in lavish public works. Sher Shah, for example, constructed forts, mosques, and caravansaries for travelers along the main highways where food and fodder were provided for troops and merchants. He also built splendid monumental tombs for his grandfather, his father, and himself to legitimize the reign of a parvenu. The tombs were placed in strategic locations as an assertion of legitimacy, and near the tombs of saints to give religious respectability.

Despite its Muslim emphasis, the Delhi regime also had substantial appeal to Hindu lords. The Muslim emphasis upon loyalty to the ruler, patron–client relations, and the virtues of service and honor were consistent with Hindu political ideals. Muslim recognition of the hierarchy of ranks validated the organization of Hindu society. Both cultures accepted the dominance of kings, though the meaning of kingship was different. For Hindus, the ruler upholds the order of the world by virtue of who he is – the *axis mundi*; for Muslims, he fulfills his role by virtue of what he does – implementing the Shari'a. Only in the fourteenth century did the Tughluq dynasty begin to absorb Hindu motifs into Muslim architecture as a symbol of the Muslim appropriation of Hindu political authority. Tughluqid architecture borrowed such design features as the Hindu *chatri*, or kiosk, heavy stone balustrades, eaves, block pillars, and capitals.

The historic task of forming a shared cosmopolitan culture was furthered in the various provincial Muslim regimes. In Bengal, Sufi writers and Muslim rulers adopted the local languages. The Hindu classic, *Mahabharata*, and Arabic and Persian classics, including stories from the *Arabian Nights*, were translated into Bengali at the order of Muslim rulers. Muslim poets also wrote in Bengali about Hindu deities and myths, using Arabic and Persian loan words. This synthesis of languages and literatures was the basis for the emergence of a new literary Bengali language. Similarly, the independent Sultans of Gujarat (1407–1572) patronized the regional languages instead of Sanskrit or Persian.

In the Deccan, Bijapur and Golconda were important centers for the synthesis of Islam and local cultures. The Bahmanid regime in Bijapur (1347–1527) ruled a land that lay between Marathi-speaking peoples to the north and Kannada speakers to the south. In each of these regions there were local devotional movements and strong attachments to local saints. In neither was the Hindu Sanskritic tradition strong. Here a Muslim regime encouraged the integration of elements of Marathi and Kannada culture and the formation of a new regional language, Dakhni, strongly influenced by Persian. The local Muslim elites developed a shared culture for the diverse linguistic and religious elements of the Bijapur state, defined in opposition to the northern regimes.

In Golconda the synthesis of Muslim and Hindu aristocracies and cultures developed under the Qutb Shah dynasty (1491–1688). This regime helped to integrate the Muslim and Telugu-speaking elites by patronizing the local warrior aristocracy, providing tax-free lands for Saivite Hindu temples, and sponsoring a regional culture based on the bilingual use of Telugu and Persian. Thus, while the Delhi Sultanate leaned to Muslim supremacy, the provincial Muslim regimes fostered the integration of Muslim and Hindu cultures and the formation of an Indian version of Islamic civilization.

CONVERSION AND THE MUSLIM COMMUNITIES

Under the cover of the conquest, Muslim scholars, scribes, Sufis, poets, and intellectuals flocked to India, seeking the patronage of the new regimes, organizing colleges and khanaqas, and opening the way for the conversion of Indian peoples to Islam. Conversion was relatively limited; it seems doubtful that more than 20 or 25 percent of the populace of the subcontinent ever became Muslim. Muslims were concentrated in the Indus Valley, northwest India, and Bengal. In the fourteenth century Islam spread across the Brahmaputra River into Assam, and was represented in the Deccan. While the aristocracy was composed of Muslims who came from Afghanistan, Iran, and Inner Asia, Indian converts were mostly from the lower classes. Conversions commonly occurred when Muslim lords endowed a mosque or khanaqa and invited scholars or Sufis to take up residence. Around the lord and his sponsored religious teachers gathered peasants and service people who took on the religion of their masters. However, the Turkish and Afghan warrior elite was probably hostile to conversions of nobles lest they compete for political power. Their position was similar to that of the early Arab regimes in the Middle East, for whom Islam signified the suzerainty and solidarity of an otherwise factious ruling caste.

Furthermore, the growth of cities broke down caste and geographical barriers to social interaction. People who had given up their social and political status, and who were ambitious to make careers under a new regime, such as itinerant merchants, workers and peddlers, fugitive peasants and vagabonds, found in Islam a unifying ideology. Sufi khanaqas were often established on the outskirts of towns and villages where they might appeal to lower-caste elements. In North India they were the centers for the birth of Urdu as the lingua franca among Muslims and between Muslims and non-Muslim populations.

In some cases conversions to Islam were correlated with important changes in regional societies. In the northwest provinces, where the Jats, a hunter-gatherer and pastoral population, were coming into contact with a state-based agricultural society and a literate form of civilization, Islam became the religion of people who were becoming peasants. In Bengal, conversion similarly represented the change of hunter-gatherer and pastoral peoples to a sedentary way of life. Before the advent of Islam, Hinduism was well established in West Bengal, where rice culture supported a Brahmin religious aristocracy and Hindu temples. In East Bengal, Brahmin and caste influences were weaker, and Buddhism was the dominant religion. Under Muslim rule, East and West Bengal were integrated under a single regime, and the new political environment was permeated by Islamic symbols. Under the leadership of Muslim landlords, warriors, and Sufis, the process of agricultural expansion continued into East Bengal, making converts out of newly sedentarized peoples.

The influence of Sufis was crucial in the spread of Islam. The story of Farid al-Din Ganj-i Shakr (d. 1245), one of the early heads of the Chisti order, is illuminating. Baba Farid settled in a place now called Pak-pattan, a village in the North Indian plain. A small dusty place of mud houses and a few shops, peopled by men reputed to be illiterate, superstitious, and quarrelsome, it had a reputation for robbing travelers. Baba Farid came to this village seeking escape from the distractions and temptations of the court in Delhi. He had for years practiced a rigorous asceticism, denying himself worldly satisfactions and concentrating his attention upon devotion to God. At Pak-pattan he stopped at the edge of the village under a clump of trees, unfolded his prayer rug, and lived for days, weeks, and perhaps months in solitude, subsisting on small gifts of food which he did not acknowledge. He spent all his time in prayer.

After a time people recognized him as a holy man. The poor came for cures and amulets, and advice on family matters. They asked him to intercede with the landlords and the tax collectors. Officials, landowners, scholars, and the rich, weary of the emptiness of the world, went to consult him. Tribal chiefs visited to ask his help in negotiating feuds. Merchants sought his protection to pass through the town unmolested. Other holy men, Muslim and non-Muslim, sat in his presence. As his reputation grew, Baba Farid acquired enough gifts to build a hospice. Disciples came to live with him. Stories circulated about his wisdom; he came to be venerated. People converted to Islam in his name. Thus an other-worldly man acquired worldly power. Renunciation was the basis of his worldly success. Because he no longer cared for the ordinary things of life, he was able to see matters in context and measure their relative importance. Because he did not care for himself, he was a good judge of other people's motives and interests; he was, therefore, successful as a teacher, healer, and mediator.

His followers did not see this as ordinary wisdom. They saw his powers as a sign of God's blessings being channeled into this world. They believed that he possessed baraka, the capacity to know things unknown and to dispense blessings which are ultimately only in God's gift. When he died, his grave became the repository of his baraka. The people visited his tomb, touched and kissed the holy place, made gifts and sacrifices, and celebrated seasonal festivals and his birth and death days.

Behind the mystical and magical powers of individual saints such as Baba Farid lay deep cultural sympathies which made the person of the Sufi and his teachings attractive to non-Muslims. The Sufi who renounced worldly gain, devoted himself to prayer, and expressed himself through poetry corresponded in the popular imagination to the Bhakti devotional preacher who had given up his past life and had access to higher wisdom. Sufism stood for detachment within the world rather than renunciation of the world. The Sufis married and raised children, cared for the community, and sought to bring justice and ethical values into human affairs. Similarly, Indic philosophies valued a detached style of life that permitted the believer to outwardly fulfill the complex requirements of the social and moral code, and yet inwardly be free for spiritual progress. The masses saw in the Sufis the kind of spiritual achievement they had come to expect from the yogis.

Sufi teachings and practices also corresponded to the Hindu metaphysical concept of the universe. The monotheism of the Sufis was not a surprise to Hindus, because the Saivite and Vaisnavite traditions had monotheistic trends. At the same time the claims of the Sufi masters to be the concrete manifestation of the powers of God were compatible with Hindu polytheism. Moreover, the Sufis did not wholly exclude the worship of local gods within and alongside Islam. Indeed, the veneration of Sufi graves and their annual festivals corresponded in some cases with the Hindu calendar. In Bengal and the Punjab Muslims celebrated Hindu festivals, worshiped at Hindu shrines, offered gifts to Hindu gods and goddesses, and celebrated marriages in Hindu fashion. Hindus who converted to Islam retained many of their past beliefs and practices; many Hindus venerated Muslim saints without change of religious identity.

Thus, in popular religious culture, the boundaries between Islam and Hinduism were more flexible than in formal doctrine. Islam entered into the Indian environment sometimes by assimilating converts into a new communal identity and religious beliefs and sometimes by being assimilated into the indigenous culture. Conversion to Islam was a subtle matter in which Islamic elements might be added to an existing complex of Hindu religious beliefs, without change of world-view or social identity, or in which the convert could make a revolutionary change in both beliefs and allegiances.

Yet, despite considerable success in the conversion of Hindus to Islam, the great majority of the subcontinent's peoples remained Hindus. While the Middle East and Indonesia were almost totally converted, India, like the Balkans, remained substantially non-Muslim. There are several reasons for this. First was the thin veneer of the Muslim conquest in India. The Muslims were small bands of warriors who were not, as in the case of the Arab or Turkish conquests of the Middle East, backed by large numbers of settlers. The Muslims established a political elite, but they could not colonize the country. Second, the pre-Islamic political structure of India remained intact. The previous regime was highly decentralized, composed of local lords and a Brahmin religious elite who retained local political power under Muslim suzerainty. The caste social structure under Brahmin leadership was also resistant to change. As in the Balkans, the thinness of the governing elite, the confirmation of local lords, and the protection of the non-Muslim populations all served to maintain a continuity of non-Muslim identities.

THE VARIETIES OF INDIAN ISLAM

The combination of migrations from the Middle East and Inner Asia and local conversions gave the subcontinent all varieties of Islam. The 'ulama' often became part of the state establishment. The Sultans appointed a chief sadr, a chief qadi, and a Shaykh al-Islam; the post of *sadr-i jahan* was created in 1248 to supervise most religious activities, including justice, prayer, markets, and endowed funds. The chief justice administered the court system, and qadis were appointed at provincial and district levels. Subordinate sadrs dealt with local land and registration matters and qadis dealt with civil and criminal cases. Preachers and prayer leaders were also state-appointed and state-paid officials. Madrasas were established and the teachers salaried by the government. The curriculums of the Mu'izzi and Nasiriya madrasas included Arabic, hadith, law, logic, theology, literature, and mysticism. However, despite the formal Muslim establishment, the influence of the 'ulama' on the general society was very limited. Rather, Sufism played the critical role in the creation of a Muslim community in India. Sufi warriors flocked to India looking for religious merit in the holy war. As on the Ottoman frontiers, they became the leaders of migrating Turkish warrior bands. The Kazaruniya order helped to establish Islam in Kashmir. Rural mystics spread the Sufi notion of the universal hierarchy of saints and the practices of veneration of tombs. Malamatis and Qalandaris, individual wandering dervishes, exemplified rejection of the worldly way of life.

The tariqat were represented by the Suhrawardiya, the Chistiya, and the Shattariya, who established extensive networks of khanaqas throughout North India.

The disciples of 'Umar al-Suhrawardi, under the leadership of Shaykh Baha' al-Din Zakariya (d. 1267), brought the order to India. Multan was their main base, but the order was also important in Uch and Gujarat. The Chisti order was introduced into India by Mu'in al-Din Hasan Chist who, born in southeastern Iran in 1141, settled in India, and died at Ajmer in 1236. His order spread throughout Rajasthan, Bengal, and the Deccan, and was especially important in the northern Gangetic plain and the Punjab. The Chisti order accepted the doctrine of Ibn al-'Arabi concerning the unity of being, and preached a non-political and non-violent philosophy.

The Shattari order was introduced into India by Shaykh 'Abdallah Shattar (d. 1485), who toured the Ganges Valley dressed like a king, with followers in military uniforms, carrying banners and beating drums, in order to propagate his beliefs. His followers regarded him as being in direct contact with the saints, the Prophet, and with God himself, a man possessed of both earthly and spiritual power and absolved by his detachment from the world from all ordinary legal and social norms. The Shattari order appealed to the rich and was closely identified with the state elites. It withered away when it lost the favor of the Mughal emperor Akbar.

The several orders represented variations on the system of Sufism that had developed in the Middle East. The distinctive feature of these movements was the organization of a brotherhood built around the total devotion and obedience of the disciples to the master. The central experience of the disciple was to be initiated into the discipline and spiritual technique taught by the master. Once the novice had been initiated there was a ceremonial passing on of the cloak, or khirqa, of the master to his disciple. The Sufis believed in the miraculous powers of their saints, and that the very order of the universe was upheld by a hierarchy of masters, the leading one of whom was called the qutb. Thus, Shaykh Nizam al-Din Auliya (d. 1325), one of the founding fathers of the Chisti order, was perceived by his followers to be the head of a spiritual hierarchy who ruled a kingdom parallel to that of temporal rulers. The great Sufi leaders presided over courts that rivaled those of temporal Sultans; the patched cloak, the prayer carpet, the wooden sandals, and the rosary were the mystics' insignias of chieftainship. The head of the order dispatched his khalifas, or lieutenants, to various provinces, and they, in turn, appointed subordinates to bring the mission to towns and cities. The chief of the whole network of Sufis was often called the Shah or Sultan to symbolize the combination of a territorial and a spiritual sphere of influence.

The khanaqa was the collective home of the Sufi community. A Chisti khanaqa consisted of a big hall called a *jama'at khana* in which the followers lived their communal life. The hall was usually a large room supported by pillars, which marked the places where the Sufis prayed, studied, and slept. Some khanaqas had rooms attached for the private use of the shaykh and the senior members. Often there was a garden, a veranda, and a kitchen. The life of a khanaqa was organized like that of a royal court. The Sufi master took a central place; his disciples hung about waiting to be invited to sit near him. The Shah received the general public, listened to petitioners, gave amulets to heal the sick, mediated disputes, and dispensed spiritual counsel.

The people attached to the khanaqa were divided between permanent residents and visitors; the permanent residents were organized in a hierarchy depending upon their spiritual standing and the duties assigned them. The disciples did personal services for the master and his family, and organized the common housekeeping tasks of the khanaqa. The visitors were numerous; they included scholars, government officials, and businessmen looking for escape from worldly burdens. Poor people came for money, advice, recommendations, or intercessions with their superiors. They came for cures, sympathy, and blessings. The mystics taught them how to worship in the manner of Islam.

Apart from the Quran and hadith, the most important religious influence on Indian Islam was the teaching of Ibn al-'Arabi and the doctrine of wahdat al-wujud, the unity of being. These teachings were spread both by the Chistis and the Shattaris, who believed that spiritual attitude was more important than specific religious laws or practices. They also saw that Islam and Hinduism shared spiritual insights, and this led to an assimilation of Sufi and Hindu beliefs about the control of emotional life as a prerequisite to the control of external behavior. The Sufis adopted Hindu ceremonies, devotional songs, and yoga techniques. Popular religious culture became a mixture of Muslim and Hindu practices. Thus, the Sufis were divided among monist, pantheist, and syncretist religious tendencies, between commitment to individual spirituality and collective Shari'a, and between universal Muslim practices and specific Indian forms of worship.

Sufism was closely connected to the vernacular languages; Sufis pioneered the absorption of Indian language, music, and poetic forms into Islamic practice. Hindi became their spoken language, and inspired the birth of Urdu, a literary version of Hindi, as a Muslim language. The earliest work in Urdu was a treatise on Sufism written in 1308. Dakhni was first used by Chistis in Golconda in the early fifteenth century and was developed further by Sufis in Bijapur and Gujarat. Mystical poetry in Sindhi and Punjabi dates back to the fifteenth century; Pashto mystical poetry to the late sixteenth century. Poetry in the vernacular languages took up the classical Persian themes of the yearning for and love of God. The love of the Prophet was also told and retold in poems, folk songs, riddles, and bridal songs. Hindu poets also wrote mystical poems using Muslim images and themes, including the honor of the Prophet and the mourning for Husayn.

Other Muslim movements veered away from the spiritualist and syncretic forms of Sufism. The Mahdawi movement was founded at the end of the fifteenth century by Sayyid Muhammad of Jawnpur. Sayyid Muhammad claimed to be the mahdi and traced his descent to Musa al-Kazim, the seventh in the "twelver" line of imams. He preached poverty, renunciation, and prayer, and sought to restore the purity of religious belief and practice, and to build a community based upon allegiance to Muslim law. His followers established *daira*, or communities, in which they lived an ascetic life, shared their earnings, and attempted to minimize their worldly involvement so as not to be distracted from their dependence upon God. The members met weekly to confess their sins. The Mahdawi movement was important in Gujarat in the sixteenth century, and was widely accepted during the reign of the great Mughal Sultan Akbar. With acceptance came a loss of missionary zeal, and with the passing of the millennium, the thousandth year of the Muslim era, the followers of Sayyid Muhammad lost their conviction of the imminent coming of the mahdi.

Yet another alternative was a "reformist" type of Islamic belief which stressed hadith as the basis of Muslim learning and pious practice. Opposed to the excesses both of legal studies and of Sufi spirituality, the hadith scholars found their master in Shaykh 'Abd al-Haqq Dihlawi (d. 1642). The Suhrawardis were committed to Muslim law, taught the doctrine of *wahdat al-shuhud* (unity of witness), and insisted upon the superiority of prophecy to sainthood. These movements would inspire Shaykh Ahmad Sirhindi (1564–1624) and the reformers of the seventeenth and eighteenth centuries.

MUSLIM HOLY MEN AND POLITICAL AUTHORITY

The relations between 'ulama', Sufis, and the state were varied. In principle, the 'ulama' were servants of the state. They benefited from state protection of Islamic religious life, enforcement of Islamic religious law, and state employment as bureaucratic officials, judges, prayer leaders, and teachers. The 'ulama' and the state had a symbiotic relationship because of the clear division of political and religious authority.

The Sufi relationship to state authority was more ambiguous. Sufi orders such as the Suhrawardi and the Chisti were themselves quasi-political societies within the Delhi Sultanate. The Suhrawardis maintained a close and collaborative relationship with the Delhi regimes, facilitated by their geographical distribution. Concentrated in the border regions of Multan, Uch, and Gujarat, remote from the center of power, the Suhrawardis were able to enjoy state patronage, gifts of land, and other favors and still maintain their autonomy as provincial notables. Their role was to mediate between the Delhi Sultanate and provincial princes and tribes. Sufism thus played an important role in integrating tribal and frontier peoples into the Delhi regime. The ability of the Suhrawardis to fulfill these political functions was the basis of their spiritual authority. Wealthy state-supported khanaqas were the worldly symbol of the Suhrawardi claim to mediate in the world to come.

The Chistis lived by a different political philosophy. Their shaykhs rejected government service, refused endowments, and expected to earn their living by cultivating wastelands or receiving unsolicited gifts from the common people. The shaykhs even refused interviews with Sultans. For ordinary disciples, however, earning a living in some simple productive way was considered meritorious. As part of their responsibility for improving the worldly condition of Muslims, they were permitted to take employment. For the order as a whole, charity and responsibility for the poor were primary values. The Chistis maintained their spiritual authority by detachment from rather than by mediation among worldly powers.

Though rejecting worldly concerns, the Chistis were after all in the midst of the world. They implicitly accepted the political structures of the Sultanate and indirectly validated the authority of the Sultans by advocating a concept of universal hierarchy which Sultans could use to validate their claims to be the heads of a temporal world order. Only wandering Qalandaris and Malamatis denounced and wholly withdrew from the world.

The relations of 'ulama' and Sufis to the state and to each other changed over time. In the course of the thirteenth century, 'ulama' influence was ascendant, but under the Khalji dynasty (1290–1320) Sufis were promoted as a counterweight to the 'ulama'. 'Ala al-Din used the latitude given him by Chisti ties to reduce the power of Turkish nobles and 'ulama' and to bring Indian Muslims into the governing elite. Muhammad b. Tughluq, however, called upon the 'ulama' and the Suhrawardis to condemn Chisti religious practices, such as *sama'*, or musically accompanied religious ceremonies. Nizam al-Din Auliya, the head of the Chisti order, had to appear in person to defend himself. The Tughluqs succeeded in forcing the Chistis to abandon their headquarters in Delhi and to disperse all over India. They were also forced to serve in military campaigns in South India and to take up missionary activities under government sponsorship. Under political pressure, the Chistis split. Some collaborated with the government and others refused. The division within the order broke the power of its all-India organization.

The political power of the Suhrawardis was also eventually broken by the authorities. Muhammad b. Tughluq gave them lands and villages, and then forbade anyone to visit their khanaqas without permission from the governors. Disputes over succession to the leadership of the order had to be brought to the Sultans for resolution. As the Suhrawardis became more dependent upon the state, their mediating powers declined. Only in Gujarat, which had an independent dynasty, did the Suhrawardis continue to be regarded as patron saints. They received gifts of landed estates and maintained their influence over public opinion. With the absorption of Gujarat into the Mughal empire in 1572, the Suhrawardis completely lost their political importance. Their decline allowed for the spread of the Naqshbandi and Qadiri orders and the eventual resurgence of 'ulama' and reformist types of Islam which demanded that state policy be based on allegiance to Shari'a rather than upon Sufi principles.

The Delhi period thus set the basis for an Islamic society with its characteristic ambiguities of Islamic and non-Islamic aspects of state ideology and popular culture. Islam in India was marked by a pluralism of religious communities which passed on to the Mughal empire.

THE MUGHAL EMPIRE

The Mughal regime and Indian culture

The Mughals completed the long struggle to create a centralized Indian empire. Founded by the victories of Babur, the empire was consolidated in the reign of his grandson Akbar (1556–1605). Akbar expanded the empire from its original territories in Hindustan and the Punjab, Gujarat, Rajasthan, Bihar, and Bengal. In the north he took Kabul, Kashmir, Sind, and Baluchistan. The Deccan was absorbed in 1600. Not until the end of the seventeenth century did the empire expand further south and absorb Bijapur, Golconda, and other hitherto independent South Indian provinces. Nonetheless, large parts of India remained outside. Rajasthan remained in the hands of local Hindu lords, and East Central India was governed by tributary tribes. The imperial government was controlled by a military and political elite which was primarily made up of Afghan, Iranian, and Turkish lords and native Indian Muslims. While the ruling elite was officially Muslim, Hindus – mostly Rajputs and Marathas – formed about 20 percent of the Mughal aristocracy. The Hindus were important as subordinate military lords, administrative officials, financiers, merchants, and landowners. Hindu officials commonly shared the Persian cultural style of their Muslim counterparts.

From the Mughal point of view, the ruling elite was held together by the loyalty and service of subordinate lineages to the dominant Mughal lineage. Indian society was a condominium of noble lineages bound to the emperor by territorial or political concessions, family ties, and ceremonial and cultural style. The aristocratic lineages were called *biradari, jati,* or *qawm*. They in turn made their clients the supporters of the Mughal state. The aristocracy was thus defined in patrimonial as well as in Muslim terms.

This ruling elite was further organized according to the *mansabdar* system. This was a military hierarchy in which each office-holder had two ranks – a *zat* rank that defined his standing in the hierarchy and a *sawar* rank that defined the number of troops he was expected to bring to battle. The mansab officers were paid either in cash or by the grant of an estate called a *jagir*, which was the equivalent of a Middle Eastern iqta'. The jagirs were awarded to the military officers of the emperor, local princes, Rajputs, and tribal leaders. Each noble maintained an administration that included a military contingent, a financial and administrative staff, a household staff, a harem, and servants. The household of a noble imitated the household of the ruler. Mughal nobles also assumed responsibility for building mosques, bridges, and caravansaries and for patronizing scientific and literary activity.

About seven-eighths of the taxable land of the Mughal empire was distributed to military assignees and about one-eighth was reserved as the personal estate of the ruler. A major administrative problem was to set the assignment of territories and revenues in proportion to the military obligation of the assignees. Changes in local conditions required constant redistribution of land in order to maintain a realistic correspondence between rated values, actual income, and military obligation. Lords were transferred from one jagir to another to prevent them from acquiring a vested interest in a particular region.

Beneath the level of the mansabdars there were numerous local chieftains. These included *zamindars*, or local notables, who had a claim to a portion of the land revenues by virtue of local conquests or caste dominance, but not, in principle,

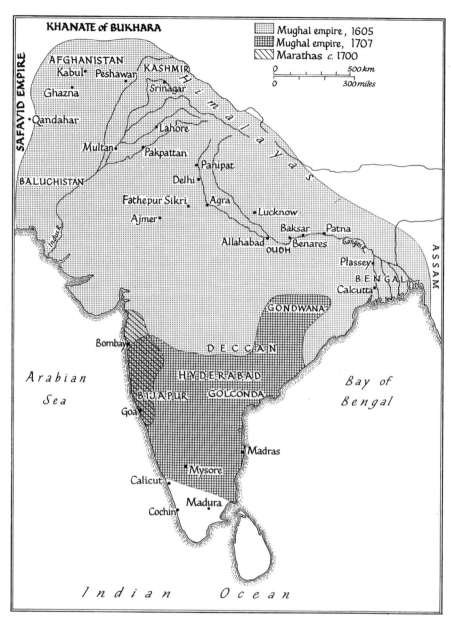

Map 19 The Mughal empire: 1605–1707

proprietary rights over the land. Still, a local zamindar had a considerable advantage in the struggle to maintain his position. Every zamindar was backed by armed retainers, who helped him coerce the peasants and who protected his interests against central government intervention. His ability to dominate the peasantry and to mediate between them and the central government gave him a strong political and economic position. The zamindars, however, were subject to the authority of the emperor and could be expelled from office. Mughal rulers often tried to displace Rajput and other Hindu lords in favor of Muslim zamindars.

Beneath the level of the zamindars there were several classes. Money lenders and grain merchants, rich peasants, small peasant landowners, landless laborers and agricultural workers of various castes, and "untouchables" made up a structured society ranked by ritual purity. Each peasant village was headed by a local official, called the *muqaddam* or *patel*, whose position was likely to be hereditary, responsible to the authorities for payment of revenues and for the prevention of crimes. Peasants were guaranteed permanent and hereditary occupancy of the land, but they were also bound to it. In an age when land was abundant, people scarce, and peasants prone to flee to uninhabited regions, physical force had to be used to keep them in place. (This is just the reverse of modern conditions, where landlords dominate an excessive number of human beings by threatening to evict them.)

The system for the collection of taxes that applied to the central provinces of the empire, including Multan, Lahore, Delhi, Agra, Oudh, and Allahabad, went back to Sher Shah, was continued by Akbar, and lasted until the end of the seventeenth century. Taxation was administered according to the *zabt* system. A fixed fee was assessed for each unit of land and paid in cash. The rate of assessment was based on the value of the crop raised and the average yield of the previous ten years. The calculation of the value of the crop was adjusted from empire-wide norms to local prices and then to estimates of cash value. The amount actually collected was ordinarily half of the total crop. Everything that could be taxed without depriving the peasants of their subsistence and their capacity to produce another crop was taken. The actual collection of taxes was entrusted to the *jagirdar*, but local functionaries representing the central administration had an important part in the tax collection. At the sub-district level, the administration was represented by a *qanungo*, who kept accounts and who was supposed to supervise the agents of the jagirdar; and a *chaudhuri*, who collected funds from the zamindars.

Akbar also set the cultural style of the Mughal era on the basis of the combined legacy of Chaghatay Inner Asia (communicated through Babur) and the Delhi Sultanate. The Chaghatay heritage stressed the role of the ruler as a warrior lord and leader of jihad. Babur added to this the sedentary urban and Persian Islamic tradition which made the 'ulama' advisors, tutors, diplomats, and administrative servants of the Chaghatay ruler. The Delhi Sultanate contributed concepts of royal authority derived from the Persian monarchical tradition, and Islamic concepts of political responsibility. The Mughals went beyond the indirect appeals of the Delhi

Sultanate to the non-Muslim elites and supported a cultural policy that was intended to create a cosmopolitan Indian-Islamic rather than an exclusively Muslim culture.

Akbar set the new pattern. While appealing to Muslim scholars by the endowment of madrasas and libraries, he also supported the Chisti order which was tolerant of syntheses between Hinduism and Islam, and started a state cult called Din-i Ilahi, or divine religion, with the emperor himself considered to be the Sufi master of a new religious order. The *Akbar-name* of Abu'l–Fazl 'Allami (1551–1602) is perhaps the best expression of the values of this reign. This book describes a court society in which the ruler is considered a philosopher-king, protector of all his subjects regardless of their religion, and a spiritual guide who brings reconciliation and love, and fosters well-being in the whole of his domain.

A broader cultural policy also sought to focus loyalty upon the ruler as the protector of a shared Hindu–Muslim elite culture in manners, dress, art, painting, architecture, poetry, and belles-lettres. The architectural style patronized by Akbar and exhibited in the major palace and fort complexes of Ajmer, Agra, Allahabad, Lahore, and Fathepur Sikri was based upon motifs drawn from both Muslim and Hindu architecture. The combination of these elements goes back to earlier Indian structures. Post and lintel construction was widely used in the domestic architecture of the Delhi Sultanate period. Serpentine brackets to support eaves, zoomorphic forms, bell-and-chain motifs, and other devices were all used in earlier mosques and palaces. Similarly, Hindu palaces and temples commonly used abstract geometric decorations and domed roofs which derived from the Muslim tradition. By the Delhi Sultanate period, Indian architecture had already assimilated diverse forms in ways that no longer retained a specifically sectarian implication. A style transcending religious and regional origins was already part of the vernacular of Indian architecture. Adopting this architectural style, Akbar fostered a common culture for a diverse elite.

Similarly, Indian painting was derived from Persian ways of figure drawing, illumination, and calligraphy, but it took on specifically Mughal qualities which emphasized line and form rather than color. While Mughal painting depicted court and hunting scenes, battles, animals, flowers, portraits, and other motifs of Persian art, it also drew inspiration from Hindu subjects and landscapes. Paintings were used to illustrate both Persian and Hindu literary works, including the *Mahabharata* and the *Ramayana*, and were produced by artists of both religious backgrounds. Indian painting, like Indian architecture, was meant to transcend sectarian implications.

In the Mughal era the Muslim population remained a minority, but not all Muslims were part of the ruling elite. They did not constitute a single community, but belonged to different ethnic groups, lineages, classes of population, and even castes. Muslims, like Hindus, were often identified with kinship and specialized occupational groups, ordered in a hierarchy that gave the highest status to warriors from Afghanistan and Inner Asia and religious families descended from the Prophet or from Iranian and Arab scholars. The craftsmen and service people were of lower status.

17 The marriage of Akbar

Islam under the Mughals

Indian Muslims formed numerous religious bodies divided by allegiance to schools of law, Sufi orders, and to the teaching of individual shaykhs, scholars, and saints. Some were Sunnis and some Shi'a, though this was not an absolute distinction, owing to the strong sympathies for the family of 'Ali among Sunnis. Sunnis were themselves divided between those committed to scripturalist Islam – to the beliefs and laws set out in the Quran, the hadith of the Prophet, and the Shari'a – and those devoted to popular Sufism, a form of religion in which veneration of saints, living and dead, with associated ceremonies of remembrance, mourning, and ritual marriages and funerals was the principal form of religious expression. One current in Indian Islam ran toward the disciplined, rational, and controlled practice of Islamic law; the other toward emotional faith and identification with the miraculous powers of saints. Into the first camp fell such diverse groups as the 'ulama', the organized schools of law, and Shari'a-minded Sufi orders. In the second camp there were the Sufi saints, and their descendants who managed their tombs, shrines, and the brotherhoods founded in their names. The two orientations led to different views about the boundaries between Muslims and non-Muslims. Popular saint worship blurred the religious distinctions among Muslims and Hindus; certain Sufi theories and cosmologies blended Hindu and Muslim concepts.

In the Mughal era, the 'ulama' were those scholars in the service of the state. The Mughals continued the Delhi Sultanate system of bureaucratic religious administration. Full control over the judiciary was given to a chief qadi. The provincial sadr was in charge of local judges, muhtasibs, preachers, prayer leaders, muezzins, and trust-fund administrators. He was responsible also for the appointment of muftis and for liaison between the government and the 'ulama'. His office provided stipends for scholars and sometimes included the power of making grants of landed property; waqfs were donated to provide income for shrines, tombs, and schools. He issued the daily allowances for religious persons and made payments out of the funds of charitable endowments. The sadr was also responsible for charities and for feeding the poor. In the course of the seventeenth century his power was checked by administrative arrangements which gave other officials control over land and by the creation of a more decentralized religious administration in the provinces. His judicial powers were also limited by rulers who involved themselves directly in religious affairs.

In the Mughal period, the influence of the Naqshbandis and the Qadiris replaced that of the Suhrawardis and Chistis. The Naqshbandis cultivated a spiritual discipline leading to the vision of God, but they also insisted upon the necessity for active engagement in worldly affairs. The histories of two Naqshbandi shaykhs of the eighteenth century illustrate the religious and social principles espoused by the order. Mirza Mazhar (c. 1700–81), the founder of the Mujaddidiya branch of the order, came from a family of soldiers and administrators, and took up the Sufi life to avoid political conflicts and to control the violent impulses in himself. He turned to Sufism as a way of finding tranquility and security in an uncertain world. His teachings stressed the harmony of the various Sufi traditions. He minimized the differences between the theosophical and legalistic forms of Sufism. His whole life was lived in cautious efforts to protect himself from contamination by food, gifts, and other worldly things which were all scrutinized for their legality and appropriateness. He also recommended celibacy. Mirza Mazhar never claimed the power to perform miracles, but his followers believed it of him anyway.

His successor was Shah Ghulam 'Ali (1753–1824), who stressed the social and political roles of the Naqshbandi shaykh, organized the khanaqa, sent disciples to proselytize in Iran and Afghanistan, and distributed charity and spiritual and moral advice to supplicants. He used his moral influence with political figures whenever possible.

By contrast, other Sufi orders stressed veneration of saints. The Chisti order was originally built upon the personal religious insights of the founding teacher, but as time passed, the charisma of the saints was taken to reside in their tombs. Their descendants then served as the managers of their shrines and the organizers of the orders that flourished around them. The *pirzadas*, the hereditary descendants and managers of the saints' tombs, supervised the festivities commemorating the birth and death anniversaries of the saints, maintained public kitchens, led community prayers, and offered amulets along with spiritual and social advice. The growth of the shrines as centers of worship led to the accumulation of properties granted and protected by the state. The Mughals awarded landed properties to the Sufis, a practice which legitimized both donor and recipient and enabled the Mughals to intervene in succession disputes and to control the managers of the shrines. They converted the pirzadas into a petty gentry sensitive to the wishes of the political authorities.

In the sixteenth century the influence of Shi'ism was also very strong. Golconda and Kashmir were ruled by Shi'i princes. The Mughals had Shi'i wives and many Shi'a held high offices. The Indian Shi'i communities included not only the "twelvers," whose teachings we have examined in the chapter on Iran, but also the Nizaris and the Bohras. The Nizaris had their origin in a schism among the Fatimids. They were the "Assassins" of twelfth-century Iran; their mission in India began in the late twelfth or early thirteenth century in Sind and Gujarat. At first the Nizari communities in India acknowledged the supremacy of the imams in Iran, but in the sixteenth century the movement split, and only some of the Nizaris maintained this connection. Eventually the imamate was transferred from Iran to India by Aga Khan I, Hasan 'Ali Shah, who moved to Bombay in 1845.

With the collapse of the Nizari state of Alamut in 1256, the mission entered a new passive phase, concentrating on the symbolic and religious rather than the political expressions of its goals. Its teaching was that God was utterly transcendent and unknowable, and that he brought into existence the world of intelligences; religious salvation was seen to come from ascending the ladder of intelligences and returning to the first intelligence through which man achieved unification with God.

18 The Taj Mahal

The Nizaris believed that the cosmic order was represented in history by prophets and imams who appeared in cyclical fashion. There were seven cycles of prophets, each cycle consisting of seven imams; the final cycle ends with the resurrection. The Bohras had their origin in the same schism that gave rise to the Nizaris. With the disappearance of their imam, al-Tayyib, in 1133, leadership of the community was turned over to the *da'i al-mutlaq*. The da'i stands in a hierarchy that includes other missionaries, including the higher-ranking *hujja*, natiq, and the imams. When the imams and the higher authorities are concealed, the da'i becomes the highest functionary in the social world. He is empowered to teach the community, resolve internal disputes, and name his successor in accordance with divine inspiration. He operates through agents called *amils* and shaykhs who are the equivalent of 'ulama'.

The Bohra branch of Isma'ili Shi'ism was first established in Yemen, and the Bohras probably came to Gujarat in the early thirteenth century. A deputy called a wali ruled in India until 1539 when the first Indian da'i was appointed. In the long history of the Bohra community, there were several major schisms. In 1846, with the death of the last da'i of the Rajput line, the authority of the da'is was compromised. The nineteenth-century Bohras tended to regard them as administrative figures rather than spiritual teachers, and their leadership was challenged by the scholars.

The diversity of Muslim religious and social groups in India inspired conflicting concepts about the social meaning of Islamic religious belief. The Shari'a-minded conceived of Muslim society as cutting across lineage and class lines. They defined Muslims not by inherited lineage, position in the state, or occupation, but by individual belief in Islam which transcended all other social ties and made men equals and brothers in religion. While they recognized the importance of the Mughal empire, Islam in their view was still a universal community. Shari'a-minded Muslims stood for state enforcement of Islamic law and state-mandated subordination of Hindus to Muslim rule by discriminatory taxes and restrictions. By contrast popular Sufism took Islam to be an integral aspect of lineage, occupational, and neighborhood ties.

These differences of religious orientation were an important political issue in the seventeenth and eighteenth centuries. While the state pursued a policy of conciliation among different Muslim groups and among Muslims and Hindus, 'ulama' critics of Akbar opposed his religious toleration, his openness to non-Shari'a religious ideas, and his assumption of the prerogatives of a Sufi. The most important opponent of imperial policies was Shaykh Ahmad Sirhindi. Sirhindi claimed to be the *mujaddid*, the renewer of Islam in his century, a man standing on the spiritual level of the early Caliphs. Initiated into the Naqshbandi order, he became the principal Indian spokesman of the Shari'a and reformist point of view. He taught that obedience to the teachings of the Shari'a was the key to its inner meaning, and modified Ibn al-'Arabi's doctrine of the unity of being and the metaphysical basis of religious syncretism, in favor of the doctrine of unity of witness. He opposed the insinuation into Islam of Sufi and Hindu practices such as worship of saints, sacrifice of animals, and religious festivals. As a reformer he waged an unrelenting crusade to persuade the Mughal authorities to adopt policies befitting an Islamic state. He regarded Hinduism and Islam as mutually exclusive; it was the obligation of Muslims to subdue non-Muslims. Thus he urged rulers and nobles to impose the poll tax on non-Muslims, to permit the slaughter of cows, to remove non-Muslims from political office, and to enforce the Shari'a in every way.

Sirhindi's great follower was Shah Waliallah (1702–63), who pursued the tradition of reform in different circumstances. In the declining age of the Mughal empire, Shah Waliallah was concerned with securing the Muslim presence in the subcontinent. After visiting Mecca, the center of reformist teaching, he stressed the importance of returning to the Prophet's teachings and the need to purge Islam of saint worship, which was subsequent to and inconsistent with the true meaning of the Prophet's life. He translated the Quran into Persian and made an argument for the use of independent scholarly judgment in the adaptation of the law to local conditions. While supporting the supremacy of Quran and Sunna, he attempted to synthesize the different schools of law and reduce the legal divergences among Muslims.

Shah Waliallah believed that reform required a Muslim state, modeled on the early Caliphate, to enforce the Shari'a. He defined the Caliph as the religious leader who is closest to the example of the Prophet, a perfect man who strives for justice and tries to use administrative and judicial techniques to lead his people to religious virtue. In Shah Waliallah's view, the will of God radiates through the Caliph into the feelings and minds of his subjects. Even in the absence of this spiritual function, a Caliph provides for the political defense of Muslim peoples and the organization of Muslim law. His duty is to enforce Islamic religious practice, collect the alms tax, promote the pilgrimage, foster study and teaching, administer justice, and wage jihad. This was a program of religious consolidation in the struggle against popular Sufi Islam and in opposition to a lax Mughal regime.

As a consequence of this pluralism, there was no sense in India of a universal or unified Muslim identity. The relation of the Mughal empire to Muslim religious life was conditioned by this pluralism. While the state patronized the small 'ulama' establishment, both 'ulama' and Sufis were generally independent. Reformist-minded 'ulama' who represented the universalistic Islamic ideal were often critical of the Mughal state for its cosmopolitan and imperial culture, its Hindu elite, and its patrimonial loyalties. Many pious Sufis withdrew altogether from political contacts, but Sufi leaders tended to be accommodationist and to accept state support and the legitimacy of the regime. Thus the legacy of pre-modern Indian Islamic organization was not state control of doctrine, teaching, or judicial administration, nor a history of well-established schools of law and 'ulama', but one of numerous autonomous and competitive Muslim religious movements.

THE DECLINE OF THE MUGHAL EMPIRE

The classic system of the Mughal empire lasted from the reign of Akbar until the reign of Aurangzeb (1658–1707). Aurangzeb was the first Mughal ruler to reverse the policy of conciliation of Hindus in favor of Islamic supremacy. In 1659 he forbade drinking, gambling, prostitution, the use of narcotics, and other vices. In 1664 he forbade *sati*, the Hindu sacrifice of widows, and abolished taxes that were not legal under Muslim law. In 1668 he banned music at court, imposed the poll tax on non-Muslims, ordered the destruction of Hindu temples, and sponsored the codification of Islamic laws called the *Fatawa-i 'Alamgiri*. He also founded Muslim colleges to promote the study of Shari'a. The religious climate of his reign reversed the tendency toward syncretism in favor of exclusivist Muslim policies. Aurangzeb's reforms antagonized Hindus but still fell short of Muslim reformist demands.

The reign of Aurangzeb also saw profound changes in the structure of the Mughal nobility. He was the first ruler since Akbar to expand the frontiers of the empire. He absorbed East Bengal, pacified the Northwest Frontier, took direct control of Rajasthan, and expanded the Mughal empire in the Deccan. The invasion of the Deccan involved the incorporation of a large number of Bijapuris, Hyderabadis, Marathas, and other Hindu lords into the imperial elite. As a result, the proportion of Hindus in the mansabdar system rose from approximately 20 to 30 percent; Marathas came to outnumber Rajput lords. While the new lords could easily be assigned a place in the rank system, there was no way to provide estates for the enlarged military elite. The result was increased competition for scarce jagirs, factionalism, and the exploitation of the peasants. In the late seventeenth century taxes began to be collected before the harvest. The poll tax on non-Muslims also increased the fiscal burden of peasants.

The decentralization of power and of the tax-collecting system allowed for the rise of new social forces. As in the Ottoman empire, land grantees, village headmen, and tax-farmers became landlords. By the eighteenth century village headmen were the key figures in the collection of village revenues and in negotiations with the government authorities. Zamindars became increasingly independent and refused payment of revenues. Mansabdars converted their jagirs into permanent zamindari tenures.

Furthermore, a new urban commercial and merchant class came into being. The breakup of the centralized state and the decline of the capital encouraged the growth of provincial towns and local elites. Rich farmers, small-town and rural shopkeepers, coin changers, money lenders, and landlords profited from the redistribution of fiscal authority. Small towns and markets throughout North India grew in commercial importance on the basis of wider market networks and rural enterprises. Sustained by aristocratic consumer demand in such growing cities as Lucknow and Benares, Hindu merchants and their clients and dependents prospered. Their commercial networks overlapped with religious sects as a rising elite sought communal solidarity and corporate protection. Similarly, decentralization of power favored the growth of Muslim families composed of local qadis, government functionaries, landowners, urban rentiers, and religious leaders who controlled the revenues of mosques, tombs, and shrines. Muslim landlords and money lenders acquired a corporate consciousness. In the *qasbahs* (small and medium-sized

towns) the leading Muslim families – sharing *ashraf* (noble Arab, Mughal, or Pashtun) status, united by intermarriage, linked to the town madrasas and academies,
and to Sufi tombs and shrines – emerged as a local elite. Peasants also organized
to resist exploitation. Castes, religious sects, and the clienteles of zamindar chiefs
provided the social basis for peasant action.

In these changing political circumstances, succession struggles after the death of
Aurangzeb and a series of feeble rulers compromised the efficacy of the Mughal
state and left it prey to internal rebellions and foreign invasions. In the early eighteenth century, several regions of the Mughal empire became independent under
the rule of local mansabdars now become *nawwabs*. The Nizam of Hyderabad
became independent in 1723. In Bengal the change of regimes destroyed the jagir
form of assignments, and the old Mughal aristocracy lost its position. Zamindars
and bankers seized control of the tax system.

In other parts of India, regimes based on Hindu lordships and popular uprisings
came to power. Hindu-governed principalities regained control of Rajasthan. In the
Punjab, religious and ethnic groups such as the Sikhs and the Jats established local
regimes. The Maratha movement, based on peasant resistance to taxation, Hindu
revivalism, and vernacular languages, and led by Shah Shahji and his son Shivaji,
defied Mughal authority. By the middle of the eighteenth century, the Marathas controlled most of South India, and had replaced the Mughals as the dominant power
in Gujarat.

By the middle of the century, Marathas, Sikhs, and Afghan tribesmen from the
north fought to control the remaining territories of the moribund Mughal empire.
The Marathas consolidated their grip on central and western India and formed five
independent and expanding states. In 1739 Nadir Shah, the conqueror of Iran, took
control of Kabul, and sacked Delhi. The helpless Mughal regime had to call upon
Maratha support to resist the Afghans, but at the battle of Panipat (1761) the Marathas
were defeated by Ahmad Shah Durrani. No Indian power proved capable of resisting the foreign invaders. As a result, the Sikhs were able to expand in the Punjab
between 1750 and 1799 and establish a new state with its capital at Lahore. The way
was also opened for the emergence of the British as the paramount power in India.

The British East India Company had been trading in India since 1600. British factories were founded at Surat in 1612, Madras in 1640, Bombay in 1674, and Calcutta in 1690. They exported Indian cotton and silk cloth, cotton yarn, raw silk,
saltpeter, indigo, and spices, and imported silver bullion and other metals. Gradually the East India Company made itself into a local government. In a long series
of eighteenth-century wars, the British defeated their French rivals. When the
nawwab of Bengal attacked the British settlement at Calcutta, he was defeated at
the battle of Plassey (1757) and again at the battle of Baksar (1764), and the British
established themselves as the de facto rulers of Bengal. In 1772 Warren Hastings,
the British governor of Bengal, took charge of the British factories of Madras and
Bombay and created a unified regime for the factories in India. Hastings' success
marks the beginning of a British Indian empire.

The transformation of the British position in India received legal recognition in the mother country and in the subcontinent. By the India Act of 1784 the British parliament required that mercantile and administrative activities henceforth be separated and that all East India Company officials in India be responsible to parliament. In Bengal, under Cornwallis (1786–93), the British established a new system of taxation and judicial administration. They took control of the courts, separated administrative and judicial jurisdictions, and established a British-officered police and army. By the so-called Permanent Settlement (1793), rural taxes were set at fixed rates – a measure which ruined the old Muslim elite and opened the way for the purchase of zamindari tenures by wealthy Hindu merchants and investors from Calcutta. At the same time British goods came to dominate the local economy. British power in Bengal was soon extended to other parts of India, and by 1818 the remaining Rajput and Maratha rulers acknowledged the British as the paramount power. The Punjab and the Northwest Frontier were absorbed at a later date. While the British in India continued to recognize the Mughal emperors as their suzerains, they had persistently and patiently acquired a new Indian empire.

Over the centuries a distinctive form of Islamic civilization had emerged in the Indian subcontinent. Like their Iranian and Middle Eastern predecessors, the Delhi Sultanates and the Mughal empire were committed to a concept of state culture that blended Islamic symbols with a royal heritage. In the Iranian case these were the symbols of ancient Iran as transmitted through the 'Abbasid Caliphate. In India royalty meant the heritage of Iran combined with Mongol, Timurid, and Chaghatay concepts and with Indian and Hindu motifs, which introduced new qualities into Islamic imperial culture.

Similarly, Muslim religious life both resembled and departed from Middle Eastern norms. Islam in India replicated the basic forms of 'ulama' and Sufi Islam. Whereas in Iran Shi'ism absorbed all levels of Islam into a monolithic establishment, in India the various forms of 'ulama' scholarship, Sufi contemplation, worship of saints, and reformist tendencies remained in open competition with each other. In India Islamic belief and practice on the popular level was manifestly mixed with local Hindu and Buddhist forms of belief and worship. The formation of a popular Muslim subculture in India was not, however, a departure from Muslim norms, but an example of a process that was universal. In the Middle East as well, Islam had been formed as a syncretism of popular Christian and Jewish religious practices with Muslim teachings, though the passage of time has concealed the syncretic nature of Middle Eastern Islam. Thus the Mughal era bequeathed to modern India a distinctive variant of Muslim institutions and cultures.

CHAPTER 19

THE FORMATION OF ISLAMIC SOCIETIES
IN SOUTHEAST ASIA

Just as Islam spread from the Middle East to Inner Asia and from Afghanistan to India, it spread from various parts of India and Arabia to the Malay peninsula and the Indonesian archipelago in the late thirteenth, fourteenth, and fifteenth centuries. In other regions, Islam was established by Arab or Turkish conquests; it was introduced into Southeast Asia by traveling merchants and Sufis. In the Middle East and India, Muslim regimes were founded by new elites; in Southeast Asia existing regimes were consolidated by conversion to Islam. The continuity of elites gave strong expression to the pre-Islamic components of Southeast Asian-Islamic civilization, and the royal culture of Java seems more local and less Muslim than the corresponding royal culture of the Mughal empire was Indian. The syncretisms of Islam and village cultures, however, were probably equally intense in the subcontinent and in Indonesia. While Muslims remained a minority in India, in Indonesia and Malaya they became the overwhelming majority.

THE DIFFUSION OF ISLAM

Indigenous pre-Islamic Southeast Asian culture formed the basis of later Islamic civilization. By the beginning of the Christian era the diverse population of Southeast Asia had developed a civilization based upon irrigated rice cultivation, animal husbandry, and metallurgy. The native cultures had their own religious beliefs and artistic accomplishments such as the wayang puppet theater and the gamelan orchestra recitals of Java and Bali. The interior of Java was a region of rice agriculture and the locus of small kingdoms. In the coastal regions of Sumatra and Java, the smaller islands, and the Malay peninsula, the populace earned its living by trade and was strongly influenced by contacts with Hindu cultures. From earliest times, there had been a tension between the agrarian hierarchical society of Java and the cultures of the coastal towns.

The early Southeast Asian societies were already state ruled, but there was no single polity. The earliest historical kingdoms on Java date from the fifth century

AD. From the fifth to the fifteenth centuries, there were several kingdoms, each a suzerainty over petty lordships maintained by control of rice and by mythic, magical, and mystical means. Each was a center for the diffusion of high culture to the surrounding countryside. The Shailendra dynasty (c. 760–860) blended indigenous Indonesian culture with Sanskrit literature and Brahmin and Saivite versions of Hinduism. Local princes borrowed Indian and Hindu political concepts to legitimize their rule. The Hindu concepts of a God King and of the terrestrial order as an analogue of the cosmic order sanctified temporal power as an expression of the spiritual universe. Great imperial palaces and Hindu and Buddhist monumental tombs were constructed by these early rulers. In the tenth century the center of culture and power in Java shifted to Mataram, which held sway from 929 to 1222. Mataram was succeeded by a number of other regional kingdoms, notably by Majapahit (1293–1389). The most important maritime kingdom was Srivijaya, first centered at Palembang and then at Jambi in Sumatra. This kingdom controlled the Malacca Straits and established a commercial hegemony between India and China. Its cosmopolitan trading connections helped establish a Hinduized culture just as it would later favor the introduction of Islam.

The advent of Islam depended upon the close trading relationships between India and Southeast Asia. Only after the consolidation of Islam on the Indian subcontinent did Muslim merchants and Sufi missionaries begin to trade and proselytize extensively. By the thirteenth century, Southeast Asia was in contact with the Muslims of China, Bengal, Gujarat, Iran, Yemen, and South Arabia. The fact that Malayan and Indonesian Islam is Shafi'i points to South India as the major source of Islamic influences.

Three theories purport to explain the acceptance of Islam. One stresses the role of Muslim merchants who married into local ruling families, and provided important diplomatic skills, wealth, and international experience for the commercial enterprises of coastal rulers. The first converts were local rulers who sought to attract Muslim traffic and win allies in the struggle against Hindu traders from Java. Coastal chiefs used conversion to legitimize their resistance to the authority of Majapahit and to throw off the suzerainty of central Javan empires.

A second theory stresses the importance of missionaries from Gujarat, Bengal, and Arabia. The Sufis came not only as teachers but also as traders and politicians who penetrated the courts of rulers, the quarters of merchants, and the villages of the countryside. They could communicate their religious vision in a form compatible with beliefs already held in Indonesia. Pantheistic doctrines were understood because of Hindu teachings. Saint worship and faith in the saint as a healer were common to both Muslims and Indonesians.

The third theory stresses the value of Islam to the common people rather than to the ruling elites. Islam provided an ideological basis for individual worth, for solidarity in peasant and merchant communities, and for the integration of parochial groups into larger societies. In an era of expanding trade Islam may have helped to create an integrated community to replace the village-scale societies disrupted by commerce and political change. It seems likely that all three factors were at work, though circumstances undoubtedly differed from place to place. While there was no single process or single source for the spread of Islam in Southeast Asia, the travels of individual merchants and Sufis, the winning of apprentices and disciples, and the founding of schools seem crucial.

The facts indicating the establishment of Islam are few. In 1282, the Hindu Malay ruler of Samudra in Sumatra had Muslim advisors. A Muslim community in Pasai in North Sumatra was reported in 1292 by Marco Polo. The tomb of Sultan Malik al-Salih in Perlak dated 1297 indicates the conversion of a local ruler. In 1345–46, Ibn Battuta, on his world tour of Muslim communities, found Shafi'i scholars in Samudra. Then, at the beginning of the fifteenth century, Iskandar, the former ruler of the trading kingdom of Srivijaya, was defeated by Javanese rivals, and forced to flee Palembang. He founded Malacca and converted to Islam. Iskandar based his political claims upon genealogical descent from past rulers, Buddhist consecration, and Islam. By such syncretism Islam was added to the panoply of Southeast Asian cultures. Malacca built up a trading empire with extensive contacts in India, Java, and China. Ships from Malacca sailed to Gujarat, Bengal, and the smaller islands of the East Indies archipelago. Malacca also attempted to build up a Malay–Sumatran territorial empire with possessions on both sides of the straits.

With the consolidation of its political and commercial prosperity, Malacca became a base for the spread of Islamic influence throughout the region. By 1474 the Malay rulers of Pahang, Kedah, and Patani were converted to Islam; on Sumatra Islam reached Roken, Siak, Kampar, and Indragiri. While Javanese students were coming to Malacca and Pasai as early as 1414 to study with Muslim teachers, the coastal principalities of Java, Demak, Tuban, Madura, and Surabaya became Muslim in the middle of the fifteenth century. These conversions were probably stimulated by their rivalry with the interior kingdom of Majapahit. By the late fifteenth century, Islam was spreading into the interior.

From its bases in Sumatra and Java, Islam spread further eastward. Ternate was converted in 1495. The Moluccas became Muslim in 1498 as a result of contacts with Java, and the coastal towns of Borneo were converted by Javanese contacts before the arrival of the Portuguese in 1511. Islamic influences from Sumatra, Ternate, and Borneo reached the Philippines. Conversions were made in Luzon, Sulu, and Mindanao. On the basis of the intersecting interests of traders and local princes, and the migrations of merchants and missionaries, Islam became the common religion of the Indies.

THE PORTUGUESE, THE DUTCH, AND THE MUSLIM STATES

The development of this newly Islamizing society was interrupted by the Portuguese, who established themselves as an Indian Ocean power in the early sixteenth century. In 1509 they defeated a combined Egyptian and Indian fleet and took Goa. In 1511 they conquered Malacca, in 1515 Hurmuz on the Persian Gulf, and in 1522 Ternate in an attempt to control the trade between China, Japan, Siam, the Moluccas, the Indian Ocean, and Europe. The Portuguese were expelled from Ternate in 1575, but they held on to other islands in the Moluccas.

Portuguese intervention paradoxically contributed to the further spread of Islam. With the fall of Malacca, Muslim teachers and missionaries migrated to northern Sumatra, Java, the Moluccas, and Borneo. In Acheh, Sultan 'Ali Mughayat Shah rallied the opponents of the Portuguese, defeated them at Pidie in 1521 and at Pasai in 1524, conquered the north coast of Sumatra, and thus set the basis for an Achenese kingdom which would be the main rival of the Portuguese. Between 1529 and 1587 Acheh made continual efforts to recapture Malacca, and finally, between 1618 and 1620, it took Pahang, Kedah, and Perak. The apogee of Achenese power was reached under Sultan Iskandar Muda (1607–36), who organized an efficient regime and established his dominance over the local lords (*uleebalang*) and village associations. Sultan Iskandar's ambition to control the whole peninsula, however, was defeated by other Malay Sultanates in 1629.

Java became the principal Muslim center of power. Between 1513 and 1528 a coalition of the Muslim kingdoms defeated Majapahit, and two new states emerged in central Java – Banten in central and western Java (founded in 1568), and Mataram in east central Java. Under Sultan Agung (1613–45) and Sultan Mangkurax (1646–77), Mataram reduced the independent princes of the island to vassals and ministers of the Mataram state, and became the ruling power on Java.

The region-wide struggle between the Muslims and the Portuguese was complicated by the arrival of the Dutch. Like the Portuguese, the Dutch came to the East Indies in quest of pepper. In 1594 Holland had won its war of independence from the Habsburg monarchy, and was excluded from access to pepper and spices in the Lisbon market. Thus, Dutch fleets sailed directly to the East Indies in 1595; in 1602 the United East India Company was chartered to control Dutch trading and to achieve a monopoly between the Cape of Good Hope and the Magellan Straits. They pushed their way into the East Indies trade by naval warfare. The Dutch defeated the Portuguese and took Amboyna in 1605. They founded Batavia in 1619, Banda in 1621, and took Ceylon in 1640. They seized Malacca in 1641.

From these fortress bases the Dutch eliminated the Portuguese and established their supremacy over the Muslim states. Acheh came under Dutch commercial control between 1629 and 1663. Treaties of 1639, 1650, and 1659 gave the Dutch two-thirds of Acheh's tin supplies. From Acheh Dutch economic power extended to the rest of Sumatra. They took Palembang in 1658, and in 1663 they obtained a monopoly of the pepper trade of Minangkabau. The Dutch defeated resistance in the Moluccas by 1658 and established a monopoly of cloves and nutmeg. In 1669 they forced Macassar to give them a monopoly of its trade, and subsequently established forts on Ternate, Macassar, and Borneo.

On Java the Dutch established themselves as territorial overlords. They consolidated their control of Batavia and the small territory around it by defeating the ruler of Mataram, Sultan Agung (1613–49), in 1629. In 1646 they forced Mataram

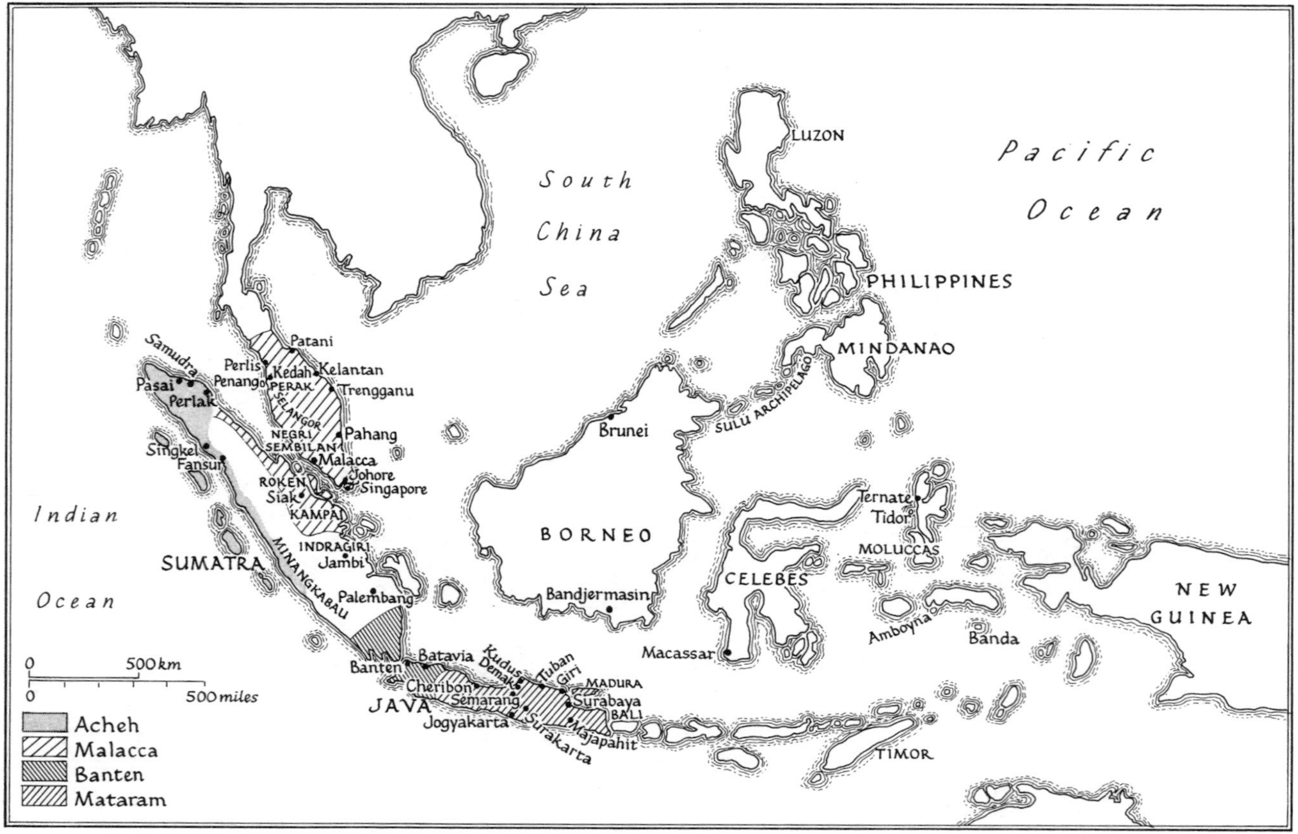

Map 20 Muslim states of Southeast Asia to 1800

PHILIPPINES

LUZON

MINDANAO

SULU ARCHIPELAGO

NEW
GUINEA

Pacific
Ocean

South
China
Sea

BORNEO

Brunei

Bandjermasin

Macassar

CELEBES

MOLUCCAS

Ternate
Tidor

Amboyna

Banda

TIMOR

Indian
Ocean

Patani

Perlis Kedah Kelantan
Penang Trengganu
PERAK Pahang
NEGRI SELANGOR
SEMBILAN Malacca
ROKEN Johore Singapore
Siak KAMPAR
INDRAGIRI
Jambi
MINANGKABAU Palembang

Samudra
Pasai Singkel
Perlak Fansur

SUMATRA

Batavia Kudus MADURA
Banten Cheribon Demak TEGRI
  Semarang Surabaya BALI
  Jogyakarta Surakarta Majapahit
JAVA

500 km
500 miles

Acheh
Malacca
Banten
Mataram

to recognize their monopolies in the spice islands. Peace prevailed until 1675, when the rivalries of Mataram and Banten required Mataram to ask for Dutch help, for which she was obliged to give the Dutch a monopoly over the cloth and opium trades. Dutch help was purchased again and again by tributes and concessions of land until, in 1755, with the partition of Mataram into two kingdoms, Surakarta and Jogyakarta, the Dutch became suzerains of both.

Thus, the spice trade required naval bases; bases needed surrounding territory; trade required empire, and by the middle of the eighteenth century the Dutch had acquired substantial control over the trade in pepper and spices by establishing forts and bases throughout the East Indies archipelago, and by forcing local rulers to grant them trading monopolies, sometimes by violence and sometimes in return for political help. With the establishment of territorial political power, Dutch interests turned from trade to a new system of economic exploitation requiring local rulers to deliver tributes. Agrarian Java replaced the spice islands as the most lucrative Dutch possession. In 1723 the Dutch required an annual quota of coffee, and native princes were expected to comply with Dutch demands for timber, cotton, and indigo. At first the local princes were autonomous intermediaries, but gradually Dutch overseers were appointed to see to the production of coffee, cloves, cinnamon, and pepper. The tributes in kind were supplemented by forced deliveries of spices at fixed prices. These goods the Dutch exported for resale in Europe.

ISLAMIC SOCIETIES IN SOUTHEAST ASIA

As in the Tatar steppes of Inner Asia, European economic and political supremacy did not prevent, but actually stimulated, the spread of Islam. While the Dutch established their commercial supremacy, Islamic loyalties, Muslim regimes, and Islamic institutions were being consolidated as the basic indigenous expression of cultural identity, political resistance, and economic competition. In each maritime Southeast Asian region, such as Acheh, Malaya, Minangkabau, and Java, a form of Islamic society developed which was at once characteristic of the particular region, reminiscent of Indonesian-Islamic societies in other areas, and recognizably Islamic in international terms.

Acheh
Acheh was the heartland of Indonesian-Islamic societies. The late sixteenth and seventeenth centuries were marked by Acheh's struggle against the Portuguese and the Dutch, contacts with the Ottoman empire, and the influx of Ottoman and Mughal scholars and Sufis. Correspondence, books, the travels of teachers, students, and pilgrims, and diplomatic missions tied Acheh directly to the international world of Islamic learning. Sufi masters formed the backbone of Achenese Islam. The indigenous Sufi tradition goes back to Hamza Fansuri, who died around 1600. He founded the Qadari order in Indonesia, wrote mystical commentaries in Malay,

and propagated the teachings of Ibn al-'Arabi and the doctrine of the unity of being. Shams al-Din Pasai (d. 1630) represented the school of Junayd, with its stress upon worldly activity and the fulfillment of the religious law. The early masters were followed by 'Abd al-Ra'uf Singkeli, who returned after 1661 to Acheh from Arabia, bringing with him the legal and mystical teachings of scholars in Medina and the Shattari order. As a result of these contacts the primary form of Islamic thought to reach the Indies was the tradition of Ibn al-'Arabi, with its emphasis on mystical unity and ecstatic experiences and its receptiveness to folk-culture versions of Islam, but at the end of the eighteenth century 'Abd al-Samad of Palembang translated al-Ghazzali's work into Malay. Achenese Islam, then, came to encompass both the ecstatic and the reformist tendencies characteristic of Islam in the Indian subcontinent and other regions. Muslim teachings became an integral part of Achenese identity.

Though we know little of Achenese society before the middle of the nineteenth century, from late nineteenth- and early twentieth-century observations we can reconstruct the role of Islam in Acheh. Achenese village society was built around lineages, or qawm. The lineage units, however, were not organized by territory; people of different lineages lived in the same villages. In each village there were two types of authority. One was the village headman who ruled in the name of customary law and represented the state. The other was the *tuanku*, a combination of Muslim scholar and Sufi adept. Ordinarily the village tuanku organized prayers, taught religious law, and performed feats of spirit healing. The two authorities represented two parallel cultural and social structures in village life: one based on kinship, custom, and political allegiance; the other based on Islamic belief and worship.

Outside the villages, the 'ulama' and Sufis maintained schools which were self-supporting agricultural communities; in these, the students not only studied but worked on the land belonging to the teachers. The schools taught ritual recitation of the Quran, Sufi beliefs, and magical formulae to students who would in turn become village teachers. These schools represented a very different world from that of the village – the world of purely Islamic social and religious obligations beyond the ties of kinship and territoriality. Islam, then, was integral to the village communities, and yet offered a radical alternative. In place of kinship, it offered brotherhood based on faith. In the political realm, Islam was the principle that legitimized and defined the organization of the state. The state in Acheh was represented by the Sultan, originally the ruler of a small capital town and the surrounding territory. He used Islamic symbols, ideas, and rituals to legitimize his regime, waged jihad against the Portuguese and the Dutch, and patronized the teaching of Islam in his domains.

Malaya

Islam in the riverine states of Malaya was also closely integrated with both village life and the state. As in Achenese villages there were two parallel authorities. The village headman, or *penghulu*, was appointed by the higher authorities to keep the

19   The Ubadiah mosque, Kuala Kangson, Malaysia

local peace, arbitrate disputes, collect taxes, organize labor, and act as a healer and spirit doctor. At the same time, the imam of the mosque, supported by a muezzin and a preacher, organized local worship and taught in the local school. The holy man was often venerated for having made the pilgrimage to Mecca and for his magical powers. Islam made an important contribution to the rituals and festivals marking the solidarity of the village community, and to the commemoration of important events in the life cycle of individuals, such as birth, marriage, and death.

Achenese and Malay villagers followed both Muslim and non-Muslim religious practices, believed in holy spirits, holy places, and saints who were venerated in both Muslim and non-Muslim guise. In the villages there were Muslim and non-Muslim holy men to offer counsel and cures. There were both Muslim and non-Muslim festivals to mark the natural cycle of life and the agricultural year. Malay and Achenese villagers considered themselves Muslims but Islam did not thereby distinguish them as a group, as a community, or as a cult separate from the total fabric of the society.

Islam was also important for the Malay state. The Sultans of the various Malay states were the heads of aristocratic lineages, who made up the political elite and were the village overlords. The Malay Sultans traced their descent to the Sultan of Malacca. A ruler was called at once *raja* (Sultan) and *yang di-pardon* (He Who Was Made Lord). His titles were Muslim and Hindu, and he was believed to be descended from ancient and divine Hindu lords as well as Muslim ancestors. His regalia symbolized his sacred and mystical personality. Drums, weapons, clothing, food, and adornments were reserved for him. While the ruler was believed to have supernatural powers, there was scarcely any public expression of his Islamic role. Apart from prayers at royal inaugurations and funerals, there were no Muslim public rituals. While Shari'a was known, it is not clear that there was a Muslim judicial administration. Religion, then, symbolized the legitimacy of the state, but did not define the operation of the political system or political practices. Compared with other Muslim states, Islam had a minimal impact. In a highly compartmentalized political system it symbolized the unity of the society based upon the allegiance of states and village communities to the same religious symbols.

Minangkabau

Minangkabau, and its colony, Negri Sembilan in Malaya, is another example of how Islam operated on several levels in Malay-Indonesian societies. Minangkabau was a region of rice agriculture and of trade in pepper and gold. Islam was introduced into Minangkabau in the sixteenth century by Sufi missionaries and Muslim traders. By the seventeenth century Islamic schools were established, and the Naqsh-bandiya, the Qadariya, and Shattariya were organized. In the eighteenth century the Shattariya became the leading Sufi order.

Minangkabau society was built on two parallel principles – one matrilineal, the other patrilineal. On the village level, clan organization, laws of marriage, land ownership, and property were defined in matrilineal terms. The village community, called *nagari*, was a grouping of a number of clans administered by chieftains called penghulus. The nagaris were integrated into still larger federations called *alaras*, under the authority of a prince or Raja. Islam represented the masculine principle. In the villages it was institutionalized in the *surau*, young men's houses, which became schools and centers of Sufi brotherhoods. In practice, however, there was a considerable overlap between matrilineal and patrilineal forms of organization. Marriage practices and inheritance laws were blends of Islamic and traditional Minangkabau norms. The two forms of law and social structure were integrated into a single society.

In the eighteenth century both economy and society in Minangkabau were radically changed. The gold and pepper trades collapsed, and coffee production expanded. In the economic upheaval some communities disintegrated while new entrepreneurs and peasants prospered. Rice and coffee producers came into conflict over land. Uprooted people sought their living in towns and markets. Traditional morality gave way to a new individualism.

The old order was challenged by a religious revival under the leadership of Tuanku Nan Tua, who militantly insisted that local religious and social practice must be reformed to meet the demands of Islam. Tuanku Nan Tua taught that it was necessary to strictly observe the rules of the Shari'a, especially in inheritance and family matters, improve mosques and dwellings, celebrate the birthday of the Prophet, and in general make the teachings of the Prophet, rather than custom, supreme. He also taught that Muslim religious law and mystical vision, Shari'a and haqiqa, should be integrated in religious life. His reform was not directed at the matrilineal village communities, but at the newly mobile merchant and peasant population to whom the Shari'a was offered as guidance for the regulation of economic conflict and moral problems. In Minangkabau, as in India, the reformist version of Islam challenged local usages.

The reform movement led to bitter civil war. In 1803 the reformers were reinforced by pilgrims returning from Mecca who had imbibed the principles current in the holy cities of Arabia. The returned pilgrims, preaching in the coffee-producing villages, called for the purification of Islamic life, adherence to the Shari'a, regularity in prayer, and an end to gambling, cock fighting, opium consumption, drinking, smoking, robbery, and violence. They called for a Muslim way of life in strict accordance with the teachings of the Prophet and opposed the magical practices that were part of the village concept of Islam. The reformist movement soon divided. While Nan Tua advocated a pacific preaching, one of his disciples, Tuanku Nan Rincheh, organized a military movement. His followers pledged to dress in white, wear beards, and abstain from bodily satisfactions. They were also prepared to wage war against the nagari, kill the penghulus, confiscate their property, and establish a new regime, headed by an imam and a qadi, and dedicated to the enforcement of Islamic law. The reformers burned the Shattariya schools.

Some penghulus accepted the Shari'a peacefully and assisted in the reform. This was especially true in merchant communities which had extensive trading connections with other parts of Malaya and Sumatra. Most of the customary chiefs, however, refused to accept the reformist movement. To defend themselves they invited the Dutch to intercede. A bitter and protracted war followed (1819–39), until the Dutch finally defeated the reformers and conquered the province. By then the internal momentum of the reform movement was spent; the Muslim factions woke up to their fate, and sought to unite to overthrow Dutch rule. Their resistance (1839–45) was unsuccessful.

Despite the final compromise between traditional leaders and reformist Muslims, the reform movement had a profound effect on Minangkabau society. While Acheh and Malaya maintained the traditional balance among village, school, and state forms of Islam, in Minangkabau the conflict between traditional village and reformist versions of Islam strengthened the practice of Shari'a Islam and succeeded in Islamizing the village communities.

Java

Islamic societies in Java were another variation upon the basic Malay-Indonesian way of synthesizing Islam with non-Islamic Southeast Asian traditions. Islamic societies in Java go back to the conversion of the coastal trading principalities, their victory over Majapahit, and the rise of Mataram. Before the consolidation of Mataram, Muslim holy men, or walis, established independent kingdoms centered around important sanctuaries or tombs, as at Giri, Cheribon, Kadilangu, and Semarang. Muslim scholars, preachers, and holy men established mosques and schools, and proselytized among Javanese. The Shattariya entered Java from Acheh in the late seventeenth century. Banten (in eastern Java), already in contact with Mecca and Medina, received the Qadiriya. By the late seventeenth century the Islamic presence was institutionalized in the form of schools and shrine complexes. A bitter struggle took place between the state and the Islamic religious centers, in which Mataram progressively destroyed the political power of the Muslim lords – though not their local religious influence. The Muslim holy men retained a charisma that could be used to rally opposition to the state. On Java Islam became both the banner of the state and the standard of the opposition.

The Mataram state combined Islamic and Hindu concepts of rule. Its rulers believed that they derived their authority directly from God – the ruler was God's representative on earth, *kalipatullah* – and indirectly from the tomb of Sunan Kalijaga, the saint and holy man who represented the spiritual presence of Islam. Despite the new layer of Islamic titulature and legitimization, the Hindu cosmological conception of the state continued to be valued. In the pre-Islamic Javan conception the universe was taken to be a single and unified phenomenon; the cosmos harmoniously ordered; the world of human beings grounded in cosmic principles. The ruler had access to cosmic powers and transmitted them to his people. For each individual the ideal of life was to cultivate an inner tranquility which made the soul correspond to the order of society and the universe.

In the Mataram conception the ruler was a sacred, indeed divine, figure; the repository of *wahyu*, divine radiance, or a luminous light which suffused his person and emanated from him. Wahyu was seen as a concrete, tangible, creative energy which flows through the universe – a force which can be accumulated, concentrated, and preserved in individuals as a result of yogic practices and extreme self-denial. Heroes concentrate power, their adversaries diffuse it. Power is also concentrated by public rituals, including mass demonstrations, powerful slogans, and the presence of thousands of submissive persons. It is concentrated by the ownership of *pusaka*, heirlooms, including spears, musical instruments, and carriages, and by control over extraordinary or deformed human beings. Power is manifest in wealth and sexual energy. Fertility, political unity, prosperity, stability, and glory of the kingdom are all considered expressions of power. However, possession of power is prior to legitimacy. Power is neither good nor evil; it is just real. Thus, in the Javanese conception of kingship the ruler was glorified by his descent from gods as well as human beings, by his possession of holy relics, and by court ceremonies where weapons and decorations symbolized his special powers. The ruler had the deepest knowledge of reality, sense of justice, and a flawless personality acquired by ritual and by observance of taboos. The king's actions were taken to be God's will.

Royal administration was conceived in terms of maintaining order and justice in the whole of the kingdom. The ruler's subordinates were fully responsible for their districts and personally accountable to him. They formed a social class called the *priyayi*, bound to their lord by *kawula-gusti*, the bond of lord and servant. The ruler must care for his officials as a father and the servants must give total love, submission, and gratitude to their lord. Officials were paid by benefices allotted to them by their patron. The central political problem for a ruler was to control the land granted to his supporters and not to allow it to become hereditary. When provincial notables built up an independent base of power, the ruler tried to use his household clients to offset their influence and to absorb or coopt them. The king and the nobility lived on the labor of the peasantry. The king was entitled to part of the produce of the land. The salaries for court workers and guards were paid for by taxes from designated districts. Peasants also labored to build water works and bridges, and provided transportation and personal services to the king and his officials.

The ideal of the Mataram aristocracy was based on individual self-cultivation. To be loyal to their lord and to fulfill their role in the cosmic order the priyayi had to cultivate an inner life of refined feeling and an outer life of polite formality. The ruling elite was distinguished from the rest of the population by a quality called *halus*, which meant smoothness of spirit, beauty, elegance, politeness, and sensitivity. The opposite of halus was *kasar*, lack of control, coarseness, and the degradation that comes from indulging in purely selfish and personal desires. Control of emotion, equanimity, patience, acceptance of fate without protest, and detachment from the external world were the most highly regarded virtues.

This inner restraint was the basis of realistic behavior. In the outer world the priyayi would express themselves by conformity to etiquette and ethics, and by speaking in correct linguistic form. Language, dance, music, and art were all channeled outer expressions of a restrained inner being. The priyayi ethic of control over the outer world protected them against inner disturbance; a balanced inner world expressed itself in outward order. The cultivation of true feeling and of true expression, both called *rasa*, was a realization of the individual's true self and a recognition of the reality of God's existence; it was also a means to worldly power through concentration and mastery of one's spiritual capacities.

Thus, Mataram society was in name Islamic but the actual organization of state, including its concepts of rulership and the personal ideal of the priyayi elite, was based on Hindu and Javanese mythical and cosmological conceptions. The strong emphasis on the Javanese and Hindu basis of Mataram culture was due to the continuity of political elites. While Muslim regimes in India, the Ottoman empire, and many other parts of the world were established by conquerors who brought their Muslim identity from without, the Mataram regime was converted from within. Though Islam had been introduced by the wars between the coastal principalities and the rulers of the interior, Mataram eventually destroyed the coastal powers, suppressed the sea trade, and made the aristocracy of the interior, rather than the commercial lords of the coast, the dominant elite on Java. Islamic identity then served to reinforce the legitimacy of the old order and allowed Javanese society to define its opposition to Dutch rule without disturbing the inherited structures of political order and personal values. The state continued its traditional, political, and symbolic functions in Islamic guise. As compared with Safavid Iran and even Mughal India, which also combined universal Islamic norms with local regional culture, Mataram leaned strongly in the direction of the non-Islamic aspects of state culture.

Alongside the state the local communal form of Islam was built around a pesantren, which was part school and part religious brotherhood. The pupils lived in dormitories, worked in the fields or at some craft that helped support the school, studied chanting of the Quran, and learned magical and mystical formulae. The influence of the 'ulama', or *kiyayis*, extended from the schools to the villages. In the villages they won a following of strict Muslim believers who looked to the teachers as their spiritual masters and who joined religious orders, ordinarily the Naqshbandiya and Qadiriya. The teachers, students, and village followers who adhered to this Muslim way of life were called *santris*.

The mass of villagers, however, were Muslim in a different sense. (Little is known about Javanese village life in the pre-modern era. The observations made here for the sake of completeness are based on mid-twentieth century research.) For most

Javanese villagers Islam was not a question of political legitimacy or doctrine but was simply part of their mentality – part of their attitude toward the world seen and the world unseen. Islam was not a religion or a sect in the sense of being an ideology and a defined social allegiance so much as a vocabulary by which people defined the sacred forces in everyday life.

Villagers called themselves Muslims, and the influence of the 'ulama' who represented conventional Islamic beliefs and practices was considerable. However, village culture was in fact compounded of animist, Hindu, and Islamic elements. The *slametan* was the primary village ritual. A slametan was given to mark such important life events as birth, marriage, illness, and death, personal and business occasions, village ceremonies of purification and solidarity, and Muslim holidays. The feast was meant to establish security and equanimity for the host, his family, and his guests, to dispel hostility and aggression, and to defend against evil spirits. Its symbolic purpose was to organize society, regulate behavior and feeling, and ward off the forces that threatened to bring disorder and chaos into everyday life. The ceremonial itself was marked by a short speech given by the host and a prayer or Quranic passage chanted in Arabic, followed by a meal. The Arabic recitation, the participation of the village religious teacher, and the choice of Muslim occasions such as the birthday of the Prophet, or the ending of the fast of Ramadan, made this multi-purpose village ceremony an Islamic occasion. The curing of disease and the warding off of evil spirits was also the function of the *dukun*, or village sorcerer, who worked his magic by spells, amulets, and herbs, sometimes giving them a Muslim orientation by chanting Quranic verses.

Islam was thus assimilated to a village religious mentality that focused on belief in a world of spirits, demons, and powers of nature. Islam in the village context was not so much a metaphysical, ethical, or legal system, or a form of social and political organization, but another metaphor for an ongoing community life based on traditional religious and social conceptions.

Thus, Islam in Java was institutionalized on three levels: that of the state, the 'ulama' community, and the village. Yet, despite the close integration of Islam with the established institutions of society, it maintained the capacity for organizing resistance and opposition to state policies. Between 1825 and 1830, Dipanegara, an aristocrat of royal lineage, rebelled in the name of Islam, with the support of Islamic teachers, against an abusive government and the growing Dutch power. Throughout the nineteenth century local kiyayis appealed to the sentiments of jihad and Islamic justice to generate peasant uprisings against local and foreign oppression. Uprisings in Banten between 1880 and 1888 were led by local religious teachers linked with the major Sufi orders. Though Islam in Java had been assimilated to a Hindu cosmological concept of an ordered universe and society, it also symbolized a principle of truth and justice which transcended the given social order and legitimized resistance to oppression.

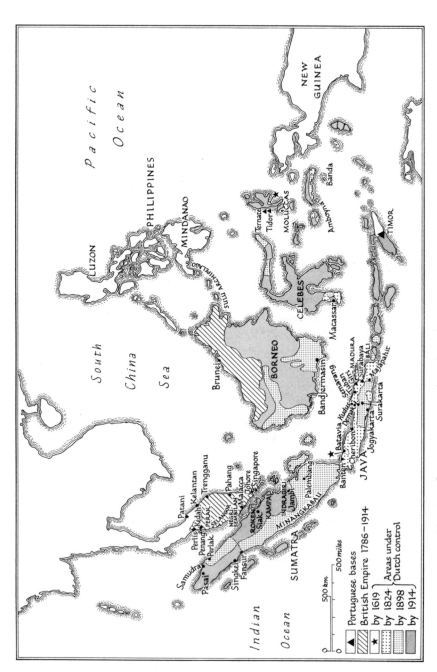

Map 21 The Portuguese, Dutch, and British empires in Southeast Asia: 1500–1914

THE NEW IMPERIALISM

While the various Islamic societies of maritime Southeast Asia had grown up under the shadow of Portuguese and Dutch commercial empires, these empires were primarily mechanisms to control trade, create monopolies, and extract tributes. The British entered the regional competition in 1786 when they made an agreement with the Sultan of Kedah to use Penang, an island off the coast of Malaya, to repair and equip fleets for the Indian Ocean, and as a base from which they could sell British goods to raise revenues for the purchase of silk and tea in China. In 1791 Penang, and in 1800 a strip of mainland called Province Wellesley, were ceded to them. Then with the conquest of Holland by France in 1795, William V of Holland turned Malacca and other Dutch colonies over to the British for use in the war against France. In 1810 Britain took control of Java. At the end of the Napoleonic wars, Britain agreed to return Dutch possessions in order to restore Holland as a buffer between Britain and France and to prevent the development of a French–Dutch alliance in the postwar period. However, the British retained control of the Malacca Straits, and established a new base at Singapore in 1819. In a treaty of 1824 the Dutch recognized India and Malaya as being in the British sphere of influence, and the British recognized Dutch predominance in Sumatra, Java, and the rest of the Indies.

The consolidation of Dutch control over Java opened the way for the expansion of Dutch administration to other parts of the East Indies. While conservatives opposed the costs of military action, Dutch officials, soldiers, and traders pressed for expansion. Between 1824 and 1858 the Dutch acquired much of Sumatra. Dutch expansion was motivated by the interest in coffee, sugar, tobacco, pepper, and spice production and, after 1870, in tin and rubber.

Commercial and military expansion brought the Dutch into direct conflict with Acheh for control of the pepper ports of northern and western Sumatra. After two campaigns in 1871 and 1874 the Dutch declared the annexation of Acheh and the abolition of the Sultanate, and demanded the unconditional surrender of the local district lords, the uleebalangs. The result was 'ulama'-led guerrilla resistance. However, Dutch control of the trade of north Sumatra, aggressive military action, and a religious policy that called for the suppression of militant Muslim opposition but the acceptance of pacific Muslim religious interests enabled the Dutch to divide the uleebalangs from the 'ulama', suppress the guerrilla resistance, and dominate Acheh by 1908.

Dutch control was also extended to the outer islands. South and central Celebes, the Moluccas, Borneo, and other places were absorbed into the Dutch empire. The Dutch either made vassals of the local chiefs or pushed them aside altogether. By 1911 they had complete control of the Indies. For the first time in history one empire ruled over the island archipelago. Thus the Dutch laid the foundation for the modern nation-state of Indonesia.

Similarly, the British were building up an empire in Malaya. Having taken control of the Malacca Straits and the port of Singapore in 1819, in 1826 they agreed with Siam to divide Malaya into British and Siamese spheres of influence. From 1824 to 1867 they attempted to maintain their trading position without extending political or territorial controls. Nonetheless, the economic development of the region generated strong pressures for further British intervention. As Malaya's tin mines were opened to exploitation, large numbers of Chinese and Indian laborers flocked into the country. After a time Malays constituted little more than half of the total population, the Chinese 35 percent, and the Indians 11 percent. Malays controlled the government and regarded the Chinese, entrenched in the economy, as an alien, threatening intrusion; the Chinese were themselves divided into warring secret societies. The Malay states were too weak and power too dispersed among local district chieftains to cope with this complex situation. Chinese and British companies based in Singapore clamored for a strong government to secure their trading interests, and urged the East India Company to take a more aggressive stance toward the Malay hinterland. The British colonial office also wanted British intervention because it feared Dutch expansion on Sumatra and the French occupation of Indo-China. Finally, in 1874 the British intervened in local wars and negotiated the so-called Pangkor engagement, by which the Sultanate of Perak accepted a British resident whose advice had to be asked on all revenue and finance questions, but not on matters of religion and local custom.

This was the beginning of colonial control. From 1877 to 1889 the British residents helped to create a centralized government in Perak, including a civil service, a police force, a court system, roads, railways, and new taxes. At the same time the British took several of the smaller Malay states under their protection. Finally, in 1896 they brought Perak, Selangor, Pahang, and Negri Sembilan into a federation of Malay states. In 1909 the federation established a council of British officers and Sultans to deal with the problems of tin and rubber development and the immigration of large numbers of Chinese and Indian workers. By World War I the federated Malay states and the various unfederated Malay states, including Kedah, Perlis, Kelantan, Trengganu, and Johore, were each subordinate to a British advisor. The Straits settlements, Singapore, and Malacca were crown colonies.

The maritime Southeast Asian societies had thus come fully under Dutch and British colonial control. The Sultans served as symbolic overlords who arbitrated disputes and reaffirmed the existence of an overarching social order in a world of innumerable village communities, but real political power was held by district and village chiefs. Though a qadi or chief judicial official was appointed at the Mataram court, there was no hierarchical organization of 'ulama' or of other Muslim religious leaders and therefore no state control of religious affairs as was the case in the Ottoman, Safavid, and Mughal empires. Nor was there any effective organization among the 'ulama' or the Sufis. 'Ulama' and Sufis were independent both of the state and of each other. Islam in Southeast Asia was organized only on a local village scale around individual teachers and holy men.

At the village level Islam specified a minimum of ritual and social practices but did not define cultural style, *mentalité*, or social affiliation. Islam for ordinary villagers was but another symbol in the complex repertoire of ideas by which they tried to protect themselves from the malevolent forces of an uncertain world. While many Muslims adhered to the high tradition defined by 'ulama' and Sufi teachings, many, if not most, lived in a mental world defined by local cultures. For most Southeast Asian villagers, Islam was an element of a more complex social and religious identity and not the exclusive symbol of personal and collective life. Nonetheless, in all its manifestations, Islamic identity, however understood, was the one shared factor in Malay-Indonesian societies.

ISLAM IN AFRICA

CHAPTER 20

ISLAM IN SUDANIC, SAVANNAH, AND FOREST WEST AFRICA

The formation of Islamic societies in sub-Saharan Africa was similar to that in Indonesia. Whereas Islamic societies in the Middle East and the Indian subcontinent were established by conquest and ordered by states, Islam in Africa was diffused by the migration of Muslim merchants, teachers, and settlers. Linked by trading networks, family connections, teacher–student relationships and Sufi fellowship, Muslim communities were established within small-scale regional states and in stateless societies. The Muslims sometimes formed peaceful minorities in non-Muslim societies. Sometimes they converted local rulers and established a joint elite of warrior rulers and Muslim merchants. In some cases they made war against local rulers and conquered them in the name of Islam. The central and western Sudanic belt was the center of a succession of Muslim empires. The Guinean savannah, Senegambia, and Mauritania were regions of Muslim communal settlement from the thirteenth to the nineteenth centuries and of Muslim jihads and state formation in the eighteenth and nineteenth centuries. In the next chapter I shall discuss the eastern Sudan and East Africa, and the establishment of European colonial empires throughout Muslim sub-Saharan Africa.

THE KINGDOMS OF WESTERN AND CENTRAL SUDAN

Before the coming of Arab and Berber Muslim tribesmen, traders, and settlers, the Sudanic region was already an agricultural and state-centered society. Herding was carried on in the Sahil, the grassy steppelands that border the Sahara. The Sudan, a broad savannah belt to the south, produced millet, maize, yams, groundnuts, cotton, tobacco, indigo, and other crops. Sudanic societies were built upon small agricultural villages or herding communities, sometimes, but not always, integrated into larger tribal and linguistic groups. The western and central Sudan was divided into a number of states, but there were also large areas that were not under state control. The Sudan region traded with other parts of Africa and the Mediterranean, often through Berber intermediaries. The Sudan exported gold, slaves, hides, and ivory, and imported copper, silver beads, dried fruit, and cloth. Gold was found at Bambuk, at the confluence of the Senegal and Faleme Rivers. For centuries the Sudan was the principal source of gold for North Africa, the Middle East, and Europe. Sudanese gold sustained the Aghlabid, Fatimid, and Spanish Umayyad regimes and later formed the economic basis of the Almoravid empire in Morocco and Spain. Trade also stimulated the growth of desert port cities such as Takrur, Kumbi (Ghana), and Gao.

The western Sudan

The oldest of the Sudanic kingdoms was Ghana, probably founded between the second and the fourth centuries AD. In the ninth and tenth centuries Ghana was both a partner and a rival of Berbers for the trans-Saharan trade. To the west of Ghana was Takrur on the Senegal River. To the east the kingdom of Kawkaw had its capital at Gao on the middle Niger River. To the south of Ghana there were no large kingdoms, but a number of small chieftainships.

Sudanic states had their origin in family groups led by patriarchs, councils of elders, or village chiefs. The state came into existence when a local elder, an immigrant warrior, or perhaps a priestly ruler established his control over other communities. The key political factor was not the control of territory but the relations that enabled the ruler to monopolize religious prestige, draw military support, and extract taxes or tributes from the subject communities. A Sudanic empire commonly had a core territory integrated by ethnic, linguistic, or similar ties and a larger sphere of power defined by the rule of a particular person, or lineage, over numerous subordinate families, castes, lineages, and village communities. The kings were believed to have divine powers and were considered sacred persons. They did not appear in public and were not to be seen carrying out ordinary bodily functions such as eating. Around the kings were numerous office-holders who helped govern the realm, and provincial and district chiefs often recruited from the junior members of the noble families.

These societies acquired an Islamic identity as a result of trade and conversion. The Arab conquest of North Africa multiplied contacts among Arab, Berber, Saharan, and Sudanese peoples. North African Berbers converted to Khariji Islam in the seventh century, and Mauritanian Berbers were converted in the ninth century. By the late tenth and eleventh centuries most of the Sudanese trading towns had a Muslim quarter, and Muslims were important as advisors and functionaries at the courts of local rulers. For the sake of administrative support, legitimization, and commercial contacts, the rulers of Kawkaw, Takrur, Ghana, and Bornu adopted Islam in the late tenth and eleventh centuries. Islam became an imperial cult and the religion of state elites and trading peoples, but the agricultural populations maintained their traditional beliefs.

From the eleventh to the sixteenth centuries several kingdoms, in different geographical locations, succeeded each other as the principal centers of political power, trade, and Islamization. Takrur was the leading state in the eleventh century. It exported gold and slaves to North Africa in return for wool, copper, and beads. Takrur was strongly committed to jihad against its non-Muslim neighbors, but came under the suzerainty of Mali in the thirteenth century and later disintegrated.

Takrur was replaced by Ghana as the preeminent center of Islam in the western Sudan. Before the conversion of its ruler the capital city of Ghana, Kumbi-Saleh, was a dual town, with one district for Muslims and one for non-Muslims. The Muslim town was equipped with mosques and religious functionaries including imams, muezzins, Quran reciters, and scholars. The Muslims provided the ruler with interpreters and officials. These local influences, reinforced by Almoravid economic, diplomatic, and cultural penetration, and by the proselytizing activities of the Almoravid leader Abu Bakr (d. 1087) and his colleague Imam al-Hadrami (d. 1096), prompted the acceptance of Islam. With the decline of the Almoravids in the twelfth century, Ghana became the richest kingdom in the Sudan, but in the thirteenth century its former tributaries freed themselves from central control and the kingdom disintegrated.

From the early thirteenth to the end of the sixteenth centuries, Mali became the dominant regime in the western Sudan and the principal center of Islam. Mali had its origin among Malinke peoples living between the Senegal and the Niger Rivers. A local chieftain, Sunjata (1230–55), of the Keita dynasty, was able to unite the Malinke chieftains, and capture the former territories of Ghana and the region between the Senegal and the Niger Rivers. The expanded territory included Bure, on the Upper Niger, the principal Sudanic goldfield, and afforded wider trading connections. The Keita dynasty ruled, with some interruptions, from 1230 to 1390. The most famous of its rulers, Mansa Musa (1307–32), made a sensational pilgrimage to Cairo in 1324, which made his kingdom legendary for its wealth in gold. Mansa Musa returned to Mali with Arab and Berber adventurers to serve in his administration. He built new mosques and palaces and introduced Arabic-style poetry to his court.

The empire he ruled may be taken as a typical West African Islamic regime. The basis of the political order was family and village units, the head of the family being both priest and chieftain. A group of villages in turn formed a *kafs*, or a territorial unit ruled by a chief called the *mansa*. The power of the mansa was originally based on election by a group of clans, but the support of his own kinsmen, clients, and slaves sometimes allowed him to escape the control of other families, usurp power, and make himself a local monarch. He could then adopt the Ghanaian and Sudanic concepts of kingship to institutionalize his power. As a ruler, he would surround himself with a bodyguard, servants, and elaborate ceremonies. A quasi-divine figure, the king was accepted as a symbol of the power of life and death.

The ruler and the royal clan were supported by a consortium of related clans. The descendants of the mansa supplied the principal functionaries. Client clans, castes of dependent craftsmen, and people allied by marriage or by past service

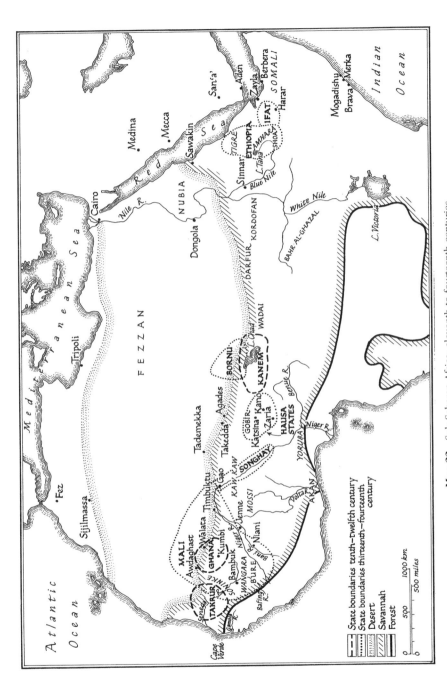

Map 22 Sub-Saharan Africa: eleventh to fourteenth centuries

also supported the ruler. Slaves and serfs worked in agricultural settlements to provide produce for the court, the army, and the administration. Taxes and tributes were extracted from dependent communities. For administrative purposes, there was a central core of territory, directly ruled by governors, and peripheral tribute-paying territories ruled by vassal chieftains.

When Islam became the royal cult, rulers built mosques, and the king and the entire court took part in public prayers held on the great Islamic festivals. The rulers of Mali brought Muslim scholars from Cairo and Fez to help establish a West African tradition of Islamic learning. The religion of the commercial classes and portions of the political elite helped unify the kingdom and gave cultural support to the dynasty. Islam was a bond of empire. Muslim festivals, however, were also occasions for the performance of pagan ceremonies and dances. This was especially important in segmented African societies where only portions of the ruling elite and the trading classes were Muslim and the mass of the agricultural population was still pagan.

By the end of the fourteenth century the Mali empire was in decline. Jenne, probably settled by Muslim traders in the thirteenth century, became the crucial link to the Akan forest region (modern Ghana and the Ivory Coast) and new supplies of gold. Timbuktu (an important Tuareg trade and religious center settled in the thirteenth century) replaced Walata as a terminus of the Saharan caravan traffic. As the trade routes changed, local chieftains became independent, and reduced Mali once again to a petty chieftaincy. The people of Mali remained identifiable as having a common dialect and customs, but the empire was no more.

With the breakup of Mali, a local leader named Sunni 'Ali (1464/65–92) founded a new empire, Songhay, in the region of the middle Niger and the western Sudan and took control of the trans-Saharan trade. Sunni 'Ali seized Timbuktu in 1468 and Jenne in 1473, and built his regime on the revenues of their trade and the cooperation of Muslim merchants. Sunni 'Ali behaved as a Muslim in giving alms and fasting during Ramadan, but he also worshiped idols and practiced non-Muslim rites.

His successor, Askiya Muhammad Ture (1493–1528), supported by Mande clans, defeated Sunni 'Ali's son, seized the state, and furthered the work of state formation by building a standing army to supplement village levies. He extended the empire into the former territories of Mali. Askiya Muhammad also tried to rally the support of Muslim religious leaders. He made Islam the official religion, built mosques, and brought Muslim scholars, including al-Maghili (d. 1504), the founder of an important tradition of Sudanic African Muslim scholarship, to Gao. The legitimization of his regime also depended upon his investiture by the Sharif of Mecca as Caliph of the lands of Takrur. Still, Islam remained the religion of the governing elite while the mass of Songhay society continued to be pagan.

The empire of Songhay was destroyed in 1591 by a Moroccan invasion, and the *arma*, or the descendants of the invading army, became the ruling elite in the Niger region. Internal warfare and the shift of trade routes from the Sahara to the

Atlantic in the eighteenth century led to the decline of the regime. Tuaregs and Bambaras established new states. By the end of the eighteenth century the process of the rise and fall of empires with different capitals came to an end, and the once great Muslim kingdoms of the western Sudan disintegrated into a plethora of small states.

Central Sudan

The central, like the western Sudan, was also the home of diverse ethnic and linguistic groups and a center of state formation. The earliest state in this region was founded by Saharan nomads at some time in the ninth century, with its capital in the region of Kanem. Trade routes from the Fezzan brought Khariji merchants into the region, and by the late eleventh century Islam was accepted as the religion of the ruling elite. Not until the thirteenth century did the rulers of Kanem make the pilgrimage and build mosques. In 1240 a madrasa was established in Cairo for Kanuri students, marking the integration of the central Sudan into the international network of Muslim scholarship. However, in the fourteenth century, the dynasty, defeated by pagan peoples living east of Lake Chad, was forced to abandon Kanem and move to Bornu west of Lake Chad. By this time the state had progressively united the various peoples subject to them into the Kanuri nation.

'Ali b. Dunama (1476–1503) founded the new capital of Ngazargamo in Bornu, and Idris b. 'Ali (1570–1602) completed the process of state formation. He developed a standing army including a cavalry corps made up of members of the ruler's household and other chiefs, and an auxiliary infantry. The elite troops were provided with firearms. Idris b. 'Ali also furthered the Islamization of the country by reintroducing Muslim law and courts, and by building mosques and a hostel in Mecca for Kanuri pilgrims. In the seventeenth century Ngazargamo became the foremost center of Islamic education in the central Sudan. It had four Friday mosques, each with its own imam; the 'ulama' engaged in learned disputations at the court of the rulers. Islam, however, did not have a substantial following outside court circles and was not the religion of the majority.

Bornu's dominant interest was the trade in gold, salt, slaves, and weapons between the central Sudan, Tripoli, and Cairo. Its major rivals were the Hausa city-states; its major ally, the Ottoman regime in Libya. In 1551 the Ottomans had seized Tripoli and in 1577 the Fezzan, which had been a vassal of the empire of Kanem-Bornu. Bornu maintained good relations with Tripoli throughout the seventeenth and eighteenth centuries. Ambassadors brought rich presents of Ottoman weapons and luxury goods in exchange for slaves and gold. Bornu also maintained close trading connections with Cairo. However, by the middle of the eighteenth century Bornu's hegemony broke down, and it was transformed from a regional empire into a smaller, relatively homogeneous Kanuri state.

Hausaland, which now makes up northern Nigeria, lay between the eastern kingdoms of Kanem-Bornu and the western empires of Ghana and Mali. As a cultural and political region Hausaland took shape in the last millennium as a result of the westward expansion of Hausa peoples. Their expansion was marked by the conversion of woodlands into open savannah and the introduction of grain cultivation and a denser peasant population.

The earliest Hausa societies were confederacies of kinship groups led by a priest-chief. The groups in the confederacy specialized in fishing, hunting, agriculture, and crafts such as blacksmithing and salt digging. Sometimes, kings emerged by the concentration of power and wealth in the hands of one priest-chief, who then expected the others to legitimize his rule. Such kings often turned to a universalistic religion, such as Islam, to acquire autonomous legitimization and to undermine the authority of their competitors. In other cases kingship was not an indigenous institution, but grew out of the dominance of a foreign trading community. In the towns of Kano and Katsina monarchical rule was established by colonies of Muslim traders who either directly seized the state or converted a local ruler. Yaji (1348–85) was the first Muslim ruler of Kano. He appointed a qadi and an imam as part of the state administration. Muhammad Rumfa (1463–99) is credited with the advancement of Islam by building mosques and schools. He commissioned al-Maghili to write a treatise on Muslim government. Other scholars from Egypt, Tunis, and Morocco turned Kano into a center of Muslim scholarship. In the sixteenth century, the new ruling dynasty of Katsina, founded by Muhammad al-Korau (d. 1541–2?), formally adopted Islam, and invited Muslim scholars from North Africa and Egypt to reside in Katsina. An 'ulama' class emerged under royal patronage. It seems probable that the new rulers tried to convert local peoples and subvert the authority of local chiefs, but were eventually obliged to compromise. Hausaland then remained divided between a Muslim cosmopolitan urban royal society and the local kinship animistic rural societies.

The city regimes were characterized by a centralized chieftainship with a fortified capital, an elaborate court, and a substantial officialdom. By the fourteenth century, Kano had acquired a powerful military machine. The *madawaki*, or chief cavalry officer, was the commander of a professional officers' corps. The Kano armies were equipped with iron helmets and coats of mail. By conquest, Kano acquired great numbers of slaves who were used as soldiers, officials, agricultural laborers, and porters on the trade routes. Colonies were created to produce agricultural revenues. The power of the state was also based on extensive trading networks. Kano became a base for the trans-Saharan trade in salt, cloth, leather, and grain, and for trade with the Ashanti and the Yorubas. Islamization generally facilitated the expansion of trade. It was the basis of an enlarged marketing network, and the 'ulama' provided legal support, guarantees, safe conducts, introductions, and other services.

In the course of the fifteenth century, under the influences of expanding international trade and intense economic and political competition with surrounding states, the Hausa system expanded to other cities and some Hausa city-states were transformed into little empires. From the time of their institutional consolidation in

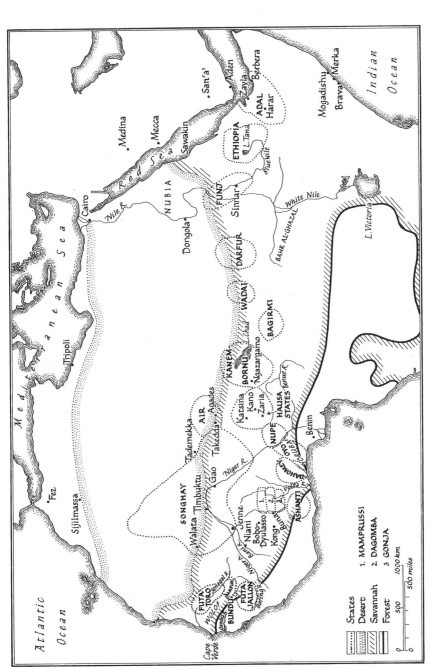

Map 23 Sub-Saharan Africa: sixteenth to eighteenth centuries

Labels on map:

Atlantic Ocean

Mediterranean Sea

Red Sea

Indian Ocean

Medina
Mecca
Sawakin
Cairo
Nile R.
NUBIA
Dongola
FUNJ
Sinnar
White Nile
BAHR AL-GHAZAL
L. Victoria
San'a'
Aden
Zayla
Berbera
Merka
Brava
Mogadishu
ADAL
Harar
ETHIOPIA
L. Tana
Blue Nile
DARFUR
WADAI
BAGIRMI
KANEM
BORNU
L. Chad
Ngazargamo
Katsina
Kano
Zaria
HAUSA STATES
Benue R.
NUPE
OYO
Benin
DAHOMEY
ASHANTI
Jenne
Niani
Bobo
Dyulasso
Kong
Bani R.
Black Volta R.
White Volta R.
Niger R.
SONGHAY
Walata
Timbuktu
Gao
Takedda
Tademekka
AIR
Agades
Tripoli
Fez
Sijilmasa
Cape Verde
FUTA TORO
BUNDU
FUTA JALLON
WOLOF
Senegal R.
Gambia R.
Bani R.

Legend:

States ▓ (dotted border)
Desert (dotted)
Savannah (hatched)
Forest (plain)

1. MAMPRUSSI
2. DAGOMBA
3. GONJA

Scale:
0   500   1000 km
0   500 miles

the fifteenth century to the end of the eighteenth century the Hausa states were at war with each other and with neighboring peoples. In the late eighteenth century the Hausa states, like those of Bornu and the western Sudan, were economically and politically exhausted.

Thus between the tenth and the eighteenth centuries a succession of Sudanic kingdoms were converted or organized under the banner of Islam. These kingdoms owed their existence to Muslim trading communities. In some cases the traders provided the economic resources, weapons, and horses that enabled local adventurers to establish states. In other cases they were themselves the conquerors. In still other cases existing Sudanic states, based upon nomadic conquests or chieftainships, found economic support and legitimization in Islam. The prayer, rituals, amulets, and magical books of the Muslim traders were as important as their financial and administrative assistance.

Muslim communities and holy men in the Sudan

The relationship between Muslim beliefs, rituals, and holy men and African chiefs was variable. In some cases the chiefs remained pagans but employed Muslims as officials, traders, and advisors. In other cases the chiefs converted to Islam but maintained a cultural style that synthesized Muslim rituals and festivals with pagan customs and ceremonies. African rulers built mosques, instituted public prayer, patronized Muslim scholars, and celebrated Muslim holidays – but ceremonial dances, recitations of poets, and the drama of court life had non-Muslim sources. In the history of a dynasty, early rulers often stressed their pagan warrior virtues while later rulers stressed their Muslim ones. They maintained a double cultural orientation to express both their Islamic and their indigenous bases of authority. African kings were not retrograde Muslims; they simply followed the universal tendency of Muslim regimes to blend Muslim and non-Muslim cultures. In cases such as Takrur and Bornu the chiefs became fully Muslim and active patrons of Muslim religious life. Whatever the degree of their attachments, when chiefs accepted Islam, their lands were regarded by Muslims as being part of the realm of Islam (*dar al-islam*).

Muslim regimes favored the work of 'ulama' and holy men. Only a small number of scholars held positions at court or as judges and prayer leaders, but their influence was considerable. The Muslim clerics presided over prayers, sacrifices, and festivals, applied Muslim law, and established a Muslim tradition of culture. Arabic thus became important not only for the diffusion of religion but for communications and trade. It was used for official correspondence in the Ghana empire before the end of the twelfth century and in Mali in the mid-fourteenth century, where the highly Islamized state of Mansa Musa had qadis and administrative departments. The earliest known Arabic texts, though, come from Bornu at the end of the fourteenth century; Arabic reached Hausaland at about the same time; fifteenth-century immigrants brought Arabic books on language and theology. Kano became a great center of Muslim learning when it was visited by al-Maghili and other North African and Egyptian scholars.

Timbuktu was probably the most important center of Arabic and Muslim studies. Its scholarly elite was drawn from a number of interrelated families representing the numerous tribal and ethnic subgroups that made up the populace of the city. While the state regimes of Mali, Songhay, and the arma of Morocco rose and fell, the scholars sustained Timbuktu society. The qadi was generally the head of the community, the principal spokesman before military regimes, and the principal mediator of internal commercial and religious disputes. His influence was maintained by his connections with trading groups, and with the families who made up the *jama'as*, or communities, of the four main (and several lesser) mosques. Due to the qadis and the scholars, Timbuktu remained an organized community and a center of Muslim scholarship regardless of the fortunes of political regimes.

The scholarly families were sustained by trade, investments in cloth, camels, cattle and urban property, contributions of rulers and state officials, and the donations of their students and disciples, who worked as traders and tailors. For centuries the 'ulama' of Timbuktu maintained a rich and vital tradition of Quranic, hadith, and legal studies, supplemented by studies in theology, linguistics, history, mathematics, and astronomy. An important biographical dictionary of late sixteenth- and early seventeenth-century scholars, written by Ahmad Baba (1556–1627), indicates a high level of Arabic and Muslim learning, and close contact with Mecca and Egypt. In the seventeenth and eighteenth centuries Timbuktu became a center of regional historical scholarship as well.

MERCHANTS AND MISSIONARIES IN THE DESERT, FOREST, AND COASTAL REGIONS

Outside the Sudanic region Muslim merchant, pastoralist, and cultivator communities, groups of warriors, traders, and religious teachers, lived in small and scattered settlements as caste-like enclaves within the larger society. After the breakup of the Songhay empire at the end of the sixteenth century, the Saharan regions from Mauritania to Lake Chad, regardless of ethnic or linguistic identity, came to be hierarchically stratified into a dominant warrior elite, usually ruled by a single lineage, and subordinated peoples. The subordinated peoples included religious lineages, artisan and slave groups. The religious lineages, called zawaya or *insilimen*, lived by pastoralism and commerce but were held in high esteem for their scholars and because they claimed Arab or sharifian descent. Each of the major caravan trading posts such as Walata, Timbuktu, and Agades was the base of a particular religious community and a center of its economic and religious networks. Knowledge of law was the basis of judicial and political authority, and the personal capacity to adapt textbook law to real situations resulted from training in Sufism. The combination of technical knowledge and personal insight, religious qualities, and the reputation for being able to perform miracles made religious leaders important as political mediators.

The Kunta family is the best-known example of a scholarly lineage with widespread influence throughout Mauritania, Senegambia, and other parts of the western

Sudan. The family's history goes back to Shaykh Sidi Ahmad al-Bakka'i (d. 1504) who established a Qadiri zawiya (Sufi residence) in Walata. In the sixteenth century the family spread across the Sahara to Timbuktu, Agades, Bornu, Hausaland, and other places, and in the eighteenth century large numbers of Kunta moved to the region of the middle Niger where they established the village of Mabruk. Sidi al-Mukhtar al-Kunti (1728–1811) united the Kunta factions by successful negotiation, and established an extensive confederation. Under his influence the Maliki school of law was reinvigorated and the Qadiri order spread throughout Mauritania, the middle Niger region, Guinea, the Ivory Coast, Futa Toro, and Futa Jallon. Kunta colonies in the Senegambian region became centers of Muslim teaching.

A student of Sidi al-Mukhtar, Shaykh Sidiya al-Kabir (1775–1868), established another Islamic network in Mauritania. Sidiya began his religious education by memorizing the Quran and then went on to studies of poetry, theology, grammar, and law. In 1809–10 he apprenticed himself to Sidi al-Mukhtar. As student, secretary, and advisor to a family that had a powerful part in the revival of the Qadiri order, extensive trading operations, and political authority in the southern Sahara, Sidiya was introduced into one of the most sophisticated of Saharan and West African societies. He studied both law and mysticism, including the works of al-Ghazzali and Ibn al-'Arabi. After some thirty-five years Sidiya returned to his home community, established his residence at Boutilimit and, as a successful mediator became wealthy from gifts of livestock, the revenues of gum and salt caravans, and the work of clients who cultivated his fields. The shaykh thus became the head of an association of believers who looked to him for guidance in political, economic, legal, and moral matters. As a successful mediator and economic organizer, Sidiya acquired a reputation as a miracle worker. After his death his eldest son, Sidiya Baba (1862/3–1926), succeeded him. Even after France occupied Mauritania, Sidiya's family was able to maintain its political influence.

A similar kind of Muslim religious community and scholarly tradition was found in the forest and coastal regions south and west of the Sudanic states – in the Volta River basin, and the Guinean forests. In this region the Muslim communities were founded by merchants and cultivators, generally known as *wangara*, or Dyula, linked by family ties and trading networks. Their communities grew up along the trade routes at the crossings of rivers, at toll posts, and at stopping places for caravans where merchants settled down to trade with the local populace. The trading communities often developed agricultural interests, and in some cases Muslims became the custodians of specialized crafts such as weaving and dyeing. Their scholars and holy men carried on the tradition of Islamic learning and offered their religious services to local chiefs.

As in the Sahara, these communities were established amidst a highly segmented society built around political lineages, age-group associations, secret societies, religious cults, occupational groups (including iron and leather workers and musicians), and different types of free men and slaves. Political units were not based upon ideology or a history of shared culture and ethnicity, but rather upon sudden conquests by small minorities. They governed heterogeneous populations which did not necessarily share a common language or customs. Heterogeneity was reinforced by rapid fluctuations in state power, migrations, and conquests, and by the movements of roving bands of refugees needing protection, warriors looking for conquests, or traders seeking profits.

The Upper Volta region attracted Muslim merchants and settlements in the fifteenth century by the opening of the Akan goldfields, and the opportunity for trade in gold, kola nuts, and salt. Some of these merchants were Soninke-speaking peoples from Timbuktu and Jenne who later adopted Malinke dialect and became known as Dyula. They settled the towns of Bobo-Dyulasso, Kong, Bunduku, and other places leading to the goldfields. Other traders came from Kanem, Bornu, and the Hausa city-states and moved into Gonja, Dagomba, and other parts of the Volta region. The most important merchant center in this area was Begho, on the edge of the Akan forest, crucially situated for the exchange of gold and kola nuts. Begho became the terminus for the trade routes connecting Buna, Kong, Bobo-Dyulasso, and Jenne. Muslims married local women and raised families, which were tied to the Muslim community through the father and to the local pagan community through the mother. The offspring of such marriages often inherited chieftainships and brought about the conversion of local peoples. They organized festivals, offered prayers and divination at local courts, distributed talismans, and participated in anti-witchcraft rituals. As a result, Muslims in the Middle Volta region were not a distinct language group but regarded themselves as part of the Dagomba, Gonja, or Mossi kingdoms.

Muslim religious influence was strongest in the kingdoms of Gonja and Dagomba. The Gonja state had been established toward the end of the sixteenth century by Mande warriors with the help of Muslim advisors and courtiers. Though the chiefs came under Muslim influence they did not formally convert to Islam. Court ceremony and culture remained a mixture of Islamic and pagan practices. The children of chiefs were circumcised and took Muslim names, but this was done in accordance with pagan and not Muslim ceremonies. Festivals followed the Muslim calendar but had no obvious Muslim features. Thus the chiefs tried to maintain elements of both pagan and Muslim ritual in order to satisfy the cultural interests of their double constituencies.

Islamic influence among the political elite spread from Gonja to Dagomba. Dagomba chiefs adopted circumcision, Muslim names, the Muslim calendar, and Muslim festivals and burial practices. Maliki law influenced customary law, and pre-Islamic pagan festivals were merged into Muslim ones. The relatively centralized political system of the Dagomba also favored the spread of Islam. Since the state was divided into territorial and village chieftainships each of which, in imitation of the royal court, sought the religious and magical support of Muslim clerics, a Muslim presence was established throughout the region. Sons of Dagomba chiefs

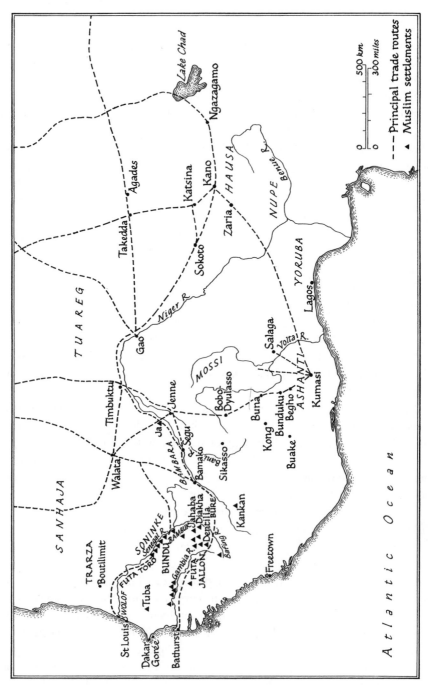

Map 24 Trade, settlements, and the diffusion of Islam in West Africa: 1500–1900

who had no prospect of obtaining ruling positions commonly converted to Islam. The chiefs also gave their daughters in marriage to Muslims in order to draw the two estates closer together.

In Dagomba Muslims came to perform important functions such as circumcision, washing the dead, officiating over festivals, and slaughtering animals for meat. By the early nineteenth century imams were widely appointed in Dagomba villages. The imam of Yendi, the capital city, held a position of particular importance as the head of the Muslim community. He was the leader of Friday prayers and the enforcer of Muslim law. By the end of the nineteenth century, though the political chiefs remained pagan, many Dagomba families had Muslim members and Muslims were considered part of the Dagomba people.

While Muslims of Gonja and Dagomba were assimilated into the general society, west of the Black Volta the Muslim trading communities remained isolated enclaves, and kept their own languages and a separate ethnic identity. Muslims maintained isolated communities built around their neighborhoods, mosques, and schools. Here Muslims were important as traders, courtiers, and religious magicians, but they had little missionary spirit and did not try to convert local peoples to Islam.

The Muslims of the Ashanti capital, Kumasi, were an example of this type. In the early nineteenth century Kumasi had a Muslim community of about a thousand, drawn mostly from neighboring Gonja and Dagomba, but also including Dyula from Senegal and Arabs from North Africa. The Muslims were headed by Muhammad al-Ghamba, who was imam and qadi, and principal of a Quran school. The Kumasi Muslims acted as agents for the Ashanti princes in the gold, kola nut, slave, and salt trades, and served Ashanti rulers as diplomats, bureaucrats, courtiers, soldiers, and religious functionaries. They provided amulets and performed rituals. Despite the importance of Muslims, Ashanti culture was not notably influenced by Islam. Muslims were not integrated into the local society, and non-Muslims were not usually converted. However, in the late nineteenth century strong reformist influences stimulated poetical and historical writing, and raised Muslim exclusivist consciousness and a sense of commitment to Islam. Classical Middle Eastern and North African Arabic works, and West African books produced outside the Ghana region were widely circulated.

Throughout the region, the Dyula communities maintained a high standard of Muslim education. A Dyula family enterprise based on the *lu*, a working unit consisting of a father, his sons, and other attached males, could afford to give some of its younger men a Muslim education. Thus there emerged an 'ulama' class known as *karamokos*, who were educated in Quran and commentary, hadith, and the life of the Prophet. A student read these works with a single teacher over a period varying from five to thirty years, and earned his living as a part-time farmer working on the lands of his teacher. Having completed his studies, a karamoko obtained a turban and an isnad, his license to teach, and set forth in search of further instruction or to start his own school in a remote village. A highly educated karamoko could become an imam or a qadi. Certain families provided scholars generation after generation. The Saghanughu was a Dyula lineage living in the northern and western Ivory Coast and in parts of Upper Volta. The lineage may be traced back to Timbuktu, but its principal figure was Muhammad al-Mustafa Saghanughu, the imam of Bobo-Dyulasso, who died around 1776–77. He produced a system of education based on three canonical texts of Quran commentary and hadith. His sons continued his teachings and spread out through the towns of Ghana and the Ivory Coast, founding Muslim schools and acting as imams and qadis.

Islam in the Senegambian region

To the west and north of Ghana and the Ivory Coast, throughout Guinea, Sierra Leone, and Senegambia, Muslims also had a complex role to play. In Senegambia the legacy of the Takrur and Mali empires was faintly kept alive in a number of small-scale states. To this was added Muslim village communities and town quarters – amidst, but politically independent of, non-Muslim peoples and states. By the eighteenth century there were important Muslim settlements in Kankan, the hinterlands of Sierra Leone, Gambia, Futa Jallon, and Futa Toro. Nineteenth-century Freetown, for example, originally a Christian settlement for liberated slaves, had colonies of Dyula migrants and Hausa and Yoruba Muslims taken from slave ships. The various ethnic groups were organized into jamats (communities) which had their own mosques and imams. Taxes were imposed on the communities to provide for religious services and to support the poor. A council of *almamis* (religious leaders) shared a Friday mosque and a joint Muslim government high school founded in 1891, and organized banquets and prayers to celebrate the birthday of the Prophet. The Muslims acquired land and political power but commonly lived under their own chiefs (*alkalis* and almamis) and pursued their own lifestyle.

The Muslim scholarly lineages were particularly important in this region. In Senegambia, the Jakhanke inhabited scattered towns and villages in Futa Jallon, Bundu, Dentilia, Bambuk, and other places. They claimed to originate in Ja on the Niger River and Jahaba on the Bafing River, from which they moved into Bundu, Futa Jallon, and Gambia. The Jakhanke were not merchants, but agriculturists supported by slave labor. The various Jakhanke villages were independent of each other and of the local chiefs. The Jakhanke were committed to peaceful coexistence and refused to become engaged in politics or war. When threatened they simply moved their villages into safer territory. Often their villages enjoyed the privileges of sanctuary, judicial independence, and freedom from military service.

The Jakhanke had a reputation for exceptional learning. They traced their spiritual ancestry to al-Hajj Salim Suwari, who probably lived in the late fifteenth century. They adhered to Maliki law although they were tolerant of customary practice. They stressed the importance of obedience to the murshid, or Sufi master, and of stages of initiation into the teachings of the community. They interpreted dreams and gave amulets for protection. They celebrated the birthday of the Prophet and the feasts of the end of Ramadan and other Muslim holidays. Though saint worship

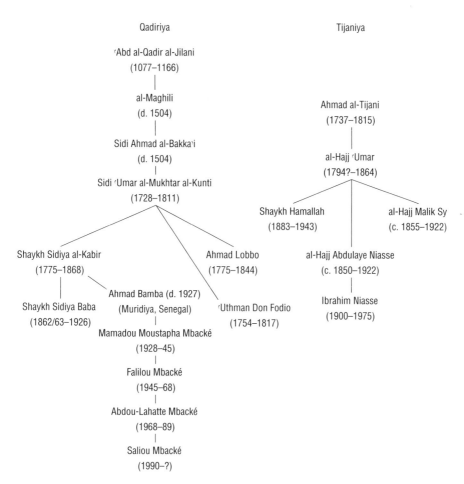

Figure 8   The Qadiriya and the Tijaniya in West Africa

was not common in West Africa, they believed that the spirits of dead saints kept guard over their followers and interceded for them before God. The graves of al-Hajj Salim and other great teachers were centers for pilgrimage. In all but name the Jakhanke extended family was a Sufi lineage.

These communities, organized by religious and lineage ties, made up, without a territorial identity or states, a self-sufficient type of Islamic society. By the end of the eighteenth century Islam in West Africa was the religion of scattered groups of Tuku-lors and Songhays, and of Dyula trading colonies, some Hausa towns, and of the domi-nant classes of the central Sudanic states. Islam also had a foothold among the Wolof, the Yoruba, and the Mossi. The Kunta, the Saghanughu, the Jakhanke, and others were closely linked by trading networks, affiliation with the Qadiriya brotherhood, and by shared religious and intellectual traditions. Other Africans were sometimes converted to Islam when traditional agricultural communities broke down and their populations were merged into larger social, political, and cultural units. Slave trading and state formation therefore favored Islam. Reciprocally, communities without extensive trading connections or political centralization found it easier to preserve a non-Muslim identity. The durability of family and village institutions, the depth of African religious culture, and the strength of traditional authorities helped to maintain a non-Islamic African majority.

The Muslim settlements were centers for the diffusion of Islamic and Arabic culture. Towns such as Timbuktu made the Quran, the sayings of the Prophet, and Islamic law familiar to local peoples. The translation of religious texts into vernacular Swahili, Wolof, Hausa, Somali, and Zenaga followed. Arabic had a strong influence upon Fulbe, Wolof, and other African languages which borrowed Arab and Muslim vocabulary and came to be written in Arabic script. Arabic was used to record family histories, dowries, debts, merchants' accounts, information about trading itineraries, and so on. It became increasingly important as an ordinary means of communication for government and merchant elites.

THE WEST AFRICAN JIHADS

Alongside peaceful Muslim colonization there was a parallel tradition of militant determination to turn small colonies into Muslim states by defeating corrupt Muslim rulers, conquering the pagan populations, converting them to Islam, and ruling them according to Muslim law. With the Almoravid movement as a shadowy precedent, the jihads burst out from Mauritania to Chad in the sixteenth century. At first the jihads rose in disparate places, but gradually they influenced each other, and culminated in a region-wide struggle to establish Muslim states. The jihads of the eighteenth and nineteenth centuries were led by Muslim scholars and teachers, itinerant preachers and their student followers, and the religious leaders of trading and agricultural communities. They took their inspiration from the militant reformers of the fifteenth century such as al-Maghili, from Islamic literary influences, and from the pilgrimage to Mecca and Medina, which may have brought West African scholars into contact with reformist Sufi circles. The jihads were finally suppressed by the British and the French at the end of the nineteenth century.

The jihad in Mauritania had its origin in the resistance of Berbers to the dominance of the Arab Banu Ma'qil. Nasir al-Din denounced the rulers for failing to perform the prayers, consorting with musicians and jugglers, and pillaging the people. He claimed to have been sent by God to stop the oppression. He called himself almami (imam) and amir al-mu'minin, the traditional title of Muslim Caliphs, proclaimed the end of time and the coming of the mahdi, and demanded that his followers conform to the teachings of the Quran. His followers swept through southern Mauritania in 1673, but Nasir al-Din was killed in 1674 and the movement defeated by 1677. The outcome of the wars was the lasting military dominance of the Arab tribes over the Berbers. Paying tribute to the Arab Hassanis, the Berbers (called zawaya) took up the roles of qadis, teachers, and spiritual counselors, and

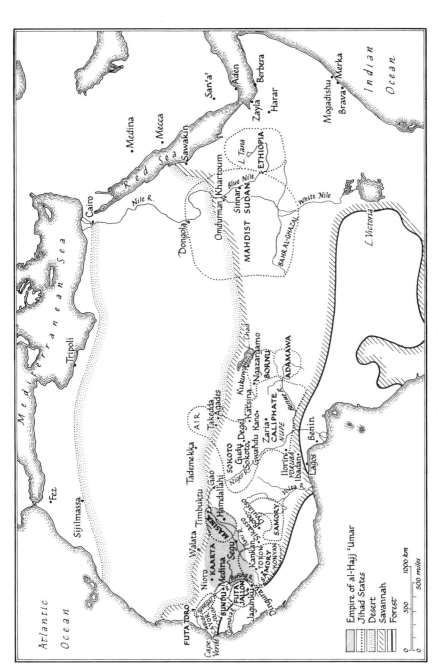

Map 25 The jihad states of the nineteenth century

were economically engaged in the mining and marketing of salt and gum arabic, maintaining wells, organizing caravans, and raising livestock. The zawaya would continue the struggle for Islamic principles, and later gave rise to both peaceful missionary movements and jihads in Senegal.

In Senegambia, Muslim jihads had their origins in the efforts of small Muslim communities to overthrow local rulers and to establish states of their own. Senegambian society was stratified into three main caste levels: the nobility, whose power rested upon training in war, the Islamic communities, and commoners engaged in crafts and agriculture. These castes were forbidden to intermarry, though one could leave either the noble or peasant caste to be initiated into the Muslim community. The basic conflict was between the military nobles and the Muslim clerics. The nobles based their claim on experience in war and the Muslims based theirs upon superior knowledge; the conflict was symbolized by the use of alcohol by the former and its rejection by the latter.

Muslim leadership came from a stratum of society called the *torodbe*: Muslim 'ulama', scholars, teachers, and students. Though they spoke Fulbe as a common language, they had no ethnic or tribal identity. Some torodbe were supported by the work of students or slaves and the contributions of artisans, but many were wandering beggars. Uprooted peoples, outlaws, vagrants, and runaway slaves were also attracted into their ranks.

The first torodbe-led jihad came in Bundu at the end of the seventeenth century, where Malik Dauda Sy founded a Muslim regime. In the 1690s he and his successors organized a state with the power to appoint and dismiss village chiefs. In the eighteenth century the rulership reverted for a time to pagans, but by then Bundu had become predominantly Muslim.

The Futa Jallon jihad was the work of the settled Muslim communities allied with Fulani pastoralists. Both groups were subordinated to the dominant Jalonke landlords to whom they paid taxes on trade and cattle. In the eighteenth century both the Muslim settlers and the pastoralists improved their economic position as a result of a growing trade in cattle and hides with Europe, and allied against the Jalonke. Islam became the banner of their solidarity and their resistance to the non-Muslim elites. In 1726 Ibrahim Musa, known as Karamoko Alfa (d. 1751), proclaimed a holy war and took the title of almami. He gathered the support of young men's gangs, renegades, and slaves and began a long struggle against the political elites. The Muslims finally prevailed in 1776, when Ibrahim Sori (1776–93) was named almami. The new state was divided into several provinces, which formed a council to elect a ruler. The almami was selected alternately from among the descendants of Ibrahim Musa and Ibrahim Sori; the former tended to represent the more pacific tradition of Muslim learning, the latter the more aggressive tradition of jihad. Under the authority of the almamis the provinces were ruled by appointed governors, and the *misidi*, or family hamlets, were ruled by local chiefs and councils of elders. The most important state activity was jihad, which was the source of slaves for export and for use on agricultural plantations. The central power, however, was gravely weakened by the emergence of a landowning aristocracy who descended from the original jihad warriors and by succession disputes between the two families that provided the almamis. Futa Jallon eventually became a French protectorate in 1881, and recognized French suzerainty in 1896/97.

In the Senegal River Valley, Futa Toro was the center of another jihad. Closely related to that of Bundu, the Muslim movement in Futa Toro was the work of the torodbe religious teachers and itinerant beggars who rebelled against the local dynasty in protest of fiscal oppression and lack of protection from Mauritanian raids. Under the leadership of Sulayman Bal (d. 1776) the torodbe established an independent territory. Sulayman was succeeded by 'Abd al-Qadir (1776–1806), a highly educated teacher, judge, and mediator, who had studied in Cayor province and thus was closely related to the widespread Senegambian and Guinean network of Muslim teachers. After his inauguration the torodbe became more militant. The new state encouraged the construction of mosques, and furthered settlement of the river frontiers with Mauritania. It invoked jihad to attack the Moors in 1786 and invaded Walo, Jolof, and Cayor by 1790. The Muslim state expanded into the upper Senegal as well. After a critical defeat in 1790, the almamate disintegrated. The torodbe intermarried with the former rulers, seized land, and became an elite of local chieftains. While almamis continued to be appointed throughout the nineteenth century, they no longer had any political power. However, memory of the early successes would again inspire jihads in the latter part of the nineteenth century.

'Uthman Don Fodio and the central Sudan

The central Sudan was another locus of jihad. Here, too, Muslim clerics and reformers dreamed of establishing an Islamic society on the model of the life of the Prophet and the early Caliphs. Such teachers as Jibril b. 'Umar had traveled to Mecca and Medina, where they were influenced by reformist Sufi views. They returned to preach the principles of the Quran and the tradition of the Prophet, uphold the rule of Shari'a, and encouraged individuals to seek personal sanctity. They also taught the doctrine of the double jihad: the inner jihad, the struggle against the corruption of the body, must precede the outer jihad, the war against pagan rulers and corrupt Muslim governments and their hired 'ulama'. Hijra, migration to a true Muslim community, and jihad, a war in the name of the faith, were the overriding obligations. Thus they introduced a universalistic and theocratic concept of Islam as the supreme arbiter of social life and as the transforming force in the lives of individuals. For them Islam was an exclusive religion incompatible with African cults. This new message was preached with messianic fervor. Throughout West and Central Africa the thirteenth Muslim century (corresponding to the nineteenth century) was expected to mark the victory of Islam over the infidel world. This was to be the age of the mujaddid, or renewer of Islam, who comes once every century, and of the Caliph of Takrur, the twelfth Caliph, whose rule would be followed by the coming of the messiah.

'Uthman Don Fodio (1754–1817) was the greatest of these new leaders. 'Uthman was a descendant of a torodbe family, well established in Hausaland, a student of Jibril b. 'Umar, an uncompromising opponent of corrupt practices, and a proponent of jihad. He began his African preaching in 1774–75, wandering from place to place as an itinerant *mallam* (religious scholar). For a time he accepted the patronage of the Hausa state of Gobir. His position was like that of the Muslim scholars who for centuries had found in the Hausa courts attractive opportunities to establish their influence, but who chafed against the restrictions placed upon them. Publicly expressing his frustration with the failure of the rulers to put Islam into practice, 'Uthman broke with the royal court. Disillusioned, he returned to Degel to preach to his followers.

The tradition of reform in which 'Uthman preached also had African origins. In the fifteenth century al-Maghili had denounced the corrupt and un-Islamic practices of West African Muslim states. He condemned illegal taxation and the seizure of private property, and denounced pagan ceremonial practices and "venal" mallams who served rulers without adequate knowledge of Arabic or Islam. Al-Maghili called for the implementation of Muslim law by a strong and committed Muslim ruler, and introduced into West Africa the concept of the mujaddid. In this vein, 'Uthman criticized the Hausa rulers for unjust and illegal taxes, for confiscations of property, compulsory military service, bribery, gift taking, and the enslavement of Muslims. He also criticized them for condoning polytheism, worshiping fetishes, and believing in the power of talismans, divination, and conjuring. Another strand in his preaching derived from the tradition of Maliki law, communicated through Timbuktu and Bornu and reinforced by reformist religious currents emanating from Mecca and Medina. 'Uthman denounced pagan customs, the free socializing of men and women, dancing at bridal feasts, and inheritance practices that were contrary to Muslim law. As in other Islamic societies, the autonomy of Muslim communities under 'ulama' leadership made it possible to resist the state and the state version of Islam in the name of the Shari'a and the ideal Caliphate.

'Uthman's influence was based on deep knowledge of Muslim law and his mystical visions. A vision in 1789 led him to believe he had the power to work miracles, and to teach his own mystical wird, or litany. He later had visions of 'Abd al-Qadir al-Jilani, the founder of the Qadiriya, and an experience of ascension to heaven where he was initiated into the silsila of the Qadiriya and the Prophet. Here he was named the imam of the walis (saints), and presented with the sword of truth. His theological writings were concerned with the concepts of the mujaddid, the hijra, the role of 'ulama' in teaching the true faith, and the role of reason and consensus in the derivation of Muslim law. All of these concerns bear on the problem of the authority of an individual scholar to challenge the established political and religious elites. Out of these concerns, 'Uthman produced numerous tracts on political theory, biographies, histories, and other works in Arabic and Fulbe. Many people regarded him as the mahdi come in fulfillment of popular prophecies. 'Uthman's appeal to justice and morality rallied the outcasts of Hausa society. He found his principal constituency among the Fulani. Primarily cattle pastoralists, they were dependent upon peasants for access to river beds and grazing lands, and were taxed accordingly. Hausa peasants, runaway slaves, itinerant preachers, and others also responded to 'Uthman's preaching.

In 1804, the conflict between 'Uthman and the rulers of Gobir came into the open. The rulers forbade Muslims to wear turbans and veils, prohibited conversions, and ordered converts to return to their old religion. 'Uthman declared the hijra and moved from Degel to Gudu where he was elected imam, amir al-mu'minin, and *sarkin muslim* – head of the Muslim community. There he declared the jihad. In the wars that followed, the Muslims rallied Fulani support, and by 1808 had defeated the rulers of Gobir, Kano, Katsina, and other Hausa states. They expanded into the territory south of Lake Chad and into Nupe and Yorubaland as far as the forest zone. By 1830 the jihad had engulfed most of what is now northern Nigeria and the northern Cameroons. The regime founded by 'Uthman is known as the Caliphate of Sokoto. 'Uthman was Caliph; his brother 'Abdallah, based in Gwandu, and his son Muhammad Bello, based in Sokoto, were his viceroys. 'Uthman retired to teaching and writing, and in 1817 Muhammad Bello succeeded him.

Sokoto was a combination of an Islamic state and a modified Hausa monarchy. Bello introduced an Islamic administration. Muslim judges, market inspectors, and prayer leaders were appointed, and an Islamic tax and land system was instituted, with revenues on the land considered kharaj and the fees levied on individual subjects called jizya, as in classical Islamic times. The Fulani cattle-herding nomads were sedentarized and converted to sheep and goat raising as part of an effort to urbanize them and bring them under the rule of Muslim law. Mosques and schools were built to teach the populace Islam. The state patronized a large community of religious scholars (mallams), some of whom were tied to the government as administrators and advisors, while others rejected worldly power and lived among the common people. The jihad movement helped to fortify the practice of Islamic law in Hausaland and also generated a theological, legal, astrological, and vernacular poetic literature in the Hausa language. Sufism became widespread and Hausa society became fully part of the Muslim world. Kano became famous for law, Zaria for Arabic grammar, and Sokoto for mysticism. The Sokoto scholars were mainly affiliated with the Qadiriya, but the Tijani order was introduced by al-Hajj 'Umar during the 1830s.

Under the authority of the Caliphate, the territories were divided into emirates appointed by and responsible to the Caliphs. Many emirates corresponded to the former Hausa states, and accepted Hausa methods of administration and palace organization. The power of the Amirs was based on military force, but they governed with the aid of the Fulani lineages and the advice of the mallams. For rural administration the emirates were divided into fiefs, some of which were controlled

20 Nigerian men and horses in quilted cloth armour

by the rulers and some by local Fulani chiefs. Village chiefs administered their subjects through appointed ward-heads and through the chiefs of organized craftsmen. The crafts were also the fiefs of officials who were responsible for the collection of taxes, observance of Muslim law, and maintenance of public property such as mosques, roads, and walls. The fact that the greater part of the territory nominally ruled by Sokoto remained in the hands of local fief-holders and chieftains meant that Islamic ideas were only occasionally applied in the provinces. Government by secular-minded Fulani chieftains led quickly away from Muslim norms, and many of the practices that had been criticized by the Muslims flourished again. Despite the claims of reform, it is arguable that the emirates were only a modified version of the older Hausa states.

The economy of the Sokoto Caliphate was based upon slave villages or plantations. First developed in the Sokoto region after 1760 (and again after the jihad of 1804–08), the plantations produced cotton, indigo, grain, rice, tobacco, kola nuts, and other crops. The state also promoted indigo and textile industries. The plantation economy flourished until the late nineteenth century, when colonial rule and the suppression of slavery allowed for a revitalization of the peasant economy.

The jihad of 'Uthman spilled out from its homeland in northern Nigeria to Bornu, the Lake Chad region, and to southern Nigeria, and inspired other jihads in the western Sudan and Senegambia. In the seventeenth century Bornu was already a center of Muslim learning, but it also had a substantial Fulani population aggrieved by landlord domination. Inspired by 'Uthman, the Fulani rose up to attack the rulers of Bornu. Bornu, however, successfully resisted the jihad by revitalizing its own Muslim credentials. Al-Kanemi, a mallam living in Ngala, helped the rulers to defeat the Fulani, and became the most powerful chieftain in Bornu. In 1814 he built his own town, Kukawa, expanded the area of his hegemony, appointed his own officials, and essentially displaced the rulers. Speaking for Bornu, he denied that jihad was legitimate when waged against Muslim peoples, regardless of whether they were good or bad Muslims.

Thus a new dynasty and a new Muslim state was, ironically, founded as a reaction against the jihad. The new regime was built upon an aristocracy consisting of the royal family, courtiers, and nobles called *kogonas*. The regime appointed qadis and imams, and professed to be as genuinely Muslim as the rival Sokoto Caliphate. It had a double structure of administration. One system was applied to the control of territories and all the resident populations; the other was directed to clans and ethnic and craft associations. The existence of both territorial and group administrations indicates a society in transition from clan lineage to territorial forms of organization.

The jihad inspired by 'Uthman also helped spread Islam into southern Nigeria. Muslim traders from Bornu, Songhay, and Hausaland came to Yorubaland in the sixteenth and seventeenth centuries and converted the first Yorubas to Islam. With the help of the Sokoto Caliphate Muslims won control of Ilorin, and Muslim quarters were formed in Abeokuta, Lagos, and other towns. Their communities were organized under the leadership of imams, who led the prayers and festivals and mediated disputes.

Still other jihads led to the formation of Muslim states south of Lake Chad in Air, north of Sokoto among the Tuaregs, and in Masina. The Masina state, led by Ahmad Lobbo, had its capital at Hamdallahi and lasted from 1816 to 1861. It was based on a highly organized army supported by a system of granaries created to provision the soldiers and spare the local population from abuse. A council of state was made up of religious teachers; the local administrative apparatus was filled with relatives and clients of the learning counselors. New legislation was introduced, including controls over women, and the suppression of fortune telling, tobacco smoking, and prostitution.

Al-Hajj 'Umar

The jihads of the central Sudan indirectly inspired a revival of jihad in the Senegambian region. The tradition of Futa Toro and Sokoto were combined to inspire al-Hajj 'Umar (1794?–1864), another great nineteenth-century leader of West African Muslim movements. Al-Hajj 'Umar was born in Futo Toro, became one of the torodbe, and in 1826 made the pilgrimage to Mecca, where he was initiated into the Tijani order and returned as the order's khalifa for the Sudan. He stayed in Sokoto from 1831 to 1837 and married a daughter of Muhammad Bello. In 1840 he settled in Jagunku on the frontiers of Futa Jallon, where he could preach to local peoples. Growing tension with the leaders of Futa Jallon forced him to move in 1851 to Dingiray, where he began the militant phase of his mission. There he organized his followers into a professional army equipped with French weapons, and in 1852 proclaimed a jihad against pagan peoples, lapsed Muslims, and European intruders.

'Umar claimed a transcendental personal authority. He denied the importance of adherence to a school of law and favored ijtihad, or personal religious judgment. He taught that a believer should follow the guidance of a Sufi shaykh who has immediate personal knowledge of the divine truth. The teachings of such a shaykh, he held, would be in full accordance with the law. 'Umar claimed the titles of amir al-mu'minin, khalifa (the successor of the Prophet), mujaddid (renewer of Islam), qutb (pole of the universe), and wazir of the mahdi. He claimed to possess *istikhara*, or divine guidance in time of difficulties. Thus he claimed virtually every form of Muslim spiritual and temporal authority. His allegiance to the Tijaniya was the basis for a break with all established Muslim authorities and for a personal appeal as shaykh and savior.

His appeal in Futa Toro, the scene of an earlier and by then aborted effort to establish a Muslim state, was enormous. 'Umar appealed to the populace on the basis of local grievances against the military elites. His followers regarded him as their almami and reviver of the eighteenth-century revolutions. His community also appealed to rootless individuals of mixed ethnic background, who found new social identity and opportunities for conquest under the aegis of Islam. He came to embody the torodbe ideal of religious revival and conquest of pagans.

His jihad began in 1852 with the conquest of Futa Toro. There he came into conflict with the French, who were attempting to establish their own commercial supremacy along the Senegal River. At Medina in 1857, they defeated 'Umar, and closed off the Senegal valley. In 1860 'Umar made a treaty with the French which recognized their sphere of influence in Futa Toro and assigned him the Bambara states of Kaarta and Segu. In quest of new territory, 'Umar and masses of followers from Futa Toro invaded Masina, thus carrying the war to Muslim peoples along the Niger bend. His enemies, led by Ahmad al-Kunta al-Bakka'i (of the Qadiri order), denounced this as an illegitimate war of Muslims upon Muslims and promoted a coalition of local states, including Masina and Timbuktu, to resist. His enemies defeated and killed him in 1864, but his followers captured Hamdallahi and established a state which lasted until 1893.

'Umar's state was officially Muslim, and forbade dancing and the use of tobacco and charms, and prohibited pagan ceremonies and the worship of idols. He was strongly influenced not only by West African reformist concepts but also by the teachings of the Tijaniya and of other reformist movements which stressed the importance of strict obedience to Muslim practice. Apart from this, its Islamic content was limited, and the primary function of the state was predatory warfare, slaving, and the accumulation of booty. The conquest state was not linked to the productive economy. The decline of the central government only accentuated the tendency to warfare, since local chieftains took to raiding to support their troops. Muslim jihad shaded over into a purely military exploitation of the surrounding peoples. 'Umar's state, in disarray, was finally overwhelmed and absorbed into a growing French West African empire in 1893.

After 'Umar's death jihad flared again in other parts of Senegambia. In the middle and latter parts of the nineteenth century the action shifted to the Wolof people of Senegal. Berber and Tukulor Muslim teachers had been active since the eighteenth century in the provinces of Walo and Cayor, where they were respected for their literacy and their magical amulets. In the nineteenth century Muslim influence increased further, owing to the suppression of the slave trade and the growth of the peanut, oil, and soap industries. The development of the new industries favored the economic and political power of Muslim peasants against the *tyeddo* slave military elites. In response to new economic and political conditions Islam provided the idiom for peasant resistance to tyeddo rule and for the integration of peasants and traders into a larger economy.

The great Senegambian jihad of this period was led by Ma Ba (1809–67), a Quran teacher and the founder of an independent settlement. Rebelling against tyeddo domination, his followers swept through Senegambia, burning villages, killing pagans, and enslaving their enemies. Ma Ba himself never actively participated in battle and retired whenever possible from political affairs, but his victories stimulated other Muslim rebellions. Lat Dior, the ruler of Cayor from 1871 to 1883, was defeated by the French and killed in 1886; despite defeat, the cumulative effect of the Senegambian jihads was the substantial conversion of the Wolof to Islam.

In the jihad period, Islam also spread in the stateless regions of the Upper Volta, the Ivory Coast, and Guinea. The most important campaigns in this region were launched in Guinea by Mori-Ule Sise, educated in Futa Jallon, who gathered bandits, vagrants, and other rootless people, built the city of Medina, and launched a jihad in 1835 in the region of Toron and Konyan. Defeated and killed in 1845, he was succeeded by a local adventurer named Samory Ture. Samory was born about 1830 of a Dyula family. He served the Medina state, engaged in various local struggles, sometimes on the pagan side, and worked relentlessly to enlarge his personal army. In 1871 he gained control over the Milo River Valley, seized Kankan in 1881, and became the principal power-holder on the upper Niger. By 1883 he had brought the local chieftains in the territory southwest of 'Umar's state under his control, and founded the kingdom of Wasulu.

This new state was governed by Samory and a council of kinsmen and clients who took on the management of the chancery and the treasury, and administered justice, religious affairs, and foreign relations. The army was the essential institution. Samory imported horses and weapons and modernized his army along European lines. At first the new state made local chieftains its vassals, but after 1878 the conquered territories were organized under military governors supported by tribute payments. In the 1880s Samory attempted to convert his regime into an Islamic state. In 1884 he took the title of almami, opened Muslim schools, forbade the use of alcohol, and required his followers to pray. He destroyed pagan sacred groves and cult symbols and forbade pagan worship. Muslim teachers and holy men were posted as officials in non-Muslim areas to enforce the Shari'a, and defeated peoples were forced to convert to Islam. Dyula traders supported Samory because of his encouragement of commerce, though they did not play a central part in the creation of the state. His Muslim policy, however, eventually led in 1888 to revolts which forced him to tolerate pagan religious associations and cults.

Samory's would-be Muslim empire was undone by the French, who pushed him eastward to Upper Volta and the Ivory Coast, where he conquered new territories and set up a new state between 1892 and 1896. In this eastern zone Samory came into conflict with both the French and the British. The French took Sikasso in 1898, and sent Samory into exile, where he died in 1900.

Jihad and conversion

With the defeat of Samory the era of eighteenth- and nineteenth-century jihads came to an end. Beginning in the western territories of Mauritania and Senegambia in the seventeenth and eighteenth centuries, they had spread throughout Sudanic and Guinean Africa. These movements represented an uprising of Muslim religious teachers and their followers against the military elites. The uprisings, however, took various forms. Most common were the revolts of Fulani pastoral peoples against landowning elites in Bundu, Futa Jallon, Hausaland, Bornu, Fombina, and other places. In some cases Muslim Fulanis formed coalitions with non-Muslim Fulani clans or with Muslim communities formed of uprooted peoples, former slaves, and oppressed peasants. In other cases the jihads represented peasant rebellions. Throughout Senegambia Muslims who opposed the tyeddo slave military elite overthrew their masters. In some of the Wolof-inhabited parts of Senegal the Muslim assault overthrew the old social structure and paved the way for massive conversions. In the Volta region, Ivory Coast, and Guinea, Dyula peoples established independent states.

Aroused Muslim populations also provided support for the expansion of Islam into new regions. The jihad of 'Uthman spilled over into the Chad region and southern Nigeria. Under the leadership of al-Hajj 'Umar torodbe elites and Tukulor peoples of Futa Toro carried jihad into the western Sudan. Similarly, Muslims supported the movement of Samory Ture in Guinea. The Muslim mission therefore involved not only local social struggles but also wars of expansion and conquest. In certain cases, such as that of Samory in Guinea, revolts in the name of Islam were the work of military adventurers manipulating Muslim symbols for the sake of a tenuous legitimacy. While some Islamic movements aimed at reform and conversion, all aimed at territorial empire. Throughout West Africa Islam had come to be the almost universal language of political ambition and moral reform.

The use of this language varied. In many cases Islam provided for the unification of heterogeneous peoples and the creation of states. Many Muslim leaders waged jihad simply in the name of Islam and of putative Muslim states, but in the case of 'Uthman, a sophisticated Sudanic African tradition of religious reform also prompted a creative literary and religious effort. Al-Hajj 'Umar turned for his religious vision to the reformist teachings of Mecca and Medina, and returned from the holy places with Sufi inspiration. Otherwise, the West African religious movements were inspired by an indigenous tradition of Muslim efforts to generate Muslim states.

As a result of the jihads, the Sokoto Caliphate took control of Hausaland and conquered satellite regions in Bornu and Chad. Muslim populations were consolidated in much of what is now northern Nigeria, Chad, and the Cameroons. New states were also founded in Masina, parts of Guinea, and Senegambia. The formation of these states led to the conversion of local peoples to Islam. Parts of Senegambia and Masina became Muslim. Converts were made among the Fulani, Soninke, and Wolof peoples. This widespread conversion of Sudanic farmers marks the breakdown of the traditional order of society under Muslim pressure and the emergence of Islam as a principal organizing force in the creation of new societies. While Islam had frequently been adopted as an imperial cult without being spread among the subjects, the nineteenth-century jihads created Islamic states which sought to include the whole population rather than a limited aristocracy, and to create a political people out of smaller groups of diverse racial, ethnic, and linguistic backgrounds.

Though great numbers of people were converted to Islam, the process of conversion was slow and the change in institutions and beliefs variable. The result was not the formation of a uniform Islamic culture but of a plethora of local variations upon Islamic practice. While we may speak about conversion and the syncretism of Islam and African practices, there was no single cultural expression of Islamic civilization in sub-Saharan Africa. Among western Sudanic peoples, Islam appeared in family festivals, spirit practices, and legends. Among central Sudanic peoples, Islam was the cult of the aristocracy and of specialized groups.

In the first stage of conversion African peoples accepted elements of Islamic culture and practice without forming a Muslim identity. Elements of Islamic material culture, including ornaments, dress, food, amulets, and some religious and mythological concepts, became part of the African cultural repertoire. In the second stage formal conversion was achieved and 'ulama' were recognized as the sole representatives of God's will. The power of communal cults waned and the worship of Allah became supreme. A third stage of Islamization involved changes in conduct and custom, as Muslim communities took on Arabic Islamic norms. At this stage Muslims recognized the supremacy of Islamic law, worshiped according to the five pillars of Islam, and incorporated Islamic practices into the rituals of circumcision, marriage, and death. Older customs and institutions were reinterpreted in Islamic terms. There may also have been legal and social changes from matrilineal to patrilineal forms of family, and from communal to private ownership of property.

At the very moment when masses of Sudanese peoples were being converted to Islam, Muslim expansion was being checked by European intervention. In the late nineteenth century the French and the British began to assert their domination. The French took possession of Senegal and of the state founded by 'Umar in 1893. They then defeated Samory in 1898. The British defeated the Sokoto Caliphate in 1903. The great century of jihad came to an end with the defeat of all the Muslim states and their absorption into European colonial empires.

CHAPTER 21

ISLAM IN EAST AFRICA AND THE RISE OF
EUROPEAN COLONIAL EMPIRES

East Africa, including the eastern Sudan, the East African coasts, and the hinterlands of Ethiopia, Somalia, and Kenya, formed another major zone of Muslim population. Here the sources of Islamic influences were primarily Egypt, Arabia, and the Indian Ocean region, rather than North Africa. While Islam in the western Sudan was essentially a royal cult and the religion of trading communities, in the eastern Sudan it was a popular religion.

SUDAN

The history of the eastern Sudan (the modern state of Sudan) was separate from that of the central and western Sudan due to the fact that Islam reached the eastern Sudan from Egypt rather than from North Africa. The Arabs occupied Egypt as far as Aswan in 641, and for centuries pushed further and further south. In the ninth century, Egyptians swarmed to the newly discovered Allaqi goldfields between the Nile and the Red Sea. In the twelfth and thirteenth centuries Arab bedouins migrated south and married into local families, and through matrilineal succession their children inherited local chieftainships. Arab penetration was followed by the Mamluk conquest of Nubia. In 1317 the church of Dongola was rededicated as a mosque. Most of the country, however, was in the hands of local Arab tribal chiefs, who continued to push south.

While Arabs were pushing south, herding peoples from the region of the Blue Nile called Funj were pushing north. The first historically known Funj ruler, Amara Dunqas, defeated the Christian kingdom of Alwa in 1504, and founded Sinnar as the capital of a Funj kingdom which reached north to the third cataract, south to the foothills of Ethiopia, and east to the desert of Kordofan. Its rulers were Muslims and used Arabic as the lingua franca of trade, though the court at Sinnar continued to speak Funj. Only in the eighteenth century did state documents appear in Arabic.

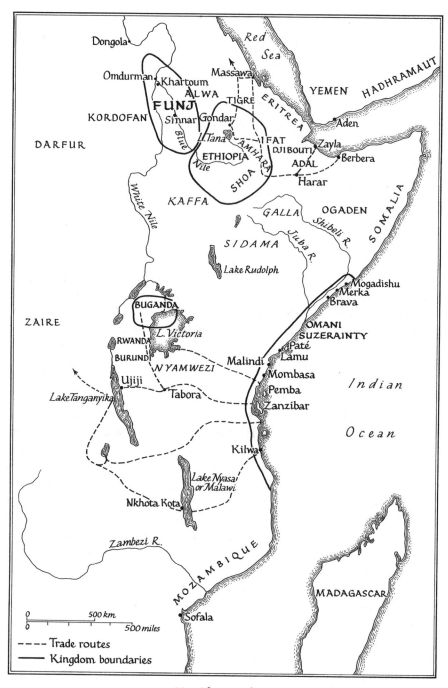

Map 26 East Africa

The Funj monarchy was a patrimonial regime built upon a Sudanese concept of semi-divine kingship. The public appearance of the Sultans was accompanied by pomp and ceremony, but Funj rulers spent most of their reigns secluded from public view. The ruler was in principle absolute, but was in practice very much under the sway of his ministers, courtiers, and family. Provincial nobles lived in castles supported by their own slave retainers. A provincial lord placed each village in his jurisdiction under the supervision of an experienced slave in order to extract taxes. Provincial nobles, however, had to appear before the Sultan each year to perform obeisance, account for their behavior, and deliver tribute. Each lesser lord was also required to take a wife from the royal family so that every vassal was related to the ruler. The ruling community formed a caste-like group which avoided intermarriage with the local population.

Islam spread in the Funj Sultanate not only as the result of its acceptance by the governing elite and the trading communities, but also as the result of the migration of Muslim scholars and holy men into the region. In the sixteenth century Funj patronage attracted scholars from Upper Egypt, North Africa, and Arabia. These holy men, known locally as *faqis*, were scholars of the Quran and Muslim law and Sufi mystics and magicians. The faqis gained considerable influence because they could intercede with and even rebuke the rulers, and because they were venerated by the common people for their magical powers. The faqis founded lineages, settled in villages, established schools, and won the populace over to Islam. Their zawiyas were residences and places of prayer in which the holy men lived surrounded by their families, servants, and disciples. Their schools (*khalwas*) taught young boys the Quran, law, and Muslim theology. In time the zawiyas grew into colonies and villages in which leading descendants of the original holy men maintained a spiritual or temporal authority. They administered Maliki law, arbitrated local disputes, and instructed the people in Islam. The eastern Sudanic faqis were also part of the Sufi brotherhoods. The Shadhiliya was brought into the Sudan in the fifteenth century, the Qadiriya in the middle of the sixteenth, and the Majdhubiya in the eighteenth.

After a long and fitful history, the Funj kingdom disintegrated in the eighteenth century. The system of marriage alliances and princely hostages upon which the power of the state depended broke down; local dynasties became autonomous. The Funj kingdom depended for its economic viability on the gold trade. All gold mined within the kingdom belonged to the Sultan, who was also the organizer of long-distance commerce. As trade expanded and foreign merchant communities in Sinnar grew larger, it became increasingly difficult to enforce the Sultan's trading monopoly. By 1700, with the introduction of coinage, an unregulated market system took hold, and the Sultans lost control of trade to a new merchant middle class. At the same time civil wars forced the peasants to look to the holy men for protection, and the Sultans lost the peasant population to the faqis. Together, the autonomy of provincial vassals, merchant communities, and faqis and their peasant clients subverted the power of the Funj Sultanate. The Funj kingdom was finally brought to an end by the Egyptian conquest of 1820–21.

The Arabization and Islamization of Funj was followed by the spread of Islam and the formation of kingdoms further south and west. In Darfur, the Keira lineage of the Fur peoples established a new dynasty in the late sixteenth century, and inherited Sudanic concepts of divine kingship. Between 1660 and 1680 Sulayman made Islam the royal cult, built mosques, and added Shari'a principles to his claims to legitimacy. Arabic became the language of the chancery; Fur remained the spoken language of the court.

At the end of the eighteenth century 'Abd al-Rahman al-Rashid (1786/87–1800/01) consolidated the Darfur Sultanate around a palace complex called al-Fashir. Al-Fashir was the hub of administration, a training ground for officers and courtiers, a center for the redistribution of goods, a final court of justice, and a stage for festivals, ceremonies, and parades. The Keira dynasty ruled their Fur subjects through a centralized administrative hierarchy, but their non-Fur subjects, the majority of the population, were divided into five provinces ruled by local chieftains. In the late eighteenth century the central government attempted to replace the traditional territorial leaders with the Sultan's slaves and clients, including merchants and Muslim holy men. The new elite progressively took control of outlying areas. The rulers also rewarded their retainers with landed estates (*hakura*) and slaves. The land grantees, however, made their holdings hereditary, married into the local elites, and emerged as a quasi-independent aristocracy. The Muslim holy men were particularly successful in consolidating their local power.

The political consolidation of Darfur was accompanied by further Islamization. Through the protection and patronage of the Sultans, and under the stimulus of trade with Egypt, traders and Sufis from the northern Sudan, Egypt, Arabia, and West Africa settled in Darfur. In eastern Darfur Muslim holy men married local women and opened khalwas and mosques. Young boys left home to study with the faqis and cultivate their fields, and they then returned home to further spread the teachings of the faith. These holy men sustained the regime by creating non-tribal communities, and by providing it with legitimizing genealogies and proper Arabic documents. Nineteenth-century Sultans attempted to bring the holy men under bureaucratic control, and after 1898 the faqis were organized district by district under the administration of muqaddams who were responsible for their discipline.

THE COASTAL CITIES AND SWAHILI ISLAM

On the coasts of the Red Sea and the Indian Ocean another form of Islamic civilization came into being as a result of the contacts of Muslim merchants and teachers with the indigenous African society. An earlier generation of scholars regarded Swahili East African coastal Islamic society as a colonial society based on the settlement of Arab or Persian migrants amidst a primitive African population. In the old view the Muslim settlers founded cities. The Swahili language and cultural style was considered the product of the assimilation of Africans into a basically Arab- or Persian-Muslim society. More recent scholarship stresses the indigenous African basis of Swahili civilization. The archeological evidence seems to show an indigenous urban society inhabiting mud and thatched-hut settlements with some stone buildings. Most of these settlements were agricultural, probably growing fruit, rice, millet, and cotton, and keeping livestock. A few, on the islands, were oriented to commerce. Some southern towns, such as Kilwa, ruled by African chiefs, traded in the Indian Ocean. The rise of an East African Islamic civilization, then, was not so much due to migration, settlement, and the founding of new towns as to contacts among merchants, the transfer of ideas and concepts, and the eventual settlement of Muslim traders.

The first Muslim settlements occurred in the ninth and tenth centuries, on the northern or Somali part of the East African coast at Mogadishu, Merka, and Brava. There were no Muslim communities on the southern coast before 1100. After 1100 the Muslim presence began to expand, stimulated by intensified trade. In the twelfth century when the first mosques were built, Zanzibar and Pemba became the most important Muslim settlements. Muslim migrants came from the towns on the Somali coast, Oman, and Iran, but the early settlers were superseded in influence in the thirteenth century by migrants from Yemen and Hadhramaut. The successive waves of migrants probably brought variant versions of Islam, including the Ibadi and Shafi'i, and Arab and Persian influences, which eventually became integrated into the East African Swahili culture.

By the thirteenth century there were some three dozen towns between Mogadishu and Kilwa, the most important of which were Malindi, Mombasa, Zanzibar, and Sofala. These towns traded with Arabia and the Persian Gulf and, via Indonesian intermediaries, with China. Kilwa exported copper; Malindi and Mombasa, iron; and Mogadishu, cloth. Tortoise shells, rhinoceros horns, amber, leopard skins, slaves, ivory, and gold were also traded. There were also extensive coconut-palm, orange, sugar-cane, rice, and sesame cultivations along the coast. As Kilwa prospered, stone palaces, city walls, and a Friday mosque were constructed; copper coins were minted. By the end of the century a stone mosque was built, with domes in the Indian style.

Little is known about the political system of these towns, but it may be surmised that they were composed of lineages. Each town may have had a council of clan chiefs, although such councils were probably superseded by a dominant lineage or by an outside Arab or Persian chief who became ruler and mediator among the local clans. The rulers were legitimized both in terms of hereditary succession and of African symbols.

Islam was also well established, for Arab and Persian migrants married into local families, and developed an Arabic-African culture in language, architecture, and dress. Ibn Battuta, who visited around 1332, saw the towns at the height of their prosperity and culture. He described Mogadishu as a Muslim community with a madrasa, scholars of Shafi'i law, and a community of descendants of the Prophet. It was ruled by officials called wazirs and amirs, and showed South Arabian influences in court ceremony. Kilwa was a Shafi'i community and possessed a school of law.

This prosperous East African society was destroyed by the Portuguese. Vasco da Gama discovered the region in 1498, and this was followed by a vigorous campaign to control the Indian Ocean and the Eastern spice trade. The Portuguese Admiral d'Almeida took Kilwa in 1505 and sacked Mombasa. By 1530 the Portuguese controlled the entire coast, basing themselves on the offshore islands of Zanzibar, Pemba, and other places. The Portuguese fought off the Ottomans and in 1542 helped defend Ethiopia against Muslim expansion. Portuguese domination lasted until Oman expelled them from the Persian Gulf region in 1650, attacked Pemba and Zanzibar in 1652, and finally took Mombasa in 1696. This conquest opened the way for a new wave of migrants from Oman and Hadhramaut, and for the restoration of Arab supremacy. The Omani presence occasioned a considerable trade in cloth, ivory, and slaves between East Africa, Oman, and India, but Omani political authority was short lived. Many of the coastal towns became independent in the course of the eighteenth century, and only Zanzibar continued to recognize the overlordship of Oman.

In the nineteenth century Omani influence in East Africa was revived by Imam Sayyid Sa'id b. Sultan (1804–56). His authority was at first accepted in Zanzibar and Kilwa, but progressively he forced Lamu, Pate, and Mombasa to recognize his regime. The new rulers appointed a *liwali* to represent them, but allowed for local autonomy through the office of the *matimim*, who was probably nominated by the local lineages. After the death of Imam Sayyid Sa'id his sons divided Oman and Zanzibar into separate kingdoms.

In this period Zanzibar became a center for a thriving East African slave trade and a market for ivory, cloves, and gum copal which were exchanged for cloth, beads, hardware, and weapons. Zanzibar's trade with the interior expanded enormously as new routes and trading towns were established. The ruler of Zanzibar monopolized the ivory and gum copal trade, encouraged Indian immigrant merchants to invest, and also stimulated the development of clove plantations based on slave labor.

The thriving slave and trading economy brought Islam to the East African interior. For centuries the Muslim presence had been confined to coastal ports, while the hinterland remained pagan, composed of self-sufficient farming communities, hardly involved in trade. From the eighteenth century, however, the growth of population and the formation of small states in the interior made it possible to organize caravans which brought Nyamwezi traders to the coast and Arab and Swahili traders to the interior. The trade was stimulated by the commercial interests of Sultan Sa'id of Zanzibar. By the 1820s and 1830s a handful of Arab and Swahili merchants and adventurers, responding to the increased demand for ivory and slaves, had become active in the interior.

Islam was carried inland along two major trade routes. A southern route connected the coastal towns of Kilwa and Malindi with the Lake Malawi region. On this route 'Abdallah b. Salim settled in Nkhota Kota, dominated its trade, and became a local chieftain. His successors instituted Arabic and religious instruction. Yao peoples living on the eastern side of Lake Malawi adopted the new religion. The first local chieftain converted in 1870; the arrival of Muslim missionaries in 1885 helped persuade other Yao of the cultural as well as the economic value of ties to the coast. Islam brought literacy, international commerce, social contacts, and administrative expertise into central Africa.

A second route was the trade network connecting Zanzibar and the coastal town of Dar-es-Salaam with the Manyema region and Buganda. On this route Tabora was the key town; from Tabora Arab traders reached Lake Tanganyika, where they established Ujiji, which in turn became the center of an Arab and Muslim community and a base for the further diffusion of Islamic influence in Zaire, Burundi, and Rwanda. In this region Arab and Swahili traders supplied local chieftains with firearms in exchange for slaves, and thus intensified the local struggle for power. Local adventurers, often supported by uprooted young-men-turned-warriors, took advantage of the situation to conquer small kingdoms. Tippu Tip, a Swahili trader and warrior, set up a small Muslim state. In Buganda, King Mutesa I Islamized his regime by observing Ramadan, building mosques, and introducing the Muslim calendar. The Islamic presence was also reinforced by the settlement of Nubians from an Egyptian military expedition.

Still, by the late nineteenth century Islam had only a scattered representation in East Africa. It spread as the result of individual conversions rather than by the conversion of tribes or lineages. Chiefs who cooperated with Arabs in trade adopted Islam. So too did slaves and porters rooted out of their home communities. Because Islam was accepted as a religion rather than a political or communal identification, Muslims, Christians, and pagans often lived in the same villages and even in the same families.

ETHIOPIA AND SOMALIA

Arab and Muslim influence on Somalia and Ethiopia goes back to the ninth century when coastal traders brought Islam to Harar on the Ethiopian plateau and founded a number of principalities. Arab merchants propagated Islam among their servants, trading partners, and in market villages. They also married into Somali pastoral lineages, and created a concept of Arab Muslim Somali identity. By the twelfth century Muslim principalities and smaller chieftainships abounded on the southwestern periphery of Ethiopia. The Muslim Sultanate of Shoa, a loose confederation of local peoples led by merchant princes, was organized by the

Mahzum family in the late twelfth century, and was annexed by the Muslim kindom of Ifat in 1285.

The Muslim principalities bordered on an ancient and powerful Christian Ethiopian civilization. The dominant population of Ethiopia spoke Amharic, a Semitic language related to south Arabian, Arabic, and Hebrew. The ancient kingdom of Axum had been converted to Christianity in the fourth century; from 451 Axum adhered to the monophysite doctrine. The head of the Ethiopian church was appointed by the Patriarch of Alexandria (until 1948). The church helped identify the Ethiopian Christian nation with the Israel of the Old Testament as a beleaguered state surrounded by the hostile pagan and Muslim neighbors. The Ethiopians were ruled by a Christian monarch bearing the title of Nejashi, who reigned over tributary local rules. By the mid-thirteenth century a revived Ethiopian monarchy challenged Muslim merchants for control of the caravan routes to the coast. Thus began a long, bitter, and still unresolved conflict among rival kingdoms, trading peoples, and religions for control of Ethiopia. To this day, the history of this region has been shaped by the struggle between Muslims and Christians.

Victory in the first phase of this struggle went to the Christians, who by 1415 had subdued the Muslim kingdom of Ifat and the lesser principalities. While some Muslims accepted Christian rule, descendants of the former rulers of Ifat founded a new Muslim kingdom called Adal along the coast of Somalia. Supported by nomadic peoples from 'Afar and Somalia, Adal resumed the war with Christian Ethiopia. Between 1516 and 1542 Muslim forces under the leadership of Imam Ahmad, supported by Ottoman troops and firearms, conquered much of southern Ethiopia; but in a decisive battle between Muslims and Christians near Lake Tana in 1542, the Portuguese intervened to help Christian Ethiopia prevail over the Muslims.

The Christian victory shattered the Muslim regimes. Only the plains of 'Afar, Somalia, and parts of southwestern Ethiopia remained Muslim. Muslim Sultanates and chieftainships disintegrated into tribal and village communities, though Harar and the coastal towns survived as centers of Islamic trade and religious activity. From the sixteenth through the eighteenth centuries, Muslims managed to propagate Islam among Galla peoples, 'Afar tribes, and some Tigre-speaking peoples of southern and eastern Ethiopia; in the mid-seventeenth century 'Ali b. Daud founded a new Sultanate of Harar. Prosperity in the Red Sea and on the Horn of Africa and trade with Zayla and the Funj Sultanate helped maintain the Harar Sultanate until the middle of the nineteenth century.

The Galla peoples, pastoralists with a common language, culture, and sociopolitical organization, had begun to move into Ethiopia in the early sixteenth century. They settled in the vicinity of Harar, slowly expanded in the Shoa and 'Afar regions, adopted Islam, and accepted the ruler of Harar as their nominal master. In practice they maintained their tribal system and an independent political hierarchy. By the early nineteenth century the Galla tribes effectively dominated the region. Harar remained a Muslim town with numerous shrines of saints, and its peoples made the pilgrimage to Mecca.

In the early nineteenth century Muslim influence began to spread again, owing to the revival of the highland trade to the Red Sea, the pilgrimage to Mecca, and the increased demand for slaves in Arabia and elsewhere. Gondar, the capital of Ethiopia, was revived by Sudanese and Ethiopian merchants, who brought European products and Maria Theresa gold thalers in exchange for coffee, wax, musk, and slaves. Merchant caravans also penetrated the Galla country of south and southwestern Ethiopia, importing copper, brass, knives, swords, spices, and cloth in exchange for coffee, skins, wax, and slaves. By the second quarter of the nineteenth century thousands of Ethiopian slaves, mostly pagans of Galla and Sidama origin, were being exported from Ethiopian ports. The trade benefited Muslims, and the penetration of Muslim caravans furthered the Islamization of Gallas.

In northern Ethiopia Gallas expanded into the Sidama highlands and the Amhara provinces. Their growing influence gave Muslim merchants and scholars a foothold in these regions. In the southwest the Galla influence was even more important. New Galla kingdoms of Limmu-Innarya and Jimma-Kakka were established. The Innarya kingdom was founded by an adventurer named Bofo Abba Gomol, who adopted Islam soon after coming to power and employed Muslim merchants and advisors. As in Sudanic Africa, a local ruler relied on Muslim officials, scribes, and financiers to consolidate his power. The capital of Innarya, Sakka, had a population of some 10,000 to 12,000, with several hundred 'ulama'. Sakka traded in ivory, skins, and incense from Lake Rudolph, musk, gold, ivory, and spices from Kaffa, and thousands of slaves. Gold was a royal monopoly.

Muslim holy men and Sufi tariqat were important to the establishment of Islam. The Qadiriya had been active in the Harar region in earlier times, and spread into Somalia and Eritrea in the nineteenth century. The reform Muslim orders also came into the region. The Salihiya were established in Ogaden after 1850. Their agricultural settlements attracted runaway slaves and detribalized individuals. The Ahmadiya were established among Somalis by 'Ali Maye Durogba, and founded agricultural settlements. The Mirghaniya in Massawa and Eritrea between 1860 and 1899 were led by Sayyid Hashim al-Mirghani. Muslim holy men married into the families of local chiefs, and reared children who succeeded to chieftainships and brought whole peoples over to Islam. These new Muslims venerated the shrines of local saints. At these shrines cultic practices showed a mixture of influences from the Meccan pilgrimage, Muslim saint worship, and pre-Islamic Galla and other local ceremonies. Thus, under the influence of trade, Muslim settlement, and Galla expansion, numerous Ethiopians converted to Islam in the troubled nineteenth century.

While Gallas occupied the Harar plateau, Somalis moving southward and westward from 'Afar took over the Ogaden. By the eighteenth century they had pushed as far as the Juba River and controlled the coastal towns of Mogadishu, Zayla, and Berbera. In the nineteenth century they moved as far south as northern Kenya. In the course of this centuries-long migration, Somalis pushed out or assimilated the original Galla inhabitants of the region. The movement of Galla and Somali lineages thus established a Muslim bloc of peoples in southern Ethiopia and on the

Horn of Africa. Thus, through tribal affiliation, a mass Islamic society comparable to that of Mauritania was created in these regions.

COLONIALISM AND THE DEFEAT OF MUSLIM EXPANSION

The spread of Islamic polities in both West and East Africa was checked at the beginning of the twentieth century by the sudden imposition of European colonial rule. While European domination was secured in a sudden burst of conquests, European involvement in Africa goes back to the fifteenth century. The Portuguese were the first Europeans to explore the African coast, establish trading stations, and open commerce between West Africa and Europe. They were eager to find gold, break the monopoly of the Muslims over the traffic of the Sudan, and convert local peoples to Christianity. In an extraordinary century of exploration, the Portuguese discovered Madeira, the Azores, the mouth of the Senegal River, and Cape Verde, visited the Gold Coast, and finally in 1482 built the fortress of Elmina as the headquarters of a garrison that enforced the Portuguese monopoly of the Gold Coast trade.

With the discovery of the Americas and the potential for growing sugar and other crops, slaves became more important than gold, and human beings became the principal African export. By the middle of the seventeenth century the Dutch had seized all of the major Portuguese bases on the Gold Coast, but in the eighteenth century the English won control of the Gold Coast and became the leading European commercial and slave-trading nation. In the meantime, the French established themselves on the Senegal River in 1637 at St. Louis and Gorée, and developed a trade in gum, wax, ivory, hides, and slaves. Europeans were almost entirely involved in exporting slaves, and had little impact on the technological or cultural development of African societies. The growth of the slave trade, however, stimulated local warfare, increased the power of African rulers over their subjects, and brought new states into being. Kings and officials became the principal slavers, exchanging slaves for weapons and other goods. Thus, most of southwestern Nigeria came under the control of the Oyo empire, and much of Ghana was ruled by the Ashanti.

In the nineteenth century, the British took the lead in suppressing the Atlantic slave trade. In 1807, an Act of the British parliament made it illegal for Britons to engage in the slave trade, and in 1833 Parliament abolished slavery in the British empire. The British used their navy to enforce the anti-slave-trade laws, and forced other countries to join in the prohibition. Behind the British resolve to abolish the trade was a combination of humanitarian concerns and the interest of manufacturers in a growing African market. From Bathurst, Freetown, fortresses on the Gold Coast, and the coast of Nigeria, British traders promoted traffic in palm oil, timber, ivory, and beeswax.

The suppression of the slave trade was also accompanied by the first European efforts to influence African societies. European explorers, missionaries, and colonists sought to convert Africans to Christianity and to create a new class of Europeanized

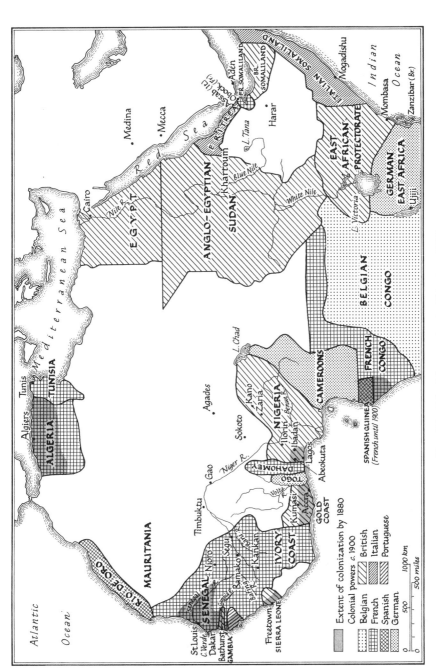

Map 27 Colonial expansion in Africa to c. 1900

Extent of colonization by 1880

Colonial powers c. 1900

Belgian
French
Spanish
German
British
Italian
Portuguese

0   500   1000 km

0   500 miles

Africans. European trade stimulated the rise of Western-educated Africans, a proto-bourgeoisie who would later become the pioneers of African nationalism. For much of the nineteenth century Europeans still held the notion that Africans could be equals once they had acquired a European education and become Christians. French and British colonies were supplied with legislative and executive councils to introduce Africans to European modes of government; Africans were prepared to hold the highest offices of state. By the end of the century, however, with their rising determination to conquer Africa, Europeans came to consider them inherently inferior.

In the second part of the nineteenth century, the British began to expand from the coasts into the interior, looking for new markets and new sources of supply. Lagos, the main port for Yorubaland, was annexed in 1861. Britain's policy was to use sufficient military and political force to protect trading interests, but not to seek commercial or political monopolies. As long as interior African states were well enough organized to hold up their end of the trade and as long as other European powers did not intervene, Britain was at first content with minimal political engagement. The British debated whether they should keep their settlements as small and inexpensive as possible or whether they should develop strong political controls to suppress the slave trade and to promote commerce and missionary work. British policies oscillated between the two alternatives, but after 1865, the British generally moved toward direct intervention and control. Traders, explorers, and missionaries, who cried out for increased political protection, won their cause. In 1874 the British made the Gold Coast a crown colony.

The French developed their colonial empire in Senegambia. After the defeat of Napoleon, St. Louis and Gorée were returned to France and became the main bases of French expansion. Suppression of the slave trade and the growth of the gum-arabic and peanut trades prompted the French to establish inland fortified trading posts on territories rented from local rulers. In 1849 they obtained rights to open factories at Joal and Kaolack. After 1851 the French adopted a more aggressive expansionist policy. Under Louis Faidherbe, military governor from 1854 to 1865, they annexed Dakar (1857) and pushed French trading posts into the African interior. They blocked the western expansion of al-Hajj 'Umar and took control of the lower Senegal River. In 1859 Faidherbe forced Sine and Saloum to guarantee freedom of French commerce and to give the French a monopoly of trade and the right to buy land. A second phase of French expansion completed the absorption of the Senegambian region. After 1863 the French laid plans to establish a series of garrisons and a railroad to link the Senegal and the Niger Rivers. They occupied Bamako in 1883, Cayor in 1886, and Nioro in 1887. The telegraph, the railroad, and the cannon assured French domination. Henceforth, the French would not only protect trade but try to assure their permanent authority by constructing roads, establishing formal administration, and introducing legal and educational policies.

Thus the European powers turned from trading interests to political annexation. As late as 1880, Britain's Lord Salisbury denied any British or European interest in African colonies, but by 1884 the expansion of the several powers, their mutual rivalries, and their competition for prestige stimulated a wave of chauvinistic nationalism in all the European countries. The winds of nationalism fanned the flames of trading interests and political rivalry into a scramble for African colonies. The French created protectorates in Senegal; the British seized Egypt in 1882; the Germans created protectorates over Togo and the Cameroons in 1884. In 1886 George Taubman Goldie's Niger Company was given a royal charter to administer law and customs in its territories, and in 1897 the company took control of Nupe, Ilorin, and Bida, and the British built a railroad from Lagos to Ibadan. Progressively, in 1885, 1891, and 1900 the British government took control of the Niger Company's territories and reorganized them under the colonial office as the Protectorate of Southern and Northern Nigeria. Between 1900 and 1906 Sir Frederick Lugard subordinated the northern Muslim emirates, and brought the Sokoto Caliphate under his control. Elsewhere, the British assumed a protectorate over the hinterlands of Sierra Leone in 1891. Having defeated the Ashanti in 1874, they took control of Kumasi and declared a protectorate over Ghana in 1896.

While the British took Nigeria, Ghana, and Sierra Leone, the French went on to complete their West African empire. By a treaty of 1889 they delineated the boundaries between French and British possessions in Senegal, Gambia, Sierra Leone, Guinea, and the Ivory Coast. By 1893 they took Masina and eliminated the state established by al-Hajj 'Umar. They pushed back Samory and established French colonies in Guinea and the Ivory Coast. From their bases in Senegal and the Ivory Coast, the French moved on to establish a protectorate over Futa Jallon in 1897, defeated Samory in 1898, and took control of the Upper Volta. By 1900 they had swept across the whole of the Sudan and conquered the Sahara as far as Lake Chad. Though fighting continued in the Ivory Coast until 1908 and in the Niger region until 1921 the French and British African empires were essentially established by 1900.

As in West Africa, European rivalries provoked a scramble for East Africa. British interests were inspired by the desire for trade, by opposition to slavery, and by Christian missionary zeal. Britain also had established interests in India, South Africa, Aden, and other Indian Ocean ports. In 1841, the British appointed a consul to Zanzibar, and by 1873 had sufficiently consolidated their influence to force the Sultan of Zanzibar to prohibit the slave trade. Britain began to look upon Zanzibar as its proxy for the penetration of explorers, missionaries, and traders. In 1890 Zanzibar became a British protectorate.

British expansion provoked Germany to seek compensation. In 1884 the Germans established protectorates in South West Africa, the Cameroons, and Togo, and between 1884 and 1888 they took control of Tanganyika, including the territories that are now Rwanda and Burundi. By agreement between the Germans and the British in 1886 and 1891, East Africa was partitioned. In 1888 the British East Africa

Company acquired Kenya, which was ruled from Zanzibar until 1904, when the Kenya protectorate received its first commissioner. Britain also created a protectorate in Uganda in 1893 by treaty with Mwanga II, the Kabaka of Buganda, by the terms of which the slave trade was prohibited. By 1914 the British had extended their control over most of the local chiefs of the region.

The British also led the way to the partition of the Somali and Red Sea coasts, primarily because of their concern for the security of traffic to Aden and the Indian Ocean. First, they encouraged Egyptian and Italian interests as a barrier to French expansion. Then in 1887 they established a protectorate on the Harar–Somali coast, and by agreement with the French defined the boundaries between their respective territories as lying between the ports of Zayla and Djibouti. In 1891 the British and Italians agreed on boundaries between British and Italian protectorates in Somaliland. Further treaties in 1897 among Ethiopia, Britain, France, and Italy regulated the Somali protectorates. Italy achieved only a nominal and disputed protectorate over Ethiopia. In the meantime, on another front, the British, who had occupied Egypt in 1882, conquered most of the Sudan in 1898 and Darfur in 1916. Thus all of Muslim Africa – indeed, all of Africa except Liberia and Ethiopia – came under European rule by World War I.

CONCLUSION: THE VARIETIES OF
ISLAMIC SOCIETY

Islamic societies from the tenth to the nineteenth centuries had a complex structure. In some cases Muslim communities were isolated pastoral, village, or urban minorities living within non-Islamic societies. Examples of this type are lineage groups united by shrine veneration in the northern steppes of Inner Asia and parts of the Sahara, and merchant communities in China or West Africa. In African societies the Muslim presence was centered around small communities such as lineage groups, teachers and disciples, Sufi brotherhoods, or networks of merchants. Merchant communities were established as early as the eleventh and twelfth centuries in the western Sudan. By the eighteenth century there were Muslim merchant enclaves in the central Sudan, Berber zawaya or insilimen holy lineages in the Sahara region, cultivator and merchant communities and scholarly lineages such as the Saghanughu (called wangara or Dyula) in the Volta River basin and Guinean forests, and Jakhanke lineages of cultivators and scholars in the Senegambia region. In East Africa Muslim communities were settled in the coastal towns. In Ethiopia and Somalia they were present among Galla and Somali peoples. In general the Muslim communities were scattered, had no territorial identity, and did not constitute governments.

The Muslim communities were connected to state formation in two ways. First, they often had great influence with military nobles. Muslim advisors gave an Islamic identity to the rulers of the ancient empires of Kawkaw, Takrur, Ghana, Bornu, Mali, and Songhay. Learned Muslim merchants served to legitimize the authority of the rulers, provide administrative services and economic resources, cultural identity, and guidance for festivals, rituals, and magic. Several of these regimes, such as the Mali and Songhay empires, became centers of Muslim worship, scholarship, and legal administration. These regimes were built on a condominium of military and Muslim merchant elites. In these societies, however, the mass of the population remained committed to their traditional religions and were not converted to Islam.

Second, Muslim communities repeatedly attempted to build states of their own. Torodbe or Muslim clerics and teachers were the leaders of these movements. They were a kind of free-floating intelligentsia hostile to the powers, sometimes outraged at their moral shortcomings and failure to implement Islamic policies, sometimes aggrieved over economic exploitation. They were backed by marginalized pastoralists and peasants, rootless wanderers, and gangs of youths. From the seventeenth century jihads were launched in Mauritania, Bundu, Futa Jallon, and Futa Toro. The most famous of these was the jihad of 'Uthman Don Fodio who created the Sokoto Caliphate in 1804, and the nineteenth-century jihad of al-Hajj 'Umar in Futa Toro. These jihads overthrew military elites, and created states in hitherto stateless regions. They were an expression of both moral reformism and political expansionism. Their greatest consequence was to bring masses of common people into the faith of Islam. The jihad states, however, were crushed by British and French colonial intervention at the end of the nineteenth century. Apart from Hausaland and Senegal they left little or no political legacy in the structuring of twentieth-century African states.

More commonly we find the various types of Muslim collectivities bound together in a larger system governed by a state. Islamic states were generally made up of numerous religious collectivities, village and tribal segmentary societies, urban jamats, Sufi brotherhoods, schools of law, and feudal principalities.

The state type of Islamic system was modeled upon the Saljuq-period form of Middle Eastern Islamic society. The early Islamic model, though modified, persisted in Iran, and Turkish migrations and conquests brought it directly to Inner Asia, India, and the Arab Middle East, and via Anatolia to the Ottoman empire in the Balkans and North Africa. Though based on the same model, in each case there were differences in state organization, religious institutions, concepts of legitimacy, and religious beliefs. In the Ottoman, Mughal, Egyptian Mamluk, and Hafsid states, the government was strongly centralized. In Iran, Algeria, Morocco, and parts of the Arab world, states were weak because they were opposed by strong tribal societies, sometimes under Sufi leadership. State control of religious elites was marked in the Ottoman empire, Safavid Iran, and the state of Bukhara, but 'ulama' and Sufis in India, Algeria, and Morocco were relatively independent. Similarly, the bases of legitimacy varied considerably. The Ottoman and Safavid empires emphasized a combination of Islamic and cosmopolitan qualities. In the Arab provinces of the Middle East and North Africa, Islamic elements predominated. Other variations occurred in the prevailing religious orientation of Muslim societies. 'Ulama' Islam was particularly strong in the Ottoman empire, Inner Asia, and Iran. Shrine-Sufism was pronounced in India and North Africa. Everywhere Islamic culture was marked by strong local syncretisms. To fully understand the variations, however, each of the regional societies has to be considered not only with regard to specific features, but also as a whole system in which state, religious, and parochial collectivities and cultures interacted.

The Iranian type of Islamic society may be understood in terms of the relations among state, religious, and tribal (uymaq) populations. The forces that gave shape to Iran go back to the Safavid conquest in 1500. The Safavids were the religious leaders of uymaq and tribal peoples, but their empire was gradually rebuilt on the basis of slave forces and a bureaucratic administration. The Safavid regime became a suzerainty superimposed upon a society parceled out into uymaq kingdoms, each region actually ruled by a tribal lord and his warriors, descended often from Mongol Inner Asian families, who organized a local government and economy and taxed the local population. In Iran political power was from the outset divided between an imperial state and tribal societies.

The central government attempted to legitimize its reign in Muslim terms. Safavid authority was based on the claim that the rulers were descendants of the seventh imam, and therefore were quasi-divine persons. As chiefs of the dominant Sufi movement, they claimed the absolute obedience of all their disciples. To bolster the prestige of the state, the Safavid dynasty sponsored an Iranian-Islamic style of culture concentrating on court poetry, painting, and monumental architecture that symbolized not only the Islamic credentials of the state but also the glory of the ancient Persian tradition. The symbolism of the regime was essentially Muslim, but included strong overtones of an independent Iranian cultural heritage.

In the course of Safavid rule, Iran was converted from Sunni to Shi'i Islam. After the Safavids conquered Iran they made Shi'ism the official religion of the country, built up cadres of Shi'i 'ulama' (mainly imported from Iraq), and ruthlessly suppressed rival religious movements. Sunni 'ulama' and Sufi movements, even including the Safavids' own supporters, were crushed or driven from the country. By the seventeenth century the Safavids had built up a virtually monolithic religious establishment, and eliminated rival forms of Islamic belief and organization.

Still, the relationship between the state and the Shi'i 'ulama' was ambiguous. The 'ulama' of Iran depended upon state support, deferred to state authority, and benefited from state appointments to political and religious offices and from state endowment of religious shrines. They played the role of intermediaries and mediators between the regime and the general populace. Altogether subordinate to the Safavid state, the 'ulama' served to legitimize and support the central regime against its tribal and religious rivals, and took the lead in the persecution of Sunnis and Sufis. There were some doctrinal and social indications, however, of an 'ulama' claim to autonomy and freedom from state control and of religious doubts of the legitimacy of the Safavid regime. With the decline and eventual destruction of the Safavids, some 'ulama' argued that the true leaders of the Islamic community were not the rulers, but the scholars themselves – the mujtahids. They had the wisdom to give guidance on spiritual matters in the absence of the true imam, and the people were bound, according to their teaching, to follow their advice.

The Iranian Shi'i 'ulama' differed from Sunni 'ulama' in several respects. One was that the 'ulama' of Iran formed a relatively cohesive body, related through the spiritual and intellectual genealogies of teachers and students, geographically defined by the boundaries of the country, and in communication with each other. Moreover, they held a large degree of authority over the common people, and did not, as did the 'ulama' of the Ottoman empire, India, or Indonesia, have important Sufi or reformist movements as competitors. Thus, Iranian society before the eighteenth century was characterized by a legitimate but not powerfully centralized monarchy, a distribution of power among tribal principalities, and a monolithic religious establishment patronized by the regime.

The Ottoman empire represented a different constellation of state, religious, and small community relations. The Ottoman regime was highly centralized. A slave military elite, bureaucratic financial administration, and Muslim religious administration gave the central government control over the subject population. As early as the fourteenth and fifteenth centuries, the Ottoman state had effectively subordinated the Turkish and Kurdish tribal populations of eastern Anatolia.

Within the Ottoman empire, however, there was considerable variation in the degree of centralization of power and in the distribution of power from province to province. While the central regime was powerful in the Balkans, most of Anatolia, the Nile Valley, Tunisia, and Algiers, much of Iraq, Upper Egypt, parts of Algeria, southern Tunisia, and Syria were dominated by segmentary populations. In these regions the authority of the central state was tenuous and the local populations were organized in tribal or Sufi-led coalitions. In Tunisia, itself a subordinate state within the Ottoman empire, the centralized state was based on a highly sedentarized and urbanized population, and tribal domains were limited to the south of the country. In Algeria, another vassal state based on a small janissary militia, the state governed some of the coastal regions, but most of the country was ruled by tribal and Sufi chiefs. The weakening of the Ottoman state in the seventeenth and eighteenth centuries allowed, in general, for a strengthening of local elites and communities.

Ottoman success in centralizing state power depended upon a number of factors. First was the power of the central regime and the relative weakness of the tribal populations. As opposed to Iran, which came under the control of the uymaqs, the Oghuz peoples who entered Anatolia in the eleventh and twelfth centuries did not bring Mongol and Chaghatay concepts of political authority, and were not organized under chiefs who controlled a large central household and smaller segmentary groups. They were dispersed peoples operating in small bands, united by successful warrior lords or by charismatic Sufi leaders. The small size of these bands made it easy for the Ottoman state to suppress them, absorb the chiefs into Ottoman administration, and deprive the Sufis of their military and political authority.

Equally important was the concept of Ottoman legitimacy. Unlike the Safavids, the legitimacy of the Ottoman regime was never questioned from a Muslim point of view. Ottoman authority was based on a Turkish tradition of patrimonial leadership, the legacy of previous Muslim states in Anatolia and the Middle East, and the conquest of the Byzantine empire. The Ottomans thus inherited the responsibilities of the historical Caliphates and the imperial aura of the ancient empires. Above all, their legitimacy was based on their success as a warrior state which fulfilled the Muslim duty of jihad, protected the Holy Cities of Arabia, and organized the pilgrimage. The kind of doubts about royal authority raised in the Safavid empire by the Shi'i 'ulama', and those raised in the Mughal empire by the accommodation of non-Muslim cultures, were minimal.

The organized religious life of Ottoman Muslims was also different from that of Iran. The Ottoman empire, like the Safavid, organized an 'ulama' bureaucracy; but unlike the Safavids the Ottomans kept the loyalty of the religious establishment. Government patronage and the creation of an elaborate bureaucracy absorbed the 'ulama' into the state machine. A graded judicial and professorial hierarchy, state salaries, and state endowments effectively committed the 'ulama' to the Ottoman regime. Even the Sufi brotherhoods, despite their large followings, were attached to the state machine and were neutralized or suppressed. The Sunni 'ulama' were totally committed to the authority of the Sultan, and stressed the legacy of religious attitudes that legitimized the state. In Iran, by contrast, the 'ulama' came to be independent of and hostile to the state.

Thus, by the eighteenth century the Ottoman empire had an institutional pattern that emphasized the centralized state, legitimized in Muslim terms, and a centralized and unified Sunni religious establishment that served virtually as a department of state. Only in bedouin-populated regions of the Arab world and North Africa was some degree of autonomy possible.

The Mughal state, like the Ottoman and Safavid empires, was a patrimonial regime. The emperor ruled through a royal household supported by a quasi-feudal elite. The armies were composed of Muslim officers, mainly of Afghan and Inner Asian descent, who were assigned tax revenues from the land in return for supplying contingents for military service. Native Hindu vassals such as the Rajputs formed an important part of the military establishment. Muslims were the original conquering elite but the Hindus were important as subordinate lords, administrative officials, financiers, merchants, and landowners. The regime was also supported by a bureaucratic administration that served to tax the subject populace and to register landed incomes. The bureaucracy was staffed by both Muslim and Hindu officials.

The Mughal regime wove together Muslim and Indian social and cultural considerations. The identity of the Muslim elites was based not only on Islam, but on noble lineage. All members of the elite were members of extended families linked by ceremonies, gifts, and concessions of property and office. Muslim peasants and pastoralists were as much subjects of the empire as were Hindus.

The Mughal empire was officially Muslim. It defended Islam, patronized Muslim religious life, and appointed Muslim judicial and other religious officials, but the Mughals also claimed the loyalty of Hindu lords and subjects and elaborated a court culture in which painting, music, literature, philosophy, and architecture embodied aspects of the Hindu as well as the Muslim heritage and blended them into a single stylistic form. In contrast to the Ottoman and Safavid regimes, the Mughal empire had a strong non-Islamic expression for its cultural and political identity.

In religious organization proper, Mughal India – as opposed to Safavid Iran – recognized no single dominant concept of Islam and no single Muslim community or religious establishment. Indian Muslims formed numerous religious bodies, divided by allegiance to points of doctrine, schools of law, Sufi brotherhoods, and to the teaching of individual shaykhs, scholars, and saints. Indian Muslims qua Muslims appeared as a congeries of religious groups rather than as a single communal body. Despite state patronage of a small 'ulama' establishment, both 'ulama' and Sufis were generally independent – and often critical – of the cosmopolitan and imperial culture, the Hindu elites, and the patrimonial loyalties of the Mughal regime. Thus, Indian Islamic society was not organized in terms of an Ottoman type of state control or an Iranian type of uniformity, but in terms of numerous independent and competitive Muslim religious movements.

Southeast Asia had a similar heritage of an agrarian and commercial economic base and a history of state regimes legitimized in terms of high religious culture, but here political fragmentation rather than imperial unity was the rule. Southeast Asia was never conquered by Muslim tribal peoples; nor were indigenous regimes able to achieve political unity. The coastal and regional states of Malaya, Sumatra, and the principalities of Java took on an Islamic identity, but they were derived historically from pre-Islamic states. Characteristically, Indo-Malay Muslim states depended heavily upon symbolic and cultural attachments to implement their rule. While Islam was woven into the symbolism of state authority, legitimization still depended upon the heritage of Hindu and Buddhist concepts. Even as compared with Mughal India, the non-Islamic cultural aspect of the political system was strongly pronounced.

The Muslim religious communities of Southeast Asia also tended to be decentralized; religious life was built around individual teachers and holy men; the Sufi brotherhoods and the 'ulama' schools were institutionally weak, and there were no significant tribal communities. Scholars functioned independently, teaching through the pesantren. The village holy men were also important influences. In Indonesia, the mass of villagers considered themselves Muslims but were not strongly influenced by Islamic rituals, concepts, laws, ethics, or institutions. They followed a customary religious and social life that had existed prior to the establishment of Islam, and assimilated Islam into this preexisting culture. Islam in Indonesia was manifest as identity rather than as social organization. Some regions were exceptions to this Indo-Malay pattern. In Minangkabau the Sufi orders were strongly organized and generated intense conflict as reformers struggled to bring Minangkabau into accord with Muslim norms.

Southeast Asian Islamic societies differed from the Middle Eastern in that there was little state participation in the organization of Muslim religious life. The village 'ulama', Sufis, and other popular teachers were wholly independent. Indeed, deep in the history of the 'ulama' of Java and the outer islands there was a tradition of resistance to state authority. The common people believed that a savior or just ruler would eventually overthrow the state to create a truly Islamic society. In India and Southeast Asia the initiative passed to independent Sufi and 'ulama' reformers and other charismatic leaders who would struggle among themselves, and with foreign and non-Islamic forces, to try to shape the Islamic destiny of the area in the modern era.

Thus the several types of imperial agrarian Islamic societies may be analyzed in terms of a pattern of institutional arrangements which involved state, parochial, and Muslim religious institutions. In each case the pattern of relations describes a variant form of Muslim society. As Muslim societies entered the modern era they would be drastically changed by internal reorganization and by the impact of European imperialism and the world commercial economy. Nevertheless, the inherited patterns would be a powerful force in the shaping of modern Islamic societies.

THE MODERN TRANSFORMATION: MUSLIM PEOPLES IN THE NINETEENTH AND TWENTIETH CENTURIES

21   The Muharram Procession, Calcutta

INTRODUCTION: MODERNITY AND THE TRANSFORMATION OF MUSLIM SOCIETIES

By the eighteenth century a worldwide system of Muslim societies had come into being. Each was built upon the interaction of Middle Eastern Islamic state, religious, and communal institutions, and local social institutions and cultures, and in each case the interactions generated a different type of Islamic society. Though each society was unique, they resembled each other in form and were interconnected by political and religious contacts and shared values. Thus they made up a world system of Islamic societies.

In the eighteenth and nineteenth centuries the evolution of these societies was diverted by European intervention. By the late eighteenth century the Russians, the Dutch, and the British had established territorial suzerainty in parts of the northern steppes of Asia, Southeast Asia, and the Indian subcontinent, and European commercial and diplomatic intervention was well advanced in other regions. In the nineteenth and early twentieth centuries, European states, driven by the need of industrial economies for raw materials and markets, and by economic and political competition with each other, established worldwide territorial empires. The Dutch completed the conquest of Indonesia; the Russians (and the Chinese) absorbed Inner Asia; the British consolidated their empires in India and Malaya, and took control of parts of the Middle East, East Africa, Nigeria, and other parts of West Africa. France seized North Africa and much of West Africa, parts of the Middle East, and other territories. Small German and Italian colonies were also founded in Africa. By the beginning of the twentieth century, the European powers (and China) had completed their conquest of almost all of the Muslim world.

These conquests were driven by rapid changes within European societies. The Industrial Revolution in Britain in the eighteenth century, and in France, Germany, and other countries in the nineteenth, the development of bureaucratic forms of economic organization, new technologies for the production of steam and electricity, and the expansion of scientific knowledge further enhanced the economic dominance of European countries.

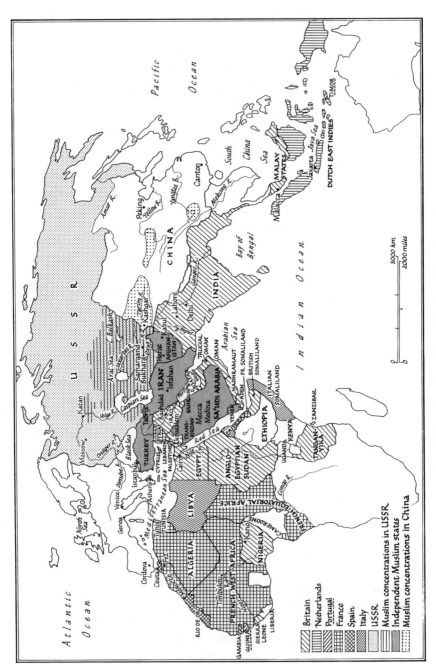

Map 28 European domination and the Muslim world: c. 1920

The American and French revolutions brought equally profound changes in the realm of politics and statecraft. They brought into being the modern nation-state built upon the relative equality and participation of its citizens, close identification of populations with the state, and a merging of national, political, and cultural identities. They also pioneered in the creation of parliamentary institutions that allowed for widespread political representation, and state structures that diffused or moderated the exercise of power in the interests of the autonomy of the civil society and the political freedom of individual citizens.

Furthermore, the European and American Enlightenments completed the historical process of secularization. Political and economic institutions were fully differentiated from religious norms. The cultivation of scientific and of humanistic mentalities relegated religion to a narrowed sphere of worship and communal activities. The scientific mentality "disenchanted" and demystified the world of nature and of human relations. Nature, society, and even the human personality became accessible to rational understanding and to the conviction that they could be modified by conscious human intervention.

Throughout the Muslim world European dominance led to the construction of centralized bureaucratic territorial states. European economic and capitalist penetration usually led to increased and often exploitative trade, stimulated the production of raw materials, and undermined local industries. The European powers forced or induced others to create modern schools, and to promote the values of European civilization, blended as best they could be with indigenous cultures. These changes in non-European societies involved the creation of new patterns of economic production and exchange and new technologies. In turn the new state and economic structures were the bases for the rise of new elites. Political managers, soldiers, technocrats, comprador merchants, intelligentsia, intellectuals, commercial farmers, and industrial workers became important forces in Muslim societies. European influence also stimulated the acceptance of new value systems – an appreciation for national identity and political participation, economic engagement, moral activism, and a new scientific world-view. All of these changes involved the adoption or recreation of the basic features of European civilization in the matrix of older Islamic societies.

In each case, however, the European impact was different – and these differences, combined with the institutional and cultural variations among the Muslim societies, would generate the various contemporary Islamic societies. Just as each Islamic society was the product of the interaction of a regional society with Middle Eastern influences, modern Islamic countries are the products of the interaction of the historical Islamic societies with Europe. Such transformations, of course, were not peculiar to the Muslim world. In the nineteenth and twentieth centuries European influence reached all civilizations, provoked profound changes, and helped shape their contemporary development.

The result was a multiplicity of societies, because there was no single European model of modern society, and because the impact of Europe was different in every part of the world. Like the great empires, religions, and civilizations of the past, Europe challenged existing elites, institutions, and cultures and forced them to define their own version of modernity. Modernity engendered plurality because it resulted from the efforts of Third World indigenous elites to reconstruct their own societies.

The role of indigenous elites, institutions, and cultures in determining the pattern of development must be emphasized because of some important differences between Muslim and European societies. In the nineteenth and twentieth centuries European societies were to a considerable extent organized in terms of economically derived social classes. In many European countries bourgeois elites were the principal forces behind economic development, state organization, and world conquest. Industrial working classes were a principal force in production. In Muslim societies economically defined social classes were relatively less significant. In these societies, the economy was embedded in and regulated by tribal, communal, associational, and state political structures. State elites – and tribal and religious notables – used political power to control land and trading resources and to extract the surplus product of peasants and other producers.

The impact of Europe on Muslim societies was mediated by the collaboration or resistance of these elites. The changes that took place in Muslim societies were forged in terms of the interests, perceptions, and responses of internal elites to the pressures and incentives generated by European power and by their desire to exploit European influences in the struggle for power within their own societies. Whatever the economic forces that impinged from without, in Muslim countries these elites had primarily a political or cultural orientation, and tended to define the problem of European intervention in sociocultural rather than economic terms. In Muslim societies economic influences commonly led to political and cultural responses. Thus, indigenous elites, institutions, and cultural codes were as important to the shape of modernity as were European imperial and economic systems.

The history of the modern transformation of Islamic societies falls into several phases and shows certain common features throughout the Muslim world. The first phase was the period from the late eighteenth to the early twentieth centuries, marked by the breakup of the Muslim state system and the imposition of European commercial and territorial domination. In this phase Muslim political, religious, and tribal elites attempted to define new ideological and religious approaches to the internal development of their own societies. Out of these responses came a second phase of development, the twentieth-century formation of national states through which the elites of Muslim countries tried to give a modern political identity to their societies and to promote economic development and social change. The phase of national state building began after World War I and persists to the present. The consolidation of independent national states in turn introduced a third phase in the development of almost all Muslim countries: the rise of Islamist or Islamic revival movements and conflict over the ultimate role of Islam in the development of these societies.

ISLAMIC MODERNISM

In almost all Muslim regions colonial rule brought new elites to the fore. Political power was taken from the hands of old elites and transferred to a new stratum of military, bureaucratic, or landowning intelligentsia – and in some countries, in a later generation, to upwardly mobile, modern-educated, middle- and lower-class intellectuals, technicians, and soldiers. In a limited number of cases the economic changes induced by European penetration promoted new strata of merchants, commercial farmers, and industrial workers. All of these new groups and classes were at first very small in size. They were the vanguard of the modernization of their societies.

These elites generated two principal responses to European pressures. One was the response of the political classes and of newly formed intelligentsias trained in Western techniques and enamored of Western cultural values and accomplishments. They favored Islamic modernist or secular nationalist concepts of the future of Muslim societies, and tended to redefine Islam to make it consistent with European forms of state and economy. The second response came from tribal leaders, merchants, and commercial farmers led by 'ulama' and Sufis, who espoused a reorganization of Muslim communities and the reform of individual behavior in terms of fundamental religious principles.

The Muslim response of course differed from place to place. In the Ottoman regions, Turkey, Egypt, the Arab fertile crescent, and Tunisia, the dominant indigenous response was that of the established political elites and the political, technical, and literary intelligentsia who rose out of the political classes. In these regions European influence was primarily diplomatic, commercial, and educational. The rivalry of the European powers in the nineteenth century allowed the Ottoman empire to survive, but made it dependent upon British and Russian diplomatic pressures and later upon German military advisors and investors. European traders extracted raw materials, and introduced European manufactures in competition with indigenous merchants and artisans. Europeans stimulated the production of cash crops such as grain, dried fruit, and cotton in Anatolia, opium in Iran, silk in the Lebanon, cotton in Egypt, and olive oil in Tunisia, and generally depressed the handicrafts and manufacturing industries. European trade promoted Christian and Jewish middlemen and depressed the opportunities of Muslim merchants. Europeans also invested in railroads, mining, and agriculture. European states and banks lent large sums to the Ottoman empire, Egypt, and Tunisia, and eventually established a foreign fiscal administration in each country. In Egypt and Tunisia this proved to be the basis for European protectorates. In the Ottoman empire, European competition weakened the Muslim bourgeoisie and helped concentrate economic power in the hands of the state elites.

The response of the political elites and intelligentsias went through a cycle of several generations. In late eighteenth-century Palestine, the early nineteenth-century Ottoman empire and Egypt, and mid-nineteenth-century Tunisia, the political elites sought to reorganize their military forces, centralize and rationalize bureaucratic administration, and promote economic activities that would increase state revenues. Political elites also recognized the need to create new schools to educate modern professional and administrative personnel. In the next "generation," Ottoman, Egyptian, and Tunisian reformers appreciated the connection between a strong state and a productive and socially integrated society, and introduced social, legal, and educational programs which undermined the traditional roles of the religious elites and created the prototypes of modern judicial and educational systems.

The formation of new intelligentsias was a critical outcome of the reform programs. In the Ottoman case, a new "generation" of Western-educated physicians, engineers, army and navy officers, and administrators was the product of professional schools and of studies in Europe. These Western-educated cadres were partially absorbed into state service, but many of them found careers in law, journalism, and literary activities, and attempted to win control of the state.

The reform program in Egypt was unusual in the degree to which the state attempted to control the economy. Muhammad 'Ali (1805–48) improved irrigation, stimulated cotton production, created trading monopolies, and invested in factories to produce military supplies. Extensive economic change created a new landowning and bureaucratic class whose scions became officials, lawyers, journalists, and politicians in the late nineteenth century. With the establishment of British rule in 1882, the domestic elites lost control of the state and were forced into lower bureaucratic functions, the liberal professions, and journalism, and from these positions formed a national movement opposed to British rule.

In the Arab fertile crescent, European political influence and commercial penetration did not lead to structural and political changes until after World War I, but educational and literary influences in the middle and latter part of the nineteenth century promoted an Arab cultural renaissance and the birth of Arab literary nationalism. In Lebanon and Syria the new intelligentsia was the product of European and modernized late Ottoman education. The formation of dependent colonial states in 1920 provoked the coalescence of an opposition intelligentsia which included Ottoman and Western-educated soldiers and officials, landowners, religious notables, and sometimes tribal chiefs and merchants. By the 1930s and 1940s further education and development had created a new generation of soldiers, technocrats, and journalists from middle- and lower-middle-class backgrounds who would rival the first generation of national leaders.

Tunisia went through a similar developmental sequence. Before the establishment of the French protectorate in 1881 the principal reaction to European economic domination came from officials who attempted to modernize and rationalize the Tunisian regime. After the establishment of the French protectorate successive generations of Western- and modern-Muslim-educated Tunisians took the lead in resisting European control and demanding political rights. From approximately 1890 to 1920 domestic leadership was provided by government officials, reformist 'ulama', and French-educated notables. In the 1930s and after, a new generation of Arab French-educated upwardly mobile intellectuals, largely from provincial small-town, middle-, and lower-class milieus, took the lead in the movement for Tunisian independence.

In all of these cases, 'ulama' and merchants played only a secondary role. 'Ulama' were auxiliaries or participants in the early phases of national movements in Egypt, Syria, and Tunisia, but were soon superseded by the Western-educated intelligentsias. Not until the 1930s did structural changes in the economy or sufficiently far-reaching changes in class structure generate a politically significant merchant or working class which could play an important political role. In no case did these new milieus disturb the dominance of the Western-educated political intelligentsias.

In other Muslim regions similar intelligentsias came into being without the mediation of the old-regime state elites and internal programs of reform, but as a result of direct European rule, the displacement of former political elites from their governing positions, and their subordination to colonial administrators. In India, British control deprived the Muslim elites of political power, generated economic changes that weakened the grip of Muslim landlords on rural revenues, and threatened to undermine Muslim culture. In response, the displaced Muslim political elite transformed itself into a modern intelligentsia. Under the leadership of Sayyid Ahmad Khan (1817–98), they founded a college at Aligarh and defined a modern Islamic education to train a new generation of officials, lawyers, and journalists. After the turn of the century Aligarh graduates became the leaders of Muslim resistance to British rule and, ultimately, the proponents of Pakistan.

In Indonesia, Dutch rule similarly transformed the historical ruling classes, the priyayi, into subordinate functionaries of Dutch administration. The Dutch themselves provided the former elites with a Western professional education in order to generate the Indonesian cadres who were needed to maintain Dutch administration. From Dutch-sponsored colleges and technical, legal, and medical schools came the officials and intellectuals who became the advocates of Indonesian national independence.

In almost all Muslim countries politicians, displaced politicians, would-be politicians, professionals, technicians, and intellectuals trained in Western techniques sought to define new political ideologies for the development of their societies. In successive generations the political elites and intelligentsias adopted Islamic modernist, secular nationalist, and sometimes socialist conceptions of national transformation.

Islamic modernism was the nineteenth-century doctrine of Muslim political elites and intelligentsias, and must be distinguished from Islamic reformism, which was a doctrine of the 'ulama'. The essential principle of Islamic modernism was that the defeat of Muslims at the hands of European powers had revealed their vulnerability, and that borrowing European military techniques, centralizing state power, modernizing their economies, and providing a modern education for their elites was essential for the restoration of their political power. It meant that the medieval forms of Islamic civilization had to be repudiated – but not that Islam itself was to be denied. Rather, it was to be reconstructed on its own inherent, but neglected, principles of rationality, ethical activism, and patriotism.

The modernist point of view was first espoused by the Young Ottomans in the 1860s and 1870s. While committed to the principles of Islam, they called upon the endangered Ottoman regime to transform itself into a constitutional government and to promote a new social morality and revived culture based on a simplified Turkish language. Similarly, in India Sayyid Ahmad Khan argued that the survival of Indian Muslims under British rule required the education of a new generation of Muslim leaders loyal to the principles of Islam but adapted to the political and scientific culture of the modern world. While the Ottoman and Indian intelligentsias were concerned with local situations, Jamal al-Din al-Afghani (1839–97) proselytized for an international union of Muslim peoples committed to the modernization of Islam and to political unity in the face of colonial oppression. Islamic modernism, then, was the ideology of elites who were concerned with the restoration of state power in terms of the indigenous social and cultural bases of political power.

The commitment of the intelligentsias to Islamic modernism was followed by a move to secular nationalism. In the Ottoman empire the Young Turks succeeded the Young Ottomans. In reaction to the pan-Islamic policies of Sultan 'Abd al-Hamid II (1876–1908) they turned from an Islamic modernist to a secular constitutionalist position. In Tunisia, the first-generation elites blended Islamic modernist and secular orientations, but were followed in the 1930s by a revived independence movement that was articulated mainly in secular nationalist terms, despite making symbolic appeals to Islam. In the Arab countries, at the end of World War I, the Damascus notables changed their emphasis from an Islamic to an Arab orientation. In Egypt, the first generation of modernist intelligentsia was superseded by secular liberal political parties. In India the Aligarh graduates were secular and modernist in lifestyle and personal religious orientation, but for reasons peculiar to the subcontinent developed a commitment to the formation of a "Muslim" national state. Only in Indonesia did the priyayi bypass the Islamic modernist phase and enter directly into a secular nationalist literary and political opposition to Dutch rule. In Indonesia, the shallow integration of Islamic values into the historical cultural orientation of the political elite helps to explain the immediate adoption of secular nationalism. In Algeria, whose migrant workers in France and rural migrants to Algerian towns formed the popular base of Algerian national movements, and in Indonesia, where the workers' movement and the Communist Party were particularly strong, nationalism was blended with socialist conceptions of state control of the economy. In general, Young Turks, Arab nationalists, pan-Turkish intellectuals, Malay aristocrats, and others set aside the Muslim dimension of their political and cultural heritage to espouse the formation of secular national types of modern society.

Nationalism came to be the preferred doctrine of the political elites and modern-educated intelligentsias for several reasons. Foremost was the influence of a Western education. Though opposed to colonial rule the first- and second-generation intelligentsias were raised in the intense glow of self-confident European supremacy, and absorbed the nationalist convictions of their colonial rulers and instructors. National and secular symbols were also particularly meaningful to a segment of society that had been uprooted from local affiliations and cast into a world of cosmopolitan education and state-centered political movements. An independent national state was the only potential homeland for people who no longer belonged to their old communities and for whom colonial political societies could only offer subordinate positions.

There were also tactical reasons for the adoption of secular nationalism as the ideology of political intelligentsias. The nationalist position helped differentiate the new segments of an intelligentsia from the established elites, and could serve as a mobilizing symbol in the competition for the support of other uprooted strata of society and as a claim to leadership of the masses. In the Ottoman empire Young Turks used the new ideology against the pan-Islamic claims of the Sultan and in opposition to more conservative and entrenched Ottoman officials. In Lebanon and Syria, nationalism was the preferred position of Christians in predominantly Muslim societies. In Tunisia, Arab French-educated intellectuals used nationalism against the established reformist oriented elites of Tunis. In Indonesia, priyayi nationalism developed partially in opposition to Muslim merchant reformist movements. Nationalism also served better than Islamic modernism to symbolize the ambiguous relationship between Muslim intelligentsias and colonial political domination. On the one hand, secularism and nationalism signified that the intelligentsias were the advanced elements of their societies and justified their demand to participate in colonial regimes. On the other hand, nationalism also legitimized resistance to foreign rule in the eyes of Europeans as well as Muslims.

ISLAMIC REFORMISM

While political elites and intelligentsias became committed to Islamic modernist, secularist, and nationalist concepts of society, an alternative set of responses came from the 'ulama' and allied merchant, artisan, and tribal milieus. In many Muslim countries the 'ulama' opposed both colonial influences and the state intelligentsias. In Iran and Indonesia the opposition came from the conventional scholars. In Iran, Russian territorial expansion and Russian and British economic penetration – in the form of monopolies and concessions, investments in mining, irrigation, and banks, and heavy loans to the Shah – met with a double response. While the state elites made attempts to modernize the military and administrative apparatus and, through new professional schools and the education of Iranians abroad, to create a small intelligentsia, the Shi'i 'ulama' protested against Russian military expansion, foreign economic penetration, and the military, administrative, and educational reform programs of the monarchy. At the beginning of the twentieth century, a coalition of 'ulama', merchants, artisans, and intellectuals overthrew the monarchy and established a short-lived constitutional regime. In Iran the heritage of a weak state and the strength of 'ulama', tribal, and guild organizations made possible a competition between alternative conceptions of an Iranian response to colonialism and an open struggle for control of the state.

In Java, where the political elites became subordinate collaborators in Dutch rule, anti-colonial resistance was led by rural 'ulama' united by the Sufi brotherhoods. In Banten (western Java) they led peasant protests, riots, and rebellions against Dutch rule and their priyayi overlords. By contrast with the Ottoman empire, where conventional 'ulama' were generally subordinate to state elites and did not play an important role in resistance or adaptation to colonial rule, in the Indies 'ulama'-led resistance was widespread.

More commonly, 'ulama' resistance was expressed in reformist terms. Islamic reformism had its origin in the seventeenth and eighteenth centuries, and preceded European domination. In Arabia and Cairo informal 'ulama' and Sufi study-groups espoused a purified version of Islamic belief and practice based on the study of the Quran, hadith, and law combined with Sufi asceticism. The imitation of the Prophet Muhammad became the ideal of a Muslim life. These reformers, aided by the conviction that God was punishing Muslims for failure to heed his will, opposed the tolerant attitude of Muslim states toward non-Muslim peoples and cultures, sought to abolish the veneration of saints and the more florid cults and ceremonies, and worked to dispel superstitious or magical beliefs and practices. The reformers espoused, instead, a religion of personal discipline, moral responsibility and commitment to a universal Muslim society. They were committed, if need be, to militant action to destroy corrupt versions of Islam and to create a just and truly Islamic community.

From Arabia and Cairo, traveling scholars, students and Sufis, merchants and craftsmen carried the reformist doctrine to India, Indonesia, and North and West Africa. The reformist discourse appealed to two milieus. First, it appealed to fragmented lineage and village societies, to whom it offered Islamic authority and leadership for the unification of diverse groups in the struggle against local rivals and states. Reformism could be used as an ideology of mobilization for conquests, the formation of new states, and for anti-colonial resistance.

The earliest example of a reformist movement in a pastoral and tribal society was the Wahhabi movement in Arabia. Born out of an alliance between a reform preacher and the Sa'udi family, the Wahhabis united diverse tribal groups into a movement that conquered most of Arabia. In West Africa, Islamic reform had both indigenous roots and international Muslim connections. While eighteenth- and nineteenth-century reformist movements in the Senegambian region represented a local tradition of Muslim resistance to non-Muslim political elites, the Fulani conquests, led by 'Uthman Don Fodio (1754–1817), who established the Caliphate of Sokoto (1809–1903) in the region between the Niger and Lake Chad, had mixed local and Arabian inspiration. International reformist influences, introduced by the

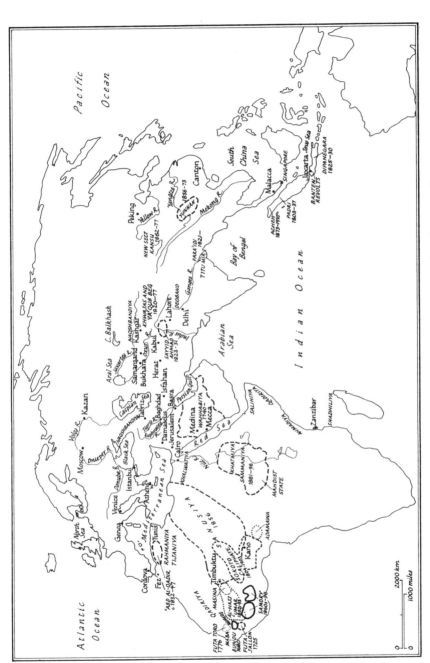

Map 29 Islamic reform and resistance movements: eighteenth and nineteenth centuries

Table 16. *Muslim reform (tajdid) movements, eighteenth to twentieth centuries*

Arabia	Reform teaching in Mecca and Medina Wahhabiya – founded by Muhammad b. Abd. al-Wahhab (1703–92); allied with Ibn Sa ud to create Sa udi state Idrisiya – founded in Mecca by Ahmad b. Idris (d. 1837)
Caucasus	Naqshbandiya – 1785–present, anti-Russian resistance
Inner Asia	Naqshbandiya – reform-oriented Sufi tariqa leads Muslim resistance to Russia and China New teaching, 1761–1877 – offshoot of Naqshbandiya, late eighteenth- and late nineteenth-century resistance to Chinese rule Khwajas and Ya qub Beg – holy Muslim lineage, formerly rulers of Kashgar, attempt to establish a Muslim state, defeated by China in 1878 Yunnan, 1856–73 – rebellion against Chinese rule and effort to establish a Muslim state *usul-i jadid* – Kazan, Crimean, and Bukharan intellectuals, notably Isma il Gasprinskii (1851–1914), sponsor new schools, combined Muslim and Russian education; modernization of Muslim peoples

India

Shah Waliallah (1703–62)

Shah 'Abd al-'Aziz (1746–1824)

Muhammad Isma'il (1781–1831)

Sayyid Ahmad Barelwi (1785–1831)   *Meccan influences*
unites Pathans to resist British and Sikhs |
          | | Fara'idi (Bengal);
Patna-Maulana Walayat 'Ali | 1818–45 anti-Hindu
          Titu Mir (Bengal)   and anti-British
Maulana Karamat   ahl-i hadith
'Ali |
          Delhi School
          |
Deoband – founded 1876. Muslim
college combined hadith studies
and Sufism and spawned
satellite schools |

          Tablighi Islam – founded 1927 by
          Mawlana Muhammad Ilyas

Southeast Asia	Padri Movement – Sumatra 1803–37 Dipanegara leads revolt on Java, 1825–30 Banten, West Java revolts, nineteenth century Kaum Muda – Sumatra and Malaya movement for reform and modernization Acheh – 1873–1908 ulama -led resistance to Dutch occupation Muhammadiya – 1912–present; educational and social reform
Egypt and North Africa	Abd al-Qadir – Qadiriya chieftain attempts to establish Algerian State, defeated by the French Rahmaniya – religious brotherhood uses networks of zawiyas in Algeria and Tunisia to resist French occupation Tijaniya – reform Sufi order inspires West and North African jihads and resistance movements Khalwatiya – reformist Sufi brotherhood Sanusiya – reformist brotherhood creates "state" in Libya, founded by Muhammad b. Ali al-Sanusi (d. 1859); resists Italian occupation Salafiya – founded by Muhammad Abduh (d. 1905), influenced islah and national movements in North Africa; Tunisia, Young Tunisians; Algeria; Ben Badis; Morocco, Allal al-Fasi

Table 16. — *Continued*

East Africa	Idrisiya spawned Rashidiya in Algeria; Amirghaniya in Sudan and Nubia; Sanusiya in Libya
	Sudan – Sammaniya gives rise to Muhammad b. Ahmad al-Mahdi (d. 1898)
	Somalia – Muhammad Abdallah Hassan leads resistance to British, 1899–1920
West Africa	Jihad of Uthman Don Fodio (1754–1817) – Northern Nigerian reformist opposition to Hausa states
	Sokoto Caliphate (1809–1903) and related jihads in Adamawa and Masina
	Al-Hajj Umar (1794?–1864) – jihad state in region of Mali and Senegal
	Bundu, Futa Jallon, and Futa Toro, reform Muslim states in the Senegambian region
	Ma Ba – nineteenth-century jihad in Senegal
	Samory (1860s–98) – Muslim adventurer founds West African state

Tijani order, spread in Algeria, Morocco, and West Africa, and interacted with local forces to inspire the formation of the regime of al-Hajj 'Umar (1794?–1864) in the regions from the Niger to Senegal. In Libya, the Sanusiya unified tribal peoples and created a loose confederation of tribes and oases which served to mediate disputes and to organize trade. Reformism also became the basis of the local struggle against colonialism in the Caucasus and Inner Asia, where the Naqshbandi order became the bearer of new religious inspiration and, ultimately, of political resistance to both Russian and Chinese expansion. In the Indian Northwest Frontier, Sayyid Ahmad Barelwi tried to organize the Pashtuns against the British and the Sikhs on the basis of reformist teaching.

Second, reformism took root in agricultural and urban merchant milieus, in direct response to European political intervention and economic changes. In Bengal the reformist Fara'idi movement was associated with the introduction of British rule and the rise of Hindu and British landlords. In northern India, British rule and the collapse of the Mughal empire led to reform movements in urban and small-town middle-class milieus. Based at Deoband, reformist 'ulama' created a network of colleges which trained cadres to proselytize, educate, and make true Muslims out of Indian believers. Deoband and subsequent reformist movements in India contributed heavily to the creation of a sense of Muslim identity throughout the subcontinent.

In Southeast Asia there were successive waves of reformism. The early nineteenth-century Padri movement in Sumatra was associated with the commercialization of coffee production. Coffee farmers were receptive to the influence of the reformist pilgrims and scholars returning to Sumatra from Mecca and Medina, who launched a movement to Islamize Muslim villages. At the end of the nineteenth century reformism became the creed of the Indo-Malay merchant communities of Singapore and other Southeast Asian ports. Enlarged world trade, pilgrimage, the creation of a capitalist plantation economy in Sumatra and Malaya producing rubber, coffee, tobacco, pepper, sugar, pineapples, and palm oil for export, the formation of a plantation and mining proletariat, commercialization, urbanization, and other forces of socio-economic change broke down traditional family and social structures, favored the growth of a Muslim merchant class in Singapore and other island ports, and of commercial planters in Sumatra and Malaya, and led to the adoption of Muslim reformism as the doctrine of new communities. These and similar milieus were the basis of the early twentieth-century Muhammadiya movement in Indonesia and the Kaum Muda (Young Group) in Malaya. In Inner Asia, merchants and intelligentsia adopted *usul-i jadid* (the New Method) in response to Russian domination, and the need to revitalize a threatened Muslim community.

Reformism could be blended with Muslim modernism. An Egyptian scholar, Muhammad 'Abduh (1849–1905), combined reformist principles – return to the Quran and the sayings of the Prophet, the right of independent judgment in religious matters, abandonment of a stifling conformity to outmoded tradition, and opposition to cultic Sufi practices – with a modernist responsiveness to the political and cultural pressures of Europe. These movements were devoted to the reform of education as a correction to shrine and saint worship and magical religious practices, and were committed to the need for adjustment to modern economic and technological conditions. They were latently, and sometimes actively, political, in that they cultivated a consciousness of the need for autonomy from European powers if the vitality of Islamic states and societies was to be restored. This blend of modernist and reformist thought inspired the Salafi movement in Egypt, the Arab Middle East, and North Africa. In North Africa the Salafi movement became the principal ideological expression of the merchant bourgeoisie of Fez and other Moroccan towns in the 1920s, and in Algeria it appealed to the urban petite bourgeoisie and uprooted rural migrants. In Morocco and Algeria reformism transcended specific class milieus and became for a time the ideology of national identity and resistance to French rule.

In short, Islamic reformism was the political and moral response of 'ulama', tribal, and urban communities to the transformation of the traditional structures of Muslim societies and to the threat of European political, economic, and cultural domination. It had its origin in the seventeenth and eighteenth centuries in response, not to European pressures, but to purely internal conditions, and it was later adapted to anti-colonial resistance. Reformism appealed to tribal societies seeking political unification and to merchant and farmer milieus undergoing commercialization and urbanization where reformist doctrine provided a cultural basis for larger-scale communities. Though often politically passive, reformism contributed to the psychological mobilization of colonized peoples and became the vehicle for the reconstruction of Muslim political identity among sub-national populations in the Caucasus, Inner Asia, India, and Indonesia and the basis for national movements in Algeria and Morocco.

Patterns of response and resistance

Thus the two principal responses to the breakdown of Muslim societies and to European penetration came from the political intelligentsias and the 'ulama', and represented, despite modifications, a striking continuity in the structures of Islamic societies. In societies with a strong heritage of state domination over the 'ulama', such as the Ottoman empire and Turkey, the political intelligentsia led the way, unopposed, to national independence; but in the more pluralist Muslim societies colonial rule precipitated a multi-sided struggle for power waged against the colonial rulers and among the various Islamic modernist secularist, nationalist, socialist, and Muslim traditional and reformist elites. In Iran, a society with a more open political structure, foreign pressures promoted a limited modernization of the state and collusion between government elites and foreign business interests, but it damaged Iranian merchant and artisan interests and 'ulama' cultural security, and provoked a coalition of 'ulama', merchant, and intellectual opposition to foreign encroachment. The result was direct conflict between state and religious elites over Iranian national identity, policies of economic development, and foreign relations.

Similarly, in India the loss of political power, economic dominance, and cultural supremacy to English and Christian rulers provoked a multiple Muslim response. From the displaced political elites, transformed by modern education into an intelligentsia, came a movement for the formation of a national Muslim state in the subcontinent. From reformist 'ulama' came repeated efforts to define the identity of an Indian Muslim population in terms of personal religious values.

Indonesia was also the center of a complex struggle among forces that had different experiences of colonial rule, different class and status interests, different historical variants of Indonesian Islamic culture, and different responses to the problems of colonialism and economic change. The priyayi were transformed by Dutch education into a secularized intelligentsia who took the lead in the Indonesian nationalist movement, while reformism became the preferred ideology of merchants and commercial farmers. In the more traditional, less disrupted parts of Java, 'ulama' (kiyayi) maintained their leadership in the countryside and led peasant resistance against Dutch rule. Indonesian politics before and since independence has been characterized by a struggle for political and ideological power among Indonesian nationalist, reformist Muslim, and conservative Muslim movements.

Algerian society similarly evinced a plural response to French occupation and colonization. The French destroyed the traditional society, but in the 1920s and 1930s urbanization and migration to the towns was the basis for the formation of a new Algerian elite. This elite was divided into three segments: the French-educated Algerians who favored cultural and political assimilation into France and the acceptance of Muslims as citizens of France; reformist 'ulama' who appealed to the petite bourgeoisie of the towns and to certain rural populations, and attempted to define an Algerian national identity in Arab and Muslim terms; and populist leaders who organized Algerian workers, both at home and in France, into a radical political movement. By the late 1940s all of these movements had failed to make significant progress toward Algerian independence, and a new generation of revolutionary soldiers took the lead in throwing off French colonialism and establishing an independent Algerian state. The new Algerian state nonetheless came to be defined by past elements of Islamic reformism and populist socialism.

Thus, in most Muslim societies the struggle among political intelligentsias, 'ulama', and other elites has given political and cultural definition to modern Muslim national states. The continuity of historic elites, institutions, and cultures in the "modernization" of these societies meant that in each Muslim country the universal features of economy and technology were expressed, organized, and interrelated in ways that yielded different versions of modernity.

NATIONALISM AND ISLAM IN THE MIDDLE EAST

CHAPTER 22

IRAN: STATE AND RELIGION IN THE MODERN ERA

Modern Iran inherited from the Safavid period (1501–1722) the pattern of state, religious, and tribal (uymaq) institutions that would shape its history to the present day. The Qajar dynasty, which ruled Iran from 1779 to 1925, resembled its Safavid predecessors in that it was a weakly centralized regime faced with strong provincial tribal forces, and an increasingly independent religious establishment. In the nineteenth century, European conquests, cultural influence, and above all economic penetration polarized state and society and led to the constitutional revolution of 1905, in which a coalition of intellectuals, 'ulama', merchants, and artisans attempted to create a parliamentary regime. The Pahlavi period, from 1925 to 1979, virtually repeated the earlier history. The Pahlavis sought to centralize state power and modernize the Iranian economy and society, and again provoked 'ulama'-led nationwide resistance in the name of Islam. For 200 years the struggle between the state and the 'ulama' was a principal feature of Iranian history.

QAJAR IRAN: THE LONG NINETEENTH CENTURY

The modern cycle began with the Qajars, who came to power after a period of anarchy and tribal struggles. Their regime was never consolidated. Their armies were composed of a small Turkoman bodyguard and Georgian slaves; the central administration was a court government too underdeveloped to tax the country effectively. The provinces they ruled were fragmented into innumerable tribal, ethnic, and local factions headed by their own chieftains. A combination of formal governmental appointments, control of land, rights to collect taxes, and the power to administer justice and mediate disputes made tribal chiefs virtually independent of the state. Khans and Ilkhans governed their own tribes. The authority of Khans was by no means absolute since it depended upon the ability to rally support from lesser chiefs who had to be coerced, cajoled, bought off, or otherwise made allies of the paramount Khans, but it was often sufficient to assure their autonomy. Town quarters and guilds also had a degree of political autonomy. The Qajars, moreover, never captured the aura of legitimacy that had surrounded the Safavids. They maintained their suzerainty by exploiting the rivalries of lesser chiefs.

While the Qajars maintained a tenuous suzerainty, the power of the religious establishment was enhanced. In the course of the eighteenth and nineteenth centuries, the 'ulama' of Iran achieved an unprecedented degree of autonomy, a strong leadership, and organizational coherence. The religious authority of the 'ulama' (known as mujtahids, or interpreters of the religious law) was vastly enhanced by the claim that they had the right to exercise independent judgment and to make new interpretations in religious matters based on their spiritual and intellectual attainments – and further, that the most pious and spiritual leaders were, in the absence of the imam, the true leaders of the Muslim community. It was a religious obligation of ordinary people to take them as their absolute spiritual guides (*marja'-i taqlid*). The Shi'i shrines, ceremonies of *ta'ziya* (the mourning of Husayn), and the passion plays that commemorated his martyrdom helped to capture the allegiance of the Iranian populace. Furthermore, these claims to an enhanced religious authority, wrested from a weak political regime, were backed by the formation of a loose system of communications which bound together the 'ulama' of Iran and the spiritual centers of Shi'ism in Iraq. The Iraqi shrines gave Iranian Shi'ism a base outside the physical control of the Qajar monarchy.

The 'ulama' also consolidated their ties with the common people through the administration of justice, trust funds, and charities, and by presiding over the prayers and ceremonies marking birth, marriage, and death. Their ties with the bazaar population of artisans, workers, and merchants were especially important. A secure financial foundation was built up on the contributions of their followers and the endowment of state lands. This religious body was not quite a church, because it lacked a formal hierarchy and regular internal organization, but it was nonetheless partially autonomous, nationwide, and capable of cohesive religious and political action.

The relationship of the 'ulama' to the Qajar regime was subtle. Despite the weakness of the regime, there were good historical precedents for the collaboration of state and 'ulama' elites. The "twelver" 'ulama' were deeply affected by a long tradition of quietism and rejection of active involvement in political affairs. Their ethos called for concentration on theological and religious matters and deference to the state in all other respects, and they depended upon the state for appointments to office, salaries, grants of land, and endowments for shrines and schools. Fath 'Ali Shah (1797–1834), whose power was precariously based on tribal forces, reconstructed the shrines, appointed 'ulama' to official positions, and respected them as mediators between the government and the populace. He tolerated the independence of leading 'ulama' notables, such as Sayyid Muhammad Baqir of Isfahan, whose power was based on substantial landed wealth, the control of religious endowments, and the support of numerous strongmen. Fath 'Ali aided in the suppression of Sufism and heretical doctrines. His reign had the double effect of binding the 'ulama' to the regime and preparing the way for their later autonomy.

European encroachment heightened the implicit tensions between the state and the 'ulama'. In the course of the eighteenth and nineteenth centuries the Russians seized control of northwestern Iran. The treaty of Gulistan (1813) confirmed the loss to Russia of Georgia, Darband, Baku, Shirvan, and other parts of Armenia. In 1826 the Russians seized Tabriz. By the treaty of Turkmanchai (1828) Russia obtained Armenia, control of the Caspian Sea, and a favored position in Iranian trade. Between 1864 and 1885 a new wave of Russian expansion culminated in the seizure of Iran's central Asian provinces. Russian conquests were counterbalanced by the British, who assumed control over Afghanistan to protect their Indian empire. Iran, which itself aspired to annex Afghanistan, was defeated in 1856 at Herat and was forced to recognize the independence of Afghanistan and to make other political and commercial concessions. The net result was to create a Russian sphere of domination in Inner Asia and the Caucasus and a British sphere in Afghanistan. Significantly, the powers did not take Iran under direct colonial rule.

After 1857 the primary form of British and Russian penetration was economic. In 1872 the Iranian government gave extensive concessions to Baron de Reuter. De Reuter was given control of customs revenues for twenty-four years, a monopoly of rail and tramway construction, exclusive rights to mine numerous minerals and metals, to construct canals and irrigation works, and rights of first refusal for a national bank, roads, telegraphs, and mills in return for royalties and a share of profits for the Shahs. In 1889 the Imperial Bank of Persia was founded under British auspices, and in 1890 a British firm was conceded a monopoly of the Iranian tobacco industry, including both domestic sales and exports. Russia made compensating economic gains. Caspian fisheries were turned over to Russia (1888), and a discount Bank of Persia was formed under Russian sponsorship (1891). In the course of the 1890s Russia became the primary investor in loans to the Shahs. Finally, in 1907 an Anglo-Russian agreement divided the country into two spheres of influence – a northern Russian and a southeastern British zone – with a neutral buffer between. In order to calm their own disputes in anticipation of a general European war, the powers allowed Iran to remain nominally independent with its monarchy intact, but effectively assumed control of the country.

As in the Ottoman empire, European political and economic intervention stimulated the Qajars to modernize and strengthen the state apparatus. Western influence created in upper-class government circles a vogue for the reform of Iran's military and governmental institutions along Western lines. A new military corps was proposed in 1826, but was vigorously opposed by the 'ulama' and by tribal forces. Nasir al-Din (1848–96) organized a military system that required each town or village to supply a quota of soldiers or to pay the equivalent of their salaries. He also tried to break the dependence of the regime on local governors, tribal chiefs, and landlords and to formalize a government administration along Russian lines. In 1851 the Dar al-Funun, or technical college, was created to train army and civil officers. In the latter part of the century missionary schools brought in Western techniques. Between 1878 and 1880 Austrian and Russian advisors helped the Iranians reorganize the cavalry and form the Cossack Brigade.

The reforms also brought into being a new stratum of Islamic modernist thinkers and Westernized intellectuals, who favored the modernization of Iran as the only effective way to resist foreign control and improve the conditions of life for the mass of its people. This stratum included people educated in Europe, high-ranking government officials in contact with foreign powers, and various religious minorities influenced by radical movements in Russian-occupied Transcaucasia. European commercial activities also generated a small Iranian bourgeoisie which prospered from the roles of middlemen in the exchanges between Europe and Iran.

Neither the governmental nor the intellectual reformers, however, had much impact on the country as a whole. Intellectual reforms reached a small milieu of court officials and Western-educated Iranian journalists, but did not touch the mass of the population. The reform program faltered because the rulers were themselves afraid that they might compromise their authority. Dependent on British and Russian help to maintain their regime, they had little incentive to strike out on their own. They found it difficult to raise money, and when they could do so, being used to thinking of state revenues as a form of private property, they were reluctant to use it in the public interest. Furthermore, tribal groups resisted centralization of military power. The 'ulama' opposed secularization. The Russians hindered railway construction. In the face of such pressures, Qajar reforms were insufficient to oppose foreign encroachment.

At the same time European intervention provoked resistance. The 'ulama' became the leading opponents of foreign influence, and of the Qajar state as a collaborator with foreign powers. Westernized intellectuals objected to the corruption of the regime and to their exclusion from power. Merchants and artisans, hurt by European competition and state-sponsored monopolies, and 'ulama', anxious over the rise of alien influences, were pushed into outright opposition. They resisted the effort to establish a Western-type army regiment along Ottoman lines in 1826, and in 1828 the Russian occupation of the Caucasus led to a nationwide agitation in favor of jihad. Muhammad Shah (1834–48) exacerbated the tension between the state and the 'ulama' by pursuing a deliberately anti-'ulama' religious policy, and by continuing the effort to adopt Western methods of government and warfare.

The tension between the state and the 'ulama' rose higher in the reign of Nasir al-Din Shah under the ministry of Mirza Taqi Khan, the Amir Kabir. The government tried to limit the jurisdiction of the 'ulama' by establishing new courts. It restricted the right of sanctuary in mosques and shrines, introduced measures to control endowments, reduced allowances, and sponsored the formation of secular schools in competition with 'ulama' schools. The state also tried to abolish the ta'ziya.

By the middle decades of the nineteenth century, the 'ulama' found themselves beset not only by the toughened attitude of the state, but also by the rise of new religious movements. The yearning for religious certainty, inherent in Shi'ism, broke out again in the preaching of Sayyid 'Ali Muhammad, who proclaimed that the believers were not in fact cut off from the hidden imam, but that there was always a human representative interpreting his will. In 1844 he declared himself to be that man, the Bab (gateway), and later proclaimed himself the true imam. This claim swept away the authority of the 'ulama', whom he denounced as venal and corrupt servants of the state. Sayyid 'Ali Muhammad further announced a new scripture, the Bayan, which superseded the Quran. His teachings included a powerful social message calling for justice, protection of property against taxes and confiscation, and freedom of trade and profit. He inspired rebellions in several Iranian provinces, but his movement was defeated and Sayyid 'Ali Muhammad himself was killed in 1850. His followers divided into two groups. One group, called the Azalis, maintained their intense hostility to the Qajars and were active in the 1905 revolution. The second group followed Baha'ollah, who in 1863 declared himself a prophet and founded the Baha'i religion. From Baha'ism came a pacifist liberal outlook which would later appeal to elements of the Westernized business classes. For the 'ulama', the only compensating development was the emergence of Shaykh Murtada Ansari as the sole marja'-i taqlid, or spiritual leader who requires the obedience of all Shi'a. For the first time the religious leadership was concentrated in a single person.

THE CONSTITUTIONAL CRISIS

The tension between the state and the 'ulama' came to a head over the de Reuter concessions. These were bitterly opposed by the 'ulama' as a sellout of Iranian interests to foreigners, and by the Russians as a sellout of Iran to the British. Under pressure they were canceled in 1873. The de Reuter agitation foreshadowed the struggle over the tobacco monopoly conceded to a British company in 1890. In 1891 and 1892 a coalition of 'ulama', merchants, liberal intellectuals, and officers organized a national boycott of the tobacco monopoly. 'Ulama'-led demonstrations were held in Shiraz, Isfahan, Tabriz, and Mashhad. A *fatwa*, or judicial opinion, issued by Mirza Husayn Shirazi, who had succeeded Shaykh Murtada, led to a nationwide boycott of tobacco products and the eventual dissolution of the monopoly. This opposition was also motivated by financial concerns. Merchants were being reduced to the role of intermediaries between foreign firms and the Iranian populace, and the livelihood of Iranian artisans, cotton cloth makers, and weavers suffered drastically from foreign imports. Ideological hostility to foreign intervention on the part of the 'ulama' and political interest in resisting the Qajars were equally important.

The opposition of 'ulama', merchants, and artisans was reinforced by the small stratum of Westernized intellectuals and Islamic modernist thinkers. Through secret societies, publications, and an extensive campaign of letter writing, they helped provoke and coordinate resistance to the tobacco monopoly. This coalition merged the century-old hostility of the religious establishment with the opposition of middle-class merchants, artisans, officials, and intellectuals to create the first "national" resistance to the Qajar monarchy.

Peasant resistance, however, was minimal. In Iran, the middle-sized landowning peasantry that in many societies has been the basis of resistance to government oppression was scarcely to be found. Most peasants were tenants and sharecroppers dependent upon their landlords. The isolation of the villages also prevented the development of class consciousness. The peasants of Iran were both too poor and too divided to participate in the insurrectionary movement.

The years between 1892 and 1905 were years of preparation for the struggle between the state and the 'ulama' that culminated in the constitutional crisis of 1905–11. While many 'ulama' resumed collaboration with the Qajar monarchy, secret societies composed of intelligentsia, 'ulama', and merchants carried on an underground agitation. The traditional religious and economic objections to government policies were merged with constitutional ideas. The existence of European parliamentary states, the formation of the Russian Diet in 1905, and above all, the modernization of the Ottoman empire and Egypt inspired Iranians to rethink the political structure of their country. Liberal and revolutionary newspapers from Russian-held Transcaucasia, circulating in Iran, also helped to promote a new climate of opinion. Popular sovereignty, rule of law, and patriotism were advanced as the principles for a modernized Persian society. Malkum Khan (1833–1908), an Armenian converted to Islam and educated in Paris, who served most of his diplomatic and political career as an ambassador in Europe, published the newspaper *Qanun* in London to espouse a modernized Iranian society. He advocated a strong monarchy with an advisory assembly to undertake a program of Westernization and the introduction of a new system of education. He argued that reform was compatible with Islam. 'Abd al-Rahim Talibov (1834–1911), a merchant who lived much of his life in Russia, also propagandized for a constitutional government and civil freedoms.

The reformers were joined by pan-Islamic agitators. Pan-Islamic thinkers presented their views in religious terms, although their long-term goal was in fact to modernize Iran. Jamal al-Din al-Afghani and Mirza Aqa Khan Kermani emphasized the political aspects of Islam as an anti-imperialist doctrine which would help revive national pride and mobilize Muslim peoples to resist Western interference. Liberal 'ulama' such as Sayyid Muhammad Taba'taba'i also embraced a Western and secular concept of government.

A treatise called *Admonition and Refinement of the People*, written by Mirza Muhammad Husayn Na'ini, embodied the position of the liberal 'ulama'. Limitations on the authority of the ruler, he argued, are essential to prevent despotism; the best mechanism for controlling rulers was a national consultative assembly. However, the possible conflicts between Islamic views and Western concepts of constitutional political organization, secular law and Muslim law, equality of citizens and Muslim supremacy over non-Muslims, and freedom of speech and the propagation of religious truth were not explored. Liberal 'ulama' adopted constitutionalism partly out of misunderstanding and partly for tactical reasons. Some of them confused the concept of constitutional assembly with the traditional Islamic notion of a court of justice. Others saw constitutionalism as a form of government that limited the power of the state and thereby reduced the prospects for oppression and tyranny. Some 'ulama' saw in a constitutional form of government a way of institutionalizing their own authority, and hoped to use parliament to gain a voice in the administration of the country. The confusion between constitutional government and traditional forms of consultation, and between institutions to enforce Islamic law and institutions of representative government, allowed the 'ulama' to form a coalition with liberals and merchants opposed to the monarchy.

The constitutional agitation came to a head in 1905 and 1906. The increasing indebtedness of the Shah to the Russians, Russian support for the Baha'is, and the appointment of a Belgian to the position of Minister of Post and Telegraph, led to protests in the bazaars, and in 1906 to the convening of a constituent national assembly. The assembly, representing a coalition of 'ulama', merchants, and Westernized liberals – 26 percent were artisan leaders, 15 percent were merchants, and 20 percent were 'ulama' – created the constitution that remained officially in force until 1979. The new constitution subordinated the Shah to a parliamentary government, but declared Islam to be the official religion of Iran. It committed the sate to the enforcement of the Shari'a, and created a committee of 'ulama' to evaluate the conformity of new legislation with Muslim law.

The promulgation of a new constitution was only the beginning of a protracted struggle. The constitutionalist side was backed by many 'ulama', merchants, artisans, and Bakhtiyari tribesmen and had strong popular support in Tabriz and Isfahan. It was opposed by the Shah, conservative 'ulama', and wealthy landowners and their clienteles. Bitter battles were fought. In 1907 and 1908 the Shah used the Cossack Brigade to close parliament; the constitutionalists resumed power from 1909 to 1911. In the second constitutional period, the coalition between liberal reformers and 'ulama' began to break up. When the reformers wanted to disestablish Islam, adopt far-reaching programs for redistribution of land, and introduce a new system of secular education, the 'ulama' became disillusioned. In any case, the Russians intervened in 1911 to destroy the new regime and to restore the government of the Shah.

The constitutional crisis of 1905 to 1911 brought into relief some of the fundamental aspects of Iranian Islamic society in the nineteenth century. Throughout the century, many 'ulama' supported the state, accepted pensions, gifts, positions at court or in government service, owned land, and identified with the ruling elites. Others adopted a quietist position out of religious and doctrinal considerations, turned their backs on the corrupt affairs of the world, and tried to preserve a measure of religious purity while waiting for the return of the hidden imam. They withdrew from political affairs to concentrate on teaching and worship, judicial administration, and charities. However, foreign influences, economic concessions, centralization of power, and state policies that restricted 'ulama' judicial and educational prerogatives provoked their opposition. This opposition was generally directed against specific policies: the 'ulama' were not in principle anti-monarchical, but were simply concerned that state policies should be consistent with Islamic religious norms. Thus, the weakness of the state and the high degree of organization among 'ulama', tribes, guilds, and local communities made possible revolutionary resistance.

TWENTIETH-CENTURY IRAN: THE PAHLAVI ERA

The twentieth century brought a new phase of historical change, but one that repeated and sharpened the basic conflict between the state and the religious establishment. While the power of the state was finally consolidated on the basis of internal reforms and even closer dependence upon European and American support, the 'ulama' continued to be the leading opponents of the state, foreign influence, and policies contrary to Iranian Islamic values. In the twentieth century the long-term conflict between the state and the 'ulama' was renewed in changing ideological, economic, and political conditions.

The modern Iranian state arose out of a period of near-anarchy from 1911 to 1925. During this period foreign intervention reached its peak. In World War I Russian troops were garrisoned in the northern provinces and British troops occupied the south. With the collapse of the Tsarist regime in 1917, all of Iran fell into British hands; the Anglo-Persian treaty of 1919 made Iran a virtual protectorate of Britain. Under the terms of this treaty Britain would train an Iranian army, finance the economic development of the country, and provide technical and managerial advisors. At the same time the Soviet Union supported separatist movements in Jilan and Azarbayjan and communist parties in Tabriz and Tehran. In 1921, however, Iran and the Soviet Union concluded a treaty of friendship on terms very favorable to Iran. The Soviets agreed to withdraw from Jilan, cancel Iranian debts and concessions, and surrender the special legal privileges afforded foreigners. The Soviets reserved the Caspian Sea fisheries and the right to intervene if Iran was threatened by another foreign power. Strengthened by the new treaty, Iran denounced the humiliating 1919 treaty with Britain.

Internally Iran was governed by a succession of ineffectual cabinets until Reza Khan, an officer in the Cossack Brigade, came to power as head of the army and Minister of Defense. He consolidated his control over the army and the police, defeated tribal and provincial forces, brought most of the country under military control, and in 1925 made himself the Shah of Iran, at once a constitutional monarch and the founder of the Pahlavi dynasty, which lasted from 1925 to 1979.

Under the rule of the Pahlavis a strong centralized government was created for the first time in Iranian history. The state was defined in nationalist ideological terms, committed under authoritarian rule to an ambitious program of economic modernization and cultural Westernization. The state gained control over the tribal societies, and even, for periods of time, over the 'ulama'.

Reza Shah's first accomplishment was to build a modern army. While the Qajars had attempted military reforms along Western lines, they had maintained the traditional pattern of competitive regiments rather than a unified corps. Reza Shah set about training a new officer corps in France, and introduced compulsory conscription. Some 33 percent of the annual government budget was spent for military purposes. Thus he built up a Westernized army which could dominate the country politically, but proved unable to prevent Russia and Britain from occupying Iran in 1941.

Bolstered by its army and an expanded administration, the new regime overcame the opposition of religious, merchant, and tribal elites. It outlawed the Communist Party and the trade unions, reduced the parliament to a rubber stamp, and censored the press. For political support it looked to the landowning classes. New laws in 1928 and 1929 recognized the de facto possession of land as proof of ownership, and required registration, which was favorable to wealthy landowners rather than to poor tenants. For the first time in history an Iranian state won complete control over the country as a whole by breaking the power of tribal communities and Khans. The tribes were forced to sedentarize, and the political power of the Khans was coopted by the state.

Though Reza Shah had come to power with the support of many 'ulama', who expected a strong government to resist foreign influence, the Pahlavi regime also diminished their power. Through the creation of a secular education system, government supervision of religious schools, and other measures the Pahlavis sought to bring the 'ulama' under state control. In 1934 the Teacher Training Act provided for new colleges, and the Ministry of Education introduced its own curriculum for theological schools. Furthermore, as an alternative to religious education, technical schools were founded by the Ministries of Education, Industry, Health, Agriculture, War, and Finance. The University of Tehran was founded in 1935, and operated with a European-educated faculty under the close supervision of the government. Many students were educated abroad and returned to spread technical knowledge and Western ideas of social relations.

A second and equally damaging blow to the 'ulama' was the reorganization of judicial administration. Though civil and criminal courts had been set up in the constitution of 1906, and new civil commercial codes promulgated in 1911 and 1915, judicial administration remained in the hands of the 'ulama'. Reza Shah, however, introduced new law codes in 1928 which replaced the Shari'a. In 1932 the parliament enacted a new law which turned registration of legal documents over to secular courts, and at a single stroke removed the most lucrative functions of the religious courts. A law of 1936 required every judge to hold a degree from the Tehran faculty of law or a foreign university, making it impossible for the 'ulama' to sit in courts of law. During the 1930s a new court system was organized, following French models, to administer a haphazard mixture of Western and Muslim legal norms. Regardless of the adequacy of the legal system, in political terms it established the supremacy of the state. Other measures were taken to ban the presentation of passion plays, pilgrimages, and sermons and to legislate modern dress codes.

The secularization of legal administration and education was part of a still larger program of state-controlled economic modernization. The infrastructure of a modern economy was developed in the 1920s and 1930s. A new customs office was established, staffed by Belgian officials. American financial missions helped organize tax collection; an Iranian national bank was founded in 1927 under the management of German financial experts. An Iranian railroad was constructed between 1926 and 1938, running from Bandar Shahpur on the Persian Gulf to Bandar Shah on the Caspian Sea. Designed in response to strategic needs, however, the railroad neglected international connections, major cities, and links between the major economic areas of the country. Similarly, postal and telegraph communications and air transportation were introduced to facilitate economic development and help extend the authority of the central government to the provinces.

After 1930, owing to lack of sufficient capital in the private economy and lack of motivation among landowners to make long-term investments in industry, the state sponsored numerous industrial projects. Priority was given to consumer substitution industries (i.e. those replacing imports with domestic products), including cotton, woolen and silk factories, sugar refining, and food-processing plants such as bakeries, canneries, and breweries. By 1941 soap, glass, paper, matches, and cigarettes were all produced in state-owned factories. The state also controlled trade and foreign exchange. In 1925 the government established a monopoly on imports of tea and sugar. It sought to regulate foreign interests. In the 1920s and 1930s, Russian and British influence remained relatively balanced. Russia was an important trading partner; Britain controlled the production of oil. To offset the influence of these two powers, Iran made use of German capital and technical assistance, and Germany maintained a strong presence by the establishment of research and cultural institutes as well as espionage and political networks. In the 1930s the Russian share of Iranian exports fell from 34 percent to 1 percent, and the German share rose from 20 percent to 42 percent. The state controlled approximately 33–40 percent of Iranian imports and exports.

Oil was first found at Masjid-i Sulayman in 1908, and in 1909 the Anglo-Persian Oil Company was founded to exploit the discovery. The British government acquired a controlling interest in 1914. The refineries at Abadan were constructed in 1915. Oil production was profitable for Iran, but was a source of bitter resentment against foreign companies for their manipulation of royalties and the absence of Iranians in managerial and administrative positions. In 1933 Iran demanded a reduction in the territories conceded for foreign exploration and a fixed income; in return, it extended the existing concessions to 1993 and exempted the oil company from taxation. These arrangements cushioned Iran in the depression years but proved contrary to Iranian interests when prosperity was restored during and after World War II.

This phase of development created a small modern sector in an otherwise backward economy and society. Manufacturing was concentrated in cities, and benefited only a small portion of the population. Agriculture remained unproductive. State centralization, economic modernization, and a new education system helped to create an elite of army officers, bureaucrats, merchants, contractors, doctors, lawyers, engineers, teachers, and writers, who adopted Western values and a Western style of life. This new elite, allied to an older generation of 'ulama' and tribal Khans, dominated an unproductive and impoverished peasant population. The modernized Iranian state defined its legitimacy in nationalist and secularist terms. A revival of interest in Persian history and themes of ancient kingship were used to legitimize the modernization of the army, the government, and the economy.

World War II put an end to this phase of the Iranian experiment in centralization of state power and economic development. Britain and Russia, concerned to keep open the supply routes across Iran to Russia, and to assure the control of Iranian oil, seized control of Iran, forced Reza Shah to resign, and made his minor son, Muhammad Reza Pahlavi, the nominal suzerain. Between 1941 and 1953, Iran passed through a period of open political struggle among its various would-be foreign protectors and internal political parties. In the late 1940s, the United States, on the edge of the cold war with the Soviet Union, eager to create a Middle Eastern barrier against possible Soviet expansion, emerged as the principal patron of the postwar Iranian regime. The United States advised the Iranian government on economic management, organized Iran's police and military forces, and supplied it with military aid. With American backing, Iran successfully resisted Soviet occupation of the northern provinces, Soviet demands for oil concessions, and Soviet sponsorship of separatist movements in Azarbayjan and Kurdistan.

In the late 1940s and early 1950s Iran also struggled to win control of the Anglo-Iranian Oil Company. In 1951, Muhammad Mosaddeq, the leader of the National Front, supported by a coalition of landowners, tribal leaders, leftist intelligentsia, merchants, and 'ulama', pushed through parliament a bill to nationalize the oil company. A bitter three-year struggle followed in which the United States refused to support Iran. The Western powers boycotted Iranian oil. The Iranian economy collapsed and the Mosaddeq coalition broke up. In the ensuing struggle for power the CIA helped the army and the Shah to seize power, dismiss Mosaddeq, and reestablish an authoritarian regime. The dispute with the oil companies was settled in 1954 by the formation of a National Iranian Oil Company and a consortium of foreign oil companies including the Anglo-Iranian Oil Company (renamed British Petroleum) and several American firms. The consortium would produce and market oil and divide the profits with the National Iranian Oil Company. Thus the foreign companies avoided nationalization and maintained control of oil pricing and marketing.

The 1953 coup also put an end to the period of open struggle for political power. The restored regime of Muhammad Reza Shah was technically a constitutional monarchy, but the Shah ruled with virtually absolute powers. He controlled the army and SAVAK, the secret police and intelligence agency, appointed the ministers, selected half of the senate, and manipulated parliamentary elections. A small elite of officers, administrators, landowners, and some wealthy merchants and religious leaders dominated Iranian political life. The Shah's regime was closely allied to the United States and was dependent upon American military and financial support. Having been brought to power with American assistance, Iran joined the Baghdad Pact (1955) and the Central Treaty Organization (1959). Iran maintained close relations with Israel. In the 1970s it assisted the Sultan of Oman in suppressing opposition, and in 1975 forced Iraq to settle disputed boundaries in the lower reaches of the Euphrates River. Close ties with the United States and even the buildup of military forces in the 1970s, however, did not prevent Iran from maintaining good relations with the Soviet Union to balance American influence and political pressure.

The Pahlavi program called not only for the construction of a centralized secular and nationalist regime, but also for the further modernization of society along Western lines. Between 1960 and 1977 the government undertook to reform the structure of landowning, modernize the industrial economy, build up military forces that would assure its regional supremacy, and reform the social structure of the country. In conjunction with agricultural reforms the Shah proposed the formation of a literacy and a health corps intended to bring the direct influence of the state into the countryside. Other reforms included the extension of voting rights to women and their employment in government offices.

A crucial aspect of the "white revolution" was land reform. In Iran the ownership of land was concentrated in the hands of a small number of families, mainly absentee landlords. The peasants were rarely owners. Most were sharecroppers and laborers. In 1962–64 and 1968, landowners were required by law to sell excess land to smallholders and tenants, but because of widespread evasion not as much was distributed as had officially been proposed. The new owners, moreover, lacked the capital, the technology, the cooperative organizations, and the government extension services necessary to maintain and increase productivity. Landless laborers, lacking the resources to farm or to pay for the land, received nothing, and, having lost their employment, had to migrate to the cities. Subsequent redistributions gave peasants benefits in ownership and tenancy rights, but did not give them adequate lands for subsistence.

In fact, the major thrust of the Shah's agricultural programs was the creation of large-scale, state-sponsored farm corporations and private agribusinesses. Farm corporations required peasants to pool their lands and take shares in the larger enterprise, often with the result that farms were mechanized and cultivators driven from the land. Private agribusinesses with heavy foreign investment also favored capital-intensive mechanized farming and forced peasants from the land. Thus, the state favored capital-intensive agriculture in a country with surplus labor. Similarly, nomads were forced to sedentarize, and pastoral livestock herding was replaced with mechanized meat and dairy farms. These farms commonly failed, and the result was falling per capita production and a large-scale movement of rural people to the big cities, especially Tehran.

As per capita agricultural production declined in the 1960s and 1970s, Iran became more dependent upon industrial development. For the first time since the limited industrialization of the 1930s, Iran experienced an industrial boom. State investments provided the infrastructure and roughly half of the capital invested in industry. The state also supported industrial growth by high tariffs, tax credits, licenses, and other devices, and promoted a boom in steel, rubber, chemicals, building materials, and automobile assembly. The huge growth of oil revenues after 1973 also enhanced the gross national product. Iranian industry, however, was too inefficient to compete in international markets, and suffered from a lack of skilled management and labor. The combination of falling per capita agricultural output, inefficient industry, and heavy purchases of foreign manufactured goods and weapons with a booming oil economy led to severe inflation and probably to a lower standard of living for all Iranians not directly involved in the modern sector of the economy.

The Shah's regime also attempted modest reforms of the position of women. As early as the 1920s a few leading intellectuals, men and women, were working for improvements in women's education, social position, and legal rights. Women, in small numbers, began to enter into teaching, nursing, and factory work. In 1936 wearing of the veil was forbidden, and women of the urban upper and middle classes began to adopt modern dress. In the crucial areas of family law and political rights, however, little was changed. Divorce remained easy for men. Guardianship of children remained the legal right of males. Polygamy and temporary marriage were still permitted. Only with the family protection laws of 1967 and 1975 were male prerogatives partially circumscribed by legislation that required divorces to be reviewed in court and wives' consent for polygamous marriages.

The program of modernization expanded the cadres of Western and modern-educated intelligentsia, officials, soldiers, business managers, and skilled workers. It also provoked first the anxieties and then the active hostility of the 'ulama', the merchants and artisans of the bazaar, and leftist intellectuals who opposed the consolidation of the Shah's power, his dependence upon foreign support, and the policies that brought economic hardship to the peasantry and to the lower middle classes. Above all, the opposition was opposed to the highly authoritarian nature of the regime.

Opposition in the 1960s and 1970s was widespread but scattered and easily defeated. The Tudeh (Communist) and National Parties were crushed by SAVAK. Kurdish, Arab, and Baluchi minorities were defeated in their bids for regional autonomy. While militant guerrilla groups, such as the Marxist Feda'iyan-i Khalq, and the Islamic leftist Mojahedin-i Khalq, opposed despotism, imperialism, and capitalism, their resistance provoked further repression and did not shake the grip of the Shah's regime.

THE 'ULAMA' AND THE REVOLUTION

Throughout this period the position of the 'ulama' was ambiguous. The politically open 1940s had encouraged 'ulama' activism in political affairs. From 1948 to 1953 Ayatollah Kashani, supported by street preachers and lower-ranking 'ulama', carried on an anti-British and anti-imperialist campaign in favor of the nationalization of the oil industry and the termination of foreign influence in Iran. For a time he supported the Mosaddeq government, but later turned against it and assisted in the restoration of the Shah.

The defeat of Mosaddeq, however, introduced a period of religious quietism and tacit collaboration with the state. The government supported 'ulama' interests through appointments at court, opportunities for enrichment through landowning, and marriage into prominent families. It increased the amount of religious instruction in public schools and periodically closed down movie houses, liquor stores, and public musical entertainments. In return, the 'ulama' accepted the Baghdad Pact and tolerated the government's policy of cooperation with foreign companies. Under the leadership of Ayatollah Burujirdi, the 'ulama' remained politically quiet – but they also consolidated their internal strength. In the 1950s and early 1960s, a national network of communications developed, with Qum as the center of Shi'i religious instruction and organization.

In the 1960s the government's economic and social policies generated intense 'ulama' opposition. The 'ulama' opposed the new land laws. Scanty evidence indicates that many 'ulama' were wealthy landowners or controlled extensive waqfs. They opposed the extension of suffrage to women; and they opposed Iran's close ties with the United States and Israel. They were also threatened by the government's proposal to establish a literacy corps which would give the state its own cadres to rival 'ulama' influence in rural areas. The quarrel between the government and the 'ulama' came to blows. In 1963 the Shah decided to call a national referendum on land reform. The proposed referendum and the police crackdown on 'ulama' activities in Qum provoked demonstrations, led by Ayatollah Khomayni, who was exiled to Iraq in 1964.

As important as renewed 'ulama' resistance to the state was the development of a religious reform movement. The reformist view was crystallized in a speech by Mehdi Bazargan in 1962, in which he went back to the Quran and to Shi'i religious traditions to justify an active political role for the 'ulama'. He said that political organization and collective struggle for a better society was the responsibility of the custodians of Islam; no longer should the 'ulama' wait passively for a return of the imam, but actively prepare the way. The reformers further proposed the formation of a council of 'ulama' to give authoritative religious advice, and the creation of a centralized financial organization to assure their autonomy from both government influence and popular pressure. Between 1967 and 1973 the reform movement took a new direction under the leadership of Dr. 'Ali Shari'ati, who formed the Husayniyah Irshad. This was an informal "university" which was intended to revitalize Shi'ism by reconciling Islamic teachings with European social sciences and thereby generate the commitment to overthrow a repressive government. For Shari'ati, Shi'ism was a religion of protest.

Ayatollah Khomayni, from his sanctuary in Iraq, became the main spokesman of opposition to the monarchy. In 1961 he advocated a parliamentary form of government, but by 1971 in his book, *Islamic Government*, he declared the monarchy an un-Islamic institution and called for a total reform of political society in which the 'ulama' would take a direct and active role. The authority of the 'ulama' would not be limited to religious and legal issues; Shi'ism as a political ideology would define the actions of the government and mold the character of the people. While based on a long tradition of 'ulama' opposition to the abuse of monarchical powers, this was, in fact, a profound innovation. Khomayni's position was the most radical statement of 'ulama' responsibilities. The traditional religious elites joined the radical intelligentsia as the spokesmen of opposition to the powers of the state. At the same time a new image of Husayn, the martyr of Karbala, took shape. He was to be not only the object of mourning and pity, but the example of courage and resistance. His image was redefined from one of passive suffering to one of protest against tyranny.

The influence of the 'ulama' spread throughout Iranian society. *Hay'at*, or informal groups of some thirty to fifty people based in a neighborhood, a factory or a bazaar, and tied to particular religious leaders, met to discuss the issues of the day. *Bazaaris*, the workers in the old-fashioned markets, and *maktabis*, the technical, managerial, clerical, upwardly mobile lower-middle-class cadres, only partially integrated into the modern sectors of the economy, were the leading recruits for revolutionary action. These groups became the basis of a mass movement in opposition to the Shah.

In the course of the 1970s the Pahlavi regime became all the more oppressive. The army and the secret police were widely feared and hated for numerous investigations, intimidation, imprisonment, torture, and assassination of potential enemies of the regime. The regime was widely perceived as being based upon American political and military support and as benefiting only a very narrow elite consisting of the Shah and his family, the army, and a cadre of prominent supporters. The government was not only hated for being a dictatorship but was resented for mismanaging the economy. Great fortunes were being earned from oil income and were being spent on weapons and for the benefit of a small elite, while inflation was undermining the standard of living of bazaar merchants, artisans, and industrial workers. The bazaar population suffered particularly from confiscations, fines, and imprisonments, as the Shah sought to contain inflation by intimidation. At the same time, the 1970s were disastrous times for masses of Iranian peasants. Millions fled the land for the cities, where they formed a huge mass of unemployed and underemployed people. By the late 1970s, Iran was importing most of its food from abroad.

In these deeply disturbed political and economic conditions, the spark for revolution was a demonstration by religious students in Qum against an alleged assassination by SAVAK. The police shot a number of demonstrators, and provoked a new demonstration to mourn the martyrs of the last. Every forty days the protests were repeated, and grew in scale until the month of Muharram (the fall of 1978), when millions of people demonstrated against the regime. The Feda'iyan-i Khalq and Mojahedin-i Khalq were revived. The oil workers refused to produce, the bazaar merchants closed their shops, and the army either would not or could not suppress the revolt. The Shah fled the country and a new regime came to power. Masses of Iranians had been mobilized by a coalition of religious and liberal leaders under the guidance of the highest Iranian religious authority, Ayatollah Khomayni.

The Iranian Islamic revolution arose out of the particular configuration of Iranian state and religious institutions, but is nonetheless a signal event in the history of all Islamic societies. It marks the culmination of an almost 200-year struggle between the Iranian state and the organized 'ulama'. In the nineteenth century, the weaknesses of the state, and the strength of non-state tribal and ethnic communities, allowed for the consolidation of a religious establishment capable of opposing the regime and of mobilizing large-scale popular support. State efforts at modernization and European penetration of the Iranian economy led to the tobacco monopoly protests of 1891–92 and to the constitutional revolution of 1906. Again, in the late twentieth century, the effort to centralize and modernize state power led to a crisis in which 'ulama', intellectuals, students, and large segments of the artisan and working population mobilized to oppose the government. The defeat of tribalism as a third force in Iranian society had led to a polarization between the state and the 'ulama', and to an Islamic revolution.

Nonetheless, the history of 'ulama'–state relations in nineteenth- and twentieth-century Iran was ambiguous. Resistance to the state was in fact sporadic, and at different times the 'ulama' have espoused both revolutionary activism and religious quietism. Within Shi'ism there is justification for both. The activist position is justified by the doctrine of commanding the good and forbidding the evil, and by the claims of the mujtahids to be spiritual advisors to all Iranians and the only legitimate authorities in the absence of the hidden imam. The example of Husayn stands as a paradigm of the obligation to confront and resist tyranny in the name of justice and Islam. Equally important, however, are the cultural traditions tending toward political pacifism. The Shi'i expectation of worldly injustice and the hope for messianic redemption works against involvement in public life.

The Iranian revolution, therefore, cannot be said to be due to an inherent religious opposition to state authority, but has to be treated as a response to specific conditions. The Russian invasion of 1826, the de Reuter concessions, the tobacco monopoly of 1891, the land reform acts of 1960 to 1963, and the economic tensions of the late 1970s impelled the 'ulama' to adopt the active rather than the passive side of their complex tradition. The constitutional revolution of 1906 and the Iranian revolution of 1979 are not expressions of a constant hostility between state and religion but the expression of a recurring possibility of confrontation between them. In Iran the weakness of the state, the organizational strength of the religious establishment, and the latent cultural permission for 'ulama' resistance have all allowed for, though they have not mandated, revolutionary struggle in the name of Islam.

The revolution also had worldwide importance. Revolution came, not primarily from the left, but from the religious establishment; not in the name of socialism, but in the name of Islam. For the first time in the modern era religious leaders have defeated a modernized regime. For the first time the revolutionary implications of Islam, hitherto manifest in lineage or tribal societies, have been realized in a modernizing industrializing society. The event shook the relations between states and religious movements, and opened doubts as to the future, not only of Iran, but of all Islamic societies.

THE ISLAMIC REPUBLIC

The victory of the revolution abolished the monarchy and established an Islamic government in Iran. The new regime was built upon the charismatic authority of Ayatollah Khomayni, the official head of the government and the authority of last resort. It was called the *wilayat al-faqih* – the rule of the jurisprudential scholar. The Ayatollah was called Imam by some of his followers, referring to his roles as head of the religion and implying the messianic function of the 'Alid Imams. A Supreme Council of *Maslaha* (public welfare) was created to oversee the activities of both the Council of Guardians and the parliament. In 1989 the constitution was revised to strengthen the hand of the President of the Republic and the government apparatus, though religious leaders, including Ayatollah Khamene'i, the successor of Ayatollah Khomayni (d. 1989) remained in principle the highest authorities and in charge of the legal system. The elite of the regime are the cadres of younger 'ulama', graduate and student activists, town and village militias, and the Islamic Republican Party – the party of the 'ulama'.

The new regime consolidated its power by eliminating coalition allies, especially the liberal nationalist, Marxist intellectuals, and the Mojahedin. Thousands of officers of the Shah's government were purged and executed by revolutionary courts. Jews, Armenians, Zoroastrians, and other minorites suffered harassment, arrest, and destruction of property, and Bahai's were relentlessly persecuted. The Westernized middle class was forced into exile. A fierce puritanism took hold. Revolutionary *komiteh*, or vigilante groups, took to the streets to police morals and to assault women who were improperly dressed or who transgressed into men's spaces. Women were forced out of many professions, and were required to be completely veiled in public. Places of entertainment, including movies and theaters, were shut down.

22   A girls' school, Tehran

Iran's foreign policy was immediately embroiled in disputes with other countries. The revolutionary government seized the United States embassy and held its personnel hostage for over a year. Iran threatened to export Islamic revolution. A Bureau of Islamic Propaganda was created to stimulate like-minded revolutionary action in other Muslim countries. Iran supported Hizballah as its proxy in the Lebanese civil war and the struggle against Israel.

In 1980 war came to Iran via an Iraqi attack on its oil-rich southwestern provinces. Iraq claimed to be defending both the Arab countries against revolutionary threats and its own Shi'i population from revolutionary contamination, but its principal motive was expansionist opportunism. Eight years of bitter warfare followed. Iran, lacking modern equipment and tactics, hurled countless youths against the Iraqis in a war reminiscent of World War I trench warfare, and Iraq fought with all means at its disposal, including chemical weapons and poison gas. The United States played an ambiguous role in the war, supplying arms and intelligence to both sides, but from 1986 weighed in on the Iraqi side to forestall an Iranian victory.

In many ways, the revolutionary government carried on the work of state building begun by the Shahs. It strengthened the ministries and the bureaucracy, and brought the army under its own control by creating new Guards Corps. While committed in theory to an Islamic state, Islamic considerations commonly yielded to *raisons d'état*. Iranian foreign policy remains driven by its national interests. The Shari'a did not become the official law of Iran, and the state remained the ultimate promulgator of law. Non-Muslims continue to be citizens of the state. In many respects, the Iranian national state absorbed its Islamic component.

Throughout the Islamic Republican period economic development has been stymied by the war with Iraq, the collapse of international oil prices in the 1980s and 1990s, and by the ongoing and unresolved struggle within the government between 'ulama' favoring a privatized market economy and those favoring government regulation in the interest of popular welfare. The economy, 80 percent controlled by the state, is mismanaged by bureaucratic bungling and by outright corruption. So-called charitable foundations, *bonyad*s, control vast resources, and use them for political and clerical favorites. Government policies favor the bazaar merchants, the mainstay of the revolution, but small-scale industries suffer from the lack of necessary foreign imports, weak exports, and black-market competition. Agriculture has generally stagnated resulting in continued importation of food supplies. In general, the Islamic state has had little impact upon the economy, the distribution of wealth, welfare, housing, and other domestic issues.

While state policy has not decisively shaped the Iranian economy, Islamist policies were forceful in shaping the media, education, and the treatment of women. The legal changes favoring women's rights introduced by the Shah were reversed and the family protection laws of 1967 and 1975 were repealed. Men have regained the right to unilateral divorce and to custody of children. Polygamy is again accepted in principle. Women are required to be veiled in public, and an unsuccessful effort was made to restrict women's employment, mainly to health care. The war with Iraq, the need in the economy for skilled workers, and the resistance of women who need the work have created more room for maneuver. Women writers, artists, and intellectuals are creating new journals to subtly push back the demands of conservative mullahs and increase the scope for women's self expression. Some women writers invoke Islam itself and contest traditional interpretations as they try to enlarge the boundaries of acceptable public discourse. For example, the journal of the Women's Society of the Islamic Revolution of Iran, *Payam-i Hajer* (Hajer's Message), denounces the extremes of intoxication with the West and the abandonment of cultural traditions, and also of blind submission to what the religious leaders call Islam. The journal interprets Islam in ways that support women's rights, and also argues that each individual has the right to interpret the Quran. The ideal woman is not passive, but knows her roles as responsible and active in society. The journal calls for the creation of a ministry of women's welfare, protests that women are excluded from being judges, criticizes polygyny and temporary marriages, and favors prenuptial agreements that may forbid a second wife and guarantee alimony in case of divorce. In 1991 and 1992 new laws allowed for prenuptial agreements of this kind. The facilities for women's education have been greatly improved, but women's participation in the workforce is still hindered by policy and social mores.

The election of Muhammad Khatami in 1997 as president of Iran, and his reelection in 2001, brought into the open the struggle between conservative mullahs defending an authoritarian Islamic society ruled by the wilayat al-faqih and more liberal reforming elements defending Islamic pluralism, democracy, and the rule of law. The clerical establishment, headed by the Supreme Leader, Ayatollah Khamene'i, controls the judiciary and large sectors of the economy. A vast apparatus of military, police, intelligence officers, morals enforcers, and organized "vigilantes" are employed to crush drug use, gambling, homosexuality, prostitution, rape, murder, spying, counter-revolutionary activities, "sowing corruption on earth," and to punish women for being improperly dressed in public. Recently, writers, journalists, and students have been beaten, tortured, and killed.

Still, the regime has not been able to check the demand for a transformation of the Islamic Republic into an Islamic democracy, a government subject to the rule of law and social justice. Post-Islamic-state liberal intellectuals such as Abdol Karim Soroush advocate a tolerant Islamic society built on the rule of law rather than the personal authority of the Supreme Leader. Students call for freedom in daily life, including choice of dress, consumption, and dating. There is a vigorous and open, though embattled, press. Elections in 2000 gave 70 percent of the seats in parliament to liberals, but they are still paralyzed by the powers of the conservatives, and it is not yet clear who will win. While the struggle is sometimes posed in terms of a conflict between Persian and Islamic identities, religion and pop culture, clerical rule and freedom, dictatorship and democracy, in this supple and sophisticated country there is still a profound underlying loyalty to the nation and to the Islamic state.

CHAPTER 23

THE DISSOLUTION OF THE OTTOMAN EMPIRE
AND THE MODERNIZATION OF TURKEY

The dissolution of the Ottoman empire was one of the more complex cases in the transition from eighteenth-century Islamic imperial societies to modern national states. The Ottoman regime was suzerain over a vast territory, including the Balkans, Turkey, the Arab Middle East, Egypt, and North Africa. Its influence reached Inner Asia, the Red Sea, and the Sahara. While the empire had gone through a period of decentralization in the seventeenth and eighteenth centuries and had begun to give ground to its European political and commercial competitors, it retained its political legitimacy and its basic institutional structure. In the nineteenth century, the Ottomans restored the power of the central state, consolidated control over the provinces, and generated the economic, social, and cultural reforms that they hoped would make them effective competitors in the modern world.

While the Ottomans struggled to reform state and society, the empire was slowly being dismembered. For survival the Ottomans depended increasingly upon the European balance of power. Until 1878 the British and the Russians offset each other and generally protected the Ottoman regime from direct encroachment. Between 1878 and 1914, however, most of the Balkans became independent and Russia, Britain, and Austria-Hungary all acquired control of Ottoman territories. The dismemberment of the Ottoman empire culminated at the end of World War I in the creation of Turkey and a plethora of new states in the Arab Middle East. As in the case of Iran, the effects of European intervention would mingle with the Ottoman institutional and cultural heritage to generate a number of different modern Middle Eastern societies.

THE PARTITION OF THE OTTOMAN EMPIRE

By the end of the eighteenth century the Ottoman empire could no longer defend itself against the growing military power of Europe, or ward off European commercial penetration. Russia had absorbed the Crimea and established itself on the

Black Sea, while Britain, after helping defeat Napoleon's invasion of Egypt in 1798, became the paramount military and commercial power in the Mediterranean. Russia wanted to absorb Ottoman territories in the Balkans and win access to the Mediterranean; Britain wanted to shore up the empire as a bulwark against Russian expansion and protect its commercial and imperial interests in the Mediterranean, the Middle East, and India. Thus, the Ottoman empire was precariously protected by the balance of European power. The stage was set for the century-long struggle over the "sick man" of Europe.

The first test of the balance of power came with the invasion of Syria in 1831 by Muhammad 'Ali, the independent Ottoman governor of Egypt (1805–48). In response, Russia and the Ottomans concluded the treaty of Unkiar Skelessi (July 1833), in which they agreed to close the Dardanelles and the Bosphorus to foreign warships. Britain, threatened by the specter of a Russian protectorate over the Ottomans and possible Russian intervention in the Mediterranean, declared for the territorial integrity of the Ottoman empire and the restoration of Syria to Ottoman control. In 1840, Russia, Britain, and Austria agreed that Muhammad 'Ali would have to retreat from Syria, and framed a new convention regulating passage through the straits. The powers agreed that no warships were to pass the Bosphorus and the Dardanelles in time of peace. Both Russia and Britain would be protected in their spheres of influence. By a supplementary agreement in 1841, the powers allowed Muhammad 'Ali to establish a hereditary regime in Egypt. Thus, the internal crisis of the empire led to a concert of European powers to regulate Ottoman affairs. The Ottoman empire had become a protectorate of Europe and a pawn of the great powers.

The balance of power and the durability of the Ottoman empire were again tested in the Crimean war, 1853–56. Provoked by Russian demands for influence in Jerusalem and a protectorate over all Ottoman Christian subjects, British, French, and Ottoman forces entered the Black Sea and took Sebastopol in 1855. By the treaty of Paris (1856) the Russians were forced to dismantle their naval forces on the Black Sea, but they were compensated by an agreement to make Romania an autonomous province under Ottoman suzerainty.

The next crisis was the revolt of Bosnia and Herzegovina in 1876 against Ottoman rule. Nationalist resistance to Ottoman rule in the Balkans had begun with the Serbian revolt of 1804–13. Between 1821 and 1829, Greece gained its independence. Serbians, Romanians, and Bulgarians also demanded autonomy. The Balkan campaigns for independence culminated in 1876 with Russian intervention. By the treaty of San Stefano (1878), the Ottomans were forced to concede the independence of Bulgaria, Serbia, Romania, and Montenegro. The huge Russian gains provoked the other European powers to call a congress of European states at Berlin in 1878. At the Congress of Berlin a new settlement was imposed. Bessarabia was ceded by the Ottomans to Russia, but in compensation for Russian gains, Austria "temporarily" occupied Bosnia and Herzegovina, and Britain obtained the use of

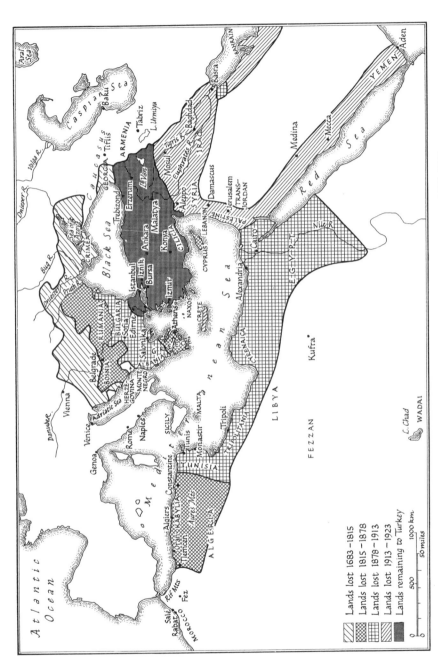

Map 30 Territorial losses and the partition of the Ottoman empire: 1683–1923

Lands lost 1683–1815
Lands lost 1815–1878
Lands lost 1878–1913
Lands lost 1913–1923
Lands remaining to Turkey

Cyprus as a base of operations. Bulgaria was reduced to a small size and Ottoman suzerainty was restored. Then, in 1882, to protect her interests in the Suez Canal and in the Egyptian debt to British and other European bond-holders, Britain occupied Egypt. Britain had changed from a policy of defense of the territorial integrity of the empire to a policy of partition in order to maintain the European balance of power. Henceforth, the Eastern Question would be handled by the further dismemberment of the Ottoman state.

Between 1878 and 1908, the partition of the empire was postponed only by the rivalries of the European powers. Britain maintained its position in Cyprus and Egypt. Germany established its influence by investing in Ottoman railroads and by supplying advisors and technicians to the Ottoman army. Big-power rivalry, however, centered on the Balkans. Austria managed to establish its diplomatic ascendancy over Serbia and good relations with Romania and Greece; Russia remained the patron of Bulgaria. Serbia, Greece, and Bulgaria, however, fought for control of Macedonia.

In 1908 an internal Ottoman political crisis upset the balance of power. Taking advantage of the upheaval in the Ottoman empire, Austria annexed Bosnia and Herzegovina. Serbia, backed by Russia, protested against the Austrian annexation, but Germany supported Austria unconditionally. The Serbians and Russians were forced to back down. The crisis, however, reopened bitter competition between Austria and Russia, and prompted the Balkan states to form their own alliances. In 1912, Serbia and Bulgaria, then Greece and Bulgaria, and finally Montenegro and Bulgaria negotiated treaties, ostensibly to keep Austria in check, but with secret clauses to attack the Ottoman empire. In October 1912, the combined Balkan armies defeated the Ottomans and took all of their remaining European territories except for a small strip around the city of Istanbul. Then in 1913 the Balkan states went to war with each other over the division of the spoils, allowing the Ottomans to regain a small part of Thrace. Within a year the rivalries of Austria and Serbia precipitated a general European war.

World War I completed the process of dismemberment. In December 1914 the Ottomans entered the war on the side of Germany and Austria. German military and economic assistance, the traditional Ottoman fear of Russia, and perhaps an ambition to restore Ottoman control over lost provinces prompted the Ottomans to join the central powers. In response, the British, the French, the Russians, and the Italians agreed to partition the Ottoman provinces. By the Sykes–Picot agreement (1916), France was to obtain a sphere of influence in Lebanon, southwestern Turkey, northern Syria, and northern Iraq, and Britain would acquire Iraq, the Arabian side of the Persian Gulf, and Transjordan. Palestine would be subject to an international regime. Russia was to obtain Istanbul and parts of eastern Anatolia. Italy was promised southern Anatolia. To promote her ambition to be the paramount power in the Near East, Britain also entered other, often contradictory, agreements. In return for Arab support against their Ottoman overlords, the British promised Sharif Husayn of Mecca that Britain would recognize an independent Arab state, with reservations for Lebanon and British and French interests. In 1917, the Balfour Declaration promised that Britain would also support the formation of a Jewish national home in Palestine.

By 1918 the European allies had defeated Germany, Austria, and the Ottoman empire; Britain conquered Palestine, Syria, and Iraq; and the allies took control of Istanbul and the straits. Britain and France agreed to divide the Middle East into a number of new states, including Lebanon and Syria in the French sphere of influence, and Palestine, Jordan, and Iraq in the British sphere. Italy was conceded southwestern Anatolia. Greece was allowed to occupy Thrace, Izmir, and the Aegean islands. Armenia was to be an independent state and Kurdistan an autonomous province. Istanbul and the straits were put under joint allied occupation. Thus, between 1912 and 1920, the Ottomans lost all of their former empire in the Balkans. New states were set up in Lebanon, Syria, Palestine, Transjordan, and Iraq. Egypt became, under a British protectorate, fully independent of Ottoman suzerainty. The political process, begun more than two centuries before, of reducing and dismembering the Ottoman empire, had reached its climax in the formation of a new system of national states.

OTTOMAN REFORM

While the European powers divided the Ottoman empire into a number of national states, the institutional organization and ideological identity of these states was shaped by the interaction of European influence and the historical legacy of the several Middle Eastern societies. In the late nineteenth-century Ottoman empire, and in the formation of modern Turkey, the primary consideration was the continuity of historical institutional and cultural forms. While European powers exerted a tremendous influence, their impact upon the internal evolution of late Ottoman and early modern Turkish societies was mediated by Ottoman and Turkish elites. Unlike other Muslim empires, the Ottomans maintained their sovereignty and were able to implement their own program of modernization and reform.

As early as the seventeenth century, Ottomans had debated the problem of how to restore the political integrity and military effectiveness of the regime. Two main positions emerged. The restorationists called for a return to the laws (kanuns) of Sulayman the Magnificent, and opposed any change that threatened to give Europeans and Christians, or European and Christian concepts and techniques, supremacy over Muslims. The modernists called for the adoption of European methods for military training, organization, and administration, and for the civil, economic, and educational changes that would be needed to support a modern state. Throughout the eighteenth and much of the nineteenth centuries these two points of view were in vigorous competition, but the dominant view came to be the one that favored modernization along European lines.

As early as the seventeenth century, Ottoman forces were being organized into new ethnic and peasant units. In the eighteenth century, European military advisors were employed to provide technical training for army officers, and a printing press was set up to publish translations of European technical, military, and geographical works. Selim III (1789–1807) introduced the first comprehensive reform program, called the Nizam-i Jedid, or New Organization, encompassing a modern army corps, increased taxation, and technical schools to train cadres for the new regime. Selim's program, however, was defeated by the opposition of the 'ulama' and the janissaries, and he was deposed in 1807.

In the decades that followed, Russian advances in the Caucasus, the rise to power of Muhammad 'Ali in Egypt, and the Greek war for independence again made the need for reform urgent. Under Mahmud II (1807–39) the reform program was revived. While Mahmud's program of military, administrative, and educational projects began on the base pioneered by Selim III, the new effort to improve military capabilities, rationalize administration, subordinate the provinces, raise revenues, and establish schools was guided by a strong Western orientation and a more radical concept of a centralized state, governed by an absolute monarch. The reforms were intended to revive the absolute authority of the Ottoman rulers supported by new elites who were technically proficient and entirely devoted to the authority of the regime. Conservative resistance was utterly crushed. In 1826 the entire janissary corps was destroyed and feudal tenures were partially abolished. The 'ulama' were weakened by the absorption of many waqf endowments, courts, and schools into new state-controlled ministries. The Bektashi religious order, associated with the janissaries, was dissolved. There would henceforth be little opposition to reform – and even considerable support from the higher-ranking 'ulama'.

This first phase of reform was followed by the Tanzimat, or Reorganization period, which lasted from 1839 to 1876. In this period the reform program was extended from military and administrative matters to economic, social, and religious affairs. As the Ottomans realized that radical changes in economy and society were needed to support a centralized state, they built factories to manufacture cloth, paper, and guns. Coal, iron, lead, and copper mining were encouraged. To stimulate agriculture, the government undertook reclamation and resettlement. Technical modernization included the introduction of a postal system (1834), telegraph (1855), steamships, and the beginning of railroad construction in 1866. Government monopolies were ended in 1838, and international commerce was stimulated by low tariffs. Though reforms in trade and banking enabled European traders and investors to achieve a dominant position in the Ottoman economy, the principle that a more productive economy was essential for state finances was established.

Important legal reforms were also undertaken. New law codes were promulgated to meet the demands of a new administration and economy, and to respond to the political pressure generated by Ottoman subjects and foreign powers. New commercial and penal codes regulating landowning and commerce were promulgated to supplement Shari'a legal principles. Western types of law courts and law codes were introduced as early as 1840. Laws of 1858 established private ownership of land. In 1870 the Ottoman government issued a new civil code, the *Mejelle*, which in substance followed the Shari'a, but nonetheless dramatically departed from tradition because it contained changes made on the personal authority of the Sultan and was administered in state rather than in Shari'a courts. The family law of 1917, by adopting a European system of personal law, made a complete break with the Muslim past.

While Ottoman educational reform began with the establishment of professional schools, a new education system, including elementary and secondary schools, was created to prepare students for higher technical education. In 1847 the Ministry of Education undertook to organize middle schools (*rushdiye*); the army created a parallel system of secondary schools. After the Crimean war, the Ministry of Education and the army began experiments in elementary education, introducing arithmetic, geography, and Ottoman history. In 1870 the first efforts were made to create a university to integrate professional, humanistic, and religious studies. Much of the program, however, remained a paper system.

Similarly, extensive reforms were made in the administration of the non-Muslim populations. While Christians and Jews formed autonomous religious communities which administered their own civil laws, the nationalist revolts made it imperative to further integrate the Christian populations and win their loyalty for the Ottoman regime. The first Ottoman response to these pressures was the Hatt-i Sherif (Noble Rescript) of Gülhane (1839), a declaration of principles of government, recognizing the rights of life, property, and honor, and the equality of all religious groups before the law. In 1856 the Hatt-i Humayun (Imperial Rescript) promised equality for non-Muslims and guaranteed their right to serve in the army. In 1867 Christians began to be appointed to state councils.

The non-Muslim communities were also reorganized to shift power from clergy to laymen. In 1850 the newly formed Protestant millet was governed by an assembly of lay members rather than by clergy. In 1863, the Gregorian Armenians were granted the right to form a national assembly with a lay majority and to elect patriarchs and councils. The Ottoman government forced the Greek clergy to form a lay assembly and then separated the Bulgarian from the Greek Orthodox Church. Behind the reorganization of the Christian communities under lay leadership was the goal of integrating the Muslim and non-Muslim populations into an Ottoman nation. No longer would religious differences be a barrier to Ottoman loyalty.

Transcending the statism of the first reforms, the Tanzimat amounted to a change in the very concept of Ottoman society. It repudiated the autonomous functioning of Islamic educational and judicial institutions, and challenged the very concept of Muslim supremacy. In the interest of a strong state, and the integration of its various religious and ethnic populations, the Ottoman authorities were tampering with the fundamental structures of Muslim society and replacing traditional educational, legal, and religious systems with secular organizations. The restoration of the empire was beginning to have revolutionary implications.

The state reforms proved revolutionary because they brought into being a new elite committed to still further change. While the Tanzimat did not deeply penetrate Ottoman society, or affect the masses of people whose lives, beliefs, and loyalties were still bound up with Islam, it created a "new class." With the destruction of the janissaries, the weakening of the 'ulama', and the adoption of the reform programs, political power in Ottoman society shifted to the *memurs*, or bureaucrats, and within that elite to the Westernized and Westernizing element – the servants of the translation bureaus and the war office who had been educated in secular schools and had traveled in Europe. This group of bureaucrats was led by Mustafa Reshid Pasha (1800–58), the son of a waqf administrator who began his career in religious schools but entered the newly reorganized administrative service of Mahmud II and became a grand vizier, and his protégés, Mehmet 'Ali Pasha (1815–71), the son of an Istanbul shopkeeper, and Mehmed Fuad Pasha (1815–69), a former medical student.

By the 1860s, moreover, Tanzimat had also generated its own opposition. While the "new class" occupied government offices, graduates of the middle and professional schools, middle-level bureaucrats, and sons of poor families who found their careers blocked by the entrenched older generation turned their energies to literature, becoming poets, writers, journalists, and editors of opposition newspapers. Resentful of the established bureaucrats, they sought allies among lower-ranking military officers, liberal 'ulama', and theological students opposed to the Tanzimat program but interested in a different program of reforms.

The new intelligentsia was represented in the 1860s by the Young Ottoman society. In the name of a synthesis of Ottoman tradition and Ottoman reform, Young Ottomans such as Namik Kemal (1840–88), Ibrahim Shinasi (1826–71), and Ziya Pasha (1825–80), were committed at once to the continuity of the Ottoman regime, the revitalization of Islam, and modernization along European lines. The Young Ottomans, dazzled by the successes of Britain, favored a constitutional regime. They believed that the ultimate value of the empire was measured by its contribution to the inherent rights of its citizens, to the security of life and property, to justice, and to the reconciliation of Christians and Muslims. In their view, the empire could not survive unless it became rooted in the masses. Moreover, a constitutional regime was the natural expression of the political and moral values that they held to be inherent both in Islam and in European culture. Thus the Young Ottoman thinkers were, without the designation, modernist Muslims. They held that Islam, properly understood, was compatible with a modern organization of society and a constitutional government. They stressed the aspects of the Islamic heritage that encouraged scientific and technical learning, the value of reason above blind faith, and the importance of an active striving for individual and social improvement. Along with their commitment to Islam, the Young Ottomans also espoused the use of a simplified version of the Turkish language to bridge the gap between the Ottoman elite and the mass of their subjects. While criticizing the program of Tanzimat as religiously and socially insensitive, they were nonetheless committed to a modernized Muslim-Ottoman society.

In 1876, taking advantage of the Ottoman defeat by Russia, the constitutionalists staged a coup d'état and brought to power 'Abd al-Hamid II (1876–1908), who was forced to accept a constitution limiting the powers of the Sultan, establishing a representative government, decentralizing administration, and mandating equality for all religious groups. 'Abd al-Hamid, however, was unwilling to surrender 500 years of Ottoman authority. Turning the tables on his constitutionalist supporters, he suspended parliament and established an authoritarian and religiously conservative regime. This regime was based on the absolute power of the Sultan, the bureaucracy, and the police. The Sultan was considered the head of Islam, and laid claim to a worldwide authority over Muslims. The new regime, however, combined conservative Islamic loyalties with the continuation of technical Tanzimat reforms. New schools, legal codes, railroads, and military techniques were introduced.

The generation of Turkish intelligentsia raised in the 1880s and 1890s took shape in reaction to the conservative regime. Continued economic and educational development swelled the ranks of the intelligentsia. The number of white-collar, technical, railroad, and telegraph workers increased. Poor and middling families were made occupationally mobile. The opportunities for communication were enlarged despite government controls and censorship. The press disseminated European ideas about science and politics, and popularized Western attitudes. Ideas spread from the capital to the provinces as students brought home a larger vision of the universe.

In 1889 exiled journalists, writers, publishers, and agitators formed the Ottoman Society for Union and Progress in Paris. The Young Turks, as they were now called, maintained their allegiance to the Ottoman dynasty, but agitated for the restoration of a parliamentary and constitutional regime. The Young Turks were divided into a group led by Ahmad Riza, who favored a strong Sultan, centralization of power, and the predominance of the Turkish-Muslim elements of the Ottoman population; and a group led by Prince Sabaheddin, who emphasized decentralized forms of Ottoman rule. The latter gave less emphasis to the Turkish and Muslim peoples of the empire, and stood for a federated society with autonomy for Christians and other minorities.

Within the empire, army officers, bureaucrats, and physicians, outraged by the inefficiency of the government, by defeats suffered at the hands of European and Balkan powers, and by their exclusion from participation in power, formed revolutionary cells in Damascus, Salonika, and elsewhere. The Fatherland Society was founded in 1905 by Mustafa Kemal, an Ottoman army officer later to be president of Turkey; a Young Turk congress created the Committee for Union and Progress (CUP) in 1907. In 1908 the CUP cell in Monastir mutinied and forced the Sultan to restore the constitution of 1876. The military coup established a facade of parliamentary government, but the new government was actually run by the CUP and by the army, and proved to be authoritarian and highly centralized. Between 1908 and 1912, a three-way struggle for power among the army, the CUP liberals, and Muslim conservatives ended with the army in control. From 1912 to 1918 the CUP ruled by decree.

In bitter reaction to the Islamic veneer of the reign of ʿAbd al-Hamid, the CUP was resolutely secular. Between 1913 and 1918 it adopted a program of aggressive secularization of schools, courts, and law codes, and passed the first measures for the emancipation of women. In 1916 the CUP government reduced the powers of the Shaykh al-Islam, transferred jurisdiction over Muslim courts to the Ministry of Justice, and control of Muslim colleges to the Ministry of Education. In 1917 a new family code based on European principles was promulgated. While the regime of ʿAbd al-Hamid had been bolstered by appeals to Islam, the opposition intelligentsia moved from the Young Ottoman position, which synthesized Islam and constitutionalism, to a more radically secular position. The struggle for power among the various segments of the Ottoman governing elite and intelligentsia led to a radicalization of the reform program along secularist lines.

The CUP program was Ottoman and secularist, but it was also increasingly Turkish-oriented. Between 1908 and 1918 the idea of Ottoman reform was overtaken by a new concept. CUP leaders began to conceive of the Ottoman empire in terms of Turkish nationality. For more than a century, Christians had pursued national goals and demanded that peoples who shared an ethnic, linguistic, and religious heritage have a territorial state of their own. By the late nineteenth century there were already several Christian nations – Greece, Serbia, Romania, Bulgaria, and Montenegro – in what had once been the domains of the Ottoman empire. Albania was soon to revolt, and Armenians were claiming territorial autonomy. For the Christians, it was easy to form a national identity in opposition to Muslim and Ottoman domination and in frank emulation of the Christian nations in the West. For the Muslims, however, it was difficult to disentangle nationalism from Islam and from the Ottoman empire. They could make no ready distinction between Muslim interests and Ottoman authority. Furthermore, the peoples we now call Turks had no concept of themselves as an ethnic group. They thought of themselves either as Muslims or as subjects of the Sultan. The word "Turk" only meant peasant, nomad, or rural bumpkin – someone without education.

Still, the idea of a Turkish nation began to take shape in the late Ottoman era. Loyalty to Islam and to the Ottoman empire came to be considered a kind of patriotism, described by the word *watan*, or fatherland. Pan-Islamic identifications inspired a sense of political unity. Muslim and Ottoman vocabularies could thus express a political concept akin to, but not identical with, the national ideal. A Turkish cultural consciousness also began to take shape. Young Ottoman writers were concerned with the reform of the Turkish language and the adaptation of the high-cultural style of Ottoman Turkish for mass use. In the 1890s, under the stimulus of European students of Turkish language and culture, and of Crimean and Inner Asian intellectuals who were refugees or students in Istanbul, the Ottomans were introduced to the idea of the "Turkish people." The press glorified Anatolia as the homeland of Turks, and peasants as the backbone of a Turkish nation. The Turkish idea was being propagated by literary clubs such as the Turkish Homeland

Society and the Turkish Hearth. These organizations waged a "national" campaign to simplify the Turkish language, make it more accessible to the masses, and persuade the populace of its own Turkish nationality. Ziya Gokalp (1875/76–1924) emerged as the spokesman of Turkish nationalism. Without regrets for the declining Ottoman empire, he celebrated the folk culture of the Turkish people, and called for the reform of Islam to make it expressive of the Turkish ethos. 'Abdallah Jevdet (1869–1932) presented a secular basis for Turkish nationalism. The Turkish concept made it possible to define a new civilization which embodied the historical identity of the Turkish people but was not Muslim, and was modern but not Western.

Between 1908 and 1918 political events put an end to the possibility of a multinational, multi-religious Ottoman empire, and made the Turkish idea more relevant. By 1908 the majority of the Christian population was already independent. Albania revolted in 1910 and its autonomy was conceded in 1912. The Balkan wars then stripped the Ottoman empire of virtually all of its European possessions, and during World War I the Armenian population of eastern Anatolia was decimated by the hardships of war, deportation, and Turkish and Kurdish massacres. Even among Muslims, Kurdish and Arab national feeling was growing, and there were Arab conspiracies against the empire. By the end of World War I all that was left of the Ottoman empire was Anatolia, with its majority Turkish population, and Kurdish and small Greek and Armenian minorities. The realities of Ottoman political life now corresponded to the nationalist concept of a Turkish people. The war had cut the Gordian knot of Ottoman loyalties by stripping away most of the non-Muslim and non-Turkish populations. It also left the remaining territories of the empire occupied and divided among the allied powers.

After the war Mustafa Kemal carried the principles of the Young Turk generation into action. Under Kemal's leadership, the national elite was able to mobilize the Turkish masses to fight against foreign occupation and to support the national idea. Kemal organized the movement for the Defense of the Rights of Anatolia and Rumelia, established a Grand National Assembly at Ankara (1920), promulgated a new constitution (1921), and established a republican regime in most of Anatolia. The new regime defeated the Armenian republic in the Caucasus, the French in Cilicia, and the Greeks in central Anatolia, and in 1923 the European powers agreed, by the treaty of Lausanne, to recognize the independence of Turkey in its present boundaries. Turkey alone of the Muslim-populated regions of the Middle East emerged from World War I as a fully independent country. Already provided with a national intelligentsia of army officers, experienced administrators, politicians, lawyers, and intellectuals, and a unified national movement, modern Turkey came into being with a coherent state structure, a unified elite, and a strong sense of its cultural and political identity.

The dominance of Ottoman military and bureaucratic elites, their turn toward nationalism, and their absolute leadership in the creation of the Turkish Republic may be better understood in terms of the historical weakness of alternative national elites. The turn toward a concept of a secular national state was abetted by the inability of Ottoman religious leaders to articulate an effective Muslim opposition. The destruction of the janissaries and the weakening of the 'ulama' in 1826 proved decisive. After that the 'ulama' continued to support the Ottoman state, the defender of Islam. The Sultan was still considered the religious chief of Muslim peoples. Selim III and Mahmud II built mosques and tombs, attended mosque prayers and Sufi ceremonies, and appointed religious teachers for the soldiers. 'Abd al-Hamid revived the identification of Sultan and Caliph, and based his authority on the claim that he was the *padishah* of the Ottomans and the Caliph of all Muslims. The Ottoman state was able to persuade Muslim opinion that the empire, despite its apparent assault on Islamic educational and legal institutions and its willingness to grant political and economic equality to non-Muslims, was still a Muslim regime.

Furthermore, many leading 'ulama' were sympathetic to the need to make Islam effective in the modern world. Spokesmen for an Islamic modernism continued to believe in the validity of their faith, but felt that it had to be revised to make it compatible with changing conditions. On one side, they opposed the traditionalists who failed to recognize the importance of the new military, economic, and technical civilization of the West. On the other side, they opposed the secularists who did not value the religious and communal inspiration of Islam. The Islamic modernists wished to persuade the traditionalists to accept modernization as consistent with Islam, and persuade the modernists to accept Islam as a moral force. The Ottoman reform program, then, was presented in a framework of loyalty to Islam and of shared concern for the adaptation of Islamic values to the modern world.

Moreover, the 'ulama' remained loyal to the Ottoman regime because they were the servants of the state and were committed to an ideology of obedience. Leading 'ulama' were also personal friends of the Sultan, enjoyed his financial favors, and were connected by family ties to the military and bureaucratic elites. Through the middle decades of the nineteenth century the only religious opposition came from lower-ranking functionaries, theological students, and rural Sufis. At the end of the century, when the initiative passed to the radical secularists, Muslim religious leaders were not in a position to resist. The tradition of subservience to state initiative, and the ambivalent recognition of the need for modernizing reforms, made it impossible for them to oppose the powerful forces, national and international, that led toward the dissolution of the Ottoman empire.

Nor did the Ottoman military and bureaucratic elites have to contend with a Muslim bourgeoisie or commercial middle class. In part this was due to the legacy of state domination of the society and in part to European economic penetration of the Ottoman empire. The Anglo-Ottoman treaty of 1838, which led to the removal of Ottoman monopolies and high tariffs, marked the full integration of the Ottoman empire into the international economy. Entry into world markets stimulated the production of cash crops such as grain, wool, raisins, tobacco, and opium, though cotton declined owing to American competition. By 1913 Anatolian agriculture provided 55 percent of the agricultural income of the Ottoman empire and

48 percent of the gross domestic product. Some 80 to 85 percent of exports were agricultural products.

Manufacturing also prospered. Though the trade treaty of 1838 is usually taken to have been a disaster for Turkish handicrafts, in fact Turkish cloth weaving and carpet making flourished in the nineteenth century, partly owing to investments by Austrian and British firms in a putting-out system of production. Industries, however, were very little developed except for state-owned factories which produced guns, clothing, and footwear for the soldiers, and sold the surplus to the general public. Ottoman efforts to create their own industries for cotton, textiles, iron, and weapons had limited prospects in the face of the high cost of imported raw materials and technicians. Nevertheless, Ottoman industrial output grew at a rate of 1.85 percent a year, about twice the rate of growth of the gross domestic product. In all, Ottoman engagement in the world economy led to intensified production for export, but to the failure of domestic industries and crafts in competition with Europe.

Ottoman engagement in the world economy also led to state indebtedness and financial dependency. The first Ottoman loans were contracted in 1854, and Ottoman economic development came to depend upon European loans for the construction of railroads, mining, and public utilities. Foreign capital also financed military expenditures and the formation of Ottoman banks. By 1882 the Ottoman state could no longer pay the interest on its debts and was forced to accept a foreign debt administration. Henceforth foreign bankers controlled the Ottoman economy. However, from 1880 to 1914 there was increased prosperity in the Ottoman empire owing to the centralization of state power, security in the provinces, and the foreign stimulus to internal investment and trade.

This foreign-stimulated and foreign-regulated economy had important consequences for the social structure of Ottoman society. It favored Greek, Armenian, Jewish, and other minorities involved in international trade, but the dependence of the Ottoman empire on the world economy did not change the distribution of political power within Ottoman society. These groups could not challenge the state elites. Control of taxation, major investments, and ideological and military power remained the prerogative of the Ottoman establishment. On the eve of the formation of the Turkish Republic, the military and administrative elites alone determined the destiny of the state.

REPUBLICAN TURKEY

Thus, the Ottoman tradition of a strong centralized state and military leadership was transmitted to the Turkish Republic. The history of modern Turkey can be divided into two phases. The period from 1921 to 1950 was the era of presidential dictatorship, religious reform, and the first stages of industrialization. From 1950 to the present is the era of a dual military rule and multi-party political system, increasing social differentiation, rapid economic change, and resumed ideological conflict.

The Kemalist period began in 1921 with the Law of Fundamental Organization which declared the sovereignty of the Turkish people. In 1923 Mustafa Kemal Ataturk was named president of the Republic for life. He was head of government, and head of the Republican People's Party. Despite brief experiments with an organized political opposition – the Progressive Party of 1924, and the Liberal Party in 1929 and 1930 – the regime proved intolerant of opposition. The party was its main instrument in the countryside, and its offices disseminated information about agricultural improvements, organized educational programs, and taught the secular and national ideology to the country people. The regime thus continued the Ottoman system in which a highly educated, urban, bureaucratic, and military elite dominated the rest of the country. 'Ulama' and local notables were excluded from political power, but landlords were allowed to retain and consolidate their economic position. It was a regime in the name of the Turkish people, but without close connections with them.

The primary goals of Kemalist Turkey were economic development and cultural modernization. In the course of the nineteenth century, European competition forced Muslim elites out of commerce and into reliance on the state as the main vehicle of economic activity. Between 1908 and 1918, however, foreign capital was withdrawn, Greek and Armenian merchants were pushed out, and the way was opened for the growth of a new Turkish commercial elite. In the 1920s, however, foreigners still controlled Turkish banks and the import–export trade.

In the 1920s, the Kemalist regime resumed state sponsorship of economic development. It promoted agricultural production by reducing taxes and by investing in roads and railways. Exports of cotton, tobacco, and dried fruit rose. The Turkish Republic also took the lead in building textile factories with Soviet loans and expertise. Traditional crafts, however, floundered. With the collapse of the export market in 1929, Turkey turned to more energetic state control of the economy and planned economic development. The inspiration was at once Ottoman and Soviet. In the 1930s the state nationalized the railroads, utilities, ports, and mines. The first five-year plan (1929–33) promoted consumer substitution industries. The Sumer Bank was founded to finance textile, paper, glass, and sugar enterprises. Great Britain helped finance the construction of iron and steel works. In the 1920s and 1930s, the foundations were set for a modern industrial economy.

At the same time, Mustafa Kemal sought to absorb the masses of the people into the ideological and cultural framework of the republican regime, break the attachment of ordinary people to Islam, and win them to a Western and secular style of life. The new regime abolished the organized institutions of Islam. The Ottoman Sultanate was abolished in 1923 and the Caliphate in 1924. Waqf endowments and 'ulama' were put under the control of a new office of religious affairs. In 1925 the Sufi orders were declared illegal and were disbanded. In 1927 the wearing of a fez was forbidden. In 1928 a new Latin script was introduced to replace the Arabic script, and an effort was begun to purify the Turkish language of its Arabic and Persian content. In 1935 all Turks were required to take surnames in the Western fashion. In the course of this period, a new family law based upon Swiss legal codes replaced the Shariʻa. "People's Houses" were set up all across the nation to teach literacy, disseminate the new ideology, and inculcate a Turkish national identity. Thus, Islam was "disestablished" and deprived of a role in public life, and the ordinary symbols of Turkish attachment to the traditional culture were replaced by new legal, linguistic, and other signs of modern identity.

Part of these changes was the transformation in the status of women. The nineteenth-century Tanzimat program had already provided elementary education for women, but at the turn of the century secular nationalists made the women's question a crucial concern. Ziya Gokalp theorized that equality of women was essential for the development of a modern Turkish society. He advocated equality in education, employment, and family life, allowing women equal rights in divorce and inheritance. In the first decade of the century urban women began to dress in European fashion. The first *lycée* for women was established in 1911, and schools for teachers, nurses, midwives, and secretaries expanded rapidly. The war years, which drained the Turkish male population, brought women into new professions and factory labor. Family legislation in 1916 and 1917 broke with the Shariʻa, restricted polygamy, and allowed women to obtain divorces in specified conditions. Still, women remained segregated in public places, including transportation. Theatrical entertainments, education, and many other activities were still carried on separately for men and women or in partitioned rooms.

The reforms of the 1920s and 1930s brought still more radical changes. Family laws of 1924 abolished polygamy, made the sexes substantially equal in rights to divorce, and required that divorce be subject to court rulings on specified conditions rather than a male prerogative. The constitution guaranteed the right of women to equality in education and employment, and in 1934 women were accorded the right to vote in national elections. In 1935 women deputies were elected to the Turkish parliament. The changes in attitude and legal principle have been the basis of an ever-expanding participation of women in Turkish public life.

Radical as were the economic and cultural policies, the Kemalist regime was not revolutionary. The position of women was improved for the sake of the state and national development rather than as a commitment to women's rights. The dominant elites and organizations retained their authority. No effort was made to mobilize the peasantry. The cultural revolution, imposed from the top, had relatively slight penetration. It served to divide the country into an urban, modernized elite, and rural peasant masses oriented toward Islam. The combination of a radical cultural policy with conservative statist political and social policies made Turkey one of the first of a new type of modern Asian nation – an authoritarian regime attempting to carry out radical economic and cultural reforms.

23   Mustafa Kemal Ataturk (left) and the Shah of Iran

The postwar Turkish Republic

The Kemalist legacy was a state dominated by a corporate elite with a monopoly of political power committed to transforming and modernizing Turkish society. When Mustafa Kemal died in 1938, the regime continued under his loyal colleague, Ismet Inonu (1938–50). The period between Kemal's death and the end of the

Inonu regime prepared the way for a new political system. Economic development generated new groups of businessmen, factory managers, rural landowners, prosperous peasants, and a new generation of intellectuals who wanted political recognition. Also, Turkish legislation after World War II relaxed government controls over commerce and the universities and increased the expectation of political participation. The Inonu government permitted the formation of the Democrat Party, and in 1950, free parliamentary elections.

Thus a new regime came into being, a representative state alongside the military bureaucratic guardian state established by Ataturk. The military, at the head of a centralized state with strong controls over the industrial economy, trade associations and labor unions, committed to secularism in cultural policy, now governed through a parliamentary system. Parliament represented the free-market sector of the economy, the ever-growing interests of independent peasants, businessmen, and professionals, who favored a mixed development policy combining state direction and market expansion, and a flexible cultural policy in which aspects of Islam, appealing to peasants, small-town populations and migrants, would be tolerated. The political parties were expected to give allegiance to Kemalism. In turn the state extended its patronage to the middle classes and the populace by a policy of legislative subsidies and welfare payments. The Turkish government became an ever more elaborate system of patronage and top-down controls.

After World War II the United States, as the main protector of Turkish political security and economic development, reinforced these trends. The USA favored a less paternalistic and more democratic multi-party system. American intervention was prompted by the expansion of the Soviet Union into Eastern Europe and the Balkans, Soviet backing for the Communist Party in the Greek civil war, and direct threats to Turkey and Iran. In 1947 President Truman declared the US determination to defend Turkey, Iran and Greece, and by 1950, the North Atlantic Treaty Organization (NATO) had been formed to counter-balance Soviet power.

The organization of the double state led to a series of crises. The opening up of the political system led to a democratization of participation, but also to a fragmentation of political parties and factions, ideological polarization, confrontations between left and right, secular and Islamist forces, Turkish and Kurdish ethnic groups, and to contradictory economic policies. The history of the Turkish Republic ran in phases of parliamentary government, each ending in a crisis in which the military seized power. Each time, the army gave new direction to the economy, suppressed political conflict, revamped the constitution, and then partially relinquished power to a civilian government. Such crises took place in 1960, 1970, and 1979-83, and again in 1997 the military intervened to ban an Islamic party from participation in the parliamentary system. Though the issues have changed, the structural problem remains unresolved.

The first phase ran from 1950 to 1960. In the 1950s the Democrat Party, led by Jelal Bayar and Adnan Menderes, took power from the People's Republican Party, founded by Ataturk. The Democrat Party mobilized a new coalition of small businessmen, landowners and their peasant dependents and clients, and middling and rich peasants. It was tolerant of Islam, and permitted religious instruction in Turkish schools. Mosques again received state support. The Sufi orders, however, were held in check and waqf endowments were not restored. The Democrat Party thus compromised the Kemalist dogma that only by secularization could Turkey become a modern country. It also favored economic modernization, and promised to curtail state intervention in the economy, transfer enterprises to private control, and increase marketing opportunities for peasants. In the course of the 1950s agriculture was modernized; production of sugar, cotton, and tobacco was increased. Turkish–American military collaboration led to the construction of roads, railroads, airfields, ports, and communications. The villages were transformed by the introduction of roads, electricity, tractors, bus transportation, and schools. Hectic and chaotic growth, however, was marked by inflation, trade deficits, and an enlarged public debt. In 1958 the International Monetary Fund forced Turkey to cut back wages and social services, and to devalue the currency.

With Turkey in economic collapse, a military coup on May 27, 1960 overthrew the Menderes government. The army, representing the Westernized elite defending Kemalist secularist policies, aligned with bureaucrats and students against the rural, small-town business, and Islamic interest groups, took control of the government. The army regime, and the National Unity Committee that it spawned, stayed in power, however, only a year. This was long enough to abolish the Democrat Party and to promulgate a new constitution and parliamentary regime and a new economic policy.

The 1960s marked the second phase in Turkey's postwar development. Turkey's economic growth then was based on state-sponsored and protected consumer industries. Industrial production and the industrial working force grew considerably. Agricultural exports and the remittances of Turkish workers in Europe contributed heavily, but these earnings failed to pay for the capital, raw materials, and other imports needed to maintain Turkey's consumer substitution industries. This led to economic unrest and another foreign exchange crisis in 1971. The army temporarily took control of the state, but soon restored a civilian government. In the 1970s the Turkish economy grew in an irregular and highly vulnerable way, dependent upon foreign loans, and provoking conflicts of interest among large and small domestic capitalists, workers, and peasants. Rising oil prices and a general slowdown in the European economy led to inflation, unemployment, foreign debts, and exchange problems, and eventually to a new International Monetary Fund program of wage freezes and imposed deflation in 1979–80.

Also, in the 1960s and 1970s Turkey returned to multi-party conflict. This was abetted not only by uneven economic development, but also by increased social and economic differentiation, and an increased tendency toward political awareness and activism. A new technical elite composed of engineers and industrial workers, a large worker movement, and militant ideological groups on both the right and the left entered the political arena. The Republican People's Party under

Bulent Ecevit came to represent the bureaucratic, intellectual, and technical elite of the country, including industrial workers and other urban groups. The party of Mustafa Kemal maintained its statist orientation, but became, in effect, a democratic socialist party appealing to a professional civil service and industrial clientele. The Justice Party, led by Sulayman Demirel, was heir to the legacy of the Democrat Party. It was oriented to large-scale private enterprise and rural development. Alongside the two major parties, new parties formed on both right and left, including the Agrarian Capitalists Democratic Party, the small-town petit bourgeois Islamist National Salvation Party, the elitist and fascist National Movement Party, and the Turkish Workers' Party and other left-wing worker, Maoist, and Soviet-oriented groups. By the late 1970s the right wing was openly at war with leftist groups. The parliamentary system failed to mediate among these conflicting interests, and again, in 1980 the army intervened to restore political and economic order. In effect, economic and cultural development has made Turkey a highly pluralistic society which lacks effective political means to give coherent economic and ideological direction to the development of the country.

In 1983, under the eyes of a watchful army and with a new constitution, the government was again returned to civilian hands under the presidency of Turgot Ozal (1983–93). The vigilance of the military was institutionalized in the National Security Council which gives the army a powerful role in the formulation of government policy and a veto over policies of which it disapproves. The new constitution is authoritarian and outlaws parties based on class, religion, and ethnicity, and restricts freedom of the press and rights of labor organization.

The 1980s also brought a return to liberal economic policies and export-based growth. Import-substitution development – that is, development based on an industrial infrastructure shielded from international competition, catering to consumer needs, and a welfare or clientism policy using industry to provide employment for government officials, managers, and workers, welfare and other services – became too costly to sustain. State intervention was reduced, foreign investment welcomed, and private enterprise encouraged. Minority interests in the Turkish airline and in hotels and telecommunications have been sold to investors. Nonetheless, the state continues to subsidize housing, and to provide benefits for the military, bureaucrats, and other favored groups. The liberalized economy remains vulnerable due to the inability of the government to effectively tax the wealthy, curb its own expenditures, or control inflation.

While economically productive, this transformation has imposed economic hardship and insecurity upon downsized segments of the population. The result is a cultural and political counter-attack in two forms: Islamism and Kurdish nationalism.

Islamic revival and Kurdish nationalism

Islam holds a nuanced place in Turkish society. The ideology of the republic is secular, and the Turkish urban educated upper classes consider Islam a symbol of backwardness. The urban 'ulama' tradition has largely been destroyed, and has no influence upon public life. However, the rural-Sufi tradition has survived and the Islamic loyalties of ordinary people were never seriously disturbed. The Turkish populace continued to identify itself as Muslim, and even in the Kemalist period continued to carry on worship in mosques and at the tombs of saints.

Moreover, the economic and political stresses of the postwar era led to the rise of new movements and parties committed to the re-Islamization of state and society. These movements appeal to students, especially in technical and medical subjects, as an expression of alienation from an authoritarian state, of concern over economic prospects, and of moral doubt which stems from social and educational mobility. They appeal to provincial small-town bazaar traders and artisans, especially in central and eastern Anatolia, and to rural or small-town populations who have migrated to the larger cities and who preserve in the new environment a small-community orientation and old values. The *gececondu* (shanty-town) migrants in Ankara and Istanbul find in Islam the basis of a new identity, social cooperation, and political representation as they struggle to organize new lives in a new environment.

One of the most important is the Said Nursi movement, founded by a religious preacher and writer, the author of the *Risale-i Nur* (Epistle of Light), which achieved a wide underground distribution in Turkey despite government opposition and the prosecution of Said Nursi for religious agitation. The *Risale-i Nur* integrates science, tradition, theosophy, and mysticism, and appeals especially to technically educated people and to a less well-educated public that is nonetheless familiar with Western scientific ideas. While Said Nursi was himself concerned about politics the movement currently postpones political action in favor of religious self-cultivation.

The National Salvation Party, also formed in the 1960s, advocated the reestablishment of an Islamic state in Turkey. It was hostile to capitalism and big business, and called upon the state to work for a moral and just society. Puritanical in moral tone, it represented both an effort to protect Anatolia's petite bourgeoisie from the encroachment of the state and large-scale economic enterprises and an effort to increase its constituency's share of economic development. The National Salvation Party won a small percentage of the vote in Turkish elections in the 1970s. The National Salvation Party rallied old Sufi networks and rural support, and expressed the political and economic grievances of its backers, but accepted the liberal, parliamentary, and human rights aspects of secular political culture.

The Refah (Welfare) Party was the direct successor of the National Salvation Party. In the 1990s this party became the vehicle not only for Islamic values but for a broader protest against economic downsizing, the unfair distribution of wealth and opportunity favoring Istanbul and Ankara rather than the provinces, government and administrative corruption, and the authoritarian controls of the state. The Refah Party, with some 20 percent of the electorate, became the country's biggest vote-getter and, taking advantage of the inability of the secular parties to agree among themselves, formed a governing coalition. In 1996 and 1997 the head of the Refah, Necmettin Erbakan, became Prime Minister of Turkey.

Still, the seeming opposition between Islamic movements and the national state is not absolute. While there are radical secularists and radical Islamists, and while Islamic rhetoric and Kemalist principles conflict, the state has also tried to incorporate Islam within the system. The initial policy of the Republic was to institutionalize Islam as a department of state by taking over courts, waqfs, and the education of imams. In the 1950s the Democrat Party lent legitimacy to Islam by setting up *iman-khatib* schools, allowing voluntary religious courses in schools, and radio broadcasts and calls to prayer in Arabic. The military regime of 1960–61 saw enlightened Islam as a bulwark against Communism. From 1965–71 the Justice Party also expanded imam-khatib schools, and encouraged Islam as a personal religion for conservatives and technocrats, and as a bulwark against the left. Post-1980s governments have tried to coopt Islam and keep it under state supervision. The state is not so much anti-Islamic as hostile to expressions of Islam not in its own control.

The second focus of opposition is the Kurdish population of the economically backward provinces of eastern Turkey, who demand cultural autonomy, self-government in a federal framework, or national independence. Kurdish-speaking peoples, who number some 20–25 million, are distributed among Turkey, Iran, Iraq, and Syria. Kurdish ambitions for a national state were blocked by the post-World War I partition of the region into the several existing states, and Kurds in each country have waged a decades-long struggle for autonomy, independence, and union. However, the Kurds fight as much with each other for leadership and for local economic and political advantages as they do against the existing states. In turn each of the states manipulates the Kurdish factions against each other, and uses them in their rivalries with other states.

Kurdish resistance to the Turkish state goes back to 1925, when Kurdish Naqshbandi chieftains fought against the Republic. Kurdish separatism became intense in the 1980s, and the Gulf War gave Kurdish separatists and nationalists a new opportunity. The Kurdish Workers' Party (PKK) intensified its ongoing violent struggle for regional autonomy and a federalized state structure for Turkey, and the Turkish government responded with repressive policies. Kurdish terrorist attacks and Turkish incitement of tribal and factional strife, relocation of Kurdish populations into so-called "strategic villages," and military attacks on Kurdish bases in Iraq, escalated into an all-out war. The capture of 'Abdallah Ocalan, the leader of the PKK in 1999, has broken militant Kurdish resistance, and forced the more radical elements of the movement to retreat from the goal of separatism to the goals of cultural autonomy and regional development.

The struggle with the Kurdish resistance creates great complications in Turkish foreign policy. Throughout the cold war era Turkey was an integral supporter of NATO's policy of containment. With the breakdown of the Soviet Union, the emergence of independent states in Central Asia, neo-nationalist wars in the Balkans, and the Gulf War (1991), Turkey has moved cautiously in several arenas. In the Balkans Turkey avoided direct engagement, though it gave strong diplomatic support to the Bosnian Muslims, because of the danger of a polarization into a Muslim – Bosnian–Albanian–Turkish coalition versus an eastern Christian – Serbian–Greek–Russian entente. In the Caucasus and Central Asia, Turkey attempted to assert its leadership for a new group of independent and underdeveloped nations. It promoted a Black Sea Economic Cooperation Council, made extensive investments in the infrastructure of the new Central Asian republics, promoted student exchanges, and took part in the creation of a new western alphabet for Central Asian Turkic languages. In this region, Turkey's influence, however, is relatively limited. Turkish initiatives have been checked by Russia which considers itself the patron power of the former Soviet states. Russia and Turkey remain rivals for the development of alternative pipeline routes for the export of regional oil and gas. Its relations with Russia are also constrained by the Kurdish problem. Russia sponsored conferences of exiled Kurds as a warning against Turkish intervention in Chechnya and the former Soviet republics. Vis-à-vis the Arab world, Turkey has several times invaded northern Iraq to try to crush the PKK. Turkey threatens to divert the Euphrates water supply and has developed ties with Israel to forestall Syrian support for the Kurds.

The Turkish modernist dream of integration into Europe is undermined by its responses to the Kurdish problem. Though Turkey is a member of the European Customs Union, and though 52 percent of Turkish exports go to and 44 percent of its imports come from the European Union countries, Turkey is held on probation for membership in the EU, many of whose members are critical of Turkey's undemocratic constitution and its human rights abuses. There are, of course, other factors in this opposition. Greece resists Turkish participation. Germany fears opening up to Turkish labor migration, and there may also be an unspoken reluctance to accept a Muslim country as part of Europe.

Militant secularist opinion in Turkey refuses to accept the legitimacy of either Islamic religious commitments or separate ethnic identities. In the high tensions of the 1990s, the army reverted to a rigidly authoritarian and secularist policy. It forced the Refah Party to relinquish its place in the government. The courts have declared it illegal, and some of its leaders have been prosecuted or banned from politics. A new group, the Virtue Party, has succeeded Refah, but its influence and voter appeal seems to have declined. Furthermore, the military opposes Kurdish demands for autonomy as a threat to the survival of the Turkish state, and so justifies tight police control over the country, and widespread human rights abuses. The military also opposes political and legal system liberalization, and implements close government controls over the media and the schools in order to maintain the secular, authoritarian Kemalist heritage. Thus, Islamic and Kurdish interests are largely excluded from the political process.

The polarization of Turkish society among secularists, Islamists, and Kurds calls into question its national identity. Behind the army's resistance to Muslim or Kurdish political and cultural demands and its repressive policies lies a concept of the Turkish nation as a unitary, homogeneous entity. Turkish nationalists do not allow for minority rights or for plural ethnic and cultural identities, and Turkey seems to be committed to the assimilation and homogenization of the population regardless of its diverse ethnic and religious backgrounds. Embedded, then, in the issue of Islam and Kurdish rights is the issue of Turkey's political identity. The repressive policies of the government and the Kurdish and Islamic challenges to its authority test Turkey's commitment to democratic and parliamentary government and the rights of citizens.

The formation of the Turkish Republic was prepared by the eighteenth- and nineteenth-century Ottoman empire. The republican bureaucratic and military elite committed to the secular modernization of the country was a direct outgrowth of the late Ottoman elite. The defeat of Islamic interests and their subordination to state control was similarly the result of the subordination of the religious establishment and the acceptance by the 'ulama' of the intrinsic legitimacy of the Ottoman regime. Furthermore, European intervention worked to strip away the Balkan Christian populations, and World War I led to the partition of the Ottoman empire in a way that substantially resolved the historical tensions between tribal and ethnic minorities and the Ottoman government. In the twentieth century, Turkish economic and social change has led to a highly pluralistic, secularized, and national society, but one in which Islam and Kurdish ethnicity continue to have profound religious and social meaning for much of the Turkish population The conflicts created by Turkish pluralism have become a test of the nation's modern identity.

CHAPTER 24

EGYPT: SECULARISM AND ISLAMIC MODERNITY

Egyptian history in the nineteenth and twentieth centuries resembles that of Turkey. Egypt also developed from an Ottoman and Islamic to a national and secular form of society. Its evolution also began with a period of state-managed reform, but its development was diverted by British occupation from 1882 to 1952. British rule cut off the consolidation of an Egyptian military and administrative elite, and made a secondary elite of landowners, officials, merchants, and intelligentsia the spokesmen for national independence. These elites, still hampered by British occupation, came to power in 1922 and ruled until 1952. Unable to surmount the dilemmas of governing under foreign rule, divided by nationalist and Islamic political orientations, the liberal elites were removed from power and replaced by a new generation of Arab nationalist military officers who instituted the military regime that governs Egypt to the present day.

THE NINETEENTH-CENTURY REFORMING STATE

Though part of the Ottoman empire, Egypt retained a separate political and cultural identity. Under Ottoman suzerainty, Egypt was ruled by local Mamluk military factions. Like the rest of the Ottoman empire, Egypt had a strong 'ulama' establishment and Sufi brotherhoods. In the course of the eighteenth century, as Ottoman control weakened, fighting among the Mamluk factions led to the decline of irrigation, excessive taxation, and increasing pastoralism and tribal autonomy. Ottoman weakness exposed Egypt to invasion by Napoleon in 1798, to British counter-intervention, and finally to the appointment of Muhammad 'Ali as governor in 1805. Muhammad 'Ali was determined to make himself an independent potentate, and founded a dynasty which ruled Egypt until 1952. He had ambitious foreign projects. He defeated the Wahhabis and established Egyptian control over western Arabia and the holy places of Mecca and Medina. He expanded Egyptian power in the Sudan, and helped the Ottomans in the Greek

512

war of independence. In 1831 Muhammad 'Ali invaded Syria and threatened the viability of the Ottoman empire.

His aggressive military regime was sustained by a far-reaching reorganization of the Egyptian state and society. He tried to create a centralized dictatorship based on an army of Turks, Kurds, Circassians, and other foreigners who were part of his personal household. With the help of Italian and French military advisors, he built a new army, for the first time recruiting Egyptian peasant soldiers. He devised a new tax system, employing salaried officials to replace the old tax-farming arrangements. Coptic scribes were employed in subordinate administrative positions. All other political forces were broken. The old Mamluk households were destroyed. The power of the 'ulama', who had risen to financial and political eminence in the late eighteenth century, was broken as Muhammad 'Ali confiscated their tax-farms and waqfs.

To support the state apparatus, the economy was totally reorganized. Muhammad 'Ali promoted sugar and cotton because they were cash crops with an international market. Major irrigation projects were undertaken to make it possible to cultivate the land all the year round. State control of agriculture and trade allowed Muhammad 'Ali to buy cotton from peasants at low prices and resell it to exporters at a profit. Machinery and technicians were imported to build factories to produce cotton, wool, and linen textiles, sugar, paper, glass, leather, and weapons. A new school system was founded to train technicians and army officers. For the sake of an effective military machine, the administration and economy of the country were totally reorganized.

Muhammad 'Ali's descendant Isma'il Pasha (1863–79) carried the development of the country still further. He continued the program of economic and technical growth, extended the railroads and telegraph, and constructed the Suez Canal and a new harbor for Alexandria. He also gave Egypt European-type law courts, secular schools and colleges, libraries, theaters, an opera house, and a Western-type press. Egypt, like the Ottoman empire, acquired the infrastructure of cultural modernity.

The effect of this reorganization was to destroy the old order of society in an upheaval even more profound than that which took place in the rest of the Ottoman empire. The whole balance of social power in Egyptian society was altered. Egyptians and Turko-Egyptian families became powerful in the army and administration. Muhammad 'Ali's economic and administrative policies promoted the development of a new landed elite. Members of the ruling family were awarded estates called *jifliks*, and tax-free lands were granted to village shaykhs who took control of taxes and corvées. The abolition of collective village responsibility made individuals responsible for paying taxes. These measures led to the concentration of land in the hands of merchants, money lenders, village headmen, and government officials. Changes in land law which abolished restrictions in private ownership of land made it possible to buy, sell, or mortgage land, and opened land to purchase by foreigners. By 1901 foreigners or Egyptians with foreign passports owned 23 percent of all estates of more than 50 acres (*faddans*). Finally, exports of cotton and sugar benefited landowners, merchants, and officials, and helped increase privately owned lands. The power of the merchant elites was also enhanced by the elimination of craft guilds. From the new class of large-scale landowners came bureaucrats and army officers, who formed a new dominant elite. While its base was in landowning, the new elite had its commercial wing, including Egyptian, Jewish, and Syrian merchants, who prospered as middlemen in the growing trade with Europe. Out of this class came the lawyers, journalists, and intellectuals who would give voice to the aspirations of the new elite.

The new economic system destroyed the village economies. Government controls and private ownership replaced village collectivities. The disruption led to peasant indebtedness, fugitivism, and to a series of peasant rebellions which swept Egypt in 1798 and 1812, throughout the 1820s, from 1846 to 1854 and from 1863 to 1865. Popular preachers who called themselves saints (*wilaya*) or mahdis appealed to Sufi conceptions and eschatological hopes. Also, the traditional guilds dissolved, and state controls replaced collective organization. A new economy promoted state control and individualism in place of the corporate structures of pre-nineteenth-century Egyptian society.

The position of the religious elites was equally transformed. In the eighteenth century, the 'ulama' of Egypt, like the 'ulama' of Istanbul, were an integral element of the ruling elite and represented the interests of the regime, acting as intermediaries between the government and the common people. In the wake of the French invasion of Egypt and the struggle for power between Muhammad 'Ali and the local Mamluks, the 'ulama' reached their maximum power. Muhammad 'Ali, in return for their support, agreed to consult them in political matters, and allowed them to grow wealthy by acquiring tax-farms and by converting endowed funds to personal uses. After Muhammad 'Ali consolidated power, he subordinated the 'ulama' to the regime, banished their leading spokesmen, abolished the tax-farms and waqfs, and made them dependent upon the ruler for their income. In the course of the nineteenth century, the 'ulama' lost their influence. They withdrew from public affairs to protect a narrow sphere of educational and judicial interests. The lack of an autonomous basis of power and a tradition of compliance operated in Egypt, as in the Ottoman empire, to confine the 'ulama' to the defense of a narrow range of traditional prerogatives.

In the course of the nineteenth and early twentieth centuries, al-Azhar became the principal 'ulama' institution, as confiscation of waqfs destroyed rival colleges, and made others administratively subordinate to the shaykh of al-Azhar. Laws of 1908 and 1911 mandated curriculum and administrative reforms which increased the authority of the shaykh over both 'ulama' and students. In a limited sphere he became principal spokesman of 'ulama' Islam and the conduit of government influence among the religious elite.

The powers of Sufis were similarly circumscribed. Whereas the Sufi orders, families, shrines, and zawiyas of the eighteenth century were independent, Muhammad 'Ali brought them under state control. In 1812 he appointed the shaykh of the Bakri lineage as chief shaykh, and made the chiefs of Sufi lineages, shrines, and brotherhoods beholden to the new chief shaykh for the payment of their stipends and waqf revenues. After 1855 the state imposed a system of licensing that gave the chief shaykh and the government the authority to define the territories in which each order could stage ceremonies and mawlids (commemorations of their revered masters), and proselytize for new members. State regulations also suppressed the most dramatic of Sufi deviances from 'ulama' religious norms. In 1881 a circular issued by the chief of Sufis prohibited music and dance performances and such spectacles as flagellation and the swallowing of hot coals. The appointment of the chief Sufi shaykh also weakened the 'ulama', as religious authority was divided between the shaykh of the Sufis and the shaykh of al-Azhar. The government was then able to manipulate the two wings of Islam against each other. In 1903 and 1905 the regulation of Sufis became the function of a government ministry. Both 'ulama' and Sufis had been made subordinate to state control.

BRITISH COLONIAL RULE

The subordination of the 'ulama' and the emergence of a new landed commercial and intellectual elite opened the way for further radical change in Egyptian society. Before these new elites could make their influence felt, however, Egypt fell under direct British rule. British interest in Egypt derived ultimately from the consolidation of the British empire in India. Napoleon's invasion of 1798, Muhammad 'Ali's attack on Syria in 1831–39, and the construction of the Suez Canal between 1859 and 1869 underlined the fact that Egypt lay on the route to India and was essential to the defense of the empire. Furthermore, Britain had acquired a major interest in the Egyptian economy. The reforms of Muhammad 'Ali made Egypt an exporter of cotton and dependent for her earnings on the world market. Reciprocally, Egypt had become an importer of British cloth. Heavy Egyptian borrowing to purchase consumer luxuries, military equipment, manufacturing machinery, and capital equipment for railroads and the Suez Canal put her into debt to European banks and governments. Egypt's economic dependence led eventually to bankruptcy, and to the imposition of a foreign-managed debt administration under Anglo-French control (1875).

The debt administration was the beginning of colonial rule. It led to open conflict between foreign interests and the new Egyptian elites. 'Ulama', landowners, journalists, and native Egyptian army officers provoked demonstrations in 1879; in 1881, led by an army officer named 'Urabi, they seized control of the war ministry and formed a parliamentary government. Britain refused to compromise with the nationalists, bombarded Alexandria, landed troops, defeated 'Urabi, and in 1882 took complete control of the country in the name of the bond-holders. Thus, the crisis of 1879–82 not only gave political shape to the new Egyptian elite of army officers, officials, journalists, landowners, and 'ulama' who opposed domestic misrule and foreign intervention, but also culminated in the British occupation of Egypt. In 1898 the British took the Sudan under joint Anglo-Egyptian rule.

From 1882 until World War I the British managed the Egyptian economy efficiently, but in the imperial interest. The British improved agricultural productivity by investments in railroads and irrigation. They built a Delta barrage and the first Aswan dam (1906), and the cropped area grew from 5.7 million faddans in 1882 to 7.7 million in 1911. This is not to say that the peasantry was notably more prosperous. The population of the country grew from 6.8 million in 1882 to 11.3 million in 1917. Also, economic development encouraged the concentration of surplus wealth in the hands of large landlords. The British improved tax collection, consolidated private property ownership, and raised adequate revenues to pay for the Egyptian budget and the foreign debt. As a result of these policies, Egypt became ever more dependent upon cotton for export. Industrialization was inhibited by the lack of British interest in encouraging competition, the unwillingness of landowners to invest, and lack of natural resources.

While British administration was in some respects favorable to Egyptian interests, there was deep resentment over the imposition of British rule by force, the displacement of Egyptian officials by British ones, neglect of education, and the exploitation of Egypt to expand the British empire in the Sudan. Under British rule the new Egyptian landowning elite and intelligentsia continued its resistance. This elite expressed itself through two related ideological positions – Islamic modernism and Egyptian nationalism. Like the Ottoman intelligentsia, the Egyptians defined first a modernist Islamic and then a secular concept of an independent Egyptian society.

THE EGYPTIAN AWAKENING: FROM ISLAMIC MODERNISM TO NATIONALISM

The most influential spokesmen for nineteenth-century Egyptian Islamic modernism were Jamal al-Din al-Afghani (1839–97) and his Egyptian disciple, Muhammad 'Abduh (1849–1905). Al-Afghani was an Iranian who later claimed to be an Afghan in order to ensure a favorable reception among Sunni Muslims. Educated as a Shi'a, he was deeply versed in Muslim philosophy. He sought to awaken Muslims to the threat of European domination and to oppose Muslim rulers who abetted Christian intervention. His political career took him to India, Afghanistan, Egypt, France, England, Iran, and finally to Istanbul, where he died. A dramatic and passionate political intriguer, an inspiring lecturer, a man of novel and imaginative ideas, he devoted his life to persuading rulers to modernize Islam. He lectured widely on theology, natural science, philosophy, and mysticism. Everywhere he was mistrusted but used and then discarded by heads of state. He inspired suspicion and fear as much as confidence and hope.

Al-Afghani's primary objective was to encourage resistance to the European powers. He dreamed of restoring the ancient and true glory of Islam triumphant. In al-Afghani's view, the struggle for independence required solidarity. Also, Muslims had to become a scientific and technically competent modern people. To restore the glory of Islam, it was essential to reform corrupt Muslim societies.

For al-Afghani, the reform of Islam was essential because religion was the moral basis of technical and scientific achievement, and of political solidarity and power. Islam was quintessentially suited to serve as the basis of a modern society. Islam was a religion of reason and the free use of the mind. The Quran, he argued, should be interpreted by reason and was open to reinterpretation by individuals in every era of history. By stressing the rational interpretation of the Quran, al-Afghani believed that Islam could be made the basis of a modern scientific society, as it had once been the basis of a medieval society built upon faith.

Islam, properly understood, he also argued, was a dynamic faith, for it encouraged an active, responsible approach to worldly affairs. The passivity and resignation that he saw in medieval Muslims were a corruption of its true teachings. Further, Islam was the basis of patriotism and loyalty to one's people. As a religion of rationality, science, activism, and patriotism, Islam embodied precisely those virtues that had made the European countries world powers. Al-Afghani saw Islam as a religion that could be the wellspring of a rationally guided, active, responsible life, compatible with modern science, dedicated to the restoration of the autonomy of Muslim nations and to the revival of the political and cultural glory of Muslim peoples. He believed that it was essential to modernize Islam, but also that faith in Islam was essential to modernity. Al-Afghani's modernism was thus akin to that of the Young Ottomans and the Aligarh school in India.

In Egypt, Islamic modernism took a different turn in the hands of al-Afghani's disciple, Muhammad 'Abduh. 'Abduh was born of an educated village family and was schooled at al-Azhar. He participated in the 'Urabi revolt of 1881, was exiled in 1882, and returned to Egypt in 1888, where he was appointed judge and later mufti, or chief of Islamic law, from 1889 to 1905. 'Abduh's endeavors as mufti were directed toward modernizing Islamic law, and revising the curriculum of al-Azhar to include modern history and geography. Like al-Afghani, he was concerned with the defense of Muslim peoples against Europeans, but for 'Abduh the central problem was not political but religious: how, when Muslims were adopting Western ways and Western values, could they maintain the vitality of Islam in the modern world?

'Abduh set about, therefore, to reformulate Islam, distinguish the essential from the non-essential, preserve the fundamentals, and discard the accidental aspects of the historical legacy. He accepted the Quran and hadith as God's guidance, but in matters not expressly treated in the Quran and hadith he argued that individual reason and judgment were essential. While the Quran and hadith always applied to matters of worship, individual judgment, or ijtihad, was essential to regulate social relations, which were governed instead by rational ideas and humane ethical considerations. In Islam he found general guidelines which had to be reinterpreted in each age, rather than an eternal, detailed blueprint for social and political organization. Thus, he denounced the slavish acceptance of past authority, which, he held, had led Muslims to believe that the political and social arrangements of the past were a religious requirement for all ages.

Behind 'Abduh's concepts lay the international movement of Islamic reform, and the eighteenth- and nineteenth-century revival of Egyptian interest in the Quran and hadith. The reform movement was associated with the diffusion of the Naqshbandi order in Syria and other parts of the Ottoman empire, and may also have been associated with the commercialization of Egypt's economy and increasing Egyptian contacts abroad. This hadith-oriented reformist Sufism made itself felt in the thought of 'Abduh. In turn, 'Abduh's Islamic reformism inspired the Salafi movement in the Arab fertile crescent, in North Africa, and as far away as Indonesia.

Under the influence of al-Afghani and 'Abduh, Islamic modernism and Islamic religious reform became the ideological programs of the Egyptian intelligentsia in the decades between the 'Urabi revolt and the turn of the century. While al-Afghani emphasized the pragmatic need for Muslim solidarity, 'Abduh pursued the same goal by emphasizing educational, legal, and spiritual reform.

In either case, the primary purpose of the Islamic movement was political revival. In Egypt, however, as in Turkey, the Islamic modernism and reformism taught by al-Afghani and 'Abduh gave way to a more secular nationalist concept of Egyptian identity and politics. The nationalist intelligentsia stemmed from the classes of landowners, officials, and Western-educated journalists and lawyers generated by earlier reforms. The leaders included Mustafa Kamil (1874–1908) who held a French law degree, Lutfi al-Sayyid (1872–1963) who came from an Egyptian village notable family and was educated in Quran schools and later in law, and Sa'd Zaghlul (1860–1928), the son of a village headman, who began his career with a religious education and then turned to secular nationalism. Other nationalists were Jewish or Christian journalists and writers who became proponents of a secular society in which minority groups could be full citizens.

National feeling seems to have come easily in Egypt. Even before nationalism became a self-conscious doctrine, Egyptian writers spontaneously identified Egypt as the watan, the motherland. The homogeneity and isolation of the country, its long history of central government, and its distinctive cultural past encouraged a consciousness of Egyptian identity. In Egypt, more than in any other Middle Eastern country, the modern national state is based on the historical existence of an Egyptian people and an Egyptian state.

In the late nineteenth century, Egyptian patriotic sentiment was blended with the idea of modernizing reform. Nationalist writers such as Mustafa Kamil propounded the idea of a unified nation, patriotic in spirit, passionate in its hatred of foreign rule, but also dedicated to a constitutional form of government and Western-type education. Lutfi al-Sayyid became the philosopher of a secular and constitutional society. Freedom, he argued, was the basis of society. Freedom from foreign rule, freedom from state control, and recognition of the inherent civil and political rights of citizens were its essential principles. For Lutfi al-Sayyid nationalism meant independence and also a new social and political system for Egypt.

The national movement began with speeches and journals, but it took political form with the formation of the Hizb al-Watani, or National Party, led by Mustafa Kamil, in the 1890s. This party and others took on formal identity in 1907. The Dinshaway episode conveyed the nationalist idea from its original middle-class milieu to students and even to the masses. In 1906 a group of British officers on a pigeon hunt got into a fight with local people. One of the officers was killed, and in retaliation the British publicly executed four peasants and flogged numerous others. The outrage awakened widespread Egyptian hostility to British rule.

World War I crystallized the determination to be independent. The declaration of a British protectorate, martial law, requisitions of Egyptian labor and manufacturing capacity, heavy migration to Cairo, and widespread hardship stiffened Egyptian opposition to British rule. At the end of the war, a delegation (*wafd*) led by Sa'd Zaghlul, inspired with hope by Woodrow Wilson's proclamations, demanded complete independence. Zaghlul was able to mobilize mass support, and in the course of a three-year struggle from 1919 to 1922 forced the British to dissolve the protectorate.

THE LIBERAL REPUBLIC

In 1922 Egypt emerged as a semi-independent state under British tutelage. An Egyptian king – of the dynasty established by Muhammad 'Ali – and a parliament governed Egyptian affairs. But foreign policy, the army, the attached region of the Sudan, and jurisdiction over all foreigners in the country was under British rather than Egyptian control. Egypt, like Turkey, came out of World War I with a secular national regime, but unlike Turkey it remained partially dependent. The difference was due partly to the fact of foreign occupation and partly to the class composition of the Egyptian elite. The Turkish elite, composed essentially of army officers, deeply rooted in a statist tradition, was capable of mobilizing the political and military potential of the Turkish nation. The Egyptian elite, composed of landowners, journalists, and politicians, was able to organize a political, but not an effective military, resistance in the struggle for independence.

Egypt entered its era of semi-independence with all the makings of a national state. It had a unified population, a history of centralized government, and a Westernized intelligentsia committed to liberal constitutionalism. The main problems facing the country were those of achieving full independence, coping with the low standard of living and the need for economic development, and creating a modern cultural and ideological identity. In most respects, the liberal regime failed. It failed to win full independence and achieve adequate and equitable economic development or provide an abiding cultural identity. It was overthrown in 1952 by army officers, who were to attempt the same objectives along new political and ideological lines.

The objective of achieving independence was complicated by a tripartite division of power between the King, the political parties, and the British. The British controlled the military and used their power at critical junctures to play the King and the parties against each other; similarly, the King and the party leaders did not try to unite against the British, but were only too glad to use British help to best their rivals.

Egyptian politics between 1922 and 1952 thus fell into a pattern. The Wafd Party, which had emerged from the struggle for independence as the most popular, would win national elections. The British and the King would conspire against the Wafd government and force it to resign. The King would, if necessary, suspend and dissolve Parliament and govern through his personal cabinet, until new elections eventually returned the Wafd to power. The game would then begin again. The King and the British were generally united against the majority party until in 1942, when the King drew too close to German and Italian interests, and the British – backed by tanks in the streets of Cairo – conspired with the Wafd to outmaneuver the monarchy. These machinations made it impossible for the liberal regime to achieve independence. The King was not eager to remove the British forces that maintained his power. The Wafd was unwilling to have any agreement negotiated by another party.

Despite these complications a treaty was worked out in 1936 which gave Egypt "independence" subject to certain reservations. The treaty provided for a twenty-year military alliance and British evacuation, except for the Canal Zone. It committed Britain to the defense of Egypt, committed Egypt and Britain to the joint defense of the Sudan, ended the special legal privileges of foreigners (such as mixed courts), and proposed that Egypt enter the League of Nations as an independent state. After the treaty, Egypt gained a greater degree of internal sovereignty, but Britain kept her predominant military position. World War II made Britain still more reluctant to withdraw. Postwar negotiations foundered over the control of the Sudan, until finally, in 1950, Egypt abrogated the treaty of 1936 and the 1899 Sudan Convention. Guerrilla war against British occupation of the Canal Zone followed, and led to riots in January, and a military coup in July 1952. This ended the reign of the Egyptian monarchy and the parliamentary system. Britain agreed finally to the evacuation of the Canal Zone.

The liberal regime also failed between 1922 and 1952 to cope with the problems of economic development. Important gains were made in the development of Egyptian consumer industries to produce processed foods, textiles, cement, paper, sugar, and other products. The Misr Bank was founded, with ownership deliberately restricted to Egyptians, in order to compete with foreign companies. In the 1920s and 1930s Egyptians began to take control of their economy out of the hands of foreigners. However, the benefits of economic progress accrued to a very small part of the population. Businessmen, skilled workers, and white-collar bureaucrats prospered to a degree, but the general standard of living fell owing to rapid population growth and the decline of world markets for cotton. Per capita food production from the late 1920s through World War II actually fell below the level of 1886. While the parliamentary regime had come to power in 1922 on the strength of peasant uprisings, once in power the nationalist parties proved to represent landowner, bourgeois, industrial, and professional class interests, rather than the general need for economic growth.

Similarly, the liberal regime also failed to define Egypt's cultural and political identity. In the 1920s Egyptian political and intellectual leaders were outspokenly secular and modernist. Many Egyptian intellectuals defended a Western orientation and liberal and national political principles. 'Ali 'Abd al-Raziq argued that Islam represented a purely spiritual community, and a code of individual behavior that had nothing to do with politics. Some writers tried to reinterpret Egyptian history in Pharaonic, but not in Muslim, terms. Taha Husayn even called Quranic and biblical history into question, espousing a thoroughgoing rationalism. Other writers attacked custom, rejected ethical ideas based on revelation and other-worldly sanctions, and advocated Western humanistic values.

Whereas the rulers of Turkey went on to implement a program of cultural modernization, Egyptian leaders could not. They lacked the absolute political power and unity essential for such a program. They were also overtaken by a growing disillusionment with Europe. World War I, the political strife of the inter-war years, the Great Depression, and, finally, World War II exposed Egyptians to the failings of the constitutional and liberal governments of Europe, the ruthlessness of the powers, their indifference to principle in manipulating non-European peoples, and their contempt for their subjects. These events shook the confidence of many Egyptians that the future belonged to the West, and left others disappointed and alienated. Furthermore, the failure of the liberal regime to win full independence and to deal equitably with the country's political and economic problems also undermined faith in parliamentary regimes and in the value of individualism.

Most important in the retreat from secularism and Westernism was the revival of popular commitment to Islam. The Islamic revival in Egypt in the 1930s and 1940s owed little to the traditional 'ulama' or Sufi brotherhoods, whose political and ideological position had left them unable to resist the state authorities. Rather, a new generation of Muslim preachers and teachers, representing youth associations, worked to teach Islamic morals and ethics, strengthen the ties of brotherhood, and restore religious law and the supremacy of Islam in public life. They appealed to people with a traditional Muslim education such as clerks, lower civil servants, shopkeepers, students, and others who had been hurt by foreign occupation and by the change from Muslim to Western education, or who had been uprooted from their position in the old order of society. Similarly, the revival appealed to a new generation of students and industrial workers who were dissatisfied with the dominance of a landowning elite committed to a foreign ideology.

The most important Islamic reform movement of this era was the Society of Muslim Brothers, founded by Hasan al-Banna in 1928. Hasan al-Banna preached the restoration of Islamic principles, and a return to the Quran and Islamic piety. He built up an extensive following divided into cells or chapters, which organized mosques, schools, clinics, and even cooperative work opportunities for their members. The movement became politically active in the 1930s, adding athletic and paramilitary groups to the other cells. Muslim Brother volunteers supported the Arab uprising in Palestine in 1936–39. In Egypt the Muslim Brothers allied with other Islamic youth movements to oppose British rule, the corruption of the Egyptian regime, and its defeat in the Palestine–Israel war. They supplied guerrilla fighters for the struggle in Suez, and sponsored violent demonstrations and strikes. By 1948–49, the movement had become the standard-bearer of Egyptian mass grievances against British rule and the failure of the liberal political system. It called for the establishment of an Islamic government based on consultation with the 'ulama' and devoted to the application of the Shari'a, proposed the regulation of the economy in accordance with a combination of Islamic and socialist principles, and promised to see to a more equitable distribution of income. Committed to the fundamental scriptures of Islam, to the assertion of an Islamic social and political identity, and to the adaptation of Islamic principles to the needs of a modern society, the Muslim Brothers were devoted to the reform of morals, education, economic projects, and the creation of an Islamic state. Islam in their minds was the blueprint for a totally modern society and an ideological and political alternative to liberalism or to Communism.

In the face of this tide of public opinion Egyptian secularists had to give way. Leaders such as Muhammad Haykal did not so much change their views as seek ways to make rationalism and scientific and secular attitudes meaningful to a mass Egyptian audience. His biography of the Prophet, and his attacks on materialism in Western culture, became the public framework of an effort to insinuate modern rational and ethical values within Islam. Thus, in the cultural atmosphere of the 1930s and 1940s, the secular intelligentsia lost the initiative, accepted an Islamic framework, and attempted to compromise between Islam and modernity. The net effect was not so much to rescue secularism as to legitimize the Muslim revival. In Egypt, as opposed to Turkey, the political elite was unable to control the national cultural agenda.

World War II and its aftermath brought the Egyptian regime to a crisis. The war further discredited British rule and intensified economic distress. Cotton prices fell, living standards declined, strikes were suppressed. Migrants from rural areas to Cairo could not find work. After the war the corruption of the Egyptian state was exposed by its failure to stop the formation of a Jewish state in Palestine. Egypt's army intervened in 1948 but was disgraced in battle, and government mismanagement and profiteering in the supply of military hardware was exposed. Soldiers returned embittered and denounced the regime for their defeat.

For a time it seemed as if the Muslim Brothers would seize power, but they were forestalled by the Free Officers. A new force had come into being in the persons of students and army officers with professional and technical educations, the sons of small-scale landowners, traders, or clerks, not implicated in the old regime. Shocked by its failure to defeat the British and by the corruption that undermined the Egyptian army in Palestine, they conspired to seize power. In 1952 the Free Officers, led by Muhammad Naguib, Jamal ʿAbd al-Nasser, and Anwar Sadat, overthrew the King and brought the parliamentary regime to an end. In the three-way struggle among the liberal, secularized older generation, the Islamic and lower-class reformers, and the new generation of technically educated army intelligentsia, the army conspirators were victorious.

THE NASSER ERA

The regime established by the Free Officers in 1952 set Egypt on the course that, with modifications, persists to the present day. It was from the outset a military, authoritarian regime, but one that would successfully cultivate mass support. The new regime broke the power of its opponents. Limits on land ownership to 200 faddans in 1953, 100 faddans in 1961, and 50 faddans in 1969 progressively undermined the economic base of the old landowning elite. The Society of Muslim Brothers was dissolved in 1956 and driven underground, while the new regime brought the University of al-Azhar, and private mosques, charities, and waqfs, under state control.

The monarchy, Parliament, and the political parties were abolished and replaced by a presidential regime and one-party system, which rested on a new political elite of army officers and bureaucrats of middle-class origin and not on the landowning and professional classes that had governed Egypt until the middle of the century. Ideologically the Free Officers' government turned from liberalism to socialism, from collaboration to anti-imperialism, and from nationalism to pan-Arabism to define the objectives of Egyptian national development. Eventually it would also claim an Islamic heritage.

In domestic affairs President Nasser was the dominant figure, basing his power on the army, the bureaucracy, and his talents for political manipulation and mobilizing public support. A major innovation was the one-party system to encourage new forms of political participation and economic cooperation for the mass of Egyptians. The Liberation Rally was formed in 1952, and was succeeded in 1955 by the National Union. The single political party helped to keep the masses responsive to decisions at the top and the upper echelons of the government in touch with the needs of the society, and served as a channel for mobility. In 1962 a national congress created the Arab Socialist Union. The Arab Socialist Union established a local party organization to influence municipal administration, to train youth cadres for eventual leadership in the party and the government, and to inculcate a socialist ideology among peasants and workers. In 1965 'Ali Sabri reorganized the party to stress youth militancy, training camps, and a more aggressive party role in local affairs. The one-party system, however, was not so important as Nasser's personal authority, charisma, and ability to balance powerful officers and officials who controlled the army, the ministries, and the major industries against each other.

The international crisis of the 1950s was crucial in defining the new regime. World War II generated a great upheaval throughout the Middle East. France was destroyed as a colonial power and Britain greatly weakened. The Middle Eastern states – Syria, Lebanon, Jordan, Iraq, Israel, and finally, in 1952, Egypt – became independent of their old colonial rulers. The United States and the Soviet Union emerged as global superpowers and immediate rivals for regional influence. They contested control of the Balkans, Turkey, and Iran, and NATO was established to contain the threat of Soviet expansion. In 1955 Iraq and Turkey were allied by the Baghdad Pact promoted by the American Secretary of State, John Foster Dulles, and Egypt came under intense pressure to join the new alliance. Nasser feared the loss of Egypt's newly won independence, the possible hegemony of Iraq within the Middle East, and the possibility of being connected, via an American alliance, to Israel. In response to these pressures, he attended the Bandung Conference of non-aligned nations, and emerged as a leading spokesman for the independence of Third World nations and for neutrality in the cold war. In 1955, Egypt refused to accept the Baghdad Pact, and negotiated Russian security guarantees and an arms deal with Czechoslovakia. In response, in March 1956, Dulles withdrew from promises to fund the construction of an Aswan dam; Nasser retaliated by nationalizing the Suez Canal. In October, Britain, France, and Israel attacked Egypt to regain control of the canal, but were forced to withdraw because of united Russian and American opposition.

The Suez crisis, Nasser's espousal of neutralism, his defiance of the United States and Britain, his arms deal with Czechoslovakia, and his survival of the British–French–Israeli assault made him the leader of the Arab world in the struggle against imperialism and Zionism. Nasserite parties were founded in several Arab countries. In 1958 a union was formed between Egypt and Syria which, it was hoped, would be the basis for a single Arab state. The union broke up in 1961, mainly because of Syrian resentment of Egyptian domination. Egypt, committed to redressing the injustice in Palestine and achieving Arab unity, continued the struggle against Israel. Defeat in the 1967 war with Israel set back the movement for Arab unity, and discredited Nasser's and Egypt's anti-Israel, pan-Arab, and pro-Soviet foreign policy.

From the late 1950s the Free Officers regime also began to organize a socialist economy. This was not done out of ideological commitment, but as a result of pragmatic efforts to find a solution to Egypt's economic problems. The basic economic problem was to check the decline in the Egyptian standard of living. From 1882 to 1960 the population of the country had risen from 6.8 million to 26 million. In the

24 President Nasser's car is mobbed by townspeople

same period the cropped area had risen from 5.7 million to 10.2 million faddans. Since it was impossible to increase agricultural production to keep pace with the rising population, the development of industry was essential. Thus in the 1950s a new strategy, based on industrialization financed by increased agricultural productivity and appropriation of the agricultural surplus, was adopted to break the cycle of impoverishment. Land was redistributed, large estates were eliminated and small ones favored, though there was not sufficient land to provide territory for all landless laborers. The government maintained private ownership of land but introduced state-controlled cooperatives in order to assure its goals. Productivity was to be increased by government provision of credits, fertilizers, and seeds, but the government requisitioned goods for export. Peasants were to be politically mobilized by opportunities to participate in local government. The state also provided vastly increased rural services in the form of roads, schools, health centers, and cottage industries.

In agriculture, however, Nasser's regime hedged its commitments. In the 1950s the regime began a program of reclamation of desert land in Tahrir (Liberation) province. Faced with the choice of distributing the new lands to individual peasants or creating state-run collective farms on the Soviet model, Sayyid Marei, the Minister of Agriculture, favored the former policy, and army officers administering the Tahrir development favored the latter. Nasser kept the issue open rather than allow either faction or either policy to win the upper hand. The result was a pragmatic and mixed economy in agriculture.

Egypt's industrial policy changed rapidly. Between 1952 and 1956 the Free Officers encouraged private entrepreneurs; however, discouraged by the hostility of the regime to large-scale private ownership in agriculture and handicapped by lack of capital and expertise, Egypt's business leaders could not make the transition from consumer to capital-goods industries. The Egyptian government believed that the policy of laissez faire had failed; its international orientation to the Third World and to the Soviet bloc made some kind of government control of the economy seem essential. Thus, between 1957 and 1960 it took control of the major banks, sequestered British, French, and Jewish property, and developed plans for agricultural reform and for the construction of the Aswan dam. Still it lacked the means to realize its objectives. In 1960 and 1961, therefore, banks and major industries were nationalized and direct government control of banking, insurance, foreign trade, transportation, construction, textile, and other manufactures was instituted. Only retail trade and housing were left to the private sector. Both foreign and Egyptian bourgeoisies were dispossessed, and the economy was nationalized and Egyptianized. The army became prominent in government administration and in management of industries, backed by a second echelon of officials, engineers, teachers, journalists, and lawyers. As the new elite became entrenched in power, it constituted a "state" bourgeoisie.

The socialized economy was expected to meet the needs of Egyptian economic development by freeing Egypt from foreign economic control, and by generating employment, higher-value products, and exports. By 1965 the public sector was providing 45 percent of the output, 45 percent of the savings, and 90 percent of the capital formation for the Egyptian economy as a whole. With the nationalization of industry came a welfare policy that promised mass education and subsidies for rents and basic commodities. The result, however, was not development but stagnation. Economic resources were channeled toward the maintenance of a large army, an ambitious foreign policy, a bloated bureaucracy, the new state bourgeoisie, and a welfare state. Excessively ambitious planning, bottlenecks, inefficiency, and corruption took their toll. Defeat in the 1967 war with Israel ruined the socialist experiment. Though Nasser lived until 1970 the 1967 war with Israel brought an end to the Nasserite style of Egyptian development. Nasser's personal charisma was shattered. It was left to his successor, Anwar Sadat (1970–81), to rethink both Egypt's foreign and domestic economic policies.

SADAT AND MUBARAK

Sadat began with fundamental political decisions: Egypt would disengage from the Soviet Union, ally itself with the United States and with the conservative Arab regimes, and resolve the conflict with Israel. The first part of this strategy was accomplished with the expulsion of Soviet advisors in 1972 – but, paradoxically, ending the struggle with Israel required one last war to give legitimacy to Sadat's regime. In 1973 Egypt surprised Israeli forces by attacking across the Suez Canal and by winning the initial battles of the war. Israel counter-attacked, penetrating Egyptian territory, but the United States intervened to stop Israel's advances and to arrange a truce. Sadat was able to break the aura of Israeli invincibility, claim a moral victory in the war, and go on, in a dramatic speech in the Israeli parliament, the Knesset, in Jerusalem, to offer Israel peace with Egypt. By the Camp David accords brokered by President Carter in 1979 Egypt agreed to recognize the existence of Israel in return for the Sinai territories conquered in the 1967 war. These gestures made Sadat an international celebrity, and won American aid and Sa'udi and Gulf state investments. The years that followed brought formal peace but a tense and unsatisfactory relationship for both Israel and Egypt.

The reorientation in foreign policy brought with it new domestic policies and political identities. Egypt turned from socialism toward a mixed economy. By 1974 this had become the policy of *infitah*, or open door to foreign investment, correlated with alliances with the United States and with conservative Arab states. Despite foreign investments, however, Egyptian prosperity continued to depend upon petroleum exports, tourism, Suez Canal tolls, and the remittances of Egyptian workers abroad. In fact, the Egyptian foreign debt grew enormously.

In agriculture, Sadat's policy was to compromise with the numerous interests involved. Some land was given to the syndicate of agricultural engineers; some was distributed to peasants who were enrolled in agricultural cooperatives; other land was sold at auction to the highest bidder, which enabled wealthy industrialists to consolidate agribusiness holdings. In general, Egypt maintained a state-dominated economy sensitive to pragmatic political considerations.

The Nasser generation of army officers, bureaucrats, and technocrats remained in power, but infitah encouraged foreign banks and joint-venture companies, and generated a new elite of import–exporters, contractors, and speculators in housing. Islamic investment companies with ties to Sa'udi Arabia and the Gulf states and local, Muslim oriented, small-scale shoe and furniture manufacturers and labor contractors flourished in the new economy. The political coalition that governed Egypt was widened to include elements of the business and professional middle classes. With the change in economic orientation Egypt also retreated from the welfare and social service goals of the 1960s and accepted a less equitable distribution of income. In the countryside, political power was transferred from large landowning families to middle-size village notables, and even to the peasant leaders of agricultural cooperatives. The rural middle class consists of a relatively small population of middle-size landowners (10–50 faddans) who, although only 3 percent of the population, own 40 percent of the land. This class, however, does not participate in national political power and is a subordinate clientele of the central state elites. An overcentralized and unresponsive municipal and agricultural cooperative administration still weighs heavily on Egyptian rural society.

Anwar Sadat was assassinated in 1981 by Muslim radicals in apparent protest against his peace with Israel and his secularist policies, but the regime remained secure. Sadat was succeeded by Husni Mubarak, his Vice-President and an air force officer who in the main continued the Sadat policies. Mubarak continued to depend upon American military and economic aid which rose to match the levels of support received by Israel. He continued close and economically supportive ties with Sa'udi Arabia and the Gulf states, and maintained a cold peace with Israel, attempting repeatedly to negotiate further agreements between Israel and the Palestinians. In the 1991 Gulf War Mubarak played a major role in mobilizing Arab support for the United Nations coalition that expelled Iraq from the occupation of Kuwait.

Under Mubarak, the Egyptian political system went through two major phases. Mubarak opened parliamentary politics to wider middle class participation. Opposition parties such as the Wafd, representing secular views, and the Muslim Brothers, representing the Muslim-oriented middle classes, were allowed to hold a minority place in parliament. Nonetheless, the state apparatus kept its dominance. The direct influence of the army in bureaucracy and business administration receded as compared with the Nasser years, but the army has been consolidated as a power enclave within Egyptian society. It runs its own economy consisting of factories, housing projects, and pension funds. The police apparatus, intelligence services, the bureaucracy, controlled labor unions, and a subordinate press assure the predominance of the government elites. Political parties, unions, and professional syndicates are manipulated by the government. Agricultural cooperatives and village councils bring government regulation to the countryside. The judiciary, however, is fairly independent, and intellectuals and students are outspoken in their disagreements with the regime. Egypt remains a highly centralized authoritarian state with a narrow base of political support drawn from the military and governmental apparatus and elements of the middle classes. It is in effect a client of the United States and oil-state interests.

Throughout the 1990s the Egyptian economy was in a precarious state. Revenues from oil, tourism, and remittances of Egyptian workers abroad, the principal sources of Egyptian foreign earnings apart from Suez Canal tolls, declined drastically. The absence of self-sustaining development makes Egypt dependent upon foreign aid. In comparison with levels of prosperity and public welfare in other developing countries, Egypt from 1980 to 1997 stands out in some respects but lags in most. There has been an increase in the incidence of poverty in both urban and rural areas. Egypt falls behind the norm in terms of increases in urban productivity, most likely because the government remains the most important employer, and efforts to privatize have faltered. Rural productivity per hectare, however, has greatly improved since the government removed production and marketing controls on wheat in 1990. Life expectancy has increased from fifty-seven to almost sixty-five years, more rapidly than the international norm, due to higher child survival rates, which in turn are due to better medical care, better quality water, and the availability of rehydration packets for children stricken with dysentery. Literacy has increased from 44 to 51.4 percent of the populace, less of a gain than other countries, as a consequence of a government policy that concentrates resources on higher education and does not invest enough in primary and secondary schooling.

The Islamic revival

This is the context in which a powerful Islamic opposition emerged. In the 1950s and 1960s Nasser's regime attempted to bring Islamic religious activity under government control. Opposition movements such as the Muslim Brothers were outlawed and the autonomy of other religious institutions was curtailed. Waqf land was taken under government control in 1960 and 1973, and private mosques were brought under government ministries. In 1961 al-Azhar was made a state university with a reformed curriculum. In the crucial field of legal administration, Egypt had already adapted new criminal and civil law codes in the nineteenth century. A new civil code based on French models was introduced in 1873; a double court system was established in 1875 to restrict the competence of Shari'a courts and to establish an alternative system of law. Yet another civil law code was introduced in 1949, and in 1955 the Egyptian government consolidated Shari'a courts and civil courts dealing with matters of personal status. The government tried to control religious life, to use the 'ulama' to support government policy, and to identify Islam with national and socialist programs.

This effort to create an apparent identity of Islam and the state was only partially successful. Muslim commitments remained independent of state control. Just as the 1930s brought a revival of Islamic sentiment in intellectual and political circles, the period from 1970 to the present has also witnessed a revival of Islam. While the 'ulama' and the official Islamic establishment remains under government control, independent preachers, missionaries, and teachers actively promote a renewed commitment to Islam. Even al-Azhar increasingly intervenes in the public sphere, and individuals on the periphery of the institution preach to the public, trying to promote a Shari'a society. The political and social atmosphere of the late 1960s and 1970s gave a new cachet to religious loyalties. The defeat in the 1967 war with Israel, the failure to solve the Palestinian problem, the burden of authoritarian government, economic failure, unfair distributions of income and power, and the collapse of old and meaningful cultures into empty nationalistic and ideological slogans led to condemnation of Egypt's secular and socialist policies. As Egyptians returned to their faith for consolation, Sadat also took up the rhetoric of Islam, and thereby lent it added respectability. Deeply felt Islamic loyalties held in abeyance among Western-educated professional and governmental elites, not fully supplanted by national, secular, or socialist loyalties, have come into the open. As secular nationalism failed to take hold, economic failures and social breakdown due to the migration of large numbers of people from rural areas to cities strengthened the potential for a new surge of Islamic identifications.

Generally speaking, contemporary Muslim revivalist groups hold the same religious and social views as the Muslim Brothers. They believe that the Quran and

Sunna must be the basis of individual morality, and stress the application of the Shari'a in all relevant matters. In social policy they hold that the primary role of women should be the care of the family. They avoid ideological positions in economic matters, but stress the importance of minimizing the differences in wealth between rich and poor. For them, social justice is more important than technological, economic, or administrative issues. In general, these groups believe that their society has been corrupted by secular values and that only a return to Islamic principles will restore morality, economic well-being, and political power.

The Islamic revival appealed especially to segments of the population that have lost out in the drive to modernization – to people who did not have a good or Western education, or a place in the modern sectors of the economy. It appealed to the old literate elite of schoolteachers and religious functionaries, and equally to artisans and shopkeepers in the bazaar economy and to small workshop and factory owners. It appealed to large numbers of uprooted migrants from rural areas attracted to the rapid urbanization of Cairo, to young professional people who found, after costly sacrifices to obtain an education, that there were no salaries and status commensurate with their ambitions.

In the 1970s Islamic revivalism appealed especially to students and professional people – engineers, schoolteachers, and white-collar workers – often from rural backgrounds and from upwardly and geographically mobile, but socially conservative, families. Student enrollment in the universities had grown from less than 200,000 in 1970 to more than half a million in 1977. The students had almost no direct instruction, and lived in extremely poor and crowded conditions. Intellectually they had become slaves of mimeographed course manuals; socially they felt oppressed and frustrated. Many young professional people also came from rural backgrounds and acquired a technical or professional skill without going through a deep process of social or cultural adjustment. In Cairo they found themselves, despite their high professional qualifications, without a place in society, living in marginal districts, alienated by inadequate salaries, and distressed by the moral corruption of a big city. They were beset by sexual tensions and were concerned about finding proper spouses. In particular, young female professional students began to wear Islamic dress, which does not reveal the figure or expose hair or limbs. This new commitment to Islamic modesty came precisely at a time when women were increasingly entering professional schools and public life. Between 1952 and 1976 the ratio of female to male students in the universities rose from 1:12 to 1:2. For women who were entering the public world dominated by men, the veil and the profession of an Islamic modesty were ways of recreating the traditional separation among young people who were otherwise – through education, travel and public transport, enjoyment of public entertainment, and political activities – thrown together. The adoption of Islamic dress implied unavailability and asexuality, and for young women from conservative rural families served as a way of controlling sexual confusion and protecting family values and marriage possibilities. Thus, while the Islamic revival in Egypt has important political aspects, it is also a mechanism for the adjustment of Muslim students to the complexities of an urban environment. The Islamic revival expresses itself in a great variety of ways and through a plethora of small groups. It is not a single organized movement. Listening to sermons or television preachers, religious worship, welfare and charitable activities, and participation in commercial associations and banks are all aspects of the larger revival. There is also a concurrent revival of Sufi Islam which represents very different moral and social principles. The *jam'at al-islamiya*, student associations dedicated to Islamization, grew up after the defeat of 1967. Ironically they were encouraged by Sadat himself as a counterweight to left-wing opposition movements. Their objective was to recreate an Islamic society on the basis of a restored Caliphate. The student jam'at began by forming poetry, painting, lecture, Quran reading, and other clubs. They were covertly aided by the police to break the power of the Communists in the universities. Apart from politics they served student interests by making copies of course syllabuses and distributing them at low cost, organizing bus services for women in Islamic dress, and providing subsidies for pilgrimage. Through independent mosques they began to preach to the common people in Cairo and the villages. They adopted the veil for women, the unshaven beard and the white dress for men, and favored public prayer demonstrations. In 1979 the jam'at became involved in hostilities with the Copts. Muslim propaganda was circulated to denounce alleged Christian aggressions, proselytizing among Muslims, and cooperation between the state and the Coptic community. There were Muslim–Christian riots. In 1981 the government dissolved the jam'at, and removed church officials in a bid for popular support. The masses were generally quiet. The student radicals had overestimated the appeal of Islam over Egyptian nationalism, and had underestimated the power of the state to keep control of the population.

In the same period, the more radical segments adopted a doctrine of direct action against the state. While the student communal groups focused on moral and social issues, the radicals held that only the overthrow of the government and the establishment of an Islamic state could lead to a truly Islamic society. They were inspired by the teaching of Sayyid Qutb (d. 1966) whose *Signs of the Road* has become an influential manifesto. This book teaches that sovereignty belongs to God and that all human authority derives from God's sovereignty. In human societies there is no middle ground between Islam and *jahiliya*, between an Islamic and a pagan way of life. Egypt in his view had become a jahiliya society, and the primary tasks of good Muslims must be retreat (hijra), as the Prophet had retreated to Medina; excommunication (*takfir*) of the false Muslims; the waging of jihad; and the reconversion of Egypt to Islam. This is an uncompromising revolutionary point of view.

In the 1970s Shukri Mustafa, the head of the Jam'at al-Muslimin (called by others *al-Takfir wa'l-Hijra*) took up this doctrine. He denounced reformist and collaborationist points of view, and excommunicated the jahiliya society led by Sadat. He formed a small group of followers who retreated from the mosques under the control of the authorities, refused all collaboration with Egyptian institutions, including the courts and schools, and even introduced a special form of marriage for the members of his community. This group, and similar ones, did not attempt to preach to the Egyptian masses but rather expected to seize power by first destroying the corrupt leadership. Such groups attempted assassinations of Egyptian political leaders in 1973 and 1977. In 1981 one of them succeeded in killing Sadat. After the assassination of Sadat the movement was not able to arouse sufficient public support, and its uprisings in Asyut and other places were put down by the army.

Today the Islamic revival movements remain very strong, especially in student milieus. The Muslim Brothers remain active as a political party. They sponsor social service projects in poor neighborhoods, and by 1992 they had control of the doctors', lawyers', engineers', and pharmacists' professional associations, university faculties, and student associations. They favor a multiple-party system, and want to participate in the formation of an Islamic state whose defining characteristic is not necessarily democracy, but rather the primacy of the Shari'a. An Islamic state would reduce but not eliminate the private sector, respect private property, and provide welfare and social security. Furthermore, the Society of Muslim Brothers in Egypt remains the homebase for numerous affiliated international chapters. Branches of the society are found in Jordan and other Arab countries, and in West Africa and Europe wherever there are growing Muslim communities. These branches uphold a revivalist version of Islam, but they are only loosely coordinated, and play different roles in different countries depending upon local educational, social, and political conditions.

In the late 1980s and 1990s the more radical groups attempted a campaign of terrorist assaults on government officials, military and police officers, Copts, and intellectuals, including the Egyptian Nobel Prize winner Naguib Mahfouz, and against cultural symbols such as cinemas and bars. A sporadic but deadly campaign was waged against foreign tourists to signify opposition to foreign influences, to hurt government revenues, and to demonstrate the failure of the state to control the country. The government has almost but not quite fully crushed the militants by a relentless military campaign, and it maintains tight controls over political parties, media, schools, and charitable associations. The Islamic opposition is highly factionalized, and has neither a common political front nor the charismatic leadership necessary to win mass support. By contrast, the Egyptian state is highly centralized and by and large legitimate in the eyes of its population. It has a monopoly of military power, commands a deep Egyptian patriotism and loyalty, and has been able to physically suppress its opponents. The radicals seem to have been checked in their drive to political power and some activists, such as Ayman al-Zawahiri, have moved abroad to take part in an international jihad, to defend Muslim communities and to weaken the United States, the principal supporter of Egypt. The polarization of state authority and violent Islamists prevents a compromise solution to the struggle between an increasingly Islamlized populace and its secular military regime. Egyptians are caught between terrorism and state repression.

The revivalist movement has also been hampered by internal factors. While Islamic revivalism is implicitly political, the revivalist groups serve many cultural and social purposes apart from politics, and they are ambivalent about the relationship of their social and cultural objectives to political power. Only a few of them are committed to political action. The rest serve the needs for moral guidance, for reassurance and self-esteem in an unsettled world, and for collective organization to serve the welfare and community needs of their members. They allow students to function successfully, and especially women students in a male environment. Meeting these moral and educational needs means that they do not necessarily direct their energies into politics.

In some ways, the Islamic revival even serves as a diversion from politics. One of the deep problems in Egyptian society is the powerlessness of masses of people. Egypt is virtually a dictatorship, and large numbers of people have no political power and few political rights. Also, Egyptian men find it hard to earn a living within Egypt. The most advantageous thing for an Egyptian worker is to go abroad. Moreover, the traditional realm of men's power in society, the family, has also been subverted. Now the state takes care of education, provides health care and social services – it even employs women. Men are no longer necessarily dominant within their households. Frustrated in the political and economic realm, men want to restore their power over the family. The result is not always political protest against the real conditions of the society, but a desire for compensation at the expense of those who are still weak. In this case, women are the weak. In many cases, the most important tenet of the Islamic revival is the restoration of symbolic and actual male supremacy over women and the curtailment of the social and educational rights that have been gained by women in the last couple of generations.

Thus, Islamic revival movements have ambiguous political implications. While some wings of the movement believe that the control of the state is essential to the success of an Islamic social and moral program, others find actual and symbolic satisfactions by turning away from politics toward moral, communal, and familial concerns. In programmatic terms, then, it is not clear that the revival gives priority to political objectives. The result is a limited impact on Egyptian public life, and a continued division of the Egyptian population between those segments that are moved by nationalist symbols and those that are affiliated with the Islamic revival.

While Egypt has been committed to modernization and secular development since the early nineteenth century, the place of Islam in Egyptian national development remains an issue for political struggle. The regimes of Nasser, Sadat, and Mubarak were committed to a moderate form of authoritarian rule, and to an economy with strong state participation. The consequence of having a political elite that rules without being able to dominate the cultural life of the country is permanent

Islamic revival. In the 1930s and 1940s the Muslim Brothers stressed the anti-imperialist aspects of Islam because it saw the British as the main enemy. In the 1950s and 1960s it stressed solidarity and justice in opposition to the corruption of the military regime. In the 1970s the Islamic reform movements emphasized personal morality and family values in response to the stresses of a changing social order. In the 1980s and 1990s, in Egypt as in Turkey, Islam has become the main vehicle of resistance to the state and its policies.

CHAPTER 25

THE ARAB MIDDLE EAST: ARABISM, MILITARY STATES, AND ISLAM

Though the Arab fertile crescent countries also had their origins in the Ottoman empire, they would develop in a different way. In the case of Turkey, the state absorbed European influences, assumed control of the reconstruction of Turkish society, and maintained its historical institutional pattern. In the Arab fertile crescent there was no history of independent states, no unified and continuing governing elite, and only the beginnings of national political movements. By the time Arab identities took form in the twentieth century they were replete with unresolved tensions among national states, ethnic identities, and Islam.

NOTABLES AND THE RISE OF ARAB NATIONALISM

The modern Arab state system and the Arab nationalist movements had their origins in the nineteenth-century Ottoman system and in the pattern of European influences on the fertile crescent. The Ottomans had ruled the fertile crescent as a number of separate small provinces. In this region, there were no units of territorial government corresponding to the Ottoman sub-states in Egypt, Tunisia, or Algeria. The principal cities, such as Damascus, Aleppo, Mosul, and Baghdad, were the main centers of government and were often the only areas under government control. In the absence of territorial states, fertile crescent societies were fragmented into family, tribal, ethnic, linguistic, religious, guild, and residential communities. Reinforcing this diversity, European influences had different impacts in different parts of the region. In the eighteenth and nineteenth centuries European trade stimulated the economic changes that led to the formation of new elites. European cultural and educational influences helped give rise to a new "nationalist" political consciousness, and European intervention created the divisions into national states that have lasted to the present day.

As early as the eighteenth century European influences stimulated important changes in the Maronite Church. Until the middle of the eighteenth century, the church had been in the control of lay Maronite landlords who appointed the Patriarch and the bishops. Eighteenth-century reformers, led by churchmen educated in Rome, attempted to free the church from lay control. The reformers established a system of church schools and attempted to propagandize the populace in favor of a church-led Maronite government. The political consequences of the Maronite revival were formidable. In 1820 there was a peasant revolt against the feudal landlords. The Maronite movement led also to increasing tension with the Druzes, who, in response to Maronite pressure, became more organized and unified. The policies of Bashir II (1788–1840), overlord of Lebanon, polarized the situation. Bashir tried to centralize power and eliminate his rivals, mainly Druze chieftains. He defeated the Druzes in 1825, and cooperated with the Egyptian invasion of Syria and Lebanon in 1831. In 1840, however, Britain and France intervened to evict the Egyptians. Bashir was removed from power, but the Maronites and Druzes remained divided and the country was ungovernable. There were Maronite–Druze wars in 1838, 1841–42, and 1845.

The Ottomans established a new government in 1843, but it lasted only until 1858, when the Maronite populace again rebelled against its feudal lords. Druze–Muslim wars against the Maronites resumed in 1859 and 1860. In 1861 the European powers forced the Ottomans to recognize Christian predominance. Under new regulations, the head of government, or *mutasarrif*, was to be a Christian, while a governing council represented the other religious communities. Lebanon became a privileged province within the Ottoman empire, with the European powers guaranteeing its security.

European influence in regional politics was accompanied by direct educational efforts. France sponsored a vigorous educational program. French Jesuits established a school at Aintura in 1728 and Maronite colleges were established at Zigharta (1735) and Ayn Warqa (1789). The Syrian Protestant College, which eventually became the American University of Beirut, was founded in 1866. Zahleh, Damascus, and Aleppo acquired new schools between 1839 and 1873. The French-sponsored University of St. Joseph was established in 1875.

In the nineteenth century trade between Europe, Lebanon, and its Syrian hinterland played a part in the complex process that led to the integration of the Levant into the world economy. Foreign trade stimulated the production of cash crops such as silk, cotton, soap, leather, and cereals wherever they could easily be transported to the coast. After 1860 Beirut flourished as an exporting center. Palestinian output and exports of cereals, fruits, olives, soap, textiles, and leather also grew with increased political control over bedouins, and because new lands were brought into cultivation. In Jabal Nablus merchant and money-lending elites and rich peasants broke the hold of old sub-district rural chiefs and their clienteles on the society. The middle peasantry increased its holdings, and eventually moved to the towns. Soap production from olive oil became the premier industry, and gave the town dominance over the surrounding countryside. The shift from textiles to olive oil linked Nablus, via Beirut, to the world economy. In Lebanon, rising population and greater economic specialization allowed silk weavers to enhance their position. Other products, such as Syrian cloths woven with silver and gold threads, which could not be imitated in Europe, maintained their hold on a specialized market. However, many craftsmen succumbed to European competition. Christian merchants active in the import–export trade became the protégés of Europeans and gained an advantage over Muslims.

These foreign commercial, educational, and religious influences, rather than internal political and economic reforms, led to the formation of a new literary intelligentsia. What the Tanzimat had done in Turkey, and what economic change did in Egypt, Western education did in Lebanon. A small vanguard took the lead in formulating a cultural renaissance. Educated Arabs became aware, not only of the West, but of their own literary heritage. The early figures in the literary revival, such as Nasif Yaziji and Butrus Bustani, were Christian-Arab writers. Bustani was a Maronite, educated at the seminary of Ayn Warqa, who compiled a dictionary to revive interest in the Arabic language. These early publicists disseminated their views through cultural and national associations, such as the Society of Arts and Sciences founded in 1847 and the Syrian Scientific Society founded in 1857, to foster the study of Arabic literature and the recollection of the glory of the Arab past. The early Arab literary thinkers also stressed modernization and reform. Their newspapers and journals presented Western European scientific and political ideas. Government, they preached, should be conducted in the interest of the governed, and provide for just and regular taxation, education, and legal reform.

By the turn of the century the intellectual revival had turned into political unrest, based upon strong anti-Turkish feeling and a strong sense of the superiority of Arab to Turkish peoples. Al-Kawakibi (1849–1903) was one of the first Arab writers to say that Arabs must take the leadership of the Muslim world from the corrupted Turks. The new literary attitude may have been promoted by a conspiracy for the restoration of the Caliphate in the person of the Sharif of Mecca, the custodian of the holy places. Behind this revival of Arab sensibility lay Islamic religious feelings channeled into pro-Arab sentiments. Arabs, after all, were the first people of Islam. The Quran was revealed in Arabic, and the glorious days of the early Islamic empires were Arab glories. Finally, Christian-Arab writers put forward the idea of secession from the Ottoman empire. Negib Azoury called for the formation of a secular Arab state in which Christians and Muslims would be equal citizens under a constitutional regime.

For very different reasons, and at a later date, Arab nationalism also took root among the Muslim notables of Damascus. Here the primary factors were not political autonomy and commercial penetration, but the very operation of the Ottoman system and a Muslim reaction against growing European – and local Christian – commercial success. Before 1860 the Damascus notables were primarily 'ulama' descended from prominent eighteenth-century families who supplied the officials for the religious posts of mufti, *khatib* (preacher), and Syndic of the Descendants of the Prophet. They also managed the waqfs, and had strong support from merchants, artisans, janissaries, and the town quarters. In the late eighteenth and nineteenth centuries these families were joined by military chieftains (*aghawat*), whose power was based on janissary clienteles, and on control of suburban quarters and the grain trade that went through them. By the late nineteenth century 'ulama' and aghawat families had merged into a combined religious and landowning elite. Rich merchants and Ottoman office-holders were also part of this elite. By this time many families were sending their sons to Ottoman professional schools and were competing for places in the Ottoman government service. The notables, however, were not a unified body, but were divided into competing families and factions.

The position of the notables was challenged but not overturned by state programs of centralization, or Tanzimat. The Egyptian occupation of Syria (1831–39) attempted to overcome local independence, establish a centralized government, and promote economic development. Ibrahim Pasha, the son of Muhammad 'Ali, attempted to disarm the local population, and introduced conscription, corvée, and a new head tax. He established monopolies for the production of silk, cotton, and tobacco, and began mining for coal. When Syria was returned to Ottoman suzerainty in 1841, the Ottomans tried to centralize power, eliminate the intermediary notables, and mobilize mass support for the state. They planned to secularize the judicial system and introduce formal equality among Muslims and non-Muslims. Yet, to offset the power of governors, they created local councils (*majlis*) and gave the notables important fiscal and administrative powers. Already threatened by European commercial competition, the growing role of Christians and Jews as intermediaries in trade with Europe, and the beginning of Christian and Jewish money lending in rural areas, the Damascus notables were hostile to Ottoman reforms.

The rise of the Ottoman Committee for Union and Progress in 1908 pushed some of the Damascus notables into adopting the Arabist intellectual and political currents of the day. The new Ottoman government first inspired great hopes, but CUP efforts to centralize power in the hands of Turks disappointed Arab leaders. In Damascus the imposition of Turkish as the language of schools and courts, Turkish controls over waqfs, and the dismissal of local officials blocked the careers and cultural self-expression of educated Arab officials, and led to the adoption of Arabism as the expression of opposition to secularization and Turkish rule. Just before and during World War I Arabism became the ideology of Damascus notables, military officers, lawyers, and those 'ulama' who were out of government favor. Arabism before 1918, however, did not mean political independence. Arab leaders generally favored an Arab–Turkish ruling condominium on the model of the Austro-Hungarian empire, and other schemes for decentralization and Arab equality.

A third current in the formation of Arabism came from Arabia. In 1915, Husayn, the Sharif of Mecca, entered secret negotiations with the British to promote an Arab revolt against Ottoman rule in Syria and Arabia. Husayn hoped, with British help, to overthrow the Ottomans and become king of an Arab state. His ambition was based upon his religious prestige as Sharif, or descendant of the Prophet, and custodian of the holy places, and upon some earlier conspiracies to make him the new Caliph of the Islamic world. Husayn carefully tried to rally Arab national and literary sentiment to his side by cultivating al-Fatat, a secret society in Damascus, which had approached him to sound out his interest in an independent Arab state allied with Britain. Britain in turn saw that Husayn could be helpful militarily and politically. Thus in a famous letter of October 1915, Sir Henry McMahon, the British High Commissioner in Egypt, implied that the British would recognize an independent Arab state, except for Lebanon and unspecified French interests. In June 1916, Husayn was declared King and attempted to seize the Hijaz. He waged guerrilla warfare against the Turks with the help of British agents and military advisors, including T. E. Lawrence. His forces took 'Aqaba in July 1917. Together the British and the Arabs took Damascus. By the end of the war, the British were in control of most of the Near East, while Faysal, the son of Husayn, established himself as governor of Damascus under British auspices. Faysal, supported by Syrian notables, demanded that the British recognize him as the monarch of an independent Arab state.

The Arab attempt to establish an independent state was aborted by the European powers. The British were not really committed to Husayn. By the Sykes–Picot agreement with France (1916), they had promised to partition the Arab Near East into two zones of direct colonial rule and two spheres of influence, and in 1917, by the Balfour Declaration, they promised to establish a Jewish national home in Palestine. In response to Husayn's protests, Great Britain assured him that the political as well as the civil and religious rights of Arabs would be protected, and in other declarations promised to assist in the formation of independent states based on the consent of the governed. At the conference of San Remo in April 1920, Britain and France nonetheless divided the Arab world in accord with the Sykes–Picot agreement. The allies created four dependent states – Iraq, Syria, Lebanon, and Palestine. France took control of Lebanon and Syria and ousted Faysal from Damascus; Britain took control of Iraq and Palestine. In 1922 Palestine was divided to create a fifth state – Transjordan. The new colonies were legitimized as mandates of the League of Nations. The turmoil surrounding the creation of these states – petitions, demonstrations, festivals, party activities, and the formation of committees of national defense – mobilized merchants, 'ulama', and street gangs whose involvement in politics was the basis of later concepts of nationalism.

Thus, as opposed to Turkey and Egypt, the British and the French, rather than local elites, held complete sway over the formation of the Arab fertile crescent states. Arab resistance was scarcely conceivable. The Arab national movement was too weak and divided to affect the fortunes of the region. Its literary wing was barely coming to political consciousness; the Arab revolt led by Sharif Husayn did not represent the modernist aspirations of the intellectuals in Lebanon and Syria. The Damascus notables were divided by faction, party, and competition for power.

While Arab ethnic and linguistic pride – and claims for autonomy or an equal place in the Ottoman empire – had been expressed, no Arab leader had a clear image of the political future. Rather, there were competing tendencies toward decentralization, toward a single Arab state, and toward regional states. In a society that had virtually no history of independent states and no history of internal institutional or economic reform, a national political movement could not but be immature. Thus the British and the French created the Arab states, gave them territorial boundaries and central regimes, and bequeathed to the future the dilemma of a cultural region partitioned into numerous small states.

ARABISM IN THE COLONIAL PERIOD

From the 1920s to the 1950s each of these states (apart from Palestine, which had special problems, to be considered shortly) was caught up in a double political struggle. Each attempted to win independence from its French or British colonial overlord, and within each there was a growing struggle for power between a dominant older-generation conservative elite and rising younger elites. Out of these struggles came political independence in the late 1940s and a conjoined domestic and international crisis over political leadership and ideological identity in the 1950s.

In the mandate period each country was in the control of a foreign power allied to a conservative domestic political elite. In Iraq, a monarch, Ottoman and Sharifian officers in the service of Faysal, and landowners and tribal chiefs composed the political elite. In Syria it included landowners, merchants, and religious leaders. In Transjordan the palace household of the Amir and the local bedouin chiefs governed the country. Lebanon was governed by the traditional landowning and sectarian bosses. The Arab population of Palestine had its clan and religious spokesmen.

In each country the political elites accepted the mandate system. Their proximate goal was the consolidation of central governments, despite the inherent fragmentation of the population into numerous tribal, ethnic, or sectarian communities; their long-term goal was independence from Britain and France. To institutionalize the newly created states, they tried to turn Arab nationalism into state-centered – Syrian, Iraqi, Lebanese – nationalism, an ideology that would define and legitimize existing states, help integrate non-Muslim minorities into the political systems, express the state structures in terms of a modern form of political identity, and justify their claim to independence from the colonial powers.

While the ruling elites appropriated the term "Arab nationalism," Arab intellectuals and educators kept alive the idea of a unified Arab nation. They defined this nation in terms of a shared language, history, and culture that could overcome the division of Arab peoples into tribes, regions, religions, and states. Sati al-Husri (1880–1968), an Iraqi Arab nationalist and educator, preached the need for unity and willingness to sacrifice parochial interests to the cause of the nation as a whole. Michel Aflaq, the founder of the Ba'th Party, gave the most romantic expression to this idea.

He defined nationalism by the Arab word *qawmiya,* which means "belonging to a group," and implies a total absorption of the individual in the nation. Only through the nation can the individual achieve true freedom and a higher mode of existence. Through solidarity and love of the nation, Arab peoples would not only realize their political objectives but attain the highest spiritual fulfillment:

> The nationalism for which we call is love before everything else. It is the very same feeling that binds the individual to his family, because the fatherland is only a large household, and the nation a large family. Nationalism, like every kind of love, fills the heart with joy and spreads hope in the soul; he who feels it would wish to share with all the people this joy which raises him above narrow egotism, draws him nearer to goodness and perfection ... It is, then, the best way to a true humanity.[1]

This appeal to romantic unity was akin to a religious mood, and pan-Arab rhetoric was suffused with words such as umma (the brotherhood of Muslims) and milla (religious community, used to mean nation). Even the mystical concept of fana', loss of self and union with the divine being, was borrowed to express the bond of the individual to the nation. Pan-Arabism was a call to overcome pluralism and worldly interests. It was a secular version of Islam. In the minds of many people, Arab nationalism and Islam could not be differentiated.

This kind of Arab nationalism appealed most profoundly to the younger generation intelligentsia of military officers, administrators, technocrats, and intellectuals. To administer the new countries, the dominant landlord, merchant, tribal, and religious elites needed people to staff the army, the administration, the schools, and the governments' technical services, and thus opened up a channel for youngsters of middle and lower middle class, often of minority backgrounds, to receive an education and a prominent place in the new nations. In Syria, 'Alawis, Druzes, Isma'ilis, and Christians went to high schools and military colleges. In Baghdad, Sunni Arabs followed this route. As in the case of the Ottoman empire and Egypt in the nineteenth century, the reorganization and centralization of state authority, the provision of modern education, and a small degree of economic and social change led to mobility from villages to cities and from rural to urban occupations. As in the nineteenth-century Ottoman empire, control of the apparatus of violence, educational achievement, technical sophistication, political awareness, social grievances against the ruling elites, and strong ambitions for personal and national glory gave the military a dominant position. This new generation also adopted the national ideology because nationalism gave identity to people uprooted from local communities and legitimized the struggle against foreign rule in terms recognized as valid by the colonial powers themselves. The new elites were determined to seize control of the state in the name of domestic reform, anti-colonialism, and Arab nationalism.

---

[1] Quoted in S. Haim, ed., *Arab Nationalism: An Anthology,* Berkeley: University of California Press, 1976, p. 242.

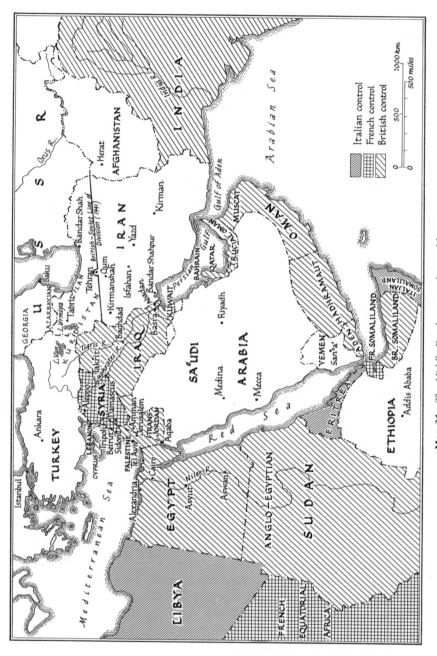

Map 31 The Middle East between the world wars

Syria in the colonial period

Syria is a principal example of the generational and ideological conflict within the Arab societies. In Syria the French secured public order, built roads and communications networks, and established the administrative infrastructure of a modern state. The French accelerated the sedentarization of the bedouins, which had begun in the late nineteenth century under the Ottomans, expanded cultivated territories at the expense of pastoralism, and converted bedouins into peasants and chiefs into landlords. After World War I the bedouins were further hemmed in by states, settlers, and roads and by heavy investment by city merchants and tribal shaykhs in land reclamation and cultivation.

In order to maintain effective administration, and to inhibit the development of a movement for independence, the French also divided Syria into ethnic and religious districts. Lebanon was made into a separate state. Latakia, which was predominantly populated by poverty-stricken 'Alawi peasants dominated by Sunni landlords, was made into a separate administrative district. The Druze areas of southern Syria, and the Jazira, the plains of northern Syria and the Euphrates region, were given regional autonomy. Alexandretta received special status because of its substantial Turkish minority, and was annexed by Turkey in 1939. Thus, France established the framework of a modern Syrian state but then reinforced ethnic and religious divisions to inhibit the formation of a cohesive national society.

Starting in the 1930s and continuing into the period of independence, the conservative elites were opposed by young army officers of middle-class backgrounds, educated in the military academy of Homs, and by Western-educated intellectuals and politicians. The most important expression of the younger generation was the Ba'th Party. The Ba'th was founded in the 1940s by Michel Aflaq and Salah al-Din Bitar, two Syrian schoolteachers educated in Paris in the 1930s. They developed a doctrine of Arab unity, social justice, democracy, and freedom. They were anti-colonialists in international orientation and socialists in domestic programs. They espoused not only a political doctrine but also a mystical feeling for the rejuvenation of the unified Arab nation. In 1949 they were joined by Akram al-Hawrani, a socialist agitator and organizer of revolts in Homs, and a conspirator with close contacts in the army.

The weakening of France in World War II opened the way to Syrian independence in 1947, and the new regime was immediately beset by a series of military coups which progressively transferred power from the old generation to the new. The process of forming a new political regime, however, was not to be completed without a protracted domestic and international crisis in the mid-1950s and early 1960s.

Iraq to 1958

Iraq was carved out of the Ottoman empire, and had a similar generational and national history. During the Ottoman period pastoralism had displaced sedentary agriculture, especially in the upper Euphrates region, the Diyala region, and in southern Iraq. In the nineteenth century the Ottoman state started the process of reducing the power of tribal chiefs. The land code of 1858 created a system that assured persons in possession of title deeds ownership of the land. These title deeds were acquired by city-dwelling merchants, tax-farmers, and some tribal leaders, who thus wrested control of the land from the tribesmen.

When the British conquered Iraq in 1917, they ruled it as a colony on the Indian model. In 1920, a revolt of Ottoman officials and landlords, Sunni and Shi'i religious leaders, and tribal groups forced them to include the Iraqi elites. The British set up a constitutional monarchy under Sharif Husayn's son Faysal, to whom they felt obligated because of his help in the war. An Anglo-Iraqi treaty of 1922 gave the British control of military, financial, judicial, and foreign affairs. In 1930, a new treaty made Iraq legally independent but allowed Britain continued control over foreign and military affairs.

British administrators helped create the infrastructure of a modern state. The British consolidated the late Ottoman land system by using rural and tribal shaykhs to take charge of tax collection and labor organization. Under the monarchy, Iraq was run by a small coalition of rural landowners, tribal chiefs, 'ulama', Shi'i religious leaders, and army officers – the latter including Ottoman officers educated in Istanbul, Sharifian officers in the service of Faysal before his arrival in Iraq, and Iraqis educated in the Baghdad Military Academy. This elite, however, was deeply divided. Between 1936 and 1941 there were a number of military coups, and World War II brought bitter struggles between pro-British and pro-German factions. In 1941 Rashid 'Ali al-Gaylani took control of the government in the interest of a pro-German policy, but British troops seized the country. From then until 1958 the King governed, often with the collaboration of his principal minister, Nuri al-Sa'id, and a small minority of landowners, 2 percent of whom owned 66 percent of the land. In the name of Arab nationalism, this elite, predominantly of Sunni background, governed a populace that was then about half Shi'i and one-fourth Kurdish.

Here too, the dominance of the old elite was challenged by a new generation of soldiers, intellectuals, and workers thrown up by a changed economy. The appropriation of land by the shaykhs and the breakup of tribal communities drove large numbers of people to the cities. A new urban generation of lower-ranking officials, junior army officers, textile workers, and displaced peasants hostile to the entrenched regime took form. The army became the effective center of the opposition. Until 1958, the regime contained this growing opposition by proposals for extensive development programs, but it did not survive to carry them out. An army coup brought an end to the monarchy in 1958.

Transjordan and Jordan

Transjordan was, even more than Iraq, a British creation. It was the most "unnatural" of the new states, corresponding to no historical province or local community. Originally it was thought to be implied in the Balfour Declaration's promise of

Palestine as a Jewish homeland, but in 1922 the British allowed Amir 'Abdallah, a brother of Faysal, to establish a government. They built up the Arab Legion and provided subsidies. Thus, the British honored their commitment to the Hashimite family and also reduced their commitment to the Zionists. A 1928 treaty established a constitutional monarchy, a legislature, and political parties, but reserved for Britain control over foreign policy and the army. In 1946 Transjordan became independent, though a treaty of 1948 reserved for Britain the right to maintain bases there. Between 1948 and 1950, as a result of the Arab–Israeli war, Transjordan absorbed parts of Palestine and was reorganized as the Kingdom of Jordan. By 1950, the state of Jordan comprised two totally different populations: the bedouins and farmers on the eastern bank of the Jordan; and, on the western side, the Palestinian population, including refugees and inhabitants of the West Bank. In order to establish an effective state, the constitution of 1952 gave representation to both elements in a new parliament. A National Guard was formed, comprising Palestinian villagers, and was later integrated into the Arab Legion.

Throughout this period Jordan was governed by a king, an elite of British army officers, Palestinian-Arab officials, Circassian palace servants, and Muslim religious leaders. In Jordan, as opposed to Iraq, the influence of tribal chiefs was rapidly reduced. While the traditional society of Transjordan was based on kinship and tribal groups, the development of the central state reduced the functions of the tribal chiefs and deprived them of their clienteles and military power. A new middle class of government officials, clerks, teachers, and merchants helped to break down their influence. By 1950, they had ceased to be a threat to the authority of the state and the army. However, in Jordan, as elsewhere, the educated middle class became a source of opposition to the governing elite. The army remained loyal to the state; the opposition was built on the intelligentsia and the Palestinians. While military-socialist regimes came to power in Egypt, Syria, and Iraq, in Jordan the opposition was defeated in 1958 with the help of British paratroopers. The regime was consolidated by the defeat of a Palestinian uprising in September 1970. King Husayn, who ruled from 1952 until his death in 1999, was succeeded by his son 'Abdallah. The regime is still based on military and bureaucratic elites, wealthy merchants, and East Bank tribal leaders, and the opposition comes from the Muslim Brothers, who are loyal to the King, but consider the liberation of all of Palestine a religious duty and reject all peace initiatives, and from more radical Islamist groups, often Palestinian. Jordan survives on American economic aid, and the balance of power among its Arab neighbors.

Lebanon

In Lebanon the struggle was not so much between generations or among military, landowning, and intellectual elites as among local political bosses and religious communities. On the eve of national state formation, Lebanon was governed by the *zu'ama'*, or bosses, usually local landowners and religious leaders, whose powers were based on the control of the peasants and on patron–client networks. The modern state of Lebanon, like Syria, was a French creation. Though France had a long history of close relations with the Maronite population, the French did not create a purely Christian state. To the old province of Lebanon, new districts, including Tripoli, Sidon, the Biqa', and South Lebanon, were added to increase the total size of the country and the proportion of Muslims. Lebanon was initially governed by a French High Commissioner, but in 1926 a new constitution divided political power among the major religious communities. It provided for a president, a ministerial government, and a bicameral legislature, in which seats were distributed in a ratio of 6:5 for Christians and Muslims. By agreement, the President would always be a Maronite, the Prime Minister a Sunni, and the head of parliament a Shi'a. Foreign affairs would be in the hands of a Christian minister; the army would be headed by a Maronite, with Muslim or Druze subalterns. The division of power was based upon dubious census data. Furthermore, the state institutions were designed to reinforce sectarian divisions rather than integrate Lebanese society. Government agencies did not build national services, but rather subsidized sectarian schools, courts, and charities. Political parties in Lebanon were expressions of the zu'ama', and popular loyalties were channeled to the leaders of clienteles rather than to the state as such.

From 1920 to 1945 Lebanon was governed on the basis of compromise among sectarian and communal bosses. In the mandate period the bosses were linked up in two main political parties: the National Bloc was substantially Maronite Christian and favored independence, but resisted ties with other Arab nationalists; the Constitutional Bloc favored close relations with Syria. In 1943 the Lebanese factions agreed on a National Pact in which the Christians and Muslims deemphasized outside political ties, whether French or Arab, for the sake of greater internal cooperation. Thus the way was prepared for the formation of an independent regime in 1945. The postwar regime continued to be based upon the allocation of government powers and resources among the bosses and confessional groups. The state existed to maintain the balance of power among them, and from 1947 to 1958 the country was ruled by a succession of coalition governments.

THE STRUGGLE FOR ARAB UNITY AND THE CONTEMPORARY FERTILE CRESCENT STATES

By the end of World War II the Arab fertile crescent states had each become an independent nation, though their future ideological and political character was yet to be determined. In each country domestic elites were still engaged in a struggle for power, but in the late 1940s and 1950s these struggles would be vastly complicated by Arab-world and global conflicts. The Arab–Israel war of 1947–48, the establishment of the state of Israel, the struggle for supremacy among Egypt and other Arab states, the drive for Arab unity, the advent of the cold war, and the maneuvering of the great powers all interacted with domestic issues to define the identity of the contemporary Arab states.

Apart from the struggles of older- and younger-generation elites, the most important factor in the postwar period was the drive toward Arab unity. While the movement for Arab unity had its origins in the pre-World War I Arab nationalist movement and in the brief and abortive effort of Faysal to establish an Arab kingdom in Damascus, with the formation of the Arab state system after World War I the concept of a single Arab nation and state survived only in the keeping of intellectuals and ideologues. It was revived in the late 1930s by the outbreak of the Arab revolt in Palestine. Between 1936 and 1939 Palestinian peasants carried on a double struggle against Jewish colonization and British rule which mobilized widespread support in Egypt and the fertile crescent countries. Also, on the eve of World War II, Britain renewed its efforts to win Arab support by declaring itself in favor of a union of Arab countries. Egypt took up pan-Arabism as a vehicle for the assertion of Egyptian leadership in the Arab-speaking Middle East. In 1945 the League of Arab States was founded under Egyptian patronage, with an Egyptian secretary-general and headquarters in Cairo. However, the Hashimite rulers of Iraq and Transjordan had their own schemes for Arab unification, and resisted Egyptian hegemony. For all practical purposes the League foundered over its failure to prevent the formation of the state of Israel in 1948.

The cause of Arab unity, however, was revived in the 1950s. By then it had been taken up by Nasser in Egypt, by the Ba'th Party in Syria, and by other elements of the new postwar Arab intelligentsia, as the banner of united opposition to Israel, to colonial and post-colonial domination by foreign powers, and to conservative domestic elites who stood in the way of social reform and economic development. Inspired by Nasser's charismatic leadership, the struggle for power in each of the fertile crescent countries was now waged in the name of Arab unity. In Egypt Nasser and the Free Officers came to power in 1952 and launched their socialist policies in the late 1950s. In Syria the Ba'th Party took power in the late 1950s and 1960s. In Iraq a coup d'état overthrew the monarchy and brought a military regime to power in 1958. In Lebanon and Jordan, however, American and British intervention helped defeat the opposition and kept the established regimes intact.

The domestic struggles were entangled in big-power rivalries. At the end of World War II Britain and France were no longer able to maintain their Middle Eastern positions, and had to concede the independence of the fertile crescent states. The United States and the Soviet Union emerged as the principal competitors for regional influence, and in the 1950s the United States attempted to align Britain, Turkey, Iran, Pakistan, and the Arab countries in an American-sponsored treaty organization. The United States was supported by Nuri al-Sa'id, the Prime Minister of Iraq, who proposed bringing the other Arab states into line. In January 1955 he and Adnan Menderes of Turkey proclaimed the Baghdad Pact. Egypt and Syria, however, opposed the Iraqi initiative, and did not want to accept American aid. After the Israeli attack on the Sinai in February 1955, Nasser emerged as the leader of the Arab struggle against imperialism and Zionism. All the Arab countries were swept by a wave of sentiment in favor of Arab unity.

The crisis of the 1950s gave the new regimes in Egypt, Syria, and Iraq their political and ideological identity. In each country the new dominant force was a military elite legitimized by its formal commitments to Arab national independence, and state-guided modernization of the economy. The political consciousness of these elites, formed in the 1950s and 1960s, was anti-imperialist, anti-Israel, and neutralist in international politics. They adopted socialist regimes which were in accord with the rejection of Western imperialism, with the support given to underdeveloped countries by the Soviet Union and its allies, and with the need to reject the previous generation that had failed to make national economic and social progress. Nevertheless, the crisis did not lead to Arab unity. Despite their common interest, the rivalries among Egypt, Syria, and Iraq prevented Arab unification.

This phase of Arab nationalism ended with the defeat of the Arab states in the June 1967 war with Israel. Nasser's leadership was discredited. The Arab states were condemned as ineffectual, and the idea of Arab unity lost its political appeal. Egypt abandoned the Palestinian cause, made peace with Israel, and allied itself with the United States and with the conservative Arabian states. The Ba'th Party in Syria and Iraq gave up the goal of Arab unity in favor of power in each separate country. In the 1970s Arabism came to be associated with oil and the economic wealth of the Gulf states and Sa'udi Arabia. A period of disillusionment with nationalism, national states, socialism, and secularism set in, and a new climate of opinion favored the reassertion of Muslim values and identities.

Syria

In many respects the new regimes in Syria and Iraq resembled that of Egypt. They were strongly authoritarian military regimes with organized bureaucratic and one-party political support, and they also depended upon patronage relationships between the leaders and a favored clientele. They subscribed to populist Arab nationalist ideologies. At the outset both adopted socialist or state-centered policies of economic development. Development not controlled, sponsored, or manipulated by the state was inhibited. In neither state were independent political parties, labor unions, or student groups allowed. In both, religiously based opposition was crushed. The Syrian and Iraqi states are different from Egypt in that neither is based upon a preexisting national society. Syria is about two-thirds Sunni Muslim, but there are strong 'Alawi, Druze, Isma'ili, and Christian minorities. Iraq is divided among a Shi'i majority (some 60 percent) and two large minorities, one Kurdish (about 20 percent) and one Sunni Arab (about 20 percent). While the Egyptian government has a broad popular base, the governments of Syria and Iraq are drawn from minority groups, and even from a limited number of families and clients within these minorities.

Since the upheavals of the 1950s, the fortunes of Syria have been shaped by the Ba'th Party and military regime. In the mid-1950s the Ba'th promoted union with Egypt to form the United Arab Republic (1958–61), a disastrous move which destroyed the civilian leadership of the party and allowed the army to take power in 1963. Since then, despite changes of personnel, Syria has been governed by a regime of army officers, and from 1966 to 2000 by only one man, Hafiz al-Asad.

To create the new regime the Ba'th Party pursued a socialist program. Agrarian reform began in 1958 with the dismantling of large estates and the limitation of ownership to a maximum of 50 hectares of irrigated and 300 hectares of unirrigated land. In 1961, lands were expropriated and redistributed to peasants. In 1966, the socialization of agriculture began in earnest, with the formation of agricultural collectives, a state monopoly of cotton production, and the beginning of the Tebke dam project which is expected to bring 640,000 hectares of reclaimed land in the Euphrates basin into cultivation. To break the patron–client ties of peasants to landlords and urban-based money lenders, new cooperatives and a peasants' union were established, which gave the state direct control of the population. The revolution, however, was not complete, for a substantial portion of the land remained in the control of rich peasants, landlords, and urban investors. These measures were followed by the nationalization of industry and commerce in 1965. Electricity, oil distribution, cotton ginning, and most foreign trade were taken under government control. Finally, in its program to defeat competing elites, the Ba'thi state took control of waqfs and appointments to religious offices.

The regime also attempted to overcome the inherent familial, ethnic, and religious factionalism of the country by creating a mass Leninist-type political machine based on middle- and lower-middle-class youths, often from rural areas, recruited from minority Isma'ilis, Christians, and 'Alawis. The party cadres monopolized officer positions in the army, government jobs, agricultural and village cooperatives, and youth organizations. Thus, the regime incorporated the minorities, broke the power of the old elites by creating new patronage networks, and extended party domination to all of Syrian society.

The creation of a mass society, however, was constrained by intra-elite struggles for power which drove the regime toward a minority- and clientele-based apparatus. Between 1963 and 1970 the army officers eliminated the civilian Ba'th Party ideologues. From 1970 until his death in 2000 Hafiz al-Asad governed the country, diminished the importance of the party, and opened new channels to political power through the army, the praetorian guard units, and the police and intelligence services, which he directly controlled. The state relied more and more on factional loyalties, especially from the 'Alawis, and within the 'Alawi community, from specific families and "tribes."

The 'Alawis are a sectarian minority considered Muslim by some Muslims but heretics by others. They were predominantly poor peasants, living in northern Syria and indentured to wealthy Sunni, Christian, or 'Alawi landowners who lived in the towns and collected rents in the villages. Many 'Alawis became involved in revolutionary movements in the inter-war years and others entered the Syrian army when the French promoted the minorities as a mechanism for controlling the majority Muslim population. Finally, 'Alawis came to power in the 1960s and 1970s under the aegis of Hafiz al-Asad.

The Syrian economy was flexibly managed to reinforce the regime. In the late 1960s and early 1970s the public sector failed to generate the resources needed to finance the state, but deficit spending financed by foreign loans and a liberalization of the economy led to a trade boom in the 1970s. By the late 1980s economic expansion led to a payments deficit, serious inflation, and a partial collapse. This politicized and fitful management of the economy favored party members and government workers, and many peasants regardless of confessional affiliation, and served to coopt 'Alawi, Aleppin, and Damascene merchants, but economic development was in the main subordinated to political objectives. Domestic investment was limited, and self-sustaining economic growth has not been achieved.

In this centralized, secular, and socialist Arab state dominated by an 'Alawi minority and its powerful military and intelligence apparatus, the majority of the population is Sunni Muslim. Islam is not mentioned in the constitutions of 1950 or 1973, and President Asad refused to officially declare Islam the religion of the state. However, it is acknowledged that the head of state must be a Muslim, and the Shari'a is embodied in the 1953 Syrian law of personal status. Religiously defined Sunni opposition has surfaced in the form of the Society of Muslim Brothers, founded in Aleppo and Damascus in the 1930s. As in Egypt, the Muslim Brothers appeal to the "old bazaar" shopkeepers, artisans, craftsmen, and their modern-educated student and intelligentsia offspring. Operating as a political party in the Syrian elections of 1961, the Muslim Brothers won 5.8 percent of the national vote and 17.6 percent of the Damascus vote. In the 1960s and 1970s, however, the Muslim Brothers turned from electoral politics to civil disobedience and armed resistance. From mid-1979 to late 1981, in response to the Syrian government's intervention against the Palestinians in Lebanon, rising inflation, and the general decline of Sunni political influence, they launched guerrilla attacks and then large-scale uprisings in Aleppo and Hama. In Hama the trigger for the resistance was the establishment of new industries in competition with local merchants, and the settlement of 'Alawi peasants in a Sunni region. These revolts were ruthlessly crushed, with widespread destruction of the historical parts of Hama. Since then there has not been notable resistance to the regime from either Sunnis or the Muslim Brothers. Thus the Islamic movement in Syria was essentially an urban reaction against a rural-based regime, an expression of Sunni hostility to 'Alawis, and a rebellion of the governed against the governing elite. It was supported by merchants and artisans, 'ulama', landowners, and other notables dispossessed by the Ba'th.

Since the advent of Hafiz al-Asad, Syria's foreign policy has turned upon complicated considerations. From 1955 until 1989 the mainstay of Syrian policy was its alliance with the Soviet Union and its consistent hostility to Israel. Syria took the line that the Arab states must mobilize to defeat and dismantle the state of Israel, and expel the European population. The only way to do this, Asad recognized, was for the Arab states to come abreast of Israel in economic, military, and organizational capacities. Syria's support for cross-border attacks upon Israel were among the critical precipitating factors in the 1967 war in which Syria lost the Golan Heights. The loss of the Golan remains to the present the central problem in Syrian–Israeli relations. Nonetheless, Syrian policy after 1967 was also carefully calculated to void premature hostilities. Syria has never permitted the Palestine Liberation Organization (PLO) to attack Israel from its territory. Syria intervened in the Lebanese civil war (1975–91), partly to forestall the emergence of a PLO-dominated Lebanon which might drag Syria into a premature war with Israel, and partly to forestall the possibility of a Lebanese–Iraqi alliance against Syria.

The collapse of the Soviet Union in 1989 led to a reorientation of Syrian foreign policy. The withdrawal of Russian military and financial support made it impossible to sustain an energetic anti-Israel policy. The formation of a USA-led coalition of Arab and European states to defeat Iraq in the Gulf War (1991) also made plain the shift to American, Egyptian, and Arabian political hegemony in the region. Hafiz al-Asad adapted himself to these new circumstances by joining the anti-Iraq coalition, pacifying Lebanon, and entering into talks with Israel over the Golan Heights. Syria, however, did not come to an agreement with Israel, and has tried to avoid decisive commitments.

The death of Hafiz al-Asad – and the succession of his son Bashar in 2000 – suggests a more relaxed regime, but in a society that is highly factionalized, where the middle classes are relatively weak, and in a situation fraught with the chronic threat of war, the Syrian political system seems locked into place.

Iraq

In many respects the development of Iraq is parallel to that of Syria. Iraq also has a narrowly based, patrimonial and highly authoritarian regime. In Iraq the old regime was also overthrown in the name of pan-Arab nationalism and domestic reform. In July 1958 a group of young army officers led by 'Abd al-Karim Qassim, representing the generation of soldiers, administrators, intellectuals, and ideologues schooled in the nationalist ideals of the 1930s and 1940s, seized power. Their hatred of Iraq's dependence on Great Britain, the Baghdad Pact, and the 1958 effort to form a conservative alliance between Iraq and Jordan precipitated a coup d'état, the execution of the King, and the formation of a Revolutionary Council.

The new regime at first favored conservative reforms in land ownership, free enterprise in industry, and strong state policies to promote health care and education. Its immediate hopes, however, were disappointed. Under Qassim's leadership, it quickly turned into a military dictatorship based on strong Communist Party support. The Ba'th Party, the Muslim Brothers, and other opposition groups were suppressed. The Qassim regime was in turn overthrown by a Ba'th Party coup in 1963, also launched in the name of Arab unity, which set Iraq on its present course. The

Ba'th nationalized the major banks and industries. In 1968 another military coup brought Ahmad Hassan al-Bakr and Saddam Husayn to power. A new constitution declared Iraq part of the Arab nation, an Islamic state, and a socialist society. The regime established in 1968 under Saddam Husayn rules to the present.

His regime is based upon the Sunni minority, and within that minority on people from the town of Takrit, within Takrit upon particular related lineages, and from within these lineages certain families who provide the officers of the government, the Ba'th Party and the Republican Guard. The men closest to Saddam are his handpicked relatives and allies, and they rule the country through the party, security and military apparatus, and by a reign of surveillance and threat. A small cadre of army officers dominates the government and the ambassadorial corps and manages the major industries. Independent lawyers, landowners, and businessmen no longer have a significant part to play in public policy. The new elite comes from middle and lower-middle class, and often conservative Islamic, backgrounds, but it is basically a state elite dependent upon the centralization of military, economic, and educational activities. The elite does not represent the majority Shi'i and substantial Kurdish populations of the country. The Ba'th regime controls all sectors of the society, and has established controls over all aspects of social and economic life. Independent agencies are not tolerated, and government controls are exercised over labor unions, businesses, the civil service, universities, and student and women's groups.

The Ba'th regime also closely controls the economy. Agriculture is regulated by the state. With the establishment of the new military regime in 1958, a program of land reform on the Egyptian model was implemented. Laws were passed to limit ownership of land to 1,000 dunums (250 hectares) of irrigated or 2,000 dunums of unirrigated land and to organize the peasantry into agricultural cooperatives to assure efficient utilization of redistributed lands. This program was successful in expropriating the old landed elite, but only after 1970 were substantial acreages redistributed and peasant cooperatives – later collectives – organized. In the 1970s, however, the main emphasis was shifted to capital-intensive irrigation and the development of mechanized farms financed by the state. The government thus adopted an agricultural policy to bypass the peasant sector. To consolidate its control of agriculture the state resisted tribal ownership of land, peasant unions, and other political forms of rural organization.

Nationalization and government controls have been applied in oil and industrial production. Oil was discovered in Iraq before World War I and was first exploited by the Turkish Petroleum Company, founded in 1912 with German, Dutch, and British participation. In 1929 the company was reorganized as the Iraqi Petroleum Company. In the course of the 1930s new concessions were granted to extend oil exploration, and in 1938 the several companies exploring for oil were merged into a single Iraqi Petroleum Company. In 1952 Iraq obtained an agreement from the international oil companies for a 50–50 share of oil profits. After 1958, the new military regime took a more radical line. In 1961 Iraq revoked the oil concessions, and in 1972 finally nationalized the Iraqi Petroleum Company. Oil production was maintained with Soviet and French help, but Iraq suffered considerable losses as a result of curtailed production.

Supported by the army and by revenues from oil production fully in its control, the state had little incentive for compromise and negotiation. State power was consolidated by a regime of terror. Informers, armed party members, and secret police were pervasive in the society. Political protesters – and also party, bureaucracy, and army members – could be summarily executed for the smallest deviance, hesitation, or suspicion of disloyalty. Political opposition was virtually eliminated. The regime was especially hostile to the Kurds, to whom it denied regional autonomy, a share in economic development, and permission to teach the Kurdish language in Kurdish schools. At the same time, the Ba'thi state managed to create a wide base of public acceptance. In the 1970s and 1980s it provided extensive subsidies for urban middle-class education and health policies, and it used the wars against Iran in the 1980s and the United States during the Gulf War of 1991 and its aftermath to win further public acquiescence.

The state has also tried to generate an Iraqi national identity. Like Egypt and Syria the new regime went through a phase of pan-Arabism. The Ba'th Party, stressing the solidarity of Arab peoples and the Iraqi state, competed with Egypt for leadership in the Arab world. By 1970 the Iraqi regime began to move toward a state-centered national identity. A new emphasis was placed upon the ancient Mesopotamian heritage of Iraq, now considered a pre-Islamic but proto-Arab civilization. Archeology, folklore, poetry, the arts, and local festivals were promoted to enhance a sense of Iraqi separateness. Islam, while retaining the strong allegiance of the population, played little part in public life until the 1990s when the regime shifted to an Islamic rhetoric for its justifications. Islam has also been the rallying call of the opposition. In the 1960s Shi'i 'ulama' formed the Da'wa al-Islamiya (Islamic Mission) to work for an Islamic state and social justice. The more militant Mujahidin (Muslim Warriors) was founded in 1979. Wherever militant opposition emerged, the regime reduced it to sporadic and ineffective terrorism.

In foreign policy Iraq's goal is to restore Arab unity under Iraqi leadership. The two prongs of this policy were competition with Egypt and Syria for Arab world leadership, and the assertion of Iraqi hegemony in the Persian Gulf. The eastern flank of Iraqi policy has led to almost two decades of warfare between Iraq and Iran, and Iraq and Kuwait and its Arab, American, and European allies.

The Iraqi–Kuwaiti problem began with the ambiguities of late Ottoman rule. The Ottomans were the actual suzerains of Iraq, but only de jure suzerains of Kuwait. After 1902 Kuwait was in fact a British protectorate. In 1920 Britain received a League of Nations mandate for both Kuwait and Iraq, and the border between the two was taken to be a line defined by an Ottoman–British treaty of 1913 which had never been ratified. When Kuwait became independent in 1961, Iraq claimed that it was a part of Iraq, and invaded in 1963. British and Sa'udi troops intervened and forced Iraq to desist, but Iraq maintained its claims to small islands in the upper Persian Gulf which were essential to keep open access to sea lanes for oil export. Another border crisis followed in 1975.

Tension with Iran over border problems was equally high. Iraq and Iran had long disputed control of the Shatt al-Arab, the single waterway that merges the Tigris and Euphrates Rivers on the last leg of their journey to the Gulf. In 1975, in return for promises that the Shah would not support Iraqi Kurdish resistance, Iraq conceded that the whole of the waterway was Iranian territory. Then in 1980, taking advantage of the revolutionary chaos in Iran, Iraq attacked western Iran. Iraq wanted to reverse its losses of 1975 and capture control of the oilfields of Khuzistan, an Arab-speaking province in western Iran. The Iraqis also hoped to forestall the spread of Iranian revolutionary influences to the Shi'a of Iraq, and perhaps to topple the Iranian regime. Iraq may have seen the war as a way of asserting Iraqi supremacy in the Gulf region and in the Arab world generally. The war, however, cost almost eight bitter and bloody years of fighting, in which vast numbers of lives were lost on both sides before a stalemate and a truce was reached in 1989.

With the end of the war against Iran, Iraq returned to its claims that Kuwait was part of Iraq, protested Kuwait's refusal to forgive its war loans to Iraq, objected to Kuwaiti drilling under a disputed and demilitarized border zone, and to excessive Kuwaiti oil production which lowered the price of oil in international markets to the detriment of Iraq's revenues. Iraq invaded Kuwait on August 2, 1991 to loot Kuwaiti resources and to gain a controlling influence in Gulf policy. Iraq's extraordinary military preparations, however, including a worldwide network to acquire materials for biological, chemical, and nuclear warfare, implied a threat to dominate Sa'udi Arabia as well. Saddam Husayn justified his invasion as an attack on a backward feudal and tribal elite. He soon linked his invasion to the Palestinian cause, calling for Israeli withdrawal from the West Bank and Gaza in return for withdrawal from Kuwait. Later he attacked Israel with ballistic missiles. Saddam's audacity and the sheer display of power had widespread appeal among Palestinians, many Jordanians, and many Arab intellectuals. He was opposed by Egypt, Syria, Sa'udi Arabia, and the Gulf states, and by a United Nations coalition led by the United States.

American intervention was governed by two considerations. The USA was opposed to any regional concentration of power that might affect long-term access to oil on favorable terms for the USA and other industrialized countries in whose economic viability America had an immediate interest. In 1953 it had helped bring down Premier Mosaddeq of Iran; it had opposed Nasser of Egypt in the 1960s and the revolutionary government of Iran in the 1980s, and now it would oppose Saddam Husayn. The USA was also concerned about the possible proliferation of weapons of mass destruction, thus far possessed only by Israel.

On January 16, 1991 the United Nations coalition launched a rapid and decisive attack on Iraqi forces. Yet the military victory was not pursued to the point of overthrowing Saddam Husayn. At the last moment the coalition forces held back from an attack upon the Republican Guard. Shi'i rebellions in the south and Kurdish rebellions in the north were abandoned by the USA and its allies, and were crushed by Saddam. Most probably the USA and its Arab allies were reluctant to destroy the Iraqi regime lest the country be fragmented. They feared Iranian hegemony over the Shi'i population of southern Iraq, and the potential subversion of Shi'i populations in eastern Arabia and Kuwait. Turkey feared the emergence of an independent Kurdish state in northern Iraq.

The cease-fire of April 1991 imposed an economic embargo and required Iraq to cooperate with a United Nations arms-inspection regime, and to destroy all stockpiles of missiles and weapons of mass destruction. Despite defeat Saddam Husayn maintains unchallenged control of the country. By 2001 the arms-control program had failed, and the embargo was being progressively undermined. Though the salaried urban middle class is ruined, and Iraqis suffer from a badly deteriorated standard of living – from shortages of food and medical supplies, and a high rate of infant mortality – the regime maintains its power based on the military, the intelligence services, the Ba'th Party, and on revived tribal loyalties and a tribalist ideology.

Lebanon

While states were consolidated in Syria, Iraq, and Jordan, Lebanon disintegrated into civil war. The mandate-period constitution of 1926 divided power among the various religious communities – Maronite, Sunni, and Shi'i – but the Lebanese government was never able to centralize power and the country was run by the zu'ama' – the bosses – through their networks of political parties, religious charities, schools, and courts. In 1943 Christian and Muslim bosses agreed to cooperate in the formation of an independent state, and formed a coalition which lasted until 1958. The regime of the bosses, however, did not allow for the rise of new strata in the society, including technocrats and bureaucrats, upwardly mobile lower-middle-class persons – often coming from rural areas to Beirut – or for Arab nationalists and lower-class urban gangs. Moreover, as Muslims became the demographic majority, they demanded a larger share of political power and economic opportunities. In 1958 Arab nationalist, pro-Nasserist elements tried to seize power, but American intervention helped restore the status quo.

In the 1960s and 1970s Lebanon was divided between those who would allow the Palestinians to use Lebanon as a base for the struggle against Israel and those who wanted to restrict Palestinian activities and avoid a confrontation with Israel. The country was polarized between conservative and leftist coalitions. The conservatives included the Phalange and other Maronite groups, and some Shi'a. The Maronite coalition was headed by Pierre Gemayl, the head of the Phalange, and by Camille Chamoun, a former President of Lebanon. Its goal was either to dominate Lebanon or to partition the country and create a Maronite state. This group favored a free-enterprise economy, and non-involvement in the struggle against Israel. Their opponents were an ideologically defined leftist coalition including Muslims, Druzes, Palestinians, and some Christian minorities. Prominent in this group was the Progressive Socialist Party, primarily Druze, led by the Jumblatt family, which supported the Palestinians, a program of socialist development within Lebanon, and neutralism in world affairs. This faction also included the Syrian Social Nationalist Party which was largely Greek Orthodox and conservative, but opposed to the separatism of the Maronites. All of these groups were united by their opposition to the status quo, to the predominance of Christians, and to the restriction of Palestinian activities.

In August 1975 the tensions among these forces ignited into civil war. The Lebanese army disintegrated, and the fighting was exacerbated by the involvement of the zu'ama' and their forces, and the *qabayan*, or lower-class street gangs. Syria intervened in the summer of 1976 on the side of the Christians when it feared that a Palestinian victory might set the stage for a Lebanese–Iraqi alliance against Syria, or for Syrian involvement in an unwanted war with Israel. With the Syrian intervention Lebanon disintegrated into sectarian enclaves. In June 1982 Israel invaded Lebanon in the hope of driving the PLO from both South Lebanon, where it had been mounting attacks against Israel, and from its headquarters in Beirut, and of shoring up a cooperative Maronite regime. The Israeli invasion succeeded in driving out the PLO, but not in creating the Maronite government it wanted. The Syrians became ever more entrenched as the arbiters of Lebanese politics.

Furthermore, Israeli occupation of South Lebanon stimulated the rise of new political forces. Among the disadvantaged Shi'a of southern Lebanon and Shi'i migrants to Beirut new parties emerged. Tinged with messianic hopes, the rise of the Shi'i underclass was part of the larger Middle East-wide Shi'i upheaval stimulated by the revolution in Iran. Led by Musa al-Sadr, a leading mullah, a new sectarian identity transcending the zu'ama' clienteles and defining a Shi'i community apart from Arab nationalism came into being. Musa al-Sadr created an infrastructure of schools and charities, rallied the newly educated and the newly rich alongside laborers, farmers, and teachers, and organized a paramilitary movement called Amal. When he disappeared during a visit to Libya in August 1978, Nabih Berri gave Amal a more secular political orientation to promote the interests of Shi'is within the framework of a Lebanese state.

In response, a rival Shi'i movement, called Hizballah (Party of God), was created by Muhammad Husayn Fadlallah, backed by Iran. Its goal was to establish an Islamic republic. This movement took the lead in the struggle against Israel. In the 1990s Hizballah became a major political party, buoyed by its successes in harassing Israeli forces and by the Israeli withdrawal in 2000 from Lebanon, and by its popular social services and infrastructure of schools and clinics. Hizballah participates in Lebanese elections and holds parliamentary seats. Despite its increasing pragmatism, in 2001 Hizballah reaffirmed its commitment to a continuing struggle with Israel as long as the Israeli–Palestinian conflict remains unresolved.

Lebanon remained mired in a chaotic and violent civil war as long as Maronite and Muslim leaders were unable to agree on a new distribution of power. Finally, in 1989 the Arab League was able to call a conference of national reconciliation in Sa'udi Arabia, rebalance the distribution of power among Christians and Muslims, and create a government of national unity. In one last spasm of ferocious warfare, General Michel Aoun tried to defeat the other major factions and create a Maronite state, but in 1991 the Syrians crushed Maronite resistance, quelled the fighting, and allowed for the emergence of the first central Lebanese government in fifteen years. Largely under the leadership of Ilyas Hrawi, and under Syrian overlordship, Beirut and Lebanon are being rebuilt.

THE PALESTINIAN MOVEMENT AND THE STRUGGLE FOR PALESTINE

Zionists and Palestinians to 1948

Palestine is the only part of the fertile crescent not to have become an Arab state. This was precluded by British support for the Zionist movement and by the formation of the state of Israel. The Zionist movement was sparked by the publication in 1896 of Theodor Herzl's *The Jewish State*, written in response both to rising Russian and European anti-semitism, and to assimilation and the loss of Jewish identity. Inspired by the ideal of a revitalized Jewish national culture, and an egalitarian and socialist society in a democratic polity, Zionism represented the transformation of a religious community into a nation conceived in terms of a shared history and culture and requiring a territorial home. The development of Jewish nationalism thus paralleled the emergence of other nationalist movements in the Balkans and the Middle East at the end of the nineteenth century. The Jewish case was complicated, however, in that the Jews wished to establish the national home in a territory where they were a tiny minority amidst an Arab-Palestinian population. Nevertheless, in 1917 the British issued the Balfour Declaration and promised to favor a Jewish national home in Palestine. The British imagined that a Jewish national home would serve as a pretext for British claims to administer the country. They also thought that they could rally the support of Russian and American Jews for their war effort and forestall similar German initiatives. In doing this they neglected their conflicting commitments to the Arabs.

The British, at the outset, allowed Jewish immigration and purchase of land, defended the Jewish community from riots, and permitted the organization of Jewish political institutions and the formation of a Jewish army. The British also suppressed the Arab-Palestinian opposition. Under British rule, the Jewish community in Palestine grew rapidly. By 1939 there were almost half a million Jews in some 250 settlements. The Jews were highly organized through the Zionist Organization, the Jewish Agency, the Vad Leumi or representative body of the Yishuv (the Jewish community in Palestine), Jewish political parties, and a Jewish labor movement.

The Palestinian movement developed in opposition to the occupation of Palestine by the British and the Jews. In 1920 most Palestinian Arabs were peasants. A middle class of doctors, lawyers, journalists, and government officials was very small. The Arab community was deeply divided by numerous clans and groups of affiliated clans, by strong class distinction between landlords, tenants, and share-croppers, and by religious divisions among Muslims and Christians. With a strong clan and religious consciousness the Palestinian Arabs had little sense of a national community and little potential for organizing a national movement.

However, in the course of the struggle against the British and the Zionists, parochial ties began to give way to a sense of regional identity. In the 1920s, Pales-tinian political awareness was cultivated by an Arab elite which tried to build a mass resistance to Zionism. This elite was divided into two segments. The first were the nationalists, who in 1918 formed the first Muslim–Christian associations to protest against the Jewish national home. They were at first allied to the Syrian national movement and envisioned a single greater Syrian-Arab state, but by 1920 Palestin-ian political activity separated itself from the general movement. The third Pales-tine Arab Congress set up the Arab Executive, which until the 1930s would be the principal spokesman for Palestinian-Arab interests.

The second Palestinian elite was Muslim. In 1922 the British established a Supreme Muslim Council to control endowed funds and the appointment of Muslim func-tionaries, and appointed al-Hajj Muhammad Amin al-Husayni to be the head of the council and Mufti of Jerusalem. Al-Husayni was also Syndic of the Descendants of the Prophet, and patron of the popular Nabi Musa festival, and he came to control both the Arab Executive and the Muslim Council. From these platforms he attempted to arouse mass support by protesting against the danger of Zionism to the holy places in Jerusalem. Al-Husayni and other religious notables organized their opposition in terms of Islam – the only idiom that was meaningful to the Palestinian population – and actively sponsored a number of demonstrations: the Nabi Musa riots of 1920, a boycott of the legislative council campaigns, the anti-land-sale campaign, and the 1929 Wailing Wall riots. They tried to make Palestine a pan-Islamic cause. In the 1920s, however, Arab leadership was highly fragmented. While al-Husayni and his followers controlled the Arab Executive and the Muslim Council, their rivals, led by the Nashashibi family, allied with mayors, landowners, and merchants, formed the National Party (1923) to contest leadership of Arab Palestine. The factional divisions led to bitter rivalries and destroyed the possibility of coordinated action.

The Palestinian movement was also beset in its early years by Muslim–Christian tensions. Christians had taken a large role in the development of Arab nationalism and in the formation of the Muslim–Christian associations, and had a heavy stake in resisting Jewish colonization. Also, Christians were important for their abilities to negotiate with and perhaps obtain support from the West. Still unity was hard to achieve. Muslims found it threatening to see Christians taking an independent role, and Christians remained suspicious of the emphasis placed on Muslim symbols. Christians did not participate in the 1929 anti-British and anti-Jewish riots.

Despite these handicaps, considerable progress was made in the 1920s. An ideol-ogy was formulated which defined the Arab nature of and the Arab right to Pales-tine. Islamic symbols of resistance to Zionism were mobilized. The Jerusalem notables emerged as leaders of the rural population, and despite religious tensions, Greek Orthodox Christians came to see themselves as part of the Palestinian Arab people. The 1930s witnessed the beginnings of a mass movement. While the factional struggle between the Husaynis and the Nashashibis smoldered, the concept of direct mass action was being fostered by militant youth groups like the Young Men's Muslim Association under the leadership of Shaykh 'Izz al-Din al-Qassam. Al-Qassam preached against British imperialism and Jewish settlement, and founded the Haifa Muslim Youth Association. He organized armed resistance cells to whom he preached a reformed Islam opposed to drinking, gambling, and prostitution. He also opposed popular religious practices such as mourning and grave visitation, and the mingling of the sexes. His was a puritanical, populist, activist notion of Islam concentrating on the appeal to save the holy land. The concepts of *mujahid* (warrior for the faith) and *shahid* (martyr) were used to generate popular participation. In the 1930s, when factional and kinship ties were all-powerful, and before the symbols of national ethnic identity had widespread appeal, only Muslim symbols could mobilize the Palestinian masses.

Al-Qassam and his followers played a large part in stimulating the Arab revolts of 1936–38. Teachers, health officers, and officials propagandized the villagers. In 1935 and 1936 a national strike begun by the Higher Arab Committee spread to the countryside. Throughout Palestine, Arab villagers, bandits, and volunteers from Syria and Egypt, operating without central direction, attacked government installations and Jewish settlements, attempting to overthrow British rule and stop Zionist colonization. The sporadic revolts were suppressed by the British in 1938. The Husaynis were removed from the Supreme Muslim Council; the Higher Arab Committee was declared illegal and a British military administration was imposed. The basic tactic of the Palestinians was to refuse cooperation with the British administration and to press the Arab cause by demonstrations, riots, and, eventually, guerrilla warfare.

From the late 1930s Britain began to change her policy in Palestine in order to win Arab support for the impending war against Germany. In the White Paper of 1939, the British decided to restrict Jewish immigration and land purchases. At the conclusion of World War II Britain refused all but a very limited immigration of Jewish refugees, despite American and Zionist pressures, and favored a renewed British trusteeship. The Jewish reaction to this change of British policy was bitter. The rise of Nazism and the destruction of European Jews in World War II had made the Zionists determined to establish a Jewish state as a refuge for the survivors. The Jews launched their own military struggle against the British mandate.

The Palestinians also regrouped. At the end of World War II al-Husayni returned from wartime exile in Europe to resume leadership of the Palestinian movement, and the League of Arab States, founded in 1945, took the initiative in defending the Palestinian cause. In 1947 Britain resigned the mandate and the United Nations partitioned Palestine into two states – one Jewish and one Arab. The Arab League forcibly resisted the formation of a Jewish state, but in the war that followed, the

Jews defeated the Arab states, and established their own state of Israel in 1948. Transjordan absorbed the portions of Palestine west of the Jordan River and Egypt took control of Gaza. A substantial portion of the Arab population of Palestine, over 700,000 people, was forced into exile. The Palestinians were scattered on the West Bank of the Jordan and exiled to Transjordan, Lebanon, Syria, and other Arab states. Though the Jews won the war and established the state of Israel, they could not win the peace. The Palestinians and the Arab states refused to acknowledge defeat. The masses of Palestinians in exile remained in refugee camps while Israel was unwilling to consider repatriation.

From 1948 to the present

Since 1948 the struggle has gone through several phases. Until 1967, the Arab states took the lead in the struggle against Israel. They imposed a trade boycott, blocked passage through the Suez Canal for goods going to or from Israel, and launched guerrilla attacks. As the Arab states found their principal patron in the Soviet Union and Israel its principal ally in the United States, the conflict escalated. In 1956 Britain, France, and Israel attacked Egypt, but were forced to desist by the objections of both the USA and the Soviet Union. A decade of border clashes culminated in the war of June 1967, in which Israel won a rapid and complete victory over the Arab states, and took possession of Gaza and the Sinai from Egypt, the West Bank from Jordan, and the Golan Heights from Syria. Israel also won control of Jerusalem. Despite the Israeli victory the struggle was not yet over. An artillery war with Egypt over the Suez Canal followed in 1969–70, and in October 1973 Egypt surprised Israel and fought another war to a stalemate. By this time, however, Egypt was really maneuvering to back out of the conflict. In October 1977, Anwar Sadat went to Jerusalem to offer peace. In 1979, Israel returned the Sinai to Egypt, and Israel and Egypt agreed to normalize relations. No agreements were reached concerning the Palestinians. This marked the end of the period of Arab state leadership in the name of the Palestinian cause.

From 1967 the Palestinians began to take responsibility for their own cause and to convert the Arab–Israeli struggle into a Palestinian–Israeli struggle. They organized a Palestinian National Council and the PLO. The PLO was a coalition. The largest group, al-Fatah, led by Yassir Arafat, an engineer trained in Kuwait, represented the Muslim- and nationalist-oriented segment of the Palestinian population, with aspirations to reconquer Palestine. Smaller, more radical Marxist-Leninist groups, such as the Popular Front for the Liberation of Palestine led by George Habash and the Democratic Popular Front for the Liberation of Palestine led by Nayyif Hawatmah, espoused not only the restoration of the Palestinians to their homeland, but the need for a revolutionary transformation of all Arab countries as a prelude to the showdown with Israel. Another important segment, Sa'iqa, was patronized and controlled by Syria. The factionalism of the PLO caused serious problems. The divisions allowed old Palestinian notable families, old-style bosses

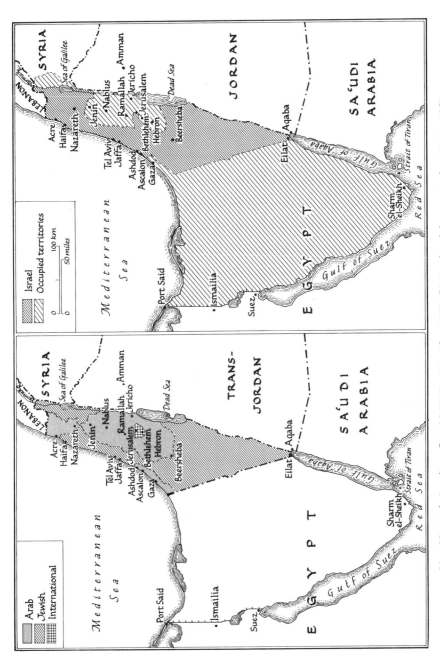

Map 32 Arab–Israeli conflict: (a) UN Partition Plan, 1947; (b) Israel and the occupied territories, 1967

(zu'ama'), and clients of other Arab states to hold a disproportionate influence within the movement. It led to the temptation for professional resistance fighters to be more comfortable in opposition than in power, and created an interest in the struggle for struggle's sake rather than in the resolution of political problems. Other divisions within the Palestinian people – between Christians and Muslims, secularists and Islamists, West Bank middle-class town populations living under Israeli occupation and lower-class Palestinians living in refugee camps – made it difficult to unite in the struggle for a Palestinian homeland.

The Palestinians also suffered from difficult relations with their nominal supporters, the Arab states. Despite strong Arab sentiment in support of the Palestinian movement, the activities of the PLO threatened the legitimacy of established states. In 1970 al-Fatah was defeated in Jordan and forced to evacuate to Lebanon. When the PLO threatened to become dominant in Lebanon, it was suppressed by Syria. The Camp David accords of 1979 were another setback in Palestinian relations with Arab patron states. They indicated the breakdown of Arab solidarity in the defense of Palestinian interests and the development of a counter-trend, as Arab states pursued their interests regardless of the Palestinians.

Nonetheless, in the late 1960s and 1970s the Palestinians made great gains for their cause. They carried on a sporadic guerrilla war against Israel. They won worldwide sympathy for their plight, and built a more cohesive national consciousness. This identity is primarily defined in nationalist and secular terms. Nonetheless, Islam penetrates Palestinian discourse through the use of such terms as jihad, shahid (martyr), mujahid, and holy land. These concepts have a specifically religious meaning but merge into the secular nationalist vocabulary. Concepts such as *thawrah* (revolution) and *fida'i* (self-sacrificing guerrilla) define national rights and dignity in words that imply redemption and resurrection. Islam helps to articulate and mobilize the Palestinians for political struggle. As in the case of Arab nationalism generally, the Palestinians have acquired a secular identity while at the same time preserving Islamic loyalties as the basis of political solidarity.

By the 1980s and 1990s Palestinian society was profoundly changed. Palestinian populations in exile were no longer only poor refugees living in camps. A majority of Palestinians had left the camps, dispersed throughout the Middle East, acquired educations, and became a middle-class population of merchants, civil servants, and professionals. The Palestinian population in diaspora was among the better-educated Arab communities.

In the West Bank and Gaza a younger generation of Palestinian notables took control. The confiscation of lands by the Israelis, the entry of Palestinian peasants into the wage-labor market, and the growth of schools and universities all helped to generate a new educated, middle-class, and professional elite. The defeat of the PLO in Lebanon and its exile to Tunisia allowed the new elite to displace the PLO and the old notables as the leaders of the Palestinian population. The new elites organized schools, social welfare agencies, agricultural relief societies, and the communal apparatus of a more organized, integrated, and nationalistic Palestinian community. The awakening in the West Bank and Gaza led in 1987 to the *intifada*, a campaign of strikes, demonstrations, riots, and stone throwing in protest against Israeli occupation, the construction of Israeli settlements on the West Bank, and administrative harassment and taxation. Local merchants protested against taxes and Israeli economic controls, and street youths took the lead in calling for the formation of a Palestinian state. The new leaders, however, were divided between those with a secular nationalistic orientation and those with an Islamic religious orientation who founded HAMAS and Islamic Jihad. Palestinian opinion in the West Bank and Gaza split between those who favored compromise with Israel as a way of ending the occupation, and those, usually the Islamists, who favored a continuing struggle for the liberation of all of Palestine. For the sake of unity the Palestinians accepted Arafat and PLO authority, and Arafat declared his readiness to recognize Israel's right to exist within its pre-1967 borders.

The period between the June war of 1967 and the Gulf War of 1991 also saw major changes in the Israeli position. Under the government of the Likud coalition and Menahim Begin (1977–83) Israel expected to prevail by military superiority rather than political compromise. After the victory in the 1967 war, the control of Jerusalem and the occupation of the West Bank and Gaza led to a rebirth of messianic hopes, and a renewed desire to take over the remainder of Palestine. Strong movements grew up within Israel calling for the colonization of the West Bank and the annexation of the West Bank and Gaza. By the 1990s there were over 140 Israeli settlements in the West Bank and Gaza. Israel expropriated land and water resources, employed Palestinians as workers, and provided most of the West Bank's imports.

In the 1980s, however, Israeli opinion divided over how to deal with the Palestinians. Despite the victory in Lebanon, the continuing occupation of South Lebanon and the rise of Hizballah made it costly for Israel in terms of soldiers' lives and political credibility. The intifada, though not militarily or diplomatically decisive, enormously raised the costs of the occupation, and raised tensions among the religious right, settlers on the West Bank, and the rest of the Israeli population. Finally, Israeli leaders became aware that the Palestinians did not constitute so grave a threat as the rising military power of Syria, Iraq, and Iran – which might threaten Israel with missiles and weapons of mass destruction. Thus, while Begin and his successor Yitzhak Shamir (1986–92) were committed to the expansion of Israeli settlements and to the eventual absorption of the occupied territories, the Labor Party increasingly favored territorial compromise and a negotiated peace.

The Gulf War provided a critical opportunity. The breakup of the Soviet Union and the defeat of Saddam Husayn allowed the USA to become the hegemonic power in the region, and the first Bush administration renewed its efforts to resolve the festering Israeli–Palestinian problem. While a formal peace conference was convened in Madrid in October 1991, secret negotiations were entered into by the PLO and Israel, leading to the Oslo accords in September 1993. The Oslo accords provided for

25 HAMAS posters for student council elections; al-Azhar University, Gaza

several stages of Israeli withdrawal and Palestinian empowerment. In the first stage Israel would turn over control of Gaza and Jericho to Palestinian administration. This was to be followed by the election of a Palestinian authority. Israel was to further withdraw its military forces from the populated area of the West Bank, and the Palestinian authority was to take control of local matters such as education, culture, welfare, tourism, and police – though Israel retained ultimate military control. The two sides were then to negotiate a permanent settlement involving the return of refugees, the status of Jerusalem, the Israeli settlements, and Israeli military occupation.

Both sides were deeply divided about the wisdom of this agreement. Arafat and the PLO favored the agreement because it restored to them the control of Palestinian affairs and because, given the political and diplomatic realities, this was the only way to an eventual Palestinian state. The agreements allowed Arafat and the PLO to set up a very authoritarian regime, built in part on the PLO militias and police, foreign aid support, favored business leaders, and the distribution of patronage to foster a political following. This regime was under strong pressure from the USA and Israel to suppress terrorism as a condition for the implementation of the Oslo accords. The Palestinian opposition denounced it because it failed to give any assurances about the eventual status of Jerusalem and the return of the refugees. Palestinian intellectuals – and many younger-generation West Bank leaders displaced from power by the return of the PLO – also opposed the peace accords, which might lead not to a Palestinian state, but to a fragmented collection of Palestinian habitats under Israeli control. HAMAS called for the formation of an Islamic state, in opposition to Arafat's secular Palestine, and for continued struggle against Israel to win Palestinian goals. In the 1990s, however, HAMAS and Arafat seem to have reached an accommodation. HAMAS modified its opposition to the regime enough to participate in Palestinian Authority institutions, and built up its social and educational services. Arafat also succeeded in reducing HAMAS's anti-Israel terrorist actions, except for a series of bombings in 1996, but he was not politically strong enough to completely suppress the opposition. Arafat dealt carefully with HAMAS, arresting and releasing its members, and temporizing in accord with political circumstances.

Israel was similarly divided. While Prime Ministers Rabin and Peres and the Labor governments believed that agreement with the Palestinians would ultimately enhance Israel's security, Likud and the orthodox and nationalist right wing did not believe that the Palestinians genuinely intended to make peace. They pointed to continuing sporadic terrorist attacks and to the potential for a Palestinian state to be used as a frontline base for renewed Arab wars against Israel. They noted continued Syrian, Iraqi, and Iranian hostility to Israel, and were convinced that Israeli security could only be assured by superior military power. In Israeli politics these divisions produced a virtual stalemate. In November 1994 Prime Minister Rabin was assassinated by a Jewish orthodox extremist. The religious parties, the settlers, and the Likud narrowly came to power in 1996 under Prime Minister Netanyahu (1996–99), and resisted further progress in negotiations with the Palestinians. Israel used the interim to expand settlements around Jerusalem.

For a time it appeared that the peace process had taken hold. In 1994 Jordan made its own peace agreement with Israel, the culmination of a decades-long relationship marked by shared interests in the division of water, the settlement of refugees, and the maintenance of a quiet border. Negotiations with Syria over the return of the Golan Heights and the ratification of peace were suspended in 1996, but President Asad was not provocative in his relations with Israel. Economic deals between Israel and the Gulf states went forward. In May 1999 Israel elected a new Labor Prime Minister, Ehud Barak, who pledged himself to peace, security, an open and tolerant Israeli society, and a resolution of the Israeli–Palestinian problem. In late 2000, however, negotiations between President Clinton, Arafat, and Barak at Camp David collapsed. Israel offered to recognize a Palestinian state in about 90 percent of the West Bank and Gaza, sovereignty over some but not all of the Arab neighborhoods of Jerusalem, and administrative jurisdiction but not sovereignty over the Muslim holy places. These offers did not meet the Palestinian demands for a return to the June 4, 1967 borders, for a sovereign capital in Jerusalem and the holy places, or for a contiguous bloc of territory not partitioned by Israeli settlements, roads, and military zones. The Palestinians also demanded Israeli recognition of the right for refugees to return to all of Palestine, with practical limitations, which was unacceptable to Israel. Instead of peace a new wave of Palestinian violence – the al-Aqsa intifada – broke out, and met with severe Israeli repression. The struggle has escalated to Palestinian suicide bombings of Israelis, and Israeli military occupation of West bank cities. In the bitterness of renewed large-scale violence, the Oslo accords have failed. Both sides are internally divided between forces that favor and those that oppose an agreement, but neither seems able to make the necessary compromises.

THE ARABIAN PENINSULA

For almost a millennium, the Arabian peninsula stood outside the mainstream of Middle Eastern developments. While the Arab conquests began a new era in Middle Eastern civilization, they left Arabia drained of much of its population, and relegated the peninsula to a marginal role in Middle Eastern history. In the Ottoman era, Egypt and the Arab fertile crescent became provinces of the empire, but with the partial exception of peripheral areas, Arabia did not. Unlike Egypt and the fertile crescent states, the peninsula was governed by family and tribal elites. Islam was a crucial factor in the unification of disparate clan and tribal groups into regional confederations and kingdoms. In the Imamate of Yemen and the Sultanates of Oman and Sa'udi Arabia, religion and state were closely identified. While the shaykhs of the Persian Gulf region did not formally claim charismatic religious authority, the rulers were considered the heads of the religion, responsible for the implementation of Islamic values. Throughout the peninsula the 'ulama', whether Zaydi, Shafi'i, Ibadi, or Wahhabi, also played an important role as political advisors to rulers, administrators of judicial and educational institutions, and a source of moral advice and political authority.

Only since World War II has the peninsula become subject to the forces that have strongly shaped the rest of the Middle East. Modern means of government organization and revolutionary political concepts have been introduced. The discovery of oil has opened the way to technical and economic modernization and the transformation of traditional values. In the last few decades Yemen has been most subjected to revolutionary nationalism and political change, while Sa'udi Arabia and the Gulf states maintain the traditional bases of political order and legitimacy in the midst of extensive economic and social transformation. As in the fertile crescent states, so in the Arabian peninsula has Arabism become the basis of social and political identity.

Yemen

Yemen has an exceptional position in the history of the peninsula because since ancient times the south has been the center of an agricultural and state-organized society, in conflict with the pastoral and tribal populations of the north. After Yemen was converted to Islam during the lifetime of the Prophet, it was absorbed into the early Umayyad and 'Abbasid empires. In the late ninth century, like other regions far removed from Baghdad, it became a center of Shi'ism. In northern Yemen a Zaydi Shi'a dynasty ruled from 893 to 1962. Southern Yemen came under the influence of Egypt. First the Fatimids and then the Ayyubids established satellite states. The Rasulid dynasty (1229–1454) organized a strong central government and won the south over to Sunni Islam. This marked the origin of the lasting division of Yemen into a Sunni agricultural population in the south and a Zaydi tribal and pastoral population in the north. After the Ottomans conquered Egypt, they occupied southern Yemen from 1539 to 1635, but the Qasimid branch of the Zaydi dynasty eventually expelled them and restored Zaydi rule. In the nineteenth century Muhammad b. 'Ali al-Shawkani (d. 1834) called for the reform and renewal of Islam, and the centralization of the state under the authority of a chief justice whose responsibility it would be to purify and renew Islam. The Qasimi imams responded to this concept, patronizing religious scholars in return for their legitimization.

In the nineteenth century Yemen was divided between an Ottoman sphere of influence in the north and a British protectorate in the south. A treaty of 1911 confirmed Ottoman suzerainty in the north, but divided administrative control between the Imam in the highlands and the Ottomans on the coast. This corresponded to the division into Zaydi and Sunni spheres of influence. With the defeat of the Ottomans in World War I, Imam Yahya won control over the whole of the country. He governed in conjunction with the Zaydi elite who were the 'ulama', governors, judges, teachers, and also merchants and military officers. They were divided into two groups: the *sada* (sayyids), a landed aristocracy of descendants of the Prophet, and

Table 17. *Regimes of the Arabian peninsula*

Persian Gulf		Oman	Central Arabia	Yemen
Bahrain	Kuwait			
Qaramita (Qarmatians), 894 to end of eleventh century	al-Sabah, 1752 to present	Ibadi imams, 796 to end of ninth century; Ibadi imams, eleventh century; Bu-Sa idis, 1741 to present		Zaydi imams (San a); Rassid line ninth century to c. 1281; Sulayhids 1047–1158; Rasulids 1229–1454; Ottomans (South Yemen) 1539–1655; Zaydi imams (Qasimid line) c. 1592–1962

Sa udis

1746 Muhammad b. Sa ud
1765 Abd al-Aziz
1803 Sa ud b. Abd al-Aziz
1814 Abdallah I b. Sa ud
1818–22 Ottoman occupation
1823 Turki
1834 Faysal I (first reign)
1837 Khalid b. Sa ud
1841 Abdallah II (as vassal of Muhammad Ali of Egypt)
1843 Faysal I (second reign)
1865 Abdallah III b. Faysal (first reign)
1871 Sa ud b. Faysal
1874 Abdallah III (second reign)
1887 conquest by Rashidis of Hail, Abdallah remains as governor of Riyadh until 1889
1889 Abd al-Rahman b. Faysal, vassal governor
1891 Muhammad b. Faysal, vassal governor
1902 Abd al-Aziz II
1953 Sa ud
1964 Faysal II
1975 Khalid
1982 Fahd
(Crown Prince Abdallah)

Sa id b. Taymur
(1933–70);
Qabus b. Sa id
(1970–)

Yemen Arab Republic 1962–90 and
People's Republic of South Yemen
1967–69; People's Democratic
Republic of Yemen 1969–90;
Republic of Yemen 1990–

the *quda*', the descendants of early judges. In the Sunni parts of the country, the Shafi'i 'ulama' held a similar position. Yemen in this period was thoroughly isolated from the outside world; there were few secular schools and few contacts with the rest of the Middle East. Every effort was made to preserve the traditional society.

Despite the efforts of Imam Yahya, social and ideological influences from the Arab Middle East began to penetrate Yemen in the 1940s. Diplomatic, military, and economic contacts with other Arab states multiplied. In 1948 Egyptian instructors were teaching in San'a', and after 1954 Yemani army officers received training in Egypt. Yemeni merchants, workers, and students also went abroad. New ideas about constitutional authority and economic enterprise began to penetrate, and Yemen went through the same process of political and ideological modernization as that experienced by Ottoman elites in the nineteenth century and Arab elites in the early twentieth.

These political and ideological changes led to the formation of rival cliques within governing circles, who used ideological distinctions to justify their competition for power. After several aborted coups, a federal union between the United Arab Republic and Yemen (1958–61) was declared. In 1962 a coalition of Zaydi army officers, Shafi'i merchants, and tribal chiefs led by 'Abdallah Sallal overthrew the Imamate. The republican regime was supported by an army from Egypt, and was opposed by tribal groups defending the prerogatives of the Imam, backed by Sa'udi Arabia. The Egyptians and the Sa'udis both withdrew from the conflict in 1967, and a new broadly based government under the leadership of Qadi 'Abd al-Rahman al-Iryani was formed.

The new government steered a middle course between Egyptian and Sa'udi influences, and promulgated a constitution for a regime based on the army, tribal forces in the north, and Sunni elites in administration and business. The constitution made Islam the official religion of the country. The new state made the Shari'a the law of the land, and accepted Sa'udi help in creating a new school system. Shawkani's status as a symbol of Yemani Islam helped introduce a new generic Sunnism as the basic religious orientation of the country. The authority of the Zaydi 'ulama' was greatly reduced. The sada' were delegitimized by the repudiation of hereditary elites, and the quda' dissociated themselves from Zaydism, professing Sunni loyalties or an undefined affiliation. In January 1974 Colonel Ibrahim Muhammad al-Hamdi overthrew the Iryani regime, but continued the policy of balance among modernists, Islamic, and tribal forces. Thus, Yemen combined an authoritarian military rule, imperious administration, tribal autonomy and disorder, judicial arbitrariness, and strong social Islamic forces.

South Yemen came under British rule in 1839; in 1937 it was made a crown colony. The British protectorate included some twenty-three Sultanates, Emirates, and tribal regimes. Under British control, the traditional Arabian clan and religious communities remained intact. The Sultans dominated the towns; the sayyids owned the land and served as mediators among the clans. Plebeian clans were organized into specialized agricultural, craft, and servant groups.

Nationalism in Aden began as a reaction against British rule. In the name of Arab nationalism and socialism a local resistance movement was founded by George Habash. In 1959 the National Liberation Front took up the opposition cause. From 1962 to 1967 demonstrations, riots, and then guerrilla warfare forced the British to withdraw. The National Liberation Front, supported by the South Arabian Federation Army, came to power and proclaimed the People's Republic of South Yemen. In 1969 the left wing of the National Liberation Front led by 'Abd al-Fattah Isma'il took control of the government and changed its name to the People's Democratic Republic of Yemen. The new government replaced the traditional elite of tribal chiefs and Muslim religious teachers with a new generation of army officers and political activists. The new elite espoused a Marxist-Leninist ideology and organized a single party, the National Front, to control all other organizations in the country. Industry was nationalized, land ownership reformed, and feudalism and tribalism condemned. Significantly, Islam remained the state religion.

In 1990, motivated by the discovery of oil in the boundary region between the two Yemens, the breakdown of the Soviet Union, economic hardship in the south, declining employment in the Gulf states, and the rising strength of Islamist parties, the Popular General Congress of the north and the Yemen Socialist Party of the south agreed to unify the country. 'Abdallah Salih and 'Ali Salim al-Bid became President and Vice President. A civil war in 1994, which resulted in the defeat of the south, left the tribal elites in control of the whole country.

Unified Yemen is very poor. Its population is about 9 million in the north and 2.5 million in the south, and grows at the extremely rapid rate of 3.5 percent per year. Oil and gas constitute about 90 percent of Yemen's exports, and 50 percent of state budget revenues. Other exports include cotton, coffee, and fish; Yemen imports machinery, cars, and consumer durables. Worker remittances made up one-third of exports until the 1990–91 expulsion of workers from Sa'udi Arabia. The underground economy in alcohol, guns, smuggled cars, and *qat*, a locally grown stimulant, is of huge importance. Since 1994 large properties confiscated by the state have been restored, and merchants and 'ulama' have prospered in a liberalized economy.

Unified Yemen has a multi-party system, a free press, and right of association guaranteed by the constitution; there were parliamentary elections in 1993 and 1997. Increased education, nationalism, and Islamism have all attenuated the Zaydi–Shafi'i distinction, and have reduced the importance and influence of the Sufi shaykhs as well, but religiously based movements have continued to be important in national politics. In 1993 the Islah party led by 'Abdallah al-Ahmar entered the government. The Islah party is a coalition of different groups including the Muslim Brothers and other Islamists, tribal chiefs, merchants and technocrat modernist-Islamists, and the coopted "men of the president." These groups are connected to the more extreme Wahhabis and Salafis. They are united in their opposition to socialism and popular Sufi Islam. Some of their more radical members may be associated with Usama bin Laden and the al-Qaeda network. In 2001 the government moved to merge the Islah schools into the public school system. Other Islamic parties include the reformed

Zaydi party, called the Hizb al-Haqq, which repudiates the Imamate, and calls for a democracy and an elected ruler who is an *ajir*, a hired servant. This party revives festivals such as Ghadir Khumm, and the birthday of Zayd b. 'Ali. Islamic movements, often financed by Sa'udi Arabia, have created a parallel education system, Islamic banks, and an education and propaganda network through the distribution of videos and audio cassettes. While the military and the tribes still dominate, the country is extremely diverse and power is widely distributed.

Sa'udi Arabia

Central Arabia has become the domain of the Sa'udi kingdom and the Wahhabi movement. In 1745 'Abd al-'Aziz b. Sa'ud (Ibn Sa'ud), the chief of a small tribal principality in north central Arabia, took up the cause of a Hanbali preacher, Muhammad b. 'Abd al-Wahhab (1703–87). Ibn 'Abd al-Wahhab had studied in Mecca, Medina, Damascus, and Basra, and returned to preach the reform principles. He insisted that the Quran and the Prophet were the only valid Muslim authorities, and proposed to return to the fundamental principles embodied in Muslim scripture. Wahhabi reformism took the extreme position of totally rejecting belief in and veneration of saints or of any human being as a form of *shirk*, or polytheism. It also rejected the common pantheistic types of Sufi theology and magical rituals. Ibn 'Abd al-Wahhab's preaching was the first political expression of a reform tendency that had developed in Mecca and would soon manifest itself throughout Islamic India, Indonesia, and North Africa.

With the conversion of Ibn Sa'ud to the Wahhabi cause, Wahhabism became the religious ideology of tribal unification. Echoing the life of the Prophet, Ibn Sa'ud and his successors waged war against the surrounding tribes, and converted them to the reformed version of Islam. As imams of the Wahhabi movement, they became the spiritual as well as the temporal chiefs of central Arabia. In 1773 they took Riyadh and made it their capital; in 1803 they captured Mecca, but they were defeated by Muhammad 'Ali, who took control of Mecca and Medina in 1812, and destroyed the Sa'udi state in 1818. During much of the nineteenth century, the Sa'udi house survived as a small tribal principality in the interior of Arabia, but in 1902, 'Abd al-'Aziz b. Sa'ud again took control of Riyadh, proclaimed himself imam of the Wahhabis, and restored the Sa'udi kingdom. The principal instrument of his power was the Ikhwan – a non-tribal military corps, settled in agricultural villages, which fought and proselytized for the Wahhabi movement. Ibn Sa'ud succeeded in unifying the tribes of central and eastern Arabia, declared himself Sultan of the Najd (1921) and proceeded to round out the boundaries of modern Sa'udi Arabia by treaties with Iraq (1922), Jordan (1925), and Yemen (1934). In 1925 he took control of the Hijaz and the holy places.

The Sa'udi regime was based on a subtle combination of political and religious powers. The Sa'udi kings were tribal chiefs who ruled by maintaining alliances and marriage ties with the families of other chiefs. The army was made up of loyal tribes. At the same time they were religious rulers, committed to upholding the laws of

Islam and protecting the pilgrimage and the holy places. The 'ulama' of the country, largely the descendants of Ibn 'Abd al-Wahhab, married into the royal family, were financially supported by the state, and had considerable influence in government circles.

The contemporary transformation of Sa'udi Arabia began with the issuing of exploration concessions to the Standard Oil Company in 1933 and 1939, and the discovery of oil. Oil production in Sa'udi Arabia began in earnest after World War II. However, only after 1973 did the price revolution in oil bring in vast riches. The Sa'udi development budget reached 40 billion dollars in 1977 and 70 billion dollars in 1980. Its programs led to the growth of cities, the construction of an industrial infrastructure, and a tremendous influx of foreign workers. In 1975, an estimated 43 percent of the population consisted of foreign workers from Yemen, Oman, Egypt, and Pakistan. Equally important was the revolution in education. By 1980 there were approximately a million children in schools, including large numbers of girls, some 40,000 students in Sa'udi colleges, and some 15,000 students abroad. By 1989 there were more than 2,500,000 students, of whom 1,160,000 were girls. There were about 100,000 students in universities. Increasing numbers of Sa'udis were trained for technical work in the petroleum industry, commerce, agriculture, finance, communications, and the military. Numerous members of the royal family have been educated in Western universities.

In the midst of these extensive educational, economic, and social changes Sa'udi society remains conservative, and the state maintains its traditional political and religious authority. The Sa'udi regime is essentially an oligarchy run by a family council, or majlis, which operates by consensus, but the regime is sensitive to the attitudes of leading bureaucrats, merchants, 'ulama', and Muslim activists. The Sa'udis maintain close family relations with important regional and tribal chieftains, and they appoint family members and loyal tribal chiefs to ministerial and administrative offices. The historical tribal societies have been restructured by sedentarization, by urbanization or the adoption of subsidized agriculture, and by the substitution of state salaries and subsidies for an independent economic life. State salaries and subsidies reach all sectors of the society. The regime has used its wealth to make clients of its own population. Reciprocally, Sa'udi subjects gain the leverage to demand subsidies and services of the government. Even in periods of declining oil revenue, as in the 1980s and 1990s, the government has been reluctant to reduce these benefits lest it lead to political unrest.

Equally important is the continuing commitment to Islam. Sa'udi society has been little affected by nationalism and secularism, and the Sa'udis cultivate their legitimacy by close attention to Islamic religious affairs and the enforcement of Islamic morals. The defining Sa'udi myth is that the ruling family is the protector of Wahhabi Islam and tribal values. The organization for "commanding the good and forbidding the evil" (the *mutawwi'in*) enforces Wahhabi concepts of morality. The successful organization of the pilgrimage is another important sign of Sa'udi legitimacy. The 'ulama' have a large voice in such matters as Islamic law and education, and they control the Ministries of Higher Education, Information, Justice, Interior, and Waqf and Departments of Legal Research, Propaganda, and Guidance and Public Morality, but their influence may not be as substantial as it sometimes appears. The power of the 'ulama' derives from their appointment by the King, and they have little say in oil, economic, and foreign policy issues. They are part of the state bureaucracy and under the supervisory control of the government. The state does not tolerate an independent religious domain.

The position of women is critical in defining Sa'udi Arabia as an Islamic society. Sex segregation outside the home is more complete in Sa'udi Arabia than in any other Muslim country, and is sustained by state policy. Women are supposed to remain in the home, raising children and inculcating them with traditional values. Women can only be educated or work in sex-segregated places, which excludes them from many professions. In political crises such as those after the 1979 assault on the mosque in Mecca or the Gulf War these regulations are ever more intensively enforced. The control of women has become an antidote to the breakdown of the functions of the traditional family, to Westernization via the media, to the creation of a technically and administratively competent middle class, and to the breakdown of traditional village and *suq* spaces in vast new urban constructions. Islamic identity, asceticism and puritanism in public, modernism and material prosperity, and ever more concessions to 'ulama' demands for a stricter Muslim lifestyle have shaped the Sa'udi nation.

Internationally, the Sa'udis have cultivated an Islamic rather than an Arab national identity. They oppose the Israeli occupation of Jerusalem, and defend the Palestinian cause. They support innumerable schools and colleges, publications and conferences, mosques and charities in countries with Muslim populations, including Britain and the United States. The Sa'udis propagate their own militant and puritanical version of Islam, and have helped foster a worldwide common practice and global Islamic identity. They have also supported insurgent movements in Kosovo, Palestine, Kashmir, and Chechnya, and most extensively in Afghanistan. Sa'udi support for Muslim insurgencies may directly or indirectly shade over into "protection" money for Jihadist movements. Sa'udi foreign policy has been governed throughout by the concerns of a wealthy but small and vulnerable state for protection from regional dangers. The Sa'udis fear terrorist attacks and, at various times, possible Egyptian, Iranian, and Iraqi interventions. They fought a proxy war in Yemen against Egyptian forces from 1962 to 1967, warded off the threat of Iranian influence among the Shi'i populations of northeastern Arabia after the Iranian revolution, and turned to the United States for protection from Iraq during its invasion of Kuwait.

Sa'udi oil policy has been managed with considerable attention to its political as well as its economic implications. The oil embargo of 1973 was an assertion of Sa'udi leadership in the Arab world and of resistance to Israel and to American influences in the Middle East. Since the 1970s the Sa'udis have taken a long-term and moderate view of the political utility of oil. They see their own best interests in cooperation with the oil-consuming powers of Europe, the United States and Japan, and have favored moderate prices in the interests of global economic stability and prosperity. Forces outside the royal family have thus far achieved little political expression. Potential political opposition exists in the new middle class of administrators, businessmen, skilled technicians, and workers who are crucial to the emerging modern economy, but who stand outside the status and political structure of the country and want a greater role in government. Religious opposition comes from groups that have been disrupted by the breakdown of tribal society and by the growth of individualism attendant upon urbanization and economic and industrial change. A bloated bureaucracy and underemployed graduates of Islamic institutions are another source of tension. Opposition has come from Shi'i workers in Aramco factories and Shi'a in the eastern province; tribal elements in the northern Najd; tribes in Asir; nationalist members of the armed forces; and, most recently, from Islamic-educated but under-employed student and graduate militants. The 1979 attack upon the Haram of Mecca was the harbinger of a new Islamic resistance, and a major trend in the 1990s was rising Islamism and the increasing influence of non-establishment 'ulama', professors of Islamic studies and graduates of Sa'udi religious universities. Al-Madina University has become a center of Sa'udi neo-fundamentalism. The radical Islamic opposition denies the Islamic credentials of the regime, and denounces it as an untribal, usurping, and corrupt government using Islam for its own purposes. It questions the morality of the rulers, and calls for a strict Shari'a state. In the 1990s the 'ulama' also became anxious about the American alliance, Western influences, and the rise of Western- and secular-educated technocrats. All the government's opponents are particularly critical of its close alliance with and dependence upon the United States, and fear this as a source of foreign cultural influences.

Nonetheless, the Sa'udi family seems to have absorbed massive economic, social, and educational changes within the political and cultural framework of tribal and Islamic legitimacy. In the 1950s and 1960s modernization of the administration and expansion of education, harsh internal security laws, control over information, repression of organized opponents, and the beginnings of a mass welfare program helped diffuse and overcome some of this resistance. Middle-class nationalists were won away from pan-Arabism, Nasserism, and Ba'thism. From the mid-1960s there was a massive expansion of education and government bureaucratic employment. The new middle classes prefer personal wealth and achievement, and do not, despite repeated promises for the granting of a *majlis al-shura* (consultative council), gain rights of political participation. The 'ulama' have been assured throughout that the Wahhabi character of the kingdom would be preserved, and the regime has steadily become religiously more conservative. In the 1990s, however, the rulers punished the 'ulama' for opposition petitions. The combination of religious identities and oil money has thus far, despite chronic latent tensions, served to maintain the regime.

The Gulf

The history of the Persian Gulf region, like that of Yemen and central Arabia, is based upon the persisting identification of political and religious authority as the basis of tribal unification. In pre-Islamic times Oman was part of a Sasanian commercial network which reached from the Persian Gulf to India. Commercial profits were invested in an Iranian type of *qanat* irrigation, and Oman became a highly agricultural society. The Arab conquests, however, introduced a large pastoral population. In 796 Oman came under the rule of Ibadi Imams, who managed to contain tribal rivalries, defend agriculture, and integrate the nomadic and settled populations. Under Ibadi leadership, Omanis founded commercial colonies in Basra, Siraf, Aden, and India, and traded on the east coast of Africa. At the end of the ninth century the Ibadi state and Omani commerce collapsed, and Egyptian-sponsored Red Sea routes took over the bulk of the Indian Ocean traffic. Oman, however, revived in the middle of the eleventh century when a second Imamate was founded, and a social system was created that lasts to the present day. Cultivators accepted a tribal concept of social organization, and thus were integrated with pastoralists into a single society. Ibadism became a full-fledged Muslim school of law, regulating personal and family behavior and political institutions. In the Ibadi system the Imam is nominated by the elders of the community, and holds power insofar as he upholds the divine law and maintains the confidence of his electors. The Imamate was thus a tribal state integrated by religious authority. The government did little to encourage investment in land. Village communities, which did not have adequate resources or organizational capacities to care for the irrigation system, were left on their own.

Oman's prosperity was revived in the seventeenth and eighteenth centuries when Omanis drove the Portuguese out of East Africa and the Sultans of the Bu Sa'id dynasty established their own trading network. Oman renewed its control over Zanzibar and other East African towns. While Zanzibar became a separate regime in 1856, the dynasty continues to rule Oman (and Muscat) to the present day. In 1955 Sa'id b. Taymur (1932–70), with British help, brought the whole country under his control. His narrow and tyrannical rule prompted several opposition movements. The Popular Front for the Liberation of Oman was formed in 1965 by embittered students; the Dhofar Liberation Front organized resistance in the personal estates of the Sultan, but was defeated with Iranian help. Until 1970, however, Sa'id b. Taymur was able to maintain complete control of the country owing to his British-officered army and the complete isolation of Oman from the outside world.

In 1970 his son Qabus b. Sa'id seized power in a palace coup. However, he did not change the government. The army is made up of Baluchi regiments and northern tribes, and leading tribal shaykhs and merchants have been incorporated into the regime. The commercial elite controls oil, finance and commerce, and the country has a more laissez faire economy than other Gulf states. Tribal elites administer social programs. A majlis al-shura was appointed in 1990, but the Sultan remains an absolute ruler with final authority over the promulgation of laws and decrees.

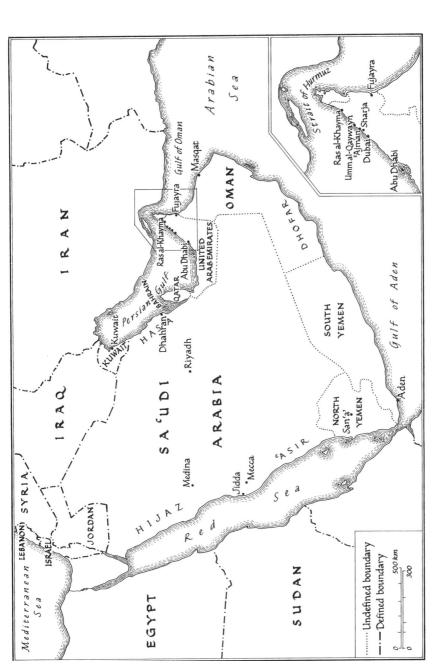

Map 33 Arabia and the Persian Gulf: c. 1974

In other parts of the Persian Gulf a new political system took shape at the beginning of the eighteenth century. In a region of fragmented lineages, the Banu Khalid became the principal tribal power, and a number of local families established their preeminence. In 1752 Sabah b. Jabr of the Banu 'Utub became the first ruler of Kuwait, and established the dynasty that rules Kuwait today. Kuwait has been a tribal state, a commercial entrepôt at the head of the Persian Gulf, and an important rival of Basra and other Persian Gulf ports. The al-Sabah family also assisted in the establishment of another branch of the 'Utub, the al-Khalifa, in Bahrain. By the end of the eighteenth century Britain had become the dominant power in the Gulf region and paramount over the small tribal regimes. In 1798 the British made the first of a series of treaties to protect British shipping in the Gulf and to install British political agents. British treaties with Kuwait, Bahrain, Oman, and the smaller "Trucial" states helped to strengthen the tribal rulers. British influence remained predominant until 1961, when Kuwait became fully independent. In 1970 and 1971, when Britain left the Gulf region, the Trucial states were severally reconstituted as members of the United Arab Emirates.

The modern transformation of the Persian Gulf region began with the discovery of oil in Bahrain in 1932, though production did not get underway in Bahrain, Kuwait, and Qatar until after World War II. In 1958 oil was found in Abu Dhabi and in 1973 in Sharja. The vast increase in oil revenues after 1973 has had the same effects in the Gulf as it has had in Sa'udi Arabia. Oil changed the distribution of power in Gulf societies. It allowed for the formation of large bureaucratic states and made the rulers independent of the merchant elites with whom they had collaborated. Rulers bought off merchant claims to political power; they assured them their money, but cultivated their own families as allies and distributed patronage benefits to the populace to wean them from client ties to the merchant elites. Shaykhs became chiefs of departments and sons of merchants the next rank in the new bureaus. The Gulf has become a highly urbanized area; the majority of the population lives in cities – including a large number of Palestinians, Jordanians, Egyptians, Yemenis, and Pakistanis, who account for as much as half, and in some places even three-quarters, of the population. The Gulf states remain small tribal principalities in which the superstructure of modern industry is carried by foreign laborers and administrators.

In each of the Gulf states the conditions of development are somewhat different. Kuwait is ruled by the al-Sabah family as a tribal state. Kinship and religious culture remain the bases of legitimacy. The secular and national aspects of Arabism are strongly present but Islam remains the basis of law and there is no pressure for secularization. A parliamentary and constitutional regime was introduced between 1962 and 1967, but was only fitfully implemented. Parliament was dissolved in 1976–81 and 1986–92. In 1992 parliament was reconvened, but the electorate was restricted to families resident from 1920 to 1959, qualifying only 80,000 voters out of a potential 600,000 Kuwaiti men. When in session the National Assembly, which includes bedouin chiefs, Islamists, progressives and Shi'a, is used by the al-Sabahs to balance the power of merchant elements. Parliament tries to enlarge scope for debate. In November 2000 it rejected a government proposal to grant women full political rights. Sunnis and tribal leaders opposed the government initiative, while Shi'a, government officials, and liberals favored it. The al-Sabahs alternate periods of open discussion and assembly with police crackdowns. While journalists and academics are largely free, broadcasting, newspapers, and NGOs require government licenses. Union activity and organizing of any sort is closely controlled.

Petroleum and petrochemicals provide 90 percent of Kuwait's government revenues and exports, and 50 percent of its GDP. Foreign workers are estimated to constitute 70–85 percent of the workforce. Per capita income has dropped steadily since the 1970s due to oil-price declines and population growth, but the great wealth of the country – in 1998 the per capita income was equivalent to over $22,000 per year – has been used to establish an extensive welfare system. The state subsidizes utilities, health care, housing, telecommunications, and education, and guarantees government employment. Islamic banking – characterized by leasing, installment sales, deferred payment sales, and equity investments – is strong in Kuwait and Bahrain. Kuwait suffered extensive damage to its oilfields in the Gulf War of 1991, but it has recuperated rapidly.

Bahrain is also a traditional chieftainship, ruled since 1782 by the al-Khalifa family. Here the ruling family represents commercial and pearl-fishing interests but not pastoral peoples. The political elite of Bahrain includes not only the ruling family but also merchants and religious leaders. Thus when Bahrain became independent in 1971 it had a historical basis for a fairly sophisticated political system. A constitutional assembly was convened in 1973, granted by the al-Khalifa family to its subjects in accord with the Muslim principle of consultation. The assembly, however, was suspended in 1975 when it threatened the dominance of the ruling Amir. The distinctive feature of Bahrain's political life is its numerous political clubs and professional societies which meet to discuss current issues. Also, owing to the early discovery of oil, Bahrain has a fairly strong union movement. As in Kuwait, the position of the ruling family is precariously balanced against the interests of a sophisticated and varied population.

Qatar has a similar political history. In pre-oil days, the ruling Shaykh depended on revenues from the merchants, but the discovery of oil enabled him to dispense with their support. Merchants were bought off by assurances of wealth, though they were not as powerful or as successful as those in Kuwait. Qatari workers, however, came from nomadic, slave, and pearl-diving backgrounds, and were factious and prone to strikes. A Qatari national consciousness has emerged, partly fostered by government patronage for historical studies and archeology. The Amir, Hamad b. Khalifa al-Thani, however, has not been able to control the bureaucracy; family members in office have created their own partially independent fiefdoms within the government apparatus. Amir Hamad, however, has become famous for his sponsorship of al-Jazira, the independent Arab television channel.

The United Arab Emirates was formed from the small Trucial states. Abu Dhabi is the principal state in the federation, along with Dubai, Sharja, Ajnan, Umm al-Qaywayn, Fujayra, and Ras al-Khayma. These states were governed by local tribal chiefs who ruled a population divided between seafaring coastal residents and inland nomadic peoples. Upon the British withdrawal in 1971, Abu Dhabi and Dubai formed a federation with the smaller states. State authority rested on the military and control of oil revenues and patronage. The United Arab Emirates has built up an administrative apparatus for finance, justice, police, and public services. There is a federal council, cabinet, and defense forces. As in the rest of the Arabian region, declining oil prices since 1980 have led to a drop in the standard of living.

Throughout the Gulf region the process of modernization remains in the hands of traditional monarchs and tribal chieftains. Nationalism has had relatively little impact in this area, and there are only sporadic pressures for inclusion of larger elements of the population in the political process. In Kuwait and Bahrain the range of political consultation has been broadened. Arabism as well as Islamic identities are stressed as the basis of social cohesion and political legitimacy. Considerable technical and economic change, a high degree of urbanization, and large numbers of foreign workers have thus far been absorbed without affecting the basic political and cultural quality of the Gulf regimes. Just as the Sa'udi regime has maintained its traditional position in the face of extensive changes, the Gulf states also show a surprising continuity of political leadership and Islamic loyalty. In these Arab countries, whose institutional heritage is tribal rather than Ottoman, secular national elites and ideologies have barely taken hold.

ARAB STATES, NATIONALISM, AND ISLAM

In the Arab countries the relationships among state organizations, Arabism, and Islam are elusive. In the Arab fertile crescent the quest for national identity and the struggle for political power has for over a century been conducted in terms of Arab nationalism. Arab nationalism was born before World War I in the literary revival of the Arabic language, the revival of Arab identification with the glories of the Islamic past, and the anti-Turkish political ambitions of Arab intellectuals. Arabism rather than Islam became the dominant discourse, displacing the traditional vocabularies of political affiliation and political action.

In the colonial period Arab nationalism became the shared ideology of both the political elites and the opposition intelligentsia. The coalescence of ideologies was based on the shared desire for independence, the need to integrate non-Muslim minorities into the political system, and the awareness of the need for a modern national form of political identity corresponding to the actual state structures. After World War II, Arab identity became the basis of political goals such as anti-imperialism, struggle against Israel, and the formation of political regimes. From the 1950s to the 1970s the two crucial themes in Arab nationalist thinking were the struggle for unity and socio-economic development. At this stage some form of socialism generally became a part of Arab nationalist ideologies.

While important in the colonial era, Islamic modernism and reformism were subsidiary currents. In Syria, the Salafi movement was interpreted in a conservative sense by Rashid Rida' (1865–1935), the foremost of Muhammad 'Abduh's disciples. Rida', like 'Abduh, held that the Quran and the teachings of Muhammad were the sole bases of Islam, but rather than stress the implications of this view for modernizing reforms, he emphasized opposition to Shi'ism and to Sufi shrines. In Rida''s view the crucial goal of an Islamic restoration was a polity, headed by a Caliph, advised by the 'ulama', which would revise the law of Islam in accordance with contemporary needs. Rida' stressed the importance of jihad – moral striving for purity and self-perfection – as the basis of loyalty and sacrifice for the common good. Other disciples of 'Abduh stressed the modernist implications of his teachings. They emphasized the importance of science and the legitimacy of social change. For the modernist writers, Islam was accepted as a true religion, but not as a touchstone for the development of a scientific civilization.

The trend toward secularism and nationalism goes back to the weaknesses of the 'ulama' in the nineteenth century. In the Arab world, as in Egypt and Turkey, 'ulama' resistance to secular trends generally came from lower-ranking religious functionaries such as prayer leaders, preachers in the smaller mosques, court clerks, notaries, Quran-school teachers, and above all students in the religious colleges. In rural areas, leadership sometimes came from Sufi shaykhs or independent preachers. This opposition proved ineffective. In general secular legal and judicial institutions have replaced Muslim law. New penal and civil codes were introduced, and a dual court system of state and Islamic courts was established in Syria and Iraq. Even when Shari'a principles continued to be accepted, they were profoundly modified by new legal procedures. Eclectic combinations of Shari'a law codes with Western criteria for evidence, cross-examination, and appellate jurisdiction changed the actual administration of Shari'a law. The effect of legal reform was to accept the modernist view that the law is not eternally fixed and that it is subject to reformulation in terms of contemporary circumstances and state interests. The dilution of Muslim legal principles and the substitution of new law codes and court systems was perhaps the single most important index of the disestablishment of Islam in the public life of Arab countries.

Despite the disestablishment of religion and the dominance of Arab nationalist sentiment, Islam continued to play a substantial role. Arab national consciousness was still bound up with Islam. Arab nationalist thinkers of the 1920s and 1930s stressed the virtual identity of Arabism and Islam. The vocabulary of Arab nationalism was infused with words such as umma (community of Muslims) and milla (religious community), which have strong religious overtones but were used to express national solidarity. Even Christian writers considered Arabism and Islam to be two expressions of the same ideal. They stressed the glory of Muhammad as a heroic leader and praised his contribution to Arab nationality, but they maintained that national ties should transcend religious ties and advocated the formation of secular states. The common people followed the nationalist thinkers in identifying the Arab nation with Islam. For them, to be an Arab was still primarily to be a Muslim. The rhetoric may have been nationalistic, but the emotional identifications were Islamic.

Islam continued to be important in ostensibly secular Arab movements. It was crucial in the mobilization of Palestinians in the 1920s and 1930s to resist British rule and Zionism; the Muslim attachment to Jerusalem remains a source of worldwide support for the Palestinian movement. Sa'udi support for the Palestinian cause does not distinguish Arab and Muslim interests. In the postwar era Arab constitutions often declared Islam the official religion of the state or required the head of state to be a Muslim.

At the end of World War II, pan-Arabism became the dominant political and cultural trend. The driving ambition in the region was to achieve the long-awaited unity of Arab peoples, dedicated to eliminating Israel and avenging the defeat of 1948. In the 1950s pan-Arabism became the banner of opposition to the elites of Syria, Iraq, and Jordan. Nasser of Egypt, the Ba'th Parties in Syria and Iraq, and Palestinian factions all proclaimed themselves custodians of the Arab dream, and fought against each other as much as they united and cooperated.

The 1967 war with Israel shattered this conflicted dream and opened a new cultural and political phase. Egypt gave up the struggle on behalf of the Palestinians. Egyptian leadership in the Arab world faded, and the initiative passed to Iraq, Iran, and the oil-producing Arabian states. The Palestinians organized to defend their own cause. Syria, though maintaining its verbal profile as a leader of the anti-Israel movement, maneuvered carefully to avoid direct conflict with Israel. Lebanon collapsed into civil war over the question of whether the Palestinians could use Lebanon as a base for their operations. Pan-Arabism receded and a new mood of national state self-assertion took hold. The more conservative Arabian peninsula and Gulf states became ever more important in Arab affairs as investors and patrons of the less wealthy Arab states. Arabism came to be identified with oil wealth. The Gulf War completed the disintegration of the pan-Arab dream. While Saddam Husayn hoped to make himself the hegemon of the fertile crescent and a dominant voice in Arab affairs, Egypt, Syria, Sa'udi Arabia, and the Gulf states allied with the United States and the United Nations to defeat him and force his evacuation from Kuwait.

As pan-Arabism declined, it became evident that despite their nationalist, socialist, and populist rhetoric, most of the fertile crescent and Arabian states are authoritarian family or military regimes. Countries such as Iraq and Syria are ruled through military, security, and party structures that are anchored in some small minority – families, clans, tribes, or sects. Others such as Egypt and the Palestinian Authority depend on military and security forces, and a dominant political party, and are not based on political coalitions within their societies. Rather, they rule by appeasing rural and traditional elites, supporting crony capitalists, and creating extensive patronage networks. In the cases of Egypt and Jordan military rule is offset by plebiscitary popular support and quasi-parliamentary institutions, which are closely controlled by the governments.

The economies of these states reinforce their political institutions. In these countries the public sector dominates. Most of these states live on rents, oil, or strategic remittances, and therefore neither tax their citizens nor represent them. Rentier states commonly use their resources to create alliances of business and administrative and even tribal elites, and to provide welfare subsides for the mass of their populations that win acquiescence to undemocratic regimes. Bank lending is the predominant source of capital, and banks are often government owned or regulated. In most of these states potential capitalists are tied to the public sector or to political networks. Property is not secure from patrimonial regimes, and both foreign and domestic investment are hampered. Military regimes resist the free flow of information and have repressed the middle classes, politicians, and intellectuals who might have created an independent civil society. On the United Nations Human Development Index, which includes education, literacy, life expectancy, and per capita income, the fertile crescent Arab countries fall below Latin America and Asia.

In the Arabian peninsula the dominant elements are extended families: the Sa'udis; al-Sabahs in Kuwait; and al-Khalifas in Bahrain and Qatar. These families have been in power, with some interruptions, since the middle of the eighteenth century, and are among the oldest governments in the world. These families rule with the support of tribal coalitions and merchant elites over societies in which a great proportion of the population are non-citizen foreign workers. For example, 80 percent of the population of the United Arab Emirates, 66 percent in Qatar, 50 percent in Kuwait, 33 percent in Bahrain and 20 percent of the Sa'udi population are guest workers, ranging from military, medical, engineering and administrative specialists to teachers, bureaucrats, and skilled workers, as well as masses of manual laborers. By their financial contributions to Egypt, Jordan, Syria, and the Palestinians they manipulate Arab world political currents to maintain their security. Culturally conservative, they have avoided the challenges of Arab nationalism and pan-Arabism; the Sa'udis in particular are sponsors of Islamic movements worldwide.

While the regimes are well consolidated, most of the Gulf and fertile crescent Arab states have weak civil societies. A critical problem everywhere is the fit between national identities and national states. Arab identity is transnational and not localized in any particular state, and thus conflicts with some two dozen state identities. Moreover, the so-called Arab states have profound internal divisions. Iraq has a large Kurdish minority, and the Arab population is divided among Sunni and Shi'i Muslims – a distinction at least as important as Iraqi national or pan-Arab identity. Syria is largely Arab, but this belies the sectarian and religious distinctions among Sunnis, Isma'ilis, 'Alawis, Christians, and Druzes. Lebanon may be Arabic speaking but its fifteen-year civil war makes clear how deep are the sectarian divides among five Muslim and seven Christian sub-communities. The Gulf states are defined as Arab, but the non-citizen population is often the majority.

Moreover, there is a deep ambiguity in the meaning of ethnic and national identity. National or ethnic identity is blended with religious identity. Turks, Iranians, Kurds, Egyptians, Algerians, Palestinians, and others believe themselves to belong to the same nation because what they have in common is Islam. While Islam is universalistic and the shared religion of peoples of many different ethnicities, it is most intensely expressed in its local and national versions.

The implied Muslim identity of Arab world states also makes for grave complications in the position of the minorities. Jews and Christians in post-independence Iraq; Greeks, Armenians, and Kurds in Turkey; Copts in Egypt; Baha'is and Jews in post-revolutionary Iran; and Christians and animists in the Sudan have all suffered religious and political persecution.

The failure of these regimes to create a coherent national identity and to win legitimacy helps account for the most important trend of the post-1967 era – the movement away from secular nationalism, liberalism, and socialism toward Islam. The 1967 war with Israel and the oil embargo of the 1970s were important turning points. The defeat of Egypt and the fertile crescent Arab states exposed not only their military limits, but highlighted the corruption of the regimes, their dependence on the United States, their failure to allow political participation or to achieve economic development, and their lack of cultural authenticity. The dramatic impact of the oil embargo turned attention to Sa'udi Arabia and the conservative Arab states. These events discredited the secular, liberal, and socialist claims of the dominant elites, and started a revival of interest in the historical culture of the region – Islam. In all sectors of society, but especially among students and the lower middle classes, a new interest in the teachings and practice of Islam became evident. Young women began to wear the *hijab*, or covering garments. Books on Islam, preaching, discussion groups, and prayer became more a part of everyday culture.

Most striking was the emergence of an active political opposition based on Islamic claims. The Society of Muslim Brothers in Egypt and Jordan, the jam'at in Egypt, HAMAS among the Palestinians, and other small militant sects opposed the rule of the entrenched elites. These were communalist movements which espoused traditional moral and social values, including the limitation of women to household and family activities, and which organized worship, instruction in schools, cooperatives, clinics and workshops, and neighborhood and social welfare services. They called for economic fairness and the reinforcement of the family, and ultimately demanded the formation of Islamic states. Their goal was to inculcate Muslim virtues in individuals and justice in society. These movements were not anti-modern so much as a populist alternative to state capitalist societies.

In general the supporters of these movements were people excluded from social and political power: bazaaris – merchants, shopkeepers, peddlers, artisans working in the old-fashioned economy of the bazaars, without government connections or access to international trade; maktabis – clerks, teachers, and minor bureaucrats without the educational opportunities to be integrated into the modernized sector of the economy; students; deracinated migrants from villages to shanty-towns in the big cities. Their protest was not only political, it also stemmed from moral confusion in face of the temptations of sexual liberty and consumerism offered by contemporary societies, and appealed to myriads of people fearful of the insubordination of women and children and the breakdown of families.

These movements pursued their goals on various levels attuned to the context and opportunities and problems of each different national society. In Iran they led to a revolutionary seizure of power. In Turkey they created a competitive political party advocating alternative policies; in Jordan, a parliamentary party; in Egypt a plethora of small groups pursued objectives ranging from moral education to terrorism. In Syria and Iraq political defiance led to crushing defeat. HAMAS functions as a competing social movement, a political opposition to the Arafat regime and a guerrilla operation against Israel. In Lebanon active Shiʻi movements, Amal, and Hizballah have become competitors for political power.

So far the radical Islamic movements have failed to come to power in the fertile crescent countries. The national state is too solidly legitimized in the eyes of its populations, and military and other elites too well consolidated to be easily dislodged. They face violent suppression by the regimes of Iraq and Syria, cooptation and manipulation in Jordan and by the Palestinian authorities. Not only do the same regimes exist in Syria, Iraq, Jordan, and the Arabian states, but as recently as 1999 and 2000 the very same people who came to power in the 1960s – Hafiz al-Asad, King Husayn, Saddam Husayn, and Yassir Arafat – still ruled. These movements also failed to come to power for reasons inherent in their character and operations. First, the Islamists are uncertain and divided about their proper goals. Is their objective to create a truly Islamic society within existing states, or is it to overthrow existing states to pave the way for a truly Islamic society? Should they work within or against the established institutions? In the struggle for power they are uncertain; lacking charismatic leadership, and are often divided into small and sectarian factions. Their protest has not undermined the established regimes. Despite profound conflicts and upheavals, the fertile crescent and Gulf states show an astonishing political stability.

CHAPTER 26

NORTH AFRICA IN THE NINETEENTH AND
TWENTIETH CENTURIES

The modern history of Arab North Africa parallels the history of the Arab Middle East. By the nineteenth century North Africa was substantially Muslim. Sufism played a large part in the organization of rural communities, and states tended to be legitimized in Muslim, rather than patrimonial, cosmopolitan, or ethnic terms. The urban populations were Arabic in speech and culture, although in the southern, Saharan, and mountain regions, Berber was the common language and the basis of social identity.

In the late eighteenth and early nineteenth centuries, the North African states were becoming more centralized and more rigorous in exacting taxes, but increased taxation provoked widespread tribal and Sufi-led resistance. European economic competition further weakened the already tenuous hold of the North African states over their rural populations. The weakened North African states all succumbed to European domination. The French invaded Algeria in 1830, and established a protectorate in Tunisia in 1881 and in Morocco in 1912. Libya was invaded by Italy in 1911. The imposition of foreign rule led, as in the Middle East, to profound changes in the structure of these societies, and to the emergence of independent national states.

ALGERIA

The French occupation

Algeria on the eve of the French conquest was governed by a regime that in many ways resembled that of Iraq and Syria. From the sixteenth century, a small force of janissaries organized the state and gave Algeria its territorial identity, but most of the country was ruled with the collaboration of tribal chiefs and Sufis who gathered their supporters on the basis of kinship or religious loyalty. By the early decades of the nineteenth century, the Algerian regime was in decline and the major Sufi brotherhoods, in reaction to fiscal burdens imposed by the central government, were in sporadic revolt.

In 1830, the government of Charles X, prompted by the need for a military victory to restore its political prestige after setbacks in the Greek war for independence, and supported by Marseilles' commercial interests, invaded Algeria. The French occupied Algiers and other coastal towns, but the defeat of the Turkish administration allowed a new Muslim state to emerge in western Algeria. In 1832 'Abd al-Qadir, whose father was head of the Qadiriya order, declared himself Commander of the Faithful and Sultan of the Arabs, and made himself responsible for applying Muslim holy law and for waging war against the French. He maintained the image of an ascetic Sufi; abstaining from alcohol, modest in dress and manner, he emulated the Prophet. However, he was careful to limit his claims so as not to offend his patron, the Sultan of Morocco. He did not have the Friday sermon delivered or the coinage minted in his name. On the basis of his religious prestige and the propaganda of the Qadiriya order, most of the regional tribes accepted his authority.

'Abd al-Qadir developed a hierarchical administration. He appointed subordinate khalifas with combined military, financial, and judicial authority. Beneath the khalifas were aghas, whose duty was to collect taxes. Below them were the qa'ids, who were chiefs of the tribes. 'Abd al-Qadir chose his officials from important religious families, and avoided using the people who had cooperated with the Turks. Alongside the state administration he organized a standing army.

From 1832 to 1841, 'Abd al-Qadir alternately waged war and made peace with the French as part of a complex struggle for the loyalty of the Algerian tribes. In 1841, however, a new French general, Bugeaud, decided to dominate Algeria absolutely, and open it to French colonization. The Moroccans intervened to protect their client, but at the battle of Isly in 1844 they were defeated, and in 1847, 'Abd al-Qadir was deported to France and then to Damascus. The way was open to complete French control of Algeria. Between 1851 and 1857 the French occupied Kabylia, and moved into the Sahara. In 1853 Wargala and the Mzab came under French suzerainty; the Mzab was annexed in 1882. In 1890 a treaty with Great Britain gave European political recognition to an expanded French Algerian empire.

The French began their reign in Algeria by adopting the Turkish and makhzan system. They combined a regional government modeled on that of the Turks with the mobilization of support from privileged tribes. After 1843, however, the French felt sufficiently in control to supervise the population directly through the Bureaux Arabes, some fifty units which combined military and civil administration. Also by the early 1840s the French embarked upon the destruction of Algerian society to make way for French colonization. General Bugeaud cut down orchards, burned crops, and destroyed peoples and villages. Great numbers of people were killed as a result of war and famine. Algerian tribes were confined to specific districts or removed and resettled in the south to make way for French colons. Between 1843 and 1870 the French undermined the tribal and religious chieftains in favor of a new generation of officials who lacked authority and were more amenable to French control. From 1874 the Muslim population was subject to the *code de l'indigénat* which made Muslims punishable for a long list of treasonable or illegal acts. These laws permitted confinement and confiscation of property.

The disorganization of Algerian society left it vulnerable to economic exploitation. Vast areas of land were confiscated. A few Muslim landowners were able to move from subsistence to a market economy, but the bulk of the population was forced into ownership of uneconomical small plots, sharecropping, labor, and destitution. While the French often argued that the poverty of the Muslims was inherent in their social and cultural limitations, or that not enough incentives had been provided to overcome a pre-market mentality, or that capitalism did not go far enough in Algeria to absorb the Muslim population, the major cause was the devastation wrought by the French invasion and the seizure of Algerian lands.

In the face of the destruction of their society, Algerian resistance was bitter but local in scale. In this resistance Muslim beliefs and loyalties played an important part. In northern Algeria there was a series of millenarian uprisings. In 1849 Bu Zian of Zaatsha, a local shaykh who had supported 'Abd al-Qadir, was impelled by a dream in which the Prophet Muhammad named him the representative of the mahdi, to resist taxation and to rebel against French control. In 1858 Sidi Sadok b. al-Haji, a leader of a Rahmaniya zawiya who had been an ally of Bu Zian in 1849, resumed the jihad, but he and eighty-eight followers were arrested. In 1860 Bu Khentash, a member of a pious and highly regarded warrior lineage, promised his followers miraculous protection against French bullets. He was killed in the same year. In 1879 Muhammad Amzian, who had fought a generation earlier on the side of Sidi Sadok, declared himself the mahdi and attacked the local officials. In southern Algeria there were also rebellions between 1851 and 1855 and 1871 and 1872 by camel-herding peoples who were attempting to protect the passages from the northern oases and to resist French officials. Sheep-herding nomads also rebelled to protect their access to markets and avoid complete economic dependence.

These insurrections were sometimes prepared by secret societies called *shartiya*, which formed within each tribe to keep watch on officials, prepare horses and weapons, and mobilize the people to fight. Preachers and Sufis, who claimed to be forerunners of the mahdi, created an atmosphere of ecstatic fervor. Sufi brotherhoods were also important. From his base in Tunisia, Shaykh Mustafa b. 'Azzuz (d. 1866) used his contacts in the Rahmaniya order, religious prestige, kinship ties, and his central position in the munitions trade to support anti-French propaganda and resistance in the Constantine region. For a time, however, the shaykh also made peace with the French. His policy was not to carry on an ideological or religious war but to make the best of the political realities.

In 1870–71 scattered local resistance finally crystallized into a massive Algerian uprising. Impelled by years of hardship and famine, by hopes that the defeat of Napoleon III in the Franco-Prussian war would make independence possible, and by fears that the rise of a republican government in France would remove all restraints upon French colonization and lead to the seizure of Algerian lands, there were revolts throughout Algeria. These rebellions were given leadership and coordination by an Algerian tribal chief named al-Muqrani, supported by the Rahmaniya brotherhood. Al-Muqrani's family had been allies of the French since the 1830s, but in 1870 their position was threatened by French efforts to replace the dominant stratum with newer, more malleable administrative cadres, and to open the way for the settlement of French colons in the Mejana and the Kabyle. Al-Muqrani was defeated. The French extracted an enormous indemnity, amounting to ten times the usual tribute, and confiscated or held for ransom hundreds of thousands of hectares of land. In historical retrospect the resistance movements were signs of Algerian determination not to accept French rule, but they were also the last phase in the defeat of Algerian society.

Muslim culture also suffered. Before the French conquest there were numerous schools and extensive properties endowed to support religious instruction. Constantine and Tlemsen, for example, had numerous primary schools, madrasas, and zawiyas with hundreds of advanced students. The colleges provided a higher education stressing grammar, law, interpretation of the Quran, arithmetic, and astronomy. French occupation, however, led to the seizure of the revenues and the destruction of many schools. In principle they were supposed to be replaced by French schools to assimilate Algerian children into European civilization, but the new school system, introduced between 1883 and 1898, reached only a small minority and essentially trained native Algerian functionaries to cooperate with the French. While many Algerian middle-class families from the Kabyle, the Aurès, and the Mzab enrolled in the new schools, the absolute numbers were small. In 1890 students enrolled in French schools amounted to 2 percent of the school-age population; in 1930 almost 9 percent of Algerian children received some education; and in 1945 approximately 15 percent. In 1954 only three-quarters of a percent of Muslims of secondary-school age were being educated. The system, minimal as it was, was resisted by the colons and by many Muslims.

Massive French colonization began almost immediately after the French conquest as companies were formed in France to speculate in Algerian land, and would-be settlers seized abandoned properties. The French government soon decided to expropriate Algerian lands on a large scale. A decree of 1843 ended the inalienability of religious endowments and allowed them to be bought and sold under European law. The French also forced tribal groups to move out of their traditional domains or to occupy smaller spaces so that the "surplus" land could be converted into colonial farms. Further regulations culminating in a law of 1873 broke down Algerian communal properties by allowing individual Muslims to sell their portions of collective tribal lands as well as family property. Vast tracts were made available to French settlers. By 1900 Europeans held 1,700,000 hectares and by 1940 2,700,000 hectares, about 35 to 40 percent of the arable land of Algeria. European settlers were nonetheless extremely dependent upon government help. Before 1870 efforts to grow grain, sugar cane, cotton, tobacco, linen, tea, and mulberries all failed. Only after a series of grape-crop failures in France did wine become the dominant European industry in Algeria.

The large European and French colony in Algeria demanded that Algeria be made an integral part of France. This was opposed by the French army, which itself wanted to govern Algeria through the Bureaux Arabes and tried to restrain the appropriation of Muslim lands and the establishment of a civilian government for the colonial population. In 1860 Napoleon III visited Algeria and was convinced that his first obligation was to protect his 3,000,000 Arab subjects. Military administration was again strengthened, but between 1864 and 1870 famines, epidemics, and tribal insurrections discredited the military administration, and the defeat of the great Muslim revolt of 1870–71 finally allowed for the establishment of a regime committed to ruling Algeria entirely in the interests of the colons. Algeria was administratively incorporated into France and reorganized as three French departments, though under a single Governor-General. The colonists were given the right to municipal government and could elect deputies to the French Assembly. In 1896 the system of direct control by French ministries in Paris was ended, and in 1898 an elected assembly, with vast European preponderance, was created. French settlers controlled local councils and the Algerian Assembly and manipulated the French parliament so that the system operated to vest control of Algeria in the hands of the colons.

The rebirth of Algerian resistance: to the end of World War II

Paradoxically, colonial rule generated the conditions for the emergence of a renewed Algerian resistance and demands for independence. The vast but disorganized and impoverished Algerian population, confined to marginal lands, its tribal leadership demolished, its religious elites co-opted, its military resistance defeated, was nonetheless to be reborn. The very economic changes introduced by the French led to the formation of new classes and a changing Algerian consciousness. As the French colonized the countryside they upset the village economies, forced rural peoples to migrate to the cities, and brought new elites into being as a result of their efforts to destroy the old. A new generation of Western- or Muslim-reform-educated men arose. They were often state employees such as teachers, postmen, pharmacists, and railway workers; sometimes they were returned war veterans. The new elites became the backbone of new organizations, including cultural associations, trade unions, and political parties. On a psychological level, French penetration came up against a hidden core of national feeling which was mobilized in symbolic ways until it eventually took political form. Popular poems and epics celebrated the past glory of Islam, destined to once again overcome the unbelievers. Disillusionment and anger were manifested in demonstrations, strikes, and sporadic violence. These were expressions of a refusal, however limited, to accept the permanence of French power.

After World War I French policy indirectly encouraged Algerian resistance. In the flush of victory and gratitude for Algerian support in the war, there were several attempts to liberalize the administration of the Muslim population. France offered Muslims French citizenship if they would give up Muslim civil law. Other legislation enlarged the representation of native peoples in local assemblies and gave suffrage to property owners, officials, and veterans. Algerian settler pressure forced the French government to renege on many of these concessions, but not before French concepts of justice, equality, and citizenship had taken hold among Muslim intellectuals.

The indigenous Algerian elite had three main components. One was the graduates of French-Arab schools who expected to be fully integrated into French society, while retaining their social and legal identity as Muslims. After the turn of the century, a small group of French-educated Muslim intellectuals organized the "Young Algerians" to press their demands. In 1927 the Fédération des Elus Indigènes d'Algérie was founded by liberal lawyers and teachers who had been elected to municipal councils. This was followed in 1930 by the organization of the federation of Muslim representatives in the department of Constantine, led by Dr. Ben Jellul. The federation became the spokesman for those Algerians who demanded equality in the army, in education, and in appointment to public office, and the abolition of all measures that discriminated against the Muslim population. The French-educated elite, however, did not demand Algerian independence. Farhat 'Abbas made the famous statement: "I have questioned history; I have questioned the living and the dead; I have visited the cemeteries. The empires of the Arabs and Islam are in the past; our future is decisively linked to that of France."

A second Algerian elite of the 1920s and 1930s was more radical and nationalist in orientation, and grew up among Algerian émigrés in Paris. In 1926 L'Etoile Nord Africaine (ENA) was established by the French Communist Party. The ENA languished until 1933, when Messali Hajj reactivated the movement. In its new incarnation the ENA stressed Algerian independence, but it played down the concept of class struggle within Algeria in the interest of generating Algerian solidarity against foreign rule. In 1936 Messali Hajj was converted to pan-Arab ideals espoused by Shakib Arslan, a Lebanese journalist living in Geneva, who called for an independent Algeria rooted in Islamic values and allied to fellow Arabs. In 1937 the ENA was transformed into the Parti du Peuple Algérien (PPA).

The PPA called for the creation of an Algerian parliament, universal suffrage, the admission of Algerians to all public functions on an equal basis, and obligatory instruction in Arabic. It called for the total political independence of Algeria, the removal of all occupying troops, and the control by the new Algerian state over banks, mines, railways, ports, and public facilities. The organization also called on Algerians to conform to the principles of Islam. The PPA was essentially a populist movement whose social base widened from its original migrant-worker supporters to artisans, small merchants, and workers. During World War II it was joined by students and graduates.

The third section of the new Algerian elite was the leaders of the Islamic reformist movement, who adapted Islamic scripturalism to Algerian nationalist needs. Muslim reformism reached Algeria as a result of contact with Muhammad 'Abduh and with Muslim reformers in Tunisia, but did not take hold until after World War I, when the position of rural Sufis was undermined. The migration of workers to the cities reduced their clientele in the countryside, and collaboration with the French reduced their prestige. The growth of an urban petite bourgeoisie and working class subverted the appeal of the magical, thaumaturgic, and mystical authority of the marabouts. The rise of the reformers in turn pushed the marabouts into cooperation with the French and thus further subverted their position. At the same time French political generosity in the aftermath of World War I provoked fears that close relations with France might tempt Muslims to assimilate. Muslims felt more acutely the need for a Muslim press and religious associations to compete with Catholic organizations and French schools.

'Abd al-Hamid b. Badis (Ben Badis), educated at the Zaytuna in Tunis, became the principal leader of the reform (*islah*) movement and of the postwar revival of Arab cultural identity in Algeria. He took his inspiration from Muhammad 'Abduh, Rashid Rida', and the Salafi movement, and emphasized the importance of returning to the Quran and hadith as the basic sources of Muslim belief and practice. He stressed belief in the unity of God, denounced polytheism, and emphasized the revealed sources of Muslim knowledge, without diminishing the importance of reason. From the Quran Ben Badis extracted the general principles of the reform: belief in the unity of God, filial piety, respect for the rights of others, proper use of worldly fortunes, honesty in commercial transactions, and purity of moral intentions. A good Muslim should emulate the virtues of the Prophet.

The emphasis on divine unity was used to launch a bitter critique of Sufi beliefs and practices. The reformers denounced the veneration of saints and beliefs in miracles and attempted to use rational arguments to demystify rural Sufism. Maraboutism, they argued, was a reprehensible novelty introduced into Islam – neither prescribed in the Quran, recommended by the Prophet, nor practiced by the early Caliphs. Thus, they tried to change the way in which the birthday of the Prophet was celebrated. In schools, clubs, and theaters, as well as mosques and zawiyas, the reformers, less ecstatic, less ritualistic and more austere, emphasized Muhammad's historical role and gave sermons on topics of current interest.

The reformers were particularly concerned with social and economic issues but conceived these issues in religious and moral terms. Thus they spoke a great deal about zakat (alms) as a source of income for the movement, and as an expression of the responsibility of the rich for the poor, but they had little to say about the conditions of urban workers and rural peasants, or about the problems of economic development and the use of capital. Following Rashid Rida' they rejected feminism, favored the use of the veil, and opposed the social interaction of men and women. They opposed giving women equality in inheritance or the right to initiate divorce. In the classical sources they found nothing to contradict modern science and technology, but while they saw Islam as compatible with the modern world, they were not principally concerned with the modernization of society. What moved them was the defeat of Muslim countries by Europeans. Only a return to the purity and vigor of early Islam would enable Muslims to assimilate modern science and remedy their cultural and political situation. The reformers' journal castigated the social ills of modern societies, including alcoholism, gambling, and all other immoral activities forbidden by religion.

The reform movement intended not only to define a new doctrine but also to create a social movement through which the new ideas could be passed on to the young. They organized conferences and discussion groups to propagate Muslim principles and Arabic culture. They sponsored a strong scout movement, and founded schools that combined teaching of the Quran, Arabic, Algerian history, and patriotic songs, plus some French, arithmetic, and geography, to inculcate the concept of an Algerian fatherland. Most of the reform schools were elementary schools but students could move on to the mosque at Constantine or the Zaytuna in Tunis for an advanced education. Only a small portion of the students actually earned an elementary certificate; few went on to higher education. The school movement reached its peak in 1954, when it had about 110 schools and 20,000 students. By then the schools were training militants for the nationalist movement, and were important in creating a sense of an Algerian national identity.

In 1931 Ben Badis also founded the Association of Muslim 'Ulama' of Algeria to sponsor preaching, publications, and schools. The strengthening of the reform movement provoked resistance from the Sufis, who founded their own Association of 'Ulama' in 1932. In 1933 the French denied the use of mosques to reformist preachers and claimed control over journals published in Arabic as well as those published in French. French controls made the reformers the only outspoken indigenous opponents of French rule. Ben Badis defended religious liberty, and the right to teach Arabic and maintain a Muslim press. After 1935 the reform movement began to slide into a more overtly political role. A joint congress of the Association of Muslim 'Ulama' and the Fédération des Elus Indigènes was held in 1936, at which Ben Badis emerged as the leading spokesman of opposition to French assimilation.

Behind the reform was a political concept: though part of the French empire, Algeria was an Arab-Muslim entity. Arabism was meant not only to combat assimilation but also to resist French efforts to divide Arabs and Berbers. Muslims should govern themselves, Ben Badis held, through a *jama'*, or permanent council, separate from and independent of states, though Muslims could also at the same time be citizens or subjects of states. His thinking distinguished cultural from political nationality, and thus allowed for a conception of a Muslim community as universal in principle and yet divided into politically and culturally distinct regional or national groups. By distinguishing religion from political nationality the reformers allowed for Algerian identity under French domination. In response to the famous declaration of Farhat 'Abbas, Ben Badis affirmed that "this Muslim nation is not France, it is not possible for it to be France. It does not want to become France, and even if it wanted to, it could not." The religious reformers popularized the notion that religiously, linguistically, and culturally, Algerians were a distinct people whose ultimate destiny was political independence.

Reformism, then, adapted itself to local circumstances in both urban and rural areas to become the most energetic and widespread cultural force in Algeria. The reform movement had strong appeal to the petite bourgeoisie of the coastal towns such as Constantine, Oran, and Algiers, and to rural areas that felt the vacuum of authority and initiative left by the decline of tribal and Sufi elites. By the late 1930s the reformers had pushed both the liberal bourgeois and the more radical worker movements to take on an Islamic aura and to legitimize themselves in Islamic terms. The death of Ben Badis in 1940 deprived the reform of its dynamism but its contribution to the creation of an Algerian national identity was lasting.

The Drive to independence and the Algerian revolution
By the mid-1930s, the cultural preparations were made, and the struggle for Algerian independence began in earnest. Algerian demands grew ever more insistent, and French responses ever more contradictory. By 1936 the various Algerian elites had coalesced in an Algerian Muslim congress which made demands for reform – maintenance of Muslim civil law, improvement in instruction and education, equality in salary and other economic matters, universal suffrage, and representation in parliament – but not independence. The French were divided as to how to respond. Some favored a conciliatory, liberal policy, but French politics made it impossible to carry this out consistently. Threatened by the new elites, the French turned to repression, closed down reformist schools and journals, and broke with the Muslim liberal bourgeoisie. For two generations the French had cultivated a small Muslim elite by holding forth the expectation that educated Muslims could become French citizens, but in 1938 the Blum–Viollette proposal to grant French citizenship to Algerians without requiring them to renounce Muslim civil law was abandoned. Liberals in Algeria lost their hope for reform and assimilation.

From the outbreak of World War II until the beginning of the Algerian revolution, nationalist groups increased their demands upon the French, who responded alternately with belated reforms and continued obstruction and repression. Throughout the war years moderate Algerian opinion backed France, but in 1943 Farhat ʿAbbas issued his Manifesto of the Algerian People, which called for an end to colonial rule and the formation of an Algerian constitution allowing for the participation of Muslims in the government of their own country. The manifesto further advocated the recognition of the Arabic language as equal to French, freedom of press and association, universal school instruction, and other liberal measures. In 1946 the new Union Démocratique du Manifeste Algérien (UDMA) was founded as the voice of Algerian bourgeois opinion. This was followed by Messali's Mouvement pour le Triomphe des Libertés Démocratiques (MTLD). In 1947 the Algerians presented the French Assembly with a plan for an Algerian republic as part of a

North African union federated with France. The French government rejected these proposals and instead passed the Statut d'Algérie in September 1947. The Statut defined Algeria as a group of departments within the French Republic administered by a Governor-General, though they were provided with an elected assembly and accorded limited financial and administrative autonomy. The Statut also provided for equality of citizenship and for recognition of the Islamic religious and Arabic language interests of the Algerian population. This plan not only fell short of Muslim proposals, but the French government manipulated Algerian elections to exclude the major Muslim parties, and otherwise postponed the implementation of the reforms. The idea of gradual and non-violent emancipation and the concept of an Algeria allied with France completely lost its value in Algerian Muslim public opinion.

Behind the maneuvering of the political elites, a new Algerian mass consciousness and political movement was in the making. In May 1945 Algerian demonstrations at Setif led to attacks on French colons and to terrible massacres of Muslims by the French. These events marked the beginning of a mass or popular nationalist sentiment. Also, within the MTLD some activists and militants concluded that armed insurrection was the only way to achieve Algerian independence. A more radical younger generation, from small towns and lower-middle-class families who had little opportunity for higher education and little contact with Europeans, but instead were stronger in their Arabic and Islamic identity – who bore a sharp sense of the misery of rural life and the injustice and indignity of French domination and a strong will to resist and to exercise power in the name of the Algerian nation – came to the fore. Within the MTLD an Organisation Spéciale (OS), led by Ait Ahmed and Ben Bella, gave the Algerian resistance a paramilitary capability. By 1949 the cadres of a military resistance were ready, but until 1954 the various Algerian liberal, radical, and revolutionary groups remained unable to agree upon such action.

Finally, in 1954 the OS organized the Front de Libération Nationale (FLN) and on November 1, 1954 launched the Algerian revolution with a nationwide campaign of guerrilla attacks. The revolutionaries organized Algeria into six provinces (wilayat); in Tunisia and Morocco they built up a strong Algerian army (ALN), commanded eventually (1959) by Houari Boumedienne. The FLN denounced the previous Algerian movements for their political failure and declared itself in favor of an independent, sovereign, democratic, and socialist Algerian state with Islamic principles – a state that could only be created by armed struggle.

The war itself brought a new generation of soldier-leaders to power. While the FLN was not officially Islamic, its supporters held strong Islamic sentiments and puritanical attitudes. The leaders of the revolution considered alcohol and tobacco to be symbols of betrayal. While they were anti-French, they were convinced that the revolution would open up for the masses the modernity that French domination had denied them. In the war itself, they were motivated by attachments to their wilayat and army units, and by a strong sense of personal responsibility. The FLN rapidly gained the political support of other movements, and by 1956 all groups had agreed on the goal of full Algerian independence.

At the congress of Summam in August 1956 the revolutionaries resolved that theirs was a struggle to destroy an anachronistic colonization but was not a war of religion, and proposed the formation of a social and democratic Algerian republic. From this point of view, the only issues to be negotiated with France were the transfer of administrative power, and subsequent cooperation in economic, social, and cultural activities. In 1958 a Gouvernement Provisionnel de la République Algérienne (GPRA) was formed to win international recognition, and was supported by Egypt and other Arab countries, the Communist states, and, to some degree, by American anti-colonialist sentiment. This international support was crucial to its eventual victory.

In response, the French reaffirmed their permanent presence in Algeria. They won the military advantage, captured Ben Bella and his companions by hijacking an airplane on which they were traveling, and under the leadership of General Massu launched the battle for Algiers. This was an urban anti-guerrilla operation which led in the middle of 1957 to the liquidation of the FLN apparatus in Algiers. The French also blocked the flow of weapons and manpower into the country from Tunisia and Morocco, and defeated the FLN in the Sahara. French tactics included massive military action and the resettlement of the Algerian population.

Though the French were winning the military victories, they could not sustain the war. On May 13, 1958, the French population of Algeria organized its own demonstrations which toppled the government of Algeria, undermined the Fourth Republic and, in June 1958, brought General de Gaulle to power. De Gaulle, however, disappointed the expectations of the colons by proposing a reconciliation between France and the FLN. He called for a referendum on a proposed new French constitution in which all residents of France and Algeria would have equal voting rights. After the referendum he proposed the Plan of Constantine for economic development, employment of Muslims, equalization of salaries, distribution of arable land to Muslim peasants, development of the school system for two-thirds of school-age children, and the construction of 200,000 housing units. This was to be financed by petroleum and gas development. Then in September 1959 de Gaulle spoke of a self-determined Algerian future, with Algerians given the right to choose between independence, autonomy in association with France, and assimilation. Thus the French government relinquished its determination to maintain Algeria as part of France. Direct negotiations with the FLN were begun in 1960, and in March 1962, at Evian, Algerian sovereignty was recognized, with France reserving bases for airplane and naval operations and for atomic testing. Future economic cooperation was agreed, and French colons were allowed to choose between French and Algerian citizenship.

Thus, after bitter struggle, terrible destruction, and massive sacrifice of human life – in spite of enormous political and administrative resources, the presence of a large European population, and a passionate desire to assimilate its colony – France lost control of its Algerian empire. Both the French right and the French left believed that the existence of France as a nation depended on its empire, but caught between leftist liberalism and rightist authoritarianism, French policy allowed Muslim dissent to crystallize, and, by repressing its manifestations, prompted further resistance. The French position was further subverted by colons, who led the French government to excesses of policy and then themselves resisted central control. The divisions in France, the numerical predominance of the Muslim population, and the growth of national consciousness made Algerian liberation inevitable.

Independent Algeria

The problems of organizing a regime, defining an economic policy, and creating a cultural identity for the new state were enormous. Algeria came to independence after the whole fabric of Algerian society had been ripped asunder. There was no unified political elite and no clear ideological direction. The Algerian elite was assembled from among liberal bourgeois professionals, reformist 'ulama', petit bourgeois radicals, and revolutionary soldiers, and was divided among the FLN, the ALN, and GPRA, and other groups. After several generations of assimilated French, reformist Muslim, and activist military leadership, the basic problem was the division within the political elite.

The outcome of the ensuing struggle for power was military dictatorship and a state bureaucratic regime. The Tripoli Congress of June 1962 formed a Political Bureau led by Ben Bella, who was named President and who promulgated a socialist constitution; the FLN became the only political party. Ben Bella and the army eliminated the wilaya commanders, and purged the FLN of his opponents. Only the Algerian Union of Workers (UGTA), a militant force in organizing railroad, post office, petroleum, municipal construction, and other workers, kept some political autonomy. The other major political bodies – the National Union of Algerian Women, the National Liberation Front Youth Movement, and the National Union of Algerian Students – were poorly organized and had little potential for political action. Control of the party and the administration, however, was not enough to save Ben Bella from a coup in June 1965 led by General Houari Boumedienne, who became President of the Republic. By 1967 the professional army officers had eliminated their rivals and taken control of the state. Military rule reached out to the larger society by creating supporting "clans" or clienteles, and Boumedienne centralized the system for distributing rents, prebends, credit, and grants to his followers. In 1978 General Boumedienne was succeeded by another military leader, Chadli ben Jadid, who maintained the regime until rising political and religious opposition led to a crisis in 1989 that required the military to temporarily accept a multi-party system.

The new elites were divided in their ideological orientation. While Ben Bella led the cadres who favored the modernization of the country and the creation of a socialist economy, and kept French as the language of government, business, and even of political discussion, Boumedienne became the chief spokesman for a Muslim and Arab identity and for close ties between Algeria, Tunisia, Morocco, and the Arab east. Reformist Islam was accepted as a legitimizing principle and its discourse infiltrated all political language. The new leaders wanted both to modernize Algeria and to deepen the religious–cultural basis of national identity. For many of the uprooted soldiers of the revolution, migrant workers returned from France, peasants residing in the towns, and mobile petite bourgeoisie, Arabism and Islam were the only common bases of social and national identity.

The state, moreover, sought to control the expression of Islam. It absorbed the independent Quran schools, controlled appointments to religious offices, and sponsored Islamic propaganda. A Ministry of Religious Affairs was created to supervise schools, mosques, religious endowments, and the training of clerics. Nonetheless, the state did not entirely capture Islam. In the 1970s there was an open debate between liberal Muslims, who held that Western science and administration could be beneficial to Muslims, and those Muslims following the more purist Muslim position of Ben Badis and the Muslim Brothers. While many devout Muslims were working within the political system, unofficial mosques and schools harbored an independent Muslim community life resisting the efforts of the state and the FLN to control the mosques. As in other Muslim countries, Islam in Algeria eluded state control and retained the capacity for articulating opposition to state policies.

Attitudes toward women became a test of cultural orientation. French rule and colonization had set a precedent for the education of women and their employment in public positions, but this had scarcely any effect on the masses. The revolution, however, made some women militant fighters, whose contribution for a time freed them from control of fathers, husbands, and brothers. With independence, women generally remained veiled and stayed away from public places. European mores were seen as incompatible with Muslim traditions.

In economic policy, the Algerian state concentrated on the development of the urban and industrial sectors of the economy by using petroleum revenues to finance an industrial revolution. State-owned steel, textile, glass, and insurance companies were founded in 1967. Algeria nationalized its gas industry in 1971; investments were made in export-oriented petrochemicals, steel, electricity, fertilizer, chemical, and plastics industries.

Agriculture was subordinated to the needs of industry. Under the socialist-military regime, abandoned French estates were nationalized and consolidated into some 2,300 farms. State decrees provided that they would be run by worker-committees, with the profits to be shared between workers and national employment and investment funds, but later measures deprived the self-managed farms of control over their own financing and marketing, and made them dependent on government ministries. Little was done, however, for the mass of the rural populace, which needed to rebuild the villages and required capital and technical assistance; nothing was done for 600,000 landless rural workers. While a small portion of the rural society was better off, the peasantry suffered from fragmentation of landownership, absentee landlordism, waqf and communal constraints on the ownership of land, sharecropping, and an inequitable distribution of income.

By 1971 demands for social justice and the need to reduce imports of food, to create a more balanced production of dairy products and grain, and to check the impoverishment of the rural population required a new agricultural policy. The new policy was supposed to consist of a redistribution of land and livestock from large to smallholders, the organization of cooperatives, and the coordination of cooperatives into a larger marketing system. The results were not encouraging. Land redistribution was very limited. Many private owners retained lands owing to exceptions in the law. The reform program extended the state-controlled sector of the economy but left the private sector with the continuing burden of an underemployed peasantry.

By the late 1970s, the failures of these policies were borne in upon the regime. A large percentage of Algeria's food supplies had to be imported. Industrial projects were often uneconomical and dependent upon foreign technicians. Housing and welfare were neglected; unemployment was high. President Chadli ben Jadid reversed the policies of the previous regime, slowed down industrial growth, tightened financial controls over industrial projects, increased consumption, and favored a greater participation of private entrepreneurs in the national economy. By and large, however, the Algerian government continued to govern through the army and a socialized economy. It encouraged the capital-intensive sectors of the economy that were under state control at the expense of the economic needs of the rural population. The revolution had ended in state capitalism.

The failure of government policies was brought home by the ever-growing strength of Muslim-led opposition. The narrow base of military and FLN party power, the failure to create a more inclusive regime, a viable economy, and a coherent cultural policy allowed for the formation of a diverse number of Muslim movements and parties. The banning of the Association of 'Ulama' in 1962 prompted the first efforts to organize Muslim teaching independently of the state. Student mosque groups recruited cadres for opposition Islamic movements. The Muslim Brothers had a strong influence. Numerous independent branches and groups – some educational, some political, some fronting for the state, some potentially violent – emerged. Frustration with economic conditions led to student demonstrations in 1982, which were suppressed by the police, bloody riots in 1985, and massive demonstrations in 1988. When the government used the army to suppress the demonstrators the regime lost all legitimacy. In 1987 the government was obliged to allow non-political associations to form publicly, and in 1989 a new constitution recognized political parties other than the FLN and envisioned open elections.

The Islamic Salvation Front (FIS), a coalition of both reformist and radical Islamic groups, but not including all such groups, became the most important party. Led by two contrasting figures – 'Abassi Madani, a cosmopolitan and flexible politician who espoused political pluralism, and 'Ali Belhadj, a purist Muslim with an Arabic and Salafi cultural background who called for the formation of an Islamic state, by violent means if necessary – the FIS adopted a nationalistic discourse in an attempt to replace the FLN as the governing party. The party not only advocated Muslim moral purity, it addressed economic issues such as employment, housing, and social and welfare services. The party won victories in a number of municipal elections, and national first-round elections in 1991 indicated that the FIS would emerge from the second round with a governing majority. In response, the military refused to accept the election results, and by a coup d'état in January 1992 removed Chadli ben Jadid and voided the elections. Since 1992 Algeria has been dominated by a small military clique called the eradicationists, who opposed any compromise with the FIS and waged full-scale war for control of the society in the name of secularism. In the 1990s a good deal of support came from the Kabyle region which opposed the Islamists and promoted Berber national identity. The regime depended largely on military power. It turned counter-insurgency over to village defense forces and militias: the result was numerous atrocities.

The opposition fought in the name of Islam, but the Islamic movement was deeply divided. The FIS failed to hold together its coalition of pious middle-class Muslims and disenfranchised youths, and splintered, with Madani favoring gradualist means and reaffirming his acceptance of the democratic process, while Belhadj called for a jihad. The movement tended to become radicalized with a strong appeal to youth, Arabophone teachers, functionaries, and imams resentful of the political predominance of Francophone elites. Some sections of the FIS formed the Islamic Salvation Army; more radical Muslims joined the Armed Islamic Groups (GIA). While the Islamic Salvation Army forces aimed their attacks on the military and its supporters, the GIA operated by racketeering, savage terrorist attacks, and assaults upon civilians that seem to go beyond any political purpose.

Thus, Algeria dissolved into a civil war, which was perhaps more extreme and bitter than anything hitherto seen in the Muslim world, a civil war in which ordinary Algerians were slaughtered by both sides in their drive to win control of the population. The indiscriminate violence led to war-weariness and to a gradual reaction against the Islamic movements and to increasing support for the government. Liamine Zeroual came to power in January 1994 and was elected to the presidency in November 1995. He was determined to crush all populist resistance and win mass support. He was able to win over moderate Muslim groups, such as the Movement for an Islamic Society (HAMAS), and middle-class bureaucrats and businessmen, and thus divide the Muslim opposition. His market-oriented approach to the economy was designed to gain foreign investment. Nonetheless, Algeria was in the process of deindustrializing; textile and food production diminished in the 1990s. Zeroual was succeeded by Abdelaziz Boutiflicka, who by 2001 was slowly maneuvering to win a popular mandate to bring the war to a conclusion on more open but undefined terms favoring continued military domination. In 2001 nominal secularism and military rule seemed to be defeating Islam and political democracy.

TUNISIA

The colonial era

In the middle of the nineteenth century, Tunisia shared the problems of the Ottoman empire and Egypt. Faced with rising European economic power and a declining internal economy, the Beys of Tunisia attempted to modernize their regime. Ahmad Bey (1837–55) founded a polytechnic school in 1838 and invited Europeans to train a new infantry corps. In 1857 Muhammad Bey (1855–59) promulgated a constitution that guaranteed security for the Tunisian population, equality in taxation, freedom of religion, and mixed European–Tunisian courts. A liberal constitution of 1861 created an oligarchic senate recruited by cooptation. These efforts at reform, however, could not be fully institutionalized, for there were never sufficiently numerous well-trained troops or administrators.

A last attempt at strengthening the state came in the administration of Khayr al-Din between 1873 and 1877. Europe was his model of efficient administration and public security. He believed that good government is the foundation of economic and social vitality, and that government should promote science, industry, agriculture, and commerce. Khayr al-Din's reforms called for political justice as the basis of progress, and made a special argument for equality among Europeans and Muslims. In practice he tried to limit public spending, to eliminate tax-collecting abuses, and to reform the administration of religious affairs. He helped to found the Sadiqi College in 1875 to train future government officials, and appointed new supervisors for the Zaytuna mosque. Under his leadership the government created new offices for the administration of waqfs and reorganized Muslim justice, especially to meet European demands for equity. The reform program included the creation of a government printing press to produce textbooks for the Sadiqi students and to reproduce classic Islamic legal treatises.

Politically, the reform effort depended upon the support of the 'ulama'. The power of the Bey, he argued, should be limited by the 'ulama', who should function as a parliament. While the 'ulama' had a limited capacity to initiate change or exercise political power, they held an important place in Tunisian society because they were the educated graduates of the principal mosques, and served as teachers and magistrates. Until the foundation of the Sadiqi College, they controlled all secondary education. Until the founding of modern newspapers they monopolized political opinion. Their social connections reinforced their influence. They pushed their sons into government service and were tied by marriage to official and merchant families, who commonly educated their children as religious scholars. The 'ulama' were also closely tied to the rural Sufis, who sent their children to the Zaytuna and who shared the same religious principles. In Tunisia there was little tension between the 'ulama' and Sufi branches of the religious establishment. The strong social influence of the religious leaders, however, was not accompanied by political power, for the Beys insisted on loyalty and passivity in return for appointments to office.

In general the 'ulama' did not oppose the technical aspects of the reform program, such as the telegraph, but otherwise they dissociated themselves from it. In 1877 Khayr al-Din was dismissed from office. Reforms in Tunisia generally followed the patterns established in Egypt and the Ottoman empire, but they did not go far enough to consolidate the power of the state.

At the same time Tunisia could no longer resist international economic and political pressures. The French, who had occupied Algeria since 1830, used border disputes as a pretext to impose French domination in 1881. The French progressively assumed the most responsible administrative positions, and by 1884 supervised all Tunisian government bureaus dealing with finance, post, education, telegraph, public works, and agriculture. They abolished the international finance commission and guaranteed the Tunisian debt, established a new judicial system for Europeans while keeping the Shari'a courts for cases involving Tunisians, and developed roads, ports, railroads, and mines. In rural areas they strengthened the local officials (qa'ids) and weakened independent tribes.

Most important was the opening of Tunisia to French colonization and the introduction of modern agriculture and education. The French encouraged colonization by selling collective lands and waqfs. Changes in land law increased state revenues by bringing land into cultivation and by guaranteeing title to European purchasers. The number of French colonists grew from 34,000 in 1906 to 144,000 in 1945, and the French occupied approximately one-fifth of the cultivable land. A French system of education was fostered by the Alliance Française and by the Catholic Church. Between 1885 and 1912 some 3,000 Tunisians studied in Paris. The French also intervened in Muslim education. In 1898 they tried to reform the Zaytuna by adding modern subjects and pedagogical methods, but the 'ulama' resisted this interference with the teaching of Muslim law. Nonetheless, some Tunisian 'ulama' and French officials cooperated in the reform of public instruction, the administration of waqfs, and the management of Sadiqi College. Rural-born and socially mobile Malikis were more willing to cooperate with the French than were their better-established Hanafi colleagues. Splits among the 'ulama' therefore allowed for an alliance between the government and some segments of the Muslim religious establishment. Tunisian elites accepted French rule without great difficulty.

Despite the relative political quiet, Tunisian officials, intellectuals, and some 'ulama' awoke to the costs of French rule. A new generation of Tunisian national leaders emerged, like the Ottoman, out of the modern-educated bureaucratic elite. From the 1880s until the 1930s Tunisian leaders came from administrative and 'ulama' backgrounds; some were educated in French schools, others imbibed reformist Islam. In 1888 graduates of the Zaytuna and the Sadiqi College created the weekly newspaper *al-Hadira* to comment on European and world events, and to discuss political, economic, and literary issues. The Khalduniya school was founded in 1896 to supplement the Zaytuna education with modern subjects. From both the reformed Muslim schools and French schools emerged the self-styled "Young

Tunisians." Fueled by eastern Arab influences, especially the teachings of al-Afghani, Muhammad 'Abduh, and the Egyptian National Party, they advocated the modernization and Westernization of Tunisian society, and a revival of Arabic culture. Inspired by Salafi values they called for the reform of Muslim legal, educational, and waqf administration. "Young Tunisians" also sponsored a reformed Quran school in which students were taught the Quran, Arabic, and the basics of arithmetic, geography, history, and French. This generation was still deeply concerned with the reform of Muslim legal administration and Arabic literary education.

The first political expression of the "Young Tunisians" came in 1907 with the founding of the journal *The Tunisian*. Secular-minded liberals and Salafiya reformers developed a national political feeling under the impetus of the Russian revolution, Woodrow Wilson's principles of self-determination, the Wafd movement in Egypt, and the formation of a popularly elected parliament in Tripolitania. Until around 1920 the nationalists demanded equal opportunity and pay in administration, and liberal freedoms of press and association. 'Abd al-'Aziz al-Tha'alibi, a leading Arab journalist and reformer, became the chief spokesman of the Destour (Constitution) Party. In the 1920s, Tunisian efforts to organize political resistance became more vigorous. In 1922 the Bey gave the French resident-general an ultimatum, but a show of French military force suppressed the Tunisian resistance. The agitation was resumed in 1924 by workers returned from France, who formed the first Tunisian economic cooperative society and the first Tunisian trade union, the General Confederation of Tunisian Workers, but Tunisian strikes were broken, and the government jailed the leaders, closed down the newspapers, and suppressed political activity.

In the 1930s a new generation of Tunisian nationalists came to the fore. For over a decade the Destour Party had been led by conservative families with a strong Muslim and Arab identity. Now representatives of small and middling provincial cities, with a combined Arabic and French education and secular socialist ideas of Tunisian society, rose to challenge the old elites. The new leaders found support among townsmen and peasant migrants and an enlarged urban population. Led by Habib Bourguiba (born in Monastir in 1903 and educated in Paris in the 1920s) and Mahmud Materi, the new leaders demanded a broadened participation in the Destour, and a more militant, organized, and ideologically coherent resistance to the French. At a Destour congress in 1932 Bourguiba demanded independence for Tunisia and offered a treaty of friendship to guarantee French interests. In 1934 the radicals took over the Destour and created the neo-Destour party with Materi as president and Bourguiba as secretary-general. The new party promptly called for a boycott of French products and for the establishment of a democratic parliamentary regime. While basically secular in orientation, the neo-Destour leaders had Muslim roots and appealed to Muslim sentiment by meeting in mosques and zawiyas. They emphasized their Muslim identity by agitating against Muslim burial rights for Tunisians who had renounced Islam by taking French citizenship. The new party broke out of the limited social stratum of the original Destour, and attempted to generate a mass movement. Yet by taking over the old party they assured continuity and national cohesion.

The neo-Destour began the twenty-year struggle that culminated in Tunisian independence. At first Tunisians had high hopes of the popular front government in France, but Tunisian demonstrations in April 1938 led to violence. The French suppressed the demonstrations, dissolved the political parties, and imprisoned Bourguiba. While Bourguiba remained in forced exile, Munsif Bey (1942–43), the Tunisian head of state, took the lead in the effort to win greater autonomy. To the French resident-general he presented Tunisian demands for the formation of a new assembly, instruction in the schools in Arabic, and expropriation by the state of large utilities and transport enterprises. In 1943 he tried to form a new ministry without the consent of the resident-general and was removed by the French, thus becoming a national hero. In 1949 a new group of Destouriens, including supporters of Munsif Bey, issued a declaration demanding self-government for Tunisia. Agricultural groups, students, feminists, and labor unions also supported the national demand. Bourguiba returned to lead the collaboration of the neo-Destour with labor unions and other groups. Despite Bourguiba's great patience and willingness to compromise, by late 1952 Tunisians were beginning to resort to urban terrorism. Finally, defeated in Indo-China, under diplomatic pressure in the United Nations, and faced with rising violence in Tunis, the French agreed in the spring of 1955 to a settlement recognizing Tunisian internal autonomy. A French–Tunisian protocol of March 1956 abolished the protectorate of 1881.

Independent Tunisia: from the 1950s to the present

The formation of an independent Tunisian government was followed by the rapid consolidation of Bourguiba's power. The 1957 constituent assembly stripped the Bey of his budget, his title, and his power; Bourguiba was made head of state, and ruled until 1987 when he was replaced by General Zine Labidine Ben 'Ali. A constitution of 1959 gave all power to the President. The new government progressively removed French officials and replaced them with party militants, though over 2,500 Frenchmen remained in Tunisian service.

In response to political pressures and economic need, the independent Tunisian regime followed a number of different economic strategies. From 1956 until 1961, it generally pursued a liberal economic policy. In 1956 and 1957 the government purchased former French lands, put waqf land under government control, and opened the way for individual ownership of collective lands. These policies, however, failed to attract capital and meet Tunisia's investment goals, and in 1962 Tunisia adopted a socialist orientation. The state became the controller, patron, and provider for the economy. European-owned land was nationalized in 1964. A system of agricultural cooperatives and state-managed farms was set up. Heavy public investment and heavy borrowing from foreign sources was to be the basis of economic development. By 1969 this policy had also failed. Tunisia could not afford both to invest and meet the demands for employment and welfare at the same time. It turned to a more open economy, but the public sector nonetheless remained over 40 percent of the total economy. A general strike and riots in 1978 marked the loss of public confidence in the policies of the regime. Bourguiba's successor, Ben 'Ali, crushed the opposition. Tunisia reverted to mixing the private, cooperative, and public sectors and encouraging private foreign investment.

Like Turkey, Tunisia pursued a complex policy of controlling the expression of Islam, and even deriving legitimacy from it, while committing itself at the same time to a drastic secularization of the society. Bourguiba brought religious institutions under the direct control of the state and used Muslim rhetoric to try to justify secularist policies. The 'ulama' were bureaucratized under the Administration of Religious Affairs, and the government took control of religious endowments. For a time, the government even allowed Islamist preaching and the expansion of missionary activities as a way of showing its support for religion. Religious schools were taken over by the Ministry of National Education. However, the new regime created a secular judiciary; the personal status code adopted in 1956 forbade polygamy and made marriage and divorce civil matters. It also favored equal rights for women. In 1960 the fast of Ramadan was denounced as a barrier to production. The neo-Destour Party (renamed the Parti Socialiste Destourien) thus became the manager of a socialist economy, the sponsor of a massive school program, the supporter of emancipation of women, the vehicle of mass political education, and the vanguard of secularization.

These modernizing and secularizing policies, however, did not fully take hold. Disillusioned by lack of economic opportunity and by lack of trust in the political elites Tunisian students and intellectuals have, since the 1960s, stressed their Arab and Muslim rather than their French-Tunisian identity. The younger intelligentsia placed greater emphasis upon socialism and democracy than upon capitalism, foreign enterprise, and European influence. They also became more strongly supportive of the Palestinian cause. Conservatives identified themselves with Islamic values, symbolized by growing attendance at worship, the emergence of religious associations, and expressions of devotion to religious leaders. Among older people and small-town dwellers there was also opposition to equalization of the rights of women. The new Islamic movement sponsored a newspaper called *al-Ma'rifa* and an association for the protection of the Quran. After 1979 the Islamists were influenced by the Egyptian Muslim Brothers and the revolution in Iran, and began to have political ambitions.

The Tunisian Islamist movement was composed of several groups. The most important party was the MTI (Harakat al-Ittijah al-Islami or Islamic Tendency Movement), founded in 1981 by Rashid al-Ghannouchi. The party called for the restoration of an Arab and Islamic identity and culture to Tunisia, a humanitarian economy, and democratic political rights. The movement was hierarchically organized, and appealed to a wide sector of Tunisian society including students, teachers, clerks, and people from rural backgrounds. The leaders were promptly sentenced to jail terms. However, in 1988 President Ben 'Ali tried a new tack, reaffirmed the Islamic identity of Tunisia, and released many activists from prison. Ben 'Ali forged a national pact with the MTI which changed its name to an-Nahda (the Renaissance Party). Al-Ghannouchi accepted the legitimacy of republican politics and renounced violence. An-Nahda ran strongly in the 1989 elections, and Ben 'Ali quickly banned Islamist political parties and jailed as many as 8,000 activists. Al-Ghannouchi was forced into exile. To the present the government continues its refusal to recognize Muslim opposition parties, and governs the country by military and police repression.

Tunisia's historical trajectory in many ways resembles that of Egypt. A highly statist Muslim society, it had come under foreign rule in the late nineteenth century. New generations of educated Tunisians responded to the loss of independence by turning to Islamic reformism and to secular nationalism. Under the aegis of a secularized nationalist elite, independence was achieved in 1956, and Tunisia attempted to develop a mixed economy and a secular society. As in Egypt and Turkey, the limitations and failures of the new regime promoted opposition voiced in terms of Muslim values and Muslim allegiances. Since 1978 Tunisia too is polarized between the regime and the Islamic resistance.

MOROCCO

Under colonial rule

Morocco represents yet another variation of North African Muslim society. It resembled Algeria, Upper Egypt, the Syrian desert regions, and eastern Anatolia in the strength of its pastoral and tribal populations, but unlike the others it was an independent state and not a dependency of the Ottoman empire. The authority of the Sultans was founded on a combination of Caliphal and Sufi attributes, but the regime nonetheless found it difficult to make its authority felt in the countryside. The authority of the Sultans was unquestioned, but their power was always challenged by tribal and Sufi chiefs. The intermediary political classes, such as the landed notables, who in other Middle Eastern societies favored centralized state controls, were in Morocco relatively weak.

European economic penetration in the late nineteenth century subverted the Moroccan state and led to the establishment of French and Spanish protectorates in 1912. The first French resident-general, Marshal Lyautey, ruled through the Sultan and the qa'ids. The government brought the tribes under control, intimidating them by military force, and cutting them off from their pasturelands. The tribes were disarmed and forced to pay taxes. The French installed military posts, and appointed officers to control the qa'ids and through them to collect taxes, organize markets, and build roads, hospitals, and schools.

The French also brought the Moroccan elites under their control. The 'ulama' and the administration of justice were subordinated to a Minister of Justice, appointed to supervise the qadis; in 1914 rules for procedures and maintenance of documents were promulgated. The French also created competing administrative tribunals, transferred penal justice to French courts, promoted Berber customary courts, and took other measures to restrict the jurisdiction of Shari'a. Most of the Sufi zawiyas accepted French authority, helped subordinate tribal regions to the central government, and kept the peace between migratory pastoral populations in the Atlas mountains. The prestige of Sufis, however, diminished as they were replaced by government administrators and their political utility declined. The Sherqawa, the Sufis of Boujad, for example, lost their intermediary roles because secular disputes could be brought to the French, and Sherqawa decisions could be appealed to French officials. They were no longer needed to protect commerce, for the protectorate gave patents for local trade. After World War II, as new economic opportunities in commerce and real estate led rural people to migrate to the cities, the Sufi clientele further diminished.

Lyautey's social and educational policies were also intended to facilitate French control. The sons of notables were to be assimilated through new schools created in Fez and other places. In 1945 a Moroccan school of administration was created. Rural primary schools, technical schools, and Muslim colleges were founded in Rabat and Fez. French policy concentrated on the education of a small elite, and by the 1950s only 6 percent of the eligible age groups were in school. Though French educational efforts were intended to produce a generation of Moroccan collaborators, they seemed only to create a hostile intelligentsia.

Furthermore, the French viewed the Berbers as non-Arabs who could be separated from the general Moroccan population and allied to France; they attempted to create a French-educated Berber elite safe from Arabic and Islamic influences. The Berber *dahir*, or decree, of 1930 proposed organizing a system of Berber courts operating under customary law (except that criminal justice was transferred to French courts), as a deterrent to the use of Islamic law and an encouragement of Berber culture. Muslims saw it as an effort to pave the way for the conversion of Berbers to Christianity and to divide the Moroccan people. There was not much chance of French success. Berber communities themselves resisted the French effort to establish customary law courts, and demanded the application of the Shari'a. Berber students learned Arabic rather than French and adopted nationalist rather than separatist sympathies. Also, improved communications, migration to the towns, and the installation of Arabic-speaking administrative officers all worked to identify Berbers with Arab Islam. The notion of an independent Moroccan Berber society allied to France proved to be a myth.

Only the territories south of the Atlas remained outside direct French control and under the jurisdiction of subordinate chieftains. The great tribal magnates, the Mtouggi, the Gundafa, and the Glawis, controlled the agricultural surplus, the passes over the Atlas Mountains, and the profits of the caravan traffic. Before 1912 the great qa'ids were able to purchase modern weapons, hire mercenaries, and build fortresses to control their districts. They were all vulnerable, however, to factionalism and personal rivalries. The French, fearing that anarchy would result from any effort to defeat the Glawis, restored their predominance and left all territories south of Marrakesh in their hands. After World War II they used the Glawis to help resist the nationalist movement.

French economic policy strongly favored the interests of French colonists. Extensive properties controlled by the Sultan and the tribes were made available for distribution. While the French held that roads and rivers, beaches, and forests were inalienable, all other properties could be bought and sold. In 1914 makhzan land was sold to European colonists, and lands assigned to tribes in payment of military service were confiscated. By the dahir of 1919 collectively owned tribal properties tended to become the private property of Europeans and tribal chiefs. European holdings grew enormously. In 1913 there were approximately 73,000 hectares cultivated by Europeans; by 1953 Europeans controlled approximately a million hectares of land. Though Europeans were barely more than 1 percent of the rural population, they controlled 10 percent of the crop land and almost 25 percent of orchards and vineyards. French taxation favored French over Moroccan interests. The *tartib*, a tax on revenue, was introduced in 1913, but rebates were given for European-type farming methods. European farmers were further advantaged by producing citrus fruits, vegetables, wine, and wheat, which could be sold for export, while Moroccans concentrated on less remunerative crops. French investment in irrigation and dams also favored Europeans. Nonetheless, the French benefited Morocco by bringing peace to the countryside and opening new markets. They also helped Moroccan farmers by introducing new seeds, crops, and breeds of livestock, and by investing in irrigation.

In industry the French favored phosphate mining and the development of flour mills, sugar refining, cement manufacture, and textile production. Moroccan workers flocked to the towns looking for employment, but wages were low and unions were proscribed by the government. French policy, on balance, created a dual economy, with a European sector favored by the administration and a relatively neglected Moroccan sector.

As in Tunisia and Algeria, French domination seemed economically and politically secure but it nonetheless generated the social and cultural conditions for the formation of an opposition movement. French rule helped to break down the traditional structure of Moroccan society. Changes in administration reduced the power of the tribal and religious chiefs. Seizure of Moroccan lands, recruitment of Moroccans into the French army, and new urban enterprises drew a substantial number of rural peoples to the towns and cities. The spread of European dress, movie theaters, and sports teams broke down local customs in favor of a more unified society. Large numbers of Moroccan workers in France also developed a Western lifestyle and political consciousness. Berber speakers were integrated into the Arab population as a result of mixing in the towns, and by the spread of the Arabic language and Arabic and Islamic education. Thus the conditions were set for a revival of Moroccan political identity and for hostility to French rule.

Moroccan opposition received early expression in the rebellion of 'Abd al-Karim in the Spanish-occupied zone. 'Abd al-Karim was an intellectual, a qadi in his early career, a teacher, and the editor of a newspaper called *Telegrama*. He was familiar with Spanish culture and had numerous European contacts. His father, a tribal leader, had been involved with German mining interests and the son had studied engineering in Spain. In 1923 'Abd al-Karim declared the Rif a republican state. The state was made up of a federation of independent tribes united by a nationalist ideology. 'Abd al-Karim denied that he was religiously inclined but nonetheless advocated the Salafi teaching and opposed saint worship. His independent republic expanded to the point where it brought France into the war on the side of Spain and resulted in his defeat in 1926. Despite this defeat, 'Abd al-Karim remained a hero to young Moroccans who aspired to overthrow French rule.

More lasting Moroccan resistance to French rule came from the religious reform movement. From the 1920s to the 1960s there was a subtle shift in the practice of Islam in Morocco. Both rural Sufis and urban 'ulama' were discredited by French control, and Moroccan religious concerns flowed into reformism. As in Egypt, Algeria, and many other places in the Muslim world, foreign rule, centralization of state power, and Muslim awareness of the need for a higher degree of communal cooperation was channeled into reform. Moroccan reformers, in Fez, Rabat, Salé, and other towns, inspired by Muhammad 'Abduh, founded schools to teach Arabic grammar, ethics, logic, Islamic history, and arithmetic, though not modern sciences. The Salafiya stressed the purification of Islam, opposition to saint worship, and defense against Western cultural encroachment.

Reformism took hold wherever the changes generated by French rule hurt the established bourgeoisie, propelling them toward national consciousness. Fez suffered a long depression from 1925 to 1940 as a result of European competition and the rise of Casablanca as a port and business center, but Fassis continued to think of themselves as the elite of Moroccan society, and resisted French rule, sponsoring religious reform movements, trade union activities, secret cultural societies, and nationalist newspapers. Wounded in pocket and pride, Fassis were driven into political action.

Around 1925 and 1926 political groups began to form around the students and educators in the new schools, and in 1927 an association of Muslim North African students was born. The Berber dahir of 1930 united Moroccan sentiment behind the reformers. The French Berber program made the preservation of Islam, and therefore of Moroccan society, a crucial issue. Communal prayers were organized, a press campaign launched, and new cells of reformists and nationalists were founded. The Moroccan proto-nationalists published a review in French called *Maghreb* in Paris, and in Fez, *L'Action du peuple*. In 1933 they proposed an annual festival in honor of the Sultan as a demonstration of Moroccan national loyalty. A year later a plan was presented to the Sultan and the French administration calling for the removal of direct French rule, appointment of Moroccan ministers, and the formation of an elected national council. The plan also called for a single judicial system based on government courts and the Shari'a. It called for the nationalization of the major industries, including mining, railroads, transport, electric power, and banks. This was the first political statement laying claim to Moroccan autonomy, if not to full independence from France. The emphasis upon Islamic reform in education was superseded by interest in administrative and legal issues, problems of land, taxation, free speech, and free press. The French rejected the reform plan, and in 1936 and 1937 some of the nationalists moved to a new stage of resistance – organizing popular demonstrations against French rule. Taking advantage of the depression, the nationalists aroused popular consciousness about the importance of defending Islam.

Here as elsewhere, World War II severely damaged the French and allowed the Istiqlal (Independence) Party, created in 1943, to come to the fore. The new party absorbed former 'ulama', administrators, and other elite persons and brought together a national elite recruited from the big cities. Its primary effort was to organize demonstrations in honor of Sultan Muhammad V, who now committed himself to an autonomous Morocco. In a speech in Tangier in April 1947, he declared Morocco an Arab state attached to the Arab League, and deliberately omitted the obligatory compliments to France. Sultan Muhammad defended Istiqlal sympathizers, and in 1949 refused to sign French-proposed legislative and administrative measures. The crisis came in 1953, when the French attempted to force the Sultan to agree to a dual sovereignty, and suppress the Istiqlal Party. Thami al-Glawi mustered large numbers of Berber tribesmen to converge on Fez and the French forced the Sultan to resign and leave the country. Istiqlal leaders were also imprisoned or exiled.

The exile of the Sultan made him a martyr and created a mass national sentiment. In his absence, many Moroccans ceased to attend the Friday prayers as a protest against an illegitimate regime. With the leading politicians in prison or exile, terrorism began in late 1953. By October 1955 al-Glawi had to yield and request the return of the Sultan. Muhammad, returned to his throne, declared that Morocco would become a constitutional monarchy and that he would conduct negotiations with France leading to independence and to a treaty of alliance. Under the leadership of Pierre Mendés-France, the French accepted Moroccan independence and signed a formal accord on March 7, 1956.

The Moroccan independence movement was strikingly different from that of Tunisia or Algeria. While in Algeria resistance was substantially the work of new elites, in Morocco the Sultan, the historical leader of the country, became the titular leader of the opposition and the embodiment of national identity. Thus he carried the old regime into the modern state. As in Tunisia and Algeria, Moroccan resistance was first associated with the Salafi reform movement, but while secular leaders took over in Tunisia and Algeria, Morocco was not easily secularized. Relatively few Moroccans had a French education.

Independent Morocco

With the restoration of independence, the Sultan remained the dominant political figure. His authority continued to be grounded in a long historical tradition. Not only did the Sultan retain his personal religious authority, but the state took control of 'ulama' activities and Muslim discourse. Councils established in 1981 gave the government control of preaching and Muslim education. Secular education also competed with Muslim. In addition ceremonies such as the bay'a and the sacrifice of 'Id reinforced the royal authority. Sultan Muhammad V (d. 1961) and his successor, Hassan (1961–99), claimed the veneration usually accorded the Sufis by sponsoring saints' festivals, taking advantage of the fact that the Sufi brotherhoods had been discredited by their collaboration with the French. Also, the Sultan judiciously appealed to the Western-educated intelligentsia and workers by using liberal and democratic rhetoric.

The protectorate also left the Sultan in an enhanced political and administrative position. The French had strengthened the bureaucracy and weakened independent rural chiefs. They left the Sultan in control of the army, the police, the Department of the Interior, the banks, and the newspapers. The Sultan, through the Ministry of the Interior, also ran a national patronage system, carrying his influence to the level of local administrators and community leaders. The Sultan also triumphed over the political parties. The hopes of Istiqlal to share in power were dashed, and the party split in 1959 into an Istiqlal wing and a new Union Nationale des Forces Populaires (UNFP). Each party created its own trade union ally. In 1962 a new constitution and parliament were created but parliament was dissolved in 1965. Since then the Sultans have governed by emergency powers.

The Moroccan regime fluctuated between absolute monarchy and manipulative flexible authoritarianism. Political parties were manipulated by the government and were allowed to be active only insofar as they accepted the system. The Sultan formed clienteles of professional, administrative, and business elites, and manipulated a myriad of factions, clienteles, interest groups, and families and tribes. He stood outside the political groupings as an arbitrator. He could muster national ideological support, and ruled by holding the balance of power among the different groups and by his control over the army, the Ministry of the Interior, and other key positions. The political elite included the bourgeoisie of Fez, which provided cadres of officials, scholars, and merchants. Leftist groups, however, were weak, and the trade unions were dependent on the state. The students were easily manipulated. Elites of rural background were important in the Ministries of the Interior, Education, and Justice, and many rural communities were brought into the system by Sufi leaders and other intermediaries. The tribes of the Rif and the middle and central Atlas, however, remained hostile to the regime, but the central government was nonetheless more strongly in control of the countryside than its historical predecessors.

The struggle to win control of the Western Sahara aroused nationalist feelings and made the Sultan ever more popular. The Western Sahara was the former Spanish colony, ceded to Morocco and Mauritania in 1976, but subject to rival claims. While Morocco claimed the territory for itself, the POLISARIO front, with Algerian support, claimed independence for a Sahrawi Arab Democratic Republic. The Sultan, mobilizing mass support and Sa'udi financing, occupied the whole territory. A United Nations peace plan of 1988 called for a referendum in the territories, which has yet to be held. Tensions remain high between Algeria and Morocco.

A segmented society built around personal ties to the Sultan and fluid coalitions, the Moroccan political system maintained stability at the price of economic development and reform. After independence, Morocco suffered from a flight of capital, though many French professional and technical workers remained. Development plans in the 1960s failed, in part, for lack of reforms in landownership. An already poor economy fell into worse hardship in the 1980s. Forced to take IMF loans in 1983 due to a balance-of-trade deficit and rising foreign debt, Morocco was obliged to undertake a program of privatization. This led to a gradual stabilization of the economy and the deficit; but while the middle class prospered, the poor have remained impoverished. Riots took place in various cities in 1981, 1984, 1990, and 1996. With a renewed downturn in the economy workers and students again protested in 1997.

In these conditions there was a strong Islamist opposition, but the Islamist movements were highly factionalized, lacked the power to overthrow the regime, and generally supported reformist and gradualist goals within the system. Islamist associations had to compromise with the regime and stress moral issues, for the Sultan retained a strong Islamic authority of his own. The lack of a unifying ideology, and competing Salafi and Sufi tendencies, allowed the Sultan to manipulate the various factions and keep them divided.

Even with the death of Sultan Hassan in 1999 and the succession of his son Muhammad VI, Morocco remains the most highly integrated and conservative of the North African Arab countries. The new Sultan, Western educated, cosmopolitan, and outward looking, appeals to the sentiments of the youth, and has proposed reforms such as a literacy program for rural women, and legal changes to replace unilateral repudiation with court-granted divorce decrees and equal division of spousal property. Islamic opposition movements have so far been contained by government authority. In Morocco, Islam is still so closely identified with the monarchy and the state that it constitutes the Moroccan national identity.

LIBYA

Ottoman rule also established the first state in the territories of Tripolitania, Cyrenaica, and the Fezzan, which make up modern Libya. Until the Ottoman occupation, Libya was a territory without a history. The invasions of the seventh century helped to Arabize and Islamize the population, but did not establish a central regime. Almohad authority was nominal; the Mamluks of Egypt had alliances with tribes in Cyrenaica which allowed them to claim that they were suzerains of the country. This claim was inherited by the Ottomans, who conquered Egypt in 1517 and Tripoli in 1551. From 1551 until 1711 Tripoli was governed by Ottoman pashas and janissary soldiers. In 1711 Ahmad Qaramanli, a local janissary officer, seized power and founded a dynasty under Ottoman suzerainty, which lasted until 1835. As Qaramanli power waned in the early nineteenth century as a result of the suppression of piracy and of growing British and French influence, the Ottomans again intervened in Libya, and brought the dynasty to an end. Ottoman governors ruled Tripolitania and were suzerains of Cyrenaica until the Italian occupation of 1911 and Ottoman withdrawal in 1912.

From 1835 to 1911 the Ottomans made extensive changes in Tripolitania. By 1858 they had defeated local resistance, established their government throughout the region, and introduced Tanzimat reforms. The Ottoman governors strengthened the central authority, encouraged the sedentarization of the bedouins, developed towns and agriculture, and helped revive the trans-Saharan trade, which flourished in Libya as the abolition of the slave traffic closed down Saharan routes going through Tunisia and Algeria. Ottoman rule encouraged local education and the formation of an intelligentsia inspired by the political and cultural life of Istanbul. In this phase of Ottoman administration, Tripolitanian officials, intellectuals, and tribal and village shaykhs acquired a sense of common identity as part of a larger provincial, Ottoman, Arab, and Muslim universe.

Cyrenaica remained a separate province under Ottoman suzerainty, and went through a similar phase of development owing to Ottoman cooperation with the Sanusiya order. The Sanusiya was founded in 1837 by Muhammad b. 'Ali al-Sanusi (1787–1859), who was born in Algeria and educated in Fez and Mecca. Al-Sanusi, under the influence of reform currents, declared that his purpose was to return to the basic precepts of the Quran and hadith, and affirmed the right of believers to use ijtihad to deduce the principles by which a Muslim life should be conducted. The Sanusiya wished to unite all of the Muslim brotherhoods, and to contribute to the spread and revitalization of Islam.

His mission led al-Sanusi to Cyrenaica, where he established a number of zawiyas before his death in 1859. The Sanusi zawiyas became centers of religious mission and teaching, but also of agricultural settlement and trade. The zawiyas, strung out along the trade routes linking Cyrenaica with Kufra and Wadai, helped organize caravans. The brotherhood progressively acquired a quasi-political authority among the bedouins of the region by negotiating cooperation in trade, mediating disputes, and providing urban services such as religious instruction, exchange of products, charity, and political representation. By the end of the century the Sanusi network of zawiyas had built up a large tribal coalition in the regions west of Egypt and the Sudan. Under Sanusi leadership this coalition resisted both French expansion in the region of Lake Chad and the Italian invasion of Libya.

After the Congress of Berlin in 1878 the Italians considered Tripolitania part of their imperial sphere of influence, and attempted to establish an economic presence in the province. Ottoman resistance to Italian economic penetration provided a pretext for an Italian invasion in 1911. The Italians occupied the towns and forced the Ottomans to concede their suzerainty over Tripolitania and Cyrenaica, but the Sanusiya also claimed to be the heirs of Ottoman authority in Libya. Only after World War I was Italy able to defeat local opposition in Tripolitania, and not until a protracted and destructive war which lasted from 1923 to 1932 were the Italians able to defeat the bedouins of Cyrenaica, seize the majority of their lands, and colonize the country. The Sanusi leaders were forced into exile, and while they retained a spiritual authority, they were obliged to accept Italian suzerainty. In 1934 the Italians completed the conquest of Cyrenaica and Tripolitania, and united the two into modern Libya.

The Italians were defeated in World War II, and Libya came under the control of Britain and France, but the United Nations decided to make it an independent country in 1951. The Sanusi leader, Amir Idris, became King, and governed the country on the basis of his family's religious legitimacy and its services in the struggle against foreign rule. He ruled with the help of urban-based officials, with the support of the bedouins rallied through the Sanusi network of zawiyas, and with the assistance of client tribal chiefs. His regime was opposed as corrupt and dependent upon foreign support by a radical younger generation of nationalist- and socialist-minded students, technicians, petroleum and dock workers, and younger army officers inspired by the pan-Arab and socialist ideologies of Nasserism and the Ba'th Party. In 1969, Libya's own Free Officers movement, comprised of middling officers and NCOs – schooled at the Baghdad Military Academy, but drawn from the poorer and weaker of Libyan tribes – led by Mu'ammar al-Qaddafi, seized power. The officers set up a Revolutionary Command Council and rapidly established an all-powerful military regime. Foreign bases were dismantled. Foreign banks and businesses were nationalized. Political parties and labor unions were outlawed. In 1973 the revolution took a still more radical turn, with the arrest of officials, professionals, and potential political opponents, and the creation of populist committees to take control of the government ministries, schools, and major enterprises. By the late 1970s the state had taken control of all important economic functions, ruined the small middle class, and substantially redistributed the country's wealth. The political effect of populism was to abolish all independent centers of wealth, and to create a system of checks on all public functionaries, thereby minimizing the prospect of opposition to Qaddafi.

Qaddafi is best known as the proponent of a radical Arab and Islamic ideology. His earliest revolutionary doctrine was a copy of Nasserite and Ba'thist ideologies and stressed Arab unity, opposition to colonialism and Zionism, and Libyan leadership in the quest for unity and in the Arab struggle against Israel. In the course of his rule Qaddafi negotiated unions between Libya and Egypt, Libya and Syria, and Libya, Sudan, and Tunisia, none of which have come to fruition. In the early 1970s he added a new dimension to his theory, in which he proposed an Arabic-Islamic mission as a Third Universal Alternative to capitalism and communism. He proclaimed an extreme form of Islamic scripturalism in which the Quran – but not the teachings of the Prophet (Sunna) – is taken as the only source of authority for the reconstruction of society. Islamic scripturalism linked with populism destroyed the authority of the 'ulama', Sufi shaykhs, bureaucrats, and technocrats, and made Qaddafi himself the central figure in this version of Islamic modernism. Also in Libya a Quranic morality forbidding gambling, alcohol, and other "Western" vices was enforced. In the international arena, the Third Universal Alternative called for jihad, or struggle, against imperialism and Zionism in the Middle East, Muslim Africa, and even in the Philippines. Implied in this theory was an unarticulated identification of domestic socialism, Arabism, and Islam. In more extreme form, and with more emphatic international implications, it represented a version of the identification of Arabism and Islam common throughout the Middle East and North Africa.

By the 1990s, however, Libya had become a mainstream North African state. A series of setbacks suffered by Qaddafi in the 1980s – including tribal opposition in Cyrenaica, falling oil prices, UN sanctions and a US embargo on oil-producing equipment and military sales to Libya as a punishment for its support of terrorist attacks – hurt the economy. Defeat in Chad and cuts in the military budget led to unrest in the army and an attempted coup in 1993. As Qaddafi retreated from his radical positions, Islamic revivalists arose to oppose him, and attacked military posts and government officials. While Qaddafi holds on to power by subsidizing the domestic economy, repressing his opponents, and cooperating with other North African states to counter the Islamist threat, his regime has sacrificed its radical mission.

ISLAM IN STATE IDEOLOGIES AND OPPOSITION MOVEMENTS

The North African Arab countries are grouped together not only because of geography but also because of similarities in their historical development. In the premodern era, there were considerable variations in the social and political structure of each region and state, but in each one, lineage communities were the basis of society and pastoralists were an important social and political force. Effective states in Tunisia and Algeria did not extend to the whole of each country. Morocco maintained a centralized state, partly by institutional means, but largely by emphasizing the legitimacy of its Sultans. Islam played a crucial political role both in the integration of tribal communities and the legitimization of regimes.

French rule led to the introduction of elements of a modern economy and education, but the continuities in the structure of states and in the role of Islam are striking. Morocco shows the greatest degree of historical continuity. French control, introduced only in 1912, seems to have had a limited impact on the Moroccan political system. The monarchy retained, with transformed meaning, its Islamic legitimacy and its political centrality. The Sultans kept both their personal charismatic and their Islamic institutional authority. They benefited by taking symbolic leadership of the Islamic reform movement, and captured the emergent awareness of Moroccan nationality by leading resistance to the French. The Sultans actually increased their administrative power by effective use of a French-consolidated apparatus and by skillful manipulation of political factions and interest groups. With independence, both the Moroccan state and society were defined in the combined terms of protectorate-influenced monarchy and Islam. Morocco, more than almost any other Muslim state, retains the impress of its historical identity.

Algeria, by contrast, is the most radically reorganized North African society. The French occupation altogether destroyed Algerian society, and the elites who emerged after World War I were a narrow and fragile stratum divided among secularists with a strong French orientation, Muslim reformers, populist leaders, and military revolutionaries with inchoate ideological leanings. The ferocity of the struggle for independence created a regime hostile to colonialism and with strong revolutionary, socialist, and egalitarian tendencies. The war for independence also gave power to a military elite in an otherwise disorganized society. The Algerian regime thus tended to pursue the development of an "enclave" state based on military power and the control of petroleum and gas resources and the industries financed by them to the neglect of the agricultural population, but it sought to bridge the gap between the elites and the masses by appeals to reformist Islam. With the destruction of the historical forms of tribal and religious organization, Islamic reformism – the religious language of national as opposed to parochial identities and the language of disciplined worldly activity – became the basis of Algerian national identity.

Libya showed a similar tendency to transform the historical structures of the society. As in Algeria, the Ottoman empire provided the rudiments of a state while Sufism was the basis for the organization of a predominantly bedouin population. In nineteenth-century Cyrenaica, moreover, Sufism was the preserve of the reformist Sanusi movement, which used its influence to organize trade, resist French and Italian colonization, and create a Libyan monarchy after World War II. The Free Officer revolutionaries, who seized power in 1969, inherited neither a strong state, nor a secular concept of monarchy, nor an integrated society. In Libya there was virtually no historical basis for a national regime. Thus the Qaddafi regime tended to be pan-Arab, Islamic, and international-revolutionary in ideological orientation, finding support for a radical reconstruction of Libyan society in universalistic terms. The Qaddafi regime at first embodied a unique combination of personal power and universalist pan-Arab and Islamic symbols, but under attack from still more radical Islamic movements it has moved to reintegrate itself into the international state system.

Tunisia was a partial exception to the North African pattern of strong Islamic identity based on the reformist movements of the late nineteenth century and the inter-war years. While state-sponsored modernism had its origins in the pre-protectorate regime, and reformism was introduced by the Salafiya during the Young Tunisian and Destour Party eras, the leadership of independent Tunisia has, by and large, been seized by a secular-oriented elite. In Tunisia, the shift from Islamic reformist to secular nationalist ideologies was, in part, due to the struggle between the old and neo-Destour leaders in the 1930s. While the older generation had a Muslim education, the younger generation was French–Arabic in education. While the older generation represented a condominium of official and 'ulama' families, the younger one represented the upwardly mobile bourgeoisie of the coastal towns. The domestic struggle for power between the two elites, combined with the struggle against the French, turned the Bourguiba generation to nationalism, though Muslim loyalties were still latent in the appeal for mass support. Also, a long history of centralized states is the basis for Tunisian national identity.

After independence the North African states entered a period of hopeful authoritarianism; in all North African countries the state derived some of its legitimacy from its control of Islamic institutions. By the 1960s and 1970s, however, the North African governments had failed to promote sufficient economic development and to modernize their societies, and kept themselves in power by turning evermore to the *mukhabarat* state, based on the police, the intelligence services, and the military. In the 1980s the North African states were all faced with demonstrations, riots, strikes, and the rise of Islamic opposition movements. After a brief period of liberalization from 1989 to 1991 police states returned to the Maghrib, in the name of suppressing the Islamic opposition.

However, state controls have nowhere deterred the Islamists, who denounce the traditional 'ulama' for their support for oppressive governments. They call for the rejection of Western mores, and the creation of Islamic states. The Islamic opposition has three forms. One is non-political, and sponsors educational, social, and cultural activities meant to Islamize society from the bottom up. Mass education, television, cassettes and radio, and an Islamic publishing industry make possible the resocialization of the people to Islam despite the educational policies of the state. These movements operate schools, clinics, and welfare programs. The second type calls for electoral, political participation as a way of taking power. The third is willing to resort to violence and terrorism. The principal movements – 'Abdelsalam Yassine's Justice and Charity in Morocco, Rashid al-Ghannouchi's an-Nahda Renaissance Party in Tunisia, and the FIS of 'Abassi Madani and 'Ali Belhadj in Algeria – belong to the second category. None of the major movements is led by traditional religious leaders, but rather all are fronted by professionals and lay intellectuals. Muslim movements have been willing to work within the system, and at times have been permitted to do so, but Tunisia and Algeria have attempted to crush them completely. Morocco bans the parties but tolerates open discussion.

Identity-based political movements may, ironically, be a consequence of state policies. The North African states derive much of their income from rents, royalties and foreign sources, and have created a pre-industrial welfare state by the distribution of patronage to clienteles built around families, and ideological and political groups. State policies do not encourage the formation of economic class and interest groups that cut across community lines. Resentment of clientism and patronage that favors small elites with educational opportunities and a high level of conspicuous consumption grows among masses of young people who are left only with "hanging out," street culture, and marginalization. The Islamic movements gain mass support not only for religious reasons but also as a protest against government failure to provide adequate employment, housing and education. The breakdown of old community ties have led to unrest, alienation, and the growth of radical Islamist sympathies. The North African societies are now polarized between their military-bureaucratic elites and popular oppositional Islamic movements.

North Africa also has to be seen in the context of the larger Arab and Middle Eastern world. Throughout the Arab Middle East and North Africa, the ideology of states has been built upon varying combinations of nationalist, pan-Arab, and Islamic symbols. Such states as Syria, Iraq, and Tunisia stress the secular-national and sometimes the socialist basis of state identity, despite such exceptions as constitutional recognition of the Islamic character of the state or latent appeals to the Muslim sentiments of the populace. The institutionally more fragile states, such as Syria, Iraq, and Libya, also heavily emphasize their pan-Arab loyalties. In these states, the Ottoman heritage of state-controlled religious establishments, and the social dominance of upwardly mobile military elites or of minority groups, has favored secular nationalism.

The Islamic element is pronounced in the official ideologies of Egypt, Algeria, and Libya. Since the turn of the twentieth century, Egypt has cultivated a strong nationalist, state-oriented self-concept with strong obeisance to Islam. The Arab and pan-Arab basis of Egyptian identity became more marked after World War II, but with the defeat of Egypt in the 1967 war with Israel, Egypt has returned to a more national state- and Islamic-centered concept of political identity. The religious loyalties of the populace and well-organized Islamic movements have made Islamic symbols a recurring part of Egypt's official ideology. Algeria and Libya are instances of a still more integral association of nationalist, pan-Arab, and Islamic symbols. In Morocco, the continuity of the monarchy and its close identification with both the Salafi movement and Sufism make Islam central to both official ideology and national identity. In all these countries Islam is particularly important in popular political identity and in the ideologies of both conservative and revolutionary regimes, just as it was in the past the basis of both Sufi-organized rural societies and anti-colonial movements.

At the same time Islam has come to play an important role in the articulation of opposition to these same regimes. Since the 1967 war with Israel, and especially since the 1979 revolution in Iran, Islam has become an ideology of political opposition and revolutionary aspirations. The Muslim Brotherhood in Egypt and Syria, the jam'at in Egypt and Tunisia, and independent religious leaders everywhere maintain the historical role of Islam as a communal and religious system apart from, and in opposition to, the state. Thus, throughout the Arab east and Arab North Africa there are profound ambiguities in the uses of Islam as an element of political identity. State regimes are organized upon the basis of fluid combinations of national, pan-Arab, and Islamic identity; opposition movements are couched in terms of Islamic aspirations. Islam, then, is an element both of state ideologies and of revolutionary utopias. It is the shared medium of political discourse grounded in the ambiguity of mass culture in which state, ethnic, national, and Islamic identities are imperfectly fused.

SECULARISM AND ISLAM IN CENTRAL AND SOUTHERN ASIA

CHAPTER 27

THE INDIAN SUBCONTINENT: INDIA, PAKISTAN, AND BANGLADESH

The contemporary history of Muslim peoples in the Indian subcontinent has its origins in the breakup of the Mughal empire and the imposition of British rule in India. The change of regimes set in motion forces that would change the religious practices and sociopolitical structures of Muslim peoples of the subcontinent and lead eventually to the formation of three national states – two predominantly Muslim, and one in which there is a substantial Muslim minority.

On the eve of its modern transformation, the Mughal empire was, like the Ottoman and Safavid empires, a patrimonial regime which strongly emphasized its Persianate cosmopolitan and Indian identity. Muslim religious life in the subcontinent was highly pluralistic and not under state control. The long century of Mughal decline, from 1730 to 1857, favored the consolidation of a provincial Muslim gentry. Literate Muslim culture, similar religious practices, and noble (ashraf) status defined the Muslim communities, which were clustered around the mosques, schools, tombs, and gentry residences of the Muslim quarters and small towns (qasbahs) of North India.

The position of this Muslim gentry and office-holding elite was gravely threatened by the rising power of the British. The decline of the Mughal regime had both symbolic and practical costs. The very existence of a Muslim regime was a charismatic guarantee of the well-being of Muslim societies. Now this assurance was gone. In many regions, such as Bengal, the concrete financial and political losses were substantial. With the reorganization of revenue and judicial administration, Europeans replaced Muslims in the top political positions, though Muslims kept their employment in subordinate posts. The Permanent Settlement in Bengal helped transfer control over landed property from Muslims to Hindus, though in the northwestern provinces Muslim landlords were able to maintain their position relative to the Hindus. Soldiers who had once served sovereign regimes were reduced to being the strongmen of the East India Company or of some British magistrate or zamindar. In Bengal, Muslim peasants subjected to Hindu landlords were deprived

620

of customary rights, and Muslim weavers suffered from the competition of Lancashire cloth.

These early losses were compounded by general economic regression between 1830 and 1857. As the British consolidated their power they began to eliminate the incomes of the great zamindars. Nobles were deprived of taxes and mint revenues, tolls, and bazaar fees. The pensions paid to princely families were subdivided among numerous heirs and pledged to money lenders. As aristocratic incomes declined, luxury consumption fell; soldiers, service people, and artisans were unemployed. While some landowners and grain merchants continued to do well, and while some districts continued to flourish, many of the gentry, minor officials, petty merchants, artisans, and laborers fared badly.

Furthermore, the new regime brought cultural as well as economic and political losses. At first the British sympathized with traditional Muslim education and the classical culture of India. By the 1830s, however, British missionaries had become more active, and British officials began to suppress religious practices that they judged barbaric. English became the language of administration and instruction. In 1835 the new school budgets reserved government funds for English instruction; in 1837 Persian was abolished as the official language of the Mughal court. Changes in the court system, and the establishment of new rules for evidence and new definitions of offenses and penalties, struck at the heart of Muslim religious law. Progressively Muslims became aware that the tide of economic and political power, impelled by Hindu merchant and British official competition, was running against them. By the 1850s the qasbah communities were in disarray. The need to come to terms with the loss of a Muslim state, with the consequences of foreign rule, and with the rising influence of Sikhs and Hindus had become acute. The failure of the Mughal empire made Muslims question whether a Muslim way of life could continue in the subcontinent, and if so, what were the practical and symbolic alternatives to the Mughal system. What kind of political institutions would be needed? What attitude should they take toward British rule? What personal religious practices would be meaningful? In what way should Muslims practice the Shari'a? Was it proper to venerate saints' shrines?

To these questions, there were three clusters of responses. The position of some religious groups such as the Barelwis and the 'ulama' of Farangi Mahall was that little new need be done but accept British rule, and transmit the traditional beliefs and practices of Islam – including respect for the Shari'a and the veneration of saints. The reformers, in the tradition of Shah Waliallah and the international movement of Muslim reform, proposed refusing collaboration with British rule and strengthening Muslim religious life by improving the practice of Islam and preventing the veneration of shrines. The third response came from the former political elites. They aimed not at the revival of Muslim tradition but at the absorption of Western science and the creation of a modern Muslim political identity. This response was represented by Aligarh and the Muslim League, and led ultimately to the formation of Pakistan. While some leaders stressed personal religion, and others political issues, the Indian-Muslim response to foreign rule was characterized, not as in the Ottoman empire by the evolution of a state policy of secularization, nor as in the Iranian case by the struggle between the state and the religious establishment, but by a multi-sided struggle among Muslims, as well as between Muslims and Hindus, and Muslims and the British, over the cultural and political future of India. Out of these struggles would come both new forms of Muslim political identity and religious practice.

MUSLIM MILITANCY FROM PLASSEY TO 1857

While the Muslim political and lineage elites were slow to adapt to the decline of the Mughal state, Muslim religious leaders were immediately galvanized into action. The Sufis and managers of shrines compensated for the loss of Mughal support by reaffirming Muslim values. The Chisti order undertook internal reforms. The reformist 'ulama' reaffirmed the need for strict adherence to the universal principles of Islam, striking a chord among Indian Muslims, who felt that the true cause of the Mughal defeat was moral and religious corruption. Muslims had fallen from God's favor for their failure to observe Islam. Without the protection of the state, exposed to infidel rule, they felt that religious and communal self-discipline and active struggle were the only answers to their plight. Thus, in 1803, a son of Shah Waliallah, Shah 'Abd al-'Aziz (1746–1824) issued a fatwa, or judicial opinion, declaring that India was *dar al-harb* (the realm of war). The unbelievers, he pointed out, administered taxation and criminal law at their discretion; India was no longer ruled by the Shari'a. The proper response to British rule, he concluded, was that Indian Muslims rise up in holy war.

His disciple, Sayyid Ahmad Barelwi (1786–1831), took up the cause. Sayyid Ahmad had begun his career as a missionary preacher in Uttar Pradesh, Bihar, and Bengal, seeking to reform religious practices. He made a three-year pilgrimage to Mecca from 1821 to 1824, and returned to India, settling finally in the Northwest Frontier province. He preached the reform program: belief in the unity of God and the elimination of polytheism and innovation in the form of shrine Sufism and Shi'ism. He sought to restore the true Islam by repudiating ordinary Indian-Muslim mystical and ritual practices, and by basing the true faith on the Quran and Sunna alone. His preaching was accompanied by a determined effort to arouse Indian Muslims to throw off the yoke of foreign rule. In the Northwest Frontier province he rallied the Yusufzai Pashtuns. The Pashtuns, hard pressed on the north by their Afghan enemies and on the south by the expanding Sikh state in the Punjab, were a disunited tribal society which Sayyid Ahmad sought to unify under a single leadership to defend their political interests and the holy cause. In 1827 he claimed the title imam, supreme religious leader, and led his people to war. Sayyid Ahmad, with a small group of followers, was killed at Balakot in 1831. The task of imposing unity and discipline on the Pashtuns was beyond reach. His religious legacy, however, remained in the form of the Tariqa-i Muhammadi (Way of Muhammad) movement, which, as we shall see, was to revitalize Indian Islam and give impetus to communal and religious reforms that survive to the present day.

Bengal was a second arena of Muslim reform and revival movements. Here the doctrinal position was similar, but the social and economic context was very different. In West Bengal, Titu Mir began his career as a disciple of the Tariqa-i Muhammadi. He had been converted to the new movement in Mecca, and considered himself a khalifa of Sayyid Ahmad. He preached the primacy of the Quran and hadith and opposed the ceremonies at Sufi shrines. Titu Mir's reform became a political cause in 1830 when the local zamindars and indigo planters tried to resist the spread of his teachings by imposing a tax on his peasant followers. In reaction, he and his followers defiled a Hindu temple. The authorities were called in, and Titu Mir was killed by the police in 1831.

The Fara'idi were a similar but unconnected movement under the leadership of Hajji Shari'atallah (1781–1840). Hajji Shari'atallah was born in Bengal, but lived for eighteen years in Mecca, absorbed in the study of Hanafi law. He was initiated into the Qadiri order and was influenced by Meccan reformist views. In 1818 he returned to Bengal to preach *tawba* (repentance) and fulfillment of *fara'id* (religious duties). Islam was to be practiced as prescribed in the Quran, the Sunna of the Prophet, and the Hanafi codes of law. The Fara'idi were not in principle opposed to mysticism, but they strenuously opposed veneration of saints, seasonal festivals, celebration of the birthday of the Prophet and of saints' "birthdays," the ta'ziya procession in mourning for Husayn, and other practices that they regarded as Hindu, Buddhist, Shi'i, or Sufi perversions of the true faith.

Between 1818 and 1838 the Fara'idi won a large following in the villages of East Bengal among peasants and workers, such as weavers and oil pressers who were being oppressed by Hindu zamindars and British indigo planters. At the death of Hajji Shari'atallah, his son, Dudu Mian, transformed the Fara'idi from a purely religious body into a movement of peasant resistance to Hindu and British exploitation. From 1838 to 1846 he organized a communal government; a khalifa was appointed for each Fara'idi village with responsibility to set up schools, teach the proper performance of Islamic rituals, dispense justice, and recruit armed gangs to defend peasant interests. Every ten villages were the responsibility of a higher official, who in turn reported to the leader of the movement.

FROM THE MUTINY TO WORLD WAR I

Thus, the first Muslim response to the imposition of British rule was characterized by the efforts of religious reformers to rally tribal and peasant populations to the defense of their interests and their religion. The Mutiny of 1857 turned Muslim activities into new directions. It began as an explosion of pent-up resentment against the accumulated insults of British rule. Hindu and Muslim recruits in British forces, the sepoys of Meerut, refused to use their newly issued Enfield rifles and cartridges because, it was rumored, the cartridges were greased with pigs' and cows' fat, an insult to men of either religion. The cartridges, however, were but a symbol of deeper cultural and political antagonisms. The Mutiny concerned not only Indian soldiers in the service of the British East India Company, but the Muslim and Hindu upper classes of central and northern India. For these classes the cost of British rule had grown heavier. The British continued to annex Indian principalities, and threatened the old Indian aristocracy, both Hindu and Muslim, with replacement by British officials. British policies also led to heavy taxation and the confiscation of estates. Equally important was the threat to Indian cultural and social values. The British had introduced the English language and Western education. British ideas about polygamy, slavery, and the freedom of women; British opposition to sati, the caste system, and other Hindu and Muslim religious practices; British interference with the operation of Muslim law; and, finally, the ever more widespread preaching, by English missionaries, of Christianity – all these threatened the self-esteem, the hallowed lifestyles, and the economic and political interests of the hitherto privileged Indian elites. As the economic and cultural price of political inferiority bore down upon Mughal India, it took only the pig-fat incident to provoke a widespread Hindu–Muslim revolt against British rule.

The revolt was bitterly suppressed and not easily forgotten. In its wake, the British reorganized the government of India. They formally abolished the Mughal empire and the East India Company in favor of direct crown government, and proceeded to consolidate their Indian regime. The British completed the introduction of legal codes, such as the Penal Code of 1860, and the Law of Criminal and Civil Procedure of 1861, and reorganized the system of judicial administration. Between 1871 and 1882 they created a new financial system, making the provinces responsible for their own revenues and expenditures. The army was reorganized with the proportion of English to Indian troops raised from one-fifth to one-half. A close-knit and professional officer corps was developed. In the half-century that followed the Mutiny, the British created the largest imperial bureaucracy in Indian history. In the same period, they began the economic modernization of India. Agricultural production was increased; trade expanded under free trade laws introduced between 1882 and 1894. The British introduced railroads, coal mining, and mechanized textile production.

The new policies rested upon a revised set of attitudes. On the one hand, the British developed an ever-increasing aloofness, superciliousness, and condescending attitude toward Indians. The late nineteenth century was the heyday of confidence in the racial superiority of Europeans and in their God-given right to bring European order to less developed peoples. An unbridgeable gulf of political, racial, and caste supremacy divided British rulers from their Indian subjects. On the other hand, some lessons had been learned from the Mutiny. The British came to understand the limits of political centralization, and to appreciate that British rule depended on the support and cooperation of Indian princes and landlords. They maintained in existence some 560 Indian princely states, restored loyalist Hindu and Muslim zamindars to their lands, and began to organize Indian municipal and advisory councils. The British also adopted a policy of non-intervention in religious matters and withdrew from efforts to reform Hindu caste or Muslim legal practices, but they continued to sponsor English education and to favor the Westernization of the Indian upper classes.

The British relationship with the Muslim population was particularly delicate. While many Britons were aware of how limited Muslim involvement in the Mutiny of 1857 had been, and how much it was a joint rebellion of the Muslim and Hindu upper classes, the British generally tended to stereotype the opposition in terms of Muslim resistance to British rule. They saw the Muslims as an entity, once the dominant elite of India, that was bound to be rebellious and had therefore to be suppressed. But the British also recognized the Muslims as a political interest entitled to special educational and electoral privileges. Until the end of the century the British continued to favor the appointment of Muslims to minor and middling government positions. By dealing with Muslims as an entity with a collective claim to political power on the basis of religious identity, they helped generate Muslim solidarity. Having defined a Muslim interest in their own mind, the British helped confirm it in the minds of Indian Muslims.

The Muslim reaction to the events of 1857 was equally consequential. At the time, qasbah political and religious elites did not think of themselves as a single political body, but all of them recognized that jihad was a failure and British rule was enduring. They agreed that their best interests lay in the cultivation of educational, religious, and cultural affairs, and in strengthening the Muslim community from within, but they were divided in practical matters. Some embraced the new regime in the hope of forming a British–Muslim condominium to govern India. Others maintained silent but deep anti-British and pan-Islamic sentiments; still others turned their backs on political issues altogether.

As the century moved on, three main strands may be distinguished in the post-Mutiny position of the qasbah elites. The first was the position of the conservative religious leaders, who recognized the futility of jihad, the need for adjustment to British rule, and the importance of preserving the traditions of Islamic religious belief and practice. The Sufi leaders and *sajjada nishins*, or heads of shrines, wanted to maintain the panoply of saint worship and festivals and the loyalty of the Muslim masses. However, Mughal decline had deprived the shrines of economic and political support; British rule had subverted their worldly political influence. To maintain their position many Sufis associated themselves with British rule and had recourse to British courts to settle land tenure and succession disputes. The sajjada nishins often delegated their religious functions to subordinates while they saw to their political interests. Other Sufis attempted to adapt theory and practice to their declining worldly authority, and stressed the purely contemplative and spiritual aspect of Sufism. They tried to preserve the inner meanings of Sufi tradition, and adopted more sober and Shari'a-oriented religious practices in the face of declining worldly authority. Conservative 'ulama' similarly attempted to maintain their traditional position; the scholars of the Farangi Mahall quarter of Lucknow and the Barelwis combined 'ulama' scholarship and Sufi shrines.

The second response within 'ulama' circles, however, was the resurgence of reformism. In North India, its most important expression in the post-Mutiny period was the founding in 1867 of the reform college of Deoband, by Maulana Muhammad Qasim Nanautawi. Deoband's curriculum combined the study of the revealed sciences (Quran, hadith, and law) with rational subjects (logic, philosophy, and science). At the same time it was Sufi in orientation and affiliated with the Chisti order. Its Sufism, however, was closely integrated with hadith scholarship and the proper legal practice of Islam.

The reform college served as an organizational focus for a Muslim community. Deoband trained its students for a public mission – to instruct the community in the true practice of Islam. Deobandis poured out, in Urdu vernacular, legal opinions on proper Islamic practice. The spread of printing made it possible for the first time to reach a mass audience. To the degree that reformism represents a long-term trend toward the adoption of normative Islamic practices, the modern era has increased the facilities for standardization. The publication, transportation, and communication facilities to reach ever-larger numbers of people have made it possible for the 'ulama' to teach the common people a high-culture version of Islam. Deoband's reach was India-wide. Many students came from Afghanistan, Central Asia, Yemen, and Arabia. Within thirty years of its founding, its graduates had established some forty branch schools, making Deoband the center of the new *maslak* – a distinctive "way" in Indian Islam.

One of the crucial principles of the school was that it should be detached from the private, familial, and local affiliations of its teachers and supporters. Deoband, unlike previous colleges in India, was organized as an independent institution, not as part of the household of the leading teachers, or as a function of the local mosque. Deliberately, it avoided both the support of rich local landowners and other Muslim nobles – and the traditional system of waqf endowments – and sought annual contributions from a wide public. Through its system of annual pledges and regular publications, Deoband cultivated widespread middle- and lower-middle-class support. By the reform and standardization of Islamic belief and practice, a program of public education, and a system of affiliated schools and public contributions, Deoband sought to unite Indian Muslims around the leadership of the 'ulama' and the schools.

The Deoband program represented a careful balance between innovative responsiveness to the new era and allegiance to traditional Muslim ideas. Many of the features of the Deoband school – the school as a physical institution with a distinct building and central library, the fixed professional staff, the ordered curriculum of study, examinations, public awards, affiliated colleges, public contributions, and missionary activities – were suggested by British practices. Deoband was thus a response to new forms of bureaucratic organization, the introduction of new secular ideals, and the competition of new elites. At the same time, it was thoroughly Muslim in terms of education, worship, and withdrawal from politics. It had been founded at the very moment that the British Raj had deprived the Muslim community of the expected protection of a Muslim state, and it represented a concept of a Muslim community without a state as a community of religious practice under the leadership of the 'ulama' whose primary institution was a system of schools. The Deobandi 'ulama' had elected to preserve and reform the personal religious practice of Muslims at the cost of giving up the political aspect of Muslim communal organization.

In Bengal the reform movement went back to the pre-Mutiny efforts of Titu Mir and the Fara'idi. Despite the impact of the earlier reform movement, most Bengali villages maintained an identity based on local dialects and a syncretic form of Muslim–Hindu folk culture. Village mullahs, prayer leaders, and teachers had little in common with the educated urban 'ulama', the ashraf who claimed Arab or Persian ethnic origin, spoke Urdu, and were separated by wealth, status, and cultural style from the *atrap*, or common people. After 1870, however, reformism began to spread again in the Bengali countryside. Though there was no focal educational institution like Deoband, public debates and revivalist meetings fostered a heightened Muslim consciousness. *Anjumans* (religious associations) were formed to link town and countryside, urban and rural 'ulama', and to teach correct Islamic practice. Most importantly, a large volume of pamphlets was published to give advice on Muslim rituals, to counsel parents on how to raise children, and to censure gambling, drinking, and smoking. The typical pamphlet, called *Nasihat-nama* (Book of Advice), tried to purge rural Islam of its basis in Bengali folk culture and to bring it into closer accord with urban high-culture Islam. The reform movement, however, weakened by the conflict between urban and rural values, had only a limited impact in rural Bengal. Instead, it was to be the 1905–11 struggle over the partition of the province by the British that would truly awaken Muslim political consciousness.

The third strand in the post-Mutiny Muslim adjustment to British rule was that of the landowning and office-holding interests. Though the British had replaced the Mughals, it was still conceivable to the political elite that they could maintain their landed, official, and status interests; but it was obvious that to do so no longer depended on the traditional kinship networks and loyalties, but upon British laws and administrative regulations. British suspicion of Muslim ambitions had to be allayed, and Muslims had to accommodate the English language and the superiority of British military, economic, and administrative technology.

For two generations, the response of the political elites was formulated by Sir Sayyid Ahmad Khan. Ahmad Khan was himself descended from a prominent family of Mughal administrators, and throughout his life continued to be posted as an officer of British administration. In his view the only adequate response to the realities of post-Mutiny India was to accept British rule. In Sayyid Ahmad Khan's view, British rule was lawful. Under British government Muslims could live in peace; the Shari'a was in fact applied, and in any case, Muslims were dependent upon British favor. In the course of his long public life he opposed pan-Islamic sentiments and Muslim participation in the Indian National Congress, which was aimed at wresting political power from, rather than simply collaborating with, the British.

His principal concern and that of his cohort was the need for Western-type education, under Muslim auspices, to train a new generation for political responsibility. The effort at cultural and educational reform began with the founding of the National Mohammadan Association in 1856 and the Mohammadan Literary Society in 1863. This was followed by the Anjuman-i Islam of Bombay and the establishment of new madrasas in Dacca and Chittagong. Sayyid Ahmad Khan himself sponsored the translation of English scientific works into Urdu, founded the Ghazipur Scientific Society in 1864, and encouraged instruction in Urdu at Calcutta University. After a visit to England in 1869–70 he published the journal *Tahdhib al-Akhlaq* (Purification of Morals) to educate Indian Muslims in the ways of modernism. The culmination of his efforts came in 1875 with the foundation of the Mohammadan Anglo-Oriental College at Aligarh, which became the training ground of the Muslim political leaders of the twentieth century.

The college at Aligarh was devoted to a combination of Islamic and English language studies. Sayyid Ahmad Khan would have preferred a modernized version of Islam, after his own fashion, but the school, for fear of scandal and loss of public support, maintained a more conservative position. The real achievement of the school, however, lay not in the curriculum or in the preparation of scholars, but in the social and moral values that it communicated to its students through the mechanisms of a new curriculum and a new form of school community. Aligarh was meant to be the Eton of India; its playing fields as much as its classrooms encouraged verbal skill, self-confidence, manly solidarity and competition, and the values of duty, loyalty, and leadership, exercised in games and in school clubs and societies, to produce young men capable of cooperation with each other in giving leadership to Indian Muslims in the context of British rule. Thus, the old ruling elites attempted to fortify their claim to continued eminence under British rule, to provide themselves with the educational and cultural style appropriate to the new era, and to train a new generation in the moral and political, as well as the intellectual, qualities needed for participation in the British Raj.

Finally, Sayyid Ahmad Khan favored the modernization of the Islamic religion so as to make it consistent with the new technical, cultural, and political order of modern times. To adapt Muslims to British rule, he had to persuade them that Western scientific thought was not antithetical to Islam. To demonstrate this, he and his contemporaries undertook the reinterpretation of the Quran. The Quran was God's revelation, and the passages that seemed difficult to understand in a modern context had to be interpreted symbolically, allegorically, or analytically to uncover their true meaning, which would always be consistent with reason and never contrary to nature. Excising the irrelevant details in favor of the main principles, stripping away the later accretions of Muslim tradition and exegesis and going back to fundamentals, Muslims have in the Quran, he argued, the source of a rational religion attuned to modern man's scientific interests.

While Sayyid Ahmad tried to persuade Muslims that the Quran allowed for scientific developments, he also attempted to convince Europeans that Islam was a reasonable religion, worthy of respect. He and his contemporaries attempted to explain the meaning of polygamy, slavery, and the place of non-Muslims and of women in Muslim societies in ways that would make Muslim social institutions acceptable to Westerners. He hoped thus to establish the worthiness of Islam in the eyes both of Muslims and of Westerners and to prepare the way for the collaboration of Muslims and non-Muslims in the government of India. Cultural and religious reform was tied to the educational and political tasks of maintaining the position of the Muslim elite in the British era.

Thus in the course of the late nineteenth century the qasbah elites of North India attempted to cope with their deteriorating social and political position and with the realities of British domination by developing new religious and cultural orientations. One wing of the qasbah elite stressed the importance of preserving the Islamic identity of Muslims, reform of religious practice, and the consolidation of larger-scale, more homogeneous Muslim communities on the bases of reformed Islam. A second wing stressed the importance of adopting the cultural style of their British overlords and thereby preserving a privileged position in the Indian state. For the time being both segments of the Muslim elite accepted the inevitability of British rule.

FROM CULTURAL TO POLITICAL ACTION

In the latter part of the century, however, the policies of loyalism and religious or modernist reform were challenged and eventually overthrown. The ambiguities in the British attitude toward the Muslims, increasing Hindu self-assertion, and the beginnings of the Indian national independence movement drove Muslim political and religious leaders toward a more aggressive anti-British policy, and brought into the open profound differences among Muslims as to their conception of the Muslim community and the goals of Muslim political action.

The British attitude toward the Muslim elites was a major factor in the eventual subversion of the loyalist policies of Sayyid Ahmad Khan. The British considered that the Muslims, as former masters of India, harbored lingering ambitions to political power, and that they had therefore to be conciliated to win their favor but repressed lest they become too powerful. They accepted the idea that the former political elite was entitled to governmental appointments and to seats on councils in proportion to their political weight rather than their absolute numbers. At the same time the British tried to reduce the proportion of Muslims employed in government. British governors sometimes deliberately favored Hindu over Muslim appointees. The administrative position of Muslims, though still substantial, deteriorated steadily.

The introduction of municipal self-government and municipal councils by the Ripon Local Council Act of 1882 and the Indian Councils Act of 1892 was also detrimental to Muslims. The electoral system favored Hindus, who were the majority of the population, and made it possible for wealthy Hindu merchants and money lenders to compete for office and to challenge the authority of the Muslim (and Hindu) landed and administrative families. While in the eastern United Provinces and Oudh the old elite maintained its position, in the western United Provinces and Doab the advantage went to aggressive Hindu newcomers.

Another factor that weakened the Muslim position was Hindu self-assertion. Hindu religious revivalism went back to the founding in 1828 of the Brahmo Samaj in Calcutta to promote theism and social reform among Hindus. In 1875 the Arya Samaj was founded to modernize Hinduism and make it a suitable faith for Western-educated Hindu merchants, officials, and intellectuals – a faith able to compete with Christianity. Among Hindus, as well as Muslims, modernizing reform was accompanied by traditionalist and orthodox revival, and was changed from an elite to a mass movement. The first cow-protection associations were founded in 1882; the first communal riots among Hindus and Muslims took place in 1893.

Of particular concern to educated Muslims was the campaign to make Hindi an official language. Hindu revivalism led to a literary renaissance, increasing numbers of newspapers with ever-wider circulation, and ultimately a Hindu crusade against the dominant place of Urdu in government affairs. Hindus campaigned to have Devanagari recognized as an official script for court and government use. The new script, they argued, would allow Hindus who did not know Persian to compete equally for government posts. The British were responsive to these demands. A British governor rejected a civil service candidates' list on the grounds that there were too many Muslims; Persian was removed from the curriculum of Allahabad University, and in 1900 the British accepted the use of Devanagari script for official purposes in the Northwest Frontier provinces and Oudh.

The beginning of the movement toward Indian national independence also brought into question the generation-old Muslim policy of loyalty to British rule. The Indian National Congress, founded in 1885, though open to Muslims, was formed by Brahmin lawyers, professionals, and middle-class intellectuals. It expressed resentment of British attitudes toward Indians, called for increased participation of Indians in the civil service and increased political representation, and opposed British economic policies that damaged Indian industries.

However, no event was more important for the change in Muslim elite opinion than the partition of Bengal. In 1905 the British, largely for administrative reasons, partitioned Bengal in a way that created an eastern province with a substantial Muslim majority; but under intense Hindu pressure Britain reversed the partition in

1911. In the eyes of many Muslims this reversal utterly discredited the policy of collaboration, and lent force to the conviction that the British were basically hostile to Muslim interests.

The first Muslim response to these challenges was to continue the policies set down in the aftermath of the great Mutiny. Sayyid Ahmad Khan reaffirmed his policy of collaboration and of using educational organizations as the spearhead of Muslim interests, but the younger generation of educated Muslim officials, lawyers, and journalists – especially those having difficulty finding suitable government employment – refused to accept the passivity of their elders. While the landowning and office-controlling elders pursued a policy of appeasement, the younger generation clamored for more direct political action In 1900 the Urdu Defense Association was formed. In 1906 a delegation of Muslim leaders from Aligarh petitioned the British viceroy, Lord Minto, for a separate Muslim electorate, and he acknowledged the Muslim right to representation in government in proportion to their assumed political importance. In 1909 the Indian Councils Act allowed for partially separate electorates. For the British this was a convenient way to satisfy the Muslim claim to political privilege; it was also a way to confirm the division of Indians into Muslim and Hindu interests and to make the British the arbiter among hostile communities.

The most important expressions of the new Muslim militancy were the founding of the All-India Muslim League in 1906, and the beginnings of political journalism. In 1908 a young journalist, Abu'l-Kalam Azad (1888–1958) began to publish *al-Hilal* (The Crescent). *Al-Hilal* preached that Muslims the world over were a single people by virtue of common religion, and that the Ottoman Caliph was their leader. Moreover, it was the duty of Muslims to work for home rule in India, and form an active political body to support the Caliphate. Another journalist, Muhammad 'Ali, a graduate of Aligarh, preached a similar creed in his paper, *Comrade*.

The new-found militancy of the Muslim political elite was paralleled by revived political activism among the reformist 'ulama' of Farangi Mahall and Deoband. Farangi Mahall was the name given to a prominent 'ulama' lineage, derived from the quarter of Lucknow which they had inhabited since the end of the seventeenth century. The quarter was renowned as one of the oldest centers of Indian madrasa education and Sufism, and the family scholars had wide networks of disciples. The Farangi Mahalli maintained a moderate version of Shari'a-Sufi Islam, combining Quranic and legal studies with mysticism. They venerated the shrines of Sufi ancestors and kept up a festival calendar of "birthday" celebrations for the saints and the Prophet; they were careful, however, to emphasize that they did not worship the saints, but rather came to the tombs in order to be closer to God. While Deobandis and other reformers criticized their Sufi practices, the Farangi Mahalli believed that their synthesis of Shari'a and Sufism was a true representation of the life and teachings of the Prophet.

One crucial principle of the school was avoidance of contact with or dependence upon government. While the Farangis had accepted Mughal gifts in the seventeenth century, by the nineteenth they had withdrawn from politics to avoid contamination by the Shi'i rulers of Lucknow and their British overlords. This apolitical stance, however, changed in the late nineteenth century. Beneath the acquiescent surface of apolitical religious activities was a smoldering resentment of infidel rule. This resentment was expressed in terms of sympathy with Muslims all over the world who were struggling against British, European, and Christian imperialism. The leaders of the Farangi Mahall played a large role in the formation of Muslim associations to support the Ottoman empire and protect the holy places in Arabia, and they were instrumental, after World War I, in launching the Khilafat movement and in the foundation of the Jami'at al-'Ulama'-i Hind (Association of the 'Ulama' of India).

Between 1876 and 1878, the years of the Russo-Turkish war and the Congress of Berlin, which witnessed the first British, as well as Russian, participation in the partition of the Ottoman empire, Indian Muslims agitated for a pro-Turkish policy. Jamal al-Din al-Afghani propagated the doctrine of pan-Islamic solidarity as the only way for Muslim peoples to throw off the yoke of European rule. In 1888 Muslim religious opposition to British rule took a new turn when the rector of Deoband issued a fatwa in favor of a Muslim alliance with the Congress Party to further the struggle against imperialism. The 'ulama' considered foreign rule to be a greater danger to Islam than domestic Hindu competition. These strong anti-colonial, anti-British, and pro-Ottoman sensibilities were stimulated in the years before World War I by the Anglo-Russian treaty of 1907 to create spheres of influence in Iran, the Italian invasion of Tripolitania, the establishment of the French protectorate over Morocco, and finally by the outbreak of the Balkan wars in 1912.

The Western-educated and the religious-educated leaders joined hands in open political action. In 1909 Mahmud al-Hasan, rector of Deoband, founded the Jami'at al-Ansar (Society of Helpers [of the Prophet]), whose ultimate objective was an alliance of Turkey, Iran, and Afghanistan to expel the British from India. In 1912-13 Maulana 'Abd al-Bari, the head of Farangi Mahall, and Shaukat 'Ali, a brother of Muhammad 'Ali, and also a graduate of Aligarh, founded the Anjuman-i Khuddam-i Ka'ba (Association of the Servants of the Ka'ba) to oppose British rule and defend the Ottoman empire. During the war Mahmud al-Hasan made the pilgrimage to Mecca, where he contacted Ottoman leaders and tried to promote the cause of a pan-Islamic Caliphate. Maulana 'Ubaydallah Sindhi traveled to the Northwest Frontier provinces and Afghanistan to explore arms manufacturers, promote unrest among the tribal peoples, and eventually set up a provisional government of India in exile. During the war, hostility to the British mushroomed into pan-Islamic, pro-Caliphal political agitation and conspiracies to weaken British rule and promote the international cause of Islam.

FROM ELITE TO MASS POLITICS

These years were marked not only by the change from passivity to active political opposition, but also by a change from elite political and educational activities to efforts to rally mass Muslim support and to weld the disparate masses of Indian Muslims into a cohesive communal and political body. The crucial reason for this change was simply the anachronism of elite self-cultivation in an era of rising Hindu political action, and the weakness of small elite groups pleading for special privileges from a powerful British state. Mass support had become essential to protect and legitimize the claims of the Muslim elite.

The whole concept of a mass Muslim society in India had only the most tenuous basis: it was perhaps stronger in the minds of the British than in those of the Muslims. The British stressed the importance of religious ties and the free exercise of religion as a cardinal principle of a liberal society, and reinforced the collective identity of religious groups by giving them the right to petition for relief of grievances and to elect their own representatives. They identified the Muslims as a religious community; then they provided the political machinery to translate that identity into concerted group action. By the Indian Councils Act of 1909 they confirmed the existence of two separate communal electorates, Hindu and Muslim, and thus gave legal and political substance to the underlying differences of language and religion.

Among Muslims the concept of a Muslim Indian society had its basis in the inherent Muslim sense of communal solidarity. It also had some basis in the cultural unity of the qasbah elites, who shared a Persian and Urdu literary education and a relatively standardized religious practice. Nevertheless, the problems of creating a mass Muslim identity were profound. The Muslim elites were divided into innumerable local family, quarter, or factional segments and were not at all unified for political purposes. They could not, as a group, provide political leadership for the mass of Indian Muslims. Moreover, despite the partial successes of the reform movement in propagating a standardized Islamic religious practice, the masses were far from sharing a common identity. Among Indian Muslims parochial family, lineage, caste, regional, and class interests commonly overrode Muslim identity. Muslim identity had always combined a universalistic sentiment with parochial loyalties, but in the late nineteenth century, there was neither the organizational basis nor the unifying symbols for a mass Indian-Muslim movement. Nonetheless, the Muslim elites, motivated by political necessity, in opposition to Hindu movements and in collaboration with British notions of politics, would attempt to bring into being a new political body – the Muslims of India. This task was never attempted in a unified way, nor fully accomplished, yet the various parallel efforts to create a shared Indian-Muslim identity and an Indian-Muslim political organization would utterly change the position of Muslim peoples in the subcontinent.

The first sign of the new orientation to mass politics was the changing character of local demonstrations and riots. Through the nineteenth century, religious festivals had served to solidify local community consciousness and to mobilize Muslims, as opposed to Hindus. By the end of the century, the formation of Islamic educational and defense associations, and increasing public debate, gave national importance to local events. The Kanpur mosque episode of 1913 became the first symbol of national Muslim politics. The British wished to move the mosque washing facilities in order to put in a new road. In other times this might have been inconsequential, but now it was seen as a threat to the safety of the mosque and, almost literally, to Islam. The desecration of the mosque crystallized a feeling of mourning, martyrdom, and defeat among Muslims. Local committees were formed to defend the mosque; Delhi- or Lucknow-based Muslim leaders took up the Kanpur cause. The defense of the mosque condemned the policy of cooperation with the government, enshrined religious symbols as the basic way of articulating Muslim identity, and crystallized a larger-scale Indian-Muslim consciousness.

The Kanpur riots were followed by Muslim riots in Calcutta in 1918, in Bombay in 1929, and again in Kanpur in 1931. These outbursts showed that an overarching Muslim identity was taking form in the minds of the urban common people, but that this symbolic identity outstripped the political structures available to organize and articulate Muslim interests. In these incidents local leadership was highly factionalized, inadequately integrated into municipal institutions, and thus unable either to direct or control popular feeling. Muslim symbols could spark large-scale demonstrations, but the factionalism among Muslim leaders prevented an organized political movement.

The closest approach to mass Muslim political action came from the Khilafat movement. In 1919 Mahatma Gandhi and the Indian National Congress were about to launch the first great campaign of non-cooperation for establishing Indian home rule and independence; Muslim leaders formed two new associations with similar goals. Muhammad 'Ali founded the Khilafat Conference to press for the restoration of the Ottoman empire, and the 'ulama' of Farangi Mahall and Deoband founded the Jami'at al-'Ulama'-i Hind to fight for Muslim religious interests and for the preservation of the Caliphate. The primary strategy of the Khilafat movement was to ally with Congress to further their joint interest in overthrowing British rule and winning political independence for India: Congress, under the leadership of Gandhi, embraced the cause of the Caliphate; Muslims pledged themselves to non-cooperation. For the first time Hindus and Muslims participated in a broad-based national movement to compel the British to return India to Indian hands.

The joint movement soon collapsed. The Muslims were divided. Some concentrated on non-cooperation, while others gave their attention to an abortive effort to move the Muslim masses to Afghanistan to set the basis for a jihad against British rule. Then, in 1923 and 1924, the independent Turkish state abolished the Sultanate and Caliphate, removing the external rationale of the movement. At the same time, the alliance with Congress foundered. The collapse of Gandhi's authority and liberal–conservative divisions within Congress compromised its commitment to a joint Muslim–Hindu movement. Hindu and Muslim extremists revived the latent antagonism between the two communities, and communal riots ensued. By 1924, the non-cooperation movement, the Khilafat movement, and Hindu–Muslim collaboration were finished.

Despite its defeat, the Khilafat movement had important consequences. It greatly enlarged the vocabulary and the shared culture of newspaper reading, poetry recitation, and public debates that conveyed anti-British and shared Muslim feeling. It created cadres to escort leaders, enforce boycotts, and maintain order at public meetings. It brought secular and religious leaders together in a common cause. Thus the movement transformed Indian Muslim politics from the maneuvers of elites to the struggle of the masses for political identity.

Despite the breakdown of the Khilafat movement, the more universalistic concept of Muslim identity continued to gain ground. Mosques and schools, and above all, the press provided arenas for debate and the dissemination of an awareness of the commonality of Indian Muslims. Muslim communal activities were directed primarily into three channels. First, spontaneous riots over Muslim issues continued to express the rallying power of Muslim symbols. Second was the revival of reformist movements and the effort to base Muslim identity upon personal religious practice. Muslim devotionalism, the love of the Prophet, and the demand for women's education all became markers of the larger and more universalistic identity of Indian Muslims. After the failure of the Khilafat effort the great mass movements of the 1920s and 1930s were the Tabligh and Tanzim.

In 1927 the Tablighi Islam movement was founded by Maulana Muhammad Ilyas, a spiritual descendant of Shah Waliallah, a graduate of Deoband, and a member of the Sabiri branch of the Chisti order. Ilyas began his career as a scholar and Sufi teacher, but gave it up to reconvert the Mewatis, a peasant community living near Delhi, to the true practice of Islam based on the Quran and hadith, observance of the Shari'a, and pious worship and meditation according to Chisti principles. He eschewed political involvement and held that only by the practice of Islam could Muslims demonstrate their stewardship of worldly affairs. His movement began by preaching to villagers, and spread throughout North India by recruiting peasant disciples to preach his message in still other villages and towns. The Tanzim movement also flourished in North India as a call for the reform of personal religious practices, and for the defense of an endangered Islam and an abused Muslim minority. Like the Tabligh movement it concentrated on the religious rather than the political aspects of the Muslim problem, and had dramatic religious and emotional appeal but no overall political organization.

THE PAKISTAN MOVEMENT

It was left to a third Muslim movement to reverse the priority of personal religious reform over political unification, stress the importance of Muslim political solidarity rather than religious practice, and create the first mass political movement based on Islamic identity. The Western-educated Muslim political elite turned the growing sense of Muslim solidarity into a political and nationalist form. With the breakup of the Khilafat movement, separatist Muslim political demands were revived. In

1924 the Muslim League called for safeguards for the religious and civil rights of the Muslim populations, and for autonomy and political predominance in Bengal, the Punjab, and the Northwest Frontier provinces. In response, the Nehru Report of 1928 favored a unified Indian state without separate electorates and without Muslim majority provinces, though it conceded that Muslims should be provided with representation in excess of proportion to population. Muslims were confirmed in their fears of Hindu domination. Muhammad 'Ali Jinnah, speaking for the Muslim League in 1929, reiterated the demand for a federal Indian state, with autonomous Muslim provinces, separate electorates, and safeguards for Muslims in law, education, and religion. Jinnah made parties, elections, and legislatures another route to the moral unity of Indian Muslims. British measures to find a compromise – the Simon Report of 1930 favoring a federal government for India, the White Paper of 1932 upholding separate electorates but depriving Muslims of parliamentary majorities in Bengal and the Punjab, and the Government of India Act of 1935, which gave British guarantees for minority rights but enlarged the franchise to the advantage of Hindu majorities – were all rejected as inadequate to the demands of one side or the other, and as unacceptable because these proposals assumed continued British rule of India. Much as the Muslims and Hindus disagreed, they were no longer willing to continue British rule as the solution to their conflict.

The elections of 1937 marked the turning of Muslim demands for separate electorates and constitutional guarantees to demands for a separate territorial nation. These elections were a defeat for the Muslim League, and afterwards Congress refused to share ministries and control of the government with Muslim League politicians. Gandhi and Nehru also attempted to appeal directly to the Muslim masses over the heads of the League politicians. Class interests, they believed, were stronger than communal ties, but Congress only reinforced Muslim fears of Hindu domination, and stimulated Muslim support for the League. In 1938, to recoup the Muslim League position, Jinnah advanced the "two nations" theory and made the first formal demand for a separate Muslim homeland, whose boundaries were not clearly defined but were understood to include the provinces of the Punjab, Northwest Frontier, and Bengal. In a 1940 resolution the Muslim League called for the formation of Pakistan.

The idea of a Muslim homeland went back only a decade – to a 1930 speech by Muhammad Iqbal, which called for the amalgamation of the Punjab, Northwest Frontier province, Sind, and Baluchistan into a single state. Muhammad Iqbal (1876–1938) was the preeminent spokesman of Indian Muslims in the twentieth century. His philosophic integration of Sufi Islam with Western thought, his understanding of Islam in universal religious terms, his commitment to the reinterpretation of Muslim principles in light of contemporary conditions, and his passionate religious and moral poetry made him the spiritual leader of Indian modernism. In this famous speech Iqbal denied that Muslims and Hindus made a single Indian nation, and called for the formation of a Muslim state, based on (unspecified) Islamic principles, to be part of a multi-national system of Muslim states. Iqbal's vision revived the basic idea of the Khilafat movement – regional Muslim populations as elements of a universal pan-Islamic community.

Chaudhari Rahmat 'Ali and his Cambridge student friends also advanced the idea of an independent Muslim state. In their conception, the new state would be a commonwealth of Indian Muslim states including regions that had majority Muslim populations, provinces ruled by Muslim princes, and areas sacred to Muslims – the conglomeration of the whole to be called Pakistan. The idea of Pakistan was a revolution in Muslim thought, for this concept of a Muslim nation did not have a specifically religious content. The Pakistan program was the program of secularized elites who were forced by disunity of the Muslim population and by competition with the Hindu majorities to call their political society "Islamic."

Muslim public opinion was not prepared for such a development. In the United Provinces, there was indeed a relatively cohesive Muslim elite and a strong sense of religious community. Here the Muslim League leaders were able to separate Islam as a symbol of political community from its traditional religious implications and to manipulate this symbol as the basis of a new political identity. In other regions, however, the process of communal political identification was not so far advanced. In the Punjab, Islamic ideological ties had developed in urban areas, but not in rural districts, where Sufi shrines and dependency on rural landlords remained the basic modes of social organization. Bengali Muslim consciousness was directed to the reform of religious practice and to agrarian social and political issues, but not to the kind of territorial polity favored by the Muslim League.

From 1938 to 1945 an energetic propaganda campaign was launched to rally Muslims to the newly defined cause. The middle classes – Muslim businessmen, landlords, government officials, professionals, and university students – were easily convinced. The 'ulama' were generally won over by their fear of Hindu competition, the perceived need for Muslim political power, and the powerful appeal of an "Islamic" state. Most important for the League cause was the support of the sajjada nishins – the Sufi elite – in the important provinces of Uttar Pradesh and the Punjab. Under British rule they had been confirmed in their ownership of land, protected from competing Hindu financial interests, and even granted additional lands. The Sufis were further allied to landowners from whom they received financial support. They married into their families, and had common interests. By 1945 the Muslim League had persuaded the religious leaders that whatever their local interests, a Muslim state, run by Muslims, to defend a Muslim way of life, was essential. The League was also able to win peasant support because of peasant anger with Hindu landlords, peasant suffering in the famine of 1943, and peasant gratitude for the League's efforts to distribute relief supplies in the countryside. The League had succeeded in capturing the symbolic attachment to Islam for the purposes of a national political movement. Yet behind the purely political use of the term there lay a profound and utopian hope, evoked by the very name "Islam," for a society in which a secure Muslim community could live in justice committed to the realization of Muslim social and personal ideals. Appealing to these deep yearnings, the Muslim League won an overwhelming victory in the elections of 1945 and became the sole representative of Muslim political interests in India.

Throughout the period from 1924 to 1947 the 'ulama' of the Jami'at al-'Ulama'-i Hind continued to resist Muslim League leadership and to advance an alternative conception of the Muslim community in India. Though very much a minority view, this conception had a profound effect upon the ideology and political situation of the millions of Muslims who remained citizens of India after the partition. The Jami'at leaders had been among the important sponsors of the Khilafat movement. With the collapse of the movement they turned their attention to the formation of Shari'a courts and to a political program demanding assurances that Muslims could continue to live according to their law and faith.

Throughout its history the Jami'at supported the concept of a united India. It opposed British rule, called for jihad, and was prepared to enter into a joint struggle with the Congress Party. Muslims could be at once Muslims and members of the same nation with non-Muslims. In their view, a united Indian nation formed with Muslim cooperation would best protect Muslim religious and communal interests. The 'ulama' imagined that this united India would provide full safeguards for Muslim law and custom. Their Saharanpur proposal of 1931 thus called for a federal state, autonomous provinces, and self-governing religious groups within the framework of a single state and constitution. According to some Muslim thinkers, the Muslim community would be headed by an Amir-i Hind, who would be a scholar of religious law and a delegate of the Caliph. The Amir would enforce Muslim law within the community, and would be selected by and bound to heed the advice of a consultative assembly of 'ulama'. He would in effect be the head of a Muslim state within an Indian union.

The Jami'at opposed the Muslim League, which it saw as collaborating in a British plot to divide Indian peoples and forestall Indian independence. The 'ulama' were also hostile to the secularism of the League's leading intellectuals. They feared that a new state, even though called Muslim, would not in fact be accountable to the 'ulama' or to the principles of Islam, and would be all the more dangerous because of its appeal to the sentiments of the populace. They also feared that the division of the subcontinent into separate states would compromise the substantial Muslim populations that were bound to remain in the majority Hindu state, and would inhibit Muslim missionary work among non-Muslim Indians. They believed that the best interests of the Muslim community would be served by maintaining the unity of the Indian Muslim population inside a single state, where weight of numbers would protect their interests and enable them to influence the policy of the Indian state on behalf of Muslim brothers elsewhere in the world. The 'ulama' of the Jami'at would rather have taken their chances in a unified Indian state than be left to the mercies of partition and secularization. They favored a powerful diaspora in India to a weak homeland in Pakistan.

In fact, with the growth of communal consciousness the differences between the Muslim League and the Jami'at were narrower than they seemed. The concept of a communal society, whether formed in traditional religious terms or in modern political terms, had won over all segments of the Muslim elites. Both the League and the Jami'at called for a separate Muslim identity. Both agreed on the need for separate electorates, for decentralized and federal forms of government, for provincial autonomy, and for guarantees for Muslim religious interests. They differed only on the question of forming a national state for Muslims. For the Muslim League, the political security of Indian Muslims was the primary consideration, and questions of religious concepts and practices were secondary. Their concept of a Muslim nation was built upon the purely political aspect of Muslim identity, which, contrary to the past history of the Muslim community, was now severed from its religious components. The Jami'at, by contrast, clung to fundamental Muslim religious ideas, but they were forced to give up the traditional idea of a Muslim state as the necessary protector of the Muslim community and as the obligatory policeman of the Shari'a. They were also forced to accept cooperation with infidels, and indeed a state that would make Muslims merely a tolerated minority in a non-Muslim state. Under the pressure of twentieth-century imperialism and nationalist reaction, traditional Islamic concepts were transformed to separate the religious and political dimensions of Muslim identity.

In the end, the tendency toward Muslim nationalism won out. It was based, despite fragmentation, upon a deep latent sense of community among the Muslims of the subcontinent. The anxieties of the Muslim upper classes threatened with political extinction, British insistence on an electoral system that divided Indians into Muslim and Hindu communities, the revivalist movements among both Muslims and Hindus which raised religious consciousness and stressed the antagonism between the two communities, and rising Muslim religious self-awareness – these forces consolidated a consciousness of Muslim-ness based on abstract symbols, such as the very name "Islam." The force of this symbolic consciousness overcame Muslim attachments to the larger Indian society. The constant efforts to reconcile Muslim and Hindu interests and to create a joint Indian political movement were frustrated by the barrier of deep mutual incomprehension and suspicion. Muslim leaders felt that the Hindus would exploit their dominant numerical position to subordinate Muslims, and Hindu leaders felt that the Muslims were angling for an opportunity to reassert Muslim supremacy. In the course of the 1920s and 1930s, every effort to form a united Hindu–Muslim political front was defeated by incompatible demands and fears which could not be allayed. In these circumstances the Muslim position evolved from a demand for protection of communal rights to the demand for a separate territorial state, regardless of the consequences for the Muslims or the peoples of the subcontinent.

After the elections of 1945 the movement toward a Muslim national state was irresistible: if there were no partition, there would be civil war. In the end there was both. In 1946 both Congress and the Muslim League rejected a British plan for a federated government; by 1947 Congress was also ready to accept partition – Congress politicians may even have seen some advantage in the division of the Muslim population rather than their unification within India. Only the question of boundaries remained. On August 14, 1947, Pakistan came into being, and on August 15 India became an independent state.

The new nations were born in the throes of one of the most terrible civil and communal wars of modern history. Millions of people were forced to leave their homes; Hindus fled Pakistan, Muslims left Hindu areas. Hundreds of thousands of people were killed in communal riots. The two nations promptly went to war over Kashmir, which was seized by India on the grounds that its ruler was Hindu, despite the claim that by virtue of its Muslim population, Kashmir should be part of Pakistan. The partition of the subcontinent thus parallels the emergence of numerous Balkan, Arab, and Turkish states in the Middle East. In each case the violence unleashed by the transmutation of religious into political–national consciousness destroyed the civilization shared among peoples of different religious persuasions.

THE MUSLIMS OF INDIA, PAKISTAN, AND BANGLADESH

India

Then some 50,000,000 strong and today more than 120 million, one of the largest Muslim national communities in the world, Muslims became a permanent minority in India. Partition gravely reduced their socio-economic standing. The economic elite was virtually wiped out by the abolition of the rights of zamindars and other gentry to incomes from land, and by the migration to Pakistan of large numbers of Urdu-speaking professionals and intellectuals, who could no longer hope to compete for positions in education or government service once Hindi was made the national language. While a new middle class of entrepreneurs, merchants, artisans, and rich peasants developed in the 1970s and 1980s, especially in medium-sized cities, the vast majority of Indian Muslims are landless laborers, marginal farmers, workers and shopkeepers. More than half of the Muslim urban population is below the poverty line, as compared with 35 percent of the Hindus. The literacy rate for Muslims (as of 1987–88) was about 42 percent, somewhat less than the national average of 52.1 percent. Indian Muslims are perceived as backward in terms of average economic welfare and education.

Under the leadership of Abu'l Kalam Azad and the Jami'at al-'Ulama'-i Hind, Indian Muslims accepted a composite nationality, considering themselves at once Muslim and Indian, a religious minority in a secular state that is culturally and religiously neutral. While most Muslims strengthened their internal communal identity, others moved toward a shared national culture with Hindus. After 1948, the so-called Congress Muslims rejected the two-nation theory and called for a much more comprehensive assimilation of Muslims into a common secular national society. After 1970 even the Jama'at-i Islami in India, under the influence of Deoband, turned its efforts

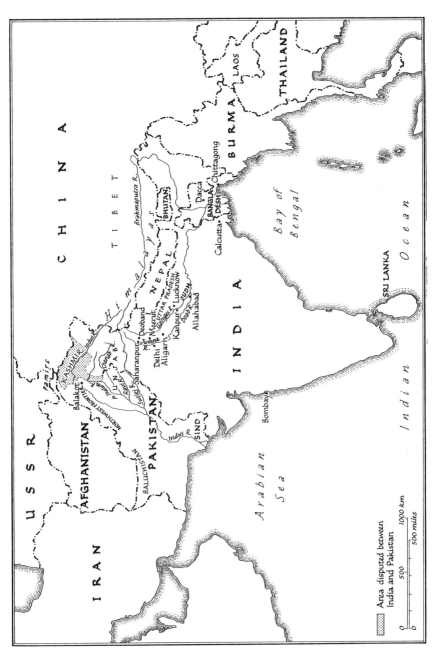

Map 34 India, Pakistan, and Bangladesh

26   Families celebrate the end of Ramadan at the Jamiʿ Masjid of Delhi

away from the formation of a Muslim state toward education, social upliftment, and acceptance of secularism and democracy as the defining traits of an Indian state protective of minority interests. Other Muslims pragmatically sought class, corporate, and interest-group alliances with non-Muslims, and many successful businessmen try to avoid ideological or communal issues. The rise of an Indian Muslim middle class elite, however, has also given a new turn to community building, through the funding of schools, colleges, mosques, and the defense of Muslim interests. In the 1980s and 1990s Sa'udi influences, the creation of madrasas, and the growing influence of the Ahl-i Hadith and the Tablighi Jama'at have stimulated Muslim self-assertion and militancy. The Tablighi Jama'at, a pietist and missionary movement to recall Muslims to the true teachings and practices of Islam, is the most important religious movement among Muslims. It has a strong appeal to educated and professional Muslims, including doctoral and engineering students, who volunteer each year to go on a preaching pilgrimage throughout the country. Because the Tabligh is not oriented toward Muslim state building, it is acceptable to the Indian government.

Nonetheless, despite cooperation with Congress and the promotion of Indian Muslims into important national positions, the Muslims of India consider themselves embattled. As a minority Muslims feel entitled to the protection of their religious beliefs and communal practices, reject the idea of a uniform national civil code, and claim autonomy in matters regulated by Shari'a, such as the family and the position of women, education, and endowments for pious purposes. They also seek to protect the use of the Urdu language, special employment and other economic opportunities, and proportional representation in legislatures and government bureaucracies. Except on the official level, Hindu–Muslim communal hostilities remain intense. Muslims suffer discrimination in employment and education, and are threatened by communal riots. Hindus, however, see Muslim demands as an insistence upon special privileges, an assertion of social superiority, and a refusal to be integrated into the general society. Behind this refusal, some believe, is an unwillingness to accept the role of citizens within the Indian national state and a lingering hope for a return to Muslim domination.

Since the 1970s the growing strength of Hindu revivalism has made the situation of Indian Muslims increasingly difficult. The Hindu revival goes back to Gandhi, who redefined Hindu identity to include the previously excluded castes, or untouchables, vastly enlarging the number of so-called Hindus, making them the great majority of the Indian population, and setting the foundation for the present claim that India is a Hindu nation, and the demand that it be declared a Hindu state. Hindu extremists reject India's Muslims as a subversive, inassimilable element of the society, and government support for the Muslim minority is denounced as a betrayal of Hindu interests. Hindu religious nationalism is stimulated by bitter intra-Hindu caste and class rivalries, and a determined effort by leaders of lesser social status to undermine Brahmin authority.

Communal movements have in turn been translated into political struggle. To contain rising Hindu demands, the Congress Party began in the 1970s to make rhetorical and then policy concessions to Hindu sentiment. In the late 1970s the Indian government hardened its position on Kashmir to avoid appearing soft on a Muslim issue. In the late 1980s the government television networks sponsored serialized presentations of the great Hindu epics, the *Ramayana* and the *Mahabharata*.

Two celebrated issues intensified both Hindu and Muslim communal feeling and undermined the secular center. One was a court decision in the Shah Bano case (1985), which upheld the payment of maintenance allowance to a divorced Muslim woman beyond the terms specified in Muslim law. Muslim leaders, defending communal rather than feminist interests, vociferously protested against the state's intervention in a matter of Shari'a. The Congress Party passed the Muslim Women's Act of 1986, in effect overturning the court's decision. In response the Hindu radical party, Bharatiya Janata Party (BJP) made this a mobilizing issue for its campaign to assert the Hindu identity of India.

The Ayodhya mosque episode escalated communal agitation to a frenzy. Ayodhya is the site of a sixteenth-century mosque named after the Mughal conqueror, Babur, but radical Hindus, claiming that the site is the birthplace of Ram, the hero of the *Ramayana*, demanded that the mosque be torn down and replaced with a *mandir* (stele) dedicated to Ram. In 1989 the BJP took part in a foundation-laying ceremony for the new temple. Three years later, in the presence of the leading Hindu party politicians, Hindu "volunteers" destroyed the mosque; this precipitated attacks on Muslims and communal riots all over India. Further terrible violence between Muslims and Hindus took place in Gujarat in 2002. State policies are ever more polarized by religio-nationalist communalism. Communalist politics are undermining the secularism and neutrality of the state.

Pakistan

Pakistan was founded on the idea that the Muslims of India formed a nation and were entitled to a territorial homeland of their own. It was made up of the territories of Sind, Baluchistan, Northwest Frontier province, and parts of the Punjab and Bengal, divided into two great territorial blocks separated by a thousand miles of intervening India. In the western part of Pakistan, more than half of the people were Punjabis, but some 20 percent were Sindhis, 13 percent Pashtuns, and 3–4 percent Baluchis. Bengal, in the east, was virtually a nation within the nation. The western region was without industrial infrastructure; the eastern region was cut off from Calcutta, its main port and processing center for jute and other agricultural products.

The crucial problem for Pakistan was to create institutions and a national identity to suit the reality of the new political boundaries and to create an acceptable and stable regime for a populace divided by sharp ethnic, linguistic, ideological, and even religious differences. While Pakistan was formed out of a deep conviction that Muslims in India required a state of their own to assure their political security and their opportunities to cultivate a Muslim style of life, since the founding of the state appeals to Islam have not been able to suppress the contradictions among a variety of Muslim identities, regional and ethnic loyalties, and class antagonisms. As in Turkey a secularized political elite descended from the older imperial elites took control of the political destinies of the country, but unlike Turkey, where the elites were avowedly secular, the Pakistani elite espoused an Islamic form of nationalism. The competition of Muslims with the Hindu population of India, and the deep particularistic, ethnic, tribal, and local divisions among Muslims, made Islam the only meaningful symbol for the unity of Pakistan.

The most pressing problem was the formation of a central state. While Congress inherited the identity and the administration of British India, Pakistan had to create an army and a revenue-extracting and administrative apparatus to govern the new country. This was undertaken in the face of communal violence and war with India over control of Kashmir. These pressures had fateful results. They led to the centralization of the state apparatus under Punjabi control, at the expense of a representative or parliamentary system, and postponed the integration of the disparate Pakistani populations. Since its creation Pakistan has had a variety of constitutions, and a number of both civilian and military regimes. The country holds together by military coercion, by strong administration, and by bargaining among various groups, but not by any deep sense of national identity.

Pakistan came into being with at least two different concepts of what it meant to be an Islamic state. The political elite considered Islam a communal, political, and national identity stripped of its religious content. Yet a large segment of the populace, led by the 'ulama' and other religious leaders, expected a state whose constitution, institutions, and routines of daily life would be governed by the Shari'a and Islamic norms. The assembly called to devise a constitution established a Board of Islamic Teaching, which recommended that the state be governed by pious Muslim leaders in accordance with the advice of the 'ulama'. The Jama'at-i Islami, led by Abul 'Ala Mawdudi, a Muslim reformer, fundamentalist, and political organizer, called for the formation of a truly Islamic state with Islamic government, banking, and economic institutions. Mawdudi appealed for a return to the Quran and Sunna and the use of rational judgment in religious matters so as to apply the principles of Islam to a modern society. The Jama'at demanded that governing officials be advised by religious councils and that non-Muslims be barred from high political posts.

The struggle over the role of Islam led to a long series of constitutional compromises. A constitution of 1956 declared Pakistan an Islamic state and made all parliamentary legislation subject to review by an Islamic Research Institute. In 1958 this constitution was abolished and a Republic of Pakistan declared, but in 1963 the Islamic provisions of 1956 were by and large restored.

While the debates over the constitution went on, the real government of Pakistan was a Punjabi elite of soldiers, administrators, and landowners. After ten years of chaotic civilian rule, the army, led by General Ayyub Khan, took control of the country. Under the Ayyub regime Pakistan continued to be ruled by its Punjabi elite. This government was highly centralized and strongly supported by landlords, business interests, officials, and also by the Sufi leaders. Though the Ayyub government centralized power, it did not integrate a divided country. Defeat in war with India in 1965 allowed demands for a reopening of the electoral system, and for provincial autonomy for Bengal. Demonstrations and riots led in 1969 to the succession of General Yahya Khan. Under military rule the resentment of Bengali East Pakistan over the military, bureaucratic, and economic predominance of West Pakistan, and the neglect of Bengali culture and literature, led to demands for autonomy. The Awami League came to power in the elections of 1970, and the Pakistan government tried to suppress Bengali opposition. The result was civil war, Indian intervention, and the transformation of East Pakistan into the independent state of Bangladesh in 1971.

In neither (west) Pakistan nor Bangladesh has the question of the relationship between the religious and political aspects of Islam been resolved. From 1970 to 1977 west Pakistan was under the leadership of Zulfiqar 'Ali Bhutto and the Pakistan People's Party. The Pakistan People's Party advocated a program compounded of agricultural and industrial reforms and the promulgation of a new constitution which defined Pakistan as an Islamic socialist republic. The president and prime minister were to be Muslims, and all laws were to be in conformity with Islam as determined by a council of 'ulama'. As Pakistan became increasingly dependent on oil-rich Arab states for loans, commerce, and employment of labor, Bhutto made further concessions to Islamic morality, such as prohibiting alcohol and gambling. However, to maintain itself in power, the Pakistan People's Party eventually succumbed to the influence of administrative and landlord groups, roused popular opposition, resorted to rigged elections, and was defeated in July 1977 by mass demonstrations and the intervention of the army.

The new military regime, led by General Zia ul-Haq (1977–88) and influenced by the Jama'at-i Islami, again attempted to base its authority on a strong pro-Islamic stance. The government reintroduced traditional Islamic punishments, prohibited gambling and alcohol consumption, and created a new judicial review system. While Islamic reform movements are usually concerned with the moral behavior of individuals, in Pakistan the emphasis was placed upon a total Islamic system, or *nizam-i mustafa*, which implies an Islamic government and economy. Pakistani planners sought to eliminate the payment and receipt of interest by the creation of profit-sharing institutions such as the National Investment Trust, which issued profit-sharing bonds; the House Building Finance Corporation, which lent money to builders and took a share of the profits from rental incomes; the Small Business Finance Corporation, which bought food and leased goods; and other similar institutions. Profit- and loss-sharing accounts were established at the nationalized banks. In their first year of operation these banks showed a return of between 8 and 15 percent, and thus proved profitable at least in the short run, though they

27 Pakistani soldiers

face the problems of limited capital and severe competition from institutions that use interest calculations.

The role of women has become a significant issue. On one side are those who favor limiting women to the household sphere, and on the other those who wish to preserve women's freedoms and opportunities in public life. Proposed changes in family law that give women certain rights in divorce and inheritance, and proposed modifications in the law of evidence, which make two women the equivalent of a single male witness, have been hotly debated.

With the death of General Zia ul-Haq in a helicopter accident in August 1988 the political situation became ever more tenuous. Civilian government was restored, with two major parties competing for power. Benazir Bhutto, the daughter of the former Prime Minister and the leader of the Pakistan People's Party, with its base of support in Sind, was the rival of the Islamic Democratic Alliance, based on Zia's Pakistan Muslim League, led by Nawaz Sharif, and supported by the Punjabi military and civil bureaucracy. The latter ruled from 1990 to 1993 and 1997 to 2000. This was not a genuinely democratic alternation of parties, because until 1997 the President was entitled by the constitution to dismiss an elected Prime Minister and parliament without any political accountability, and did so five times The parties failed to provide stability or prosperity as the already desperate Pakistani standard of living was further eroded by inflation. Factional conflict among Punjabi and Sindhi landlords, sectarian street battles among Sunnis and Shi'a, and between Sindhi- and Urdu-speaking muhajirs (emigrants from India), and massacres in Karachi and Lahore made the major cities ungovernable. In 2000, the military, led by General Pervez Musharaff, again took power.

Islamic parties were very strong in Pakistan. The principal parties were the Jama'at-i Islami, dedicated to the formation of an Islamic state, the Jami'at-i 'Ulama'-i Islam, affiliated with the reformist Deoband movement, and the Jami'at-i 'Ulama'-i Pakistan, founded in 1948 and affiliated with the Barelwis. The Da'wat-i Islam, founded by Muhammmad Tahir al-Qadiri, is a missionary and social service movement which has founded schools, libraries, and publications to promote unity among Muslims, and the practice of Islam according to the teachings of the Prophet. In the 1980s and 1990s the demand for Islamization came from the military elites supported by some segments of an activist, urban population, and was closely tied to the ambitions of authoritarian regimes to maintain themselves in power. Yet the principal Islamic parties have played an indecisive role in the governance of the country. The Jama'at-i Islami, which persuaded General Zia to declare Pakistan an Islamic state, did not actually fare well under the military Islamic or the subsequent electoral regimes, though it remains an influential, albeit small, party. The declaration of an Islamic state allowed for the proliferation of sundry rival Islamic parties, splitting the popular vote, and engagement in practical politics brought out a number of inherent contradictions in the Jama'at. The party was revealed to be a top-down movement with a strong intellectual authority but little mass support; engagement in politics caused splits within the movement over questions of tactical advantage and adherence to principle. In the summer of 1998 the embattled Prime Minister, Nawaz Sharif, again called for the implementation of Islamic law, and the Jama'at-i Islami found itself in the position of protesting that there were Islamic laws enough; too little adherence was the problem. While Islam was being used to generate national solidarity, the tensions among Punjabi, Pashtun, and Sindhi interests, and the divisions between Sunnis and Shi'a were not resolved by the reassertion of Islamic values.

Pakistan's principal foreign policy also reflected the interpenetration of state interests and Islamic religio-national identity issues. In the 1980s Pakistan became the principal supporter of Islamic movements in Kashmir and of the Afghan resistance to Russian occupation. It may be seen as carrying on the nineteenth-century British defense of the subcontinent against Russian expansion, but it also sought to ward off Iranian-Shi'i influences, forestall Indian pressures on its frontiers, and divert the Pashtun demand for an independent state, which might be carved out of Pakistan and Afghanistan. Its policy was also intended to make Afghanistan a client state and bridgehead to Central Asia. The anti-Russian component of this policy garnered American support, and the Islamist orientation not only served regional purposes but mobilized Sa'udi and Gulf state support. This policy bore the price of sheltering millions of Afghan refugees, and allowing a lawless frontier open to radical Islamic ideological currents, and active arms and drug markets. With the retreat of the Soviet Union, Afghanistan was plunged into anarchic factional fighting. Pakistan supported the Taliban (student) drive to unify Afghanistan as an Islamic state. The Taliban, supported by the Jami'at-i 'Ulama'-i Islam who control the madrasas from which they come, dominated the country from 1994 until their defeat by American intervention in late 2001.

The mountain valley of Kashmir remains a bitter bone of contention between India and Pakistan. Kashmir, though largely Muslim in population, was turned over to India in 1947 by the ruling Maharaja, Hari Singh. India and Pakistan went to war over Kashmir, and in January 1949 a United Nations-brokered cease-fire left two-thirds of the province in Indian and one-third in Pakistani control. From 1947 to 1953 Indian Kashmir was allowed a considerable internal autonomy under the leadership of Shaykh Muhammad 'Abdallah and the National Conference, but in 1953 the Indian government arrested Shaykh 'Abdallah and gradually brought the province under closer rule. From 1975 to 1984 Kashmir was again permitted free elections and was ruled by Shaykh 'Abdallah and his son Faruq 'Abdallah, but by the mid-1980s trust between Delhi and local leaders had again broken down, and Kashmiris began a fully fledged armed insurgency led by the Jammu and Kashmir Liberation Front, calling for an independent and secular Kashmir. As the military struggle went on, Muslim–Hindu antagonism rose; the Sikh movement gave new examples of religious nationalism, and Kashmiris began to define themselves in Muslim terms. In 1987 India refused to allow the Muslim United Front to come to power by elections. Pro-Muslim and pro-Pakistan sentiment became more important than secularism, and the leadership of the insurgency shifted to the Harakat and the Hizb ul-Mujahidin. Sa'udi influences, more militant forms of Islam, and the backing of the Pakistani intelligence services gave the struggle in Kashmir the aura of a jihad. The fighting escalated with the deployment of more than 500,000 Indian soldiers to suppress the resistance. The dispute over Kashmir, which has already led to two India–Pakistan wars, now provokes chronic frontier skirmishing and threats of war. In 1998, nuclear weapons were tested by both India and Pakistan as they sought to intimidate each other. In early 2002 India mobilized a massive army to force Pakistan to retreat from its support of the Kashmiri resistance. For India it is essential to control Kashmir as a demonstration of the viability of a religiously mixed society and as an assertion of Indian pride against the threat of further partition. Pakistan claims the right of a Muslim nation to inherit contiguous territories with a Muslim population. Kashmiris, who once supported regional independence, have moved from secularism to Islamism, and from desire for autonomy toward incorporation into Pakistan.

Bangladesh

Bangladesh came into being as a separate state in 1971, and at first stressed the national rather than the religious aspect of Bangladeshi identity. It had been formed with strong Indian support, and had a large Hindu minority. The national emphasis served to repudiate the Pakistani insistence on a Muslim identity, and the preference of religious groups for continued union. Bangladeshis were also able to use the new national emphasis to justify taking over the jobs and properties of West Pakistanis. The constitution of 1972 proclaimed secularism a basic principle and outlawed political action by religious groups; a Bengali literary revival also stressed the Bengali rather than the Islamic aspects of national identity. But like Pakistan, Bangladesh has never quite succeeded in overcoming the basic poverty of the country, the initial lack of political institutions, and the ambiguities of political identity.

By the late 1970s, the ruling Awami League under the leadership of General Zia ul-Rahman found it increasingly important to reaffirm the Islamic aspect of Bangladeshi identity. In order to highlight the differences between Bangladeshis and the Bengalis of West Bengal who are part of the state of India, and to reduce the influence of West Bengali intellectuals on the new state, the constitution of 1977 relaxed the ban on Islamist activities, and replaced the principle of secularism with a reference to trust in God. This tendency was reinforced by the coup of 1982 which brought General Ershad to power. Still, the governing Bangladesh Nationalist Party overwhelmingly defeated the Islamic parties in the elections of 1979 and 1991 and maintained a secular program of development combined with a generalized sense of Islamic religious affiliations. The party continues to take the middle line between the secularism of the Awami League and the thoroughgoing Islamic position of the Jama'at-i Islami. The public holds strong Muslim sympathies, marked by the strength of the Tabligh movement, and the controversy surrounding the feminist writer Taslima Nasreen, who was forced to leave the country after charges that she had blasphemed against the Quran. Bengali identity has both an ethnic-national and a Muslim aspect, and one or the other may be emphasized, depending upon changing political conditions.

CONCLUSION

The formation of the three Muslim societies of the Indian subcontinent can be understood in terms of the complex legacy of a Mughal state whose legitimacy was defined in Muslim, cosmopolitan, and Indian terms, and of a Muslim religious establishment which was both independent of the state and disunified. The pluralistic structure of Mughal society allowed for alternatives to Muslim identity expressed in tribal, caste, occupational, or ethnic terms. When this society faced the great shocks of European domination in the nineteenth and twentieth centuries, its pluralistic political and religious elites were divided over whether to define their interests in terms of ethnic, national, or religious identity; and, when they chose religious terms, whether to emphasize the communal-political or the personal-ethical aspects of Islam.

In the subcontinent the complexity of the Muslim institutional and cultural heritage has allowed, according to circumstances, for all possible variations of contemporary Islamic identities and relations among Islam and states. In India Muslims face the dilemma of how to live a Muslim life without the protection of a Muslim regime. The Muslims of India have tended to remain socially and religiously conservative. Indian-Muslim religious leaders stress individual religious commitment and present Islam in devotional rather than collective terms. They resist Indian state efforts to modify legal and educational institutions as an unwarranted interference with religious rights. In Pakistan, by contrast, the state is officially Muslim and emphasizes Islam as a collective identity. The state bears responsibility for the integration of Islam with a modern state and economy, and promotes more radical policies and departures from traditional Muslim practice than is seen in India. In Bangladesh political identity oscillates between the poles of national and religious symbols without defining the directions for Muslim social and religious practices.

CHAPTER 28

ISLAM IN INDONESIA, MALAYSIA, AND THE PHILIPPINES

By the middle of the nineteenth century, the Muslim peoples of Southeast Asia were not yet part of a unified culture or empire, but were divided into many ethnic and linguistic populations and numerous states. Holland and Britain had established their empires, but only in the late nineteenth century did Dutch and British domination lead to profound transformations in political and economic life and provoke both nationalist and Muslim reactions to foreign intervention. As in South Asia, foreigners controlled the state and the dominant responses to changing political and social conditions came not from government institutions, but from autonomous sectors of society. The traditional 'ulama' and Sufi teachers, the former political elites, new strata of Indonesian administrators and intellectuals, Muslim reformers, and eventually radical military leaders rose up to lay claim to the future of Southeast Asian societies. Secular nationalist, Communist, Islamic traditionalist, and reformist Islamic movements were pitted against Dutch and British rule, and against each other, in the struggle to define the shape of this region in the twentieth century.

DUTCH RULE AND THE CAPITALIST SYSTEM IN THE INDIES

Between 1795 and 1815 the Dutch and the British experimented in Java with various systems of state control and compulsory cultivation, and with free peasant agriculture, capitalist agriculture, and different policies of free and controlled trade. Before 1795 the Dutch extracted produce, such as coffee and pepper, by forced deliveries for sale in Europe, but the defeat of Holland by France in 1795 and the collapse of the Dutch East India Company in 1799 turned the Dutch to centralized political control to maximize the extraction of tributes. In 1806 Governor Daendels was sent to subordinate local lords, and encourage cotton and coffee production. When the British took control of Java in 1811, Sir Stamford Raffles introduced a capitalist type of economic development, conferred private ownership of land upon Indonesians, and devised a new tax system which substituted a cash tax, equivalent to two-fifths of the value of the produce, for forced deliveries. Raffles also tried to introduce wages instead of forced labor, and, in general, to promote a monetary economy, and build up the consuming power of the natives so that British goods could be sold in the Indies. When the Dutch returned in 1816 they reverted to direct controls. In 1825 they established the Nederlandsche Handel Maatschappij (NHM), a monopoly company, to organize trade between the East Indies and Holland. In 1830 Governor Van Den Bosch centralized political and economic controls. He divided Java into administrative districts called "residences," and further subdivided the residences into regencies. A Dutch controller supervised the local princes, or regents, whose position was made hereditary but reduced in actual effectiveness. In the course of the century the regents were deprived of their share of tax revenues. In 1867 their lands were confiscated, and in 1882 they were denied the labor and personal services once owed them by the peasants. The regents were reduced from independent princes to salaried local officials.

The economy was organized under "the culture system." This was a form of taxation which required the peasants to devote one-fifth of their land to government-assigned crops – usually sugar, indigo, coffee, tea, tobacco, cinnamon, and cotton – and to deliver the produce as a tribute in kind, in lieu of other rents or taxes. In addition, they were required to contribute their labor: to build irrigation canals, roads, and bridges, clear wastelands, and otherwise build up the economic infrastructure of the island. Though the system was supposed to assure the peasants a fixed obligation, they were in fact subject to further extortion, rents, and corvées. The goods delivered by the culture system were sold to the NHM at contract prices and were shipped to Europe in Dutch cargo ships. Imports to Java also came primarily from Holland. During the 1840s, the culture system was overexploited, and could not produce adequate revenues. Peasant welfare declined, and the Indies suffered from famines. The Dutch did not prosper because of competition from British and Chinese merchants.

Furthermore, in Holland the revolution of 1848 brought to power a new merchant class with a liberal capitalist ideology, and led to the formation of a parliamentary government which in 1864 assumed control of the Indies budget. Also, in the course of the 1850s and 1860s, Dutch public opinion underwent important changes. The publication of Dekker's *Max Havelaar*, and sugar-contract scandals, discredited the culture system and brought a demand for a new colonial administration based on liberal principles. The liberals wanted to abolish state controls in favor of free enterprise and eliminate the system of forced deliveries in favor of direct taxation. In the course of the 1860s, state cultivation of pepper, cloves, nutmeg, indigo, tea, cinnamon, and tobacco was abolished, and the sugar law of 1870 mandated the progressive establishment of a free market in place of the traditional system of consignments. To bolster the new system of private enterprise, state lands were leased on a long-term basis, and new laws permitted long-term leasing of smallholdings and of village lands to capitalist entrepreneurs. Corvée labor was abolished and wage labor implemented in 1882. The new policy stimulated capitalist forms of development, the expansion of the sugar industry, irrigation, and railroad construction. By the end of the nineteenth century control of the Javanese economy had substantially shifted from Dutch government officers to private capitalist entrepreneurs.

These policies had profound consequences. In Java the culture system led to the cycle of development called "agricultural involution." The primary crops, sugar for export and rice for subsistence, were complementary. They could be grown in adjacent fields or alternated in the same fields when seasonally appropriate, and be maintained by the same labor of terracing and irrigation. This complementarity made it possible to provide at once for exports, government revenues, and food production. Moreover, since both sugar and rice output could be increased by ever more intensive investments of labor, a cycle of development was entrained in which increased food production could sustain a larger population that could in turn increase both food and sugar production and thereby sustain further population increases. As population rose and rice production reached its limits, the system could be kept going by growing maize, soybeans, and other foods on lands unsuitable for rice and sugar. Java entered a cycle of growth that led to ever higher populations and more intensive agricultural exploitation – a cycle which increased Dutch revenues from sugar output but also kept the native population at a subsistence level. As the population of Java rose from approximately 7 million in 1850 to 28.4 million in 1900, there was no rise in the per capita standard of living. An egalitarian, labor-intensive society was meshed into a capitalistic and machine-intensive colonial economy, but village communities were left socially undisturbed.

Whereas in Java the capitalist economy could be superimposed upon and integrated with a peasant society, in Sumatra the introduction of a capitalist economy led to profound social changes. In the early nineteenth century, Sumatra was an important source of agricultural and forest commodities for export, and a market for textiles, hardware, and other foreign goods. The new economic developments also led to an extensive commercialization of the Sumatran economy. New towns were founded for new settlers. Dutch schools were introduced. A network of village banks called the People's Credit System was established. Newspapers were printed. As opposed to Java, capitalism entered into the fabric of the traditional society to create new classes among the population. Dutch control led to the introduction of tobacco, palm, tea, rubber plantations, and tin-mining enterprises. While tobacco and food crops could be intertwined because tobacco was believed to require a long fallow period and because food crops were cultivated by very simple methods, rubber, palm, tea, and similar plantations were incompatible with growing rice and corn, and peasants were driven off the land. The plantation and mining economy in Sumatra (and Malaya) created a laboring proletariat. Capitalist development also created a smallholder class of farmers who changed from slash-and-burn agriculture to fixed gardening operations, producing part of the rubber and coffee crop for export.

28 Dawn prayer to celebrate the end of Ramadan, Jogyakarta, Indonesia

In the outer islands, and in Malaya, the expansion of private land ownership broke down the values that regulated the communal economy. While the Javanese village collectivity was protected by the peculiarities of wet rice ecology, in the outer islands traditional collective and family controls over land were weakened.

The involution of agriculture in Java, and the growth of a capitalist and commercial economy on the outer islands, led to an important redirection of Dutch administrative policy at the turn of the twentieth century. Despite the premises of liberal theory, the expansion of capitalist agriculture and industrial enterprises required state intervention. Even though Dutch capitalists and settlers were opposed to central government controls, they favored military expansion and investments in police, schools, irrigation, railroads, agricultural experimentation, and other services. Also, Dutch surveys of 1888 and 1891 uncovered abuses such as extortion, arbitrary demands on peasant labor services, and excessive appropriation of land by village officials. By 1900 it was clear that the liberal capitalist policy had favored individual capitalists, but had harmed native welfare, reduced government revenues, and injured Dutch manufacturers' interests in a prosperous Indonesian economy.

Humanitarians, liberals, and missionaries joined in the call for economic reform, protection of native interests, and the education and employment of Javanese officials in government service. Liberals held that it was Holland's duty to take responsibility for the welfare of the native population and even to repay Indonesia for centuries of economic exploitation. Some imagined that Dutch rule would be built upon the cooperation of Dutch and local peoples; others called for the assimilation of Indonesians into European culture and the creation of a unified Dutch–Indonesian elite to govern the country. The critics of government policy called for a revolution in the government of the Indies, and for the creation of a welfare state with Indonesian participation. This was called the Ethical Policy. Though well intentioned, it was entirely Euro-centered, and presupposed Dutch domination. The Ethical Policy was a Dutch version of the white man's burden.

After 1900, a combination of capitalist needs and humanitarian concerns reversed the laissez-faire policy of the previous generation in favor of state stimulation and management of economic development. State enterprises were to build up the agricultural, mineral, and industrial resources of the country. Railroads, roads, and shipping lines were to be developed; irrigation was to be extended. The state worked tin and coal mines, laid out rubber plantations, and established agricultural credit banks. It contributed agricultural, medical, and veterinary specialists to help in economic enterprises. Native welfare was promoted through education, public health, and the protection of peasants and workers from capitalist exploitation. The Ethical Policy thus entailed extensive government involvement in village affairs. Throughout Java and the outer islands, the new policy meant a more direct involvement of Dutch officials in the daily routines of Indonesian communities, and a tremendous expansion of the civil service.

The Dutch were especially active in the creation of new schools for Indonesians. In the early nineteenth century Indonesian aristocrats were educated in the homes of Dutch settlers, and the first Dutch school to train Indonesians for civil service jobs was founded in 1848. By 1851 there were schools for clerks and health officers which trained low-ranking priyayi for government service. Then, between 1902 and 1908, numerous technical schools were established to train Indonesian officials. An agricultural school was opened in 1903; medical and veterinary schools were in place by 1907; a law school was opened in 1908. By 1914 Western-type education was extended to the high-school and elementary-school levels, where Indonesians were introduced to a curriculum that included the study of Dutch, English, science, mathematics, and drawing. In the 1920s schools for law, engineering, and specialized administrative jobs were introduced.

Finally, the new policy meant the centralization of Dutch political control over the whole of the archipelago, and the formation, in 1914, of a single government for all of the Indies. Mixed European and Indonesian local councils were formed; in 1916 the Dutch introduced a new representative assembly, the Volksraad. This was an advisory assembly which included both elected and appointed Dutch and native representatives. In 1922 a new fundamental law gave the government of the Indies greater autonomy from Holland and made the Volksraad a legislative body for the colonial region. However, the new freedoms were offset by increasing the proportion of European representatives.

Dutch administrators also introduced new law codes. A code for foreign orientals was introduced in 1848 and a criminal code for native Indonesians in 1872. Between 1904 and 1927 the Dutch attempted to bring all customary native law into accordance with European norms, and to establish a unified system of legal administration. However, after 1927 Dutch policy reverted to a dualistic law system which attempted to maintain the customary Indonesian legal systems alongside European codes and procedures. Despite the policy of preserving customary, or *adat*, law, considerable inroads were made by statutory enactments. The Dutch gave Indonesia a legal system compounded of adat, Muslim, and Dutch statute law.

After centuries in which the Dutch had merely skimmed the profits of the Indies without touching the underlying structure of society, they began the modern transformation of Indonesia. The historical balance among the state elites, the 'ulama', and the peasantry was deeply disturbed. Dutch rule had sapped the authority of the priyayi, and brought into being new classes to compete with the established elites for political and social power. In Java Dutch policies created medical, engineering, legal, and teaching professionals, and technically trained civil servants in the forestry, mining, agricultural, railway, telegraph, and health administrations. The new professionals and administrators were drawn from the lesser-ranking priyayi families, the scions of the newly rich in Minangkabau and the outer islands, the children of provincial chieftains, and Ambonese and Mendanau Christians. These newly educated professionals and administrators interposed themselves between the old aristocracy and the peasantry, competed with the village 'ulama' and headmen, and laid claim to an expanded political role.

These new classes were also hostile to the Dutch government that had spawned them. Despite benefiting from policies that attempted to integrate Indonesians into Western culture and Dutch administration, the new administrators were opposed to European domination. The new priyayi clamored for increased educational opportunities and for more political power. For their part, the merchants, landowners, and religious leaders of the outer islands opposed Dutch restrictions on trade and pilgrimage, and the competition of Christian missionaries. The merchants of Sumatra, Singapore, and Malaya, tied to a Muslim system of international economic and cultural exchanges, opposed Dutch rule as a threat both to their commercial and to their religious interests.

The emergence of these new and frustrated strata of the Malay–Indonesian populations was the basis of an ideological and political renaissance in the early twentieth century. Out of these several milieus came new programs for secular nationalism, socialism, and Islamic revival, each of which aspired to an independent and modern form of Malayan and Indonesian civilization. Nationalism was the position of the new priyayi bureaucrats and intellectuals, and it also appealed to Javanese peasants. The Communists represented lesser priyayi, student, and worker interests. Islamic reformism spread most widely in urban and middle-class milieus, and in many villages, especially in the outer islands. Islamic conservatism was the creed of rural kiyayi ('ulama') and their peasant followers. Much as all of these movements were devoted to Indonesian independence, they were profoundly at odds with each other. Muslim middle-class leaders fought priyayi elites; intellectuals opposed the old aristocracy; reformers opposed customary community leadership; left-wing intellectuals and workers fought the bourgeoisie. From 1912 until the achievement of independence, these movements struggled as much with each other as against the Dutch.

INDONESIAN TRADITIONALISM, NATIONALISM, AND ISLAMIC REFORM

The earliest reaction to consolidated Dutch rule and the decline of the aristocracies came from Muslim milieus. The changing balance of power allowed for a resurgence of 'ulama' challenges to the authority of the priyayi elites. Ever since the consolidation of Mataram in the early seventeenth century, the Javanese aristocracy had been divided into two groups – the priyayi, conditioned by Javanese values, who governed, and the kiyayi, who represented Islamic religious faith and community loyalty. With the absorption of the priyayi aristocracy into the Dutch colonial administration, the kiyayi became the only independent representatives of Javanese society. Their authority, numbers, and influence were vastly enhanced. Moreover, pilgrimage to Mecca and extensive journeys for religious study in Arabia brought Malay Indonesian Muslims into contact with reformist teachings, heightened their consciousness of Muslim identity, and made them aware of Muslim worldwide opposition to European colonialism. The *hajjis* brought back a commitment to the improvement and intensification of Muslim religious life, a desire to rouse their people from torpor and misguidance to a proper Muslim worship, and a commitment to political autonomy.

'Ulama' and peasant resistance

'Ulama'-led peasant resistance began with the Java wars of 1825–30. In Jogyakarta the Dutch had alienated both the nobility and the common people by a land policy that canceled leases instigated by previous Dutch administrations, and forced the rulers to pay compensation to the lessees. These same rulers also had to lease lands to the Dutch government, which were then turned over to European cultivators. In 1825 local resentment burst into a civil war led by Prince Dipanegara, a member of the ruling family who had been passed over for succession and had devoted himself to religious studies. The corruption of the court and its subservience to the Dutch made him a spokesman for Muslim religious virtues. It became his mission to oppose the corruption of the aristocracy and purify Islam. Prince Dipanegara allied with religious leaders to lead a peasant revolt that lasted for five years. Though it was eventually put down, Dipanegara became a symbol of national resistance to foreign rule.

In the Banten region of Java, kiyayi and peasant resistance was virtually endemic. Banten had been conquered in the fifteenth and early sixteenth centuries by Muslims who set out the system of wet rice cultivation and established a system of feudal rule. The rice fields were cultivated by peasants on condition that they paid a tribute and performed labor services, such as constructing roads. Some categories, called *abdis*, were obliged to perform personal services in the households of the sovereign or the lords as well. The lords' rights to personal services led to frequent abuses, as people were commandeered to clean gardens, collect firewood, gather fodder for horses, and do other household tasks.

The Dutch annexed this stratified society in 1808 and retained the Sultans until 1832. To compensate for the loss of political autonomy, the old nobility began to take service in the colonial administration. There, they had to compete with civil servants of non-noble origin. Then in 1856 and 1882 the Dutch passed new laws to reduce, and then abolish, personal services and to replace them with a capitation tax, but the peasants were nonetheless obliged to serve. As a result, all elements of the population resented Dutch rule. Deprived noble families, religious leaders, village elders and chiefs, and abused peasants all had reason to revolt in the name of the old Sultanate or in the name of Islam. There were insurrections in 1820, 1822, 1825, 1827, 1831, 1833, 1836, and 1839. In 1845 peasant rebels put on white clothes to indicate that they were fighting a holy war. There were further revolts in 1850, 1851, 1862, 1866, and 1869.

In the 1840s and 1850s, Banten was swept by a religious revival. This included increased observance of Muslim rituals and pilgrimage, the establishment of schools, and enrollment in the religious brotherhoods. The Qadiri order enlisted the independent kiyayis into a unified movement and strengthened the ties between the religious leaders and their followers. The orders preached a reformed version of Islam with insistence upon strict observance of Quranic rules, and combined religious revivalism with strong hostility to foreign rule. Equally important were expectations of the coming of the mahdi. Letters were circulated purporting to bear signs of the end of the world and the last days. Wandering preachers stimulated the fervor. Many kiyayis came to be venerated as miracle workers who could foretell the future and heal the sick. Religious hopes turned upon the conviction that the territory of Islam would be freed from foreign subjugation and that an independent Muslim state would come into being.

This religious revival built up to the Great Insurrection of 1888. In an atmosphere of bitter hostility to foreign rule, resentment against the corrupt aristocracy, and passionate hopes for the founding of an Islamic state, peasant gangs attacked Dutch officials and Javanese administrators. The government managed to suppress the rebellions. Elsewhere in the Indies, the Padri movement in Minangkabau, the Banjermasin war of 1859, and the Acheh wars of 1871–1908 all involved 'ulama'-led peasant resistance to the expansion of Dutch authority and the authority of the local political elites.

The initial Dutch reaction to these developments only served to encourage them. By 1825 the Dutch had already identified the Muslim kiyayi as their main opponents. To counteract their influence, they attempted to ally with the local priyayi and customary chiefs, and curtail the pilgrimage, which they recognized as a principal stimulus to Indonesian resistance. The protracted Acheh wars and the massive Banten revolt finally forced a reexamination of Dutch policy. Upon the recommendation of Christiaan Snouck Hurgronje, the Dutch distinguished Islam as a religion from Islamic political militancy. They decided to allow greater freedom to make the pilgrimage to Muslims who accepted Dutch rule. At the same time they maintained their surveillance. Anti-Dutch political action was ruthlessly suppressed. Thus, while Islamic religious opposition did not shake Dutch rule, Islam became more deeply rooted in Indonesian rural society.

Priyayi and worker nationalism

While Islamic kiyayi and peasant resistance was rooted in the traditional structures of Indonesian society, Indonesian nationalism had its origins in the late nineteenth-century reaction of the priyayi aristocracy to the consolidation of Dutch rule. The first priyayi response to the stripping away of royal authority and aristocratic privileges was a backward-looking revival of local court cultures. Then, inspired by the Russo-Japanese war and by the Indian and Chinese nationalist movements, and threatened at home by Chinese political competition, Western-educated Indonesians banded together to promote Indonesian cultural and political awareness.

Budi Utomo (Noble Endeavor), founded in 1908, was the first Javanese cultural association dedicated to education and the revival of the Hindu–Buddhist culture of old Java in the hope of recreating the refinement and stability that had been lost through excessive Westernization. Budi Utomo at first accepted the Dutch Ethical Policy and was loyal to the government, but in 1917 it moved from culture to politics by calling for autonomy and a parliamentary regime. A more radical Indische Partij was formed by Efi Douwes-Deckker in 1911 to represent the interests of the "Indos" of mixed European and Indonesian descent and to present their claim for equality with Europeans. This was the first party to claim political independence for a united Indonesia. Taman Siswa (Garden of Learning), founded in 1922, was devoted to an educational program to restore Javanese arts and culture. The association founded some 250 schools and tried to create a community of students and teachers – a nationalist brotherhood – to symbolize the maturation of the Indonesian nation and its aspirations to independence. *Pudjangga Baru* (New Poet), founded in the 1930s, was a literary journal whose writers and readers attempted to deal with the problems of integrating Indonesian and Western values. Their ideal was to generate a national language that could express the Western content of their education.

Progressively, these cultural and educational groups became politicized, but only in the late 1920s and early 1930s did national political parties come into being. In 1927 the Indonesian Nationalist Party (PNI), was formed out of a study group led by Sukarno. In 1939 the federation of Indonesian political parties, GAPI, was formed to give cohesion to the nationalist movement. While the nationalist groups continued to operate within the framework of Dutch rule, more radical opponents to colonialism emerged. The labor union movement was established soon after the turn of the century. In 1905 a government railroad workers' union was founded, followed by unions of tramway workers, customs officers, teachers, pawnshop employees, and public works and treasury officials. Radical political leadership was supplied first by the Indische Sociaal Democratische Vereeniging, founded in 1914, which introduced socialist and Communist ideas into Indonesian politics. The Communist Party of Indonesia was established in 1920. In 1925 and 1926 the Communists provoked a series of strikes in Semarang and revolts in Jakarta and other parts of Java and Sumatra. These revolts were easily crushed, and the Communist Party was declared illegal and forced underground.

Thus, the nationalist movement developed in two wings – one representing the interests of the Western-educated priyayi civil service and professional milieus and the other representing worker and radical intelligentsia ambitions for political power and Indonesian independence. In both wings the national movement stressed secular values and the combination of the Indonesian heritage with international and Western ideals.

Islamic revivalism

In the same period new forms of Islamic religious, social, and political action were born in the major ports of Sumatra, Java, and Malaya among Muslim merchants sensitive both to the pressures of the expanding colonial powers and to the currents of reformist thinking emanating from Mecca and Cairo. Singapore, a melting-pot of Southeast Asian peoples, became the principal center of Islamic reformism and modernism. It harbored a large Malay population, immigrants from Minangkabau, Javanese laborers in transit to and from the rubber plantations of Malaya, and other Indonesians who passed through in the course of their pilgrimage to Mecca. Dutch restrictions on the hajj made British-ruled Singapore the major port for Indonesian pilgrims. Singapore also had significant Arab and Indian Muslim communities.

The Arab settlement was especially important. Many Arabs worked in Singapore as brokers arranging the pilgrimage traffic. Shaykhs and sayyids from Hadhramaut had great prestige, and were respected for their religious probity. They formed a commercial elite, owned land and houses, invested in plantations and trade, and had control of the batik, tobacco, and spice trades. This group built mosques, organized festivals, and worked to cultivate Arabic and Muslim cultural sophistication. The Jawi Peranakan, the offspring of Malabari Indian traders and Malay women, were also among the leaders of the cultural life of Malaya and helped generate a revival of the Malay language and an incipient Malay national consciousness. They worked as clerks, interpreters, schoolteachers, and merchants, and ranked after the Arab community in prestige and authority. In 1876 the Jawi Peranakan began to publish a Malay newspaper which was used as a teaching device in Malay schools. They sponsored the publication of Malay romances, poetry, tales, and translations of Arabic religious literature. A society for linguistic knowledge worked out Malay equivalents for English terms and absorbed Arabic words into Malay usage. Out of these efforts came a shared language and a new Malay consciousness, transcending specific localities.

The Arabs, Jawi Peranakan, and Malays also sponsored the diffusion of Islamic reformism and of the Naqshbandi and Qadiri orders. They contributed to the development of a cosmopolitan Muslim religious consciousness no longer tied to particular localities. In the port towns, Islam was not the religion of a village community but of mobile individuals united in an international association. From Singapore reform Islam spread throughout Southeast Asia by trade, pilgrimage, and by the movement of students, teachers, and Sufis.

Reformism was stimulated elsewhere by commerce, urbanization, and education. In Java, several Islamic movements were founded between 1905 and 1912. The most important of these was Muhammadiya, which was founded in 1912 by Hajji Ahmad Dahlan for the reform of the practice of Islam and the betterment of the Muslim community. Dahlan was the son of a religious official, a pilgrim to Mecca, a mosque officer, and a trader in batik. His movement appealed to poor and middling traders operating outside the traditional social structures.

Muhammadiya advocated a pious life based on the duties described in the Quran and the sayings of the Prophet, but rejected the medieval Muslim legal and philosophic systems and the authority of Muslim saints in favor of ijtihad, or individual reasoning in religious matters. Muhammadiya discouraged elaborate birth, circumcision, wedding, and funeral rituals, and opposed the worship of shrines, but not Sufism as such. It stressed the importance of ethics, purification of the soul, controlling base desires, and the deepening of wisdom and moral understanding. While Muhammadiya has sometimes been considered a modernist form of Islam, its primary concerns place it in the tradition of Muslim reformism.

Muhammadiya taught that personal virtue had to be expressed in social action. Its primary project was the creation of modern-type religious schools. While the pesantren were devoted to recitation of sacred scriptures and mystical formulae, the Muhammadiya schools taught basic Muslim religious principles, the Arabic language, Dutch, and secular subjects. They introduced a graded program of study, rationalized methods of instruction, and emphasized comprehension and reasoning rather than memorization, attempting to adjust Muslim values to contemporary educational and social needs. By 1929 Muhammadiya had founded sixty-four village schools and several teacher-training colleges, and many libraries, clinics, orphanages, hospitals, and poor-houses. A women's movement, and youth and scouting groups, were attached to Muhammadiya. The main function of the various Muhammadiya-related societies was *tabligh,* or evangelical teaching of the reformed Muslim faith.

Persatuan Islam, founded in West Java in 1923 by merchants led by Hajji Zamzam and Hajji Muhammad Yunus, was also dedicated to religious studies, the proper practice of Muslim rituals, and the observance of Muslim law. For this movement too the Quran and hadith were the only bases of Muslim belief and behavior, but they could be adapted to new conditions by the independent judgment of qualified persons. Persatuan Islam opposed popular Indonesian religious practices such as the use of amulets and recourse to magic for healing. It opposed Sufism wherever it encouraged improper rituals, saint worship, or belief in the intercession of holy men with God. Persatuan Islam also denounced the wayang puppet theater because it represented Hindu values and encouraged the freedom of women. Though reformist, Persatuan Islam denied the need for adaptation to contemporary developments and held that Islam was inherently progressive. It also opposed secular nationalism because it represented a deification of the nation. In its view, only by a return to true Muslim principles could the political power and the freedom of Indonesian and other Muslim peoples be restored. The movement founded colleges to train missionaries and published the journal *Pembela Islam.* Numerous tracts were published in standard Indonesian, and study-groups were formed to educate Muslims in their religious responsibilities.

The Islamic religious and educational revival also had political dimensions. In response to Chinese commercial competition and Christian missionary activities in central Java, Hajji Samanhudi formed an Islamic training association in 1911. With the aid of 'Umar Sa'id Tjokroaminoto, he transformed his group into the Sarekat Islam in 1912. Tjokroaminoto soon turned the party into the premier political movement in Indonesia. The Sarekat Islam congress of 1917 declared that Islam required Indonesians to exert themselves in the faith and to avoid resignation to poverty. It made demands for the improvement of agriculture, government subsidies for education, the abolition of feudal privileges, and the extension of electoral rights to Indonesians. This combination of Islamic and political appeals made Sarekat Islam the first mass Indonesian political party. Not only middle-class and urban people but also 'ulama' and peasants supported the movement. Many peasants believed that Sarekat Islam was a harbinger of the coming of the *ratu adil* (the just prince) and the mahdi.

Minangkabau was another center for revitalized Islamic religious and social action. Minangkabau's history of Islamic reform began early in the nineteenth century with the Padri movement, which attempted to bring custom into accord with Shari'a. That struggle ended in Dutch rule, but reformist Sufis, especially of the Naqshbandi order, continued to denounce customary practices and to insist on the reform of Islam.

In Sumatra and Malaya, the economic and political impact of Dutch capitalism and the intrusion of new ideas from Singapore, Mecca, and Cairo also generated renewed debate. The bearers of new ideas were called the Kaum Muda, or Young Group, and some of them were concerned with the modernization of customary law along Western and secular lines. The Young Malay group (1906), Usaha (Association of Endeavor, 1912), and the Young Sumatran Union (1918) were founded to promote modern education and to incorporate Western ideas into the old adat. Other Kaum Muda were oriented to Islamic reformism. Shaykh Ahmad Khatib (1855–1916), who had studied in Mecca and had been introduced to the ideas of Muhammad 'Abduh, returned to raise a new generation of Sumatran and Malayan scholars who in turn founded new schools, publications, and religious missionary movements. Shaykh Muhammad Tahir (1867–1957), who had also studied in Mecca and absorbed the ideas of Muhammad 'Abduh, founded the newspaper *al-Imam* in Singapore. *Al-Imam* tried to awaken Muslims to the need for education. It taught that the decline of Islam was due to neglect of the divine law and that submission to the Quran and hadith would uplift the lives of individual Muslims and help bring about a renaissance in the Muslim community. *Al-Imam* stressed the importance of using reason in religious matters and challenged customary beliefs and practices. It brought into public debate such religious questions as whether *talkin* prayers should be recited over graves, whether the correct procedure in prayer was to recite the *niya* (intention) aloud or silently, and whether savings banks and cooperatives were legitimate. In the 1920s Penang became the center of reformist thought, owing to the work of Sayyid Shaykh al-Hadi, who founded the Madrasa al-Mashhor in 1919 and the Jelutong Press in 1927 to publish books on the subject of the emancipation of women and other reform issues. The reformist schools combined a religious curriculum with a secular program of studies in history, geography, mathematics, and other modern subjects. By the 1920s there were 39 such schools and 17,000 students in Sumatra. These reformers opposed, as did their counterparts in Java and Singapore, popular Sufi practices such as celebrations of the death days of saints, challenged adat marriage, funeral, and holy-day ceremonies, and denounced the practices both of the traditional 'ulama' and of the village penghulus (customary chiefs).

The movement for religious reform eventually became a challenge to the Dutch as well. Between 1918 and 1923 several efforts were made to unify the various Kaum Muda groups and channel them into political action. Radical intellectuals penetrated the Sumatran student movement to preach against capitalism and imperialism, oppose government taxes and forest policy, and call for independence both from the feudal rule of local notables and from the imperialistic rule of the Dutch. The Sumatran student groups appealed to petty traders and to smallholding peasants, and eventually provoked scattered rebellions, which were put down by the Dutch in 1926 and early 1927. Thus, the Islamic movement began with a religious and reformist orientation focused on correct belief and practice of Islam, and through educational and social action cultivated a political consciousness in opposition to Dutch rule and the authority of the traditional aristocracies.

The formation of movements that emphasized religious reform, educational modernism, and political action provoked a counter-movement among the traditional 'ulama'. In 1921 a Union of 'Ulama' of Minangkabau was formed, and it was followed in 1926 by the Nahdatul 'Ulama' (Union of 'Ulama') of Java. Nahdatul 'Ulama' was built around a network of religious notables centered on the pesantren of Jombang in East Java. The NU defended traditional religious principles, and reaffirmed the Shari'a, the schools of law, and the Sufi practices that were at the core of their spirituality. They rejected the reformist emphasis upon the Quran and Sunna in favor of the traditional practice of Islam. However, the adoption of organizational techniques borrowed from Muslim reform and nationalist movements led to modern forms of political action. The kiyayi, who in the nineteenth century had organized resistance to Dutch rule and priyayi administration through the Sufi tariqat, in the twentieth century entered the struggle over the shape of Indonesian society as a political party.

The differences between the old and new forms of Islam were manifold. The traditionalists viewed the world as unchanging; the reformers saw it as ever changing in history. The traditionalists viewed religion as a mystical and magical disposition of mind. Traditional religion was oriented to ritual, to states of feeling, and to passive acceptance of reality. Prayer, fasting, and recitation were intended to create inner peace and bring about harmony between the believer and the truth. By contrast, the reformers stressed active mastery of the self, and defined religion in terms of individual responsibility for moral and social reform. Their religion was inner-directed, ethical, and intellectual. Whereas traditional religion maintained its commitment to a concept of the harmony of the individual with his community, the community with the state, and the state with the universe, reformist religion sought to create a Muslim utopia. To achieve these goals, the reformers adopted Western organizational and educational methods, accepted scientific ideas and the use of vernacular languages, and waged a vigorous campaign in the press. Scout movements, schools, orphanages, and hospitals were essential in making Islam an active force in society.

From the 1920s, the several nationalist and Muslim parties provided ideological and political direction for Indonesian communities. They reorganized the urban administrative, commercial, and working population into new social units called *aliran*, built around the major religious and political movements. In the villages the parties provided ideological and cultural clarification, and organized schools, charities, youth and women's groups, and social clubs. Nationalist, Communist, and Muslim movements generated their own parochial followings tied to an array of social and religious activities. While many villages remained the preserve of one or another movement, others were polarized among the competing forces. From the local point of view, national parties were more than ideologies. They were a new form of community which channeled everything from entertainment to political action into a single movement.

COMPROMISE AND COMPETITION: 1900–1955

From 1900 to approximately 1920 Dutch policy indirectly favored the rise of the nationalist and Islamic movements. The Dutch supported education; Indonesians were employed in administration; political parties were legalized; freedom of the press was allowed. By 1917 Sarekat Islam had emerged as a mass political movement and the main force in Indonesian opposition to Dutch rule, but in the course of the next decade and a half, it broke up over differences of ideology and political orientation. The rise of a socialist wing polarized the party. In 1923 the movement split; the leftists were forced out, and with them Sarekat Islam lost the mass of its followers. It also lost its ascendancy over Indonesian peasants when it was challenged by Nahdatul 'Ulama'. In the 1920s Sarekat Islam adopted the non-cooperation policy – a militant Islamic, anti-Communist, and anti-Dutch orientation. By the late 1920s, however, the pan-Islamic idea had failed to rally significant support, and Sarekat Islam turned to a nationalist line, changing its name to Partai Sarekat Islam Indonesia. This politically activist position led to a falling out with Muhammadiya. Muhammadiya, primarily concerned with educational and missionary activities, was willing to cooperate with the government, and its members were forced by a party decision in 1929 to choose between the two movements. In the 1930s, the Muslim movement remained divided among activist, reformist, and conservative religious wings, but the apolitical reformist Muslim position remained the most important. A single mass movement was still not possible, given the ideological and cultural divisions within Indonesian society. Nonetheless, the parallel activities of the various Muslim groups generated widespread support and created a broad base for their ultimate claim to form an independent and Muslim Indonesian state.

With the political decline of the Muslim movements, the initiative shifted to the nationalists. With the founding of the PNI in 1927, Sukarno became the leading spokesman of Indonesian unity, independence from Holland, and the separation of state and religion. He wrote extensively on the question of Islam and the state, and urged a solution resembling Ataturk's Turkey, in which Islam would be permitted as a private religion but would not be allowed to influence national politics. He thus presented a vision of Islam as a personal religion in the context of a secularized national state.

In response to the growing nationalist and Muslim opposition, the Dutch retreated from the Ethical Policy and turned to repression and renewed centralization of power. They tried to hamper the Muslim movements by establishing state control of education, through the so-called "guru" ordinances (1905 and 1925) which required that Muslim instruction be licensed by the regents. A law of 1932 required government permission for non-state schools. Priyayi were given control over the legal administration of marriages, to the chagrin of the Muslims. Christian missionaries were supported by state subsidy for travel and schools. In 1935 the Dutch assumed the right to proscribe political parties; finally, in 1940, they banned political meetings.

In the face of nationalist competition and Dutch policies, the Muslims generated a new wave of political activism which was to last through the war years until 1955. While Muhammadiya gave priority to moral and educational reform, the Persatuan Muslimin Indonesia, founded in 1930, campaigned against imperialism and capitalism, and called for Indonesian independence as an essential condition for both Islamic reform and economic prosperity. The Partai Islam Indonesia similarly combined Muslim, anti-imperialist, and anti-capitalist slogans. This party called for reform of Islam, independence from Holland, the formation of a unified Indonesian parliamentary state, and state control of vital economic enterprises. Indonesian Muslim parties formulated new demands for a parliamentary regime that would include a ministry of Islamic affairs and in which two-thirds of the ministers would be Muslim.

The Japanese occupation (1942–45) gave tremendous encouragement to the Muslims. The Japanese undermined the old domestic aristocracy, and rapidly brought the Muslim movement under their control. While they suspended many of the political parties, they allowed Muhammadiya and Nahdatul 'Ulama' to function. They established a religious affairs and propaganda office to take control of all Muslim education above the primary level. They also formed Muslim militias with a flag featuring a crescent and rising sun to signify the identification of jihad with Japan's war against the West. Special training courses for intellectuals and kiyayis were established. In November 1943 the Japanese founded Masjumi to unify and coordinate the whole of the Muslim movement. Under the aegis of Masjumi they created a religious bureaucracy staffed by Muslims to connect the central administration with the villages.

The administrative and military functions assigned to the Muslims greatly enhanced their political power and enlarged the clientele for later Muslim political action. A coalition of middle-class merchants, rich peasants, and village 'ulama' had been mobilized to cooperate with the Japanese. The formation of labor and military battalions created new military and religious leaders from proletarian backgrounds. Thus, the Japanese gave the Muslims important advantages in the forthcoming struggle to determine the political and cultural principles of an independent Indonesian state.

Having destroyed the Dutch, the Japanese were in turn defeated in 1945. On August 17, 1945, Sukarno proclaimed Indonesian independence, but the struggle to make that independence actual took five years more. With British help the Dutch attempted to regain control of the Indies; only in August 1950, under Indonesian military and United Nations political pressures, were the Dutch finally obliged to recognize an independent republic.

The Indonesian Republic

The government of the new republic was formed by a coalition of Muslim and nationalist parties including Masjumi, Nahdatul 'Ulama', PNI, and the Communist Party (PKI). Despite the great organizational gains made by the Muslims in the war years, the Muslim demands for the constitution and institutions of the new republic were only partially met. The Muslims first demanded the formation of a *negara islam* (a Muslim state). To Muslim conservatives this meant that most ministers would be Muslims and that a parliament of kiyayis would be formed to review legislation and pronounce on its conformity to Islamic law. To Muslim reformers it meant a general proclamation of the principle that the state was in accord with Islamic law. The Muslims were able to insert into the Jakarta charter the stipulation that it was "an obligation for the Muslims to carry out the Shari'a." The nationalists, however, were in favor of the *pançasila*, or five principles, which included belief in God, nationalism, humanitarianism, democracy, and social justice. The nationalist program pointedly omitted any direct reference to Muslim symbols and emphasized secular concepts instead. In the constitution of the republic, the pançasila was enshrined as the symbol of the new order and the phrases identifying the new state as Muslim were omitted.

To satisfy Muslim interests, the constitution provided for the formation of a Ministry of Religion. The ministry was commissioned to protect religious freedom and to maintain harmonious relations among the different religious communities, but its primary purpose was to administer Muslim religious affairs, including marriage and divorce, endowments, mosques, and the pilgrimage. Its Bureau of Religious Education managed government-sponsored religious schools; the Bureau of Religious Propaganda distributed books and pamphlets and otherwise promoted Islamic missionary efforts. The Bureau of Religious Justice regulated Shari'a courts. The new ministry was also a vast bureaucratic apparatus that linked the central government to the villages and provided an important source of patronage and influence for the Muslim political parties. It satisfied Muslim interests in having state support for Islam and encouraged hopes for the eventual realization of a Muslim state.

On the outer islands, however, various Muslim groups refused to accept the compromise and determined to fight for the immediate realization of an Islamic state. During World War II Sumatra had gone through a revolution which destroyed the power of the feudal chiefs in Acheh, Minangkabau, and the East Coast residency. In Acheh the 'ulama' defeated the local uleebalang aristocracy and consolidated its own political position. Muslim groups in the Celebes and Kalimantan also insisted on the immediate formation of an Islamic state. In some of these cases, the concern for an Islamic state may have been a front to win the autonomy of outer islands from the central government in Java.

The most important of these rebel Islamic movements was the Dar ul-Islam, founded by a former Sarekat Islam activist named Kartosuwirjo. In 1940 Kartosuwirjo founded the Suffah Institute as a propaganda and training center to produce cadres for Muslim missionary work and for the Muslim military unit, Hizballah, organized by the Japanese under Masjumi auspices. In 1945 he was put in charge of Masjumi military units in western Java. He fought against the Dutch in 1947. In 1948 he refused to accept the Renville Agreement truce between Indonesian and Dutch forces, and appointed himself the Imam of an Islamic provisional government, Negara Islam Indonesia. His Islamic state was declared to be based upon the Quran, and was in constitutional form a republic with an elected parliament. The Imam, elected by the parliament, was the head of state. The new state proclaimed that it would guarantee equality before the law, the right to a decent standard of living, and freedom of worship, speech, and assembly for all citizens. All important civil and military positions were reserved for Muslims. Armed struggle against the Dutch and later against the Indonesian Republic continued until it was finally suppressed in 1962.

The defeat of Dar ul-Islam transferred the struggle over the political identity of Indonesia to the political sphere. From 1950 to 1955 the PNI and Masjumi quarreled over the role of Islam and of the Communists. But the Muslims were also divided. In 1952 Nahdatul 'Ulama' withdrew from Masjumi and became a separate political party. There were divisions between Muhammadiya and Nahdatul 'Ulama'. The unresolved struggles among the political parties led to a national election in 1955, which proved to be a critical moment in Indonesian history. It consolidated the aliran as the basic form of Indonesian ideological and social organization. The PNI and PKI appealed mainly to villages led by former aristocrats, landowners, and spirit healers. The Muslim parties appealed to different traditionalist and reformist village constituencies. In most cases the competition divided the villages into factions led by the traditional headmen and those led by the kiyayi.

More immediately, the election results were a decisive check to the campaign for the formation of an Islamic state. In Java the vote was split among the PNI, Masjumi, NU, and PKI. On the outer islands, in the strong Muslim areas of Sumatra, South Kalimantan, and North Sulawesi, the vote was substantially Muslim but was divided between the reformers and the conservatives. In the national tally as a whole, however, the Muslim parties combined polled only 42.5 percent of the vote, and fell short of the majority essential to form a parliamentary Islamic state. From 1955 to the present the Muslim parties have had to adjust to the fact that though Indonesia is overwhelmingly Muslim, the Muslim parties are a political minority.

INDONESIA FROM 1955 TO THE PRESENT

Sukarno and a secular Indonesia: 1955-1965

With the defeat of Muslim aspirations, control of the state was taken over by President Sukarno and the army. In 1957 Sukarno attempted to bypass the parliamentary system by creating a Guided Democracy. He proposed the formation of a cabinet including the Communists and a national council to represent worker, peasant, youth, and regional interest groups. The shift in power created widespread apprehension of Communist influence, provoked fears of Javanese domination of the outer islands, and frustrated Muslim ambitions for regional autonomy. Army leaders on Sumatra and Sulawesi and Muslim spokesmen representing Masjumi, including Muhammad Natsir, the leader of the party, opposed the new program and formed a revolutionary government of the Republic of Indonesia. The revolutionary government was defeated, and in July 1959 Sukarno dissolved the constituent assembly and declared a return to the constitution of 1945, which provided for a strong presidential regime.

President Sukarno devised new institutions which gave a leading role to the army and the civil service. Major sections of the economy were nationalized, and the army took control of important industries. Authoritarian controls were set up over political parties, labor unions, and newspapers. The new regime was buttressed by a new ideological program called Nasakom, in which Sukarno attempted to synthesize nationalism, religion, and Communism as the symbols of a highly centralized regime and centrally planned economy. In 1960 Masjumi was disbanded, and its leaders arrested and imprisoned. Nahdatul 'Ulama', however, maintained close ties with Sukarno. While Masjumi represented outer-island reformist, urban, and commercial interests, Nahdatul 'Ulama' represented a Javanese peasant constituency. It was willing to accept Sukarno's authority, with its strong overtones of traditional Javanese statecraft, and suspend the ultimate goal of an Islamic state in return for control over the Ministry of Religion and for the protection of its political position in the Javanese countryside. While Masjumi was broken because of its ideological demands, Nahdatul 'Ulama' was able to retain political and tactical flexibility.

Sukarno soon alienated the intellectual and artistic elites by the suppression of cultural and political expression. He furthermore brought the country to virtual economic ruin as a result of excessive spending and the accumulation of staggering foreign debts. The new regime also gave the Communists an important opportunity to consolidate their political position. The Communists threatened army control of the corporations nationalized in 1957 and 1958, and embarrassed it in its relations with its main supplier, the United States. They succeeded in bringing about a land-reform program in 1963, and then attempted by direct action to expropriate the estates of large landowners, mostly belonging to PNI and to NU. The Communist challenge, however, provoked an alliance between the conservative Muslim parties and the army. In 1964 and 1965 there were direct clashes between Communist and Muslim youth gangs. In late 1965 an attempted Communist coup triggered a massive civil war in East and Central Java and the slaughter of innumerable Communists.

The Suharto regime: state and Islam 1965-1998

With the defeat of the Communists, General Suharto established a new military regime at the end of 1965, edged Sukarno out of power, and assumed the presidency in 1966. General Suharto came to power on the basis of a coalition of Indonesian army officers, Islamic community organizations, and Protestant and Catholic minorities, with the support of the professional and bureaucratic middle class and the Westernized academic intelligentsia. His regime was based on the military and ruled through a nationwide network of relatives, clients, protégés, and loyalists who controlled the major positions in the government and the economy. A government political party, called Golkar, which drew support from elements of former Communist, PNI, and Masjumi activists, was created to manipulate the national elections in 1971 and 1977. With the help of advisors educated in the United States, he adopted a free-enterprise program of development. The Suharto regime took a strong secular cultural line, with emphasis upon the pançasila as the basic principles of state and society, and Bahasa Indonesian as the common language.

However, the Suharto regime moved further and further toward coercion. The policies of the Suharto government toward the Muslim movements were an echo of those introduced by the Dutch toward the end of the nineteenth century. The Dutch distinguished between the religious and the political aspects of Islam, tolerating the former and repressing the latter. Throughout the 1960s, 1970s, and 1980s, the Suharto regime kept close control over Muslim parties. The army resisted the effort to rehabilitate Masjumi, convinced that militant Islam introduced religious concerns into politics, divided the nation, and distracted it from the problems of modernization. Muslim insistence that the state enforce Islamic religious laws kept alive army fears that Muslims would use their mass support to control the state. Nonetheless, in 1968 President Suharto permitted the formation of the Partai Muslimin Indonesia on condition that all former Masjumi leaders were excluded from the executive of the new party. In 1969 the government also established its own center for Indonesian-Islamic *da'wah*, or Muslim missionary activities, to take away the fire of the independent Muslim missions. In 1973 four Islamic parties were fused into the United Development Party (PPP), which was denied a Muslim name and was closely regulated by the government.

Not only were Muslim political ambitions checked, but Muslim identities were challenged by nationalist secular ideologies. The pançasila principles were an Indonesian and Javanese alternative to Islam. Under the banner of secularism the state began to encroach upon Islamic law. A marriage reform bill of 1974 proposed secular inheritance and adoption laws in competition with Shari'a. In reaction,

Muslim courts resisted reform, but Muslim judges were poorly trained, lacked authority, and suffered from the competition of civil courts.

A second challenge came from Kebatinan, or Javanese mystical groups. After the 1965 anti-Communist civil war religious affiliation became necessary to avoid the suspicion of belonging to the Communist Party, and Kebatinan groups claimed that their practices constituted a religion in the same sense as Christianity, Hinduism, or Islam. Kebatinan supporters also tried to identify Javanese mysticism with the pançasila. The mystical groups were attempting to become a new national religion. Equally important was the threat of Christian proselytizing. The government allowed Catholics and the World Council of Churches to build schools and hospitals, though Indonesian law forbade missionary activities among Hindus, Buddhists, or Muslims. The exclusion of Islamic groups from political power legitimized the drift away from Muslim identity.

Despite these political and cultural setbacks, the basic strength of the Muslim movements remained considerable. Nahdatul 'Ulama' was willing to cooperate with secular regimes, and maintained its influence. It was still basically concerned with religious practice rather than political opposition, and cooperated with the government through the Ministry of Religion and through 'ulama' councils in Acheh, West Java, and West Sumatra. However, its position was weakened in the 1970s and 1980s by the appointment of a reformist Muslim as the Minister of Religion, by competition from reformist Muslim schools, and by the creation of the United Development Party. NU congresses accepted that pançasila, without reference to Islam, were the basic principles of Indonesian society. Nonetheless, at the local level, the 'ulama' remained a prominent political force. In West Java and Sumatra, the kiyayi exerted a substantial influence upon family, agricultural, and other village affairs. Through 'ulama' and school networks, regional councils, national religious parties, and the Ministry of Religion the kiyayi were able to influence the government. The rural 'ulama' were at once religious scholars and national politicians.

Furthermore, the Ministry of Education promoted Muslim education and publications. Under the direction of Mahmud Yunus, the ministry devised a comprehensive Islamic school program including six-year elementary, four-year intermediate, and four-year senior high school education. Religious instruction was added to the curriculum of all government schools. An Islamic State University, founded in 1951, was consolidated into the State Institute of Islamic Religion in 1960, with faculties of theology, law, education, and humanities. Since 1960 religion has been a compulsory subject at college and university levels. The Ministry of Religion supervised innumerable madrasas and pesantrens and helped them reform their curricula.

Another factor in Islamic strength was the continuing vitality of the reformist and modernist movements. Muhammadiya remained important in providing a personal ideal of rational, efficient, and puritanical behavior, a concept of community, and a model of an ongoing Islamic society. Muhammadiya claimed an active membership numbering millions.

The Muslim activists responded to government secularism in a variety of ways. In the outer islands, frustrated by the high degree of centralization of power on Java and the lack of political and economic autonomy, many Muslims intensified their demand for the formation of an Islamic state. By contrast, other Muslims responded to political and cultural pressures by accommodating the secularization of state and society. Muslim politicians were willing to put aside ideological objectives and operate in a pluralistic political system as one group among many. For these politicians, who had wide business, regional, or professional contacts, Islam was only one element of identity. Intellectuals withdrew from political competition and distinguished worldly from spiritual values. The Indonesian Students' Association's (HMI) 1971 charter accepted the secularization of society and the concept of Islam as a personal religion. Its main spokesman was Nurcholish Majid, who saw Islam as a private belief system rather than a communal and political one, and stressed cooperation with non-Islamic groups. He argued that worldly matters are not regulated by divine law. For thinkers in this vein, the Quran served to inspire and motivate behavior, but did not provide precise rules for daily life.

Most Muslim activists, however, held that only a long-term cultural approach could allay the suspicions of the military, and foster the practice of Islam. The major Muslim movements avoided politics, but continued to work for an Islamic society by moral, religious, and social action. Some promoted da'wah, or preaching; others worked for Muslim social welfare, and some technocrats worked within the government for a development-oriented Islam. In 1967 the Dewan Da'wah Islamiyah Indonesia was sponsored by Muhammadiya and former members of Masjumi to distribute literature, preach to public meetings, organize mosque and library construction, and sponsor irrigation and forestry projects. The Congress of 'Ulama' of Acheh was formed to see that Muslims worshiped properly and maintained Islamic precepts in family and business matters. The general goal of these movements was to imbue Indonesians with Islamic values, strengthen the brotherhood of Muslims, and progressively convert nominal Muslims into dedicated and active participants in a Muslim community. For Muslims with this orientation, political activity declined in favor of an upsurge of prayer, fasting, and other religious practices.

By the late 1970s a major Islamic revival was under way. The 1970s saw the growth of the Salman movement on campuses, led by Imaduddin Abdulrahim, promoting a student life strict in prayer, fasting, and almsgiving, but easy in dress and amusements. The younger generation accommodated political realities by making religion a matter of personal conviction, but in 1981 the military regime alienated the students' association. To express its dissent from authoritarian rule and the pançasila ideology, the students' association reaffirmed a concept of Islam both as a personal religion and as the basis of the sociopolitical order. Student interest in Islam spread through the educated middle classes, who now saw in Islam a response to urban anomie and secularist corruption. They carried their convictions into the country's bureaucratic, educational, and economic institutions. Islamic influence in public life was reinforced by the breakdown of the historical distinctions of *abangan* (traditionalist) and *santri* (reformist), NU and Muhammadiya. Muslims were moving toward a synthesis of views. The expansion of state schools, commercial success, the influence of Nurcholish Majid and his insistence that each person must understand Islam for himself, and that many forms of government are compatible with Islam, have helped create a broader consensus on Islamic values.

From the late 1970s the Suharto regime began to respond to the rising middle-class commitment to Islam. Suharto's policy remained the promotion of personal piety and the suppression of political activity, but the government made some concessions to reinforce Muslim courts, and banned Christian missionary activity. The Ministry of Religion built mosques, schools, and prayer halls, and strengthened the Islamic Institute Colleges. Permission was given to wear the *jilbab* (head covering). Islamic think tanks, and research and conference centers, were opened. In 1987 the government relaxed its control over missionary preachers. In 1990 Suharto himself made the hajj. NU made its way back into influence by its mediating role between government and society. It remained committed to a national ideal in which Islam is a moral influence rather than to a totalistic Islamic state program, and was rewarded for its cooperation by many tokens of increased legitimacy.

In the 1990s the government turned from containment to support for Muslim movements. In 1990 Suharto reversed previous policy, and created the Association of Indonesian Muslim Intellectuals (AIMI) to promote the Islamization of Indonesia. Though still authoritarian and under close political control, Islam was now declared integral to Indonesian national identity. However, many Muslim leaders opposed the new organization, fearing that it would crush Islam under bureaucracy or undermine variety and tolerance in the Indonesian practice of Islam. A still more cynical view saw the AIMI as a strategy to coopt the Islamic movements, and to completely control the political system by bringing together representatives of Golkar, the PPP, and other parties in order to assure Suharto's reelection in 1998. This effort at co-optation failed when in 1998 Dr. Amin Rais, the head of Muhammadiya, declared that the Islamic movements would no longer tolerate the corruption of the Suharto regime.

The collapse of the Indonesian economy in 1997 brought an end to the reign of Suharto. The collapse impoverished vast numbers of Indonesians and exposed the corruption and self-serving economic policies of the government. After demonstrations and riots, Suharto resigned in May 1998. His demise was followed by political instability, and a quick succession of presidents including Habibie, a client of Suharto, Abdurrahman Wahid (1999–2001), the former head of NU, and Megawati Sukarnoputri, the daughter of Sukarno. The weakening of the central government and the discrediting of pançasila opened the way for separatist movements in the outer islands. After bloody suppression, East Timor won its independence with United Nations assistance. There were secessionist movements in Acheh, ethnic warfare in Irian Jaya and Kalimantan, Muslim–Christian riots in Ambon, and many other signs of the disintegration of state power and of the cohesion of Indonesian society. In 2000, as state power and the military weakened, Muslim political parties, student groups, and militias grew more powerful. Such groups as the Army of Allah and the Islamic Youth Front attacked bars and brothels, and Laskar Jihad sent volunteers to fight against the Christians in the Moluccas. The Star Moon Party is hostile to the Chinese and calls for the government to favor Muslim businessmen. NU and Muhammadiya, however, take a moderate position and favor diffusing racial tensions. Since the terrorist attacks of September 11, 2001 on New York and Washington, the Indonesian government is under great American pressure to suppress radical Muslim groups, while it strives to keep its balance in a fragmented and politically volatile Indonesian society.

BRITISH MALAYA AND INDEPENDENT MALAYSIA

The consolidation of the British empire in Malaya at the turn of the twentieth century also entailed the creation of centralized states and a capitalist economy concentrating upon agricultural and extractive industries. Sugar was introduced in the 1830s, coffee in the 1880s, and rubber at the end of the century. Pineapples and oil palm became important in the first decade of the twentieth century. Tin mining was important in Perak and Selangor. Gold and iron were also mined. The mining industry was generally owned by Chinese and worked by Chinese labor. Penang and Singapore became the main ports for the export of Malayan tin and the import of Chinese and other foreign laborers. By 1910 Malaya, like India, was exporting raw materials to Britain and Europe.

These developments had profound effects upon the organization of religious life and the relationship between Malay states and Muslim communities. In the traditional era, the Sultans were the foremost religious and political functionaries, and symbolized the Muslim nature of Malayan society. They had, however, a very limited role in the actual administration of Muslim law, education, and worship. The village 'ulama' were the principal representatives of Islam. They maintained worship, taught Islamic lore, presided over ceremonies of marriage and death, arbitrated disputes, healed the sick, controlled communal property, and collected Islamic taxes. Their influence was consolidated by marriages with other 'ulama' and wealthy landlord families. Despite the occasional appointment of a qadi to the central administration, the 'ulama' were basically individual functionaries not subject to state control. Though they belonged to the Shafi'i law school, and often to a mystic order, there was no central religious organization. The Sufi orders may have facilitated some standardization of religious views and education, but they did not actually create a collective body of religious teachers.

British domination drastically changed this system. When British residents consolidated the apparatus of centralized government, they deprived Malay Sultans of their authority in all matters except those bearing on religion and custom. The

Sultans, therefore, tried to strengthen their influence in these areas, and extend state control over village religious life. As early as 1880, a state *kathi* was appointed in Perak. Between 1884 and 1904, Raja Muda Sulayman, the ruler of Selangor, codified marriage and divorce laws, appointed qadis, and enacted Muslim penalties in civil and criminal matters. In Kelantan there was similarly an official reorganization of Islamic religious life due to local fears for the safety of Muslim tradition. Between 1888 and 1894, an official, styled *maha menteri*, insisted on the universal observance of Shari'a, required Muslims to attend the Friday prayers, provided for public readings of hadith, and centralized control of the state over local imams. Under his administration the government began to take a portion of the charity taxes, and a constabulary was created to enforce religious norms. Between 1905 and 1909, however, the British strengthened the central government of Kelantan, favored civil courts at the expense of Shari'a courts, and removed the imams from revenue administration. The mufti, however, was given control of the village mosques and revenues. He was made a salaried member of the government and head of the Muslim religious court system.

In 1915 the *Majlis Ugama* (Religious Council) was created to take full authority over religious courts and village mosques. The Majlis also took control of three-fifths of the zakat revenues and four-fifths of the head tax ordinarily collected by village religious leaders. In later years the Majlis sponsored education in English, Arabic, and Malay, prepared texts and translations, and otherwise provided state leadership for the reform of Islamic religious life. Throughout the Malay peninsula, centralized administration of religious affairs and the creation of chief qadis, councils, and Shari'a committees brought Islamic legal, educational, ritual, and financial affairs under state control. State control gave a strong conservative bias to Islamic affairs but proved to be a factor for political stability until the 1950s.

The changes introduced by British imperial controls and by the development of the Malayan economy further stimulated the Kaum Muda, or reformist and modernist Muslim movement. The rise of the Kaum Muda was a grave challenge to both state and village Muslim elites. Traveled merchants and students came back to their villages to challenge the authority of local imams and Sufis and the state administration of Islam. In the late 1920s journals produced by students in Cairo broached the issues of pan-Islamic and pan-Malayan unity and anti-colonialism. In the 1930s the Kaum Muda became politically militant; the very name came to imply nationalist opposition to foreign rule. In response to this challenge several Malay states censored or banned publications and forbade the teaching of Islam without the permission of the Sultans. Religious officials condemned the new views.

In the 1920s and 1930s the initiative passed to secular nationalists. The English-educated scions of the dominant Malay aristocracy, motivated by fear of rising Chinese influence, formed Malay associations. Many of these associations called upon the Sultans and the British to protect Malay privileges against Chinese competition; they laid claim to future leadership in Malayan politics. Other intelligentsia, however, began to speak against British rule and against the established aristocracy. The graduates of the Sultan Idris Training College, often of lower-class origin, strongly influenced by left-wing Indian nationalism, formed the Kesatu Melayu Muda in 1938 as the vehicle of their anti-British and anti-aristocratic program.

Nonetheless, the nationalist movement was relatively little developed in this period, in part because the Malay aristocracy was reasonably content with and dependent upon British control, and in part because the 1920s were relatively prosperous. The availability of jobs for educated Malays in the civil service inhibited the formation of nationalist parties. The hostilities among Malays, Chinese, and Indians made it difficult to crystallize a Malayan national movement conceived in territorial rather than in communal terms, and the absence of basic economic and political changes affecting the mass of the population made it impossible to generate mass support for opposition to British and aristocratic Malay rule. Thus, opposition was limited to very small groups of modernist Muslims and modern-educated Malays.

The years following World War II brought profound changes to Malayan political life, not as a result of nationalist opposition, but due to the formation of an independent Malayan state governed by its traditional elites. Independent Malaya had its origins in 1946, with British proposals for the creation of a Malayan union of the federated and unfederated Malay states, Singapore, Malacca, and Penang. The British proposed bypassing the Sultanates, setting up a central government for the whole of the region, and giving immigrant Chinese and Indian communities access to political power. These proposals were bitterly opposed by the Malay aristocracy, who in 1946 formed the United Malay National Organization. The strong resistance led the British to modify their proposals in 1948 in favor of a Federation of Malaya, which preserved the separate existence of the several Malay states and guaranteed the supremacy of Malay interests.

This federation, however, was attacked by the Malayan Communist Party, largely supported by Chinese workers. The Malayan Communist Party had organized anti-Japanese resistance in the 1940s; after the war it launched a guerrilla movement against the new federation and the continued British influence that it implied. In reaction the United Malay National Organization, the Malayan Chinese Association, and the Malayan Indian Association formed an alliance. In 1957 an independent Malayan state was formed with the support of Malay officials, Chinese merchants, and Indian intellectuals under the leadership of Tunku 'Abd al-Rahman. Under the new constitution, the dominance of Malays in education and the state bureaucracy and of non-Malays in the economy was confirmed. Islam was declared the official religion of Malaya, but freedom of worship was guaranteed. A ten-year grace period was given before Malay was to replace English, Chinese, and Tamil in state schools. In 1963 the federation of Malaya was reorganized to include North Borneo and Singapore (though Singapore withdrew in 1965), and the extended federation was officially renamed Malaysia.

The Malaysian state and Islam in a multi-ethnic society

In independent Malaysia, the ruling United Malay National Organization (UMNO) was a secular party stressing the ethnic dimension of Malay-Muslim identity. Malays received preferential treatment in the distribution of scholarships, licenses in certain businesses, and positions in public service, but ethnic Chinese and Indians were part of the ruling coalition. In the federation period religion was a local concern, and most Malay states maintained a department of religious affairs involved in mosque construction, enforcement of moral and criminal codes, and the collection of alms taxes. Teaching heretical doctrines was punishable, and laws were passed to penalize individuals for failure to attend Friday prayers or keep the fasts. In 1957 independence gave the federal government some role in religious matters. Islam was made the official religion of the federation. Schools were required to give Muslim religious instruction when there was a minimum number of Muslim students.

Several forces tended to further promote the Muslim dimension of Malay identity. The first Islamic opposition party emerged in Kelantan and Trengganu. The Pan-Malayan Islamic Party became the chief spokesman for Muslim communal hostility to the Chinese and Indians, and the first to call for an Islamic state to implement Islamic law. In Kelantan, the Pan-Malayan Islamic Party (PMIP) rallied strong support from a coalition of village imams and religious leaders who were resisting centralized administration and the loss of tax authority, and young nationalist radicals and small peasant landowners who were hurt by increasing rents, falling prices, and the threat of losing their land. For these peasants and local elites, the PMIP's Islamic orientation symbolized not only economic concerns but anxiety over losing an Islamic way of life that depended upon a combination of ownership of land and Muslim religious authority. The appeal to Islam legitimized the defense of worldly interests by invoking collective solidarity and moral principles; it dignified the struggle to protect the peasant way of life by invoking a moral vision of a society grounded in justice – justice identified with peasant and village interests. The rhetoric of the PMIP thus fused class interests with higher moral and social concerns.

The PMIP's success was telling. In 1959, it defeated the Alliance coalition in Kelantan and Trengganu, and built up the apparatus of Islamic administration under its own control. It strengthened the offices of qadi and mufti and suppressed immoral activities and competing religious sects. In response to the growth of the PMIP, the UMNO attempted to recruit religious leaders and pledged itself to promote Islamic interests. The UMNO's movement toward an Islamic position, however, threatened to undermine the coalition with Chinese and Indian groups. Also, throughout the 1960s, Malays reinforced their position in education and the civil service, and began to demand a larger role in the national economy. Young Malay leaders claimed support for Malay state capitalism, and raised the question of whether Malayan society would be Muslim or pluralistic in ideological orientation. The elections of 1969 increased the pressures on the dominant parties. The PMIP gained in strength, and Chinese radicals attacked the complacent attitude of the Malayan Chinese Association toward their deteriorating situation and demanded equality for Chinese. The balance of power broke down into communal riots in 1969.

In reaction an emergency regime was installed. The new national front included much the same conservative forces. Again it attempted to maintain some balance among the communities, and yet to satisfy Malay economic grievances and reinforce a nationalist concept of Malay identity. A new economic policy, focused on the expansion of government investment and public enterprises, and financed by foreign capital and export earnings from petroleum, rubber, timber, and palm oil, was instituted in the 1970s; it aimed at promoting Malay involvement in the economy. Its goal was 30 percent Malay ownership and employment in Malaysian businesses, and the formation of a state-capitalist Malay economic elite. In 1972 the PMIP, under the new name of Islamic Party of Malaysia (PAS), was drawn into the national front. The UMNO had tried to coopt it, but this only led to the penetration of the government bureaus and economic and educational institutions by committed Muslim activists.

Despite these efforts to diffuse Islamic influence, the forces promoting an Islamic identity gained in strength. Increasing urbanization and migration to cities, and above all the growth of the student population brought a new Muslim consciousness to the fore. The decline of the PAS as a spokesman for a radical Islamic position led to the rise of *dakwah* (missionary and educational movements). White-collar workers, teachers and students, usually of secular educational background, became increasingly conscious of the corruption of their society and the need for Muslim reforms. Attending lectures, adopting Muslim dress, calling for a return to the guidance of the Quran and personal morality, they denounced the West as the principal source of evil. They also appealed to Malay ethnic chauvinism. In place of the traditional rural leadership the new movements were led by urban-based, university-educated, and sometimes foreign-educated Muslim Malays, and they appealed to urban workers, students, and lower-level professionals. Education abroad, the dissemination of Muslim publications, and the rise of Islamism elsewhere has had a strong impact. Islamic training camps, seminars, and discussion groups, and agitation over events in Palestine, Lebanon, and Afghanistan also promoted the new consciousness. The adherents of the dakwah movements were identified by dress: loose-fitting robes, veils, and sometimes turbans. They were puritanical, and opposed the traditional spirit cults, shamanism, feasting to consolidate local communities, and adat, or local custom and customary law. Dakwah in Malaysia was part of a global movement to define a standardized Islam.

The Islamic revival spawned three major groups. The Malay Muslim Youth League (ABIM), founded in 1971, led by Anwar Ibrahim, was dedicated to the Islamization of the individual, the family, the umma, and the state, and the education of a God-fearing Malaysian youth. A second dakwah group, Darul Arqam, sponsored cooperatives, workshops, clinics, and schools and stressed independence through economic activity such as agriculture and small-scale manufacturing. Darul Arqam was dedicated to living by Quranic and Arabic customs, including the segregation of the sexes. It represented an egalitarian and utopian program, but was forced out of Malaysia by charges that it was a messianic authoritarian cult. A third movement, the Tabligh, a preaching movement, appealed to well-educated people. These activist groups, fundamentalist in religious orientation and reformist in political affairs, threatened to upset the delicate balances of the Malaysian state.

In response the government of Prime Minister Mahathir b. Muhammad has since 1981 maintained a tight control over the country. The regime is highly authoritarian. The Mahathir government curbed the more radical Muslim demands, arrested individuals as provocateurs of inter-ethnic strife, and regulated publications. It responded to dakwah by attempting to coopt it. In 1982 Anwar Ibrahim accepted a place in the UMNO, and the government declared its desire to absorb Islamic values. The state treated Islam as a kind of civil religion, legitimizing state policies. At the same time the state also lent its support to a purely secular Malay nationalist movement, Bumiputera (Indigenous Sons of the Earth), which cultivated an ethnic Malay consciousness committed to technical and economic modernization. Government policy stressed both Muslim religious and Malay ethnic cultural orientations.

Domestically, Mahathir declared Malaysia to have an Islamic economy and founded an Islamic bank, insurance and other companies, though Bank Islam Malaysia remains on the edge of the banking system and the impact of Islamic norms upon banking has been marginal. The government has increased support for Muslim schools and broadcasting, created an Islamic university, and raised the status of Muslim judges to be equal to those of the civil courts. The regime also brought a high level of prosperity to the country, shifting Malaysia from an economy of tin, rubber, and palm oil to microchips and contemporary industrial products. The country has developed an extensive infrastructure of highways, airports, dams, and mass transit. In foreign policy Mahathir gave strong support to Arab interests, the PLO and the Afghan resistance. Malaysia cultivated business ties to Uzbekistan, Kuwait, and Sa'udi Arabia, but was circumspect in dealing with Iran, Libya, and Syria.

Thus, the Malaysian state is trying to find its own mode of Islamic correctness which keeps a balance among the demands for an Islamic state, the pressures of the international economy, and the needs of a multi-ethnic society. The Islamists have forced the government to take increasingly pro-Islamist positions and have greatly raised the tensions with non-Muslim, non-Malay ethnic groups, especially the Chinese, and with rural Malays still committed to folk Islam. The regime hovers between the need to cultivate Malay support and the need to maintain the collaboration of the Chinese. The more it stresses Islam, the more it threatens the non-Malay populations.

Still the Islamists face major barriers to the formation of an Islamic state. While radical groups calling for the complete Islamization of state and society remain very strong, the state threatens to absorb the dakwah movements. As the Islamic discourse is adopted by politicians, 'ulama', Muslim activists, and others, it becomes more diffused as the basis of Malay political identity, but less specific as a political program. Moreover, substantial Chinese and Indian populations, Western secular ideas of constitution and democracy, state patronage of ethnic Malays, and the free-enterprise capitalist-based structure of the economy give great institutional depth to a pluralistic society.

The role of women in society is hotly debated. The UMNO calls for the integration of women in employment and a modest form of dress. The PAS wants to limit women to the nurturing professions – teaching, nursing, and social work – and calls for purdah. A women's movement called Sisters in Islam argues that the Quran has been misinterpreted, and tries to defend gender equality on Islamic grounds.

Since 1998 Malaysia has been in a latent political crisis. Prime Minister Mahathir's credibility has been damaged by the removal of Anwar Ibrahim from office and his prosecution for sodomy. This high-handed suppression of his rival has provoked protests against Mahathir's economic policies, business cronyism and corrupt contracts, and the lack of an independent judiciary. At the end of 2001 the tensions surrounding Malay identity had not been resolved.

THE PHILIPPINES

Muslims make up about 4–7 percent of the Philippine population, but are concentrated in the southern islands. Mindanao was the principal center of Muslim population. Despite numerous wars, the Spanish failed to conquer the southern Sultanates. Muslims were not Hispanized, and the Spanish were not able to give an overarching identity to the region. Nor did a shared Muslim identity or political cooperation emerge in opposition. Muslims were divided into three major and ten minor ethno-linguistic groups. They were ruled by local *datus* (feudal lords), who maintained large clienteles.

After the Spanish–American war the United States took control of the islands in 1899. The American administration introduced the idea of a trans-ethnic Muslim identity. Najeeb M. Saleeby argued for a unification of the Muslim populations to transcend the feudal, chieftain-led structure of the society, and to facilitate colonial administration and community development. His views influenced Lawrence Kuder, superintendent of schools in the Muslim regions of Lanao, Sulu and Cotabato, who wanted to create a Western-educated Muslim elite of civil servants, lawyers, and politicians to represent their people in the Philippine state. A new generation, regardless of local langauges, was taught an ethnic identity, that of Muslim-Filipinos.

When the Philippines became independent in 1946, the state was dominated by a Christian majority prejudiced against its non-Hispanicized Muslim population. It encouraged a large-scale immigration of Christians into the southern islands. The first local resistance came from the younger intelligentsia, educated in Manila and abroad, allied to local merchants and smugglers. They were divided into two wings. One stressed an Islamic identity and the construction of Muslim communities around mosques, schools, and pilgrimage. The second was a nationalist separatist movement which appropriated the name Moro from the Spanish colonial discourse, but with a new positive meaning, to refer to the Muslim population in an ethnic sense of the term Muslim. The Philippine-Muslim National League was announced in 1968; resistance escalated with ethnic riots in Cotabato in 1970, and after the declaration of martial law in 1972, became armed secessionism led by the Moro National Liberation Front, founded by Nur Misuari in 1971. The self-declared nationalist movement called for a Muslim homeland (Bangsamoro). This was a rebellion against both the state and the traditional nobility. Datus and the older-generation elites generally opposed the violence, and allied themselves with the Manila government. The Marcos regime responded by a declaration of martial law, and an on-and-off war for regional autonomy in the name of a Muslim population against a repressive Philippine state continues to the present.

The movement had two dimensions. One was the struggle for the autonomy of a regional population, and the other was a struggle for the creation of a common reformed Islamic identity. Sa'udi, Egyptian, and Libyan money flowed in to promote Islamic learning and to support the Moro resistance. Missionaries from al-Azhar established madrasas.

A peace settlement in 1977 calling for an autonomous region was never implemented. Separatism reemerged in the 1980s in the form of an unarmed Islamic movement led by Muslim clerics calling for religious reform and political autonomy. The 'ulama' defined a society based on political autonomy, judicial equality, and reformed Islamic practice. In 1984 the Moro Islamic Liberation Front (MILF), led by Hashim Salamat, was formed to continue the struggle, now for both regional independence and the formation of an Islamic state. Islamic renewal became the basis of new coalition of Moro separatists, Islamic clerics, and Muslim politicians. With the collapse of the Marcos regime in 1986 and the withdrawal of the army to fight Communist rebels, government vigilantes wrought havoc in the region. The Moro National Liberation Front made a new peace with the Philippine government in 1996. Nur Misuari became governor of the Autonomous Region for Muslim Mindanao. The MILF signed a cease-fire in 1997. Today it calls for a Timor-style referendum on Mindanao and the Sulu archipelago, but more radical splinter movements continue the armed struggle in the name of Islam. The Abu Sayyaf group, founded in 1991 with funding from private Sa'udi sources, engages in armed raids and kidnapping to raise ransom money for its cause.

The common people themselves have their own, different, views about their goals. They backed the Muslim resistance movement because they saw in it protection against the army, but did not identify themselves as part of a Moro Muslim nation. Nor did they practice Islam in the fashion of the reformed clerics. They believe in magic, amulets and spirits; celebrate the traditional wedding, mortuary, and remembrance feasts, and resist the demands of the reformed 'ulama' that they practice Islam in accord with Middle Eastern customs. They are Muslims, but refuse the cultural and ethnic identity constructed for them by the elites. Within Moro society there are debates among traditional and reformed Muslims, traditional and Muslim defined political leaders, as well as between regional Muslims and the Christian-controlled Philippine state.

CONCLUSION

The structures of contemporary Southeast Asian societies represent a coming together of the historical institutional and cultural patterns of the region and the influences generated by Dutch, British, and American colonial rule. In the nineteenth century the Dutch and the British introduced radical economic and political changes. These changes, in the long run, generated a conflict between Southeast Asian secular and Muslim identities. In the Indies, Dutch economic and trade policies stimulated Muslim merchants to create the Islamic modernist movements. Dutch educational and administrative measures were also conducive to the formation of priyayi-led nationalist and Communist movements. These positions reflected the historical division between those people who saw the world in Javanese and Indonesian cultural terms and those who viewed it in Muslim terms. The twentieth-century history of Indonesia was the history of the revived struggle of Islam against other forms of Indonesian culture. For the last half century, Sukarno and Suharto held off the demand for an Islamic state, but the Islamic revival has had substantial success in redefining the religious and ideological commitments of the Indonesian state.

In Malaysia, as in Indonesia, dakwah movements have raised Muslim consciousness. The state has made important concessions to the Muslim interests and Muslim identity of the Malay majority, but also tries to defuse the political pressures and to accommodate its Chinese and Indian minorities and the capitalist structure of the economy.

In the Philippines trans-ethnic Muslim identity is not the expression of a historical culture, but is a modern phenomenon, resulting from American rule and educational policies, and a reaction against an abusive Philippine state. Strongly influenced by Islamic reformism from abroad, the Moro movements wage a struggle for an independent Islamic state.

CHAPTER 29

INNER ASIA UNDER RUSSIAN AND CHINESE RULE; THE CAUCASUS AND AFGHANISTAN

By the end of the nineteenth century the Muslim populations of Inner Asia had come under Russian and Chinese rule. Like the Portuguese, the British, the French, the Germans, and the Dutch, the Russians and the Chinese became rulers of Muslim peoples. In their cases, however, colonial expansion took place on territories contiguous with the imperial homelands and were not regarded as foreign domains which would eventually win their independence, but as integral parts of the conquering empires. From the Russian and Chinese points of view the "colonial" problem took the form of a "minority" problem. How best could Inner Asian peoples be governed and eventually assimilated into the body politic of imperial and then Soviet Russian, and Communist Chinese, societies? From the Muslim point of view the problem became how to define Muslim identity in the face of pressures for assimilation into foreign civilizations. In the 1990s, the collapse of the Soviet Union unexpectedly allowed for a new wave of state formation among the Muslim peoples of Inner Asia and a redirected quest for religio-ethnic identities.

TSARIST RULE AND JADID

The first stages of Russian rule in the nineteenth century paralleled other colonial situations. The Russian conquests gave Inner Asia a new territorial and administrative organization. The Russians dismantled the Muslim states and divided the region into two large governorates – one for the Kazakh steppes and one for the territory that would henceforth be known as Central Asia or Russian Turkestan. Autonomous vassal states remained at Bukhara and Khiva.

The Russians were at first favorable to Muslim religious organizations. In Bukhara, a highly organized, state-supported religious establishment retained its economic and social cohesion. Muslim education continued to be the preserve of the *maktab* (elementary Quran school) and the madrasa. The supervisors and teachers were appointed by the local rulers. The Shaykh al-Islam and the qadis were responsible for the supervision of the schools. Students and faculty received stipends from waqfs, and graduates usually went on to take positions as teachers, imams, muftis, and judges. Muslim holy men continued to function among tribal and rural peoples. The veneration and visitation of shrines remained a central aspect of Inner Asian Muslim worship.

In territories under direct Russian rule, the Tsars actually promoted Muslim religious organizations in order to bring them under their control. In 1788 Catherine the Great established the first Muslim religious administration at Ufa for European and Siberian Muslims. Another "muftiat" was organized in the Crimea in 1794. In 1872 separate Sunni and Shi'i boards were established in Transcaucasia. The Russian authorities appointed the Shi'i Shaykh al-Islam and Sunni mufti, the qadis, and the heads of religious assemblies. The Tsar's administration regulated the appointment of muftis to local mosques (leaving many of them vacant), paid their salaries, supervised their activities, and required them to be politically loyal. The regime also supervised Muslim publications. The Tsarist policy was similar to that of the Muslim rulers of Bukhara and the Ottoman empire, save that it was carried out under the auspices of a non-Muslim regime.

In rural and nomadic areas 'ulama' and schools were of secondary importance. Qadis were appointed by the Khans but they had only a limited impact on the application of the Shari'a to inheritance, land, water, and family problems. Independent Sufi holy men, called *ishans*, held the allegiance of the populace, and espoused a form of Muslim belief centered upon veneration of saints expressed in pilgrimages and festivals which combined Muslim and shamanistic practices. In Turkmenistan, for example, the people were organized by lineage and tribal affiliation; venerated Sufis acted as intermediaries among the warring tribes and between the Khans and the tribes. Sometimes Sufis were the leaders of Turkmen rebellions against Iranian or Khivan authority. Sufis also served as caretakers of holy places, teachers, cemetery directors, intermediaries with dead saints, and practitioners of folk medicine. The ishans did not own property in land or water rights, but earned their living by selling talismans and amulets and by receiving payments for religious performances.

Most striking in Turkmen society were the evliads, or holy lineages believed to descend from the Prophet and the first four Caliphs. The descendants of Muhammad and of the Caliphs 'Uthman and 'Ali by Muhammad's daughters, called sayyids, and the descendants of Abu Bakr and 'Umar, called khwajas, were believed to have inherited the religious powers of their holy ancestors. The lineages in fact descended from intermediary Sufi masters. For example, Gezli Ata, the likely founder of the Ata lineage, was a fourteenth-century Sufi connected with the Yasavi order. In Turkmenistan, as in Egypt, Morocco, and many other places in the Muslim world, Sufi allegiance and Prophetic lineage were combined. These lineages were believed to possess shamanistic powers capable of driving out evil spirits. Their dhikr ceremonies effected spirit cures and were marked by trances and frenzies. Veneration for the holy lineages by ordinary Turkmens was similar to the pre-Islamic cult of ancestors.

The creation of a Russian imperial administration, the settlement of Russian garrisons, the opening of the region to Russian trade, and the introduction of Russian education and cultural policies led to profound changes. The implications of Russian rule, however, were different in each of the regions they controlled, depending upon the local objectives of Russian policy, and the nature of the local Muslim societies.

In Turkmenistan Russian occupation led to important changes in the religious structure. The Russians pacified Turkmen feuds, encouraged private property in land, promoted a shift to sedentary life, and thus undermined the need for tribal solidarity and religious mediation. At the same time mosques, qadi courts, schools, and pilgrimage became more common. With sedentarization and the centralization of political power, even under infidel auspices, there was a shift from the mediating role of Sufis to an organized leadership of the 'ulama' type. This was similar to the changes in Morocco and India, where the introduction of European rule reduced the authority of rural Sufis in favor of the 'ulama'.

In the Kazakh regions, the Russians attempted to break up the old social structure and to implant a colonial society. The introduction of a market economy and taxation in cash undermined the Kazakh nobility by exposing it to both Russian rule and competition from Tatar merchants and clerks. The introduction of the scythe made it possible to cut hay for winter fodder and reduced the need to nomadize; Russian laws made communal lands and collective rights to hay and fodder into private properties. Russian rule improved security for nomadic peoples, and allowed them to expand into new areas and survive on less extensive territories.

As the nomadic populations were forced to sedentarize, Russian colonists began to occupy "unused" fertile lands. Before 1868 the Russian government favored only the settlement of Cossacks or farmer-soldiers, but after the conquest of Turkestan Russia permitted peasant colonization as well. Between 1868 and 1880 some 4,000 Russian families settled in the Semirech'e and additional Tatar and Uzbek colonists came from Turkestan. Until 1889, the Russian government attempted to restrain colonization, but the establishment of a Russian settlement administration in 1896, the construction of the trans-Siberian railroad, and government support for the seizure of unoccupied or surplus Kazakh lands led to great waves of Russian immigration, especially after 1905. By 1912 more than 1.5 million Russians made up 40 percent of the population of the Kazakh steppes. In a continuing cycle, the ever-growing Russian population forced the Kazakhs into smaller spaces and the contraction of the Kazakhs encouraged Russian colonization still further. From the Russian point of view, colonization made it possible to convert the fertile steppe region from pastoral to agricultural uses, to secure it against possible revolts, and to reduce population pressure in western and central Russia. From the Kazakh point of view it meant the destruction of their society. The Kazakhs were forced into daily conflict with Russian settlers and were deprived of their migration routes, water, and land.

In Turkestan, by contrast, the Russians adopted a minimalist policy to assure military control and dominance in trade, and otherwise did not interfere with local economies, social organization, education, and cultural life. While the Russians administered all the higher levels of territorial government, they allowed some measure of self-government at local levels. They instituted a three-year term for village elders and required district headmen to be elected by the natives, though they could be dismissed by Russian officials. Muslim and customary law courts continued to function. Though limited at the local level, Russian administration still made village and religious chiefs subordinate to central control.

The Russian impact on the economy of Turkestan, however, was the critical lever for the changes that were to follow. While the Krasnovodsk Caspian–Samarqand (1881–88)–Tashkent (1898) Railroad was mainly of military importance, the Tashkent–Orenburg line, completed in 1906, opened the way for the immigration of Russian administrators and skilled workers and for the construction of modern Russian cities adjacent to old Muslim ones. Tashkent, the capital of Turkestan, was provided with schools, museums, libraries, newspapers, an observatory, and other institutions – a model of Russian modernity in Inner Asia. Other towns in Transcaspia and Semirech'e also acquired large Russian populations. Russian colonization in rural areas, by contrast with the Kazakh steppes, was limited by the fact that Turkestan was already densely occupied by a native peasant population.

Railroad construction also led to a tremendous increase in cotton production. With railroads, northern wheat could be brought from the Ukraine and western Siberia to make up for Central Asian lands turned over to cotton. As a result cotton acreage in Farghana rose from 14 percent of cultivated land in 1885 to 44 percent in 1915, displacing wheat, sorghum, alfalfa, and rice. For Turkestan as a whole, however, only 13 percent of arable land was committed to cotton, owing to a lack of adequate irrigation and drainage, the use of land by nomads, and large tracts of undeveloped land owned by the ruler of Bukhara. In 1912 Turkestani cotton accounted for 63.6 percent of all Russian cotton supplies, and was vital to the industrialization of Russia. Thus, under Russian control, Turkestan came to have a one-crop economy supplemented by silk, dried fruit, grapes, wine, and sugar beets. Industrialization in Central Asia before 1917 was largely limited to cotton-processing industries in which all the skilled workers were Russians. Turkestan was treated as a colonial economy whose raw materials were extracted for the benefit of the imperial power and whose industrialization was subordinate to export interests.

Russian land policies also had important long-term implications. In 1886 the Tsarist regime made waqf lands the property of their tenants, and required that new waqfs have official approval. In 1913 it declared all occupied lands the property of tenant producers, and all grazing and unused lands state property. By 1913 about 50 percent of irrigated land in Turkestan had become the property of small owners. While the changes in land law made peasants proprietors, it also made them vulnerable to the money economy and to the vagaries of the world market. Peasants had to find capital for tools, oxen, and seed, as well as funds to tide over bad years in the cotton market. As a result many went into debt, lost their land to money lenders, and reverted to the status of sharecroppers. The overall result of changes in the land law was a reconcentration of ownership in the hands of a new class of landlords, merchants, usurers, and – occasionally – successful older gentry. Concentration of land in Turkestan led to the consolidation of a new bourgeois landowning elite, and was not in the long run beneficial to the peasantry.

In the protectorate of Bukhara, Russian intervention had similar effects. The construction of railroads opened Bukhara up to Russian capital, and linked it closely to the Russian economy. Permanent settlements of Russian railroad workers were founded in Bukhara, Tirmidh, and other towns, and Russian business firms and banks were opened. Russia displaced Iran and India as Bukhara's principal trading partner. Bukhara exported cotton, lambskins, wool, silk, hides, dried fruits, and carpets, and imported Russian textiles, metals, sugar, and chinaware. Russia assumed control of Bukharan customs, and introduced Russian coinage. The reorientation of trade benefited Bukharan merchants and peddlers, but penalized local artisans and textile producers. Carpet and silk production was henceforth restricted to the luxury trades. Russian capital also undermined the Bukharan peasantry. To survive in the world cotton market, Bukharan peasants had to take out loans at high rates of interest, and sell the cotton crop in advance at low prices. Many would lose their land. While the bourgeoisie prospered in trade, as an intermediary between the Russians and the native population or as agents of Russian commercial firms, and acquired land, the artisans and peasants suffered.

The common people and the new bourgeoisie had different responses to Russian rule. By and large, the common people suffered passively. Despite the sedentarization and impoverishment of the nomads, there was virtually no military resistance in the Kazakh steppes between 1869 and 1916, and none in Transcaspia between 1881 and 1916. Only in Transoxania and Farghana was there scattered Sufi-led opposition and peasant banditry. There were riots in Tashkent in 1892, provoked by medical measures taken to resist a cholera epidemic which included inspection of women and restrictions on burials in Muslim cemeteries. In 1898 Ishan Muhammad al-Khalifa Kabir (1856–98), called Ishan Madali, led about two thousand rebels to almost instant defeat. Madali had acquired a local reputation, first as a simpleton and then as a holy man. He made the pilgrimage to Mecca in 1884 and returned to organize charities for the poor. With the help of his followers he built a school, a mosque, warehouses, kitchens, and a residence for his wives clustered in a big compound. Disgruntled 'ulama' and former office-holders became part of his following. In 1898 his people attacked several Russian garrisons, planning to evict the Russians and reestablish the Khokand Khanate. They were quickly dispersed, and Madali was executed. Resistance in Turkestan, however, was not entirely quelled. Between 1906 and 1910 sporadic banditry in the countryside increased, as peasants who had been pushed off the land by usurers attacked Russian settlers.

World War I precipitated the first widespread Muslim rebellions. In 1916, at the height of the cotton-harvesting season, the Russians attempted to mobilize 240,000 Muslim workers to serve in labor battalions. The resistance was strongest in regions that had large numbers of Russian colonists and where there had been forced sedentarization and seizure of lands. No doubt, long-suffered economic misery fueled the outburst. Kazakhs attacked government buildings, schools, post offices, rail and telegraph lines, and Russian civilians, but Russian peasants retaliated by seizing the property of natives and forcing them to flee. There were terrible communal massacres on both sides. Kirgiz peoples rebelled, and many moved to China. The other Muslim regions were generally quiet.

Jadid reformism

Rather than resist, the middle classes became the bearers of a new cultural and political consciousness. Since the early nineteenth century the University of Kazan had been the principal center for the communication of Russian culture to Tatars and Kazakhs, and after the middle of the century the Russians vastly expanded their educational effort. Nicholas Il'minskii created schools that would give Tatars a Russian and European education, imparted by native instructors using native languages. While some Tatars resisted this program because they feared forced Russification, and some Russians were concerned about an education that would encourage national languages and separatism, many Tatars welcomed the new education as a means of spreading modernism and of entering into the life of the Russian state.

In Turkestan, Russian education came to Muslims as a result of different policies. Here Governor-General von Kaufman decided to create schools for Russian settlers (1876) that had no religious or confessional bias, and wait for Muslims to voluntarily enroll and adopt a superior Russian civilization. In 1884 the first Russian native school to teach Russian language, arithmetic, geography, history, literature, and other secular subjects in the morning, and Muslim religion and local languages in the afternoon, was founded. A small number of schools sufficed to create a cadre of Muslim translators, teachers, and intellectuals. Generally, however, Muslims found them unsatisfactory because of their poor teaching of Muslim subjects and the fear that their children would be weaned away from Islam. By 1917 Muslim education was still mostly in the hands of the 'ulama'.

However, Russian conquests and colonization led to the development of a native bourgeoisie, and Russian education favored, as in colonial situations the Muslim world over, the emergence of a small intelligentsia. Under the influence of Russian education, and of new ideas from Turkey and Iran, this intelligentsia began to demand reform of Muslim practices, self-improvement, cultural enlightenment, and, eventually, political autonomy. Some of the new intelligentsia stressed national development, and others religious reform. After the turn of the century there would be advocates of socialism as well.

The most significant of the new cultural tendencies was the *usul-i jadid*, or New Method, a program of educational reform that gradually developed into a political movement. The usul-i jadid had its origin among wealthy and highly Europeanized Kazan and Crimean Tatars, often educated at the University of Kazan, who had not only become assimilated to Russian culture but sensitive to their own Turkish and Muslim heritage, and aware of their backwardness. The Volga and Crimean Tatar bourgeoisie carried the new concept into Kazakhstan, Turkestan, and Bukhara.

The Tatar intellectual revival began early in the nineteenth century under the leadership of Abu Nasr al-Kursavi (1783–1814), a young Tatar theologian and teacher in a madrasa in Bukhara, who proclaimed the primacy of reason over dogma. He was exiled, but his views were taken up by Shihab al-Din Marjani (1818–89), who called for freedom of independent judgment in religious matters, the abandonment of the fixed dogmas of the past, a new education based on the teaching of the Quran, hadith, and the history of Islam, and instruction in Russian language and modern science. His program was oriented toward a reform of Islamic belief and teaching and to a modernization and integration of Islam with Russian culture. Marjani thus represented a combination of the reformist and the modernist orientations.

A principal contributor to the creation of a Muslim literature which could communicate modern ideas was 'Abd al-Qayyim Nasiri (1824–1904), the son of a village religious teacher, educated in the madrasas of Kazan and Bukhara, learned in Arabic, Persian, and Chaghatay, who taught himself Russian and taught for a time in a Russian theological seminary. In 1871 he left the seminary and opened his own school. Basing his work on his own pedagogical concepts, he taught not only Muslim subjects, but the Russian language, arithmetic, geography, history, music, and drawing. For this enterprise Nasiri created his own texts, including a syntax for Tatars trying to learn Russian, and a Tatar–Russian dictionary. He also wrote on European sciences, and published material on trade and industry. A folklorist who accumulated Tatar songs and legends, he preserved the knowledge of pre-Islamic beliefs. Though he was opposed to the conservative religious leaders and their concept of education, he was in fact a devout Muslim and published numerous religious works, including studies of the life of the Prophet and stories of Muslim saints. In his own lifetime he was largely ignored, but as an encyclopedist and popularizer he was a pioneer in joining Muslim reform to Muslim modernism.

The most famous jadid leader was Isma'il Gasprinskii (1851–1914), a Crimean Tatar who had a European education and worked as a journalist in Istanbul and Paris. In 1883 he began to publish *Tarjuman*, which became the principal expression of the jadid campaign for the modernization and unification of Muslim peoples. Gasprinskii became a proponent of the modernist rather than the reformist orientation. He argued that Muslims must borrow from the West to revitalize their intellectual and social life. While Islam could remain a philosophic and theological system, Muslim peoples had to become part of modern technical civilization. He held up the positive example of the small Tatar community in Poland which was Muslim in religion but otherwise wholly assimilated, and the negative example of Bukhara as a benighted and backward Muslim society.

Gasprinskii pioneered in sponsoring jadid schools. By 1905 Kazan, Orenburg, Bagtchesaray, and Baku had become important centers of jadid education. He also tried to develop a standard Turkish literary language based on Ottoman to replace Arabic, Persian, and Chaghatay. Gasprinskii's ultimate objective was to transmit European culture to Muslim peoples and to unify them on the basis of a common language, a rational form of religion, and a shared modern civilization.

Tatar merchants and intellectuals introduced the jadid schools to Tashkent and Bukhara, where they were taken up by local cotton merchants and money lenders who had a Russian education or had been exposed to Russian ideas. Tashkent schools and the *Turkestan Native Gazette*, an official government publication produced in literary Uzbek with a Russian translation, were the main vehicles for the spread of interest in modernization. Stimulated by the Iranian revolution of 1906 and the Young Turk coup of 1908, Bukharans themselves founded additional schools which emphasized religion and provided supplementary studies of the Russian language, arithmetic, geography, physics, and chemistry. These contrasted with the reformist schools in Crimea and Kazan, which stressed secular rather than religious instruction. In 1910 a new society called the Union of Noble Bukhara was founded to print a journal and distribute literary materials. These Yeni Bukharlar (Young Bukharans) included intellectuals of merchant and 'ulama' background, many of whom were educated in Istanbul. They combined Young Turk-type reformism, Tatar jadidism, pan-Islamic, anti-Russian, and anti-feudal sentiments.

The leading ideologue of the Bukharan reform was 'Abd al-Rauf Fitrat. He argued that Muslim civilization in Bukhara was in decline and that the conservative 'ulama' were responsible. The 'ulama', he argued, had distorted the teaching of the Prophet, put Islam at the service of the privileged classes, and made it hostile to progress. He was equally opposed to popular religious practices and the worship of saints. He argued that the regeneration of the Muslim community would depend upon a new understanding of Islam which rejected ignorant leadership and blind fidelity. Fitrat believed that the rebirth of the Muslim community could only be realized by a spiritual renovation of individuals, based on a reformed education, and by a social and political revolution which would bring an end to foreign domination and to a corrupt political elite. He was the first Bukharan thinker to emphasize political action and to propound an Islamic identity based on the concept of *vatan* (fatherland) and millet (nation).

The jadid movement in Tsarist Russia was similar to modernist movements in other parts of the Muslim world. In social origin it was a collection of intelligentsia drawn from bourgeois and merchant strata of society, a movement not of a displaced but of an aspiring political elite. While it echoed 'ulama' reformism by its emphasis upon the Quran, Sunna, and ijtihad, jadid was primarily a modernist movement which attempted to transform Islam into another version of modern technical and national civilization. It seems closer to the modernism of the Ottoman empire and Sayyid Ahmad Khan in India than to the reformism of the Sufis.

Cultural concerns, moreover, soon led to politics. Within the jadid movement, and alongside it, the Tatars began to discuss their political identity and to debate whether Tatars were Turks or a separate nation. Emigrés in Turkey took the pan-Turanian view that Tatar, Turkish, Mongolian, and Finno-Ugric peoples formed a single nation glorified by the conquests of Attila, Chinggis Khan, and Timur. Tatars within Russia generally held that they formed a distinct nation (millet), and aspired to assimilation into Russian society. They demanded individual equality of Muslims with Russians and imagined a future of cooperation between the two peoples. Rashid Ibragimov imagined a Russian–Muslim federation on the Austro-Hungarian model. Socialist ideas also began to spread among Muslim intellectuals in Kazan, Kiev, Tiflis, and Orenburg. As a dispersed population without much hope of territorial separation from Russia, Tatars were most likely to support pan-Islamic or pan-Turkish causes.

Kazakhs had equally advanced nationalist and assimilationist conceptions. A small number went to Russian schools and served in the Russian army and administration. Hostile to Tatar merchants and cultural influences, they were willing to collaborate with Russian educators. Il'minskii and his student Ibragim Altynsarin (1841–89) collaborated in introducing a Russian-type education in the Kazakh language and in opening teacher-training schools that used the Cyrillic alphabet. Altynsarin founded four Kazakh schools between 1879 and 1883, followed by a Kazakh teachers' college to train a native vanguard. This period of Kazakh–Russian collaboration ended with the first great wave of Russian colonization between 1896 and 1910. From then on Kazakh intellectuals began to cultivate a separate national consciousness. Alash Orda (named after a mythic Kazakh horde) was founded in 1905, though it did not become politically active until 1917. In 1907 the first newspapers were published. Kazakh intellectuals continued to favor European and modern education but opposed cultural Russification and Russian colonization. Among the radicals the first murmurs about Kazakh liberation and political autonomy were to be heard.

The Russian revolutionary years of 1904–05, the formation of a *duma*, or legislature, in 1906, and temporary freedom of organization, press, and assembly stimulated a burst of Muslim newspapers, political parties, and congresses. A number of Muslim and socialist parties were created, primarily by Tatars and Azarbayjanis. In 1904 the Tatar students of the Muhammadiya madrasa founded al-Islah (Reform) to press the concepts of cultural jadid into the struggle for political rights. In 1905 a Marxist-nationalist party, Berek (Unity), was organized by graduates of the teachers' school. Berek combined with al-Islah to create the Tangchylar (Morning Star), which had a populist or socialist revolutionary orientation. Al-Islah people created a Kazan branch of the Russian Social Democratic Party. Other Tatars founded the Tatar Social Democratic Group in 1907. A Crimean party, Milli Firqa (National Party), was formed about the same time.

In 1905 Kazan Tatars, Crimeans, and Azarbayjanis held an illegal all-Russian Muslim congress in Nizhnii Novgorod, which led to the founding of the Russian General Muslim Party (Ittifaq al-Muslimin). At three Muslim congresses of 1905 and 1906 Tatar leaders attempted to create a union of the Muslims of Russia to work for a constitutional monarchy, equality and cooperation between Russians and Muslims, freedom of Muslim instruction, press, and publications, and respect for private property. Despite the superficial unity of the congresses, the delegates were in fact deeply divided. Gasprinskii and older Tatar leaders opposed political action and wanted to concentrate on religious and cultural affairs. Muslims close to the Russian socialists opposed a religious party. The majority favored Muslim political action on a national-religious basis and a platform calling for civil rights, toleration of minorities, equality of peoples, and cultural autonomy, but not territorial independence.

In Azarbayjan, Armenian and Russian influence combined with the conservatism of the Shi'i 'ulama' to promote a radical and anti-religious intelligentsia. Hummet (Endeavor), founded in Baku in 1904, was affiliated with the Bolsheviks. Baku was the ideal location for a Muslim proletarian party since it had an industrial working class employed in the oil industry, a liberal Muslim tradition, and abundant contacts with radical political currents in the outside Muslim world.

By 1907, however, Russia's brief liberal period was succeeded by a reaction, and the Muslim intelligentsia was left politically isolated. Its efforts to ally with Russian liberals broke down, and it had no support from the Muslim masses. Despite the traumas suffered by Kazakh herdsmen displaced by Russian colonists, and Turkestan peasants impoverished by Russian land administration and cotton policies, the mass of the people continued to live in lineage and village communities under the authority of tribal and religious chiefs. On the eve of the 1917 revolution the Muslim intelligentsia was minuscule in size, divided by religious, socialist, and nationalist ideologies, and without popular support.

THE REVOLUTIONARY ERA

The outbreak of the Russian revolution in 1917 provoked a struggle for power among Russians and between Russians and Muslims. The Russian provisional government established in February 1917 gave way in October to a Soviet regime. Officially, Communist Party doctrine proclaimed the right of all colonized peoples to self-determination and assured them the right of secession. The Commissariat for Nationality Affairs, established in 1917 with Joseph Stalin as chairman, was at first prepared to think in terms of cultural or political autonomy, but by 1919 the party was determined to assert its rule over Muslim populations. The Communists found themselves heir to regions inhabited by numerous Russians and to territories and peoples of great strategic and economic importance which they were loath to surrender. Russian populations in Inner Asia, regardless of political views, were also ready to fight to maintain Russian ethnic predominance.

While Russian Reds and Whites were embroiled in civil war, the Muslim intelligentsia and other regional and local leaders sought to take advantage of the breakdown of the Russian state. From 1917 to 1920 Muslims of Bashkiria, Kazakhstan, Azarbayjan, and the Caucasus struggled for regional independence. In the Urals, the Bashkirs, a people closely related to the Tatars, who earned a living from stock raising, forestry, and some agriculture, fought to stop Russian colonization and return Russian-occupied lands to Bashkir owners. In 1917 they formed the Bashkir National Council and withdrew from the All-Russian Muslim Congress. Stalin at first favored the formation of a Bashkir republic as an example of how the Soviets would support Muslim peoples; but local Tatars, who dreamed of a unified Tatar state, opposed Bashkir autonomy. The Bashkirs, too weak to win on their own, allied first with White and then Red Russians, but in 1920, supported by the Red Army, local Russians and Tatars destroyed the short-lived republic.

In Kazakhstan, the third All-Kazakh Congress in December 1917 proclaimed an autonomous region with capitals at Semipalatinsk and Jambeyty, and organized an independent Kazakh Muslim spiritual administration. Kazakhs demanded a halt to Russian colonization and the return of colonized lands. They came under attack from both the Bolsheviks and from Turkestani pan-Islamic critics, and found themselves involved in a complex civil war involving both White and Red Russians. In the end Alash Orda was defeated and an Autonomous Soviet Socialist Republic was declared in 1920. In Azarbayjan and the Caucasus local autonomy movements came to a similar end.

In other regions the Muslims strove not for full independence, but for cultural and partial political autonomy within a Russian-Soviet framework. In the Volga region Muslims formed moderate bourgeois and socialist parties which were often the outgrowth of associations that had developed after the 1905 revolution. Muslim congresses, held at Moscow and Kazan in May, July, and November 1917 were divided over whether they should seek cultural autonomy within a Russian state or form a federation of Muslim states. Successive congresses created a national council (*Milli Shura*) and an executive committee, a military council under Tatar and Bashkir leadership, and finally a constituent assembly, which declared the formation of an Idel-Ural Tatar state. This would-be state was dissolved by the Bolsheviks in 1918. Through the Central Commissariat for Muslim Affairs, Stalin succeeded in absorbing the Tatar socialists and national Communists into the Russian party, and in 1920 the Soviets organized a Tatar Autonomous Soviet Socialist Republic. In the Crimea Soviet rule was similarly established as a result of a coalition between the Russian Communist Party and the Milli Firqa party. The Democratic Tatar Republic, founded in 1917, came under Soviet control, and was reorganized in 1921 as the Soviet Republic of the Crimea.

In Turkestan, the path to Soviet rule was tortuous. The revolution of February 1917 led to the formation of an entirely Russian provisional government. In response, Muslim intellectual leaders called a congress in April 1917, in an atmosphere governed by the brutal suppression of the 1916 insurrections, famine, and open conflict between Muslims and Russians for control of the land. Most of the participants were Russian-educated intellectuals and Tatar merchants who favored cultural autonomy rather than political independence. Bolder delegates wanted territorial autonomy within a federated Russian state. All the delegates took a conciliatory attitude in the hope of future alliances with both liberal and radical Russians. They also feared the strength of conservative religious leaders who might well control any independent Muslim movement and defeat the reformist intellectuals. As a result, the congress split into two groups. One formed an Islamic council, which represented the jadid orientation and was committed to the formation of a modern state federated on an equal basis with the Russian state; the other organized an association of 'ulama' which was primarily concerned with the supremacy of the Shari'a.

In October 1917 the Soviets took power in Turkestan, and rejected Muslim participation in the government on the grounds that the Muslims did not represent the proletariat. In reaction, in November 1917 Muslims proclaimed an Autonomous Republic of Turkestan with its capital at Khokand – a republic based on the Shari'a, to be federated with Russia. The Khokand government, in its brief lifetime, opened new schools, created a militia, returned land to the peasants, redistributed waqfs, and gave grain to the poor, but in February 1918 it was overthrown by Russian forces. Thus of the two revolutions in Turkestan, the European proletarian and the Muslim bourgeois, the superior military power won out. Turkestan was declared an Autonomous Soviet Socialist Republic.

In 1919, concerned about Russian chauvinism and the hostility of Muslims to the narrowly Russian regime, Moscow sent a special commission to centralize power and to create some basis for cooperation with local people. In order to win jadid support the Russians now guaranteed religious freedom, and appointed a commissariat for Turkestani self-administration. Jadid leaders flocked to join the Communist Party, and worked to modify Russian policies to meet the needs of the Muslim population. Their priority was to cope with famine and disease.

While jadid intelligentsia tried to penetrate the regime from within, bandit-like resistance took hold in the countryside. Embittered former Khokand military units, landowners, merchants, village and clan notables, tribal chiefs, Sufis, unemployed tenant farmers, and workers were behind the so-called *basmachi* (rural bandit) resistance in the name of the Shari'a, the Prophet Muhammad, and the Muslim obligation of jihad. By 1920 the numerous and factious basmachi groups were driven by the Russians into the most remote rural areas. The basmachis, however, were not crushed. The introduction of anti-Muslim religious policies spurred renewed resistance. In 1921 and 1922 Enver Pasha, the former Ottoman minister of war, attempted to unify the movement. Enver, however, was killed in August 1922 and the opportunity was lost. In the meantime the Russians realized that military measures would not suffice to suppress the basmachis and decided to make political concessions. Waqf lands were restored, madrasas were reopened, and Shari'a courts were allowed to sit. Requisitions of cotton and other crops were suspended. Weakened by their own internal divisions, subverted by Soviet concessions, and overwhelmed by Russian military power, the basmachis were defeated. Sporadic resistance flared again in the late 1920s and early 1930s, but by 1924 Turkestan was effectively under Soviet control.

Bukhara and Khiva went through similar experiences of Soviet–Muslim collaboration and eventual reorganization and absorption into the Soviet state. The struggle in Bukhara began with the long-standing opposition between the Amir, the conservative Muslim administrative and religious elites, and the jadid reformers. The February revolution emboldened moderate jadidists to seek the formation of a salaried civil service, the separation of the treasury and the privy purse, and the removal of the chief qadi, who was a barrier to constructive reforms. The Young Bukharan radicals demanded the establishment of a parliament to limit the powers of the sovereign, freedom of teaching and publication, and exclusion of reactionary ministers from the cabinet. Allied with the Tashkent Soviet they tried to force the adoption of their program, but were defeated by a massive counter-demonstration led by conservative mullahs. However, in 1920 – with Russian military help – the Bukharan radicals established a Bukharan People's Soviet Republic, supported by wealthy merchant families. The new regime was declared a popular democracy committed to Islam and the Shari'a. It guaranteed rights of property, and freedom of association, publication, and religious conscience, and made promises of political reform, distribution of land, and enfranchisement of women. These promises, however, proved impossible to implement since the new regime lacked the personnel to replace the old elite.

The Russian–Bukharan coalition was soon superseded by full Communist rule. The consolidation of Soviet power began with the penetration of Russians and Tatars into the army, school system, customs services, militias, police, and administrative services. Trade treaties gave the Soviets a virtual monopoly of Bukharan commerce. In 1923 a Central Asiatic Economic Council was formed to integrate Bukharan territories into the monetary, transport, and communications networks of the Soviet Union. The Russian Communist Party accused the Bukharan party of bourgeois nationalist, pan-Islamic, and pan-Turkish tendencies, arrested Bukharan government officials, purged the party, and organized a new proletarian party hostile to Islam and to bourgeois influences. Incorporation into the Soviet Union as a Soviet Socialist Republic followed in 1924. Khiva had already been assimilated in 1923.

In most of these cases, the Muslim intelligentsias had to collaborate with the Russian Communist Party, for the Muslims lacked the political power to realize their cultural and ideological goals independently. They were deeply divided among themselves, and lacked organizational strength, military power, and direct contact with the masses. Besides, they were at odds with local chiefs and notables and with the conservative religious leaders. While some were hostile to the Russians, many were fully assimilated and imagined a cooperative future in the relations of Muslims and Russians. Vladimir Ilich Lenin's promises of self-determination, the diplomatic skills of Stalin, who held open the hope of a federal Russian system, and the hope that the Communists would give equality to Muslims brought them into the party. Some mistakenly identified the Russian revolution with jadid reform. Thus many former feudal nobles, rich merchants, reformed 'ulama', and intellectuals joined the Bolshevik party with the expectation that they would achieve equality with Russians and national liberation. Among the most important leaders to cooperate with the regime were Mir Said Sultan Galiev (1880–1928?), a Volga Tatar; Ahmad Baytursun (1873–1937), a Kazakh writer and founder of Alash Orda; 'Abd al-Rauf Fitrat (d. 1938), one of the ideological leaders of the Young Bukharans movement; Fayzullah Khoiaev (1896–1938), a young Bukharan; and Nariman Narimanov (1870–1933), an Azari social democrat and founder of Hummet.

Sultan Galiev and other Muslim Communists understood Communism not as a theory of proletarian revolution but as a practical doctrine which explained how to organize an underground movement, agitate, educate the masses, gain political support, and articulate national rights. They set aside the Marxist emphasis upon class struggle and the centrality of the proletariat to argue that colonial peoples, regardless of internal divisions, were proletarian nations and that their principal task was to win their independence. National revolution had to precede class struggle. The revolution, in their view, would be led by peasants rather than workers and would center on the countryside rather than on the cities. National liberation would enable Muslim countries to bypass the capitalist stage of historical development and enter directly into socialism. Sultan Galiev, expressing the almost universal mistrust of Russians, was skeptical of the Russian claim that socialism would put an end to colonialism, and held that a former capitalist oppressor nation, under socialism, would be a socialist oppressor nation. Emphasizing the national component of his political views, he believed that socialism and Islam were compatible and should be integrated into national Muslim societies.

This doctrine of international revolution and liberation of colonized peoples had important implications within the Soviet system. The national Muslim version of Communism enabled Muslim leaders to resist Russian interference in local affairs and to oppose policies promoting class struggle on the grounds that Islam minimized class antagonism and that national liberation from colonial rule had priority. It also articulated the desire to expel Russian colonists and be free of Russian political control. Some Muslim nationalists also harbored ambitions to infiltrate Muslims into the Communist Party, win control of education, and promote pan-Islamic and pan-Turkish ideals.

The Russian Communist Party vigorously opposed the Muslim national orientation. To counteract the Muslim Communists, Stalin worked assiduously to build up organizations that would assimilate the Muslim groups. Stalin's view – that there could be only one Communist Party in the Soviet Union, that class struggle was intrinsic and prior to national struggle, and that revolution would have to be pursued first in Europe rather than in Asia – prevailed. In 1923 the twelfth congress of the Russian Communist Party denounced the Georgian national Communists and demanded the subordination of regional parties to central interests. Sultan Galiev was vilified and expelled from the party as an opponent of centralized political power, a danger to Soviet security in the border regions, and a promoter of local nationalisms. In 1928 he was sent to a prison camp and disappeared.

Thus, in regions where Soviet and Muslim nationalists had formed an alliance, Russians ousted their Muslim rivals, and defeated armed resistance. While Muslim nationalist and reformist leaders in most Third World countries had generations to consolidate their position, mobilize mass support, achieve independence, and generate a national identity on their own terms, in the Soviet Union, Muslim leaders were quickly defeated. By 1920 the Soviets had established Tatar, Crimean, Kazakh, Turkestani, and Azarbayjani Soviet Socialist Republics, and two People's Republics in Khiva and Bukhara. The latter were changed into Soviet Socialist Republics in 1923 and 1924. In 1924 Turkestan, Bukhara, and Khwarizm were territorially regrouped, and four Inner Asian republics – Uzbekistan, Turkmenistan, Kazakhstan, and Kirgizia – were organized. They were founded on the basis of ethnic and linguistic similarities among the populations, but part of the plan was to divide the Muslims and forestall the development of a pan-Turkish national movement. The republics all belonged to the Union of Soviet Socialist Republics. In principle they were independent states federated for the purposes of defense, foreign policy, and economic management, but according to the Soviet constitution, Soviet law prevailed over local law, and all territories were considered the sovereign domain of the Soviet Union. In practice the republics were closely controlled by the Communist Party and the central state administration.

The system of "autonomous" national regimes was extended to other Muslim groups. According to Soviet classifications, Muslim nations (*natsii*, peoples who shared a common history, language, cultural identity, and political-territorial organization), comprising more than 300,000 members, included Uzbeks, Tatars, Kazakhs, Azaris, Tajiks, Turkmens, Kirgiz, Bashkirs, Chechens, Ossets, Avers, Lezghins, Kabardes, and Karakalpaks. Other smaller groups, based on the unification of tribal people by shared language, but not having all of the characteristics of nations, were classified as nationalities (*narodnosti*). From 1936 to the dissolution of the Soviet Union in 1991 the various nations and nationalities were organized into six Soviet Socialist Republics (Uzbekistan, Azarbayjan, Kazakhstan, Turkmenistan, Tajikistan, and Kirgizia) and eight Autonomous Soviet Socialist Republics, including Tataristan, Bashkiria, Daghestan, and other Caucasian units. There were also four lesser-scale autonomous provinces in the Caucasus.

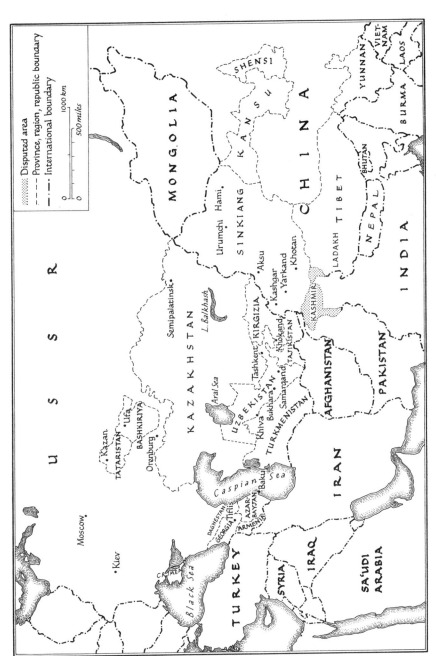

Map 35 Soviet and Chinese Inner Asia to 1990

Disputed area
Province, region, republic boundary
International boundary

1000 km
500 miles

Moscow
Kiev
Black Sea
CRIMEA
TURKEY
SYRIA
IRAQ
SA'UDI ARABIA
IRAN
DAGHESTAN
GEORGIA
ARMENIA
AZARBAYJAN
Tiflis
Baku
Caspian Sea
Aral Sea
Khiva
Bukhara
TURKMENISTAN
UZBEKISTAN
Samarqand
TAJIKISTAN
Khokand
Tashkent
KIRGIZIA
Kazan
TATARISTAN
Ufa
BASHKIRIYA
Orenburg
KAZAKHSTAN
L. Balkhash
Semipalatinsk
MONGOLIA
Urumchi
Hami
SINKIANG
Aksu
Kashgar
Yarkand
Khotan
KASHMIR
AFGHANISTAN
PAKISTAN
LADAKH
TIBET
NEPAL
BHUTAN
INDIA
CHINA
KANSU
SHENSI
YUNNAN
BURMA
VIET-NAM
LAOS

U   S   S   R

SOVIET MODERNIZATION

The pre-World War II era

The organization of a system of Soviet Socialist Republics opened the way for a radical effort to modernize the conditions of life and the consciousness of Inner Asian peoples, and to integrate them into Soviet society. To achieve these goals the Soviets subordinated Inner Asian peoples to Russian bureaucratic and political machinery, and undertook the economic transformation of native societies. Soviet political and economic policies were accompanied by direct efforts to subvert religious and family culture in order to promote instead Soviet-oriented "national" cultures.

The 1920s and 1930s were the crucial first phase in this process. In this period the Soviets worked out a system of governmental and party controls to assure the dominance of the central regime. Starting in 1922 and 1923 they began to remove the Muslim old guard and bourgeois nationalists in the Communist Parties of Turkestan, Bukhara, Khiva, and other regions, and replace them with more dedicated Russian and local "proletarian" cadres. By 1928 the Communist Parties of Tataristan and the Crimea had also been purged. All of the literary, cultural, and scientific institutions of the Volga region were brought under Soviet control. In the 1930s the Communist Parties of Kazakhstan, Uzbekistan, Kirgizia, Tajikistan, and the Crimea were systematically purged. By 1937 and 1938 the older generation of Muslim national Communists had been totally destroyed. Despite paying lip service to the rights of national minorities, the Soviets asserted the absolute primacy of the central party and central government ministries. "The right to self-determination cannot and must not serve as an obstacle to the exercise by the working class of its right to dictatorship" was the policy implemented by Stalin.

Communist Party purges in the 1920s and 1930s raised the problem of finding politically loyal and technically proficient cadres. In Uzbekistan and other republics the Russians oscillated between efforts to promote native cadres in the interest of "affirmative action" and the employment of Russian experts. By the middle and late 1930s, however, the party had to acknowledge the educational deficiencies that hampered the training and employment of local peoples, and switched to a policy stressing Russian experts and the use of Russian as an international language. The lack of an adequately educated local population, and the desire of Europeans to command the government institutions meant that, in varying degrees, Russian personnel dominated the government and party apparatuses of the Inner Asian republics.

Economic development in Inner Asia had to begin virtually from scratch. From 1914 to 1920, civil war, famine, brigandage, and government confiscations had taken a tremendous toll. Untold numbers of people died in the revolutionary years. Agricultural and manufacturing output fell to minuscule levels. To restore the economy to pre-revolutionary levels the Soviets had to go back on their initial proposals to institute collective farming and adopted the New Economic Policy (NEP). They returned confiscated lands to their Muslim owners, and encouraged the reconstruction of irrigation works, the replacement of draft animals, and other measures to repair the damages of the civil war period. The Soviets de-nationalized many enterprises and dropped forced requisitions. For a long time the government gave up trying to settle nomads, but assigned them fixed pastures – a measure that was conducive to partial sedentarization. The greatest efforts were made to increase cotton production at the expense of rice and other crops. By 1928 the NEP had brought agricultural and industrial production to about 70 percent of 1913 levels.

With the mending of the Inner Asian economies the Soviets launched a program of land reform. In Turkestan they began by seizing the land and water rights of landlords and waqfs. In 1924 they determined to eliminate "feudal and tribal survivals," seize all large properties and the "excess" properties of middle and small landowners, and redistribute the land among the poor and landless peasants. The goal was to increase the well-being of the poorest stratum of peasants, to break the political backbone of both the secular and religious rural elites, and to open the society to the more drastic reorganizations to follow. Land reform was carefully prepared by the organization of an agricultural workers' propaganda movement called Koshchi, which tried to undermine respect for traditional authority, encourage the peasants to drive out landowners, and promote class warfare. This was difficult because the economic and social gap between large and small owners was not in fact clearly demarcated and because of the close cultural and religious ties between the larger owners and the poorer peasants. Cooperatives and unions were also intended to accustom peasants to collective organization.

The great drive for collectivization of agriculture and the industrialization of the Inner Asian republics (and the whole of the Soviet Union) began in 1928. State farms and collectives were introduced that year. Between 1929 and 1934 a new trade union of agricultural and forestry workers was organized. In 1934 machine tractor stations were introduced to centralize state control over agricultural production and promote more efficient utilization of mechanized resources. Peasants on collective farms were closely regimented. A new elite of collective-farm administrators and a new proletariat of agricultural workers came into being. By 1937 collectivization was about 95 percent complete. Tajikistan, for example, was transformed from a subsistence area to a producer of cotton, grain, fruit, and livestock for export.

Kazakhstan was a special case. Here land reform began in 1921 and 1922 with the distribution of water rights among the poor settlers; in 1926 and 1927 some 2,000,000 acres were taken from wealthy landowners and given to the poor. This was followed in 1928 by a redistribution of herds, forced sedentarization, and forced collectivization that squeezed the nomads into livestock collectives and state farms. By 1932 the sedentarization of Kazakhs was considered complete, but the costs were enormous. The Kazakh population declined by some 900,000 in the 1930s owing to executions and emigration to China, and there was a catastrophic collapse in the size of animal herds.

Industrial development in Inner Asia was of primary importance in long-term Soviet plans but of limited impact in the 1920s and 1930s. From 1917 to 1922, civil war and nationalizations led to the collapse of the cotton-processing industry, but this was restored, and from 1928 to 1941 the Soviets introduced mechanized textile production and engineering industries, and increased the production of coal and electric power, which served as a basis for further industrialization. Development in Kazakhstan was limited to the restoration of agricultural processing, and meat-packing, wool, and canning industries.

While economic development was limited, the Soviets achieved an educational miracle by providing mass education in Inner Asia to the same standards that prevailed throughout the Soviet Union. The scope and success of this effort is unrivaled in any colonial regime or any independent Muslim country. In 1930 primary education was made universal and compulsory, and a literacy campaign to educate adults between the ages of sixteen and thirty was launched. Local languages were used for instruction, though in 1938 Russian was made obligatory in minority schools. Until the 1940s the main objective was to make the population literate and to promote the acceptance of Soviet society. After that, emphasis was placed upon occupational training.

The literacy campaign was accompanied by an intensive effort to promote national cultures as the vehicle for the inculcation of a socialist mentality. The Soviet regime had divided the Muslims into a number of national states in an attempt to break down both sub-national tribal loyalties and supra-national religious or ethnic consciousness, and to encourage national identities that could be integrated into the Soviet political order. The concept of nation, however, had scarcely any precedent in pre-Soviet Muslim political culture. Most Muslims considered themselves members of a particular tribe, town, or village; only the elites identified themselves with territorial states such as Khokand or Bukhara; only jadidists accepted the idea of a pan-Turkish or pan-Islamic political identity. Now, in the framework of the national republics an intense socialization and indoctrination program was carried out through schools, political meetings, theaters, clubs, newspapers, lectures, folk art, and parades led by a new generation of party activists, writers, and teachers. In the cultural field the Soviets attempted to blend regional culture into Soviet culture, using local history, languages, epics, folklore, and arts to carry the socialist message.

The most important changes were language and literature reforms. In 1926 the Soviets decided at a Turkological congress held in Baku to eliminate Arabic script and introduce the Latin alphabet for all Turkic languages. The new alphabet had complex political implications. While it cut Muslim peoples off from the literatures of the past, it put Inner Asian Muslims in contact with Turkey, which also used the Latin alphabet. The Latin alphabet, furthermore, made it difficult to learn Russian. Thus in 1939 and 1940 the Soviets introduced a new Cyrillic script, and attempted to modernize Inner Asian languages by promoting an ever-increasing use of Russian terms, some of which are international technical and scientific words modified to conform to Inner Asian phonemes and grammar.

The Soviets also made intensive efforts to modernize literature. In 1925 they called for the formation of national, as opposed to pan-Turkish or pan-Islamic, cultures. In 1934 they created a writers' union to define new criteria for writing and publication, and to oblige writers to follow the party line. The introduction of political controls over nationality literatures led to a tortuous struggle between the writers and the censors. In the 1920s and 1930s minority nationality writers responded to Soviet pressures by generating a new form of Soviet socialist realism in local languages, but Inner Asian writers also attempted to preserve the traditional and classical cultures while acknowledging only the most important Soviet themes. The purges of the late 1930s, however, destroyed the nationalist poets and intellectuals.

At the same time that the Soviet regime helped promote national cultures, it made strenuous efforts to undermine Islam as an organized religion and as an influence in social and cultural affairs. Religion was considered a barrier to the full assimilation of citizens into Soviet society. Soviet policy toward Islam was inherently antagonistic, and favored the "dying out" or eradication of religious belief. In the civil war period from 1918 to 1920, the Soviets attempted to destroy all of the public aspects of Islam, including Muslim judicial administration, religious properties, and schools, but their decrees were not effectively implemented. The 'ulama' opposed revolutionary concepts as atheistic, and stirred popular resistance to Soviet policies. The basmachi resistance and pressure from local elites forced the Soviets to restore Muslim schools, colleges, mosques, and endowments. A *makhama-i shari'a*, or Muslim Directorate, was established in Tashkent to supervise the administration of schools, the training of teachers, and the appointment of mosque functionaries. The Soviets had to concede that Islam had retained its hold on the beliefs and identity of the people. Nonetheless, from their point of view some progress had been made; the influence of the 'ulama' decreased in urban areas and Muslims began to rely more and more upon secular schools and courts.

The creation of the national republics in 1924 opened the way for a new Soviet effort at secularization, this time with lasting effect. In 1923 the separation of church and state was again proclaimed. Between 1923 and 1928 new laws were passed to deny religious organizations the right to exist as corporate bodies or own property, confiscate large religious endowments, abolish religious courts, and eliminate religious education. A government agency took over complete control of waqfs, and by 1930 effectively legislated them out of existence. This was similar to what happened in most Muslim countries. While qadi and customary courts continued for a time to apply Muslim law concerning polygamy, bride price, and legal procedures, portions of Shari'a that contradicted Soviet law were progressively declared invalid, and in practice Muslims were obliged to turn to Russian courts. In 1926 the Shari'a courts were reduced to voluntary agencies, and by 1927 they had virtually disappeared.

About this time most Muslim schools were forced to close. These measures were accompanied by intense anti-religious propaganda by the League of Militant Atheists, including attacks on belief in God, the Quran, and upon prayer and fasting. In 1929 Muslim religious leaders were arrested. Many were killed, and the Muslim religious administration was suppressed.

A major part of the Soviet anti-religious campaign was directed toward family law. Between 1924 and 1926 a new family law was promulgated which provided for equality of women's rights in divorce and property. The new law made the legal age of marriage sixteen for females and eighteen for males, abolished the bride price, prohibited polygamy and abduction, and gave women full rights to participate in the labor force. The practice of wearing the veil or *paranja*, which totally covers face and body, was denounced. Social pressures within the Muslim community, however, prevented women from changing traditional practices and asserting their legal rights. While stressing women's proper role in the labor force, by 1936 the Soviets conceded the importance of the "socialist" family and the roles of wife and mother. By this time, however, the whole institutional structure of Islamic worship, education, justice, and property had been destroyed.

Post-World War II

After World War II, the Soviet Union continued its basic program of political and economic assimilation of the Muslim populations, but its religious and cultural policies were significantly modified, especially after the death of Stalin in 1953. Russians continued to dominate controlling positions in the party, the political police, the army, planning, communications, local industry, irrigation, transport, finance, and banking, but certain "representative" posts, such as first Communist Party secretary, chairman of the council of ministers, or membership in the presidium of the Supreme Soviet, were reserved for Inner Asians. Powerful positions in both governmental and party organizations were staffed by Russians or by Muslim functionaries with Russian (or other European) "doubles." One common arrangement was the appointment of nationals as first secretaries and Russians as second secretaries to control the party functionaries. Russian domination was partly a question of political reliability and partly a problem of the recruitment of adequately trained native cadres. Russians were suspicious of the technical and educational qualifications of local people and of their social and cultural style.

There was a similar long-term continuity in policies of economic development. During World War II the Soviet government further built up Uzbekistan, Kazakhstan, and the Urals in order to create an industrial base behind the battle lines. After World War II fertilizer, steel, electric power, coal, oil, and natural gas were developed. Substantial irrigation programs added millions of hectares to the arable land of Turkestan, but backward methods of agriculture, and lack of fertilizer and machinery, inhibited the development of the cotton industries. By the end of the 1960s the substitution of machines for hand labor in cotton harvesting made it possible to cultivate newly irrigated land and increased the productivity of labor. Nikita Khrushchev's (1953–64) virgin lands program in Kazakhstan completed the process of turning the region from nomadic pastoralism to agriculture.

While there was considerable industrialization in Inner Asia, most of it was concentrated in cotton and textile production, food processing, hydro-electric development, copper mining in Kazakhstan, and oil extraction in Baku. Moscow extracted valuable raw materials including cotton, metals, and fuels from its still relatively underdeveloped Inner Asian regions, but in return subsidized industrial and agricultural investments. Large numbers of Russian and Ukrainian workers provided the managerial and skilled working cadres. Economic changes generated new institutions such as factories, collective farms, and unions, and brought a large number of workers into a modern economy. Under Soviet rule Inner Asia achieved a higher standard of living than almost any other Asian-Muslim country. By the 1950s diet was adequate and in the 1960s housing was improved. The Muslim population, which had declined in the bitter revolutionary and civil war years and stagnated between 1917 and 1959, began to grow rapidly. It rose from 24,000,000 in 1959 to 47,000,000 in 1970. It grew four to five times as fast as the Slavic population owing to a large increase in fertility, which was not checked by rising incomes, education, or urbanization. The Soviet government tolerated private initiative in food production, marketing, contracted services, and housing.

The maturation of the Soviet education system led to an ever-increasing employment of Muslims in government, party, and technical positions, diminishing the role of Russians, Jews, and other Europeans. Local participation was vigorously promoted, and native cadres were rapidly integrated into the Soviet state and party organizations. By 1975 Muslim technicians formed 57.6 percent of the workforce in Uzbekistan. Educationally and socially less developed regions, such as Tajikistan, had proportionally smaller native cadres. Despite this rapid integration, however, Muslims neither aspired to social integration nor suffered from discrimination. They had a status structure of their own, looking down upon lower classes of Russian settlers as uneducated and uncultivated people.

After Stalin's death, the Soviet government became more tolerant of non-Russian cultures. While Khrushchev advocated an internationalist and unitary Soviet society, he recognized that the fusion of nations was not likely to be soon accomplished. After Leonid Brezhnev assumed power in 1964, official pronouncements and speeches tended to stress the shared values of Soviet peoples, but not the assimilation of nationalities. Ideology and similar socio-economic principles defined the Soviet people, but national and ethnic differences were accepted as part of political reality. In practice this meant that the minorities were accorded a measure of cultural autonomy in return for their acceptance of the primacy of Russian language and culture.

Thus, Stalin's death allowed for a revival and recreation of national cultures. Inner Asian oral literatures had survived in the forms of songs for weddings and funerals, tales, legends, and epic poems, and continued to be published and discussed. Historical novels and epic poems dealing with the glories of the past were published, and literary and anthropological studies recognized the eastern heritage of Uzbeks, Kazakhs, and other Asian peoples. The schools taught a modified form of their literary and historical past. Periodicals were published in Kazakh, Uzbek, Azeri, Tatar, Turkmen, Kirgiz, Tajik, Bashkir, and other languages. *Mirasism*, or "rediscovery of the pre-revolutionary national patrimony," became an important cultural trend. Despite this liberalization, a vast number of books printed in Turkish and Inner Asian languages had primarily a Russian and European content, and novels and other literary works were constrained by Soviet political supervision.

The overall effect was to consolidate a new sense of nationality. While Uzbeks became politically loyal citizens of the Soviet Union, integral members of the administrative and technical workforce, fluent speakers of Russian, and European in public dress and manners, they still identified themselves as Uzbeks and condemned the effort to "pass" or assimilate completely into a Russian identity. Similarly, Kazakh intellectuals tried to reconcile political loyalty and ethnic identity, and to reinterpret their national past in ways consistent with their Soviet present. Soviet Muslims were highly acculturated but not assimilated into Russian society.

In the postwar era, Soviet policy toward Islam also moderated, but the official position was still hostile. From 1941 to 1953, in order to pacify Muslim opinion and win support for the war effort, the Soviet regime allowed the 'ulama' to rebuild Islamic religious organizations under state control. In 1943 the muftiat, or Directorate of Muslim Peoples, was reestablished in Tashkent with jurisdiction over Uzbekistan, Kazakhstan, Kirgizia, Tajikistan, and Turkmenistan. Separate departments of religious affairs were recognized at Baku for Azarbayjan, at Ufa for Russian and Siberian Tatars, and at Makhachkala (in Daghestan) for the North Caucasus. Each of these boards was headed by an elected mufti, but the North Caucasus had two chiefs, a Sunni mufti and a Shi'i Shaykh al-Islam. Councils of 'ulama' and mosque representatives were called to give fatwas, or legal decrees, concerning religious and ritual matters, such as laws of marriage, divorce, and circumcision. Local mosque congregations were administered by an elected *mutawalliyat* or administrative committee, which controlled the mosque's buildings and other property, and by an elected auditing commission. Elected lay members of the congregation took over the authority of the imams. They reported to the Council for the Affairs of Religious Cults, which had been established in 1944, and religious activity outside the control of these organizations was deemed illegal.

The Muslim Board for Central Asia and Kazakhstan was the most important, and its influence and authority extended throughout the Soviet Union. It managed a number of mosques. The board also administered the only two madrasas in the Soviet Union that trained students to be religious functionaries, the Mir-i Arab Madrasa of Bukhara and the more advanced Imam al-Bukhari Islamic Institute in Tashkent. Apart from the two colleges there were no Muslim schools, no Shari'a courts, and no endowed waqfs.

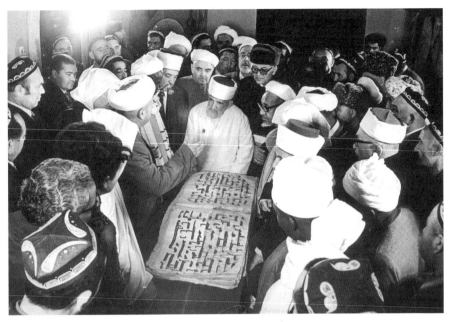

29 'Ulama' study the Quran in Tashkent

The Tashkent board was an active publisher of religious materials. Its publications included collections of hadith, classical texts, and the only Muslim periodical published in the Soviet Union, *Muslims of the Soviet East*. This journal was published in English, French, Russian, Arabic, Persian, Dari, and Uzbek. It published historical and literary notes, reviews of religious texts, and discussions of the preservation of monuments. It gave religious advice on such questions as observance of Ramadan and the birthday of the Prophet, and visits to saints' shrines.

Despite the organization of Muslim administration, a strong anti-religious campaign was carried out under Khrushchev from 1954 to 1964; it involved the "deregistration" of Muslim clerics and the suppression of mosques. After Khrushchev's demise the Soviet regime adopted educational and persuasive methods, instead of administrative or police measures, to restrict religious activity. An elaborate anti-religious propaganda campaign, including publications, films, radio broadcasts, and reports of research institutes, assailed Islam. Soviet academic writers treated Islam as an archaic residue of an outmoded society. In the 1970s there was a fresh anti-Islamic campaign directed at Sufism in the Caucasus. The campaign stressed the incompatibility of religion and modern science, and the superiority of Communist to Muslim morals.

In response, Muslim religious leaders attempted to demonstrate the compatibility of Islam, modernity, and socialism. They praised Soviet society for its economic achievements and published photographs of power plants next to those of mosques. They also defended the Soviet Union against its Western critics, and strongly supported Soviet foreign policy with articles on fraternal delegations from Muslim countries, reports on disarmament and anti-nuclear conferences, and strong advocacy of the Palestinian struggle against Israel. 'Ulama' played an important part in Soviet foreign affairs by receiving delegations, making official visits abroad, and propagandizing for the advantages of Islam under socialism. Their very position required them to support the Soviet system and to adapt Islam to the requirements of a socialist society. They were also sensitive to the needs of a secular, technically trained Muslim population for whom religious belief had to be justified and made meaningful in contemporary terms. Moreover, the Muslim religious leaders were themselves Soviet-educated citizens, participating in a Soviet society through part-time employment in the workforce and through marriage and family ties. Their own identity depended upon a blending of Soviet modernity and Islam. The maintenance of an official religious establishment indicated a tacit collaboration between the government and the 'ulama'. The government sponsored the Muslim administration in the hope of winning Muslim support, and for fear that disestablishment would reinforce underground Islamic movements. The leaders of official Islam lent their support to the Soviet regime in return for the opportunity to maintain a Muslim organization.

Alongside official or state-administered religion, there also flourished a "parallel Islam," or unofficial Muslim religious activity, which was especially strong in rural areas. Sufi brotherhoods, highly decentralized, were still important in the tribal regions of Turkmenistan, Kirgizia, Kazakhstan, and the Caucasus. Pilgrimage to shrines and saints' graves played an important part in preserving an unofficial Muslim religious life. Among less-educated people animistic practices survived under the guise of Islam. Amulets were used to ward off spirits, exorcise demons, and heal injuries. The cult of ancestors, sometimes inherited from pre-Islamic sanctuaries, and shamanism continued to be practiced. Alongside the Sufis there were numerous healers, wandering shamans, and other holy men. In family affairs there were strong survivals of pre-Islamic rituals marking the births of children, and magical ceremonies on the occasions of marriages and funerals. In these cases, the persistence of traditional beliefs may be related to the persistence of communities that were not absorbed into the mainstream of Soviet economic and political life. In general, however, urbanization associated with industrialization, higher levels of formal education, and the incorporation of women into the workforce tended to secularize Soviet-Muslim populations. This secularization, especially among professionals and skilled workers, meant a declining attention to prayer, fasting, mourning, and other religious ceremonies. Still, even the educated intelligentsia remained strongly attached to their native languages, ethnic identities, and religious customs. They did not intermarry with Russians, and they resisted assimilation by practicing traditional customs in relation to women, Ramadan observances and festivals, and Muslim rituals in birth, circumcision, marriage, and burial ceremonies.

While some of the Muslim elite was coopted by the Soviet system, the masses were not assimilated. Muslims maintained a distrustful sense of separateness, an identity based on multiple and sometimes conflicting loyalties directed to clan and tribe, national republics, the universal Muslim community, and the Soviet federal regime. Muslims held a modulated concept of political identity involving Soviet citizenship, minority nationality, and an Islamic heritage.

Thus, the Muslims of the former Soviet Union experienced intensive economic and social modernization and the inculcation of new values through Soviet scholastic and political education. In the Soviet Union traditional social structures were broken down, traditional elites eliminated, and traditional religious educational, legal, and ritual practices constrained or abolished. The 'ulama' establishment was made dependent upon the state. Independent Sufi brotherhoods existed only as clandestine organizations and probably had a limited following, except in parts of the Caucasus. Even on the level of personal belief, Islam diminished, as the worldview of Muslim citizens of the Soviet Union came to be formed by Soviet political and scientific concepts. At the same time the Soviets helped cultivate secularized national identities as a bridge to the integration of Muslims into a multi-national Soviet political society.

Though Islam was disestablished on a political level, Muslim belief and identity remained important. Even politically assimilated Muslims – who considered themselves Soviet citizens, who were loyal to the state and accepted its socialist political and economic values, who spoke Russian, wore European dress, and assumed European manners, and who possessed modern technical and administrative skills – maintained a separate identity on the level of ethnic and family culture and self-image. Cultivated by language and ethnic consciousness, Islam continued to have a subjective hold on Soviet populations of Muslim background. In rural areas, among rural migrants to cities, and among older persons not affected by the process of social and economic change, Muslim belief remained in full force. Though there was a strong continuity of regime in Turkey, and the greatest possible break with the historical past in the Soviet Union, in both cases modern secular states pressed Islam into becoming a religion of personal faith and social identity.

NEWLY INDEPENDENT STATES IN FORMERLY SOVIET INNER ASIA

The breakup of the Soviet Union in 1991 put an end to decades of struggle over Muslim religious and national identities, but the formation of independent states did not lead to a clarification of these issues. Rather, it led to an intensification of conflicts over political power, economic resources, and national, regional, and religious identities.

By the time of Mikhail Gorbachev (1986–91), nationality minorities were beginning to protest against Soviet policy and authority. In 1988 there were anti-government riots in Kazakhstan. Nationalist protests demanding the use of Kirgiz broke out in 1989. In Uzbekistan there was ethnic conflict in the Farghana Valley, and Russians began to leave the region. Between August and December 1991 the Central Asian states declared their independence and on December 9, 1991 Soviet leaders meeting in Minsk officially declared an end to the Soviet Union and formed the new Commonwealth of Independent States, with promises of military and economic cooperation among the now separate and sovereign members.

Though newly independent, the Central Asian states (Uzbekistan, Tajikistan, Kyrgyzstan, Turkmenistan, and Kazakhstan) are all governed by their former Communist Party bosses, now self-declared nationalists and secularists. All the new regimes are highly authoritarian, and are based on closely controlled political and police institutions. Their opponents look to a variety of populist, tribal, ethnic, and religious agendas.

With independence the regional economies broke down. The Soviet economy had centered on cotton production, mining, and other resource extraction. Cotton production pushed out food crops and made the region dependent upon imported supplies. Pesticides and fertilizers polluted the land. Irrigation used up valuable water supplies and contributed to the shrinking of the Aral Sea. Productivity actually fell in the last years of the Soviet regime. Moreover, the Central Asian states were exploited as colonies. While they produced much of the Soviet cotton, they produced little of the cloth. Hydro-electric power projects supplied both the region and European Russia with electricity, but Central Asian oil and gas reserves, apart from Kazakhstan, were neglected. Universal literacy was a great achievement, but social welfare and health services lagged behind the already poor Soviet standards. The Soviet legacy – combined with inflation, food shortages, high unemployment, mafia-like control of businesses, corruption, and political instability –has contributed to an economic disaster. While the new states have promised a liberalization of the economy, little land has been distributed to individual owners.

The Central Asian region is rich in oil and gas supplies – Kazakhstan, Turkmenistan, and Azarbayjan have promising reserves – but the new states cannot export their oil or gas without going through the territory of other countries. Regional competition has blocked the economic opportunities of all. Russia attempts to control the pipeline routes that already cross its territory and to tap supplies that Turkmenistan and Kazakhstan would rather sell for higher prices in Europe. For new pipelines Russia favors routes across its own territories to the Black Sea. Turkmenistan, dreaming of becoming another Kuwait, prefers new lines via Turkey and Iran. Turkey, however, backed by the United States, objects that the Black Sea routes require passage through the Straits which are already dangerously overcrowded, and favors the construction of new pipelines that would bring resources directly to the Mediterranean. The shortest export routes would cross Iran, but this is opposed by the United States for political reasons. In the meantime there is considerable uncertainty over the extent of Caspian Sea oil and gas reserves, and whether the required investments would be profitable. Political instability and numerous local conflicts also deter foreign investors.

In most of the newly independent Central Asian states national identities are contested and hard to consolidate. Governments favor a national and secular definition

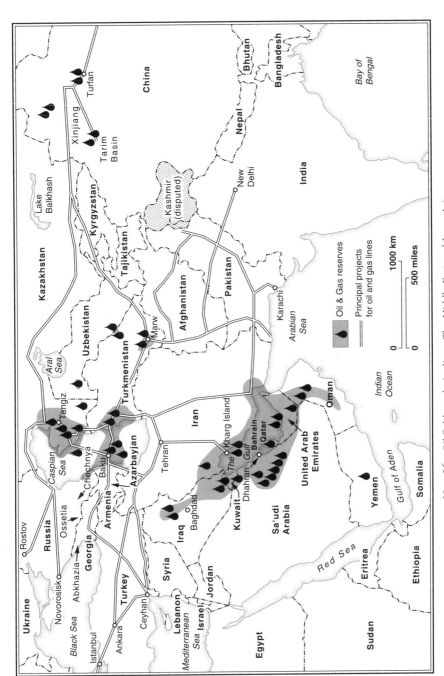

Map 36 Oil fields and pipelines: The Middle East and Inner Asia

of identity, and are hostile to Islamist movements, but the former Communist Party regimes are opposed by a variety of factional, ethnic, nationalist, and Islamic groups. Tensions run high in all the newly independent states between the resident Russian populations and the non-Russian native populations. In each country the majority ethnic population would like its own language to be the national language, and they have taken measures to declare Turkmen, or Uzbek or Kazakh – as the case may be – the national language, but they have nonetheless been obliged to recognize a special status for Russian due to the large Russian populations, the critical role played by Russians in the economy and administration, and the importance of their Russian ally. There are conflicts between the majority and ethnic minorities in each country. In some cases local, tribal, and clan polities oppose the central governments. No unifying political parties have emerged.

In all the Central Asian states, the formation of national identities is complicated by the Islamic revival. In the last moments of the Soviet Union Islam was still tightly controlled by the Soviet state, with only two madrasas functioning in the whole of the Soviet Union to train clerics, and only a handful of selected delegates permitted to make the pilgrimage to Mecca and Medina. With the demise of the Soviet Union a host of hitherto suppressed tendencies emerged, including militant movements aimed at the formation of Islamic states, often inspired by influences from abroad, pan-Islamic and pan-Turkish teachings, jadid-type reformism, energetic local 'ulama' leadership in the construction of mosques and schools, and revived Sufism. With strong external support from Sa'udi Arabia, the Gulf states and Pakistan there is a so-called Wahhabi revival, preaching a reformist or scripturalist version of Islam, hostile to local Sufism, and particularly active in building mosques and schools and sponsoring Islamic religious instruction. The so-called Wahhabi movements, however, have found it difficult to cross ethnic lines and have raised deep local suspicions because of their reputation for having promoted civil conflict in Afghanistan and Tajikistan. At the same time a Sufi revival restores the traditional Sufi functions of worship, healing, and instruction, and popular Muslim beliefs and practices. Finally, Islamic political parties have emerged in Tajikistan and Uzbekistan, committed to the founding of an Islamic state. In the newly independent states the ruling elites have tried to coopt the religious leaders. The Kazakhstan Religious Board, created in imitation of the Soviet Central Asian Religious Board, sponsors religious education, repairs mosques, and sends delegates on the pilgrimage. Uzbekistan and Turkmenistan have similar religious bodies.

The Muslim situation is a microcosm of all the varieties of Muslim belief, practice, and organization found throughout the world. The diversity of the Islamic revival in Central Asia means that no unified or politically decisive movement has emerged. Nor does Islam unify the various ethnic communities; each of them has its own schools, mosques, shops, and cafes.

The political situation in each of the major countries is profoundly unsettled. In Kazakhstan, Nursultan Nazarbayev runs a presidential regime, but one that steers carefully amidst the pressures of a substantial Russian population, the escalating demands of Kazakh nationalism, intense international pressures to cope with Kazakhstan's nuclear weapons, and an enormous potential for the development of the Tengiz gas and oilfields, which cannot be fully realized until a pipeline outlet is decided upon. President Nazarbayev tries to keep good relations with Moscow, but promotes Kazakh cultural identity to ward off militant Kazakh nationalism. The opposition parties – Azat, the Freedom Party, and the anti-nuclear and Green party called Semipalatinsk-Nevada – which opposed the continuation of the old Communist Party elite, and extremist Kazakh nationalist and Islamic parties, now mostly underground, have been crushed. Islam still holds considerable appeal as the basis of an independent Kazakh identity. The Qadi of Alma Ata, Radbek Nisanbai, attempted to lead a religious revival, translating the Quran into Kazakh, opening a madrasa, printing a newspaper, and building numerous mosques. Islam appeals even more to non-Kazakh minorities, who see it as a way to differentiate themselves from both Kazakhs and Russians.

Uzbekistan is ruled by President Islam Karimov, the former head of the Uzbek Communist Party, now called the National Democratic Party. Karimov runs an authoritarian regime, which imposes tight political and economic controls, and aspires to be the leader of all the Central Asian states, but the Uzbek economy founders, and the World Bank and foreign investors avoid this dictatorial regime. The political opposition is extremely varied, and fragmented. There have been clashes between Uzbek nationalists and various minority groups, especially in the Farghana Valley. Karimov has banned Birlik, the Uzbek nationalist movement that calls for his removal, separation from Russian influence, and a pan-Turkish alliance. Muslim opposition is fragmented. The official Islamic hierarchy faces opposition from the Sa'udi-supported Ahle Sunna, which builds mosques and madrasas, the militant Islamic Movement of Uzbekistan, which may have several thousand fighters and calls for the formation of an Islamic state, and the Islamic Democratic Party, which calls for the implementation of the Shari'a but opposes violence. The Islamic reformist and political movements denounce popular Sufism as a Zionist and Turkish conspiracy against Islam. Sectarianism and divisions among Muslims subverts their potential power, and the government suppresses both Islamic political and social and moral reform movements. The American intervention in Afghanistan has further strengthened President Karimov's position vis-à-vis the Islamists.

Kyrgyzstan is ruled by Askar Akaev, a former physicist who was elected as a liberal leader in 1991 on the basis of promises to privatize the economy. In July 1994 Akaev disbanded parliament, shut down the opposition press, assumed dictatorial powers, and in practice abandoned the program for privatization and market development. While Muslim movements remain active in the principal cities of Beshkeh and Osh, building mosques and schools, Islamic political parties have been suppressed.

Turkmenistan is ruled by Saparmurad Niyazov, called Turkmenbashi, also a former Communist Party chief who declared his country's independence in August

1990 and was elected President in 1991. The Communist Party, now called the Democratic Party of Turkmenistan, is the sole active party under an essentially dictatorial regime.

Unlike the other Central Asian states, Tajikistan has disintegrated into civil war. Rakhmon Nabiev, the former Communist Party governor of the country, tried to maintain the old Communist Party hierarchy, and to consolidate his power by repressive measures. Nabiev was opposed by a strong Islamic Renaissance Party, which called for the formation of an Islamic state. While he was able to hold this party in check, rival regional and tribal elites, Afghan- and Iranian-sponsored factions, and Russian and Uzbek interventions broke down civil order. After a series of bitter and destructive conflicts a new regional coalition led by forces from Kuliab province was able to elect Emamli Rakhmonov as President in November 1994. Tajikistan remains the most embattled of the new Central Asian states.

Russia, Turkey, and Iran all maneuver to maintain or generate spheres of influence and to support factions and policies favorable to their own interests. In the Caucasus and Central Asia, Turkey has attempted to assert its leadership by promoting a Black Sea Economic Cooperation Council, making extensive investments in the infrastructures in the new Central Asian Republics, student exchanges, television broadcasts, and by sending volunteer technical and professional experts. It has also taken part in the creation of a new Western alphabet for Central Asian Turkic languages. Turkey's influence, however, is relatively limited. Turkish initiatives in this area have been checked by Russia, which considers itself the patron power of the former Soviet states. The Russians have negotiated a mutual assistance treaty with Uzbekistan and other republics, and have intervened in disputes between Uzbekistan and Tajikistan. Russia and Turkey remain rivals for the development of alternative pipeline routes for the export of regional oil and gas.

Iran also has an important role to play in Central Asia. It has close cultural ties with Persian-speaking Tajikistan. It has sponsored an Association of Persian Languages, a Caspian Sea Economic Organization, and has funded the Islamic Renaissance Party in Tajikistan. Iran has rail links and proposed oil and gas links to Turkmenistan. It is a key player in the Caspian Sea region.

THE CAUCASUS

The Caucasus region lies outside Inner Asia, but it too was absorbed by Russia in the late eighteenth and nineteenth centuries. Historically, Caucasian peoples were ruled by nobles who dominated free peasants and various categories of serfs and slaves; some groups were organized in lineages or small confederations of clans. Islam was first introduced to Azarbayjan and other areas south of the Caucasus by the Arab conquests of the seventh century. It was reinforced by Saljuq migrations in the eleventh century. In the twelfth and thirteenth centuries the Golden Horde introduced Islam to the northern Caucasus, and the influence of the Crimean Khans and the Ottoman empire helped spread Islam in the sixteenth and seventeenth centuries. Naqshbandi Sufis appeared in Daghestan in the eighteenth century. Studying in Mecca and Medina, teaching in Damascus and Aleppo, local scholars were connected to the international community of 'ulama' and Sufis. Yet on the eve of Russian domination, only part of the Caucasian population of about one-and-a-half million, divided into some twenty different Turkish, Iranian, and Caucasian language groups, was Muslim. In many cases the elites were Muslim while the common people remained animists.

The Chechens were an important element of this population, but in the nineteenth century they did not have a concept of a unified nation. They recognized the people of a common language (*vainakh*, our people), but they were grouped into tribes (*teip*) made of clans (*gars*). The teip were grouped into *tuqums*, tribal unions consisting of a group of villages. The head of each family was an absolute authority in his home, but a council of elders spoke for the tuqum. Islam entered the region from Daghestan, either by the conquests of local princes, or by the preaching of *qumyg* – seasonal shepherd-missionaries. In any case, in the early nineteenth century the few local mullahs had very little influence and the legal system was based primarily on adat or custom rather than Shari'a. For example, women could annul marriages on their own initiative.

The Russians began to penetrate the region in the early eighteenth century. With the breakup of the Safavid empire the Russians took northern Daghestan in 1723 while the Ottomans occupied eastern Georgia and southern Daghestan. Russia annexed Georgia in 1801–04.

In the late eighteenth and nineteenth centuries, a succession of Naqshbandi imams led the resistance of free peasant landowners to the Russians and the local lords allied with them. Shaykh Mansur (c. 1760–91) tried to reinforce Islam, bring an end to feuds, and convert pagan peoples. After having visions of horsemen sent to him by the Prophet Muhammad, he proclaimed himself Imam. He wore a veil to conceal his radiant holiness, and forbade the drinking of wine or the smoking of tobacco. Four main principles inspired his movement: the return to a purified Islam, the struggle against non-Islamic religious practices, the rule of Shari'a, and holy war against the infidels. Mansur raised a coalition of free peasants and local notables, but, deserted by the nobles, was defeated in 1787 and captured in 1791.

Despite this defeat his efforts deepened the hold of Islam and prepared the way for later Sufi preachers who would make the Caucasus a bastion of Islamic resistance to the Russians. Shamil (active 1834–59) was the most famous leader of the effort to create a common state transcending tribal confederations. He tried to replace blood feud with Shari'a rules and to implement Muslim laws on inheritance, marriage, divorce, and criminal offenses, and banned alcohol, music, and the smoking of tobacco. He opened Quran schools. There was great resistance to his efforts to assume authority over a confederation or to impose taxation. His state was built on the backbone of his Khalifas and warriors, or *murids* (the Safavi pattern), and was successful mainly in areas already prepared by the Naqshabandis. Shamil was defeated in 1859 by the Russians and by tribal antagonism.

In spite, or perhaps because, of defeat, Sufism continued to flourish. The conviction that Sufis could communicate with supernatural beings, ward off evil spirits, and serve as guardian intermediaries between men and God grew stronger. The graves of saints – and other holy places such as crossroads, hills, caves, and stones that commemorated battles fought against the Russians – were visited by pilgrims seeking cures, aid in pregnancy, and other kinds of worldly good fortune. Alongside the Naqshbandiya, the Qadiriya gained adherents and introduced their own dhikr based on loud recitation, dancing, music, and drumming. The two orders joined in a great revolt in 1877–78, but this also was crushed by the Russians. During the revolution the Muslims of the Caucasus again made a vigorous effort to expel the Russians and to establish an autonomous state. In 1917 a congress of 'ulama' elected an imam, who led resistance from 1920 to 1925. The Russians defeated this resistance, arrested the religious leaders, disarmed the people, and liquidated Muslim institutions and Shari'a courts. Nonetheless, there were new revolts between 1928 and 1936 and from 1940 to 1944. During World War II the whole population of Chechen-Ingushia was deported to Kazakhstan and Siberia, and the territory was jurisdictionally divided among the Russian and Georgian Soviet Republics. (Also in 1944, on the basis of allegations that the Tatars had collaborated with the Germans, the Russians deported the entire Tatar population of the Crimea to Inner Asia and incorporated the region into the Ukraine.)

At the end of the Soviet era, Caucasians remained closely attached to Islam, observed the fast of Ramadan, and made pilgrimages to tombs of saints. There were still numerous Quran schools and Sufi teachers officiating over prayers and family rituals. The survival of the Sufi brotherhoods was partly due to the discipline exerted by the leaders over their followers, and partly due to the identification of the Sufi brotherhoods with families and clans (*teip*). In some cases a group of families living in a village would consider themselves both the members of a Sufi brotherhood and the descendants of a common ancestor. From the 1970s, however, a religious revival began in the region. Muslim missionaries went to Daghestani and Chechen villages preaching the purification of Islam from innovation, reliance on Quran and Sunna, and criticizing the Sufis for visits to saints' shrines, mawlid celebrations, and the use of talismans and charms.

With the decline of the Soviet Union General Dudayev founded the Chechen National Congress in 1990, seized power by coup in September 1991, and declared independence in November 1991. In 1994 Russia, saying it had to defend its territorial integrity and protect itself against bandits, attacked Chechnya and, in severe fighting, destroyed the capital, Grozny. Russia, exhausted by heavy military losses and internal divisions over the wisdom of its strategies, agreed to a peace which gave Chechnya de facto independence, though nominally within the framework of the Russian state. Chechnya declared itself an Islamic republic in 1996. Some

"Wahhabi" groups established Islamic village republics under Muslim law, to provide for local security, and to take marriage, inheritance, and land disputes under their own control. In 1998 they declared a jihad in the name of an Islamic caliphate in the Caucasus. In 1999, led by Shamil Basayev, they attacked villages in neighboring Daghestan, and precipitated the second Russian–Chechnyan war. Russia reinvaded and militarily reoccupied Chechnya. A guerrilla war continues. In a heavily armed and factionalized region, with local clans and gangs competing for power, and Russia determined to maintain political control but uncertain of how much military and political effort it can afford to invest, the situation remains unstable.

In neighboring Daghestan Muslims are also divided into numerous competing forces, with two main religious tendencies. The official Muslim Spiritual Board of Daghestan sponsors mosques, schools, charities, publishing, and holiday celebrations and pilgrimage. The Wahhabis, representing the more scripturalist and less local type of Islam, try to Islamize social and ritual practices in daily life. There are separatist movements in other parts of the Caucasus as well. Georgia has Muslim Abkhazian and Ossetian minorities who have claimed reunion with Russia or territorial independence. Both have partially achieved their objectives with Russian help.

Azarbayjan

Azarbayjan has been part of the Soviet Union since 1924. Soviet rule destroyed civil society and left the country in the hands of competing bureaucratic mafias with regional or clan bases. In 1989 Azari nationalists demanded independence, calling for a return to Azari Turkish culture and an end to the use of Cyrillic script. A nationalist uprising was put down by Russian troops in Baku in 1990, but Azarbayjan became independent upon the official demise of the Soviet Union.

The critical problem for Azarbayjan is the war with Armenia over Nagorno-Karabakh, an autonomous district with an Armenian ethno-religious population, within the territory of Azarbayjan. In 1988 Armenia claimed Nagorno-Karabakh, and in response in November 1990 Azarbayjan abrogated the autonomous status of Nagorno-Karabakh, claiming the rights of a territorially sovereign state over its populations. War between Armenia and Azarbayjan followed. Azarbayjan was defeated, and after a succession of presidents, a military coup brought Haidar Aliyev to power in 1993, in effect a restoration of the old Communist Party elite and of Russian influence.

Aliyev is opposed by numerous parties and factions representing powerful bosses or warlords rather than ideological or political principles, and the country faces grave problems in creating a coherent national identity in the face of ethnic differences, rivalries of family and regional bosses, factionalized political parties, economic dislocation, and Russian and other international manipulations. Azarbayjani economic and oil development is stymied by rivalries within the elite over who will control the deals, and by rivalries over the pipeline routes. In cultural terms, the elites stress Turkish connections, but there are close ties to Iran as well. The breakup of the Soviet Union has allowed for the expression of Muslim desires for mosques and pilgrimages. While there are Muslim movements representing parties committed to an Islamic state and parties of moral reform, Islam seems to be of secondary importance in Azari politics.

Despite two centuries of Russian influence and all the Soviet programs for education, legal rights, and employment for women, Azarbayjan maintains the traditional and Muslim patterns of family culture. The jadidist generation called for the emancipation of women as essential to the progress of the nation. The Soviet Union encouraged literacy, high educational levels, and employment, though most women remained employed in agriculture or lower-skill jobs. Also, while the Soviet Union ostensibly opened up new roles for women it did not provide the housing and child-care facilities that were need to maintain their independence. Women had to go back to their extended families to find support. In the Soviet era too there was a tacit bargain with local elites that in return for their political support the Soviet Union would overlook continued male dominance in the family – their "honor" would be respected. In effect, a dual culture emerged – in public, Soviet; in private, Azari. With the collapse of the Soviet Union women have lost what meager gains they had made, and have to depend upon kinship ties for protection. Women are again expected to be moral exemplars, defer to men, and not smoke, drink, or appear in public without a chaperon. They are used as symbols of national and ethnic identity and Muslim modesty.

AFGHANISTAN

Throughout history Afghanistan was located in the interstices between the great empires of West, Central, and South Asia. A poor, mountainous, and inaccessible country, it was never conquered as a whole by any of the surrounding empires. The population is extremely varied, divided among ethnic Turks in the north, Pashtuns in the east, Baluchis in the south, and Turkomans in the west. Tajiks are the second-biggest ethnic group, followed by Uzbeks and Hazaras, who are considered socially inferior and who in recent decades have migrated to Kabul to work as laborers. Most (85 percent) of the population was involved in raising wheat, cotton, fruit, sheep, goats, and cattle. Half the population speaks Pashto, and Farsi is the common language of the non-Pashtun population. Farsi and Islam are the only common cultural elements, and the population is intensely parochial, tribal, and sectarian.

Historically, the country was ruled by the tribal khans, whose power varied greatly. In some cases they were the landowners as well as chiefs and the rest of the tribesmen were serfs or tenants; in some cases power was more equally distributed. Some tribes dominated subordinate ethnic groups, who supplied labor. Within the tribes the dominant value was consensus and cooperation. The *jirga* existed as a larger-scale convocation of tribal elders, but in general Afghan society

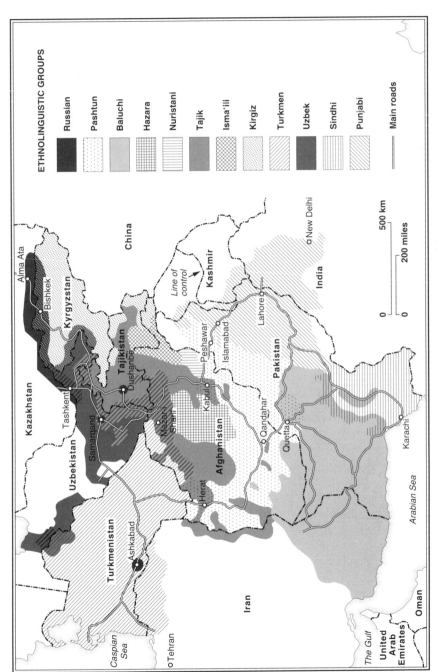

Map 37 Ethnic populations in Inner Asia and Afghanistan

ETHNOLINGUISTIC GROUPS

- Russian
- Pashtun
- Baluchi
- Hazara
- Nuristani
- Tajik
- Isma'ili
- Kirgiz
- Turkmen
- Uzbek
- Sindhi
- Punjabi
- Main roads

500 km

200 miles

China

Alma Ata

Bishkek

Kyrgyzstan

Kazakhstan

Tashkent

Samarqand

Uzbekistan

Tajikistan

Dushanbe

Mazar-i Sharif

Turkmenistan

Ashkabad

Caspian Sea

Tehran

Iran

Herat

Afghanistan

Kabul

Qandahar

Quetta

Peshawar

Islamabad

Line of control

Kashmir

Lahore

Pakistan

New Delhi

India

Karachi

Arabian Sea

The Gulf

United Arab Emirates

Oman

was highly conflicted due to blood feuds, intra- and inter-tribal rivalries, and the antagonisms of tribes of different ethnic, language, and religious orientations. The most important conflicts were those between tribes and would-be central states. To survive, central rulers had to mobilize tribal support, manipulate tribes against each other, and motivate them to attack external enemies. As a central government consolidated it put out new military outposts, built roads, established communications, such as the telegraph, and followed up with tax collectors and schoolteachers. As a central government weakened, the tribes refused payment of taxes, raided outposts, attacked small towns for arms and loot, and disseminated religious propaganda against the central government. Islam played a great social role. Mullahs had great influence in community matters such as property and honor, and many were worldly, wealthy, and prestigious. They were men of knowledge and property, and power-brokers in political affairs. Sufi *pirs* (holy men) formed extensive networks including prominent political and social leaders; these networks were the basis of their fund-raising and political influence.

Ghaznavids, Ghurids, Mongols, and Timurids in succession have all been rulers of Afghanistan. Mughals, Uzbeks, and Safavids partitioned it in the sixteenth to the eighteenth centuries. In the eighteenth century rising Pashtun tribes pushed out the Safavids and fought the Mughals. Then began a long and often-repeated effort to create a centralized state. In this effort the most important Pashtun tribes, the Durranis and the Ghilzais, played the leading roles. A Durrani chieftain, Ahmed Shah Sadozai, created a small suzerainty over the tribes of Afghanistan and northern India, including the Punjab, Multan, and Kashmir (1747–73). After the death of his son Timur, Sadozai's rivals partitioned his domains. Dost Muhammad (1835–63), founder of the Muhammadzai dynasty, reestablished a central government. After his victory over the Sikhs in 1837 he called himself amir al-mu'minin, Commander of the Faithful, the historical title of Muslim rulers.

In the middle of the nineteenth century, the bordering empires – British and Russian – became rivals for control of Afghanistan. The British saw it as the key to the defense of their Indian empire, and invaded in 1839–42. They found this strategy too costly, and then attempted to force the amirs to pacify the Pashtuns and prevent raids into India. Russian conquests in Central Asia led the British to a more "forward" policy, and another invasion in 1878–80. The British wanted an Afghanistan strong enough to be a barrier to Russia but not so strong as to threaten India. Again they had to resort to supporting the Afghan amirs as the best vehicle for controlling the tribes. In the 1880s Britain and Russia came to terms over boundaries. In 1885 the Lumsden Commission negotiated a northern border with Russia, and in 1893 the Durand Agreement defined the borders with British India. In 1907 a British–Russian treaty ratified Afghanistan's position as a buffer state.

The long process of "modernization" began with Amir 'Abdur Rahman (1880–1901) who, with British help, undertook to unify the country and consolidate royal authority. He conquered Hazaras, Shi'is, and *kafirs* (non-Muslims), and then claimed to rule by

30 The Mosque of Mazar-i Sharif, Afghanistan

divine right, and not by tribal delegation. 'Abdur Rahman created the first modernized state apparatus. Centralized military rather than tribal levies were used to defeat local resistance. The government was organized into functional departments. The mullahs were made to serve in government offices and to run state courts as the state coopted the 'ulama' by patronage, appointments to offices, and the endowment of waqfs. 'Abdur Rahman adopted his own version of the Tanzimat to build up the army and administration, and military workshops and industries. Under Habibullah (1901–19) professional schools were created to train army officers, administrators, and teachers, producing the first members of a modernist and nationalist intelligentsia. Mahmud Beg Tarzi was the principal promoter of the new modernism.

Amanullah (1919–29) carried the Tanzimat into social and economic reforms. In the early years of his reign he introduced a new legal, judicial, and administrative framework, and in 1928–29, returning from a visit to Europe, proposed more radical reforms, such as the unveiling of women, the wearing of Western dress at court, the abolition of slavery, and secular education. Amanullah planned to give women virtually equal rights in marriage, divorce, and inheritance, and diminish the role of the mullahs in law and education. These proposals provoked open rebellion by tribal leaders who feared the centralization of power, and by Mujaddadi Naqsh-bandi religious chieftains, who denounced him as an infidel ruler. The rebels forced him out of power, and a Pashtun general, Nadir, became Shah, succeeded by Zahir Shah (1933–73). His uncle, Prince Da'ud, held effective power from 1953 to 1979.

Zahir Shah promulgated a new constitution, and struggled to get control over the religious leaders, and offset their opposition to reforms. The new regime stressed its Islamic identity, but stimulated economic growth, strengthened the army, and expanded education. Afghanistan saw its first political parties and free press in the last decade of Zahir's reign. Reforms on behalf of women resumed in 1959. Women in Kabul went to school and work, unveiled, but the countryside remained conservative.

The dominant themes of the regime had been the same for a century: centralization of state power vs. tribal autonomy; modernization, especially the position of women, in the face of conservative and religious opposition. The Afghan elite in the monarchical period included the royal family, the army, landowners, some capitalists, religious and tribal leaders, and the Western-educated intelligentsia. Tribal leaders were often assigned governorships, and military and other leading roles. The government offices were generally run by family and clientele groups. In the 1950s all the new sectors of the economy, transport, roads, irrigation, and power – except cotton and sugar processing – were developed by the government. The largest project was a vast scheme to irrigate the Helmand Valley. The United States and the Soviet Union, each unwilling to see the other dominate the country, provided considerable foreign aid.

In the 1960s and 1970s the cold war and the international balance of power were crucial to the fate of Afghanistan. The rise of the Pashtunistan movement, calling for unification of all Pashtuns including those living in Pakistan, alienated Afghanistan from Pakistan and the United States and forced Afghanistan closer to the Soviet

Union. The Soviets became the principal suppliers of economic aid and education for the young Afghan elite, and built up strong support in the military and government services, and among intellectuals. In 1973, Prince Da'ud removed Zahir Shah from power, and with the support of the army and the Communist Parcham Party instituted a presidency and a republican state. This was a coup designed to reduce Soviet influence in Afghanistan, and was accomplished with the financial and political assistance of Pakistan, Sa'udi Arabia, and Iran.

The Soviet Union, however, was dissatisfied with Sultan Da'ud's tilt towards the Islamic states, and supported a coup d'état by the People's Democratic Party of Afghanistan, aided by Marxists seeded throughout the army and the bureaucracy. The party was divided into two factions: Khalq – mainly Pashtun and rural; and Parcham – mainly urban and non-Pashtun. The Khalq and Parcham factions then fought each other, eliminating a series of leaders, until Khalq was victorious in 1979. The new regime sought to subordinate Afghanistan to a Leninist party. It proposed land and social reforms, especially enhancing the rights of women, but without popular support and ideological acceptance it depended almost entirely upon the Soviet Union. A resistance movement backed by the United States, Pakistan, and Sa'udi Arabia sprang up. The United States was eager to back an Afghan resistance, albeit Islamist, in order to harass the Soviet Union. Sa'udi Arabia was pursuing a pro-Sunni policy which it hoped would create an alliance of conservative Islamic states and radical military activists and offset Iranian influence. Pakistan wanted to use Afghan Sunnism as part of a drive to protect itself against the rise of Iranian and Shi'i influence in Afghanistan, to outflank India in the struggle for Kashmir, to offset the influence of the Pashtunistan movement, and to win influence in Central Asia. The Soviet Union, unwilling to see a foreign-backed regime on its borders, and perhaps with its own ambitions to advance toward the Persian Gulf, intervened to save its puppet. The Russians removed the Khalq leader, Hafizullah Amin, and installed Babrak Karmal, head of the Parcham faction, and Russian forces invaded the country. Thus began a war that lasted until the Russian withdrawal in 1989, and a civil war, which continued through 2001.

The war was organized in the name of Islam, which came to play a new and unprecedented role in Afghan politics. Historically, Islam was not crucial in the formation of the Afghan monarchies. The state derived its legitimacy and power from the support of the tribal – especially Pashtun – aristocracies. Mullahs were generally subordinate to the tribal chiefs and landlords, though the monarchies tried to cultivate the support of high-ranking mullahs by appointments to offices, endowments, and using them as policy advisors. The position of mullahs, Sufi pirs, and sayyids was weakened by the centralization of the state, the introduction of secular education and courts, and the rise of a modernist discourse. For educated people Islam became one ideology among many.

In the 1960s and 1970s, a new type of Muslim intelligentsia, the counterpart of the new generation of secular and Marxist intelligentsia, came to the fore. The modern-educated Islamist intellectuals were more political and ideological than the traditional Muslim religious leaders. They formed study circles influenced by the Society of Muslim Brothers and the Jama'at-i Islami. Islamist groups created a Muslim student union, and won control of the Kabul University campus in 1969. By uniting with 'ulama' in 1973 a nationwide organization was formed, which insisted on the implementation of the Shari'a.

The Islamist movement, however, was composed of very different groups. One of the most important was the Hizb-i-Islami, led by Gulbuddin Hikmatyar and supported by detribalized middle-class students. Hizb-i-Islami was a highly authoritarian and ideologically purist party; its goal was to create an Islamic state. A second movement was the Jami'at-i-Islami, led by Burhanuddin Rabbani, which had strong support in the north and northeast among Uzbeks, Turkomans, and Tajiks. There were also several traditionalist parties based upon older 'ulama' and Sufi networks. The Milli Islami Mahaz (National Islamic Front), led by Sayyid Ahmad Gailani, had links with tribal chiefs, landowners, Sufi shaykhs, and had US and Sa'udi support. Various Shi'i parties were backed by Iran.

After the Communist coup, the Islamists became active in opposition, and demanded the implementation of the Shari'a as the civil law of Afghanistan and the formation of an Islamic state. The resistance, however, was locally based, divided by region, clienteles, parties, tribes, the ambitions of chieftains, and Muslim ideologies, and was unable to form a unified movement. While some leaders, such as Ahmad Shah Mas'ud, succeeded in creating cross-ethnic and regional alliances, Islamic resistance was basically organized on ethnic lines. The intensification of non-Pashtun ethnic identities only created further barriers to national unity since Pashtuns loathed the idea of non-Pashtun leadership. Hazara Shi'is were divided between traditionalists and Islamists, and often fought each other. Isma'ilis stood aside altogether. Separate Uzbek and Turkoman parties took form. Field commanders operated on their own without full coordination with the political parties. The Naqshbandiya and the Qadiriya played an important role in the resistance, indicating the continued vitality of the Sufi movements, but many Sufis supported the Islamists. The Jabha-i Najat-i Milli Afghanistan (National Liberation Front of Afghanistan) led by Sibghatullah Mujaddidi played an important political role, but favored the return of Zahir Shah. The result of the civil war was a general breakdown of integrative institutions and a reinforcement of regional, sectarian, and ethnic ties.

The Islamic movements in Afghanistan afford a striking example of the interconnection of parochial, national, and religious identities. The Hizb-i-Islami was a very sectarian revivalist movement, and a political action party, perhaps even a religio-political gang, composed of middle-class students, from one ethnic sector of Afghan society (the Pashtun), which fought for power in a national state while defining its goals as the establishment of an Islamic state and the implementation of the Shari'a. Rabbani's Jami'at-i-Islami was similarly a sectarian political action party, largely Uzbek, Tajik, and Turkoman in composition, fighting for national power in the name of universalistic Islamic principles.

The war was a disaster for all the participants. Its destructiveness was extreme. Millions of Afghans were killed, and millions more forced into exile. Military defeat and the demoralizing repercussions of the war forced a Soviet withdrawal in 1989, and eventually compromised the Soviet Union itself. The Soviets left a Marxist regime under General Najiballah but this collapsed in April, 1992. After the demise of Najiballah, an Uzbek–Tajik–Mujahidin coalition took control of the state under the nominal presidency of Rabbani, but the rifts among Islamists and secularists, Islamist factions, Islamists and traditionalists, ethnic, regional, and warlord factions and militias made it impossible to govern. Internal divisions encouraged external interventions, and since 1992 the United States, Pakistan, Iran, Sa'udi Arabia, and Uzbekistan have all tried to influence developments in Afghanistan. With the emergence of the newly independent Central Asian states, Afghanistan looks more than ever to be the key to trade and the opening of oil and gas routes to Pakistan and the Gulf.

Of the competing forces, the Taliban came closest to conquering and unifying the whole of Afghanistan. The Taliban were religious students in rural schools and madrasas of the Northwest Frontier province. Many fought in the Islamic resistance. Supported by Pakistan and Sa'udi Arabia, and by various Islamist parties, in 1994 Mullah Muhammad Omar rallied the students to fight criminals and bandits, won popular support, and took control of Qandahar. The movement then received the support of the Jami'at-i 'Ulama'-i Islam in Pakistan, which sent its students to join the Afghan volunteers. The Taliban took Kabul in 1994 and then moved against Shah Mas'ud and the northern warlords, but never quite won control of the whole of the country. The Taliban was reinforced by non-Afghani volunteers for jihad and, since 1996, by Usama Bin Laden and his al-Qaeda network. The Taliban suppressed the non-Pashtun and Shi'i parts of the population, imposed an extreme Islamic discipline, and barred women from schools and workplaces. Its leaders destroyed all the Buddhist monuments in the country and required Hindus to wear identifying yellow badges.

The attack on the United States on September 11, 2001 opened a new phase of warfare. The United States resolved to overthrow the Taliban regime and to prevent the use of Afghanistan as a base for international terrorism. The USA bombed the Taliban and al-Qaeda forces from the air and supported the forces of the Northern Alliance on the ground. By the end of 2001 the Taliban regime was defeated, but the political future of Afghanistan was still unresolved.

THE MUSLIMS OF CHINA

China's Muslim population falls into two main groups. The Hui are those Muslims spread throughout the regions of Han population who in physical appearance and language are Chinese, but consider themselves a separate people because they do not eat pork, worship ancestors, gamble, drink, or smoke opium. They are descended from Persian, Arab, Mongolian, and Turkish Muslims who settled in

China at various times in the past. The Hui commonly recognize the principle of Qing Zhen, which means "pure and true," and refers first of all to the avoidance of pork, and then to religious values, ethnic descent, and lifestyle. Hui commonly give very different interpretations to the principle of Qing Zhen, and have never been organized as a single body, or been in strong network communication. They typically work in private commerce and transport.

The Hui identify themselves by a number of factors, some of which overlap, but none of which are held by every Hui community. In the northwest, in Ningxia province, the Hui stress their Islamic beliefs and orthodoxy. There is increasing strictness of practice, affiliation with the Khufiya Sufi order, separation of men and women in the fields, madrasa education, and celebration of Muslim festivals. Mosque and graveyard are the centers of the community. In the suburbs of Beijing Hui communities see themselves in terms of occupation, market economy, schooling, and above all endogamous marriages. Hui women never marry Han men, and people find spouses in their brigade and district and via a network of connections to other Hui communities. In Beijing's Oxen Street, Hui identity is not ideologically defined, but is indicated by choices of schooling, occupation, spouses, avoidance of pork, and eating in Hui restaurants. In the southeast, in Chendai, Islam scarcely plays any part in Hui identity, and the Hui stress their common descent from Arab-Muslim ancestors and the veneration of ancient tombs, giving a lineage identity to people who are otherwise indistinguishable from local Hans. Among other Hui, secular associations such as restaurants, schools, and clubs define group identity and neither religion nor ancestry is given much weight. In some communities the mosque remains important for social functions such as marriages and funerals rather than worship. Government recognition and policies have helped forge Hui ethnic self-awareness. Now Islam is becoming more important to Hui identities.

The other Muslims are Inner Asian peoples, including Uighurs, Kazakhs, Kirgiz, and other minority groups, most of whom speak Turkic languages and are not assimilated to a Chinese cultural style. These peoples were absorbed into the Chinese state in the late nineteenth century when the Chinese defeated Chinese-speaking Muslims resident in Yunnan, Shensi, and Kansu provinces, and Uighurs and Kazakhs in Xinjiang. In the republican period (1911–49) China's relations with its Muslim minorities were based on the expectation that they would be totally assimilated and incorporated into Chinese society.

Xinjiang, however, preserved a considerable autonomy, and was ruled by a succession of independent warlords. Yang Tseng-hsin became the first governor (1911–28) under the republican regime. To support his administration he mobilized both Chinese and Muslim soldiers to maintain a local balance of power, counteract Chinese secret societies, and forestall the possibility of Muslim forces being used to create an independent state. Yang gave the local chieftains autonomy, spared the province heavy economic burdens, and thus managed to maintain Chinese suzerainty and his personal control. In 1924 he signed a treaty with the Soviet Union which exchanged Chinese consulates in Soviet Central Asia for Soviet consulates in eastern Turkestan, and thus bolstered the autonomy of the region from central government control. Yang was assassinated in 1928 and in 1933 Xinjiang was taken over by Sheng Shih-ts'ai. Sheng also followed a policy of maintaining close ties with Russia and of rallying local non-Chinese support. He encouraged newspapers in local languages, stabilized the currency, and, with Russian investments, improved communications, built factories, and set up an oil refinery. The German invasion of Russia, however, cut off Russian support and obliged Sheng to restore Xinjiang to the control of the Chinese government.

World War II and the defeat of the regime of Chiang Kai-shek allowed for Kazakh and Uighur rebellions in 1944. The Soviet Union helped to negotiate the return of the province to China in 1946, and the rebel groups agreed to subordination to China in return for local autonomy and a reformed administration. The nationalist Chinese regime, however, forfeited its opportunity to win local goodwill, the Muslims failed to unite to maintain their independence, and the Chinese Communists were able to absorb the province in 1949.

Under Communist rule, China's Muslim minorities have received a great deal of political attention because they are often frontier populations, or live in resource-rich regions that contain a great part of China's minerals as well as meat, milk, and wool supplies. They also make an entrepreneurial contribution to the Chinese economy, and could serve as an alternative base of political power in a very fractured society. For reasons of defense and economy, as well as national pride, the Chinese government is eager to win their loyalty, but there have been frequent changes in Chinese policy. The original Chinese goal was the disappearance of ethnic and national differences in a Chinese proletarian culture. Muslims were encouraged to cultivate traditional customs and beliefs, and yet to participate in the Chinese Communist Party, state bureaucracies, and other mass organizations. In the 1920s and 1930s the party followed the Russian line in promising self-determination to minorities. In 1938 Mao Zedong abandoned his support for self-determination in favor of a policy of autonomy within a unified Chinese state. Mao declared that minorities would receive equal rights with Chinese. Hui were taken into the party and the Red Army, and Muslims were promised that their religious interests would be protected. Upon coming to power the Chinese Communists continued their policy of accommodation with Muslim communities. They ordered that Muslim customs be accepted in workplaces and government agencies. Muslim circumcision and marriage practices were permitted. A Chinese Islamic Association was founded in 1953 and a Chinese Institute of Islamic Theology, which trained religious scholars, was founded in 1955. Leading Muslims were confirmed in regional political positions and autonomous political areas were set up in Xinjiang and other provinces. Medical and educational work was begun. Scientific agricultural and stock-breeding

31 A Mosque in Inner Mongolia

techniques were introduced, and strenuous efforts were made to promote production with the help of Chinese workers who assisted local peoples. From 1949 until 1955 the Chinese government concentrated on the integration of its minority regions.

By 1956 party leaders were convinced that it was time to move to a new stage of development and to speed up the socialization of the minority populations. Muslim leaders were encouraged by the Hundred Flowers Campaign to express their criticisms of the Communist Chinese regime. This revealed strong separatist tendencies, a desire to be unified with fellow Muslims inside the Soviet Union, hopes for an Islamic state, and criticisms of Chinese control. Muslims had grievances due to food shortages, confiscation of mosques, and dissemination of Marxist education and propaganda. While they were not persecuted, Muslims felt a narrowing of the boundaries of their autonomy.

These revelations brought a severe Chinese reaction. In 1957 the Chinese Communists began more aggressive efforts to assimilate the minority populations. This included emphasis upon class struggle, the abolition of special customs, and limitations on regional autonomy. Local nationalisms were denounced as a form of ingratitude, and the Chinese decided to replace the traditional elites by cadres with an acceptable class background, to create cooperatives, and to socialize production. Minority languages, festivals, and customs were attacked, and pressure was put on the Hui to eat in common dining halls and intermarry with Chinese. Special Muslim restaurants and bathing facilities were closed. Women were obliged to put aside traditional clothing and go to work, and mosque properties were confiscated. Mixed-nationality communes were formed, and Han youth were sent to colonize minority areas. The Chinese Islamic Association was disbanded in 1958.

These measures provoked military resistance in Ningxia province with the objective of establishing a Muslim republic. Kazakhs emigrated across the border into the Soviet Union. Thus it was evident that the campaign for assimilation had gone too rapidly and had to be repudiated. Resistance made the Chinese elites aware of the extent to which they had been misled by lower-level cadres and how cultural pressures that had no economic relevance could be counter-productive. Also, the concern of the Chinese regime to protect its borders with the Soviet Union and to win the diplomatic support of Muslim Middle Eastern, African, and Asian states hastened the end of the Great Leap Forward. Some communes were dissolved, the Hui were permitted independent dining halls, and the special characteristics of minority populations were recognized as acceptable.

In 1966, however, the Cultural Revolution and the mobilization of the Red Guards reopened the struggle against the special privileges of minorities. The Red Guards demanded that mosques be closed, Quran study prohibited, and Muslim circumcision and marriage practices forbidden. Despite these pressures, by 1969 Hui schools were again functioning and religious festivals were being observed. A new constitution of 1970 recognized minority languages and customs but did not give particularly warm assurances about their protection. While policy toward the minorities was moderated for tactical reasons, many party activists continued to favor assimilation.

After 1975 the Chinese government reaffirmed the right of minorities to develop their own culture within the framework of the Chinese state. With the death of Mao and the overthrow of the Gang of Four in 1976, Muslims were more fully rehabilitated and allowed to rebuild schools, operate restaurants, and pursue religious activities. In 1980 the Chinese Islamic Association held its first meeting since 1963. Since the 1980s, with the opening of the Chinese economy and the absence of foreign threats, minorities have increasingly asserted their demands for autonomy and the government has been more positive in response. Government policy grants minority populations special considerations such as autonomous administrative districts, and permission to have more than one child. At the same time, however, the Chinese government seeks to suppress movements for independence in Xinjiang and Tibet, pursues policies that would integrate Muslims into local administration, and tries to dilute Muslim power in the provinces by resettling large numbers of Chinese peasants in northwestern Muslim regions. The Chinese government also threatens to destroy counter-revolutionaries operating under the cover of religion. Frequent changes of direction indicate that the Chinese leadership itself is divided over what policies would lead ultimately to fusion of national minorities in Chinese society.

Xinjiang, which harbors a substantial portion of the non-Han Muslim population, remains a special case. Chinese Communist authority was established there in 1949, and separate administrative regimes were set up for Kazakhs and Uighurs. The Chinese formed the Ili-Kazakh Autonomous Chou and the Xinjiang Uighur Autonomous Chou in 1955 for a population of some 3,500,000 people living in the Tarim basin and in the vicinity of Kashgar, Aksu, and Khotan. The Chinese destroyed the traditional elites, collectivized agriculture and herding, introduced new schools, and favored economic development. They invested in irrigation and reclamation projects and increased the output of wheat, cotton, corn, and rice. In Kazakh districts they developed coal, iron, and petroleum. The government also tried to settle the nomads by persuading them of the advantages of sedentary livestock herding. Large numbers of Chinese settlers were moved into the region with the completion of the Hami railroad in 1959. By now Han peoples constitute more than 40 percent of the total population.

The Chinese government maintains a two-pronged policy towards the region. Xinjiang is given priority in Chinese plans for economic development. China cultivates good trade relations with the surrounding Inner Asian states in order to reduce tension within Xinjiang, and to create an incentive for neighboring states to suppress support from across the borders. At the same time, Muslim leadership and dissidents within Xinjiang are suppressed. Nonetheless, an Islamic educational revival and contacts with the outside stimulate Muslim self-awareness and regional separatism. Throughout the 1990s there were reports of underground movements, assassinations, and riots in Kashgar.

CONCLUSION

Russian and Chinese control of Inner Asian peoples differed from that of European imperial regimes in other parts of the Muslim world. These imperialisms were a direct expansion of the Russian and Chinese states onto contiguous territories, and allowed for the migration and settlement of Europeans and Chinese into the conquered territories without either the colonial or conquered peoples regarding the newcomers as temporary residents. In Soviet Inner Asia the presence of a large European population led to an unprecedented integration between the colonizing and the colonized societies. Probably no other Muslim region was as highly modernized. This did not mean a full equalization of Russians and Muslims. Muslim populations remained subordinate to de facto Russian controls both in the government and the party apparatus. Independence, however, has not brought any political or economic advantages to the region. In China, though some sectors of the Muslim population have been assimilated for centuries, the Hui did not lose their identity or become fully absorbed into Chinese society. Separatist tendencies remain strong among Inner Asian Muslims.

CHAPTER 30

ISLAM IN WEST AFRICA

To the end of the nineteenth century Islam had spread in Sudanic, savannah, and forest West Africa by virtue of a combination of forces. Migrant trading communities and missionary teachers had formed scattered Muslim communities throughout these regions. In parts of the Sudan and East Africa these communities converted local rulers and helped establish Muslim states. In other cases Muslim 'ulama' and holy men waged jihad to form new states. At the very end of the century European invaders defeated, subordinated, and broke up existing states and imposed their own regimes. Muslim state formation was checked and Muslim peoples became subject to new European-generated political and economic pressures.

COLONIALISM AND INDEPENDENCE: AFRICAN STATES AND ISLAM

The French and the British empires between them largely determined the political configuration of modern African societies. By 1900 the French empire comprised a vast region including the Atlantic coastal territories of Senegal, Guinea, the Ivory Coast, and Dahomey. Between 1899 and 1922 the interior was organized into the large colonies of French Sudan, Niger, and Mauritania. Upper Volta was formed in 1919, but in 1932 it was divided among the Ivory Coast, Niger, and the Sudan, and then reconstituted in 1947. The French Central African empire included Muslim populations in Chad. The British organized protectorates for Gambia, Sierra Leone, Ghana, and the northern and southern regions of Nigeria. The Nigerian protectorates were united as the colony and protectorate of Nigeria in 1914.

In the government of both British and French territories, one basic principle applied. The populations were ruled through intermediary local chiefs supervised by foreign officials. This principle was implemented in different ways. The French favored highly centralized and authoritarian means of control. In Senegambia and the Sudanic regions they broke the potential for Muslim resistance, dissolved the larger states and paramount chieftainships, displaced the older aristocracies, and favored local-level district chiefs who were easy to subordinate to the central administration. These local chiefs were not men of traditional importance, but rather newcomers promoted by the French to collect taxes, organize corvée, and administer the French judicial code.

The British sought political control by the policy of "indirect rule." They accepted a much larger scale of native administration than the French, and guaranteed the authority of the dominant elites. In northern Nigeria they bypassed the Sokoto Caliphate, and made the Amirs, advised by British residents or divisional officers, responsible for administration, tax collection, and justice. British officers supervised the Amirs but did not intervene between them and their subjects. However, the British also rationalized local administration in northern Nigeria, and replaced feudal tenures by direct administration, established a territorial system of native courts, and greatly strengthened the Muslim judiciary. They protected the region from the direct impact of European rule by laws that forbade Europeans to purchase land and prohibited Christian missionaries from entering predominantly Muslim areas.

Throughout West Africa the establishment of colonial regimes led to profound economic and social changes. The principal interest of the colonial powers was to stimulate exports of cash crops such as peanuts from Senegal, timber from the Ivory Coast, and palm oil from Dahomey. The French collected taxes in cash to force increases in agricultural production, and used forced labor on banana, cocoa, and coffee plantations. The British developed cocoa, timber, rubber, manganese, aluminum, and gold exports from the Gold Coast. Nigeria, which exported palm oil, cocoa, rubber, and peanuts, had high gross export earnings but a low per capita income.

Railroads were built to link the interior with international markets. The French built railways from St. Louis to Dakar and from Dakar to Bamako, linking the Niger River and the Atlantic. Railroads in Guinea, the Ivory Coast, Dahomey, Sierra Leone, and Nigeria tied the producing regions of the interior to the ports, but did not link the interior territories with each other. The railroads destroyed the trans-Saharan traffic, and ended the long struggle between Saharan and European peoples, begun by the Atlantic slave trade, for control of the commerce of Africa. Henceforth international trade would move by rail to the coast rather than by camel across the desert.

Trade, moreover, was controlled in the interest of the European companies. Currency, banking, navigation, customs, and legal arrangements ensured the domination of a few large colonial banks, shipping lines, and other firms. French restrictions on the domestic economy of their African colonies made prices in French West Africa higher than world levels, and French West Africa ran a consistently unfavorable balance of trade. Africans were ruined by European competition, and eliminated from the export business. Arabs, Greeks, and Indians migrated to the French colonies and often took local retail trade out of African hands. Until the 1930s neither the British nor the French invested in the colonies, but expected them to pay the costs of their administration. Only in reaction to the Depression did the colonial powers begin to regard it in their interest to finance economic development, and not until after World War II did the British and the French invest more heavily.

Political and economic change in the West African colonies was accompanied, as elsewhere in the Muslim world, by the formation of new economic classes and social and political groups. Changes in the economy broke down lineage bonds, brought individuals into large-scale market arrangements, promoted mobility, and generated a demand for individual, as opposed to collectively shared, wealth. Economic changes promoted seasonal or migrant labor and wage employment, and encouraged the growth of urban centers with their relative freedom from traditional authority and concepts. Changing patterns of trade and administration brought Africans to capital and port towns. Out of these uprooted populations new elites and new communities came into being.

In the cities an African bourgeoisie emerged as Western education equipped small minorities to serve as doctors, teachers, lawyers, journalists, interpreters, and government officials. Education, however, was very limited. In the French empire only about 3 percent of African students were enabled to go to school. In Nigeria, British education generated a small Western-educated elite which was mostly southern in origin. In the decade before 1942 some 300,000 students went to primary schools, but only 2,000 to secondary schools. Almost all of these schools were in the south, and a large proportion were Christian missionary schools. With a few exceptions Christian missionaries and Western schools were excluded from northern Nigeria.

Colonial administration and education also generated a subordinate elite of mechanics, transport workers, bricklayers, clerks, cash-crop farmers, and others. Clerks had a particularly close acquaintance with the workings of a modern administration and economy, and were important as liaisons between the sub-elites and higher-level government officials. Clerks and schoolteachers became important spokesmen in clubs and tribal, trade union, and political movements. The new elites asserted themselves through a myriad of new associations. Tribal, ethnic, mutual-aid, trade union, and debating societies, and, ultimately, political clubs were the product of migration and urbanization and the basis for the emergence of political parties. Student and youth associations were particularly important for the ultimate formation of African nationalist movements.

The Depression and World War II gave these new elites an opportunity to press their demands. The war fatally damaged the political power and moral authority of the European powers, and allowed African leaders to claim self-determination and political independence. Though French administration was assisted by local councils with advisory powers and local chambers of commerce, high-ranking African chieftains, rich traders, property owners, and war veterans were the only people eligible for political participation. The French fought a long rearguard action to moderate African demands and to maintain the subordination of the colonies. At the Brazzaville conference in 1944 they acknowledged their obligation to invest in African economic development, to build bridges, ports, and agricultural facilities, and to improve health services and education. The conference also adopted a new political goal. In place of the French concept of the assimilation of individual Africans to French citizenship, it proposed an association of African societies within a French union, and the formation of territorial assemblies which would be entitled to send representatives to the French parliament.

Territorial assemblies led to political parties. Some of these were personal factions, or coalitions of smaller associations, but some were mass parties with wide bases of support. The most important was the Rassemblement Démocratique Africain (RDA), formed in 1946 as an anti-imperial congress-type movement, uniting professional elites, trade union leaders, and youth organizations under the leadership of Félix Houphouet-Boigny. Under French rule the RDA was the principal party in the Ivory Coast, Sudan, Niger, and Guinea. In Senegal it was displaced by the African branch of the French Socialist Party and the Bloc Démocratique Sénégalais (BDS), founded in 1949, led by Léopold Senghor and renamed Union Progressiste Sénégalaise in 1951. In 1958 General de Gaulle proposed a referendum which offered African states a choice between immediate independence and self-government within the French community. Most of the West African states, obliged by economic dependence, voted to remain attached to France. Only Guinea voted for immediate independence without linkage to France, but by 1960 France conceded independence for the Ivory Coast, Dahomey, Niger, Upper Volta, and the Islamic Republic of Mauritania.

Ghana, under the leadership of Kwame Nkrumah and the Convention People's Party, was the first British dependency to achieve independence. In Nigeria, the movements that led to independence had their origin among Western-educated Africans in the aftermath of World War I. In Nigeria, the British favored older elites and excluded the small, Western-educated elite from the higher branches of government administration. Encouraged by their education to believe that they would ultimately control the society, the new elites became anti-colonial nationalists and claimed the right to speak for the mass of the people. On behalf of the sub-elites of clerks, technicians, traders, and landowning farmers, they demanded equality in wages with European workers, equality in participation in the colonial regimes, and, ultimately, independence. In the 1930s, trade unions, worker associations, occupational and professional groups, and kinship and tribal unions were formed in great numbers and became channels for political agitation. In Nigeria the combined pressures of student and nationalist leaders and a British change of heart about colonial rule led to the first Nigerian constitution in 1946. The Richards Constitution provided for a Nigerian legislative council and four provincial units – the Lagos Colony and the Western, Eastern, and Northern provinces – each with a house of assembly recruited from the existing native authorities. The constitution promoted regional and ethnic rivalries among Yorubas and Ibos, northern Muslims and southerners, and between the dominant and minority groups in each region, over the distribution of regional and central authority. The Muslim north in particular feared subordination within a Nigerian state dominated by the south. The federation as a whole finally became independent in 1960. The former British possessions of Sierra Leone and Gambia became independent in 1961 and 1965.

In the newly independent states, territorial boundaries, administrative structures, dominant elites, and ideological conceptions were all the products of the colonial era. Most Sudanic and West African peoples were and are ruled by narrow – often military – elites, in the name of interests and ideologies that do not, with some exceptions, reflect the values and identities of the masses. The new elites were commonly non-Muslims and were primarily concerned with political and economic modernization. They accepted Islam as a "personal religion" on a par with Christianity and not necessarily as relevant to the political order.

Nonetheless, while European rule promoted secular elites, it also aided the peaceful spread of Islam. Colonial administration indirectly favored the spread of Islam by creating peace and order and by stimulating trade. Europeans broke down the traditional structures of society, introduced new educational and social ideas, opened markets, attracted migrant Africans to growing cities, and thereby indirectly promoted Islam as a form of authority and as an expression of cohesion among displaced peoples. The colonial powers also regarded Muslims as culturally and educationally more advanced than non-Muslim Africans, and appointed Muslim chiefs and clerks as administrators in non-Muslim areas. They subsidized Muslim religious teachers, who were allowed to pursue their missionary, community organizing, and instructional activity. In some cases colonial authorities helped organize Islamic law courts.

In both the colonial and independence periods there were significant conversions to Islam among pagan peoples. Between 1900 and 1960 the Muslim population of West Africa approximately doubled, and continues to grow substantially. In the region of Mali, 3 percent of the Bambaras were Muslims in 1912. French pacification opened new trading opportunities and led to widespread conversion, until by the 1960s 70 percent of the Bambara were Muslims. Mali is today about 90 percent Muslim. In northern Nigeria, where the British recognized Islam as the religion of the state, Hausas converted in large numbers. For example, the Bauchi emirate, which was 50 percent Muslim in 1920, was 75 percent Muslim in 1952. Ilorin was 43 percent Muslim in 1931 and 63 percent Muslim in 1952. Islam was spread south by Hausa migrants and by the large-scale conversion of Yorubas. According to the Nigerian census of 1963 over 40 percent of the population of Lagos and the western region was Muslim. By 1970 Nigeria as a whole was more than half Muslim.

Islam also made new converts in the Guinean and coastal regions. In Upper Volta at the end of the nineteenth century there were only some 30,000 Muslims, but by 1959 there were 800,000, approximately 20 percent of the population. Today Muslims make up about half the population of Burkina Faso. In the Ivory Coast the Muslims formed 7 percent of the populace in 1921, 22 percent in 1960, and 33 percent in 1970; at present they are about 60 percent. The Muslim population of Ghana has risen since independence from about 15 to about 30 percent. Sierra Leone was about 35 percent Muslim in 1960 and is about 60 percent Muslim today. Muslims are a great majority in Mauritania, Senegal, Mali, Nigeria, Gambia, Guinea, Niger, and Somalia. They make up half or more of the population of Nigeria, Ivory Coast, Burkina Faso, Sierra Leone, Chad, Guinea-Bissau, Ethiopia, and Sudan, and are a substantial minority in Ghana, Cameroon, Tanzania, and other countries.

Colonial rule not only favored the spread of Islam, but also created the conditions that shaped the social character, religious practices, and communal identity of Muslims. European rule forced the Muslims to abandon their eighteenth- and nineteenth-century political aspirations and to accept foreign domination. In many cases Muslims not only accepted but also collaborated with foreign or secular rulers. Muslim leaders, such as the Amirs of northern Nigeria or the Sufis of Senegal, became the foremost participants in colonial and post-independence regimes. Muslim religious leaders commonly preached acceptance of these regimes and helped recruit manpower for European armies, collect taxes, and even suppress Muslim dissidents. As in India, they saw themselves as an elite, the natural allies and the likely beneficiaries of cooperation with the state. Whereas in North Africa, the Arab Middle East, India, and Indonesia, Muslim associations were transformed into political movements, in Sudanic, savannah, and forest West Africa this was not usually the case.

Many Muslims, however, refused cooperation and withdrew from contact with Europeans. While Muslim resistance to colonial expansion in the nineteenth century was militant, after the consolidation of the European empires there was little armed resistance. Mahdists in Nigeria, Tuaregs in Niger, and Sufi-led warriors in Mauritania and Somalia were the only major exceptions. Muslim opposition to foreign rule could generally be expressed only indirectly through schools, reform movements, and Sufi-led brotherhoods. The Bamidele movement in Ibadan (Nigeria), for example, insisted on preserving Arabic usage, Muslim dress, and reformed Islamic practices. Muslim ethnic groups such as the Hausas and Yorubas were organized to protect Muslim identity. Educational associations were formed among urban and "modernized" Muslims.

The Hamalliya expressed opposition to foreign rule by symbolic means. The Hamalliya, founded by Shaykh Hamallah (1883–1943), was a Sufi brotherhood based in Nioro; it was an offshoot of the Tijaniya, and it condemned the parent order for having corrupted the true teachings of the founder. Shaykh Hamallah himself lived in seclusion, taught only in his own mosque, and never solicited gifts, though he accepted contributions from people who visited him. His followers held up his humility and gentleness against the greed and pride of the regular Tijaniya. His very withdrawal, however, had important political implications. Shaykh Hamallah refused to speak of political matters, and to publicly acknowledge French authority. His followers took his refusal to imply hostility to French rule. The French – ruling through a small number of administrators who had little understanding of African languages or peoples, and dependent upon clerks, interpreters, informers, and spies – harbored an almost paranoid suspicion of what the natives were doing. The French were eager to control the activity of Muslim religious leaders, and put them all under close surveillance. Outraged at the refusal of Shaykh Hamallah to give them political recognition, they deported him in 1925. In response he began to use an abbreviated prayer, and his followers turned to pray in the direction of his internment rather than Mecca. This symbolized the absence of a legitimate government.

The movement taught the social equality of all castes, and appealed strongly to runaway slaves, youth, and people without tribal or social standing. In the 1940s the Hamalliya divided into two wings. One refused to recognize the local religious authorities and was constantly involved in hostilities with the regular Tijaniya. A second wing, led by Tyerno Bokar Salif Tall (d. 1940), stressed the intellectual and mystical teachings of the master, egalitarianism, and rejection of foreign rule. Only after Hamallah's death did his followers begin to organize politically and to clash with the French.

Thus, the colonial heritage was complex. Britain and France had organized the territorial and administrative structure of the present African states. They had also promoted, albeit inadvertently, the spread of Islam and Muslim religio-communal organizations. The processes of Islamization, however, were very uneven. While some African states, such as Mauritania, Senegal, Niger, Mali, and Somalia, soon acquired large Muslim majorities, in many other states the population was partly Muslim, partly Christian, and partly African animist. Where Muslims were approximately half of the total population, as in Nigeria, Burkina Faso, the Ivory Coast, Cameroon, Sudan, and Ethiopia, this proved to be a recipe for conflict and even civil war. In many other cases, Muslims remained a minority and evolved political and communal structures fitting their demographic situation.

Furthermore, Muslims were themselves divided by conflicts of political ideology, religious cult, and differences of class and milieu. In the last half-century Muslims have embraced at least five principal orientations: there have been secularized Muslims, 'ulama'-defined and led communities, Sufi tariqat, reformist (sometimes called Wahhabi) movements, and Islamist or radical political Islam. There are, of course, many groups within each category. As we examine several African-Muslim societies, we will see major variations in the structure of national and Muslim political and communal organization, and in the Muslim adaptation to the larger African civilization.

MAURITANIA

Among African states, Mauritania shows the closest integration of state, national, and ethnic identities. The population of Mauritania is wholly Muslim, and the state identifies itself as Islamic. Mauritania is thus closest to Somalia or northern Sudan

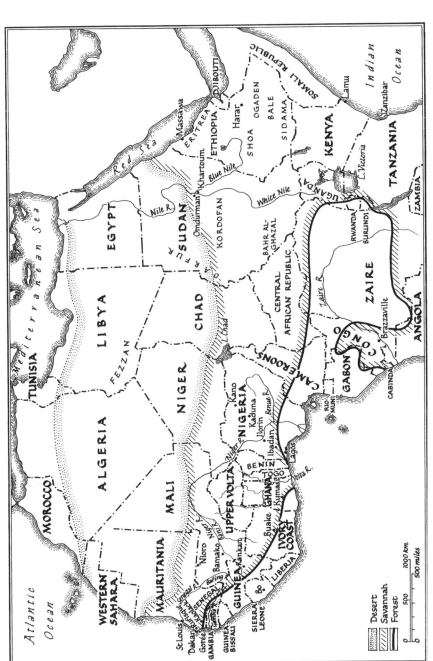

Map 38 Northern and Sudanic Africa: c. 1980

in the blending of popular Arab and Muslim identity and closest to Algeria and Libya in the integration of state and Islamic identity.

Historically, Mauritanian society was highly stratified. It was organized in a hierarchy of tribal groups. The Hassan or Arabs, descendants of the Bani Hassan conquerors, were the warriors. They raided, plundered, and collected tributes. The zawaya tribes were the descendants of the Sanhaja and the religious elites; they managed learning, trade, agriculture, and animal herding. These groups dominated tributary artisans, freedmen, and slaves. The Mauritanian population was also divided between the Arabophone tribes in the north and the black, Senegalese-related African population in the south, which had its own system of stratification. Since the eighteenth century, Sufi fraternities have been the principal expression of Muslim social organization. Shaykh Sidi al-Mukhtar al-Kunti and Shaykh Sidiya al-Kabir of Boutilimit were the founding fathers of Mauritanian Islam, though the Tijaniya became important in the nineteenth century.

Modern Mauritania was born out of French rule. A French protectorate was declared in 1904, but between 1902 and 1934 there were frequent Mauritanian rebellions. These were all suppressed, and eventually most of the Muslim religious leaders accepted collaboration with the French to protect their religious and economic interests. The French considered the Hassani tribes as the political elite, paid them subsidies, and institutionalized their authority as intermediaries between the French government and the general populace, but they also suppressed their traditional raiding activities obliging the Hassanis to take up stock raising and commerce. Thus they deprived the zawaya (religious) tribes of their traditional functions of political mediation, economic negotiation, and the organization of production. While believing they were preserving the traditional order of society, the French broke down the symbiosis among the Mauritanian tribes.

In 1946 the French separated Mauritania from Senegal and attempted to create a new political structure for the country. A local assembly was created in 1947, and Mauritanian political parties – the Entente Mouritanienne, formed in 1948, the Union Progressiste Mouritanienne (UPM), and the Association de la Jeunesse Mouritanienne (1951–52) – came into being. The parties represented a split in Mauritanian society between the traditional elites and the modern type of politician. A major issue in the 1950s was how to preserve Mauritanian identity by avoiding absorption into the Arab-Moroccan north or the Senegalese and Sudanese south.

Mauritania became independent in 1960, under the leadership of Mukhtar ould Daddah, the leader of the UPM, a cousin of Shaykh Sidiya, and a former collaborator with the French. In 1964 his renamed Mauritanian People's Party was made the only legitimate party. This was essentially an Arab regime which gave little political power to black African Halpular- and Sarkole-speaking agriculturalists and other southern ethnic groups. The ruling party represented the traditional political elites, and was drawn mainly from the zawaya tribes. In the new structure some non-tribal associations such as trade unions, women's organizations, and schools have been introduced; changing patterns of economic activity have allowed a new class of entrepreneurs to rise in influence. Though there has been some movement toward the formation of ideological political parties and an Islamist movement, in any governmental or business transaction family connections remain a critical factor. Merchants, bureaucrats, and tribal leaders are closely related. Though Islam is the common religion it does not in a practical sense unify the country.

In 1978 the regime was overthrown by a military coup, introducing a period of instability – and a succession of military rulers – which lasts to the present. Mukhtar ould Daddah had laid claim to the disputed Western Sahara, and shared in a short-lived partition of the region with Morocco, but the POLISARIO movement forced Mauritania to retreat, and provoked the coup of 1978. Tribalism and regionalism have become ever more important. Black African protests against political exclusion, organized by the Forces de Libération Africaine de Mauritanie (FLAM), founded 1983, led to the expulsion of blacks from the bureaucracy, the military, and the universities. Masses of villagers fled to Senegal and Mali in 1989–90. Mauritania receives help from Iraq and other Arab countries, and basically lives on foreign aid.

Islamic political parties are outlawed, and a coalition of traditional religious leaders and government authorities resists militant Islamic movements. The government promotes Islam to reinforce its authority. A charter of 1985 declared Islam the religion of the state and the people, and the Shari'a the only valid source of law. In 1991 an Islamic High Council was created, which includes both leading 'ulama' and leaders of the tariqat. The Tijaniya and Qadiriya both support the government, and the authority of the marabouts rose after they played an important role in resolving the hostilities between Senegal and Mauritania. The state also controls religion through mosques, schools, and institutes for higher education.

SENEGAL

Senegal is also an overwhelmingly Muslim society, but the state has a very different relationship with Islam. The Senegalese state was organized in accordance with European political institutions and led by a non-Muslim elite, but the bulk of the population was encadred in Sufi brotherhoods. Senegal is held together by the collaboration of state and Sufi elites, and thus represents a recreation of the classic pattern of relations between Muslim states and Muslim communal organizations.

The Senegalese pattern had its origins in the late nineteenth century, when the Muslim jihads and French conquest transformed the traditional bases of Senegalese society. In the wars of the late nineteenth century, the tyeddo slave military elite and the ruling pagan families were eliminated – though many old families maintained their position by producing a Sufi master or by marrying into Muslim families. Soldiers, peasants, and artisans dependent on the former chiefs, as well as liberated slaves, turned for leadership to Muslim holy men. A changing economy, which made peanut production rather than slave owning the basis of social power, assisted the transition. Thus a large portion of the Wolofs, the principal language group in Senegal, accepted Islam. For example, by 1913 close to half of western Saloum and three-quarters of lower Saloum was Muslim. By 1960 about half of the Serers had also converted to Islam. Today Senegal is over 90 percent Muslim.

French rule also helped promote the spread of Islam. The French saw the Muslims as advanced in civilization, productive in economic life, and skilled in administration. They used Muslim clerks and chiefs as intermediaries and allowed them to administer Muslim law. Under French rule Muslim holy men traveled from place to place, teaching, founding schools, and building communities. The French, however, also feared the Muslims as potential political rivals, and attempted to keep them under control. A law of 1903 required schoolteachers to be licensed and to be capable of teaching French. In 1908 the French forbade the circulation of Arabic newspapers. In 1911 French was made mandatory for use in Muslim courts, and Muslim holy men were forbidden to collect alms.

These policies, however, were never consistently applied, and after World War I the French switched to a policy of selective support for and manipulation of Muslim leaders. In turn, the Sufis helped the French keep the peace, raise troops, collect taxes, and encourage agricultural production. The Muslim elites adapted to French rule by giving up political militancy in favor of worship, education, and economic enterprise, and built up a new structure of Muslim brotherhoods. The Fadiliya were organized by Sa'ad Bouh (1850–1917), the Qadiriya by al-Hajj Malik Sy, and the Tijaniya by Ibrahim Niass (1900–75), the scion of a Senegalese Tijani family, who founded his own branch of the order and claimed in the 1930s to be the "savior of the age." His message was particularly attractive to Muslims attempting to adjust to migration and urban settlement.

The most important and well known of the Senegalese brotherhoods is the Muridiya, founded in 1886 by Ahmad Bamba (1850–1927), a holy man of Wolof and Tukulor descent, whose reputation was based on asceticism, piety, and lack of self-interest. He recognized that war against the French was futile, and took charge of the former followers of Ma Ba, Lat Dior, and others, urging them to turn from war to work. This reclusive and peaceful mystic was supported by Shaykh Ibra Fall (1858–1930), a former warrior who gave his allegiance to Ahmad in 1886, and worked to recruit his military followers into the Murid movement. Ibra Fall's submission marks the acceptance by the tyeddo of colonial domination and of Muslim leadership as the necessary conditions for the survival of Wolof society. The complementarity of marabout and warrior, of spiritual and worldly power, helped make the new order persuasive to numerous Senegalese. Ahmad Bamba was for a long time feared by the French as having territorial and political aspirations. He was exiled between 1895 and 1902 and again until 1907, but in 1912 the French accepted him as a spiritual and economic leader and allowed him to return to Diourbel.

The Murids integrated themselves into the French-dominated regime. Successive leaders of the order came to their positions with French support, and became clients of the French government. The primary activity of the order was to move labor teams into new lands along the edges of the deserts, organize agricultural colonies, and reclaim them for peanut cultivation. The leaders of the order owned the fields and peasants worked on them either in teams or on a weekly contributory basis. The order attracted landless, unemployed young men who often served an apprenticeship from the ages of nine to twenty-five in *daira*, or farming groups. By 1912 the order had 68,000 and by 1960 some 400,000 followers; by that time, one of every three Wolofs and one of every eight Senegalese was a member. Work was a form of withdrawal from politics, and at the same time a form of adaptation to modern life. By turning to economic activity, a defeated people found new dignity.

In religious terms the Murids gave themselves – body, soul, and property – to the master, who then protected them and interceded for them before God. The order stressed total obedience and regular payments of labor. The khalifa was the custodian of the founder's tomb. Beneath him were some 300–400 shaykhs, who arbitrated disputes, but did not usually teach or officiate in prayers. Their position depended upon public recognition as being persons with magical powers. The order was extremely hierarchical, with lesser leaders owing allegiance to the higher.

Traditional Islamic practices were not emphasized. Though Ramadan was observed, ordinary prayers and fasts were not scrupulously attended. Wolofs in general know little about the theological or mystical teachings of Islam, do not follow the Muslim law of divorce, and continue to employ a system of justice emphasizing family responsibility in marriage and property matters. The Fall branch of the Murids is ostentatiously unorthodox and nonconformist. The descendants of Ibra Fall do not observe prayer or other Islamic rituals, but believe that through work, charms, and magical practices, they may attain religious blessing.

At the same time that Senegalese society was being organized by Sufi brotherhoods, an urban non-Muslim, French-educated, professional and political elite took the lead in the struggle for independence. Senegal has a history of politically sophisticated elites going back to the middle of the nineteenth century, when the French extended citizenship to the residents of St. Louis, Dakar, Gorée, and Rufisque. Senegalese elites participated in French administration and worked for European businesses.

Senegal became independent in 1960. It is a secular state, and its institutions – the constitution, republican government, the civil code, administration, education and the judiciary – all come from the French model. Political discourse is replete with symbols of Islam, but the *état laïc* is universally accepted. The elites are defined by the use of French. Senegal is a relatively unified African society because the Wolof language is spoken by about 80 percent of the people and because most Senegalese are Muslims. National administration is centralized and hierarchical. The government has strong ambitions to educate, develop, and control society in the interest of its eventual secularization.

From 1960 Senegal was ruled by Léopold Senghor, the head of the Union Progressiste Sénégalaise, who dominated the country until he retired in 1980. By 1964 he had eliminated his rivals, and in 1966 he declared Senegal a one-party socialist state. From 1976 to 1980, possibly anticipating his retirement, Senghor permitted the creation of a multi-party system and national elections. The Socialist Party, the successor of the UPS, continued to win the overwhelming majority of the votes. After Senghor's retirement, for the first time, a Muslim, Abdu Diouf, was elected president, and remained in office until 2000.

Behind its institutional facade Senegal was organized into Sufi brotherhoods under the authority of their marabouts, who both resisted state power and facilitated governmental control. Though rivals for authority, state officials and marabouts cooperate. The marabouts legitimize the regime, and serve as auxiliaries in administration. The state sponsors projects that are of economic benefit to the marabouts, and provides them with honor and resources. These resources, and their ability to get jobs and mediate with the government, help the marabouts build a following of people who look to them for employment, medical and social support, spiritual counsel, and help in family and social relations. Popular support enables the marabouts to both shape state policy and to subtly challenge state authority.

While officials and Sufis collaborate, there are tensions between them. The farming practices of the Murids were criticized for over-cultivation of peanuts, neglect of rotation with other crops, deforestation, and exhaustion of the soil. The government attempted to create peasant cooperatives in order to improve agricultural techniques and to win control of the peanut industry. The Murids, however, continued to open up new territories without regard to soil conservation, the use of machinery, or modern agricultural methods. Recently, they have moved from peanut production into urban trade, and control small shops, electrical contracting, haulage, rice distribution, and other markets. Similarly, when the state adopted a new civil code in 1972 the marabouts simply refused to implement it. They also manipulated the dates of festivals to show symbolically that the state does not control them. Marabouts, unlike Islamists, do not contest the power of the state, but limit it through the creation of a religiously defined "civil society."

In each locality, the Sufi daira is the neighborhood or workplace unit of organization. It organizes festival and collects monies. The festivals are the critical demonstrations of numbers and strength. Individuals get the benefit of social insurance-type help, and may use the economic connections of the marabout to earn a living. In practice, however, the tariqat do not really control their members. While everyone has a marabout, loyalty is not exclusive. Commerce and marriage are not kept within the tariqa. People send their children to Quran schools at their convenience, regardless of their marabout. The marabouts instruct their followers on how to vote, but many disciples ignore or abstain from voting. Marabouts have to be careful of the sentiments of their followers when dealing in politics.

Urbanization in Senegal has led to the growth of a middle class, including professionals, bureaucrats, and teachers, who question the magical authority of the rural leaders. In the towns there has been a resurgence of interest in the Arabic language and in the Islamic beliefs that stress regular prayer, pilgrimage, ethical deportment, and intellectual interests coupled with the repression of religious emotion. Dyula traders, other migrants from the countryside to the towns, and returned students from the Middle East created the Muslim Cultural Union in 1953, which sponsored Arabic and Muslim school instruction and opposed colonialism, capitalism, and the power of the rural Sufis. A Muslim Association of African Students was founded in 1954, and a movement for the teaching of Arabic in Senegal in 1957. The National Federation of Muslim Cultural Associations, founded in 1962, lobbies for educational improvements and expansion of the teaching of Arabic and the Quran. In the 1970s the growth of Arabic economic and cultural influences stimulated calls for an Islamic constitution.

The reformers, primarily returned students and teachers of Arabic, however, have a very limited influence. The Mustarshidin, founded in 1980 by Shaykh Tidiane Sy, combines tariqa in its organization, reformism in its teachings, and Islamism in its denunciations of corruption and the West, and has mobilized alienated youth to oppose the government. Generally, however, the Islamists have been coopted into the Senegalese political system. The Senegalese respect Arabic as a sacred language, but do not consider it as part of their national identity, and the reformers have had to ally themselves either with the government or with the Sufi elites. Thus far, despite a Muslim president and the strength of Islamic feeling, the country is too divided among religious brotherhoods, urban and rural peoples, and traditionalists and modernists to generate a broad movement to turn Senegal into a Muslim state.

In Senegal the situation of women is ambiguous. The spread of Islam gave women family and inheritance rights they had not previously possessed, but the diffusion of the Sufi brotherhoods also led to the removal of women from positions of authority. Western influences have helped Senegalese girls attain some degree of education, though to a much smaller extent than boys. Women have been allowed to vote since 1956. By 1993 women made up about 15 percent of the legislature and the civil service. A Senegalese law of 1972 bans marriages under the age of sixteen, prohibits unilateral repudiation by the male, and provides that spouses must agree at the time of marriage whether the marriage is to be polygamous or monogamous. State law, however, is not enforced by the marabouts, who are the controlling local authorities. Muslim radicals who favor the formation of an Islamic state generally call for the veiling, seclusion, and withdrawal of women from public life.

NIGERIA

Northern Nigeria until independence

By contrast with Mauritania and Senegal, the unification of northern and southern Nigeria under British rule created a religiously pluralistic society. In northern Nigeria Islam had been the religion of the state elites since the fifteenth century. The Sokoto Caliphate brought it to a large proportion of the population. The Amirs were responsible for the implementation of justice. They appointed mallams to lead the prayers, preside over festivals, and advise them on Muslim law. Unofficially, they arbitrated local disputes. British rule tended to consolidate this Muslim society. In 1931 the British set up a conference of Amirs and chiefs of northern Nigeria, and protected them from Christian missionaries. While the British opposed the expansion of education because of lack of money and trained staff, the Amirs were eager to have English rather than Arabic taught in the schools, and sent their own children to the few schools that were available. Thus, there were no modern secondary schools until Katsina College was founded in 1922. English was made a compulsory subject in middle schools in 1930–31, and Arabic became part of the curriculum in 1932. Quranic instruction was provided by government-paid mallams. The Kano Law School had a fully Islamic curriculum. By the 1940s the British had changed their policy and sought to provide the modern kind of education given in the south, but by the time of independence only a minuscule number of northerners had been exposed to Western and secular values.

British rule, while politically conservative, stimulated important economic and social changes. The introduction of roads and railroads, and the promotion of export crops such as peanuts and cotton, brought the northern Nigerian peasantry into the international market economy. Vulnerable to changing world prices and excessive debt, many peasants lost their land and were forced to migrate to the cities.

This may have been one reason for the conversion of many Hausa peasants to Islam. The overall rate of conversion is not known, but studies of individual and communal experiences show that many converts were attracted by commercial opportunities. Successful trade depended on networks of relatives, friends, creditors, and customers. Traders therefore converted to Islam when their business enterprises had outgrown local markets and required the support of the larger-scale Muslim networks. Converts often moved from village to city levels of trade, and broke off ties with their village kin and the land. When a pagan Hausa converted he appeared before a Muslim judge and went through a ceremonial ablution. He was then given a gown, a turban, and a jug to hold the ablution water. This transition was fraught with dangers, which were conceptualized in terms of fear of evil charms and attack by spirits. Converts attempted to safeguard themselves by giving alms, having discussions with mallams, and taking medicines. Women ceased farm work, entered into seclusion, and became the financial responsibility of their husbands, though many earned an income from crafts or trade. Though they became Muslims, Hausa converts often continued to believe in spirits, which they equated with the Muslim jinn.

The development of a commercial economy led to important changes in the social structure of northern Nigeria's principal city, Kano. At the turn of the century about 77 percent of the population of Kano city was Hausa, but in rural areas the population was about two-thirds Hausa and one-third Fulani. There was an Arab minority. The populace was thus divided along linguistic, ethnic, and class lines. The class structure consisted of a ruling-class Fulani elite, rich Hausa merchants, senior civil servants, middle-class traders, and the common people or *talakawata*. Occupational groups were organized into communities, which were a combination of labor unions, welfare societies, and family councils. Throughout the nineteenth century religious activity was under the aegis of separate Hausa, Fulani, and Arab clans. Since the 1920s there has been a dramatic increase in population as a result of the introduction of a railroad, peanuts as a cash crop, and international air travel – developments which made Kano the principal market for northern Nigeria, and the center of a flourishing merchant class. By 1950 Kano was almost altogether Muslim, although non-Muslims from other parts of Nigeria dominated modern industries and government administration.

The integration of this populace took place on the basis of a shared Hausa language and shared Muslim religious affiliations. Common economic interests drew together Hausa merchants and Fulani administrators, and Hausa and Fulani craftspeople in similar trades. The revival of Muslim brotherhoods also served to bring Hausas, Fulanis, and Arabs into trans-ethnic religious associations, marking the change from a fragmented to more integrated local identity. The most important vehicle of these changes was the spread of the reformed Tijani order in the 1930s.

The Tijaniya were introduced into northern Nigeria in the nineteenth century by al-Hajj 'Umar, who married the daughter of Muhammad Bello, but there were few Tijani amirs or mallams until the conversion of Amir 'Abbas (1903–19). Muhammad Salga became the imam of the first Tijani mosque in Kano. The allegiance of his following was later given to Ibrahim Niass, a Wolof residing in Kaolack (Senegal), who was regarded as the khalifa, the seal of saints and the mujaddid, or reformer, of the century. Some of his followers believed that he was also the mahdi or messiah. They believed that Ibrahim had succeeded al-Hajj 'Umar, the reformer of the thirteenth Muslim century, and 'Uthman Don Fodio, the reformer of the twelfth. The reformed order was further reinforced by the formation of the Youth of Islam and the Society of Young Muslims as the expression of younger-generation activists. By the 1960s about 60 percent of the mallams of Kano belonged to the reformed Tijaniya. Kano in turn became the base for the further expansion of the reformed order to other northern Nigerian cities such as Katsina and Kaduna and to rural areas. Throughout Nigeria and West Africa the order organized religious ceremonies, such as the recitation of dhikr and the celebration of the birthday of the Prophet. The order sponsored numerous schools and contributed to a revival of Arabic and Muslim education in opposition to Western schools. The Tijaniya network made it possible for traders and travelers to find housing, jobs, and other assistance. Ibrahim had a strong following among women because of his reputation for baraka and the conferral of blessings. The Qadiriya similarly became a mass organization, including Hausas as well as Arab and Fulani scholars, emphasizing collective prayers and celebrations.

The transnational affiliations of the Sufi brotherhoods, pilgrimages to Mecca, and studies in Cairo linked Kano to the outside Muslim world. By the time of independence, northern Nigerian and Kano identity, in particular, had several inter-related levels. On one level there were still the remnants of the nineteenth-century concepts of community. The Fulani elite had perpetuated its power, and Fulani, Hausa, and other ethnic identities remained strong among the common people. At the same time there was a tendency to redefine social identity in Muslim terms. The Amirs stressed their Islamic functions; the Sufi brotherhoods and political parties stressed the Muslim aspirations of the merchants and the common people.

Building on Sufi religious consolidation, the northern elites wanted to unify northern Nigeria, and make Muslims dominant in the country as a whole. In 1948 they formed the Nigerian People's Congress to represent the interests of the north-ern political establishment. Ahmadu Bello was the principal leader of this effort. As the leader of the People's Congress he promoted an informal governing network of politicians, military officers, bureaucrats, bankers, intellectuals, and business-men, the so-called Kaduna Mafia, who supported administrative, judicial, and edu-cational reforms. In the 1960s he tried to mobilize popular support by founding a new "trans-Sufi" movement under the name Usmaniya (a reference to 'Uthman [Usman] Don Fodio). Outside support came from Sa'udi Arabia and Kuwait. After Bello's assassination in 1966 the movement splintered, and was ultimately paralyzed.

In competition, younger members of aristocratic families, newly prosperous merchants, and others founded the Northern Elements Progressive Union (NEPU, 1947–50). The NEPU was led by mallams who had a Western as well as an Arabic education. Aminu Kano, who had studied Quran interpretation, wrote Hausa plays criticizing the abuses of the ruling elite. His criticism was directed not only against Britain but also against the native establishment. The party rallied teachers, clerks, servants, petty traders, craftsmen, workers, and lesser 'ulama' to oppose autocratic colonial rule. Just as Muslim brotherhoods became the expression of the middle classes, new Islamic political movements emerged to consolidate petit-bourgeois and lower-class opposition to the state and merchant elites. In northern Nigeria, state, merchant, and populist opposition were all committed to Muslim symbols, interpreted in varying ways.

Southern Nigeria

While in northern Nigeria Islam was the pervasive idiom of social organization and political conflict, in southern Nigeria, Islam did not define the society as a whole but was the religion of specific minorities. In southern Nigeria the first Yoruba con-verts were made by Muslim traders from Bornu, Songhay, and Hausaland. In the nineteenth century liberated slaves from Sierra Leone and Brazil established colonies in Lagos, and Muslims from the north settled in Ilorin, Ibadan, and other towns on the basis of ethnic or other local affiliations.

Lagos had for more than a century been the center of important Muslim com-munities. In 1861 it became a British colony. The British helped to resolve disputes among Muslims, and acquired a reputation for being impartial in internal Muslim affairs. British officials even patronized mosques. The British also posed a great challenge to Muslims by introducing Western and Christian education. Christian schools had great appeal, as Western education was a key to commercial and professional career advancement, but many Muslims were afraid it would subvert family beliefs. Thus, the Muslims formed their own educational societies. The Egbe killa society of Lagos was founded in the 1880s. The Ahmadiya, a missionary Muslim association from India, began proselytizing during World War I; the Ansar ud-deen was founded in 1923. By 1960 it had some 50,000 members, teacher-training colleges, high schools, and primary schools. Other associations were founded to serve the need for the education of women. Thus Lagos became a center of Muslim modernism.

Ibadan, before Nigerian independence, had two Muslim communities, one Yoruba and one Hausa. The Yoruba-Muslim community was organized under the authority of a chief imam. A council of ten scholars, who inherited their positions and were supported by contributions, ran the mosques and community affairs. The Yoruba Muslims supported a Quran school and a higher Muslim academy, but they did not live in an exclusive setting, and had close social relationships with non-Muslim Yoruba, including the sharing of churches, mosques, and ceremonies.

Alongside the Yoruba there was also a Hausa-Muslim community. The Hausas came to Ibadan as migrant traders, teachers, beggars, porters, and workers. They were primarily engaged in long-distance trade, in which they imported peanut oil, dried meat, fish, milk, and cattle from the north, and exported kola nuts, sugar, iron, salt, and manufactured goods from the south. The trade was conducted in a traditional framework – without banks, insurance companies, civil courts, or even legal documents. Success depended upon the trust developed within a close-knit minority community. At the beginning of the twentieth century Hausa businessmen living in Ibadan formed a quarter of their own, inhabited by migrant northerners and their wives and prostitutes. The British and the majority Yoruba favored the formation of such a quarter under the control of a Hausa chief as a way of regulating a restless migrant community that included not only peddlers and merchants, but beggars, thieves, and other troublemakers.

The chief of the quarter played an indispensable part in the life of the Ibadan community. He acted as judge, officiated at marriages, mediated inheritance and custody disputes, appointed headmen for occupational sub-groups, maintained public services, and policed the activity of strangers. He was an essential reference for creditworthiness, and for the legitimization of land and property ownership. Every man owed the chief direct personal allegiance, which was signified by kneeling down in front of his office. There were also sub-chiefs to regulate the cattle market, the butchers, and the guilds of beggars. The beggars were organized into three sub-groups under a chief of the blind, a chief of the lame, and a chief of the lepers. Begging was a regular occupation, to which no stigma was attached. Each beggar was assigned a workplace, and paid his Friday earnings to the chief.

Landlords had a crucial economic function; they were hotel and rooming-house keepers for itinerant workers. They acted as intermediaries for their guests, arranging deals, advancing capital, holding deposits, and advising on business conditions. A wealthy landlord had a clientele of workers – including his sons, foster-sons, and others – who carried on the business of his firm. He helped generate the personal contacts that facilitated trade.

In the late 1940s and 1950s this society of chiefs and landlords was subverted by the rise of the nationalist movements. Faced with competition from the Yoruba and the rise of Nigerian nationalism, the Hausas had to identify their own group interest in ways that would both exclude the Yoruba and be consistent with the new emphasis on national solidarity. Thus between 1950 and 1952 after an inspiring visit by Ibrahim Niass, virtually the whole of the Hausa community joined the Tijaniya.

The new religious awareness also changed the nature of authority within the Hausa community. As teachers of correct Muslim practice, the mallams became important. They provided for education; they advised the chiefs and the merchants as to whether it was propitious to undertake particular activities, and were believed to know the right religious and magical formulae to achieve practical results. They were also believed to have the purity of heart that was essential to mystical power. Members of the Tijaniya looked to their ritual masters for protection against evil spirits, and consulted them on matters of family, business, and daily behavior. Anxious landlords, particularly sensitive to changing market conditions, looked to the mallams for social and moral support. The chiefs and the landlords signified their acceptance of this new religious authority by making the pilgrimage to Mecca and earning the title hajji. They became more sensitive to public pressures, especially those due to the practice of "public scandalizing," or denunciation of individuals for unacceptable behavior. Community organization, community authority, and community identity were restructured in Muslim terms.

Independent Nigeria

The formation of a Nigerian national state in 1960, bringing north and south into the same political framework, profoundly altered the political meaning of Islam. Owing to intense ethnic, religious, and regional differences, a true union of north and south was not achieved. The crucial problem was the antagonism between the Muslim north, the Yoruba west, and the Ibo east. Though the north had political predominance, the south had the oil and the bulk of the nation's administrative cadres. In 1966 the rising power of the north, and resistance to central government authority in the west, prompted the military, led by General Ironsi, succeeded by General Gowon, to seize power. The Ibo east, however, refused incorporation into the new regime and proclaimed the Republic of Biafra. A bitter civil war was fought until the defeat of the eastern provinces in 1970.

Between 1966 and 1979 a succession of military governments sought to reintegrate the country. Southern fears of northern domination, revived by cooperation among the northern states and a census showing that the north had a majority of the population, contributed to a new uprising. In 1976 the Gowon regime was overthrown and replaced by a new military government headed by Olusegun Obasanjo (1976–79). The country was returned to civilian government, and in the elections of 1979 the National Party of Nigeria, representing the Muslim elites of the north, prevailed. Al-Hajji Shehu Shagari became the President of Nigeria's second republic. The north, having accepted integration into the national political system, became the predominant power. Their only opponent was the People's Revolutionary Party, which had the support of workers, craftsmen, and traders in Kano and Kaduna.

In 1984 another coup inaugurated a period of military rule, which lasted until 1999. The military regimes of this era were noteworthy for their corruption, exploitation of the country's oil resources for private gain, and widespread lawlessness throughout the country. The death of General Abacha in 1998 paved the way for the election of former General Obasanjo to the presidency. Despite this instability, the post-1966 military regimes progressively strengthened the Nigerian state. The exploitation of Nigeria's oil reserves gave the federal government vastly increased revenues. The federal state also had major investments in the petrochemical, gas, fertilizer, cement, automobile, paper, and sugar industries, and the government took a major role in the regulation of the banks and the economy. State policies favored the formation of a Nigerian economic elite. A decree of 1972 reserved large areas of the economy for native Nigerians and prohibited foreign firms without a minimum Nigerian participation. Government banks began to allocate a substantial proportion of their loans to Nigerian businessmen and civil servants, who were able to become entrepreneurs. Clientage relations between capitalists and clerks, artisans, and agents sometimes enabled the common people to prosper.

Islam in post-independence northern Nigeria

The political context profoundly altered the role of Islam in northern Nigeria, and in the nation as a whole. With the formation of a military regime in 1966 the political power of the northern Amirs was reduced, and their ceremonial and religious functions became correspondingly more important. They became patrons of Muslim religious groups, helped to sponsor the translation of the Quran into Hausa, and diffused Islamic reform attitudes in order to integrate Arabic- and Hausa-speaking Muslims. Internal differences among Muslims were deemphasized in favor of a shared Islamic identity. New reformist movements – representing the more universalist, scripturalist, and radical versions of contemporary Islam, and closely allied to the northern elites – arose to challenge the predominance of the Tijaniya and Qadiriya. Muslim and Arabic education sponsored by the reformers helped produce a new counter-elite. Most madrasa graduates became teachers of Islam, and a few became qadis. Their goal was to establish a Shari'a society. They regarded women as intellectually and morally inferior, resisted women's education, and called for their seclusion in the household.

In the 1960s Shaykh Abubakar Gumi, Grand Qadi of northern Nigeria from 1960 to 1966, became the leader of this tendency. Gumi, originally a protégé of Ahmadu Bello, attacked the Sufi brotherhoods as a form of *bid'a*, or illicit innovation, criticized common practices such as the veneration of saints and conspicuous consumption at marriages and festivals, promoted a modern Muslim education, and worked to integrate the Shari'a into all secular jurisdictions including the constitution of Nigeria. Gumi also favored the education of women and female suffrage, in part because he saw this as a way of increasing the voting and political power of the Muslim north in national politics. His followers founded the Yan 'Izala in 1978, an acronym for the Association for the Removal of Innovation and the Establishment of the Sunna. The movement had financial support from Sa'udi Arabia and Kuwait. It spread by intensive preaching, and cassette and radio propaganda. The reformist program appealed to a modernizing, educated, but anti-Western milieu of functionaries, businessmen, intellectuals, and students for its advocacy of Muslim solidarity, equality, and its opposition to corruption. Yan 'Izala and reformism shaded into Islamism, a program for Islamic ideological identity and Islamic political institutions. Yan 'Izala militants were involved in violent clashes with supporters of the Sufi brotherhoods. The violent elements also saw themselves at war with a Judeo-Christian Western world.

The 1970s also witnessed a counter-trend toward integration of the north into the nation. In the 1970s, the northern Muslim elites had to ally with non-Muslim southerners to maintain their political position. The close economic ties between the Hausa north and the Yoruba south, the economic interdependency of Kano and Lagos for transportation and the marketing of agricultural products, and federal subsidies laid the foundation for interregional cooperation. The media also emphasized national Nigerian identity, as opposed to religious and regional ties.

The 1980s, however, brought increased Muslim militancy. The oil boom of the 1970s stimulated both Islamic revival and religious conflicts. An important politicizing moment for Nigerian Muslims was the promulgation of the Universal Primary Education scheme in the 1970s, which was perceived as increasing the influence of Western-Christian and diminishing Islamic values. As Muslims increasingly improved their attendance at mosques, opened schools, and dressed in conservative fashion, the northern states encouraged Islam in the media and the schools. Muslim movements also worked for the unification of the Muslim population, and for national policies recognizing Islam. The Council of 'Ulama', founded in 1986, called for recognition of Friday and Islamic festivals as national holidays, a less Western-oriented foreign policy, termination of diplomatic relations with the Vatican and Israel, and Nigerian membership in the international Organization of the Islamic Conference (OIC). The Nigerian Supreme Council for Islamic Affairs (NSCIA) also advocated introduction of an Islamic calendar, a national Shari'a court of appeal, and other Islam-related policies. Eventually three judges versed in Islamic law were appointed to the Federal Court of Appeals, though a separate Muslim court was not established. Under Muslim influence the national education system provided for the teaching of Islam and the Hausa language. As Muslims were better integrated into national life, Muslim activists propounded Islam as a blueprint for the social order as well as for personal religious behavior. While the Yoruba west was much more accommodating and tolerant, it also harbored strong reformist movements and demands for the Islamization of the political system.

In the new atmosphere, Muslims became increasingly politicized and assertive. Muslim radicals in the north came to see themselves as an embattled minority threatened by non-Muslim predominance in the south and by Western influences, and at the same time as bearers of a holy mission to universalize the Sokoto Caliphate, and to make the north a Muslim holy land from which all non-Muslims were to be eliminated.

Muslim militancy contributed to a high level of tension with the Christian populations. In 1987 the Muslim Students' Society and the Fellowship of Christian Students in Kaduna fought street battles over a presumed insult to the Quran. Fighting spread to the township, then to villages, and to the entire state of Kaduna. Churches and mosques were destroyed. Relations between Muslims and Christians have become even more delicate since the end of military rule in May 1999, and subsequent moves by the northern states to implement the Shari'a. In 1999 Zamfara became the first Nigerian state to adopt Shari'a. The Kano state assembly approved the introduction of the Shari'a. Niger passed bills introducing Shari'a. By November 2001 twelve northern states had adopted Islamic law. There were murderous and destructive Muslim–Christian riots. President Obasanjo opposed the movement toward Shari'a, but the northern states are slipping out of federal control.

Nigerian women live in a very conservative setting. Seclusion of women is the normative practice in Nigeria. This implies that men and women do not mix socially. Girls tend to marry between the ages of eleven and fourteen, and most work at home in food preparation, sewing, knitting, and similar activities. Generally, women require their husbands' permission to undertake outside educational or economic activities. Still, there is some scope for autonomous women's activities. Women were enfranchised in 1976. The Agency for Mass Education was started in 1977 and provides adult-education classes for women. Learned women teach privately and a few teach at the Women's Arabic Teachers College in Kano, founded in 1978. In 1979 the People's Redemption Party, which came to power in Kano and Kaduna, supported universal primary education, including education for girls, and had two women appointed to government posts. There are also feminist organizations, including the Federation of Muslim Women's Associations of Nigeria that support the establishment of Shari'a law and defend women's rights in inheritance, child custody, and education as defined in Islamic law.

While Islam was becoming a national religion it was also becoming the religion of lower- and middle-class opposition to the dominant elites. In the 1950s the Northern Elements Progressive Union opposed the emirate system and the aristocracy in the name of the middle-class intelligentsia, the common people, and Islamic values. With the consolidation of state economic and political elites in the 1970s, Islam was revived as the banner of the opposition. In Kano, for example, laborers, factory workers, petty traders and craftsmen – many of whom were itinerant Quran students and downwardly mobile mallams (religious teachers) – found in Muslim values an outlet for their concerns about wage exploitation, inflation, and a declining standard of living for the common people. The mallams were particularly important, for they provided interpretive leadership for fellow workers. In working-class milieus the mallams and the students taught the Quran, behaved in the exemplary Hausa-Muslim manner, cultivated courtesy, modesty, patience, and honesty, advocated social solidarity and Muslim justice, and articulated the resentment of the poor at low wages, the excesses of consumption by the rich, and political oppression. In Muslim terms they expressed a lower-class demand for justice. These mallams, however, once a respected social category, became redefined as an embarrassing, dangerous, and immoral class by the newly wealthy elites. Universal Primary Education undermined traditional modes of Islamic learning and lessened the need for mallams. Homeless and unemployed Quran students displaced from construction jobs and burdened by rising food and housing costs threw themselves into the Yan Tatsine movement, a millenarian outburst that led to riots throughout northern Nigeria from 1980 to 1985. Another radical Islamic movement was inspired by Iran's revolution. They called themselves Shi'a, but they were not religiously connected to historical Shi'ism. Most of the activists were students of Quran schools who had no more than a primary education. For them Shi'aism was not a belief system so much as a protest movement that implied a return to the pristine values of Islam.

Just as Islam symbolized the fusion of Hausa and Fulani ethnicity and the complex interweaving of local Kano, northern regional, and Nigerian national identity, it symbolized the class conflict between the dispossessed and the elites. All parties find in Islam the symbols and the organizational basis for the struggle for political power. As in other Muslim countries, Islam in northern Nigeria has become a universal idiom, an encompassing basis for social identity with sufficient internal differentiation to articulate conflicting interests in a complex society.

THE WAHHABIS AND REFORMIST MOVEMENTS

In other parts of West Africa, Muslims are minorities and have not shaped the governing regimes. Most West African states have been and are ruled by one-party systems, military regimes, and similar concentrated governments, while Muslim communal life is built around schools and scholars, clerical lineages such as the Jakhanke and the Saghanughu, Sufi brotherhoods, and minority ethnic groups.

The older forms of community are being challenged by reformist and modernist movements which seek to transform both the practice of Islam and the politics of their societies. Modernist movements, however, are not localized in particular countries, but spread all across West Africa, reflecting growing urbanization and the need for moral order and social controls in changing societies. The pressures of city life under colonial rule brought out a conflict of interest between well-established elders, who wanted to appropriate family wealth, and younger family members and workers, who turned to modernist and educational reform movements as an expression of protest. Most of the members were small and middling traders and petty functionaries. Disillusionment with Sufism because of its collaboration with colonial and state authorities also fueled these movements.

The Wahhabiya, centered in Bamako, is a good example. The name signifies their reformist intentions – not an identity of beliefs with the Sa'udi Arabian movement. The Wahhabiya was introduced by students who had gone to al-Azhar and Cairo Universities, where they came into contact with the Muslim Brothers and other neo-Islamic movements. Pilgrimage to Mecca and Medina was also an important source of reformed religious ideas. One of these pilgrims, al-Hajj 'Abdallah Mahmud, returned to Bamako imbued with reform ideas. He called on his fellow Muslims to study the Quran and the sayings of the Prophet, to adhere to the Maliki school of law and ascetic forms of Sufism, and to eschew saint worship and animistic religious practices. He attacked the local mallams for cultic rituals and for collaboration with colonial rulers. Al-Hajj 'Abdallah founded a school in 1949, and organized the Subbanu al-Muslimin (Society of Young Muslims) in 1951. The prime function of this association was the education of children to prevent their assimilation of French values and to promote Islam. While a colonial-sponsored education in French symbolized dependency, an Arabic one signified opposition to Westernization. The graduates were generally reformist in the Salafi sense, in favor of the implementation of the Shari'a, and hostile to the old-fashioned 'ulama' and the traditional marabouts.

The movement spread rapidly over the trade routes of West Africa, with branches in Kankan, Bo, Buake, and other towns in Mali, Guinea, Gambia, Sierra Leone, and also the Ivory Coast, Senegal, Upper Volta (Burkina Faso), and the Niger region, especially where there were no strong Tijani or Qadiri communities. In the 1950s, the French–Arabic schools and Arabic madrasas generated a new elite. The development of the reformist groups led to conflicts with other Muslims, disputes over the control of local mosques, and often to the formation of separate mosques in each town.

From the 1970s contact with the Arab Middle East further spread Islam and Arabic instruction. Sa'udi Arabia, Libya, Tunisia, and Egypt support this tendency with money for mosques, madrasas, and scholarships. The Sa'udis created the Muslim World League (Rabitat al-'Alam al-Islami) in 1962, the World Assembly of Muslim Youth in 1973, and several international Islamic Universities. Libya created an Association and Faculty for Call to Islam (Da'wa al-Islamiya), gave scholarships to African students, sent missionaries to other African countries, and sponsored conferences. Iran had a similar program. Sudan built an International University of Africa and a University of the Quran. Mosques, madrasas, cultural centers, and clinics were built in Senegal, Niger, and Nigeria. Islamic associations proliferated. Pilgrimage, scholarships, financial assistance, endowments, and conferences reached people deprived of a Western education.

In the 1980s Islamism became more important. While reformism was dedicated to the purification of the life of the individual, Islamism was aimed at the formation of an Islamic state. The Islamists created social welfare movements to replace ineffective states in the provision of schools, mosques, and social and health services. Islamic universities have been created in Senegal and Nigeria. These movements are closely tied to the politics of each country. In the 1950s and 1960s the rise of the reform movement was closely associated with the RDA political party in Sudan, Guinea, and the Ivory Coast. The reformers and RDA shared a common opposition to French colonial rule, and to forced labor and other forms of taxation. Both were opposed to the conservative rural chiefs and religious leaders, and both were supported by modernizing commercial groups. They shared principles of social justice and equality which could be expressed in either secular or Muslim terms. The RDA politicians often used the Muslim vocabulary and readings from the Quran to appeal for Muslim support. Thus, the cultivation of reform Islamic religious principles was a way of raising political consciousness; conversely, nationalism was motivated by Muslim feeling.

The association of Islam with national identity has become closer in many states. In Mali in the 1960s, President Modibo Keita suppressed the reformist associations, but the growth of Arabic and Islamic education, closer ties to the Arab states, and grants from Sa'udi Arabia and Kuwait helped reverse earlier policies. His successor, Mousa Traore, sponsored a Malian Association for Islam's Unity and Progress and used it to control Muslim affairs. Madrasa education expanded enormously in the 1970s, and by the 1980s madrasas had been accepted as a major branch of the national education system. Numerous government posts in the Ministries of Education, Justice, Interior, Religious Affairs, and Foreign Service were given to Arabic speakers even though the state elites were still secular and Francophone. The Islamists argue that Islam expresses the inherent nature of Africa, in opposition to the imperialism of the West. Islam has become, in effect, the national religion of Mali.

In 1987, Upper Volta was renamed Burkina Faso. After a succession of military coups, a constitutional republic was established in 1991. In Burkina Faso the Arabist and Islamist movement is a counter-culture to the European style of modernity, and also a way of integrating the disparate ethnic groups that make up the Muslim population of the country. Madrasa education, which began just after World War II, now serves half of the Muslim population, though only tiny minorities reach the secondary level. Islam is also strengthened by the construction of mosques, preaching on national television, official recognition of Muslim festivals, and support from the Arab world. Madrasa education appeals to the lower middle classes, excluded from political power, who favor a state based on the Shari'a. The Islamic movements, however, are divided into numerous factions.

32 The Friday mosque at Mopti, Mali

The Ivory Coast

In the Ivory Coast, Wahhabism not only changed national politics, but transformed the very definition of ethnicity and Islamic identity. Here the Dyula were the established Muslim community. They lived in the Koko quarter of Korhogo, and made their living in weaving and trade. They were organized in *kabila*, or wards, which were patrilineal descent groups. The Dyula were divided into moieties – the *mory* were the clans who strictly observed Islam, and were the learned custodians and transmitters of Arabic texts; their isnads traced back to al-Hajj Salim Suwari in the fifteenth century. The *tun tigi* were the clans that participated in Muslim festivals but did not strictly observe Islamic laws – the people of warfare and politics, but not of religious knowledge. The scholars held that Islam was separate from politics, and supported the existing regimes; all other Dyula were free to belong to any faction or party. The Tijaniya and Qadiriya founded branches among the Dyula, but they were not organized corporate groups. Membership was voluntary, and the joiners were usually older men seeking recognition for religious merit.

As new people of different ethnic groups converted to Islam, it ceased to be an ethnic-minority religion, and became the religion of large numbers of people throughout the nation. To be Muslim was redefined, no longer in terms of belonging to Dyula mory and tun tigi lineages, but in terms of observance of Islamic law. The tun tigi clans came under pressure to upgrade their observance; sermons replaced dancing as the typical Muslim ceremony.

This change was fostered by Wahhabism, which was introduced into the Ivory Coast in the late 1940s. The movement spread along the trade routes and established itself in the principal towns, especially Abidjan, Bouake, and Bamako, and the earliest converts were *nouveaux riches* merchants, shippers, entrepreneurs, and their dependent workers. Wahhabis tended to be pro-Arab and anti-colonial, and were involved in the struggles for national independence. The new intellectuals devalued the mory lineage culture, and stressed the universality of Islam rather than traditional kinship and ethnic loyalties. Wahhabi preachers denounced magic, saint worship, and the traditional special rituals for life-cycle events. Though the Wahhabis had begun as a movement of the well-to-do, they progressively became a movement of lower-class, recent converts, to whom their universalism and indifference to race, caste, and social origin appealed. A good proportion were Guinean migrants. By the 1990s the radicalism and sectarianism of the Wahhabis had diminished, and they began to pray with other Muslims. At least externally there was a return to Muslim unity.

With the growing strength of Islam, Houphouet-Boigny, who had a strong pro-Catholic orientation, created an Islamic Superior Council to integrate Muslims into the government. Imams supported him for reelection in 1990. After his death in 1993, however, the Muslim north and the predominantly Christian and animist south began to struggle for power. There have been riots, assaults upon Muslims, and the burning of mosques in Abidjan.

Ghana

Kumasi provides another example of the older type of Muslim community and the challenges posed by reformism. In the nineteenth century it already had a strong Muslim community, which provided the Ashanti government with scribes, ambassadors, political advisors, soldiers, and religious magicians. The Muslims had considerable influence because of the value attached to their amulets, and they intermarried with the Ashanti elite. In addition to the local Muslims there were Hausa and Mossi traders who brought cattle, leather, and cloth to Kumasi in return for gold dust, salt, and kola nuts.

In 1896 the British conquered the Ashanti empire, took Kumasi, and in 1900–01 declared a protectorate over northern Ghana. They developed the gold mines and cocoa plantations on the Gold Coast, opened the way to unrestricted northern immigration to the south, and attracted hundreds of thousands of workers from northern Ghana, Hausaland, Upper Volta, Togo, Dahomey, Niger, and Mali. Many of the migrants were not Muslims, but soon adopted Islam and the Hausa language. This populace was concentrated in the Zongo or Muslim quarter of Kumasi. Ethnic differences were perpetuated through lineages, which appointed their own headmen. The headmen were vital because they helped the sick and poor, provided food and lodging, took care of orphans, supervised inheritances, performed marriages and burials, and adjudicated disputes on the basis of Islamic and customary law. The British recognized the community headmen, allowed them to organize courts, and appointed a *sarkin*, or chief, of the Zongo. With independence, the Muslim community was restructured. In 1957 Kwame Nkrumah removed the headmen from office and created a direct link between the government and the communities by the appointment, under the authority of the Minister of the Interior, of a man named Mutawakilu as Sarkin Zongo. The Muslim Council was created as an instrument of government control. With the removal of Nkrumah in 1966 the Muslim communities again set up their own headmen.

Since 1966 the community structure of the Zongo has evolved to emphasize its common Muslim identity. Ethnic ties were generally stronger among first-generation immigrants, but second- and third-generation residents identify with wider Muslim rather than with more parochial groups. Neighborhood, school, and youth groups are formed on a multi-ethnic basis. The Hausa version of Islam has become standard. Marriage and naming ceremonies tend to follow the Hausa pattern. Festivals, funerals, ceremonial days, and worship in the common mosque also serve to reinforce a trans-ethnic solidarity. Progressively, the old ethnic-lineage headmen were challenged by modernizing movements led by a younger generation of urban-born, educated leaders. In Ghana these movements included the Ahmadiya, the Ghana Muslim Mission, the Islamic Research and Reformation Center, the Islamic Solidarity Association of West Africa, the Supreme Council for Islamic Affairs in Ghana, and the Ghana Muslim Representative Council – all of which sponsor English–Arabic schools and missionary activities.

Muslims of South Africa

There are three main groups of Muslims in South Africa, who make up about 2 percent of the population – about 325,000 people. Cape Malays came from the Indonesian archipelago in the seventeenth century. Indian Muslims came as indentured laborers, traders, merchants, and hawkers in the nineteenth century. After 1860 Muslim laborers came from Malawi and Zanzibar. There are some local converts.

The first group of Muslims came from the Southeast Asian islands after the Dutch East India Company established itself in the Cape in 1652. These first Muslims were Amboyan Mardyckers, who were brought to protect the Dutch settlement against the indigenous San and Khoi. The Dutch also brought Muslim slaves from all over Africa and Asia, as well as Muslim convicts. Under the Dutch, Muslims could not worship publicly, which meant that they relied on Sufi traditions and practiced Islam mainly at home. Only in 1798, under British rule, was the first mosque permitted. More mosques were established in the nineteenth century, usually around an individual imam. In one case, Malay Muslims were awarded land for a mosque after assisting the British in fighting the Xhosa in the east. However, in general, Muslims in the Cape maintained an oppositional relationship with the state. In the twentieth century, Muslims in the Cape were affected by apartheid laws. Most Muslims were relocated from the city center and from business areas to the suburbs of Cape Town. New mosques were built in the residential areas. Various efforts to unify Muslims under a single umbrella organization, such as the Muslim Judicial Council (MJC), which was formed in 1945, failed. The MJC wanted to make Shari'a the law of the Muslim community, but this was resisted by the independent imams.

The Muslims in the Transvaal primarily came from India as indentured workers, hawkers, and traders during the British era. The earliest mosque in Transvaal was built in Pretoria in 1887. Most of the religious leaders were brought from India, and in general they were very conservative. The 'alim, or scholar, of each mosque decided religious issues, but committees of influential traders and hawkers controlled the relationship of the mosques to the state authorities. There are also many Muslims in Natal, whose ancestors came from India to work on the sugar plantations.

In present-day independent South Africa Muslims are assured religious rights. Muslims can demand rescheduling in schools or offices to attend religious services. New organizations, such as the Muslim Youth Movement, the Call of Islam, and Qiblah have been formed.

CHAPTER 31

ISLAM IN EAST AFRICA

The East African states are here grouped together for convenience, but the experience of each country was in fact very different. The history of the Sudan resembles that of North Africa and the Middle Eastern Arab countries. For a century and a half, the Sudan has been consolidating a modern state. The northern part of the country has an Arabic-speaking population, a Muslim identity, and strong Islamic movements, but the southern part encompasses a non-Muslim African population which resists assimilation on Arab, Muslim, and central-state terms. Somalia also resembles the Sudan, the Arab Middle Eastern and North African countries, and Mauritania in that tribal, Muslim, and Arab identity have become part of Somali national identity. Ethiopia also has a long history of state consolidation, but this has taken place under Christian rather than Muslim leadership. In Ethiopia the Muslim populace has resisted incorporation into a non-Muslim state, but until recently its resistance was expressed in secular rather than religious terms. The histories of Kenya, Tanzania, Uganda, and other East African countries, by contrast, follow a West African pattern in which the dominant consideration in the twentieth century has been the formation of colonial regimes and their replacement by secular national states. In these countries Islam is the basis of local communal and social organization but not of state power or national identity.

SUDAN

By the nineteenth century the regions that comprise the modern state of Sudan already had a long history of Muslim Sultanates, substantial Muslim populations, and developed Muslim religious institutions. In the nineteenth and twentieth centuries the process of territorial unification and consolidation of state power proceeded relentlessly. It began with the Egyptian conquest of the Sudan by Muhammad ʿAli, nominally the Ottoman governor of Egypt, but already an independent ruler, who conquered the Funj Sultanate in 1820, and founded Khartoum as a new capital in

1830. Later Egyptian rulers expanded their territory to include the Upper Nile and equatorial provinces in 1871, Bahr al-Ghazal in 1873, and Darfur in 1874.

The new regime set out to administer the Sudan in accordance with the Tanzimat, or modernization principles already being applied in Egypt. A local army was recruited from the southern population, and the country was divided into administrative districts whose officials collected taxes from village headmen. The Egyptians organized a state trading monopoly, and slave raiding became a state business. When the state trading monopolies were ended in the reign of Muhammad Sa'id (1854–63), Europeans flocked to the Sudan to take over the gum arabic, ostrich feather, and ivory trade. In 1863 Isma'il Pasha formed the Sudan – later the Egyptian – Trading and Commission Company to build and operate the railroads, steamships, and telegraph. A prosperous economy was the basis of large state revenues and the centralization of administration.

Egypt also attempted to subordinate the Muslim religious elites. The Egyptians canceled the special financial privileges of the local faqis, and suppressed some of the Sufi tariqat. Instead they encouraged an 'ulama' establishment primarily staffed by Egyptians, though it incorporated local Sudanese students who were graduates of al-Azhar. The Egyptian religio-legal administration applied Hanafi law even though most of the local religious leaders were Malikis. The Egyptians also created a court (*majlis mahalli*) in the major towns and a court of appeals (*majlis al-ahdan*) in Khartoum.

The weakening of local holy men and tribal chiefs by a foreign regime led to the spread of the reformed tariqat. By the late eighteenth century reformist brotherhoods, inspired by pilgrims returning from Mecca and Medina, were making headway. The Sammaniya order was introduced by Shaykh Ahmad al-Tayyib b. al-Bashir, who returned around 1800. The reform teaching of Ahmad b. Idris al-Fasi (d. 1837) was introduced into the Sudan by Muhammad al-Majdhub (1796–1833), a descendant of an established holy family, who remade the order according to new principles. The Khatmiya was introduced through the teaching of Muhammad 'Uthman al-Mirghani (1793–1853). These orders represented a new concept of Islamic religiosity, committed to formal Islamic law and hostile to the traditional veneration of the faqis as miracle workers and holy men. The tariqat quickly became politically important. The Khatmiya established a nationwide organization and cooperated with the Egyptian regime. The Sammaniya also established a widespread network, but held aloof from the rulers and took the side of the local population. The Majdhubiya offered militant resistance. Thus, despite Egyptian efforts to impose a state form of Islamic administration, Sufism remained the basis of local opposition to Egyptian rule.

A half-century of Egyptian rule eventually provoked violent resistance to oppressive Turkish officials, when Shaykh Muhammad Ahmad (1848–85), a pious member of the Sammaniya order, declared himself the Mahdi, the expected savior, and called for a restoration of the true Islam. By divine inspiration he gave instructions on such matters as the seclusion of women and distribution of land, and attempted to modify customary Sudanese religious practices in accordance with the teachings of the Shari'a. He was opposed to the wearing of amulets, consumption of tobacco and alcohol, the wailing of women at funerals, music in religious processions, and the visiting of saints' tombs. In imitation of the migration of the Prophet, he and his followers retreated to the mountains of Kordofan, called themselves the Ansar (Helpers of the Prophet), and created a revolutionary state with an army, treasury, and legal administration. The early supporters of the Mahdist revolt included pious disciples, Baqqara nomads who made up the bulk of the army, and various tribes.

In 1885 the Mahdists defeated General Gordon and took Khartoum. Upon the death of the Mahdi, 'Abdallah b. Muhammad, his khalifa, or designated lieutenant, assumed the task of building a state. His succession marked the transformation of the charismatic revolutionary movement into a conventional regime. The Mahdists, who began by rebelling against Egyptian rule, continued the movement toward the centralization of state power. The new ruler concentrated on building up military power, adopting the Turko-Egyptian fiscal system, and restoring the government's authority over rural areas. In practice this meant a return to the bureaucracy and corruption of the past. The Mahdists also sought to reform Islamic practice in accordance with international standards, and suppressed local faqis and local forms of the veneration of saints. In reaction, a local Muslim faqi in Darfur named Abu Jummayza attempted to revive the influence of the local faqis and tribal peoples against the encroachment of the state and the international reformist religious brotherhoods.

The Mahdist state also had to deal with expanding Italian, French, and British power. In 1898 an Anglo-Egyptian army defeated the Mahdists at the battle of Omdurman. The conquest led to the Anglo-Egyptian Condominium (1899–1955), or joint Anglo-Egyptian sovereignty. Egypt financed the army and the administration of the country, but left a British governor-general in full military and civil control. Under Lord Kitchener and his successor, Sir Reginald Wingate (1900–16), the British defeated the remaining opposition, and in 1916 incorporated the Darfur province into the Sudan. They set up a provincial administration with British officials at the head and Egyptians and Sudanese in the lower offices. Despite their defeat, however, the Mahdists retained wide support. They had helped overcome tribal particularism and would later be an important base for the development of Sudanese nationalism and a Sudanese state.

Despite being non-Muslims, the British reverted to the religious policy of the previous Egyptian regime. In the north they attempted to rebuild the 'ulama' establishment by creating a board of 'ulama' in 1901. They financed mosques and pilgrimages, and encouraged the application of Muslim law in Muslim courts, staffed by Egyptian judges and some Sudanese trained at al-Azhar. Sudanese legal scholars graduated from Gordon College and from the Institute of Learning in Omdurman

33 The tomb of the Mahdi, Omdurman, Sudan

(founded in 1912). While favorable to the 'ulama', the Condominium government was hostile to Sufism. Where the Mahdists had destroyed local shrines, the British refused to permit them to be rebuilt. However, they were unable to enforce their anti-Sufi policies, and the tariqat set up new mosques and schools.

During World War I the British relented and began to promote the Khatmiya in order to win political support. Despite the vacillations in British policy, the Mahdists accepted – and even supported – British rule. The Ansar broadened their appeal from rural to town populations, published a newspaper, and urged a peaceful jihad. By 1924 the Khatmiya were sufficiently disturbed by the success of their rivals to declare that they would prefer continued British rule to a restoration of the Mahdist state. At the same time a secular nationalist movement was born. The Sudan Union Society was formed in 1920, calling for self-determination; the White Flag League, supported by army officers, followed, and there were nationalist demonstrations in 1924. The intelligentsia, however, was split between the two religious movements, and by the 1940s had failed to become an independent third force.

Disturbed by the increasing influence of the religious leaders and the nationalist ferment, in 1924 the British adopted a new administrative policy to counterbalance the urban and religious elites by increasing reliance on tribal and rural chiefs. They reduced the size of the bureaucracy in order to avoid educating and employing an urban elite, and encouraged English education in the south to foster regional separatism. By 1936, however, they realized that indirect rule could not work because there was not a strong enough tribal organization in rural areas. Having failed to cultivate adequate rural support, they returned to the urban intelligentsia, and thus increased the opportunities for national and religious resistance. In 1938 the Graduates General Congress was formed to give Sudanese officials a voice in administration, and by 1943 it had been taken over by the Mahdists. The first political party, the Ashiqqa, an offshoot of the Khatmiya, was formed in 1943. In 1944 the leader of the Mahdists, Sayyid 'Abd al-Rahman, the son of the Mahdi, formed the Umma Party, which favored independence, but was nonetheless friendly with the British. Thus, as the problem of Islamic localism receded and the problem of national independence became central, the Islamic religious movements became the basis of nationalist political parties. The Muslim religious leaders were the only ones who could mobilize mass support.

The path to independence, however, remained tortuous. Britain was reluctant to concede its colonial powers, but in 1947 proposed the formation of a national legislative assembly and executive council, reserving a veto for the British governor-general. Southern leaders were doubtful about their place in a national union but accepted the idea at the Juba Conference of 1947. Northern Sudanese religious and nationalist groups were bitterly divided over the further question of union with Egypt. The National Union Party (NUP), representing the Khatmiya and the urban and riverine areas, feared a Mahdist restoration and favored an Egyptian alliance. The Ansar or Mahdists favored immediate independence and opposed a union of

Egypt and the Sudan. The elections of 1953 showed that the country was completely divided. The NUP dominated the Sudanese parliament, but the Umma Party (Mahdists) was strong in the Darfur, Kordofan, Blue Nile, and southern provinces. The Umma made it clear by massive public demonstrations that the pursuit of union with Egypt would lead to civil war. In turn the NUP became disillusioned with Nasser and suspicious of Egyptian intentions. In January 1954 the British transferred power to the Sudanese, and in 1956 Sudan became officially independent.

Independent Sudan has not been able to establish a stable national regime. One factor is the religious and factional divisions within the country, and the deep splits between those movements committed to an Arabic-Islamic conception of Sudanese identity and the military elites committed to a secular concept of Sudanese nationhood. Another critical factor is the split between the Arab-Muslim north and the non-Muslim south. About 40 percent of the Sudanese were Arab-Muslims, but Nilotic, Nilo-Cushitic peoples, including the Dinka, Nuer, Shilluk, and others, made up more than half the population. Northerners virtually excluded southerners from pre-independence politics and from the negotiations with Egypt and Britain. Thus the non-Arab southerners formed political parties, such as the Sudan African National Union (SANU), which called for regional autonomy and even independence. The conflict between the unitary Arabic-Islamic concept of the Sudan and a pluralistic African concept, including Christian and animist Sudanese, continues to the present.

The parliamentary regime formed in 1954 was soon overtaken by a military coup led by General Ibrahim 'Abbud. In 1958 a council of the armed forces seized control of the government, abolished the political parties and the trade unions, and, with the blessing of the Khatmiya and the tolerance of the Ansar, set out to impose central control and Arabic and Islamic identity on the southern regions. The military regime provoked southern, Communist, Muslim brotherhood, and student resistance, which led to guerrilla war in the south and student demonstrations and railroad strikes in the north. In 1964 'Abbud was forced to resign and was replaced by a civilian coalition government. This new government ruled from 1964 to 1969, but it too failed to cope with the problems of religious and secular identity and of north and south, and succumbed to a military coup led by Ja'far Numayri.

Numayri dissolved the parliament, formed a revolutionary command council, and renamed the country the Democratic Republic of the Sudan. Between 1970 and 1972, he disbanded the Communists, crushed the Khatmiya and the Ansar parties, and determined to deal with the south by recognizing its African identity and autonomy. Numayri allowed the Bahr al-Ghazal, Equatorial, and Upper Nile provinces to become a self-governing region, though the national government maintained control of defense, foreign policy, and currency. After 1976 the Numayri regime went through several phases. For a time it became Western oriented. It rebuilt its ties with the Mahdists, maintained good relations with Egypt, and sponsored large-scale agricultural development along the Nile.

In September 1983 Numayri switched direction, and launched an effort to totally Islamize the Sudan. While there were precedents for this – going back to General

'Abbud, who in 1964 Arabized the administration and the school system and expelled foreign missionaries, and to a 1968 draft constitution which made Islam the official religion, and Arabic the official language of the state – Numayri's program went beyond declarations. He reinstituted the *hudud*, or Islamic punishments, strengthened Islamic courts, and declared himself the infallible imam. He also resumed the struggle to Islamize the south. Numayri was overthrown in 1985, and for four years there was a moderate coalition government led by Sayyid Sadiq al-Mahdi. Then in 1989 Hassan al-Turabi, the leader of the National Islamic Front (NIF), and his military allies led by General 'Umar al-Bashir, seized power.

Turabi was an idealist who dreamed of an international Islamic order, though channeled through national states, and an exceptionally skillful politician who from the outset appreciated the importance of the state as an instrument of Islamization. In his early writings he proposed an Islamic charter, a government committed to the divine law, and to the reformation of Islam. Only Islam, he believed, would mobilize the masses. He called for a democratic and presidential system of government, and a state that would manage the key sectors of the economy while respecting private property. The state, in control of the media, would be the educator of Muslims. Turabi was a modernist in that he believed in the utility of modern technologies, the need to adapt Muslim law to historical circumstances, and the full participation of women in contemporary life.

From the mid-1980s, Turabi built up a considerable network in the military, the legislature, the student movements, and the professions. The NIF sponsored schools, clinics, and mosques, the Faisal Islamic Bank, and such agencies as the Islamic Da'wa Organization and the Islamic African Relief Agency. By 1995 Turabi had consolidated his hold on the state. Once in power he established an autocratic and repressive regime. Opposition leaders were imprisoned. All criticism was suppressed, and a regime of indoctrination and control was implemented. The civil service and the unions were purged of non-Islamists, who were replaced with NIF cadres. Arabic instead of English was mandated in the schools.

Government policy toward women changed drastically. When Sudan became independent, women were valued for their potential contribution to the development of the country as civil servants, doctors, and teachers. The NIF government, however, rejected women's emancipation as an imitation of Western values, and women were removed from senior positions. In the NIF view women may work, but not if their jobs threaten the power of men. Health, welfare, and nurseries are considered suitable areas of employment for women. Women's organizations have been banned. The government has proscribed the teaching of art and music, forbidden men and women from dancing together, and segregated the sexes in public places. Women have been flogged for violating the Islamic dress code.

The Turabi regime took an uncompromising position toward the south, and insisted upon Arabizing and Islamizing the non-Muslim population. Southerners, represented in part by the Sudan People's Liberation Movement, define themselves as Africans and Christians, and call for a pluralistic state with protection for the rights of minorities. The Sudanese opposition, largely in exile, under the banner of the National Democratic Alliance, also favors an ethnically and religiously pluralistic society. There seems to be no way to reconcile these conflicting agendas. A bitter civil war of genocidal proportions is being fought, with tactics that include starving the civilian populations and forcing them to migrate. The discovery of oil raised the stakes in the conflict, and has led government forces to drive southerners from the land. As the struggle continues a political crisis was sparked by General Bashir's coup of December 12, 1999. He dismissed Turabi, and dismantled parliament two days before it was expected to reduce Bashir's presidential powers.

SOMALIA

Somalia is reminiscent of Mauritania in that the state overlies an Arab-Muslim tribal society. By the eighteenth century the tribes of Somalia were largely Muslim and Arab. Somalia began to acquire the shape of a modern state in 1891, when it was divided between Britain and Italy. The Italian protectorate was administered in a highly bureaucratic way and favored the development of irrigation, railroads, roads, and schools. With the outbreak of World War II, however, the British conquered Italian Somaliland, and assumed control over the whole of what was to be the future Somali state. The first Somali opposition to colonial rule was expressed by the formation of the Somaliland National Society in 1935, which was devoted to modern education, overcoming Somali particularisms, and unifying the population. A Somali Officials' Union was formed in 1937 and a Somali Youth League in 1943. In 1950 Somaliland was returned to Italy as a United Nations Trusteeship, and the northern and southern regions were unified in 1960, when Somaliland became an independent country. The new government managed to integrate the former British and Italian sectors with great rapidity.

The Somali people are a single cultural and linguistic nation. They are all Muslims but are divided into two lineage groups – the Somali and the Sab – who are further subdivided by a complex segmentary system into numerous confederacies, sub-confederacies, tribes, and tribal sections. The tribe is the most common political organization; its chief is both warrior and rainmaker, and is believed to have religious and magical powers. Without being ethnic Arabs, the tribes have a strong Muslim identity and trace their descent to Muhammad. The political parties formed in both Italian and British Somalia in the 1950s were thus clan based. The Somaliland National Society was based on the Isaq group, and the United Somali Party was based on the Dir and the Darod. However, the development of a new script for the Somali language helped create a symbolic focus for national identity.

The Somalis were also adherents of three main Sufi brotherhoods – the Qadiriya, the Ahmadiya, and the Salihiya. The Qadiriya was introduced into Harar as early as the fifteenth century. One of its branches, the Uwaysiya, is active throughout

East Africa. The Ahmadiya was founded by Ahmad b. Idris al-Fasi (1760–1837) and was brought to Somalia by ʿAli Maye Durogba. The Salihiya, founded by Muhammad b. Salih in 1887, is the order that gave rise to Muhammad b. ʿAbdallah (Abdille Hassan), who returned from Mecca to preach the purification of Islam. He declared war against Christians and against British rule, but in 1908 concluded a temporary peace which allowed him to run a small quasi-autonomous state within Somalia. The British finally defeated his movement in 1920.

Among northern Somalians, who tended to be pastoralists, the Sufis were considered client tribes, and were supplied with land to cultivate. They were adopted into the lineages of the dominant tribes, who regarded their ancestors as Sufi saints. In these cases the Sufi communities were commonly established on the boundaries between tribal groups where they could serve as mediators.

In the southern parts of Somaliland, where there was more farming and less pastoralism, tribal structure was weaker and state organization stronger. Since lineage was less important, Sufis played a larger role in giving cohesion to the agricultural society and had a relatively more secure political position vis-à-vis the tribes. The Sufis served the tribes as teachers and judges, administering Muslim law in matrimonial, property, and contract matters. They also acted as mediators and arbitrators. When a local Sufi saint died, his tomb often became a venerated place, the object of pilgrimages, and was sanctified by his reputation for baraka. Besides the Sufi brotherhoods and the shrines, there were innumerable holy men, who provided religious services and were the objects of veneration. The religious leaders were bridges between otherwise competing tribes and allowed some degree of unification across clan and tribal lines.

The Somali government tried to integrate all of the major factions and local kinship units into the national state. Despite the hostilities among them, all major groups considered themselves as belonging to the larger Somali nation. The fluidity of the tribal structure allowed for flexible political bargaining and coalition making. Thus segmentation could be made to operate not only as a divisive force but also as a force for unification.

In 1966 General Siyad Barre staged a coup d'état, and the army took control of the government. He proclaimed Somalia's commitment to scientific socialism and turned to the Soviet Union for support. The government attempted to suppress lineage and tribal affiliations, and appealed for national cooperation. A cult was created around the person of the head of state. Muslim religious leaders were executed in 1975, and women were given equal legal rights with men. Vigorous efforts were made to promote literacy, and to resettle the nomads on state farms or collectives. However, lineage loyalties endured, and the government considered itself both socialist and Muslim.

The most difficult political issue for Somalia was its claim to territory occupied by Somalian peoples in Kenya, Djibouti, and Ethiopia. These claims were resisted by the neighboring states, and the Organization of African States was loath to recognize any demands for border changes. With the withdrawal of the French from Djibouti and the outbreak of the Ethiopian revolution, Somalian guerrillas in Eritrea, Bale, and the Ogaden tried to wrest these provinces from Ethiopian control. In the regional and international struggle that followed, the Soviet Union abandoned Somalia in favor of Ethiopia, and Ethiopia – with Russian and Cuban support – was able to resist the Somalian attack. The war with Ethiopia intensified the emphasis upon the Islamic identity of Somalia. Siyad Barre was overthrown in 1991 and since then Somalia has been without a central government. Clan-based militias rule the country, and United Nations and American interventions have accomplished nothing.

ETHIOPIA AND ERITREA

Like the Sudan, Ethiopia is sharply divided between Muslim and non-Muslim populations; today the Muslim population is between a third and a half of the total. Muslim and Christian groups have been in conflict for centuries. In the late eighteenth and early nineteenth centuries the territorial expansion of Islam and the rising power of Muslim principalities threatened to undermine Christian control of Ethiopia, but in 1831 Teodros came to the Ethiopian throne with a program of reuniting the Christians, conquering Jerusalem, Mecca, and Medina, abolishing Islam, and bringing the kingdom of peace. After his death (1867) Teodros was succeeded by Menelik II (1867–1913), the ruler of Shoa, who in 1889 became King of Kings. A consolidated Christian-Ethiopian kingdom set out again to absorb the Muslim minorities in Harar, Sidamo, Arussi, Bale, and Eritrea. The revived Ethiopian kingdom also managed to check the threat of European colonialism. In 1885 the Italians occupied Massawa on the Red Sea coast, and in 1896 concluded the treaty of Uccialli which Italy regarded as a treaty of protectorate although Menelik maintained his independence.

After Menelik's death in 1913, there was a long interregnum until Haile Selassie ascended the throne in 1930 and resumed the effort to centralize the Ethiopian state. He attempted to bypass the power of the nobility by building up cadres of educated commoners. His work was interrupted by the Italian invasion of 1934 and 1935, which forced the Emperor to flee and led to the creation of an Italian East African empire, including Ethiopia, Eritrea, and Somalia. In 1941 the British helped to organize an Ethiopian resistance and returned Haile Selassie to the throne. The process of centralization resumed as Selassie defeated provincial rivals, curbed the power of the church, made the clergy subordinate to the Emperor, and deprived the nobility of its position as a military and tax-collecting elite. Despite this centralization, local ruling families commonly remained powerful.

As in many Third World countries, political centralization led to social change. Selassie brought to power a new class of officials drawn out of the old nobility. In the 1950s these were superseded by a younger generation of army officers, secondary school and university graduates, labor union leaders, and others. The post-1950 elites were impatient with the corruption of the older generation. In 1974 a mutiny of soldiers, followed by widespread strikes and riots, led to the creation of a new regime run by the Coordinating Committee of the Army, or *Derg*, which dismantled the imperial government and deposed the Emperor. In 1975 the Derg was taken over by radicals who announced a Marxist-Leninist ideology, nationalization of property, land reform, and the abolition of the lineage system in the north and of tenancy in the south. In 1978 Mengistu Haile Mariam created the People's Democratic Republic of Ethiopia with Soviet and Cuban help. Widespread revolts followed. A new constitution of 1994 divided the country into semi-autonomous ethno-linguistic states, but the breakup of the central state only opened the way for chaotic local fighting.

In this confused situation some Muslims seized the opportunity to resist the Ethiopian state. Since the nineteenth century, Muslims under Ethiopian rule had been excluded from public posts, though the 1931 constitution established equal rights and allowed Muslims to acquire land, hold official positions, and receive official recognition for Muslim festivals. Muslim dissatisfaction, however, came into the open in the Bale province, where Somali and Galla peoples revolted. Backed by Sa'udi Arabia, the Sultan of the 'Afars rebelled in the Ogaden. The Western Somalia Liberation Front opened its drive for autonomy. The Ethiopians defeated much of the opposition, and repulsed a Somalian invasion. In other parts of the country, however, Christians and Muslims are not necessarily divided by religion. They share saints and pilgrimages, intermarry, move freely from one religion to the other, and are joined by family ties.

Eritrea, which is also about half Muslim and half Christian, became the main focus of continuing opposition. Its borders were first defined by the Italians, and the Muslim population, consisting mainly of Tigray tribes, began to acquire political consciousness only in the 1940s. In 1952 Eritrea was federated with Ethiopia on the basis of regional autonomy, but Selassie worked to integrate it into Ethiopia. In 1957 Arabic and Tigriniya were abolished as official languages. This led to the formation of the Eritrean Liberation Front (ELF), composed of students, workers, and intellectuals. By 1962 this movement had been suppressed and Eritrea was formally annexed by Ethiopia. In response the ELF was reorganized, without a specific ideological identity, by exiled leaders in Cairo and by local soldiers supported by tribal and religious leaders. Then, in 1970, dissatisfied factions with a more radical ideological bent formed the Eritrean People's Liberation Front (EPLF), and on the basis of radical ideology rather than Muslim identity, created a coalition with Eritrean Christians hostile to the domination of the Amharic Ethiopian elite. The EPLF called for a national democratic revolution, a people's war, and the revolutionary transformation of society. In 1977 the EPLF and ELF agreed on independence as a common goal. Eventually Ethiopian and Eritrean resistance defeated Mengistu, and a referendum of 1993 established the independence of Eritrea under the leadership of Isayas Afework, the head of the EPLF. Another war, over boundaries, was fought with Ethiopia from 1998 to 2000.

SWAHILI EAST AFRICA

By the nineteenth century the East African coast was the home of a Swahili Muslim civilization. The principal center of Muslim culture was Zanzibar, which had been conquered by Imam Sayyid Sa'id b. Sultan, the ruler of Oman (1804–56), and was the capital of the only Muslim state in the region. The Muslim population was concentrated in the coastal towns and on the offshore islands, and consisted primarily of Swahili-speaking peoples, and enclaves of Indian Muslims who formed their own communities (jamatbandis). Zanzibar had qadis and muftis, most of them south Arabian in origin. Zanzibar and Lamu had madrasas and served as centers of higher education. In the interior the Somalis had been converted to Islam, but otherwise there were only occasional Muslim enclaves along the trade routes leading to the Lake region and the Congo. The Muslims of the interior were mainly Bantu speakers under Swahili influence.

At the end of the nineteenth century European protectorates were established over Zanzibar, Tanganyika, Kenya, Uganda, and other territories, and gave new direction to the political history of the region. As in West Africa, colonial regimes gave rise to secular national states in which Muslims were substantial minorities but did not determine the ideological and political character of the regimes. Also as in West Africa, colonial administration, white settler colonization, and Christian missionary influence actually hastened the diffusion of Islam. Trade brought interior peoples to the coastal towns, where they were converted to Islam and from where they returned to proselytize in their home countries. European administration also favored the spread of Islam because the British and the Germans employed Muslims as government officials, policemen, soldiers, and schoolteachers. During World War I the Germans, who were allied with the Ottoman empire, acted as patrons of Muslim interests. It seems likely that the spread of Islam was facilitated by political instability, by the need for a common identity for heterogeneous peoples, and by the need for new bases of social and political organization. The spread of Islam was also favored by the use of Swahili as a lingua franca in Kenya, Tanganyika, Uganda, Northern Rhodesia, Madagascar, the eastern Congo, and other East African regions.

The spread of Muslim allegiances was accompanied by the spread of Sufi orders. In the course of the colonial period the large Muslim minorities of East Africa were organized into Sufi-led brotherhoods. The Shadhiliya, led by Muhammad Ma'ruf (1853–1905), established missionary centers along the coast and introduced reformed Islamic practice. The Qadiriya, represented by the sub-order of the Uwaysiya, founded by Shaykh 'Umar Uways al-Barawi (1847–1909), was based in

Zanzibar but carried on missionary activity in Tanganyika and Kenya and as far as the eastern Congo. The Uwaysiya were active among Swahili and Bantu-speaking peoples, winning Muslims to the brotherhood and converting pagans to Islam. They also led Muslim anti-German resistance in southern Tanganyika. Shaykh Uways became famous for his polemic with the Salihiya brotherhood over the question of whether it was legitimate to visit saints' tombs and whether deceased saints could be mediators between men and God. Uways took a conservative tolerant view of these practices in opposition to reformist teachings. He was assassinated for these views in 1909.

Zanzibar

The situation of Muslims differed in each colonial territory. Zanzibar was dominated by its Arab population, which owned most of the arable land, filled the civil service, and controlled the government and police, forming a closed aristocratic society. An Indo-Pakistani community controlled trade. The indigenous African majority were mainly craftsmen, fishermen, and workers, and called themselves Shirazis, though they were divided into numerous tribal groups. Migrants from mainland East Africa were concentrated in Zanzibar town, and developed a strong sense of political unity. The Arabs resisted any attempts by the Africans to raise their status or political influence. Zanzibar was the center of 'Alawiya, Shadhiliya, and Qadiriya Sufi brotherhoods. It had a strong tradition of 'ulama' scholarship, but ziyarat (visits to saints' tombs), mawlids (celebration of the "birthdays" of saints), and festivals were common.

While the British intended to rule through the established Sultanate and the Arab elites, they nonetheless promoted far-reaching changes in the structure of society and the balance of power within it. The British reduced the power of the Sultan and destroyed the economic base of the Arab elites by the abolition of slavery. The Arabs lost control of the plantations to Indian money lenders and merchants. At the same time, the British tried not to disrupt the clove plantations. Slaves were made into semi-servile peasants owing labor service, and Nyamwezi workers were imported. The freeing of the slaves allowed a new African elite and community to take shape. Africans began to obtain ownership of land. In the 1930s political associations for Arabs, Indians, Shirazis, and migrant mainland Africans were formed.

World War II brought a movement toward independence and open political struggle among the different segments of Zanzibari society. At the end of World War II the island Arab and African populations became increasingly politicized as a result of the return of soldiers from the war and the news of events in Egypt and Palestine. British political reforms and the dock workers' strike of 1948 also had a mobilizing effect. The Zanzibar National Party, founded in 1956, became the principal proponent of the Arab interest, and the Arab minority – united on the basis of shared language and culture, Muslim piety, ethnic pride, and former political dominance – attempted to expel the British and to create an Arab-Islamic state. The

Afro-Shirazi Union founded in 1957 became the expression of both native peasants and migrant mainland workers.

With the creation of a party-political system in the 1950s, the Arabs struggled to win at least enough African support to control the government. They tried to create a climate of opinion conducive to a multi-national state and solidarity based on Islam. Finally, the Arab parties won the 1961 and the 1963 elections. However, in 1963 the government party weakened itself by attempting to suppress opposition and dismiss the African police force and to replace it with Arabs and Asians. The Arab position was also weakened because it was no longer based on a military and landowning elite but on a younger generation of civil servants, journalists, and politicians.

This rigid regime was attacked immediately after independence (December 1963) by African revolutionaries who seized the government, nationalized the land and the major businesses, opened foreign ties with Eastern-bloc countries, and decimated the Arab community. The coup led to the merger of Zanzibar and Tanganyika in 1964. Zanzibar as a province of Tanzania maintains an Islamic but not an Arab identity. Quran schools and an Islamic institute perpetuate Muslim and Arabic-language instruction. Madrasa instruction is being strengthened in response to the growing presence of Islamic reformist influences.

Tanzania

Tanganyika was given its first territorial government by Germany, which declared a protectorate in 1885. German rule was established in the face of intense local resistance. The Bushiri revolt was led by slave traders attempting to protect their interests against German taxation and control. The resistance of the Yao peoples of the Makonde plateau lasted until 1889. The Unyanyembe of Tabora fought the Germans until 1893; the Hehe kingdom battled with the Germans for control of the trade routes until 1898. With the defeat of the Hehe kingdom the Germans were able to begin systematic administration and taxation. They established a government consisting of a central governor and twenty-two provincial districts with their own police and judicial services. *Akidas*, or officials of Arab and Swahili origin, were appointed where there were no local chiefs. The Germans experimented with plantations producing coffee, sisal, rubber, and cotton. Africans were forced to grow cash crops so that they could pay taxes. In some districts German settlement was encouraged, and the whites used forced African labor. Economic exploitation led to new rebellions. The Maji Maji revolt in southeastern Tanganyika began in 1905 and attracted widespread support. This revolt was savagely repressed, but later German governors tried to mitigate African hostility by forbidding corporal punishment and by instituting educational and health reforms.

After defeating the Germans in World War I, the British took control of most of Tanganyika in 1919 as a League of Nations mandate. Rwanda and Burundi were given to Belgium, and Kiyunga was annexed to Mozambique. The British also encountered active African resistance, though in more peaceful form. British agricultural and educational policies helped form a new elite, and African welfare organizations were formed by civil servants, rich peasants, and educated youths in rivalry with traditional chiefs. In the 1920s and 1930s they evolved into nationalist political organizations. The Tanganyika African Association (founded in the 1920s), supported by farmers concerned about state agriculture and marketing policies, was in 1954 renamed the Tanganyika African National Union (TANU) and reorganized, on the model of Ghana's Convention People's Party, as a national political coalition. It took the lead in creating a mass movement to win self-government on the basis of Tanganyikan unity, ignoring ethnic, racial, and religious divisions. The TANU won national elections in 1958 and 1959, and Tanganyika became independent in 1961.

Under the leadership of Julius Nyerere, Tanganyika was one of the most successful African states in creating a concept of a national society dedicated to the welfare and dignity of its citizens. Tanzania adopted the values of equality, democracy, decentralized administration, socialism, and full communal participation in the political society. The doctrinal concept was summed up in the term *ujamaa*, or community. However, there was constant tension between these ideals and the tendency of the TANU to centralize power, create a strong civil service, and attempt a disciplined control of the masses. In the Arusha Declaration of 1967, Nyerere reaffirmed his vision of a democratic political society. He tried to define a truly African orientation in terms of decentralization of the economy and popular participation in political power. He also attempted to curtail the bureaucratic elite and to encourage labor-intensive agricultural development and independence of foreign loans and influence. New programs of village development were undertaken in the 1970s, but the results were meager.

As opposed to Zanzibar, Muslim communities in Tanganyika were not organized under state auspices. Though the British cut Tanganyika off from the official Islamic establishment of Zanzibar, Sufi Islam spread throughout the region as a form of native reaction to foreign rule. The tariqat became the principal Muslim organizing institutions, though the rivalries among the brotherhoods also spread dissension among the Muslims. The Muslim brotherhoods were then progressively linked to a national political movement. In 1934 the Muslim Association of Tanganyika (MAT) was formed, and through it Sufi leaders became active supporters of the TANU. In 1957 an All-Muslim National Union of Tanganyika was founded to give expression to purely Muslim interests, but the majority of the Muslim population continued to back the national party. In the 1960s the government created the Supreme Council of Tanzanian Muslims, as a way of coopting the Muslim elites.

The case of Shaykh Ramiya of Bangamoyo is illustrative of both the local role of Sufism and its integration into national politics. Shaykh Ramiya was a former slave who became a merchant and landowner, pursued religious studies, and won great local respect. He collaborated with the British and was appointed a liwali, or district officer. From his combined economic, religious, and political position, Shaykh

Ramiya established a branch of the Qadiriya order. Most of his followers were Africans who benefited from the social solidarity of the brotherhood and from their allegiance to a powerful patron. In 1938 his son and successor Shaykh Muhammad declared that the Prophet was not an Arab but a man of all races – an expression of the African identity of this Muslim community. Shaykh Muhammad encouraged his followers to join the national political party and himself became a local representative. After independence Nyerere appointed him *hakim*, or local governor. Shaykh Muhammad was thus an African-Muslim religious leader who displaced the political power of older Shirazi lineages and became part of the Tanzanian national political elite. By organizing his followers into a religious brotherhood, he linked local communal structures to the national political regime. The Tanzanian state showed its recognition of Muslim political support by appointments to the Ministry of Justice and to local judgeships. Muslims make up about one-third of the country's population.

When Nyerere retired in 1985, the failures of his policies were evident. His experiment in nation building was undermined by economic stagnation, unemployment, and growing communal antagonisms among Asian Shi'a, Omani Arabs, Shirazis, and Africans. A new government under 'Ali Hassan Mwiniyi, the former president of Zanzibar, reversed Nyerere's policies. It created a multi-party system and began the privatization of the economy, but this led only to economic collapse. There were anti-Christian riots and attacks on Christian schools in 1993. With the collapse of the secular national state, there was revived competition among Muslims over the definition of Muslim identity. Sufi shaykhs who had supported the TANU were discredited, and the influence of Arab-world-trained reformist teachers has grown considerably.

Kenya

While Tanganyika developed as an African society, Kenya became a white settler society. It was acquired by the British East Africa Company in 1888, made a separate protectorate in 1904, and declared a crown colony in 1918. Between 1900 and 1919 the country was subjugated by force and organized for European settlement. Whites from South Africa, Britain, New Zealand, Australia, and Canada were settled in the highland territories, and Africans were moved into native reserves. From 1923 to 1952 the British pursued a policy of segregated development, manipulating African reserves to secure the best lands and mineral resources for white exploitation. It also favored the whites in medical, educational, and economic services. Despite discrimination, an African elite emerged from British missionary schools and military service, and formed the East African Association, the Cavirondo Taxpayers' and Welfare Association, and, in 1944, the Kenya African Union under the leadership of Jomo Kenyatta. Africans demanded adequate employment, educational opportunities, and access to land. In 1952 the Mau Mau revolt, a guerrilla war against whites and white rule, broke out. The struggle led in 1959 to the removal of internal racial and territorial boundaries and to the formation in 1963 of an independent Kenyan state under the leadership of the Kenya Africa National Union Party. Kenyatta died in 1978, and was succeeded by Vice President Daniel arap Moi, who was still in power at the end of 2001.

The Muslim population of Kenya is about 6 percent of the total, but it is also very diverse, representing numerous African, Asian, and Arab communities. In the coastal regions the Muslim population is closely related to Zanzibar. The interior population includes Kikuyu, Masai, and Maru peoples, who converted to Islam after World War I as a result of trading contacts with the coast. There are numerous Muslim associations, such as the Kenya Muslim Welfare Society, which sponsors schools and clinics. The influence of Muslims is limited because of their concentration on the coast in Swahili-speaking areas, and the absence of Sufi brotherhoods as a base of recruitment and political network formation. Nonetheless, some Muslim groups have been assertive in promoting education and da'wa, and students returning from Sa'udi Arabia oppose local practices such as funeral orations and celebration of mawlids. In 1992 more radical elements created the Islamic Party of Kenya (IPK). The Supreme Council of Muslims has made a point of assuring government authorities of their opposition to the IPK.

Uganda

In Uganda the organization of a colonial state also set the terms for the eventual emergence of an independent Uganda. Buganda became a British protectorate in 1893, and the Uganda agreement of 1900 brought the whole country under British rule. By 1914 the British brought the remaining local chiefs under their control. In the struggle for power the British were closely allied with the Protestants and encouraged the spread of Christianity as a barrier to Islam. Under British rule, a Ugandan education system was set up, divided along religious lines. Catholics and Protestants were favored by government grants of land, and the Muslims were discriminated against in appointments to office and in government support of mosques and schools. As opposed to Kenya, the British kept white settlers out of the region and favored a peasant economy based on cotton and coffee production. A small urban population, largely foreign in origin, included Indians, Europeans, and Arabs, who had come to trade.

African protest developed early. In the 1920s the Young Baganda Association called for African participation in government. A Uganda African Farmers' Association was organized to protect African peasants' interests against Indian and European merchants. The development of nationalism and militant resistance to the British, however, was limited, since in Uganda Africans did not suffer from large-scale alienation of land and were buffered from foreign interference by the British system of indirect rule. Nonetheless, in 1952 the Uganda National Congress called for independence. The Kabaka of Buganda, the most prominent local ruler, and the Protestant elites, emerged as the most powerful forces in the country. In 1960 the Uganda People's Congress was formed to represent the interests of other chieftains and population groups. The 1962 elections brought Mutesa II, the hereditary ruler of Buganda, to power, but in the next few years the Uganda People's Congress consolidated its grip on the civil service, subverted the trade unions, and built up the army. In 1966, using the army, Milton Obote seized power, abrogated the 1962 constitution, and assumed the office of executive president. While Uganda still had a civilian administration from 1966 to 1971, it was in fact under military rule. In January 1971 an army coup d'état brought General Idi Amin to power. Idi Amin's power was built on the support of Nubian forces in the Ugandan army. Originally from the Sudan, they came to consider themselves a tribal group – superior to, separate from, and resentful of the rest of the population.

While British administrative policy in Uganda was inimical to Islam, Islam still spread as the result of the influence of Arab traders, Sudanese soldiers, and Swahili contacts. By 1930 there were approximately 122,000 Muslims. Mbogo, former Kabaka of Buganda, became the chief patron of the Muslim community. He had relatively little success, however, in promoting Muslim interests, and failed to acquire government land for the support of mosques. After he died in 1921 the Muslims split into two sects, the Kibuli and the Butambla, which were divided over competition for leadership and over the doctrinal question of whether it was necessary to say the noon prayers in addition to the congregational prayers on Friday. Also at issue was the authority of marriage registrars and teachers. The sectarian split inhibited the reform of Muslim education and the overall development of the Muslim community. By World War II strong efforts were being made to settle the dispute. In 1944 the Ugandan Muslim Education Association was founded to overcome factionalism and unify educational programs, and the parties were reconciled in 1948. The East African Muslim Welfare Society also constructed schools and mosques and provided fellowships for Muslim students. With development of the independence movement in the 1950s, Muslims were accorded a larger role in government, but by 1965 they still had little political influence. Some Muslims served as intermediaries between the state and the Muslim population, but these politicians did not have any deep legitimacy in the Muslim community. Thus the state could not control the Muslims any more than the Muslims could influence the state. In general the state acted as arbitrator in disputes among Muslim groups and as patron for Muslim demands such as funds for education, appointment of ministers, or symbolic recognition.

Under the regime of Idi Amin (1971–79), who was himself a Muslim, Muslims enjoyed government support. The Uganda Muslim Students' Association and the Uganda Muslim Supreme Council were formed as vehicles for the organization of the Muslim community under state tutelage. Amin carried on a pro-Arabic and pro-Islamic policy. Property seized from expelled Asians was given to the Uganda Muslim Supreme Council. Still, Amin had no more success than previous governments in mobilizing the Muslim community. They were neither united nor subordinated to the state apparatus. When he was ousted many Muslims fled the country, and many mosques and schools were destroyed by their opponents. Since 1986 the regime of

Yoweri Kaguta Museveni and the Uganda Patriotic Movement has stabilized the internal politics of the country. Muslims are about 15 percent of the population.

In the 1960s other former colonial territories in East Africa such as Rwanda, Burundi, Malawi, and the Congo also emerged as independent states. Muslim minorities had been established under the influence of Arab and Swahili traders, East African missionaries, and post-World War II Pakistani merchants. In these countries the Muslim populations are small, poor, ill educated, and play little role in national politics.

The Shi'i communities

The East African-Muslim population also includes small but important communities of Indian origin, including Isma'ilis, Bohras, Ithna-'ashari Shi'a, and Ahmadis. Indian Muslims were first attracted to Zanzibar by Sayyid al-Sa'id (1804–56), who appointed Indians as customs collectors and financial advisors, and encouraged them to trade. The British similarly encouraged trade and the migration of Indians from Gujarat and other Indian provinces. Indians commonly came to work as laborers or shop assistants, learned Swahili, saved a little money, opened their own shops, returned to India to marry, and brought back relatives to help in their businesses. With the opening of the interior by British and German railroads many Isma'ilis migrated inland. Between 1900 and the 1960s they became a highly developed community with collective investments in modern enterprises. Secularly educated women are free from purdah. The community maintains clinics, sports clubs, libraries, meeting halls, hospitals, schools, and other facilities. The community has also formed investment trusts for insurance, agriculture, and housing projects. The Aga Khan governs the community through a hierarchy of councils. In principle, his authority is absolute and his approval is required for all appointments, but the Isma'ili community and its agencies are actually run by a small elite. A new generation of educated doctors, engineers, and professionals is gradually replacing the older commercial aristocracy. A constitution of 1954 created agencies for secular and religious affairs, education, health, property, alms and tax collection, and industrial development. The constitution also included a personal law which dealt with family and marriage matters. As revised in 1964 it explicitly prohibited polygamy, set a minimum marriage age of sixteen years for females and eighteen for males, and granted substantial equality to women in divorce. Matters such as guardianship, adoption, and legitimacy were adjusted to correspond with territorial law in East Africa.

The Bohra Shi'a are highly active in trade. They include metalworkers, watchmakers, and merchants. The Bohra community is organized in a hierarchical way. The high chief for all of East Africa resides in Mombasa; local amils supervise the mullahs, who teach in the schools and perform local religious services. Between 1951 and 1955, a new congregation was formed, called the Da'udi Bohra Jamat Corporation, which consists of all males over eighteen years old, and elects a managing council which administers community property, including mosques, assembly houses, schools, clubs, clinics, and real estate. The community is supported by endowments, gifts, and taxes on the membership.

The Ithna-'ashari Shi'i community also has a strong organization. Local congregations are organized as jamats, each with an executive council, a board of trustees, and committees to administer the various communal properties and activities. There is a supreme council for East Africa representing the local jamats. The Ahmadis, a Muslim sect founded in northern India at the end of the nineteenth century, also have a small but active following in East Africa and are strongly interested in missionary activity. They are the first to have translated the Quran into Swahili. While the Asian communities are highly modernized, they are also close-knit and sectarian, and have not been integrated into the general African society.

Thus the Muslim communities in East Africa are highly diverse and fragmented by ethnic origins, religious belief, and sectarian organization. Throughout East Africa, excluding Sudan and Somalia, Muslims are a political minority in the sense that they do not control state power. Nor do East African regimes identify themselves as Islamic. In Tanzania the Muslim population is held under strict political control. In Uganda it has been defeated in the recent struggle for power. As a political minority, Muslims concentrate on religious matters and have formed numerous associations for educational and welfare purposes.

UNIVERSAL ISLAM AND AFRICAN DIVERSITY

Throughout the nineteenth century, Muslims were expanding as traders, missionaries, and warriors. In the Sudanic region, Muslim regimes were consolidated and new populations converted to Islam. From the Sudan Muslims penetrated the Guinean forest and coastal territories of West Africa. Large numbers of people in Nigeria and Senegal were Islamized. In East Africa Gallas, Somalis, and other peoples were converted to Islam.

The militant expansion of Islam was brought to a halt by European conquest between 1882 and 1900. The establishment of colonial rule, however, did not stop the spread of Islam by peaceful means. In fact, colonial rule facilitated the diffusion of Islam by providing political security and expanded commercial opportunities, and by stimulating urbanization and the migration of merchants and workers. At present Muslims constitute the overwhelming majority in Mauritania, Senegal, Guinea, Mali, Niger, and Somalia. They make up half or more of the population of Nigeria, Burkina Faso, the Ivory Coast, and Sierra Leone, and are a substantial minority in Ghana and Tanzania.

The rapid diffusion of Islam had important consequences for Muslim beliefs, communal organization, and the relation of Muslims to states and national societies. While the principal goal of many nineteenth-century Muslim movements was to establish Muslim states and a comprehensive Islamic society, colonial rule led rather to the consolidation of secular or non-Muslim national states. Almost all the independent African regimes have adopted a secular national identity based on non-religious ideologies. Only where there are substantial Arab populations or claims to Arab identity – as in Mauritania, northern Sudan, and Somalia – is national identity expressed in Islamic terms. Only Sudan has declared itself an Islamic state. In Nigeria Muslim identity has been integrated into the national political system, and Muslim communal organizations and concepts of justice play an important role in the internal struggle for political and social power. Elsewhere, secular elites treat their Muslim populations, however large or small, as communal constituencies. All African-Muslim populations are organized as communal groups seeking state protection and patronage for their economic, educational, and foreign policy interests.

Muslim communities are organized in various ways. The traditional forms of 'ulama' and law-school organization are found only in Sudan. Elsewhere, Sufi brotherhoods are the principal form of Muslim association. In Mauritania, Senegal, Guinea, Mali, Nigeria, Somalia, Tanzania, and other parts of sub-Saharan Africa, they serve on a local basis to integrate diverse ethnic populations, as in Kano, or diverse tribes, as in Somalia. They also serve to organize their members for worship and spiritual comfort, for economic competition, as in the case of the Muridiya of Senegal or the Hausa of Ibadan, or for political administration as in the case of the Tijaniya of Senegal and Nigeria, the Qadiriya in Tanzania, the Khatmiya in the Sudan, and the Sanusiya in Libya.

Apart from the organized brotherhoods, Sufi families, lineages, and individual holy men also play an important social role. In Somalia, Sufi lineages serve as a link between tribal groups. In Guinean and coastal West Africa educated missionary families are the basis of Muslim settlements and Muslim education. In many parts of Guinean West Africa, Sudan, and Tanzania, Muslim communities are built around individual holy men and revered local shrines.

In African cities and towns there has been an extraordinary proliferation of Muslim associations, fraternities, and clubs. Some are the expression of minority groups, such as the Isma'ili or Bohra communities in East Africa, which form jamatbandis with a high degree of internal diversification for religious, welfare, educational, and economic activities. Other associations are the expression of ethnic minorities, such as northern migrants in southern Nigeria, Ghana, and Sierra Leone. Such associations, however, are not separated from, but are merged into, family, tribal, and ethnic groups. For the Dyula communities and Muslim-led missionary settlements in West Africa, Islam is part and parcel of a familial, occupational, and linguistic identity which distinguishes Muslim merchant groups from the peoples among whom they settle. Similarly, Islam is coupled with Hausa ethnicity to define Muslim communities in southern Nigeria. Among Arab peoples of Mauritania, Somalia, and the Sudan, Islam is fused with tribal, ethnic, and linguistic traits. To be Arab-Somali or zawaya Berber is by definition to be a Muslim. In these cases, too, Islam is fused not only with ethnicity but with nationality insofar as the Mauritanian, Sudanese, and Somali political societies consider themselves Islamic.

Not all Muslim urban associations, however, are ethnic in quality. Many are small clubs built around the leadership of a particular teacher who organizes study groups, discussions, and communal activities which may be as serious as managing a school or as playful as cafe conversation. The most striking type of urban association are the modernist groups devoted to Muslim reform and education. The Wahhabiya in Sudanic Africa and various Nigerian modernist groups are the principal examples, but such associations are found throughout the region and form the backbone of Muslim efforts to combine modern education with religious commitments. In recent decades the influence of so-called Wahhabiya or reformist associations, often with the financial and logistical backing of Sa'udi Arabia and other Arab countries, has grown enormously. These associations work, depending upon the context, for the reform of social and religious practices, and for the creation of Islamic states. In many areas where Muslims are minorities, as in Uganda or the Congo, educational associations have become the principal form of Muslim communal organization.

Muslim communal structures, then, range from traditional forms of local kinship and village groups, to Sufi lineages, brotherhoods, educational associations, and modernist reformist congregations. Islamic communal organization both reinforces minority ethnic identity and serves to link together different tribal and ethnic groups. It serves political purposes varying from collaboration with state authorities to passive withdrawal, passive resistance, active engagement, and even revolutionary action. Muslim belief and identity is highly adaptive to social context, and particularly responsive to the realities of political power.

While Muslims have accepted non-Muslim states as the political background for their communal organizations, in recent decades the relationships between Muslim communities and states have become problematic. Since the 1970s Muslims in Nigeria, Senegal, Guinea, Somalia, Sudan, and elsewhere have demanded that the state systematically promote Muslim education, apply Muslim law, and assume a Muslim identity. Guinea, for example, which was ruled by Sekou Toure and the Parti Démocratique and had a long history of efforts to modernize the country and improve the position of women, began to organize Muslim festivals and invoke the militant Muslim legacy of Futa Jallon. In Nigeria and Senegal there is considerable tension between states and Muslim communal leaders, who demand that the state represent a Muslim ideal. In the Sudan Numayri and Turabi attempted to impose an Islamic identity on the southern parts of the country. In Ethiopia and Chad Muslim minorities are fighting for political autonomy or control of the state.

Muslim religious orientations are as diverse as the forms of social organization. Some forms of popular Islam are highly syncretic and merged with African animist and spirit worship. In these mergers the Muslim calendar, festivals, and rituals to celebrate births, circumcisions, marriages, and to mark deaths tend to be adopted outright. Otherwise, though Islam in principle challenges African belief systems, in practice it seems to rationalize and Islamize existing beliefs rather than totally change the mentality of African peoples. While Islam emphasizes the absoluteness of God, it is also host to a variety of subsidiary powers, and accepts divination, magic, witchcraft, and sorcery. African spirits are identified as jinn and spirit cults – such as the Holey of the Songhay, the Bori cult of the Hausa, and the Zar cult in Ethiopia, Somalia, and Sudan – have special appeal to Muslims. They supply catharsis and spiritual consolation for women in particular. Muslim belief sanctions magical practices directed toward the cure of disease and the search for prosperity. Pagan ceremonies and artistic representations also serve to provide emotional comfort. Muslim religious leaders recognize the necessity of balancing strict religious principles with the practical needs of the common people for magical sustenance.

Alongside accommodationist, assimilationist, or syncretic forms of Islam, there is the standard Shari'a-based Muslim practice and belief. Shari'a has had important effects, for example, in criminal law and in dealing with problems of injury and death. It has tended to reinforce patriarchal and patrilineal family organization and inheritance. Because it favors individual over communal interests, Shari'a is preferred by new converts who wish to extract themselves and their wealth from family control. However, where there is a strong corporate interest in land or livestock, as among the Somali, the Fulani, and others, Shari'a considerations tend to be ignored. The spread of Shari'a, then, depends upon local social structures, and the interests of individuals and contending parties. In some cases, for example, it is possible to gain an advantage in commercial or property matters by applying Shari'a rather than customary law.

Shari'a has had a strong influence on marriage practices. It defines marriage as a voluntary contract between individuals and assigns basic responsibilities to each. It also simplifies divorce for men. The Muslim marriage gift, or *mahr*, has been adopted by various African peoples as a gift, or promise of a gift, payable directly to the wife upon divorce or the death of the husband. It supplements the ordinary payment of a bride price to the bride's kin and guardians. Despite Shari'a, however, widow inheritance and replacement by sisters continue to be important wherever marriage is primarily conceived as an alliance among kinship groups.

Reformist Islam is another important version of Islamic belief and practice. While accommodationist and Shari'a-oriented Islam both seek to penetrate and transform African social ideals and behavior, the reformist trend stands altogether outside the African tradition. Relying wholly on the Quran and Sunna, hostile to African spirit worship and belief in amulets, the reformers bring to Africa an international standard Muslim belief and practice. Reformist movements have become increasingly vocal with the growth of education in the Arab world, the creation of a new Muslim intelligentsia, the founding and expansion of madrasas, and the diffusion of new religio-educational associations. People of Muslim education and commitments increasingly demand the reform of the religious practices of fellow Muslims and the replacement of secular regimes by Islamic states. Reformism, however, sometimes blends into modernism. The educational associations of Freetown, Lagos, and Dakar are committed to the adaptation of Muslim identity to modern and Western civilization, and to the integration of Muslims into secularized national African societies.

Finally, there are the sectarian forms of Islam – those minority groups of Muslims committed to particular doctrines. These include the Asian Isma'ili, Bohra, and other minority communities. From a pan-African perspective, Islam is not a single religion but a constellation of religious communities which share, however remotely, a sense of common identity.

The diversity of sub-Saharan African Islam implies a great range of political and social behavior. While Muslim believers in the nineteenth century strove primarily to create Muslim states in Sudanic and West Africa, only where Muslim populations were relatively homogeneous (and Arab), as in Sudan, Mauritania or Somalia, do avowedly Muslim states exist today. Whereas Islam in principle is committed to a comprehensive political order, the traditional Islamic ideal has been adapted to political actuality. Muslim communities in Africa are in the main associations for worship, education, and welfare. Whereas Islam is in principle a religion that shatters all lesser loyalties, in Africa it is an integral part of Hausa, Berber-Somali, Arab, Mossi, Dyula, and other linguistic and ethnic affiliations. While in principle Islam is a universal religion based on a revealed scripture, in Africa it takes on an infinite variety of local forms. Everywhere, however, there is a growing pressure to assert the universalistic dimensions of Islam against African particularisms.

ISLAM IN THE WEST

CHAPTER 32

MUSLIMS IN EUROPE AND AMERICA

The Muslim populations of Europe and America are extremely diverse, and it is largely for geographical convenience that we consider them all in one chapter. They are diverse in origins, in living conditions, in customs, and in their concept of themselves as Muslims and their place in Euro-American societies. In Europe the critical distinction is between – on the one hand – the Muslims of the Balkans, who have their origin in the Turkish conquests and migrations of the fourteenth and subsequent centuries, and in the indigenous populations who converted to Islam in Ottoman times, and – on the other hand – those of Western Europe, who are for the most part recent immigrants. After World War II Pakistanis, Indians, and, to a lesser extent, Arabs came to Britain; North Africans and smaller numbers of West Africans, Turks, and Iranians to France; Turks to Germany; there were also many others, either refugees from the breakup of the former colonial empires or temporary workers. Most have remained in their new countries, and have established or reunited families, and now constitute a small but significant and growing part of the population of Western Europe. A trickle of immigrants came to the United States before and after World War I, but most of the present Muslim population are immigrants from India, Pakistan, Palestine, Lebanon, Iran, Iraq, and other countries, who came to the United States in the last few decades. The USA differs from Western Europe in that there has been a considerable conversion of Americans, mostly black Americans, to Islam.

EASTERN EUROPE

In the 1990s there were approximately 8,250,000 Muslims in the Balkans. They made up about 13 percent of the population. Some 70 percent of the population of Albania, 45 percent of Bosnia-Herzegovina, 30 percent of Macedonia (mostly Albanians), 20 percent of present-day Yugoslavia (including Albanians in Kosovo and Serbo-Croatian-speaking Slavs in the Sandjak), 13 percent of Bulgaria, and tiny minorities in Romania (Tatars) and Greece are Muslims. Albanians altogether number more than 4,000,000; Bosnians 2,350,000, and Turks 1,050,000 in Bulgaria, Macedonia, Greece, and Romania.

In this region the present situation of Muslims derives from the decline of the Ottoman empire and the rise of Orthodox Christian nationalisms in Greece, Serbia, Romania, and Bulgaria in the nineteenth century. Muslims lost their political protection, and large numbers migrated to the Ottoman empire or Turkey after the Russo-Turkish war of 1878, after the Balkan wars of 1912–14, and again after World War I. In the post-World War I settlement, Muslims from Greece were moved to Turkey and orthodox Christians living in Anatolia were transferred to Greece. Still, large concentrations of Muslims remained as minorities in states whose majorities considered the state the possession of the Christian population. In all the Balkan countries there were strong trends towards secularization of Muslims. The Muslim population came to include both peoples who continued to practice Islam and those who did not but considered themselves Muslim by ancestry or by virtue of culture and ethnicity.

After World War II many of the Balkan states were taken over by Communist parties who persecuted Muslims and tried to suppress Islam. Bulgaria and Yugoslavia suppressed the practice of Islam. Albania under Enver Hoxha (1946–85) uprooted Islamic institutions. With the collapse of the Communist regimes, their programs for creating homogeneous nations failed, and there has been a revival of ethno-religious identifications and conflicts. In Yugoslavia, the death of Tito in 1980 allowed for increasing tensions among the component states of federated Yugoslavia. Albanians demanded local autonomy or "republic" status for Kosovo, and clashed with Serbian nationalists for control of the province. In 1991 Macedonia declared its independence, followed by Slovenia, Croatia, and Bosnia-Herzegovina. Only Montenegro and Serbia remained in the Yugoslav federation, led by Slobodan Milosevic until his downfall and arrest in 2000. Serbia and Croatia went to war. Bosnia was engulfed in civil war. Euro-American NATO intervention finally brought an end to the fighting in 1995 and new efforts at the reconstruction of the war-torn region. Further conflicts engulfed Serbs and Albanians in Kosovo, also ending in NATO intervention and occupation of the province. Macedonia under NATO political guidance teeters on the edge of a new civil war between Albanians and Slavs.

Bosnia

After centuries of Ottoman rule, Bosnia became part of the Austro-Hungarian empire in 1878. For Bosnian Muslims the Ottoman empire had been a refuge and Ottoman withdrawal a deep disappointment. The Austrians organized Bosnian Muslims under the authority of a *ra'is al-'ulama'*, paid his salary, and created an advisory committee which assumed control of waqfs. In 1909 the Muslim administrative apparatus became autonomous. The Bosnian elites kept the Ottoman language as a sign of high status and of Muslim identity. At the same time the expansion of secular education and the formation of reading and political clubs developed a new intelligentsia. From both religious and secular intellectuals there came a Bosnian concept of ethnic identity, partly religious, partly national, which was separate from Serbian and Croatian identities. The common people resisted the efforts of both Serbs and Croats to "nationalize" them. They spoke Bosnian and wrote it either in Arabic or in Cyrillic script.

With the founding of Yugoslavia in 1918, Bosnians formed the Yugoslav Muslim Organization, which demanded autonomy and the maintenance of Muslim educational and judicial institutions, but after the coup of 1929 King Aleksander pursued a policy of Serbianization, and partitioned Bosnia-Herzegovina out of existence. The province was absorbed by Croatia during World War II. Caught between the Ustasas Croats and Chetnik Serbs, tens of thousands of Bosnians were killed during the war.

The formation of a Communist regime in 1945 promoted further Bosnian emigration to Turkey. The Communists banned the Sufi orders in 1952, closed down Muslim schools and mosques, and took control of the income of waqfs. From 1957 to 1969, however, the Muslim hierarchy was reorganized. After 1966 President Tito adopted a tolerant nationalities policy, and recognized Bosnians as a separate and equal nationality within the Yugoslav state. Sufi tekkes reopened, and a Muslim revival of mosque and school building began – though it did not change the basically secular character of Bosnian-Muslim identity. The new policies were evidently intended to offset local Serbian and Croatian political pressures, since Muslim identity was not encouraged among Albanians and Turks or among Muslims living in predominantly Serbian provinces.

With the collapse of the Communist government in 1990, the Bosnian Muslim Party of Democratic Action, headed by Alija Izetbegovic, called for an independent, secular, multi-national Bosnian state. The declaration of Bosnian independence led Serbs living in Bosnia and Herzegovina to declare their own Serbian republic, make war on the Muslims, and attempt by "ethnic cleansing" to drive them out of the region. The war was marked by horrifying episodes of torture, rape, and mass murder of Bosnian Muslims. The Serbian assault was also directed against mosques, historic buildings, and other artifacts in an effort to eradicate all signs of Bosnian identity. The United Nations attempted to intervene, but a UN arms embargo worked only to the advantage of the Serbs, and its peace-keeping forces were ineffectual. Eventually a Croatian–Bosnian alliance, with NATO air support, brought an end to the war. By the Dayton Accords of November 1995, Bosnia was divided into two states, one Muslim and Croatian, the other Serbian. NATO forces still occupy the province in an effort to create political stability and allow the several nationality groups to live together.

The war intensified the identification of Bosnian Muslims with Islam. The breakup of Communist rule, international support from Muslim countries, and UN and NATO support for minority rights helped consolidate Muslim identities. A Muslim vocabulary using such concepts as jihad and shahid (martyr) became part of Bosnian discourse. Muslim teaching and practice resumed; Sarajevo has become an important center of Muslim publishing.

Albanians

In Albania Islam and Muslim identities have not been an issue, and Islam is not equated with Albanian nationality. About 55 percent of the population of Albania is Sunni; 15 percent is Bektashi. The Ghegs who populate the north are divided between Sunnis and Catholics, and the Tosks in the south between Bektashis and Greek Orthodox. From 1967 to 1990 all religious activities were banned, but they were restored in 1990 by President Ramiz Alia. With considerable help from Sa'udi Arabia, the Gulf states, Turkey, and Malaysia – and support from Albanians abroad – mosques, madrasas, Sufi tekkes and shrines, and libraries are being rebuilt, but attendance is still sparse. Bektashis receive some help from Iran. The Islamic cultural and religious revival notwithstanding, political identities are expressed in nationalist terms, and there is an increasing interest in an encompassing Balkan Albanian state to integrate the Albanian populations of Albania, Kosovo, and Macedonia.

In the Kosovo region of Yugoslavia Albanians never accepted the Yugoslav state as did Bosnians, and maintained their separate identity and territorial claims. Kosovo-Albanian identity was also defined in ethnic rather than in religious terms. While the 1974 Yugoslav constitution recognized Kosovo as an autonomous region within the Yugoslav federation, the 1980s saw an intensification of Albanian–Serb conflict for control of Kosovo. By 1990 Albanians made up 85 percent of the population, and schools, courts, and media were all Albanian. Schools were the center of opposition to integration into Yugoslavia. While Albanians had cultural autonomy, nationalist ambitions for independence or for the creation of a greater Albania still smoldered.

Then, in 1989, Slobodan Milosevic, the President of Yugoslavia, stripped Kosovo of its autonomy. Police repression and the dismissal of Albanians from media and other important positions followed. The Serbs wanted to colonize the region, and force Albanians to emigrate. In response Albanians created an underground government, led by Ibrahim Rogova, which demanded independence; more radical elements organized the Kosovo Liberation Army. As the fighting escalated, and repeated diplomatic efforts to pacify the region failed, Serbian assaults against Albanians finally led to NATO intervention. From March to June 1999, the USA and its allies bombed Serbia, while Serbian forces made a last effort to drive out the Albanian population. NATO eventually forced Serbia to accept a NATO occupation, and the province is now under allied administration. Most Albanians maintain an ethnic nationalist identity, and some reject Islam as an outmoded Ottoman heritage, but other Kosovo Albanians have begun to define themselves in Islamic-nationalist terms.

Macedonia is the most recent of the Balkan states to undergo inter-ethnic and religious strife. Formerly an autonomous part of the Yugoslav Republic, Macedonia became independent in 1991. Muslims make up about 30 percent of the population, including Albanians (about 20–25 percent), and Turks (about 4–5 percent). Other Macedonian Muslims, who are ethnically and linguistically Slavs, called Pomaks or Torbeshi, and Roma (Gypsies), tend to identify themselves either as Turks or Albanians. Albanian demands for cultural autonomy, recognition of

Albanian as a national language alongside Serbian, and partner status in a state defined as a condominium of ethnic groups have met with stern resistance from Slavic-Macedonian nationalists. In 2000 and 2001 NATO was attempting to forestall the outbreak of civil war, and to arrange a political compromise. The conflict in Macedonia is expressed in nationalist rather than religious terms.

Bulgaria

Muslims in Bulgaria number about 1.25 million, or 13 percent of the population, most of whom are Turks with substantial numbers of Roma and Pomaks. Muslims in Bulgaria have gone through waves of discrimination and persecution. After Bulgaria became independent in 1878 its new leaders were determined to Westernize the country and wipe out the Ottoman heritage, and many Muslims left for the Ottoman empire in 1878 and 1912–13. The Turkish village population, however, was unscathed since it was not considered a political rival to the Christian elites. When the Communist Party came to power in 1944, it tried to suppress religious identity in favor of secular and socialist identities. From the late 1950s to 1985 the state tried to undermine the separate ethnic identity of Muslims. Muslim religious and cultural practices were forbidden. Turkish-Muslim names and public use of the Turkish language were forbidden, and the Communists tried to promote assimilation by the education of a Turkish secular elite. Repression led to migrations in 1950–51, and to the mass emigration of half a million people in 1989.

The breakup of the Communist regime was an opportunity to reconsolidate both the religious and ethnic forms of Muslim identity. After 1989 the Pomaks, who generally identify themselves as Bulgarians, maintained their separateness by keeping strong kinship and work ties, and by reviving Islamic instruction and practices. Their distinct identity is also protected by the fact that they are concentrated in remote villages, and have generally (apart from construction work) avoided occupations such as peddling or trading which separate the men from their families. Economic hardship is now the greatest danger to these communities.

Balkan Muslims look to Turkey for political protection and refuge, and Turkey sees itself as a kindred state because of religion and the remembrances of Ottoman history. Turkey intervened militarily, seizing part of Cyprus in the name of protecting the Muslim-Turkish community and preventing the unification of Cyprus with Greece, made agreements with Greece about Muslims in Thrace, and accepted refugees from the Balkans, but otherwise has been very cautious in dealing with the region. Turkish foreign policy makers are aware of the danger of an extreme polarization of the Balkans into Christian and Muslim alliances.

WESTERN EUROPE

While in Eastern Europe Islam is a deeply rooted indigenous presence, it was only in the nineteenth century that Muslims began to go to Western Europe. Bosnians went to Vienna, and Turks to Paris, as diplomats and students. Indian soldiers in the British armed forces and Yemeni and Somali seamen settled in Liverpool and London. Algerian workers went to Marseilles before World War I, and during and after the war France brought Algerian recruits to the metropole, and later allowed for the opening of a mosque in Paris and a Muslim cemetery in Bobigny. In the inter-war period students from colonized countries made their way to colonial capitals. Muslims from Russia and later the Soviet Union, captured in the two World Wars, sometimes ended up in German armies.

An intensive migration of Muslims to Western Europe began in the 1950s and 1960s, partly because of the breakup of colonial empires, but largely due to European economic prosperity and the consequent recruitment of laborers. These were mostly unskilled or low-skilled workers in agriculture and construction, and typically they came without families. After 1973 a European-wide recession led to efforts to stop labor migration, and even to induce foreigners to return to their home countries. Governments then permitted families to join workers already in Europe, prompting a new wave of immigration. From the 1980s, the predominant sources of immigrants were illegal aliens seeking work and political refugees seeking asylum. These immigrants had much greater difficulty integrating into the labor force in a period of economic stagnation, though some of them benefited from periodic efforts to regularize the status of illegal aliens. Conversely, migrants in the 1990s included professionals recruited for their high skills, typically in the computer and software industries.

The incorporation of Muslims into Western Europe

Each generation and type of migrant has a different relationship to the host country, but for all of them the critical formative influences are the policies of the host countries toward citizenship, the attitudes of the already settled populations toward immigrants, and the institutional mechanisms for the incorporation of immigrants into the larger society.

European and American attitudes toward immigration differ considerably. The United States is historically a country of immigration with the expectation of permanent settlement and assimilation into American society. Assimilation has historically entailed the loss of the languages of country of origin, a downplaying of ethnic differences in the public realm, and a devaluation in public symbols of the specificity of immigrant cultures. This has been counterbalanced by the acceptance of religious identity in the private sphere as compatible with American political identity in the public sphere. The USA seems to be in transition toward the recognition of Islam as an indigenous religion, part of the Judeo-Christian–Islamic tradition. Politicians have begun to refer to the triumvirate of church, synagogue, and mosque.

In many European countries immigration has not historically been thought to lead to permanent settlement and integration into the national population, but over time it has become evident that Muslim immigrants are not temporary workers, but permanent residents. This has forced Europeans to rethink their citizenship policies and to reformulate their ethnic, religious, and national identities. In their need to cope with large immigrant populations, European states have adopted a variety of policies. Legal requirements, which differ in each country, define the requirements and possibilities of citizenship. In Britain and France immigrants may become citizens after five years of residence, and in Germany after eight years. In all three countries there are requirements for knowledge of the language and civic traditions and for good character, but in practice citizenship is most easily attained in Britain. France demands a high degree of assimilation. German law gives officials a wide discretion to restrict citizenship in the national interest.

Laws concerning children of non-citizen parents also differ. In the United States a child is automatically a citizen by virtue of being born in the country. In Britain the child of non-citizens is a citizen only if one parent is "settled" or legally resident without limit of time, but children of non-settled residents can become citizens after ten years of residence or if a parent becomes settled. In France a child is eligible for citizenship if one parent was born in France, but by recent legislation must be five years resident in France between the ages of eleven and eighteen, and formally request French citizenship. In Germany since January 2000 a child is a citizen at birth if at least one parent has been legally resident for eight years. This is a major change in policy. Until the new law came into effect, Germany required German ethnic ancestry for citizenship. The United States, Britain, and France permit dual citizenship to naturalized citizens who are citizens of another country by virtue of ancestral ties, but German law requires a person born in Germany to choose one or the other citizenship by the age of twenty-three.

Apart from efforts to obtain citizenship, immigrants in each country have adopted a variety of strategies to become integrated into their new homelands. Where immigrants are citizens – as in the United States, Britain, and France – they have normal political channels to press their interests. In the United States Muslims form associations to lobby for immigrant interests. In Britain, participation in and influence upon local governments, the formation of interest-group lobbies, and demands for public recognition are the typical means to press for inclusion in the society. Muslims demand to be free of discrimination in employment. They ask for the protection of the anti-blasphemy laws, and for their religious identity to be recognized as legitimate in the public sphere. In France the trade unions and anti-racial discrimination movements are the routes to a place in French society. In Germany the principal vehicles of incorporation are the unions, vocational institutes and schools, and the educational policies of the some of the more liberal German federal states, such as Berlin and Bremen.

Equally important are the prevailing cultural attitudes and the policies derived from them. The degree of acceptance, assimilation, and accommodation differs in different countries. Belgium and the Netherlands institutionalize parallel religious confessional communities within the structure of the state. Sweden, Britain, and the United States seem to be the most open to multiculturalism. Britain is multi-culturalist in that it accepts and publicly supports the expression of a variety of racial and ethnic identities, but there is strong resistance to the acceptance of religion, as opposed to race, in defining a minority community. The multi-culturalist societies hover between cultural pluralism and multiculturalism – between acceptance of a variety of communities in the private sphere and their validation in the public sphere.

France maintains the ideal of a secular, civic society of individuals, and resists multiculturalism in favor of individualism. In France immigrants may become "French" but only on condition of complete linguistic assimilation and acceptance of French *laïcité*, or the confinement of religion to the private sphere. France has little tolerance for communal collectivities within the body politic. Germany is divided between liberals who accept immigrants and rightists who protest against the state's immigration, employment, and welfare policies.

The host societies have had great difficulty in finding a modus vivendi with their unanticipated immigrant populations. Large numbers of immigrants, now permanent residents, test the capacity of European societies to assimilate individuals, and to recognize group identities and the collective rights of different religions and cultures. Many Europeans think of Muslims as a single ethnic group, and regard Islam as a fundamentalist religion which threatens separatism in the body politic. The presence of large numbers of Muslims has raised questions about the compatibility of Islam with European institutions, and reciprocally about Europe's capacity to accept pluralistic societies. International events such as rise of Qaddafi and Khomayni to power, terrorist episodes, and the rise of the Taliban in Afghanistan have raised anti-Muslim feeling. The Salman Rushdie affair (see below) led many to believe that Muslim values were incompatible with European liberal values.

From the late 1970s to the early 1990s there was a strong reaction against the presence of immigrants. Strong right-wing parties emerged in France, Germany, Austria, Italy, and other countries, protesting against immigration, the employment of immigrants, and social and financial support for immigrant communities. There are conflicts over the distribution of jobs and other resources. Many Europeans see immigrants as they saw colonial subjects – as lower peoples who have to be assimilated by education – and assume that their civilization will be defined only on European terms. Behind these concerns lies the larger threat of the globalization of economies, unchecked immigration, and the loss of national cultures. These tensions seem to have diminished in the later 1990s, probably due to a combination of relative prosperity, strong repression of criminal attacks upon immigrants and of racist political parties (as in Germany), and perhaps a gradual reconciliation with the fact of a permanent Muslim presence in Europe.

How well Muslims have fared as individuals and as communities differs from country to country and within each country. It varies enormously with differences of institutions, political context, and social attitudes in each host country – combined with equally numerous variations in the cultures, identities, and objectives of the immigrant populations. On the part of immigrants the process of settlement raises questions about the practice of social and religious customs, legal behavior, communal organizations, and relations to the host societies. Immigrants have to deal with differing traditions regarding women's dress, education, and employment. They have to face conflicting influences upon their children, and children who begin to resist parental authority in their choices of language, religious practice, education, social mores, and relations with the opposite sex. Immigrants turn to the European host societies for accommodation in their efforts to cope with these problems, asking for mosques, schools, acceptance of special Muslim needs such as halal meat, headscarves for girls, recognition of Muslim family law, access to resources and social services, governmental protection, political acceptance, and public tolerance.

Legal issues are especially complicated. Muslim immigrants brought with them not just one legal system, but the various different systems found within each home country – Shari'a, customary law, modern legislation, and current administrative practice. In family disputes conflicts arise over whether real-life practice, or Shari'a, or the legal code of the country of origin, or that of the country of residence should apply. Custody and inheritance disputes arise from mixed marriages.

To cope Muslims formed mosques, community centers, and social organizations. The first were local, village, regional, and ethnic-based associations. Governments, political parties, and movements in the home countries formed branches in Europe. Sa'udi Arabia and Libya, for example, sponsored mosques and community projects, and sent imams to the Muslims in Europe. The Diyanet, or Turkish Ministry of Religion, sought both to promote and supervise Turkish Muslim religious and educational activities in Germany. Finally, European governments in Britain, Belgium, and France have established associations and councils to organize and represent the immigrant communities. Such groups fall short of comprehensive inclusion or representation of Muslims, and have been hampered by internal fragmentation as well as institutional and political resistance in the host societies.

France

As a result of colonial recruitment, Algerian soldiers and workers first came to France at the time of World War I. After the Algerian war of independence Algerian supporters of the French, called Harkis, were evacuated to France in 1962. North Africans came in large numbers after World War II and until 1974. In the 1970s Turks, and black Africans from Mali, Mauritania, and Senegal, increased the Muslim presence. Only after 1974 did North African and sub-Saharan immigrants begin to think of themselves as permanent residents; only after 1989 did the Turks. By the 1980s there was a tendency for Maghribis born in France to assimilate to French public identity, but Turks, Malays, and Pakistanis held on to the dream of returning to their home countries. By 1990, there were over three million Muslims in France, mostly concentrated in the industrial towns of Marseilles, Lyon, Paris, and Lille. These included 850,000 Algerians, 400,000 Harkis, 450,000 Moroccans, 200,000 Tunisians, 200,000 Turks, 100,000 Senegalese, Malians, and other West Africans, and 450,000 *beurs*, or people born to Muslim families in France.

Immigrants to France tended at first to define themselves in ethnic and national terms, but French law provides for freedom of religious association, and Muslims quickly established numerous prayer rooms, mosques, and communal associations, albeit on an ethnic basis. Many of these were linked to governments and political parties in their countries of origin. Reciprocally, governments and parties of the home countries tried to organize their compatriots in France. The FIS from Algeria, an-Nahda from Tunisia, the Sultan of Morocco, and the Turkish Diyanet are all active among immigrants in France. West Africans tend to be affiliated with Sufi brotherhoods, and Turks with Naqshbandis. Religious and political associations with an Islamic rather than an ethnic orientation are also active. These include the Tabligh, the Mosque of Paris, the Association of Muslim Students (affiliated with the Society of Muslim Brothers), the Union of Islamic Organizations, a federation of mosques, and the National Federation of Muslims (Moroccan). There is some pressure to create a national association of all Muslims because of French political practice, but it has been very difficult to establish an overall coordinating body. Government efforts to structure the Muslim communities create the paradox of an assemblage of ethnic minorities organized as a religious community by a secular state.

Education is the critical issue for Muslims. The state school system is firmly secular, and France has a long tradition of using education to socialize children to the non-religious values of the French Republic. Though French law allows religious bodies to receive a state subsidy for their schools, no Muslim schools have been founded under this system. In France the mosques provide supplementary Arabic and religious instruction.

The "headscarves" incident was the most contentious indication of the unsettled relations between Muslim students and the French school authorities. The principal of a French high school in the town of Creil asked Muslim girls to remove headscarves. The laïcist conceptual framework did not allow for differences in the public sphere. The girls refused and were expelled. The Council of State at first allowed each school to make its own policy, but then reversed its ruling, and ordered girls to be allowed to go to class with headscarves. This created a public furor, and polarized Muslim and French public opinion. French secularists defended the ideological commitments of the school system. Muslims defended their religious liberty. The debate radicalized Muslim self-awareness, and more and more girls came to school with headscarves. French public opinion begin to fear this as political statement of sympathy with Algerian fundamentalists, or as a sign of the oppression of women, and a barrier to integration. A right-wing anti-immigrant movement led by Jean-Marie Le Pen made striking gains in local elections. The issue was settled in 2000 by the French Constitutional Council, which ruled that the wearing of headscarves was acceptable if not accompanied by proselytizing. French public opinion is now more tolerant of the Muslim presence, but does not have a positive overall view of Islam.

Muslims in France are in process of losing their old cultures, and of developing, not one new unified identity, but a variety of identities. Second- and third-generation

Maghribis who go to French schools develop values different from those of their families. Groups that are socially and economically assimilated tend toward Gallicization and integration, while retaining religious practices on an individual basis. Some studies find that immigrants are becoming socially and professionally integrated, experience a high degree of intermarriage, want to be seen as individuals, have little sense of community with other Muslims or Arabs, and have no interest in creating a reformulated Arab identity.

Surveys in the 1990s showed that 70 percent of Muslims interviewed expected to be integrated into French society and to practice Islam as a private religion. About 25 percent of the total were completely secular, and did not have any Islamic identity in public. About 25–30 percent wanted public visibility of Islam and are in favor of minarets, festivals, Ramadan, and halal food. A recent poll, in *Le Monde*, in October, 2001, found that 16 percent of respondents identified themselves only as being of Muslim origin; 36 percent said they were non-practicing believers; and 42 percent practicing believers. Non-practicing Muslims tend to come from the technical or administrative middle class. The practicing Muslims include persons with both the least and the most education. The numbers who respect Ramadan have been rising. Muslims seem to have concluded that integration without giving up Islam is possible.

A forceful counter-trend, however, is the emergence in the 1990s of a neo-Islamic identity, community separatism, and withdrawal from French society. Islamism as a political alternative is most likely to gain in areas of failed integration. Religious associations try to bring structure to the anomie of towns, mediate relations with the political authorities, and create a "Muslim" ethnicity. Excluded, unemployed, segregated Arab and black youths are developing their own neo-communalist sub-culture in Islamic form. In some respects the neo-Islamic revival is a protest of the disadvantaged against the prejudices of French society, the hardships of unemployment, and the loss of cultural authenticity. Students, workers, and youths link up across ethnic lines in a new pan-Muslim identity. In this sub-culture brothers want to control sisters (girls tend to become assimilated more readily) and to replace failed parents. Typically they insist that women wear a conservative style of "Muslim" dress to mark the community, though men do not have a distinctive Muslim look. Control of women has become essential to their cultural identity. Muslim lay preachers, often foreign, elite immigrants – and even the French government – are trying to find communal interlocutors, and to shape this identity. All find it hard to cope with the lack of organization and the spirit of revolt. Neo-Islamic demands are a gesture of refusal, a counter-rejection to an exclusive French society.

The new Islamist identity in France has other meanings. It is also a form of political mobilization for Maghribis who do not accept their nationality of origin as their basic identification and thereby refuse the right of home country political authorities to speak for them. It is in part an effort to find an alternative to Western values and identities. In part the revival is promoted by the emergence of a transnational, global Muslim sense of affiliation, and by such international movements as the Tabligh, which preach a pietist and devotionalist form of Islam, and the Muslim Brothers, who promote a politically activist form of Islam.

While there is a French Muslim population, there is no nationwide Muslim community. Whether the urban disinherited or the assimilating milieu will define the identity of the rest of the Muslim immigrant population and their roles in French society remains an open question.

Germany

In Germany most foreign guest-workers came from Turkey in the 1960s. They were recruited as part of a deliberate government–industry initiative, and by the collaboration of German and Turkish authorities. Immigrant Turks and Kurds settled in the industrial belt from Cologne to Essen, and in Hamburg, Stuttgart, Karlsruhe, and Frankfurt. Numerous Iranian, North African Arab, and Yugoslav refugees came at later dates. Germany provided limited social benefits for Turkish workers, but did not accord citizenship rights on the assumption that they would be there temporarily, but not permanently settled, and in accordance with German laws which allowed citizenship only to people of ethnic German descent. After 1974 Germany stopped the influx of new workers but permitted the reunification of families, and thus set the basis for permanent immigrant residence. Estimates of the Muslim population vary from two to three million Muslims in a total population of about eighty million.

Turkish and other Muslim immigrants in Germany, as elsewhere in Europe, face discrimination, and sometimes overt hostility on the part of Germans who see them as competitors for jobs and for cultural recognition. Turkish immigrants call for equality of opportunity, protection from harassment and discrimination, equality of status for Islam with other religions, and above all access to German nationality. Turks want to maintain a double citizenship, becoming German citizens while remaining citizens of Turkey. Recent German legislation has permitted the naturalization of residents, but requires the renunciation of foreign citizenship.

While pursuing these public demands, individuals have adopted numerous different versions of Muslim identity. In Germany, as in other parts of Europe, "Muslims" denotes a cultural group, not necessarily implying religiosity. Underlying presumed Muslim identities are Turkish, Kurdish, and other ethnic and national affiliations. Immigrant youths are still marginalized in German society, but seem to be moving toward a cultural synthesis. Neither German nor Turk, they combine headscarves and jeans.

The organization of the Turkish community was facilitated by German laws which recognize religious associations as corporations with public status and rights to administer instruction and be represented in public institutions such as hospitals, the army, prisons, and the media. In effect the state considers religious associations as subcontractors for welfare matters, and distributes tax revenues to churches, nurseries, hospitals, and other charities. Muslims, however, are not fully

incorporated into the system. While they have created the legally required registered associations and foundations, they have not yet achieved recognition as a
united representative public law corporation.

Turkish immigrants have instead created a widespread network of associations
which operate even more freely in Germany than in Turkey. These associations
include the Turkish state Diyanet, the Turkish Ministry of Religious Affairs, which
promotes a Turkish-Muslim identity and forms of Islam compatible with Turkish
state secularism. It works to prevent the assimilation of Turks in Europe and to
maintain their loyalty to the fatherland. The Diyanet sponsors mosques and school
instruction, appoints imams, and distributes religious publications. Only imams
approved by the Diyanet are officially accepted in Germany. Since the Diyanet
encourages a secularist tendency in education, many parents prefer to send their
children to mosque schools.

Non-state movements based in Turkey compete for influence among Turkish
immigrants. These include the Sulaymancis, the Milli Gorus, linked to the Refah
(Welfare) Party, the Nurcis, the Naqshbandi Turkish Islamic Centers, and the pan-
Turkish nationalist Federation of Turkish-Democratic Idealist Associations. Milli
Gorus promotes the idea of an Islamic state and wants Turkey to adapt Islamic law.
It claims 200,000 members. A Caliphal State movement led by Metin Kaplan has about
1,300 members, and advocates the formation of an Islamic government in Turkey
unified with the rest of Muslim world. These two movements represent separatist
communities in exile oriented to the politics of Turkey rather than Germany. Other
Muslim movements in Germany include the Society of Muslim Brothers and representatives of the Algerian FIS and GIA, Hizballah, HAMAS, Shi'i missions, the Muslim
World League, the Ahmadiya, and possible Bin Laden recruits among alienated youth
and foreign students. These groups offer religious services, pilgrimage, education,
help with German bureaucracy, and courses in everything from Arabic to comput-
ers. Efforts to create a unified Muslim organization have thus far failed to take hold.

Education remains a critical problem for Muslim communities. German federal
states (*Länder*) are responsible for providing teachers and instruction in religion and
foreign languages in the state schools. Religious groups supply the curriculum. In
the states of Bremen and Berlin religious communities have full responsibility for
programs, including teacher training, but the state provides financial support and 80
percent of teachers' salaries. State education authorities, however, have to approve
standards for teachers and classroom syllabuses, and have resisted the actual implementation of such programs for Muslims. German officials have also resisted setting
up independent Muslim schools similar to church schools. The primary concern is
political activism in the mosques. German judges have raised questions as to
whether Muslim education represents a genuine religious tradition or is a form of
political or ideological indoctrination. In Berlin in 1998 a court ruled that the Islamic
Federation could participate in the school system, but this has not been implemented
because of connection of the Islamic Federation to Milli Gorus, which has political

objectives and is resisted by the Diyanet. Muslim demands for prayer in the schools, or the separation of the sexes in biology classes, also meet with resistance from German public opinion because they are suspected of serving political rather than strictly religious ends, and because of the implied gender inequality.

As negotiations continue Muslim community groups are under pressure to adjust their curricula to satisfy the authorities. This shapes their beliefs, and tends to promote Islam as the private beliefs of individuals rather than Islam as a collectivity. For example, in February 2000 a Berlin court recognized the Alevis as a religious group entitled to provide religious instruction in the public schools. The Alevis, who had depended on a tradition of verbal communication of beliefs from elders to disciples, had virtually lost their religious identity in the 1980s. Now to keep a community identity they have had to create a teachable religion.

A case study of Muslims in Augsburg shows that Muslims who do keep a religious identity and affiliations to religious communities have different religious and political orientations. Some movements, such as the Nurcis, who cultivate a reformed type of Sufi mysticism, and the Tabligh, who represent an inner-worldy socially active religiosity, have a purely religious orientation. The Nurcis believe that consciousness raising has to precede politics, and stress the importance of adhering to principles and avoiding compromises. They make no effort to raise mass support, appeal mainly to intellectuals, and foster strong ties between teachers and disciples. The Tabligh, a missionary preaching movement, represents a purist scripturalist position, separating religion and politics to avoid compromising religious values.

Other scripturalist movements hold that religious and worldly concerns cannot be separated. Religious awareness has to be based on political power. Movements with inner-worldly aims typically have a cadre structure, and a hierarchically organized inner group, distinguished from ordinary adherents and sympathizers. The Sulaymancis try to support their Quran schools by pragmatic policies such as alignment with the Turkish Party of the Right Way, led by Suleyman Demirel. The National Sight Party, an affiliate of the Welfare Party, is also strategically oriented, and willing to participate in politics to promote its identity objectives.

Though the tactics are different, the common purpose of these Turkish Muslim movements is the Islamization of society in Turkey. All the groups in Augsburg are interested in struggling for their cause at home, and in protecting their German base for that struggle, but show much less concern for the immediate problems of Muslims in Germany.

German society remains strongly divided over the place of immigrants. Liberal Germans defend their rights to security and cultural identity, and residents are permitted to vote in local elections, but many Germans refuse to accept people who are not ethnic Germans as true citizens. A strong rightist movement protests against immigration, as well as employment and welfare benefits for migrants. These tensions rose markedly in the 1990s with the stresses accompanying German reunification. A neo-Nazi current, especially in underemployed and still depressed eastern Germany, has led to violent attacks upon and murders of immigrants. Though punished severely in the courts and threatened with political suppression, anti-immigrant violence remains a critical problem.

The situation of Muslims in Switzerland resembles that of Germany. Turks lean toward ethnic-heritage forms of Islam, and affiliate with movements, such as the Diyanet, Milli Gorus, Sulaymancis, and Nurcis, that are based in Turkey. Arabs lean toward universalistic Islam. The Muslim Brothers and Sa'udi mosques in Geneva promote a "born again" individualistic Muslim identity to be combined with participation in Swiss public life.

Britain

After World War II emigration to Britain was opened to citizens of the British commonwealth, and immigrants began to arrive as laborers in the 1950s. In anticipation of restrictions imposed in 1962 there was a massive immigration of Pakistanis, Gujaratis, Kashmiris, Punjabis, Turkish Cypriots, Malaysians, Moroccans, Yemenis, and West Africans. In 1968 further restrictions were imposed on British passport-holders who could not show a family connection to Britain, and the emphasis in immigration policy shifted to family reunification. Then, in the 1970s, a great wave of South Asians came from East Africa. A census of 1986 showed almost a million Muslims in Britain, and there are now probably about 1.5 million. Most live in London, Birmingham, and Bradford in Yorkshire.

Among first-generation migrants, religion is subsumed as part of ethnic identity. For example, Pakistanis have their own food and clothing stores, television and radio programs, mosques, and schools. Muslim immigrants affiliate with a variety of religious movements which are registered as organized charities. South Asians follow either the Barelwi or the Deobandi tradition. Bangladeshis worship at the Brick Lane mosque, which is Barelwi; social and community needs are handled by the Bangladesh Welfare Association. Pakistanis attend the East London mosque, which is Deobandi, and receives support from Sa'udi Arabia and Pakistan. It is allied to the Muslim Youth Organization which provides its social outreach. The Tablighi Jama'at, affiliated with the Deobandi mosques, helps create an international identity for mobile Muslims. It urges Muslims in new countries to be responsible citizens. The Jama'at-i Islami in Britain is a pressure group organized to influence policy toward Muslims. Linked with the Islamic Foundation, the UK Islamic Mission, and the Young Muslims, it tries to propagate its own ideology, but has little grass-roots support. There are also Sufi tariqat.

Most Muslim organizations, however, are local and are concerned with school, mosque, food, and burial issues. In Bradford and Leicester Muslims are organized on a city-wide basis. The Bradford Council of Mosques is a coordinating body created to give a common voice to the various Muslim communities. It negotiates with school authorities for the special needs of Muslim students. There are various national organizations such as Union of Muslim Organizations and the Council of Mosques, but Muslims in Britain, as elsewhere in Europe, are not unified and generally do not recognize comprehensive allegiances.

34 An Anti-Rushdie demonstration, London

Since the 1980s Muslims in Britain have tended to reaffirm the religious dimensions of their identity. Participation in Friday prayers, observance of Ramadan, and consumption of halal meat have become ever more common. The first engagement in public issues came in the 1980s with demands for schools for Muslim youth. While considering education highly desirable to pave the way for a better livelihood, Muslim parents were dissatisfied with the secularism of British schools, and saw their cultural neutrality and social diversity as a challenge to Muslim convictions about the truth of their own religion. They feared the exposure of their children to racist attitudes and the mixing of the sexes. They wanted to establish Muslim schools, classified as voluntary schools under religious control but subsidized by state funds, similar to Church of England, Catholic, and Jewish schools. In places where Muslims are in a local majority, they have tried to bypass the local authorities and receive direct subsidies from the central government as allowed in the Educational Reform Act. In the public arena, Muslims call for laws to meet their religious and educational needs and to protect them against discrimination. Some demand the application of Muslim family law in Britain.

The trend toward the assertion of Muslim identity also has a transnational dimension. Muslim activists insist that Muslims overcome their ethnic and national divisions, and accept common religious practices and beliefs. A small minority of Islamic activists insists on strict devotions, and completely rejects a Western way of life. There is also a Muslim community in Norwich which refuses to accept health services, schools, and the jurisdiction of British courts in family law.

The Rushdie affair was a crystallizing moment in the evolution of the position of Muslims in Britain. The publication of *The Satanic Verses* with their implied insults to the Prophet Muhammad united Muslims in anger, and generated demands for protection under British blasphemy laws, and for the withdrawal of the book from circulation. Led by the Bradford Council of Mosques, Muslims staged a ritual book-burning ceremony, and were joined by Muslims the world over in their protest. Ayatollah Khomayni of Iran condemned Rushdie to death. British public opinion reacted to these expressions of outrage by defending freedom of speech; there was a perception that Muslims were a fundamentalist bloc with anti-British, anti-liberal, and anti-modern views. Muslims further alienated British opinion by their open support for Saddam Husayn in the Gulf War. Muslims and other Britons did not understand each other's positions or grasp the depth of each other's anger over the Rushdie affair.

Nonetheless, in the 1990s Muslims in Britain still participated in politics, and won increasing recognition in British public life. An umbrella Muslim council of Britain was created in 1997, and the first Muslim MP was elected. Three Muslims have been appointed to the House of Lords. In 1998 Muslims won the same rights to state-funded schools as Christians and Jews; the 2001 census included a religious affiliation question; and Islamic studies are burgeoning in British universities. There is an active Muslim press. Despite these gains the sense of alienation remains very strong, as do antagonisms between Muslims and other Britons. Recent riots in Leicester reveal the depth of unresolved social and political problems.

The development of Muslim identities has been explored through recent fieldwork among Pakistanis in Waltham Forest Borough, London. This is a very conservative community where elders maintain kinship and local networks in their home country and try to prevent the assimilation of their children into the larger British society. Fathers, brothers, and mothers want to control the dating and marriages of their daughters and sisters, which is an issue of honor as well as community boundaries. Conversely, young people want to expand their freedom of action; many want to enjoy a British lifestyle, but still respect their families. They also find their assimilation blocked by British racism and Islamophobia. Coming from tight-knit Pakistani communities, yet living in and adapting to a Western society that is in its turn doubtful about them, they are ambivalent about their mixed identities.

One outlet for identity dilemmas is an increasing commitment to Islam. The renewed commitment to Islam is defined by reading and discussing Quran and hadith, participation in mosque prayers, observance of Ramadan, avoiding alcohol or pork, eating only halal foods, and social behavior that eschews nightclubs, and restricts or renounces dating members of the opposite sex. While some young men do not practice Islam, they nonetheless affirm Islam as their identity and a total life system. They see it as a source of guidance, morality, discipline, and compassion. Women believe that Islam, properly understood, is favorable to them. Perhaps the fundamental underlying factor in the renewed devotion of young men and women in Britain is that it provides an anchor of certainty and unchangeable truths in a very fluid cultural situation. Moreover, the emphasis upon the universal principles of Islam and the global identity of Muslims allows young British Muslims to reject more narrow ethnic cultures. Islamic identities allow young people to separate from their parents, and to participate in a larger community. Religion enlarges their horizons without betraying the fundamentals of identity.

Alternatively, instead of affiliating with Islam, many young people think of themselves as British Pakistanis or British Asians. While young British Pakistanis are closely bound to their parents' authority and culture, they widen their horizons by subtle adjustments. There is growing resistance to intra-family marriages, especially since these often involve arranged marriages with partners still in Pakistan. Outside the home people speak English. Asian rap is popular. Bhangra music – a fusion of Punjabi and Western styles – symbolizes this movement toward a broader identity. Turning to Asian identity and to Islam opens a larger world without compromising ties to family and community.

The Netherlands

In the Netherlands Muslim immigration began in the 1960s. Recruitment of workers and family unification plans promoted by the Dutch government in bilateral agreements with Turkey, Tunisia, Morocco, and Yugoslavia brought Muslim workers and their families into the country. By 1989 there were about 400,000 Muslims in Holland. Here too Muslims represented a great diversity of orientations. Several Turkish Islamic associations, several Moroccan associations and Sufi orders, and the Tabligh movement are active in the Netherlands. Instruction in mosque schools is very popular, and by 1990 Muslims were able to open state subsidized schools in parallel with those of other religious groups.

The Dutch government has moved from a concept of immigrants as temporary guest-workers to one that sees them as ethnic minorities, and its policy aims at promoting multi-culturalism, equality before the law, and overcoming social and economic deprivation. Dutch policy tries to preserve the distinctive cultural heritage of immigrant groups, and allows government support for religious private schools, radio and television broadcasting, and community organizations. Under the latter rubric there are even subsidies for mosques. However, the Dutch authorities have decided to curb the recruitment of imams from abroad for fear that they discourage the integration of Muslims, oppose careers for women, and represent a form of foreign control over the Muslim population. A plan of 1998 calls for the creation of training institutes for imams in Holland, but Muslims are trying to create private universities to accomplish this on their own terms.

Sweden

Sweden has a Muslim population of Turks, Arabs, and Pakistanis. About half the people of Muslim origin in Sweden are not religious at all, and about 35 percent are moderately observant. Sweden subsidizes religious schools in parallel with its support for the state church, but refuses to recognize any official relationship with home countries.

Deeply grounded in Protestant values, Swedes had assumed that immigrants could be assimilated as individuals, but now they are confronted with the demand for recognition of collective rights, which Muslims see as the only way to preserve their values and culture. Sweden is sorely taxed by the demand to switch from the French Enlightenment and British liberal notions of a society of individuals with universally valid, equal rights to a society that recognizes the rights of ethnic and religious communities as groups.

The condition of Muslims varies in other European countries. In Belgium the state recognizes religious authorities as intermediaries in schools, hospitals, and welfare agencies. The problem here is for Muslims to win the status of a recognized religious community. Austria makes Muslim instruction available as part of the state curriculum. Italy has only just begun to recognize that it has to deal with the presence of hundreds of thousands of Muslims from Albania and from North and East Africa.

IMMIGRANT IDENTITIES IN EUROPE: A BROAD SPECTRUM OF RESPONSES

The central issue for Muslims is how they will define themselves in the European context. Will they maintain a separate communal and legal life and demand recognition as autonomous communities? Will they support a more radical adversarial political Islam? Will they become part of a multi-cultural society? Will they be assimilated as individuals? It is difficult to answer these questions precisely. Though there are case studies, there is little or no statistical data on identity preferences and on Muslim opinion about public issues broken down by socio-economic class or by generation.

In this complex situation, in which both immigrant and host societies are ambivalent about their relationships, Muslim identities have evolved in a number of directions. In the first generation the predominant tendency was to maintain close cultural, social, religious, and political ties with the home country. Immigrants maintained their ethnic identity by keeping up languages, customs, and religious rituals. Pakistanis in Britain kept up marriage, trade, and religious networks with their home communities, and sponsored Barelwi and Deobandi mosques, often with the local chapters representing a village or neighborhood in the old country. Turks and Kurds in Germany divided their loyalties among the Diyanet, the Milli Gorus, the Sulaymancis, Nurcis, and other movements representing the Turkish government, opposition parties, or Sufi brotherhoods in Turkey. Algerians, Moroccans, and Tunisians in France typically organized mosques by national groups, with overt or covert home government or political party affiliations. They tended to think in terms of collective solidarity rather than individual mobility, and fell back on traditional ethnic or national cultures to cope with their new environment. Many immigrants, however, went in the opposite direction, and assimilated to – and even disappeared into – the host society. This was especially true for second-generation immigrant families in France.

For assimilating persons who maintain a Muslim identity, there are a variety of options. Some migrants assimilate to the public domain of their host countries, but remain Muslims by personal identity though they may not follow Islamic rituals or keep a communal affiliation. Others, though assimilated in the public domain, consider themselves pious Muslims, whether they regularly practice Islamic rituals or not. Still other assimilated Muslims may reinterpret Islamic values and behaviors to synthesize Islam and European values, creating a new hybrid Western–Islamic identity, a Euro-Islam, a liberal form of Islam accommodating European secular, individualistic, and civic values. These Muslims define a middle course between ghettoization and assimilation by formulating a syncretic, diaspora version of Islamic culture. Islam for such people is a secularized, privatized religion of individuals who choose their own level of observance and identifications, without a necessary connection to umma, jama'a, or state.

Among active and practicing Muslim believers there are various possibilities. One option is to practice Islamic rituals and attend mosques but avoid political involvement. Tablighi Jama'at, a missionary movement founded in India and active in Europe and the USA, repesents this position. Its first mission to Britain took place in 1946; to the United States in 1952, and to France in 1962. Following the migrations of South Asian Muslims, the Tablighis have established mosques in London, Paris, Brussels, and Toronto. In the 1980s they held a world congress in Dewsbury in England. Tablighis, who leave their routine lives to travel on missions, believe in the absolute superiority of Islam over Western civilization and eschew materialism and consumer culture, but avoid political involvements. Missionaries and militants proselytizing for Islam consider it a universal religion apart from parochial cultures; they separate Islam from specific ethnic communities and religion from culture, but also claim for individuals the right of ijtihad, which can serve as a mechanism for adjustment to life in Europe.

Another option is to practice Islam in a communal context. Some Muslims have formed separatist enclaves within Europe or America, utopian small communities withdrawn from the general society, that require separate facilities such as schools and the recognition of their collective organization and legal systems. Their goal is the preservation of distinct identities in multi-cultural societies. Other Muslims in Europe consider their sojourn a temporary exile, and remain focused on the struggle for improvement in their home countries or in the Dar al-Islam. Some undertake missionary work and use their residence as a base for converting Europeans to Islam.

A powerful recent trend is to turn ethnic-Muslim identities toward a universalistic Muslim identity based on the worldwide commonalities in Muslim belief. The second generations of immigrant families often reject the ethnic or national Islamic customs of their parents. As Muslims of different backgrounds interact, traditions are reconsidered and common Islamic norms rediscovered. Neo-Islamic movements break ties to home countries and to parochial cultures. The universalistic Islamic identity has paradoxical implications. While it creates a worldwide sense of Muslim affiliation, it is in fact a stripped-down version of Islam with little of the historical cultural content. Furthermore, despite its transnational character, it serves to facilitate integration into new host societies because it bypasses foreign ethnic and national loyalties and fits the prevailing Euro-American concept of religious identity in multi-religious national societies. Yet Muslims also use the transnational, cosmopolitan, global Muslim identity to break away from European values. This choice is often the preference of intellectuals and students and the outlet of marginalized, excluded elements of the immigrant population who combat discrimination or problems of delinquency, drugs, unemployment, and violence, or make up for the failure of public services, by building an alternative Islam.

Finally, there are neo-Islamists who emphasize political goals rather than pious practices as a path to the restoration of the unity and power of Muslim peoples. Pan-Islamic social and political solidarity, hostility to the West, and commitment to jihad – and to terrorism – also stem from Islam as a form of political protest. The weakness of schools, political parties, and unions among immigrants gives greater scope to religion to define collective identity.

MUSLIMS IN AMERICA

The American-Muslim population is composed both of immigrants and a substantial number of American converts. A trickle of Muslim immigrants came to the USA before the end of World War I, mainly from Palestine, Lebanon, and Syria. Generally single men and unskilled workers, they tended to intermarry and assimilate. American laws of 1921 and 1924 cut off the flow of immigrants, but after World War II the Immigration Act of 1947 allowed for increased numbers. A new wave of Muslim migrants consisted of students and professionals who came between 1945 and 1967. They also tended to intermarry, and downplay or lose their Muslim identity. The Immigration Act of 1965 finally abolished the earlier quota systems, opening the way to the large contemporary influx. Political crises sent waves of immigrants from India, Pakistan, Bangladesh, Palestine, Lebanon, Iran, and Kuwait to the USA. Shi'a, including small numbers of Bohras and Nizaris, have come from India, Iraq, and Iran. The population of Muslims in America is estimated at about 5.5 million, approximately 30 percent African American, 33 percent Arab, 29 percent South Asian, 5 percent Turkish, and 3 percent Iranian.

New York has a population of some 300–600,000 Muslims, living mostly in Queens and Brooklyn. A pre-World War I generation of Polish, Russian, and Lithuanian Muslims has been joined by Pakistanis, Bangladeshis, Albanians, Egyptians, and Indonesians. Metropolitan Detroit has a population of about 300,000 Arabs, including both Muslims and Christians; Lebanese Muslims have a big community in Dearborn. Chicago has a Muslim population of about 300,000. The first Chicago Muslims came from Lebanon, Palestine, and Syria at the end of the nineteenth century. More recently the partition of the Indo-Pakistan subcontinent, Middle East wars, the separation of Bangladesh from Pakistan, the breakup of the Soviet Union, and the war in Bosnia have sent successive waves of refugees to Chicago. These immigrants tend to be well-educated professionals, doctors, engineers, educators, independent businessmen, and students. They have created substantial community facilities, such as mosques, schools, cultural and community centers, and a bookstore.

Los Angeles is home to an estimated 500,000 Arabs, Indo-Pakistanis, and Iranians. There are two principal Islamic centers in Los Angeles: the Islamic Center of Southern California, which has a reputation for adapting Islam to conditions in America; and the Islamic Society of Orange County. There are numerous separate mosques for different schools of Muslims – Sunnis, Ithna-'asharis, Nizaris, Ahmadiya, and others – and even separate mosques for ethnic and national communities. There are separate Shi'i mosques founded by Lebanese, Pakistanis, East Africans, Iraqis, and Iranians. Even within ethnic communities there are deep religious and social differences. Furthermore, the boundaries between ethnic and religious identities are unclear. Most Iranians in the United States are not Muslims. Iranian Muslims are mainly political exiles, and identify in secular and national terms. There are substantial Muslim populations in the San Francisco Bay area as well, including Arabs, Iranians, Turks, and Afghans. San Diego has some 20–50,000 immigrant Muslims, segmented among Kurds, Somalis, Afghans, Arabs, and South Asians. Albanian Muslims have two religious institutions: the mosque, at which there are weekly prayers, celebrations of the 'ids (festivals), and marriages and funerals; and the Bektashi tekke, with branches in Chicago, New York, Detroit, and other places which serve for worship, personal prayers, and social support.

American converts

A second element in the Muslim population in the USA is American converts. These include people attracted to Sufism through the movements of Idris Shah, Hazrat Inayat Khan, Subud, and the Bawa Muhaiyaddeen, and through extensions of the traditional Middle Eastern Sufi orders such as the Nimatullahi and the Naqshbandi. Americans have also joined non-orthodox movements such as the Nation of Islam and the Ahmadiya. African Americans make up a substantial part of the converted population; they have turned to offshoots of Islam to escape the stigmatized identity forced upon them by white Americans. Islam appeals to African-Americans as an alternative to white-Christian culture, for its egalitarianism, and its links to a universal community.

The Moorish Science Temple of America was the first African-American group to define itself in Muslim terms. Noble Drew Ali was its founder. He held that the afflictions of blacks were due to the oppression of whites, and that black people would have to recover their true Muslim and Asiatic identity, discarding slave names for their true names, return to their true culture and religion, and restore their material condition.

The second group was the Nation of Islam (NOI), founded by Wallace D. Farad, who moved to Detroit in 1930. He sought to restore the pride of African Americans by teaching that they were the chosen of God – the descendants of the tribe of Shabazz, an Asiatic people, God's original people, and the founders of civilization – kidnapped and enslaved in America. Blacks, he taught, were superior to whites because they were the God's own creation, while whites were the creatures of an inferior demon. Master Farad was regarded by his followers as God incarnate and Elijah Poole, renamed Elijah Muhammad, was his prophet. In 1932 Master Farad disappeared, and Elijah Muhammad took over the leadership of the NOI; he further developed the mythology that identifies the blacks as God's chosen people of strength and goodness and whites as morally degenerate. Elijah Muhammad enforced a pure lifestyle, and encouraged black-owned businesses to support the community. The movement was intended to restore a culture destroyed by Westernization, and to create a separate black nation.

Malcolm X, who started life as a petty gangster, was a typical convert – a man rescued by faith from a debased life, who went on to become a fiery preacher of black separatism and hatred of whites. In a pilgrimage to Mecca, however, the hospitality and acceptance of white Muslims led him to believe that the ideology of the NOI deviated from the true Islam as understood worldwide, and that the true Islam could transcend race and include both whites and blacks. In 1964 he broke with the NOI and established his own Muslim Mosque Inc. On February 25, 1965 he was assassinated in New York; three NOI members were convicted of his murder.

With his death the NOI split into two wings. The majority, the followers of Warith Deen Muhammad, son of Elijah, abandoned the separatist concept and moved towards integration with the practices and beliefs of global Islam, acceptance of whites, and a return to emphasis upon the African connections of blacks. The name of the movement was changed to the American Muslim Mission. Louis Farrakhan, however, declared himself the prophet of the Messiah Elijah. Farrakhan revived the NOI with its emphasis upon black supremacy, nationalist separatism, and hostility to whites and Jews. The movement brought discipline into the lives of its members, including a strict dress code for women, and forbade alcohol, drugs, and gambling. The Fruit of Islam was its proto-militia. Farrakhan, however, has recently moved toward standard Islam, adopting Friday prayers and Ramadan. In February 2000 he participated in a joint rally with Warith Deen Muhammad and declared himself in favor of the unity of Muslims. While the NOI moves externally toward mainstream Islam, its theologians still distinguish between the external and the internal Quran, and defend their religious differences. Farrakhan tries both to assert a separatist legacy and to ally with traditional Muslims.

Other African-American movements echoed these positions. Some were Sunni movements affiliated with worldwide Islam such as the Hanafi Madhhab and the Darul Islam movement. A group of American converts established Darul Islam in the late 1940s and early 1950s as a utopian community, to restore African-American pride. They combined belief in Islam with an African-American nationalist political consciousness. Centered around a succession of mosques in Brooklyn, New York, the community spread to some thirty affiliated chapters along the east coast. Distrustful and disengaged from American society, Darul Islam dissolved into a Sufi movement in 1982.

There were also offshoots of the NOI that mixed Islam, black nationalism, and other American religious traditions. The Allah's Nation of the Five Percenters was a break-off group from the NOI, founded by Charles "Pudding" 13X, who was killed in 1969. This sect mixed Islamic symbolism, black supremacy, and popular culture, and communicated with young African Americans through rap music. The Five Percenters considered themselves the remnant of the truly righteous. They taught a mystical theology based on interpretations of letters and numbers in sacred texts. The group reached its high point in the 1960s and 1970s. African-American Muslims thus include black nationalist separatists, religious separatists who are Sunni Muslims but not nationalists, and assimilationists such as Warith Deen Muhammad.

The NOI is widely respected, especially among African Americans, for its programs of rehabilitation and stabilization of communities, but is very controversial for its strong anti-white and anti-semitic positions. The African-American establishment views Islamic separatism and Islamic nationalism as romantic and utopian, and favors assimilation and integration. There is also tension with Afrocentric secular nationalists who are hostile to Islam and look to establish the concept of an African and Nilotic heritage for American blacks. Similarly, there are high tensions between American-born black Muslims and immigrants. American Muslims tend to be of evangelical background, more individualistic and free in interpretation of scriptures, while immigrants tend to be more ethnic and collectivist in approach. American Muslims accuse the immigrants of racism and argue that they confuse true Islam with ethnic customs, and the immigrants say the blacks are not true practitioners of Islam. Sunni Muslims also reject American black nationalism and separatism.

Muslim identity issues in America

Regardless of ethnic background Muslims have diverse responses to the American situation and different tendencies to assimilation, accommodation, and separatism.

There are intense debates over questions such as: Can Muslims be part of American society without losing their identity? Will Americans accept Islam as a positive force in a multicultural society? Can Muslims ask for equal rights and still maintain a separate identity?

Two trends are noteworthy. The first is the trend to assimilate and even to disappear into the broader American society. Immigrants before World War II, such as Turks and Kurds in Detroit, have largely been absorbed into the American mainstream. Isma'ilis from the Indian subcontinent and from East Africa tended to adopt American social norms in family and business behaviors and social dress, even though they have maintained close ties to their countries of origin. Post-1960s immigrants, however, tended to reject such accommodations and wanted to maintain their traditional lifestyles. The large post-World War II inflow allowed immigrants to settle in communities that maintained close ties to their homelands, ethnic identity, and Muslim customs and social practices. Traditionalist immigrants wanted to practice Islam as understood in their home countries, making few distinctions between Islam and ethnic customs. Many defined themselves in terms of national, ethnic, or even regional and village origins, and maintained political and religious loyalties to families, communities, and governments in their home countries.

While some immigrants were concerned to preserve ethnic identity and customs, the strongest tendency is to be ever more Muslim to compensate for living in the new environment. This attitude leads to a great variety of positions on Muslim identity and the role of Muslims in America. Some Muslim leaders believe that there is no permanent place for Muslims in America, and counsel return to their homelands to work for an Islamic state. They see their presence in the USA as a hijra, an emigration, like that of the Prophet to Medina, to reorganize and return to create Islamic societies in their home countries. Others see themselves in the USA permanently with the eventual goal of converting America to Islam. Da'wa, the reconversion of Muslims to the true practice of Islam, or the dissemination of the faith and conversion of non-Muslims, has active proponents in the USA. Da'wa movements include the Tablighi Jama'at, the Salafiya sponsored by Sa'udi Arabia, and the Kho'i foundation, which is Shi'a. This view sometimes leads to the position that Muslims should live in the USA in separate enclaves centered on mosques and schools without assimilation into the broader society. Their focus should be on strengthening Muslim institutions. Isma'il Faruqi was an important spokesman for promoting Muslim intellectual institutions to provide leadership, and saw Muslims as bringing morality and salvation to the USA. A more common view is that America can be a legitimate homeland. The early twentieth-century theologian and reformer Rashid Rida' is cited as an authority for the idea that Muslims should remain in non-Muslim lands to practice Islam and possibility convert their peoples. If Muslims can practice their religion, the new country may be considered part of the Dar al-Islam. In such circumstances Muslims should not harm the host state; they may earn interest in bank accounts and be employed in government jobs.

Other Muslims call for an energetic participation in American social and political life, stressing the common monotheistic values. Fazlur Rahman was a leading proponent of a modernist Islam and amicable relations among peoples of different faiths. Sayyid Hosein Nasr has promoted Sufism as a route to an Islamic identity within North American society. Accommodationists want to practice an Islam adapted to the American way of life.

Muslim reformism, Salafiya, and transnational Sunni Islam draw ever more support, especially from youths, as a form of religious identity that binds people to the highest and most universal principles of Islam, and to the fellowship and solidarity of Muslims worldwide. The Shari'a-minded Sunnis deemphasize ethnic and parochial differences and tend toward a unified Muslim identity. Sunni universalism fits well with the American emphasis upon separation of church and state, and American acceptance of legitimate religious differences among otherwise assimilated populations.

The broad questions of the relation of Muslims to American identity, their degree of separateness and degree of assimilation translates into daily concerns. The most pressing family problem is the autonomy of children and the fear that they will stray from the community or be corrupted by the temptations of American life. Immigrant communities try to preserve parental control over multi-generational families. Parents commonly participate in the choice of spouses for their children, and arranged marriages are frequent. Girls are often raised in the home, restricted in outside activities, and commonly forbidden to date, though young men – who must have an education to earn a living – are given more leeway. Spouses are often found in the home country. A survey in the 1970s showed a strong tendency among young people to accept parental authority, restricted dating, and arranged marriages. This has to do with fact that economic and status ambitions among already middle-class and professional people do not create strong pressures to leave the confines of the family and the community.

Education is an absorbing issue. Some parents have chosen Islamic schools. These provide separate schooling for their children, and do not allow them to socialize outside the community. Schools are increasingly set up to keep the young within their faith and culture of origin. Others send their children for supplementary evening and weekend schooling. Some work for the improvement of the public schools, and try to educate public-school teachers about Islam. They defend the importance of sending their children to public schools in order to prepare them to cope with life in America, and will permit their children to have friends outside the Muslim community. There are now a few Muslim colleges and graduate schools in the USA intended to train community leaders.

There are big differences, however, between immigrant and native American communities in their views about the status and behavior of women. Though it is widely agreed that women should dress modestly and that they should have free choice in social demeanor and not be dictated to by their men, immigrant communities tend to be more traditional and restrictive of women's activities. A survey of women's attitudes in Dearborn showed that men, often brothers and other male relations as well as fathers, took a patriarchal attitude toward women, insisting on female modesty and restricting work opportunities away from home. Among Yemenis, the "rich-peasant" mentality kept women from work, and upheld male authority. Among Palestinian-Americans, young men are expected to become educated and to do well in business and the professions. They often assimilate to the general society and find American wives. Palestinian-American women, however, tend to be closely controlled. They have to maintain the family honor, and are raised to marry men from the homeland. Palestinian men, however, often strongly ideological, are suspicious of Palestinian-American women as too Americanized, too assertive, and too lacking in Palestinian consciousness to serve for the perpetuation of national identity. This creates a marriage problem for Palestinian-American women.

Female converts to Islam distinguish between Islamic principles and foreign cultural ideals in the treatment of women. While they try to adjust to the expectation of their husbands' families and home culture, most Muslim-American women believe that women should have careers, though on terms that will not interfere with their family roles. Though women are almost never allowed to pray with men or serve as imams, some mosques seat men and women in parallel facing the *mihrab* (the niche indicating the direction of Mecca), separated by a curtain. In some mosques women sit in the rear; in some on a balcony; and some broadcast the services by television to a separate room.

The head covering is important as an indicator of gender relations among Muslims, but wearing a head cover also declares the community's intention to preserve its identity, and tests the tolerance of the wider society for Muslim customs. State courts in the USA have tended to consider a distinctive head dress a threat of proselytism, or a threat to the separation of church and state, or a challenge to secular education, and have favored state regulation rather than individual choices.

The effort to create an appropriate Muslim architecture to express the particular needs of Muslims and symbolize Muslim faith in America is particularly challenging. Muslims began by creating mosques in storefronts, offices, homes, and former churches which they "Islamize" by providing facilities for ablutions, marking the direction of prayer, and decorating with Arabic calligraphy. The first newly built dedicated mosque in America was the Islamic Center in Washington D.C., opened in 1957, and since then over a hundred mosques have been built and many hundreds of other buildings converted for use as mosques. Most are in New York and California, and some are in Michigan, Illinois, and Texas. Mosques generally include a school, community and conference rooms, libraries, and recreational centers. Immigrant communities tend to favor mosques that replicate traditional home country or some generalized traditional images, such as those in the Islamic Cultural Center in

Washington. Some combine ethnic tradition with American features such as the Islamic Cultural Center in New York. In New Mexico, Indiana, and Oklahoma there are innovative mosques which attempt to fit into the local environment, without iconic references to traditional architecture; buildings that are designed to fulfill Islamic requirements for multi-ethnic congregations, without showing a preference for any single ethnic group. These differences reflect the diversity of identities among Muslims in America.

The problems that face Muslim communities raise the question of leadership. In the USA imams are not only called upon to lead prayers and give legal advice, but like rabbis and ministers are asked to provide pastoral care, organize community activities, run schools, arbitrate disputes, and promote an understanding of Islam in the outside world. Hitherto most muftis and imams have been imported from the old world because they are very knowledgeable about religion, but these imams are not adapted to American circumstances. They also pose problems because of the influence of foreign contributors which tie American Muslims to the religious, ideological, and political interests of the donors. Imams raised in the USA are not yet well enough trained in Islam. A critical need is the training of American imams and *fiqh* (legal) counselors in both classical religious studies and social sciences and humanities. The Fiqh Council of America now deals with questions about dress, marriages, divorce, and other issues.

Prosperity and freedom attracted Muslims to America, but they are alienated by prejudice, discrimination, suspicion, and the negative attitudes of Americans toward Islam. As a result of the Iranian revolution, the Rushdie affair, the Gulf War, the rise of the Taliban in Afghanistan, and the September 11 attacks on the World Trade Center and the Pentagon, the anxieties of Muslims have increased. While many Americans have attempted to reassure them of their welcome, Muslims find the present atmosphere hostile to Islam. Muslims are also challenged by the American demand for civic and patriotic assimilation. For Muslims there are special problems concerned with voting, participation in the military, differing marriage and divorce laws, and banking and business practices. Muslims are also challenged by the absence of provision for Muslim holidays in American work and school regulations, and by American social mores, including less controlling social practices toward girls and dating, and the weakness of patriarchal authority.

In response to such problems, Muslims have attempted to create organizations and lobbies to defend their common interests. The Arab Anti-Discrimination Committee was one of the earliest political lobbies. The transition from ethnic to pan-Muslim internationalism is signaled by the formation of the multi-ethnic Islamic Circle of North America, the Muslim Public Affairs Council, 1988; the American Muslim Council, 1990; the American Muslim Alliance, 1994; and the Council on American Islamic Relations. The American Muslim Political Coordination Council is the umbrella for groups trying to make Muslim weight felt in politics. The Islamic Society of North America provides nationwide educational materials, libraries, workshops, a housing and marriage bureau, trust funds, and publications, but it mainly serves immigrant communities and is viewed by blacks as uninterested in their needs. Nationally, the Federation of Islamic Organizations is an umbrella movement for mosques and communities, sponsored by Sa'udi Arabia. The Muslim Students' Association plays a role in promoting a single Islamic identity beyond national, ethnic, and linguistic allegiances. On a local level some coalescence occurs. In New York, Sunnis and Shi'a share the same mosques. Since the 1990s an annual Muslim World Day parade and prayer on Lexington Avenue has marked a united Muslim presence. Still, the absence of a single recognized authority or a tradition of hierarchy makes it difficult to unify Muslim communities and to define an Islamic identity transcending ethnic groups and sectarian differences.

CONCLUSION: SECULARIZED ISLAM
AND ISLAMIC REVIVAL

For nearly five thousand years Middle Eastern and Islamic societies have been based upon the constellation of lineage, tribal, religious, and political institutions first evident in the ancient cities of Mesopotamia in the third millennium BC. This configuration of institutions was the basis of pre-Islamic Middle Eastern societies and was the template upon which Middle Eastern Islamic societies were constructed. In Mecca 1,400 years ago the Prophet Muhammad received the revelations that would infuse the ancient patterns of society with new meaning. The new religion was institutionalized in Arabian tribal communities. After the Arab conquest of the Middle East, it was embedded in the ruling political institutions such as the Caliphates and Sultanates, and in Islamic religious communities such as Sunni schools of law, Sufi brotherhoods, and Shi'i sects. It was also embedded in both literary culture and popular concepts and mores. The institutionalization of Islam gave rise to a new civilization.

The religious basis of this new civilization was faith in Islam as revealed in scripture and law, as understood in theology, and as practiced in mysticism. Islam provided a concept of the universe, ethical rules, legal norms for daily behavior, ritual prescriptions for mediating the relation of human beings and God, mystical methods of self-cultivation, and symbols of self-identity. In fact, Islam embodied not one but several religious ideals. Sunni-Sufis cultivated ethical and spiritual living within the world. The Shi'a looked to the imams for guidance and salvation. By veneration of saints, Muslims sought to win divine blessing through the intercession of holy men. Gnostic philosophers and mystics sought escape from worldly actualities through rational and spiritual concepts of religious salvation.

Conquering tribesmen, traveling merchants, and wandering Sufis brought Islam to peoples outside the Middle East. The diffusion of Islam and the conversion of new peoples brought Islamic societies into being in Inner Asia, India, Southeast Asia, Turkey, the Balkans, North and West Africa, and other regions. These societies were formed by the integration of the local pre-Islamic civilizations with the universal aspects of Islam to create a new family of human communities. The religious way of life and identity borne by the 'ulama' and the Sufis again became articulated in parochial associations such as lineage, tribal, village, and urban communities, and states. By the seventeenth century Islamic societies were fully institutionalized throughout much of Asia, Africa, and Eastern Europe. Each had a distinctive *gestalt*, but each was intelligible as a variation upon an earlier Middle Eastern pattern of concepts and institutions.

Whatever the variations, Islam was never the sole organizing principle of pre-modern Islamic societies. Each inherited and maintained cultural identities, social organizations, political institutions, and economies defined in non-Islamic terms. The military and bureaucratic institutions, systems of taxation, and cultural legitimizations of "Muslim" states always had a non-Islamic dimension inherited from the pre-Islamic culture of each region. Nor were social organization, ethnic identity, and elite leadership of parochial communities Islamic. The economies of Muslim peoples were almost never organized in Muslim terms except for certain modifying ethical concepts such as opposition to usury and demands for fairness, justice, and charity. In all Muslim societies the prevailing culture was a mixture of Islamic concepts and symbols and non-Islamic institutions and identities. However important, Islam always remained but one aspect of complex societies.

THE INSTITUTIONAL AND CULTURAL FEATURES OF PRE-MODERN ISLAMIC SOCIETIES

A central feature of these societies was the structure of state and religious organizations. We commonly say that in Muslim societies state and religion are unified and that Islam is a total way of life, which defines political as well as social and familial matters. This is the Muslim view embodied in the ideal of the Prophet and the early Caliphs, who were rulers and teachers, repositories of both temporal and religious authority, and whose mission was to lead the community in war and morality. This ideal inspired the efforts of reformist, revivalist, and "Caliphal" movements to create an integrated Muslim state and society. Such movements were common in lineage communities, in which adherence to Islam led to tribal unification, conquest, and the formation of new empires, as in the case of the Fatimid, Almoravid, and Almohad movements in North Africa, the Safavid movement in Iran, and others. In the eighteenth and nineteenth centuries reformist movements with similar intentions led to conquests and state formation in such cases as the Sokoto Caliphate in what is now Nigeria and the Mahdist state in the Sudan. In different terms the ideal is invoked by contemporary neo-Islamic movements.

Most Muslim societies did not and do not conform to this ideal, and were and are built around separate state and religious institutions. By the eighth and ninth centuries, the early Caliphate was already evolving into an imperial and secular political regime, while Muslim populations were being formed into a multitude of religiously defined communal groups. These included schools of law, reformist movements, Sufi lineages, brotherhoods, shrine communities, Shiʻi sects, and ethnic associations. Such groups were or became independent of states; most withdrew from participation in government, and were primarily concerned with solidarity, worship, education, law, personal morality, and upholding the public symbols of Islam. The separation on an institutional level of state institutions and religious associations became the norm for the late ʻAbbasid Caliphate, the Saljuq and Mamluk Sultanates, the Ottoman, Safavid, and Mughal empires, and other Muslim regimes.

This separation, however, was neither clear-cut nor complete. While the separation was well defined on an institutional level and in terms of organizations, personnel, and ethos, in cultural concept there was a deep ambiguity about both states and religio-communal associations. On the one hand, Muslim states were considered instruments of worldly secular power and were legitimized in terms of patrimonial claims to superior ancestry, state-patronized artistic and literary cultures, and appeals to universal cosmological or philosophical concepts. Their culture derived from the pre-Islamic and non-Islamic substrates of the societies they ruled. On the other hand, these states also had a Muslim religious value derived from historical continuity with the early Caliphate, or based on their role as defenders, patrons, and supporters of Muslim worship, education, law, and jihad. They also had an inherent sacred value, for in many Muslim societies the state was conceived as the direct expression of God's will for the ordering of human affairs. Their religious worth was derived both from service to Islam and directly from divine decree.

Similarly, Muslim religious associations, though basically committed to small communal and individual religious pursuits, were involved in politics. While Muslim religious leaders were in fact committed to an apolitical form of religiosity, in concept they could not imagine their associations as entirely independent of an all-embracing Islamic political order. In concept a Muslim state was necessary for a complete Muslim way of life.

Conceptual ambiguities were translated into a variety of institutional patterns in the relationship between states and religious associations. In the Ottoman and Safavid empires, the states themselves controlled Muslim judicial, educational, and social functions. The Ottoman and Safavid monarchies were strongly supported by an ʻulamaʼ bureaucracy. In these empires Muslim religious associations became virtual departments of state, though in Iran the religious elites were eventually able to assert their autonomy. In Mughal India, or Mataram Java, Muslim religious leaders, associations, and activities were largely autonomous, and often critical of state policies and state-patronized culture.

Thus in the pre-modern era there were two alternative concepts of Islamic society. One was the "Caliphate," which integrated the state and the community, the realms of politics and religion, into an inseparable whole. The second was the "Sultanate," or secular state, which ruled over the quasi-independent religious associations that were the true bearers of Muslim religious life. In one image the state was the all-encompassing expression of an Islamic society; in the other, an Islamic society was divided into separate state and religious institutions. The relationship between Muslim communities and states was variable and ambiguous. The former were sometimes subordinate and committed, sometimes independent and hostile. Sometimes they accepted the inherent legitimacy of ruling regimes; sometimes they rejected them as antithetical to a truly Muslim society. Most often they regarded states with detachment. While accepting the necessity of political order, they disdained political involvement, and withdrew into communal and personal religious affairs. While accepting political realities, they were nostalgic for the better days of the true Caliphate and yearned for the era of justice. The legacy of pre-modern societies to the modern era, then, was not a defined structure of state and society, but a spectrum of variation and an inherent ambiguity about the relations between the two.

THE NINETEENTH- AND TWENTIETH-CENTURY TRANSFORMATION OF MUSLIM SOCIETIES

This legacy was transmitted through nineteenth-century changes into the twentieth-century structure of Muslim societies. In response to the impact of European imperialism and commercial domination, Muslim political and religious elites proposed alternative concepts for the reconstruction of their societies, each a variation upon past orientations toward the relationship of state and religion. The political elites, transformed into intelligentsias, adopted first Islamic modernist, then secular nationalist, and sometimes socialist, conceptions of national transformation, and became committed to secular or even Western concepts of state and society. In one sense these concepts were a profound departure from the historical political culture, but in another sense they were consistent with aspects of the historical culture that accorded the state an inherent legitimacy regardless of its relationship to Islam. In the nineteenth and twentieth centuries, the state intelligentsias did not so much change their fundamental position as shift from traditional to modern expressions of political identity. The adoption of Western ideologies and of Western political methods was for the political elites a continuation of the tradition in which domination was symbolized in non-Muslim cosmopolitan terms.

The response of the religious elites to the breakdown of the Muslim state system and to European domination was Islamic reformism or Islamic renewal. With the decline of Muslim states, the rise of European influence, and a changing balance of forces in Muslim societies, reformism gave lineage, village, and tribal communities new opportunities to resist state control, and helped village, artisan, and merchant milieus undergoing economic and commercial change to define new identities.

The reformist movements adopted the ambiguous attitude of the historical religious associations toward political actualities. Some of the movements tended to be apolitical and to concentrate upon educational and religious practices. This was true of movements backed by the commercial middle classes such as Deoband,

Tanzim, and Tabligh in India, and Muhammadiya in Indonesia. Some movements, however, tended to turn the energies generated by religious reform into political efforts to reconstruct an Islamic state. This was true in tribal milieus and anti-colonial movements such as the Sanusiya and the West African jihads.

Nations, nationalism, and Islam

The struggles against colonial domination, and the conflicts among the various Muslim elites, each bearing within itself a variant version of the historical Muslim political culture, gave shape to modern Muslim societies. In the states that became independent after World War I and World War II, and up until the 1970s, the outcome of these struggles was a threefold structure of society. This included a secularized state, correspondingly differentiated non-political Muslim religious associations, and opposition movements that favored the reconstruction of an integrated Muslim state and society.

The dominant trend in the first three-quarters of the twentieth century was the consolidation of national states under the auspices of the political intelligentsias and their legitimization in secular terms. Some derived from the transformation of earlier regimes such as the Ottoman empire, the Iranian monarchy, and Tunisian, Moroccan, Egyptian, and other Sultanates. Some were due to the construction of new territorial entities such as Syria, Iraq, Jordan, Indonesia, Malaysia, Nigeria, and Senegal, where colonial rulers commonly crushed feudal, tribal, and religious opposition, and brought varied territories under state control. The former Soviet Union and the People's Republic of China absorbed Muslim populations into large non-Muslim empires. The new states were commonly based on military elites, as in Syria, Iraq, Egypt, Jordan, Algeria, Pakistan, Indonesia, Nigeria, Sudan, Libya, and many smaller African states. In almost all cases the central state was strengthened by its control over the economy. Military elites, as in Egypt, Syria, Iraq, and Algeria, generated a state capitalism or socialism in the interests of the new dominant class. In Algeria, Libya, Iraq, Sa'udi Arabia, the Gulf states, Indonesia, and Nigeria, the elites were supported by state-controlled petroleum revenues.

From independence until the 1970s, the state elites in most countries favored a secular ideological identity. With the notable exceptions of Sa'udi Arabia and Morocco states generally separated themselves from Muslim religious concepts and institutions. Many states attempted to neutralize Muslim activities by bringing them under official control. Government ministries in Egypt, Indonesia, Tanzania, and in the Soviet Union coopted Muslim leaders and used them as intermediaries to control Muslim populations. In general, Islam was disestablished, and law and education passed out of religious hands into state control or were left as parallel but secondary systems of private adjudication and instruction. Sufism as a system of organizing tribal peoples for political purposes virtually disappeared. Centralization of state power also destroyed or neutralized tribal communities in Turkey, Iran, Inner Asia, Egypt, Syria, Algeria, and other places.

This transformation of relations between state and society was accompanied by new nationalist, liberal, and socialist ideologies and symbols of legitimization. In part this was due to the fact that the elites who took the lead in the struggle for independence were disposed by experience of colonial rule, education, and acquaintance with Europe, and by the struggle against older feudal and religious elites, to define their concept of an independent society in national and ethnic rather than traditional imperial or religious terms. Even modernist and reformist Muslim leaders, as in the Ottoman empire or Algeria, blended their hopes for Islamic reform with the realities of political struggle to give them a national definition. In areas where movements toward independence were cut off, as in Inner Asia, Muslim modernism was redirected toward the cultivation of ethnic and national identity and to integration into state-dominated societies. By maintaining a non-Islamic identity, political elites tried to distance themselves from the embrace of Islamic religious authority. By regulating state affairs in accordance with secular norms and symbolizing them in secular terms, the state elites shielded themselves from Islamic religious precepts. Thus, the ideological orientation of modern Muslim states also derived from the historical practice of Muslim imperial regimes in the Middle East, South and Southeast Asia, and Africa which were legitimized, in part, by non-Islamic concepts and symbols.

The change to a nationalist consciousness became important in the late nineteenth and early twentieth centuries as a rhetorical and polemical tactic to assert the claims of a new intelligentsia. For cosmopolitan, mobile, educated persons who had been taken out of the matrix of small, family-centered communities, and launched into the world of cities, international contacts, foreign languages, and global political concerns; for people who no longer belonged to the old order, and for whom the colonial political societies could only offer positions of subordination to a foreign elite, nationalism became a homeland of the mind. The national idea expressed the opposition of a new elite to the imperial and religious elites of their own societies and to their colonial rulers. Nationalism was an irresistible argument against colonial masters precisely because Europeans accepted it as the basis of political society. National symbols also made it easier to bring non-Muslim minorities into the anti-colonial struggle, and implied a claim to superiority and leadership over the masses. On the basis of their secular, national vision, the intelligentsias claimed a right to rule as the enlightened exemplars of modernity.

With independence, nationalism was diffused from the elites to the masses. In premodern Muslim societies political and social identities were formed on several levels. Each individual had at once political loyalties to a governing elite, a local familial, lineage, tribal, or village membership, and an Islamic religious identity. Linguistic and ethnic consciousnesses were usually subsidiary features of social self-awareness. Modern nationalisms, however, emphasized the hitherto subordinate factors. In the case of Turks, Arabs, Iranians, Malays, Uzbeks, Tajiks, Kazakhs, Bengalis, Pashtuns, and others, contemporary identity was rebuilt upon a fusion of historical lineage, ethnic, linguistic, and Islamic symbols, recast in linguistic-ethnic and nationalist terms. Nationalism served to replace loyalties to parochial family, village, and religious associations, and committed peoples to a broader concept of political identity. The masses too began to see themselves in ethnic, national, and state political terms.

State formation was itself a source of national consciousness. Strong Tunisian, Egyptian, Algerian, Bengali, and Indonesian identities have all been shaped by nation-states. In theory, national states may seem contrary to the universalism of Islam, but in fact they were easily accepted. Indeed, the breakup of the early Caliphate constituted a precedent for and legitimization of separate Muslim states. To many Muslims who were born and educated in (and who derived their security and livelihoods from) the new states, they seemed a fitting framework for educational and missionary activity on behalf of Islam. While Islam is not in principle territorial, national states commonly define the boundaries of Muslim identities.

Despite the tendencies toward secularization, national movements in Muslim countries always retained an important and subtle intermixture of Islam. The Islamic orientations of nineteenth-century Sufism and Islamic modernism were absorbed into national movements. Young Ottoman modernists gave way to Young Turk nationalists. Aligarh modernists and the Muslim League, led by the scions of the former Muslim elites of the subcontinent, turned to the formation of a national state. The Egyptian disciples of Muhammad 'Abduh began as early as the 1890s to think in national Egyptian terms. Damascus notable families changed from an Islamic reformist expression of regional anti-Ottomanism to Arab nationalism after World War I. The Destour in Tunisia, originally inspired by Salafi reformism, yielded to neo-Destour secularism in the 1930s. Islamic reformism also became the basis for anti-colonial movements and the formation of national states in Libya, Algeria, and Morocco. Muslim reformism helped create national political movements by calling for allegiance on the basis of Muslim principles which transcended purely local identifications. By turning Muslims from local sects, shrines, and mediators to the abstract principles of the faith, reformism set the foundations for the unification of large populations in national political struggles. Reformism provided the cultural standards and educational and egalitarian sentiments that served, like nationalism, as the basis of modern political regimes.

Moreover, much of the emotional power of nationalism in the Muslim world comes from the capacity of national movements to parochialize Islam and channel the force of Muslim faith into nationalism. For example, what makes Turks Turkish in the minds of many is Islam. Turkey's leaders brought the Republic into being determined to transform it into an ethnically defined secular society, and resolutely denied Islam a role in the constitution of the state, but the Turkish people continued to identify with it. In practice most Turks maintained a dual identity, both Turkish and Muslim, or understood their Turkish nationality as an expression of their Muslim identification. Algerian nationality is understood to mean a combination of Arab ethnicity and Muslim religion. Palestinians show an interlocking of national and religious identities. The PLO defines the Palestinian state as a secular national state and of course includes Christian Palestinians, but for many decades the allegiance of Palestinians to a Palestinian national entity has been cultivated in terms of Muslim symbols and affiliations. Conversely, HAMAS, which defines itself as an

Islamic movement and its goal as an Islamic state, is a Palestinian movement opposed to the PLO and Israel. Islam and Palestinian national identity are not quite interchangeable, but they are not separable either. Then there are Malay-Muslim, Bosnian-Muslim, and other ethnic- and language-based, hyphenated Muslim identities. Conversely, Sa'udi Arabia, Morocco, Iran, Sudan, and Pakistan define themselves as Islamic states, but their citizens are Iranians, Moroccans, and so on.

Indonesia illustrates another variation in the conjunction of national and Muslim identities. Here the anti-colonial struggle was carried on by parallel secular national and Muslim movements. The priyayi of the Indonesian National Party advocated a secular Indonesian state, while the 'ulama' and Muslim intellectuals formed Sarekat Islam and Nahdatul 'Ulama', two political parties calling for an Islamic state. The result was a virtually continuous unresolved crisis over how to integrate the national secular and Muslim components of Indonesian identity. The secular and Islamic anti-colonial parties joined forces in the struggle against the Dutch and won independence in 1947, but in post-independence Indonesia they fought each other for power until the elections of 1955 showed that the Muslim parties collectively could not win a majority. Under Sukarno Indonesia was defined as a secular state according to the pançasila, or five principles: belief in God, nationalism, humanitarianism, democracy, and social justice. (These five principles employ universalist humanistic, as opposed to universalist religious, ideas as the bases of national identity.) Yet even under the officially secular rule of Sukarno and Suharto, Islam was favored by state ministries, and Muslim reformist and educational movements were tolerated. In its last decade the Suharto regime coopted a major Muslim movement and restored the integral connection of the state with Islam. In 1999 for the first time the leader of a Muslim movement, Abdurrahman Wahid, was elected President. Politically contested, the role of Islam in the constitution of the state is still not fully resolved.

Thus, national identity was neither rigorously secular nor exclusively religious. Nationality involved concepts of citizenship, ethnicity, and religion in an ambiguous connection to each other so that it was possible for different people to share the same nationality on the basis of one or another of these factors or some combination of them, or to modify their concept of identity in response to changing political situations.

In the first decades after independence, the new states profoundly affected the organization, practice, and conception of Islam. In increasingly secularized societies there were strong tendencies for Islam to become less a religion of customary collective practice and more one of individual quest and commitment. As religion played a smaller role in the public world or in explaining nature, it played a larger role in meeting ethical and psychological needs. Islam as private belief and as social identity were becoming dissociated from the communal and political institutions in which such belief and identity had once been embedded. In Indonesia, Turkey, the former Soviet Union, and other highly secularized societies, Islam was becoming a religion of personal beliefs without political implications. Conversely, in other cases it became a form of personal or ethnic identity without a religious meaning. Many people were "Muslims" without being believers. They were Muslim by virtue of ancestry and family, or affiliation with a nationality group, or as a consequence of individual choice without implying personal piety.

The secularization of Muslim states also had important implications for Muslim religious associations. It often reinforced their already inherent tendency to concentrate on communal and individual religious needs rather than political goals. While older forms of tribal and Sufi organizations disappeared in West Africa, Egypt, Indonesia, and Malaysia, ethnic associations, modernist religious congregations, and clubs multiplied to meet the need for collective worship, education, charity, and for simple sociability and discussion. In many cases the local cells were independent, but in some they were linked up in larger movements, such as the Tijaniya in West Africa. Some of these movements were reformist or Salafi movements, such as Muhammadiya in Indonesia, intended to inculcate the correct practice of Islam, provide for community welfare, and foster solidarity among Muslims. These associations had a strong appeal to students, intellectuals, technicians, professionals, and merchants. Some of these movements were da'wa, or missionary movements, such as Tablighi Islam, which worked to convert non-Muslims to Islam, and nominal Muslims to the correct practice of Islam. These movements sponsored educational and social welfare activities, including schools, clinics, cooperatives, and businesses.

Many of these reformist and modernist associations played an important role in the adaptation of Muslim populations to national states and economies. Reformist principles favored delayed emotional gratification and stressed self-control and obedience to abstract rules and authorities as the basis of religious fulfillment. They directed pent-up emotions into a sense of individual responsibility to remake the world in accordance with Islam. They facilitated the transfer of popular loyalties from tribal and parochial communities and from saintly religious authority to national regimes. They were also congruent with modern industrial societies because of their egalitarianism and emphasis upon universal education, and with urbanized societies, for they favored disciplined behavior. Muslim reform movements were not merely an accommodation to the secularization of Muslim societies but a creative adaptation to the development of a more complex and highly integrated type of social system. Though reformism disposed believers to worldly activity, it was not necessarily a Muslim equivalent of the Protestant ethic. The doctrinal basis of radical Protestantism – the evil nature of human beings and predestination – is not found among Muslims; the psychological tension over the sinfulness of human beings is muted.

THE ISLAMIC REVIVAL

Thus, the most common outcome of independence was the formation of secular states with Islamo-ethnic societies. Contemporary nationality was built on a Muslim substrate, and conversely, Muslim identity was translated into ethnic and national loyalties which commonly outweighed the Muslim ones. However, since the 1970s latent Muslim identifications have begun to assert themselves in a worldwide Islamic revival. This revival is commonly characterized as "Islamic fundamentalism." This term has some validity, in that many movements so labeled do indeed seek to return to the Quran and the teachings of the Prophet, but otherwise it is at best only an umbrella designation for a very wide variety of movements, some intolerant and exclusivist, some pluralistic; some favorable to science, some anti-scientific; some primarily devotional and some primarily political; some democratic, some authoritarian; some pacific, some violent. We shall use the term "Islamic revival" to cover the whole range of newly founded and active Islamic movements. The terms "reformist," "Salafi," and "Wahhabi" refer to those movements committed to the reform of Islamic belief and practice. "Islamist" refers to those with primarily political agendas and "jihadist" to those for whom violence is the principal tactic.

In religious terms the revival encompasses schools of philosophical and religious thought, movements to promote personal piety and prayer, and educational movements dedicated to the reform of Muslim religious practice. Many have a social activist, community-building orientation. In political terms it includes movements that are engaged in national politics as parties and lobbies, some of which have auxiliary paramilitary forces. On the extreme are movements that use assassination, bombing, and other assaults as part of an effort to seize political power by coups d'état. Some of these movements are broad-spectrum organizations whose activities cover the range from prayer to politics. These movements may be national or international. Perhaps the principal division is between those reformist movements that accept the political status quo and those that believe it necessary to overthrow existing regimes. The former expect that they will ultimately transform their societies by the cumulative effect of educational and missionary activities. By contrast, the politically oriented groups hold that control of the state is the key to a truly Islamic society.

In cultural terms the Islamic revival is a counter-attack against European and American values such as individualism, materialistic consumerism, the independence of women, sexual liberty, religious and moral relativism, and pop culture. These movements are motivated by the fear that Western influences will undermine the authority of fathers, religious teachers, and rulers, and subvert Islamic beliefs and Muslim cultures. American television and movies, sexual and consumer mores – symbolized by McDonald's, Coca-Cola, jeans, and other icons of American style – are seen as a profound threat.

Among the revivalist movements liberal Islam is important in Iran, Egypt, Europe, and the United States. It is characterized by its stress upon the need for independent thought on religious matters, ijtihad, and the integration of Islam and modern societies. The liberal approach accepts that there are necessarily a variety of ways to interpret Quranic texts. Where the Shari'a is silent, liberal thinkers see a divine intention to leave a space for the discretion of Muslims. Among the leading spokesmen of this position are Muhammad Arkoun in Paris and Abdol Karim

Soroush in Iran. Both wish to reconcile the eternal truths of the revelation with the changing conditions of the world. In Soroush's view religion is eternal, but the human understanding of it changes with circumstances. He argues against the identification of Islamic teachings with Shari'a. Legalistic literalism is not the core of Islam: mystical love is its essence. He favors an Islamic democracy for Iran, and condemns the ideologizing of Islam, its reduction to political and identity purposes. The liberal thinkers argue that the norms of modern government, and universal human values such as rationality, justice, freedom, and human rights are not inherently matters of religion but can be compatible with religious truth. Modern Islam must integrate the truths of religion with the values of contemporary societies.

Liberal Muslims such as Arkoun think of Islam as a personalized religion, and do not think that Muslims should be subjected to communal control, or public affairs subordinated to Islamic norms. Nonetheless, liberal Muslims have taken positions on political issues. In the 1980s they favored Muslim movements that tried to enter national politics by forming parties and contesting elections. They justified demands for political participation in the name of the early Islamic principles of shura (consultation) and 'ijma (consensus). Liberal Muslim thinkers also favored the education and political participation of women. In the face of repressive domestic or colonial regimes, however, Muslim liberals have accepted armed struggle as a necessity. Thus, HAMAS, Hizballah, and FIS, after the voiding of the Algerian elections in 1992, were considered legitimate. The Taliban, however, represented the antithesis of liberal Islamists, who condemned the repression and virtual house arrest of women, the suppression of minorities, and the demand that Muslim men grow beards.

More widespread are the revivalist movements that promote Islam as a comprehensive blueprint for a modern way of life and call for the formation of Islamic states to enforce an Islamic morality. The earliest of these, the Society of Muslim Brothers in Egypt and the Jama'at-i Islami in Pakistan, go back respectively to the 1930s and 1940s.

The revivalists generally advocate the teaching of Arabic and Quran, strictness in the observance of Muslim rituals, and denounce local customs derived from Sufi practice, tradition, or magical beliefs. They look to the formation of a totalistic Islamic society as an alternative to nationalism, capitalism, or socialism, a society which would bring fulfillment in terms both of personal piety and collective life. For these movements Islam is the design of a total and exalted way of life which contains all individual and social good. The Islamic movements want to derive from Islam a position on every issue of private and public concern – women, education, economy, social structure, and government – to demonstrate that all modern needs can be met by the central symbols of their own tradition. The branches of these movements sponsor the teaching of Arabic and Quran, and call on their governments to adopt an Islamic posture. Disillusionment with secularism and the quest for indigenous rather than foreign values have propelled these efforts to define a post-modern concept of Muslim society.

The utopian aspirations of the Islamic movements evoke the Muslim ideal of the Caliphate, but in many respects they are an altogether novel adaptation of Islamic concepts to modern conditions. The new Islamic movements have little of the traditional scriptural, legal, theological, or mystical content. While they may derive from previous reform tendencies, they are led by preachers who are not themselves 'ulama' or Sufis. No longer based on schools of law or Sufi brotherhoods, they are organized through study groups, scout groups, women's auxiliaries, athletic clubs, economic enterprises, political parties, and paramilitary units.

Since the 1970s educational, missionary, and revivalist movements have become ever more important. In West Africa the Wahhabiya movement is widespread in Mali, Guinea, the Gambia, Sierra Leone, the Ivory Coast, Senegal, Ghana, and Burkina Faso. In Nigeria it is represented by the Yan 'Izala. In South Asia we find the Da'wat-i Islam in Pakistan and the Ahl-i Hadith in India. Similar views are held by the Jam'at in Egypt, Muhammadiya in Indonesia, and the Malay Muslim Youth League and other groups. With the breakup of the Soviet Union the "Wahhabiya" have become active in the newly independent states of Inner Asia, and in Chechnya where they have founded village-scale Islamic republics under the rule of Shari'a. In Jordan, the Salafi movement espouses a return to the Quran and Sunna as the sole sources of Islam, and operates informal study groups, classes, lectures in homes and mosques, and distributes publications and cassettes through its bookshops. In Egypt the Society of Muslim Brothers is built around a structure of formal organizations – charitable, professional, and social – culminating in a political party.

These movements have constructed great numbers of mosques, schools, and community facilities. They sponsor meetings, publications, and conferences, and they have generated ever-growing numbers of graduates of madrasas and other Muslim schools who form a body of committed opinion, cadres for teaching, missionary work, and political leadership. A new elite, indeed a counter-elite, to both Western-educated and traditionally educated Muslim leaders has emerged. Sa'udi Arabia and the Gulf states have played a leading part in the sponsorship of revivalist movements, and Sudan, Libya, and other Muslim states have contributed too. Iran supports Shi'i activities.

Revivalism appeals to new and varied clienteles. Throughout West Africa it has appealed to merchants, professionals, and to migrants. In Kano in Nigeria it has appealed to peasant migrants, who organized Islamic groups under the leadership of rural religious teachers to press their economic interests as laborers. In Malaysia small-scale peasant landowners organized under the banner of Islam to resist the pressures that were depriving them of ownership of land. In Egypt, Turkey, and Iran, it has appealed to the old strata of artisan and merchant classes, and to the lower level of Muslim-educated teachers and clerks who were threatened by competition from new enterprises and with displacement by Western-educated elites. It has also appealed to the new intelligentsia of socially mobile but economically insecure students, intellectuals, technicians, middling bureaucrats, and professionals. In Egypt

Islamic radicalism also won strong support among students of medicine, engineering, pharmacy, and other highly professional clienteles. In Turkey Islamic student groups and parties were strongest in the technical faculties while socialist groups predominated in the arts faculties. In Iran student leadership was crucial in the internal revival until the revolution. Separated by their education from traditional communities, they were not part of the political elites. Like uprooted peasants and bazaaris, these strata turn to Islam to symbolize their anxieties, and their hostilities to the powers – domestic and foreign – that thwart them and their dreams of a more perfect future.

In parallel with the growth of reformist movements there has been a dramatic upsurge in political movements. Many of these are extensions of teaching and missionary work. Their supporters believe that an Islamic society cannot be built by education alone, but requires political power. Politically activist Islamist movements include movements of a democratic type which profess to compete, or be willing to compete if permitted, for influence and votes within the political system, such as the Welfare Party and its successor, the Virtue Party in Turkey, an-Nahda, or the Renaissance Party, in Tunisia, the Society of Muslim Brothers in Egypt and Jordan, Jama'at-i Islami in Pakistan, PAS in Malaysia, PPP in Indonesia, and other parties.

Everywhere the revivalist movements have transformed state and popular identities. In many countries national identities, built on a compound of religious and ethnic loyalties, have shifted from emphasis upon the secular ethnic to the religious aspects. While ethnic identities remain very strong among Kurds, Berbers, and others, many Indonesians, Malaysians, Iranians, Turks, Egyptians, Algerians, Tunisians, and other Muslims now lay greater emphasis upon the Islamic rather than the political or ethnic component of their identities. In deference to popular pressure governments commonly adopt a more positive attitude toward Islam, and relax earlier demands for secularism. Bangladeshi and Malay identity, for example, have shifted to emphasis upon Islam, and correspondingly the governments of these countries have declared themselves patrons, supporters, and protectors of Islam. Indonesia in the last decade of Suharto's reign accepted the Muslim sentiments of the populace, and tried to coopt the Muslim movements and identify the regime as a patron of Islam. Since Zulfiqar 'Ali Bhutto, Pakistani regimes have rededicated themselves to the formation of an Islamic system. The Taliban made Afghanistan an Islamic state until their defeat in late 2001. Sudan until December 1999 was avowedly an Islamic state in the control of Hassan al-Turabi and the National Islamic Front. Mauritania has declared the Shari'a the only valid source of law. In Nigeria Muslim demands have led to declarations that Shari'a is the law of several of the northern federal states. In Egypt, Morocco, and Jordan governmental elites have reaffirmed their personal Muslim commitments and have made Muslim movements part of the political process.

In other cases revivalist political movements have led to violent contests for political power. Iran, Afghanistan, Egypt, and Algeria have been through bitter civil wars.

Small factions attempt assassinations, coups d'état, or violence against tourists, minorities, and others in their efforts to disrupt regimes. Jihadist or militant neo-Islam has been stimulated by the return of veterans from the Afghan war against Russian occupation who believe in takfir – declaring Muslim enemies apostates – and in the use of violence to seize power. In Egypt the government seems to have suppressed decades-long violent efforts to seize and Islamize the state, but Islamic Jihad and other terrorist groups remain underground. In Algeria the military has in the main suppressed the violent opposition of the FIS and GIA. In Indonesia the collapse of the Suharto regime has opened the way for the formation of a plethora of small radical Islamist movements that back separatist movements in the outer islands, battle with Christians, attempt to enforce Islamic morality, and call for the formation of an Islamic state. These groups include Laskar Jihad, the Army of Allah, and the Islamic Youth Front. In Uzbekistan and Tajikistan the Islamic Movement of Uzbekistan and the Islamic Renaissance Party try to destabilize the governments.

Militant and violent Islamic movements also commonly appear in anti-colonial struggles. In Afghanistan numerous Muslim groups fought a long and successful war against the Soviet Union, but then fought each other, and were eventually crushed by the Taliban. Chechnya also has numerous resistance movements to Russian rule, which is maintained at great cost only by a full-scale military occupation. In Kashmir Hizb ul-Mujahidin and other groups have waged a terrorist war against Indian control. In the Philippines the Moro Islamic Liberation Front and the Abu Sayyaf group continue a battle for regional autonomy. Hizballah, HAMAS, and Palestinian Islamic Jihad fight against Israel. There is active resistance to the Chinese in Xinjiang.

In states with divided Muslim and non-Muslim populations there has been an upsurge of political struggle, riots and demonstrations, and even civil war. This is the case in Lebanon and Nigeria, where there has been Muslim–Christian fighting, and the Sudan, where the Muslim and Arab north has been engaged in a genocidal civil war to dominate the Christian and animist south. Tensions are high in Chad and Ethiopia, both divided between Muslim and Christian populations. Islamist militancy is also a factor in Sunni–Shi'i tensions in Bahrain, Iraq, and Sa'udi Arabia.

Islamic revivalism has been an important development of the late twentieth century, but it also reflects longer-term structures in Islamic history. Ever since the ninth century, there has been a de facto separation of state and religion in Islamic societies. Historically, the state was regarded as a secular institution, an instrument for the exercise of power, yet intended and required to protect, cultivate, and foster the Islamic way of life. The modern state inherits this position. While its secular self-definition is inherently appropriate to the political and economic functions of the state, nationalist ideologies – so compelling for political elites, anti-colonial movements, state formation, and the legitimization of the Muslim states – have proved to be weak in transcendental appeal, and leave Muslim populations uneasy about their political loyalties and unsettled in their aspiration for a higher destiny. Correspondingly, for many centuries, Islam has been the organizing principle of individual behavior and of small-scale community life, but only indirectly an influence upon the state. Yet Muslims yearn for an ideal world in which the state, as well as the small community and the individual, is built around Islamic principles – a yearning for an integral Islamic universe. Thus the primary goal of Islamic movements are moral and social, but control of the state turns out to be an ideal – if not, in practice, an essential – part of their program.

Thus, the Islamic revival reanimates the tradition that integrates religion and politics. That tradition has now become the discourse of urban working- and middle-class populations as well as of rural lineage and tribal communities. In the past, states and empires were legitimized in religious terms and were supposed to defend the religious interests of Muslims and uphold religious law, but religious leaders distanced themselves from politics. By contrast, the neo-Islamic movements channel religious belief and solidarity into politics. In the contemporary era religious feeling becomes the basis of total commitment to political causes. The merger of religion and politics is a classical Islamic ideal, but in the recent era they have again been brought together.

Transnational Islam

The rise of these movements has also helped to create an ever-growing worldwide consciousness of the common features of Muslim belief and ever deeper universalistic Muslim sympathies and identifications. The Islamic revival has strengthened transnational (or international) Muslim movements committed to a variety of goals, including the educational consolidation of true Islamic practice, the creation of a Caliphate or global Islamic society, and the victory of Islam over non-Islamic – especially Western Christian and Jewish – cultures.

On one level transnational Islam manifests itself in the form of a growing universalistic Islamic identity. The increasing integration of world societies as a result of enhanced communications, media, travel, and migration makes meaningful the concept of a single Islam practiced everywhere in similar ways, an Islam which transcends national and ethnic customs. The hajj, the pilgrimage, remains the primary example of this identity, but there is an ever more widely shared Islamist revival call for a return to the Shari'a. Common political concerns, such as the position of Muslim minorities, or the conflicts involving Muslims in Afghanistan, Palestine, Bosnia, Chechnya, and elsewhere, generate Muslim identifications transcending political boundaries. The global identification has become important to Muslim youths in Europe and the United States.

This sentiment is reinforced by a proliferation of organized transnational Muslim movements. These movements include publication and propaganda organizations such as the Rabitat al-'Alam al-Islami (Muslim World League); or the Jami'iyat al-Da'wa al-Islamiya (Islamic Call Society) promoting the study of the Quran; missionary (da'wa) societies, such as the Tablighi Islam; and Sufi brotherhoods, such as the Qadiriya and Tijaniya in sub-Saharan Africa. Muslim banks, the World

Assembly of Muslim Youth, the Institute for Muslim Minority Affairs, emigrant communities with international ties, and other such organizations are part of the global phenomenon. In this array of organized transnational groups, the majority are primarily religious associations.

Banks are particularly important, since they are part of a global system of finance. They allow for investments and transfers of money to and from any part of the world. Islamic banks are based on the principle that the Shari'a condemns the taking of interest, and are structured as joint stock companies. Depositors do not receive a fixed rate of interest, but rather participate in the investment profits of the bank. Borrowers share equity ownership with the banks rather than paying interest. However, in competition with standard banks Islamic banks are becoming increasingly pragmatic. In place of a stipulated rate of interest, investments take into account the value of money over time, and many loans are made on the basis of a predetermined return. Many banks employ Western fund managers under the supervision of a board of Islamic scholars, and invest in international markets. Some Western banks have set up Islamic branches. Islamic banking is a global phenomenon, but more and more has the aspect of a marketing scheme for a self-identified Muslim public.

There are, however, weighty limitations upon universalistic Islam. Global Muslim identity does not necessarily or even usually imply organized group action. Even though Muslims recognize a global affiliation, the real heart of Muslim religious life remains outside politics – in local associations for worship, discussion, mutual aid, education, charity, and other communal activities. Moreover, many movements that operate internationally are really sponsored extensions of national states. For example, the Organization of the Islamic Conference, which has worldwide outreach and sponsors relief efforts, political interventions, and the Islamic Development Bank, are the collective agencies of national governments. The Muslim World League is Sa'udi sponsored; the Islamic Call Society is Libyan. International movements such as the Ikhwan al-Muslimin or the Jama'at-i Islami have branches in several countries, which give intellectual, logistical, and financial support to each other, but nonetheless operate independently within the political framework of their home countries. While the sentiment of a worldwide brotherhood of Muslims – the umma – is very strong, and while there are numerous associations that operate for religious purposes, most Islamic political groups are in fact localized in national states. On the political level, Islamic universalism and national state particularism are not opposed, but rather are joined together.

Transnational military and terrorist organizations

The growth of universalistic or transnational Islamic movements has its violent dimensions as well. In the 1980s and 1990s Islamic opposition in many countries was domesticated and integrated into national political systems, sometimes in the form of political parties or by the creation of Islamic-nationalist ideologies, and sometimes by the declaration of Islamic states. The Islamist movements have been brought into the political system in Turkey, Malaysia, and Indonesia. In Sa'udi Arabia, Egypt, and Algeria, violent Islamic opposition, while not eliminated, was politically crushed. Coopted or defeated, the neo-Islamic movements had two main options. One was continued pursuit of educational objectives, reformist and Salafi teachings to promote religious transformation from within by peaceful means.

The second was to continue the struggle by supporting anti-colonial movements in Algeria, Egypt, Lebanon, Palestine, Sudan, Chechnya, Afghanistan, Kashmir, Pakistan, the Philippines, Malaysia, and Indonesia. A new kind of activist arose, mobile transnationals moving from one jihad to another, commonly non-Afghan veterans of the Afghan war against the Soviet Union, able to supply fighting assistance, logistical support, money, and organizational help to each other. The non-Afghan "Afghanis" were trained in Mujahidin camps supported by Sa'udi Arabia, the Pakistani intelligence services, and the CIA. "Afghans" trained for the war against the Soviet Union have gone on to fight in the Gulf War with Iraq, the GIA in Algeria, the Kashmiri Harakat al-Ansar, the Yemeni Jihad, and have joined other radical groups in the Philippines, Chechnya, Egypt, and Bosnia. Other transnational jihad fighters include disaffected Sa'udis, Egyptians, and Algerians, some of whom had been part of opposition movements in their home countries. Some cells operated in Europe and in the United States. Many are unnamed groups; some are under the umbrella of the Egyptian Anathema and Exile or the Algerian Salafist Group for Preaching and Combat. The struggle is also waged against the USA on the grounds that it is the principal international supporter of corrupt governments in the Muslim world. The bombing of the World Trade Center in New York in 1993, of the American embassies in Tanzania and Kenya, of the USS *Cole*, attacked in Aden harbor, and the airplane attacks on the World Trade Center and the Pentagon of September 11, 2001 are examples of a worldwide jihad against the most powerful of the Western nations.

Usama bin Laden, the organizer of the al-Qaeda network, is widely thought to be the mastermind behind these assaults. His movement is called the World Islamic Front for the Struggle against Christians and Jews. Broadly speaking its goal is to overthrow enemy governments and establish an Islamic regime (or regimes) for their populations. In political terms it calls for the removal of American forces from Sa'udi Arabia, protection for the people of Iraq from American and allied bombing, help for the Palestinians in their struggle against Israel, and support for Islamist movements worldwide. The great enemy of Islam is the United States, which supports repressive and un-Islamic regimes the world over. Jihadist Islamists, encouraged by their victory over the Soviet Union in Afghanistan, seek to humble and drive the USA out of the Islamic world. Bin Laden called upon all Muslims to rise up and wage jihad against Americans – both military personnel and civilians – and their allies everywhere.

Bin Laden's role, however, was not clearly defined. It does not seem likely that he had a direct operational role, but was rather an inspiration and a hero to Islamist militants, a spokesman for their grievances, the principal theorist of Islamic jihad,

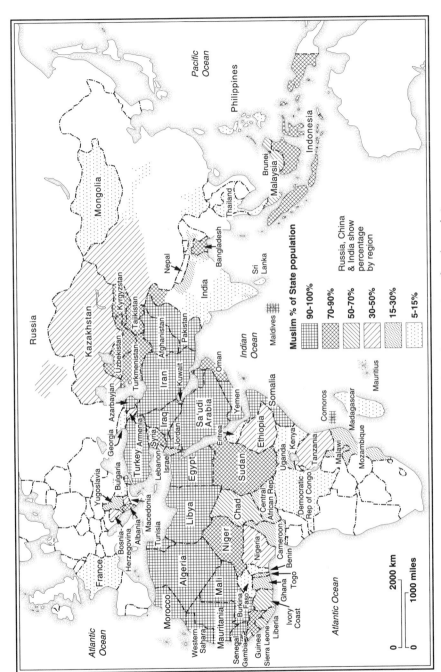

Map 39 Muslim population by percentage of total population

The map shows the following labels:

Atlantic Ocean
Pacific Ocean
Indian Ocean
Russia
Mongolia
Kazakhstan
Kyrgyzstan
Uzbekistan
Tajikistan
Turkmenistan
Azerbayjan
Georgia
Armenia
Turkey
Bulgaria
Yugoslavia
Macedonia
Albania
Bosnia-Herzegovina
France
Tunisia
Morocco
Algeria
Libya
Niger
Mali
Mauritania
Western Sahara
Senegal
Gambia
Guinea
Sierra Leone
Liberia
Ivory Coast
Burkina Faso
Ghana
Togo
Benin
Nigeria
Cameroon
Chad
Central African Rep
Sudan
Egypt
Lebanon
Israel
Syria
Iraq
Jordan
Sa'udi Arabia
Kuwait
Iran
Afghanistan
Pakistan
Oman
Yemen
Eritrea
Ethiopia
Somalia
Uganda
Kenya
Democratic Rep of Congo
Tanzania
Malawi
Mozambique
Madagascar
Comoros
Mauritius
Nepal
India
Bangladesh
Sri Lanka
Maldives
Thailand
Brunei
Malaysia
Indonesia
Philippines

Muslim % of State population

- 90–100%
- 70–90%
- 50–70%
- 30–50%
- 15–30%
- 5–15%

Russia, China & India show percentage by region

0   2000 km
0   1000 miles

Table 18. *Muslim population by countries*[1]

Name	Total population (in 1,000s)	Date of data	% of Muslims	Muslim population (in 1,000s)
Afghanistan	25,889	1997	99	25,630
			84 Sunni	21,750 Sunni
			15 Shi i	3,880 Shi i
Albania	3,490	1995	70	2,440
Algeria	30,554	1990	99.5	30,400
Armenia	3,810		43	164
Austria	8,091	1995	2.1	161
Azerbaijan	8,051	1995	93.4 (mostly Shi i)	7,520
Bahrain	691	1991	81.8	560
			61.3 Shi i	420 Shi i
			20.5 Sunni	140 Sunni
Bangladesh	129,194	1991	88.3	114,080
Belgium	10,249	1995	2.5	256
Benin	6,396	1992	20.6	1,318
World Fact Book			10.0	640
Bosnia & Herzegovina	3,836	1999	43	1,650
Brunei	336	1991	67.2	226
Bulgaria	8,172	1995	13.1	1,070
Burkina Faso	11,946	1994	50	5,970
Burundi	6,055	1990	1.6	97
World Fact Book			10.0	605
Cameroon	15,422	1990	21.8	3,360
Canada	30,770	1991	0.9	290
Central African Republic	3,513	1995	15	530
Chad	8,425	1993	53.9	4,540
China	1,265,207	1980	1.4	18,000
World Fact Book			2–3	25,236–37,854
Comoros	578	1995	99.3	574
Congo, Democratic Republic of the	51,965	1995	1.4	730
World Fact Book			10	5,196
Croatia	4,252	1997	1.3	50
Turkish Republic of Northern Cyprus	192	1996	96.4	184
Denmark	5,339	1995	1.5	180
Djibouti	451	1995	97.2	440
Egypt	65,871	1990	90	59,284
World Fact Book	68,359		90	61,523
Eritrea	4,136	1995	69.3	2,870
Ethiopia	64,117	1994	32.9	21,094
World Fact Book			45–50	32,058
Fiji	819	1986	7.8	64
France	58,835	1997	5.5	3,240
The Gambia	1,367	1993	95	1,300
Georgia	5,020	1995	11	550
Germany	82,225	1995	2.4	1,973

[1] The figures in the table are taken from the *Britannica Book of the Year 2001*, (Encyclopedia Britannica, Inc. Chicago, London, 2001). Numbers are also quoted from the *World Fact Book, 2001* (CIA) wherever there are significant discrepancies. Both sources have inconsistencies and are to be used with caution.

Table 18. *Muslim population by countries* (continued)

Name	Total population (in 1,000s)	Date of data	% of Muslims	Muslim population (in 1,000s)
Ghana	19,534	1991–2	14.4	2,812
World Fact Book			30	5,860
Greece	10,562	1995	1.3	140
Guinea	7,466	1983	86.9	6,350
Guinea-Bissau	1,286	1991	46	590
Guyana	792	1995	9	71
India	1,014,004	1995	12	121,680
			9 Sunni	91,000 Sunni
			3 Shi i	30,000 Shi i
Indonesia	209,342	1990	87.2	182,546
Iran	67,704	1996	99.6	67,433
			93.9 Shi i	63,547 Shi i
			5.7 Sunni	3,859 Sunni
Iraq	22,676	1994	97	21,995
			72.5 Shi i	14,170 Shi i
			34.5 Sunni	7,820 Sunni
Israel	6,107	1999	14.9	910
Italy	57,723	1996	1.2	700
Ivory Coast	15,981	1988	38.7	6,180
World Fact Book			60	9,588
Jordan	4,982	1995	96.5	4,810
Kazakhstan	14,913	1995	47	7,010
Kenya	30,340	1995	6	1,820
Kuwait	1,984	1995	85	1,686
			45 Sunni	893 Sunni
			40 Shi i	793 Shi i
Kyrgyzstan	4,895	1997	70	3,426
Lebanon	3,578	1995	55.3	1,980
			34 Shi i	1,220 Shi i
			21.3 Sunni	760 Sunni
Liberia	3,164	1995	16	506
Libya	5,115	1995	97	4,960
Macedonia	2,041	1995	30	610
Madagascar	15,506	1997	7	1,090
Malawi	10,386	1995	20	2,080
Malaysia	23,260	1980	52.9	12,300
Maldives	285		100	285
Mali	10,686	1995	90	9,620
Mauritania	2,668	1994	99.5	2,650
Mauritus	1,184	1990	16.3	190
Mongolia	2,399	1995	4	100
Morocco	29,067	1995	99.8	29,008
Mozambique	19,105	1995	28.2	5,390
World Fact Book			20.0	3,820
Myanmar (Burma)	41,735	1983	3.8	1,600
Nepal	24,702	1991	3.5	870
The Netherlands	15,896	1997	4.3	690
Niger	10,076	1995	88.7	8.940
Nigeria	123,338	1995	43	53,035
World Fact Book			50	61,669

Table 18. *Muslim population by countries* (continued)

Name	Total population (in 1,000s)	Date of data	% of Muslims	Muslim population (in 1,000s)
Oman	2,416	1993	87.7	2,120
Pakistan	141,553	1993	95 75 Sunni 20 Shi i	134,475 106,170 Sunni 28,310 Shi i
Philippines	76,320	1996	4.6	3,490
Qatar	599	1995	95	570
Romania	22,435	1992	0.2	45
Russia	146,001	1995	10	14,600
Rwanda	7,229	1996	1	70
Sa udi Arabia	22,024	1992	96.6 93.3 Sunni 3.3 Shi i	21,275 20,550 Sunni 725 Shi i
Senegal	9,987	1988	92	9,190
Sierra Leone	5,233	1993	60	3,140
Singapore	3,278	1995	14.9	489
Somalia	7,253	1995	99	7,240
South Africa	43,421	1991	1.1	477
Spain	40,128	1995	1.2	460
Sri Lanka	19,246	1981	7.5	1,450
Sudan	35,080	1992	72	25,258
Suriname	431	1995	19.6	85
Syria	16,306	1992	86 74 Sunni 12 Shi i	14,023 12,066 Sunni 1,957 Shi i
Tajikistan	6,312	1995	85 80 Sunni 5 Shi i	5,370 5,050 Sunni 320 Shi i
Tanzania	35,306	1997	37	13,060
Thailand	62,423	1996	5.3	3,308
Togo	5,019	1993	15	750
Tunisia	9,593	1995	99.5	9,540
Turkey	65,667	1994	99.8 80 Sunni 19.8 Shi i	65,535 52,533 Sunni 3,002 Shi i
Turkmenistan	4,885	1995	87	4,250
Uganda	23,318	1995	16	3,731
United Arab Emirates	3,022	1995	96 80 Sunni 16 Shi i	2,901 2,417 Sunni 484 Shi i
United Kingdom	59,714	1995	2.6	1,552
United States	275,372	1995	1.9	5,232
Uzbekistan	24,756	1995	88	21,790
Yemen	17,479	1995	99.9 60 Sunni 40 Shi i	17,460 10,487 Sunni 6,974 Shi i
Yugoslavia	10,662	1995	19	2,030
Zambia	9,582	1995	1	95

Total
    minimum   1,270,735
    maximum 1,324,393

and an organizer of terrorist training. He played an important role in sponsoring and financing – and possibly coordinating – jihad groups. He was sheltered by the Taliban in Afghanistan, and was in turn a principal military and financial supporter of their regime until the defeat of that government in December 2001 by the United States and the Northern Alliance, a coalition of Afghan forces. In response to his movement, the United States has launched its own global effort to crush the terrorist networks.

Terrorism has an ambiguous status in the contemporary Muslim world. Most Muslims repudiate the terrorist attacks launched in their name, but the militant radicals have widespread sympathy because they articulate the grievances of many Muslims against American policy. The radicals also share the beliefs of the broader political–communal movements which sponsor teaching of reformed and true Islam, and create schools, mosques, clinics, social services, relief organizations, and charities. Missionary, teaching, and charitable activities and the promotion of Salafi or Wahhabi Islam is backed worldwide by Sa'udi and Gulf state financing and by Arab teachers, missionaries, and organizers from the Middle East. Though it is denounced as un-Islamic, terrorist violence is indirectly an extremist expression of this broader movement to promote Islamic belief and practice and the expansion of the domain of Islam.

In some respects the emergence of extremist political Islam is the outcome of the historical processes of the last century. Islam used to be one element of the multilayered sense of self held by most Muslims. Islam was joined to family, village, patronage network, clan, tribe, language-group, religious sect, and political identities. Complex cross-cutting identities were a moderating factor in political behavior. However, the destruction of historical forms of small communities and the reduction of peoples to an undifferentiated mass mobilized for political struggle, the decline of 'ulama' and Sufi authority and the emergence of a new radical religious intelligentsia, and the global forces of media and migration have for many people reduced the choice of identity to one between Islam and the secular world of nation-states. This polarization has had devastating worldwide consequences.

CONTEMPORARY PATTERNS IN THE RELATIONS BETWEEN STATES AND ISLAMIC SOCIETIES

The precise relationships between states, apolitical Muslim religious associations, and politically active Islamic movements vary from country to country. These variations strikingly correspond to the historical configurations of state and religious institutions in each society, and seem to derive from the conflicts among political and religious elites and intelligentsias in the nineteenth and early twentieth centuries.

Most Muslim societies became independent after World War I or World War II and began the era of self-rule with a highly secularized regime, strong apolitical forms of Muslim communal life, relatively weak neo-Islamic movements, and limited penetration by Islam into national political identity. With the rising influence of revivalist

Table 19. *Muslim population by region*

Areas	Number of Muslims	Proportion of Muslims to total population	Chief languages spoken by Muslims
Arab countries Arabia, the fertile crescent, Egypt, Sudan, Maghrib (Libya to Morocco)	c. 284,000,000	Great majority Muslims; Christian minorities in many countries	*Arabic* (in various vernaculars), some Berber
Iranian highlands Iran (and Azarbayjan), Afghanistan, Tajikistan	c. 106,000,000	Almost entirely Muslim; some Christian, Jewish, and Zoroastrian minorities	*Persian*, Pashto, Baluchi, Kurdish, Turkish
Turkey and Southeast Europe Turkey (Anatolia), the Balkans, Crimea	c. 74,000,000	Muslim majority in Turkey, otherwise majority is Christian; Jewish minority	*Turkish*, Slavic, Albanian, some Greek
Inner Asia Volga Basin, Siberia; Kazakhstan, Uzbekistan, Turkmenistan, Kyrgyzstan, etc.	c. 12,000,000	Muslims are a minority along Volga and in Kazakhstan; republics are largely Muslim but recent Russian influx	*Turkish* in various forms
Indian subcontinent Pakistan, Bangladesh, Indus Valley, Ganges plain, Deccan, south India, Ceylon	c. 317,000,000	Majority in those areas which became Pakistan and Bangladesh; minority elsewhere among Hindus, Christians, Sikhs; Muslims about 1/4 of all Indic population	*Urdu*, Punjabi, Kashmiri, Bengali, Gujarati, Sindhi, Telegu, Tamil, Malayalam
Malaysia and Indonesia From Burma to Indonesia and the Philippines	c. 204,000,000	Great majority in most islands; minorities in Indochinese lands divided among Buddhists and some Hindus and Christians	*Malay* (Indonesian), Sudanese, Javanese
China All provinces but especially Kansu, Yunnan, Xinjiang	c. 18–35,000,000	Minority among Buddhist-Taoists	Chinese, Turkish
Sub-Saharan Africa East coast, western and central Sudan, and scattered	c. 1,300,000	Almost entirely Muslim in large parts, shading to a minority divided among animists and Christians	Swahili, Hausa, Somali, etc.
Western Europe	c. 9,000,000	Minorities	Various
North America	c. 5,500,000	Minorities	Various

* Based on M. G. S. Hodgson, *Venture of Islam*, Chicago, 1974. Population figures from *Britannica Book of the Year 2001.* (Encyclopedia Britannica, Inc., Chicago, London, 2001)

and political Islamic movements since the 1970s, Turkey, Tunisia, Senegal, and Egypt, with some concessions, have maintained their secular identity. Algeria affords the paradox of a state with a Muslim national identity and an anti-Islamic policy. Many states, such as Malaysia, Indonesia, Mali, Mauritania, and Bangladesh, have evolved toward an Islamo-nationalist identity, while others, such as Iran, Libya, Pakistan, Sudan, and Afghanistan, have declared themselves Islamic states – in addition to Sa'udi Arabia and Morocco, which have long had Islamic identities. Here we shall review a few cases to explore these variations and their relation to historical institutions and cultures.

Secularized states and Muslim societies: Turkey, Tunisia and Senegal

Turkey is prototypical of the secularized Muslim societies. It has disestablished Islam in public life and has created a pluralistic political system, but in many ways the modern form of development depends upon the institutions of the Ottoman empire. By the eighteenth century the Ottoman empire had a centralized state regime, legitimized in both Muslim and non-Muslim terms, and a centralized and unified Sunni religious establishment. Through bureaucratic administration, the millet system, and guilds, the Ottoman regime controlled its subjects to a degree unparalleled among pre-modern Muslim societies. The eighteenth and nineteenth centuries brought important changes to Ottoman society, but these changes served to carry the pattern of state domination into the twentieth century. Foreign and domestic pressures provoked the Ottoman elites to modernize along Western lines – by improving military capabilities, rationalizing administration, restoring the authority of the central government, and making the social and cultural changes necessary to support a centralized state. These reforms brought into being a new intelligentsia – the graduates of military, medical, engineering, and diplomatic schools – each successive generation of which espoused a still more radical program of reform. By World War I the ruling "Young Turks" were committed to secularization in place of Ottomanism and Islam. The parts of this elite that survived the defeats of World War I, under the leadership of Mustafa Kemal, undertook the creation of the Turkish Republic.

The Ottoman religious elites could offer no effective response either to European intervention or to the determination of the state elites to create a secular national state. The religious elites were subordinate functionaries of the state, committed to the authority of a regime which for centuries had been a warrior state and protector of Muslim peoples. Nor were the Ottoman commercial classes sufficiently developed to be a rival for political power. Whatever the opinion of the 'ulama', and whatever the shock to the feelings of masses of Turkish Muslims, the voice of the Westernized political establishment was the only one heard at the foundation of the Turkish Republic.

The Republic thus inherited the Ottoman tradition of centralized government and competent military leadership, a long history of nineteenth-century reform and modernization, and an intelligentsia of army officers, administrators, engineers, technical experts, and intellectuals. Modern Turkey came into being with a coherent state structure and a strong commitment to a state-directed society. The new regime transformed Turkish society and culture in ways that submerged the traditional religious organizations and Islamic identity. In the 1920s and 1930s Turkey set the foundations for a modern industrial economy, and sought to absorb the masses of the people into the cultural framework of the republican regime. It attempted to break the attachment of ordinary people to Islam and to win them over to a Western and secular style of life. Economic development generated a more differentiated social structure, including new groups of businessmen, factory managers, rural landowners, prosperous peasants, engineers, industrial workers, and intellectuals. In the post-World War II era Turkey acquired a parliamentary regime complete with competing political parties and an elected parliament, but the true government of the country remained the military. The army intervened in national politics in 1960, 1970, and from 1980 to 1983 when a new constitution was written creating a National Security Council which gave the military an official channel through which to direct the development of the country.

However, the cultural changes imposed from the top had relatively slight penetration. They divided the country into a modernized urban elite and rural masses whose Islamic loyalties have never been seriously disturbed. While the state is secular, the Turkish populace has continued to identify itself as Muslim, and throughout the republican era carried on worship in mosques and at the tombs of saints. In the 1960s and 1970s movements and parties committed to the re-Islamization of state and society grew stronger. The Said Nursi movement, Naqshbandi Sufis, and the National Salvation Party, which favored the reestablishment of an Islamic state, grew increasingly active. In the 1980s and 1990s the state again tried to institutionalize Islam via the control of courts, waqfs, and the education of imams. President Ozal sought to coopt the Islamic movements. State tolerance for Islam, however, only encouraged the growth of Islamic opposition. Competing within the Turkish political system, the Refah or Welfare Party, the successor to the National Salvation Party, led by Necmettin Erbakan, with the support of students, small-town bazaaris, provincial businessmen, and rural migrants to the large cities, won 20 percent of the vote – making Erbakan, for a time in 1996 and 1997, Prime Minister of Turkey. He was forced out of power by the military in 1997. The Welfare Party was banned, and votes for its successor, the Virtue Party, fell to about 10 percent. From the point of view of the military the Islamic parties represent a threat of a radical "Iranian"-type revolution and the destruction of the secular Turkish republic founded by Ataturk; the opposition presents itself as a coalition of provincial, peasant landowners, small-town businessmen, pious Muslims, and Kurds opposed to the unfair distribution of resources and power in contemporary Turkey.

At the same time, the Turkish government waged a long – and by 2001 seemingly successful – war to suppress Kurdish demands for autonomy and national independence. The long struggles, however, and the polarization of Turkish society among secularists, Islamists, and Kurds calls into question its national identity. Behind the army's resistance to Muslim or Kurdish political and cultural demands lies a concept of the Turkish nation as a unitary, homogeneous entity. Turkish nationalists do not allow for minority rights or for plural ethnic and cultural identities. The repressive policies of the government and the Kurdish and Islamic challenges to its authority have pushed Turkey to a crisis of political identity. Is it to be a democratic society or a military state? Is it a unified homogeneous secular society, is it an Islamic society, or is it a pluralistic society which can accept autonomous ethnic and religious sub-communities?

Tunisia also has an Ottoman heritage, and shows similar tendencies to secular national identity. Like Turkey, Tunisia in the nineteenth century had a strong central state and a state-controlled 'ulama' establishment. The breakdown of the commercial economy and an accumulation of foreign debt allowed for the establishment of a French protectorate in 1881. In the 1920s French- and Muslim-educated bureaucrats and intelligentsia opposed French rule in the name of Islamic reformism and a constitutional regime, but failed to achieve their political goals. Therefore, in the 1930s, a younger generation representing the upwardly mobile French and Arab intellectuals of the Sahil region seized control of the Destour Party. In opposition to the old elite and in the name of independence, nationalist rhetoric superseded Islamic reformism. In 1956 the Destour, led by Bourguiba, came to power, maintained its nationalist orientation, and generated first a socialist and then a mixed economy.

Tunisia, however, also retained Islam as part of the identity of the common people. This persisting Islamic identity allowed for an Islamic revival in the 1970s in reaction to the failures of the state and a lagging economy. An Islamic Party led by Rashid al-Ghannouchi, renamed an-Nahda, or the Renaissance Party, in 1988, ran strongly in the 1989 elections on a platform renouncing the use of violence, accepting republican politics, and affirming the Islamic, humanitarian, and democratic identity of Tunisia. The party was promptly banned by the government, and its leader was forced into exile. Thousands of activists were jailed. Thus Tunisia, like Turkey, has a history of centralized state power which allows for the formation of a modern state and a history of colonial occupation that has given the state elites a secular identity, but maintains secular rule only through repression of strong Islamist movements.

Senegal affords the striking counterpoint of a secular regime which rules over an avowedly Muslim society. Pre-modern Senegal was divided into numerous non-Muslim kingdoms within which Muslim communities formed segregated enclaves. In the late eighteenth and nineteenth centuries the Muslims fought to win control of the Senegambian region, establish Muslim states, and convert the populace to Islam. Senegal was the scene of the great jihads of Futa Toro, al-Hajj 'Umar, Ma Ba, and others. These last Senegalese echoes of the "Caliphal" tradition of a unified Islamic state and society were overthrown by the French conquest at the end of the nineteenth century.

The French created an entirely new political structure – a Senegalese territorial state in which the Muslim communities were reorganized as Sufi brotherhoods. The Tijaniya, the Muridiya, and other Sufi tariqat organized the populace into brotherhoods which provided social leadership, spiritual meaning, and organized economic activity. As organized communities, the Muslims worked out a pattern of cooperative relations with the French. When Senegal became independent in 1960, the state was taken over by a Western-educated Senegalese political elite which resumed a collaborative relationship with Senegalese religious notables. Thus the modern structure of Senegalese society is based on the historical division between state and religious elites and on the cooperation between them, while the population has retained a Muslim identity. Only recently has there been minority pressure for the Islamization of the state, coming from urban professionals, bureaucrats, and teachers who affirm an Arabic and Islamic identity. The revivalist demands, however, do not shake the political system, and the Islamist movements have had either to transform themselves into Sufi orders or ally with the government.

Islamic nationalism: Egypt and Algeria

Egypt and Algeria illustrate a different relationship between the "secular" state and Islamic identity. Both have moved toward Muslim-national identities, but both have been beset by bitter civil wars in which the state has crushed the Islamist opposition.

The basic structures of Egyptian society also derived from the eighteenth- and nineteenth-century Ottoman model, but differed in the degree to which Islam remained part of the Egyptian political process. In the early nineteenth century Egypt went through a phase of centralization of power and economic development which created new landowning elites and made the 'ulama' and Sufis subordinate to the state administration. Egypt, however, unlike the central provinces of the Ottoman empire, came under direct British rule in 1882. British occupation provoked the formation of a new intelligentsia, committed first to Islamic reform and modernism and then to secular nationalism as the ideological basis for independence. In 1922 native Egyptian landowners, officials, journalists, and lawyers won partial autonomy and established a constitutional monarchy based on liberal principles. The liberal regime, however, failed to win full independence from Britain, and failed to cope with the grave problems of economic inequality. Nor could the Egyptian elites, who lacked direct continuity with the Ottoman heritage and the military capability, self-confidence, and authority of the Turks, carry through the kind of drastic secularization achieved in Turkey. Instead, in the 1930s and 1940s, the authority of the political elites was challenged by the Society of Muslim Brothers, which proposed the establishment of a government devoted to the application of Islamic law, a regulated economy in accordance with a combination of Islamic and socialist principles, and the adoption of Islam as an ideological and political alternative to liberalism or Communism.

The failed monarchy and liberal regime was overthrown in 1952 by the Free Officers' coup led by Naguib, Nasser, and Sadat. The new Egyptian regime was committed to a moderate form of authoritarian rule, centralized management of the economy, and a socialist ideology. In the 1950s and 1960s it attempted, as had the liberal regime of the 1920s, 1930s, and 1940s, to bypass the influence of Islam and pursue a secular policy of development. Strong efforts were made to bring Islamic religious activity under government control. Opposition movements such as the Society of Muslim Brothers were outlawed, and the autonomy of religious institutions was curtailed. Though Muslim law continued to be applied in Egypt, legal codes were brought under government jurisdiction. In general, the government tried to control religious life, to use the 'ulama' to support its policies, and to identify Islam with national and socialist programs.

This effort to create an apparent identity between Islam and the state was only partially successful. Just as the 1930s brought a revival of Islamic sentiments in intellectual and political circles, the 1970s witnessed a revival of Islam appealing to middle-class students and young professional people. While the 'ulama' and the Islamic establishment remained under government control, independent preachers, missionaries, and teachers actively promoted a revived commitment to Islam. Also, the 1967 defeat in the war with Israel, the failure to resolve the Palestinian problem, and the failure to develop economically led to the condemnation of Egypt's secular and socialist policies. Islamist groups within the universities, reformist and missionary groups, and violent political groups proliferated. Militancy grew in the 1980s. The Society of Muslim Brothers established itself as a dominant influence in the universities and in the professional associations. It sponsored community service for the poor and elected members to the Egyptian parliament. A jihadist Islamist group assassinated President Sadat in 1981. There were clashes between Muslim radicals and Copts, and in the 1990s a terrorist campaign to assassinate government officials, military officers, secular intellectuals, and tourists. The government has largely crushed the radical opposition, but the result is nonetheless a substantial shift of public opinion toward the Islamic dimension of Egyptian identity.

Algeria, also a former province of the Ottoman empire, evolved in a manner closer to Egypt than to Turkey or Tunisia. The historical Algerian state and its core of 'ulama' controlled only a small part of Algerian society, while organized tribal and Sufi-led communities dominated the rest. Moreover, in Algeria, French colonialism had a more drastic impact than in any other part of the Middle East or North Africa. French occupation and massive European colonization led to the total destruction of the old society and its elites, seizure of the land, impoverishment of the people, and the ruin of its educational facilities and culture. Only after World War I did a new intelligentsia take shape, consisting of a small elite of French-educated intellectuals, Communist-led worker radicals, and Muslim reformist educators.

Whereas the national elites in Turkey, Egypt, and Tunisia were relatively unified, in Algeria none of the subgroups was able to give political and ideological leadership to the country as a whole. In the course of the Algerian struggle for independence, militant revolutionary soldiers took charge. The soldiers who won Algerian independence then established a highly centralized military-bureaucratic regime and socialized economy in a shattered society. The military and technocratic elite concentrated upon the development of large petrochemical and associated industries, and neglected agricultural development and the peasant population. In a society shattered by colonialism and war, the political elite appealed to the one enduring aspect of the Algerian heritage – Islam – and tried to integrate reformist Islam with socialism. The state ministries tried to control schools, mosques, waqfs, and the training of clerics, but Muslim groups maintained their autonomy. Popular frustration with a deteriorating economy prompted demonstrations and riots throughout the 1980s, until the government was forced to recognize political parties and to hold elections. The victor in the 1990 elections for local offices was the FIS, a coalition of Muslim parties, but the military refused to accept the results or to hold further elections. There followed a vicious civil war which seems to have resulted in the maintenance of military rule after the loss of some one hundred thousand lives. The army remains in power; the Islamic opposition, defeated, remains latent. As in Egypt, Islamic-national identity has not prevented a lasting split between the state and the opposition, each invoking the name of Islam.

Islamic-national societies in Southeast Asia

The Muslim societies of Southeast Asia became independent under the aegis of secular national regimes, but these regimes were coupled with active and competing Islamic movements, and have gradually evolved from secular to Islamic-national identities. The Southeast Asian combination of secular state and Islamic challenge had its origins in the historical structures of Indonesian societies as modified by the Dutch. Whereas in the territories of the former Ottoman empire, modern secular states were built upon a historical legacy of strong state regimes which dominated the religious elites – a legacy which could be transformed into legitimate secular state domination in the twentieth century – in Southeast Asia the historical states were weak and decentralized but were firmly legitimized in non-Muslim cultural terms. Their non-Islamic cultural identity, rather than their political strength, formed the basis for the secularization of Indonesian twentieth-century national society. Similarly, the historical segmentation of Indonesian and Malaysian societies into separate state, religious, and village milieus permitted autonomous religious movements based on non-state communal structures.

The Dutch empire generated the transition from the old to the new forms of state and society. It set the geographical and administrative foundations for the modern state of Indonesia. Under Dutch tutelage, the Indonesian priyayi received a modern education and adopted secularist concepts. Thus they combined the non-Muslim aspects of priyayi culture with a Western orientation to become leaders of the nationalist movements. In reaction to the nationalism of the aristocrats, the Communist Party organized Indonesian intellectuals and workers to fight for a secular but socialist society.

At the same time extensive economic changes throughout the Indonesian archipelago and the Malay peninsula brought forth competing elites. In the Indonesian outer islands, Singapore, and the Malayan ports, economic change stimulated the rise of merchant groups and independent landowners who expressed their cultural and political interests in terms of reformed and modernized Islam. In Indonesia the reformist sensibility led in two directions. One was toward religious and educational reform as typified by the Muhammadiya movement. The other was political action as exemplified by Sarekat Islam. In response to the modernist movement, the rural 'ulama' organized their own political parties to defend village Islamic culture. Each of these movements built up a national following based on the aliran, or integrated community. By the time of independence Indonesian society was divided into several ideologically defined and competing communities.

The Indonesian movements waged a successful war to free Indonesia from Dutch rule, and then a post-independence struggle to define the identity of the independent Indonesian state. The nationalist and Communist politicians, supported by the army, sought to define the Indonesian nation in accord with the pançasila principles. The various Muslim movements wished to have Indonesia declared an Islamic state. In the decisive elections of 1955 the Muslims failed to win a majority, and between 1955 and 1960 were driven from political power. Then in the wake of civil war and the massacres of 1965 in which the Communists were virtually annihilated, a secular-oriented military elite led by General Suharto took power.

The military regime coopted Nahdatul 'Ulama', the party of the religious leaders, which accommodated secular rule in return for the protection of its interests in the Ministry of Religion and the villages, and brought other Muslim political groups under close government supervision. While some reformist Muslim associations remained active opponents of the regime and aspired to the formation of an Islamic state, most turned from politics to da'wa, or educational preaching and religious reform. They accepted the dominance of the military secular state and defined Islam as a communal religion and a personal belief system rather than a political movement, but they continued their campaign to imbue Indonesia with an Islamic identity. In the late 1970s and 1980s Islam became the base of a rising middle class, and the government gradually gave way to demands for schools and mosques, conference centers and think tanks. Nahdatul 'Ulama' regained its influence as a sponsor of Islamic morals, and in 1990 Suharto indicated his recognition that Islam was central to Indonesian identity by the creation of the Association of Indonesian Muslim Intellectuals to promote the Islamization of Indonesia. The collapse of the Suharto regime in 1998, however, left a political vacuum, weakened the military, opened the way for Muslim–Christian conflicts, and led to further demands by radical Muslim students and militias for the creation of an Islamic state.

Malaysia has also evolved toward an Islamic identity. It is divided between a majority Malay-Muslim population and substantial Chinese and Indian minorities.

Since independence the government and the ruling United Malay National Organization have tried to maintain a secular identity, giving preferential assistance to ethnic Malays but incorporating the minority communities into the political system. The Muslim dimension of Malay identity became ever more important, however, with the victories of the Pan-Malayan Islamic Party in the provinces of Kelantan and Trengganu and the eventual incorporation of its successor, the Islamic Party of Malaysia, into the national front in 1972. At the same time the migration of the rural population to the cities, and a growing student and middle-class urban population, led to an increased Muslim consciousness. The dissemination of Islamic education and propaganda, and the rise of missionary and revival movements, forced the state to redefine itself in Muslim terms. Under Prime Minister Mahathir (1981–present) Malaysia has increased its support for Islamic education at all levels, developed Islamic financial institutions, and defends Muslim interests in its foreign policy. While still trying to maintain a balance with the Chinese and Indian minorities, and a posture consistent with Malaysia's economic development as part of a global economy, Islam has become the salient dimension of Malay identity and Malaysian state policies.

THE NEO-ISLAMIC STATES

While the majority of modern national states in regions with substantial Muslim populations have adopted a secular or an Islamic-national identity, certain states are avowedly Muslim. These have included revolutionary Iran, Pakistan, Afghanistan, and Sudan and the conservative monarchies of Sa'udi Arabia and Morocco. Though all these states are nominally Muslim, they are Muslim in very different senses and for very different reasons.

Iran

Iran has a deep historical basis for the conflict between state and religious elites that has led to the present revolutionary regime. Unlike the Ottoman empire, where the state dominated the 'ulama' and controlled modern development, in Iran there has been a steady conflict between a relatively weak state and a relatively strong 'ulama' establishment. With the decline of the Safavid regime, and the succession of the Qajars, who ruled Iran for 150 years but were never able to control the country effectively, the power of the religious establishment was enhanced. By the end of the nineteenth century the state and religious establishments were in conflict over how to cope with Russian and British expansion. The 'ulama' and other intelligentsias organized mass protests against the government's surrender to foreign pressures. These confrontations culminated in 1891–92 in protests against the tobacco monopoly granted to British financiers, and in 1905–11 in the constitutional revolution that led to the creation of a short-lived parliamentary regime. The historical weakness of the state and the autonomy of religious, tribal, and other local communities made it possible to organize a revolutionary movement under Islamic auspices.

Iranian history in the twentieth century repeated the conflict of state and religion but changed the role of tribal and ethnic communities. The modern Iranian state was created by Reza Khan (later Shah), who came to power in 1925 and established a regime in the name of secular modernity and Persian nationalism. He built up a centralized army and administration, and laid the foundations for an industrial economy and for Western-type educational and legal systems. Above all he broke the power of Iran's tribal communities. Reza Shah was forced to abdicate in 1941 and was replaced by his son, Muhammad Reza Shah, who reigned until 1979. The restored regime was technically constitutional but the Shah ruled with virtually absolute powers. In 1963 he launched the "white revolution," for land reform, for the construction of a centralized secular national regime, and for the modernization of economic, educational, and social life along Western lines.

The Pahlavi regime diminished the power of the 'ulama', but not decisively. Secular education, government supervision of religious schools, new legal codes, reductions of funds, and other measures brought the 'ulama' for a time under state control. In the 1950s there was even a period of cooperation as the government lent tacit support to 'ulama' interests, including appointments at court and opportunities for enrichment through landowning and marriage into prominent families. In return the 'ulama' accepted the Baghdad Pact, and tolerated the government's policy of cooperation with foreign oil companies. The white revolution caused a break in this cooperative relationship, for it aroused 'ulama' concerns about the strengthening of state authority and provoked their hostility to the particular measures proposed. Equally important was the development of a reform movement which urged the 'ulama' to take collective responsibility for a better society. From Iraq, Ayatollah Khomayni became the main spokesman of the opposition to the monarchy.

The revival of Islamic religious and political consciousness, centered around 'ulama', intellectuals, students, and politicians, soon became a movement of mass opposition to the Shah. The deterioration of the Iranian economy in the 1970s, political oppression, and the scandal of its overt dependence on American support led to the formation of a coalition of radical guerrilla groups, liberal politicians, and 'ulama', who were able to mobilize mass support for a series of demonstrations that eventually brought down the Shah's regime. The revolution abolished the monarchy and established an Islamic government in Iran. Thus the long conflict between the state and the religious institution ended in the formation of an Islamic state.

Nonetheless, the Islamic Republic of Iran from 1980 to the present remains a national state, though in Islamic guise. The country is ruled by a double regime: on the one hand, an elected president, now Muhammad Khatami, and a liberal majority in parliament, favor a pluralistic democratic, and legally regulated modern Islamic society; on the other hand, a clerical elite headed by Ayatollah Khamene'i maintains an authoritarian control over the state through the institutions of the

Council of Guardians and the Office of the Superior Interests of the Islamic Republic, councils which can review the conformity of parliamentary legislation with Shari'a and overturn parliamentary laws and governmental regulations. The 'ulama' control the military and the intelligence services, the morals police and gangs of "vigilantes," and important sectors of the economy. Despite its defeat in national elections the clerical establishment still holds the upper hand in the control of the country. Under the Islamic regime the economy founders, but close controls are exerted over the appearance and activities of women. Despite its Islamic elite the new regime is driven by a strong sense of Iranian state interests, especially in foreign policy and by strengthened bureaucratic and military institutions. There is considerable continuity with the pre-Islamic regime of the Pahlavi Shahs.

The history of Iran thus differs from that of the Ottoman empire, where the state elites, committed by nineteenth-century changes to a secular concept of society, did not have to contend after World War I with serious tribal or ethnic opposition, could dominate the religious elites, and could create a modern Turkish state in their ideological image. In Iran, by contrast, the state, weakened by the tribal communities, could not prevent the consolidation of a religious establishment capable of opposing it. In the twentieth century the elimination of tribalism as a crucial third force led to a polarization between the state and the general society led by the 'ulama'. Thus in the Ottoman empire the historical strength of the state and the subordination of the religious establishment allowed the state elites to govern the direction of twentieth-century development, while in Iran the historical weaknesses of the state and the autonomy of the religious establishment allowed for national revolutionary struggle in the name of Islam. Owing to its peculiar historical balance of institutional powers, Iran has yielded an Islamic variant of a modern national state.

Pakistan

While Iran is a revolutionary Islamic state, Pakistan is dominated by a conservative military Islamic regime. Pakistan had its origins in the interaction of state, religious, tribal, and ethnic institutions embedded in the Mughal empire. The Mughals presided over a highly autonomous and pluralistic society organized into Muslim, ethnic, or tribal groups. When the empire was finally destroyed by the British there was no continuing Muslim state in the subcontinent to channel the further development of the society and no organized religious establishment to speak for its values.

The Muslims took a variety of positions, reflecting the class, religious, and ethnic structure of Mughal society. The Muslim bureaucratic and landowning lineages accepted the reality of British rule, and tried to maintain their class position. The former Mughal political elite adopted a Western-type education and advocated the modernization of Islam to make it consistent with the technical, cultural, and political order of the times. Out of this milieu came Aligarh, the Muslim League, and the Pakistan movement. This was the program of a secularized elite of landowners, office-holders, politicians, and journalists, who were not necessarily committed to the religious tradition, but were forced by their struggle against the British and competition with the majority Hindu population, combined with the deep-set ethnic, tribal, and local differences among Muslims, to promote an Islamic form of nationalism as a unifying symbol.

The Muslim religious leaders had their own program. They attempted to reconstruct Muslim society through the rational, disciplined practice of Islam based on the Quran and the teaching of the Prophet. While many religious leaders were hostile to the secularism of the League's leading politicians, the reform movement helped to create a sentiment of Muslim identity throughout the subcontinent. Thus, the political elites sought to define an essentially secular position in terms of Muslim political symbols – the only symbols capable of rallying the fragmented Muslim society confronted with Hindu opposition – while the religious elites concentrated upon moral and communal reform.

Despite its Muslim identity Pakistan was divided by profound ethnic and regional differences. Created out of the territories of Sind, Baluchistan, the Northwest Frontier provinces, West Punjab, and Bengal, it had an ethnic population consisting of Punjabis, Bengalis, Pashtuns, Sindhis, Baluchis, and others. The main problem of the state was to create a national identity to match the reality of new political boundaries and to generate an acceptable regime for a populace divided by a myriad of ethnic, linguistic, and ideological distinctions. With the fissure of Pakistan and Bangladesh, Bengali separatism prevailed over national unity.

Furthermore, Pakistan came into being with widely divergent concepts of what was meant by an Islamic state. The political elite considered Islam a communal and national identification, but a large segment of the populace, led by the 'ulama' and other religious leaders, believed that the new state should be dedicated to the formation of a society whose constitution, institutions, and routines of daily life were governed by Islamic law. To maintain their legitimacy, successive Pakistani regimes have declared their commitment to Islam. In the early 1970s Prime Minister Zulfiqar 'Ali Bhutto declared Pakistan an Islamic socialist republic, with all laws in principle in conformity with the Shari'a. His successor, General Zia ul-Haq, tried to legitimize a weak military state by calling for the creation of a total Islamic system, nizam-i mustafa, with Islamic politics, Islamic banking, and Islamic taxation, following the program of the Jama'at-i Islami. After his death in 1988, a chaotic decade of civilian rule ended in another military coup, and the current regime of General Pervez Musharaff, who has supported the Taliban in Afghanistan, and Muslim jihadists in Kashmir. Only under intense American pressure after the attacks on the World Trade Center and the Pentagon has he turned against the Taliban. Islam continues to be essential to a fragile national solidarity, and at the heart of both Pakistani identity and government policies.

Pakistan, then, is the product of a history different from that of Turkey and Iran. Unlike the Ottoman empire and Turkey, the state lacked power; unlike Iran, the religious elites lacked unity; unlike both, the ethnic minorities were very powerful. In

Pakistan no coherent national identity has emerged. The state continues as in 1947 to appeal to Islam to overcome the pluralistic heritage of the subcontinent. In Pakistan, in contrast to Iran, the Islamic revival has politically conservative implications.

Afghanistan

While the Islamic states of Iran and Pakistan are expressions of a national state structure, the emergence of Afghanistan as an Islamic state gave a contemporary turn to a profound history of ethnic and tribal divisions. Afghanistan is Pashtun in the east, Baluchi in the south, and Turkish, Tajik, Turkoman, Uzbek, and Hazara in the north. Historically, kings have been weak, and the country has been ruled by tribal Khans. In the late nineteenth century the Muhammadzai dynasty began a nearly century-long episode of consolidation and modernization of the society. 'Abdur Rahman (1880–1901) started a program of Tanzimat reforms to create a modern military and state bureaucracy, and his successors created schools to educate a new elite, reform the economy, and transform the status of women. In the cold war era of the 1960s and 1970s the United States and the Soviet Union competed for influence with the monarchy and with an ever larger but highly factionalized intelligentsia. As a result of factional struggles Communist intellectuals of the Khalq faction formed a pro-Soviet government in 1979. This government was opposed by an equally factional Afghan resistance, led by rival Muslim intellectuals whose goal was the establishment of an Islamic state, and who were supported by the United States, Pakistan, and Sa'udi Arabia. The opposition included Pashtun warriors affiliated with the Hizb-i-Islami, and Uzbeks, Hazaras, and Tajiks organized in the Jami'at-i Islami led by Burhanuddin Rabbani. Supported by jihadists from the Arab world and elsewhere, the Islamic resistance defeated the Soviet-backed government and drove the Russians from the country. They then fell to civil war among themselves, until eventually the Taliban, students from the religious schools of Pakistan's Northwest Frontier province, supported by Pakistan and the al-Qaeda network of Usama bin Laden, won control of most of the country. They consolidated an Islamic state, enforcing a punitive discipline upon women. In late 2001, as a consequence of the airplane attacks on the World Trade Center and the Pentagon, the United States went to war with Afghanistan, and overthrew the Taliban. In Afghanistan the creation of rival secular and Islamic intelligentsias, and the meddling of foreign powers, has led both to an Islamic state and to the destruction of most of the country.

Sa'udi Arabia

The conservative monarchical Muslim states such as Sa'udi Arabia and Morocco represent yet other types of historical development. The Sa'udi regime has its origins in an eighteenth-century movement of religious reform which enabled the family of Ibn Sa'ud to create a coalition of tribes which would dominate the Arabian peninsula. The Wahhabi movement legitimized a chieftainship based on the integration of lineage and religious authority. Though the Sa'udi state disintegrated in the nineteenth century, it was reconstructed and expanded in the twentieth on similar social and ideological lines. The continuity of religious legitimization was reinforced by the Saʿudi seizure of Mecca and Medina in 1926 and the assumption of the custodianship of the holy places. Despite the extraordinary economic transformation of the country, the Saʿudi state continues to be governed as the property of the ruling family. Their great oil revenues have allowed the Saʿudis both to employ and subsidize all sectors of the society, to make clients of their own population, and to patronize Muslim teaching and religious activities all over the world. Their control of education and public opinion means that Saʿudi society has been little affected by the waves of nationalism and secularism that have borne heavily upon other Arab countries. To maintain its authority the royal family leans to an ever more conservative form of Islam, conceding control of public morals to the mutawwiʿin, or morals police, and control of education and information to the ʿulamaʾ.

Nonetheless, an Islamic opposition has arisen which criticizes the regime for its corrupt lifestyle, for its military alliance with the United States, and for the intrusion of Western influences. In Saʿudi Arabia a tribal state given political cohesion by its advocacy of Islamic reformism, and transformed by its extraordinary oil revenues, renews emphasis upon Islam to legitimize the ruling family while its opponents appeal to the same Islam to overthrow it.

Morocco

Morocco, like Saʿudi Arabia, continues to be defined as an Islamic society. Like Saʿudi Arabia, its Islamic identity depends upon the continuity of its monarchy from the pre-colonial era to the present. As early as the fifteenth and sixteenth centuries the Sultans of Morocco emerged as religious leaders venerated for their descent from the Prophet and their Sufi achievements. For centuries they maintained a weakly centralized territorial state against the powerful tribal–Sufi coalitions that dominated the countryside. In the nineteenth century European commercial penetration – and finally, French occupation – subverted the state and led to the imposition of a foreign protectorate in 1912. The French, however, kept the Sultan as a figurehead for their rule, and behind this facade actually strengthened the state apparatus and undermined the political power of the tribal coalitions and the Sufi brotherhoods.

Moroccan resistance and the Moroccan struggle for independence were led by the young sons of established bourgeois families. The reformers mobilized intellectuals and urban workers for the struggle against the French, and by the 1940s the Sultan himself had become the titular head of the national resistance. To his traditional Sufi charisma the Sultan added the role of patron of Islam and the nation. With the coming of independence in 1956, his authority, reinforced by his role in the struggle for independence, made him as never before the principal Moroccan political figure. Islam, nationality, and monarchy became fully identified. While the Sultans also depended on the French centralization of state powers, Morocco bypassed the development of a secular intelligentsia and the transformations of regime and economy that have broken the historical continuity of other North African and Muslim societies. The Moroccan state may then be considered a modified traditional Islamic state which coopts and deflects Islamic opposition, like the Sa'udi, rather than a national-Islamic state like Iran and Pakistan.

MUSLIMS AS POLITICAL MINORITIES

A number of Muslim societies, however, have not been encadred under indigenous states but remain political minorities within states created by outside forces. This is the case for Muslims in China, India, and much of Africa, where they are a demographic and political minority.

These cases also fall into several types. In some cases the central issue is whether the Muslim populations will be able to define the political identity of mixed Muslim and non-Muslim societies on their own terms. Sudan is divided between a Muslim north and a non-Muslim south. The Arab-Muslim north attempts to extend its political control and religious identity to the other region. In Nigeria the northern emirates became committed to an Islamic identity in the nineteenth century. The commercialization of the northern economy and its new links to international markets further assisted the spread of Islam as a religion of traders, merchants, workers, and other mobile people. In the 1930s and 1940s Sufi brotherhoods helped integrate the various northern Nigerian ethnic and occupational groups into a more embracing society. The British, however, made the old Sokoto region part of a larger Nigerian state. With the coming of independence in 1960, the northern Muslim regions joined a secular national state in which Muslims formed a near majority. For two decades there was intense regional and ethnic conflict in Nigeria, but the 1970s brought a consolidation of the Nigerian federal state on the basis of military rule and the control of oil revenues.

In the complex struggle for power, Nigerian and Islamic identities have become ideological alternatives. Vis-à-vis the south, the north defines itself as Muslim. Northern elites, however, accept Nigerian nationality in order to collaborate with the non-Muslim southerners with whom they share control of the central government. To the extent that the elites stress Nigerian identity, the common people and student groups adopt Islam as the banner of resistance to military rule, economic injustice, and cultural confusion. In northern Nigeria Islam is now part of the political identity of all classes, but it has a different significance for each class or milieu, and is used both to legitimize the state and to motivate the opposition.

The 1980s and 1990s have witnessed increased Muslim militancy. The oil boom of the 1970s stimulated an Islamic revival. Muslims became increasing observant of Islamic norms for prayer, education, and social behavior, and increasingly by insistent that Shari'a law, Muslim festivals, and Muslim foreign policy interests be recognized by the national state. Muslim radicals want to make Nigeria a Muslim holy land. While Muslims in the Yoruba region are much more accommodating than Hausas, they also harbor strong revivalist movements and demands for the Islamization of the political system. Since 1999 numerous northern states have adopted Shari'a as their legal code. Muslim militancy contributes to a high level of tension with Christians. Since the 1980s, and especially since the end of military rule in May 1999, there have been riots and street fighting between Muslim and Christian mobs throughout the northern provinces.

In other situations, the problem for Muslim communities within non-Muslim societies is how to maintain their identity. The case of India, where Muslims form a minority of some 140,000,000 in a total population of more than a billion, is particularly important. Constant conflict between Hindus and Muslims has greatly increased Indian-Muslim awareness of their minority status. Despite some efforts toward assimilation or alliances with the Hindu majority, Indian Muslims have responded in the main by consolidating a separate communal identity stressing the maintenance of Shari'a, the endowment of Muslim schools, and the defense of Urdu and of their distinctive religious practices. In the 1980s and 1990s Sa'udi influences, and the growth of Muslim movements such as the Tabligh and the Ahl-i Hadith, stimulated Muslim self-assertion. Muslim parties have been formed to defend Muslim political interests, and Muslims bargain with the major political parties to gain support for privileges in employment, schooling, and cultural affairs. A corresponding Hindu revival, however, has generated demands that the state become a Hindu state. Hindu extremists call for the rejection of the Muslims as an unassimilable minority. India is polarized by religio-national communal identities. The secularity and neutrality of the state and its protection of Muslims seem ever more diminished.

China represents yet another type of Muslim minority situation. In the People's Republic of China the Muslim population falls into two main categories. The people of Xinjiang and other Muslim areas conquered in the nineteenth century have maintained a separate non-Chinese ethnic and communal identity under Chinese rule. Since the 1980s the state has tried to cultivate minority support with various benefits, while still trying to win control of minority regions by the settlement of Han Chinese. Nonetheless, underground resistance and demands for regional separatism have been growing in Xinjiang throughout the 1990s.

A second Chinese Muslim population are the Hui, who have for centuries been fully assimilated into the larger Han Chinese society to the extent of being physically and in public manners indistinguishable from Han Chinese. Yet the Hui maintain a persistent consciousness of separateness through their food customs, family rituals, occupations, memberships in clubs and associations, and self-proclaimed religious identity. In this case the crucial issue is not separateness, but the degree of acculturation or assimilation of the Muslim populations and the meaning of Muslim identity in a multi-national society.

THE ROLE OF WOMEN IN MUSLIM SOCIETIES

One of the most difficult issues in the contemporary transformation of Muslim societies is the role of women. Throughout the Muslim world important changes are taking place in the concept of male and female identity, in family roles, and in the place of women in public life. But our understanding of the nature of these changes is still extremely limited, partly due to a lack of adequate information and partly because the issues are clouded by intense and often ideological debate. Muslims differ profoundly among themselves. For outsiders it is difficult to separate their own values from the conceptions of dignity, security, and love that prevail in Muslim societies. Here we shall attempt only a tentative summary of some of the principal considerations in the contemporary discussion of the role of women in Muslim societies. These remarks are based primarily on the situation of Muslim peoples in the Middle East; other regions differ considerably.

The pre-modern Middle East to the eighteenth century

The pre-modern structures of Middle Eastern families, women's roles, and the concept of women's identity are little known, but there are a number of guiding considerations. In ancient pre-Islamic Near Eastern societies, the lives of women in the ruling classes were marked by seclusion and veiling. While the wives of kings, public officials, and warriors occasionally rose to unofficial positions of prominence, and substituted for men in moments of crisis, war, politics, and worship were men's work. Women of other classes were not secluded or veiled, and their roles were defined as household and craft work, care of children, and light agriculture, while heavy agricultural work, including plowing and irrigation, was done by men. Women's status, and their political and legal rights, probably deteriorated with the formation of the ancient temple communities and empires, though their economic roles, including property ownership, did not change. The monotheistic religions added a rationale for the inferiority of women and the need for their subordination to men; divorce rights tended to favor men.

Arabian and Quranic ethics both placed a higher value on the position of women in society. In pre-Islamic Arabia they were in various situations. In lineage groups organized on a patriarchal agnatic basis, women were indeed lesser beings, virtually chattels of the clans. In other communities they were much more independent, often living with their own tribes, with husbands as visitors. Women were also engaged in commerce. The Prophet's own wife Khadija was an independent businesswoman.

The Quran found a middle ground between the conflicting Arabian precedents. In general it strengthened the patriarchal clan, and left the prerogatives of men largely intact, but it also enhanced the status of women. Women were no longer seen merely as the mothers of warriors, but were recognized as persons of religious importance, entitled to modesty, privacy, and dignity. The Quran provided women with property rights, and rights to support in the case of divorce while pregnant. The Quran also favored mutuality in the relationships between husbands and wives, and counseled against hasty and willful divorces.

The period in which Quranic values defined Muslim mores, however, was short lived. After the Arab conquests, prior Byzantine and Sasanian concepts and practices prevailed over Arabian and Quranic values. Conquest and slavery enforced a turn toward polygamy, harems, and the subordination of women. Later Turkish and Mongol conquerors, among whom women had had prominent social roles, also succumbed to the Middle Eastern norm.

In the Islamic era from the seventh to the eighteenth centuries, in ideology and theory – and to a large degree in behavior – Middle Eastern societies made a relatively sharp division between men's and women's roles. The family and household was the domain of women. Though women were commonly employed in domestic crafts, agriculture, and stock herding, the middle- and upper-class ideal was isolation from the marketplace, politics, and social life with men. The pre-modern societies also assumed the dominance of men over women and public deference of women to the authority of men. In extended families and lineages women were subject to the authority of fathers, brothers, husbands, and husbands' male kin.

Male dominance was strongly supported by legal and social structures. Marriages were commonly arranged by families; a bride's male guardians were ultimately responsible for her welfare. A bride would ordinarily move to the house of her husband and reside with his kin. In Muslim law men had vast prerogatives to initiate divorce, while women had few. In the case of divorce, children beyond a certain age belonged to the husband and his family. In Muslim law, however, women had important economic rights. In many cases they could exercise these rights and maintain control over their own property, but in many other instances social practice restricted their opportunities to accumulate or inherit property. Contrary to Muslim law, customary law often allowed families to refuse women their Islamic right to inherit their share of the properties of husbands or other relatives.

The ideological and conceptual world of pre-modern Middle Eastern Muslim societies also required and legitimized male dominance. The prevailing ideologies held that men were physically stronger, more intelligent, and more suited to action, and must rule over women, who were more subject to their emotions. Women were identified with the undisciplined forces of nature; men with the order imposed by culture. The rule of men should, of course, be gracious and protective. This basic attitude was reinforced by the belief that the honor of a man and his family, lineage, or tribe depended upon the honorable conduct of the women. As a consequence of these attitudes, in men's eyes, women's sexuality was the essential aspect of their femininity.

However, this concept of the relations between men and women has to be modified to take into account important economic and social realities. The relations between the sexes were more complicated than is implied in the simple concepts of male dominance and social segregation. While women had a lesser role in the "public" sphere, the "public" domain was much smaller in pre-modern than in modern societies, and families played a much larger part in economic life and politics. Women were commonly the custodians of the family social status, and they had the principal roles in arranging marriages and maintaining reciprocal relations with other families. Educated upper-class women taught the Quran and the sayings of the Prophet to the girls in their family networks. The nominal domain of women was thus more consequential than it would seem today.

Other factors could also give women considerable autonomy – and even dominance – in domestic affairs. In the direct relations between husbands and wives, wives' personal influence, manipulation of husbands, women's conspiracies and intrigues, threats to humiliate husbands by denouncing them for neglect or impotence, and setting sons against fathers all worked to subvert the domestic power of the males. The dependence of men upon domestic life and the opinion of their neighbors and kin also helped to equalize the relationship between husbands and wives. Furthermore, women had their own bases of social and personal autonomy in women's friendships and social gatherings. The world of women was full of symbols and rituals that belittled and excluded men.

Moreover, the relationships between men and women and women's standing in the public world were not fixed by the culture system, but varied with context. In the Ottoman era, upper-class women were more likely to be confined to the harem or household, but they also had the resources and opportunities to take control of their lives and advance their interests. They became property owners through inheritance, dower, and as beneficiaries of waqfs. They endowed waqfs and held timars, tax-farms, and business partnerships. In the Ottoman household they exercised a measure of the state's sovereignty. In Mamluk Egypt they controlled tax-farms, endowments, land, and residential and commercial property. In Aleppo they owned houses and commercial properties. Wherever power was localized in households, they had more than was possible in bureaucratic states. Educated women were often valued for their opinions on religious, family, and political matters.

Lower-class women also had a measure of independence because of economic activities. Women played a significant economic role in animal husbandry, agriculture, home crafts, and cottage industries. Rural women produced tents, bedding, clothing, mats, rugs, sacks, pottery and baskets, both for the household and the market. They acted as healers, midwives, cooks, prostitutes, musicians, savants, and traders. In the towns women did embroidery, and washed, carded, and spun wool. Women's lending and marketing networks were a source of income. While there were important variations by region and class, the economic contributions of women's incomes and assets, and their control over the distribution of family food and other resources, gave them a considerable familial and social power. Lower-class women also had more mobility. In eighteenth-century Mosul, for example, women visited tombs and took part in Sufi ceremonies. In Cairo they went on picnics and visited tombs.

Even in legal terms, the practice of the courts created situations different from the texts of the law. Wealthy women used the courts to get marital advantages not envisioned in strict Shari'a, such as opportunities for divorces and annulments, control of dower, custody of children, and restricting a husband's rights to take another wife. Seventeenth- and eighteenth-century fatwas from Syria and Palestine show that even though qadis believed in the gender superiority of men, they helped women by enforcing their rights and widening the grounds for divorce or annulment granted at the woman's initiative. The law schools also differed considerably in their norms for family relations, and could be manipulated to gain advantages in given situations. Though Malikis insisted on a guardian for a first marriage, Hanafis allowed women to marry by themselves. While Hanafis had little leeway for annulment, Malikis allowed for it for desertion, non-maintenance, or bodily harm. Nonetheless, women's options were much more limited than those of men. Women still had to operate within the framework of unequal power and unequal legal rights, and find whatever amelioration they could.

Thus the personal relations and attitudes of men and women toward each other had several dimensions, corresponding to the complexity of their social and economic roles. Women were not only erotic objects, but to some degree were partners in earning a living and in family relations. While, from an outside point of view, men were dominant, women cannot be thought of as an oppressed class. They did not see themselves as forming a collectivity with interests opposed to those of men. They saw themselves as playing a valued, legitimate, and important role in family and social life, one that differed from but was complementary to that of men.

Women and the emergence of the national state system: 1900 to the 1970s
The late nineteenth and twentieth centuries brought major changes in the position of women. Women were profoundly affected by the impact of European imperialism, by domestic political and economic reforms, by the entrance of the Middle East into new economic orbits, and by the introduction and circulation of new ideas about marriage and gender. In Egypt and Syria, the growth of European trade and the spread of the cash economy heightened the sexual divisions of labor, with men working in the fields and women doing household economy work. Over time, however, the importation of European textiles destroyed many local industries, and drove women from household work into mills, and carpet, silk, and lace-making factories. Twentieth-century changes tended to push women further out of agriculture and pastoralism as these become wage activities, and made them more into consumers and workers in handicraft production geared toward export. Wage labor reduced women to piece-work, took them out of home or neighborhood workshops, and raised moral questions about their exposure to strange men.

As the European powers extended their economic, military, and political control over the region, they brought with them a host of ideas about the allegedly backward position of women in the Islamic world, and used those notions to justify and legitimize their dominion. Travelers, merchants, and colonial officials alike recorded their impressions of such things as the harem, polygamy, and the veil, and colonial officials determined that the region's political and economic reform would be complete only if women were rescued from the harem, unveiled, and given the legal rights (including the right to monogamous marriages) that Western women enjoyed. As ruling elites in Istanbul, Cairo, and the Arab provinces struggled to consolidate and maintain their power they introduced new standards and ideas about women, marriage, and the family.

Drawing on their education, contacts with Europeans, and on the policies of colonial administrations, a new generation of Egyptian intellectuals, professionals, and civil servants began discussing the role of women in the economic and political futures of their societies. Schools, student missions to Europe, and print journalism disseminated their ideas. Westernized intelligentsias proposed the emancipation of women and their integration into the society as full equals of men, and opposed veiling, seclusion, and the lack of education for women. The education of women would save them from idle and empty lives, fit them for employment, and train them for harmonious marriages and the raising of children. Only through a modern education, they argued, could women fulfill their domestic roles as mothers and the educators of modern youth. They argued further that the freedom of women was essential for the freedom of the whole society, and that their emancipation – and the equality of men and women in public roles – was necessary for the creation of modern national states. Reformers favored the nuclear family as a necessary condition of a moral and modern society.

The intelligentsias took up the cause of women for several reasons. First, it was part of their attempt to secularize Muslim societies, separate state and religion, reduce the domain of Islamic law, and repudiate established political authorities. Intelligentsias desired, by playing up the condition of women, to show their own emancipation and modernity, and to affirm the value of individuality expressed through personal achievement. The condition of women was used to highlight the backwardness of society. A change in women's status was a symbol of their demands for a change in the whole social order.

Yet early modernizers and nationalists discussed the "woman question" without regard for real women, treating them only as symbols of their political projects. To replace the Ottoman Islamic identity with a new Turkish identity, Ziya Gokalp presented women as the embodiment of ancient Turkish society, which had been smothered by Islam. Ataturk too promoted the emancipation of women as the condition for a new era of democracy and liberation. Through the education of women Turkey would come to its true self without having to imitate the West. In Egypt, Qasim Amin adopted the European trope that the education of women was the key to the reform of the nation. He argued that nations would progress or fail as a consequence of the position of women. In turn-of-the-twentieth-century Iran, too, women were in the minds of male theorists a symbol of modernity rather than the beneficiaries of liberation. Nationalism often used women but failed to improve their condition.

The earliest practical reforms came in nineteenth-century Ottoman society, where the first demands for the modernization of the position of women called for monogamy in the royal household, the elimination of concubinage, and greater freedom for women in marriage and social activity. The first school for girls was established in 1863, and it was followed by a spate of missionary schools in the 1870s. Between 1908 and 1919 numerous secondary schools were inaugurated, and the university was opened to women in 1915. During World War I, women had to work in factories, banks, the postal service, municipal offices, and hospitals, and their experience opened the way for later reforms. In 1924 education was made compulsory for both sexes. In Turkey, the companionate monogamous nuclear family was advanced as an ideal, and came to be accepted in practice as well. Polygamy was abolished in 1924, and women were given the same rights to divorce as men, marking the emergence of the educated woman and the monogamous couple along with the birth of modern Turkey.

In Egypt Isma'il Pasha (1863–79) opened primary schools for girls, and the first secondary school in 1873. At the same time, missionary and private schools opened all over Egypt, and even those upper-class Egyptians who were reluctant to send their daughters to school had them privately tutored by Westerners. Despite the fact that the colonial government in Egypt spent as little money as possible on education, the system of public education continued to grow, and to introduce Egyptian boys and girls to European-style curricula. By 1913 there were about 2,600 girls, about 12 percent of the students, in primary schools. Finally, in 1929 women were allowed to enter the university. In Iran, upper- and middle-class women were more frequently educated, though women continued to lead segregated lives. As in Turkey and Egypt, missionary and foreign private schools began to educate the daughters of the elite from the turn of the century, and the first public school for girls was opened in 1918. When Reza Shah Pahlavi took the throne, he, like Ataturk, made reform of the status of women the project of a modernizing state.

As the result of educational reforms, women began to speak on their own behalf, and to articulate platforms that had to do with the needs and desires of "real" – as opposed to "symbolic" – women. Women's newspapers emerged in Egypt, Turkey, Iran, and Syria. *The Young Woman* was founded in Alexandria in 1892 and was followed in 1895 by the Turkish-language *Ladies' Own Gazette*. Women's educational and charitable organizations were founded in conjunction with publications. Educated, middle-class women also started social clubs and salons. Thus, the first movements to advance women's interests came into being. In the Ottoman empire, Fatma Aliye Hanem, daughter of a Tanzimat reformer, used the press to advance her ideas about women as wives, mothers, and Muslims, publishing a book on women as early as 1891. In the period between 1908 and 1916, a number of women's societies were formed, including the Society for the Elevation of Women and the Society for the Defense of the Rights of Women in 1908. Such organizations engaged in philanthropic activities, and encouraged the advancement of women's position in Ottoman society. In Egypt Huda Sha'rawi founded the Muhammad 'Ali Organization to provide schools, workshops, residences, and a dispensary for poor women. In Iran, women's organizations and periodicals advocated women's education, hosted debates on veiling, and promoted women's professional training. The Women's Freedom Society, founded in 1906, provided women with a forum in which to debate and discuss such topics as the differences between women in Eastern and Western societies and the position of women in Iran.

Social activism was followed by political engagement. Some women were content to play the idealized roles of wives and mothers, while others wanted to be free to participate in the politics of independent nations. Women joined in the nationalist movements, working alongside men for emancipation from colonial rule, without challenging patriarchal ideas or presenting a feminist agenda. In Turkey, the mobilization of men for World War I meant that women were needed for labor, allowing for unparalleled opportunities in the workforce. In Egypt separate women's political groups were formed in conjunction with the Wafd. In the 1920s Women's Committees to Defend Palestine engaged in demonstrations. In 1923 Egyptian women founded the Egyptian Feminist Union. In Iran, women were active in the Tobacco Rebellions of 1890 and the constitutional revolution of 1905–11. The National Ladies' Society of 1910, for example, participated in strikes and boycotts, and called for the ejection of foreigners from Iran. It was only with the assumption of power by Reza Khan Pahlavi in 1925 that feminist agendas were subsumed by the state.

In the decades after World War I newly independent states, such as Turkey and Iran, became the most powerful forces in changing the condition of women. States and ruling elites used the family issue to help consolidate their power, mobilize women for the labor force, undermine tribal communities, and create a symbolic identity for new nations. The nuclear family was seen as more compatible with industrialization and the centralization of state power than was the extended family. Under the auspices of the Turkish state, the University of Istanbul was made coeducational in 1921; primary education was made compulsory for both sexes in 1924. Women were given the same legal rights as women in Europe by the adoption of the Swiss civil code in 1926. The new family law enshrined the principle of monogamy, the right of women to obtain divorces, and their formal equality in inheritance matters. They were given the right to vote in municipal elections in 1930 and in national elections in 1934.

In Iran, Reza Shah similarly promulgated measures to modernize the status of women. In the 1930s education and public entertainments were opened to women. The veil and the *chador* were outlawed. While men retained important legal privileges in family matters, the age of marriage was standardized, marriages had to be registered in court, and child marriages and temporary marriages were made more difficult. However, less was accomplished in fact than on paper. The reforms of the Pahlavi regime did not go far enough to undermine patriarchal culture, and all independent women's organizations were replaced by a state-sponsored Women's Center. The Shah's abdication in 1941 destroyed almost all of the gains made in the previous two decades. In the 1950s and 1960s, however, women again benefited from the authoritarian Pahlavi regime. New family laws were promulgated in 1967 and 1973; these discouraged polygamy and made it harder for men to obtain unilateral divorces. They gave women equal rights to institute divorce proceedings, though the criminal code still allowed a man to murder his adulterous wife, sister, or daughter in the name of family honor. Women, moreover, did not usually have the economic power to activate legal rights. While the presence of women in the civil service rose to 28 percent – mainly in teaching, nursing, and clerical jobs – laws regulating working conditions did not apply to small shops with fewer than ten employees, and so did not benefit poor working women. In Iran the modernization process did not go far enough to transform the structures underlying male domination and female subordination. The lack of democratic institutions also impeded the formation of a genuine women's movement.

In Egypt the reforms inaugurated by Nasser resulted in what is considered the golden age of women's rights in the Middle East. In order to industrialize, modernize, and secularize Egypt, Nasser provided for women's suffrage, education, and employment. Women entered all the professions, assisted by maternity leave and childcare. They were elected to public office. Nonetheless, because there were no women in the military they were excluded from the highest positions of the state. Sadat overturned the single-party system created by his predecessor, and further expanded women's participation in government, especially for upper-class women who had education, organizing skills, and experience in voluntary organizations. In 1979 Sadat introduced a quota system to allocate thirty parliamentary seats and 10–20 percent of seats on government councils nationwide for women. When Mubarak repealed Sadat's quota system in 1986, women turned to the syndicates of lawyers, doctors, and engineers for representation.

In several Arab Middle Eastern countries, women have been educated and integrated into the labor force in varying degrees. In Arab countries such as Egypt, Iraq, Lebanon, and Tunisia women are employed in industrial labor. Iraq, for example, facilitated the employment of women by providing state-subsidized housing and childcare. Female workers are enrolled in unions and federations, but these organizations are closely controlled by the state. Women with professional skills in government, teaching, and medicine find employment in state bureaucracies in Egypt, Kuwait, and elsewhere. Women, of course, continue to work in the informal sector at home, in local workshops, peddling, and other enterprises. Most importantly, however, the state has not only changed the economic position of women, but by the promotion of educational, health, and social welfare programs, has usurped traditional family roles. Women have become clients of the public sector; state employees have been substituted for the male members of the family as the principal source of important services. Women increasingly have dealt with men who are not kin as employers, teachers, bureaucrats, and colleagues.

In politics women have been important in the revolutionary struggles of Iran, Algeria, and Yemen, and in the Palestinian movement. These movements mobilized women to demonstrate, organize, make speeches, and even to fight, but the post-revolutionary period in several of these countries brought a reaction and a withdrawal of women from active politics. In general women's roles were construed as auxiliary to men's, and women were denied full rights of political participation. Iran in the 1930s, Iraq, and Egypt all made women's organizations dependent upon the state and forbade autonomous activities. Nationalist movements in opposition tended to be supportive of feminist objectives; in power they viewed them as subversive. Only in Egypt and Iran in the 1960s were women given the right to vote.

In the Palestinian case, women have served both as symbols of the ideals of the community and as fighters in the struggle against Israel. Women played an active role in the Palestinian uprising of 1936–39, sometimes on the front lines, oftentimes providing medical care, smuggling arms, sewing uniforms, and collecting funds. After 1948, women came under pressure to represent the moral and cultural values of the Palestinian past, rather than play an activist political role. The two intifadas, or uprisings against Israel's military occupation of the West Bank and the Gaza Strip, however, brought women fully into the public realm, relaxing traditional gender and familial roles. During both uprisings, women engaged in the fighting, even as suicide bombers. At the same time, as men were killed, arrested, deported or imprisoned, women had to act as heads of family, household, and community.

The relaxing of gender roles in the struggle for Palestinian independence meets with resistance from men, and Palestinian feminists fear that women will be forced back into traditional roles once the struggle is over. Under the Palestinian National Authority women have been subsumed under men's groups, and both secular and Islamist groups have coopted or demoralized women's movements. Palestinian citizenship is defined in patrilineal terms.

In legal and family matters, the tendency in Muslim countries from the 1950s to the 1970s was to ameliorate the position of women, but in matters of family law, no Arab country has followed the example of Turkey and completely eliminated Muslim religious law as the basis of modern civil law. (Tunisia is the closest approximation.) Arab countries reinterpreted Shari'a in order to accommodate it to contemporary needs rather than reject it altogether in favor of foreign legal systems. States implemented legal reforms, sometimes by legislation, sometimes by new procedural requirements, sometimes by picking and choosing among the provisions of the traditional law schools.

Generally, the conjugal family was strengthened against wider kinship ties by requiring a woman's personal consent to a marriage, legislating a minimum age to avoid child marriage and to minimize parental domination, removing male guardians, and by providing court relief for abuse, and improved custody rights. Polygamy was restricted, but only Turkey, Tunisia, Israel, and the Soviet Union denied it to their Muslim populations. Morocco and Lebanon did not directly restrict polygamy, but made it possible for women to insert restrictive clauses into marriage contracts. Tunisia required the consent of both potential spouses for a valid marriage, but in Morocco a guardian might still speak for a woman. Divorce regulations were changed to increase the power of women, and most countries curtailed the freedom of husbands to repudiate a marriage. In many cases divorce has been taken out of the hands of husbands by laws that require a court to issue a decree of dissolution of marriage. Only Iran (before the revolution) and South Yemen abolished unilateral repudiation completely.

Inheritance laws remained unchanged except to allow orphaned grandchildren to become legal heirs. In Egypt this was done by permitting grandfathers to mandate inheritance in their wills; in Pakistan it was done by assigning a direct share to orphaned grandchildren. Similarly, there were tendencies to consider the welfare of children in custody provisions. Many countries gave the courts the right to grant custody of a child at their discretion, though Islamic law specifies that after a certain age the children come into the possession of the husband.

Alongside state formation, economic development, urbanization, and modern bureaucratic and industrial organizations also helped break down traditional families, promoted nuclear households, and favored the incorporation of women into the workforce. Contemporary societies gave women important roles in NGOs, charities, and syndicates. At the same time the mass media generated new values, tastes, fashions, and fads, and above all the awareness of Western lifestyles. Middle Eastern and Muslim women began to value individual autonomy, choice in marriage, independent households, and self-fulfillment through love and work.

The degree of change differed in the various Middle Eastern countries. In most countries the trends toward emancipation of women from the household and toward increased education and employment affected the urban upper and middle classes. In Turkey, for example, there was virtually complete legal equality but only upper- and middle-class women in urban areas actually received secondary or higher education and were professionally employed. Turkish women made up a substantial percentage of the medical, legal, and other professional workforces. The position of lower-class women was also changed, but in less attractive ways. Female migrants to the cities sometimes became laborers. Lower-class women in rural areas engaged in agriculture when men left home to work in Europe.

In the Arab countries compulsory education was instituted for both boys and girls, but women still lagged behind men in education and literacy. Many people felt that education for girls came at the expense of necessary household labor and childcare, or that it would ruin a girl's morals and her chances for a good marriage. There were also strong objections to integrated schools, though schools for girls were insufficient in number. In such countries as the Sudan, Iraq, and Egypt, however, there was a very high proportion of female students in higher education, and in scientific and technical professions, especially in teaching and nursing. While there have been important gains in the employment of women, women in Arab countries seemed to participate less in the workforce than women in other less developed countries such as those of Latin America. In general, family and social attitudes and low educational attainment continued to depress the absorption of women into the workforce.

Arab family practices were also changing between the 1950s and the 1970s, but only to a limited extent. The impetus for this adjustment was not so much economic and industrial change as Western cultural influences, the spread of egalitarian concepts, and nationalist ambitions for a larger contribution from women to the general society. In Lebanon, Jordan, and other Arab countries the extended family, once the ideal, was much diminished in practice. Marriages were less commonly arranged by parents; daughters were more usually consulted. The age of marriage for women was rising. There were still, however, strong preferences for endogamy, and for marriages among cousins or within a neighborhood or village. Even where families were fully nucleated there were strong social and residential ties to extended families. Polygamy was declining, but it was still found in rural areas and among the well-to-do classes.

Thus, the first half of the twentieth century posited new levels of women's integration into public life through unveiling, education, employment, and political participation. The modern national state attempted to redefine family structure and women's roles in order to enhance its powers, break down opposition kin groups, and mobilize workers for the labor force. It also generated a more intense set of obligations for women within the family, where they were supposed to become scientific managers of the household and raise children to fit the new world. The bourgeois nuclear family became the ideal in the interest of the rationalization of family and work.

In general, the barriers to change were formidable. The traditional status of women worked against further change. Limited education, illiteracy, economic dependency, lack of employment opportunities, social segregation, and male hostility to the social or political involvement of women inhibited the new trends. Some of the deepest barriers to change were the cultural values with which both men and women were imbued from childhood. In most Middle Eastern societies the traditional concepts of male superiority and family honor remained potent. Correspondingly, the highest values assigned to women were related to fertility and motherhood, and women were imbued with the expectation of security, protection, and esteem in the family context – values that do, in fact, bring emotional and social gratification. Furthermore, deep within Middle Eastern cultures is the fear of uncontrolled sexuality. These attitudes reinforced the political and economic forces that inhibited further change.

How much did women actually benefit in practice from reform? In many cases the state gave token rights but actually deprived women of the economic and political means to realize those rights and in some cases continued to enforce patriarchal laws and cultural values. Women were not so much liberated as subjected to another mode of regulation. Whether women could actually make use of legal and social changes depended very much on their immediate family and communal con-

texts. Women often would not claim their legal or social rights lest it hurt their overall position in the family or community.

Thus, there were no universally accepted models for women's roles in society,
and no widely enough accepted values to legitimize one system of practice or
another. Change therefore generated doubt, anxiety, and conflict: conflict between
generations over the right to choose a spouse, conflict between mothers-in-law and
wives for the allegiance of sons and husbands, and conflict between men and
women over educational and employment opportunities. In many countries men
found themselves economically and socially oppressed, often humiliated by political helplessness, and wanted to be compensated by control over women, precisely
at a moment when women were asserting their own rights to a fuller public life.

Women and the Islamic revival

At this uncertain juncture in the 1970s, the Islamic revival reopened the debate
about the role of women. The debate over women has become the battleground
for the broader issues of secularization versus Islamization, state power versus
communal autonomy, and Westernization versus cultural authenticity. Can there be
indigenous projects of modernity that define new roles for women without their
becoming Western? Can there be an indigenous, even an Islamic, modernity? This
debate is highly politicized, and all the positions reflect political, ideological, and
religious agendas.

The critical debates have been between traditionalist interpreters of the Quran,
modernist interpreters of the Quran, and more radical feminist critics, who all differ
on questions of polygamy, veiling, the economic rights of women, inheritance, and
employment. The traditionalists argue that the Quranic texts are normative and
specify eternally valid rules, but even they differ in their judgments about the social
roles of women. Some believe the Quran requires that women be lodged in the
home and have no public role; they should be subordinate to men in order to
protect their modesty. Islamist movements generally espouse these values. Radical
Islamists in Algeria, Sudan, Afghanistan, Iran, Morocco, Nigeria, and elsewhere
have tried to ensure separateness by restricting the freedom of movement of
women in public spaces unless they are fully covered. They condemn the employment of women outside the home, oppose political participation, and denounce
contrary values as a sign of Westernization. They favor a return to Islamic family
law, which enhances gender differences and the disparity of legal rights. In many
countries there has in fact been a reversal of the legislation of earlier decades, and
a re-Islamization of law. In Algeria, for example, the legal code of 1984 recognized
the rights of male guardians in marriage arrangements, permitted polygamy, and
gave husbands the right of unilateral divorce.

Other traditionalists, equally committed to the Quran and hadith, accept public
roles for women. More nuanced views are expressed in Egypt. While the association of feminism with capitalism, colonialism, and Western influence has made it

suspect, traditionalists and Islamic revivalists approve the twentieth-century idea of the nuclear family. Their call for a return to the home means to a twentieth-century home defined by bourgeois marriage ideals. Since the core of the feminist and modernist project turns on the breakdown of the extended family and of the women's societies that interfere with the concentration of husband and wife on each other and their children, Islamists, in effect, accept the basic concept of modernity. Islamists also accept women's education. They are not quite sure about employment. Some see work outside the home as a source of temptation, but many recognize that two working persons are necessary for a middle-class lifestyle. They often accept women's employment with strictures about proper dress and conduct.

There is also a broad range of Muslim "feminist" opinion. A new kind of Islamist women's movement has emerged in Egypt. Women studying Muslim ethics are imbued with Sufi concepts of spirituality. They discuss the problems of daily life and try to make ethical judgments on Muslim terms. These women are conservative in their social views, and do not wish to disrupt the historical male prerogatives, but they nonetheless take responsibility for their behavior and seek to shape their family life in accord with Muslim ethics. They are independent female actors without feminist or modernist goals.

Other Muslim feminists, however, hold that Islam is in principle favorable to active roles for women in contemporary societies. They argue that the Quran is descriptive of a given time and place, and that with changes in historical and social conditions new adaptations are necessary. Quranic norms concerning women's status in the family have to be treated as ethical injunctions rather than legal requirements. They see the Quran as being supportive of the integration of women in society now that this has become essential to the fulfillment of family functions.

A more conservative version of this sort of "feminism" holds that Islam inculcates a high standard of sexual and marital morality, provides for the protection and security of women, and guarantees many legal and property rights. In its historical context, and in the present, Islam has had an uplifting and civilizing effect upon the actual relations between men and women in Middle Eastern societies. Such feminists call for education and work roles for women, but are not interested in unveiling. They accept the Islamic discourse on the differences between men and women.

Yet another variant of an Islamist modernity for women, or Islamist feminism, emerged in the 1980s in Turkey among provincial women who demanded education and work, but wore the hijab to facilitate their entry into the public world. Egyptian women similarly see the hijab as a statement of the right to be present in public places. Throughout the Muslim world the adoption of hijab, which is supposed to be a sign of submissiveness to Islam, also serves to legitimize and facilitate trips to hammam or beauty salon, school, and work.

More radical Muslim feminists attempt to reinterpret the Quran in a way favorable to the full equality of women. They use Islamic arguments based on the Quran and the reinterpretation of the Shari'a to legitimize women's education and employment. They hold that early Islam enhanced the position of women in Arabian society, and that not Islam itself, but the historical conditions of Middle Eastern societies, are to blame for the subordination and segregation of women. A full and equal role for women is inherent in the true Islam. This type of feminism is most common among Muslim women outside the Middle East or South Asia. In most cases, feminist projects have to tack between indigenous values and Western examples.

Some feminists, however, are highly critical of their societies. There is widespread agreement that female segregation and subordination is in part the product of patriarchal authority and male-based kinship groups which think of women as part of a group and act on their behalf, though they note that Middle Eastern Muslim societies do not from this point of view much differ from Mediterranean European or Latin American societies. Many critics see Islam as reinforcing this subordination. They argue that the most profound teaching of Islam is the subordination of human beings to God and avoidance of any life experiences in politics, art, or love that compete with this ultimate religious demand. The Islamic concept of man as the slave or servant of God, the humble, unassuming devotee of the divine being, is the model for the relations between males and females. Islam, they say, requires male control over females because of the perceived threat of uncontrolled sexuality and because of the potential for women to create allegiances that compete with man's obligation to God. From this point of view Islam is intrinsically hostile to the equality of women and to the development of a full person-to-person love relationship between men and women. The teachings of the Quran, Islamic law, and the moral attitudes carried by the 'ulama' have further cultivated a climate of opinion leading to the subordination of women.

Iran today is the principal battleground over the roles of women in contemporary Muslim societies. The Iranian revolution at first attracted widespread female support. Intellectuals identified the true Islam with modernity, including progress, autonomy, freedom, education, and justice. Women who supported the Islamic revolution came from three groups: lower-class women following their men interested in the betterment of material conditions – poor women attracted by the provision that husbands are responsible for the care and feeding of their wives; middle-class bazaari families accepting their men's values; and educated women hostile to foreign influences. Women who participated in the revolutionary demonstrations believed that they were defying the West and that the revolution would lead to democracy. The revolution also appealed to a fascist consciousness: subordination to the leader, dogmatism, lower-middle-class populism, and association of homeland with family and religion.

Once in power the revolution rapidly implemented a radical Islamist program. Women were immediately required to wear the hijab in the workplace. Men and women were segregated in schools. Public flogging and stoning were instituted for men and women accused of committing adultery. The minimum age for marriage for women was lowered from eighteen to thirteen, and restrictions on polygamy were removed. The family protection laws were rescinded, making it easy for men to repudiate a marriage, and very difficult for women to do so. A woman could obtain a divorce only if her husband was economically incapable of supporting a wife, impotent, infertile, insane, or absent for more than six months. These measures were part of a family policy meant to stabilize marriages and encourage the birth of children. The government sponsored matchmaking, and financial assistance was given to newlywed couples. The state declared itself in favor of motherhood. Marriage was pronounced a "divine" institution, for God had given men economic power, and women reproductive power. Huge families were encouraged, and were called "Islamic." The new laws, however, proved to be counterproductive and led to an increase in divorces. In 1989 Iran tried to strengthen the position of women somewhat by giving them broader rights to stipulate conditions for a divorce in marriage contracts and by requiring that all divorces be registered with the courts.

In public life women kept the right to vote, to be elected to parliament, and to hold cabinet positions, but they were excluded from the courts. After 1982 only certain university subjects were deemed proper for women: nursing, education, and theology. Women were excluded from vocational education in fields such as agriculture, veterinary medicine, geology, and engineering, though after 1990 women were allowed to reenter technical professions when the state realized that there was a shortage of trained personnel. Conversely, men were barred from fashion design, gynecology, and nursing. These constraints were justified by a discourse that said that the disciplining of women's instincts was necessary for social order. Islamic discourse is backed by Iranian popular culture, with its traditional images of women's weakness, segregation, and gender hierarchy.

The greatest efforts to restrict the activities of women have promoted the most energetic feminist reaction in the Muslim world. Educated women were repelled by the Khomayni program, but no one could publicly defy or reject Islamic norms – it would be blasphemy and treason at the same time. Iranian women instead have found private ways to express their dissent. They find subtle language and gestures to protest against misogyny. They make their own interpretations of the life of Fatima, the daughter of Muhammad. Women's magazines such as *Payam-i-Hajar* call for relief for working women. *Zanan* advocates reinterpreting the Quran, and calls into question male clerical interpretations. Within the Islamic framework, women are becoming more active. There are female preachers. They are present in mosques, discussing the Quran. Iranian feminists are trying to create a new form of Islamic feminism which transcends the opposition of secularism and Islam, Westernism and indigenous culture.

The question of the veil, or more accurately women's clothing which covers both face and the shape of the body, has become the focal issue of debate in the current Islamic revival. The veil is usually taken as a symbol of the domination of women by men, but in fact it symbolizes the complexities of their relationships. The wearing of the veil was not, and is not, universal among Middle Eastern and

Muslim women. It was commonly worn by urban and middle-class women but not by working, peasant, and nomadic women. Indeed, upward social mobility and urbanization stimulated the wearing of the veil.

Nowadays, wearing or not wearing hijab has become an important political symbol. Secular nationalism called for the removal of the veil as a symbol of the emancipation of women from traditional restrictions. The Islamist opponents of national states favor restoring "covering" as a sign of the power of men, the return of women to their family roles, and their opposition to the authority of the state. Yet "covering" has a paradoxical meaning, and implies both a return to tradition and the integration of women into the public life of contemporary societies. "Covering" is at once a sign of modesty, unavailability, virtue, and commitment to indigenous values and a mechanism to facilitate women's education and work. Moreover, it is an ambiguous form of social communication. It is understood as a shield, protecting women against men, and society against the danger of temptation represented by women, but while it secludes and conceals women, it also creates mystery and attractiveness, and gives women freedom of movement. It has an ambivalent significance in terms of purity and passion, autonomy and subordination, and dependence and independence. Perhaps more than any other issue the "women's question" sums up the complexities of Islamic modernity.

CONCLUDING REMARKS

In the shaping of the modern Islamic world there have been two contradictory trends: the trend toward global integration, which favors universalistic Islam, and the trend toward the consolidation of national states, which favors the parochialization or localization of Islam. Universalistic Muslim concepts, norms, and practices have been on the rise ever since the eighteenth-century reform movements called upon Muslims to abandon local practices and to conform to the common texts of Islam – the Quran, selected hadith, and the principle of Shari'a. In the eighteenth and nineteenth centuries, hostility to the veneration of shrines and popular Sufi ceremonies; in the twentieth century, hostility to Western cultural practices and norms are the bases of religious authority and political action. Also, since the eighteenth century there has been a tendency for universalistic Islam to become more standardized. Local cultic practices are being increasingly marginalized as folk cultures not authentically Islamic, and the traditional legal, theological, and philosophic scholarship in all its rich detail and specificity is less widely pursued. We see an increasingly global Muslim identity based on common beliefs, rituals, and social practices. Islam is defined more and more by simple and abstract symbols and slogans common to all Muslims, and by ever more widespread acceptance of the Shari'a as the necessary law for a Muslim life. Common political concerns such as the position of Muslim minorities, or the conflicts involving Muslims in Afghanistan, Palestine, Bosnia, Chechnya, and elsewhere, generate identifications transcending political boundaries. This is encouraged by contemporary communications, media, transportation, and migrations. The universalistic identity is reinforced by a proliferation of organized transnational or global Muslim movements including such diverse groups as publication and propaganda organizations, missionary (da'wa) societies, Sufi brotherhoods, banks, youth associations, emigrant communities with international ties, and others. There are international political action groups calling for the formation of a Caliphate or Islamic states, and informal networks committed to violent action. In this array of organized transnational groups, the majority are primarily religious associations, but radical political forms of Islam, and international terrorist networks, are increasingly important.

A profound legacy of cultural expectations, carried from generation to generation, supports these universalistic tendencies. The deepest of these is the image of the Prophet as an active leader who not only calls people to believe in his teachings, but strives to create a society that fulfills in daily practice the laws, ethics, and rituals of Islam. Out of the legacy of the Prophet comes a profound impulse toward social activism and personal responsibility to restore the true Islam. Moreover, historically, Muslims have expected that righteous leaders would periodically arise to guide and direct the community, and that individual holy men would be the bearers of worldly transformation, sweep away corruption, command the good and forbid the evil, return the community to the teachings of the Prophet, and restore the glory of Islam. The tradition of self-anointed charismatic leaders assuming responsibility for a religious movement has been inherited in the contemporary world by self-declared wagers of jihad, purifiers of Islam, the leaders of radical Islamic movements. Cultural preferences for individual moral and religious self-assertion, charismatic authority, devotion of disciples to masters, and small-group loyalties so critical in historical Sufism are translated today into modern radical organizations. Moreover, traditional Islamic vocabulary still defines the political goals of contemporary movements. The goal of establishing a Caliphate and the vocabulary of jihad are still widespread.

These trends toward the more universalistic expressions of Islam are also the product of an ever-growing tendency toward globalization in the world economy, with its attendant systems of transport, communications, and technology. The steamship, the airplane, the radio, the cassette recording, and the internet are the instruments of a worldwide Muslim cohesiveness. Trade, the growth of the hajj, emigration, and other population movements have created a more interlocking Muslim world. So too the shared experiences of the breakdown of old Muslim empires, incorporation into European empires, and the subsequent anti-colonial movements have helped create a global Muslim self-awareness and a pressure for shared ways of expressing Islamic identity. In this respect, while transnational movements are not new to the Islamic world, the scope and variety of these movements is growing.

However, the precedents and forces that favor the incarnation of Islamic universalism in particularistic settings are equally strong. There are weighty limitations upon universalistic Islam. Global Muslim identity does not necessarily or even usually imply organized group action. While Muslims recognize a global affiliation, the real heart of Muslim religious life remains outside politics, in local associations for worship, discussion, mutual aid, education, charity, and other communal activities.

Moreover, Muslim identity is rarely found in isolation from other kinds of identity. Muslims are at one and the same time Muslims and loyal adherents of families, tribes, ethnic groups, or states. Their religious identity gives them universal affiliations; their secular identity roots them in particular communities; the combination leads to such phenomena as tribal Islam and Islamic nationalism. The absorption of Islamic movements in national or particularistic contexts derives from within Islamic culture itself – from the inherent ambiguity as to whether the fulfillment of Islam requires an Islamic state or only devoted individuals and small communities. It is never fully decided whether an Islamic society is to be reached through the hearts of individuals or through controls of the state; whether Islam is a religion of individuals or a political society. This ambiguity leads to a tendency for Islamic movements to oscillate between political and cultural-social goals, and between universalistic principles and rootedness in particularistic contexts.

These ambiguities rest on a still deeper cultural template: the relationship between spiritual reality and worldly existence. The fundamental metaphor of Islam is the distinction between this earthly world and the divine world of the life to come – *dunya* and *din* – the two totally separate realms which are nonetheless connected by the human soul. In Islam the divine truth has to be manifest in worldly realities. The Shari'a defines the practice of everyday life. The Prophet and the great Sufis bring divine revelation and spiritual vision into the world.

In the contemporary world, the enormous consolidated power of national states feeds upon this inherent cultural ambiguity. States resist the political challenge of Muslim movements but accept, validate, and imitate their religious, cultural, and social goals. National states try to shift Islamic discourse and action toward non-political goals consistent with their own existence. Ethnic associations, educational, da'wa (missionary), welfare, and charity enterprises provide an outlet for Muslim activism and form a counterpoint to politicized national or transnational action. The historical apolitical culture of Islam and the structures created by national states work together to favor a modern model of international apolitical Islamic missionary work and non-political forms of Islam in domestic politics.

As in the past, political institutions define the field of action for religious groups. Empires have disappeared, and the consolidation of national states has, in the main, eliminated local-level tribal polities. The historical role of Islamic reform in the creation of new tribal coalitions and states is no longer viable. National states have absorbed all territorial political space, and control the machinery of political power. They have extraordinary power to intervene in the lives of their citizens. Islamic movements have to reckon with that power. Furthermore, the complexity of societies, the overlapping domains of political organization and economic activity, the multiplicity of social bodies, and the complications of identities also reinforce the inherent cultural ambiguity and lead to the ever-varied relations of Islam as a universal religion and as a national and local phenomenon. Thus both historical precedents and contemporary practice generate Islamic movements that are both universal and particularistic, local and global, national and transnational.

Finally, the linkages of Islamic universalism and Muslim particularisms are also reinforced by the symbolic construction of meaning. Symbols interconnect related concepts, and religious ideas are particularly powerful connectors. Belief in God is a symbol of the totality and the unity of all being. In addition, as Durkheim pointed out more than a century ago, religious symbols articulate – indeed, they constitute, they construct – the existence of a community, the body social, a force present, powerful, all-absorbing and yet invisible and intangible, beyond the apprehension of the senses. The community is symbolized as transcending its individual members. It is attached to the highest being, the greatest and most powerful being, the totality of all being, to perfection in all its aspects, and especially to perfect goodness. In the minds of individuals, the symbol of the divinity constitutes the personal self as well. Religious faith links the self, community, polity, the highest good, the totality, and the unity of the world, and thus can generate passionate devotion to communal and national identities.

Secular nationalist symbols exert a very similar appeal. Nationalisms are not only political identities, but, like religions, are comprehensive systems of meanings and values. They fuse personal and collective identities. National as well as religious symbols have the power to invoke deep loyalty, devotion, sacrifice, love of community, and a sense of the fulfillment of transcendental purposes. Religion and nationalism work together because they are overlapping systems of meaning. As much as the interweaving of Islamic universalism and Islamic particularism is a function of a particular historical culture, and a response to contemporary political economies, it also embodies a profound and perhaps universal symbolic process.

These reflections suggest that the structures of lineage, religious, and state institutions derived from the ancient Near East and Islamic religious culture are enduring, though modified, templates for the contemporary evolution of Islamic societies. The old tripartite structure of state, religious, and parochial institutions has been transformed by the destruction of independent lineage and tribal communities and the increasing integration of territorial populations into national states. The identity of Muslim peoples has been redefined in either nationalist or reformist Islamic terms. The contemporary era has also witnessed the transformation of the historical structures of state and religious institutions. States tend to be more highly secularized; religious associations tend to be reoriented to communal and personal interests. At the same time there is a strong reaction against the trend to secularization and a resurgence of Islamic religious and political movements, some of which give an ideological and political interpretation to Islam, but aspire to a utopian reintegration of all levels of personal, communal, and political life.

The ambiguities of secularization and Islamization and the conflict between secular and Islamic concepts of political and moral order reveal a profound continuity in the institutional structures of Islamic societies. In some cases, contemporary Islamic states and Islamic religious movements are simply the direct continuations of past ones. The Iranian mullahs have been part of an organized institution since the sixteenth century. Morocco and Sa'udi Arabia have regimes founded respectively in the seventeenth and eighteenth centuries. The Salafi reformers of the late nineteenth and early twentieth centuries have contributed to the creation of national identity and national states in Egypt, Tunisia, Algeria, and Morocco. The contemporary patterns of relations between states and religious institutions in Turkey, the Arab world, North Africa, Pakistan, Indonesia, Malaysia, Senegal, and other countries are recognizable variations upon the historical relationships between state and religious institutions in those societies. While the political elite preserves the syncretism between cosmopolitan and Islamic forms of culture, the Islamic revival evokes the heritage of personal religious identity and communal responsibility. This conflict reflects a similar nineteenth-century struggle between secularized and religious elites, and echoes the eighteenth-century pre-modern structures of Muslim societies. It may be traced back as far as the ninth-century differentiation of state from religious institutions within the early Islamic empire, which in turn was based on a still more ancient distinction between political and religious life characteristic of almost all Middle Eastern and Mediterranean societies since ancient times. Even the earliest civilization of Mesopotamia in the third millennium BC had differentiated temple and state institutions.

Apart from social institutions, Islam remains in the hearts and minds of individual Muslims an essential component of personal and political identity. To be a Muslim, after all, is not only a matter of states, 'ulama', colleges, and Sufi hospices, but of individual morality, beliefs, and personal and social identity. Islam is the name of the primordial sentiment that defines for the individual believer both personal existence and the existence of a truly human community. Thus the Islamic revival movements are not only grounded in institutions but in the cultural and symbolic meanings of Islam.

Today these ancient templates are being transformed by two fundamental forces. First is the increasing reach of the global economy, which leads not only to economic integration but to the breakdown of cultural barriers and the diffusion of global lifestyles. In the history of these societies I have played down the material, technological, economic, and ecological factors, and have considered them as embedded in pre-modern state, 'ulama', Sufi, and tribal institutions and collectivities, and in the formation of contemporary social classes, ideologies, and states. I have not treated material and economic change as causal historical forces. My basic position has been, as indicated in the preface, that ancient agricultural, artisanal, and commercial technologies and economies had already shaped the institutional structures of human societies before the advent of the Islamic era, and that despite the rise and fall of human fortunes the basic "modes of production and exchange" in Muslim countries did not fundamentally change until European colonialism and industrial·capitalism made themselves felt in the nineteenth and twentieth centuries.

However, even if we give priority to such institutional and cultural considerations, the course of nineteenth- and twentieth-century developments inevitably raises the question as to whether the forces of technology and economy associated with the development of industrial capitalism, the creation of an integrated world economy, and the diffusion of new global cultures, including the cultures of consumerism and of democratic rights, will not in the end break down the historical political and religious institutions. For example, in Turkey changes in industrial development, and the emergence of a proletariat and new strata of bourgeois entrepreneurs, seems to have undermined the historical structures of state and religious organization. In the former Soviet Union radical political and cultural change transformed Islam, for many Muslims, into a religion of private belief and national identities. Similar forces are operative everywhere from Europe and America to Indonesia.

Second is the rise of the new Islamist discourses, which threaten from within to transform the historical identity of Muslim societies. The Islamist discourses define a new type of Islam, one which is highly political, often reduced to a limited number of religious ideas, and stripped of the panoply of religious beliefs, practices, and symbols that have historically structured Muslim life. In many respects, the new Islamism would be hardly recognizable to past generations. Everywhere the forces of secularization and of neo-Islamic integration represent important departures from historical templates. In many Muslim regions an active struggle is being waged to create a post-modern form of Islamic society whether defined in liberal, political, ideological, or universalistic revivalist terms. With these changes it has become open to question whether the Islamic institutional and cultural heritage may not in some cases be giving way to modern political, technological, and economic forces, and in other cases to new forms of Islam, and whether Muslim peoples still constitute, and will continue to constitute, Islamic societies as known to history.

GLOSSARY

'abd: slave; property rights in a person, regulated by law and Quranic ethics. In Muslim countries slaves were commonly employed as household servants and soldiers. *See also ghulam, mamluk.*

adab: habit, upbringing, behavior, refinement of manners, literary cultivation, urbanity; the ideal behavior of a scribe or spiritual cultivation of a Sufi.

adat: in Indonesia and Malaysia, custom or customary law as opposed to Shari'a or Muslim law.

'adl: justice; in law, the quality required to be a legal witness; in religion, the state of personal perfection of one who fulfills God's teaching; in philosophy, the harmony among the faculties of the soul.

agha: Turkish word for elder brother, chief, or master; in Ottoman usage the title of a high-ranking military official; in Algeria, the head of the janissary corps.

ahl: people who occupy a tent; family or community.

ahl al-bayt: people of the house, family of the Prophet.

ahl al-dhimma: the people of the covenant; Jews, Christians, and others accepted as subjects under Muslim rule and entitled to legal protection in return for payment of taxes; also called *ahl al-kitab*, or people of the book.

ahl al-hadith: partisans of hadith as a principal source of Muslim law and morals; a term for the supporters of the Hanbali school of law.

ahl-i hadith: a community in India and Pakistan which professes to follow only the Quran and hadith as sources of Muslim law and does not accept the traditional schools of law.

akhi: member of fourteenth-century Anatolian groups of young men who held to the ideals of *futuwwa* (q.v.); generally urban, artisan, and middle class.

akhlaq: ethics; Greek ethics conveyed into Islamic thought by the translation of Aristotle and Galen and incorporated into the writings of Miskawayh, al-Ghazzali, and others.

'Alids: descendants of the Prophet's cousin 'Ali; the family that claims to be the heirs of the Prophet's religious and political legacy and the rightful heads of the Muslim community.

'alim (pl. *'ulama'*): a learned man, particularly in Muslim legal and religious studies; occurs in varying forms such as *mallam, mullah,* etc.

amin: trustworthy; title for the holder of an official position such as the head of a guild.

amir: title of a military commander, governor, or prince; commonly transliterated "emir"; equivalent of the Turkish *bey* or *beg*.

amir al-mu'minin: Commander of the Faithful, the proper title of the Caliph or successor to the Prophet.

amir al-umara': supreme commander; title used for the military rulers who took over 'Abbasid government.

amsar: see *misr*.

anjuman: assembly; refers to religious, educational and political associations of Muslims, especially in Iran, India, Pakistan, and Turkey.

ansar: "helpers" of Muhammad at Medina; later used as designation for members of Muslim religious and political associations.

'aql: reason, reasoning, intelligence; the rational faculty as opposed to the lower faculties of body and soul.

'asabiya: spirit of kinship or faction; the tribal solidarity that enables a small pastoral community to conquer city-dwellers and create new empires; the political solidarity of ruling elites.

ashraf: people who trace their lineage to the Prophet or his companions; in India, the noble classes; *see also sharif*.

'ashura: supererogatory fast day on the tenth of Muharram, the first month in the Muslim calendar; commemoration of the martyrdom of Husayn.

atabeg: the tutor of a Saljuq prince, his principal military advisor; later, independent governors.

a'yan: local notables; in late Ottoman times, holders of officially recognized political power.

ayatollah: miraculous sign of God, the highest-ranking scholar of law in the "twelver" Shi'i religious hierarchy.

'ayyarun: vagabonds; tenth- to twelfth-century urban gangs who subscribed to *futuwwa* (q.v.) ideals and often appeared as military opponents of state regimes.

baba: Turkish for father, old man, Sufi leader.

baqa': survival in God, the divinely granted attribute of the mystic, who experiences the unity of God but returns to the world of daily activity.

baraka: blessing; the divine power emanating from a holy man.

batin: the inner, esoteric meaning of a text.

bay'a: contract; oath of allegiance recognizing the authority of a Caliph.

bayram: see '*id*.

bey: Turkish title for army officer, official, or ruler of small principality; also transliterated *beg*; *see also amir*.

Bohras: a Muslim community in India, mainly Isma'ilis. Most are merchants but many are Sunnis and peasants.

Caliph: *see khalifa*.

da'i: "summoner"; propagandist or missionary for Shi'i movements; usually the lowest-ranking figure in a Shi'i hierarchy.

dar al-harb: the land of war, territory not under Islamic law and subject to conquest by Muslims; contrasts with *dar al-Islam*, the lands in which Islamic law prevails.

dargah: royal court or residence; shrine and tomb of a Sufi master.

da'wa: the summons to acknowledge religious truth and join a religious community; missionary movement; used in the variant forms *da'wah* in Southeast Asia.

da'wah: see *da'wa*.

dawla: dynasty; by extension, government or state.

devshirme: Ottoman levy of Christian youths to be trained as janissaries and court officers.

dhikr: reminding the self; continuous and rhythmic repetition of the name of God, a Sufi form of prayer which varies with the different Sufi orders.

dhimma: contract of hospitality and protection for peoples of the revealed religions; *see also ahl al-dhimma*.

dihqan: landowner, village chief, the local notables of the late Sasanian and early Muslim empires.

diwan: a collection of poetry or prose; a register, the name applied to government bureaus which keep tax, military, and other records.

evliad: used in Inner Asia to refer to the Sufis descended from the Prophet and the early Caliphs.

falasifa: wise men, philosophers, the Muslim proponents of Greek philosophy.

fana': in Sufi usage, annihilation of the self, the state that precedes the experience of the unity of God.

faqi: poverty-stricken mendicant who lives only for God; *see also Sufi*.

faqih (pl. *fuqaha'*): scholar of Islamic law, jurist; *see also 'alim*.

fata (pl. *fityan*): young man, member of a group or gang devoted to the ideals of *futuwwa* (q.v.).

fatwa (pl. *fatawa*): an opinion on Islamic law given by a *mufti* (q.v.); collected legal opinions form a corpus which modifies the application of the early codes of Islamic law.

fiqh: understanding, jurisprudence, Islamic religious law.

firman: command, edict of a ruler.

fitra: inherent original state of the soul before it is vested in the body.

fityan: *see fata*.

futuwwa: virtues or qualities of young men, including bravery and nobility; the ideology of fraternities and young men's street gangs; *see also 'ayyarun, akhi*.

ghazal: love song; an Arabic poetic form which passes with variations into Persian, Turkish, and Urdu poetry.

ghazi: a frontier warrior for the faith.

ghulam: a young male slave in military or palace service; *see also 'abd, mamluk*.

ghulat: Shi'a who hold "extreme" views of the spiritual qualities of the imam.

hadith: a report of the sayings or deeds of the Prophet transmitted by his companions; collections of hadith are second in authority to the Quran as a source of Muslim belief and practice.

hajib: chamberlain, chief of palace administration, and sometimes head of government.

hajj: the annual pilgrimage to Mecca required of every Muslim at least once in his lifetime.

hal: a Sufi term for a spiritual state received by the grace of God; opposed to *makam*, a station on the way toward mystical union achieved by the Sufi's own effort.

hanif: an Arabian believer in the unity of God before the revelation of Islam.

haqiqa: in Sufism, truth or reality which is experienced through union with God; ultimate reality.

haram: the portion of a house reserved for the women, from which males are excluded.

hijra: the emigration of the Prophet from Mecca to Medina in 622, the base year of the Muslim era.

hikma: the wisdom attained through philosophy, science, or occult knowledge.

hila (pl. *hiyal*): legal stratagem.

hilm: forbearance, moderation, tranquility in the face of passion.

himaya: commendation or protection given by nomads to settlers, landlords to peasants, the powerful to the weak, in return for payment; the protection of European consuls for local clients.

hujja: proof; the person through whom God's presence becomes accessible; a rank in the hierarchy of Shi'i missionaries; *see also da'i*.

'ibada (pl. *'ibadat*): obedience to ritual religious practices, including ablutions, prayer, fasting, pilgrimage, etc.

'id: the Muslim festivals; *'id al-fitr*, the breaking of the fast of Ramadan, and *'id al-adha*, the sacrificial festival of the tenth of Dhu al-hijja; in Turkish called *bayram*.

ijaza: a certificate given by a teacher to a student certifying his capacity to transmit a particular text.

ijma': consensus of legal scholars or of the community as a whole; a basis of Muslim law.

ijtihad: "exerting oneself" in Islamic law; reasoning by analogy, free from received opinions, in order to reinterpret Islamic law; *see also mujtahid*.

'ilm: knowledge, especially of religious truths; the knowledge that guides behavior.

iltizam: a form of tax-farm in the Ottoman empire and Egypt.

imam: the supreme leader of the Muslim community; the successor to the Prophet, used commonly by the Shi'a for 'Ali and his descendants.

imamzada: a descendant of a Shi'i imam; the shrines of sanctified descendants of 'Ali revered by pilgrims, who believe they have miraculous qualities.

iman: faith, fidelity, belief.

imaret: in Ottoman usage, an endowed complex of religious and charitable facilities, commonly including a place for prayer, a college, library, soup kitchens, etc.

insilimen: a term used in the Sahara for religious scholars and venerated holy lineages; *see also zawaya*.

iqta': a grant of the rights to collect taxes from land conceded in return for development or administrative and military service; *see also jagir, timar*.

ishan: an honorific used in Inner Asia as the equivalent of a Sufi shaykh or spiritual leader.

islah: reform, purification, and revitalization of the Muslim community based on a return to the first principles of the Quran and hadith; *see also tajdid*.

islam, Islam: submission, unconditional surrender to God, the name of the religion of Muslims, the institutions and cultural style of states and societies formed by the Islamic religion.

Isma'ilis: a branch of the Shi'a who look to the leadership of Isma'il, a son of Ja'far, and his descendants; this branch includes the Fatimids; later divided into several branches, including the Nizariya who spread from Syria and Iran into India; subcommunities include the Khojas, Bohras, and others.

isnad: a chain of authorities, the series of transmitters of hadith (q.v.) whose names guarantee their validity.

ithna 'ashari: the branch of the Shi'a who believe in the twelve imams descended from 'Ali, the last of whom disappeared and went into hiding in 873 and will return as the messiah; the branch of Shi'ism to which the majority of the populace of Iran adheres.

jagir: an assignment of revenues in Mughal India in lieu of payment of salary; *see also iqta', timar*.

jama'a: meeting, assembly, the community of believers, the umma (q.v.).

jamatbandi: a collectivity or small community; used especially of the Shi'i sects.

jami': mosque for Friday prayers.

janissary: member of the Ottoman infantry corps, the elite regiments of the Ottoman regime.

jihad: striving; effort directed toward inner religious perfection and toward holy war of the Muslims against the infidels.

jinn: spirit beings, composed of vapors or flames, who are imperceptible but malevolent influences.

jizya: the poll tax levied on non-Muslims in a Muslim-ruled society.

Ka'ba: the central sanctuary of Islam, located in Mecca, the principal object of the hajj.

kafir: an unbeliever, one who is ungrateful to God for his gifts.

kalam: theology, the subject that attempts to give rational proofs for religious beliefs; deals with the problems of the divine unity, attributes, human free will, self-determination, etc.

kanun: state-promulgated administrative regulations or codes of law, usually dealing with financial and criminal matters; in contemporary usage, all codes of law promulgated by governments.

karamoko: a West African title for scholar and teacher; *see also 'alim*.

kasb: economic gain; in theology, the technical term for acquisition of responsibility and of reward or punishment for good or bad deeds.

kashf: lifting of the veils, the realization or vision of God as ultimate reality.

khalifa: successor of the Prophet and head of the Muslim community; the Caliph; in Sufism the disciple of the master authorized to transmit prayers, initiate new members, and act as a deputy or head of the Sufi order.

Khan, khan: a Turkish title, originally the ruler of state but then applied to subordinate chiefs and nobles; also a caravansary.

khanaqa: a building for Sufi activities where the shaykh may live, instruct his disciples, and carry on Sufi worship; *see also ribat, tekke, zawiya*.

kharaj: the tax on land.

Kharijism: early religio-political movements whose followers held that the Caliph should be elected by the community.

kharja: *see muwashshah*.

khatib: official preacher who presents the Friday sermon; in principle, the representative of the ruler.

khirqa: the patched cloak worn by Sufis and passed from master to initiate as a symbol of the communication of the blessings inherited from the Prophet.

Khojas: a sect of Nizari Isma'ilis in India.

khwaja: a title variously used by merchants, scholars, and officials; in modern Turkish, *hoja*, a professional man of religion.

madhhab: a Muslim school of law; the four principal schools are the Hanafi, Maliki, Shafi'i, and Hanbali.

madrasa: a college whose primary function is the teaching of law and related religious subjects.

mahalla: a town quarter.

mahdi, Mahdi: the "guided" one; the person who will appear on the last day and establish Islam and the reign of justice.

mahr: in Muslim law, the gift that the bridegroom gives the bride, which becomes her personal property.

majlis: a gathering, assembly, or council.

makhzan: Moroccan central government administration; royal court, army, and provincial officials.

maktab: an elementary school for teaching children recitation of the Quran and the basics of reading and writing.

mallam: the term used in West Africa for a religious scholar; *see 'alim.*

mamaluk: a slave or freedman in military service.

maqam: a station on the Sufi path to unity with God acquired by the Sufi's own efforts.

marja'-i taqlid: source of imitation; in Iran, just and learned scholars of law qualified to give authoritative legal opinions; the common people are obliged to accept them as absolute religious authorities.

masjid: a mosque or place of prostration and prayer; a center for Muslim communal affairs.

masnavi: an epic poem in Persian and related literatures.

ma'sum: a person who possesses *'isma*, infallibility, freedom from committing sins.

mawali: *see mawla.*

mawla (pl. *mawali*): client or freedman, servant; the word also applies to the patron or master.

mawlid: the celebration of the birth of the Prophet; also applies to celebrations at saints' shrines.

mihrab: the ornamented niche in the wall of a mosque that indicates the direction of prayer.

millet: religion or religious communities; in contemporary usage, nation.

minaret: the tower of a mosque from which the call to prayer is proclaimed.

minbar: the high seat or chair in a mosque from which the preacher delivers the sermon.

mi'raj: the ascent of the Prophet to heaven in Jerusalem after the miraculous night journey from Medina.

misr (pl. *amsar*): the military camps and garrisons constructed in the early Islamic conquests; administrative capitals for the conquered provinces.

mobad: a Zoroastrian clergyman.

mu'amalat: Muslim laws pertaining to social relations.

mufti: an expert in Muslim law qualified to give authoritative legal opinions.

muhajirun: the emigrants who accompanied the Prophet on the *hijra* (q.v.) from Mecca to Medina.

muhtasib: an official who supervises fair market practices and public morals.

mujaddid: "the renewer"; the scholar or holy man who comes once every century to restore the true knowledge and practice of Islam.

mujtahid: a person qualified to exercise *ijtihad* (q.v.) and give authoritative opinions on Islamic law.

mullah: a learned man; often used in the Indian subcontinent; the equivalent of *'alim* (q.v.).

murshid: guide; a Sufi master and teacher; *see also Sufi*.

muwashshah: love poem; form of Arabic verse popular in Spain, commonly ending in a *kharja*, or refrain of Romance origin.

nafs: soul; the animal faculties as opposed to the rational or angelic faculties.

naqib: a syndic or headman.

naqib al-ashraf: the syndic or headman of the groups of descendants of the Prophet found in many Muslim countries.

nasiha: faithful advice to a ruler; exhortation to do good.

nass: in Shi'i usage, the explicit designation of a successor to the imamate, which confers upon him knowledge and power appropriate to the office.

niya: intention, necessary state of mind for the validity of religious actions.

padishah: a nineteenth-century title for the Ottoman Sultans.

pançasila: the five principles of Indonesian independence.

penghulu: headman, used in Indonesia as a title of a village administrator.

pesantren: in Indonesia, a school or seminary for Muslim students.

pir: a title for a Sufi shaykh.

pirzada: the descendant of a pir or saint, or the manager of his tomb.

priyayi: the governing and scribal class; the elite of pre-modern Indonesian society.

qadi: judge, the Caliph's designated representative to adjudicate disputes on the basis of Shari'a.

qa'id: a tribal, district, or military chief; term widely used in North Africa.

qalb: in Sufism, the heart, the soul, the seat of conscience and knowledge.

qanat: an underground irrigation canal, commonly used in Iran.

qasaba: a fortified castle, residence of government officials; a chief town; in India, *qasbah*.

qasbah: *see qasaba*.

qasida: the classical Arabic ode which often eulogizes the tribe of the poet or a great man; the Persian *qasida* is a lyric poem.

qawm: lineage, tribe, religious community, nation.

qibla: the direction of the Ka'ba (q.v.) in Mecca, which Muslims face during prayers.

Quran: Muslim scripture, the book containing the revelations of God to Muhammad.

qutb: the pivot around which something revolves; the head of the invisible hierarchy of saints upon whom the order of the universe depends.

ra'is (pl. *ru'asa'*): a person of high rank, a headman or chief.

Ramadan: the ninth month of the Muslim calendar, the month of annual fasting.

Rashidun: the rightly guided, a title applied to the first four Caliphs.

ribat: a frontier fortress and residence for Muslim warriors and mystics.

ruh: soul, sometimes the equivalent of *qalb* (q.v.).

rustaq: an administrative district comprising a town and subordinate villages.

sabr: steadfastness, patience, endurance in fulfillment of religious obligations.

sadaqa: voluntary alms, sometimes a synonym for *zakat* (q.v.).

sajjada nishin: "one who sits on the prayer carpet"; the successor to the leadership of a *khanaqa* (q.v.) or the custodian of a Sufi shrine.

salat: Muslim ritual prayer performed five times daily; in Persian called *namaz*.

sama': Sufi musical session intended to inculcate states of ecstasy.

santri: in Indonesia, a student of Islam; devout and correct Muslim.

sarkin: a Hausa title for headman, ruler.

sawafi: crown estates seized by the Umayyad dynasty from former Sasanian royal and noble landowners.

sayyid: prince, lord, chief; a descendant of Husayn, the son of 'Ali.

shahada: "witnessing"; the Muslim profession of faith.

Shah-en-shah: king of kings, a Persian title of the emperor.

shahid: witness; martyr.

Shari'a: the path to be followed; Muslim law, the totality of the Islamic way of life.

sharif (pl. *ashraf* or *shurafa'*): noble; a descendant of the Prophet.

shaykh: an elder, head, chief, respected man of religion, Sufi leader, teacher.

shaykh al-Islam: a chief jurisconsult or *mufti* (q.v.); the head of the religious establishment in the Ottoman empire.

Shi'a: the group of Muslims who regard 'Ali and his heirs as the only legitimate successors to the Prophet, divided into sects according to allegiance to different lines of 'Alid descent.

shirk: polytheism, associating other beings with God, the ultimate blasphemy.

shura: council; specifically the council established by the Caliph 'Umar to choose his successor.

shurafa': see *sharif*.

silsila: the sequence of Sufi masters reaching back to the Prophet through whom a particular Sufi acquires his knowledge.

sipahi: a cavalry soldier in the Ottoman empire; appears in India as "sepoy."

Sufi: a Muslim mystic; named after the early ascetics who wore garments of coarse wool; *see also ishan, murshid, pir, shaykh.*

sultan, Sultan: "power," authority, the title of a Muslim monarch.

Sunna: "the trodden path," custom, the practice of the Prophet and the early community which becomes for all Muslims an authoritative example of the correct way to live a Muslim life.

Sunnis: those who accept the Sunna (q.v.) and the historical succession of Caliphs, as opposed to the 'Alids (q.v.); the majority of the Muslim community.

sura: a group of Quranic verses collected in a single chapter.

tafsir: commentary and interpretation, the exegesis of the Quran.

tajdid: renewal, applied to the post-eighteenth-century movement to revive the true practice of Islam based on the Quran and hadith; *see also islah*.

talakawata: a Hausa term for the peasants and working poor.

taljia: commendation; *see also himaya*.

Tanzimat: reorganization, the name for the Ottoman reforms of the nineteenth century.

taqlid: "imitation," the principle of following the established doctrines of the Muslim schools of law; the opposite of *ijtihad* (q.v.).

tariqa: a way, the Sufi path; the system of beliefs and training transmitted by particular schools of Sufis; a brotherhood of Sufis.

tasdiq: faith, affirmation of the truth of God's existence.

tawakkul: trust in God.

tawba: repentance, turning to God.

tawhid: unity, the oneness of God's being and the unity of the mystic with the divine being.

ta'wil: allegorical exegesis of the Quran.

ta'ziya: the lamentation for a martyr, the mourning for Husayn displayed in processions and mystery plays in the month of Muharram; also refers to a model of Husayn's tomb at Karbala kept in imamzadas (q.v.).

tekke: the Turkish name for a Sufi residence; *see also khanaqa*.

timar: Turkish and Ottoman term for a grant of tax revenues to support a military retainer of the Sultan.

tyeddo: the name of the warrior slave elite in Senegambia.

'ulama': the collective term for the scholars or learned men of Islam; *see also 'alim*.

uleebalang: an intermediary administrative official in the Malayan Sultanates.

umma: people or community; the whole of the brotherhood of Muslims.

'ushr: the tenth of the produce levied on Muslim-owned lands.

uymaq: in Iran and Inner Asia a chieftaincy under the authority of a headman supported by military retainers and allied lineages.

wahdat al-shuhud: unity of witness.

wahdat al-wujud: unity of being, existential monism.

wali: a protector, a benefactor, a companion, a governor; a friend of God, a saint or a Sufi whose tomb is visited for its blessing; the legal guardian of a minor, woman, or incapacitated person.

waqf: an endowment, an irrevocable grant of the income of property set aside in perpetuity for a religious or charitable purpose.

watan: country, motherland.

wazir: "a helper," the chief secretary of a ruler; head of the bureaucracy; prime minister.

wilayat: a legal competence; power delegated to a governor or *wali* (q.v.); in Ottoman usage, a term for an administrative district.

wird: a litany or patterned devotion chanted by Sufis.

yasa: Mongol law.

zahir: the external, literal meaning of a text, as opposed to *batin* (q.v.), its inner significance.

zakat: a legal alms tax raised from Muslims.

zamindar: a landowner; under the Mughals, a person with a right to collect revenues from the land.

zandaqa: a body of dualistic or heretical beliefs.

zawaya: Berber North African religious lineages.

zawiya: a building that functions as a Sufi residence, place of prayer, school, and the tomb of a saint; *see also khanaqa*.

ziyara: a visit to the tomb of a saint or holy man to pray for intercession before God.

BIBLIOGRAPHY

INTRODUCTION

This bibliography is intended as a guide to further reading and includes the most important translations and scholarly works. Most of the citations are to English-language works, but important materials in French, German, and other languages are suggested. Readers will find further bibliographical references in many of the cited works. J. D. Pearson, *Index Islamicus*, Cambridge, 1958–, covers the periodical literature of all Islamic regions from 1906 to the present and book literature from 1976 to the present.

The following abbreviations are used in the bibliography:

AIEO	*Annales de l'institut des études orientales*
BEO	*Bulletin d'études orientales*
BSOAS	*Bulletin of the School of Oriental and African Studies*
CMRS	*Cahiers du monde russe et soviétique*
IJAHS	*International Journal of African Historical Studies*
IJMES	*International Journal of Middle East Studies*
JAH	*Journal of African History*
JAOS	*Journal of the American Oriental Society*
JESHO	*Journal of the Economic and Social History of the Orient*
JRAS	*Journal of the Royal Asiatic Society*
REI	*Revue des études islamiques*
ROMM	*Revue de l'Occident musulman et de la Méditerranée*
RSO	*Revista degli studi orientali*
SI	*Studia Islamica*
ZDMG	*Zeitschrift der deutschen morganländischen Gesellschaft*

PART I

Introduction

On Islamic history as a whole see M. G. S. Hodgson, *The Venture of Islam*, 3 vols., Chicago, 1974. Hodgson is particularly sensitive to religious and literary issues and to the existential meaning of Islamic discourses. The *Encyclopaedia of Islam*, new edn, ed. H. A. R. Gibb et al., Leiden, 1960 is an inexhaustible reference work on all topics related to this volume. The following atlases are useful reference works: R. Roolvink, *Historical Atlas of the Muslim Peoples*, Amsterdam, 1957; F. Robinson, *Atlas of the Islamic World since 1500*, Oxford, 1982; J. L. Bacharach, *A Middle East Studies Handbook*, Seattle, 1984; C. F. Beckingham, *Atlas of the Arab World and the Middle East*, New York, 1960; D. E. Pitcher, *An Historical Geography of the Ottoman Empire*, Leiden, 1972; J. E. Schwartzberg, *A Historical Atlas of South Asia*, Chicago, 1978; G. S. P. Freeman-Grenville, *A Modern Atlas of African History*, London, 1976; and J. D. Fage, *An Atlas of African History*, New York, 1978; H. Kennedy, *An Historical Atlas of Islam*, Leiden, 2002.

On early Islamic history and civilization see J. J. Saunders, *A History of Medieval Islam*, London, 1965; H. A. R. Gibb, *Mohammedanism*, 2nd edn, London, 1969; F. Rahman, *Islam*, 2nd edn, Chicago, 1979; G. E. von Grunebaum, *Medieval Islam*, 2nd edn, Chicago, 1956. In French there is L. Gardet, *L'Islam, religion et communauté*, Paris, 1967; R. Mantran, *L'Expansion musulmane, VIIᵉ–IXᵉ siècles*, 2nd edn, Paris, 1979; C. Cahen, *Les Peuples musulmans dans l'histoire médiévale*, Paris, 1977. See also F. Robinson, *The Cambridge Illustrated History of the Islamic World*, Cambridge, 1996; J. Esposito, ed., *The Oxford History of Islam*, Oxford, 2000; J. Bloom and S. Blair, *Islam: A Thousand Years of Faith and Power*, New Haven, 2002.

Chapter 1

A useful introduction to pre-Islamic Arabia is I. Shahid, "Pre-Islamic Arabia," *Cambridge History of Islam*, I, ed. P. M. Holt, A. K. S. Lambton, and B. Lewis, Cambridge, 1970, pp. 3–29. The pre-Islamic kingdoms of Yemen may be studied in J. Ryckmans, *L'Institution monarchique en Arabie méridionale avant l'Islam*, Louvain, 1951. On Arabian bedouin society see H. Lammens, *Le Berceau de l'Islam*, Rome, 1914; H. Lammens, *L'Arabie occidentale avant l'hégire*, Beirut, 1928; A. Musil, *Arabia Deserta*, New York, 1927; F. Gabrieli, *L'antica società beduina*, Rome, 1959. On the bedouinization of Arabia: W. Caskel, *Die Bedeutung der Beduinen in der Geschichte der Araber*, Cologne, 1953; W. Caskel, "The Bedouinization of Arabia," *American Anthropologist*, Memoirs, 76 (1954), pp. 36–46.

Pre-Islamic Arabian poetry is the principal literary source of our knowledge of Arabian peoples: see C. Lyall, tr. and ed., *Translations of Ancient Arabian Poetry*, London, 1885; C. Lyall, tr. and ed., *The Mufaddalīyyat*, 2 vols., Oxford, 1918–21; C. Lyall, tr. and ed., *The Poems of 'Amr son of Qami'ah*, Cambridge, 1919.

On pre-Islamic Arabian religion see B. Farès, *L'Honneur chez les Arabes avant l'Islam*, Paris, 1932; G. Ryckmans, *Les Religions arabes préislamiques*, 2nd edn, Louvain, 1951; J. Chelhod, *Le Sacrifice chez les Arabes*, Paris, 1955; J. Chelhod, *Introduction à la sociologie de l'Islam: De l'animisme a l'universalisme*, Paris, 1958, which gives an important evolutionary theory; J. Chelhod, *Les Structures du sacré chez les Arabes*, Paris, 1964; T. Fahd, *La Divination arabe*, Leiden, 1966; T. Fahd, *Le Panthéon de l'Arabie centrale à la veille de l'hégire*, Paris, 1968; M. M. Bravmann, *The Spiritual Background of Early Islam*, Leiden, 1972.

Arabian family and social institutions are the subject of W. R. Smith, *Kinship and Marriage in Early Arabia*, New York, 1979; G. H. Stern, *Marriage in Early Islam*, London, 1939; W. M. Watt, *Muhammad at Medina*, Oxford, 1956, pp. 261–302.

Mecca is the subject of H. Lammens, *Le Mecque à la veille de l'hégire*, Beirut, 1924, which develops the theory of the importance of Mecca as a trading center. On Meccan society and commerce: M. J. Kister, *Studies on Jahiliyya and Early Islam*, London, 1980.

Chapter 2

The most important source for the rise of Islam is the Quran itself. A vivid but not always literal translation is A. J. Arberry, tr., *The Koran Interpreted*, New York, 1955. More literal translations include J. M. Rodwell, tr., *The Koran*, London, 1939; E. H. Palmer, tr., *The Koran*, London, 1951. Introductions to the Quran include R. Bell, *Introduction to the Qur'an*, Edinburgh, 1953; A. Jeffries, *The Qur'an as Scripture*, New York, 1952; R. Blachère, *Introduction au Coran*, 2nd edn, Paris, 1959. R. Roberts, *The Social Laws of the Quran*, London, 1971 is a convenient compilation of all the texts dealing with social issues.

The earliest authoritative Muslim biography of the Prophet is made up of the traditions collected in the second century after his death by Ibn Ishaq, and edited by Ibn Hisham, *Life of Muhammad*, tr. A. Guillaume, Lahore, 1955. The most important Western biography is W. M. Watt, *Muhammad at Mecca*, Oxford, 1953; and W. M. Watt, *Muhammad at Medina*, Oxford, 1956. See also M. Rodinson, *Mohammed*, tr. A. Carter, London, 1971.

The relationship of the Quran to the Bible and of Muhammad to Jewish and Christian tradition is the subject of Tor Andrae, *Les Origines de l'Islam et le Christianisme*, tr. Jules Roche, Paris, 1955, summarized in English in Tor Andrae, *Mohammed: The Man and his Faith*, tr. T. Menzel, London, 1956; R. Bell, *The Origins of Islam in its Christian Environment*, London, 1968; H. Speyer, *Die biblischen Erzählungen im Qoran*, Hildesheim, 1961; C. C. Torrey, *The Jewish Foundation of Islam*, New York, 1933. The most important contributions to understanding the Quran in its Arabian context are T. Izutsu, *Ethico-Religious Concepts in the Qur'an*, Montreal, 1966; and T. Izutsu, *God and Man in the Koran*, Tokyo, 1964.

Chapters 3 and 4

On the Arab conquests and settlement see al-Baladhuri, *Futah al-Buldan*, Leiden, 1866; P. K. Hitti and E. C. Murgotten, tr., *The Origins of the Islamic State*, 2 vols., New York, 1916–24; Fred M. Donner, *The Early Islamic Conquests*, Princeton, 1981; E. Shoufany, *Al-Riddah and the Muslim Conquest of Arabia*, Toronto, 1972. The classic history of the Umayyad period is J. Wellhausen, *The Arab Kingdom and its Fall*, Calcutta, 1927. A good recent general history is M. A. Shaban, *Islamic History*, I, Cambridge, 1971, with fresh but sometimes controversial interpretations. A useful collective work is G. H. A. Juynboll, ed., *Studies on the First Century of Islamic*

Society, Carbondale, Ill., 1982. On the transition from ancient to Islamic times see M. Morony, *Iraq after the Muslim Conquest*, Princeton, 1983. E. L. Peterson, *'Ali and Mu'awiya in Early Arabic Tradition*, Copenhagen, 1964 is of exceptional historiographical importance.

On the Umayyad Caliphs see G. Rotter, *Die Umayyaden und der zweite Burgerkreig, 680–692*, Wiesbaden, 1982; F. Gabrieli, "Il califfato di Hisham," *Mémoires de la Société royale d'archéologie d'Alexandrie*, VII, Alexandria, 1935. Fiscal administration is the subject of D. B. Dennett, *Conversion and the Poll Tax in Early Islam*, Cambridge, Mass., 1950.

Art and architecture: K. A. C. Creswell, *Early Muslim Architecture*, Oxford, 1969; J. Sauvaget, *La Mosquée omeyyade de Médine*, Paris, 1947; O. Grabar, *The Formation of Islamic Art*, New Haven, 1973; O. Grabar, *City in the Desert: Qasr al-Hayr East*, 2 vols., Cambridge, Mass., 1978. See also Grabar's dissertation, "Ceremonies and Art at the Umayyad Court," Princeton, 1954; and his collected papers, *Studies in Medieval Islamic Art*, London, 1972.

On Umayyad urbanism see Salih al-'Ali, *Al-Tanzīmāt al-ijtimā'iya wa'l-iqtiṣādīya fī'l-Baṣra*, Baghdad, 1953; and I. M. Lapidus, "Arab Settlement and Economic Development of Iraq and Iran in the Age of the Umayyad and Early 'Abbasid Caliphs," *The Islamic Middle East, 700–1900: Studies in Economic and Social History*, ed. A. L. Udovitch, Princeton, 1981, pp. 177–208, with further references.

The anti-Umayyad movements to 750: S. M. Jafri, *Origins and Early Developments of Shi'a Islam*, London, 1979; W. M. Watt, "Shiism under the Umayyads," *JRAS* (1960), pp. 158–72; W. M. Watt, "Kharijite Thought in the Umayyad Period," *Der Islam*, 36 (1961), pp. 215–31. The messianic movements of the late Umayyad era may be studied in G. Van Vloten, *Recherches sur la dominion arabe, le chiitisme et les croyances messianiques sous le khalifat des Omayades*, Amsterdam, 1894; B. Lewis, "An Apocalyptic Vision of Islamic History," *BSOAS*, 13 (1950), pp. 308–38. The 'Abbasid revolution is the subject of M. Shaban, *The 'Abbasid Revolution*, Cambridge, 1970; F. Omar, *The 'Abbasid Caliphate*, Baghdad, 1969; C. Cahen, "Points de vue sur la révolution 'abbaside," *Revue historique*, 230 (1963), pp. 295–338.

The first century of the 'Abbasid empire is covered by H. Kennedy, *The Early 'Abbasid Caliphate*, London, 1981; and J. Lassner, *The Shaping of 'Abbasid Rule*, Princeton, 1980.

'Abbasid urbanism is treated in I. M. Lapidus, "The Evolution of Muslim Urban Society," *Comparative Studies in Society and History*, 15 (1973), pp. 21–50; J. Lassner, *The Topography of Baghdad in the Early Middle Ages*, Detroit, 1970. For 'Abbasid military institutions see P. Crone, *Slaves on Horses: The Evolution of the Islamic Polity*, Cambridge, 1980; D. Pipes, *Slaves, Soldiers and Islam*, New Haven, 1981. 'Abbasid administration: the legal sources are translated by A. Ben Shemesh, *Taxation in Islam*, 3 vols., Leiden, 1958–69; D. Sourdel, *Le Vizirat 'abbaside*, 2 vols., Damascus, 1959–60; S. D. Goitein, "The Origin of the Vizierate and its True Character," *Islamic Culture*, 16 (1942), pp. 255–392; E. Tyan, *Histoire de l'organisation judiciaire en pays d'Islam*, Leiden, 1960; and his summary, "Judicial Organization," *Law in the Middle East*, ed. M. Khadduri and H. Liebesny, Washington, D.C., 1955, pp. 236–78. For provincial tax administration see F. Hussein, *Das Steuersystem in Ägypten, 639–868*, Frankfurt am Main, 1982; A. K. S. Lambton, *Landlord and Peasant in Persia*, London, 1953; C. Cahen, "L'Evolution de l'iqta' du IXe au XIIIe siècle," *Annales ESC*, 8 (1953), pp. 25–52.

Provincial histories: for Iran see the *Cambridge History of Iran*, IV, ed. R. N. Frye, Cambridge, 1975; W. Barthold, *Turkestan Down to the Mongol Invasion*, London, 1968; G. H. Sadiqi, *Les Mouvements religieux Iraniens au IIe, et au IIIe siècle de l'hégire*, Paris, 1938; C. E. Bosworth, *Sistan under the Arabs: From the Islamic Conquest to the Rise of the Saffarids*, Rome, 1968, and the relevant articles in his collected *Medieval History of Iran, Afghanistan and Central Asia*, London, 1977. For Egypt see G. Wiet, *L'Egypte arabe*, Paris, 1937; Z. M. Hassan, *Les Tulunides*, Paris, 1933.

Chapter 5

The theory of the Caliphate is reviewed by T. Arnold, *The Caliphate*, London, 1965; E. Tyan, *Institutions du droit public musulman*, I, Paris, 1954; L. Gardet, *La Cité musulmane*, Paris, 1954; H. A. R. Gibb, "Constitutional Organization," *Law in the Middle East*, ed. M. Khadduri and H. Liebesny, Washington, D.C., 1955, pp. 3–28; D. Sourdel, "Questions de cérémonial 'abbaside," *REI*, 27 (1960), pp. 121–48.

Reviews of the development of Arabic literature include R. Blachère, *Histoire de la littérature arabe des origines à la fin du XVe siècle de J.-C.*, 3 vols., Paris, 1952–66; A. F. L. Beeston et al., eds., *Arabic Literature to the End of the Umayyad Period*, Cambridge, 1983; H. A. R. Gibb, *Arabic Literature: An Introduction*, 2nd edn, Oxford, 1963; G. E. von Grunebaum, *Themes in Medieval Arabic Literature*, London, 1981; A. Hamori, *On the Art of Medieval Arabic Literature*, Princeton, 1974; M. Zwettler, *The Oral Tradition of Classical Arabic Poetry: Its Character and Implications*, Columbus, Ohio, 1978. For Arabic literary criticism see V. Cantarino, *Arabic Poetics in the Golden Age*, Leiden, 1975; K. Abu Deeb, *Al-Jurjani's Theory of Poetic Imagery*, Warminster, 1979.

On Persian literature see G. Morrison, J. Baldick, and S. Kadkani, *History of Persian Literature from the Beginning of the Islamic Period to the Present Day*, Leiden and Cologne, 1981. J. Rypka, *History of Iranian Literature*, Dordrecht, 1968 is the classic work in the field. See also G. Lazard, ed. and tr., *Les Premiers poètes persans*, Tehran, 1964.

Adab, or courtly literatures of the 'Abbasid era, are treated in F. Rosenthal, *Knowledge Triumphant: The Concept of Knowledge in Medieval Islam*, Leiden, 1970; G. E. von Grunebaum, *Medieval Islam*, Chicago, 1946; J. C. Vadet, *L'Esprit courtois en Orient dans les cinq premiers siècles de l'hégire*, Paris, 1968; V. Monteil, *Abu-Nuwās: Le vin, le vent, la vie*, Paris, 1979.

For Ibn al-Muqaffa', see D. Sourdel, "La Biographie d'Ibn al-Muqaffa' d'après les sources anciennes," *Arabica*, 1 (1954), pp. 307–23. Ibn Qutayba (d. 889) is the subject of G. Lecomte, *Ibn Qutayba: L'Homme, son oeuvre, ses idées*, Damascus, 1965. A partial translation of Ibn Qutayba's major work is provided by J. Horovitz, "Ibn Quteiba's 'Uyun al-Akhbar," *Islamic Culture*, 4 (1930), pp. 171–98, 331–62, 488–530, 5 (1931), pp. 1–27, 194–224. For Jahiz: C. Pellat, ed. and tr., *The Life and Works of Jahiz*, Berkeley, 1969; C. Pellat, *Le Milieu Basrien et la formation de Jahiz*, Paris, 1953.

A brief overview of Islamic philosophy may be found in W. M. Watt, *Islamic Philosophy and Theology*, Edinburgh, 1962; R. Walzer, *Greek into Arabic*, Oxford, 1962. On Shi'i philosophy see H. Corbin, *Histoire de la philosophie islamique*, Paris, 1964. The transmission of Greek thought into Arabic is discussed in D. L. E. O'Leary, *How Greek Science Passed to the Arabs*, London, 1949; F. E. Peters, *Aristotle and the Arabs*, New York, 1968.

For the major Arab philosophers: G. N. Atiyeh, *Al-Kindi: The Philosopher of the Arabs*, Rawalpindi, 1966; *Al-Kindi's Metaphysics: A Translation of "On First Philosophy,"* tr. A. L. Ivry, Albany, N.Y., 1974; J. Jolivet, *L'Intellect selon Kindi*, Leiden, 1971; al-Farabi, *Idées des habitants de la cité vertueuse*, tr. R. P. Jaussen, Cairo, 1949; al-Farabi, *Fuṣūl al-Madanī: Aphorisms of the Statesman*, tr. D. M. Dunlop, Cambridge, 1961; al-Farabi, *Philosophy of Plato and Aristotle*, tr. M. Mahdi, New York, 1962.

Chapter 6

Hadith and law: al-Bukhari, *Al-Sahih: Les Traditions islamiques*, 4 vols., tr. O. Houdas, Paris, 1903–14. A convenient later collection of hadith is al-Khatib al-Tibrizi, *Mishkat al-Masabih*, 4 vols., tr. J. Robson, Lahore, 1960–65. Important studies on hadith include W. Graham, *Divine Word and Prophetic Word in Early Islam*, The Hague, 1977; G. H. A. Juynboll, *Muslim Tradition: Studies in Chronology, Provenance and Authorship of Early Hadith*, Cambridge, 1983. The classic studies in the field are I. Goldziher, *Muslim Studies*, 2 vols., tr. C. R. Barber and S. M. Stern, London, 1968–71; I. Goldziher, *Le Dogme et la loi de l'Islam*, Paris, 1973; I. Goldziher, *Introduction to Islamic Theology and Law*, tr. A. Hamori and R. Hamori, Princeton, 1980; J. Schacht, *The Origins of Muhammadan Jurisprudence*, Oxford, 1959. Good summary reviews of these findings are found in J. Schacht, *An Introduction to Islamic Law*, Oxford, 1964; N. J. Coulson, *A History of Islamic Law*, Edinburgh, 1964. Two important texts in the development of Muslim legal theory are M. Khadduri, tr., *Islamic Jurisprudence: Shafi'i's Risala*, Baltimore, 1961; Malik b. Anas, *Al-Muwatta'*, tr. A. A. Tarjumana and Y. Johnson, Norwich, 1982. Important collections of articles on Islamic law include N. J. Coulson, *Conflicts and Tensions in Islamic Jurisprudence*, Chicago, 1969. For commercial law, see A. L. Udovitch, *Partnership and Profit in Medieval Islam*, Princeton, 1970. For law of war and peace: M. Khadduri, *War and Peace in the Law of Islam*, Baltimore, 1955; al-Shaybani, *The Islamic Law of Nations*, tr. M. Khadduri, Baltimore, 1966.

On theology (*kalam*): L. Gardet and M. Anawati, *Introduction à la théologie musulmane: Essai de théologie comparée*, Paris, 1948; P. Morewedge, *Islamic Philosophical Theology*, Albany, N.Y., 1979; L. Gardet, *Dieu et la destinée de l'homme*, Paris, 1967. For the origins and first century of Muslim theology see W. M. Watt, *The Formative Period of Islamic Thought*, Edinburgh, 1973; J. van Ess, *Zwischen Hadit und*

Theologie, Berlin and New York, 1975; J. van Ess, *Anfänge muslimischer Theologie*, Beirut, 1977; M. Cook, *Early Muslim Dogma: A Source-Critical Study*, Cambridge, 1981; A. J. Wensinck, *The Muslim Creed: Its Genesis and Historical Development*, London, 1965. On Mu'tazilism see J. van Ess, *Frühe Mu'tazilitische Haresiographie*, Beirut, 1971; A. Nader, *Le Système philosophique des Mu'tazila*, Beirut, 1956. For al-Ash'ari see M. Allard, *Le Problème des attributs divins dans la doctrine d'al-As'ari et de ses premiers grands disciples*, Beirut, 1965; al-Ash'ari, *The Theology of al-Ash'ari*, tr. R. J. McCarthy, Beirut, 1953.

Important works on special problems in Muslim theology include T. Izutsu, *The Concept of Belief in Islamic Theology*, Tokyo, 1965; L. Gardet, "Les Noms et les statuts: Le Problème de la foi et des oeuvres en Islam," *SI*, 5 (1956), pp. 61–123.

Sufism: M. G. S. Hodgson, *The Venture of Islam*, I, Chicago, 1974, pp. 359–409 gives a good general introduction. For a Muslim convert's point of view, see T. Burckhardt, *An Introduction to Sufi Doctrine*, tr. D. M. Matheson, Lahore, 1959. On early Sufism the pathbreaking work of L. Massignon, *Essai sur les origines du lexique technique de la mystique musulmane*, 2nd edn, Paris, 1954; L. Massignon, *La Passion d'al-Husayn ibn Mansour al-Hallaj*, 2 vols., Paris, 1922, tr. H. Mason as *The Passion of al-Hallaj*, 4 vols., Princeton, 1982; and P. Nwyia, *Exégèse coranique et language mystique*, Beirut, 1970 are indispensable. For other good general histories see A. Schimmel, *The Mystical Dimensions of Islam*, Chapel Hill, N.C., 1975; G. C. Anawati and L. Gardet, *La Mystique musulmane*, Paris, 1961. On the relation of Sufism to other mysticisms see L. Gardet, *Expériences mystiques en terres non-chrétiennes*, Paris, 1953; R. C. Zaehner, *Hindu and Muslim Mysticism*, New York, 1969; R. C. Zaehner, *Mysticism, Sacred and Profane*, Oxford, 1957.

Translations and works dealing with the principal early Sufi masters include H. Ritter, "Studien zur Geschichte der islamischen Frömmigkeit; Hasan el-Basri," *Der Islam*, 21 (1933), pp. 1–83; J. van Ess, *Die Gedankenwelt des Harit al-Muhāsibi*, Bonn, 1961; M. Smith, *An Early Mystic of Baghdad. A Study of the Life, Teaching and Writings of al-Muhasibi*, London, 1935; M. Smith, *Rabi'a the Mystic*, Cambridge, 1928; al-Kharraz, *The Book of Truthfulness [Kitāb al-sidq]*, tr. A. J. Arberry, London, 1937; A. H. Abdel-Kader, *The Life, Personality and Writings of al-Junayd*, London, 1962; al-Niffari, *Kitāb al-mawāqif wa-l-mukhatabat*, ed. and tr. A. J. Arberry, London, 1935; M. I. el-Geyoushi, "Al-Tirmidhī's Theory of Saints and Sainthood," *Islamic Quarterly*, 15 (1971), pp. 17–61.

For 'Abbasid-period Shi'ism, see H. Laoust, *Les Schismes dans l'Islam*, Paris, 1965. For Isma'ilism see B. Lewis, *The Origins of Isma'ilism*, Cambridge, 1940; T. Nagel, *Frühe Ismailiya und Fatimiden*, Bonn, 1972; W. Madelung, "Das Imamat in der frühen ismailitischen Lehre," *Der Islam*, 37 (1961), pp. 43–135.

Chapter 7
On the political and religious struggles of the reign of al-Ma'mun, see I. M. Lapidus, "The Separation of State and Religion," *IJMES*, 6 (1975), pp. 363–85, where references may be found to earlier literature.

Chapter 8

On the century of 'Abbasid decline see H. Bowen, *The Life and Times of 'Ali ibn 'Isa, the Good Vizier*, Cambridge, 1928; M. Forstner, *Das Kalifat des Abbasiden al-Musta'in*, Mainz, 1968; W. Hellige, *Die Regentschaft al-Muwaffaqs*, Berlin, 1936; A. Popović, *La Révolte des esclaves en Iraq*, Paris, 1976.

Chapter 9

For the history of Iran in the late 'Abbasid, Saljuq, and Mongol eras see the *Cambridge History of Iran*, IV, *The Period from the Arab Invasion to the Saljuqs*, ed. R. N. Frye, Cambridge, 1975, and V, *The Saljuq and Mongol Periods*, ed. J. A. Boyle, Cambridge, 1968. See also R. Frye, *Islamic Iran and Central Asia (7th–12th centuries)*, London, 1979; A. K. S. Lambton, *Theory and Practice in Medieval Persian Government*, London, 1980; D. S. Richards, ed., *Islamic Civilization 950–1150*, Oxford, 1973.

For the Buwayhids see M. Kabir, *The Buwayhid Dynasty of Baghdad*, Calcutta, 1964; H. Busse, *Chalif und Grosskönig, die Buyiden im Iraq*, Beirut, 1969. R. Mottahedeh, *Loyalty and Leadership in an Early Islamic Society*, Princeton, 1980 deals with the concepts that underlay Buwayhid social and political practices. On the Ghaznavids see C. E. Bosworth, *The Ghaznavids*, Edinburgh, 1963. A regional history of the Caspian area is V. Minorsky, *A History of Sharvan and Darband in the 10th–11th Century*, Cambridge, 1958.

On the Saljuq period see C. Cahen, "The Turkish Invasion: The Selchukids," *A History of the Crusades*, I, ed. M. W. Baldwin, Philadelphia, 1958, pp. 135–76; C. Cahen, "The Historiography of the Seljuqid Period," *Historians of the Middle East*, ed. B. Lewis and P. Holt, London, 1962, pp. 59–78; E. Tyan, *Institutions du droit public musulman: Sultanat et califat*, II, Paris, 1957; Nizam al-Mulk, *Siyasat-Nama: The Book of Government*, tr. H. Darke, London, 1960. On the Khwarazmshahs see H. Horst, *Die Staatsverwaltung der Grosselgūqen und Hōrazmšāhs, 1038–1231*, Wiesbaden, 1964.

Political and cultural geography is the subject of X. de Planhol, *Le Monde islamique: Essai de géographie religieuse*, Paris, 1957; X. de Planhol, *Les Fondements géographiques de l'histoire de l'Islam*, Paris, 1968; A. Miquel, *La Géographie humaine du monde musulman jusqu'au milieu du XI⁰ siècle*, Paris, 1967. On economy and technology see R. Bulliet, *The Camel and the Wheel*, Cambridge, Mass., 1975; A. M. Watson, *Agricultural Innovation in the Early Islamic World: The Diffusion of Crops and Farming Techniques, 700–1100*, Cambridge, 1983; M. Lombard, *Les Textiles dans le monde musulman du VII⁰ au XII⁰ siècle*, Paris, 1978.

On the economic history of the Middle East from the origins of Islam to the thirteenth century see A. L. Udovitch, ed., *The Islamic Middle East, 700-1900: Studies in Economic and Social History*, Princeton, 1981; E. Ashtor, *A Social and Economic History of the Near East*, London, 1976; D. S. Richards, *Islam and the Trade of Asia*, Oxford, 1970.

The basic history of Mediterranean trade through the late Middle Ages is W. von Heyd, *Histoire du commerce du levant au moyen âge*, 2 vols., tr. F. Reynaud,

Amsterdam, 1959. The study of Mediterranean trade in the early Middle Ages was for decades dominated by H. Pirenne, *Mohammed and Charlemagne*, New York, 1958. The controversy that followed is summed up in a pamphlet by A. F. Havighurst, *The Pirenne Thesis*, 3rd edn, Lexington, Mass., 1976. Important revisions include A. R. Lewis, *Naval Power and Trade in the Mediterranean*, Princeton, 1951; E. Eickhoff, *Seekrieg und Seepolitik zwischen Islam und Abendland. Das Mittelmeer unter byzantinischer und arabischer Hegemonie (650–1040)*, Berlin, 1966. For the period of the Crusades see E. H. Byrne, *Genoese Shipping in the Twelfth and Thirteenth Centuries*, Cambridge, Mass., 1930.

Chapter 10

For the social organization of the 'ulama' see R. P. Mottahedeh, *Loyalty and Leadership in an Early Islamic Society*, Princeton, 1980; R. W. Bulliet, *The Patricians of Nishapur*, Cambridge, 1972; J. Gilbert, "Institutionalization of Muslim Scholarship and Professionalization of the 'Ulama' in Medieval Damascus," *SI*, 52 (1980), pp. 105–34. For the madrasa see G. Makdisi, "Muslim Institutions of Learning in Eleventh-century Baghdad," *BSOAS*, 24 (1961), pp. 1–56. A. L. Tibawi, "Origin and Character of al Madrasah," *BSOAS*, 25 (1962), pp. 225–38 is a rebuttal of Makdisi's views. Also important are D. Sourdel, "Reflexions sur la diffusion de la madrasa en Orient du XIe au XIIIe siècle," *REI*, 44 (1976), pp. 165–84; G. Makdisi, "Ash'ari and the Ash'arites in Islamic Religious History," *SI*, 17 (1962), pp. 37–80, 18 (1962), pp. 19–39.

For religion and politics in the Saljuq era see H. Laoust, "La Pensée et l'action politiques d'Al-Mawardi," *REI*, 36 (1968), pp. 11–92; H. Laoust, *La Politique de Gazālī*, Paris, 1970. On Hanbalism see G. Makdisi, *Ibn 'Aqil et la résurgence de l'Islam traditionaliste au XIe siècle*, Damascus, 1963; and G. Makdisi, "Hanbalite Islam," *Studies on Islam*, ed. M. L. Swartz, New York, 1981, pp. 216–74.

On the social history of Sufism see J. S. Trimingham, *The Sufi Orders in Islam*, Oxford, 1971. On veneration of saints see I. Goldziher, "Veneration of Saints in Islam," *Muslim Studies*, II, London, 1971, pp. 253–341; J. Sourdel-Thomine, "Les Anciens lieux de pèlerinage damascains," *BEO*, 14 (1952–54), pp. 65–85.

On urbanism see I. M. Lapidus, "The Early Evolution of Muslim Urban Society," *Comparative Studies in Society and History*, 15 (1973), pp. 21–50; I. M. Lapidus, "Muslim Cities and Islamic Societies," *Middle Eastern Cities*, ed. I. M. Lapidus, Berkeley, 1969, pp. 47–79; and I. M. Lapidus, *Muslim Cities in the Later Middle Ages*, Cambridge, 1984. Collective works devoted to cities include A. Hourani and S. M. Stern, *The Islamic City*, Oxford, 1970; L. C. Brown, *From Madina to Metropolis*, Princeton, 1973; M. Haneda and T. Miura, eds., *Islamic Urban Studies*, London, 1994.

S. D. Goitein, *A Mediterranean Society: The Jewish Communities of the Arab World as Portrayed in the Documents of the Cairo Geniza*, 4 vols., Berkeley, 1967–78 portrays the Jewish communities of the Mediterranean but throws light on

Muslim societies as well. On the Muslim merchant classes see S. D. Goitein, "The Rise of the Near-Eastern Bourgeoisie," *Journal of World History*, 3 (1956), pp. 583–604; M. Rodinson, "Le Marchand musulman," *Islam and the Trade of Asia*, ed. D. S. Richards, Oxford, 1970, pp. 21–36; M. Rodinson, *Islam and Capitalism*, tr. B. Pearce, Austin, Tex., 1978. For guilds and working classes see R. Brunschvig, "Métiers vils en Islam," *SI*, 16 (1962), pp. 41–60; S. D. Goitein, "Artisans en Méditerranée orientale au haut moyen âge," *Annales ESC*, 19 (1964), pp. 847–68.

Futuwwa, 'ayyarun, and urban young men's gangs: C. Cahen, "Mouvements populaires et autonomisme urbain dans l'Asie musulmane du moyen âge," *Arabica*, 5 (1958), pp. 225–50, 6 (1959), pp. 25–56, 233–65; F. Taeschner, "Das Futuwwa-Rittertum des islamischen Mittelalters," *Beiträge zur Arabistik, Semitistik und Islamwissenschaft*, ed. R. Hartmann and H. Scheel, Leipzig, 1944, pp. 340–85.

Non-Muslim peoples under Muslim rule: A. Fattal, *Le Statut légal des non-musulmans en pays d'Islam*, Beirut, 1958; A. S. Tritton, *The Caliphs and their Non-Muslim Subjects*, London, 1970; S. D. Goitein, *Jews and Arabs: Their Contacts through the Ages*, New York, 1964; N. A. Stillman, *The Jews of Arab Lands*, Philadelphia, 1979; A. S. Atiya, *A History of Eastern Christianity*, 2 vols., London, 1968–69; P. Rondot, *Les Chrétiens d'Orient*, Paris, 1955; M. Morony, "Religious Communities in Late Sassanian and Early Muslim Iraq," *JESHO*, 17 (1974), pp. 113–35.

Conversion to Islam has been little studied. See N. Levtzion, ed., *Conversion to Islam*, New York, 1979; R. Bulliet, *Conversion to Islam in the Medieval Period*, Cambridge, Mass., 1979; I. M. Lapidus, "The Conversion of Egypt to Islam," *In Memoriam S. M. Stern (Israel Oriental Studies)*, 2 (1972), pp. 248–62.

Chapter 11
Important overviews of the literature are E. I. J. Rosenthal, *Political Thought in Medieval Islam*, Cambridge, 1958; W. M. Watt, *Islamic Political Thought*, Edinburgh, 1968. On juristic political theory see A. K. S. Lambton, *State and Government in Medieval Islam*, Oxford, 1981; Y. Ibish, *The Political Doctrine of al-Baqillani*, Beirut, 1968; al-Mawardi, *Les Statuts gouvernementaux*, tr. E. Fagnan, Algiers, 1915; Ibn Taymiya, *Ibn Taymiyah on Public and Private Law in Islam*, Beirut, 1968; H. Laoust, *Essai sur les doctrines sociales et politiques de Takī-d-Dīn Ahmad b. Taimīya*, Cairo, 1939.

Translations of the works of al-Farabi on political theory include *Idées des habitants de la cité vertueuse*, tr. R. P. Jaussen, Y. Karam, and J. Chlala, Cairo, 1949; *Fuṣūl al-Madanī: Aphorisms of the Statesman*, ed. and tr. D. M. Dunlop, Cambridge, 1961; *Philosophy of Plato and Aristotle*, tr. M. Mahdi, New York, 1962. Averroes' principal political work is the *Commentary on Plato's Republic*, ed. and tr. E. I. J. Rosenthal, Cambridge, 1966.

Translations of Mirrors for Princes include al-Jahiz, *Le Livre de la couronne*, tr. C. Pellat, Paris, 1954; Nizam al-Mulk, *The Book of Government or Rules for Kings*, tr. H. Darke, 2nd edn, London, 1978; al-Ghazzali, *Book of Counsel for Kings*, tr.

F. Bagley, London, 1964; Kai Ka'us b. Iskandar, *A Mirror for Princes: The Qābūs Nāma*, tr. R. Levy, New York, 1951; see also G. Richter, *Studien zur Geschichte der älteran arabischen Fürstenspiegel*, Leipzig, 1932.

The *Muqaddima* or *Prolegomena* of Ibn Khaldun is translated by W. M. de Slane, *Les Prolégomènes d'Ibn Khaldoun*, 3 vols., Paris, 1934–38; F. Rosenthal, *Ibn Khaldun, The Muqaddimah*, 3 vols., New York, 1958. Among recent scholarly works on Ibn Khaldun see M. Mahdi, *Ibn Khaldun's Philosophy of History*, London, 1957; W. J. Fischel, *Ibn Khaldun in Egypt*, Berkeley, 1967; Y. Lacoste, *Ibn Khaldoun: Naissance de l'histoire passé du Tiers-Monde*, Paris, 1966; M. M. Rabi, *The Political Theory of Ibn Khaldun*, Leiden, 1967; P. von Sivers, *Khalifat, Königtum und Verfall: Die Politische Theorie Ibn Khaldūns*, Munich, 1968; A. al-Azmeh, *Ibn Khaldūn in Modern Scholarship: A Study in Orientalism*, London, 1981; and A. al-Azmeh, *Ibn Khaldun: An Essay in Reinterpretation*, London, 1982.

Chapter 12

On ethics see M. Arkoun, "L'Ethique musulmane d'après Māwardī," *REI*, 31 (1963), pp. 1–31; M. Arkoun, *Contribution à l'étude de l'humanisme arabe au IVe/Xe siècle: Miskawayh (320/325–421–932/936–1030), philosophe et historien*, Paris, 1970; Ibn Miskawayh, *Traité d'éthique*, tr. M. Arkoun, Damascus, 1969; Muhammad Abul Qassem, *The Ethics of al-Ghazali*, Petaling Jaya, 1975.

The post-945 development of Sufism is represented by al-Kalabadhi, *The Doctrine of the Ṣūfīs*, tr. A. J. Arberry, Cambridge, 1935; al-Sarraj, *The Kitab al-Luma' fi'l-Tasawwuf of Abū Naṣr*, tr. R. A. Nicholson, London, 1963; al-Hujwīrī, *The Kashf al-Mahjūb*, tr. R. A. Nicholson, London, 1911; S. de Laugier de Beaurecueil, *Khwādja 'Abdullāh Anṣārī mystique hanbalite*, Beirut, 1965.

For al-Ghazzali, see M. Bouyges, *Essai de chronologie des oeuvres d' al-Ghazali*, Beirut, 1959; H. Laoust, *La Politique de Gazzali*, Paris, 1970; H. Lazarus-Yafeh, *Studies in al-Ghazzali*, Jerusalem, 1975. The works of F. Jabré explore al-Ghazzali's conceptual vocabulary: *La Notion de certitude selon Ghazali*, Paris, 1958; *La Notion de la ma'rifa chez Ghazali*, Beirut, 1958; *Essai sur la lexique de Ghazali*, Beirut, 1970.

Translations of al-Ghazzali include W. M. Watt, *The Faith and Practice of al-Ghazali*, London, 1953; a translation of the autobiography, *Deliverance from Error: The Book of Knowledge*, tr. N. A. Faris, Lahore, 1962; *The Alchemy of Happiness*, tr. C. Field, London, 1980; *Al-Ghazali's Book of Fear and Hope*, tr. W. McKane, Leiden, 1965; G. H. Bousquet, *Ihya': ou Vivication des sciences de la foi, analyse et index*, Paris, 1955 – a résumé of al-Ghazzali's principal work; *Tahafut al-Falasifah* [Incoherence of the Philosophers], tr. S. A. Kamali, Lahore, 1958. On Suhrawardi al-Maqtul (d. 1191) see S. H. Nasr, *Three Muslim Sages*, Cambridge, Mass., 1964; H. Corbin, *Les Motifs zoroastriens dans la philosophie de Suhrawardi*, Tehran, 1946; and H. Corbin, *Suhrawardi d'Alep*, Paris, 1939. Translations include *Opera metaphysica et mystica*, tr. H. Corbin, I, Istanbul, 1945, II, Tehran, 1952.

On Ibn al-'Arabi (d. 1240) see A. E. Affifi, "Ibn 'Arabi," *History of Muslim Philosophy*, I, ed. M. M. Sharif, Wiesbaden, 1963, pp. 398–420; A. E. Affifi, *The Mystical Philosophy of Muhyid Dīn Ibnul-'Arabi*, Cambridge, 1939; H. Corbin, *Creative Imagination in the Sufism of Ibn 'Arabi*, tr. R. Manheim, Princeton, 1969; T. Izutsu, *A Comparative Study of the Key Philosophical Concepts in Sufism and Taoism*, Berkeley, 1984.

Translations of Ibn al-'Arabi's works include *Sufis of Andalusia. The Rūh al-quds and al-Durrat al-fākhirah of Ibn 'Arabī*, tr. R. W. J. Austin, Berkeley, 1977; *La Profession de foi*, tr. R. Deladrière, Paris, 1978; *The Bezels of Wisdom*, tr. R. W. J. Austin, New York, 1980; *The Seals of Wisdom*, tr. A. al-Tarjumana, Norwich, 1980; *Journey to the Lord of Power: A Sufi Manual on Retreat*, tr. T. Harris, New York, 1981.

On the philosophy of Ibn Sina see L. Gardet, *La Pensée religieuse d'Avicenne (Ibn Sīnā)*, Paris, 1951; A. M. Goichon, *La Philosophie d'Avicenne et son influence en Europe médiévale*, 2nd edn, Paris, 1951; A. Afnan, *Avicenna: His Life and Works*, London, 1958; H. Corbin, *Avicenna and the Visionary Recital*, tr. W. Trask, New York, 1960. Translations include *Avicenna on Theology*, tr. A. J. Arberry, London, 1951; *Livre des directives et remarques*, tr. A. M. Goichon, Beirut, 1951; *Avicenna's Psychology*, tr. F. Rahman, London, 1952; *The Metaphysica of Avicenna*, tr. P. Morewedge, New York, 1973. Translations of Ibn Rushd include *Tahafut al-Tahafut* [The Incoherence of the Incoherence], 2 vols., tr. S. van den Bergh, London, 1954; *On the Harmony of Religion and Philosophy*, tr. G. Hourani, London, 1961; *Averroes' Three Short Commentaries on Aristotle's "Topics," "Rhetoric," and "Poetics,"* tr. C. E. Butterworth, Albany, N.Y., 1977.

For special topics in Islamic philosophy see M. Fakhry, *Islamic Occasionalism and its Critique by Averroes and Aquinas*, London, 1958; A. J. Arberry, *Revelation and Reason in Islam*, London, 1957; F. Rahman, *Prophecy in Islam*, London, 1958; S. H. Nasr, *An Introduction to Islamic Cosmological Doctrines*, Cambridge, Mass., 1964; I. R. Netton, *Muslim Neoplatonists: An Introduction to the Thought of the Brethren of Purity*, London, 1982.

The transmission of Arabic and Hebrew philosophy to Europe and the development of Christian scholasticism are the subjects of F. van Steenberghen, *Aristotle in the West: The Origins of Latin Aristotelianism*, tr. L. Johnston, Louvain, 1955; F. van Steenberghen, *The Philosophical Movement in the Thirteenth Century*, Edinburgh, 1955; E. Gilson, "Les Sources gréco-arabes de l'Augustinisme avicennisant," *Archives d'histoire doctrinale et littéraire du moyen âge*, 14 (1929), pp. 5–149; M. Steinschneider, *Die europäischen Übersetzungen aus dem Arabischen bis mitte des 17. Jahrhunderts*, Graz, 1956. For relations between Islam and the West more generally see R. W. Southern, *Western Views of Islam in the Middle Ages*, Cambridge, Mass., 1978; N. Daniel, *Islam and the West: The Making of an Image*, Edinburgh, 1960; N. Daniel, *The Arabs and Medieval Europe*, 2nd edn, London, 1979; J. Kritzech, *Peter the Venerable and Islam*, Princeton, 1964; K. I. Semaan, ed., *Islam and the Medieval West*, Albany, N.Y., 1980.

PART II

Chapter 13

For Iran under the Mongols see the relevant chapters of the *Cambridge History of Iran*, v, ed. J. A. Boyle, Cambridge, 1968; C. Cahen, "The Turks in Iran and Anatolia before the Mongol Invasions," *History of the Crusades*, II, ed. R. L. Wolff and H. W. Hazard, Madison, Wis., 1969, pp. 661–92; C. Cahen, "The Mongols and the Near East," *ibid.*, pp. 715–34; B. Spuler, *Die Mongolen in Iran: Politik, Verwaltung und Kultur der Ilchanzeit, 1220–1350*, Berlin, 1968. On Mongol art see D. N. Wilber, *The Architecture of Islamic Iran*, Princeton, 1955; O. Grabar and S. Blair, *Epic Images and Contemporary History: The Illustrations of the Great Mongol Shahnama*, Chicago, 1980. See bibliography for chapter 17 for further references to Mongols and Inner Asia.

For the political system of Iran in the fifteenth century see J. E. Woods, *The Aqquyunlu: Clan, Confederation, Empire*, Minneapolis, 1976. On the rise of the Safavid dynasty see M. Mazzaoui, *The Origins of the Safawids*, Wiesbaden, 1972. A general history of the Safavid period in English is R. Savory, *Iran under the Safavids*, Cambridge, 1980. L. L. Bellan, *Chah 'Abbas*, I, Paris, 1932 covers the principal reign of the dynasty. For Safavid and later Iranian relations with Europe see R. K. Ramazani, *The Foreign Policy of Iran: 1500–1941*, Charlottesville, Va., 1966.

Safavid state organization: A. K. S. Lambton, *Landlord and Peasant in Persia*, London, 1953. For the theory of Iranian monarchy see A. K. S. Lambton, "Quis custodiet custodes? Some Reflections on the Persian Theory of Government," *SI*, 5 (1956), pp. 125–48, 6 (1956), pp. 125–46. For Safavid art and architecture see S. C. Welch, *A King's Book of Kings: The Shah-nameh of Shah Tahmasp*, London, 1972; S. C. Welch, *Persian Painting: Five Royal Safavid Manuscripts of the Sixteenth Century*, New York, 1976; J. Bloom and S. Blair, *Art and Architecture of Islam, 1250–1800*, New Haven, 1994.

The relations between state and religion in Safavid Iran are the subject of J. Aubin, "Etudes safavides: I, Šāh Ismā'īl et les notables de l'Iraq persan," *JESHO*, 2 (1959), pp. 37–81; J. Aubin, "La Politique religieuse des Safavides," *Le Shī'isme imāmite,*Colloque de Strasbourg, Paris, 1970, pp. 235–44; S. Arjomand, "Religion, Political Action and Legitimate Domination in Shi'ite Iran: 14th to 18th Centuries," *European Journal of Sociology*, 20 (1979), pp. 59–109; S. Arjomand, "Religious Extremism (Ghuluww), Sufism and Sunnism in Safavid Iran: 1501–1722," *Journal of Asian History*, 15 (1981), pp. 1–35.

Iranian illuminationist philosophy has been examined by S. H. Nasr, "The School of Isfahan," *A History of Muslim Philosophy*, II, ed. M. M. Sharif, Wiesbaden, 1966, pp. 904–31; H. Corbin, *En Islam iranien*, 3 vols., Paris, 1974; and H. Corbin, *La Philosophie iranienne islamique aux XVIIe et XVIIIe siècles*, Paris, 1981. See also F. Rahman, *The Philosophy of Mulla Sadra (Sadr al-Din al-Shirazi)*, Albany, N.Y., 1976.

The work of James Reid on *uymaq* and tribal structures has contributed to my interpretation of the dynamics of Iranian history. See his *Tribalism and Society in*

Islamic Iran, 1500–1629, Malibu, Calif., 1983; "The Qajar Uymaq in the Safavid Period, 1500–1722," *Iranian Studies*, 11 (1978), pp. 117–143; and "Rebellion and Social Change in Astarabad, 1537–1744," *IJMES*, 13 (1981), pp. 35–53.

On the Iranian economy see R. Quiring-Zoche, *Isfahan im funfzehnten und sechzehnten Jahrhundert*, Freiburg, 1980; M. Keyvani, *Artisans and Guild Life in the Later Safavid Period*, Berlin, 1982.

For the eighteenth-century collapse of the Safavid regime see L. Lockhart, *The Fall of the Safavi Dynasty and the Afghan Occupation of Persia*, Cambridge, 1958; L. Lockhart, *Nadir Shah: A Critical Study*, London, 1938; and J. R. Perry, *Karim Khan Zand: A History of Iran, 1747–1779*, Chicago, 1979. Other studies of Turko-Iranian tribal societies in the eighteenth and nineteenth centuries include G. Garthwaite, "Pastoral Nomadism and Tribal Power," *Iranian Studies*, 11 (1978), pp. 173–97; R. Loeffler, "Tribal Order and the State: The Political Organization of the Boir Ahmad," *Iranian Studies*, 11 (1978), pp. 144–71.

Chapter 14

The classic history of the Ottoman empire is H. Inalcik, *The Ottoman Empire: The Classical Age, 1300–1600*, tr. N. Itzkowitz and C. Imber, London, 1973. H. A. R. Gibb and H. Bowen, *Islamic Society and the West*, 2 parts, Oxford, 1950, 1957, despite out-of-date sections, is still an indispensable introduction. See also N. Itzkowitz, *The Ottoman Empire and Islamic Tradition*, New York, 1972; S. J. Shaw, *History of the Ottoman Empire and Modern Turkey*, 2 vols., Cambridge, 1976.

On pre-Ottoman Turkey see C. Cahen, *Pre-Ottoman Turkey, 1071–1330*, tr. J. Jones-Williams, London, 1968. Important studies of the Turkish principalities include B. Flemming, *Landschaftsgeschichte von Pamphylien, Pisidien und Lykien im Spätmittelalter*, Wiesbaden, 1964; P. Lemerle, *L'Emirat d'Aydin: Byzance et l'Occident. Recherches sur "La Geste d'Umur Pacha,"* Paris, 1957; P. Wittek, *Das fürstentum Mentesche*, Amsterdam, 1967; S. Vryonis, Jr., *The Decline of Medieval Hellenism in Asia Minor*, Berkeley, 1971; and S. Vryonis, Jr., "Nomadization and Islamization in Asia Minor," *Dumbarton Oaks Papers*, 29 (1975), pp. 41–71.

On Ottoman conquests see P. Wittek, *Rise of the Ottoman Empire*, London, 1938; F. Babinger, *Mahomet II, le Conquérant, et son temps*, Paris, 1954; S. Runciman, *The Fall of Constantinople*, Cambridge, 1965. Ottoman wars with the Austro-Hungarian empire: D. Vaughan, *Europe and the Turk: A Pattern of Alliances, 1350–1700*, Liverpool, 1954; C. M. Kortepeter, *Ottoman Imperialism during the Reformation: Europe and the Caucasus*, New York, 1972; S. A. Fischer-Galati, *Ottoman Imperialism and German Protestantism*, Cambridge, Mass., 1959. For Ottoman expansion in the Crimea see H. Inalcik, "The Origin of the Ottoman–Russian Rivalry and the Don–Volga Canal (1569)," *Annales de l'Université d'Ankara*, 1 (1946–47), pp. 47–106; W. E. D. Allen, *Problems of Turkish Power in the Sixteenth Century*, London, 1963.

On Ottoman expansion in the Mediterranean see F. Braudel, *The Mediterranean and the Mediterranean World*, 2 vols., tr. S. Reynolds, New York, 1972; A. Hess, *The Forgotten Frontier: A History of the Sixteenth-century Ibero-African Frontier*,

Chicago, 1978. For Ottoman–Safavid wars see E. Eberhard, *Osmanische Polemik gegen die Safawiden im 16. Jahrhundert. nach arabischen Handschriften*, Freiburg, 1970. A useful collection of documents is J. C. Hurewitz, *Diplomacy in the Near and Middle East: A Documentary Record, 1535–1914*, I, New York, 1956. For Ottoman rule in the Balkans see P. F. Sugar, *Southeastern Europe under Ottoman Rule, 1354–1804*, Seattle, 1977; N. Beldiceanu, *Le Monde ottoman des Balkans (1402–1566)*, London, 1976.

For the institutions of the Ottoman state see A. D. Alderson, *The Structure of the Ottoman Dynasty*, Oxford, 1956; I. M. Kunt, *The Sultan's Servants: The Transformation of Ottoman Provincial Government, 1550–1650*, New York, 1983; H. Inalcik, "Military and Fiscal Transformation in the Ottoman Empire, 1600–1700," *Archivum Ottomanicum*, 6 (1980), pp. 283–337. B. Miller, *The Palace School of Muhammad the Conqueror*, Cambridge, Mass., 1941 depicts the education of the janissaries.

For Islamic religious elites see H. A. R. Gibb and H. Bowen, *Islamic Society and the West*, Oxford, 1950–57, I, pp. 19–38, II, pp. 70-261; J. Birge, *The Bektashi Order of Dervishes*, London, 1937.

On the non-Muslim populations: F. W. Hasluck, *Christianity and Islam under the Sultans*, 2 vols., Oxford, 1929; T. Ware, *Eustratios Argenti: A Study of the Greek Church under Turkish Rule*, Oxford, 1964; N. J. Pantazopoulos, *Church and Law in the Balkan Peninsula during the Ottoman Rule*, Thessaloniki, 1967; S. Runciman, *The Great Church in Captivity*, London, 1968; L. Arpee, *A History of Armenian Christianity from the Beginning to our Own Time*, New York, 1946. On the Jewish communities see M. A. Epstein, *The Ottoman Jewish Communities and their Role in the Fifteenth and Sixteenth Centuries*, Freiburg, 1980; C. Roth, *The House of Nasi: The Duke of Naxos*, New York, 1948. The relations between Ottomans and Europeans are discussed in B. Homsy, *Les Capitulations et la protection des chrétiens au Proche-Orient aux XVIe, XVIIe et XVIIIe siècles*, Paris, 1956; C. A. Frazee, *Catholics and Sultans: The Church and the Ottoman Empire, 1453–1923*, Cambridge, 1983. A major reinterpretation of the "millet" system is advanced by B. Braude, "Foundation Myths of the Millet System," *Christians and Jews in the Ottoman Empire*, I, ed. B. Braude and B. Lewis, New York, 1982, pp. 69–88.

For the development of Istanbul see B. Lewis, *Istanbul and the Civilization of the Ottoman Empire*, Norman, Okla., 1963; R. Mantran, *La Vie quotidienne à Constantinople au temps de Soliman le Magnifique et de ses successeurs*, Paris, 1965. Balkan cities are the subject of N. Todorov, ed., *La Ville balkanique sous les Ottomans, XVe–XIXe siècles*, London, 1977. On the small towns of Anatolia see S. Faroqhi, *Towns and Townsmen of Ottoman Anatolia*, Cambridge, 1984.

The demographic and economic development of Anatolia is treated by M. A. Cook, *Population Pressure in Rural Anatolia, 1450–1600*, London, 1972. See also H. Islamoglu and S. Faroqhi, "Crop Patterns and Agricultural Production Trends in Sixteenth-Century Anatolia," *Review* (New York), 2 (1979), pp. 401–36. Ottoman trade: H. Inalcik, "Bursa and the Commerce of the Levant," *JESHO*, 3 (1960), pp.

131–47; H. Inalcik, "Capital Formation in the Ottoman Empire," *Journal of Economic History*, 29 (1969), pp. 97–140; H. Islamoglu-Inan, *State and Peasant in the Ottoman Empire*, New York, 1994. The struggle for control of the international spice trade is the subject of S. Y. Labib, *Handelsgeschichte Ägyptens im Spätmittelalter (1171–1517)*, Wiesbaden, 1965. For the rise of Europe and the transformation of the world economy see I. Wallerstein, *The Modern World System*, 2 vols., New York, 1974–80; P. Pachi, "The Shifting of International Trade Routes in the 15th–17th Centuries," *Acta Historica*, 14 (1968), pp. 287–321; R. Mantran, "Transformation du commerce dans l'Empire Ottoman au dix-huitième siècle," *Studies in Eighteenth-Century Islamic History*, ed. T. Naff and R. Owen, Carbondale, Ill., 1977, pp. 217–35.

The growth of European commerce in the seventeenth and eighteenth centuries is studied in P. Masson, *Histoire du commerce français dans le Levant au XVIIe siècle*, Paris, 1896; P. Masson, *Histoire du commerce français dans le Levant au XVIIIe siècle*, Paris, 1911; N. G. Svoronos, *Le Commerce de Salonique au XVIIIe siècle*, Paris, 1956; A. C. Wood, *A History of the Levant Company*, London, 1935. See also D. Goffman, *Izmir and the Levantine World*, Seattle, 1990; E. Eldem, D. Goffman, and B. Masters, *The Ottoman City between East and West*, Cambridge, 1999.

On Turkish art and literature see E. Atil, ed., *Turkish Art*, Washington, D.C., 1980; G. Goodwin, *A History of Ottoman Architecture*, Baltimore, 1971; O. Aslanapa, *Turkish Art and Architecture*, London, 1971; M. And, *A History of Theatre and Popular Entertainment in Turkey*, Ankara, 1963–64; M. And, *Turkish Miniature Painting*, Ankara, 1974; E. Atil, *Turkish Miniature Painting*, Tokyo, 1960.

On the seventeenth and eighteenth centuries see S. J. Shaw, *Between Old and New: The Ottoman Empire under Sultan Selim III, 1789–1807*, Cambridge, Mass., 1971; T. Naff and R. Owen, eds., *Studies in Eighteenth Century Islamic History*, London, 1977. Specialized studies on the internal condition of the Ottoman empire include W. J. Griswold, *The Great Anatolian Rebellion: 1000–1020/1591–1611*, Berlin, 1983; K. Barkey, *Bandits and Bureaucrats: The Ottoman Route to State Centralization*, Ithaca, N.Y., 1994.

Ottoman military and political relations with Europe in the eighteenth century are treated in M. S. Anderson, *The Eastern Question, 1774–1923*, London, 1966; L. Cassels, *The Struggle for the Ottoman Empire, 1717–1740*, London, 1966; A. W. Fisher, *The Russian Annexation of the Crimea, 1772–1783*, Cambridge, 1970; B. H. Sumner, *Peter the Great and the Ottoman Empire*, Oxford, 1949; G. S. Thomson, *Catherine the Great and the Expansion of Russia*, London, 1947.

Chapter 15

For Fatimid art see K. A. C. Creswell, *The Muslim Architecture of Egypt*, 2 vols., Oxford, 1952–59; O. Grabar, "Imperial and Urban Art in Islam: The Subject Matter of Fatimid Art," *Colloque international sur l'histoire du Caire*, Cairo, 1973, pp. 173–89; J. M. Bloom, "The Mosque of al-Hakim in Cairo," *Muqarnas*, 1 (1983), pp. 15–36; C. Williams, "The Cult of Alid Saints in the Fatimid Monuments of Cairo," *Muqarnas*, 1 (1983), pp. 37–52; M. Canard, "Le Cérémonie fatimite et le cérémonie byzantin," *Byzantion*, 21 (1951), pp. 355–420; and M. Canard, "La Procession du nouvel an chez les Fatimides," *AIEO*, 10 (1952), pp. 364–98.

For Syria in the early Islamic era see K. S. Salibi, *Syria under Islam: Empire on Trial, 634–1097*, Delmar, N.Y., 1976; M. Canard, *Histoire de la dynastie des Hamdanides de Jazīra et de Syrie*, Paris, 1953. Histories of the Crusades include S. Runciman, *A History of the Crusades*, 3 vols., Cambridge, 1951–54; H. E. Mayer, *The Crusades*, tr. J. Gillingham, London, 1972; J. Prawers, *Crusader Institutions*, Oxford, 1980; H. W. Hazard, *The Art and Architecture of the Crusader States*, Madison, Wis., 1977.

For the history of Muslim Syria in the crusading era the fundamental work is C. Cahen, *La Syrie du Nord à l'époque des croisades*, Paris, 1940. Good general accounts may be found in K. M. Setton, ed., *A History of the Crusades*, 2nd edn, 4 vols., Madison, Wis., 1969–77. See also N. Elisseeff, *Nūr ad-Dīn: Un grand prince musulman de Syrie au temps des croisades (511–569 H/1118–1174)*, 3 vols., Damascus, 1967; E. Sivan, *L'Islam et la croisade*, Paris, 1968.

Useful translations of Arabic sources include F. Gabrieli, ed., *Arab Historians of the Crusades*, Berkeley, 1969; F. Gabrieli, *Recueil des historiens des croisades*, Académie des inscriptions et belles-lettres, 14 vols., Paris, 1966–67; Ibn al-Qalānisī, *The Damascus Chronicle of the Crusades*, tr. H. A. R. Gibb., London, 1932; Usāmah ibn Munqidh, *An Arab-Syrian Gentleman and Warrior in the Period of the Crusades*, tr. P. K. Hitti, New York, 1929.

Isma'ilism in the Crusades period is the subject of M. G. S. Hodgson, *The Order of Assassins*, The Hague, 1955; B. Lewis, *The Assassins*, London, 1967. See especially M. G. S. Hodgson, "The Isma'ili State," *Cambridge History of Iran*, v, ed. J. A. Boyle, Cambridge, 1968, pp. 422–82.

For Egypt and Syria under Saladin and the Ayyubids see A. Ehrenkreutz, *Saladin*, Albany, N.Y., 1972; R. S. Humphreys, *From Saladin to the Mongols*, Albany, N.Y., 1972. Ayyubid military organization is treated by S. Elbeheiry, *Les Institutions de l'Egypte au temps des Ayyūbides. L'organisation de l'armée et des institutions militaires*, Paris, 1971; R. S. Humphreys, "The Emergence of the Mamluk Army," *SI*, 45 (1977), pp. 67–100, 46 (1977), pp. 147-82. Ayyubid administration has been extensively studied by C. Cahen, *Makhzūmiyyāt: Etudes sur l'histoire économique et financière de l'Egypte médiévale*, Leiden, 1977.

For Syrian Muslim towns see E. Ashtor-Strauss, "L'Administration urbaine en Syrie médiévale," *RSO*, 31 (1956), pp. 73–128; C. Cahen, "Mouvements populaires et autonomisme urbain dans l'Asie musulmane du moyen âge," *Arabica*, 5 (1958), pp. 225–50, 6 (1959), pp. 25–56, 233–65; and the relevant chapters of J. Sauvaget, *Alep*, Paris, 1941. On the 'ulama' and the schools of law in Syria see N. Elisseeff, *Nūr ad-Dīn: Un grand prince musulman de Syrie au temps des croisades (511–569 H/1118–1174)*, 3 vols., Damascus, 1967.

Ayyubid architecture is treated by F. Herzfeld, "Damascus: Studies in Architecture," *Ars Islamica*, 9 (1942), pp. 1–53, 10 (1943), pp. 13–70, 11 (1946), pp. 1–71, 13–14 (1948), pp. 118–38; J. Sauvaget, M. Ecochard, and J. Sourdel-Thomine, *Les Monuments ayyoubides de Damas*, Paris, 1938–50.

An extensive bibliography of works on the Mamluk era in Egypt and Syria is found in I. M. Lapidus, *Muslim Cities in the Later Middle Ages*, Cambridge, Mass., 1967, with supplements in the 2nd edn, Cambridge, 1984.

The history of Egypt under Ottoman rule is given by P. M. Holt, *Egypt and the Fertile Crescent, 1516–1922*, London, 1966; S. J. Shaw, *The Financial and Administrative Organization and Development of Ottoman Egypt, 1517–1798*, Princeton, 1962; S. J. Shaw, *Ottoman Egypt in the Eighteenth Century*, Cambridge, Mass., 1962. The economy of Ottoman Egypt: A. Raymond, *Artisans et commerçants au Caire*, 2 vols., Damascus, 1973–74; A. Raymond, "The Economic Crisis of Egypt in the Eighteenth Century," *The Islamic Middle East, 700–1900: Studies in Economic and Social History*, ed. A. L. Udovitch, Princeton, 1981, pp. 687–707; G. Baer, *Egyptian Guilds in Modern Times*, Jerusalem, 1964.

On Egyptian Islam see A. L. Marsot, "The Ulama of Cairo in the Eighteenth and Nineteenth Centuries," *Scholars, Saints and Sufis: Muslim Religious Institutions since 1500*, ed. N. R. Keddie, Berkeley, 1972, pp. 149–65; M. Winter, *Society and Religion in Early Ottoman Egypt*, New Brunswick, N.J., 1982.

On the Arab provinces under Ottoman rule see H. Laoust, *Les Gouverneurs de Damas sous les Mamlouks et les premiers Ottomans*, Damascus, 1952; M. A. Bakhit, *The Ottoman Province of Damascus in the Sixteenth Century*, Beirut, 1982; K. K. Barbir, *Ottoman Rule in Damascus 1708–1758*, Princeton, 1980; A. K. Rafeq, *The Province of Damascus, 1723–1783*, Beirut, 1966.

For the 'ulama' and Sufism in Syria see M. Winter, "Sheikh 'Alī ibn Maymūn and Syrian Sufism in the Sixteenth Century," *Israel Oriental Studies*, 7 (1977), pp. 281–308; A. Hourani, "Sheikh Khalid and the Naqshbandi Order," *Islamic Philosophy and the Classical Tradition*, ed. S. M. Stern and V. Brown, Columbia, S.C., 1972, pp. 89–103; J. Voll, "Old 'Ulama' Families and Ottoman Influence in 18th-century Damascus," *The American Journal of Arabic Studies*, 3 (1975), pp. 48–59.

Palestine has been the subject of U. Heyd, *Ottoman Documents on Palestine, 1552–1615*, Oxford, 1960; A. Cohen and B. Lewis, *Population and Revenue in the Towns of Palestine in the Sixteenth Century*, Princeton, 1978; M. Ma'oz, ed., *Studies on Palestine during the Ottoman Period*, Jerusalem, 1975; A. Cohen, *Palestine in the Eighteenth Century*, Jerusalem, 1973. On Lebanon see K. S. Salibi, *The Modern History of Lebanon*, London, 1965; I. F. Harik, *Politics and Change in a Traditional Society: Lebanon, 1711–1845*, Princeton, 1968; B. Doumani, *Rediscovering Palestine: Merchants and Peasants in Jabal Nablus*, Berkeley, 1995.

On Iraq see T. Nieuwenhuis, *Politics and Society in Early Modern Iraq (1802–1831)*, The Hague, 1982; S. H. Longrigg, *Four Centuries of Modern Iraq*, Oxford, 1925.

Chapter 16

General histories of North Africa include J. M. Abun-Nasr, *A History of the Maghrib*, 2nd edn, Cambridge, 1975; A. Laroui, *The History of the Maghrib*, Princeton, 1977; L. Valensi, *On the Eve of Colonialism: North Africa before the French Conquest*, New York, 1977; C. A. Julien, *History of North Africa: Tunisia, Algeria, Morocco, from the Arab Conquest to 1830*, New York, 1970.

The Arab conquests to the thirteenth century: H. R. Idris, *La Berbèrie orientale sous les Zīrīdes*, Paris, 1962; G. Marçais, *Les Arabes en Berbèrie du XIᵉ au XIVᵉ siècle*, Paris, 1913; M. Talbi, *L'Emirat aghlabide: Histoire politique*, Paris, 1966. For the Fatimids see the previous section on Egypt and Syria. Kharijism has been studied by T. Lewicki, "La Répartition géographique des groupements ibādites dans l'Afrique du Nord au moyen âge," *Rocznik orientalistyczny*, 21 (1957), pp. 301–43; and T. Lewicki, "The Ibadites in Arabia and Africa," *Journal of World History*, 13 (1971), pp. 51–130.

The origin of the Almoravid movement has been reinterpreted by P. F. de Moraes Farias, "The Almoravids: Some Questions Concerning the Character of the Movement during its Periods of Closest Contact with the Western Sudan," *Bulletin de l'Institut français d'Afrique Noire*, 29 (1967), pp. 794–878; H. T. Norris, "New Evidence on the Life of 'Abdullāh b. Yāsīn and the Origins of the Almoravid Movement," *JAH*, 12 (1971), pp. 255–68; V. Lagardere, "Esquisse de l'organization militaire des Murābitūn à l'époque de Yūsuf b. Tāšfīn, 430 H/1039 à 500 H/1106," *ROMM*, 27 (1979), pp. 99–114; N. Levtzion, "'Abd Allāh b. Yāsīn and the Almoravids," *Studies in West African Islamic History*, I, ed. J. R. Willis, London, 1979, pp. 78–112.

The impact of the Hilali invasions is much debated: H. R. Idris, "L'Invasion hilālienne et ses conséquences," *Cahiers de civilisation médiévale*, 11 (1968), pp. 353–69; J. Poncet, "Prospérité et décadence ifrikiyennes," *Cahiers de Tunisie*, 9 (1961), pp. 221–43; J. Poncet, "Le Mythe de la 'catastrophe' hilālienne," *Annales ESC*, 22 (1967), pp. 1099–1120.

On Saharan, North African, and Mediterranean trade see N. Pacha, *Le Commerce au Maghreb du XIᵉ au XIVᵉ siècle*, Tunis, 1976; J. Devisse, "Routes de commerce et échanges en Afrique Occidentale en relation avec la Méditerranée," *Revue d'histoire économique et sociale*, 50 (1972), pp. 42–73, 357–97.

The basic study of Tunisian society from the thirteenth to the sixteenth centuries is R. Brunschvig, *La Berbèrie orientale sous les Hafsides*, 2 vols., Paris, 1940–47. See also L. C. Brown, "The Religious Establishment in Husainid Tunisia," *Scholars, Saints and Sufis*, ed. N. R. Keddie, Berkeley, 1972, pp. 47–91; J. Abun-Nasr, "The Beylicate in Seventeenth-Century Tunisia," *IJMES*, 6 (1975), pp. 70–93; J. Pignon, "La Milice des janissaires du Tunis au temps des Deys (1590–1650)," *Cahiers de Tunisie*, 4 (1956), pp. 301–26.

For the economic history of Tunisia in the eighteenth and early nineteenth centuries see L. Valensi, "Islam et capitalisme, production et commerce des Chéchias en Tunisie et en France aux XVIIIIᵉ et XIXᵉ siècles," *Revue d'histoire moderne et contemporaine*, 16 (1969), pp. 376–400; L. Valensi, *Tunisian Peasants in the Eighteenth and Nineteenth Centuries*, Cambridge, 1985; M. H. Cherif, "Expansion européenne et difficultés tunisiennes de 1815 à 1830," *Annales ESC*, 25 (1961), pp. 714–45; L. C. Brown, *The Tunisia of Ahmad Bey, 837–1855*, Princeton, 1974.

For Algeria under the Turks see P. Boyer, *L'Evolution de l'Algérie médiane*, Paris, 1960; P. Boyer, *La Vie quotidienne à Alger*, Paris, 1964; W. Spencer, *Algiers in the Age of the Corsairs*, Norman, Okla., 1976. On piracy and trade in the Mediterranean from the sixteenth to the nineteenth centuries see G. Fisher, *Barbary Legend: War, Trade and Piracy in North Africa, 1415–1830*, Oxford, 1957; P. Masson, *Histoire des établissements et du commerce français dans l'Afrique barbaresque (1560–1793)*, Paris, 1903; A. E. Sayous, *Le Commerce des Européens à Tunis*, Paris, 1929.

On Algerian society see P. Boyer, "Contribution à l'étude de la politique religieuse des Turcs dans la Régence d'Alger (XVIe–XIXe siècles)," *ROMM*, 1 (1966), pp. 11–49. R. Gallissot, *L'Algérie pré-coloniale: Classes sociales en système précapitaliste*, Paris, 1968; R. Gallissot, "Pre-colonial Algeria," *Economy and Society*, 4 (1975), pp. 418–45; J. C. Vatin, "L'Algérie en 1830: Essai d'interprétation des recherches historiques sous l'angle de la science politique," *Revue algérienne*, 7 (1970), pp. 977–1058; A. Nouschi, "La vita rurale in Algeria prima de 1830," *Studi Storici*, 4 (1963), pp. 449–78. Morocco's history is covered by the work of H. Terrasse, *Histoire du Maroc*, 2 vols., Casablanca, 1950; E. Lévi-Provençal, *Les Historiens des Chorfa: Essai sur la littérature historique et biographique au Maroc du XVIe au XXe siècle*, Paris, 1922. On the Moroccan economy before the nineteenth century see P. Berthier, *Les Anciennes Sucreries du Maroc*, 2 vols., Rabat, 1966; A. Hammoudi, "Sainteté, pouvoir et société: Tamgrout aux XVIIe et XVIIIe siècles," *Annales ESC*, 35 (1980), pp. 615–41.

For Moroccan urban society, see K. Brown, *People of Salé*, Manchester, 1976; R. Le Tourneau, *Fes avant le protectorat*, Casablanca, 1949; R. Le Tourneau, *Les Villes musulmanes de l'Afrique du Nord*, Algiers, 1957; R. Le Tourneau, *Fez in the Age of the Marinides*, Norman, Okla., 1961; J. S. Gerber, *Jewish Society in Fez, 1450–1700*, Leiden, 1980.

On North African Sufism see A. Bel, *La Religion musulmane en Berbèrie*, Paris, 1938; G. Drague, *Esquisse d'histoire religieuse du Maroc: confréries et zaouias*, Paris, 1951; P. J. André, *Contribution à l'études des confréries religieuses musulmanes*, Algiers, 1956; J. Abun-Nasr, *The Tijaniyya*, London, 1965; R. G. Jenkins, "The Evolution of Religious Brotherhoods in North and Northwest Africa 1523–1900," *Studies in West African Islamic History*, I, ed. J. R. Willis, London, 1979, pp. 40–77; C. Geertz, *Islam Observed*, New Haven, 1968; V. J. Cornell, "The Logic of Analogy and the Role of the Sufi Shaykh," *IJMES*, 15 (1983), pp. 67–93.

Introductory accounts of Muslim Spain include A. Chejne, *Muslim Spain*, Minneapolis, 1974; J. O'Callaghan, *A History of Medieval Spain*, Ithaca, N.Y., 1975; and the classic E. Lévi-Provençal, *Histoire de l'Espagne musulmane*, 3 vols., Paris, 1950–53. Important interpretations of the economic and social bases of Spanish and Muslim civilization are T. Glick, *Irrigation and Society in Medieval Valencia*, Cambridge, Mass., 1970; T. Glick, *Islamic and Christian Spain in the Early Middle Ages*,

Princeton, 1979; P. Guichard, *Structures sociales, orientales et occidentales dans l'Espagne musulmane*, Paris, 1977. See also D. Wasserstein, *The Rise and Fall of the Party-Kings*, Princeton, 1985.

Muslim urban communities and the supervision of markets are treated in the work of P. Chalmeta Gendrón, *El "señor del zoco" en España*, Madrid, 1973; L. Torres Balbás, "Les Villes musulmanes d'Espagne et leur urbanisation," *AIEO*, 6 (1942–47), pp. 5–30; L. Torres Balbás, "Extensión y demografia de las ciudades hispano musulmanas," *SI*, 3 (1955), pp. 37–59.

On Islam in Spain see H. Mones, "Le Rôle des hommes de religion dans l'histoire de l'Espagne musulmane jusqu'à la fin du Califat," *SI*, 20 (1964), pp. 47–88. For Spanish Sufism see P. Nwyia, *Ibn 'Abbād de Ronda (1332–1390)*, Beirut, 1961.

For the Reconquista and relations between Muslims and Christians see R. Burns, *Islam under the Crusaders: Colonial Survival in the Thirteenth-Century Kingdom of Valencia*, Princeton, 1973; R. Burns, *The Crusader Kingdom of Valencia: Reconstruction on a Thirteenth-Century Frontier*, 2 vols., Cambridge, Mass., 1967; J. Boswell, *The Royal Treasure: Muslim Communities under the Crown of Aragon in the Fourteenth Century*, New Haven, 1978; J. Edwards, *Christian Cordoba: The City and its Region in the Late Middle Ages*, Cambridge, 1982.

On Arabic literature see the contributions of J. Monroe, *The Shu'ubiyya in al-Andalus: The Risala of Ibn Garcia and Five Refutations*, Berkeley, 1969; J. Monroe, *Hispano-Arabic Poetry*, Berkeley, 1974; S. Stern, *Hispano-Arabic Strophic Poetry*, Oxford, 1974; L. Compton, *Andalusian Lyrical Poetry and Old Spanish Love Songs*, New York, 1976. A vivid interpretation of Spanish architecture and its cultural significance is O. Grabar, *The Alhambra*, London, 1978.

Chapter 17

For the dynamics of steppe empires see R. Grousset, *The Empire of the Steppes: A History of Central Asia*, tr. N. Walford, New Brunswick, N.J., 1970. D. Sinor, *Introduction à l'étude de l'Eurasie centrale*, Wiesbaden, 1963 contains ample bibliographies. O. Lattimore, *Inner Asian Frontiers of China*, New York, 1951 is an imaginative interpretation of the formation of nomadism in Inner Asia and its relation to sedentary empires. L. Krader discusses Inner Asian social organization: *Peoples of Central Asia*, Bloomington, 1963; and *Social Organization of the Mongol-Turkic Pastoral Nomads*, The Hague, 1963.

On the Mongol, Chaghatay, and Timurid periods in Inner Asia see P. Brent, *The Mongol Empire: Genghis Khan, his Triumph and Legacy*, London, 1976; V. V. Bartold, *Histoire des Turcs d'Asie centrale*, Paris, 1945; V. V. Bartold, *Four Studies on the History of Central Asia*, tr. V. Minorsky and T. Minorsky, 3 vols., Leiden, 1956–62; J. A. Boyle, *The Mongol World Empire, 1206–1370*, London, 1977. Two important early histories have been translated: Rashid al-Din Tabib, *The Successors of Genghis Khan*, tr. J. A. Boyle, New York, 1971; and M. Haydar (Dughlat), *A History of the Moghuls of Central Asia (Tarikh-i Rashidi)*, tr. E. D. Ross, New York, 1970.

For the Golden Horde see G. Vernadsky, *The Mongols and Russia*, New Haven, 1953. For the Russian conquest: A. S. Donnelly, *The Russian Conquest of Bashkiria, 1552–1740*, New Haven, 1968; C. Lemercier-Quelquejay, "Les Missions orthodoxes en pays musulmans de Moyenne et Basse Volga, 1552–1865," *CMRS*, 8 (1967), pp. 363–403; H. Carrère d'Encausse, "Les Routes commerciales de l'Asie Centrale et les tentatives de reconquête d'Astrakhan," *CMRS*, 11 (1970), pp. 391–422. For the Crimea see A. Bennigsen et al., *Le Khanat de Crimée dans les archives du Musée du Palais de Topkapi*, Paris, 1978; A. W. Fisher, *The Russian Annexation of the Crimea*, Cambridge, 1970.

On Kazakhs see R. Majerczak, "Renseignements historiques sur les Kazaks ou Kirghizes-Kazaks depuis la formation de la Horde Kazak jusqu'à la fin du XIXe siècle," *Revue du monde musulman*, 43 (1921), pp. 54–220; A. Hudson, *Kazak Social Structure*, New Haven, 1938; T. G. Winner, *The Oral Art and Literature of the Kazakhs of Russian Central Asia*, Durham, N.C., 1958; E. Bacon, *Central Asia under Russian Rule*, Ithaca, N.Y., 1966.

Bukhara and the Central Asian Khanates: M. Holdsworth, *Turkestan in the Nineteenth Century: A Brief History of the Khanates of Bukhara, Kokand and Khiva*, London, 1959; H. Carrère d'Encausse, *Réforme et révolution chez les musulmans de l'Empire russe: Bukhara, 1867–1924*, Paris, 1966. On Central Asian culture see E. Knobloch, *Beyond the Oxus: Archaeology, Art and Architecture of Central Asia*, London, 1972; N. Chadwick and V. Zhirmunsky, *Oral Epics of Central Asia*, London, 1969.

On Islam in Inner Asia see H. Algar, "The Naqshbandi Order: A Preliminary Survey of its History and Significance," *SI*, 44 (1976), pp. 123–52. Important Russian scholarship on Sufism in Turkestan and Turkmenistan includes S. M. Demidov, *Sufizm v Turkmenii: Evolutsiia i perezhitki* [Sufism in Turkmenia: Evolution and Remnants], Ashkhabad, 1978; M. B. Durdyev, "Dukhovenstvo v sisteme obshchestvennykh institutov turkmen kontsa XIX–nachala XX v." [The Clergy in the System of Social Institutions of the Turkmen at the End of the Nineteenth – beginning of the Twentieth Century], *Vestnik Moskovskogo Universiteta* [Moscow University Review] (1970), pp. 27–42; S. M. Demidov, "Magtymy" [The Magtyms], *Domusul'manskie verovanie i obriady v srednei azii* [Pre-Muslim Beliefs and Rites in Central Asia], Moscow, 1975; V. N. Basilov, "Honour Groups in Traditional Turkmenian Society," *Islam in Tribal Societies: From the Atlas to the Indus*, ed. A. S. Ahmed and D. M. Hart, London, 1984, pp. 220–43.

For the Muslims of China before the Chinese occupation of eastern Turkestan see M. Rossabi, *China and Inner Asia*, New York, 1975; M. Rossabi, "The Muslims in the Early Yuan Dynasty," *China under Mongol Rule*, ed. J. Langlois, Princeton, 1981, pp. 257–95; R. Israeli, "The Muslim Minority in Traditional China," *Asian and African Studies*, 10 (1974–75), pp. 101–26; and R. Israeli, "The Muslims under the Manchu Reign in China," *SI*, 49 (1979), pp. 159–79.

The *khwajas* of Kashgar and the nineteenth-century struggle for eastern Turkestan are the subject of T. Saguchi, "The Eastern Trade of the Khoqand Khanat,"

Memoirs of the Research Department of the Toyo Bunko, 24 (1965), pp. 47–114; H. G. Schwarz, "The Khwajas of Eastern Turkestan," *Central Asiatic Journal*, 20 (1976), pp. 266–96; T. Yuan, "Yakub Beg (1820–1877) and the Moslem Rebellion in Chinese Turkestan," *Central Asiatic Journal*, 6 (1961), pp. 134–67. On other nineteenth-century Muslim rebellions see R. Israeli, "The Muslim Revival in 19th-Century China," *SI*, 43 (1976), pp. 119–38; Wen-djang Chu, *The Moslem Rebellion in Northwest China*, The Hague, 1966.

Chapter 18
For an overview of the history of Muslims in India see P. Hardy, *The Muslims of British India*, New York, 1973. See also H. G. Behr, *Die Moguln: Macht und Pracht der indischen Kaiser von 1369–1857*, Vienna, 1979. For histories written in the subcontinent see S. M. Ikram, *Muslim Civilization in India*, New York, 1964; M. Mujeeb, *The Indian Muslims*, Montreal, 1967; I. H. Qureshi, *The Muslim Community of the Indo-Pakistan Sub-continent, 610–1947*, Karachi, 1977; S. M. Haq, *Islamic Thought and Movements in the Subcontinent, 711–1947*, Karachi, 1979.

On the Delhi regime see V. D. Mahajan, *The Delhi Sultanate*, Delhi, 1981. Provincial regimes: S. Dale, *Islamic Society on the South Asian Frontier: The Mappilas of Malabar 1498–1922*, Oxford, 1980; R. M. Eaton, *Sufis of Bijapur 1300–1700: Social Roles of Sufis in Medieval India*, Princeton, 1978; J. F. Richards, *Mughal Administration in Golconda*, London, 1976; A. Karim, *A Social History of the Muslims in Bengal down to AD 1538*, Dacca, 1959; R. M. Eaton, *The Rise of Islam and the Bengal Frontier*, Berkeley, 1993.

On Mughal administration see I. Habib, *The Agrarian System of Mughal India 1556–1707*, Bombay, 1963; W. H. Moreland, *The Agrarian System of Moslem India*, Delhi, 1968; M. Athar 'Ali, *The Mughal Nobility under Aurangzeb*, Bombay, 1966; J. F. Richards, *Kingship and Authority in South Asia*, Madison, Wis., 1978.

For Islamic religion and culture see Aziz Ahmad, *Studies on Islamic Culture in the Indian Environment*, Oxford, 1969; Aziz Ahmad, *An Intellectual History of Islam in India*, Edinburgh, 1969; A. Schimmel, *Islam in the Indian Subcontinent*, London, 1980; B. D. Metcalf, ed., *Moral Conduct and Authority: The Place of Adab in South Asian Islam*, Berkeley, 1984; A. Schimmel, *Mystical Dimensions of Islam*, Chapel Hill, N.C., 1975; J. A. Subhan, *Sufism: Its Saints and Shrines*, Lucknow, 1960; S. A. A. Rizvi, *A History of Sufism in India*, New Delhi, 1978.

On Islam under the Delhi Sultanate the principal contributor is K. A. Nizami: see *Some Aspects of Religion and Politics in India during the Thirteenth Century*, Aligarh, 1961; and *Studies in Medieval Indian History and Culture*, Allahabad, 1966. On Sufism in the Mughal period see A. A. Rizvi, *Muslim Revivalist Movements in Northern India in the Sixteenth and Seventeenth Centuries*, Agra, 1965. Sirhindi is the subject of Y. Friedmann, *Shaykh Ahmad Sirhindi: An Outline of his Thought and a Study of his Image in the Eyes of Posterity*, Montreal, 1971. For translations and works concerning Shah Waliallah: Shah Waliullah, *Sufism and the Islamic Tradition: The Lamahat and Sata'at of Shah Waliullah*, tr. G. N. Jalbani, London,

1980; S. A. A. Rizvi, *Shah Wali-Allah and his Times: A Study of 18th Century Islam, Politics and Society in India*, Canberra, 1980.

Commerce in India and the Indian Ocean is the subject of M. N. Pearson, *Merchants and Rulers in Gujarat: The Response to the Portuguese in the Sixteenth Century*, Berkeley, 1976; A. Das Gupta, *Malabar in Asian Trade: 1740–1800*, Cambridge, 1967; A. Das Gupta, *Indian Merchants and the Decline of Surat c. 1700–1750*, Wiesbaden, 1979; O. P. Singh, *Surat and its Trade in the Second Half of the 17th Century*, Delhi, 1977.

On Muslim "sects": S. C. Misra, *Muslim Communities in Gujarat*, Bombay, 1964; A. Nanji, *The Nizari Ismaili Tradition in the Indo-Pakistan Subcontinent*, Delmar, N.Y., 1978.

Indian architecture and art are the subjects of S. C. Welch and M. C. Beach, *Gods, Thrones and Peacocks: Northern Indian Painting from Two Traditions: Fifteenth to Nineteenth Centuries*, New York, 1965; P. Brown, *Indian Architecture: Islamic Period*, Bombay, 1968; G. Hambly, *Cities of Mughal India*, New Delhi, 1977; R. Nath, *History of Sultanate Architecture*, New Delhi, 1978. On Mughal poetry see R. Russell and K. Islam, *Three Mughal Poets: Mir, Sauda, Mir Hasan*, Cambridge, 1968.

The decline of the Mughal empire and the transition to the British era are interpreted in C. A. Bayly, *Rulers, Townsmen, and Bazaars: North Indian Society in the Age of British Expansion*, Cambridge and New York, 1983; R. B. Barnett, *North India between Empires: Awdh, the Mughals, and the British, 1720–1801*, Berkeley, 1980.

Chapter 19

A survey of Southeast Asian peoples is given by H. Geertz, "Indonesian Cultures and Communities," *Indonesia*, ed. R. T. McVey, New Haven, 1963, pp. 24–96. Brief historical introductions are to be found in H. J. Benda, "The Structure of Southeast Asian History: Some Preliminary Observations," *Journal of Southeast Asian History*, 3 (1962), pp. 106–38; W. Roff, "South-East Asian Islam in the Nineteenth Century," *Cambridge History of Islam*, II, ed. P. M. Holt, A. K. S. Lambton, and B. Lewis, Cambridge, 1970, pp. 155–81. For a fuller history see B. H. M. Vlekke, *Nusantara: A History of Indonesia*, The Hague, 1959. On trade and society see J. C. van Leur, *Indonesian Trade and Society*, tr. J. S. Holmes and A. van Marle, The Hague, 1955; B. J. O. Schrieke, *Indonesian Sociological Studies*, 2 vols., The Hague, 1955, 1957; W. F. Wertheim, *Indonesian Society in Transition*, The Hague, 1959.

Origins and diffusion of Islam in Indonesia: C. A. Majul, "Theories on the Introduction and Expansion of Islam in Malaysia," *Sulliman Journal*, 11 (1964), pp. 335–98; M. C. Ricklefs, "Six Centuries of Islamization in Java," *Conversion to Islam*, ed. N. Levtzion, New York and London, 1979, pp. 100–28; C. C. Berg, "The Islamisation of Java," *SI*, 4 (1955), pp. 111–42; A. H. Johns, "From Coastal Settlement to Islamic School and City: Islamization in Sumatra, the Malay Peninsula and Java," *Hamdard Islamicus*, 4 (1981), pp. 3–28.

For Southeast Asian trade see O. W. Wolters, *The Fall of Srivijaya in Malay History*, Ithaca, N.Y., 1970. For Dutch and British commerce and colonial empires see

F. S. Gaastra, J. R. Bruijn, and I. Schoffer, eds., *Dutch–Asiatic Shipping in the Seventeenth and Eighteenth Centuries*, 3 vols., The Hague, 1979; K. Glamann, *Dutch–Asiatic Trade, 1620–1740*, Copenhagen, 1958; A. Reid, *The Contest for North Sumatra: Atjeh, the Netherlands, and Britain, 1858–1898*, Kuala Lumpur and New York, 1969; J. S. Bastin, *The Changing Balance of the Early Southeast Asian Pepper Trade*, Kuala Lumpur, 1980; J. S. Bastin and R. Roolvink, eds., *Malayan and Indonesian Studies*, Oxford, 1964; J. S. Furnivall, *Colonial Policy and Practice: A Comparative Study of Burma and Netherlands India*, Cambridge, 1948; J. S. Furnivall, *Netherlands India: A Study of Plural Economy*, Cambridge, 1944.

For Java see C. Geertz, *The Religion of Java*, Glencoe, Ill., 1960; B. Anderson, "The Idea of Power in Javanese Culture," *Culture and Politics in Indonesia*, ed. C. Holt, Ithaca, N.Y., 1972, pp. 1–69; S. Moertono, *State and Statecraft in Old Java: A Study of the Later Mataram Period, 16th to 19th Century*, Ithaca, N.Y., 1968.

Minangkabau and the Padri movement have been studied by C. Dobbin, *Islamic Revivalism in a Changing Peasant Economy: Central Sumatra 1784–1847*, London, 1983; P. E. Josselin de Jong, *Minangkabau and Negri Sembilan: Socio-Political Structure in Indonesia*, Leiden, 1951. C. S. Hurgronje, *The Achenese*, 2 vols., tr. A. W. S. O'Sullivan, Leiden and London, 1906 is the classical study of this North Sumatran Muslim society.

On Sufism there are several articles by A. H. Johns: "Muslim Mystics and Historical Writing," *Historians of South-East Asia*, ed. D. G. E. Hall, London, 1961–62, pp. 37–49; "Islam in Southeast Asia: Reflections and New Directions," *Indonesia*, 19 (1975), pp. 33–55; "Friends in Grace: Ibrahim al-Kurani and 'Abd al-Ra'uf al-Singkeli," *Spectrum: Essays Presented to Sultan Takdir Alisjahbana on his Seventieth Birthday*, ed. S. Udin, Jakarta, 1978, pp. 469–85.

The history of Malaya is treated by J. Kennedy, *A History of Malaya, AD 1400–1959*, London and New York, 1962; K. G. Tregonning, *Papers on Malayan History*, Singapore, 1962; R. O. Winstedt, *The Malays: A Cultural History*, London, 1961; R. O. Winstedt, *A History of Classical Malay Literature*, Kuala Lumpur, 1969. For political institutions see J. M. Gullick, *Indigenous Political Systems of Western Malaya*, London, 1965.

Chapter 20

Two good bibliographies are P. E. Ofori, *Islam in Africa South of the Sahara: A Select Bibliographic Guide*, Nendeln, 1977; S. M. Zoghby, *Islam in Sub-Saharan Africa: A Partially Annotated Guide*, Washington, D.C., 1978. Valuable introductory histories include R. A. Oliver and J. D. Fage, *A Short History of Africa*, 3rd edn, Harmondsworth, 1970; *The Cambridge History of Africa*, 8 vols., Cambridge, 1975– ; J. S. Trimingham, *The Influence of Islam upon Africa*, Beirut, 1968. Important collections of articles include I. M. Lewis, ed., *Islam in Tropical Africa*, London, 1966; and J. Kritzeck and W. H. Lewis, eds., *Islam in Africa*, New York, 1969. Studies of special topics with Africa-wide scope are J. N. D. Anderson, *Islamic Law in Africa*,

London, 1954; A. G. B. Fisher and H. J. Fisher, *Slavery and Muslim Society in Africa: The Institution in Saharan and Sudanic Africa, and the Trans-Saharan Trade*, London, 1970; C. Meillassoux, ed., *L'Ésclavage en Afrique pré-coloniale*, Paris, 1975. For histories of Islam in West Africa see J. S. Trimingham, *A History of Islam in West Africa*, London and New York, 1962; J. D. Fage, *History of West Africa*, Cambridge, 1969; D. McCall and N. Bennett, *Aspects of West African Islam*, Boston, 1971; C. Meillassoux, *The Development of Indigenous Trade and Markets in West Africa*, London, 1971; J. F. A. Ajayi and M. Crowder, eds., *History of West Africa*, 2 vols., London, 1976; J. R. Willis, ed., *Studies in West African Islamic History*, London, 1979; P. B. Clarke, *West Africa and Islam*, London, 1982. An unusual study of the integration of pagan and Muslim culture in West Africa is R. A. Bravman, *Islamic and Tribal Art in West Africa*, London, 1974. For the Almoravid movement see the bibliography for chapter 16.

On Mali, an early Muslim empire, see C. Monteil, *Les Empires du Mali*, Paris, 1930; D. T. Niane, *Sundiata: An Epic of Old Mali*, tr. G. D. Pickett, London, 1965; N. Levtzion, *Ancient Ghana and Mali*, London, 1973. For the Songhay empire see J. Boulnois and B. Hama, *L'Empire de Gao*, Paris, 1954.

Timbuktu is the subject of H. M. Miner, *The Primitive City of Timbucktoo*, Garden City, N.Y., 1965; S. M. Cissoko, *Tombouctou et l'empire Songhai*, Dakar, 1976; M. Abitbol, *Tombouctou et les arma*, Paris, 1979; E. N. Saad, *Social History of Timbuktu: The Role of Muslim Scholars and Notables, 1400–1900*, Cambridge, 1983.

For Hausaland from the fourteenth century to the jihad of ʿUthman Don Fodio see M. G. Smith, "The Beginnings of Hausa Society, AD 1000–1500," *The Historian in Tropical Africa*, ed., J. Vansina, R. Mauny, and L. V. Thomas, London, 1964, pp. 339–57; F. Fuglestad, "A Reconstruction of Hausa History before the Jihad," *JAH*, 19 (1978), pp. 319–39; J. E. G. Sutton, "Towards a Less Orthodox History of Hausaland," *JAH*, 20 (1979), pp. 179–201; M. Hiskett, "An Islamic Tradition of Reform in the Western Sudan from the Sixteenth to the Eighteenth Century," *BSOAS*, 25 (1962), pp. 577–96.

For Bornu see A. Schultze, *The Sultanate of Bornu*, tr. P. A. Benton, London, 1968; L. Brenner, *The Shehus of Kukawa: A History of the Al-Kanemi Dynasty of Bornu*, Oxford, 1973.

Mauritania: D. G. Lavroff, *Introduction à la Mauritanie*, Paris, 1979; C. C. Stewart with E. K. Stewart, *Islam and Social Order in Mauritania*, Oxford, 1973; H. T. Norris, *Shinqiti Folk Literature and Songs*, Oxford, 1968; and H. T. Norris, *The Tuaregs: Their Islamic Legacy and its Diffusion in the Sahel*, Warminster, 1975.

On Muslim merchants and scholars: P. D. Curtin, *Economic Change in Precolonial Africa*, Madison, Wis., 1974; P. E. Lovejoy, "The Role of the Wangara in the Economic Transformation of the Central Sudan in the Fifteenth and Sixteenth Centuries," *JAH*, 19 (1978), pp. 173–93; C. C. Stewart, "Southern Saharan Scholarship and the *Bilad Al-Sudan*," *JAH*, 17 (1976), pp. 73–93. L. O. Sanneh stresses the clerical rather than the commercial groups: *The Jakhanke: The History of an Islamic Clerical People of the Senegambia*, London, 1979.

On Islam in Ghana the principal contribution is N. Levtzion, *Muslims and Chiefs in West Africa*, Oxford, 1968. On Muslims in the Ashanti empire of Ghana see I. Wilks, *The Northern Factor in Ashanti History*, Legon, Ghana, 1961; and I. Wilks, *Asante in the Nineteenth Century*, London, 1975.

For Sierra Leone see D. Skinner, "Islam and Education in the Colony and Hinterland of Sierra Leone (1750–1914)," *Canadian Journal of African Studies*, 10 (1976), pp. 499–520; and D. Skinner, "Mande Settlement and the Development of Islamic Institutions in Sierra Leone," *IJAHS*, 11 (1978), pp. 32–62.

Important studies of the great eighteenth- and nineteenth-century jihads include J. R. Willis, "Jihad fi Sabil Allah: Its Doctrinal Basis in Islam and Some Aspects of its Evolution in Nineteenth Century West Africa," *JAH*, 8 (1967), pp. 395–415; M. Hiskett, "The Nineteenth-Century Jihads in West Africa," *The Cambridge History of Africa, 1790–1870*, v, ed. J. E. Flint, Cambridge, 1976, pp. 125–69; M. Last, *The Sokoto Caliphate*, New York, 1967; H. A. S. Johnston, *The Fulani Empire of Sokoto*, London, 1967; M. Hiskett, *The Sword of Truth: The Life and Times of the Shehu Usuman Dan Fodio*, New York, 1973. For the Sokoto Caliphate: M. G. Smith, *Government in Zazzau, 1800–1950*, London and New York, 1960; R. A. Adeleye, *Power and Diplomacy in Northern Nigeria, 1804–1906*, London, 1971; V. N. Low, *Three Nigerian Emirates*, Evanston, Ill., 1972. On the trade and economy of northern Nigeria in this period see J. P. Smaldane, *Warfare in the Sokoto Caliphate*, Cambridge, 1974; P. E. Lovejoy, "Plantations in the Economy of the Sokoto Caliphate," *JAH*, 19 (1978), pp. 341–68.

The eastern offshoots of 'Uthman's jihad are treated in S. Abubakar, *The Lamibe of Fombina: A Political History of Adamawa, 1809–1901*, Zaria (Nigeria), 1977; A. D. Babikir, *L'Empire de Rabeh*, Paris, 1950. On the western offshoots: A. H. Ba and J. Daget, *L'Empire peul du Macina*, Paris, 1962.

For the jihads in Senegambia and Mauritania see M. A. Klein, "Social and Economic Factors in the Muslim Revolution in Senegambia," *JAH*, 13 (1972), pp. 419–41; J. R. Willis, "The Torodbe Clerisy: A Social View," *JAH*, 19 (1978), pp. 195–212.

For al-Hajj 'Umar see B. G. Martin, *Muslim Brotherhoods in Nineteenth-Century Africa*, Cambridge, 1976, pp. 68–217. For the Umarian state see B. O. Oloruntimehin, *The Segu Tukulor Empire*, London, 1972; Y. Saint-Martin, *L'Empire toucouleur, 1848–1897*, Paris, 1970; R. L. Roberts, "Production and Reproduction of Warrior States: Segu Bambara and Segu Tokolor, c. 1712–1890," *IJAHS*, 13 (1980), pp. 389–419; J. R. Willis, *In the Path of Allah: The Passion of Al-Hajj 'Umar*, London: 1989. For comparative purposes see D. Forde and P. M. Kaberry, eds., *West African Kingdoms in the Nineteenth Century*, London, 1967.

The principal contributions to the study of the Senegambian region in the nineteenth century are M. A. Klein, *Islam and Imperialism in Senegal*, Stanford and Edinburgh, 1968; Charlotte A. Quinn, *Mandingo Kingdoms of the Senegambia*, Evanston, Ill., 1972; P. D. Curtin, *Economic Change in Precolonial Africa: Senegambia in the Era of the Slave Trade*, Madison, Wis., 1975; D. W. Robinson, *Chiefs and*

Clerics: Abdul Bokar Kan and Futa Toro, 1853–1891, Oxford, 1975; T. Diallo, *Les Institutions politiques du Fouta Dyallon au XIXe siècle*, Dakar, 1972. See also L. G. Colvin, "Islam and the State of Kajoor: A Case of Successful Resistance to Jihad," *JAH*, 15 (1974), pp. 587–606. The conversion of the Wolof is discussed in L. Behrman, "The Islamization of the Wolof by the End of the Nineteenth Century," *Western African History*, IV, ed. D. McCall, N. Bennett, and J. Butler, New York, 1969, pp. 102–31. On French policy in Senegal at the beginning of the colonial era see G. W. Johnson, *The Emergence of Black Politics in Senegal: The Struggle for Power in the Four Communes, 1900–1920*, Stanford, 1971.

The principal study of Samory is Y. Person, *Samori: Une révolution dyula*, Dakar, 1968–75.

On Muslim brotherhoods and religious teaching in West Africa see J. M. Abun-Nasr, *The Tijaniyya: A Sufi Order in the Modern World*, London and New York, 1965; B. G. Martin, *Muslim Brotherhoods in Nineteenth-Century Africa*, Cambridge, 1976.

Chapter 21
For overviews of East African history see R. Oliver and G. Matthew, eds., *History of East Africa*, I, Oxford, 1963; V. Harlow and E. M. Chilver, eds., *History of East Africa*, II, Oxford, 1965; *The Cambridge History of Africa, 1050–1600*, III, ed. K. Oliver, Cambridge, 1977; *The Cambridge History of Africa, 1600–1790*, IV, ed. R. Gray, Cambridge, 1975.

On the early history of Muslim settlement see H. N. Chittick, *Kilwa: An Islamic Trading City on the East African Coast*, Nairobi, 1974; P. S. Garlake, *The Early Islamic Architecture of the East African Coast*, Nairobi and London, 1966; G. S. P. Freeman-Grenville, *The Medieval History of the Coast of Tanganyika*, London and New York, 1962. An important revision of the subject is under way. See R. L. Pouwels, "The Medieval Foundations of East African Islam," *IJAHS*, 11 (1978), pp. 201–26, 393–409; J. de V. Allen, "Swahili Culture and the Nature of East Coast Settlement," *IJAHS*, 14 (1981), pp. 306–34; J. C. Wilkinson, "Oman and East Africa: New Light on Early Kilwan History from the Omani Sources," *IJAHS*, 14 (1981), pp. 272–305.

On Zanzibar and the development of coastal trade with the interior see C. S. Nicholls, *The Swahili Coast: Politics, Diplomacy and Trade on the East African Littoral, 1798–1856*, London, 1971; L. Farrant, *Tippu Tip and the East African Slave Trade*, London, 1975; N. R. Bennett, *Mirambo of Tanzania ca. 1840–1884*, New York, 1971.

For Ethiopia see J. S. Trimingham, *Islam in Ethiopia*, London, 1965; M. Abir, *Ethiopia: The Era of the Princes*, New York, 1968; J. Cuoq, *L'Islam en Ethiopie des origines au seizième siècle*, Paris, 1981.

On Somalia see I. M. Lewis, *Peoples of the Horn of Africa, Somali, Afar and Saho*, London, 1969; D. D. Laitin, *Polity, Language and Thought: The Somali Experience*, Chicago, 1977; L. V. Cassanelli, *The Shaping of Somali Society: Reconstructing the History of a Pastoral People, 1600–1900*, Philadelphia, 1982.

For the Sudan see J. S. Trimingham, *Islam in the Sudan*, London, 1965; P. M. Holt and M. W. Daly, *The History of the Sudan from the Coming of Islam to the Present Day*, 3rd edn, London, 1979; Y. F. Hasan, *The Arabs and the Sudan: From the Seventh to the Early Sixteenth Century*, Edinburgh, 1967; R. S. O'Fahey and J. L. Spaulding, *Kingdoms of the Sudan*, London, 1974; R. S. O'Fahey, *State and Society in Dar Fur*, London, 1980.

For African society on the eve of colonialism see E. Colson, "African Society at the Time of the Scramble," *Colonialism in Africa: The History and Politics of Colonialism 1870–1914*, I, ed. L. H. Gann and P. Duignan, Cambridge, 1969, pp. 27–65 and other essays in this volume. On the rise of colonial domination see M. Crowder, "West Africa and the Europeans: Five Hundred Years of Direct Contact," *Colonial West Africa: Collected Essays*, London, 1978, pp. 1–25; P. Ehrensaft, "The Political Economy of Informal Empire in Pre-Colonial Nigeria, 1807–1884," *Canadian Journal of African Studies*, 6 (1972), pp. 451–90. The diplomatic background of the European scramble for Africa is included in R. Robinson and J. Gallagher, *Africa and the Victorians*, New York, 1961; J. D. Hargreaves, *Prelude to the Partition of West Africa*, London and New York, 1963.

PART III

Introduction

On the contemporary Islamic world see J. Voll, *Islam: Continuity and Change in the Modern World*, 2nd edn, Syracuse, N.Y., 1994; M. Ruthven, *Islam in the World*, 2nd edn, New York, 2000.

Chapter 22

Of the general histories of modern Iran, N. R. Keddie, *Roots of Revolution: An Interpretive History of Modern Iran*, New Haven, 1981 is well balanced. Iran's foreign relations are discussed in M. E. Yapp, *Strategies of British India: Britain, Iran, and Afghanistan, 1798–1850*, Oxford, 1980; R. K. Ramazani, *Iran's Foreign Policy, 1941–1973*, Charlottesville, Va., 1975; S. Chubin and S. Zabih, *The Foreign Relations of Iran*, Berkeley, 1974; F. Kazemzadeh, *Russia and Britain in Persia, 1864–1914: A Study in Imperialism*, New Haven, 1968.

On nineteenth-century Iran under the Qajars see S. Bakhash, *Iran: Monarchy, Bureaucracy, and Reform under the Qajars, 1858–1896*, London, 1978; N. R. Keddie, "The Iranian Power Structure and Social Change, 1800–1969: An Overview," *IJMES*, 2 (1971), pp. 3–20; E. Abrahamian, "Oriental Despotism: The Case of Qajar Iran," *IJMES*, 5 (1974), pp. 3–31.

Iran's economic history is covered by C. P. Issawi, ed., *The Economic History of Iran, 1800–1914*, Chicago, 1971; A. Ashraf and H. Hekmat, "Merchants and Artisans and the Developmental Processes of Nineteenth-Century Iran," *The Islamic Middle East, 700–1900: Studies in Economic and Social History*, ed. A. L. Udovitch, Princeton, 1981, pp. 725–50.

Iran under the Pahlavis: A. Banani, *The Modernization of Iran, 1921–1941*, Stanford, 1961; E. Abrahamian, *Iran between Two Revolutions*, Princeton, 1982; J. Bharier, *Economic Development in Iran, 1900–1970*, London, 1971; J. Amuzegar and M. A. Fekrat, *Iran: Economic Development under Dualistic Conditions*, Chicago, 1971. Post-World War II institutions and political struggle are treated in R. W. Cottam, *Nationalism in Iran*, Pittsburgh, 1964; L. Binder, *Iran: Political Development in a Changing Society*, Berkeley, 1962; M. Zonis, *The Political Elite of Iran*, Princeton, 1971; J. A. Bill, *The Politics of Iran: Groups, Classes, and Modernization*, Columbus, Ohio, 1972; S. Zabih, *The Mossadegh Era: Roots of the Iranian Revolution*, Chicago, 1982; E. J. Hooglund, *Land and Revolution in Iran, 1960–1980*, Austin, Tex., 1982.

Relations between 'ulama' and the state are the subject of H. Algar, *Religion and State in Iran, 1785–1906: The Role of the Ulama in the Qajar Period*, Berkeley, 1969; H. Algar, "The Oppositional Role of the Ulama in Twentieth-Century Iran," *Scholars, Saints and Sufis*, ed. N. R. Keddie, Berkeley, 1972, pp. 231–55; N. R. Keddie, *Religion and Rebellion in Iran: The Tobacco Protest of 1891–1892*, London, 1966; H. Algar, *Mirza Malkum Khan: A Study in the History of Iranian Modernism*, Berkeley, 1973. On the constitutional revolution of 1906–11: N. R. Keddie, "Iranian Politics 1900–1905: Background to Revolution," *Middle Eastern Studies*, 5 (1969), pp. 3–31, 151–67, 234–50; S. Arjomand, "The Shi-ite Hierocracy and the State in Pre-Modern Iran, 1785–1890," *European Journal of Sociology*, 22 (1981), pp. 40–78; S. Akhavi, *Religion and Politics in Contemporary Iran: Clergy–State Relations in the Pahlavi Period*, Albany, N.Y., 1980; Y. Richard, *Le Shi'isme en Iran: Imam et révolution*, Paris, 1980; P. J. Chelkowski, ed., *Ta'ziyeh, Ritual and Drama in Iran*, New York, 1979; M. M. J. Fischer, *Iran: From Religious Dispute to Revolution*, Cambridge, Mass., 1980; Ayatollah Ruhollah Khomeini, *Islamic Government*, tr. Joint Publications Research Service, New York, 1979.

Stimulating assessments of the revolution include the work of S. A. Arjomand: "Shi'ite Islam and the Revolution in Iran," *Government and Opposition*, 16 (1981), pp. 293–316; "Traditionalism in Twentieth-Century Iran," *From Nationalism to Revolutionary Islam*, ed. S. A. Arjomand, London, 1984, pp. 195–232; T. Skocpol, "Rentier State and Shi'a Islam in the Iranian Revolution," *Theory and Society*, 11 (1982), pp. 265–83; N. R. Keddie, "Iranian Revolutions in Comparative Perspective," *American Historical Review*, 88 (1983), pp. 579–98.

On social structure see P. W. English, *City and Village in Iran: Settlement and Economy in the Kirman Basin*, Madison, Wis., 1966; J. I. Clarke, *The Iranian City of Shiraz*, Durham, 1963; M. E. Bonine, *Yazd and its Hinterland: A Central Place System of Dominance in the Central Iranian Plateau*, Austin, Tex., 1975; P. G. Ahrens, *Die Entwicklung der Stadt Teheran. Eine städtebauliche Untersuchung ihrer zukünftigen Gestaltung*, Opladen, 1966. An outstanding book on a declining pastoral society is F. Barth, *Nomads of South Persia: The Basseri Tribe of the Khamseh Confederacy*, Boston, 1961.

On the place of women in Iranian society see G. Nashat, ed., *Women and Revolution in Iran*, Boulder, 1983; E. Sanasarian, *The Women's Rights Movement in Iran,*

New York, 1982; F. Azari, *Women of Iran: The Confict with Fundamentalist Islam*, London, 1983; A. K. Ferdows, "Women and the Islamic Revolution," *IJMES*, 15 (1983), pp. 283–98; Z. Mir-Hosseini, *Islam and Gender: The Religious Debate in Contemporary Iran*, Princeton, 1999;

On the Islamic Republic see H. Omid, *Islam and the Post-Revolutionary State in Iran*, New York, 1994; J. Foran, ed., *A Century of Revolution: Social Movements in Iran*, London, 1994; N. R. Keddie, *Iran and the Muslim World*, New York, 1995; F. Moghadam, *From Land Reform to Revolution: The Political Economy of Agricultural Development in Iran, 1962–1979*, London, 1996; S. Rahnema and S. Behdad, *Iran after the Revolution*, New York, 1996; J. Amuzegar, *Iran's Economy under the Islamic Republic*, London, 1997; E. Sciolino, *Persian Mirrors: The Elusive Face of Iran*, New York, 2000; W. Buchta, *Who Rules Iran? The Structure of Power in the Islamic Republic*, Washington, D.C., 2000; R. Wright, *The Last Great Revolution: Turmoil and Transformation in Iran*, New York, 2000.

Chapter 23
Turkey's relations with Europe are the subject of M. S. Anderson, *The Eastern Question, 1774–1923*, London, 1966; S. J. Shaw, *Between Old and New: The Ottoman Empire under Sultan Selim III, 1789–1807*, Cambridge, Mass., 1971; C. K. Webster, *The Foreign Policy of Castlereagh, 1812–1815*, London, 1931; H. W. V. Temperley, *The Foreign Policy of Canning, 1822–1827*, London, 1966; C. K. Webster, *The Foreign Policy of Palmerston, 1830–1841*, London, 1951; J. C. Hurewitz, "The Background of Russia's Claims to the Turkish Straits: A Reassessment," *Belleten, Türk Tarih Kurumu*, 28 (1964), pp. 459–97; V. J. Puryear, *England, Russia and the Straits Question, 1844–1856*, Berkeley, 1931; F. E. Bailey, *British Policy and the Turkish Reform Movement: A Study in Anglo-Turkish Relations, 1826–1853*, London, 1942.

On the Crimean war, Russia, and the Balkans see B. H. Sumner, *Russia and the Balkans, 1870–1880*, Oxford, 1937; H. Temperley, *England and the Near East: The Crimea*, London, 1936; W. L. Langer, *The Diplomacy of Imperialism, 1890–1902*, 2nd edn, New York, 1960; W. L. Langer, *European Alliances and Alignments, 1871–1890*, 2nd edn, New York, 1962; D. Harris, *A Diplomatic History of the Balkan Crisis of 1875–1878: The First Year*, London, 1936; E. M. Earle, *Turkey, the Great Powers, and the Baghdad Railway*, New York, 1935.

World War I and the partition of the Ottoman empire: H. N. Howard, *The Partition of Turkey: A Diplomatic History, 1913–1923*, Norman, Okla., 1931; E. Kedourie, *England and the Middle East: The Destruction of the Ottoman Empire, 1914–1921*, 2nd edn, London, 1987; F. G. Weber, *Eagles on the Crescent: Germany, Austria and the Diplomacy of the Turkish Alliance, 1914–1918*, Ithaca, N.Y., 1970; C. Jelavich and B. Jelavich, *The Establishment of the Balkan National States, 1804–1920*, Seattle, 1977; P. Helmreich, *From Paris to Sèvres: The Partition of the Ottoman Empire at the Peace Conference of 1919–1920*, Columbus, Ohio, 1974; H. N. Howard, *Turkey, the Straits and US Policy*, Baltimore, 1974. On the Armenian question see R. G. Hovannisian, *The Armenian Holocaust: A Bibliography Relating to the Deportations, Massacres, and Dispersion of the Armenian People, 1912–1915*, Cambridge, 1980; R. G. Hovannisian, *Armenia on the Road to Independence*, Berkeley, 1984; R. G. Hovannisian, *The Republic of Armenia*, 2 vols., Berkeley, 1971, 1982.

The development of the Middle Eastern economy: R. Owen, *The Middle East in the World Economy, 1800–1914*, New York, 1981. See also C. Issawi, ed., *The Economic History of Turkey, 1800–1914*, Chicago, 1980; C. Issawi, ed., *The Economic History of the Middle East, 1800–1914*, Chicago, 1966; D. Quataert, *Social Disintegration and Popular Resistance in the Ottoman Empire 1881–1908*, New York, 1983; H. Islamoglu-Inan, ed., *The Ottoman Empire and the World Economy*, Cambridge, 1987.

On reform and modernization of the Ottoman empire: B. Lewis, *The Emergence of Modern Turkey*, 2nd edn, London, 1968; N. Berkes, *The Development of Secularism in Turkey*, Montreal, 1964; R. H. Davison, *Reform in the Ottoman Empire, 1856–1876*, Princeton, 1963; R. Devereaux, *The First Ottoman Constitutional Period: A Study of the Midhat Constitution and Parliament*, Baltimore, 1963; S. Mardin, "Power, Civil Society and Culture in the Ottoman Empire," *Comparative Studies in Society and History*, 11 (1969), pp. 258–81.

Works concerning institutional modernization include C. V. Findley, *Bureaucratic Reform in the Ottoman Empire: The Sublime Porte, 1789–1922*, Princeton, 1980; S. S. Omar, "The Majalla," *Law in the Middle East*, I, ed. M. Khadduri and H. J. Liebesny, Washington, D.C., 1956, pp. 292–308; G. Baer, "The Transition from Traditional to Western Criminal Law in Turkey and Egypt," *SI*, 45 (1977), pp. 139–58; A. M. Kazamias, *Education and the Quest for Modernity in Turkey*, Chicago, 1966; S. J. Shaw, "The Origins of Representative Government in the Ottoman Empire: An Introduction to the Provincial Councils, 1839–1876," *Near Eastern Round Table, 1967–1968*, ed. R. B. Winder, New York, 1969, pp. 53–142.

On the Ottoman intelligentsia see S. Mardin, *The Genesis of Young Ottoman Thought*, Princeton, 1962; E. E. Ramsaur, *The Young Turks: Prelude to the Revolution of 1908*, Princeton, 1957; F. Ahmad, *The Young Turks: The Committee of Union and Progress in Turkish Politics, 1908–1914*, Oxford, 1969; D. Kushner, *The Rise of Turkish Nationalism, 1876–1908*, London, 1977.

Ottoman 'ulama' and the state are the subject of U. Heyd, "The Ottoman 'Ulemā and Westernization in the Time of Selim III and Mahmud II," *Studies in Islamic History and Civilization*, ed. U. Heyd, Jerusalem, 1961, pp. 63–96; R. L. Chambers, "The Ottoman Ulema and the Tanzimat," *Scholars, Saints and Sufis*, ed. N. R. Keddie, Berkeley, 1972, pp. 33–46.

For Ataturk and the Turkish Republic see R. D. Robinson, *The First Turkish Republic*, Cambridge, Mass., 1965; Lord Kinross, *Ataturk: The Rebirth of a Nation*, London, 1964; C. Keyder, *The Definition of a Peripheral Economy: Turkey, 1923–1929*, Cambridge, Mass., 1981.

For Turkish politics and economy since World War II see K. H. Karpat, *Turkey's Politics: The Transition to a Multi-party System*, Princeton, 1959; K. H. Karpat, *Social*

Change and Politics in Turkey: A Structural-Historical Analysis, Leiden, 1973; F. Ahmad, *The Turkish Experiment in Democracy, 1950–1975*, Boulder, 1977; E. K. Trimberger, *Revolution from Above*, New Brunswick, N.J., 1978; J. M. Landau, *Radical Politics in Modern Turkey*, Leiden, 1974. On Turkish economic development see B. Berberoglu, *Turkey in Crisis: From State Capitalism to Neo-colonialism*, London, 1982.

On local politics see J. S. Szyliowicz, *Political Change in Rural Turkey: Erdemli*, The Hague, 1966; K. H. Karpat, *The Gecekondu: Rural Migration and Urbanization*, New York, 1976. See also A. P. Sterling, *Turkish Village*, London, 1965; M. Makal, *A Village in Anatolia*, ed. A. P. Stirling, tr. Sir W. Deedes, London, 1954, a touching account of the efforts of a teacher to bring the revolution to rural Turkey; M. E. Meeker, "The Great Family Aghas of Turkey: A Study of a Changing Political Culture," *Rural Politics and Social Change in the Middle East*, ed. R. Antoun and I. Harik, Bloomington, 1972, pp. 237–66.

The revival of Islam: U. Heyd, *Revival of Islam in Modern Turkey*, Jerusalem, 1968; S. Mardin, "Religion in Modern Turkey," *International Social Science Journal*, 29 (1977), pp. 279–97; J. Landau, "The National Salvation Party in Turkey," *Asian and African Studies*, 11 (1976), pp. 1–57; I. Sunar and B. Toprak, "Islam in Politics: The Case of Turkey," *Government and Opposition*, 18 (1983), pp. 421–41; S. Mardin, *Religion and Social Change in Modern Turkey: The Case of Bediuzzaman Said Nursi*, Albany, N.Y. 1989.

On the role of women see N. Abadan-Unat, "The Modernization of Turkish Women," *Middle East Journal*, 32 (1978), pp. 291–306; N. Abadan-Unat, *Women in Turkish Society*, Leiden, 1981; E. Ozdalga, *The Veiling Issue, Official Secularism and Popular Islam in Modern Turkey*, Richmond, 1998.

Turkish politics and economy in the 1990s: S. Bozdogan and R. Kasaba, eds., *Rethinking Modernity and National Identity in Turkey*, Seattle, 1997; J. Pettifer, *The Turkish Labyrinth: Ataturk and the New Islam*, London, 1997; H. Poulton, *Top Hat, Grey Wolf and Crescent: Turkish Nationalism and the Turkish Republic*, London, 1997; Z. Onis, *State and Market: The Political Economy of Turkey in Comparative Perspective*, Istanbul, 1998.

Turkish foreign policy: A. Z. Rubinstein and O. M. Smolansky, *Regional Power Rivalries in the New Eurasia: Russia, Turkey and Iran*, Armonk, 1995; V. Mastny and R. C. Nation, eds., *Turkey between East and West*, Boulder, 1996.

For the Kurdish question see R. Olson, ed., *The Kurdish Nationalist Movement in the 1990s*, Lexington, Ky., 1996; E. O'Ballance, *The Kurdish Struggle 1920–1994*, Basingstoke, 1996; D. McDowall, *A Modern History of the Kurds*, London, 1997; R. Olson, *The Kurdish Question and Turkish–Iranian Relations from World War I to 1998*, Costa Mesa, 1998; M. M. Gunter, *The Kurdish Predicament in Iraq: A Political Analysis*, Basingstoke, 1999.

Comparative studies: J. Waterbury, *Exposed to Innumerable Delusions: Public Enterprise and State Power in Egypt, India, Mexico and Turkey*, Cambridge, 1993;

A. Oneu, C. Keyder, and S. Ibrahim, eds., *Developmentalism and Beyond: Society and Politics in Egypt and Turkey*, Cairo, 1994; J. Saeed, *Islam and Modernization: A Comparative Analysis of Pakistan, Egypt, and Turkey*, Westport, Conn., 1994; D. Waldner, *State Building and Late Development*, Ithaca, N.Y., 1999.

Chapter 24
General histories of Egypt in the nineteenth and twentieth centuries include P. M. Holt, *Egypt and the Fertile Crescent, 1516–1922: A Political History*, London, 1966; J. Marlowe, *A History of Modern Egypt and Anglo-Egyptian Relations, 1800–1956*, 2nd edn, Hamden, Conn., 1965. Collected articles dealing with the social transformation of Egyptian society are found in P. M. Holt, ed., *Political and Social Change in Modern Egypt*, London, 1968; G. Baer, *Studies on the Social History of Modern Egypt*, Chicago, 1969. Also see J. Abu-Lughod, *Cairo: 1001 Years of the City Victorious*, Princeton, 1971. The classic description of Egyptian society is E. Lane, *An Account of the Manners and Customs of the Modern Egyptians*, London, 1842, republished as *The Modern Egyptians*, London, 1908.

Books dealing with the economic development of Egypt in the nineteenth century: D. S. Landes, *Bankers and Pashas: International Finance and Economic Imperialism in Egypt*, New York, 1958; E. R. J. Owen, *Cotton and the Egyptian Economy, 1820–1914*, Oxford, 1969; A. Richards, *Egypt's Agricultural Development, 1800–1980: Technical and Social Change*, Boulder, 1982. On the long-range patterns of Egyptian economic development: C. Issawi, "Egypt since 1800: A Study in Lopsided Development," *Journal of Economic History*, 21 (1961), pp. 1–25; P. O'Brien, "The Long-term Growth of Agricultural Production in Egypt: 1821–1962," *Political and Social Change in Modern Egypt*, ed. P. M. Holt, London, 1968, pp. 162–95; A. Richards, "Growth and Technical Change: 'Internal' and 'External' Sources of Egyptian Underdevelopment, 1800–1914," *Asian and African Studies*, 15 (1981), pp. 45–67.

Muhammad 'Ali and nineteenth-century reforms: P. Gran, *Islamic Roots of Capitalism: Egypt, 1760–1840*, Austin, Tex., 1979 is suggestive but not reliable. See H. H. Dodwell, *The Founder of Modern Egypt: A Study of Muhammad 'Ali in Egypt*, Cambridge, 1931; H. Rivlin, *The Agricultural Policy of Muhammad 'Ali in Egypt*, Cambridge, Mass., 1961. Muhammad 'Ali's foreign policy: V. J. Puryear, *Napoleon and the Dardanelles*, Berkeley, 1951; Shafik Ghurbal, *The Beginnings of the Egyptian Question and the Rise of Mehmet Ali*, London, 1928. Isma'il Pasha and Egypt in the mid-nineteenth century: G. Douin, *Histoire du règne du khédive Isma'il*, 3 vols., Rome, 1933–41.

Egypt under British rule, 1882–1922: A. Scholch, *Egypt for the Egyptians: The Socio-political Crisis in Egypt, 1878–1882*, London, 1981; A. L. al-Sayyid Marsot, *Egypt and Cromer: A Study in Anglo-Egyptian Relations*, New York, 1968; J. Berque, *L'Egypte, l'imperialisme et révolution*, Paris, 1967.

For the 'ulama' and Sufism in the nineteenth century: A. L. al-Sayyid Marsot, "The Role of the 'Ulama in Egypt during the Early 19th Century," *Political and Social*

Change in Modern Egypt, ed. P. M. Holt, London, 1968, pp. 264–80; A. L. al-Sayyid Marsot, "The Beginnings of Modernization among the Rectors of al-Azhar, 1798–1879," *Beginnings of Modernization in the Middle East*, ed. W. R. Polk and R. L. Chambers, Chicago, 1968, pp. 267–80; F. de Jong, *Ṭuruq and Ṭuruq-linked Institutions in Nineteenth-Century Egypt*, Leiden, 1978; P. Kahle, "Zār-Beschwörungen im Egypten," *Der Islam*, 3 (1912), pp. 1–41.

Egypt under the parliamentary regime: M. Deeb, *Party Politics in Egypt: The Wafd and its Rivals, 1919–1939*, London, 1979; A. L. al-Sayyid Marsot, *Egypt's Liberal Experiment, 1922–1936*, Berkeley, 1977. Egyptian nationalism and Islam in the inter-war years: J. Heyworth-Dunne, *Religious and Political Trends: Modern Egypt*, Washington, D.C., 1950; N. Safran, *Egypt in Search of Political Community*, Cambridge, Mass., 1961; C. Wendell, *The Evolution of the Egyptian National Image: From its Origins to Ahmad Lutfi al-Sayyid*, Berkeley, 1972; C. D. Smith, *Islam and the Search for Social Order in Modern Egypt*, Albany, N.Y., 1983; Taha Husayn, *Stream of Days: At the Azhar*, 2nd edn, tr. H. Wayment, London, 1948; P. Cachia, *Taha Husayn: His Place in the Egyptian Literary Renaissance*, London, 1956.

For introductions to modern Egyptian literature see H. Kilpatrick, *The Modern Egyptian Novel*, London, 1974; H. Sakkut, *The Egyptian Novel and its Main Trends from 1913 to 1952*, Cairo, 1971.

Egypt under Nasser and Sadat: A. Abdel-Malek, *Egypt: Military Society: The Army Regime, the Left and Social Change under Nasser*, tr. C. L. Markmann, New York, 1968; A. Abdel-Malek, *Idéologie et renaissance rationale: L'Egypte moderne*, Paris, 1969; R. W. Baker, *Egypt's Uncertain Revolution under Nasser and Sadat*, Cambridge, Mass., 1978. For issues of political economy see J. Waterbury, *The Egypt of Nasser and Sadat: The Political Economy of Two Regimes*, Princeton, 1983; R. Mabro and S. Radwan, *The Industrialization of Egypt, 1939–1973: Policy and Performance*, Oxford, 1976; R. Mabro, *The Egyptian Economy, 1952–1972*, Oxford, 1974; P. K. O'Brien, *The Revolution in Egypt's Economic System: From Private Enterprise to Socialism, 1952–1965*, London, 1966; R. Springborg, *Family, Power and Politics in Egypt: Sayed Bey Marei: His Clan, Clients and Cohorts*, Philadelphia, 1982.

On rural development see G. Saab, *The Egyptian Agrarian Reform: 1952–1962*, London, 1967; J. Mayfield, *Rural Politics in Nasser's Egypt: A Quest for Legitimacy*, Austin, Tex., 1971; H. Fakhouri, *Kafr el-Elow: An Egyptian Village in Transition*, New York, 1972; I. Harik, *The Political Mobilization of Peasants: A Study of an Egyptian Community*, Bloomington, 1974; L. Binder, *In a Moment of Enthusiasm: Political Power and the Second Stratum in Egypt*, Chicago, 1978.

On Islam in the era of Nasser and Sadat see M. Berger, *Islam in Egypt Today: Social and Political Aspects of Popular Religion*, Cambridge, 1970; M. Gilsenan, *Saint and Sufi in Modern Egypt*, Oxford, 1973. On the Muslim Brotherhood see C. Wendell, ed. and tr., *Five Tracts of Hasan al-Banna (1906–1949)*, Berkeley, 1978; R. P. Mitchell, *The Society of the Muslim Brothers*, London, 1969; S. Qutb, *Social Justice in Islam*, tr. J. B. Hardie, Washington, D.C., 1953.

On the current Islamic revival: S. E. Ibrahim, "Anatomy of Egypt's Militant Islamic Groups," *IJMES*, 12 (1980), pp. 423–53; F. El-Guindi, "Veiling *Infitah* with Muslim Ethic: Egypt's Contemporary Islamic Movement," *Social Problems*, 28 (1981), pp. 465–85; G. Kepel, *Le Prophète et Pharaon: Les mouvements islamistes dans l'Egypte contemporaine*, Paris, 1984; P. Gaffney, *The Prophet's Pulpit: Islamic Teaching in Contemporary Egypt*, Berkeley, 1994; V. J. Hoffman, *Sufism, Mystics and Saints in Modern Egypt*, New York, 1995; M. Zeghal, *Gardiens de l' Islam: Les Oulemas de al-Azhar dans l'Egypte Contemporaine*, Paris, 1996; G. Starrett, *Putting Islam to Work: Education, Politics, and Religious Transformation in Egypt*, Berkeley, 1998; D. J. Sullivan and S. Abed-Kotob, *Islam in Contemporary Egypt: Civil Society vs. the State*, Boulder, 1999.

Egyptian society and economy in the 1990s: D. Singennan, *Avenues of Participation: Family, Politics and Networks in Urban Quarters of Cairo*, Princeton, 1995; W. Armbrust, *Mass Culture and Modernism in Egypt*, Cambridge, 1996; S. Soliman, *State and Industrial Capitalism in Egypt*, Cairo, 1999; R. Bush, *Economic Crisis and the Politics of Reform in Egypt*, Boulder, 1999.

Chapter 25

For a deep historical perspective see A. Hourani, *A History of the Arab Peoples*, Cambridge, Mass., 1991. A large literature deals with the diplomatic, economic, and social problems of the Middle East as a whole. Here we shall indicate books that concentrate on the Arab East, though some contain discussions of Iran and Turkey. On the role of the big powers in the nineteenth century and during World War I see the bibliography for chapter 23. On the Arab world since World War I see B. Lewis, *The Middle East and the West*, New York, 1966; W. R. Polk, *The United States and the Arab World*, Cambridge, Mass., 1969; E. Monroe, *Britain's Moment in the Middle East, 1914–1956*, Baltimore, 1963.

England's role in the partition of the Ottoman empire and its diplomatic relations with France, Sharif Husayn, and the Zionists is the subject of E. Kedourie, *England and the Middle East, 1914–1921*, 2nd edn, Hassocks, 1978; E. Kedourie, *The Chatham House Version*, London, 1970; G. Antonius, *The Arab Awakening*, London, 1938. T. E. Lawrence tells his own story in the brilliant *Seven Pillars of Wisdom*, Garden City, N.Y., 1935, and is the subject of a rewarding biography by J. E. Mack, *A Prince of our Disorder*, Boston, 1976.

On the economic history of the Middle East see R. Owen, *The Middle East in the World Economy, 1800–1914*, New York, 1981. Three important collections of articles are C. Issawi, *The Economic History of the Middle East, 1800–1914*, Chicago, 1966; A. L. Udovitch, ed., *The Islamic Middle East, 700–1900: Studies in Economic and Social History*, Princeton, 1981; and M. A. Cook, ed., *Studies in the Economic History of the Middle East*, London, 1970. For the development of the region since World War II see C. Issawi, ed., *An Economic History of the Middle East and North Africa*, New York, 1982. From a dependency theory point of view, see S. A. Amin,

The Modernization of Poverty: A Study in the Political Economy of Growth in Nine Arab Countries, 1945–1970, Leiden, 1974; S. A. Amin, *The Arab Economy Today*, London, 1981. On Middle Eastern oil see P. R. O'Dell, *Oil and World Power*, 5th edn, Harmondsworth, 1979; M. Abir, *Oil, Power and Politics*, London, 1974; M. A. Adelman, *The World Petroleum Market*, Baltimore, 1972.

On Arab nationalism and Arab thought see A. Hourani, *Arabic Thought in the Liberal Age*, Cambridge, 1983. This may be supplemented by S. Haim, ed., *Arab Nationalism: An Anthology*, Berkeley, 1976; H. Sharabi, *Arab Intellectuals and the West, 1875–1914*, Baltimore, 1970. On Arab nationalism at the time of World War I see Z. N. Zeine, *Arab–Turkish Relations and the Emergence of Arab Nationalism*, Beirut, 1958; Z. N. Zeine, *The Emergence of Arab Nationalism*, Delmar, N.Y., 1973; C. E. Dawn, *From Ottomanism to Arabism: Essays on the Origins of Arab Nationalism*, Urbana, Ill., 1973; P. S. Khoury, *Urban Notables and Arab Nationalism: The Politics of Damascus, 1860–1920*, Cambridge, 1983; H. Kayali, *Arabs and Young Turks*, Berkeley, 1997.

Arab nationalism in the inter-war years: W. Cleveland, *The Making of an Arab Nationalist: Ottomanism and Arabism in the Life and Thought of Sati' al-Husri*, Princeton, 1971. Postwar statements of the Arab position include al-Bazzaz, *Al-Bazzaz on Arab Nationalism*, London, 1965; H. Nuseibeh, *The Ideas of Arab Nationalism*, Ithaca, N.Y., 1956; F. A. Sayegh, *Arab Unity: Hope and Fulfillment*, New York, 1958.

On Arab ideology and politics see L. Binder, *The Ideological Revolution in the Middle East*, 2nd edn, New York, 1979; M. C. Hudson, *Arab Politics: The Search for Legitimacy*, New Haven, 1977; F. Ajami, *The Arab Predicament: Arab Political Thought and Practice since 1967*, Cambridge, 1981; A. Abdel-Malek, *La Pensée politique arabe contemporaine*, 3rd edn, Paris, 1980; F. Ajami, *The Dream Palace of the Arabs*, New York, 1998.

On the Salafi movement see E. Kedourie, *Afghani and 'Abduh*, London, 1966; N. R. Keddie, *Sayyid Jamal ad-Din al-Afghani: A Political Biography*, Berkeley, 1972; C. C. Adams, *Islam and Modernism in Egypt*, London, 1933; M. H. Kerr, *Islamic Reform: The Political and Legal Theories of Muhammad 'Abduh and Rashid Rida*, Berkeley, 1966.

On Islam in the period since World War II see H. A. R. Gibb, *Modern Trends in Islam*, Chicago, 1947; W. C. Smith, *Islam in Modern History*, Princeton, 1977; E. Kedourie, *Islam in the Modern World*, London, 1980; J. J. Donohue and J. L. Esposito, eds., *Islam in Transition: Muslim Perspectives*, New York, 1982.

Studies of the role of Islam in the functioning of contemporary societies include R. Peters, *Islam and Colonialism: The Doctrine of Jihad in Modern History*, The Hague, 1979; E. I. J. Rosenthal, *Islam in the Modern National State*, New York, 1965; S. A. Arjomand, ed., *From Nationalism to Revolutionary Islam*, London, 1984; M. Rodinson, *Islam and Capitalism*, tr. B. Pearce, Austin, Tex., 1978; M. Gilsenan, *Recognizing Islam: Religion and Society in the Modern Arab World*, New York, 1982;

I. M. Abu Rabi', *Intellectual Origins of Islamic Resurgence in the Modern Arab World*, Albany, N.Y. 1996.

On Arab world politics see W. Laqueur, *The Middle East in Transition*, New York, 1958; M. H. Kerr, *The Arab Cold War: Gamal 'Abd al-Nasir and his Rivals*, 3rd edn, London, 1971. The military in the Middle East: E. Be'eri, *Army Officers in Arab Politics and Society*, tr. D. Ben-Abba, New York, 1969; J. C. Hurewitz, *Middle East Politics: The Military Dimension*, New York, 1969; V. J. Parry and M. E. Yapp, eds., *War, Technology and Society in the Middle East*, London, 1975.

On the social structure of the Arab Middle East see G. Baer, *Population and Society in the Arab East*, tr. H. Szoke, London, 1964; D. Eickelman, *The Middle East: An Anthropological Approach*, Englewood Cliffs, N.J., 1981; A. Hourani, *A Vision of History: Near Eastern and Other Essays*, Beirut, 1961; A. Hourani, *The Emergence of the Modern Middle East*, Berkeley, 1981.

On land tenure, rural development, and politics see D. Warriner, *Land Reform and Development in the Middle East: A Study of Egypt, Syria and Iraq*, 2nd edn, London, 1962; G. Baer, *Fellah and Townsman in the Middle East*, London, 1982; R. Springborg, "New Patterns of Agrarian Reform in the Middle East and North Africa," *Middle East Journal*, 31 (1977), pp. 127–42; R. Antoun and I. Harik, eds., *Rural Politics and Social Change in the Middle East*, Bloomington, 1972; L. J. Cantori and I. Harik, eds., *Local Politics and Development in the Middle East*, Boulder, 1981. On nomadism see C. Nelson, ed., *The Desert and the Sown: Nomads in the Wider Society*, Berkeley, 1973.

A number of lively books with insight into the conditions of town and village life include H. Ammar, *Growing up in an Egyptian Village*, London, 1954; H. Ayrout, *The Egyptian Peasant*, tr. J. Williams, Boston, 1963. Ivo Andrić, *The Bridge on the Drina*, tr. L. Edwards, New York, 1959 is a revealing historical novel about a town in Bosnia under Ottoman rule.

Urbanization is the subject of a brief overview by C. Issawi, "Economic Change and Urbanization in the Middle East," *Middle Eastern Cities*, ed. I. M. Lapidus, Berkeley, 1969, pp. 102–21. See also G. H. Blake and R. I. Lawless, eds., *The Changing Middle Eastern City*, New York, 1980; V. F. Costello, *Urbanisation in the Middle East*, Cambridge, 1977.

Introductions to changes in Islamic law include N. J. Coulson, *Conflicts and Tensions in Islamic Jurisprudence*, Chicago, 1969; J. N. D. Anderson, *Islamic Law in the Modern World*, Westport, Conn., 1975; N. J. Coulson, *Succession in the Muslim Family*, Cambridge, 1971; H. Liebesny, *The Law of the Near and Middle East*, Albany, N.Y., 1975.

On Arabic literature see the bibliographical review by R. Allen, "Arabic Literature," *The Study of the Middle East*, ed. L. Binder, New York, 1976, pp. 399–453. On poetry see M. Khouri and H. Algar, eds., *An Anthology of Modern Arabic Poetry*, Berkeley, 1974; S. Jayyusi, *Trends and Movements in Modern Arabic Poetry*, 2 vols., Leiden, 1977; M. Badawi, *A Critical Introduction to Modern Arabic Poetry*, Cambridge, 1976.

For drama and theater see T. al-Hakim, *The Sultan's Dilemma in Arabic Writing Today: The Drama*, ii, ed. M. Manzalaoui, Cairo, 1968; J. Landau, *Studies in the Arabic Theater and Cinema*, Philadelphia, 1958.

On the role of women in Middle Eastern societies see E. Fernea, *Guests of the Sheik*, Garden City, N.Y., 1965; L. Beck and N. Keddie, eds., *Women in the Muslim World*, Cambridge, Mass., 1978; James Allman, *Women's Status and Fertility in the Muslim World*, New York, 1978; F. Hussain, *Muslim Women*, London, 1984; J. I. Smith, ed., *Women in Contemporary Muslim Societies*, London, 1980; E. W. Fernea and B. Bezirgan, eds., *Middle Eastern Muslim Women Speak*, Austin, Tex., 1977. On changing Muslim law see J. L. Esposito, *Women in Muslim Family Law*, Syracuse, N.Y., 1982. On the Arab countries see D. J. Gerner-Adams, "The Changing Status of Muslim Women in the Arab World," *Arab Studies Quarterly*, 1 (1979), pp. 324–53; E. T. Prothro and L. N. Diab, *Changing Family Patterns in the Arab East*, Beirut, 1974. From a feminist point of view there are a number of controversial works, including G. Tillion, *The Republic of Cousins: Women's Oppression in Mediterranean Society*, Thetford, 1966; F. Mernissi, *Beyond the Veil: Male–Female Dynamics in a Modern Muslim Society*, Cambridge, Mass., 1975; N. El-Saadawi, *The Hidden Face of Eve: Women in the Arab World*, tr. S. Hetata, London, 1980; F. A. Sabbah, *Women in the Muslim Unconscious*, New York, 1984.

Also see the section on women in the Islamic world in the conclusion.

Nineteenth-century Syrian economic development and political change: M. Ma'oz, *Ottoman Reform in Syria and Palestine, 1840–1861*, Oxford, 1968. Valuable articles on this subject by D. Chevallier, S. Shamir, A. Hourani, and R. S. Salibi are included in *Beginnings of Modernization in the Middle East*, ed. W. R. Polk and R. L. Chambers, Chicago, 1968. On long-term relations between nomadic and settled peoples see N. Lewis, "The Frontier of Settlement, 1800–1950," *The Economic History of the Middle East 1800–1914*, ed. C. Issawi, Chicago, 1966, pp. 258–68.

Syria in the mandate period: S. H. Longrigg, *Syria and Lebanon under the French Mandate*, London, 1958; P. S. Khoury, "Factionalism among Syrian Nationalists during the French Mandate," *IJMES*, 13 (1981), pp. 441–69. The rise of the Ba'th Party: J. F. Devlin, *The Ba'th Party: A History from its Origins to 1966*, Stanford, 1976; K. S. Abu Jaber, *The Arab Ba'th Socialist Party: History, Ideology and Organization*, Syracuse, N.Y., 1966.

Independent Syria and the Ba'th regime: S. Heydemann, *Authoritarianism in Syria: Institutions and Social Conflict, 1946–1970*, Ithaca, N.Y., 1999; P. Seale, *The Struggle for Syria: A Study of Post-war Arab Politics, 1945–1958*, London, 1965; N. Van Dam, *The Struggle for Power in Syria: Sectarianism, Regionalism and Tribalism in Politics 1961–1978*, London, 1979; I. Rabinovich, *Syria under the Ba'th, 1963–66: The Army-Party Symbiosis*, Jerusalem, 1972. The Ba'th party machine is treated in R. Hinnebusch, *Party and Peasant in Syria: Rural Politics and Social Change under the Ba'th*, Cairo, 1979; H. Batatu, *Syria's Peasantry*, Princeton, 1999. On Islam and politics in Syria see H. Batatu, "Syria's Muslim Brethren," *MERIP Reports*, 110 (1982), pp. 12–20.

Political economy and economic development: S. Amin, *Irak et Syrie, 1960–1980: Du projet national à la transnationalisation,* Paris, 1982; A. G. Samarbakhsh, *Socialisme en Irak et en Syrie,* Paris, 1980; F. H. Lawson, *Why Syria Goes to War? Thirty Years of Confrontation,* Ithaca, N.Y., 1996.

Syria in the 1990s: I. Rabinovich, *The Brink of Peace: The Israeli–Syrian Negotiations,* Princeton, 1998; L. Wedeen, *Ambiguities of Domination: Politics, Rhetoric and Symbols in Contemporary Syria,* Chicago, 1999.

Geographical and anthropological studies of Syrian towns and cities include D. Chevallier, *Villes et travail en Syrie du XIXe au XXe siècle,* Paris, 1982; J. Gulick, *Tripoli: A Modern Arab City,* Cambridge, Mass., 1967; L. Sweet, "Tell Toqaan: A Syrian Village," Ph.D. thesis, University of Michigan, 1958.

An outstanding work on modern Iraq is H. Batatu, *The Old Social Classes and Revolutionary Movements of Iraq,* Princeton, 1978. On political issues see D. Pool, "From Elite to Class: The Transformation of Iraqi Leadership, 1920–1939," *IJMES,* 12 (1980), pp. 331–50; P. A. Marr, "Iraq's Leadership Dilemma: A Study in Leadership Trends, 1948–1968," *Middle East Journal,* 24 (1970), pp. 283–301; S. Jawad, *Iraq and the Kurdish Question, 1958–1970,* London, 1981; H. Batatu, "Iraq's Underground Shi'a Movements: Characteristics, Causes and Prospects," *Middle East Journal,* 35 (1981), pp. 578–94. On social change in rural areas: R. A. Fernea, *Shaykh and Effendi: Changing Patterns of Authority among the Shabana of Southern Iraq,* Cambridge, Mass., 1969.

On the regime of Saddam Husayn: S. al-Khalil, *The Monument,* Berkeley, 1991; L. Lukitz, *Iraq: The Search for National Identity,* London, 1995; K. Makiya, *Republic of Fear: The Politics of Modern Iraq,* Berkeley, 1998.

On Jordan see P. J. Vatikiotis, *Politics and the Military in Jordan: A Study of the Arab Legion, 1921–1957,* London, 1967; P. Gubser, *Politics and Change in al-Karak, Jordan,* London, 1973; P. Mazur, *Economic Growth and Development in Jordan,* London, 1979; S. H. Fathi, *Jordan – An Invented Nation? Tribe–State Dynamics and the Formation of National Identity,* Hamburg, 1994; A. Shryock, *Nationalism and the Genealogical Imagination: Oral History and Textual Authority in Tribal Jordan,* Berkeley, 1997; M. Boulby, *The Muslim Brotherhood and the Kings of Jordan, 1945–1993,* Atlanta, 1999.

Lebanon: nineteenth-century conflict is studied in I. Harik, *Politics and Change in a Traditional Society: Lebanon 1711–1845,* Princeton, 1968; W. R. Polk, *The Opening of South Lebanon, 1788–1840,* Cambridge, Mass., 1963; D. Chevallier, *La Société du Mont Liban à l'époque de la Révolution Industrielle en Europe,* Paris, 1971; L. T. Fawaz, *Merchants and Migrants in Nineteenth-Century Beirut,* Cambridge, Mass., 1983.

Interpretations of the Lebanese political system in the postwar period: M. C. Hudson, *The Precarious Republic: Political Modernization in Lebanon,* New York, 1968; L. Binder, ed., *Politics in Lebanon,* New York, 1966; R. Owen, ed., *Essays on the Crisis in Lebanon,* London, 1976; D. Gilmour, *Lebanon: The Fractured Country,* Oxford, 1983. The Maronites and the Kata'ib movement are treated in J. P. Entelis,

Pluralism and Party Transformation in Lebanon: Al-Kata'ib, 1936–1970, Leiden, 1974; S. Joseph, "Muslim-Christian Conflicts: A Theoretical Perspective," *Muslim–Christian Conflicts: Economic, Political and Social Origins*, ed. S. Joseph and B. Pillsbury, Boulder, 1978, pp. 1–60.

Lebanon in the civil war and after: F. Ajami, *The Vanished Imam*, Ithaca, N.Y., 1986; W. Phades, *Lebanese Christian Nationalism: The Rise and Fall of an Ethnic Resistance*, Boulder, 1995; E. Salem, *Violence and Diplomacy in Lebanon: The Troubled Years 1982–1988*, London, 1995; M. Ranstorp, *Hizballah in Lebanon: The Politics of the Western Hostage Crisis*, Basingstoke, 1996; M. Gilsenan, *Lords of the Lebanese Marches: Violence and Narrative in an Arab Society*, London, 1996.

Studies of town and village communities include J. Gulick, *Social Structure and Culture Change in a Lebanese Village*, New York, 1955; S. Khalaf and P. Kongstad, *Hamra of Beirut: A Case of Rapid Urbanization*, Leiden, 1973; F. I. al-Khuri, *From Village to Suburb: Order and Change in Beirut*, Chicago, 1975; E. L. Peters, "Aspects of Rank and Status among Muslims in a Lebanese Village," *Mediterranean Countrymen*, ed. J. Pitt-Rivers, Paris, 1963, pp. 159–200.

The most balanced account of Zionist settlement and Arab resistance from World War I to 1950 is J. C. Hurewitz, *The Struggle for Palestine*, New York, 1976. On the Arab-Palestinian population in the British mandate period see J. Migdal, ed., *Palestinian Society and Politics*, Princeton, 1980; Y. Porath, *The Emergence of the Palestinian-Arab National Movement, 1918–1929*, London, 1974; Y. Porath, *The Palestinian Arab National Movement: From Riots to Rebellion, 1929-39*, London, 1977; A. Lesch, *Arab Politics in Palestine, 1917–1939: The Frustration of a Nationalist Movement*, Ithaca, N.Y., 1979; Y. N. Miller, *Government and Society in Rural Palestine, 1920–1948*, Austin, Tex., 1985.

Post-1948 Arab-Israeli relations: C. K. Zurayk, *The Meaning of the Disaster*, tr. R. B. Winder, Beirut, 1956; D. Peretz, *Israel and the Palestine Arabs*, Washington, D.C., 1958; W. R. Polk, D. Stamler, and E. Asfour, *Backdrop to Tragedy: The Struggle for Palestine*, Boston, 1957; W. Khalidi, ed., *From Haven to Conquest: Readings in Zionism and the Palestine Problem*, Beirut, 1971; N. Safran, *The United States and Israel*, Cambridge, Mass., 1963; N. Safran, *From War to War: The Arab-Israeli Confrontation, 1948–1967*, New York, 1969; I. Lustick, *Arabs in the Jewish State: Israel's Control of a National Minority*, Austin, Tex., 1980; N. Johnson, *Islam and the Politics of Meaning in Palestinian Nationalism*, London, 1982.

Palestinians in the era of Oslo: H. H. Ahmad, *Hamas from Religious Salvation to Political Transformation*, Jerusalem, 1994; M. Darweish and A. Rigby, *Palestinians in Israel: Nationality and Citizenship*, Bradford, 1995; Aziz Haidar, *On the Margins: The Arab Population in the Israeli Economy*, London, 1995; R. Khalidi, *Palestinian Identity: The Construction of Modern National Consciousness*, New York, 1997; G. Robinson, *Building a Palestinian State*, Bloomington, 1997.

On the history of Zionism and Israel: W. Laqueur, *A History of Zionism*, New York, 1972; H. M. Sachar, *A History of Israel: From the Rise of Zionism to our Time*,

New York, 1976; D. Peretz, *The Government and Politics of Israel*, 2nd edn, Boulder, 1983.

Arabian peninsula: for the Wahhabi movement and the Sa'udi state see C. S. Hurgronje, *Mekka in the Latter Part of the Nineteenth Century*, tr. J. H. Monahan, Leiden and London, 1931; R. B. Winder, *Saudi Arabia in the Nineteenth Century*, New York, 1965; G. Troeller, *The Birth of Sa'udi Arabia: Britain and the Rise of the House of Sa'ud*, London, 1976; J. S. Habib, *Ibn Sa'ud's Warriors of Islam: The Ikhwan of Najd and their Role in the Creation of the Sa'udi Kingdom*, Leiden, 1978.

Sa'udi Arabia to 1980 is the subject of W. A. Beling, ed., *King Faisal and the Modernisation of Saudi Arabia*, London and Boulder, 1980; C. M. Helms, *The Cohesion of Saudi Arabia: Evolution of Political Identity*, London, 1981; R. El-Mallakh, *Saudi Arabia, Rush to Development: Profile of an Energy Economy and Investment*, London, 1982; W. B. Quandt, *Saudi Arabia in the 1980s: Foreign Policy, Security, and Oil*, Washington, D.C., 1981; W. Ochsenwald, "Saudi Arabia and the Islamic Revival," *IJMES*, 13 (1981), pp. 271–86; S. Altorki, *Women in Saudi Arabia*, New York, 1986.

Sa'udi Arabia in the 1980s and 1990s: M. Abir, *Saudi Arabia: Government, Society and the Gulf Crisis*, London and New York, 1993; J. W. Wright, *Islamic Banking in Practice: Problems in Jordan and Saudi Arabia*, Durham, 1994; A. H. Cordesman, *Saudi Arabia: Guarding the Desert Kingdom*, Boulder, 1997; G. Simons, *Saudi Arabia: The Shape of Client Feudalism*, London, 1998.

For the life of the bedouin see H. R. P. Dickson, *The Arabs of the Desert: A Glimpse into Badawin Life in Kuwait and Sa'udi Arabia*, 2nd edn, London, 1951; W. Thesiger, *Arabian Sands*, New York, 1959, a great travel adventure.

The Gulf region in the nineteenth and early twentieth centuries, and the role of Great Britain, is covered in A. M. Abu Hakima, *History of Eastern Arabia, 1750–1800: The Rise and Development of Bahrain and Kuwait*, Beirut, 1965; T. E. Marston, *Britain's Imperial Role in the Red Sea Area, 1800–1878*, Hamden, Conn., 1961; J. B. Kelly, *Britain and the Persian Gulf, 1795–1880*, Oxford, 1968; B. C. Busch, *Britain and the Persian Gulf, 1894–1914*, Berkeley, 1967. For Oman see R. Said-Ruete, *Said bin Sultan (1791–1865): Ruler of Oman and Zanzibar*, London, 1929; R. G. Landen, *Oman since 1856*, Princeton, 1967.

Accounts of the Gulf states in the first decades of independence include J. D. Anthony, *Arab States of the Lower Gulf: People, Politics, Petroleum*, Washington, D.C., 1975; E. A. Nakhleh, *Bahrain: Political Development in a Modernizing Society*, Lexington, Mass., 1976; J. C. Wilkinson, *Water and Tribal Settlement in South-East Arabia: A Study of the Aflaj of Oman*, Oxford, 1977; J. Townsend, *Oman: The Making of a Modern State*, London, 1977; R. S. Zahlan, *The Origins of the United Arab Emirates: A Political and Social History of the Trucial States*, London, 1978; J. E. Peterson, *Oman in the Twentieth Century: Political Foundations of an Emerging State*, London and New York, 1978; M. W. Khouja and P. G. Saadler, *The Economy of Kuwait: Development and Role of International Finance*, London, 1979; F. I. Khuri, *Tribe and State in Bahrain*, Chicago, 1980; A. J. Cottrell, ed., *The Persian*

Gulf States: A General Survey, Baltimore, 1980; T. Niblock, ed., *Social and Economic Development in the Arab Gulf*, New York, 1980; R. El-Mallakh, *The Economic Development of the United Arab Emirates*, London, 1981.

Kuwait in the 1990s: J. Crystal, *Oil and Politics in the Gulf: Rulers and Merchants in Kuwait and Qatar*, Cambridge, 1995; A. N. Longva, *Walls Built on Sand and Migration: Exclusion and Society in Kuwait*, Boulder, 1997; A. H. Cordesman, *Kuwait: Recovery and Security after the Gulf War*, Boulder, 1997.

Other Gulf states in the 1990s: Ian Skeet, *Oman: Politics and Development*, New York, 1992; M. Asher, *The Phoenix Rising: The United Arab Emirates*, London, 1996; C. H. Allen, Jr. and W. L. Rigsbee II, *Oman under Qaboos*, London, 2000.

For Yemen see A. S. Bujra, *The Politics of Stratification: A Study of Political Change in a South Arabian Town*, Oxford, 1971; R. W. Stokey, *Yemen: The Politics of the Yemen Arab Republic*, Boulder, 1978; C. Makhlouf, *Changing Veils: Women and Modernisation in North Yemen*, Austin, Tex., 1979; S. G. Caton, *Peaks of Yemen I Summon*, Berkeley, 1990; P. Dresch, *Tribes, Government and History in Yemen*, Oxford, 1989.

Yemen since unification: B. Messick, *The Calligraphic State*, Berkeley, 1993; M. Mundy, *Domestic Government: Kinship, Community and Policy in North Yemen*, London, 1995; J. Kostiner, *Yemen: The Tortuous Quest for Unity, 1990–1994*, London, 1996; S. Carapico, *Civil Society in Yemen: The Political Economy of Activism in Modern Arabia*, Cambridge, 1998; R. Leveau, F. Mermier, and U. Steibach, eds., *Le Yemen contemporain*, Paris, 1999.

Middle East regional issues: F. Goldberg, R. Kasaba, and J. Migdal, *Rules and Rights in the Middle East: Democracy, Law and Society*, Seattle, 1993; D. Garnham and M. Tessler, eds., *Democracy, War, and Peace in the Middle East*, Bloomington, 1995;. J. Kemp and R. E. Harkavy, *Strategic Geography and the Changing Middle East*, Washington, D.C., 1997; B. Maddy-Weitzman. and E. Inbar, eds., *Religious Radicalism in the Greater Middle East*, London, 1998; C. M. Henry and R. Springborg, *The Politics of Economic Development in the Middle East and North Africa*, Cambridge, 2001.

Chapter 26

An outstanding contribution to the analysis of development in North Africa is E. Hermassi, *Leadership and National Development in North Africa*, Berkeley, 1972. On North Africa under French rule and the rise of nationalism see J. Berque, *French North Africa: The Maghrib between Two World Wars*, tr. J. Stewart, New York, 1967; R. Le Tourneau, *Evolution politique de l'Afrique du Nord musulmane, 1920–1961*, Paris, 1962; C. R. Ageron, *Politiques coloniales au Maghreb*, Paris, 1972; A. al-Fasi, *The Independence Movements in Arab North Africa*, tr. H. Z. Nuseibeh, Washington, D.C., 1954.

Comparative studies of independent North Africa include M. Brett, ed., *Northern Africa: Islam and Modernization*, London, 1973; M. Halpern, *The Politics of Social Change in the Middle East and North Africa*, Princeton, 1963; D. E. Ashford, *National Development and Local Reform: Political Participation in Morocco,*

Tunisia, and Pakistan, Princeton, 1967; I. W. Zartman, ed., *Man, State and Society in the Contemporary Maghrib,* New York, 1973; L. Anderson, *The State and Social Transformation in Tunisia and Libya, 1830–1980,* Princeton, 1986. On Islam see P. Shinar, "'Ulama', Marabouts and Government: An Overview of their Relationships in the French Colonial Maghrib," *Israel Oriental Studies,* 10 (1980), pp. 211–29. The imposition of the Tunisian protectorate is the subject of J. Ganiage, *Les Origines du protectorat français en Tunisie, 1861–1881,* 2nd edn, Tunis, 1968. On French rule in Tunisia see J. Poncet, *La Colonisation et l'agriculture européennes en Tunisie depuis 1881,* Paris, 1961. Tunisian state and society in the late nineteenth century: L. C. Brown, tr., *The Surest Path, by Khayr al-Din al-Tunisi,* Cambridge, Mass., 1967; A. H. Green, *The Tunisian Ulama 1873–1915,* Leiden, 1978.

The Tunisia nationalist movement: N. Ziadeh, *Origins of Nationalism in Tunisia,* Beirut, 1969; A. Mahjoubi, *Les Origines du mouvement national en Tunisie (1904–1934),* Tunis, 1982. A. Memmi, *The Pillar of Salt,* tr. E. Roditi, New York, 1955 is a sensitive novel portraying the impact of colonialism upon a Tunisian Jewish boy.

General books on independent Tunisia include C. Micaud et al., *Tunisia: The Politics of Modernization,* New York, 1964; C. H. Moore, *Tunisia since Independence,* Berkeley, 1965; J. Duvignaud, *Change at Shibeika: Report from a North African Village,* tr. F. Frenaye, Austin, Tex., 1977; M. E. Hamdi, *The Politicisation of Islam: A Case Study of Tunisia,* Boulder, 1998; A. Ghanmi, *Le Mouvement Feministe Tunisien, 1978–1989,* Tunis, 1993.

Histories of Algeria under French rule include P. Boyer, *L'Evolution de L'Algérie médiane (ancien département d'Alger) de 1830 à 1956,* Paris, 1960; C. R. Ageron, *Histoire de l'Algérie contemporaine (1830–1964),* Paris, 1966; C. A. Julien, *Histoire de l'Algérie contemporaine,* Paris, 1964; C. R. Ageron, *Les Algériens musulmans et la France (1871–1919),* 2 vols., Paris, 1968.

For Algerian society on the eve of the French invasion see the bibliography to part II. For the resistance of 'Abd al-Qadir see R. Danziger, *Abd al-Qadir and the Algerians,* New York and London, 1977. Later Algerian resistance movements have been studied by A. Nadir, "Les Ordres religieux et la conquête française (1830–1851)," *Revue algérienne des sciences juridiques, politiques et économiques,* 9 (1972), pp. 819–68; P. Von Sivers, "The Realm of Justice: Apocalyptic in Algeria (1849–1879)," *Humaniora Islamica,* 1 (1973), pp. 47–60; F. Colonna, "Cultural Resistance and Religious Legitimacy in Colonial Algeria," *Economy and Society,* 3 (1974), pp. 233–52; F. Colonna, "Saints furieux et saints studieux ou, dans l'Aurès, comment la religion vient aux tribus," *Annales ESC,* 35 (1980), pp. 642–62; J. Clancy-Smith, "Saints, Mahdis and Arms: Religion and Resistance in Nineteenth-Century North Africa," *Islam, Politics, and Social Movements,* ed. E. Burke and I. M. Lapidus, Berkeley, 1991, pp. 60–80.

On Muslim culture see H. Masse, "Les Etudes arabes en Algérie (1830–1930)," *Revue Africaine,* 74 (1933), pp. 208–58, 458–505; F. Colonna, *Instituteurs algériens: 1833–1939,* Paris, 1975; J. P. Charnay, *La Vie musulmane en Algérie: d'après la jurisprudence de la première moitié du XXe siècle,* Paris, 1965.

The French colonization and its impact upon the economic well-being of the Muslims: J. Reudy, *Land Policy in Colonial Algeria: The Origins of the Rural Public Domain*, Berkeley, 1967; M. Launay, *Paysans algériens: La terre, la vigne et les hommes*, Paris, 1963.

The birth of Algerian nationalism: A. Nouschi, *La Naissance du nationalisme algérien*, Paris, 1962; E. Sivan, *Communisme et nationalisme en Algérie, 1920–1962*, Paris, 1976. For Muslim reformism see A. Merad, *Le Reformisme musulman en Algérie de 1925 à 1940*, The Hague, 1967; P. Shinar, "The Historical Approach of the Reformist 'Ulama' in the Contemporary Maghrib," *Asian and African Studies*, Jerusalem, 7 (1971), pp. 181–210; P. Shinar, "Ibadiyya and Orthodox Reformism in Modern Algeria," *Scripta Hierosolymitana*, IX, ed. U. Heyd, Jerusalem, 1961, pp. 97–120; P. Shinar, "Traditional and Reformist Mawlid Celebrations in the Maghrib," *Studies in Memory of Gaston Wiet*, ed. M. Rosen-Ayalon, Jerusalem, 1977, pp. 371–413. For Sufi Islam see J. Carret, *Le Maraboutisme, et les confréries religieuses musulmanes en Algérie*, Algiers, 1959; M. Lings, *A Moslem Saint of the Twentieth Century: Shaikh Ahmad al-'Alawi, his Spiritual Heritage and Legacy*, London, 1961.

The revolutionary struggle: D. Ling, *The Passing of French Algeria*, London, 1966; W. B. Quandt, *Revolution and Political Leadership: Algeria 1954–1968*, Cambridge, Mass., 1969; D. Ottaway and M. Ottaway, *Algeria: The Politics of a Socialist Revolution*, Berkeley, 1970; T. Smith, *The French Stake in Algeria, 1945–1962*, Ithaca, N.Y., 1978; Frantz Fanon, *The Wretched of the Earth*, tr. C. Farrington, New York, 1963; I. L. Gendzier, *Frantz Fanon: A Critical Study*, New York, 1973.

Post-independence Algeria: J.-C. Vatin, *L'Algérie politique*, 2nd edn, Paris, 1983; M. Lacheraf, *L'Algérie: Nation et société*, Paris, 1965; A. Gauthier, *L'Algérie: Décolonisation, socialisme, industrialisation*, Montreuil, 1976; M. Lazreg, *The Emergence of Classes in Algeria*, Boulder, 1976; J. R. Nellis, "Socialist Management in Algeria," *Journal of Modern African Studies*, 15 (1977), pp. 529–54. On the structure of Algerian society: P. Bourdieu, *The Algerians*, tr. A. C. M. Ross, Boston, 1962; P. Bourdieu, *Sociologie de l'Algérie*, 3rd edn, Paris, 1963.

Algeria's civil war in the 1990s: A. Touati, *Algerie, Les Islamistes à l'assaut du pouvoir*, Paris, 1995; A. Djazair, *Les Integristes contre l'Algerie*, Paris, 1998; W. B. Quandt, *Between Ballots and Bullets: Algeria's Transition from Authoritarianism*, Washington, D.C., 1998; A. Dahmani, *L'Algerie a l'epreuve: Economie politique des reformes, 1980–1997*, Paris, 1999.

The basic structures of Moroccan rural society are treated in a number of brilliant and conflicting works: J. Berque and P. Pascon, *Structures sociales du Haut-Atlas*, 2nd edn, Paris, 1978; E. Gellner, *Saints of the Atlas*, Chicago, 1969, supplemented by his *Muslim Society*, Cambridge, 1981; D. F. Eickelman, *Moroccan Islam: Tradition and Society in a Pilgrimage Center*, Austin, Tex., 1976; C. Geertz, H. Geertz, and R. Rosen, *Meaning and Order in Muslim Society: Three Essays in Cultural Analysis*, Cambridge, 1979. Other valuable studies include: V. Crapanzano, *The Hamadsha: A Study in Moroccan Ethnopsychiatry*, Berkeley, 1973; R. Jamous, *Honneur et baraka: Les Structures sociales traditionelles dans le Rif*, Paris, 1981; P. Rabinow, *Symbolic*

Domination: Cultural Form and Historical Change in Morocco, Chicago, 1975; D. Hart, *Dadda 'Atta and his Four Grandsons: The Socio-Political Organisation of the Ait 'Atta of Southern Morocco*, Cambridge, 1981; D. Seddon, *Moroccan Peasants: A Century of Change in the Eastern Rif, 1870–1970*, Folkestone, 1980. On Islam see the classic E. A. Westermarck, *Ritual and Belief in Morocco*, 2 vols., New Hyde Park, N.Y., 1968.

On Moroccan political society and its response to the French occupation: R. E. Dunn, *Resistance in the Desert: Moroccan Responses to French Imperialism, 1881–1912*, London and Madison, Wis., 1977; E. Burke, *Prelude to Protectorate in Morocco*, Chicago, 1976. See also E. Burke, "Morocco and the Near East: Reflections on Some Basic Differences," *Archives européennes de sociologie*, 10 (1969), pp. 70–94; D. Seddon, "Tribe and State: 'Approaches to Maghreb History,'" *The Maghreb Review*, 2 (1977), pp. 23–40.

The French protectorate is treated in C.-A. Julien, *Le Maroc face aux impérialismes, 1415–1956*, Paris, 1978; R. Landau, *Moroccan Drama, 1900–1955*, San Francisco, 1978; R. L. Bidwell, *Morocco under Colonial Rule: French Administration of Tribal Areas 1912–1956*, London, 1973; G. Maxwell, *Lords of the Atlas: The Rise and Fall of the House of Glaoua, 1893–1956*, London, 1966. The development of an Islamic-national resistance is covered by A. Laroui, *Les Origines sociales et culturelles du nationalisme marocain (1830–1912)*, Paris, 1977; J. P. Halstead, *Rebirth of a Nation: The Origins and Rise of Moroccan Nationalism, 1912–1944*, Cambridge, Mass., 1967.

For the Moroccan economy see C. F. Stewart, *The Economy of Morocco, 1912–1962*, Cambridge, Mass., 1964; J. L. Miege, *Le Maroc et l'Europe (1830–1894)*, 4 vols., Paris, 1961–63; J. Waterbury, *North for the Trade: The Life and Times of a Berber Merchant*, Berkeley, 1972.

On the politics of independent Morocco see I. W. Zartman, *Morocco: Problems of New Power*, New York, 1964; J. Waterbury, *The Commander of the Faithful: The Moroccan Political Elite*, London, 1970; K. E. Mourad, *Le Maroc à la recherche d'une révolution*, Paris, 1972; A. Benhaddou, *Maroc, les élites du royaume: Essai sur l'organisation du pouvoir au Maroc*, Paris, 1997; A. Hammoudi, *Master and Disciple. The Cultural Foundations of Moroccan Authoritarianism*, Chicago, 1997.

A good introduction to the historical background of modern Libya is L. Anderson, "Nineteenth-Century Reform in Ottoman Libya," *IJMES*, 16 (1984), pp. 325–48. The Sanusiya are discussed in the classic E. E. Evans-Pritchard, *The Sanusi of Cyrenaica*, Oxford, 1949. On the Qaddafi regime see J. L. Wright, *Libya: A Modern History*, Baltimore, 1982; M. Djaziri, *Etat et société en Libye: Islam, politique et modernité*, Paris, 1996; M. O. El-Kikhia, *Libya's Qaddafi: The Politics of Contradiction*, Gainsville, Fla., 1997; D. J. Vandewalle, *Libya since Independence: Oil and State-Building*, London, 1998.

On contemporary Islamic movements see J. Ruedy, *Islam and Secularism in North Africa*, New York, 1994; E. E. Shahin, *Political Ascent: Contemporary Islamic Movements in North Africa*, Boulder, 1997; J. P. Entelis, *Islam, Democracy and the State in North Africa*, Bloomington, 1997.

Chapter 27

For the principal histories of the Muslim populace of India see part II above. See also S. M. Ikram, *Modern Muslim India and the Birth of Pakistan, 1858–1951*, 2nd edn, Lahore, 1970; A. Ahmad, *Islamic Modernism in India and Pakistan*, London, 1967; A. Ahmad and G. E. von Grunebaum, eds., *Muslim Self-statement in India and Pakistan, 1857–1968*, Wiesbaden, 1970.

The nineteenth-century Muslim reform movements in Bengal: M. A. Khan, *History of the Fara'idi Movement in Bengal, 1818–1906*, Karachi, 1965; R. Ahmad, *The Bengal Muslims, 1871–1906: A Quest for Identity*, Delhi, 1981; S. Ahmad, *The Muslim Community of Bengal 1884–1912*, Dacca, 1974. On the college of Deoband: B. D. Metcalf, *Islamic Revival in British India: Deoband, 1860–1900*, Princeton, 1982; see also F. Robinson, "The 'Ulama' of Farangi Mahall and their Adab," *Moral Conduct and Authority*, ed. B. D. Metcalf, Berkeley, 1984, pp. 152–83.

Indian Muslim modernist movements are treated in D. Lelyveld, *Aligarh's First Generation*, Princeton, 1978; F. Robinson, *Separatism among Indian Muslims: The Politics of the United Provinces' Muslims, 1860–1923*, Cambridge, 1974; G. Minault, *The Khilafat Movement: Religious Symbolism and Political Mobilization in India*, New York, 1982; M. Hasan, ed., *Communal and Pan-Islamic Trends in Colonial India*, New Delhi, 1981. The position of the 'ulama' is explained by P. Hardy, *Partners in Freedom and True Muslims*, Lund, 1971; M. Anwarul Haq, *The Faith Movement of Mawlana Muhammad Ilyas*, London, 1972.

The development of Muslim communalism and Pakistan to 1947: M. Iqbal, *The Reconstruction of Religious Thought in Islam*, Lahore, 1962; M. Iqbal, *Poems from Iqbal*, tr. V. G. Kiernan, London, 1955; P. Moon, *Divide and Quit*, Berkeley, 1962; D. Gilmartin, "Religious Leadership and the Pakistan Movement in the Punjab," *Modern Asian Studies*, 13 (1979), pp. 485–517; David Gilmartin, "Partition, Pakistan and South Asian History: In Search of a Narrative," *The Journal of Asian Studies*, 57 (1998), pp. 1069–95.

Muslims in India since partition: T. N. Madan, *Muslim Communities of South Asia*, New Delhi, 1976; R. E. Miller, *Mappila Muslims of Kerala*, Madras, 1976; I. Ahmad, ed., *Family, Kinship and Marriage among Muslims in India*, New Delhi, 1976; I. Ahmad, ed., *Caste and Social Stratification among Muslims in India*, 2nd edn, New Delhi, 1978; I. Ahmad, ed., *Ritual and Religion among Muslims in India*, New Delhi, 1981; G. Krishna, "Indian Muslims in the Nation-Formation Process," *Contributions to South Asian Studies*, 2nd edn, Delhi, 1982, pp. 110–45; M. Hasan, *Legacy of a Divided Nation: India's Muslims since Independence*, Boulder, 1997; S. Bose and A. Jalal, *Modern South Asia*, London, 1997; S. Bose, *The Challenge in Kashmir*, New Delhi,1997.

On Pashtuns and the Northwest Frontier provinces see A. S. Ahmed, *Pukhtun Economy and Society: Traditional Structure and Economic Development in a Tribal Society*, London, 1980; A. S. Ahmed and D. Hart, eds., *From the Atlas to the Indus: The Tribes of Islam*, London, 1981; F. Barth, *Features of Person and Society in Swat*, London, 1981.

For the political economy of Pakistan see K. B. Sayeed, *The Political System of Pakistan*, Lahore, 1967; R. S. Wheeler, *The Politics of Pakistan*, Ithaca, N.Y., 1970; S. J. Burki, *Pakistan under Bhutto, 1971–1977*, London, 1980; K. B. Sayeed, *Politics in Pakistan*, New York, 1980; H. Gardezi and J. Rashid, eds., *Pakistan; The Roots of Dictatorship: The Political Economy of a Praetorian State*, London, 1983; A. Jalal, *Democracy and Authoritarianism in South Asia: A Comparative and Historical Perspective*, Cambridge, 1995; R. E. Looney, *The Pakistani Economy: Economic Growth and Structural Reform*, Westport, Conn., 1997; S. Shafqat, *Civil Military Relations in Pakistan: From Zulfikar Ali Butto to Benazir Butto*, Boulder, 1997; H. Iftikhar Malik, *State and Civil Society in Pakistan: Politics of Authority, Ideology and Ethnicity*, Oxford, 1997.

Islam and politics in Pakistan: L. Binder, *Religion and Politics in Pakistan*, Berkeley, 1961; on Mawdudi see S. A. A. Maudoodi, *First Principles of the Islamic State*, tr. K. Ahmad, Lahore, 1960; S. A. A. Maudoodi, *Towards Understanding Islam*, tr. K. Ahmad, Lahore, 1974; C. J. Adams, "The Ideology of Mawlana Mawdudi," *South Asian Politics and Religion*, ed. D. E. Smith, Princeton, 1966, pp. 371–97; S. V. R. Nasr, *The Vanguard of the Islamic Revolution: The Jama'at-i Islami of Pakistan*, Berkeley, 1994; S. V. R. Nasr, *Mawdudi and the Making of Islamic Revivalism*, New York, 1996; A. S. Ahmed, *Jinnah, Pakistan and Islamic Identity: The Search for Saladin*, London, 1997; H. I. Malik, *Islam, Nationalism and the West: Issues of Identity in Pakistan*, Oxford, 1999.

Chapter 28

On Indonesian history see M. C. Ricklefs, *A History of Modern Indonesia, c. 1300 to the Present*, Bloomington, 1981; H. J. Benda, *The Crescent and the Rising Sun*, Ithaca, N.Y., 1955; "South-East Asian Islam in the Twentieth Century," *Cambridge History of Islam*, II, ed. P. M. Holt, A. K. S. Lambton, and B. Lewis, Cambridge, 1970, pp. 182–208. On Indonesian society see C. Geertz, *The Religion of Java*, Glencoe, Ill., 1960; W. F. Wertheim, *Indonesian Society in Transition: A Study of Social Change*, 2nd edn, The Hague, 1959; J. L. Peacock, *Indonesia: An Anthropological Perspective*, Pacific Palisades, Calif., 1973; J. C. van Leur, *Indonesian Trade and Society*, tr. J. Holmes and A. van Marle, The Hague, 1955. On the rise of the Indonesian nationalist movement see R. Van Niel, *The Emergence of the Modern Indonesian Elite*, The Hague, 1960.

Muslim peasant resistance to Dutch rule is treated in S. Kartodirdjo, *The Peasants' Revolt of Banten in 1888*, Amsterdam, 1966; J. M. Van der Kroef, "Prince Diponegoro: Progenitor of Indonesian Nationalism," *Far Eastern Quarterly*, 8 (1948), pp. 424–50; J. M. Van der Kroef, "Javanese Messianic Expectations: Their Origin and Cultural Content," *Comparative Studies in Society and History*, 1 (1959), pp. 299–323.

Muslim reformism is discussed in D. Noer, *The Modernist Muslim Movement in Indonesia, 1900–1942*, Singapore and New York, 1973; J. L. Peacock, *Purifying the Faith: The Muhammadiya Movement in Indonesian Islam*, Menlo Park, Calif., 1978; J. L. Peacock, *Muslim Puritans: Reformist Psychology in Southeast Asian Islam*,

Berkeley, 1978; H. M. Federspiel, *Persatuan Islam: Islamic Reform in Twentieth Century Indonesia*, Ithaca, N.Y., 1970; T. Abdullah, *Schools and Politics: The Kaum Muda Movement in West Sumatra (1927–1933)*, Ithaca, N.Y., 1971.

The relations between religion, national consciousness, and social change are studied in C. Geertz, *The Social History of an Indonesian Town*, Cambridge, Mass., 1965; C. Geertz, *Peddlers and Princes*, Chicago, 1963; C. Geertz, *Agricultural Involution: The Process of Ecological Change in Indonesia*, Berkeley, 1966; D. H. Burger, *Structural Changes in Javanese Society: The Supra-Village Sphere*, Ithaca, N.Y., 1956; B. J. O. Schrieke, *Indonesian Sociological Studies*, 2 vols., The Hague, 1955–57; R. R. Jay, *Religion and Politics in Rural Central Java*, New Haven, 1963; L. Castles, *Religion, Politics, and Economic Behavior in Java: The Kudus Cigarette Industry*, New Haven, 1967. J. T. Siegel, *The Rope of God*, Berkeley, 1969 analyzes the social structure and mentality of Acheh.

The politics of independent Indonesia is covered in G. M. Kahin, *Nationalism and Revolution in Indonesia*, Ithaca, N.Y., 1952; H. Feith, *The Decline of Constitutional Democracy in Indonesia*, Ithaca, N.Y., 1962; H. Hill, ed., *Indonesia's New Order: The Dynamics of Socio-Economic Transformation*, St. Leonards (Australia), 1994.

On the role of Islam see B. J. Boland, *The Struggle of Islam in Modern Indonesia*, The Hague, 1971. On Muslim legal administration see D. S. Lev, *Islamic Courts in Indonesia*, Berkeley, 1972; A. A. Samson, "Religious Belief and Political Action in Indonesian Islamic Modernism," *Political Participation in Modern Indonesia*, ed. R. W. Liddle, New Haven, 1973, pp. 116–42; D. Noer, *Administration of Islam in Indonesia*, Ithaca, N.Y., 1978; M. K. Hassan, *Muslim Intellectual Responses to New Order Modernization in Indonesia*, Kuala Lumpur, 1980; T. Taher, *Aspiring for the Middle Path: Religious Harmony in Indonesia*, Jakarta, 1997.

On Islam in Malaysia see W. R. Roff, *The Origins of Malay Nationalism*, New Haven, 1967. Clive Kessler gives revealing insights into Muslim symbols and politics: *Islam and Politics in a Malay State: Kelantan 1838–1969*, Ithaca, N.Y., 1978. See also M. Yeger, *Islam and Islamic Institutions in British Malaya: Politics and Implementation*, Jerusalem, 1979; B. W. Andaya and L. Y. Andaya, *A History of Malaysia*, London, 1982; J. Nagata, *The Reflowering of Malaysian Islam: Modern Religious Radicals and their Roots*, Vancouver, 1984; H. Muttalib, *Islam and Ethnicity in Malay Politics*, Singapore, 1990; H. Muttalib, *Islam in Malaysia: From Revivalism to Islamic State*, Singapore, 1993; R. L. M. Lee and S. F. Ackerman, *Sacred Tensions: Modernity and Religious Transformation in Malaysia*, Columbia, 1997.

On the political economy of Malaysia see H. Osman Rani, Jomo Kwame Sundaram, and I. Shari, eds., "Development in the Eighties: With Special Emphasis on Malaysia," *Bangi: Jurnal Ekonomi Malaysia*, 2 (1981); Hua Wu Yin, *Classical Communalism in Malaysia. Politics in a Dependent Capitalist State*, London, 1983; E. T. Gomez and K. S. Jomo, *Malaysia's Political Economy: Politics, Patronage and Profits*, Cambridge, 1997.

Philippines: T. M. McKenna, *Muslim Rulers and Rebels*, Berkeley, 1998; G. C. Delasa, *The Quranic Concept of Umma and its Function in Philippine Muslim Society*, Rome, 1999. Comparative and regional studies include: R. Hefner and P. Horvatich, *Islam in an Era of Nation States: Politics and Religious Renewal in Southeast Asia*, Honolulu, 1997; A. Bowie and D. Unger, *The Politics of Open Economies: Indonesia, Malaysia, the Philippines and Thailand*, Cambridge, 1997; F. S. Atlas, *Democracy and Authoritarianism in Indonesia and Malaysia: The Rise of the Post-Colonial State*, Basingstoke, 1997; J. S. Kahn, ed., *Southeast Asian Identities: Culture and the Politics of Representation in Indonesia, Malaysia, Singapore and Thailand*, Singapore, 1998.

Chapter 29

Inner Asia up to the revolution is covered by the general works indicated in part II. In addition see R. A. Pierce, *Russian Central Asia, 1867–1917: A Study in Colonial Rule*, Berkeley, 1960; S. Becker, *Russia's Protectorates in Central Asia: Bukhara and Khiva, 1865–1924*, Cambridge, Mass., 1968; H. Carrère d'Encausse, "Tsarist Educational Policy in Turkestan, 1867–1917," *Central Asian Review*, 11 (1963), pp. 374–94.

A number of general books deal with the Soviet period and the Muslim population: A. Bennigsen and C. Lemercier-Quelquejay, *Islam in the Soviet Union*, London, 1967; A. Bennigsen, *Les Musulmans oubliés: L'Islam en Union Soviétique*, Paris, 1981. See also H. Carrère d'Encausse, *Decline of an Empire: The Soviet Socialist Republics in Revolt*, tr. M. Sokolinsky and H. A. LaFarge, New York, 1979; S. Akiner, *Islamic Peoples of the Soviet Union*, London and Boston, 1983.

The jadid movement is treated in S. A. Zenkovsky, *Pan-Turkism and Islam in Russia*, Cambridge, Mass., 1960; C. Lemercier-Quelquejay, "Abdul Kayum al-Nasyri: A Tatar Reformer of the 19th Century," *Central Asian Survey*, 1 (1983), pp. 109–32; A. Bennigsen and C. Lemercier-Quelquejay, *La Presse et le mouvement national chez les Musulmans de Russie avant 1920*, Paris, 1964. On Muslim national Communism see A. Bennigsen and C. Lemercier-Quelquejay, *Les Mouvements nationaux chez les Musulmans de Russie*, Paris, 1960; A. Bennigsen and S. E. Wimbush, *Muslim National Communism in the Soviet Union: A Revolutionary Strategy for the Colonial World*, Chicago, 1979.

The revolutionary epoch is treated in A. G. Park, *Bolshevism in Turkestan, 1917–1927*, New York, 1957; R. E. Pipes, *The Formation of the Soviet Union: Communism and Nationalism, 1917–1923*, Cambridge, Mass., 1964; E. E. Bacon, *Central Asians under Russian Rule: A Study in Culture Change*, Ithaca, N.Y., 1966. Controversial but informative accounts are given by B. Hayit: *Turkestan im XX. Jahrhundert*, Darmstadt, 1956; and *Sowjetrussische Orientpolitik am Beispiel Turkestans*, Cologne, 1962. Questions of national identity and Soviet policy are treated in E. Allworth, *Uzbek Literary Politics*, The Hague, 1964; E. Allworth, *The Nationality Question in Soviet Central Asia*, New York, 1973; J. R. Azrael, ed., *Soviet Nationality Policies and Practices*, New York, 1978.

The impact of Soviet rule upon Muslim populations in terms of education, employment, acculturation, and political relations is the subject of T. Rakowska-Harmstone, *Russia and Nationalism in Central Asia: The Case of Tadzhikistan*, Baltimore, 1970; W. K. Medlin, W. M. Cave, and F. Carpenter, *Education and Development in Central Asia: A Case Study on Social Change in Uzbekistan*, Leiden, 1971; G. Hodnett, *Leadership in the Soviet National Republics: A Quantitative Study of Recruitment Policy*, Oakville, Ontario, 1978; M. Rywkin, *Moscow's Muslim Challenge: Soviet Central Asia*, Armonk, N.Y., 1982; E. Allworth, ed., *Central Asia: 130 Years of Russian Dominance*, Durham, N.C., 1994.

The Soviet scholarship on Islam includes: T. Saidbaev, *Islam i obshchestvo: opyt istoriko-sotsiologicheskogo issledovaniia* [Islam and Society: An Experiment in Historico-Sociological Research], Moscow, 1978; N. Ashirov, *Evoliutsiia islama v SSSR* [The Evolution of Islam in the USSR], Moscow, 1973; N. Ashirov, *Islam v SSSR: Osobennosti protsessa sekuliarizatsii v respublikakh sovetskogo vostoka* [Islam in the USSR: The Particularities of the Process of Secularization in the Republics of the Soviet East], Moscow, 1983; S. M. Demidov, *Turkmenskie ovliady* [The Turkmen Evliads], Ashkhabad, 1976.

Two general books on Islam in China are R. Israeli, *Muslims in China: A Study in Cultural Confrontation*, London and Malmo, 1980; J. T. Dreyer, *China's Forty Millions*, Cambridge, Mass., 1976, an account of the minorities policies of the People's Republic of China. For Xinjiang see R. Yang, "Sinkiang under the Administration of Governor Yang Tseng-Hsin, 1911–1928," *Central Asiatic Journal*, 6 (1961), pp. 270–316; O. Lattimore, *Pivot of Asia: Sinkiang and the Inner Asian Frontiers of China and Russia*, Boston, 1950; G. Moseley, *A Sino-Soviet Cultural Frontier: The Ili Kazakh Autonomous Chou*, Cambridge, 1966; Dru Gladney, *Ethnic Identity in China*, New York, 1998.

Post-Soviet Inner Asia: A. Rashid, *The Resurgence of Central-Asia: Islam or Nationalism*, London, 1994; H. Malik, *Central Asia: Its Strategic Importance and Future Prospects*, New York, 1994; K. Dawisha and B. Parrott, eds., *Conflict, Cleavage and Change in Central Asia and the Caucasus*, Cambridge, 1997; John Anderson, *Kyrgyzstan: Central Asia's Island of Democracy?* Amsterdam, 1999; A. Rashid, *Jihad: The Rise of Militant Islam in Central Asia*, New Haven, 2002.

Afghanistan: V. Gregorian, *The Emergence of Modern Afghanistan*, Stanford, 1969; L. B. Poullada, *Reform and Rebellion in Afghanistan*, Ithaca, N.Y., 1973; O. Roy, *Afghanistan: From Holy War to Civil War*, Princeton, 1995; R. Rubin, *The Fragmentation of Afghanistan: State Formation and Collapse in the International System*, New Haven, 1995; C. Noelle, *State and Tribe in Nineteenth Century Afghanistan*, Richmond, 1997; L. P. Goodson, *Afghanistan's Endless War*, Seattle, 2001; A. Rashid, *Taliban: Islam, Oil and the New Great Game in Central Asia*, London, 2000.

The Caucasus: A. Zelkina, "Islam and Society in Chechnia," *Journal of Islamic Studies*, 7 (1996), pp. 240–64; C. Gaal and T. De Waal, *Chechnya: Calamity in the Caucasus*, New York, 1998; Sebastian Smith, *Allah's Mountains: Politics and War in the Russian Caucasus*, London, 1998; J. B. Dunlop, *Russia Confronts Chechnya: Roots of a Separatist Conflict*, Cambridge, 1998; C. van der Leeuw, *Storm over the Caucasus: in the Wake of Independence*, Richmond, 1999.

Chapter 30
For Muslim peoples in West Africa see J. S. Trimingham, *Islam in West Africa*, Oxford, 1959; J. S. Trimingham, *A History of Islam in West Africa*, London, 1962; V. Monteil, *L'Islam noir*, Paris, 1980; R. L. Moreau, *Africains musulmans: des communautés en mouvement*, Paris, 1982.

For the European scramble for Africa see part II. A comprehensive survey of the era of colonial rule may be found in L. H. Gann and P. Duignan, eds., *Colonialism in Africa, 1870–1960*, 5 vols., London, 1969–75; M. Crowder, *West Africa under Colonial Rule*, Evanston, Ill., 1968; M. Crowder, *West African Resistance: The Military Response to Colonial Occupation*, London, 1971; M. Crowder, *Colonial West Africa: Collected Essays*, London, 1978. A leading French historian is J. Suret-Canale: see *French Colonialism in Tropical Africa*, tr. T. Gottheiner, London, 1971; and *Afrique noire: occidentale et centrale*, 3 vols., Paris, 1961–64. On German colonialism there is M. E. Townsend, *The Rise and Fall of the German Colonial Empire, 1884–1914*, New York, 1930.

The transition to independence is treated in T. L. Hodgkin, *Nationalism in Colonial Africa*, New York, 1957; W. H. Morris-Jones and G. Fischer, eds., *Decolonisation and After: The British and French Experience*, London, 1980; J. Hargreaves, *The End of Colonial Rule in West Africa*, London, 1979; E. Mortimer, *France and the Africans 1944–1960: A Political History*, London, 1969; W. J. Foltz, *From French West Africa to the Mali Federation*, New Haven, 1965. A very brief but effective account of the gaining of independence in French West Africa is I. Wallerstein, "How Seven States Were Born in Former French West Africa," *Africa Report*, 6, 3 (1961), pp. 3ff.

On the independent African states see G. M. Carter, ed., *African One-party States*, Ithaca, N.Y., 1962; J. S. Coleman and C. G. Rosberg, eds., *Political Parties and National Integration in Tropical Africa*, Berkeley, 1964; A. R. Zolberg, *Creating Political Order: The Party-states of West Africa*, Chicago, 1966; L. Kuper and M. G. Smith, eds., *Pluralism in Africa*, Berkeley, 1969; R. I. Rotberg and A. A. Mazrui, eds., *Protest and Power in Black Africa*, New York, 1970; M. Crowder and O. Ikime, eds., *West African Chiefs: Their Changing Status under Colonial Rule and Independence*, tr. B. Packman, New York, 1970; G. N. Brown and M. Hiskett, eds., *Conflict and Harmony in Education in Tropical Africa*, London, 1975.

Recent overviews of West African history: N. Levtzion, *Islam in West Africa: Religion, Society and Politics*, Brookfield, Vt., 1994; B. Callaway and L. Creevey, *The Heritage of Islam: Women, Religion and Politics in West Africa*, Boulder, 1994; M. Hiskett, *The Course of Islam in Africa*, Edinburgh, 1995; L. O. Sanneh, *The Crown and the Turban: Muslims and West African Pluralism*, Boulder, 1997; G. M. Okafor, *Christianity and Islam in West Africa: the Ghana Experience*, Wurzburg, 1997; N. Levtzion and R. L. Pouwels, eds., *The History of Islam in Africa*, Athens, Ohio, 2000.

Mauritania: F. de Chassey, *Mauritanie 1900–1975: De l'ordre colonial à l'ordre néo-colonial entre Maghreb et Afrique noire*, Paris, 1978; P. Marchesin, *Tribus, ethnies et pouvoir en Mauritanie*, Paris, 1992.

On Ghana see I. M. Wallerstein, *The Road to Independence: Ghana and the Ivory Coast*, Paris, 1964; D. Austin, *Politics in Ghana, 1946–1960*, London, 1964. An important study of the Muslim populace of Kumasi, Ghana is E. Schildkrout, *People of the Zongo: The Transformation of Ethnic Identities in Ghana*, Cambridge, 1978.

On the Muslims in the Volta River region see E. P. Skinner, *The Mossi of the Upper Volta: The Political Development of a Sudanese People*, Stanford, 1964; J. Adouin, *L'Islam en Haute-Volta à l'époque coloniale*, Abidjan, 1975. For Sierra Leone see B. E. Harrell-Bond, A. M. Howard, and D. E. Skinner, *Community Leadership and the Transformation of Freetown (1801–1976)*, The Hague, 1978; M. Kilson, *Political Change in a West African State: A Study of the Modernization Process in Sierra Leone*, Cambridge, Mass., 1966. Cameroon: G. M. Okafor, *Christians and Muslims in Cameroon*, Wurzburg, 1994. Chad: A. Le Rouvreur, *Sahéliens et Sahariens du Tchad*, Paris, 1962; J. Le Cornec, *Histoire politique du Tchad, de 1900 à 1962*, Paris, 1963. South Africa: A.Tayob, *Islam in South Africa: Mosques, Imams, and Sermons*, Gainesville, Fla., 1999.

Senegal: E. J. Schumacher, *Politics, Bureaucracy and Rural Development in Senegal*, Berkeley, 1975; M. Crowder, *Senegal: A Study of French Assimilation Policy*, London, 1967. The Murids have inspired an extensive literature: C. T. Sy, *La Confrérie sénégalaise des Mourides*, Paris, 1969; L. C. Behrman, *Muslim Brotherhoods and Politics in Senegal*, Cambridge, Mass., 1970; D. B. Cruise O'Brien, *The Mourides of Senegal: The Political and Economic Organization of an Islamic Brotherhood*, Oxford, 1971; D. B. Cruise O'Brien, *Saints and Politicians: Essays in the Organisation of a Senegalese Peasant Society*, London, 1975; J. Copans, *Les Marabouts de l'arachide: La Confrérie mouride et les paysans du Senegal*, Paris, 1980; K. Mbacke, *Soufisme et confrérie religieuses en Senegal*, Dakar, 1995; L. A. Villalon, *Islamic Society and State Power in Senegal*, Cambridge, 1995; S. Gellar, *Senegal: An African Nation between Islam and the West*, Boulder, 1995.

The history of Nigeria: M. Crowder, *The Story of Nigeria*, London, 1977; J. S. Coleman, *Nigeria: Background to Nationalism*, Berkeley, 1958. For the post-1966 military regimes and political economy see S. K. Panter-Brick, ed., *Nigerian Politics and Military Rule*, London, 1970; S. K. Panter-Brick, ed., *Soldiers and Oil: The Political Transformation of Nigeria*, London, 1978; R. Melson and H. Wolpe, eds., *Nigeria: Modernization and the Politics of Communalism*, East Lansing, Mich., 1972. See also A. Ozigi and L. Ocho, *Education in Northern Nigeria*, London and Boston, 1981; M. Bray, *Universal Primary Education in Nigeria: A Study of the Kano State*, London and Boston, 1981.

On Islam and society in northern Nigeria see J. N. Paden, *Religion and Political Culture in Kano*, Berkeley, 1973; R. Loimeier, *Islamic Reform and Political Change in Northern Nigeria*, Evanston, 1997; M. H. Kukah and T. Falola, *Religious Militancy and Self-Assertion: Islam and Politics in Nigeria*, Aldershot, 1996. On the relations between Islam and the political-economic structures of Nigerian society: P. Lubeck, *Islam and Urban Labor in Northern Nigeria: The Makings of a Muslim Working Class*, Cambridge, 1986.

Migrant Hausa merchants and workers are treated in A. Cohen, *Custom and Politics in Urban Africa: A Study of Hausa Migrants in Yoruba Towns*, London, 1969. For Islam among the Yoruba see T. G. O. Gbadamosi, *The Growth of Islam among the Yoruba, 1841–1908*, Atlantic Highlands, N.J., 1978; P. J. Ryan, *Imale, Yoruba Tradition: A Study of Clerical Piety*, Missoula, Mont., 1977. See also S. F. Nadel, *A Black Byzantium: The Kingdom of Nupe in Nigeria*, London, 1942; S. F. Nadel, *Nupe Religion*, Glencoe, Ill., 1954.

On reformist and Wahhabiya movements see L. Kaba, *The Wahabiyya: Islamic Reform and Politics in French West Africa*, Evanston, Ill., 1974; R. Launay, *Islam and Society in a West African Town*, Berkeley, 1992; R. Otayek, *Le Radicalisme islamique au sud du Sahara*, Paris, 1993; O. Kane and J.-L. Triaud, *Islam et islamismes au sud du Sahara*, Paris, 1998.

Other studies of Islam in West Africa are H. J. Fisher, *Ahmadiyyah: A Study in Contemporary Islam on the West African Coast*, London, 1964; P. Alexandre, "A West African Islamic Movement: Hamallism in French West Africa," *Protest and Power in Black Africa*, ed. R. I. Rotberg and A. A. Mazrui, New York, 1970, pp. 497–512; L. Brenner, *West African Sufi: The Religious Heritage and Spiritual Search of Cerno Bokar Saalif Taal*, Berkeley, 1984; N. Levtzion and H. Fisher, *Rural and Urban Islam in West Africa*, Boulder, 1987; H. T. Norris, *Sufi Mystics of the Niger Desert*, Oxford, 1990; L. Brenner, ed., *Muslim Identity and Social Change in Sub-Saharan Africa*, Bloomington, 1993; C. B. Yamba, *Permanent Pilgrimage in the Lives of West African Muslims in the Sudan*, Washington, D.C., 1995.

Chapter 31

Muslim peoples in East Africa are the subject of J. S. Trimingham, *Islam in East Africa*, Oxford, 1964; P. H. Gulliver, ed., *Tradition and Transition in East Africa*, Berkeley, 1969; A. I. Richards, *The Multicultural States of East Africa*, Montreal, 1969; B. A. Ogot, ed., *Zamani: A Survey of East African History*, 2nd edn, Nairobi, 1974; D. A. Low and A. Smith, eds., *A History of East Africa*, III, Oxford, 1976. See also W. Arens, ed., *A Century of Change in Eastern Africa*, The Hague and Chicago, 1976; R. L. Pouwells, *Horn and Crescent: Cultural Change and Traditional Islam on the East African Coast, 800–1900*, Cambridge, 1987.

On the Swahili-speaking coastal population see J. W. T. Allen, ed. and tr., *The Customs of the Swahili People*, Berkeley, 1981; H. B. Hansen and M. Twaddle, *Religion and Politics in East Africa*, London, 1995; on Zanzibar: N. R. Bennett, *A History of the Arab State of Zanzibar*, London, 1978; A. Clayton, *The Zanzibar Revolution and its Aftermath*, Hamden, Conn., 1981; A. Clayton, "The Zanzibari Revolution: African Protest in a Racially Plural Society," *Protest and Power in Black Africa*, ed. R. I.

Rotberg and A. A. Mazrui, New York, 1970, pp. 924–67; C. Grandmaison and A. Crozon, *Zanzibar aujourd'hui*, Paris, 1998.

For Tanzania see R. Yeager, *Tanzania: An African Experiment*, Boulder, 1982; J. Iliffe, *A Modern History of Tanganyika*, London, 1979; A. H. Nimtz, Jr., *Islam and Politics in East Africa: The Sufi Order in Tanzania*, Minneapolis, 1980. For Ugandan history and politics see S. R. Karugire, *The Political History of Uganda*, Nairobi, 1979; F. B. Welbourn, *Religion and Politics in Uganda, 1952–1962*, Nairobi, 1965; N. King, A. Kasozi, and A. Oded, *Islam and the Confluence of Religions in Uganda, 1840–1966*, Tallahassee, Fla., 1973; A. Oded, *Islam in Uganda: Islamization through a Centralized State in Pre-Colonial Africa*, New York, 1974. The Asian Muslim minorities are the subject of G. Delf, *Asians in East Africa*, London, 1963.

Somalia: I. M. Lewis, *A Modern History of Somalia: Nation and State in the Horn of Africa*, London, 1980; I. M. Lewis, "Sufism in Somaliland: A Study in Tribal Islam," *BSOAS*, 17 (1955), pp. 581–602; I. M. Lewis, *Blood and Bone: The Call of Kinship in Somali Society*, Lawrenceville, 1994; J. M. Ghalib, *The Cost of Dictatorship: The Somali Experience*, New York, 1995; P. Woodward, *The Horn of Africa: State Politics and International Relations*, London, 1996.

On Ethiopia see J. S. Trimingham, *Islam in Ethiopia*, London, 1952; G. K. N. Trevaskis, *Eritrea: A Colony in Transition, 1941–52*, London, 1960; R. L. Hess, *Ethiopia: The Modernization of Autocracy*, Ithaca, N.Y., 1970; B. Habte Selassie, *Conflict and Intervention in the Horn of Africa*, New York, 1980; J. Young, *Peasant Revolution in Ethiopia: The Tigray People's Liberation Front, 1975–1991*, Cambridge, 1997.

Sudan: A useful overview of the history of the Sudan is P. M. Holt and M. W. Daly, *The History of the Sudan from the Coming of Islam to the Present Day*, 3rd edn, London, 1979. See also R. L. Hill, *Egypt in the Sudan, 1820–1881*, London, 1959; P. M. Holt, *The Mahdist State in the Sudan, 1881–1898*, Oxford, 1958; H. Shaked, *The Life of the Sudanese Mahdi*, New Brunswick, N.J., 1978. Sudan under British rule: M. W. Daly, *British Administration and the Northern Sudan, 1917–1924*, Istanbul, 1980; G. Warburg, *Islam, Nationalism and Communism in a Traditional Society: The Case of the Sudan*, London, 1978.

For the politics of independent Sudan see P. K. Bechtold, *Politics in the Sudan: Parliamentary and Military Rule in an Emerging African Nation*, New York, 1976. On Islamic movements see J. S. Trimingham, *Islam in the Sudan*, London, 1965. For the conflict between north and south see D. M. Wai, ed., *The Southern Sudan: The Problem of National Integration*, London, 1973; L. P. Sanderson and N. Sanderson, *Education, Religion and Politics in Southern Sudan, 1899–1964*, London and Khartoum, 1981.

Arab tribal organization: T. Asad, *The Kababish Arabs: Power, Authority and Consent in a Nomadic Tribe*, London and New York, 1970; A. G. M. Ahmad, *Shaykhs and Followers: Political Struggle in the Rufa'a al-Hoi Nazirate in the Sudan*, Khartoum, 1974.

Sudan in the 1980s and 1990s: A. El-Affendi, *Turabi's Revolution: Islam and Power in Sudan*, London, 1991; S. Hale, *Gender Politics in Sudan: Islamism, Socialism, and the State*, Boulder, 1996; S. E. Hutchinson, *Nuer Dilemmas: Coping with Money, War, and the State*, Berkeley, 1996; A. M. Lesch, *The Sudan: Contested National Identities*, Bloomington, 1998; G. N. Anderson, *Sudan in Crisis: The Failure of Democracy*, Gainsville, Fla., 1999; D. Peterson, *Inside Sudan: Political Islam, Conflict and Catastrophe*, Boulder, 1999.

Chapter 32

The Balkans: Mark Pinson, ed., *The Muslims of Bosnia and Herzegovina*, Cambridge, Mass., 1993; T. Bringen, *Being Muslim the Bosnian Way: Identity and Community in a Central Bosnian Village*, Princeton, 1995; H. Poulton and S. Taji-Farouki, eds., *Muslim Identity and the Balkan State*, London, 1997; G. Duijzings, *Religion and the Politics of Idenity in Kosovo*, London, 1998.

Western Europe: B. Lewis and D. Schnapper, *Muslims in Europe*, London, 1994; G. Nonneman, T. Niblock, and B. Szajkowski, eds., *Muslim Communities in the New Europe*, Reading, 1996; G. Kepel, *Allah in the West: Islamic Movements in America and Europe*, Cambridge, 1997; T. Modood and P. Werbner, eds., *The Politics of Multiculturalism in the New Europe: Racism, Identity, and Community*, London, 1997; S. Vertovec and C. Peach, eds., *Islam in Europe: the Politics of Religion and Community*, Basingstoke, 1997; J. Alwall, *Muslim Rights and Plights: the Religious Liberty Situation of a Minority in Sweden*, London, 1998; J. S. Nielsen, *Toward a European Islam*, Basingstoke, 1999.

France: S. Boumama and H. S. Saoud, *Familles Maghrebins de France*, Paris, 1996; S. Bencheikh, *Marianne et le Prophete: L'Islam dans la France laïque*, Paris, 1998; N. Venel, *Musulmanes françaises: des Pratiquantes Voilées a l'université*, Paris, 1999; A. Lamchichi, *Islam et Musulmans de France: Pluralisme, laïcité et citoyenneté*, Paris, 1999.

United Kingdom: T. N. Basit, *Eastern Values, Western Milieu: Identities and Aspirations of Adolescent British Muslim Girls*, Aldershot, 1997; J. Jacobson, *Islam in Transition: Religion and Identity among British Pakistani Youth*, London, 1998; L. Newbigin, L. Sanneh, and J. Taylor, *Faith and Power: Christianity and Islam in "Secular" Britain*, London, 1998.

United States: Y. Haddad and J. Smith Adleman, eds., *Muslim Communities in North America*, Albany, N.Y., 1994; E. McCarus, ed., *The Development of Arab-American Identity*, Ann Arbor, 1994; K. M Moore, *Al-Mughtaribun: American Law and the Transformation of Muslim Life in the US*, Albany, N.Y., 1995; B. D. Metcalf, *Making Muslim Space in North America and Europe*, Berkeley, 1996; R. B. Turner, *Islam in the African-American Experience*, Bloomington, 1997; E. Shakir, *Bint Arab: Arab-American Women in the US*, Westport, Conn., 1997; L. S. Walbridge, *Without Forgetting the Imam: Lebanese Shi'ism in an American Community*, Detroit, 1997; J. Smith, *Islam in America*, New York, 1999; Y. Yazbeck and J. L. Esposito, eds., *Muslims on the Americanization Path?*, New York, 2000.

Conclusion

Islam – beliefs and communities: J. Esposito, *Islam: The Straight Path*, Oxford, 1998; E. Sirriyeh, *Sufi and anti-Sufis: The Defence, Rethinking and Rejection of Sufism in the Modern World*, Richmond, 1999; F. De Jong and B. Radtke, eds., *Islamic Mysticism Contested: Thirteen Centuries of Controversies and Polemics*, Leiden, 1999; R. Firestone, *Jihad: the Origin of Holy War in Islam*, New York, 1999. On the Ismaʻilis see F. Daftary, *The Ismaʻilis: Their History and Doctrines*, Cambridge, 1990; F. Daftary, *Mediaeval Ismaʻili History and Thought*, Cambridge, 1996.

Political thought and ideology: M. Arkoun, *Rethinking Islam*, Boulder, 1994; O. Roy, *The Failure of Political Islam*, Cambridge, 1994; J. L. Esposito, *The Islamic Threat: Myth or Reality*, New York, 1995; A. E. Mayer, *Islam and Human Rights*, Boulder, 1995; Mir Zohair Husein, *Global Islamic Politics*, New York, 1995; G. E. Fuller and I. O. Lesser, *A Sense of Siege: The Geopolitics of Islam and the West*, Boulder, 1995; W. E. Shepard, *Sayyid Qutb and Islamic Activism: A Translation and Critical Analysis of Social Justice in Islam*, Leiden, 1996; D. F. Eickelman and J. Piscatori, *Muslim Politics*, Princeton, 1996; J. Esposito, ed., *Political Islam: Revolutionary Radicalism or Reform*, Boulder, 1997; F. Hoveyda, *The Broken Crescent: the "Threat" of Militant Islamic Fundamentalism*, Westport, Conn., 1998; Bassam Tibi, *The Challenge of Fundamentalism: Political Islam and the New World Disorder*, Berkeley, 1998; M. Monshipouri, *Islamism, Secularism and Human Rights in the Middle East*, Boulder, 1998; C. Kurzman, ed., *Liberal Islam: A Source Book*, Oxford, 1998; F. Rahman, *Revival and Reform in Islam: A Study of Islamic Fundamentalism*, ed. Ebrahim Moosa, Oxford, 2000; M. Sadri, *Reason, Freedom and Democracy in Islam: Essential Writings of Abdulkerim Soroush*, Oxford, 2000; G. Kepel, *Jihad: The Trial of Political Islam*, Cambridge, Mass., 2002.

Women and gender: A. A. Sonbol, *Women, the Family and Divorce Laws in Islamic History*, Syracuse, N.Y., 1996; Y. Y. Haddad and J. Esposito, eds., *Islam, Gender and Social Change*, New York, 1998; L. Abu-Lughod, *Remaking Women: Feminism and Modernity in the Middle East*, Princeton, 1998; G. R. G. Hambly, *Women in the Medieval Islamic World*, New York, 1998; H. Bodman and N. Tohidi, *Women in Muslim Societies*, Boulder, 1998; L. A. Brand, *Women, the State and Political Liberalization*, New York, 1998; G. Nashat and J. E. Tucker, *Women in the Middle East and North Africa*, Bloomington, 1999; M. L. Meriwether and J. E. Tucker, *A Social History of Women and Gender in the Modern Middle East*, Boulder, 1999.

INDEX